ISBN 978-1-5281-4186-4
PIBN 10981234

1 MONTH OF
FREE
READING

at

www.ForgottenBooks.com

By purchasing this book you are eligible for one month membership to ForgottenBooks.com, giving you unlimited access to our entire collection of over 1,000,000 titles via our web site and mobile apps.

To claim your free month visit:

www.forgottenbooks.com/free981234

REPORTS OF CASES

DECIDED IN THE

SUPREME COURT

OF THE

STATE OF GEORGIA

AT THE

OCTOBER TERM, 1899

VOLUME 109

STEVENS AND GRAHAM

REPORTERS

ATLANTA

Rec. Sept. 18, 1900.

Electrotyped, printed, and bound by
THE FOOTE & DAVIES COMPANY,
Atlanta, Ga.

THE SUPREME COURT.

Hon. THOMAS J. SIMMONS, Chief Justice.

Hon. SAMUEL LUMPKIN, Presiding Justice.

Hon. WILLIAM A. LITTLE, Associate Justice.

Hon. WILLIAM H. FISH, Associate Justice.

Hon. ANDREW J. COBB, Associate Justice.

Hon. HENRY T. LEWIS, Associate Justice.

GEORGE W. STEVENS, Reporter.

JOHN M. GRAHAM, Assistant Reporter.

Z. D. HARRISON, Clerk.

LOGAN BLECKLEY, Deputy-Clerk.

JAMES W. VAUGHAN, Sheriff.

JUDGES OF THE SUPERIOR COURTS.

CIRCUIT.	JUDGE.	RESIDENCE.
ALBANY	Hon. W. N. Spence	Camilla.
ATLANTA	Hon. J. H. Lumpkin	Atlanta.
ATLANTIC	Hon. Paul E. Seabrook	Pineora.
AUGUSTA	Hon. Edward L. Brinson	Waynesboro.
BLUE RIDGE	Hon. George F. Gober	Marietta.
BRUNSWICK	Hon. Joseph W. Bennet	Brunswick.
CHATTAHOOCHEE	Hon. W. B. Butt	Columbus.
CHEROKEE	Hon. A. W. Fite	Cartersville.
COWETA	Hon. Sampson W. Harris	Carrollton.
EASTERN	Hon. Robert Falligant	Savannah.
FLINT	Hon. E. J. Reagan	McDonough.
MACON	Hon. William H. Felton Jr.	Macon.
MIDDLE	Hon. Beverly D. Evans	Sandersville.
NORTHEASTERN	Hon. John B. Estes	Gainesville.
NORTHERN	Hon. Seaborn Reese	Sparta.
OCMULGEE	Hon. John C. Hart	Union Point.
OCONEE	Hon. C. C. Smith	Hawkinsville.
PATAULA	Hon. H. C. Sheffield	Arlington.
ROME	Hon. W. M. Henry	Rome.
SOUTHERN	Hon. Augustin H. Hansell	Thomasville.
SOUTHWESTERN	Hon. Zera A. Littlejohn	Cordele.
STONE MOUNTAIN	Hon. John S. Candler	Edgewood.
TALLAPOOSA	Hon. Charles G. Janes	Cedartown.
WESTERN	Hon. Richard B. Russell	Winder.

JUDGES OF THE CITY COURTS.

ALBANY ....Hon. Richard Hobbs........Albany.
ATHENS...................Hon. Howell Cobb..........Athens.
ATLANTA ....Hon. H. M. Reid...........Atlanta.
    Criminal Court......Hon. Andrew E. Calhoun *..Atlanta.
BARNESVILLE ....Hon. Charles J. Lester.....Barnesville.
BAXLEY..................Hon. Thomas A. Parker....Baxley.
BRUNSWICK ....Hon. J. D. Sparks †.........Brunswick.
CAMILLA.................Hon. J. H. Scaife..........Camilla.
CARROLLTON ....Hon. W. F. Brown..........Carrollton.
CARTERSVILLE..........Hon. J. W. Harris..........Cartersville.
CLARKESVILLE ....Hon. J. B. Jones ....Clarkesville.
COLUMBUS ....Hon. James L. Willis.......Columbus.
DAWSON ....Hon. James G. Parks.......Dawson.
DOUGLAS .... Hon. F. Willis Dart.......Douglas.
EASTMAN...............Hon. James Bishop Jr......Eastman.
ELBERTON ....Hon. Pulliam P. Proffitt...Elberton.
FLOYD COUNTY.........Hon. John H. Reece§ ......Rome.
FORSYTH..............Hon. William M. Clark....Forsyth.
GREENVILLE ....Hon. W. R. Jones.......... Greenville.
GRIFFIN.................Hon. E. W. Hammond.......Griffin.
GWINNETT COUNTY‡....Hon. Samuel J. Winn ......Lawrenceville.
HALL COUNTY...........Hon. Garland H. Prior .....Gainesville.
JEFFERSON ....Hon. W. W. Stark...........Harmony Grove.
LA GRANGE..............Hon. Frank P. Longley....La Grange.
LEXINGTON ....Hon. Philip W. Davis......Lexington.
MACON ....Hon. W. D. Nottingham.. ..Macon.
NEWNAN........ ....Hon. Alvan D Freeman.....Newnan.
RICHMOND COUNTY.....Hon. William F. Eve.......Augusta.
SAVANNAH...............Hon. Thomas M. Norwood.. Savannah.
SWAINSBORO ....Hon. Alfred Herrington....Swainsboro.
VALDOSTA ....Hon. W. H. Griffin........Valdosta.
WASHINGTON ....Hon. William H. Toombs....Washington.
WAYCROSS...............Hon. J. S. Williams.......Waycross.
WRIGHTSVILLE.........Hon. Vernon B. Robinson...Wrightsville.

*Successor to Hon. John D. Berry.
†Successor to Hon. Samuel C. Atkinson.
§Successor to Hon. George A. H. Harris.
‡ Abolished by act of December 19, 1899. Acts 1899, p. 380.

TABLE OF CASES REPORTED.

Acme Brewing Company v. Fletcher.......................... 463
Alexander v. State............................... 805
American Freehold Land Mortgage Company v. Dodge... 394
American Trust and Banking Company v. Maddox........ 787
Americus Manufacturing and Improvement Co. v. Mize... 359
Angier v. Equitable Building and Loan Association....... 625
Anthony v. Birch.................................... 349
Ashley v. Cook...................................... 653
Aspinwall v. Chisholm & Company.......................... 437
Atlanta Banking Company v. Floyd........................ 778
Atlanta Consolidated Bottling Company v. Hutchinson... 550
Atlanta Consolidated Street Railway Company v. Bagwell. 611
Atlanta Guano Co. v. Davis Sulphur Ore Co................ 606
Atlanta National Bank v. George...................... 682
Atlanta National B. & L. Association v. Stewart............ 80
Austin v. Farmers Mutual Insurance Association........... 689
    Velvin.................................... 200
Bagley v. Hanesley.................................... 346
Bagwell v. Atlanta Consolidated Street Railway Co......... 611
Bank of Forsyth v. Gammage............................ 220
Bank of Richland v. Bivins............................ 342
Barfield v. Macon County........................... 386
Barge v. Weems................................... 685
Barker v. Cunningham.............................. 613
Barnett v. City of Atlanta............................ 166
Barron v. Gentry................................... 172
Barrow v. Smith................................... 767
Barry v. Cherokee Iron Company 175
Baxter & Company v. Suwannee Turpentine Company... 597
Bell v. Bowdoin.................................... 209
Berger v. Saul & Company............................ 240
Bice v. State...................................... 117

Biggers v. State... 105
Birch v. Anthony.. 349
Bishop v. Mathews & Company.................................. 790
Bivins v. Bank of Richland.. 342
Blanton v. Osborn & Walcott Manufacturing Company... 196
Blocker v. Boswell... 230
Bloodworth & Company v. Hudgins........................... 197
Blue & Stewart v. Collins... 341
Boswell v. Blocker... 230
Bowdoin v. Bell... 209
Branan v. Warren.. 835
Brantley Company v. Lee.. 478
Brinson & Ingram v. Central of Georgia Railway Co...... 354
British America Assurance Company v. Nicholas........... 621
Brown v. Drake.. 179
           Holton... 431
           State... 570
Broznack v. State... 514
Bruce v. Conyers... 190
Brunswick and Western Railway Company v. Petty....... 666
Bullock v. Wilcox Lumber Company........................... 532
Burch v. Daniel........... 256
Burton v. State... 134
Bush v. State.. 120
Butler v. Mountain City Mill Company....................... 469
Cade v. Larned.. 292
Callaway & Company v. McCord Company.................. 796
Carter v. Peoples National Bank................................. 573
Central of Georgia Railway Co. v. Brinson & Ingram..... 354
                                         Hall...................... 367
                                         Hammond.............. 383
                                         Ricks...................... 339
                                         State...................... 716
Chamblee v. Pirkle.. 32
Channell v. State... 150
Chapman v. State.. 157
Charland v. Marshall... 306
Cheney v. State.. 503

Cherokee Iron Company *v.* Barry.............................. 175
Chisholm & Company *v.* Aspinwall........................... 437
City Council of Augusta *v.* Mutual Reserve Fund Asso.... 73
City of Atlanta *v.* Barnett............................. 166
     Columbus *v.* Hartfield................................. 112
         Wiley..................................... 295
     Elberton *v.* Long............................... 28
Cleveland *v.* State.................................... 265
Coachman *v.* Knowles................................ 356
Cole *v.* McClendon.................................... 183
Collins *v.* Blue & Stewart............................ 341
Collum *v.* State..................................... 531
Columbus Fertilizer Company *v.* McDaniel.................. 284
Conley *v.* Redwine.................................... 640
Conyers *v.* Bruce.................................... 190
Cook *v.* Ashley..................................... 653
     Simmons................................... 553
Cosby *v.* Weaver.................................... 310
Cowart *v.* McDaniel................................. 419
Cox *v.* McMillan.................................... 42
Craven *v.* State.................................... 266
Crosby *v.* King Hardware Company.................... 452
Cross *v.* Southern Railway Company 170
Cunningham *v.* Barker.............................. 613
     United States Savings and Loan Co....... 616
Daniel *v.* Burch.................................... 256
Davis Sulphur Ore Co. *v.* Atlanta Guano Co............... 607
Dawson *v.* Equitable Mortgage Company.................... 389
Delegal *v.* State........... 518
Dent *v.* Parkman..................................... 289
Dodge *v.* American Freehold Land Mortgage Company... 394
Donaldson *v.* Roberts............................... 832
Donehoo *v.* Huff 638
Dover *v.* State 485
Downing Company *v.* Ridgeway........................ 591
Drake *v.* Brown.................................... 179
     Drewry.................................... 399
Dyson *v.* Southern Railway Company 103

Echols v. State.. 508
Elder v. Foute.. 713
Ellis v. Poe & Brother 422
Embry v. State.. 61
English v. S. P. Richards Company............................ 635
Epps v. Story... 302
Equitable Building and Loan Association v. Angier........ 625
Equitable Mortgage Company v. Dawson...................... 389
Ethridge v. Mayor and Council of Forsyth 156
Farmers Mutual Insurance Association of Ga. v. Austin .. 689
Felton v. Grier.. 320
Fletcher v. Acme Brewing Company 463
Flournoy v. Ozburn.. 704
Floyd v. Atlanta Banking Company........................... 778
Ford v. Gill 691
Fountain v. Napier Brothers 225
Foute v. Elder.. 713
Fuller v. State.. 809
Fulton County v. Turner... 633
Gammage v. Bank of Forsyth................................... 220
Garrett v. Wade.. 270
Gentry v. Barron 172
George v. Atlanta National Bank............................... 682
Georgia Loan, Savings and Banking Company v. Morris... 12
Georgia Northern Railway Co. v. Tifton, T. & G. R. Co... 762
Georgia Railroad and Banking Company v. Roughton.... 604
Georgia Southern and Florida Railway Co. v. Jossey...... 439
Georgia State Building & Loan Association v. Savannah... 63
Gibson v. Interstate Building and Loan Association....... 460
Gill v. Ford... 691
Glynn County v. Milburn 473
Gordon v. Gordon 262
Green v. State.. 536
Grier v. Felton.. 320
Griswold v. Rutherford.. 398
Haines v. State..... 526
Hall v. Central of Georgia Railway Company............... 367
Hamilton v. Mutual Benefit Life Insurance Company..... 381

Hammond v. Central of Georgia Railway Company........ 383
Hanesley v. Bagley.. 346
Harris v. State.. 280
Hartfield v. City of Columbus................................... 112
Haunson v. Nelms.. 802
Henderson v. Heyward.. 373
Hiles Carver Company v. King................................... 180
Hodge v. Little Rock Cooperage Company.................... 434
Holliman v. Mayor etc. of Hawkinsville...................... 107
Holmes v. Otis Brothers & Company.......................... 775
Holton v. Brown 431
          State 127
Howard v. Pope.. 259
          State.. 137
Hudgins v. Bloodworth & Company........................... 197
Huff v. Donehoo... 638
Hunnicutt v. McMillan 699
Hutchinson v. Atlanta Consolidated Bottling Company... 550
Imperial Fertilizer Company v. Tiedeman & Brother...... 661
In re Kenan, solicitor-general................................... 819
Interstate Building and Loan Association v. Gibson 460
Irvine's Georgia Music House v. Wynn 287
James v. Taylor.. 327
Jenkins v. Southern Railway Company 35
Jewell v. Walker 241
Johnson v. State... 268
Johnston & Company Limited v. Woodson 454
Jossey v. Georgia Southern and Florida Railway Co....... 439
          Rushin 319
Kassell v. Mayor and Aldermen of Savannah............... 491
Kelly & Jones Company v. Moore............................. 798
Kenan, solicitor-general, In re................................. 819
King v. Hiles Carver Company................................. 180
King Hardware Company v. Crosby........................... 452
Knowles v. Coachman... 356
Langston v. State.. 153
Larned v. Cade.. 292
Lee v. Brantley Company....................................... 478

Leman & Company v. Penn Tobacco Company 428
Little Rock Cooperage Company v. Hodge................... 434
Long v. City of Elberton.. 28
Lowery v. Powell.. 192
Lowman v. State.. 501
Macon County v. Barfield... 386
Maddox v. American Trust and Banking Company........ 787
　　　　　　Strauss.. 223
Marcrum v. Washington.. 296
Marshall v. Charland.. 306
Mathews & Company v. Bishop.................................. 790
Mayor of Forsyth v. Ethridge. 156
　　　　Hawkinsville v. Holliman............................. 107
　　　　Macon v. Wood.. 149
　　　　Moultrie v. Patterson 370
　　　　Savannah v. Georgia State B. & L. A................. 63
　　　　　　　Kassell. 491
McCain v. Sutlive 547
McClendon v. Cole.. 183
McCombs v. State......... ....496, 500
McCord Company v. Callaway & Company.................. 796
McDaniel v. Columbus Fertilizer Company.................. 284
　　　　　Cowart.. 419
McElveen & Hardage v. Southern Railway Company 249
McMillan v. Cox 42
　　　　Hunnicutt... 699
Merritt v. Williams..213, 217
Milburn v. Glynn County 473
Miller v. State... 512
Mize v. Americus Manufacturing and Improvement Co... 359
Mohr–Weil Lumber Company v. Russell...................... 579
Monroe v. Stiger... 457
Moore v. Farmers Mutual Insurance Association of Ga.... 689
　　　　Kelly & Jones Company............................. 798
　　　　Wheeler 62
Morris v. Georgia Loan, Savings and Banking Company.. 12
　　　　State... 351
Mountain City Mill Company v. Butler....................... 469

Mozley v. Reagan.. 182
Mutual Benefit Life Insurance Company v. Hamilton..... 381
Mutual Reserve Fund Life Association v. Augusta......... 73
Napier Brothers v. Fountain 225
Nelms v. Haunson.. 802
Nicholas v. British America Assurance Company........... 621
O'Brien v. State... 51
Offerman & Western R. Co. v. Waycross Air-Line R. Co.. 827
Osborn & Walcott Manufacturing Company v. Blanton.... 196
Otis Brothers & Company v. Holmes 775
Ozburn v. Flournoy.. 704
Page v. Pitt... 557
Paille v. Plant... 247
Parker v. Steele... 791
Parkham v. Dent.. 289
Patterson v. Mayor etc. of Moultrie............................. 370
Penn Tobacco Company v. Leman & Company............... 428
Peoples National Bank v. Carter.................................. 573
Petty v. Brunswick and Western Railway Company....... 666
Phelps v. State.. 115
Pirkle v. Chamblee 32
Pitt v. Page.. 557
Plant v. Paille 247
Poe & Brother v. Ellis.. 422
Pope v. Howard... 259
Powell v. Lowery... 192
Preston v. Walker.. 290
Ralph v. Ward... 363
Ray v. Ray.. 465
Reagan v. Mozley... 182
Redwine v. Conley 640
Reid v. Whitton... 174
　　　　Wilson Brothers.. 424
Rice v. Ryan... 448
Ricks v. Central of Georgia Railway Company.............. 339
Ridgeway v. Downing Company................................... 591
Roberson v. Simons... 360
Roberts v. Donaldson.. 832

Robinson *v.* State.................................506, 564
Ross *v.* State...................................... 516
Rosser *v.* Sutton................................. 204
Roughton *v.* Georgia Railroad and Banking Company..... 604
Rushin *v.* Jossey 319
Russell *v.* Mohr–Weil Lumber Company..................... 579
Rutherford *v.* Griswold.............................. 398
Ryan *v.* Rice...................................... 448
Saul & Company *v.* Berger......................... 240
Schmitt *v.* Schneider.............................. 628
Sewell *v.* Suttles................................ 707
Simmons *v.* Cook.................................. 553
Simons *v.* Roberson..... 360
Smith *v.* Barrow................................... 767
          State 227, 479
Southern Bell Telephone Company *v.* Stewart.............. 80
Southern Express Company *v.* Stewart..................... 80
Southern Home B. & L. Association *v.* Stewart............. 80
Southern Railway Company *v.* Cross........................ 170
                              Dyson...................... 103
                              Jenkins.................... 35
                              McElveen & Hardage...... 249
                              Wingard 177
S. P. Richards Company *v.* English 635
State *v.* Alexander............................... 805
          Bice...................................... 117
          Biggers.................................. 105
          Brown................................... 570
          Broznack................................ 514
          Burton................................... 134
          Bush 120
          Central of Georgia Railway Company.............. 716
          Channell 150
          Chapman 157
          Cheney 503
          Cleveland................................ 265
          Collum 531
          Craven................................... 266

State v. Delegal... 518

Dover.. 485

Echols.. 508

Embry... 61

Fuller.. 809

Green.. 536

Haines... 526

Harris... 280

Holton............................. 127

Howard.. 137

Johnson... 268

Langston.. 153

Lowman.. 501

McCombs..496, 500

Miller 512

Morris.. 351

O'Brien... 51

Phelps. 115

Robinson..506, 564

Ross.. 516

Smith..227, 479

Sumner... 142

Teasley... 282

Thompson.. 172

Tinsley... 822

Tripp... 489

Trust Company of Georgia............................ 736

Steele v. Parker.. 791

Sterling Cycle Works v. Willingham.......................... 559

Stewart v. Building, Express, and Telephone Companies. 80

Stiger v. Monroe.. 457

Story v. Epps.. 302

Strauss v. Maddox.. 223

Sumner v. State... 142

Sutlive v. McCain.. 547

Suttles v. Sewell 707

Sutton v. Rosser.. 204

Suwannee Turpentine Company v. Baxter & Company.... 597

Taylor v. James.................................. 327
Teasley v. State... 282
Thompson v. State.. 272
          Wright. 466
Tiedeman & Brother v. Imperial Fertilizer Company....... 661
Tifton, Thomasville & Gulf R. Co. v. Ga. Nor. R. Co...... 762
Tinsley v. State 822
Tripp v. State. 489
Trust Company of Georgia v. State of Georgia............... 736
Turner v. Fulton County 633
Union Fraternal League v. Walton............................   1
United States Savings and Loan Co. v. Cunningham.....,.. 616
Velvin v. Austin 200
Wade v. Garrett. 270
Walker v. Jewell .... 24.
          Preston 290
Walton v. Union Fraternal League..............................   1
Ward v. Ralph 363
Warren v. Branan 865
Washington v. Marcrum............... 296
Waycross Air-Line R. Co. v. Offerman & Western R. Co.. 827
Weaver v. Cosby 310
Weems v. Barge.. 5
Western and Atlantic Railroad Company v. Wilkes......
Wheeler v. Moore...
Whitton v. Reid..
Wilcox Lumber Company v. Bullock............................ 535
Wiley v. City of Columbus...................................... 295
Wilkes v. Western and Atlantic Railroad Company....... 794
Williams v. Merritt 213, 217
Willingham v. Sterling Cycle Works........................... 559
Wilson Brothers v. Reid... 424
Wingard v. Southern Railway Company 177
Wood v. Mayor and Council of Macon......................... 149
Woodson v. Johnston & Company Limited................... 454
Wright v. Thompson... 466
Wynn v. Irvine's Georgia Music House 287
          Wynn.. 255

GEORGIA CASES CITED BY THE COURT.

Adams v. Rome, 59/769.	48
Akin v. Ordinary, 54/59.	477
Akridge v. ˙ ˛tillo, 44/585.	197
Allen v. Cravens, 68/554.	548
Allen v. Sharp, 62/183.	309
Allen v. State, 51/264.	109
Almand v. Ga. R. Co., 102/151.	204
American Car Co. v. Atlanta City Street Railway Co., 100/254.	550
Anderson v. Faw, 79/558.	548
Anderson v. Taylor, 41/10.	197
Ansley v. Wilson, 50/418.	646
˛rnett v. Griffin, 60/349.	103
Athens City Waterworks Co. v. ˙thens, 74/413.	67
Atlanta City Street Railway Co. v. American Car Co., 103/254.	775
Atlanta and Florida Railroad Co. v. Kimberly, 87/161.	594
Atlanta and West Point Railroad Co. v. Newton, 85/517.	370
Aug˙ ˛ National Bank v. Mer- ˌ3˙ ˛nts Bank, 104/857.	548
˛˛˙ ˙ ˙. Aug. Ry. Co., 108/671.	30
˙˙ ˙ Walker, 77/338.	31
˙˙ ˙. State, 103/388.	54
˙˙ T ˛ ˙˙ State, 97/452.	674
˛˛˛˛˛ ˛o v. McLeod, 63/162.	299
Barfield v. Jefferson, 84/609.	221, 339
Barksdale v. Bunkley, 26/398.	585
Barron v. State, 74/888.	542
Bazemore v. Davis, 55/504.	335
Beardsley v. Hilson, 94/52.	39
Beck v. Henderson, 76/360.	345
Bedell v. R. & D. R. Co., 94/22.	254
Bell v. State, 91/227.	826
Biggers v. Bird, 55/650.	243, 655
Bird v. Burgsteiner, 100/486.	640
Black v. Harper, 63/752.	197
Black v. State, 36/447.	571
Black v. Walker, 98/31.	292
Blacker v. Dunlop, 93/819.	339
˙˙˙ckman v. State, 80/785.	276
Blackwell v. Broughton, 56/390.	621
Bleyer v. Old Hickory, 70/724.	265
Blocker v. Boswell, 109/230.	240
Blount v. Edison Co., 106/197.	552, 777
Bohler v. Schneider, 49/195.	77
Bolden v. State, 64/361.	490, 542
Bostwick v. Duncan, 60/383.	446
Bowen v. Johnson, 12/9.	665
Boyd v. McFarlin, 58/208.	643
Boyd v. Spencer, 103/828.	341
Boynton v. McDaniel, 97/400.	446
Brady v. Brady, 71/71.	219, 578
Braswell v. McDaniel, 74/320.	337
Broach v. Powell, 79/79.	578
Brobston v. Penniman, 97/527.	27
Brooks v. Rooney, 11/423.	644
Brooks v. State, 96/353.	500
Broome v. Davis, 87/584.	334
Brown v. Social Circle, 105/834.	380, 495
Brown v. State, 58/214.	512
Brown v. State, 76/626.	529
Brown v. State, 95/481.	137
Brown v. State, 104/525.	60, 823
Brumbalo v. Baxter, 33/81.	41
Brunswick R. Co. v. Clem, 80/539.	680
Bryan v. Walton, 33 Supp./11.	834
Buchanan v. State, 24/282.	145
Buice v. Mining Co., 64/769.	801
Burch v. Daniel, 101/228.	257
Burch v. Savannah, 42/600.	77
Burns v. Chandler, 61/385.	621
Burns v. Eq. B. & L. A., 108/181.	628
Butler v. Durham, 2/414.	632
Butler v. R. & D. Co., 88/594.	675
Caldwell v. State, 101/557.	54
Cameron v. Phillips, 60/434.	655
Cameron v. Sheppard, 71/781.	548
Campbell v. Met. Co., 82/320.	388
Carnes v. State, 28/192.	541
Carr v. Ga. Loan Co., 108/757.	396
Carswell v. Hartridge, 55/412.	655
Carswell v. Macon Co., 38/403.	392

Caswell v. Bunch, 77/504. 392
Cathing v. State, 62/244. 603
Cecil v. Gazan, 65/689. 656
Cedartown v. Freeman, 89/451. 266
Cedartown Improvement Co. v.
  Cherokee Imp. Co., 99/122. 652
Central Ga. Bk v. Iverson, 73/19. 834
Central R. Co. v. Collins, 40/582. 727
Central R. Co. v. Gleason, 69/200,
  72/742. _795
Central R. Co. v. Hasselkus, 91/385. 253
Central R. Co. v. Macon, 43/642. 751
Central R. Co. v. Perry, 58/461. 795
Central R. Co. v. Pool, 95/412. 176
Central R. Co. v. Thompson,
  76/770. 795
Central R. Co. v. Wood, 51/515. 606
Chapman v. State, 18/736. 106
Cheeney v. Ocean S. Co., 92/726. 455
Cherry v. North & S. R., 65/633. 623
Cherry v. Smith, 51/558. 197
Chicago Building Co. v. Summer-
  our, 101/820. 446
City Council v. Bank, 47/562. 79
City Council v. Dunbar, 50/387. 87
City Council v. R. Co., 74/658. 830
City Council v. R. Co., 78/119. 94
City of Albany v. R. Co., 71/158. 94
City of Atlanta v. Gate City Gas
  Light Co., 71/106. 373,766
City of Atlanta v. Green, 67/386. 387
City of Atlanta v. R. Co., 74/16. 94
City of Atlanta v. Smith, 99/462. 784
Clark's Cove Co. v. Steed, 92/440. 360
Clayton v. Wallace, 41/268. 344
Cobb v. Smith, 102/585. 150
Coleman v. Maclean, 101/303. 244
Coleman v. Slade, 75/61. 309
Collier v. Elliott, 100/363. 634
Columbus R. Co. v. Wright, 89/574. 94
Comm'rs v. Tabbott, 72/89. 150
Conley v. Arnold, 93/823. 642
Conley v. Buck, 100/187. 427, 642
Conley v. Buck, 102/752. 642
Conley v. Maher, 93/781. 642
Conley v. Redwine, 103/569. 642
Conley v. State, 83/496 ; 85/348. 642
Conley v. Thornton, 81/154. 642
Cook v. Eq. B. & L. A., 104/814. 628

Cooper v. State, 103/405. 109
Cosnahan v. Johnston, 108/235. 704
Cotting v. Culpepper, 79/792. 639
County of Houston v. Central R.
  Co. 72/211. 94
County of Pulaski v. Thompson,
  83/274. 753
Cox v. Murphy, 82/623. 606
Crabb v. State, 88/584. 825
Crane v. Barry, 47/476. 197
Cranston v. Augusta, 61/572. 149, 167
Crawford v. May, 49/43. 621
Cruger v. Tucker, 69/557. 41
Cumming v. Clegg, 52/605. 578
Cunningham v. Griffin, 107/690. 495
Cunningham v. State. 103/239. 509
Cutliff v. Albany, 60/599. 78
Cutts v. Scandrett, 108/620. 239
Davis v. Bennett, 72/762. 265
Davis v. Comer, 108/117. 647
Davis v. E. T. R. Co., 87/605. 831
Davis v. Lumpkin, 106/585. 299
Davis v. Morgan, 96/518. 347
Davis v. Muscogee Co., 106/126. 606
Davis v. State, 40/229. 53
Dawson v. Garland, 70/447. 222
Decker v. McGowan, 59/805. 103
DeLoach v. Trammell, 72/198. 264
Denson v. Denson, 94/525. 304
Dew v. Hamilton, 23/415. 392
Dickson v. State, 62/583. 572
Dixon v. Baxter, 106/180. 599
Dodd v. Glover, 102/82. 454
Dodd v. Thompson, 63/393. 333
Dorsey v. Miller, 105/88. 238, 240
Doyal v. State, 70/134. 504
Drawdy v. Littlefield, 75/215. 344
Dumas v. State, 62/58. 126
Dumas v. State, 65/475. 276
Dunagan v. Stadler, 101/474. 298
Duncan v. State, 97/181. 482
Dutcher v. Hobby, 86/198. 658
Dykes v. McVay, 67/502. 656
Dyson v. Pope, 71/209. 404
East T. R. Co. v. Hayes, 83/558. 675
East T. R. Co. v. Markens, 88/60. 369
Eberhart v. State, 47/598. 276
Edison Co. v. Blount, 96/272. 552
Edwards v. State, 53/428. 143

Embry v. State, 109/61.	62
Empire Co. v. Main, 98/183.	632
Eq. Life v. Paterson, 41/338.	8, 11
Evans v. State, 78/351.	165
Eve v. Cross, 76/693.	337
Everett v. Westmoreland, 92/670.	789
Exchange Bk. v. Loh, 104/446.	18
Exchange Bk. v. Macon Co., 97/1.	828
Ex parte Craig, T. U..P. C. 159.	191
Farley v. Bloodworth, 87/110.	834
Farmer v. State, 91/720.	153
Fears v. State, 102/274.	376
Ferguson v. New M. Co., 51/609.	624
Fidelity Co. v. Kangara Co., 92/172.	797
Fisher v. State, 78/258.	542
Fla. C. R. Co. v. Ragan, 104/353.	624
Fletcher v. Perry, 97/369.	655
Floyd v. Eatonton, 14/354.	169
Fogarty v. State, 80/464.	148
Foley v. Abbott, 66/115.	431
Forbes v. Hall, 102/47.	646
Forbes v. Turner, 54/252.	197
Foster v. Jones, 23/168.	702
Franklin v. State, 85/570.	572
Fry v. Calder, 74/7.	602
Fuller v. Buice, 80/395.	446
Fuller v. State, 73/412.	568
Fulton County Street Railroad Co. v. McConnell, 87/756.	595
Gaines v. State, 108/772.	266
Gallery v. State, 92/463.	487
Gammage v. Powell, 101/540.	708
Garrison v. Atlanta, 68/64.	168, 372
Gartrell v. Linn, 79/700.	249, 358
Gault v. Wallis, 53/677.	372
Gentry v. Walker, 101/123.	172
Georgia Ice Co. v. Porter, 70/637.	674
Georgia R. Co. v. Lybrend, 99/431.	424
Georgia S. R. Co. v. Trust Co., 94/306.	674
Georgia State B. & L. Association v. Savannah, 109/63.	103
Glover v. State, 105/597.	503
Godwin v. Maxwell, 106/194.	715
Goodwin v. Savannah, 53/414.	79, 88
Gould v. Atlanta, 55/678.	76, 89
Grant v. State, 97/790.	368
Green v. Ansley, 92/647.	600
Greer v. Burnam, 69/734.	240
Greer v. Fergerson, 104/555.	181
Gresham v. Johnson, 70/631.	208
Groves v. Williams, 68/598.	318
Groves v. Williams, 69/614.	655
Gunn v. Gunn, 74/555.	427
Gunn v. Knoop, 73/510.	471
Hadden v. Larned, 87/634.	396
Haley v. Evans, 60/157.	446
Hall v. Matthews, 68/490.	208
Hall v. State, 100/311.	199
Halloran v. Bray, 29/422.	197
Hamilton v. Phenix Co., 107/728.	178
Hamilton v. State, 97/216.	360
Hanks v. Phillips, 39/550.	41
Hardin v. Almand, 64/582.	197
Harrell v. Pickett, 43/271.	619
Harris v. Amosk. Co., 97/465.	423
Harris v. Cannon, 6/382.	600
Harris v. Central R. Co., 78/526.	369
Harris v. Perryman, 103/816.	413
Harrison v. Kiser, 79/588.	593
Hart v. Hatcher, 71/717.	222
Hart v. Respess, 89/87.	393
Hartridge v. Wesson, 4/101.	241
Hatcher v. Jones, 53/208.	578
Hawkins v. Jonesboro, 63/527.	103
Hazlehurst v. Freeman, 52/244.	829
Heard v. Phillips, 101/691.	348
Helms v. O'Bannon, 26/132.	224
Henderson v. Cen. R. Co., 73/718.	606
Henderson v. Pope, 39/361.	344
Henderson v. Williams, 97/709.	48
Hendrick v. Davis, 27/167.	644
Hendrix v. Mason, 70/523.	178
Henry v. McAllister, 93/667.	309
Herndon v. Black, 97/327.	423
Herz v. Claflin, 101/615.	675
Hightower v. George, 102/549.	175
Hill v. Dalton, 72/314.	376, 494
Hill v. Decatur, 22/203.	377
Hines v. Rutherford, 67/607.	656
Hill v. State, 64/454.	153
Hinkle v. Burt, 94/506.	777
Hodgkins v. Marshall, 102/191.	434
Holliday v. Griffith, 108/803.	438
Holmes v. Martin, 10/503.	725
Holmes v. Pye, 107/784.	204
Home Ins. Co. v. Augusta, 50/530.	76

Hood v. Von Glahn, 88/405.   494
Hornsby v. Butts, 85/694.   777
Hudgins v. State, 61/182.   148
Hudson v. Hudson, 87/678; 90/581.   316
Hudson v. Hudson, 98/147.   312
Hufbauer v. Jackson, 91/301.   240
Huff v. State, 104/524.   481
Hughes v. Griswold, 82/299.   306
Hughes v. Hughes, 72/174.   304
Huie v. McDaniel, 105/319.   675
Humphrey v. McGill, 59/649.   646, 709
Humphries v. State, 100/260.   278
Imboden v. Etowah Co., 70/86.   674
Inman v. Estes, 104/645.   548
Irvine v. Wynn, 107/402.   288
Jack v. Kehler, 55/639.   821
Jacobs v. State, 20/841.   541
James v. Sams, 90/404.   392
James v. Smith, 62/345.   230
Jeffries v. Bartlett, 75/230.   645
Johnson v. Dooly, 72/301.   710
Johnson v. Dorough, 99/644.   292
Johnson v. Franklin, 63/378.   333
Johnson v. Reese, 28/353 ; 31/601.   645
Johnson v. State, 48/117.   500
Johnson v. State, 76/76.   513
Johnson v. State, 90/441.   58, 154
Johnson v. State, 98/78.   509
Johnson v. State, 109/268.   500
Johnston v. Tatum, 20/775.   195
Jolly v. Lofton, 61/154.   339
Jones v. Hurst, 91/338.   104
Jones v. Newman, 110/   .   288
Jones v. Rountree, 96/230.   285
Jones v. State, 48/163.   163
Jones v. State, 90/616.   278
Jones v. State, 105/649.   500
Jones v. Sullivan, 33/486.   41
Jones v. Thacker, 61/329.   557
Jones v. Warnock, 67/484.   264
Joseph v E. T. R. Co., 92/332.   290
Joseph v. Milledgeville, 97/513.   77, 89
Jessey v. Ga. So. R. Co., 109/439.   627
Kahn v. Macon, 95/419.   493
Kaufman v Ferst, 55/350.   264, 826
Keck v. Gainesville, 98/425.   493
Keen v. Waycross, 101/588.   640
Kelly v. Jackson, 67/274.   178
Kirtland v. Davis, 43/318.   621

Kiser v. Carrollton Co., 96/761.   797
Kupferman v. Buckholts, 73/778.   333
Kyle v. Montgomery, 73/337.   355
Lambert v. Smith, 57/25.   801
Lane v. Macon R. Co., 96/630.   591
Lathrop v. Soldiers' Asso., 45/483.   619
Lee v. Hale, 77/1.   207
Leonard v. Collier, 53/387.   219
Lester v. Callaway, 73/731.   197
Lester v. McIntosh, 101/675.   288
Little v. Sexton, 89/411.   602
Little Rock Cooperage Company
   v. Hodge, 105/828.   435
Lockwood v. Barefield, 7/393.   191
Loid v. State, 104/726.   58
Lopez v. Downing, 46/120.   338
Love v. Anderson, 89/612.   339
Lovett v. Moore, 98/158.   602
Lowry v. Parker, 83/343.   221
Lunsford v. Malsby, 101/39.   552
Lynch v. Pollard, 40/173.   621
Mack v. State, 63/696.   143
Macon Sash Co. v. Macon, 96/23.   114
Maddox v. Gray, 75/452.   38
Malsby v. Young, 104/205.   175
Mansfield v. Turpin, 32/260.   307
Marchman v. Todd, 15/25.   358
Markham v. Huff, 72/874.   392
Marsh v. Lazenby, 41/153.   620
Marshall v. Charland, 106/42. 294, 307
Mason v. Comm'rs, 104/35.   587
Massey v. Ins. Co., 70/794.   446
Mathis v. Bagwell, 101/167.   204
Mayor of Hawkinsville v. Ethridge,
   96/326.   150, 167
Mayor of Leesburg v. Putnam,
   103/110.   378
Mayor of Marietta v. Alexander,
   86/455.   149
Mayor of Macon v. Macon Con-
   struction Co. 94/201.   71, 99
Mayor of Macon v. Wood, 109/149. 168
Mayor of Rome v. McWilliams,
   52/251.   89
Mayor of Savannah v. Hartridge,
   8/23.   77, 89
Mayor of Savannah v. Weed,
   84/683.   67, 79, 96
Mays v State, 91/720.   153

McAlpin v. Bailey, 76/687. 309
McAlpin v. Lee, 57/282. 41
McAlpin v. Purse, 86/271. 572
McCalla v. Am. F. Co., 90/113. 655
McClendon & Co. v. Hernando
  Phosphate Co., 100/223. 623
McCord v. Laidley, 87/221. 610
McCrory v. Hall, 104/668. 182
McGowan v. Lufburrow, 82/523. 701
McGowan v. Sav. Asso., 80/515. 66,102
McLaren v. Bradford, 52/648. 191
McLaws v. Moore, 83/177. 221
McLendon v. Harrell, 67/440. 556
McLendon v. LaGrange, 107/356. 68
McMahon v. Paris, 87/660. '317
McMillan v. Bell, 105/496. 401
McPherson v. State, 22/488. 490
McVicker v. Conkle, 96/595. 498
Merchants Bk. v. Haiman, 80/624. 603
Merchants and Mechanics Bank v.
  Tillman, 106/55. 658
Merritt v. Merritt, 66/324. 219
Miller v. Desverges, 75/407. 715
Miller v. Ennis, 107/663. 261
Miller v. Miller, 105/305. 261
Miller v. Redwine, 75/130. 48
Miller v. State, 94/1. 813
Miller v. State, 99/207. 129
Millirons v. Dillon, 100/656. 631
Minter v. State, 104/743. 119
Mitchell v. State, 71/128. 126
Mitchell v. State, 110/ . 484
Mitchum v. State, 11/615. 124
Mize v. Americus Co., 106/140. 359
Mohrman v. Augusta, 103/841. 168
Moncrief v. State, 99/395. 674
Monroe v. Foster, 49/514. 326
Moore v. Atlanta, 70/611. 388
Moore v. Medlock, 101/93. 392
Moore v. State, 96/309. 108
Moran v. Atlanta, 102/840. 493
Morgan v. Fidelity Co., 101/391. 585
Morgan v. Printup, 72/66. 777
Mundy v. VanHoose, 104/292. 67, 96
Murray v. State, 85/381. 145
Mut. Asso. v. Augusta, 109/73. 103
Nat. Bk. v. Danforth, 80/55. 655
Newton M. Co. v. White, 42/148. 828
Norton v. Paragon Co., 98/468. 479

O'Brien v. State, 109/51. 61, 63
Ocean S. Co. v. Cheeney, 95/381. 455
Oellrich v. Ga. R. Co., 73/389. 655
O'Kelley v. Faulkner, 92/521. 316
Osborne v. Hill, 91/137. 656
Overby v. Thrasher, 47/10. 197
Palmer v. Moore, 82/177. 50
Papworth v. Fitzgerald, 106/378. 380
Papworth v. Ryman, 108/780. 548
Papworth v. State, 103/36.
  57, 61, 63, 822
Parker v. Belcher, 87/110. 834
Parker v. Glenn, 72/637. 710
Parks v. State, 105/242. 503, 524
Patton v. State, 80/714. 826
Paulk v. Sycamore, 104/24. 168, 373
Paulk v. Sycamore, 104/728. 380, 495
Pearce v. Augusta, 37/597. 75
Pearson v. Brown, 105/802. 675
Perdue v. Ellis, 18/586. 376
Perkins v. State, 78/316. 490
Pettee v. Flewellen, 2/236. 789
Phinizy v. Clark, 62/623. 656
Phillips v. St. Mt., 61/386. 168, 372
Phipps v. Tompkins, 50/641. 197
Phœnix Ins. Co. v. Gray, 107/110. 108
Planters' Bk. v. Padgett, 69/159. 674
Plumb v. Christie, 103/686. 60
Ponder v. Shannon, 54/187. 639
Poullain v. Brown, 80/28. 312
Powell v. State, 101/9.
  123, 481, 488, 502, 524
Price v. Amis, 58/604. 578
Price v. Baynes, 57/176. 197
Price v. State, 72/441. 487
Prince v. State, 30/27. 490
Pritchett v. Davis, 101/236. 337
Pritchett v. Inferior Ct., 46/462. 473
Pryor v. Leonard, 57/136. 219
Pulliam v. Dillard, 71/598. 360
Radcliffe v. Biles, 94/480. 445
Rainey v. State, 100/82. 385
Rakestraw v. Lanier, 104/188. 726
Randle v. Stone, 77/501. 471
Ray v. Home Co., 106/492. 392
Ray v. Ray, 106/260. 465
Ray v. Strickland, 89/840. 191
Redding v. State, 91/231. 826
Reese v. Kirby, 68/825. 624

Reeves v. Graffling, 67/512. 211
Reinhart v. Blackshear, 105/799. 675
Richmond Co. v. Childress, 82/719. . . 612
Richmond Co. v. Shomo, 90/498. 254
Roberts v. Dickerson, 95/727. 261
Roberts v. State, 55/220. 165
Robinson v. Alexander, 65/406. 655
Robinson v. Donehoo, 97/702. 385
Robinson v. State, 84/680. 490
Robuck v. Harkins, 38/174. 833
Roe v. Maund, 48/462. 41
Rogers v. Kingsbery, 22/60. 834
Rogers v. Rogers, 78/688. 863
Roland v. Coleman, 76/652. 243
Rolfe v. Rolfe, 10/143. 159
Ross v. Campbell, 73/309. 38
Rothschild v. Darien, 69/503. 493
Rounsaville v. McGinnis, 93/579. 392
Rountree v. Lathrop, 69/539. 360
Rountree v. Rutherford, 65/444. 222
Rucker v. State, 97/205. 674
Russell v. Mohr-Weil Lumber
    Company, 102/563, 593. 580
Rutherford v. Ex. Com., 9/54 313
Ryan v. Am. Mge. Co., 96/322. 294
Ryan v. State, 45/128. 129
Saffold v. Wade, 56/174. 211
Salter v. Glenn, 42/64. 385
Sanderlin v. Willis, 94/171. 292
Sanders v. Bell, 56/443. 709
Sanders v. State, 60/126. 542
Sav. R. Co. v. Morton, 71/24. 94
Sawyer v. Cargile, 72/290. 646
Scarborough v. Hall, 67/576. 624
Schnell v. State, 92/459. 278
Schofield v. Woolley, 98/548. 665
Scoville v. Calhoun, 76/263. 415
Seymour v. Almond, 75/112. 413
Sharp v. Findley, 71/654. 701
Sharp v. Loyless, 39/678. 834
Sharpe v. Kennedy, 51/263. 627
Shattles v. Melton, 65/464. 337
Shaw v. State, 83/92. 385
Sheffield v. Clark, 73/92. 197
Shuman v. Smith, 100/415. 266
Sibley v. Mut. Asso., 87/738. 426
Singer Co. v. Wright, 97/114. . . 79, 228
Skellie v. Central R. Co., 81/56. 423
Skidaway Co v. O'Brien, 73/655. 606
Skipper v. Johnson, 21/310. 777

Small v. State, 63/386. 571
Smalls v. State, 99/26. 423
Smith v. Brown, 96/274. 182
Smith v. Champion, 102/92. 626
Smith v. Cuyler, 78/654. 602
Smith v. Eason, 46/316. 715
Smith v. Floyd County, 85/420. 387
Smith v. Green, 34/180. 222
Smith v. Smith, 36/190. 313
Smith v. State, 63/168. 532
Smith v. State, 88/627. 812
Smith v. State, 105/724. 56
Smith v. State, 106/673. . . . . 503, 524
Smith v. State, 109/227. 463
Smith v. Wilkes County, 79/127. 388
Smith v. Willis, 105/840. 264
Solomon v. Peters, 37/251. 645
Southern Star Lightning Rod Co.
    v. Cleghorn, 59/782. 664
Sparks v. Dunbar, 102/129. 828
Sparrow v. Pate, 67/352. 472
Spence v. Steadman, 49/133. 326
Springer v. State, 34/379. 385
Stafford v. State, 93/207. 490
Stancell v. Kenan, 33/56. 368
Stancell v. Ga. Loan Co., 96/227. . . . 306
Stansell v. Massey, 92/436. 240
Starke v. State, 93/217. 109
State v. Atkins, 35/319. 402
State v Central R. Co., 109/716. 751
Steam Laundry Co. v. Thompson,
    91/47. 345
Stephens v. Gas Co., 81/150. 801
Stewart v. State, 58/577. 815
Stewart v. Stisher, 83/300. 221
Stiles v. State, 57/183. 124
Stokes v. State, 73/816. 490
Story v. Brown, 98/570. 434
Strauss v. Waycross, 97/475. 495
Strong v. Atlanta Consol. St. Ry.
    Co., 97/695 285
Stroup v. Sullivan, 2/275. 833
Studstill v. State, 7/2. 540
Sullivan v. Hernden, 11/294. 644
Suttles v. Sewell, 105/129. 708
Suttles v. Sewell, 109/707. 805
Sutton v. McLeod, 29/589. . . . . 41, 655
Talmadge v. Interstate B. & L.
    Association, 105/550. 652
Tarver v. State, 95/222. 500

Taylor r. Gray, 20/77. 202
Taylor v. State, 105/847. 266, 675
Teal v. State, 22/75. 487
Teasley r. State, 104/738. 502, 524
Thomas v. State, 90/437. 130
Thomas v. State, 91/207. 522
Thomas v. State, 96/311. 53
Thompson v. Etowah Co., 91/538. 347
Timothy r. Chambers, 85/267. 335
Toler v. Passmore, 62/263. 578
Tomlinson v. Hardwick, 41/547. 197
Tompkins v. Cooper, 97/681. 632
Towns r. Mathews, 91/546. 207
Treadwell v. State, 99/779. 515
Trustees v. Atlanta, 76/189. 78
Upchurch r. Lewis, 53/621. 655
Vandigrift v. Potts, 72/665. 261
Varnedoe v. State, 75/181. 126
Verdery v. Summerville, 82/138. 67, 93
Vornberg v. Owens, 88/237. 207
Wade v. Weslow, 62/562. 333
Walden v. County of Lee, 60/296. 103
Walker v. Maddox, 105/255. 424
Walker v Sanford, 78/165. 412
Wallace v. Trustees, 52/167. 645
Walter v. Kierstead, 74/25. 801
Waring v. Savannah, 60/93. 77, 89
Watkins r. Angier, 99/519. 453
Wayne r. Myddleton, 2/383. 48
Weatherly r. Hardman, 68/592. 427
Weaver v. State, 89/639. 79
Welch v. State, 50/128. 480
Wells v. E. T. R. Co., 74/548. 355

Wells r. Savannah, 87/400. 67
Wells r. State, 102/658. 278
Werner r. Rawson, 89/619. 447
Western and Atlantic Railroad
    Co. v. Burke, 97/560. 680
Western & Atlantic R. Co. r. Ohio
    Valley Co., 107/512. 254
Western Union Tel. Co. v. Am.
    Union Tel. Co., 65/160. 726
Western Union Telegraph Co. r.
    Michelson, 94/436. 674
White r. Bleckley, 105/173. 548
White v. Int. Asso., 106/146. 294
White r. State, 100/659. 123
White Star Line Co. v. County of
    Gordon, 81/47. 238
Whitlow v. State, 74/819 815
Whitt v. Ketchum, 84/128. 261
Wilkerson v. State, 91/729. 123
Williams v. Augusta, 4/509. 169
Williams v. Barlow, 49/530. 646
Williams v. State, 69/13. 815
Williams v. Orient Insurance
    Company, 100/791. 243, 655
Willis v. State, 93/208. 813
Wilson v. Dozier, 58/602. 427
Wood v. McGuire, 21/576. 600
Wood v. State, 46/322. 53
Wood v. State, 48/192. 154
Woodson v. Veal, 60/562. 655
Wright v. Atlanta, 54/645. 77
Yahoola Co. v. Irby, 40/479. 41
Zellers v. Beckman, 64/747. 337

CASES

DECIDED IN THE

SUPREME COURT OF GEORGIA

AT THE

OCTOBER TERM, 1899.

UNION FRATERNAL LEAGUE *v.* .WALTON.

109
s112 31
f112 54
f112 54
f112 54
j112 54
109   1
d122 56

1. While a valid contract of insurance can not lawfully be taken on the life of another by one who has no insurable interest therein, because it contravenes public policy, yet, as one has an insurable interest in his own life, he may lawfully procure insurance thereon for the benefit of any other person whose interest he desires to promote. Such a contract can not be defeated because of the want of insurable interest in the beneficiary, when it appears that the person whose life was insured acted for himself, at his own expense and in good faith, to promote the interest of the beneficiary, in taking out the policy. A contract so entered into is in no sense a wagering or speculative one. LUMPKIN, P. J., dissenting.
2. A contract entered into by a benefit society with a member is executory, and its terms will be ascertained from the certificate issued to the member, in connection with the charter and laws of the society, subject to the law of the State under which it was created; and if nothing exists which restricts the appointment of a beneficiary to receive the benefit fund, the member may, at the time he executes the contract, legally designate whomsoever he pleases as beneficiary, and his right to do so can not be questioned.

Argued May 10, — Decided October 25, 1899.

Action on insurance certificate. Before Judge Hart. Laurens superior court. January term, 1899.

Anderson, Felder & Davis, for plaintiff in error.
Charles Z. McCord, contra.

LITTLE, J.   R. Annie Walton instituted an action against
the Union Fraternal League, an insurance corporation of the
State of Massachusetts, doing business in Georgia, to recover
the sum of two thousand dollars besides interest, being the
amount of a certain certificate of membership insurance issued
by the defendant company on the life of Sid A. Pughsly Jr.,
in which the plaintiff was named as the beneficiary.   The certificate was taken out by Sid A. Pughsly Jr. on his own life and
upon his own application, and kept in force at his own expense
as a member of the local lodge of the defendant company
doing business in Laurens county, Georgia.   To the petition
was annexed a copy of the certificate of membership and insurance, by which it appears that the defendant company undertook to pay, out of its beneficiary fund of the class in which
the certificate was issued, a sum of money not exceeding two
thousand dollars to Mrs. R. Annie Walton on the death of
Pughsly.   In the certificate the beneficiary, Mrs. Walton, is
named as "cousin."   Attached to the certificate are a number
of conditions to which no particular reference need be made.
Certain tables of designations and figures are also printed on
the back of the certificate, and in reference to them is a collection of rules designated as "laws on the foregoing table," which
seem to be more in the nature of explanation than of arbitrary
rule.   Among these we find the following: "Speculative risks
will not be tolerated, nor will any benefits be paid to other
than blood relatives, or dependents on the member."   "The
foregoing Plan of Family Protection is devised to insure permanent success, and to restrict the admission of undesirable
people."   It appears from the certificate that the defendant is
a Massachusetts corporation, and the signatory clause recites
that it was executed in Boston, Massachusetts.   It does not,
however, otherwise appear whether the contract was executed
in Georgia or Massachusetts, nor does the record contain the
charter of the defendant company, nor any part of its constitution or by-laws.   The defendant filed a demurrer to the petition, on the sole ground that it set forth no cause of action,
because it did not appear that the said Mrs. R. Annie Walton,
the beneficiary named in the certificate of insurance, had any

insurable interest in the life of the insured Pughsly, it being admitted as a fact on the hearing that the beneficiary was not related to the assured on whose life the insurance was taken out by himself for her benefit. The demurrer was overruled, and error assigned to that judgment. One question only arises for determination under the record in this case; that is, whether a beneficiary, named by a member of a fraternal or benevolent association which provides for life-insurance, is entitled, after the death of such member, to recover the amount of the benefit without showing any insurable interest in the life of the deceased. The contention of the plaintiff in error is that the contract under consideration must be governed by the principles of law applicable to ordinary contracts of life-insurance, and the legal proposition is submitted that a policy in favor of one who has no insurable interest is void, as it is a wager contract and against public policy. We can not assent to the correctness of this proposition.

A contract of life-insurance is defined by our Civil Code, § 2114, as one by which the insurer for a stipulated sum engages to pay a certain amount of money if another dies within the time limited by the policy. The last paragraph of this section is in the following words: "The life may be that of the assured, or of another in whose continuance the assured has an interest." Taken together, the meaning of the section is, that one may insure his own life without qualification ; that he may not insure the life of another unless he has an interest in the continuance of the life of that other. Necessarily, in the first instance, the amount of the policy is to be paid to some one other than the insured, because ordinarily under the contract the amount is not payable until his death. By section 2116 of the Civil Code it is provided that the assured may direct the money to be paid to his personal representative, or to his widow, or to his children or to his *assignee*; and it is further provided that when the insurer gives such directions, no other person can defeat the same, and that the assignment is good without such assent. We are aware that there is a seemingly irreconcilable conflict between the adjudicated cases as to whether the assignee of a life policy takes anything under the

assignment unless he has an insurable interest in the life insured.   But it will be noted that under the provisions of our
code no such qualifications are made essential to the validity
of the assignment, nor do we think under sound reasoning any
can exist.   The rule which restricts the execution of a valid
contract of insurance on the life of another to one who has an
insurable interest in that life is founded alone on public policy,
and it may be stated in general terms that where one has an
interest in a life that interest is insurable.   Beyond all controversy a man has an insurable interest in his own life,
and we fail to see, when having that interest he enters into
a contract with an insurer by which, for a stipulated sum
which he periodically pays, the insurer becomes liable to pay
a given sum of money at the death of the insured, why he who
is most interested, whether actuated by the ties of relationship,
motives of friendship, gratitude, sympathy or love, may not
make the object of his consideration the recipient of his own
bounty.   If it be replied that a temptation is extended to the
beneficiary by improper means to hasten the time when he
should receive the amount of the policy (and it is for this reason that such contracts will only be upheld when the idea of
temptation is rebutted by the natural ties of blood or affinity),
we might well ask ourselves why executory devises, bequests,
provisions for support and maintenance provided for friends
and even strangers are not subject to the same inhibition, as being against public policy.   But while, as we have before said,
many adjudicated cases, frequently contrary to natural justice,
clearly hold that unless the beneficiary or assignee has an insurable interest in the life of the insured the policy or assignment is void, we shall undertake to show by authority that
such is not the rule of the law.

Mr. Greenhood, in his treatise on the Doctrine of Public
Policy in the Law of Contracts, pp. 279, 280, lays down two
rules so abundantly supported by adjudicated cases as to make
their citation impractical here. The first is: " A policy of insurance issued on the life of one in whose life he to whom the policy is issued has no insurable interest, unless he is a mere trustee for the life-assured ; or a policy issued to one upon his own

life, if he be merely the agent of another who is without interest, for whose benefit the insurance is thus taken, although upon the face of it it is payable to such person, is void." The second is: "But one may insure his own life for the benefit of any person, although the latter may have no insurable interest in the life of the former." In support of the rule last laid down, the author quotes from a leading case, Provident Life Ins. Co. v. Baum, 29 Ind. 240, the following strong and expressive language: "It can not be questioned . . that a person has an insurable interest in his own life, and that he may effect such insurance, and appoint any one to receive the money in case of his death during the existence of such policy. It is not for the insurance company, after executing such a contract, and agreeing to the appointment so made, to question the right of such appointee to maintain the action. If there should be any controversy as to the distribution among the heirs of the deceased of the sum so contracted to be paid, it does not concern the insurers. The appellant's contract with the insured is to pay the money to the appellee, and upon such payment being made, it will be discharged from all responsibility. So far as the insurance company is interested, the contract is effective as an appointment of the appellee to receive the sum insured."

Mr. Joyce in his Treatise on Insurance, vol. 2, § 918, declares that "the weight of authority seems also to favor the proposition that if a person effects a valid insurance upon his own life, and the transaction is bona fide and not intended to circumvent the law, the assignment to another will be upheld, even though the assignee has no insurable interest in the life insured." In the case of Amick v. Butler, 111 Ind. 578, Mitchell, J., delivering the opinion, refers to this question in the following language: "It has never been seriously questioned but that a person may insure his own life, and by the terms of the policy appoint another to receive the money upon the event of the death of the person whose life is insured; or, having taken a policy valid in its inception, that he may in good faith assign his interest in such policy, as in any other chose in action." For which he cites: 51 Ind. 24; 53 Ind. 380; 3 Sim. 149; 138 Mass. 24; 11 R. I. 439. He further says, "In either

case the essential point is that the transaction be bona fide, and
not merely a cover for obtaining wagering or merely speculative insurance, and a device to evade the law," citing 29 Ind.
236 ; 85 N. Y. 593; 98 Mass. 381; 94 U. S. 457; 80 Ill. 35; 70
Pa. St. 450. And in relation to the conflict between such rulings and the adjudicated cases which seem to hold otherwise,
he says: "The cases which hold invalid the taking or assignment of insurance policies turn upon the fact that in each case
the transaction was found to be merely colorable, and a scheme
to obtain speculative insurance," citing 41 Ind. 116 ; 15 Wall.
643; 104 U. S. 775. Mr. Justice Bradley, in the case of Conn.
Mut. Life Ins. Co. *v.* Schaefer, 94 U. S. 460, in discussing what
is an insurable interest, says: "But precisely what interest is
necessary, in order to take a policy out of the category of mere
wager, has been the subject of much discussion. In marine and
fire insurance the difficulty is not so great, because there insurance is considered as strictly an indemnity. But in life insurance the loss can seldom be measured by pecuniary values.
Still, an interest of some sort in the insured life must exist. A
man can not take out insurance on the life of a total stranger,
nor on that of one who is not so connected with him as to make
the continuance of the life a matter of some real interest to
him. It is well settled that a man has an insurable interest in
his own life, and in that of his wife and children ; a woman in
the life of her husband; and the creditor in the life of his
debtor. Indeed, it may be said generally that any reasonable
expectation of pecuniary benefit or advantage from the continued life of another creates an insurable interest in such life.
And there is no doubt that a man may effect an insurance on
his own life for the benefit of a relative or friend ; or two or
more persons, on their joint lives, for the benefit of the survivor
or survivors. The old tontines were based substantially on this
principle, and their validity has never been called in question."

In the case of Loomis *v.* Eagle Life Ins. Co., 6 Gray, 399,
Chief Justice Shaw, delivering an opinion which involved the
question of insurable interest, used this language: "All, therefore, which it seems necessary to show, in order to take the
case out of the objection of being a wager policy, is that the

insured has some interest in the life of the *cestui que vie*; that his temporal affairs, his just hopes and well-grounded expectations of support, of patronage, and advantage in life will be impaired; so that the real purpose is not a wager, but to secure such advantages, supposed to depend on the life of another; such, we suppose, would be sufficient to prevent it from being regarded as a mere wager. Whatever may be the nature of such interest, and whatever the amount insured, it can work no injury to the insurers, because the premium is proportioned to the amount; and whether the insurance be to a large or small amount, the premium is computed to be a precise equivalent for the risk taken. Perhaps it would be difficult to lay down any general rule as to the nature and amount of interest which the assured must have. One thing may be taken as settled, that every man has an interest in his own life to any amount in which he chooses to value it, and may insure it accordingly." In the case of Sabin *v.* Phinney, 134 N. Y. 423, it was held that a member of the Ancient Order of United Workmen of New York can legally direct the sum due at his death to be paid to a stranger who has no insurable interest in his life. The true rule, as we take it on the authority of a very large number of cases collected in a note to the case of Morrell *v.* Trenton Ins. Co., a Massachusetts case reported in 57 Am. Dec. 102, is, that one may insure his life and make the amount of the policy payable to whom he pleases, provided the contract is not made at the expense and for the benefit of the person designated as the beneficiary, as a cover for a mere wagering contract. In the same note authorities are cited for the proposition, "that the insurable interest which one has in his own life is what supports the policy in such a case." As laid down in Field's Lawyer's Briefs, § 417, the rule is that "Any person may insure his own life for the benefit of his creditors, relatives, friends, or even strangers. But if the insurance is effected by some other person, it is essential that he have a pecuniary interest in the life of the assured." To the same effect see Robinson *v.* U. S. Accident Association, 68 Fed. Rep. 825; 85 N. Y. 593; 38 Conn. 294; 51 Vt. 625. We think also that this court has recognized the doctrine for which we

are contending, in the case of *Equitable Life Assurance Society*
v. *Paterson*, 41 *Ga.* 338, where McCay, J., declared that the
law which prohibits the insurance of a life by another who has
no interest in the continuance of that life is founded on a
sound public policy, and that it was intended to prevent gaming policies and to avoid that inducement to crime which
would exist if it were permitted. In the case then under consideration it appeared that a woman who contracted marriage
had at the time a living husband, making, of course, the last
contract of marriage void. While living together under such
void marriage, the supposed husband procured a policy of insurance on his life in favor of the woman with whom he was
then living. Payment of the policy was resisted on the ground
that she had no insurable interest in the life of the person insured. This court there held that such a contract of insurance
did not come within the reason of the law which prohibited
gaming policies, nor was it open to the objection that it offered
an inducement to crime. Judge McCay in his opinion, on this
subject, said: "Though the marriage was illegal, yet in fact
the woman had an interest, and a deep interest, in the life of
the husband. He treated her as his wife. He supported her
as such, she passed in society as such, and she was dependent
upon him for support as such. It was the husband who in
fact effected this policy. It was his own method of extending
to this woman his assistance and protection, after he should
himself be dead. Here is no gaming, since the very person
whose life is insured is himself the actor in the transaction.
So, too, as to the temptation to crime, offered to the beneficiary
of the policy. It would seem, when the person whose life is
insured is himself the actor in the matter, the amount of
temptation held out to others to take his life, may, as a general rule at least, be left to his discretion." Further on in the
same opinion, referring to the provision now found in our code
which expressly permits the insured to direct the money to be
paid to his assignee, he says, "and if he may do this, we do
not see that an insurance effected by him, as the assured of another, for that other's benefit, is not equally good."

We have entered into the discussion of this case at length,

because of the fact, as stated in the outset, that the adjudicated cases are in conflict. But we feel assured, both by reason and the long line of adjudicated cases to which only partial reference has been made, that the true rule which should obtain in such cases is, that where one obtains a contract of insurance on his own life and keeps up the same out of his own means, and directs the amount of the policy to be paid at his death to another whom from love, friendship, or any other reason he desires to benefit, the named beneficiary is entitled to recover on such contract, notwithstanding it may not be shown that he or she has any other insurable interest in the life of the deceased than exists in his good will and emanates from his expressed wish to benefit. It is, after all, but a gift from him to one whose interests he desired to promote and whose welfare he wished to protect when he was dead. Such a contract is in no sense a mere hazard, and is composed of none of the elements which make up a wagering policy, and it is only these that the law, mindful of the best interests of the citizen, prohibits. There is, however, another view to be taken of the question which arises in this case. Differences exist between contracts entered into under the plan of ordinary life-insurance and those made by benefit societies. We only call attention, however, to those differences which exist in the selection of the beneficiary. A contract entered into by a benefit society with a member is, of course, executory, and its terms and conditions are ordinarily manifested by the certificate of membership. In addition to such, the charter of the society, its constitution and by-laws necessarily form a part of such contract. 29 Ohio St. 557; 94 N. Y. 580; 44 Md. 429. The law which provides for the organization of a benefit society usually specifies the classes of persons who may be made beneficiaries of the insurance; and where the organic law of the society, or the charter procured from the State under that law, prescribes what classes of persons may become beneficiaries of its insurance, it is not in the power of the society or one of its members, or both, to enlarge or restrict these classes; for the society has no authority to create a fund for a person who does not belong to one of such classes, and the member has no right or power to

designate such person as his beneficiary. Niblack on Accident
Insurance and Benefit Societies, § 158, citing 76 Mich. 146;
13 Bush (Ky.), 489; 146 Mass. 286. Under an act of the State
of Michigan which authorized the organization of societies to
secure to the family or heirs of any member upon his death a
certain sum of money, it was held that no other person than a
member of the family or an heir of the person insured could
be made a beneficiary, and an old army comrade and intimate
friend who had been designated by the member as the beneficiary could not take. Mutual Benefit Society *v.* Hoyt, 46 Mich.
473. A large number of adjudicated cases supporting this
principle may be found in Bacon's Treatise on the Law of
Benefit Societies and Life Insurance, § 237; and the reason
which underlies the rule is, that the member of the society has
under his contract no interest nor property in the benefit, but
has simply the power to appoint some one to receive it. If,
however, there is nothing in the charter or by-laws of the organization, nor in the statutes of the State, restricting the appointment, the member may designate whomsoever he pleases,
and no one can question the right. 1 Bacon, Ben. Soc. § 246;
Massey *v.* Mutual Relief Society, 102 N. Y. 523; Knights of
Honor *v.* Watson (N. H.), 15 Atl. Rep. 125; Walton *v.* Odd
Fellows Society, 42 Minn. 204.

In the present case, while it appears on the face of the certificate that the plaintiff in error is a Massachusetts corporation, none of the provisions of the charter appear in the record, nor any portion of its constitution or by-laws is set out,
nor can it be now determined whether the contract of insurance is to be governed by the laws of the State of Massachusetts or by those of Georgia. Hence, no restriction of the
power of the member to name the beneficiary is made to appear, and the certificate evidencing a contract of life-insurance
similar to those entered into by mutual companies, the case
will be determined under the general law applicable to insurance contracts. It is true that on the back of the certificate
appears a condensation of certain explanations in which it is
asserted that speculative risks will not be tolerated nor benefits paid to other than blood relatives or dependents. It does

not appear, however, unqualifiedly, as it is arranged, that it is one of the conditions referred to in the certificate, and without further explanation we are not able to say that it is. Therefore, so far as the record appears, there was nothing to restrict the designation of the beneficiary by Pughsly at the time he entered into the contract, and by the terms of the contract the benefit fund is made expressly payable to the defendant in error. Being so, and treating this contract as subject to the law which fixes the insurable interest of a beneficiary where the policy is taken out and maintained by the insured, no reason appears why the defendant in error was not entitled to maintain her action; and the judgment of the court below in overruling the demurrer is

Affirmed. All the Justices concurring except

LUMPKIN, P. J., dissenting. A policy of life-insurance naming as the beneficiary thereof one who has no insurable interest in the life of the insured is a wagering policy, and therefore void, although taken out by the insured at his own expense. Independently of adjudications rendered outside of this State, I am of the opinion that the question raised in this case is settled by section 2114 of the Civil Code, which reads as follows: "An insurance upon life is a contract by which the insurer, for a stipulated sum, engages to pay a certain amount of money if another dies within the time limited by the policy. The life may be that of the *assured,* or of another in whose continuance the *assured* has an interest." That is to say, the life insured may be that of the beneficiary named in the policy, or the life of another person in the continuance of which life the beneficiary has an insurable interest. "The beneficiary of an insurance policy may be defined as the party to whom the proceeds are made payable by the terms of the contract;" and "beneficiary" and "assured" are synonymous terms, though the former is the more commonly used. 3 Am. & Eng. Enc. L. (2d ed.) 926.

The question at issue was neither made in nor passed upon by this court in the case of *Equitable Life Assurance Society* v. *Paterson,* 41 *Ga.* 338. It is true the report of that case discloses that in the requests to charge, made by counsel for the defendant, this question was presented to the trial judge for his determination; but the motion for a new trial, the denial of which was the only ruling excepted to, did not in the remotest manner invoke a decision of the question whether one can take out a valid policy of insurance on his own life for the benefit of a stranger; nor is any such question dealt with in the synopsis of the points decided, which, under our statute, is the official announcement of the decision rendered. Accordingly, the remarks of Judge McCay upon the subject of insurable interest should be treated as merely obiter and in no sense binding as authority.

MORRIS, administrator, *v.* GEORGIA LOAN, SAVINGS AND BANKING COMPANY *et al.*

1. A creditor of a person having his life insured, who takes an assignment of the policy to secure his debt, is only entitled to retain after collection of the policy such an amount as is sufficient to pay the debt together with all advances the creditor has made to keep the policy in force. If a balance remains, the payees named in the policy are entitled to receive it. Accordingly, where the amount of the debt is in issue, it must be ascertained, like any other question of fact, by the verdict of a jury.
2. Where an individual has an interest in a promissory note which he knows was given without consideration, and such individual as cashier of a bank, having full authority and control of the discounts of the bank without reference to or consultation with any other officer of the bank, discounts such note with the funds of the bank, the latter is not a bona fide purchaser of the note, without notice. If it ratifies the act of its officer and claims title to the note, it must take it subject to the knowledge which the officer who discounted it had at the time.
3. It was error to have granted a nonsuit in this case, there being evidence from which the jury might have found a verdict for the plaintiff.

Argued May 25, — Decided October 25, 1899.

Complaint. Before Judge Reid. City court of Atlanta. January term, 1899.

Anderson, Felder & Davis and *Arnold & Arnold,* for plaintiff. *Dorsey, Brewster & Howell,* for defendants.

LITTLE, J. Morris, as administrator of Ragland, instituted an action against Cassin, Purtell, and the Georgia Loan, Savings and Banking Company, a corporation doing business in the city of Atlanta, to recover the sum of $4,556.31, with interest, which he claims the defendants to be due to him under the following alleged facts: In May, 1895, Ragland procured from the Connecticut Mutual Life Insurance Company a policy of insurance upon his own life, for the sum of five thousand dollars, on which the annual premium was $103.15; the premiums were payable quarterly, and Ragland paid such premiums as were due on May 27 and August 27, 1895. Being unable to continue the payment of the premiums, Cassin and Purtell agreed to advance to him the amounts necessary to pay the same as they became due, and, to secure payment of the amount so advanced, Ragland assigned the policy to Cassin and Purtell, who required and received of Ragland his promissory note dated December 11, 1895, for $4,300 principal, to become due one year after date. This pretended debt was fictitious except as to the premiums advanced by Cassin and Purtell. At the time of these transactions Cassin was the cashier of the defendant banking company. After the execution of the note, Cassin and Purtell indorsed it in blank and made a pretended transfer of it to the defendant banking company, which took the same with notice of its character. On November 5, 1896, Cassin and Purtell also transferred the policy of insurance to the banking company. A short time thereafter Ragland died. Cassin, as cashier of the banking company, made out and forwarded proofs of death, and on the 31st day of December, 1896, the insurance company paid to the banking company the face value of the policy, five thousand dollars, which was consented to by the plaintiff under notice that he as administrator would claim from the banking company the amount so paid, less what had been advanced to Ragland by Cassin and Purtell. Of the five thousand dollars the banking company retained $4,663.11, and $309.89 was received by Ragland's administrator. By the terms of the policy the amount insured was payable to the representatives of Ragland, and the only claim that Cassin and Purtell and the banking company have on the fund is the amount of one premium, $106. No services were rendered, accepted, or contracted for from Cassin, Purtell, or the banking company. Defendants answered, admitting certain allegations, and denying others which raised an issue as to the good faith of the defendants in taking the note and assignment of the policy. It was also admitted that Cassin was cashier of the defendant banking company. On the trial the policy of insurance was introduced in evidence, being for the sum of five thousand dollars, dated May 27, 1895, providing for an annual premium of $103.15, insuring the life of Hudson E. Ragland, and payable to his executors, administrators, or assigns, and containing other stipulations not necessary to be enumerated. To this policy were attached certain assignments, one from H. E. Ragland to H. A. Cassin and J. H. Purtell, dated December 11, 1895, consideration five dollars; the second, by Cassin and Purtell to the banking company, reciting a consideration of $4,609.60. Certain letters were also introduced, written by the insurance company to Cassin in 1896, acknowledging the receipt from the latter of two payments of $26.55 for premiums on the policy of insurance, and of copy of assignment of the policy, and later of the receipt of the policy with releases duly executed.

The oral testimony was, briefly stated, as follows: Mr. Felder, one of the counsel for the plaintiff in error, testified, that he knew Ragland, who was stenographer for the witness's firm. Ragland died about December, 1896. He received from $25 to $30 per month for his services as a stenographer; he was very poor, and witness never saw any signs of his having any large amount of money at any time; he had no visible property up to the date of his death. There was no evidence of his having any more money than what he received from his salary. Witness's firm had an office in the building known as "Temple Court"; the defendant banking company, Cassin, and Purtell were just across the street. Purtell had an office which was either connected with some company that Cassin was following, or in the back room of the bank building. Cassin had an office designated by the sign "Cashier," the bank business being immediately in rear of it. "I went over to see Cassin to talk with him about this matter of insurance; I knew him

very well. Purtell was present on one occasion. We had prepared the petition in this suit. I said to Cassin that I supposed he did not desire the petition filed, that as a matter of
course he did not let Ragland have the money, and I did not
think he could insist on keeping it. I told him he was not
entitled to anything more out of the policy than he put into it.
He said he thought he was, that he was entitled to it without
reference to the amount of money he put in the policy, and
said he was going to contend for it, or words to that effect. I
said, 'Cassin, you didn't put into this policy any more money
than the premiums advanced.' He said either he or Purtell
or both had given Ragland something additional, $25 or $30
above the premium. I told him that if he could stand the
suit we could, and that I would file the petition. He then
asked me to wait until the next day, so that he could see a
lawyer and get advice as to whether or not they could hold the
money. I did not call again, but was sent for, and Cassin
said that he had discussed the matter with Purtell, and they
had been advised that they had a right, without reference to the
amount of money advanced to Ragland, to keep the whole proceeds of the policy. He did not mention paying anything except
the premium and a small amount of $25 or $30. I told him that
any claim that he let Ragland have any money was absurd,
and he admitted it. The conversation occurred in the office
of the Georgia Loan, Savings & Banking Company. No one else
was present, and no one higher in authority than Cassin. Cassin represented the bank, was acting as cashier." Witness further stated that the occasion of his visit was to see both Cassin
and the bank; his understanding was that Cassin was the bank;
had been there several times, and had never seen any one else
doing anything. "Cassin or Purtell told me they had transferred the policy to the bank for a valuable consideration. The
conversation was after the death of Ragland, and the money
had been collected. Ragland was not a robust, vigorous man;
he was a very small, delicate young man."

Herrington testified, that he was security on the bond of
Morris as administrator; he went to the bank at different times
with and also without Morris; whenever he went there Cassin

represented the bank; no one else acted on behalf of the bank
in paying the money, or claimed to be interested for the bank,
except Cassin; no one seemed to be over him or to have charge
of him on the subject. "When I went there Cassin said he
would pay the difference between the note and the policy, and
that was all he would do. I enquired of him about the note
and how he came to obtain it, and he gave me to understand
that I need not pry into his business. I asked him how the
boy [Ragland] came to give him the note; he said, 'The note
will speak for itself.' That was in the place of business of the
bank." Moyers testified: Knew Cassin and had some knowledge of the Georgia Loan, Savings & Banking Co., and some
dealings with it. "Since I have known the company Cassin
was in charge of it so far as I could see and know; have known
it for 8 or 9 years. They were originally in an upstairs room
at the corner of Alabama and Whitehall; Cassin was in charge.
They then removed to the corner of Loyd and Alabama; Cassin still had charge, so far as I know. From there they moved
to 24 South Pryor. My office was in the adjoining building. I
saw that place of business repeatedly during the day, and, so
far as I could know, see, and judge, Cassin was in charge of it
then. I did not know of any one else having active control of
affairs; had many business dealings with the bank; Cassin
acted in its behalf, and I recall no transaction I ever had with
it that he did not immediately act. Knew some of the directors; knew Grant who was president when I first got ac-
quainted with the institution, also knew Gress by sight. I do
not mean to say that Cassin was the owner of the bank, but
the Big Boss, so far as his conduct was concerned." Smith testified: Was related to Ragland by marriage; he died about
September, 1896, had no property and no means and no income, except his salary as stenographer, that witness knew.
Gress testified: He was president of the Georgia Loan, Savings
& Banking Company in 1895 and 1896; Cassin was the cashier. Witness took no part with Cassin and Purtell in getting
the note and insurance policy from Ragland; had nothing to
do with discounting the note; was out of the city; knew the
paper was in there, but didn't know whose it was; he found it

afterwards in the assets of the bank before it was due. We had papers on a large number of borrowers; didn't know anything about the people.

This evidence being submitted, defendants moved for a nonsuit. The plaintiff then offered to amend his petition by averring that the note of $4,300 was given by Ragland for an advance of $106, and that $4,194 of the sum was usury, and that the bank is affected with notice thereof. The amendment was objected to, disallowed by the court, and a judgment was then rendered granting a nonsuit in the case, to which the plaintiff excepted. An exception is also taken to the refusal of the court to require the defendant banking company to produce its books under a subpœna duces tecum.

1. It is insisted on the part of the plaintiff that there was evidence before the court which would have authorized the jury to find that, having made a valid contract of insurance on his life, payable to his executors, administrators, and assigns, Ragland was induced by the two defendants Cassin and Purtell to transfer and assign the policy to them for a consideration of $25 or $30 in addition to the payment of certain subsequent premiums as they fell due, and that the note of $4,300 delivered by Ragland to the assignees was really without any consideration and made as a cover to conceal the nakedness of the transfer. An examination of the evidence contained in the record shows that the policy was issued to Ragland on May 27, 1895, and that the assignment of the policy to Cassin and Purtell was made on December 11, 1895, more than six months thereafter. It does not appear that Cassin paid any premiums until May subsequent to the assignment, and for aught that appears in the record the policy evidences a good and valid contract insuring the life of Ragland. If it be true that there was no consideration for the note of $4,300, and that the same was executed and delivered by Ragland only for the purpose of enabling the assignees to claim the entire amount of the policy, it must fail to accomplish that result; for as a matter of law an assignment of a policy of life-insurance to a creditor by the insured, and for the purpose of securing his indebtedness, is valid only in the amount of the debt and the expenses incurred by the cred-

2

itor in keeping up the policy.   In 2 May on Insurance, § 459
A, it is said, "A creditor's claim upon the proceeds of insurance
intended to secure the debt should go no further than indemnity, and all beyond the debt, premiums, and expenses should
go to the debtor and his representatives, or remain with the company, according as the insurance is upon life or on property."
And in 13 Am. & Eng. Enc. L. (1st ed.), 648, it is declared, on
the authority of adjudicated cases cited, that, "Where the assignment is for the purpose of securing a creditor, although he
is entitled to recover the face of the policy, he can not hold
what is not necessary for his indemnity.   The legal representatives of the debtor will be entitled to the balance."   A case
which seems directly in point is that of Cammack *v.* Lewis, 82
U. S. 643, where it appeared that L. was indebted to C. in
the sum of $70, and at C.'s suggestion L. took out a policy on
his life for $3,000, for which C. paid the premium.   Imme-
diately after the policy was issued, L. gave to C. a note for
$3,000, and assigned to him the policy of insurance.   A short
time thereafter L. died, and the widow filed a bill to recover
the amount of the policy (or rather such a part of it as she
had not theretofore received).   In delivering the opinion of
the court, Mr. Justice Miller said: "We think that Cammack
could, in equity and good conscience, only hold the policy as
security for what Lewis owed him when it was assigned, and
such advances as he might afterwards make on account of it,
and that the assignment of the policy to him was only valid
to that extent."   See also the case of *Exchange Bank of Macon*
v. *Loh,* 104 *Ga.* 446, where this court held that a creditor has,
for the purpose of indemnifying himself against loss and for
no other, an insurable interest in the life of his debtor, and
that the insurance will be available to the creditor to no greater
extent than the amount of his insurable interest at the time
the insurance was effected, viz., the amount of the then existing indebtedness.   So that, if it be true that at the time he
executed and delivered the promissory note for $4,300 and
assigned the policy of insurance to Cassin and Purtell, Ragland was in fact a debtor to the assignees in an amount less
than the face of the policy, the effect of the assignment was

to vest in the assignees title to so much of the fund collected as equalled the amount of the true indebtedness. The original contract of insurance made the executors and administrators of Ragland, as well as his assigns, the payees of the policy after payment of the debt his assignment secured. The administrator would in law be entitled to have the balance. But it is urged that, even if the note was without consideration, the inference is legally irresistible that the purpose of the parties in the execution of the note and the assignment of the policy of insurance was an accommodation. How this is we, of course, do not know. Only a jury under proper instructions should determine that fact.

2. It is further insisted by counsel for defendants, that the evidence showed that the banking company was a bona fide holder of the note and transferee of the policy of insurance, for value, before due, and that this fact precludes a recovery by the administrator. A bona fide holder of a negotiable promissory note receiving the same before due, for value, is protected against a plea of failure of consideration. But the subject-matter of the present action is to recover from the defendants a sum of money which it is alleged they collected and which belongs to the plaintiff. The collection of the money and its retention by the defendants can not be based on the fact that they are innocent holders of a promissory note of the insured received before due, for value; the money for which suit was brought did not come into the hands of the defendants as the proceeds of any negotiable instrument; and their right to collect the policy and to hold the amount as payment of the note depends upon the assignment of the policy, and not upon the manner in which they hold the note. A policy of insurance is a contract which is not negotiable, but is assignable, and the law which protects the bona fide holder of a negotiable promissory note, when received before due and for value, in no sense applies to the transfer or assignment of a contract of insurance. Unless the assignor has a right or interest in the contract which he is capable of assigning, the assignee takes nothing by the assignment, and that he has such right and interest the assignee must determine at his peril. "A policy of insurance

is assignable as well absolutely as by way of mortgage or
pledge to secure a debt." It is a "chose in action, governed
by the same principles applicable to other agreements involving pecuniary obligations." Bliss on Life Insurance, § 328.
Being a chose in action, a contract of this character may be
assigned so as to vest the title in the assignee, but the latter
takes it subject to the equities existing between the assignor and
debtor at the time of the assignment. Civil Code, § 3077.
However, we are not disposed to omit from our consideration
the important legal question on which the parties are at issue,
and which must ultimately control the disposition of the fund
arising from the collection of the policy of insurance. It is
contended by counsel for the plaintiff, if the note given by
Ragland was without consideration and received by the payees as a cover under which they might hold the policy by
transfer, that the knowledge of Cassin, one of the payees, of the
character of the note must be imputed to the bank of which
he was cashier. This contention is denied by counsel for the
defendants, who insist that even if the theory of the plaintiff
be correct as to the origin of this note and the scheme which
Cassin is charged with having engineered, then the bank is not
chargeable with any notice or knowledge of Cassin; and that
if it discounted the note before due and for a valuable consideration, the law will not impute to it the knowledge of Cassin.

Assuming, for the sake of the argument, that the note at its
execution was without consideration, invalid, and part of a
scheme to defraud, it becomes important to ascertain what
business relation Cassin, one of the payees, bore to the banking
company, and in what manner the note was negotiated. One
of the witnesses testified that he had known the banking company for eight or nine years; that Cassin was apparently in
charge of affairs; that witness knew of no one else having active control of affairs besides Cassin ; that witness had a great
many business dealings with the bank; that Cassin acted for
the bank whenever such dealings were had, and he does not
recall any transaction ever had with the bank where Cassin
did not act. The president of the bank testified that he knew
nothing about any of the notes or any of the parties to any of

the bank notes, and had nothing to do with the discounting of
them; he was out of the city when Ragland's note was discounted; he afterwards found it in the assets of the bank. For
aught that appears in the record, no other officer of the bank
ever knew of or had anything to do with the note of Ragland
and the policy of insurance until after the former was discounted and the latter transferred. Therefore, what was done
for the bank was done by Cassin without consultation. And
just here we may call attention to the difference which existed
in the manner of conducting the business of this banking company and that of ordinary banks of discount. Usually, in the
latter, the question of discounting paper comes before the
board of directors or a committee, and the cashier is but the
executive officer to carry out their decision; his duties are ordinarily strictly executive. It is, however, nevertheless true
that, beyond his inherent powers, the cashier may be authorized to act for the bank by the organic law, by action of the
stockholders, by a vote of the board, by usage and tacit approval. 1 Morse on Banks and Banking, § 165. If it be assumed in this case that the duties inherent in the office of
cashier do not fix the status of Cassin as such officer of the
bank for the discounting of commercial paper as would make ·
the bank chargeable with a notice to him, the evidence fully
warrants the conclusion that he in fact, by permission of those ·
interested in the bank, did exercise those duties, and that no
one else did. Our Civil Code, § 3027, declares that notice to
the agent of any matter connected with his agency is notice to
the principal; and, under this established rule of law, it is insisted that when Cassin represented the bank and discounted
the note of Ragland payable to himself and Purtell, he did it
as the agent of the bank and with full knowledge at that time
that it was entirely without consideration, and that therefore
the bank is not a bona fide holder without notice. While conceding the general rule, counsel for the defendants insist that
it is qualified by a well-recognized exception, and that the
true rule is clearly set out in the opinion in the case of Bene-
dict v. Arnoux, 154 N. Y. 715, as follows: "So long as the
agent acts within the scope of his employment, in good faith,

for the interest of his principal, he is presumed to have disclosed to his principal all the facts that come to his knowledge; but just as soon as the agent forms the purpose of dealing with his principal's property for his own benefit and advantage, or for the benefit or advantage of other persons who are opposed in interest, he ceases in fact to be an agent acting in good faith for the interest of his principal, and such purpose is deemed to be in fraud on the rights of his principal, and the presumption that he discloses all facts that have come to his knowledge no longer prevails."

We are not prepared to admit that, where the agent has notice, the doctrine of implied notice to the principal rests alone on the presumption that the agent will disclose his knowledge to his principal. Many adjudicated cases place it there; others do not; and we shall take occasion presently to cite some of the latter, and present some of the reasons why the Arnoux case, supra, falls short of settling the rule applicable to the case at bar. We may say here, that we find it impracticable to review in detail the many interesting and pertinent cases cited by counsel for defendants. Necessarily, in stating the reasons which impel our conclusions, we, to some extent at least, discuss the principles which they enunciate. Taking the rule of constructive notice as stated in our code to be fully established, and considering in connection therewith the exceptions to this general rule urged by counsel, we call attention to the view of Judge Story as expressed in his work on Agency, § 140. He says: "Notice of facts to an agent is constructive notice thereof to the principal himself, where it arises from, or is at the time connected with, the subject-matter of his agency; for, upon general principles of public policy, it is presumed that the agent has communicated such facts to the principal; and if he has not, still, the principal having entrusted the agent with the particular business, the other party has a right to deem his acts and knowledge obligatory upon the principal; otherwise, the neglect of the agent, whether designed or undesigned, might operate most injuriously to the rights and interests of such party." In discussing the duty of the agent to communicate the knowledge which he has to the principal, Mr. Wade, in his treatise on the Law of Notice, § 690, says: "The restriction of the rule to cases where there is a probability that the agent will communicate the knowledge seems to have had its origin in a total misapprehension of the purposes for which the rule was established. It tends to defeat the application of the doctrine to cases where it is most essential in the promotion of good faith and fair dealing;" and cites the following case as an example: A solicitor acted for both parties in preparing a deed which contained a covenant against prior incumbrances. The same solicitor had previously prepared a mortgage on the identical property. The court held that the fact that the solicitor was employed by the party whose interest it was to conceal the prior mortgage was sufficient evidence that it was concealed from the principal, and he was therefore unaffected by the knowledge of his agent. Further referring to this case, the author says: "Leaving out of consideration the probable event of its being utterly impossible for the agent to communicate the knowledge in time, the case cited above fairly illustrates the danger of resting the rule upon the presumption that the agent communicates the knowledge of which he is possessed, unless such presumption is conclusive. The doctrine announced in this case is against the weight of authority, both in England and in this country." Again, this author in § 683b declares, upon authority, that "A corporation will always be affected when the notice comes to it through an officer within whose special line of duty the matter in question lies," and that "The cashier of a bank is the particular officer who has charge of the ordinary business of the bank, and for this reason notice of facts affecting its business will bind the corporation." In treating of the effect of notice to directors and other officers of a corporation, the same author in section 683a declares: "And where he [the officer] acts for the corporation in the transaction of the business in respect to which it is sought to charge it with notice; as where he, as one of the board of directors, authorizes the discount of a note procured by fraud, of which he had notice, the bank would be bound as though his knowledge had been communicated to the entire board. When the fact in question comes to the knowledge of a director or other officer when he is making authorized official inquiry, or is otherwise engaged officially for his principal, it can be of no consequence that he fails to communicate it"; citing 121 Mass. 490; 2 Hill, 454; 25 Conn. 446; 34 N. Y. 30; 27 N. H. 157. Mr. Pomeroy (2 Equity Jur. § 666), after declaring that the rule which we are considering alike includes and applies to the positive information or knowledge obtained or possessed by the agent in the transaction and to actual or constructive notice communicated to him therein, says: "The *rationale* of the rule has been differently stated by different judges; by some it has been rested entirely upon the presumption of an actual communication between the agent and his principal; by others, upon the legal conception that for many purposes the agent and principal are regarded as one."

We admit the existence of many adjudicated cases which seemingly support the contention of the defendants as to the exception to the general rule under which they claim that the banking company is entitled to hold the note of Ragland, freed from any implied notice of Cassin's fraud, if such there be. But a distinction must be drawn in these cases between the exception and the rule. We concede it to be a sound proposition that where an officer or agent of the corporation, as a party in interest for himself, deals with the corporation, the latter is not charged with notice of the information possessed by such officer or agent so dealing, but it is because in such a transaction the assumed agent is in realty the adverse party and is not to be treated in so dealing as an agent of the corporation at all. And many, if not a majority, of the cases which announce the doctrine that when the agent has an interest in the transaction which would be prejudiced by the disclosure of the information, the presumption of its communication does not prevail, will be found to be where the agent or officer acts in his individual capacity and treats with some other officer or agent of the corporation. In these cases the two parties to the contract are the corporation and the individual who happens to be an officer of the corporation but acting in the prosecution in his individual capacity. But the principle involved in those cases can not be fully applicable to a case where one party, having knowledge of the invalidity of a paper of which he is the ostensible owner, discounts it in a bank of which he is the duly authorized agent, and is himself the only actor for the bank and by his act enables the bank to collect and retain the proceeds of such paper against the rights of the true owner. In such a transaction he is either the agent of the bank to discount the paper, or he is not. If he is not, then the discounting was illegal, and the owner is entitled to it or its proceeds. If he is the agent of the bank and the facts insisted on here existed, his action would be a fraud upon the rights of the owner, of which the bank can not take advantage. In the case of First National Bank *v.* New Milford, 36 Conn. 93, it appeared that Conklin was at the same time treasurer of the town and cashier of the bank; that he took $3,000 from the bank for his own use and executed a note to it for the amount as treasurer of the town, he having been allowed and accustomed to make loans for the bank without consulting the directors. The money he received was put to his personal use; none of the officials of the town knew of the existence of the note until afterwards when the defalcations of Conklin became public. At the date of the note the town was not in need of money. On the question of the knowledge of the bank, the court in that case said: "If Conklin, as agent of the town, had applied to the directors for a loan, offering the note and telling them that he had drawn it, not for the benefit of the town, but for his own benefit, without consulting the officers of the town, and when there was a sufficient supply of money in the treasury, it must be conceded that the board would in making the loan have been *particeps criminis* in the fraud, and the bank could not recover. . . We can not perceive that that case would differ from this. The contract, if any was made, was made by Conklin on behalf of the bank. No other mind but his met the mind of the agent of the town in making the contract. He as agent of the bank had full knowledge, therefore, of the fraud; and now the bank, if they ratify his contract and confirm his agency, must accept his knowledge and be bound by it, precisely as if the loan had been made and the knowledge had by the board of directors."

The Supreme Court of New Hampshire has ruled, that if one without authority assume to act as the agent of another, and the latter take the benefit of the unauthorized act by claiming rights under it, or otherwise ratifying the acts of his self-appointed agent, he must take such benefit with notice of such matters as appear to have been within the knowledge and recollection of the agent at the time of the transaction.   13 N. H. 145.   And it seems to be established that where one is an officer of two corporations which have business transactions with each other, his knowledge can not be attributed to either corporation in a matter in which he did not represent it.   If he did represent one or both, his action would be binding and his knowledge would attach to the one represented.   Smith *v*. Farrell, 66 Mo. App. 14; 118 Ill. 625; 47 N. W. Rep. 402; 2 Hill, 451; 72 N. Y. 286; 11 S. C. 396.   In a case reported in 134 Mass. 453, it appeared that B. as trustee held certain trust funds; that as an individual he owned a bank.   F. was the cashier of the bank and was also agent of B.   F. as agent was in possession of certain moneys belonging to B.'s trust fund, and wrongfully paid the same in discharge of a private indebtedness which B. owed the bank, either to himself as cashier or to the teller.   On a bill filed by the cestui que trust the court ruled, that the bank must restore the money; that F.'s knowledge was the knowledge of the bank; that the bank could not receive the trust funds except charged with the knowledge that the cashier had, and subject to the responsibilities which that involved; and said: "If F. was the instrument of B. in committing a fraud on the bank by unlawfully transferring to it the securities of another, whether he concealed this fact or not, the bank could not take the securities from his hands or hold them in its custody except with the knowledge he had.   The only authority the bank could have to hold or sell them was under the contract made by or through Fuller, its cashier."   In the case of Davis Co. *v.* Davis Co., 20 Fed. Rep. 699, where the transaction was had between one, who was an officer, with other agents of the corporation, two propositions are discussed and decided which refer to the distinction above suggested.   The first is, that "A corporation is charged with notice of facts known to a director who is an active agent of the corporation in the transaction affected by his knowledge, although he acquired his knowledge unofficially." The second is, that "A corporation is not charged with notice of facts known to its officer or agent in a transaction between him and the corporation in which he is acting for himself and not for the corporation." In the case of *Brobston* v. *Penniman*, 97 *Ga.* 527, it appeared that three persons formed a partnership. Two of the three were, respectively, president and cashier of a bank. The two persons holding said offices, without the knowledge of the third, executed and delivered to the bank in which they were officers a promissory note in the name of the partnership, to raise a sum of money which they had agreed to put in the partnership business. It was held that the knowledge of the president and cashier of the facts mentioned was the knowledge of the bank itself, and that the bank was not entitled to recover against the partnership. See also 72 N. Y. 286; 19 Hun, 354. It was held In re Millward-Cliff Cracker Co., 28 Atl. Rep. 1072, that "the fraud of a bank president in contriving and negotiating in his bank fraudulent notes of a corporation, for his own use, imputes knowledge to the bank, and it has no claim against the corporation."

3. It is our opinion that, under the evidence submitted, a jury would have been authorized to find that the insurance policy was a good and valid contract; that the execution of the promissory note and the transfer of the policy of insurance by Ragland to Cassin and Purtell were without consideration and in fraud of the payees of the policy, the executors and administrators of Ragland, and that the defendant banking company took the note and the transfer of the policy of insurance with the knowledge of Cassin that the same was fraudulent and without consideration. We do not, of course, mean to be understood as intimating that these facts are conclusively established by the evidence, but only that a jury could under the evidence have found them to be true, and if they had the plaintiff in the action would have been entitled to recover. The court having granted a nonsuit, thereby refusing to permit the jury to render a verdict under the evidence in the case, committed error, and the judgment is

Reversed. All the Justices concurring.

LONG v. CITY OF ELBERTON.

1. The erection of a prison by the municipal authorities of a city within the limits thereof is not an invasion of the property rights of the owner of adjacent lands, and, therefore, not the foundation of an action for damages against the city.
2. After the erection of such a building, it is the duty of the public authorities to use and maintain the same in a proper and orderly manner ; and if they permit it to be so negligently kept as to create a nuisance, the damage caused thereby may give a right of action to one who sustains special and particular injury, not for the erection, but for such negligent maintenance.

Argued June 7, — Decided October 28, 1899.

Action for damages. Before Judge Reese. Elbert superior court. September term, 1899.

J. P. Shannon and *P. P. Proffitt*, for plaintiff.
I. C. VanDuzer and *J. N. Worley*, for defendant.

LITTLE, J. The plaintiff instituted an action to recover damages against the City of Elberton. He alleged, that he was the owner of a hotel building in said city, and eight brick storehouses adjoining and opposite his hotel ; that he expended a large sum of money in the erection of said buildings, which before the damage complained of were worth a large amount of money ; that he and his family reside in the hotel, and that the same was made comfortable and pleasant for his family as well as his guests ; that during the year 1897 the City of Elberton, without the consent of petitioner and against his protest, erected within one hundred feet of his property a building known as the city prison, which is a brick structure containing offices for the city and a number of prison cells and lockups in which violators of the city laws are confined ; that these are frequently drunk, boisterous, profane, obscene, and offensive, and that frequently crowds of objectionable persons are gathered around the city prison to the annoyance of the neighborhood ; that the building is not provided with waterworks or sewers, and that slops and filth are carried therefrom daily in full view of the public; that the prison emits foul air and unwholesome stenches, and the inmates make discordant and savage noises, and that the city convicts are kept therein; that this building is so situated that it stands broadside to the hotel building, with no obstruction between the two buildings, and all the unpleasant accompaniments of the prison are in full view of the windows and piazzas of the hotel and of persons dwelling therein or on the grounds attached thereto. He alleges that the same is a nuisance; that he endeavored to induce the city authorities not to construct the building at that place, informing them that it would injure his business, and the value of his property, but they did so over his protest. He alleges that the erection of the prison was a violation of the public duty and a reckless disregard for his rights, and the maintenance of the same as situated is a gross wrong; that it renders his home undesirable and his hotel building less desirable for a hotel, his storerooms less valuable for business, and has injured the market value of all his property above described, whereby he has been damaged the sum of five thousand dollars; that the city authorities could easily have erected said prison elsewhere where the damage it would cause would have been insignificant; that he himself offered to the city a lot in rear of his property, which was convenient in every respect, but they refused to erect the prison on that lot; that it was located in its present place as the result of bad faith and on account of ill will to petitioner. He alleges that the prison and the manner in which it is used and kept is a nuisance and has greatly damaged his property, and that its erection was, and its maintenance is, a direct invasion of his rights, for which he is entitled to recover damages under the constitution and laws of this State. The petition, as amended, was demurred to generally. The court sustained the demurrer, and the plaintiff excepted.

It is claimed by counsel for the plaintiff, that since the adoption of the constitution of 1877 a municipal corporation is liable to an individual for damages to private property, to the same extent and under the same circumstances that it is liable for property taken for public purposes; and we understand the present action is based on the provision of that constitution which declares that private property shall not be taken or *damaged* for public purposes without just and adequate compensation being first paid.   Civil Code, § 5729.   It is contended that the erection of the city prison in Elberton, and the use of said building for the confinement of violators of the law, in close proximity to the property of the plaintiff, has depreciated the value of said property, and therefore damaged it in the sense contemplated by the constitution.   It is not necessary in this case that the meaning of the word *damaged* in the constitution shall be either considered or discussed.   It was passed on by this court in the case of *Austin* v. *Augusta Terminal Railway Company*, 108 *Ga.* 671.

The simple erection of a necessary prison building can not, without more, so injure adjacent property as to entitle the owner to have damages for such erection.   No one is so hindered in the use of his property and so restricted as to the character of buildings he shall put upon it, as to make it necessary to consult adjacent lot owners in reference to the improvements to be made.   The lot being his own property, the owner may put it to such use as he sees proper, provided the buildings and improvements made by him do not infringe the legal right of his neighbor to the similar enjoyment of his own property.   A log house on a fashionable street may be built alongside of a palace, and by its erection the value of the latter may be depreciated, but that depreciation is *damnum absque injuria.*   The owner of the lot has as much right to erect the hut as the other has to build his palace — no more, no less; but if the hut or the palace be so used as to interfere in the lawful enjoyment of his property by the other, there the damage with a right to compensation exists.   If noxious gases from a business carried on in either befoul the air which the other is entitled to have without it — if the flow of poisonous fluids from a manufactory carried on at either place sterilizes the land of the other — if offensive smells emanate from the one and affect the health of those dwelling in the other, then there is a cause of injury which the law will redress, because the use which brings about any of these things is an infringement on the right of the other; but none can be allowed for the character of the building.   The municipal authorities of the

City of Elberton, being invested with certain powers of government, had a legal right (being necessary to the exercise of those powers) to erect a building for the purpose of furnishing public offices and maintaining a prison in which might be securely kept violators of the law; and the rule is clearly established, that a corporation authorized by the law to do a particular thing, so long as it keeps within the scope of the power granted, is completely protected from proceedings either at law or in equity in behalf of the public therefor (2 Wood on Nuisances, §753), and that if in the discharge of a duty imposed by law it proceeds in a careful and prudent manner, the damages resulting therefrom to individuals are *damnum absque injuria.* 99 U. S. 635; 88 Pa. St. 309; 69 Mo. 341; 38 Mich. 315.

In the case of *Bacon* v. *Walker*, 77 *Ga.* 338, this court, Chief Justice Jackson delivering the opinion, said: "It is true that nobody would be pleased at the erection of a jail in the vicinity of his residence, but it must be built somewhere. It is a public necessity. It is authorized by law. In no sense, or rather in no legal sense, is it a nuisance. Nothing that is legal in its erection can be a nuisance *per se*; much less can that which public necessity demands be one." It "must be built in some part of the city and near to somebody's house . . ; and equity will not stop the public works because of such damage." And in the case of *Pause* v. *Atlanta*, 98 *Ga.* 103, this court through Atkinson, J., said: "A distinction should be borne in mind between those cases where one seeks to recover because of the appropriation by the public to the public use of private property, and damages to one's property sustained in consequence of the construction of such public improvement, and that other class of cases in which, though one's property be neither appropriated nor damaged, yet in consequence of the construction of such improvement one suffers damage resulting from personal inconvenience, and consequent damage in the conduct of one's business. In the former cases the right of compensation is a matter of principle; the amount of damage, a mere matter of degree. However slight or however great one's damage may be, he is nevertheless entitled to compensation. In the latter class of cases something more must appear than mere damage or inconvenience. It must be made to appear that in the construction of such an improvement the municipal authorities have been guilty of negligence, omission of duty or negligent commission of an act authorized by law, in order to authorize a recovery." Under the authority of the cases cited, the plaintiff was not entitled to recover for the erection of the prison. Undoubtedly, it added nothing which was desirable to the neighborhood, and detracted much from it, but this and similar inconveniences are to be borne by the citizen in the vicinity of whose property such public buildings are located, and for his inconvenience and depreciation in values in property so occasioned the law affords no compensation. It does not, however, follow, because the erection of such a building was a public necessity and, the authorities had the right to select the lot upon which it was erected, that it can be so maintained as to perpetuate a nuisance. While the authorities have a right to use and maintain it for the purposes intended, the duty rests upon them to maintain it in a proper manner, and if such maintenance after its erection should prove a nuisance, it is the right of any citizen of Elberton, or other person interested, either to abate the same, or, if special and particular damage is caused to him, to obtain proper compensation for his injury. 2 Wood on Nuisances, § 748. Inasmuch, however, as the petition seeks to recover damages from the city for the erection and maintenance of the building as a prison, and the law nowhere authorizes such to be given under the circumstances detailed in his petition, the court committed no error in sustaining the demurrer thereto, and the judgment is

Affirmed. All the Justices concurring.

PIRKLE et al., administrators, v. CHAMBLEE.

Presumptively, one who signed as surety a promissory note which had been previously signed by two other persons apparently as joint principals undertook to contract as surety for both of these persons, and the burden of showing that one of them was himself a mere surety for the other, and that the last signer so knew at the time of signing the paper, was on him who asserted that such was the fact.

Submitted June 10, — Decided November 1, 1899.

Application to make proof of suretyship. Before Judge Kimsey. Hall superior court. December 12, 1898.

S. C. Dunlap, G. H. Prior, and *F. M. Johnson*, for plaintiffs in error. *M. L. Smith, H. H. Perry*, and *H. H. Dean*, contra.

LUMPKIN, P. J. This case was here at the March term, 1897. See 101 *Ga.* 790. A new trial was then ordered on the ground that the court erred in rejecting certain testimony. Subsequently a verdict was returned finding that George L. Chamblee was a cosurety with A. R. Cooper, deceased, upon the promissory note given to Davie. The administrators of Cooper moved for a new trial; the motion was overruled, and they excepted. There was practically no dispute as to the facts of the case as developed at the last trial, and it turns upon the law as announced in the foregoing headnote. It appears that James M. Chamblee and George L. Chamblee signed the note in question, apparently as joint principals. After their signatures had been affixed to it, A. R. Cooper signed the same as a surety, which fact appeared upon the paper itself. There was no evidence tending to show that he had any knowledge of the true relation of the two Chamblees to the instrument, other than that derivable from the fact that upon the paper itself, as presented to him to sign, they appeared to be joint principals. We are of the opinion that, in the absence of any information to the contrary, Cooper had a right to assume that they were such, in which event he surely could not be held liable as a cosurety with George L. Chamblee, even though in point of fact, as between the two Chamblees, George L. undertook to become bound as a surety only. When he signed the note apparently as a principal with a knowledge that Cooper was thereafter to be invited to sign as a surety, it was incumbent upon the former to give notice to Cooper of the real truth of the matter; for otherwise, George L. Chamblee would occupy the position of one who, by representing himself to be a principal, has misled another and induced him to sign an instrument to which, had he been informed of the facts in the case, he might have declined to affix his signature. In other words, if Cooper signed the note upon the faith of what appeared upon

3

its face to be the contract he was asked to enter into, George L. Chamblee would be estopped from setting up an essentially different contract, to the end that he might be relieved in part of the liability he apparently undertook to assume, by imposing upon Cooper a liability he never consented to incur.

In the motion for a new trial complaint is made of the following charge of the court: "The administrators of Cooper say that suppose, for the sake of argument, that Chamblee was surety, he has got no right to set it up as against Cooper; that is their contention. I will give you the law on that subject. Estoppels must be mutual between the parties. I charge you that the burden would be on Cooper's administrators to show an estoppel as against Chamblee, and that burden could be carried by a mere preponderance of testimony." It is alleged that this charge was erroneous, because "the burden was on George L. Chamblee to show that Cooper knew that George L. Chamblee was security, and not principal, when he, Cooper, signed said note." The charge excepted to is at least susceptible of a construction rendering it open to the criticism made thereon. Otherwise, it would be difficult to ascribe any significance to the words: "that burden could be carried by a mere preponderance of testimony." Inasmuch as George L. Chamblee signed apparently as a principal, and thus held himself out as such, the burden was clearly upon him, if he was merely a surety, to show that this fact was known to Cooper before he signed the instrument. Otherwise, as we have endeavored to show, Chamblee would not be in position to insist that relatively to Cooper his liability upon the paper was that of a surety only. There was no evidence even remotely tending to establish such knowledge on the part of Cooper; and this being so, Chamblee failed utterly to carry the burden of proof resting upon him. In view of this fact, it results not only that the above-quoted charge was erroneous, but also that the verdict in his favor was without evidence to support it.

Judgment reversed. All the Justices concurring.

JENKINS *v.* SOUTHERN RAILWAY COMPANY.

1. Even if, in order to invest an infant of tender years with the title to land, it may not be absolutely essential that there should be in every instance a manual delivery to such infant himself, or to a third person as his agent, of a voluntary conveyance in which he is named as grantee, yet no effect can be given to an instrument of that character which the maker thereof, after signing and acknowledging in the presence of witnesses, retains in his own custody, in the absence of satisfactory proof that it was his intention that such instrument should operate to immediately convey to the infant grantee the legal title to the premises therein described. In the case at bar, the charge of the court upon this subject was certainly as favorable to the plaintiff as he had any right to expect; and, under the facts and circumstances disclosed by the evidence, a finding in favor of the opposite party was fully warranted.

2. The doctrine that recitals in a deed are binding upon the parties thereto and their privies has no application whatsoever to the facts of the present case, and accordingly can not be invoked to overcome the defendant company's defense that it held under a third person who, subsequently to the execution of the voluntary deed relied on by the plaintiff, in good faith and without notice thereof bought the premises from his grantor, and therefore acquired all the rights of a bona fide purchaser for value.

3. As has been repeatedly ruled by this court, to defeat a plaintiff in ejectment, the defendant need only show a paramount title outstanding in a third person, without going further and connecting his own possession with that title.

Argued June 10,—Decided November 1, 1899.

Complaint for land. Before Judge Kimsey. Habersham superior court. November 15, 1898.

W. I. Pike, J. J. Strickland, Oscar Brown, and *A. P. Wofford,* for plaintiff. *Dorsey, Brewster & Howell, Sanders McDaniel, Arthur Heyman,* and *J. J. Bowden,* for defendant.

FISH, J. 1. The plaintiff in this case, J. H. Jenkins, based his claim of title to the premises in dispute upon a deed of gift to himself and his mother, alleged to have been duly executed by his grandsire, Noah Ballew, in 1868. At that time the plaintiff was an infant about two years of age. It was shown on the trial that this deed had never been recorded and was lost or destroyed. The plaintiff's mother, who appeared as a witness, testified as to its contents, however, and swore unequivocally that the grantor had formally delivered the deed to her in person, and she had "kept it for several months, prob-

ably a year." On the other hand, Ballew, who testified in behalf of both the plaintiff and the defendant, denied most positively that there had ever been any delivery, either actual or
constructive, to the plaintiff, and gave the following account
concerning the matter: He procured a justice of the peace to
draw up the instrument in question, and signed the same in
the presence of two witnesses, but retained it in his possession.
Shortly thereafter, with the intention "that it should operate
and enure as a muniment of title to [his] daughter and grandson," Ballew tendered this instrument to his son-in-law, Pick
Jenkins, the father of the plaintiff. Jenkins, however, declined
to accept the same, telling Ballew "to keep it." The latter,
having gained the impression from the manner of Jenkins's refusal to accept the deed "that he thought it was not worth anything and did not want it," thereupon placed the same among
his other private papers and retained custody of it until some
time during the year 1888, when it was either lost or stolen.
No further attempt was made by Ballew to effectuate his intention of making a formal delivery of the instrument. On the
contrary, in 1873 he sold the premises to one Morton, having
in the meantime decided "to give [his daughter] and her son
another piece of land in lieu of the land in question." He accordingly gave them a larger tract of land in the upper part of
the county, to which place Jenkins removed his family, aban-
doning possession of the premises in dispute, upon which he
had resided both before and after the signing of the instrument
above referred to. Upon this branch of the case, the trial judge
charged the jury: "If the grantor, at the time of the execution of the deed, had the determination to deliver it, and although he may have declared before the witnesses that this was
his purpose, and then attempted to deliver it to the grantee, or
some one for him, and failed to deliver it for or on acount of
the failure of the one to whom presented to accept it on any
account, and then changed his purpose as to the delivery of
the deed, this would not be a good delivery." "The grantee
need not be present at the time to accept it, and it need not be
delivered to the infant, but may be delivered to some one for
it, or kept and held by the grantor for such infant, if that was

his intention to pass title to such infant, and finally at the proper time to pass the deed to him, unless this intention was abandoned. How did the grantor regard it? Did he attempt to deliver it and failed, and then abandoned that intention and regarded it as his and treated it as such? If so, there would be no delivery."

Exception is taken to this portion of the court's charge, for the reason, as contended by the plaintiff, "that the rule announced, while applicable to adults, is not applicable to minors, when an offer has been made to deliver for his benefit." We are aware that, with a view to jealously guarding the rights of infants, in some jurisdictions the courts have gone to the extent of giving effect to a deed of gift made in behalf of one of tender years, although it appeared there had been no "manual delivery at all, the grantor retaining the deed among his own papers." See 1 Dembitz on Land Titles, § 51. But it is to be observed that in every case where such an instrument has been upheld, notwithstanding the grantor did not actually part with its custody, the courts have justified their position upon the ground that the peculiar facts and circumstances brought to light disclosed an intention on his part to make a final disposition of the property named in the instrument. Thus, in Newton v. Bealer, 41 Iowa, 334, wherein it appeared that "a father had executed a conveyance of realty to his infant son, but had retained the deed in his possession, and had in various ways indicated his intention that the property in question should be thus bestowed at his death, it was held that effect should be given to this intention," after his decease, the court saying (page 339): "Where one who has the mental power to alter his intention, and the physical power to destroy a deed in his possession, dies without doing either, there is, it seems to us, but little reason for saying that his deed shall be inoperative, simply because during life he might have done that which he did not do." Again, in Colee v. Colee, 122 Ind. 109, 17 Am. St. Rep. 345 (a case upon which the plaintiff in error mainly relies), it was disclosed by the evidence that "A wife, for the purpose of putting land beyond the reach of her husband, signed and acknowledged a deed in which the land was con-

veyed to her children, all of whom but one were infants." She
thereafter "caused it to be recorded, and then took possession
of it, intending to retain the deed and the land in her possession until her death." It further appeared that "by the terms
of the deed she reserved to herself a life-estate in the land," so
her retention of the instrument was not at all inconsistent with
the idea that she intended that it should immediately take effect
as a conveyance. Accordingly it was held that "The making
of a voluntary conveyance, absolute in form and beneficial in
effect, by a father or mother to one who is not sui juris, and
placing it upon record, is deemed to evince an unmistakable
intention on the part of the grantor to give the deed effect and
pass the title to the grantee, the assent of the latter, if nothing
further appears, being presumed from the beneficial character
of the transaction."

. In the present case, aside from the signing and acknowledgment of the instrument in the presence of witnesses, the only
evidence of the intention of Ballew at all contradictory to what
he swore as a witness was proof of certain declarations alleged
to have been made by him to the effect that he had given the
land in controversy to his daughter and her minor son. The
instrument was never recorded, nor did the grantor named
therein evince an intention to become the custodian of it until
the infant became of age, otherwise than by preserving the
same. The plaintiff attained his majority on September 7,
1887, yet, although Ballew remained in life and then retained
the paper in his custody, he made no attempt or offer to deliver
it. On the contrary he had, some fourteen years previously,
apparently abandoned entirely his intention of making the
gift and had sold the land to another person, at the same time
deeding to the plaintiff and his mother a larger tract located
elsewhere in the county. Clearly, therefore, were an adult
named in the instrument as grantee, it could not properly be
given the effect of a conveyance duly delivered. See *Maddox* v.
Gray, 75 *Ga.* 452, and *Ross* v. *Campbell*, 73 *Ga.* 309. The mere
fact that the plaintiff was an infant of tender years at the time
of the signing of the paper in question can not, it would seem,
supply the place of satisfactory evidence that his grandsire in-

tended this instrument to immediately operate as a conveyance. Nevertheless, as has been seen, the trial judge fairly submitted to the jury the question whether or not, although Ballew retained the paper in his own custody, he really intended that it should forthwith operate to pass title to the plaintiff. Certainly the charge excepted to was as favorable to him as he had any right to expect. The circumstance that Ballew formally offered and tendered the instrument to the plaintiff's father, to be accepted in behalf of the grantees therein named, counts for nothing in the plaintiff's favor, for his father expressly declined to accept this proffered delivery. In this connection see *Beardsley* v. *Hilson*, 94 *Ga.* 52–54. Indeed, this circumstance would seem to indicate that Ballew never originally contemplated becoming himself the custodian of the instrument, treating himself as the trustee of the plaintiff to hold in the latter's behalf the evidence of an executed gift, but rather that Ballew, after signing the paper, still considered it as belonging absolutely to himself, and expected thereafter to finally put into effect his intention to bestow upon the plaintiff the proposed gift by selecting for him an agent to accept, in his behalf, a written conveyance thereof. If this was really Ballew's intention, he clearly was at liberty to abandon it at any time before it was fully executed, and Jenkins's refusal to accept the tender made to him left Ballew precisely in the situation he occupied prior to making the offer, i. e., the position of one who, having parted with nothing, may or may not, at his option, take further steps to carry into effect his benevolent purpose of bestowing upon another a voluntary gift. We may add, before concluding this branch of the discussion, that we are entirely satisfied with the finding returned by the jury, even though, as may be true, they based their verdict solely upon the conclusion that there had not been either an actual or a constructive delivery of the instrument upon which the plaintiff relied as a muniment of title. There was, however, as we will now undertake to show, another view of the case upon which the jury might very properly have predicated their finding against him.

2. Evidence was introduced in behalf of the defendant railway company affirmatively showing that Morton, to whom

Ballew sold the land in 1873, was an innocent purchaser for
value, without notice of the alleged unrecorded deed of gift
previously executed in favor of the plaintiff. He sought to
overcome the defense thus interposed, by testimony to the effect
that Morton had fraudulently procured possession of his deed
from Ballew, which had been delivered in escrow to a third
person, without paying in full the purchase-price. The issue
of fact thus raised might, under the conflicting evidence bearing thereon, have been determined by the jury either way, but
apparently the preponderance of proof, taken in connection
with the circumstance that Ballew, so far as appears, never
made any attempt to collect that portion of the purchase-price
alleged to have been unpaid or to disturb Morton in his possession of the premises under his deed, constrained the jury to
find, as they did, in favor of the defendant. It does appear
from the record before us that in a deed from Ballew to one
Kimsey, "dated January, 1873, which deed was recorded in
1873," the grantor described the premises thereby conveyed as
being "all the land of lot 149 except" some forty acres previously sold, and "also thirty-five acres, more or less, heretofore
deeded to Jerusha Jenkins [the plaintiff's mother] and her
heirs." The deed from Ballew to Morton, the latter testified,
was executed in the "summer of 1873." No attempt appears
to have been made to show that he had actual knowledge of
the above recital in the deed to Kimsey, or that this deed was
put on record before Morton purchased the premises in dispute;
so the jury would not have been authorized to find that he had
even constructive notice of the contents of that instrument.
Nor, as is contended by the plaintiff in error, can the recitals
therein be regarded as binding upon Morton and his privies in
estate. He certainly was not a party thereto, nor did he derive title thereunder, either directly or through the grantee
therein named. This being so, he would not, simply because
his grantor was the same person who had previously executed
that instrument, be estopped from denying the truth of the recitals therein contained. "Recitals in a private deed only bind
parties and privies, and are not evidence against one not claiming under the deed." The doctrine that one asserting title

under a conveyance is estopped to deny the truth of its recitals is based upon the "rule of common sense" that he is not at liberty to "claim under it and deny it at the same time."
Hanks v. *Phillips*, 39 *Ga.* 550, 553. To the same effect, see *Yahoola River Mining Co.* v. *Irby*, 40 *Ga.* 479, and *Cruger* v. *Tucker*, 69 *Ga.* 557, 562. Accordingly, it would be an unpardonable perversion of both law and justice to hold that, in a contest between the holder of an unrecorded deed of gift and one occupying the attitude of a subsequent bona fide purchaser for value and without notice of such voluntary conveyance, the doctrine of estoppel which the plaintiff in error seeks to invoke has any application whatsoever.

3. As to a portion of the premises in dispute, upon which were located certain tracks of the defendant company referred to by counsel as its "Y," the plaintiff in error concedes that it showed a regular chain of titles back to Morton. As to that portion traversed by its main line, however, the company failed to show title derived from any source. Counsel for the plaintiff accordingly insisted here that the trial judge committed grave error in his charge to the jury upon the law relating to the rights of innocent purchasers for value without notice of a prior voluntary conveyance, in that he did not limit the defense thus interposed by the company to that part of the land occupied by its "Y," but expressly instructed the jury, in effect, that the company could successfully defend the action by showing that Morton was a bona fide purchaser for value and therefore became invested with the paramount title to the land in controversy. This position is clearly untenable. "A defendant in ejectment may defeat a recovery against him by showing a paramount outstanding title to the premises in a third person." *Brumbalo* v. *Baxter*, 33 *Ga.* 81. And, to the same effect, see *Jones* v. *Sullivan*, Ibid. 486; *Roe* v. *Maund*, 48 *Ga.* 462; *McAlpin* v. *Lee*, 57 *Ga.* 282. It is not at all necessary that the defendant should introduce evidence "connecting his possession with that title." *Sutton* v. *McLeod*, 29 *Ga.* 589. For, as was pertinently remarked by Judge Lumpkin in the case last cited (page 594): "The possession of the defendant is a protection against all who seek to disturb it, until the true owner comes

to assert his right.   To him the defendant is answerable for mesne profits.   And it is enough for him to show that the party suing is not the true owner, but that the paramount title is outstanding in another.   This principle is hoary with age.   We bow to it reverently."   It follows, necessarily, that there is no merit in the additional complaint of the plaintiff in error that, notwithstanding the defendant company signally failed to prove it had any interest whatever in that portion of the premises over and along which its main line of railway extended, the trial court charged the jury, in substance, that it was incumbent upon the plaintiff, in order to make out a case entitling him to a recovery, to establish by proof his alleged title as to the entire tract of land in controversy.

Judgment affirmed.   All the Justices concurring.

McMILLAN *v.* COX.

1. When by the terms of a will real and personal property is given to the wife for life with remainder to the children of the testator, a power conferred on the executrix, who was the wife of the testator, to sell any or all of the property devised and reinvest the proceeds, expressed in language which plainly and unequivocally limits the purpose for which any sale can be made to that of reinvestment only, does not, notwithstanding the will may contain broad and liberal provisions as to the manner in which this power may be exercised, empower the executrix to mortgage the property devised, nor to convey the title of such property as security for a debt created by her.

2. When, after expressly conferring such a power, the will also declares that "no part of the corpus of said estate is to be spent unless in the judgment of my said wife the same shall be necessary for the proper maintenance and education of my minor children," nothing more than an implied authority to use a portion of the corpus, if necessary for the maintenance and education of the testator's minor children, is given.   The language quoted can not be construed so as to confer upon the executrix authority to borrow money for any purpose.

3. The court erred in holding that the will authorized the executrix to borrow money and secure the same by a mortgage on property of the estate, and in appointing a receiver, and granting the injunction.

Argued May 27, — Decided November 2, 1899.

Injunction and receiver.   Before Judge Lumpkin.   Fulton superior court.   April 15, 1899.

Dorsey, Brewster & Howell and *Arnold & Arnold*, for plaintiff in error. *Abbott, Cox & Abbott*, contra.

LITTLE, J. Mrs. Cox filed an equitable petition in which she made the following case: McMillan died testate in Fulton county, and the first item of his will, which was duly probated, is as follows: "I give and bequeath all of the property of every kind whatsoever, both real and personal, that I may own or to which I may be entitled at the time of my death, including all land, movable property, money, notes or other choses in action, rights or credits of whatever character or description, and no matter where or in what shape the same may be, to my beloved wife Janie H. McMillan during her life, and at her death to be divided equally among my children, to wit: Lula, Harry, William, John, Archie, Jennie, Nannie, Robert, and an infant daughter now three months old, with full power in my said wife without any order of court to sell and convey in her discretion any or all of said property upon such terms as to her may seem proper, and reinvest the proceeds, subject to the same limitations, the purchaser from her receiving the fee-simple title unincumbered by any remainder interest, and her said power to sell and reinvest continuing and running through all subsequent investments made by her, the remainder interest of my said children attaching to all property purchased by her and lost upon all sold by her. This wide discretion is vested in my wife with the belief that she will use it for the best interest of herself and my children, so that my said estate shall be taken care of and kept together while my wife lives, and then be divided among my children. No part of the corpus of said estate is to be spent, unless in the judgment of my said wife the same shall be necessary for the proper maintenance and education of my children." Janie H. McMillan was appointed executrix of the will and guardian of the minor children. Testator died in October, 1882. At the time of his death, McMillan was possessed of a large and varied estate, consisting of merchandise, book accounts, and the undivided one-half interest in the notes and accounts of the firm of McMillan & Snow, and also an undivided one-half interest in lot number twenty-five (25) on Marietta street in the City of Atlanta,

Georgia, together with other lands; also money and solvent
debts.   In 1892 the executrix induced petitioner to loan her
the sum of six thousand dollars, for which she gave a promissory note signed "Janie H. McMillan, executrix of J. C. Mc-
Millan," becoming due March 1, 1897, and also executed and
delivered certain interest notes for two hundred and forty dollars each.   For the purpose of securing said loan, Janie Mc-
Millan, individually and as executrix of the will of her testator, made and delivered to petitioner her deed conveying an
undivided one-half interest in lot number 25 on Marietta street
in the City of Atlanta, on which was situated a storehouse.
The petition alleges, that the loan obtained from petitioner was
for the purpose of improving the estate left by the testator, by
erecting buildings and making other improvements rendering
the estate productive; that the principal borrowed, six thousand dollars, is now due, together with interest on the same according to the contract.   The defendant now sets up that she
had no power, as executrix, to bind the estate of her testator
for the payment of the sum borrowed, nor to convey title to
the land as security, and she therefore refuses to pay the same.
By proper conveyances from certain of the remaindermen, Janie H. McMillan individually has now a one-third interest in
the land conveyed, in fee simple.   She is insolvent, is in possession of the property and receiving the rents.   Her individual
interest therein is not sufficient to pay petitioner the amount
which is due.   She has not paid the taxes on the property, but
has wasted and squandered the income.   The plaintiff prays
for a receiver to take charge of the property conveyed, and to
collect the rents; that the defendant be enjoined from interfering with such property; that the interest in the property belonging to Janie McMillan individually be sold and the proceeds applied to the payment of the indebtedness; that two
thirds of an individed one-half in the land conveyed be decreed to be bound for the payment of such balance as may be
due petitioner after the sale of the individual interest of said
Janie McMillan.   There was also a prayer for general relief.

The defendant answered, and denied that she had any power
to bind the estate by contracts for improving the same.   She

admits that the loan was made to her individually, but denies that the estate is bound; admits the execution of the deed, and avers that the money was borrowed for her own purposes, and was used in operating a store, and was of no benefit to the estate.   She denies that she has any life-estate which can be disposed of, her only interest being as trustee for her children during her life, and alleges that the income during her life belongs to the children.   The deed from McMillan to Mrs. Cox was executed on March 1, 1892.   It purports to convey the undivided one-half interest in the lot on Marietta street, and recites that it is made under section 1969 of the Code of Georgia, for the purpose of securing a loan of six thousand dollars, which is obtained for the purpose of improving the estate left by J. C. McMillan under his will, by building and other improvements, rendering said property productive, and obviating the necessity of sale and reinvestment for such purpose.   On the hearing, this deed was put in evidence; also the promissory notes, and the will of McMillan.   It was also shown that Mrs. McMillan had neglected to pay the premiums for insurance on the property; that the State and county taxes for a number of years were not paid by the executrix, but were transferred to different parties, and are still outstanding.   It was agreed that Mrs. McMillan was insolvent, and that three of the children, remaindermen under the will, are yet minors. The presiding judge appointed a receiver for a one-half undivided interest in the land, and the receiver was directed to collect the rents and hold the property for the further order of the court.   An injunction was also granted; and to these rulings of the trial judge the plaintiff in error excepted.

1. The question made and passed upon by the judge in the court below was, whether the power conferred on Mrs. McMillan by the will of her husband authorized her to borrow money for the purpose of improving the estate left by the testator in his will, by building and making other improvements, rendering said property productive and obviating the necessity of sale and reinvestment for such purpose.   The judge of the superior court held that the powers conferred did so authorize the executrix, and under that construction he appointed a receiver for

the entire interest in the property purporting to be conveyed
by the deed. One of the prayers of the original petition was
that the interest belonging to Janie H. McMillan individually
should be sold and the proceeds applied to the payment of the
indebtedness due the petitioner. Inasmuch as the separate
question as to what interest Janie McMillan individually owned
in the property, and whether it, under the terms of the will,
passed by her deed, was not considered and passed upon by
the trial judge, we confine ourselves to the consideration of the
construction of the will to ascertain whether the executrix had
the power to convey the interest for the purposes expressed in
the deed. If she did, then the ruling made below and the appointment of the receiver was proper. If she did not have such
power, then the court committed error in appointing the receiver and granting the injunction.

It is said that the power given to the executrix is very broad,
and that the language shows that the testator intended to trust
very much to her discretion. This is undoubtedly true, but,
as we read the first item of the will, while the discretion given
the executrix is very broad, its exercise is limited to a narrow
field. Undoubtedly by the terms of the will the wife took a
life-estate in all of the property of the testator, and the children took as remaindermen. To arrive at the intention of the
testator, it is necessary that the whole will shall be construed
together. We find that the testator, after the devise to his
wife and children and after conferring the powers named on
the executrix, declares, "No part of the corpus of said estate
is to be spent unless in the judgment of my said wife the same
shall be necessary for the proper maintenance and education
of my minor children." Here is a declaration that but one
contingency shall authorize the diminution of the corpus of
the estate, that is, when it becomes necessary to properly maintain and educate the minor children. True, the judgment of
the executrix must determine when such maintenance and education require the use of a part of the corpus, but that judgment can not be exercised in conveying away any part of the
estate except for maintenance and education of the children.
When properly construed, we think, there is no other clause

of the will which gives the wife any power to diminish the corpus of the estate. She is invested with full power, and in her discretion without any order of court, to sell and convey any or all of the property on such terms as she may see proper, and reinvest the proceeds. If the power is exercised according to the evident intention of the will, then the discretion vested in the executrix only enables her to exchange property of the estate for other property to belong to the estate, because, immediately following the provision granting power to sell and convey and reinvest the proceeds, the will in terms requires that the property in which the proceeds are invested shall be subject to the same limitations which qualified the devises to the wife and children. It is said, however, that in the exercise of this power of sale and reinvestment the grantee in a conveyance from her would not be bound to see to the actual investment. This is undoubtedly true, because the power to invest was entrusted to her discretion, with which the grantee has nothing to do; besides, the will provides that the purchaser who receives from her a fee-simple title takes it unincumbered. But it is nevertheless true that the power of sale is by this portion of the will confined to the purposes of reinvestment. We do not undertake to say, if she had conveyed any portion of this property for the declared purpose of reinvestment, that title would not have passed, notwithstanding the reinvestment never was made. But how can the petitioner take any benefit from the power given to sell for the purpose of reinvestment? It is not claimed at all that the defendant in error purchased the property attempted to be conveyed. The purpose specified in the deed which she received was not a sale for the purpose of reinvestment, but a loan of money to be used for building upon the land and otherwise improving the property. Therefore, without regard to the question as to whether the money borrowed was devoted to building and making other improvements of the property, it does not seem to have been authorized under a power which limited the right to sell and convey to a purpose of investing the proceeds, after such sale, in property which should belong to the estate.

But it is claimed that a power to sell and convey carries

with it the right to create a mortgage. In his learned and able
opinion the judge who presided on the hearing in this case
says that he "does not find it necessary to hold that as a rule
a simple power to sell, in a deed or will, without more, necessarily includes a power to mortgage." Much might be said to
the contrary. In the case of *Adams* v. *Rome,* 59 *Ga.* 769, Judge
Bleckley uses this language: "If the power to sell and convey
stood alone, it would *probably* comprehend the power to mortgage"; citing 2 *Kelly,* 404; 3 P.Wms. 9. Counsel for plaintiff in
error has cited us to the cases of *Wayne* v. *Myddleton,* 2 *Ga.* 383,
Miller v. *Redwine,* 75 *Ga.* 130, and *Henderson* v. *Williams,* 97
Ga. 709, to support the contention that the power to sell and
convey in this case carries with it a right to create a mortgage
on the property. It appeared in the case of *Wayne,* that certain
slaves were given to a trustee for the use of the grantor's wife
during her life, and after her death to her children. The cestui
que trust, with the approbation of her trustee, purchased a
tract of land, growing crop, stock, cattle, etc., and a payment
was secured by a mortgage on the four slaves conveyed by the
deed of trust, and also by a mortgage on the land. The crop,
cattle, etc., and the services of hired slaves, were received by
the cestui que trust. The mortgage was foreclosed, and the
slaves sold. It was held that the cestui que trust was competent to make the contract. The deed authorized the cestui que
trust, with the consent of her trustee, to sell and dispose of
the trust estate whenever she should deem it proper to do so,
and to reinvest the proceeds upon like trusts. It will be noted
that the power given in this case was to sell and dispose of the
trust estate at any time the cestui que trust thought proper to
do so, and to reinvest. The facts of the case show that as consideration for the debt which she secured by mortgage she received other property, not, it is true as it turned out, of the
full value of her note, but a very considerable amount. In the
case of *Miller* v. *Redwine,* supra, the lease of a hotel, the furniture contained in it, and the live stock about it, were conveyed
by will to a daughter-in-law and her children through the
medium of a trustee, with the right in the trustee "to sell said
property and reinvest the same for the benefit of his cestui que

trust at any time, without an order of court for that purpose."
It was held that the mortgage to Redwine was legal, it having
been made to raise money to carry on the hotel business, and
this decision was placed on the ground that the trustee is invested with sufficient power to execute the trust, and in order
to determine the power, the court will look to the character of
the trust estate. In the case of *Henderson* v. *Williams*, the trustee had power and authority to allow the corpus of the estate
to be used on the written consent of the cestui que trust, when
it became desirable to use any part of the corpus of the trust
estate for the improvement thereof or for the more comfortable
support of said cestui que trust. Under this power the trustee
procured supplies to enable him to make a crop, and with the
written consent of the cestui que trust made a deed to secure
the payment of the note so given. This was held to be a
proper exercise of the power.

Whether these cases rule the principle clearly and explicitly, that a power to sell includes the power to mortgage, is a
question we do not now have to decide. The decision in each
of them seems to be made upon the facts as shown, rather than
to settle the principle broadly; but they do not, in our opinion, afford authority which will support the deed made by
Mrs. McMillan, under the powers and restrictions of the will.
Of this we are clear. If A. should give to B. a power of attorney to sell a piece of property, it could hardly be claimed
that B. under such power could execute a mortgage on the property to secure a loan. We think that the true principle is, that
a power to sell and convey *may* include the power to mortgage,
but it does not necessarily do so; and whether such power is
or is not included depends upon the character of the estate,
the words granting the power, and the purposes for which the
debt was created. We are satisfied, however, that when by
the terms of a will the power of sale is given *only* for the purpose of reinvestment, with a provision restricting the expenditure of the corpus of the estate to a single purpose, and the
further provision that the same uses and restrictions which attached to the property devised should also attach to the property purchased with the proceeds of property which should be

4

sold under the power given, no right or power is given to the executrix to create a mortgage on the property of the estate to secure a loan of money. The intention to grant that power is not consistent with the restricted power of sale given by the will and the expressed purpose of the testator to limit the expenditure of the corpus of this estate to one other purpose.

2. It may be further said that, as a general rule, an executor can not contract debts which will bind the estate he represents. *Palmer* v. *Moore*, 82 *Ga.* 177. In order to make such debts valid charges on the estate he represents, there must be express authority so to do; and if the executrix in this case had the right to borrow money and charge the estate she represented with its payment, she must have had express power to do so. The power given by the will is that which we first quoted, that no part of the corpus is to be spent unless in the judgment of the executrix it became necessary to do so for the maintenance and education of the children. Certainly it can not be claimed that power to borrow money was conferred by this clause of the will. It was but an effort on the part of the testator to prevent making his estate liable for any debt, and preventing any part of his property from being expended unless it became necessary for the maintenance and education of his children. There is no condition of the will which authorizes the executrix to spend any portion of the corpus of the estate, except when necessary for the maintenance and education of the children. The intention gathered from the entire will is, that his wife and children shall be supported from the rents and profits of the estate of which he was possessed; that inasmuch as it was probable that the estate would remain under the control of his executrix for a considerable length of time, and as some of his children were young and had to be reared and educated, if such rents and profits were not sufficient to maintain and educate the children, then he gave the power to his executrix to sell such a part of his estate as was necessary for this purpose. In the meantime, if it became desirable to sell any particular pieces of property, or all of it, and with the proceeds to procure other property, power was given to the executrix so to do, for the benefit of his devisees; but the testator nowhere in his

will used language which, fairly construed, showed that he intended to give his executrix power to borrow money or contract debts with the incident risk of dissipating an estate which he set aside for the support and maintenance of those whom he left dependent upon it.

Judgment reversed. All the Justices concurring.

O'BRIEN *v.* THE STATE.

109
d112
112
109
114
114
114
|109
|116
109
123

1. An indictment which simply charges the accused with a misdemeanor, in that he, on a day named, in a designated county, did "unlawfully sell spirituous and intoxicating liquors, contrary to the laws of said State," etc., in effect charges him with violating a law prohibiting and making penal the sale of liquors in that county; and if there be no such law, it charges him with no offense at all. Upon a trial under such an indictment, no matter what the evidence may be, the accused can not legally be convicted of a violation of a statute prohibiting and making penal the sale of such liquors within three miles of a designated church in such county, nor of a violation of a statute regulating the granting of licenses to sell intoxicating liquors by the ordinary of the county and providing a penalty for a violation of its provisions, nor of the offense of selling liquor without a license.
2. The act of February 27, 1877 (Acts of 1877, p. 33), making lawful, in any county of this State, the sale of domestic wines, in quantities of not less than one quart, by the manufacturers of the same, being a general law, and such wines being "intoxicating liquors," a subsequent act which by its terms undertakes to "prohibit the sale and furnishing of spirituous, malt, or intoxicating liquors," within the limits of a designated county, is unconstitutional. LITTLE and LEWIS, JJ., dissenting.

Argued May 15, 1899. — Decided January 24, 1900.

Indictment for selling liquor. Before Judge Reese. Warren superior court. April term, 1899.

Horace M. Holden and *E. T. Shurley*, for plaintiff in error.
R. H. Lewis, *solicitor-general*, by *Harrison & Bryan*, contra.

FISH, J. The defendant in the court below was tried and convicted upon a special presentment which simply charged him with a misdemeanor, in that he, on the 25th day of May, 1898, did, in Warren county, "unlawfully sell spirituous and intoxicating liquors, contrary to the laws of said State," etc. He admitted that on the day named he did, in that county, sell such liquors, but contended that he had violated no law in so doing. In view of the fact that the State, in effect, contends that under this presentment the conviction of the defendant was lawful, if his admission and the evidence in the case showed that he had violated the provisions of *any* statute in reference to the sale of such liquors which was of force in Warren county, it becomes important to first determine what is the proper legal construction of this presentment. It charged the accused with unlawfully selling spirituous and intoxicating liquors in Warren county. The charge was not that he had sold such liquors, in that county, under designated circumstances which rendered the sale unlawful, but the charge imported that a sale of such liquors in Warren county, was per se unlawful, and that the defendant, having sold them in that county, was guilty of a misdemeanor. For if a mere sale, without more, was not unlawful, and the purpose of the State was to rely for a conviction upon proof that the defendant sold such liquors in that county, at a place, or under circumstances, which, under the provisions of some particular penal statute, rendered the sale unlawful, then the presentment should have contained, in addition to the allegation that the defendant sold such liquors in Warren county, such essential averments of facts as to the place or the circumstances of the sale as, taken in connection with the sale, would show a violation of the statute in question.

1. It is an elementary rule of criminal procedure that the indictment shall contain a complete description of the offense charged, and it follows that there can be no conviction for the commission of a crime an essential element of which is not charged in the indictment. Nor can a defective indictment be helped out by the evidence at the trial, nor be aided by argument and inference. Clark's Crim. Proc. §§ 325, 509; 1 Whar. Crim. P. & P. § 166; 10 Enc. P. & P. 473 et seq.; Black, Intox. Liq. §§ 437, 440, 448, 463, 476, 477; and cases cited by all these authorities. While, under section 929 of our Penal Code, an indictment is sufficiently technical and correct if the offense be charged in the terms and language of the code, or so plainly that the nature of the offense charged may be easily under-

stood by the jury, yet this court has frequently held that the indictment should leave nothing to inference or implication, but its statements should be so plain that a common man may without doubt or difficulty, from the language used, know what is the charge made against the accused. See cases cited under the section. As said in *Johnson* v. *State*, 90 *Ga.* 441, this section was not intended to dispense with the substance of good pleading, nor to deny to one accused of crime the right to know enough of the particular facts constituting the alleged offense to be able to prepare for trial, nor to deprive him of the right to have an indictment perfect as to the essential elements of the crime charged. It is true there was a special demurrer in that case; but where the indictment fails to allege an essential element of the crime charged, such defect will not be cured by verdict, and a motion in arrest of judgment will prevail.

In *Wood* v. *State*, 46 *Ga.* 322, it was held that an indictment for burglary, which fails to charge the intent with which the accused broke and entered, is fatally defective. McCay, J., in delivering the opinion, said: "If the intent is material, it is necessary to allege it. It is a prime ingredient in the offense, and an indictment fails to charge the offense of burglary unless the intent of the breaking, etc., be set forth." In *Thomas* v. *State*, 96 *Ga.* 311, it was held that "It is indispensable to the maintenance of a conviction for larceny, that the indictment allege the ownership of the property stolen, or that the owner thereof is unknown; and the indictment failing to allege either, a motion in arrest of judgment should be sustained." In that case Atkinson, J., said: "That the goods taken and carried away should be the property of a person other than the one so taking and carrying them away, is as essential to the commission of the offense of larceny as the taking and carrying away itself. This is one of the essential ingredients of the offense inhering in the very definition of larceny." So in *Davis* v. *State*, 40 *Ga.* 229, it was held that in an indictment for larceny it is necessary to allege the value of the stolen article, and if no value be alleged the judgment will be arrested after verdict. In the case under review, the offense alleged, if there

be such an offense, is either selling spirituous and intoxicating
liquors, or selling such liquors in Warren county.   There is
no statute of force in this State under which the sale of spirit-
·uous and intoxicating liquors in the State is per se unlawful.
Therefore, unless there is a statute applicable to Warren county,
under the provisions of which a sale of such liquors in that
county is unlawful, this presentment did not allege any offense
at all against the defendant.   There is a special statute which,
as amended, undertakes to prohibit and make penal the sale
of such liquors in Warren county, and we think that a proper
construction of this presentment is that it intended to charge
the accused with a violation of this particular statute.   See
Caldwell v. *State*, 101 *Ga.* 557.   This statute, which we will
consider in the next division of this opinion, is claimed by
the plaintiff in error to be unconstitutional.   Counsel for the
State insists that it is constitutional, but contends that, even
if it be held unconstitutional, the accused was guilty of the
charge made against him in the presentment, because he violated the provisions of an act which makes it a misdemeanor
"for any person or persons to engage in the sale of intoxicating,
spirituous, or malt liquors, wines, beer, or cider within three
miles of the Methodist church at Barnett, Warren county, Ga."
(Acts of 1884–5, p. 547), as, under the evidence in the case, he
.sold spirituous and intoxicating liquors within the territory
therein designated.   The plaintiff in error, in reply to this,
contends that this act is also unconstitutional, and, in support
of this contention, cites the decision of this court in the case of
Bagley v. *State*, 103 *Ga.* 388.   While, under the decision in the
Bagley case, there seems to be much force in this contention
of the plaintiff in error, in the view which we take of this case,
as indicated above, the question whether this act is or is not
constitutional is not before us, for the simple reason that the
defendant in the court below was not charged with a violation
of its provisions.

The accused was charged with a misdemeanor, in that, in
Warren county, he unlawfully sold spirituous and intoxicating
liquors.   He was not charged with a misdemeanor, in that he,
in Warren county, sold such liquors within three miles of the

Methodist church at Barnett, nor was there anything whatever in the presentment which indicated a purpose on the part of the State to charge him with a violation of the provisions of this particular statute. It is true that, if this act is constitutional, and he did in Warren county sell spirituous and intoxicating liquors within three miles of this church, he would, in a general sense, have unlawfully sold such liquors in Warren county; but, as we have seen, he could not legally be convicted of the distinct offense of selling such liquors within three miles of the Methodist church at Barnett, under a presentment which did not charge him with this particular offense. With as much reason the State might claim the right to convict the accused, under this presentment, if by the evidence it were shown that he had sold liquor, in Warren county, on an election day, or to a person intoxicated, or to a minor without the written consent of his parent or guardian, or that he had, in that county, violated any other law in reference to the sale of such liquors, which was of force therein; for, in either event, he would have unlawfully sold liquor in Warren county. The State can not be permitted to formulate a general charge of this character and, under its cover, sweep the whole range of the criminal liquor statutes, in an effort to prove that the accused has violated some one of them. To allow the State to do this would put the defendant to a great disadvantage. The indictment against him would only put him upon notice that the State expected to prove that he had violated some one of the various penal statutes in reference to the sale of liquor, but what particular charge, or charges, the prosecution would spring on him during the progress of the trial he would have no means of ascertaining. An indictment should be sufficiently certain to put the defendant upon notice of the nature of the offense charged, in order that he may prepare to meet the charge against him, and to enable him to plead any judgment which may be rendered in the case as a bar to any subsequent prosecution for the same offense. The present case well illustrates how unfair to a defendant it would be to allow the prosecution to pursue such a course as this. For counsel for the State contends, first, that, under the admission of the defendant in the court below, it was shown that he had violated a statute which makes it unlawful to sell spirituous or intoxicating liquors anywhere in Warren county; second, that if the conviction can not be sustained under this statute, it was proved that he was guilty of having violated another statute which makes it a misdemeanor to sell liquor within three miles of the Methodist church at Barnett; third, that if the conviction can not stand under either of these statutes, the evidence showed that the defendant violated the law against selling liquor without a license; fourth, that if none of these positions is tenable, the testimony showed that he violated the provisions of an act approved February 28, 1874, which prescribes upon what conditions licenses to sell liquors can be granted by the ordinary of Warren county, and provides a penalty for a violation of its provisions, and that the conviction should be upheld under this last-mentioned statute. Under the authorities cited, such contentions are manifestly unsound. Such offenses are so different in their material elements that a conviction or an acquittal of one of them could not be pleaded in bar of a prosecution for another. *Smith* v. *State*, 105 *Ga.* 724. We hold that the legal effect of the presentment under which the accused was tried was to charge him with having violated a law prohibiting the sale of spirituous and intoxicating liquors anywhere in Warren county; and a general verdict of guilty rendered upon such a presentment can apply only to this charge.

2. Is there any law prohibiting the sale of spirituous and intoxicating liquors in Warren county? It is not pretended that the provisions of the general local option liquor law have ever become operative in that county. The legislature has, however, undertaken to prohibit the sale of intoxicating liquors in that county. In 1882 the General Assembly passed an act entitled, "An act to prohibit the sale and furnishing of spirituous, malt, or other intoxicating liquors in the county of Warren, and to provide a punishment for a violation of the same, and for other purposes"; which was approved by the Governor on December 12, of that year. By a proviso to this act, the 159th district, G. M., of that county, in which district the town of Barnett is

situated, was exempted from the operation of this act, until the act should be ratified by the voters residing in the district, at an election held for that purpose.   It appears from the evidence in the case that no such election has ever been held.   In 1897 the legislature amended this act by striking this proviso therefrom.   The State contends that since the passage of the amendatory act the sale of spirituous and intoxicating liquor has been unlawful in any part of Warren county.   The plaintiff in error contends that the original act of December 12, 1882, is unconstitutional for the same reason that this court, in *Papworth* v. *State*, 103 *Ga.* 36, held an act which undertook to entirely prohibit the sale of intoxicating liquors in Irwin county to be unconstitutional.   In the *Papworth* case it was held that, "There being on the 26th day of September, 1879, a general law of force in this State, rendering lawful, in any county thereof, sales of domestic wines, in quantities of not less than one quart, by the manufacturers of the same (Acts of 1877, p. 33), and such wines being 'intoxicating liquors,' an act approved on the day above mentioned, which by its terms undertook to 'entirely prohibit the sale of spirituous or intoxicating liquors,' within the limits of a designated county, was unconstitutional.   As its effect would be to render penal, in that county, all sales of domestic wines, it was violative of that clause of the constitution prohibiting special legislation in any case for which provision has been made by an existing general law."   The act of 1877 herein referred to was of force on December 12, 1882, and for that matter is still of force, in this State.   The act now under consideration undertook by its terms to immediately prohibit the sale of spirituous, malt, or other intoxicating liquors in all of Warren county except one district thereof, and to prohibit the sale and furnishing of such liquors in that district also whenever the act should be ratified by the voters of the district.   By the amendatory act the prohibition provided for in the original act is made to apply to the whole county.   It is very apparent that, under the decision just cited, this act is unconstitutional.   With but very slight and immaterial alterations, the headnotes and opinion in the *Papworth* case would precisely fit the present case, so far as the point now under consideration is concerned. As there is no valid law which prohibits and makes penal the sale of spirituous and intoxicating liquors in Warren county, it necessarily follows that the verdict finding the accused guilty was contrary to law, and the trial judge erred in not granting a new trial.

Judgment reversed. All the Justices concurring, except Little and Lewis, JJ., who dissent.

LEWIS, J. I agree with Justice Little in the views expressed in his dissenting opinion in the case of *Papworth* v. *State*, 103 *Ga.* 39-42, and hence with him dissent from the opinion of the majority of the court in this case. Since the decision in the *Papworth* case was rendered, this court, in the case of *Loid* v. *State*, 104 *Ga.* 726, decided that it can not take judicial cognizance of the fact that domestic blackberry wine is necessarily intoxicating. It was held error in that case because the court below did not submit that as a question of fact for the jury to pass upon. I can not see, therefore, how it can be ruled by the court, as a matter of law, that the word "intoxicating" in an act necessarily includes domestic wine. There is no more reason for saying domestic blackberry wine is not included in the words "intoxicating liquors" than there is in saying that domestic grape wine is not so included. But even conceding that the views of the majority of my brethren are correct, that the local act in question by the use of the words "intoxicating liquors" necessarily included domestic wines, I think the views of the majority are based upon a misconception of the true meaning of that provision in the constitution which prohibits special legislation in any case for which provision has been made by an existing general law. Before a local act becomes obnoxious to this clause in the constitution, there must be some general law which either provides substantially for the same thing sought by the local act, or which provides some means for obtaining the local relief sought other than by local legislation. The constitution does not declare or intimate there shall be no local legislation for a county the effect of which would be to suspend the operation of a general law in that county. Legislation touching the liquor traffic is founded upon the police power of the State, and that power is constantly exercised with reference to particular localities in a State, changing in such localities the operation of the general law. This system doubtless proceeds on the policy that it is often the case that certain police regulation is required for one community, city or county, on account of its peculiar environments, which is not generally demanded throughout the State. Now the purpose of the constitution was simply to declare that no special legislation should be had touching matters for which substantially the same relief can be obtained by virtue of a general law. But if there be no general law making provision for such relief, then a local act on the subject is not violative of the provision in the constitution. The object of a local law is really to substitute for a certain locality something in lieu of, and entirely different from, what is provided in the general law. This is certainly true of local legislation with reference to the sale of liquor. There has always been some general law touching the liquor traffic in Georgia. If the domestic wine act of 1877 had never been passed, this local law for Warren county would have amounted to a repeal of the general liquor law on the subject of permitting by license the sale of intoxicants. This court has decided that the "local option law" is a general law, and, therefore, a local act prohibiting the sale in a county, passed after the local option measure, is unconstitutional. Why? Simply because the general local option law made provision for the accomplishment of the same thing, to wit, prohibition of the liquor traffic by an election. But in this case there was no provision in the domestic wine law, nor was there in any other general law of this State, providing for any relief of the kind sought by this local act for Warren county when that act was passed. Suppose, for instance, instead of the domestic wine law of 1877, the legislature had passed an act legalizing throughout the State the sale of all spirituous as well as other intoxicating liquors; could it be said that such a general act would prevent subsequent legislatures from passing special laws prohibiting such sale in given communities or counties? Manifestly not, if the general law, instead of making provision for obtaining such local relief, makes provision exactly to the contrary.

In the case of *Brown* v. *State*, 104 *Ga.* 525, the question as
to the validity of a local act prohibiting the sale of intoxicating liquors in a certain district in Carroll county was involved.
That act was passed since the adoption of the present constitution.   In the opinion on p. 528 the following language is
used: "The effect of the act of 1881 was not only to repeal
the act of 1875, but also to suspend the general law of the
State upon the subject of the sale of liquors in so far as the
714th district G. M. of Carroll county is concerned."   In the
dispensary cases, *Plumb* v. *Christie*, 103 *Ga.* 686, the point was
made that that local act for Terrell county was unconstitutional, because contrary to the section of the constitution
declaring that no special law shall be enacted for which provision has been made by an existing general law.   There is
no question that this local dispensary act repealed the general law of the State upon the subject of the liquor traffic
in the county of Terrell; yet this court held the act was constitutional, for the simple reason that there was no provision
in the general law for the sale of liquors through the medium
of dispensaries.   I think the principle in that case necessarily
controls this; the only difference being that in one instance
there was a general law providing for the sale of liquors in
Terrell in a certain way, and a local law in effect repealing a
general statute, by making special provision for its sale in that
county in an entirely different manner.   In this case there is
a general law authorizing the sale of domestic wines throughout the State.   There is a special law which, under the construction of the majority of the court, prohibits the sale of
domestic wines in a particular county.   This local act is not
more effectual in suspending the operation of the general law
than was the dispensary act in the case above cited.   I therefore think the local prohibitory acts for Warren county were
constitutional, that the defendant was legally convicted, and that
the court did right in refusing a new trial.   Even if said acts
are unconstitutional, as decided by the majority, I can not
agree with them that under this indictment the defendant
could not have been found guilty of the violation of any law
making penal acts of selling liquor.   There was no demurrer

filed to the indictment. The State made out its case by an admission of the defendant in open court that he sold liquor in that county, and there was no contest or defense made on the trial below that, under the allegations in the indictment, he could not be convicted for the violation of any law making his acts of selling liquor penal.

LITTLE, J. In addition to the reasons given in my dissenting opinion in the case of *Papworth* v. *State*, 103 *Ga*. 39, I fully concur in the reasons given by Justice Lewis in his dissent to the opinion of the majority of the court.

EMBRY *v.* THE STATE.

FISH, J. There being, on September 5, 1883, a general law of force in Georgia declaring that "it shall not be unlawful for any person, who shall manufacture or cause to be manufactured in this State any wine from grapes, the product of any vineyard in this State belonging to such person, to sell or offer to sell, anywhere in the State, such wine at wholesale, or in quantities not less than one quart" (Acts of 1877, p. 33), and such wines being "intoxicating liquors," an act approved on that day, which undertook to prohibit and make penal "the sale of spirituous, malt, or other intoxicating liquors, in the counties of Glascock and Paulding," was unconstitutional. *Papworth* v. *State*, 103 *Ga*. 36 ; *O'Brien* v. *State*, ante, 51. It follows, therefore, that where one was indicted and tried for a violation of the provisions of such an unconstitutional local statute, a verdict of guilty was unauthorized by law, and a motion for a new trial, alleging that it was contrary to law, should have been sustained.

Judgment reversed. All the Justices concurring, except

LITTLE and LEWIS, JJ. We dissent from the opinion of the majority of the court in this case, upon the grounds set forth in our dissenting opinions in the *Papworth* and *O'Brien* cases, supra.

Submitted January 15,—Decided January 26, 1900.

Indictment for selling liquor. Before Judge Janes. Paulding superior court. August term, 1899.

A. L. Bartlett, for plaintiff in error.

W. T. Roberts, solicitor-general, contra.

109 61
109 69

109 61
d112 291
m112 401
109 6
114
114
109
123

MOORE *v.* WHEELER, sheriff.

One indicted and tried under an unconstitutional statute may, even after
final conviction, obtain his discharge from custody on a writ of habeas
corpus. LITTLE and LEWIS, JJ., dissent on the ground that, in their
opinion, the statute in question is not unconstitutional.

Argued October 9, 1899. — Decided January 26, 1900.

Petition for habeas corpus.   Before Judge Janes.   Paulding
county.   August 24, 1899.

A. L. Bartlett and *L. M. Washington*, for plaintiff.

LUMPKIN, P. J.   The grand jury of Paulding county returned an indictment against Moore, charging that, on a day
named, he did in that county "unlawfully sell spirituous
liquors, malt liquors, and other intoxicating liquors." He entered a plea of guilty, and was sentenced. Subsequently he
sued out a writ of habeas corpus, whereby he sought to be discharged from custody. In his application for the writ he
alleged that the indictment was void, because based upon the
act of September 5, 1883 (Acts of 1882–3, p. 570), prohibiting the sale of spirituous, malt, and other intoxicating liquors
in the counties of Glascock and Paulding, and that this act was,
for reasons alleged, unconstitutional. On the hearing the judge
remanded the prisoner to custody, and of this he complains.

In *Embry* v. *State*, this day decided, ante, 61, the unconstitu-
tionality of this statute was declared. As the indictment
against Moore was evidently framed under this act, the sentence
against him, though based upon a plea of guilty, was a mere
nullity, and he ought to have been discharged. It seems to
be now well settled that where one is indicted and tried under
an unconstitutional statute, he may, even after final conviction
and sentence, obtain his discharge from custody on a writ of
habeas corpus.   See Ex parte Siebold, 100 U. S. 371; Ex
parte Clarke, Ibid. 399; Ex parte Yarbrough, 110 U. S. 651;
Ex parte Royall, 117 U. S. 241; In re Ziebold, 23 Fed. Rep.
791; In re Tie Loy, 26 Fed. Rep. 611; In re Ah Jow, 29 Fed.
Rep. 181; In re Payson, 23 Kan. 757, 760; Ex parte Burnett,
30 Ala. 461; Ex parte Rollins, 80 Va. 314; Ex parte Rosen-

blatt, 19 Nev. 439; Ex Parte Mato, 19 Tex. App. 112; Brown
v. Duffus, 66 Iowa, 193; Fisher v. McGirr, 1 Gray, 2; Whit-
comb's case, 120 Mass. 118. "An unconstitutional enactment
is never a law; and if there can be a case in which a conviction is illegal and without jurisdiction, it seems that such a
case is presented when it appears either that there is no law
making criminal the alleged crime, or authorizing its prosecution in the court wherein the sentence has been imposed." 2
Freeman on Judgments, § 624, p. 1092.

Judgment reversed. All the Justices concurring, except
LITTLE and LEWIS, JJ., dissenting. We dissent from the
opinion of the majority of the court in this case, upon the
grounds set forth in our dissenting opinions in the cases of
Papworth v. *State*, 103 Ga. 39, and *O'Brien* v. *State*, ante, 51.

GEORGIA STATE B. & L. ASSOCIATION v. MAYOR AND ALDERMEN OF SAVANNAH et al.

When by the terms of an act the president of a building and loan association is required to return to the tax-receiver of the county where such
association is located, at its true market value, the stock owned by the
stockholders thereof upon which no advance has been made, the tax so
imposed is not a tax against the corporation, but is against the property
of the individual holders, and is a plan adopted by the legislature to
conveniently reach this class of stock in the hands of the owner, and is
not imposed as a franchise, but a property tax. When the same act provides that the taxes so required shall be in lieu of all other taxes and
licenses, whether State, county, or municipal, against said associations
(except a business license), the latter provision is inoperative and void,
and is in violation of the constitutional provision requiring all taxation
to be uniform and ad valorem.

Argued June 8, 1899.—Decided January 26, 1900.

Petition for injunction. Before Judge Falligant. Chatham
county. March 30, 1899.

C. G. Tiedeman, and *Saussy & Saussy*, for plaintiff.
Samuel B. Adams, for defendants.

LITTLE, J. The Georgia State Building and Loan Association of Savannah presented to the judge of the superior

court of the Eastern circuit a petition making substantially
the following case: Petitioner is an interstate building and
loan association, chartered under the laws of the State of
Georgia, having its principal office in the City of Savannah,
and having stockholders residing in a number of States, including the State of Georgia.   The business of petitioner is strictly
that of a building and loan association, that is, lending its
funds to its members only, and all securities held by it represent advances made by it to its stockholders upon real estate
and stock collateral, and its other property consists of office
furniture and real estate acquired by purchase upon foreclosure of liens for advances, or which has been taken in settlement of indebtedness due by its members.   Petitioner has
made its return for taxes to the State and county for the year
1898, in accordance with the requirements of the act of the
General Assembly, and has paid to the Mayor and Aldermen
of the City of Savannah, a municipal corporation of said county
and State, the license fee demanded for the year 1898, and has
paid said corporation all taxes legally demanded of it for the
year 1898.   The City of Savannah assesses the value of real
estate for taxation without return of the same by the owner,
and requires each resident to make an annual return of personal property to its board of tax-assessors.   During the month
of January, 1898, petitioner made a return, fixing the value
of its office furniture at five hundred dollars, and the value of
its mortgages and liens at twenty-seven thousand dollars.   The
return as to the value of mortgages was made without an admission that the municipal authorities had a right to assess and
levy a tax upon such securities, but as a matter of compromise
and in accordance with a plan agreed on between the municipal corporation and petitioner.   The tax-assessors of the city
declined to receive the return as to mortgages and liens, and
arbitrarily assessed the mortgages held by petitioner at the
sum of two hundred and fifty thousand dollars, and the
municipal corporation has levied a tax in accordance with such
assessment.   Petitioner has refused to pay that tax, because it
is illegally assessed, and the city has caused a tax fi. fa. to be
issued and levied on the real property and office furniture of

petitioner situated in the City of Savannah, and is proceeding to advertise and will sell the same to satisfy the fi. fa., unless restrained. Petitioner alleges that said municipal corporation has no power to levy or assess any taxes against building and loan associations except upon their real estate, and if the city ever had such power it has been abridged, suspended, and revoked by the act of the General Assembly which reserved to the State the exclusive right to tax such association in a particular manner, and has expressly rescinded the right and power of the municipality to impose a tax on the property of such associations. The tax assessed is contrary to the laws of the State and violative of the legal rights of petitioner. It prays that the writ of injunction do issue, restraining the city, its agents and servants, from interfering with the property of petitioner under said tax fi. fa.; that the said assessment and levy of tax be declared illegal and void; and that the tax fi. fa. be decreed to be canceled. In answer to the rule to show cause, the Mayor and Aldermen of the City of Savannah set up that the tax execution assailed is legal and valid, and that petitioner is subject to the tax demanded. On the hearing, after the introduction of evidence tending to support the allegations of fact made in the petition, the judge of the superior court refused to grant the injunction, and to his order so refusing the plaintiff excepted.

A number of questions of greater or less importance are made or suggested in the pleadings and urged in the briefs of counsel; but the main question presented for our determination is, whether section seven of the tax act of 1896 (Acts 1896, p. 27) is violative of par. 1, sec. 2, art. 7 of the constitution of this State, which declares that all taxation shall be uniform upon the same class of subjects, and ad valorem on all property subject to be taxed within the territorial limits of the authority levying the tax, and shall be levied and collected under general laws. This section provides for a tax upon certain shares of stock of building and loan associations, in the following words: "The president of all building and loan associations, or other associations of like character, shall be required to return to the tax-receiver of the county where such associa-

5

tions are located, at its true market value, the stock of such associations owned by the stockholders thereof (upon which, as shown by the books of such associations, no advance has been made or money borrowed thereon by the individual stockholders therein), to be taxed as other moneyed capital in the hands of private individuals is taxed; *provided*, that no tax shall be required of building and loan associations to be paid upon any portion of their capital which has been loaned or advanced to a shareholder upon real estate, upon which real estate tax is payable by said shareholders; *and provided further*, that the taxes required by this section shall be in lieu of all other taxes and licenses, whether State, county, or municipal, against said association, except a business license by the town or city in which the principal office of any such association is located, and except a fee required to be paid the State treasurer by act approved October 19, 1891." It is contended by the City of Savannah, that the second proviso of said section in effect exempts from municipal taxation the property of the building and loan associations which is held or located in the City of Savannah, and that for this reason the said section of the act is unconstitutional and void. On the contrary, three propositions are submitted by counsel for the plaintiff in error, as a basis for the contention that this method of imposing taxes on building and loan associations is not violative of the constitutional provision. These are: (1) That the proviso to the section creates no exemption of property from taxation, but, as a municipal corporation can impose no tax without an express grant of power, the proviso found in the section operates as a limitation of the right of the city to impose a tax on the property of building and loan associations. (2) That this proviso is a legislative declaration against double taxation. (3) That the tax imposed is a franchise and not a property tax.

It may be well to note, in passing, that the general tax act of 1884 contains an exactly similar section, saving and excepting the second proviso, and that in the case of *McGowan* v. *Savannah Mutual Loan Association*, 80 *Ga.* 515, the terms of the section were construed by this court; but the ruling did not involve the question of the constitutionality of the method of taxation there adopted, but only the construction of the body of the section together with the only proviso found therein; and it is not necessary for our purposes further to consider the ruling in that case, as the question in the case at bar turns largely upon the legal effect of the second proviso, which declares that the taxes required by the section shall be in lieu of all other taxes and licenses, whether State, county, or municipal, with the exception of a license tax by the city in which the principal office of the association is located.

It would be a work of supererogation at this late day to enter into a discussion, or cite authorities, to show that under the system of taxation prescribed by our constitution the property of all persons and corporations, unless exempted, is not only to be taxed but must be taxed on the basis of value. Under its provisions, property of every kind, real estate, money, choses in action, movables, are, as a rule, not only subject to tax but, taking value as a basis, subject to the same rate of tax; that is to say, the owner of land of the value of one thousand dollars must pay to the government, as a contribution for protection and support, the same number of dollars as the owner of personal property of the value of one thousand dollars pays —no more, no less; and property of all kinds is, by a proper interpretation of our statute, placed in one class as a subject of taxation. And not only so, but taxation shall be uniform on all property subject to be taxed; and this is true whether the tax is imposed by the State, by the county, or by a municipal corporation. The fundamental object sought to be accomplished under the provisions of our law in relation to taxation is equality, and that the rich man, the poor man, the corporation, the association, shall alike contribute to the support of the government on the basis of the value of the property owned, and that all taxation imposed in this State shall be on this equitable plan; and any method of the taxation of property which is not uniform and ad valorem is illegal and contrary to the plain mandates of the law. *Verdery* v. *Summerville*, 82 *Ga.* 138; *Athens City Waterworks Co.* v. *Athens*, 74 *Ga.* 413; *Mayor and Aldermen of Savannah* v. *Weed*, 84 *Ga.* 686; *Wells* v. *Savannah*, 87 *Ga.* 400; *Mundy* v. *Van Hoose*,

104 *Ga.* 292; *McLendon* v. *LaGrange*, 107 *Ga.* 356.   Par. 2,
sec. 2, art. 7 of the constitution declares what property is exempt from taxation. These subjects are purely religious, charitable or educational, and, except as named, no property in this
State is free from the burden of taxation. Taking the principles above announced as true, we come now to consider
whether the legal effect of the section of the tax act brought
under review is to exempt the property of building and loan
associations from this general rule of taxation, or whether the
General Assembly, in the passage of the act, sought to limit
the power of the municipal authorities of the City of Savannah in imposing a tax on the property of building and loan
associations. In an appendix to the Code of 1882, laws having reference to the City of Savannah were codified. These
laws, where they have not been changed by the General Assembly, are in full force, and by section 4847 of that code it
will be found that the General Assembly invested the municipal authorities of the City of Savannah with "full power and
authority to make such assessments, and lay such taxes, on
the inhabitants of said city and those who hold taxable property within the same, and those who transact or offer to transact business therein, as said corporate authorities may deem
expedient for the safety, benefit, convenience, and advantage
of said city, and may enforce the payment of such assessments
and taxes in such manner as said mayor and aldermen may
prescribe. Besides real and personal property, said mayor and
aldermen may tax capital invested in said city," etc. So that,
by the laws of the State, the municipal authorities of the City
of Savannah are, and have long been, invested with full power
and authority to levy and collect a tax for the benefit of said
city, on the real and personal property therein, which tax,
since the adoption of the constitution of 1877, is to be laid and
collected under the provisions of that instrument. *Verdery* v.
Summerville, supra. It is hardly to be presumed that the General Assembly, in the passage of the tax act of 1896, either intended or endeavored to withdraw from the authorities of the
municipal corporations of the State any of the powers in relation to taxation which had theretofore been conferred, and.

which are so necessary for the maintenance of the municipal government. Certainly no such intention is expressed in clear words, and no inference that it existed can be drawn except from the inhibitory proviso; and if such could be conceived to have been the intention of the framers of that act, it is somewhat singular that it existed only as to the property of building and loan associations and one or two other particular classes of corporations. It may not be amiss to say, that if it was the intention of the General Assembly to limit the power of the municipal authorities to tax the property of the corporations referred to, then a serious question would arise as to the power of the municipality to tax similar property of other corporations and persons under the general legal duty to tax all property alike; and we can not assume, from the language of this section, that it was the purpose of the General Assembly to make such a distinction in the taxing power of municipal corporations as would entail this serious consequence.

The section of the act under consideration provides for a tax on such shares of stock of building and loan associations as have not been advanced on. These shares are property, and the section in general terms declares that they shall be taxed as other property. By implication, no tax is to be imposed on such shares as have been advanced on, presumably for the reason, as stated by Chief Justice Bleckley in the *McGowan* case, supra, that shares advanced on have no value. We will not stop to discuss the question whether such shares have value, but will only say that if they have, they are taxable, and if they have none, they are not. We call attention to the fact that, after declaring that taxes shall be imposed on the shares of stock described, it is further declared that such taxes "shall be *in lieu* of all other taxes and licenses, whether State, county, or municipal, against said corporations" (except a business license, etc.); that is to say, that the taxes imposed shall, as to the association, be in place of all other taxes—that not only cities, towns, and counties, but even the State shall impose no further tax; and if the words used are to be construed as a withdrawal of the power of a city to impose a tax on the property of the association, it would likewise be a declaration of

the withdrawal of the right of the State to tax in any other
way.   Manifestly a conclusion reaching this result is not good;
but, construing section 7 as a whole, the better interpretation
is that the purpose of the legislature was to fix a tax upon certain shares of the association, which it deemed a fair and equitable mode of taxation, and that having paid a tax to the State
on this basis, no other tax of any kind or character should be
imposed upon it either by the State or by any county or city.
In other words, by this act, the General Assembly undertook
to fix an arbitrary basis of taxation against these associations,
which should stand in the place of any other property tax,
evidently upon the idea that the taxing power had a right, in
raising the revenue necessary for the support of the government, to classify subjects of taxation.   This our constitution
forbids, when applied to property.   We are not prepared to
say that, from the nature of the property to be taxed, a plan
may not be devised for assessing and collecting taxes otherwise than by direct imposition of the rate upon specific items
which together constitute an industrial or transportation enterprise.   Whether it may or may not be done is a matter with
which we are not now concerned; but if done, the plan, to be
legal, must contemplate an assessment which is the equivalent
of the rate on other similar property on the basis of value.
Certainly this was not contemplated, nor accomplished, by the
section of the tax act which is now under consideration.   That
act, so far as building and loan associations are concerned,
made but one item taxable, that is to say, shares of stock.   If
the association is possessed of other property, land, houses,
bonds, mortgages, office furniture, etc., why should not this
property also bear its proportion of the burden imposed by the
government?   Similar property of individuals and other corporations is taxed, and we not only know of no rule of law by
which such property can be free of this burden, but we know
of no moral reason why it should.   But it is said that the section is a legislative declaration against double taxation.   There
are, in general, four methods of taxing corporate interests.
These are—1st, by a tax on the franchise; 2d, on the capital stock; 3d, on the real estate and personal property of the

corporation; 4th, by a tax on the shares of stock in the hands of the stockholders. 1 Cook on Stock, etc., (3d ed.) § 561. See also 2 Redf. Rwys. 453, and authorities cited. It is not incumbent on the taxing power to impose a tax on each, but it may do so; and while, as a rule, double taxation is properly not favored, whether it will be imposed or not rests with the taxing power—originally the legislature. The decision in *Mayor of Macon* v. *Macon Construction Co.*, 94 *Ga.* 201, is not in conflict with the doctrine here announced. There this court was construing an act which only empowered the municipality to tax property and capital employed, which is, of course, itself property; and it was merely held that the capital stock of a corporation was not a part of its property or assets. But whether or not the object of the legislature in imposing the tax laid by the words of the statute be in fact a declaration against double taxation, yet such declaration can not avail in the presence of the declaration of a superior power, that in all events the property owned by the corporation must be taxed.

But it is argued that the shares upon which no advance has been made are in the nature of capital stock, and that the capital stock of corporations represents the property of such corporations. It is not necessary, in this case, to enter into an argument as to whether taxation of capital stock is the equivalent of an imposition of a tax on property of the corporation. The true rule on that subject, in cases where the doctrine can be applied, seems to be, that unless it is clearly manifest from the terms of the act, taken all together, that it was the intention of the lawmaking power, in imposing a tax on the capital stock, that such stock should represent the property of the corporation, it will not be held to be an equivalent for the tax on the property. Railroad Companies *v.* Gaines, 97 U. S. 697. But in the case we are considering, the capital stock of the corporation, as such, is not taxed at all. The words of the act are, that the president shall be required to return the stock of such associations owned by the stockholders thereof on which no advance has been made. This is not a tax against the corporation. The shares owned by the stockholders are the individual property of the stockholders, and are liabilities

of the corporation and not assets. *Mayor of Macon* v. *Macon Construction Co.*, 94 *Ga.* 201. It may be that under such circumstances the corporation would make payment of this tax a charge on its own funds, but it is not bound to do so. As was said by Chief Justice Bleckley in the case of *McGowan*, supra, "Of course, while the association is taxed upon this stock, it has or may have recourse to the owners for reimbursement .
. ; the corporation is required to return it and pay the tax on it; but if it is necessary to equalize the matter as among the stockholders, the corporation can require the stockholder to pay the tax to it. This is simply a scheme to reach this class of stock conveniently, by making the corporation return it and pay taxes upon it, instead of the owner of the stock;
. . the adjustment of the matter to reach equality among the stockholders being left to the corporation and the stockholders to make among themselves.". So that the tax imposed by this section is against the individual stockholder on his property, and, as a matter of law, there is no provision made for any kind or character of taxation by the act we are considering, against the property of building and loan associations. Judge Cooley, in his work on Taxation (2d ed.), 231, says: "A tax on the shares of stockholders in a corporation is a different thing from a tax on the corporation itself or its stock, and may be laid irrespective of any taxation of the corporation when no contract relations forbid." Citing 1 Cush. 142; 26 N. J. 181; 47 Pa. St. 106; 21 N. Y. 449; 39 Ill. 130; 15 Ind. 150; 3 Wall. 573; 15 Wall. 300; 8 Lea, 406; 32 La. An. 157. There can, therefore, be nothing in the claim in this case that the shares of stock taxed represent the property of the corporation; nor from its nature, as above shown, can it be successfully contended that the tax provided for is anything else but a direct tax on property. We have very carefully considered the elaborate briefs of the able counsel representing the parties in this case, and have only failed to review many of the points made and authorities cited because, in our judgment, the case, under the provisions of our constitution, turns on a few principles which, as we think, have been clearly settled. Necessarily, if we are right in ruling that the tax imposed by the act is in legal

effect a tax against the owners of shares and not against the corporation, no argument is required to meet the proposition that such is a franchise and not a property tax.   As we view the case in its entirety, the seventh section of the act of 1896 imposes no tax whatever against the property and effects of a building and loan association, but it simply provides for the assessment and collection of taxes against the holders of free shares therein ; and when it declares that such taxes shall be in lieu of all other taxes against said association except a business license, the conclusion is irresistible that the act contravenes the plain language of our constitution and is obnoxious to the system of taxation which is therein adopted, and that it affords no obstacle to the levy and collection of taxes on the property of such associations in the same manner and at the same rate which is imposed on like property of individuals and other corporations.   Whether the amount assessed against the plaintiff in error be just or not is another and a very different question, susceptible of easy solution.   As, however, no special stress was laid here upon that question, but the case was made to turn on the constitutionality of the act of 1896, it must, for the reasons stated, be ruled that the judge committed no error in refusing to grant the injunction.

Judgment affirmed.   All the Justices concurring.

MUTUAL RESERVE FUND LIFE ASSOCIATION *v.* CITY COUNCIL OF AUGUSTA *et al.*

A tax imposed by a municipal corporation on the gross premiums of an insurance company doing business in the city where the tax is imposed is not a property tax in the sense of the constitution, so as to require the ad valorem system to be applied. While by a municipal ordinance a tax on the gross premiums of an insurance company doing business in the city, at a given rate per cent., may be lawfully imposed if the authority to do so be clearly given, an ordinance which by its terms only imposes such tax on non-resident companies, and expressly excludes resident companies from its operation, is void for the want of the uniformity required by the constitution.

A license tax of a given sum imposed upon every agent of a fire or life-insurance company is payable by an agent of an association which has no capital stock but insures the lives of its members under the assessment

plan, and this is true notwithstanding such agent is the employee of
the company and does not represent any other company.

Argued June 1, 1899. — Decided January 30, 1900.

Petition for injunction. Before Judge Brinson. Richmond
county. March 13, 1899.

King & Anderson, for plaintiff.
William H. Barrett, for defendant.

LITTLE, J. The Mutual Reserve Fund Life Association
made application to the judge of the superior court of Richmond county, to enjoin the City of Augusta from proceeding
to collect from it certain taxes and license fees which the city
alleges that petitioner and the agent of the petitioner doing
business in the City of Augusta are due to it. By an ordinance
duly passed, the city imposed a tax of one and a quarter per
centum "on the gross premiums of every insurance company
not located in this city," and under this ordinance executions
have been issued against plaintiff in error for the years 1894,
1895, 1896, and 1897. In addition to the tax so levied, the
city through its officials demands of petitioner that it pay into
the city treasury an annual license tax of one hundred dollars.
Petitioner alleges that the ordinance imposing the tax on its
gross premiums is unconstitutional, illegal and void, and that
its agent in the City of Augusta is its employee, and not a
broker representing different life-insurance companies, and the
license fee of one hundred dollars is demanded under an ordinance of said city which provides that a license tax shall be
assessed "upon every agent of a fire or life insurance company,
for each company, of one hundred dollars," and that under
said ordinance it is not legally liable to pay said sum. It was
admitted that one and one quarter per centum, the rate charged
on the gross premiums of insurance companies not located in
Augusta, is the same as the rate charged upon real and personal property in said city, and that there is no insurance company with its principal office in the City of Augusta. It was
also admitted that the petitioner had been licensed to do business in the State of Georgia as a mutual life association furnish-

ing insurance upon the assessment plan, and that it had complied with all the laws of the State entitling it to do business. On the hearing, the judge denied the injunction, and the plaintiff in error excepted.

In order to properly determine whether the plaintiff in error is liable for the payment of the tax imposed upon its gross premiums, it may be well to consider whether such a tax is to be classed as a tax on property or a tax on business. The history of the legislation of this State, since the present system of taxation was adopted, will show that the General Assembly has invariably treated a tax upon sales or receipts as a business tax. In each of the general tax acts since the adoption of the present constitution, and for a number of years prior to that time, a tax has been imposed upon the gross receipts of insurance, sleeping-car, telegraph, and express companies, and at a rate different from that which is imposed by the State upon property in general. If these provisions of our general tax laws should be considered as a property tax, there would be but little question that they would be obnoxious to the provisions of our constitution, which declares that taxation shall be uniform and ad valorem. But if they are to be considered as a business tax, then, under previous adjudications made by this court, if all subjects belonging to the same class were made subject to the same rate of taxation, such provisions would not come within the constitutional inhibition. Leading text-writers, and adjudications of other States, with a considerable degree of unanimity, declare such a tax to be a business tax and not a property tax. 1 Desty on Taxation, 229, 303, 304, 375, citing a large number of adjudicated cases. The Supreme Court of Pennsylvania has directly passed upon the questions involved, and held, in the case of Insurance Company of North America v. Commonwealth, 87 Pa. St. 181, that a tax upon the gross premiums of insurance companies was a business and not a property tax.

There is, however, a seeming conflict in some of the cases passed upon by this court, where this question was involved. In one case, that of *Pearce, Wheless & Co.* v. *Augusta*, 37 *Ga.* 597, it was apparently held, that a tax on gross sales of cotton, and on the gross amount of all sales of goods, and on the gross receipts for storage, and on every one hundred dollars of commissions received by commission merchants and cotton factors, was a property tax. Subsequent rulings, to which we shall hereafter refer, held such a tax to be a business tax. This conflict was referred to by Chief Justice Bleckley in the case of *Gould* v. *Atlanta,* 55 *Ga.* 678, but in the decision in the latter case no attempt was made to reconcile the conflict, nor was the question now in issue directly decided. If the decision rendered in the Augusta case, supra, be critically examined, it will be easy, we think, to show that the ruling of the court can not be held as authority for the proposition that the tax imposed by the ordinance being considered was a property tax. The ruling made was, that the City Council of Augusta, under its charter, had the power and authority to enact the ordinance under which the taxes were imposed, and to assess and collect the same. It is true that Chief Justice Warner, who delivered the opinion, in the discussion of the question treated the tax imposed as a property tax; but, unless the decision of the court held it so to be, the words used in the reasoning of the judge are not sufficient of themselves, to adjudicate that the tax imposed by the ordinance was a tax on property. The part of the charter invoked to support the ordinance levying the tax vested the City Council of Augusta with "power and authority to make such assessments on the *inhabitants* of Augusta or those who held taxable property within the same, for the safety, benefit, convenience and advantage of the said city, as shall appear to them expedient." In the case of *Home Insurance Company* v. *Augusta,* 50 *Ga.* 530, this court held that the words in the charter above quoted were broad enough to authorize the city to tax occupations, businesses, etc., as well as property; so that it was not at all essential to the conclusion arrived at by the court to rule that the tax was one on property, in order to sustain the ordinance. As we have said, the court did not in terms so hold, and, as the charter was sufficiently broad to enable the city to place a tax on business and occupation, the ordinance passed in pursuance of the power was legal. As a matter of fact, the ordinance did not refer to the class in which the tax should be placed, but simply designated that a given rate per cent. should be imposed on the gross premiums of certain insurance companies doing business in the city. So, undoubtedly, the decision was correct, and the reasons given by the judge in coming to the correct conclusion are not to be regarded as authoritative expressions of the court. So construing the decision in that case, it is, as we shall presently see, not at all in conflict with subsequent decisions on the subject.

In the case of *Joseph* v. *Milledgeville*, 97 *Ga.* 513, a tax upon all gross sales of goods, wares, and merchandise was treated and considered as a business tax, and the effect of that decision is to practically hold it as such. As bearing on the point, see also the following decisions of this court: *Burch* v. *Savannah*, 42 *Ga.* 600; *Bohler* v. *Schneider*, 49 *Ga.* 195; *Home Ins. Co.* v. *Augusta*, 50 *Ga.* 530; *Wright & Hill* v. *Atlanta*, 54 *Ga.* 645. In the case of *Waring* v. *Savannah*, 60 *Ga.* 93, Chief Justice Jackson so pertinently deals with the question as to make his remarks valuable here. He says: "But are gross earnings and interest, coming in from any source, labor, capital, investment of any sort, money loaned,—are these things property in the sense of the constitution, and to be taxed as real, genuine property—such as real estate and personal effects,—or are these really *income?* Certainly the gross earnings of a laboring man are nothing but his income; so, it would seem, the earnings of a salaried officer are income; and so the income from capital employed in a bank, or railroad, or manufactory, would seem to be income only." In the case of *Mayor &c. of Savannah* v. *Hartridge*, 8 *Ga.* 28, Judge Lumpkin said that "The subject of taxation has been, very properly, divided into three classes—capitation, property, and income; . . and when one or more is mentioned or treated of, the other is never intended." And it was ruled in that case that a charter which authorized a municipal corporation to tax real and personal estate does not necessarily confer the right to tax income. We think, from the authorities to which reference has been made, that it may now be regarded as settled in this State that a tax imposed upon gross premiums of an insurance company is a business tax and not a property tax, and, being so, it may be imposed by a municipal corporation when clearly authorized so to do by its charter; but such power must appear by express words or unavoidable implication. 8 *Ga.* supra, cited approvingly in the case of *Trustees* v. *Atlanta,* 76 *Ga.* 189. We do not find it necessary to closely examine the acts incorporating the City of Augusta, for the purpose of ascertaining whether this power has been conferred, because, under a view of this ordinance which we shall presently take, it must be held to be unconstitutional and inoperative, whether the power has or has not been conferred. It will be seen, by reference to the terms of the ordinance, that the tax of which complaint is made is imposed only on the premiums of such insurance companies as are not located in the City of Augusta. It is, however, shown that no insurance company has its principal office in the City of Augusta, but this fact can not affect the legality of the ordinance. It must stand or fall, in this regard, upon its compliance with the constitutional requirements. Its legal effect is to impose a tax on the gross premiums of non-resident insurance companies, and exempt the gross premiums of resident companies, if such are now or should hereafter become established in the City of Augusta while the ordinance remains in force. On the legal question involved Judge Cooley in his work on Taxation, page 99, says: "The Federal constitution provides that the citizens of each State shall be entitled to all the privileges and immunities of citizens of the several States. The obvious purpose is to preclude the several States from discriminating in their legislation against the citizens of other States. A State law, therefore, which imposes upon citizens of other States higher taxes or duties than are imposed upon citizens of the States laying them, is void." Citing 14 Ala. 627; 22 Ark. 556; 11 Allen, 268.

In construing the constitutional provisions as to the uniformity and ad valorem system to be enforced in this State, this court has repeatedly held that one business may be taxed and not another. But the requirement as to this kind of taxation is, that it shall be uniform upon all business of the same class. *Cutliff* v. *Albany,* 60 *Ga.* 599; *Burch* v. *Savannah,* 42 *Ga.* 600; *Bohler* v. *Schneider,* 49 *Ga.* 195; *Home Ins. Co.* v.

Augusta, 50 *Ga.* 530; *Goodwin* v. *Savannah*, 53 *Ga.* 414;
Mayor etc. of Savannah v. *Weed*, 84 *Ga.* 683; *Weaver* v. *State*,
89 *Ga.* 639. A classification for taxation may be made, but
it must be reasonable and not arbitrary, and, in order to be
valid, must be natural. As an instance, we think the City of
Augusta, assuming it had legal power, might properly classify
the business of insurance, but a classification which applied
only to particular insurance businesses for the purposes of taxation would not meet the constitutional requirement. The
General Assembly of this State, in the exercise of its right to
classify the subjects upon which a business tax may be levied,
has provided that insurance companies, including resident as
well as non-resident companies, should be placed in a class.
In the case of *Gould* v. *Atlanta*, 55 *Ga.* 678, this court held:
"The power in the charter of Atlanta to tax itinerant traders
is not lawfully exercised by the adoption of an ordinance
to tax those itinerant traders only who are non-residents of the
city. No tax can be imposed on non-resident traders of
the same class." See also *Singer Company* v. *Wright*, 97
Ga. 119; *City Council of Augusta* v. *Planters Bank*, 47 *Ga.*
562. It must, therefore, be held that the ordinance is invalid,
and that no legal tax could be imposed under it, because of
the discrimination made against non-resident companies and
in favor of home companies. In relation to the imposition of
the license tax of one hundred dollars, we are equally clear
that the contention of the plaintiff in error should not prevail.
This ordinance is placed upon every agent of a fire or life-insurance company, and is a license or business tax on the occupation of the agent. Notwithstanding the plaintiff in error
is engaged in the business of life-insurance on the assessment
plan and has no capital stock, it is nevertheless engaged in the
business of life-insurance, and, being a corporation, it acts
through its agents, and notwithstanding the agent who represents it in the City of Augusta is not a broker, nor represents
other insurance companies, he yet represents this insurance
company, and is therefore, in contemplation of the law, an
agent of a life-insurance company, and is embraced in the terms
of the ordinance. Inasmuch as the judge denied the applica-

tion for injunction, we must, in view of what has been said, reverse that judgment; but we do so only to the extent of the tax executions issued upon the assessment on the gross earnings of the plaintiff in error, and rule that he did not err in refusing to restrain the City of Augusta in collecting the license tax imposed on the agent.

Judgment reversed. All the Justices concurring, except Simmons, C. J., who was disqualified.

ATLANTA NATIONAL BUILDING AND LOAN ASSOCIATION *v.* STEWART, tax-collector.

SOUTHERN HOME BUILDING AND LOAN ASSOCIATION *v.* STEWART, tax-collector.

SOUTHERN EXPRESS COMPANY *v.* STEWART, tax-collector.

SOUTHERN BELL TELEPHONE AND TELEGRAPH COMPANY *v.* STEWART, tax-collector.

1. The constitution of 1868 provided that "taxation on property shall be ad valorem only, and uniform on all species of property taxed." As long as that constitution was of force the General Assembly had power to exempt one species of property and tax another; and this exemption could be either express or result from a failure to provide that a given species of property should be taxed.

2. The constitution of 1877 provides that "all taxation shall be uniform upon the same class of subjects, and ad valorem on all property subject to be taxed within the territorial limits of the authority levying the tax, and shall be levied and collected under general laws." Under this constitution the General Assembly can not lawfully either expressly exempt from taxation, or accomplish this result by a failure to tax, any property except that which in the constitution itself the General Assembly is expressly authorized to exempt.

3. The tax of $1.00 for each telephone station or box, which is imposed by paragraph 2 of section 9 of the general tax act of 1896 upon telephone companies, is an occupation or business tax, and not a tax upon property.

4. The tax of two and one half per centum on the gross receipts of express companies, imposed by paragraph 1 of section 9 of the general tax act of 1896, is an occupation or business tax, and not a property tax.

5. Whether occupations shall be taxed, and if taxed how they shall be classified, are questions referred by the constitution to the General As-

sembly ; but all such taxes when levied shall be uniform upon the same class of subjects.

6. As the General Assembly has no power to exempt property from taxation by simply failing to provide proper machinery for the collection of the tax, a tax act will not be construed as failing so to provide unless such construction is absolutely demanded by the terms of the act.

7. The General Assembly has no power to declare that an occupation or business tax shall be levied upon certain classes of corporations, which when collected shall be received in lieu of all other taxes upon the property of such corporation.

8. All property of every nature whatsoever, except that which the constitution expressly declares the General Assembly has power to exempt from taxation, within the limits of this State, whether belonging to individuals or corporations, is not only subject to taxation but must be taxed, and the General Assembly has no power to declare otherwise. "Once for all, the constitution has enumerated the two classes of property, which enumeration the legislature, the courts, and the citizens must recognize as exhaustive ; property, whatever its species, is simply exempt or subject to be taxed. If exempt, it pays nothing ; if subject, the amount it shall pay is measured by multiplying the fixed rate into the actual value. The result will be, in every instance, that all persons who own taxable property of equal value will pay the same amount of taxes, and all who own more than others will pay more, and all who own less will pay less."

9. When a tax act provides machinery ample in its nature to bring under taxation all of the property of an individual, such machinery may be used to bring under taxation the property of corporations.

10. When a tax act provides machinery suitable to be used in bringing under taxation the property of all private corporations, such machinery may be resorted to for bringing under taxation the property of a corporation which the same paragraph of the law has unconstitutionally declared shall not be taxed in the manner therein prescribed.

11. The general tax act for 1896 provides for machinery which is ample in its nature to bring under taxation all such property of incorporated companies as is involved in the present cases.

12. Has the General Assembly the power to levy a tax upon the property of certain classes of individuals and corporations, and withdraw from the various counties of the State the power to tax the same?

13. The tax imposed upon the stock of the stockholders of building and loan associations under section 7 of the general tax act of 1896 is a tax on the shares as the property of the shareholders, and is not a tax on the property of the corporations.

14. The General Assembly has power to levy a tax upon the shares of stock of an incorporated company as the property of the shareholders, and also a tax upon the property of the corporation.

15. The General Assembly has no power to provide that a tax shall be levied and collected upon the shares of the members of a private corporation and that such tax shall be received in lieu of all other taxes against such corporation.

6

16. The obligation which a borrowing member of a building and loan association has assumed to such association is an asset of the corporation ; and to the extent of its market value, whatever that may be, it is subject to the ad valorem tax which has been levied upon all property within the State.

17. Has the General Assembly the power to declare that certain designated property has no value, and therefore shall not be returned for taxation?

18. As the officers having in charge the affairs of a county are authorized to levy certain taxes without a recommendation of the grand jury, it is incumbent upon one who attacks a levy for county tax made by such officers without the recommendation of the grand jury, in excess of fifty per cent. of the State tax, to distinctly allege and prove that the excess was levied for some purpose for which such officers had no right to levy the tax without the recommendation of the grand jury.

19. The provisions of section 400 of the Political Code, to the effect that it is the duty of the county authorities "to see that by the time of the organization of [the] grand jury [at the spring term] they shall have prepared by their county treasurer, under their supervision, a statement of the financial condition of the county, and the amount of tax required to discharge the county liabilities for that year, which shall be by the treasurer presented to the foreman of the grand jury on the first day of court, for inspection of that body," are merely directory and not mandatory, and the failure of the county authorities to comply therewith does not affect the validity of the tax levy made during the year.

20. A chose in action owned by a resident of this State, although the debtor is a non-resident, is taxable as property in this State, no matter where the evidence of the debt may be actually located. There is nothing in the "interstate commerce clause" of the constitution of the United States, or the laws passed in pursuance thereof, which would have the effect of prohibiting the taxation of such property by the authorities of this State.

Argued December 22, 1899. — Decided January 30, 1900.

Petitions for injunction. Before Judge Lumpkin. Fulton superior court. October 21, 1899.

Ellis & Ellis, W. A. Wimbish, Burton Smith, F. G. duBignon, Dorsey, Brewster & Howell, and *Arthur Heyman,* for plaintiffs. *Luther Z. Rosser,* for defendant.

Cobb, J. The four corporations named as plaintiffs in error each filed its petition in the superior court of Fulton county, alleging that the tax-collector of Fulton county was attempting to enforce the collection of taxes which they were respectively not required by law to pay, and praying that he be enjoined from so doing. The injunction was refused in each case and the plaintiffs excepted.　The following sections of the general tax act of 1896 are involved in the discussion which will follow :

"Section 1. Be it enacted by the General Assembly of the State of Georgia, that the Governor be authorized and empowered, with the assistance of the comptroller-general, to assess and levy a tax on the taxable property of the State, for each of the fiscal years eighteen hundred and ninety-seven and eighteen hundred and ninety-eight, of 3 45-100 mills; and the Governor be, and is, hereby authorized and empowered, by and with the assistance of the comptroller-general, to assess and levy, in addition to the foregoing general State tax, a tax of 2 50-100 mills, for each of the years eighteen hundred and ninety-seven and eighteen hundred and ninety-eight, on all taxable property of this State, for the purpose of raising·the funds necessary to meet the appropriations of this General Assembly for educational purposes in instructing children in the elementary branches of an English education only."

"Sec. 3. Be it further enacted by the authority aforesaid, that the taxes provided for in paragraphs 1 and 2 of this act shall be returned to the tax-receiver in the county of the residence of the person liable to such tax, and shall, by the receiver of tax returns, be entered upon his digest of taxable property."

"Sec. 7. Be it further enacted by the authority aforesaid, that the president of all building and loan associations, or other associations of like character, shall be required to return to the tax-receiver of the county where such associations are located, at its true market value, the stock of such associations owned by the stockholders thereof (upon which, as shown by the books of such associations, no advance has been made or money borrowed thereon by the individual stockholders therein), to be taxed as other moneyed capital in the hands of private individuals is taxed; *provided*, that no tax shall be required of building and loan associations to be paid upon any portion of their capital which has been loaned or advanced to a shareholder upon real estate, upon which real estate tax is payable by said shareholders; *and provided further*, that the taxes required by this section shall be in lieu of all other taxes and licenses, whether State, county, or municipal, against said associations, except a business license by the town or city in which the principal office of any such association is located, and except a fee required to be paid the State treasurer by act approved October 19, 1891."

"Sec. 8. Be it further enacted by the authority aforesaid, that the presidents of manufacturing and other incorporated companies, or their agents, other than railroad, insurance, telegraph, telephone, express, sleeping and palace car companies, shall be required to return all their property whatever of their respective companies at its true market value to the tax-receiver of the county where the same is located, or where the principal business of each company is located, to be taxed, save and except that all canal or stock water navigation companies shall make, through their respective executive officers or stockholders in possession of the same, returns to the tax-receiver of each county in which the same is located, or through which the same shall pass, in whole or in part, of the right of way, locks and dams, toll-houses, structures, and all other real estate owned or used by the company or the stockholders thereof; *provided,* this act shall not make subject to taxation any property of canal or navigation companies which is not subject to taxation by the laws of this State as now existing."

"Sec. 9. Be it further enacted by the authority aforesaid, that all persons or companies, including railroad companies doing an express or telegraph business and charging the public therefor, in this State, shall pay 2½ per centum on their gross receipts, and all persons or the superintendent or general agent of each telegraph or express company, or the president of each railroad company doing such business in the State, shall make a quarterly return under oath, as follows: On the last day of March, June, September, and December, in each year, to the comptroller-general, showing a full account of their gross receipts during the quarter ending on such date; and said taxes herein levied upon said gross receipts as shown by said quarterly returns shall be paid by the respective persons or companies to the comptroller-general at the same time of making such returns. The gross receipts herein named shall, be construed to mean the full amount of all money received from all business done within this State. If any person, superintendent, agent, or president, as the case may be, whose duty it is to make returns under this section, shall fail to do so within thirty days after the time herein required, such persons, superintendent, agent, or president shall be liable to indictment, and upon conviction shall be punished as prescribed in section 1039 of volume III of the Code of 1895. Second. That each telephone company or individual operating telephone in this State shall pay a tax of one dollar for each telephone station or box, with instruments complete, rented or used by their subscribers, and the superintendent or general manager of the company shall make returns under oath, and payments to the comptroller-general on the dates named in the first paragraph of this section."

"Sec. 15. Be it further enacted by the authority aforesaid, that in returning property for taxes all property shall be returned at its value; promissory notes, accounts, judgments, mortgages, liens of all kinds, and all choses in action shall be given in at their value, whether solvent or partially solvent."

With the order refusing to grant the injunction the judge filed a written opinion, which is in the record. We have arrived at the same conclusion that the learned and able judge of the Atlanta circuit reached in regard to the law of these cases; and as his opinion is so complete and satisfactory on every material branch of the case, we adopt the same as the opinion of the court and do not deem it necessary to add anything to what he has said. That opinion is as follows:

"Four cases are before me, all involving the collection of State and county taxes for the year 1898.

"First. The Southern Bell Telephone Company filed its bill to enjoin the enforcement of an execution issued by the tax-collector of Fulton county for State and county taxes. The company has made returns to the comptroller-general, as provided in the general tax act of 1896, in division 2 of section 9, as to the number of boxes or stations rented or used by its subscribers, and has paid a tax of one dollar for each station or box. It has made no returns of property for taxation to the tax-receiver. The tax-collector of Fulton county issued an execution against the American Bell Telephone Company for State and county taxes, on the ground that it was a defaulter, having failed to return certain property for taxation. The Southern Bell Telephone Company files its petition alleging that it is the lessee of the property referred to from the American Company, and that under its contract of lease the duty of paying any tax devolves upon it, and that the execution issued against the American Company should be enjoined. This is the first case.

"Second. The second case is that of the Southern Express Company. It alleges that it has made returns as required by section 9 of the tax act of 1896, and paid a tax of two and one half per cent. on its gross receipts, and that it is not liable for any further tax. It has made no return to the tax-receiver; and thereupon the tax-collector of Fulton county has issued against it an execution for State and county taxes, on certain property located in this county. That is its case.

"Third. The other two cases are based on the same principles, and are substantially alike. These are the cases of the building and loan associations. They allege that they have made returns as provided in section 7 of the tax act of 1896, and that they have returned to the tax-receiver of Fulton county, at its true market value, the stock of the association owned by the stockholders thereof, upon which, as shown by the books of the association, no advance has been made or money borrowed by the individual stockholders, and have been taxed upon this. They have also returned certain other property. The tax-collector has issued against these associations respectively, for State and county taxes, tax executions, alleging that they have failed to make returns of their taxable property; and against the enforcement of these executions, petitions seeking injunction have been filed. These make up the cases respectively.

"I will not stop to discuss, comparatively speaking, what may be termed the minor points in the cases; though, standing alone, they might be of considerable importance. For instance, the question whether the Southern Bell Telephone Company has any status to file a petition to enjoin an execution against the American Bell Telephone Company on the ground that it is a lessee; or the question raised by the Southern Express Company as to the valuation put upon its property; or on the question raised as to whether the interstate commerce laws have anything to do with the case. As to the last, I will deal with it no further than to say that if a man in New York owes a man in Georgia on a promissory note, or a mortgage, 1 know of no reason why the Georgia man is relieved from paying taxes upon it. I do not perceive that the interstate commerce laws have anything to do with it. The fact that the creditor resides in one State and the debtor in another does not free the creditor from paying on his property in the State and county of his residence. *City Council of Augusta* v. *Dunbar,* *50 Ga.* 387, 392. These questions I will not stop to discuss at length, because, comparatively speaking, they are of minor importance; but will pass at once into the great questions involved in the case.

"These cases involve several questions, but the most important may be reduced to two: (1) Do certain provisions of the general tax act of 1896 impose or seek to impose property or valuation taxes; or do they impose business or occupation taxes? (2) If they seek to provide for property taxation, or to exempt property from other taxes by valuation, are they unconstitutional? The first question applies more especially to the cases of the Telephone Company and the Express Company; and the latter applies to those cases, and also to that of the Building and Loan Associations. For convenience, let us take up the case of the Telephone Company first. The provision of the act of 1896 on this subject is contained in section 9, subsection 2, which reads as follows: 'That each telephone company or individual operating telephones in this State shall pay a tax of one dollar for each telephone station or box, with instruments complete, rented or used by their subscribers; and the superintendent or general manager of the company shall make returns under oath, and payments to the comptroller-general, on the dates named in the first paragraph of this section.' Can this be claimed to be a tax on property? There is not the slightest hint that the value of the box or station has any connection with the tax. For a station or box worth twenty-five dollars the company would pay one dollar; for another costing or worth a thousand dollars it would pay exactly the same. No effort is made to ascertain value, or to deal with property as to its value. The company might have buildings and real estate worth a million of dollars, and furniture and other property worth ten thousand dollars, or it might have no property and operate with rented property, but this clause has no reference at all to property, and would be the same in either case. It simply refers to the number of stations or boxes rented or used. A tax on a person, graduated according to the number of a certain kind of articles, apparatus, or machines employed by him or it, without regard to value, is unquestionably not a property tax, but an occupation tax. *Goodwin* v. *Savannah*, 53 *Ga.* 410, 414. This view is strengthened by the fact that the same tax is levied alike on éach telephone company or *individual* operating telephones. Will it be claimed that if an individual operates a telephone business, all of his property of every sort and kind is free from taxation, except to pay one dollar a box for the telephones operated by him? I conclude that the tax imposed upon telephone companies, or individuals operating telephones, of one dollar per box or station, is an occupation tax, and has no relevancy to the property tax which each individual or company must pay like all other persons. Further, the returns are to be made quarterly to the comptroller-general, not annually to the tax receiver or collector. The whole mode and method of returns and collections is entirely different from property taxation.

"Next let us consider briefly the case of the Express Company. Here the charge is measured by gross receipts. This, too, is an occupation or business tax. It has no reference whatever to the amount of property of the company, or its value. It deals with the amount of business done; not with the amount of property owned. Suppose the company should own no property, but continued business with rented property on which the owner paid the tax, would it not be liable to this tax on gross receipts? If so, clearly it is not a tax upon property, but is a tax upon occupation or business. *Waring* v. *Savannah*, 60 *Ga.* 93; *Mayor etc. of Rome* v. *McWilliams*, 52 *Ga.* 251, 273‑5; *Joseph* v. *Milledgeville*, 97 *Ga.* 513; *Mayor etc. of Savannah* v. *Hartridge*, 8 *Ga.* 23; Cooley on Taxation (2d ed.), 571. In *Gould* v. *Atlanta*, 55 *Ga.* 678, a query was put, but no ruling made. Even if a tax graded by receipts from sales, i. e., the purchase-price, may be closely assimilated to a tax on the thing sold, this could not apply to receipts, not from sales, but from business done not involving selling. The act provides 'That all persons or companies, including railroad companies doing an express or telegraph business, and charging the public therefor, in this State, shall pay $2\frac{1}{2}$ per centum on their gross receipts,' etc. Now suppose an individual or company worth one million dollars in property should do a small express business, receiving say one thousand dollars per annum. Will it be contended that the payment of two and one half per centum on this thousand dollars would relieve him or it wholly from all property taxation? But perhaps it may be suggested that it applies to such property as may be in some way used in connection with the express business. Let us see: Suppose a railroad company should do a little express business (and, for the purpose of taxation, the smaller the business the better for the .company), would the payment of two and one half per cent. on the receipts relieve it from taxation on its road-bed, depot, and rolling-stock, although all of them were used in connection with the storage and carriage of express matter? It will be observed that the act, as already stated, says, 'all persons or companies, including railroad companies doing an express or telegraph business,' and therefore puts a railroad company doing that business on an equality with express companies. If all were not exempt, what part would be? The engines pull the expressed freight for long distances, just as the horses for short distances; the cars haul the freight on its long journey, as the wagons do in delivery. The engines and cars can not move or haul express matter without a road-bed, and the freight can not be stored except in depots or warehouses. Where is the line to be drawn? Shall it be said that if the business is done by a railroad company, the tax imposed by this section is a business tax and does not give it relief from property taxation, but if done by another company that it is a property tax, or has the effect of exempting its property or taking the place of taxation on its property? Is it a property tax if done by one kind of corporation, and a business tax if done by another kind of corporation?

"Again, the returns and payments are to be made quarterly, and a failure to make such returns for thirty days is an indictable offense. It is quite common to make a failure to obtain a license, or the doing of business without a license, or without the payment of a license or occupation tax, penal; but if it has ever been sought, in the history of this State, to enforce the return and payment of taxes on property by indictment, I have not heard of it. It has been held in one case that a municipality could not tax income, although its charter authorized it to levy a tax on all property, and that the two were not identical. *Mayor etc. of Savannah* v. *Hartridge*, 8 *Ga.* 23. I am of the opinion that the taxes imposed on express and telegraph companies, under section 9 of the general tax act of 1896, are not property taxes at all, nor have anything to do with property taxation. If it be said that the payment of these taxes, and also of ad valorem property taxes, would be oppressive and burdensome, the reply is, that, if this be true, the matter of classifying and regulating occupation taxes is left by the constitution to the legislature, with the single restriction that there must be uniformity within the class. If an occupation tax is too high as to any class, the legislature can lower it; if too low, they can raise it. But the constitution confers no power on the legislature to say that "we have charged you too high an occupation tax; therefore we will exempt your property from taxation." Let it be noted that, as to the two classes of companies above referred to, there is not the slightest indication that there is any effort in the act to arrive at the value of their property, or to tax their capital, or their stock, or anything as a representative or equivalent of property value. But as to them it is a plain, bald charge upon their business or occupation, arrived at in the one case by counting the number of boxes or stations, and in the other by the amount of business done, or receipts therefrom, regardless of property owned. If it be said that the intention of the legislature was to accept this in lieu of an ad valorem tax, it seems to me that the constitution of this State does not authorize a tax on property to be measured in any way except ad valorem; that is, according to value. Civil Code, § 5883. I will discuss the constitutional question somewhat further in considering more particularly the cases of the building and loan associations; but suffice it for the present to say that, if I have made it clear that the amounts charged against these companies under the act of 1896 are fixed entirely without reference to the amount of property owned by them in this State, or its value, then either it is an occupation tax and has no reference to property taxation, or else it is a property tax graded not according to the value of the property, while the constitution says that all taxes on property shall be according to value. To hold that these are occupation taxes leaves them to stand as constitutional taxes; and the question of collecting additional property taxes will not affect them. To hold that they are property taxes, and not according to valuation, would make the whole tax unconstitutional. I think it proper to give the section a construction which will hold it constitutional. Thus construing the act, we have valid, constitutional business or occupation taxes imposed on express and telephone companies.

"The next question is whether anything in the act prevents taxation of the property of these companies within the taxing district. On this point there are two contentions on behalf of the companies: (1) That the legislature intended these taxes to take the place of, or as a substitute for, or commutation of ad valorem taxes. But a moment's thought will show that this is only another way of saying that, while it is true the constitution provides that all property shall be taxed according to value, and no property shall be exempted (except as specified in it), nevertheless the legislature may levy a tax or accept a sum for or in lieu of a property tax, without reference to value; or may accept a business tax and exempt the property of the person paying it. The legislature can not do this. (2) The second contention is, that, even if the position thus contended

for by the companies be untenable and not in accordance with
the constitution, nevertheless there is no machinery provided
for the collection of an ad valorem tax against these companies.   The eighth section of the act provides that the presidents of manufacturing and other incorporated companies, or
their agents, other than certain companies named, including
express and telephone companies, shall make returns to the
tax-receiver of the county where it is located, or its principal
place of business is located, of 'all their property whatever of
their respective companies, at its true market value,   .   .   to
be taxed for State and county purposes, as other property in this
State is taxed.'   It is said that this excludes or excepts these
companies from making such returns, and leaves no method
of collecting ad valorem taxes from them; in the language of
the briefs, 'no machinery' for doing so.   An effort is made
in argument to separate the State and county tax, and, on the
assumption that no ad valorem tax is due the State, to attack
the county as without power or means to proceed.   But if
what I have said above be correct, the State stands side by
side with the county as to this ad valorem tax.   If the construction contended for be correct, then we would have a general tax act providing a mode and machinery for collecting ad
valorem taxes on only a part of the taxable property of the
State, and the result would be that the whole act would be unconstitutional and void; for an act which provides for an ad
valorem tax on only a portion of the taxable property of the
State would plainly be contrary to the provisions of the constitution.   If the construction contended for were correct, therefore, the State would have no valid tax act, and the whole tax
system of the State would be unconstitutional.   No such construction will be put upon the act unless necessary.   What is
the correct construction, then?   This: The act of 1896 does
provide for the assessment and levy of a uniform ad valorem
tax on all the taxable property within the State.   This does
furnish authority sufficient to cover all taxable property, and
it is expressly so declared.

"Section 1 of the tax act provides, 'That the Governor be
authorized and empowered, with the assistance of the comp-

troller-general, to assess and levy a tax on the taxable property of the State,' covering the taxable property of the State. Section 2 provides, 'That, in addition to the ad valorem tax on real estate and personal property as required by the constitution and provided for in the preceding section, the following specific taxes shall be levied,' and so forth; thus covering all the property in the State, the taxation of which is contemplated by the constitution. Section 15 provides that, in returning property for taxation, all property shall be returned at its value, etc. If, then, there is an act broad enough to cover all property, and there is an attempt to except some from it, the act will stand, but the exception will fall. In the case of *Verdery* v. *Summerville*, 82 *Ga.* 138, Chief Justice Bleckley, delivering the decision, on page 142 says, in dealing with an ordinance which taxed realty only: 'By taxing realty only, the ordinance by necessary implication exempts personalty, and the tax officers whose function it might be to collect taxes for the municipality would be compelled to treat personalty as beyond the purview of the ordinance. Were the terms of the ordinance comprehensive enough to embrace all property of both kinds, and then by some further provision one kind were expressly exempted, the latter provision might be treated as void, and the tax on both kinds collected.' It may be doubted whether the legislature could constitutionally pass an act that the county should not impose an ad valorem tax on certain special property within its territory. It was contended by the attorney for the county that it could not be done, and it may be questioned, if the State can withdraw from counties the power to tax certain property, or the property of certain persons natural or artificial, why not of all? Where is the limit? It is asked, if the State may reserve to itself and withdraw from the county the right to tax property of telephone or express companies within its limits, why not that of brokers, private bankers, wholesale merchants, retail merchants, etc., etc., etc., ad libitum? It may also be suggested that possibly there may be a difference between the legislative power as to municipal corporations (which may be created, or abolished, or changed by the legislature), and as to counties, which under the constitution of 1877 the legislature can neither create nor abolish.   But without stopping to discuss whether the legislature can exclude a county from taxing certain property within its limits, in these cases, I have sought to show that, in so far as the act seeks to exempt or except certain property, the exception is not a mere withdrawal of the county's authority, but applies to the ad valorem taxation of the State as well as the county, and is altogether void to the extent of the exception.   The ruling as to taxation of railroads in *Columbus So. R. Co.* v. *Wright,* 89 *Ga.* 574, is quite different from this case. There the purpose was to arrive at a fair valuation for taxing purposes of property partly located and partly shifting, such as rolling stock and the like; and the mode of arriving at it, while in some respects different from the usual mode, was yet in substantial accord with it.

"If a legislature can not exclude certain property directly from taxation ad valorem, it would seem that it can not do so indirectly by some process of withdrawing 'machinery.'   To say that a legislature can not pass a constitutional act exempting a piece of property, but can effect the same purpose by saying to the taxing authorities, 'You shall not use the ordinary machinery of taxation or any other mode as to that property,' is a mere variation of terms, and not a variation, it seems to me, in substance.   The general tax laws furnish general machinery.   An unavailing effort to withdraw one cog from the machinery will not stop it, but it will grind on the same.   The cases of *Sav., Fla. & W. R. Co.* v. *Morton,* 71 *Ga.* 24, *City of Albany* v. *S., F. & W. R. Co.,* 71 *Ga.* 158, *County of Houston* v. *Central R. Co.,* 72 *Ga.* 211, *City of Atlanta* v. *Ga. P. R. Co.,* 74 *Ga.* 16, and *City Council of Augusta* v. *Central R. Co.,* 78 *Ga.* 119, did not discuss or decide any constitutional question, and, so far as the reports indicate, no constitutional question was raised in them, but they arose merely on the construction of acts of the legislature.   It is suggested in argument that the Supreme Court would not have held as they did had the acts been unconstitutional; but it is well known that neither the Supreme Court nor any other court is in the habit of raising constitutional questions affecting the validity of legislative acts, ex mero motu, especially where the revenue of the State is involved and when they are simply asked to construe an act. Indeed, courts do not generally decide on the constitutionality of an act at all, unless it is necessary to do so. The rulings of the Supreme Court are, of course, to be accepted as correct, but they are to be accepted as rulings upon the points which were before them, viz.: what was the construction to be given to those acts, and whether under those acts the counties and towns were given authority with respect to those railroad taxes.

" I now come more especially to consider the case of the building and loan associations. In argument it was contended that the tax imposed on building and loan associations was in fact a property tax, and that the act provided an equitable mode of arriving at a valuation of the association's property, and was not contrary to the uniform and ad valorem clause of the constitution of the State. In construing constitutional provisions which change former provisions, as in construing other laws, there are certain guiding rules. Among these I may mention a few. One is, to consider the old law, the mischief, and the remedy; another is, to consider the words of the instrument; another is to consider its reason and spirit. Let us look for a moment at the present constitutional provisions as to property taxation, in the light of these rules.

"The constitution of 1868 contained the following clause (section 5019, Code of 1873): 'The power of taxation over the whole State shall be exercised by the General Assembly only to raise revenue for the support of government, to pay the public debt, to provide a general school fund, for common defense, and for public improvement; and taxation on property shall be ad valorem only, and uniform on all species of property taxed.' The last words of the section may well be repeated, 'and uniform on all species of property taxed.' This was the old law. What was the mischief arising under it? It gave the legislature power to classify, not only occupations or business for taxation, but also property (as has been ruled by the Supreme Court). Its uniformity clause only extended to uniformity within the classes, but left power in the legislature to create a diversity of classes. Thus some property might be taxed one way, and some another, and some not at all. *Waring* v. *Savannah*, 60 *Ga.* 93. I do not stop to discuss whether legislatures did prefer one class of property of persons natural or artificial to another, in taxing property. They had the power, and that was enough, in the opinion of the framers of the new constitution, to call for a remedy. What was the remedy? In 1877 the people of the State held a constitutional convention, prominent among the members of which were those two great Georgians, Robert Toombs and Charles J. Jenkins, and a new constitution was adopted which contained the following provisions: 'All taxation shall be uniform upon the same class of subjects, and ad valorem on all property subject to be taxed within the territorial limits of the authority levying the tax, and shall be levied and collected under general laws.' Civil Code, § 5883.

"Section 5884 states what property the legislature may exempt from taxation. Section 5886 provides that 'all laws exempting property from taxation, other than the property herein enumerated, shall be void.' (See also *Mundy* v. *Van Hoose*, 104 *Ga.* 297.) Section 5887 provides that 'the power to tax corporations and corporate property shall not be surrendered or suspended by any contract or grant to which the State shall be a party.' The language would seem to be plain, its purpose unmistakable, to require all property to be taxed not only uniformly, but ad valorem. It left no loophole to escape. There was to be no classifying of property; no exempt property except that specifically allowed to be exempted by the constitution. The rule was absolute: Property, tax according to value.

"In the case of *Mayor etc.* v. *Weed*, 84 *Ga.* 683, the court makes use of the following language: 'The legislature or municipal authorities may classify all subjects of taxation exclusive of property, and may tax or exempt any or all such classes, with a uniform rate upon the whole of each class taxed. Taxation on property must be upon all not exempted in the constitution, with a uniform rate upon all kinds.' In the opinion, on page 686, the present Chief Justice says: 'If property is taxed, all of it must be taxed except that exempted in the constitution. The legislature or municipal authorities can make no exemption as to property; it must be taxed, and taxed according to its value. Though property is a subject of taxation, the constitution treats it as but one subject, and prescribes the rule of uniformity as to it by saying that all of it subject to be taxed shall be taxed ad valorem.' In *Verdery* v. *Summerville*, 82 *Ga.* 138, and following pages, the opinion was rendered by Chief Justice Bleckley. On page 139, he makes use of the following language : 'Property subject to be taxed is treated as one single class, and the only division of it contemplated or allowable is by territorial lines, coinciding with the territorial limits of the various authorities by which the taxes upon it are levied.' On page 140, discussing the difference between the constitution of 1868 and that of 1877 on this subject, he says : 'Another important difference between the two constitutions tends to show that property subject to be taxed is all to be taxed alike when any of it is taxed. That difference is, that the older constitution did not limit or prohibit exemptions, but the younger does. It specifies certain property that may be exempted, and then declares that laws exempting any other shall be void. Thus, the only classification of property, relatively to taxation, that is made or authorized, is into exempt property and property subject to be taxed; and taxation on all property subject to be taxed is required to be ad valorem, that is, according to value. Once for all, the constitution has enumerated the two classes of property, which enumeration the legislature, the courts, and the citizens must recognize as exhaustive; property, whatever its species, is simply exempt or subject to be taxed. If exempt, it pays nothing; if subject, the amount it shall pay is measured by multiplying the fixed rate into the actual value. The result will be, in every instance, that all persons who own taxable property of equal value will pay the same amount of taxes, and all who own more than others will pay more, and all who own less will pay less.' If this is not a clear, plain, and pointed statement, I despair of attempting to express the idea more strongly. If any part of the act of the legislature is contrary to the constitution, that instrument in express terms provides that it shall be the duty of the courts to so declare it. Civil Code, § 5733.

"I am not prepared to hold, nor is it necessary in this case to hold, that where property is transitory in its character, like much of that belonging to railroad and sleeping-car companies, the legislature may not fix some just and equitable rule by which to arrive at a valuation at the time for taxation. Possibly it may be competent to provide against taxing the shares of stock where all the property which gives them value has been taxed. I do not decide as to this, because it is not before me directly. But in this case, the act provides in terms, not for relieving shareholders against what might be claimed to be double taxation, if the company had paid on everything conferring value on the share; but, on the contrary, it provides for the company to pay only on the market value, not of its property, but of shares belonging to certain of its stockholders on which no loans have been made. It is exactly a reverse proceeding. Suppose it be true that, if all the property which gives shares of stock a valuation has been paid upon, it is equivalent to paying on the shares, and the owners need not pay again, or at least that the legislature may provide that they need not pay again, the provision of this act is that if the company will pay on the market value of the shares of some of its stockholders it need not pay on any of its property. It will be perceived that the two things are not identical, or even similar. Does this represent the value of all the property or assets of the company? Is it a rule for arriving at a just and fair valuation of the property of the company? If a stockholder in any other corporation borrows money and pledges to it his stock or mortgages land as security, is not his debt an asset of the company? It is true he occupies a dual position of stockholder and debtor, but that does not make the debt any the less an asset of the company, although as a stockholder he may be affected pecuniarily by the tax. Again, suppose a loan is only made on shares to half their value, surely they have some value left. Yet, under the terms of section 7 of the act, they are not to be considered at all. It only provides for returning for taxation shares on which no loans have been made. Under the modern system of building and loan associations, loans are not confined to the old method of being made solely

by 'selling' the money, or equivalent methods, and made to
the full value of the stock; and I believe it appears in the
record that in these companies loans have been made in a number of cases on stock alone, and not on real estate security.
Now, there is no rule of law that the associations are bound to
lend to the full value of the stock. Indeed, ordinary business
experience would indicate that they would probably not do so;
but that they would lend to half the value of the stock, or one
third the value, or the like, where no real estate security was
taken, and the only security was the stock itself. Nevertheless, under the terms of this section of the act they are to exclude altogether from taxation such stock, or what the company
holds as its representative value.

"Every person who knows anything about these associations,
knows that whenever a borrowing stockholder defaults in payment, and is sued by the association as a corporation, it gets a
judgment against him and his property; and yet that claim is
not to be considered as an asset—a loan on which suit can be
brought, judgment obtained, and property sold, is treated as
not an asset. It is not a mere advance of his share. It is an
actual loan, and he is sued and his property sold if he does
not pay it. It seems to me that the market value of shares
owned by stockholders, on which no loans at all have been
made, does not and can not represent the market value of the
entire property of the company—it does not furnish a rule for
so doing. That stock as such is not synonymous with the
property of the company or its assets, see *Mayor etc. of Macon*
v. *Construction Co.*, 94 *Ga.* 201. In making up the amount
a borrowing member is due at any time, when he is sued, certain charges are made against him, and he is credited with
something before judgment is taken. What? The value of
his stock. Yet here is stock with an actual value, and a value
which is credited to the defendant when he is sued on his loan,
and yet it is totally excluded from the return under this section of the act. The most positive proof that the market value
of shares of non-borrowing members is no criterion or measure
of the total property of the association is to be found by referring to the petition itself. Turning to the petition of the

Southern Home Building and Loan Association against Stewart, tax-collector, we find that in section 4 there is the following allegation: 'That in compliance with the requirements of this act, petitioner returned for taxation ·by the State and county for the year 1898 the market value of all its unadvanced shares within the jurisdiction of the authority levying the tax, and in addition thereto returned for separate and independent taxation by the State, county, and city all of its other property located within the jurisdiction and not represented in the market value of taxable shares (excepting as hereinafter stated),' so that it concedes that there is property not represented in the market value of shares on which no loans have been made.   Also in paragraph 5 it is stated that 'Petitioner failed to return for taxation for year 1898 the value of its office furniture and fixtures, which it is now advised by its counsel it should have done.   Petitioner avers that its office furniture and fixtures on the taxing day in the year 1898 were of the value of $1,400, which at the tax rate for that year amounts to $——— due the State of Georgia, and $——— due the county of Fulton as a tax thereon, which several sums with penalties and costs it has tendered to the tax-collector of said county, and now here tenders and offers to pay in court.'

"The act specifically limited the return required to the market value of the shares not borrowed on, and declared that this should be in lieu of all other taxes.   If the section of the act is unconstitutional, can it be helped or rendered constitutional by saying that this does not represent the property of the association except in part, but the association is willing to pay on some more which they concede they have?   When they apportioned the assets on their books so as to give a value to the shares, did they apportion nothing to shares of borrowers?   If not, how will the whole stock ever mature?   If they did so apportion any amount to shares borrowed on, then palpably the market value of non-borrowing shares does not represent the total assets so apportioned.   It is suggested that the act intended that all other property not going to make up the market value of stock according to its system of bookkeeping was not sought to be excepted.   But such is not the language of the act. Nor do I understand that an act can be made constitutional or not as bookkeeping may vary. It is to be remarked that, while this association may perhaps loan exclusively to members, an act has been passed which, if valid, authorizes these associations to loan to others than members at more than eight per cent. Civil Code, § 2388. The section of the tax act under consideration takes no account of this. Building and loan associations, as they now exist, bear little relation or resemblance to the original associations. Section 2398 of the Civil Code provides as follows: 'The name "building and loan association," as used in this article, shall include all corporations, societies, or organizations or associations doing a savings and loan or investment business, on the building society plan, viz., loaning its funds to its members, whether issuing certificates of stock which mature at a time fixed in advance or not.' If this means what it says, it looks very much like declaring corporations, societies, organizations, or associations which do a business of loaning its funds to the members, without regard to maturing stock, to be building and loan associations. How is section 7 to be applied to them? Note that this section of the tax act includes not only building and loan associations, but 'other associations of like character.' If every corporation or association that loans money to its members regardless of maturity of stock is a building and loan association, and a building and loan association may also lend to outsiders, adding principal and interest together and dividing the whole into monthly payments, what sort of an institution is an association 'of like character'? I have looked with some degree of curiosity, and I have only found the expression, outside the tax act, in the section of the code referred to, to wit section 2388, where it provides that building and loan associations and 'other like associations' may lend not only to members, but to parties not members, in a manner which the Supreme Court has recently held was usurious in others. There may be other places where the expression is used that I have overlooked, but this is the only place I have found where is added to building and loan associations the expression 'other like associations,' or 'of like character.' The only thing of 'like character' referred to in section 2388 seems to be the right to charge usury.

"It is true Chief Justice Bleckley, in *McGowan* v. *Sav. Mut. Loan Asso.*, 80 *Ga.* 515, after deciding the point raised, discussed somewhat the question of the constitutionality of the proviso of the act then considered as to real estate loans, and suggested a construction as a possible solution.   The constitutional question does not seem to have been directly involved in the case, and yet even an expression of opinion from so able a jurist is worthy of serious consideration, whether it be a direct adjudication or not.   But in the wide diversity of plans adopted by building and loan associations now, I hardly think he would hold as a matter of law that all borrowing shares were loaned on to their full value, or had no value.   He would, I suggest with great respect, hold that whether a share (whether borrowed on or not) has a market value is not a question of law, but a question of fact for the taxing authorities. If market value of shares is to be taken as a measure of value of all property of the association, should it not be the value of all shares, leaving the question whether any particular shares were of value to be determined as a matter of fact and not a matter of law?   Can an act of the legislature declare that certain property has no value?   People's L. & H. Asso. *v.* Keith, 28 L. R. A. 65.   I may remark that Chief Justice Bleckley treated the proviso as of doubtful constitutionality, and only to be sustained by so construing it as to exclude nothing which it appeared ought to be included.   The act as it then existed has been added to by a second proviso, expressly declaring that this shall be in lieu of all other taxes; and also the act of 1891 has been passed defining building and loan associations as above stated.   So that since that decision there have been two very marked and material changes.   The first is that the doubtful proviso has been rendered more doubtful by the second proviso excluding what Judge Bleckley seemed to think ought to be included, and also by an act of the legislature defining what building and loan associations are, and very much broadening the definition.

"I have found some difficulty on the question (raised by

the building and loan associations alone) on the county tax levy; but as they recognized it and paid a portion of the tax assessed under it, and as the charges are not very specific as to what excess over a legal levy there was, if any, and the year when a new levy could be made, if this be invalid, has passed, and except in a clearly made out case courts do not incline to grant ad interim injunctions against the collection of tax executions, I decline one in this case. *Decker* v. *McGowan,* 59 *Ga.* 805; *Hawkins* v. *Jonesboro,* 63 *Ga.* 527; *Walden* v. *County of Lee,* 60 *Ga.* 296; *Arnett* v. *Griffin,* 60 *Ga.* 349; *Verdery* v. *Summerville,* 82 *Ga.* 138. I think section 400 of the Political Code, if applicable to these commissioners, only directory, and that the entire right of the county to collect any revenue for the year will not be lost by a failure to comply with it. Besides, the petitions seek to enjoin the collection of certain executions as a whole, in which are included both State and county taxes. Now, if I have succeeded in showing that, under the law, the defendants owed State taxes, then these executions would certainly not be enjoined entirely, if at all."

In this connection see *Georgia State B. & L. Asso.* v. *Savannah,* ante, 63; *Mutual Reserve Fund Life Asso.* v. *Augusta,* ante, 73.   *Judgment affirmed. All the Justices concurring.*

SOUTHERN RAILWAY COMPANY *v.* DYSON.

109
a113
113
109
119
109
f 127
d128

When the petition in an action against a railway company for damages alleged to have been sustained by the plaintiff's unlawful expulsion from a train insufficiently describes the ticket presented to the conductor as the evidence of the former's claim of a right to passage, it is erroneous to overrule a special demurrer properly pointing out the defectiveness of the petition in this respect. FISH and LEWIS, JJ., dissenting.

Argued June 15, Reargued October 6, 1899. — Decided January 31, 1900.

Action for damages. Before Judge Gober. Cobb superior court. November term, 1898.

Dorsey, Brewster & Howell, E. W. Frey, and *H. M. Dorsey,* for plaintiff in error. *Mozley & Griffin,* contra.

LUMPKIN, P. J.   Mrs. Dyson brought an action against the Southern Railway Company, for damages alleged to have been sustained by her unlawful expulsion from a train of the defendant.   Her petition alleged that she purchased from an agent of the company "a ticket from Mableton to Atlanta, Georgia, for first-class passage to Atlanta, Ga., over defendant's line, paying therefor the sum forty-seven cents."   The character of the ticket was not otherwise indicated, nor did the petition contain any allegation that it was good for passage at the time when presented.   Her complaint was, that the conductor refused to recognize this ticket as valid and accept it for passage.   The defendant demurred to the petition generally and specially.   One ground of its special demurrer was as follows: "Defendant demurs specifically, because there is no description given of the ticket; because it is not stated what writing or printing or stamp appeared on said ticket, nor any of the conditions, dates, or anything going to show the character of said ticket."   The demurrer was overruled, and a trial had, resulting in a verdict in favor of the plaintiff.   The defendant moved for a new trial, which was denied, and by its bill of exceptions complains both of the overruling of its demurrer and of the refusal to grant a new trial.   We shall deal only with the question presented by the special demurrer; for, as we have reached the conclusion that the same ought to have been sustained, all the proceedings in the trial court subsequently to the overruling of the company's demurrer are to be treated as wholly nugatory.   *Jones* v. *Hurst*, 91 *Ga.* 338.

The character of the ticket was of the utmost importance in determining whether or not the plaintiff was legally entitled to ride upon the train from which she was expelled.   She claimed to be a passenger of the company under a contract with it evidenced by this very ticket, and surely the defendant, when it by special demurrer called for a description thereof, was entitled to have the same.   The petition did not allege that the price paid for the ticket was at the maximum rate allowed by law, or that it was unlimited as to time.   Although it would have been a simple and easy matter to comply with the defendant's proper and reasonable demand, plaintiff's counsel made no offer to amend. The failure to make an appropriate amendment ought to have resulted in a dismissal of the action. As the plaintiff chose to stand upon her petition as filed, and thus deny the defendant information essential to its defense, her rights in the premises are to be thereby tested; and we have reached the conclusion that she ought not to have been allowed to force the defendant company to a trial on the merits upon such indefinite and insufficient pleadings in respect to a matter of such vital importance.

Judgment reversed. All the Justices concurring, except

FISH and LEWIS, JJ., dissenting. Even if, in such an action, it was necessary to describe the ticket at all, the description in the present petition was sufficient. The special demurrer assumed that the ticket contained conditions, when it did not appear from any allegation in the petition that such was the fact; and therefore, in this respect, the demurrer was in effect what is termed a "speaking demurrer."

BIGGERS v. THE STATE.

109
116
—
109
127

Where a person indicted in the name of "Biggers" pleaded in abatement that his true name was "Bickers," and that he had never been known and called by the name of "Biggers," such a plea was properly determined against him on the doctrine of *idem sonans*.

The verdict of guilty was demanded by the evidence, and there was no error in overruling the motion for a new trial.

Submitted October 3, — Decided October 25, 1899.

Indictment for gaming. Before Judge Nottingham. City court of Macon. June term, 1899.

John R. Cooper, for plaintiff in error.
Robert Hodges, solicitor-general, contra.

LITTLE, J. Plaintiff in error was indicted in the superior court of Bibb county, for the offense of gaming, and tried in the city court of Macon and found guilty. He pleaded a misnomer in abatement, and alleged that his true name is not John Biggers but that his name is John Bickers. By consent the plea was submitted to the judge for determination, who adjudged that "Upon hearing the evidence I find 'Bickers' and 'Biggers' are *idem sonans*, and find against the plea." He moved for a new trial, on the ground that the verdict was contrary to law and the evidence. The evidence was clear and overwhelming that the defendant was guilty of the offense of playing and betting for money, within the statutory limit of time before the finding of the indictment, at a game known as "craps," played with dice; and the only question is, whether or not the court committed any error in his finding upon the plea of misnomer. We think not. The two names Bickers and Biggers have a very similar sound, and the rule laid down by Mr. Bishop in his Criminal Procedure (4th ed.), vol. 1, § 688, is, that the law does not regard orthography, that no harm comes from misspelling a name, provided it is *idem sonans* with the true spelling. He cites a number of cases to support the doctrine. In the 21 Mo. 504, "Blackenship" was held to be *idem sonans* with "Blankenship." In 18 Ill. 52, "McInnis" was held to be *idem sonans* with "McGinnis." In 2 Greene (Iowa), 88, "Conly" was held *idem sonans* with "Conolly." In the 18 *Ga.* 736 (*Chapman* v. *State*), it was held that "Hudson" was *idem sonans* with "Hutson." In delivering the opinion in that case, Lumpkin, J., said: "*Idem sonans* is no longer an infallible test. *Identitate personæ*, and not *identitate nominis*, is and should always have been the true and only issue." There was no pretense in this case that the person on trial was not the person who was guilty of the offense charged in the bill of indictment. His plea was that he was not indicted by his right name, and while in all cases the accused has the right not to be held to answer to an indictment framed against another person, nor against himself in any other than his true name or one by which he is known, such immaterial error in orthography as is alleged to exist in this case will not be favorably considered. There was no error in finding against the plea.

Judgment affirmed. All the Justices concurring.

HOLLIMAN v. MAYOR etc. OF HAWKINSVILLE.

|109 1
|112
f112

109 1
120 15

1. Where a petition for certiorari distinctly sets forth the errors therein complained of, a bill of exceptions alleging that the court erred in overruling or refusing to sustain the certiorari contains a good assignment of error.

2. A bill of exceptions sued out to review a decision overruling a certiorari to a judgment of a municipal court, convicting one of a violation of a municipal ordinance, need not be served upon the solicitor-general of the circuit.

3. When one is prosecuted under a municipal ordinance for doing business without a license, and defends on the ground that he is a disabled Confederate soldier, and therefore exempt from the payment of such license, a certificate from an ordinary, such as is provided for in section 1642 of the Political Code, is at least prima facie evidence that he is a disabled soldier, and becomes conclusive of the fact when there is no evidence to the contrary.

(a) The statute exempting Confederate soldiers from paying a license tax is applicable to those soldiers who are either disabled or indigent, and it need not appear in a given case that the soldier is both disabled and indigent.

(b) In such a case it need not appear that the person's disability was brought about by service in the army.

(c) Whether a disabled Confederate soldier would be authorized to do business in more than one place, or by agents, are questions not involved in the present case.

4. When a case has been tried before a mayor and appealed to the council, it is improper for the mayor to appear in the attitude of counsel for the municipality; and certainly, when he does, it is grossly improper in the council to allow him in his argument to make prejudicial statements against the accused not warranted by the evidence, and still more improper not to allow the accused to controvert the same by evidence.

Argued October 6, — Decided October 25, 1899.

Certiorari. Before Judge Smith. Pulaski superior court. August term, 1899.

W. L. & Warren Grice and *Hardeman, Davis & Turner*, for plaintiff in error. *J. H. Martin*, contra.

COBB, J. Holliman was tried in the police court of Hawkinsville for "the offense of doing business without a license." Upon conviction he entered an appeal to the council of the city. The case came on to be tried before the mayor pro tem. and the other members of the council, the mayor, who presided in the police court, not participating as a member of the court on the trial; and the accused was again convicted. He

carried the case by certiorari to the superior court, and upon
the judgment of the council being affirmed, he excepted and
brings the case here for review.

1. When the case was called in this court a motion was
made to dismiss the writ of error, one of the grounds being that
there was no sufficient assignment of error, the bill of exceptions alleging merely that the court erred in overruling the
certiorári.   Upon reference to the petition for certiorari it appears that there are a number of clear and distinct assignments
of error which must have been passed upon by the judge when
he overruled the certiorari, and an assignment of error in the
bill of exceptions that the judge erred in overruling the certiorari is equivalent to saying that he erred in refusing to sustain the certiorari on each and every ground thereof.   The case
of *Phœnix Ins. Co.* v. *Gray*, 107 *Ga.* 110, is controlling upon
this question of practice.   In that case it was held that an assignment of error in a bill of exceptions, that the judge erred
in overruling the certiorari, was sufficient, notwithstanding the
errors complained of in the petition for certiorari were not set
out in full therein but were embodied in a motion for a new
trial which was attached thereto.

2. Another ground of the motion to dismiss the writ of
error was, that the bill of exceptions had not been served upon
the solicitor-general of the circuit.   The constitution declares
that "It shall be the duty of the solicitor-general to represent
the State in all cases in the superior courts of his circuit, and
in all cases taken up from his circuit to the Supreme Court,
and to perform such other services as shall be required of him
by law."   Civil Code, § 5862.   It has been held that when
application is made for a writ of certiorari by a person who
has been convicted in a county court of a violation of a criminal law of this State, notice of the sanction of the writ and
of the time and place of hearing should be given to the solicitor-general of the circuit instead of to the solicitor of the
county court.   *Moore* v. *State*, 96 *Ga.* 309.   It has also been
held that a bill of exceptions alleging as error the overruling
of a certiorari which complains of a conviction for a criminal
offense in a county court should have been served upon the

solicitor-general of the circuit. *Starke* v. *State*, 93 *Ga.* 217, and cases cited. The case of *Allen* v. *State*, 51 *Ga.* 264, holding the contrary, has never been followed, and with that one exception the uniform ruling has been as above stated. It has also been held that a bill of exceptions sued out to review a judgment of the superior court, reviewing on certiorari the judgment of a city court convicting one of a criminal offense, must be served upon the solicitor-general of the circuit. *Hall* v. *State*, 100 *Ga.* 311. This would not, of course, be true where the act establishing a city court otherwise provides. See *Cooper* v. *State*, 103 *Ga.* 405. The reason why the solicitor-general is the proper officer to receive notice or service in the cases referred to is, that the State is a party in the superior court to such cases. As the State is not a party to a case originating in the police court, even though such a case should reach the superior court by certiorari, the duty of representing it does not devolve upon the solicitor-general under the constitutional provision above referred to. We know of no statute requiring the solicitor-general to represent municipal corporations either in the superior court or in this court in cases which originate in the police court of such corporation; and consequently a failure to serve this officer with the bill of exceptions in such a case is no ground for dismissing the writ of error. It is true that section 1076 of the Penal Code provides that, "in a criminal case, the copy bill of exceptions shall be served upon the solicitor-general." That section, we think, deals with "criminal cases" in which the State is a party; and even though the trial of a person in a police court of a town for a violation of one of its ordinances may for some purposes be considered "a criminal case," it is not such a criminal case as the section above quoted deals with; and consequently a bill of exceptions complaining of the overruling of a certiorari sued out to review the judgment of such a court need not be served upon the solicitor-general.

3. The accused contended that he was improperly convicted, because he was a disabled Confederate soldier and as such entitled to conduct business in the town of Hawkinsville without a license for the privilege of so doing. The law under which he

claimed this exemption is as follows : "Any disabled or indigent
Confederate soldier or soldiers of the Seminole, Creek, or Cherokee Indian War, or Mexican War, who are residents of this State,
may peddle or conduct business in any town, city, county or counties thereof without paying license for the privilege of so doing;
and a certificate from the ordinary of any county stating the
fact of his being such disabled or indigent Confederate soldier
or soldiers of the Seminole, Creek or Cherokee Indian War, or
Mexican War, who are residents of this State, shall be sufficient proof."   Political Code, § 1642; Acts 1897, p. 24.   Upon
the trial the accused admitted that he had been and was doing
business in the city of Hawkinsville without a license from that
city.   He introduced in evidence three certificates signed by
the ordinary of Laurens county, one to the effect that he was
a Confederate soldier, and that the ordinary had before him
the certificate of a physician showing that he was disabled.
The second was in these words: "I certify that W. S. Holliman is a disabled Confederate soldier."   The third stated that
Holliman entered the Confederate service in 1864 and continued in active service until the close of the war, and that he
contracted hernia in the service of the Confederacy.   In passing the law above quoted the General Assembly intended to
exempt two classes of Confederate soldiers from paying the
license therein mentioned, viz.: (1) disabled soldiers, whether
indigent or not ; (2) indigent soldiers, whether disabled or not.

The law declares that the certificate of the ordinary that a
soldier is disabled or indigent shall be "sufficient proof" of
these facts.   The certificate of the ordinary is certainly prima
facie evidence of these facts.   As two of the certificates introduced by the accused stated unequivocally that he was a disabled Confederate soldier, there was before the court prima facie
evidence, at least, to show that the accused was entitled to the
exemption claimed by him.   The law does not require that the
disability should have resulted from service in the Confederate
army, and therefore it was not necessary that the certificate
should state this fact.   There was no evidence whatever to contradict the statements made in the certificates of the ordinary
to the effect that the accused was a Confederate soldier and

that he was disabled at the time he claimed the exemption. This being true, his conviction for the offense charged was unauthorized, and the certiorari should have been sustained.

It was contended by counsel for the defendant in error that, even conceding that the accused was a disabled Confederate soldier, as the evidence showed that he was conducting a business as a merchant both in the city of Dublin and in the city of Hawkinsville, and as the privilege of conducting business without a license, given by the law to disabled Confederate soldiers, was personal and could not be carried on by agents, the conviction was proper. Whether this position is well taken or not it is not necessary for us to decide in this case, as no such question was raised in the municipal court; the answer of the mayor pro tem. to the petition for certiorari distinctly stating that "there was no issue made or tried except as to whether or not he was exempt from paying tax by reason of being [a] disabled or indigent Confederate soldier, and, there being no evidence to show that he was either, he was adjudged guilty."

4. Complaint is made in the petition, that, after the evidence was concluded and the case argued by counsel for the accused, the mayor, who had rendered the decision appealed from, was permitted by the council to argue the case against the accused, and made the following remarks: "A good deal has been said about the amount of this fine. My reason for making it one hundred dollars was that Mr. Holliman told me the town authorities of Dublin permitted him to do business there without a license and without paying tax, and I am informed on good authority that he was fined a hundred and fifty dollars by the Dublin authorities for doing business without a license, and that he afterwards compromised the matter by paying one hundred dollars. When a man undertakes to deceive me in my court and is convicted, I give him the full extent of the law, and I told Mr. Holliman my only regret was that I could not make the fine more. I told him this after leaving the court-room, and in answer to his question if I could not make the fine higher." The mayor pro tem., in answer to the writ of certiorari, says: "It is not true that the Hon. S. A. Way was permitted to argue the case against the defendant.

It is true that the mayor made a statement explaining his action in imposing the fine upon Holliman, and used in substance the language set forth in the petition. He also stated, as a further reason, that the pension law was abused, that Holliman was worth a considerable sum; and this statement was simply in explanation of his action in imposing the fine which had been criticised." The decision of the mayor being under review in the trial before the council, he was disqualified from acting as a member of that court. Civil Code, § 4045. The mayor recognized this, and did not preside over the council. The policy of the law in disqualifying the mayor from presiding on the appeal from his decision would seem to require that he should abstain absolutely from interference in any way or connection of any kind with the case when it is tried on the appeal. It does not seem proper for a judge whose decision is under review to appear in the appellate court in the attitude of counsel to endeavor to sustain the rulings made by him as judge. But even if it was lawful and proper for the mayor to appear before the council in the attitude of a prosecuting attorney, he should have been kept within the bounds of legitimate argument, and not permitted, under the guise of argument, to state facts which were irrelevant and of a character calculated to prejudice the accused. Especially would remarks of the character above quoted furnish ground of complaint when the record discloses, as it does in this case, that the council refused to hear the accused in contradiction of the statements made by the mayor.

Judgment reversed. All the Justices concurring.

HARTFIELD *et al. v.* CITY OF COLUMBUS (two cases).

1. A disabled or indigent Confederate soldier holding the proper certificate from an ordinary may, except as to those kinds of business in which he is not by virtue of such certificate authorized to engage, lawfully conduct as many lines of business as he is able to carry on in his own name and upon his own account, without paying to any municipal corporation a license tax upon any particular business so carried on or upon any subordinate branch thereof.

2. An agent, servant, or employee of a Confederate soldier lawfully operat-

ing under such a certificate is not amenable to a city ordinance imposing a penalty for "doing business without license."

Argued October 5, — Decided October 27, 1899.

Certiorari.   Before Judge Butt.   Muscogee superior court.
May term, 1899.

Cameron & Hargett, for plaintiffs in error.
Francis D. Peabody, contra.

LUMPKIN, P. J.   The plaintiffs in error, Hartfield and Salter,
were separately convicted, in the recorder's court of the City
of Columbus, of the offense of "doing business without license."
Each sued out a certiorari, which was overruled, and he excepted.   In this court the two cases were argued together, and
may be disposed of in the same manner.   The facts are substantially as follows: J. R. Christian and William A. Adams were
indigent Confederate soldiers, and each of them had received
from the ordinary of Muscogee county a certificate authorizing
him to conduct business without any license for this privilege.
Christian was carrying on within the City of Columbus a draying business, in the conduct of which he employed Hartfield
as a driver.   The latter had no interest in the business or in
the property used in carrying on the same, but was simply
working for wages as the servant of Christian.   Adams was
the owner of a wood-yard and carried on the business of retailing wood in the city.   Salter was a mere employee of Adams,
having no interest in the business but working for wages,
which he earned by driving a wagon belonging to Adams and
delivering wood to the customers of his employer.   On some
occasions, Salter carried wood about the city for sale in small
quantities, found purchasers for the same, and collected the
price thereof, his so doing being an incidental feature of the
business of Adams.   The two cases, in the view we take of the
law, stand upon substantially the same footing.   Section 1642
of the Political Code, as amended by the act of December 9,
1897 (Acts of 1897, pp. 24–5), authorizes any indigent or disabled Confederate soldier residing in this State to "peddle or
conduct business in any town, city, county or counties thereof,
without paying license for the privilege of so doing, . . pro-

vided that this section shall not authorize peddling or dealing in ardent and intoxicating drinks." By the act of December 20, 1898 (Acts of 1898, pp. 46–7), this section was further amended so as to prohibit soldiers operating under certificates from the ordinary from "running a billiard, pool, or other table of like character, or dealing in futures, or peddling stoves or clocks, or carrying on the business of a pawnbroker or auctioneer, or dealing in lightning-rods."

The position of counsel for the city was, that under the law a Confederate soldier could not carry on more than one kind of business by virtue of his certificate from the ordinary; and further, that even if a Confederate soldier engaged in only one particular business having subordinate branches which were the subjects of municipal taxation, he was not exempt from paying the license imposed by the tax ordinance of the city upon each of such branches. In this connection it was urged that as the city levied an occupation tax of ten dollars on a dealer in wood, and also a specific license tax on each wagon or dray used by such dealer in connection with his business, a Confederate soldier engaged in such business, while exempt from paying the ten dollars as an occupation tax, would be liable for the specific tax levied on each wagon or dray used by him. The case of *Macon Sash Company* v. *Macon*, 96 *Ga.* 23, was cited in support of the contention that a general license to conduct a given business does not exempt a person carrying on the same from paying an additional license tax on each of the subordinate branches thereof. We do not think, however, the decision in that case is at all applicable to those now under consideration. The fundamental mistake of counsel for the city lies in the proposition advanced by him, that the certificate of the ordinary limits the holder of the same to the transaction without license of one particular kind of business only. We are firmly of the opinion that under the law the holder of such a certificate is authorized to engage in business generally, and therefore to carry on as many different lines of business as he may be able with his own means to conduct in his own name and on his own account. Of course, he could not legally transfer his privilege, directly or indirectly, to another. We ac-

cordingly hold that a Confederate soldier having a proper certificate from the ordinary may carry on a draying business
without paying any license for the privilege of so doing, and
also without paying any specific taxes upon the drays used by
him in connection therewith; and further, that he may engage
in selling wood and delivering the same by wagons without becoming liable for any municipal tax either upon his occupation or upon the vehicles by means of which his business is
conducted.   As a matter of course, his servants and employees
are also protected by the certificate under which he operates,
and can not themselves be called upon to pay for any license
covered by the exemption granted to him.

It follows from the above, that the conviction of the plaintiffs in error was unlawful, and that the superior court erred
in holding to the contrary.

Judgment in each case reversed.   All the Justices concurring.

PHELPS *v.* THE STATE.

1. A written contract for the dissolution of a partnership between two persons, wherein it was, among other things, stipulated that in consideration of a specified sum to be paid by one to the other within a stated
number of days the latter agreed to transfer his interest in the firm and
its assets to the former, who was to execute to the seller " a thirty-day option to purchase the business " at a designated price, was apparently executory, and certainly did not by its terms operate to immediately effectuate the contemplated dissolution.   In order for it to have this effect, it
was, in any event, essential that both parties so understood and intended.
2. If shortly after the execution of such a contract, and before payment in
full to the selling partner of the price agreed upon for his interest in the
partnership, a debtor thereof, voluntarily and without solicitation, paid
to him a sum due the firm, a proper determination of the question
whether or not he received this money in the belief that it was still his
right, as a member of the firm, to make the collection, would depend
largely upon his understanding of the true intent and meaning of the
contract with reference to the time when the dissolution was to take
effect.
3. Accordingly, the mere facts that such a contract had been executed, and
that the partner who thereby agreed to sell out had received money due
the firm as above indicated, would not of themselves warrant the conclusion that in so doing he acted with a fraudulent intent, nor justify a
jury in convicting him of a larceny of the money, even though he might,

after receiving the price of his interest in the partnership and after signing another instrument by which the dissolution was unquestionably
accomplished, have failed to pay over or account for the sum so collected.
4. Some of the instructions complained of in the motion for a new trial
were out of harmony with the rules above laid down, and therefore erroneous. For this reason, and upon a general view of entire case as presented by the record, there should be another trial.

Argued October 3, — Decided October 26, 1899.

Accusation of simple larceny. Before Judge Calhoun.
Criminal court of Atlanta. May 27, 1899.

Hunt & Golightly and *J. D. Humphries*, for plaintiff in error.
J. F. O'Neill, solicitor, H. C. Erwin, Howard Van Epps, and
Beverly W. Wrenn Jr., contra.

COBB, J. Phelps was placed upon trial in the criminal
court of Atlanta, on an accusation charging that he had committed the offense of simple larceny by stealing "two dollars
and thirty-seven cents in money, the property of E. E. G. Roberts." The evidence showed that Phelps and Roberts had
been copartners in a mercantile business under the firm name
of W. C. Phelps & Company, and that on February 11, 1899,
they entered into a written agreement, the material parts of
the same being as follows: "This agreement witnesseth that,
for and in consideration of fifty dollars to be paid to W. C.
Phelps within seven days, I hereby agree to transfer to Mr.
E. E. G. Roberts my interest in the firm of W. C. Phelps and
Co., said Roberts to assume all and relieve me of all liabilities
of said firm, and in further consideration of the transfer said
Roberts is to execute to Mr. W. C. Phelps, a thirty-day option
to purchase the business for seventeen hundred and fifty dollars." When this paper was signed Roberts paid to Phelps
fifty cents, and on the evening of the 13th day of February
the two persons signed another paper of which the following
is a copy: "The firm of W. C. Phelps & Co., composed of
W. C. Phelps and E. E. G. Roberts, is hereby dissolved, the
said W. C. Phelps retiring from the business and E. E. G.
Roberts continuing the same and assuming all of the old firm
liabilities." On the same day Roberts paid to Phelps $49.50,
the balance due by the terms of the paper first above quoted,

$2 of the amount having been previously paid. On that day and before the paper last referred to was signed, Phelps called at the store of Shirley for the purpose of soliciting an order for goods for the firm of Phelps & Company, and while there Shirley, noticing that an account owing by him to that firm was due on that day, voluntarily and without solicitation on the part of Phelps, paid him the amount of the account and Phelps receipted for it in his individual name. According to the testimony of Roberts, Phelps never disclosed to him that he had collected this account and never accounted to him for the amount thereof in any settlement that he made with him. Phelps in his statement asserted that he had accounted to Roberts for this money along with other collections made by him. The jury, under the charge of the court, returned a verdict of guilty, and the plaintiff's motion for a new trial having been overruled, he excepted.

The rules of law applicable to the case under consideration are stated in the headnotes. The charge of the court is not in entire harmony with these rules, and for this reason a reversal of the judgment is necessary. Conceding that the testimony for the State disclosed the truth of the transaction under investigation, the issue to be determined was whether the accused, when he collected the money and failed to pay it over to Roberts, knew that he was acting without authority and intended to appropriate to his own use property which was not his own and which he had no right to control; or whether he was acting in good faith, believing he had a right to collect the money, and that his failure to account for the same to his former partner was of such a character as to render him only civilly liable for the wrong done by him.

Judgment reversed. All the Justices concurring.

BICE *v.* THE STATE.

The provision of law which prohibits carrying to a church, or other place where the people have assembled for divine worship, any liquor or intoxicating drink, is violated when one attending such exercises at a named church has in his buggy a bottle containing whisky, and the buggy is left standing within one or two hundred yards of the church building during the exercises. The defense that such liquor was carried there to be used by the wife of the person carrying it, in case of a sudden attack of illness, will not avail against the plain words of the statute, which itself furnishes the only exceptions allowable to the operation of the law.

Argued October 16, — Decided October 26, 1899.

Indictment for carrying liquor to church. Before Judge Reagan. Monroe superior court. August term, 1899.

Persons & Persons, for plaintiff in error.

O. H. B. Bloodworth, solicitor-general, contra.

LITTLE, J. Bice was indicted for the offense of carrying liquor to a church, and found guilty. He moved for a new trial, which was refused, and he excepted. It was shown that Bice went to Hopewell church in Monroe county, carrying his wife in a buggy. On arriving there he detached his mule and left the buggy one or two hundred yards distant from the church. He had some whisky in a bottle which he left in his buggy when he and his wife went into the church building where a religious meeting was in progress. This was on a Sunday in August, 1899. The defense relied on by the accused was, that his wife for two years had been troubled with heart disease, and that a physician furnished him the whisky and told him it was necessary to take it along for her. The motion for new trial is based on the grounds, that the verdict is contrary to law and against the evidence; and that the court in effect charged the jury that it was unlawful for the defendant to carry liquor to a church even under the direction of a physician who had prescribed whisky as a medicine for his wife who accompanied him, that no one can carry liquor to church even as a medicine, except a physician, that in cases of accident or misfortune liquor may be carried to a church and used, but not otherwise than by a physician, etc.

Two points are raised in the brief of counsel for plaintiff in error: first, that the place at which the liquor was carried and left was several hundred yards from a church or place where people assembled for divine worship, and that this did not constitute a violation of the law; second, that taking spirituous liquor to a church, for the use of a sick person who might need

it, was not within the contemplation of the statute. Neither
of these contentions is, in our judgment, sound. Section 438
of the Penal Code positively forbids any person from carrying
to a church, or other place where the people have assembled
for divine worship, any liquor or intoxicating drink. To this
mandatory provision of the law certain exceptions are made in
section 441 of the Penal Code. The exceptions named are,
that it shall not be unlawful to use intoxicating liquors at such
places in case of accident or misfortune, nor are practicing
physicians prohibited from carrying and using such liquor as
they may deem necessary in their regular practice. It is contended that these sections of the code should be strictly construed. We think so, too, but not so strictly as to defeat the
evident purpose which was intended to be accomplished. The
object of this provision of the law was to absolutely prevent
the indulgence in intoxicating liquors at a church where people were assembled for worship, and such object would be defeated if the provision were so construed as to permit persons
to take such liquors to a point within one or two hundred yards
of the church building within ready reach of the thirsty. It
was hardly contemplated that the statute would only be violated by taking the liquor into a church. Certainly its purpose was to preserve order and promote that decorous conduct
on the part of those who attend the services as befits the occasion, and to absolutely prohibit the introduction into the assembly of an influence which might defeat these objects. Taking into consideration the purposes of the act on which the section of the code is founded, a fair and even strict construction
requires us to hold that, when it forbids carrying intoxicating
liquor to a church, it means also to forbid its introduction to
a place in such immediate proximity to the church building
as to make it readily accessible to those who may desire to use
it. This court has ruled that an indictment charging one with
disturbing a congregation "at" a named church is supported
by proof that the congregation was disturbed at a bush-arbor
near such church. *Minter* v. *State*, 104 *Ga.* 743. The principle as to place, there ruled, governs the first point made by
the plaintiff in error.

Nor do we think the charge of the court complained of was error. It is well enough to provide against sickness, not only in the form of heart disease, but of colic, cramps, and the like as well; but, under the statute we are considering, such a provision can not lawfully be made by carrying the medicine to church, if such medicine be whisky or other intoxicating liquor; and if one should unfortunately be subject to any of these ills, he must either stay at home, or, if he wishes to provide against sudden attacks, take with him some other kind of medicine. A practicing physician may lawfully carry and use at a church such intoxicating liquor as he may deem necessary in his regular practice, but a layman can not, even when advised so to do by a physician. As to this matter, the privilege given by law to the physician is by the same law withheld from the layman. The statute itself fixes the exceptions to the operation of the law. To these we can not make any addition. In our judgment, the plaintiff in error violated the law, he was properly convicted, and the court committed no error in overruling his motion for a new trial.

Judgment affirmed. All the Justices concurring.

BUSH v. THE STATE.

1. When, in passing on a motion to continue a criminal case because of the absence of two material witnesses, the presiding judge directed the trial to proceed, with the statement that he would send for the witnesses and if he did not procure their attendance he would then entertain a motion to continue from the defendant, and when during the progress of the trial an officer returned with one of such witnesses, reporting that the other could not be found, and the defendant did not renew the motion, but without objection the case proceeded to verdict, a new trial will not be granted because the continuance was thus refused.
2. There was no error in excluding the answer to a question relating to character, the question itself not being in proper legal form. Had it been otherwise, this court could not have considered the point thus sought to be made, because the ground of the motion does not state what the witness would have answered had he been permitted.
3. Such conversation and conduct of the parties as are properly parts of the res gestæ of the homicide may lawfully go to the jury in a dying declaration made by the deceased.

4. When in a prosecution for a homicide dying declarations are sought to be admitted, the judge must first determine from preliminary evidence whether prima facie they are competent as such, and were made under circumstances entitling them to admission ; but, having been admitted, it is for the jury to finally pass on the question whether or not such declarations of the deceased were conscious utterances in the apprehension and immediate prospect of death. A charge which does not so instruct the jury, but may be so construed as that the jury will infer that they must take such admissions as a part of the evidence in the case, without a qualification that they must finally determine whether such declarations were made and, if they were, at a time when the deceased was in the article of death and conscious of his condition, was error.
5. No other errors requiring a reversal of the judgment appear in the motion for new trial.

Argued October 3,—Decided October 27, 1899.

Indictment for voluntary manslaughter. Before Judge Spence. Miller superior court. April term, 1899.

W. D. Sheffield, *C. C. Bush*, and *R. H. Powell & Son*, for plaintiff in error. *John R. Irwin, solicitor-general*, by *King & Anderson* and *Lewis W. Thomas*, contra.

LITTLE, J. Bush was indicted for the offense of voluntary manslaughter, and found guilty. He made a motion for a new trial, which was refused, and he excepted.

1. One of the assignments of error is that the court refused to continue the case on the showing made by the accused. This showing was based on the absence of four witnesses. It does not satisfactorily appear, by the evidence submitted on the motion to continue, that two of the witnesses had been subpœnaed; the other two had, and at the conclusion of the evidence on the motion the court stated that he refused the motion as to the two witnesses who it appeared had not been subpœnaed; that the other two witnesses, Spooner and Thompson had been sent for by the court, and that if they should be brought in after the case had been ruled to trial he would allow them to be sworn at any time; that if they did not come, a motion from the defendant, even after the case had gone to trial, to continue it on account of their absence, would be entertained. Before the consideration of the case was concluded, the witness Spooner was brought into court and sworn.

The officer who had been sent for Thompson returned and stated that he could not be found. No further motion was made by counsel for defendant to continue on the ground of the absence of Thompson, and, without any further reference to the question of continuance, the case proceeded to verdict.

It must be conceded that the action of the court in conditionally refusing the motion to continue was irregular. Very much the better practice would have been to postpone the trial of the case until the two witnesses Spooner and Thompson had been sent for, and failing to respond, the judge should have then passed absolutely upon the motion submitted. It was not shown that the other two witnesses had been subpœnaed, and of course there should not have been any continuance on account of their absence. When the judge in response to the motion to continue for the absence of the two subpœnaed witnesses stated that he would send for the witnesses, and if they were not brought into court that he would then entertain a motion from the defendant to continue, it was such an intimation that he would continue the case unless he was able to procure the attendance of the witnesses as required the counsel, when it was ascertained that Thompson could not be found, to renew the motion if they then desired to continue. No further suggestion in relation to continuance was made. It must therefore be assumed that if, under the circumstances stated, the motion had been renewed, the court would have continued the case, and that the judge was justified in supposing, in the absence of any renewal of the motion, that the defendant was satisfied to proceed, having procured the testimony of one of the witnesses. While this manner of passing on a motion to continue is irregular and unsatisfactory, it does not afford any ground for a reversal of the judgment.

2. It is further complained that the court sustained an objection to a question propounded in the following form: "Mr. Corbett [deceased] was a man of violent disposition, wasn't he?" We suppose that this question was intended to elicit information that the deceased bore the character of being a man of a violent disposition. There are several objections to the question as propounded. One sufficient one is that it was

not in proper and legal form.   For aught that appears in this
ground, the witness had not testified that he knew the character of the deceased, nor does the ground of the motion state
what answer the witness would have made to a proper question on this subject.   Under these circumstances, the court
committed no error in refusing to admit the evidence.   See
Powell v. *State*, 101 *Ga.* 9.

3. It is complained in another ground of the motion, that
the court committed error in admitting as evidence to the
jury certain statements made by the deceased and offered as
dying declarations.   These statements were that at the schoolhouse Bush had cursed him for a G— d— son of a b—, and
told him that he was going to kill him.   To the admission of
this evidence defendant objected on the ground that dying declarations could .only be admitted to prove who was the slayer,
and the res gestæ of the homicide.   Dying declarations of the
deceased, as to the cause of the death and the person who killed
him, are admissible in evidence in a prosecution for the homicide.   Penal Code, § 1000.   In the case of *Wilkerson* v. *State*,
91 *Ga.* 729, Mr. Justice Lumpkin, delivering the opinion of the
court, said : " In our opinion, the words 'as to the cause of his
death' are sufficiently broad to include all relevant facts embraced in the *res gestæ* of the homicide.   The object of the law
in permitting such declarations to be received would be defeated
if they were confined to the immediate physical cause of the
death, and the name of the slayer.   The conversation or conduct of the parties at and immediately preceding the homicide,
and constituting the *res gestæ* of the occurrence, such as a witness would be permitted to relate, may, we think, be proved
by the dying declarations of the person killed." And in the case
of *White* v. *State*, 100 *Ga.* 659, this construction of what might
be received as dying declarations was approvingly referred to.
So that we may now consider it as established, for the reason
stated by Mr. Justice Lumpkin, that all relevant statements
which are a part of the res gestæ of a homicide are admissible as
dying declarations.   The question then arises whether the statements objected to were so nearly connected with the act of homicide as to be free from suspicion of device or afterthought.   Penal

Code, § 998. It is a difficult matter in many cases to determine whether the declarations are so nearly connected with an
act as to become part of the res gestæ. In the case of *Stiles* v.
State, 57 *Ga.* 183, this court held that where a difficulty commenced at one groggery and terminated at another, the same
night in the same village, all that transpired at both groggeries
is admissible as res gestæ, though some interval of time intervened between the beginning and end of the rencounter. And
it was said in the case of *Mitchum*, 11 *Ga.* 615, that declarations, to be contemporaneous with the act, are not required to
be precisely concurrent in point of time. If the declarations
spring out of the transaction — if they elucidate it, and if they
are made at a time so near to it as to preclude reasonably the
idea of deliberate design, they are to be regarded as contemporaneous. In the case above cited, Nisbet, J., delivering the
opinion, said, referring to what was the res gestæ, that: "No
definition could be found so comprehensive as to embrace all
cases; hence it is left to the sound discretion of the courts what
they shall admit to the jury along with the main fact, as parts
of the res gestæ." Whether the statements made in the declaration which was admitted as a dying declaration as to what the
accused said and did were parts of the res gestæ of the homicide
must be determined under the above rules. If they were,
then, under the authority of the *Wilkerson* case, supra, they
could properly be included in a dying declaration. If they were
not, then, under the law governing the admission of dying declarations, they could not. We find it difficult as a matter of
law to determine whether they were or not, because of the want
of sufficient information. The interval of time which elasped
between the altercation, if there was any, which occurred at the
window of the schoolhouse, and the homicide, does not appear
with sufficient certainty to enable us to decide; and as a
new trial is to be had on another ground, we refrain at this
time from expressing an opinion on that point. If in another
trial this time is shown, together with the actions of each of
the parties following until the homicide, we will be better able
to judge, if it should come to us for decision; and from what
has been said above, if occasion requires, it can readily be

determined whether the statements sought to be admitted are a part of the res gestæ and therefore admissible as a part of the act of homicide. We are not unmindful that a sound rule governing the admission of evidence requires that dying declarations should be received with caution. Nevertheless, under the rule promulgated, they are properly admissible when they come within the terms prescribed.

4. Another ground of the motion assigns error in admitting in evidence the alleged dying declarations, without submitting to the jury for their determination the question as to whether such declarations were actually made, whether they were made in articulo mortis, and whether the deceased was conscious of his condition at the time they were made. In connection with this ground of the motion, the plaintiff in error sets out a portion of the charge of the judge, as follows: "The dying declarations of any man, when they are made in article of death, when he is conscious of his condition, can go to the jury as evidence, and should be considered with all the other evidence in the case in determining what the truth of the case is, that being the peculiar province of the jury, and then take the law from the court, and apply it to that state of facts as you find them, and then let that be the basis of your verdict." From this charge the conclusion might be drawn by the jury that, inasmuch as the judge had admitted the declarations, it was their duty to consider the same as evidence, and to weigh them with the other facts in arriving at their verdict. It might also be inferred by the jury that, inasmuch as the evidence had been admitted, it was not necessary for them, in order to determine their value, to first find whether the declarations were in fact made in the article of death, and that the deceased was conscious of his condition at the time they were made. The ground of the motion is properly certified to by the presiding judge, and we find in the charge no reference to the duty of the jury to consider whether the declarations were made when the party was in a dying condition and whether he knew that fact. We are quite sure that this necessary and important condition was momentarily overlooked by the presiding judge, but the failure to so instruct might have had the effect of allowing the

jury to consider the dying declarations as evidence without determining its value by the ascertainment of these preliminary facts. Under the evidence in the record, there was no error in admitting the dying declarations to be considered by the jury. The rule is, that this character of evidence can not be admitted until the presiding judge is satisfied, from the preliminary examination, that the requirements of the statute have, prima facie, been met. If they have, the evidence goes to the jury primarily for their determination whether the declarations were made, and if so, were they made at a time and under such circumstances as make them evidence? The jury are at liberty to weigh all the circumstances under which the declarations were made, including those already proved to the judge, and to give the testimony such credit as upon the whole they may think it deserves. Following this rule, it was held in the case of *Dumas* v. *State*, 62 *Ga.* 58, that: "The court must judge of the preliminary evidence in the first instance, and, deeming it prima facie sufficient, should admit the declarations to the jury, instructing the jury afterwards to pass finally for themselves on the question, whether or not the declarations were conscious utterances in the apprehension and immediate prospect of death." To the same effect, see *Mitchell* v. *State*, 71 *Ga.* 128; also *Varnedoe* v. *State*, 75 *Ga.* 181. We must rule, therefore, that the charge set out in this ground of the motion for a new trial, when applied to the alleged dying declarations which had been admitted in evidence, standing by itself, was error. As an abstract proposition of law, the charge was correct; but in connection with such charge the jury should have been instructed that, notwithstanding the admission by the court of the alleged dying declarations on the preliminary evidence submitted, yet it was for the jury, in passing upon the value and weight of this evidence, to determine whether the deceased was in articulo mortis and conscious of his condition at the time they were made. If they should be of the opinion that he was in the article of death when they were made, but not conscious of his condition, then, notwithstanding the admission, they should reject the evidence as dying declarations.

5. A number of assignments of error, other than as above indicated, are set out in the motion. A careful consideration fails to disclose any material error, or one authorizing the grant of a new trial, other than above appears; and only because of the failure of the judge to properly instruct the jury in reference to the consideration of dying declarations, as above indicated, is a new trial awarded.

Judgment reversed. All the Justices concurring.

HOLTON v. THE STATE.

1. False representations acted on by another, in consequence of which he was cheated and defrauded, must, to be the basis of a prosecution for cheating and swindling, relate either to the present or to the past. A promise relating to the future can not be the basis of a prosecution for this offense. But where there is both a false pretense and a promise which acted together on the mind of the person defrauded and induced him to part with a thing of value, and he would not have done so on the promise without the pretense, such a pretense, if false, is sufficient to support a conviction for being a common cheat and swindler.
. 2. A representation by one that he has title to a named lot of land, made for the purpose of inducing another to purchase it, if false within the knowledge of him who makes the representation, is within the statute against cheating and swindling.
3. If by deceitful means or artful practices one is induced to give to another his negotiable note promising to pay a given sum at a named date, whether as a matter of fact the maker is or is not insolvent, he is nevertheless defrauded and cheated.
4. There was no error in the charges, nor in the refusals to charge, nor in the rulings of the court of which complaint is made. There was ample evidence to support the verdict, which was not contrary to law.

Submitted October 4, — Decided October 27, 1899.

Accusation of cheating and swindling. Before Judge Williams. City court of Waycross. June term, 1899.

G. J. Holton & Son and *J. Walter Bennett*, for plaintiff in error. *J. L. Crawley, solicitor*, and *L. A. Wilson*, contra.

LITTLE, J. 1. An accusation was preferred in the city court of Waycross against the plaintiff in error, charging him with the offense of cheating and swindling. On the trial of the case the evidence of the State tended to establish the following facts: Holton approached M. S. and J. L. Lee and asked them to purchase a certain lot of land in Ware county, being a wild lot, and represented to them that it was owned by one Conally, and that he had a power of attorney from Conally to sell the land. He represented the title of Conally to be a good and genuine title, superior to any other claim of title to the lot, Holton promising at the same time to defend the title if any adverse claim should be made against it. The purchasers relied upon the representations that the title was good, and also upon the promise of Holton that he would defend the title to the same. Under these representations and this promise, M. S. and J. L. Lee purchased the land for four hundred dollars and gave their promissory notes for the same, one for $150, all of said notes being due in the future and at different dates. During the negotiations M. S. Lee told Holton that he had heard that the Southern Pine Company had a claim on the lot. Holton stated in reply to Lee that the title he had was superior to any claim of title by the Southern Pine Company or any one else. Soon after they entered into possession of the land the Southern Pine Company applied for an injunction restraining them from cutting the timber. Lee called on Holton, who lived in Appling county, to defend the title. He referred Lee to a firm of lawyers in Waycross, whom Lee consulted, and was advised that the chain of title which he received from Holton was forged. Lee interposed no defense. The injunction was granted. In the meantime Holton had traded off one of the promissory notes of Lee and received in exchange therefor his own personal obligation. This note was sued upon, and a judgment obtained thereon against M. S. and J. L. Lee. Neither of them had ever paid any money on the judgment, and it was probable that they were insolvent. At the time of the trade for the land, Lee called Holton's attention to the fact that he did not have the original plat and grant; to which Holton replied that it was at his home, and that Lee could get it any time he came for it. On the trial of the case it was admitted that all of the deeds received by Lee from Holton were forged, with the exception of that made to Lee. There was much other evidence to which, for the purposes of this opinion, it is not necessary to make reference. The defendant contended, that if the title was forged he had no knowledge of it, and that when the application for injunction was filed he proposed to the brothers Lee that if they would convey the title to him he would defend it. He denied making any promise, and otherwise controverted many of the statements made by witnesses for the State. The jury returned a verdict finding the defendant guilty. He made a motion for a new trial, which was overruled, and he excepted. Besides the general grounds that the verdict was contrary to law and the evidence, certain rulings and charges of the trial judge were alleged to be error, in the motion for new trial. These, however, can be disposed of by the determination of certain contentions urged in the brief of counsel for plaintiff in error, which are: First, if the purchasers bought the land on the faith of a promise made by Holton in the nature of a false representation that he would defend the title, a prosecution for this offense would not lie. Second, whether the title which Holton had was the true title or not was a matter of opinion, and was so recognized by the purchasers when they took Holton's promise to stand between them and all damage. Third, it was not shown either that Holton got a thing of value, or that the brothers Lee suffered any loss.

The statute for the violation of which the plaintiff in error was charged declares that any person using any deceitful means or artful practices, other than those which are expressly mentioned in the code, by which an individual or the public is defrauded and cheated, shall be punished as for a misdemeanor. It is a sound proposition of law, that false representations, to be the basis of a prosecution for cheating and swindling, must relate either to the past or to the present. *Miller* v. *State*, 99 *Ga.* 207. It therefore follows, that any promise or statement as to what may occur in the future, however false, will not serve as a basis for such a prosecution, because a promise is not a pretense. *Ryan* v. *State*, 45 *Ga.* 128. But it by no means follows that a prosecution may not be maintained, when in connection with a promise a false representation has been made. On this subject Mr. Bishop, in his work on Criminal Law (vol.

9

2, § 424), says: "It would be difficult to find in actual life
any case wherein a man parted with his property on a mere
representation of fact, whether true or false, without an accompanying promise. If, therefore, we look at the promise
simply as a nullity, it does not impair a simultaneous false pretence, considered as a foundation for an indictment." And,
citing a number of cases, he says, in section 427, that "The conclusion to which the foregoing views leads us accords with what
the English judges have held, that where the blended pretence
and promise, acting together on the mind of the defrauded
person, were the inducements to part with his goods, and he
would not have done it by reason of the pretence alone without
the promise, the case falls still within the statute." This point
has, however, been exactly decided in the case of *Thomas* v.
State, 90 *Ga.* 437, where the court held that the offense of cheating and swindling may be committed by a false representation
of a past or existing fact, although a promise be also a part of
the inducement to the person defrauded to part with his property. We understand from the evidence that the purchasers of
the land testified that they would not have given their notes and
received a deed if plaintiff in error had not represented to them
that the title which he held was the true and genuine title and
superior to any outstanding, nor would they have purchased
even under this representation but for the promise that he
would defend the title in the future. Under the authorities
above cited, the promise may be rejected as being of no avail
in this prosecution and entirely insufficient to support a conviction, but, having eliminated it, the representation as testified to
remains, and if false, and the purchasers were defrauded and
cheated, that representation, even though accompanied with
the promise, was sufficient to support the conviction.

2. It is further contended, however, that whether the title
which Holton had to the land was the true and genuine title
was a matter of opinion, and any representation, however
false, which expresses the opinion of the person, can not be
made the basis for such a prosecution. It is an established
rule that a pretense, to be criminal, must be of a fact as distinguished from the state of the speaker's mind, and of a nature

to be known by him. 26 Iowa, 262; 41 Tex. 65; 84 N. C. 751; 35 Mich. 36. But if one represents a thing to be true when he knows it is not, such representation falls within the statute, because it is a pretense of the facts and not a mere opinion. 64 Me. 157; 95 N. C. 663. Mr. Bishop in discussing this question says, in his Criminal Law, vol. 2, §454: "When two men are negotiating a bargain, they may express opinions about their wares to any extent they will; answering, if they lie about their opinions, only to God, and to the civil department of the law of the country. But when the thing concerns fact, as distinguished from opinion, and a man knowingly misstates the fact, his words amount to a false pretense."

It has been several times ruled that the false pretense of having title to property, or of its being unencumbered by mortgage, made by one offering it for sale, is within the statute. 1 Mo. 248; 11 Allen, 233; 11 Cox C. C. 270. See also 65 Iowa, 452. And this is equivalent to ruling that a representation as to ownership of property, when false, is a representation of a fact and not of opinion, and therefore sufficient to support a prosecution.

3. But it is contended that, even if the representations were false and so known, it is not shown that Holton got a thing of value, or that the purchasers of the land suffered any loss. In other words the proposition is, that a promissory note of an insolvent person obtained by means of false pretenses is not such a defrauding and cheating of the maker of the note as will support a prosecution for cheating and swindling. It will not be doubted that if one by deceitful means or artful practice is deprived of any valuable thing, the one so deprived is both defrauded and cheated. In the case of State v. Thatcher, 6 Vroom (N. J.), 445, Van Syckel, J., in discussing what property must be obtained in order to constitute the offense, said: "Is the maker's own note or contract of suretyship a valuable thing? The signing of the name was an act—the name when signed was a thing. Was it a thing of any value? While it remained locked up in his secretary, it was of no value to the maker, but *eo instanti* it passed out of his hands by the fraud, it became impressed with the qualities of commercial paper,

and possessed to him the value which it might cost to redeem it from a bona fide holder. . . Can it, therefore, be said that a paper which imposed such a risk was of no value to the maker? Its value to him consisted, not in what it would put in his pocket if he retained it, but in what might be taken out of his purse by the delivery of it to the defendant." See also 5 Dutcher, 13; 7 Metcalf, 475. In the case of People *v.* Reed, 70 Cal. 529, in construing a section of the Penal Code of California which declared that "Every person who knowingly and designedly, by false or fraudulent representation or pretenses, defrauds any other person of money or property, . . and thereby fraudulently gets into possession of money or property, . . is punishable," etc., it was held that a promissory note is personal property and may be the subject of the offense of obtaining property under false pretenses; it being shown in that case that the accused by false pretenses induced another to make and deliver to him his promissory note for a given sum. And in the case of State *v.* Porter, 75 Mo. 171, it was held that to procure the making and delivery of a promissory note by false pretenses, without regard to the value of the note, or whether it is negotiable or not, was a violation of the statute of the State of Missouri which made it a misdemeanor for any person who, with intent to cheat or defraud another, should designedly . . obtain from any person any money, personal property, right in action, or other valuable thing or effects whatsoever, etc., it being held that such a note was a valuable thing within the meaning of that section. While these rulings of other courts, construing other statutes, are not binding authority on us in the construction of our statutes, they are precedents founded on sound reason and emanating from judges of ability, after careful consideration. It will not do to say that a written promise to pay money is valueless because the maker is not at the time possessed of property. It is his obligation. Upon it a judgment may be rendered carrying with it a lien on all future-acquired property. We are, therefore, of the opinion that this contention of the plaintiff in error is not sound, but that the promissory note made by the brothers Lee to Holton was, without regard to whether the makers were solvent or insolvent, a thing of value; and that where such a thing is obtained from another by deceitful means or artful practice, that other is defrauded and cheated in the sense of the statute.

4. The jury were authorized to believe the evidence adduced by the State, and it is clearly established not only that the representations were made, but that the purchasers of the land acted thereon, in connection with the promise. It was admitted by the defendant on the trial that the deeds which constituted the chain of Conally's title were forgeries. So that, at the time the defendant executed a conveyance of the land to Lee, Conally had no title. It was further shown that the title was at that time vested in the Southern Pine Company. As a matter of course, if the accused did not know that the deeds were forgeries, but in good faith sold property under the belief that they were genuine, he would not be guilty of any offense. As to whether he knew or did not know this fact was for the jury alone to determine under the evidence. The defendant neither by proof nor by his statement identifies Conally in any way. He simply said that he received the papers by mail, and whether Conally is a myth or a person in esse can not be determined under his statement. He admits selling the land to Lee, and the conveyance shows he sold it as attorney in fact for Conally. It was, therefore, incumbent upon him to at least give some explanation as to who Conally was, where he resided, and the circumstances under which he consented to act as attorney in disposing of the land. The duty of a satisfactory explanation of these matters was put upon him by the evidence, to which he failed to respond. Further, although he conveyed the land as the property of Conally, he not only took the notes payable to himself, but the evidence showed that he traded one of such notes before it matured, in exchange for his own personal debt. The jury were fully authorized from the evidence to find that the accused knew that the title which he represented as genuine was forged, thus completing all of the elements to sustain a verdict of guilty.

Judgment affirmed. All the Justices concurring.

BURTON v. THE STATE.

184
521

One can not legally be convicted of the offense of assault with intent to
murder, alleged to have been committed with a pistol, upon proof which
merely shows that he drew the weapon from his hip-pocket, and, in consequence of its being caught in the lining of his coat, did not make any
actual attempt to inflict with the pistol an injury upon the person alleged
to have been assaulted.

Argued October 4, — Decided October 27, 1899.

Indictment for assault with intent to murder. Before Judge
Brinson. Richmond superior court. April term, 1899.

The plaintiff in error was indicted for and convicted of the
offense of assault with intent to murder. He made a motion
for a new trial, on various grounds, which being overruled, he
excepted. Only two witnesses testified in the case, both of whom
were introduced by the State. One of these testified as follows:
Witness was a baggage-master on the Georgia Railroad. On
the date the offense is alleged to have been committed, he
started out of Augusta, Ga., on the night express. He started
to the front end of the baggage-car, to see if any one was out
there, and met the porter coming in, who said that two men
were out on the front. Witness then went out and asked them
to come inside, and one of them got off. The other, the accused, refused to come in, but finally came up on the platform
near the witness, who caught hold of his arm, to pull him inside, and, when he did that, the accused "threw his hand back
to his hip-pocket and jerked out a pistol, and it got caught in
the lining of his coat, which was torn, and the pistol fell on
the floor." In the language of this witness, "His manner in
pulling out that pistol was, that he just run his hand back
there very quick, like he was in a big hurry, and jerked it out
that way [illustrating with a quick motion to his hip-pocket
and thence up to his waist]. I was trying to get him in the car
when he did that. When the pistol fell he jumped at the pistol and attempted to pick it up again, and I attempted to keep
him off it, and there was a tussle there between him and me,
and I finally got him back off the pistol. . . He was doing
all he could to get the pistol, and I was doing all I could to

keep him from getting it, and the porter was standing there
and picked up the pistol about that time. . . When I told
him to come into the car he refused, and I caught him by
the arm and endeavored to bring him into the car. At that
time he reached for a pistol. When I caught hold of his arm,
he jumped by me in the car door, and threw his hand back
there [indicating to hip-pocket] and drew a pistol. That pistol was not in his coat pocket; it was in his pants pocket. He
jerked loose from me. It all happened in about a second."

The train porter testified that he discovered two men, one of
whom was the accused, on the front end of the baggage-car,
and told them that they would "either have to come back
through the train or get off"; that the accused said to his companion, "Don't get off, but stay up here with me." Witness
then said, "Come on in, come on in, or get off." Whereupon the
accused said, "No, by God, I am not going to come in and I am
not going to get off." The witness succeeded in getting the
man with the accused to get off the train, and, failing in his
efforts to get the accused to do likewise, went inside for assistance
and reported the matter to the baggage-master. Then — quot-
ing from the report of this witness's testimony contained in the
record — "He [the baggage-master] started out to the front,
and he says, 'Hey, boys, what are you doing out there?' So
they were talking there, and I heard him say, 'Come on in, we
don't haul passengers out there'; and they gave each other
some pretty stiff talk out there, but of course I didn't hear exactly what that was. So he reached out and grabbed this fellow by his hand, and pulled him inside the door, . . and
when he pulled him inside the car door this fellow [defendant]
reached back with his hand to his pocket, just so [indicating hip
pocket], and, as his elbow got inside the car door, he pulled
his pistol out, and it got hung in the lining of his coat, and as
he went to bring his hand around, the lining of his coat
snatched it out of his hand, and it fell on the floor, and Mr.
Chandler [the baggage-master] and that man [defendant] was
in a scuffle, and they both was trying to get it, and while they
were scuffling I went down and got it, and after I got it he
says, 'Well, boys, you all have got it on me; if I had got it on

you I would have used it, and you can use it on me or not.'"
The witness further testified that the pistol was loaded.

C. E. Dunbar and *E. H. Callaway,* for plaintiff in error.

W. H. Davis, solicitor-general, by *Anderson, Felder & Davis,*
contra.

FISH, J. In the view which we take of this case, it is only
necessary to consider that ground of the motion which alleges
that the verdict was contrary to law and the evidence. In our
opinion, the evidence, which is set out in the reporter's statement, is not sufficient to sustain the conviction. The drawing
of the pistol by the accused from his pocket was neither preceded by nor accompanied with any threat whatever. What
he would have done with the weapon, if it had not caught in
the lining of his coat and fallen from his grasp, is mere matter for conjecture. His saying, after the porter had picked up
the pistol, and after the struggle between himself and the baggage-master for its possession was over, "Well, boys, you all
have got it on me; if I had got it on you, I would have used
it," did not necessarily show that at the time that he drew the
weapon from his pocket he intended to kill the baggage-master with it, nor that he then intended to use it upon the latter's
person at all. It is just as reasonable to suppose that, by this
expression, he simply meant that if he had succeeded in getting the pistol back into his possession he would then have used
it. The intention to use it might have been formed during the
struggle for its possession between himself and the baggage-
master. How he would have used the pistol does not appear.
If he had retained his hold on the pistol, perhaps he would
have attempted to shoot the baggage-master, or, to make it
stronger, suppose we say that he probably would have done so.
But the question is not what he might have done, nor what he
probably would have done; but it is, what did he actually do?
He made no attempt to shoot. He neither cocked the pistol,
nor pointed it toward the person alleged to have been assaulted,
nor did he even raise the pistol in a position which indicated
an intention to strike him with it. Did he, when he drew the
pistol from his pocket, intend to shoot the baggage-master, or

did he intend to strike him with the weapon, or did he merely
intend to intimidate him by the show of a deadly weapon?
Can it be said, beyond a reasonable doubt, that he manifestly
intended to kill and that he had actually begun to execute this
intention? We think not. All that can be said from the evidence
is that, by drawing his pistol from his pocket, he was prepared to
commit a violent injury.   But it takes more than mere preparation to commit such an injury upon the person of another to
amount to even an assault. *Brown* v. *State*, 95 *Ga.* 481. He did
not try to use the pistol upon the person alleged to have been
assaulted; and so long as he did not attempt to thus use it, it
matters not why he did not make such an attempt.   In Lawson
v. State, 30 Ala. 14, it was decided that "the drawing of a pistol, without presenting or cocking it, is not an assault." We
are clearly of opinion that the evidence in this case is not sufficient to support a verdict finding the accused guilty of the
offense of assault with intent to murder.

Judgment reversed.   All the Justices concurring.

HOWARD *v.* THE STATE.

1. One may be an accessory before the fact to the offense of wilfully and
maliciously setting fire to and attempting to burn a house which may be
the subject-matter of the crime of arson.
2. Such a house is sufficiently described in an indictment averring that it
was "a certain guard and jail house" in a named village, and was the
property of that village.
3. On the trial of one charged with being an accessory before the fact to the
commission of a particular crime, evidence tending to show that the accused had a motive for desiring this crime to be committed, and that he
had actually endeavored to induce one other than the person named in
the indictment as principal to commit it, was admissible for the State.
4. On such a trial, the free and voluntary declarations or admissions of the
alleged principal are admissible to show his guilt; but neither declarations nor admissions of an alleged principal which merely tend to incriminate the alleged accessory are admissible against the latter, if made
after the completion of the criminal enterprise.
5. A charge which gave to evidence of the character last indicated in the
preceding note the same effect as the sworn testimony of an accomplice
was erroneous.

Argued October 5,—Decided October 27, 1899.

Indictment for attempt to commit arson.   Before Judge
Bennet.   Pierce superior court.   May term, 1899.

J. L. Sweat, W. A. Milton, and *A. E. Cochran,* for plaintiff
in error.   *J. M. Terrell, attorney-general, John W. Bennett, solicitor-general,* and *Estes & Walker,* contra.

Lumpkin, P. J.   The grand jury of Pierce county returned
a bill of indictment against John Ford and J. R. Howard, containing two counts.   In the first, both were charged with "the
offense of an attempt to commit arson, for that the said John
Ford and J. R. Howard . . unlawfully, wilfully, and maliciously did set fire to and attempt to burn a certain guard and
jail house in the city, town, and village of Patterson, in said
county, the same being then and there the property of the said
city, town, and village."   The second count charged Howard
"with having committed the offense of being accessory before
the fact to the offense of an attempt to commit arson, for that
the said John Ford . . did unlawfully, wilfully, and maliciously
set fire to and attempt to burn" the house in question, and
Howard, "being absent at the time the said crime of an attempt
to commit arson was committed, as aforesaid, did then and there
unlawfully, maliciously, and wilfully procure, counsel, and command the said John Ford to commit said crime as aforesaid."
Howard was put on trial, and, before pleading to the merits, demurred to the indictment as follows: "(1) Because said defendant is not charged in said indictment, in either of the
counts thereof, with any crime under the laws of Georgia.   (2)
Because there is no such offense, under the laws of Georgia, of
an attempt to commit arson, as charged in the first count of said
indictment.   (3) Because there is no such an offense, under the
laws of Georgia, of accessory before the fact to the offense of an
attempt to commit arson, as charged in the second count of said
indictment.   (4) Because the house described in the first and
second counts of said indictment, upon which it is alleged the
offense of an attempt to commit arson was perpetrated, is described as a certain guard and jail house in the city, town, and
village of Patterson, the same being then and there the property
of the said city, town, and village of Patterson; said description

being too general and indefinite and such as is unauthorized and not warranted by law." The demurrer was overruled, and Howard was convicted. He excepted to the refusal of the court to sustain his demurrer, and also to a judgment denying him a new trial.

1. Section 136 of the Penal Code defines arson as "the malicious and wilful burning of the house or outhouse of another." The next section declares that "the wilful and malicious burning, or setting fire to, or attempting to burn, a house in a city, town, or village, whether the house be the property of the perpetrator or of another, shall be punished" as a capital offense. It will thus be seen that the act of "setting fire to," or the act of "attempting to burn," a house in a city, town, or village, if wilfully and maliciously committed, is made by law an offense punishable in the same manner as the wilful and malicious burning of such a house. In the first count of the indictment both Ford and Howard are accused of setting fire to and attempting to burn the jail house in Patterson. Logically, and from the standpoint of common sense, the charge thus made against these persons really meant that they set fire to the house and in this manner attempted to burn it. In the second count Ford was charged with setting fire to and attempting to burn the house, and this count contained the further averment that Howard procured, counseled, and commanded Ford "to commit said crime as aforesaid." The plain meaning of this is, that Howard incited Ford to set fire to and attempt to burn the jail. Inasmuch as setting fire to this house was a distinct offense, and as it was an act the doing of which could be incited by another, we have no difficulty in holding that the indictment was good. It is true that no section of the Penal Code may contain the phrase "attempt to commit arson," but, as we have shown, section 137 does make punishable the act either of feloniously setting fire to, or attempting to burn, a house in a city, town, or village, the doing of either of which necessarily constitutes an attempt to commit arson. So far, therefore, as the first three grounds of the demurrer are concerned, it deals with a mere play upon words and is entirely without merit.

2. The ground of the demurrer alleging insufficiency in the

description of the house is also without merit.   Indeed, the
demurrer is itself defective, in that it fails to point out in
what respects the description is incomplete.   Certainly, one
accused of setting fire to, or inciting another to set fire to, a
jail and guard house of a designated village, the same being
the property of that village, could never for an instant doubt
to what particular building the indictment referred.

3. Complaint is made that, during the progress of the trial,
the court, over objection of counsel for the accused, admitted
the testimony of a witness to the effect that, shortly before the
attempt to burn the jail was committed, the accused had endeavored to induce the witness to burn the building, and had
expressed a determination to have the same burned because he
had once been imprisoned in it.   This evidence was admissible.
It tended to show a felonious intent formed by the accused to
commit the offense with which he was charged. . His expressions, as testified to by the witness, were in the nature of a threat,
and disclosed, moreover, a motive for procuring the crime to
be committed.

4. It appeared on the trial that Ford was detected in the act
of setting fire to the jail, and that while attempting to make
his escape he was shot down and arrested.   Over the objection
of Howard, the court allowed a witness to testify to certain declarations made by Ford after he had been taken into custody,
to the effect that he came there to burn the jail at the instance
of Howard, who had loaned him his pistol and incited him to
become the chief actor in the commission of the criminal enterprise.   Such parts of these declarations as embraced incriminating admissions or confessions on the part of Ford tending
to show his guilt were admissible in evidence; for it was necessary for the State to prove that Ford was guilty as a principal
in order to establish the guilt of Howard as an accessory, and
any pertinent testimony tending to show this essential fact was
certainly admissible.   It makes no difference that the State
may have had other and stronger proof of Ford's guilt; for
it was undeniably the right of the prosecution to introduce all
relevant evidence at its command.   On the other hand, the
declarations of Ford, in so far as they implicated Howard,

were not admissible. They were not declarations of a conspirator made during the pendency of the criminal enterprise, nor did they constitute a part of the res gestæ of the offense with which either Ford or Howard was charged; for it distinctly appears, as will have been seen, that the felonious act which Ford intended to commit, and did commit, was fully completed, that he voluntarily started to leave the scene of his crime, and that the declarations with which we are now dealing were made while he was in custody. Clearly they were not immediately connected with the act of setting fire to the jail; for they did not escape from him while engaged in the prosecution of that act, and the circumstances under which they were uttered completely negative all idea that they so closely followed that act in point of "time as to be free from all suspicion of device or afterthought." See Civil Code, § 5179. Accordingly they are to be treated as amounting to neither more nor less than a mere narrative of something which had occurred in the past between Ford and Howard.

5. It seems, however, that the trial court regarded these declarations as if they stood upon the same footing as would the sworn testimony of an accomplice introduced against the accused; for in a portion of its charge to the jury, of which complaint is made, instructions were given them upon that branch of the law which relates to the corroboration of the testimony of an accomplice. No witness professing to be an accomplice was sworn, and these declarations constituted the only basis for such instructions. It is evident, therefore, that the law bearing upon the testimony of accomplices and the corroboration thereof was entirely inapplicable to the facts of the present case, and no instructions upon the subject should have been given.

The motion for a new trial presents other questions of minor importance, but the case upon its substantial merits is disposed of by what is said above.

Judgment reversed. All the Justices concurring.

SUMNER *v.* THE STATE.

1. In a trial under an indictment for murder, it is the duty of the presiding judge to give in charge to the jury the law relating to voluntary manslaughter when there is any evidence which would support a verdict for that offense. In the present case, while much of the evidence tended to show that the homicide might have been legally graded as murder, yet there was evidence which, if credible, might reduce the offense from murder to voluntary manslaughter. The court therefore, properly charged the law relating to voluntary manslaughter, and the jury having returned a verdict finding the defendant guilty of that offense, it can not be said that such verdict was contrary to the law or the evidence in the case.

2. A charge in the following words, "On the other hand, if you are satisfied, after a careful consideration of all the evidence in the case, testimony and other sources of information," etc. (as to the guilt of the defendant), might, if standing alone, authorize the inference that the jury in making their verdict could regard other sources of information than the evidence and the statement of the accused; but when it appears by reference to the entire charge that the jury were repeatedly instructed in arriving at their verdict to only regard the evidence in the case and the statement of the prisoner, it is not cause for a new trial that such inference might be drawn from this detached portion of the charge. Taking the whole charge together, the words, "other sources of information," could not be fairly understood as applying to anything except the prisoner's statement.

3. When a new trial of a criminal case is asked on the ground that one of the jurors who tried the case was not a fair and impartial juror, and in support of such ground an affidavit of only one person is presented tending to show that prior to the trial the juror made statements showing that he was prejudiced against the defendant, a new trial, without more, will not be ordered. The juror, having qualified on his voir dire is to be presumed to have rightly done so until the contrary is shown by more than one witness.

4. The grounds of the motion for new trial not dealt with above present no sufficient cause for a reversal of the judgment.

Argued October 5, — Decided October 28, 1899.

Indictment for murder. Before Judge Spence. Worth superior court. April term, 1899.

J. W. Walters and *Frank Park*, for plaintiff in error.

W. E. Wooten, solicitor-general, by *Harrison & Bryan,* and *J. J. Forehand,* contra.

LITTLE, J. L. M. Sumner was indicted for the murder of James Powell, and was found guilty of the offense of voluntary manslaughter. His motion for a new trial was overruled by the presiding judge, and he excepted to that decision.

1. One ground of the motion alleges error because the court gave in charge to the jury the law of voluntary manslaughter; and inasmuch as the verdict was for voluntary manslaughter, this ground will be considered in connection with the first two grounds, that is, that the verdict was contrary to law and the evidence. If a verdict for voluntary manslaughter could not have been sustained under any of the evidence in the case, then the law relating to that offense should not have been given in charge to the jury, nor can a verdict for that offense be sustained. On the contrary, if there was evidence from which the jury trying the case might have determined that the homicide was committed as the result of passion, and there were facts which in law justified the existence of that passion, then the law relating to the offense of voluntary manslaughter should have been given in charge, and a verdict for that offense must stand. The determination of the question involved, therefore, necessarily requires, to some extent at least, an examination of the law of voluntary manslaughter, as well as reference to some parts of the evidence. Under our law it is requisite, in order to reduce a homicide from murder to voluntary manslaughter, that it shall be shown not only that the homicide was without malice and was the result of a sudden heat of passion, but also that the deceased must have done something to the defendant to justify the passion which prompted the act. Penal Code, §§ 64, 65. The latter section prescribes that, in order to justify the excitement of passion, there must be some actual assault upon the person killing, or an attempt by the person killed to commit a serious personal injury on the person killing, or other equivalent circumstances, that is, circumstances equivalent to an assault, or equivalent to an attempt to commit a serious personal injury. None of these things justify the killing, but some of them must exist to justify the passion which causes the killing, in order to make the offense voluntary manslaughter. It has been held in the case of *Edwards* v. *State*, 53 *Ga.* 428, that the equivalent circumstances referred to in the statute do not include words, threats, menaces, or contemptuous gestures, and in the case of *Mack* v. *State*, 63 *Ga.* 696, it was said that while the law furnishes this standard, it

leaves the jury to make the comparison as to what are circumstances equivalent to an assault and equivalent to an attempt
to commit a serious personal injury.   Keeping these principles
of law in view, we now seek from the brief of evidence to ascertain whether there were present at the commission of the homicide any circumstances which the jury could believe excluded
the idea of deliberation or malice in the commission of the
homicide and which justified the excitement of passion on the
part of the accused, necessary to reduce the grade of the homicide from murder.   It may be said in a general way, without
discussing the evidence, that it was shown clearly that at the
time and immediately preceding the act of homicide, bad blood
toward each other was manifested by both the deceased and the
accused; that they cursed each other in a shocking manner
and quarrelled violently; and, while it appears that the accused
placed himself in a defensive position and it was the evident
intention of the deceased to attack the accused, that nevertheless the passions of both were greatly aroused.   •

Henderson Powell, a witness for the defendant, testified,
among other things, that the deceased cursed the accused, and
the latter came walking towards the deceased and said, "Powell, you know G— d— well that I am not scared of you," and
then the deceased began trying to get to him.   I had hold of
Powell at the time, and turned him loose, and when Powell
got within two steps of the accused the latter raised his hand
and went to shooting.   Did not see Powell have any knife, but
saw a knife on the floor open.   The accused told the deceased
several times to let him alone, that he did not want to hurt
him and he did not want the deceased to hurt him.   Could not
tell whether Powell was standing still when he was shot or not.
Edwards testified, that he went into the store and saw that
something was the matter; that he spoke to the accused and
asked him what did it all mean; that he replied to him,
"Don't talk to me, talk to the other man."   He then went to
Powell and told him to go out of the store and have no row.
Powell had his knife out.   Powell did go out of the store, and
then returned.   The accused was then behind the counter, and
Powell was on the outside of it.   Witness held to Powell, and

he swung his knife around and cut his coat; he then turned
Powell loose, who began cursing the accused and got in about
3 or 4 feet of the counter with a knife in his hand, and the accused then shot him. Sheppard said that Powell was doing
the cursing; that several tried to get him out; that the accused
was behind the counter, and the deceased with a knife in his
hand made a rush up to the counter behind which the accused
was, and accused shot him. He got pretty close to accused,
but the counter was between them. Among other things, Dunn
testified that Powell cursed Sumner and stepped out in the little
gate and walked a step or two towards the accused and cursed
him again. The accused said nothing. The deceased made a
start and accused commenced shooting him. Persons present
tried to get Powell to stop; they turned him loose, and he went
right towards accused and was in 5 or 6 or 7 feet of the counter. Witness did not see him have a weapon. One witness
testified that there were four shots fired very rapidly; that
Powell was struck three times, once on the back of the head,
another wound was under the arm, etc.

We do not refer to any part of the evidence, which is very
voluminous, except such as would seem to authorize a charge
and verdict of voluntary manslaughter; but it appears that the
parties were involved in a difficulty, that the accused placed
himself behind the counter, that the deceased advanced on
him, some of the witnesses say with a knife, some did not see
any. It is apparent from much of the evidence that at the
time of the shooting the accused was not in imminent danger;
but from it the jury, we think, might have considered that the
deceased made an assault on the accused, and, if not an assault,
that the circumstances attending his advance to the accused
were the equivalent of an assault sufficient to arouse passion
which prompted the shooting. If so, a verdict of manslaughter would be supported, and it was the duty of the presiding
judge to charge the law of that grade of homicide. As to what
are equivalent circumstances, see *Murray* v. *State*, 85 *Ga.* 381.
Where the attempt to commit an injury is between provocation
by words and an attempt to commit a felony, the verdict for
manslaughter is proper. *Buchanan* v. *State*, 24 *Ga.* 282. A

careful review of the evidence induces us to think that the verdict rendered was the lowest that could properly have been rendered.

2. Complaint is made that the court erred in giving the following charge to the jury: "On the other hand, if you are satisfied, after a careful consideration of all the evidence in the case, testimony and other sources of information; satisfied beyond a reasonable doubt that there was no necessity for the killing at the time it occurred, that it was not necessary to protect his person from a felony which was about to be committed upon it, the circumstances were not sufficient to excite the fears of a reasonable man that his own life was in imminent peril, and that it was not necessary for him to take human life in order to save his own life; satisfied beyond reasonable doubt that the circumstances were not sufficient to excite the fears of a reasonably brave man of a felony being committed upon his person, then it would be your duty to convict him." The specific error alleged in this charge is, that it did not confine the jury to the issues in the case as disclosed by the evidence, but instructed the jury that they could consider other sources of information, without explaining what they were, and that the jury were thus left free to consider any kind of information derived from any source. As set out in the motion, this extract from the charge, if taken alone, might be susceptible of the construction given to it by counsel for the plaintiff in error, and, if it could thus be construed, it would be error; for, as a matter of course, the jury in the trial of a criminal case must, in determining the facts, regard only the evidence and the statement of the prisoner. In endeavoring to ascertain what was the meaning of the judge when he referred to "other sources of information," and how it might have been taken or construed by the jury, we have carefully examined the entire charge, and we find that the judge opens his charge with this statement: "It is your duty, gentlemen, to try this case by the evidence. Take the law from the court, and apply the law to the facts as you find them. You will not be controlled or influenced by anything outside the evidence in the case. Consider it in connection with the statement of the defendant, which he has a

right to make under the law." And again, further on in his charge he says: "Your own responsibility, gentlemen, is to try this case by the testimony, by the evidence in the case, consider it along with the statement of the defendant, and to find a truthful verdict." Again he charges: "Take the case, gentlemen, and consider it carefully as its importance demands at your hands, consider all the evidence in the case, and determine what is the truth of the transaction — what are the facts." The direction to determine the truth of the case under the evidence and statement of the accused is repeated in a number of other places in the charge. It is apparent that the portion of the charge excepted to, standing alone, would be error, but that when taken in connection with the other parts of the charge the jury could not understand that they were to look to any other source but the evidence and the statement of the prisoner, in order to determine the guilt or innocence of the defendant. Indeed, from the language used in different parts of his charge where the judge referred to the evidence and the statement of the prisoner in the same connection, the words "other sources of information" were evidently intended by him, and so understood by the jury, to refer to the statement of the defendant. So construing the charge, it affords no ground for a reversal of the judgment.

3. Another ground of the motion is, that Lewis, one of the members of the traverse jury who tried the case, was not, at the time that he qualified, a fair and impartial juror, because he had formed and expressed an opinion as to the guilt of the defendant, and was prejudiced against him. In support of this ground of the motion an affidavit of G. B. Edwards was filed, who deposed that, during the week preceding the trial of the accused, he had a conversation with W. H. Lewis who was afterwards on the jury which tried the case against Sumner, and that Lewis remarked that Joe M. Sumner ought not to help his son Leonard at all, that he ought to let him go, and that Oscar Sumner, Leonard's brother, ought to have been fined a thousand dollars for selling cider to Sumner; that if he, Lewis, were on the jury that would try Sumner, he could not help him a bit; that he thought he ought to be allowed to go on

without help; that the people of Worth county ought to hang
a few and stop all this killing business. This was the only
affidavit submitted to show the disqualification of the juror.
In the case of *Fogarty* v. *State,* 80 *Ga.* 464, this court, citing
the case of *Hudgins* v. *State,* 61 *Ga.* 182, approvingly quoted
from the opinion in the last-named case the rule there laid
down, in the following language: "After verdict, to disqualify a juror who tried the case and swore that he had not formed
and expressed an opinion, and had no bias or prejudice, and
was perfectly impartial, there should be the affidavits of at
least two witnesses, or what is equivalent thereto, against such
oath of the juror; otherwise it is but oath against oath, and
the verdict will not be set aside on the ground of the incom-
petency of the juror." The ruling made in that case settles
this ground of the motion against the plaintiff in error.

4. Other grounds complaining of different portions of the
charge of the court appear in the motion for new trial. We
have considered these in connection with the entire charge of
the court, and, so considered, the errors committed, if any, are
in our judgment so immaterial as not to require elaboration,
and present no sufficient cause for a reversal of the judgment
refusing the new trial. We find in the record affidavits from
jurors in relation to the manner in which their verdict was
made, together with certain affidavits of outside parties concerning the same. Jurors can not, of course, be heard to impeach their verdict. The State met these with counter-affi-
davits, and the whole matter was submitted to the determination of the trial judge. He heard and passed upon all the
questions so raised, and we are satisfied that the conclusions
reached by him ought to stand. After giving the reasons assigned by the plaintiff in the grounds not specifically mentioned,
why a new trial should be granted, careful consideration, we are
constrained to believe that no material error was committed
either in the rulings or the charge of the presiding judge, and that
the circumstances of the homicide failed to support the defense
of justifiable homicide. The judgment of the court below is
                    Affirmed.   All the Justices concurring.

MAYOR AND COUNCIL OF MACON v. WOOD.

The decision of the superior court on certiorari reversing the judgment of a
  municipal court convicting one of a violation of a municipal ordinance
  is not subject to review by this court.

Argued October 8, — Decided October 28, 1899.

Certiorari.   Practice in the Supreme Court.

Minter Wimberly, for plaintiff in error.
M. Felton Hatcher, contra.

COBB, J. Wood was tried and convicted in the recorder's
court of the City of Macon, for the violation of a municipal
ordinance.   Upon the hearing of a writ of certiorari sued out
by him, the judge of the superior court passed an order directing that "the certiorari be sustained and the defendant discharged."   To this order the Mayor and Council of the City
of Macon excepted.   When the case was called in this court
a motion was made to dismiss the writ of error, on the ground
that in such a case a writ of error would not lie at the instance
of the mayor and council.

In the case of *Cranston* v. *Augusta*, 61 *Ga.* 572, it appeared
that Cranston had been tried in the recorder's court and
acquitted.   Upon certiorari the decision of the recorder was
reversed, and direction given that Cranston be punished in
accordance with the ordinance of the city which he was alleged
to have violated.   To this judgment he excepted, and the
judgment of the superior court was reversed upon the ground
that a municipal corporation can not have a writ of certiorari
to review a judgment rendered by the corporation court under
which the accused was discharged from custody.   In the opinion
Mr. Justice Bleckley says: "As the law now stands, the city,
like the State, must acquiesce in judgments of discharge rendered on final trial in police or criminal proceedings."   In the
case of *Mayor etc. of Marietta* v. *Alexander*, 86 *Ga.* 455, the
accused was convicted in a police court, and a certiorari sued
out by him was sustained and a new trial ordered.   To this
ruling the municipality excepted.   When the case was called
in this court, a motion was made to dismiss the same upon the

ground that the municipality had no right to sue out a writ of error in such cases. The point raised by this motion was, however, not decided, it being distinctly left an open question. In *Mayor etc. of Hawkinsville* v. *Ethridge*, 96 *Ga.* 326, the accused was convicted in a police court, and carried his case by certiorari to the superior court. When the certiorari came on for a hearing in that court a motion was made to dismiss the same, which the court overruled. To this judgment overruling the motion to dismiss the municipality excepted. The writ of error was dismissed upon the ground that a municipal corporation could not sue out a bill of exceptions to this court in such a case. Even if the fact that in the *Cranston* case the accused was acquitted in the police court distinguishes that case from the present one, where the accused was convicted in the police court and his discharge from custody was due to the judgment of the superior court, the *Ethridge* case is directly controlling here, because in that case the accused was convicted in the police court, and a writ of error, complaining of the refusal of the superior court to dismiss his certiorari, was dismissed for want of jurisdiction in this court to entertain the same. See, in this connection, *Commissioners* v. *Tabbott*, 72 *Ga.* 89; *Cobb* v. *Smith*, 102 *Ga.* 585.

> *Writ of error dismissed.   All the Justices concurring.*

CHANNELL *v.* THE STATE.

150:
435

1. The removal of an officer from the county for which he was elected to another county in this State does not vacate the office until the fact has been judicially ascertained. A challenge by a defendant in a criminal case, therefore, to the array of jurors, because of such non-residence of a jury commissioner who participated in drawing the jury list was demurrable, it not appearing that the fact of such non-residence had been judicially determined.

2. One who deliberately kills another, not for the purpose of preventing any impending wrong, but in revenge for a past offense, however heinous such an offense may be, is guilty of murder. The undisputed evidence in this case showing such to be the motive of the killing, the law of manslaughter was not involved.

Argued October 6,—Decided October 28, 1899.

Indictment for murder. Before Judge Smith. Montgomery superior court. April term, 1899.

H. B. Simmons, Allen Fort, and *C. D. Loud,* for plaintiff in error. *J. M. Terrell, attorney-general, J. F. DeLacy, solicitor-general,* and *E. D. Graham,* contra.

LEWIS, J. W. T. Channell was placed on trial in Montgomery superior court, under an indictment charging him with the murder of W. H. Thompson. Before proceeding to trial on the merits of the case, the accused challenged the array of jurors, upon the ground that the list of jurors was illegally made up, because one of the jury commissioners who participated in preparing the list was not a jury commissioner at the time, as he had moved from the county of Montgomery to the county of Laurens. The State's counsel demurred to this challenge, and to the judgment of the court sustaining the demurrer the accused filed exceptions pendente lite. The accused pleaded not guilty. The record discloses substantially the following facts developed in the progress of the trial: Some time during the year previous to the killing the accused brought suit for divorce against his wife, charging her with adultery with Thompson, the deceased. Not having sufficient evidence to sustain this charge, the suit was abandoned. From the time it was instituted up to the time of the killing in March, 1899, the accused and his wife lived apart. She finally left the town where they were living and moved to De Soto, where she was when the homicide occurred. After the dismissal of the divorce suit, and a short while before the homicide, the accused made repeated threats against the deceased, stating to one witness that as soon as he arranged his business he would kill Thompson, assigning as the reason that he had come between him and his wife. Arming himself with a shotgun, he came within a few feet of where the deceased was sitting engaged in conversation with three other persons in a quiet manner, and hailed Thompson with the remark, "Come across." The deceased asked an explanation of what he meant, and the accused replied, "You have come between me and my wife." As Thompson was rising unarmed, without any demonstration of making any attack or doing any harm to the accused, he was shot down while in a half bent position, the accused having the gun pointed toward him before he began to rise. The accused was begged by one of the witnesses present not to shoot again, but fired his gun again after Thompson had fallen. The accused then endeavored to make his escape by going off, but was followed and arrested. Such was, in substance, the evidence introduced by the State. The defendant introduced no testimony, but made a statement in which he admitted the facts of the killing, and said that when he fired the accused had his hand in his pocket or behind him; and further assigned as a reason for the killing a letter that he had received in which the writer stated that he could testify to the adultery between the wife of the accused and Thompson. The jury returned a verdict of guilty. A motion for a new trial was made and overruled, and the bill of exceptions alleges error on the judgment overruling the motion, and also on the judgment sustaining the demurrer to the challenge made to the array of jurors.

1. Section 229 of the Political Code prescribes how offices in this State may be vacated, and one of the methods (see subdivision 5) for vacation is, "By the incumbent ceasing to be a resident of the State, or of the county, circuit, or district for which he was elected. In the first case the office shall be vacated immediately; in the latter cases, from the time the fact is judicially ascertained." It is manifest from this provision that when an incumbent of an office has moved from the county for which he was elected to another county in this State, the office is not thereby immediately vacated, and does not become so until the fact has been judicially ascertained. The challenge to the array of jurors made in this case was clearly insufficient, in that it recited no facts showing that the office of the jury commissioner had been vacated; and hence there was no error in sustaining the demurrer to this challenge.

2. Besides the general grounds in the motion for a new trial, that the verdict was contrary to law and evidence, it is further alleged that the court erred in failing to give in charge to the jury the law of voluntary and involuntary manslaughter.

There is not a fact or circumstance developed by the sworn testimony as it appears from this record which would have authorized the court to instruct the jury upon either one of these grades of homicide. We do not think that even the statement of the accused could, by any fair construction put upon it, reduce the killing below murder. But even if it were susceptible of such a construction, there was no request to charge the law of manslaughter, and an omission to instruct the jury upon any theory of the defense sustained only by the statement of the accused, without a request, is not reversible error, as has been repeatedly held by this court. This killing was the result of express malice. It was from hatred, not fear; for revenge, and not for protection; to redress a past alleged wrong, and not to defend against a threatened or impending injury. There was not a single fact in the testimony which in the remotest degree tended to show any legal cause whatever for the excitement of that sudden heat of passion that, under the law, would reduce the killing from murder to manslaughter. There was not even any evidence in this case that the deceased was ever guilty of illicit intimacy with the wife of the accused. But even if evidence to this effect had been of the most positive character, the killing was not for the purpose of preventing, but avenging a past wrong. If there is any principle of criminal law well established by repeated rulings of this court, it is, that the deliberate killing of another, not for the purpose of preventing any impending wrong, but solely for the purpose of avenging a past offense of debauching the slayer's wife, involves no element of manslaughter whatever, but is a case of absolute murder. *Hill* v. *State*, 64 *Ga.* 454; *Mays* v. *State*, 88 *Ga.* 402; *Farmer* v. *State*, 91 *Ga.* 720.

Judgment affirmed. All the Justices concurring.

LANGSTON v. THE STATE.

109 153
113 1149
109
123
109 i
124 21

An indictment which charges the accused with seducing a virtuous unmarried female "by persuasion and promises of marriage, and by other false and fraudulent means," is demurrable for failure to set forth by what means other than persuasion, accompanied by promises of marriage, the alleged seduction was accomplished. LITTLE, J., dissenting.

Submitted October 6, — Decided October 28, 1899.

Indictment for seduction. Before Judge Henry. Floyd superior court. July term, 1899.

M. B. Eubanks, for plaintiff in error.
Moses Wright, solicitor-general, contra.

LUMPKIN, P. J. The only question for decision in this case is whether or not the court erred in overruling a special demurrer to the indictment. It charged the accused with the offense of seducing one Emma Oliver, "by persuasion and promises of marriage, and by other false and fraudulent means." The main point presented by the demurrer was, that the indictment failed to set forth what were the "other false and fraudulent means" employed by the accused in accomplishing the alleged seduction. In our judgment, this point was well taken. Section 387 of the Penal Code specifically declares that the offense of seduction may be committed either by "persuasion and promises of marriage," or by "other false and fraudulent means;" that is, means not consisting of mere persuasion accompanied by promises of marriage. This court, in the noted case of *Wood* v. *State,* 48 *Ga.* 192, distinctly and in terms recognized the distinction between seduction accomplished by persuasion and promises of marriage, and seduction brought about by false and fraudulent means of a different character. While section 929 of the Penal Code provides that "Every indictment or accusation of the grand jury shall be deemed sufficiently technical and correct which states the offense in the terms and language of this Code, or so plainly that the nature of the offense charged may be easily understood by the jury," yet, as has been held by this court, the purpose of this section was not to dispense with good pleading or to deny to one accused of an offense which may be committed in more than one way a statement of the facts relied on to establish his guilt sufficiently full and complete to put him upon reasonable notice of what he is called upon to meet. *Johnson* v. *State,* 90 *Ga.* 441, 444. A man charged with seducing a virtuous unmarried female by means of persuasion and promises of marriage would, without further detail, understand the precise nature of the charge preferred against him, and could very well anticipate the character of proof upon which the State would rely for a conviction. But a man accused generally of seduction, in that he used false and fraudulent means other than persuasion and promises of marriage, would be completely in the dark as to how the State expected to establish his guilt, and therefore at a loss how to prepare his defense. Accordingly, when a man is indicted for committing this offense by such other false and fraudulent means, and by special demurrer demands the information to which he is, as just pointed out, fairly entitled, he should not be forced to trial upon an indictment wanting in such essential particulars.

It seems that the judge below upheld the indictment in the present case upon the idea that the words "and by other false and fraudulent means" could be treated as mere surplusage. We can not concur in this view. These words were vital, pregnant, and full of significance; they carried a distinct and serious charge against the accused, not embraced in the averment that he had employed "persuasion and promises of marriage." Doubtless they might well have been omitted from the indictment, but, as they were inserted in it, a demand for a statement of their full intent and meaning could not be met by adjudging, in effect, that they had no meaning whatever.

Judgment reversed.   All the Justices concurring, except

LITTLE, J., dissenting. The only point of difference between a majority of the court and myself rests on the construction of the bill of indictment. Further than this I do not dissent from any proposition of law announced by my brethren. The statute on which the bill of indictment was based declares that if any person shall, "by persuasion and promises of marriage or other false and fraudulent means, seduce a virtuous unmarried female," etc., he shall be punished by imprisonment and labor in the penitentiary. The offense is complete if one seduces such a female by persuasion and promises of marriage, and it is also made out if such seduction is accomplished by false and fraudulent means other than by persuasion and promises of marriage. The bill of indictment contains but one count. That charges the defendant with having seduced Emma Oliver "by persuasion and promises of marriage and by other false and fraudulent means." I understand, from the reasoning of my brethren, that if the words "and by other false and fraudulent means" were left out of this charge, the indictment would be good. While the additional words do not, of course, add any force to the charge that the female was seduced by persuasion and promises of marriage, certainly they do not take anything away from the effect of the charge made in the words of the statute. They qualify them in no way, and by the words in the bill of indictment a charge is distinctly made that the female was seduced by persuasion and promises of marriage. The added words were not used for the purpose of charging that the defendant accomplished the seduction by other means than by persuasion and promises of marriage. If they stood alone, the indictment would not be good, because the means charged to be false and fraudulent are not set out. But I know of no reason, in law or logic, why, when an offense is charged in the words of the statute, additional words which do not qualify them, nor in themselves set out an offense, would render the charge, as made, illegal. It is, therefore, my opinion that the demurrer was properly overruled by the trial judge, and that the verdict should not be set aside.

ETHRIDGE *v.* MAYOR AND COUNCIL OF FORSYTH.

Averments in an affidavit attached to a petition for certiorari, that the same is not filed for delay, and that the affiant believes he has good cause for certiorari, necessarily mean that the petition is not filed for delay "only," and that the affiant "verily" believes his petition is meritorious. The omission, therefore, from such an affidavit of the above-quoted words does not afford cause for dismissing the certiorari "on account of the insufficiency of the affidavit of the petitioner."

Argued October 16, — Decided October 28, 1899.

Certiorari. Before Judge Reagan. Monroe superior court. August term, 1899.

Stone & Williamson, for plaintiff in error.

Persons & Persons, contra.

LUMPKIN, P. J. After conviction in the municipal court of Forsyth of a violation of an ordinance of that city, Ethridge sued out a certiorari. It was in the superior court dismissed "on account of the insufficiency of the affidavit of the petitioner." An inspection of the affidavit shows a manifest intention to comply with the provisions of section 4638 of the Civil Code, which prescribes the form of affidavit to be made in all cases of certiorari except to the court of ordinary. The only criticisms upon the affidavit suggested in the argument here were, that the word "only" did not appear after the word "delay," and that the word "verily" was not inserted before the word "believe," so as to make the affidavit conform to the language of the form prescribed by that section. We think there was a substantial compliance with the requirements of the law. One who swears that he does not sue out a certiorari for the purpose of delay necessarily avers that it is not sued out for "delay only." Indeed, an affidavit omitting the word "only" is really stronger in this respect than the law requires; for a general affirmation that the petition is not filed for delay completely negatives the idea that mere postponement entered at all into the motives of the affiant in seeking to take his case up. We are further of the opinion that one who swears he believes a thing in effect swears he "verily" believes it. It is inconceivable how a party can believe he has good cause for certiorari without at the same time "verily" entertaining that conviction. We therefore hold that the court below erred in dismissing the certiorari.

Judgment reversed. All the Justices concurring.

CHAPMAN *v.* THE STATE.

1. It was error to admit in evidence, against one on trial for a criminal offense, a declaration made by his wife in his presence before the offense was committed, the same being offered as tending to show a threat on his part, when the language used by the wife was not affirmatively approved

109 15
s112 5

109 1
115 5
115 (

109 1
119 1

109
e124

109
125

by him, and was not such as to call for a disclaimer by him of any criminal intent or purpose.

2. When the evidence as to threats introduced on the trial of one charged with a crime is by no means clear or satisfactory, it is error for the court to instruct the jury that evidence has been introduced "tending to show threats."

3. After specifying the three statutory methods prescribed in the code for impeaching witnesses, it was error for the court to instruct the jury that it was their duty to believe a witness who had not been impeached by some of these designated methods, there being other legal ways in which a witness may be discredited.

4. In the trial of a criminal case where the State relied upon evidence of an accomplice and claimed that it had been corroborated, it was error for the court to charge the jury as follows: "Slight evidence that the crime was committed by the defendant and identifying him with it will corroborate the accomplice and warrant a finding of guilty."

5. The grounds in the motion for a new trial not dealt with above are without merit, there being no error of law committed except as above indicated.

Argued October 3, — Decided November 1, 1899.

Indictment for arson.   Before Judge Russell.   Hall superior court.   June 19, 1899.

Estes & Jones, W. B. Sloan, J. C. Boone, and *B. H. Hill,* for plaintiff in error.

W. A. Charters, solicitor-general, and *Dean & Hobbs,* contra.

LEWIS, J.   The plaintiff in error was placed on trial in Hall superior court, under an indictment containing two counts, the first charging him and one Reuben Priest as principals in the commission of the offense of arson by burning a millhouse not situate in a city, town or village; the second count charging plaintiff in error as being an accessory before the fact to said offense, alleging that he had procured and counseled Reuben Priest to commit the offense of arson.   To this indictment the defendant Reuben Priest pleaded guilty, and Tom Chapman, the plaintiff in error, was placed on trial under the issue formed by his plea of not guilty.   In the prosecution the State relied for a conviction of Chapman upon the second count of the indictment.   The jury returned a verdict of guilty, with recommendation to mercy, and the defendant assigns error in his bill of exceptions on the judgment of the court overruling his motion for a new trial. The State relied upon the testimony of Priest for a conviction, claiming that it had been sufficiently corroborated by the facts and circumstances proved on the trial. Priest swore positively to a state of facts which, if true, fastened upon the accused the charge against him, of being accessory before the fact to the crime of arson. D. T. Quillian appeared as prosecutor. The house burned was on his plantation, and was alleged to belong to him and another. On the trial a witness for the State testified in substance that he was at the defendant's house a short while before the burning, and while sitting around the fire talking with reference to a prosecution for an illegal sale of liquor against the defendant, who was present with his wife, she remarked, "You will hear of Quillian's losing as much as we have by being prosecuted for selling liquor." This testimony was admitted by the court over the objection of defendant's counsel; and this is one ground of complaint in the motion for a new trial.

1. It is the policy of the law to receive with caution and care even a voluntary confession of guilt made by one charged with crime. Whenever it is insisted that the admission or confession of a party is to be inferred from his acquiescence by silence in the statements of others made in his presence, it is still more important that such testimony should be received with great caution. This is true when the statement directly and clearly charges a criminal offense or criminal purpose, and naturally calls for a denial on the part of the accused. It follows, from this caution with which the law declares the jury should receive such evidence, that unless the declarations of another naturally call for some reply from the accused, they should not be admitted at all. This principle is clearly recognized in the case of *Rolfe* v. *Rolfe*, 10 *Ga.* 143, and, as far as we have investigated, is recognized by all authorities on evidence, and by the adjudications of all the courts on the subject. See 1 Gr. Ev. (16th ed.) § 98 et seq.; 1 Am. & Eng. Enc. L. (2d ed.) 672-4, and numerous cases cited; Abbott's Trial Brief (Criminal Causes), §§ 651-2; Commonwealth *v.* Kenney, 12 Metcalf, 235, 46 Am. Dec. 672-4. In the case of Moore *v.* Smith, 14 Serg. & R. 392, Duncan, J., announcing the opin-

ion of the Supreme Court of Pennsylvania on this subject, says: "Of all evidence, loose, hasty conversation is entitled to the least weight." Applying this principle of law to the question of the admissibility of the wife's declaration in this case, we think the court erred in overruling the objections made thereto by counsel for the accused. The language used by the wife carries with it no definite or certain significance whatever. It is insisted in behalf of the State that it was susceptible of the construction that the accused would inflict some injury upon the prosecutor. The State claimed that the motive for the burning was revenge on account of a prosecution for an illegal sale of liquor against Priest and the accused on trial, and that the prosecutor, whose house was burned, and others, interested themselves in this prosecution. There may have been some ground of *suspicion* that the wife had reference to some injury that would be inflicted by her husband on the prosecutor, but this is not sufficient to construe his silence into an admission of any criminal intent on his part. The language itself has not necessarily such meaning. It might, with equal propriety, be insisted that the wife, in the hasty conversation around the fireside, was simply predicting that a loss would overtake the Quillians in the course of the dispensations of Providence, or that in a moment of excitement she thoughtlessly made the remark without having any definite idea herself of exactly what she meant. Even if she did entertain the idea of doing a wrong or of causing a loss to the prosecutor or his family, there is nothing in what she said, or under the circumstances in which her statement was made, which would lead to the inference that her husband entertained the same thought and reflection that was in his wife's mind. He was simply silent. We think there was nothing in what was said to naturally call for a denial on his part; for the language used did not necessarily imply anything that would tend to inculpate him with a criminal intent or purpose; and the admission of this testimony, therefore, was error.

2. Exception is taken in the motion for a new trial to the following charge of the court: "There has been some evidence allowed to go before you, tending to show threats." A fair

inference to be drawn from this expression is, that the language quoted had direct reference to the party on trial, and that the court meant there was evidence tending to show he had made threats. We fail to find in the brief of evidence any testimony of a positive threat made by the accused either against the prosecutor or any one else. As above indicated, the declarations made in his presence do not even tend to prove a threat. The only other testimony bearing upon the subject was that of a witness who presented to the defendant, before the burning, a petition for money to be paid one who lived on the prosecutor's land. To this the accused replied that "he had got in some trouble and had money to pay out, and that corner had a good deal to do with the trouble, and they were going to be sorry for it." While we think this testimony, in the light of the other evidence in the record, was properly admitted by the court, as being susceptible of the construction that the accused intended to do the prosecutor a wrong, yet it by no means necessarily required such a construction. The words employed were uncertain in their meaning. The accused may have had no reference to the prosecutor, and may not have contemplated the commission of any offense. As to what he meant, in the light of other facts and circumstances in evidence, was purely a question for the jury. Considering, then, the charge of the court complained of, in connection with all the testimony bearing upon the subject of threats by the defendant, it embodied an expression of an opinion by the court as to the weight of the evidence on this vital point in the case. Section 4334 of the Civil Code makes it reversible error for a judge of the superior court in his charge to the jury to express or intimate an opinion as to what has or has not been proved. The expression that there is evidence "tending to show" a given fact necessarily implies the idea that the testimony points to such a conclusion, at least to the extent of having a tendency to establish its correctness. Counsel for the State contends that the words used by the court simply meant that evidence was introduced for the purpose of showing a threat. We do not think this is at all a legitimate construction of the word "tending," as used in this connection. The trial judge, in a note to

11

this ground of the motion, states that "the jury no doubt understood the court, from various things that occurred on the trial, to mean what he intended to say, 'for the purpose of,' instead of 'tending to.'" We see nothing in the record that would throw any different light upon the meaning of the charge excepted to than what would be implied from the ordinary meaning and acceptation of the terms used. It was earnestly insisted by counsel for the plaintiff in error that there was no evidence even tending to show any threat on the part of the accused. On the other hand it was contended that the evidence did tend to establish such a threat. The record itself indicates that this involved between the parties, to say the least of it, a debatable question upon a material fact at issue, the correct solution of which depended largely upon the proper construction to be given uncertain and ambiguous language admitted in evidence. We think, therefore, it was manifest error for the court to instruct the jury that the evidence tended to establish the particular theory of either party. The question might have been different had there been positive and uncontradicted evidence of a threat made by the accused. But in this case the most that could be contended for by counsel for the State was that the circumstances proved tended to show a threat by the accused, or a purpose on his part to wrong the prosecutor. The circumstances relied upon to sustain such a contention were of such a nature as to render plausible an argument to the contrary. In view, therefore, of the close issue of fact presented upon this particular branch of the case, we think any expression of the court as to what side of the issue the evidence tended to establish was, within the true spirit and meaning of section 4334 of the Civil Code, a clear intimation of what had or had not been proved. As above indicated, there is no positive proof of any threat in this case. All the evidence relied upon to sustain the theory of such a threat is purely of a circumstantial nature. As to what facts such circumstances tend to establish is always a question for the jury, and for the court to intimate what they tend to show in any given case we think clearly invades the province of the jury.

3. Error is assigned in the motion for a new trial upon the

charge of the court to the effect that witnesses "are to be believed unless they are impeached by some method known to the law." The court then enumerates in the charge excepted to the three methods provided by law for impeachment of witnesses, namely: "First, by disproving the facts testified to by a witness. Second, by proof of contradictory statements, the attention of the witness being first called to the time and place, etc. Third, by proof of general bad character, as where witnesses appear and testify that the character of a witness is bad, and they would not believe him on oath." To this charge the court added, "Unless impeached by some of these methods, it is the duty of the jury to believe a witness." While it is true the court pointed out in his charge the only methods indicated by the statute for the impeachment of witnesses, it does not follow that unless he has been impeached by one or more of these methods the jury can not discredit the witness for other reasons not contemplated by the statute on the subject of formal impeachments; for instance, the feelings or prejudices of the witness either for or against the parties litigant, the reasonableness or unreasonableness of his tale, his manner of testifying, and many other things may be considered by the jury in passing upon his credibility. A witness, for example, may testify to a state of facts the happening of which any person of ordinary intelligence would know to be physically impossible. Although no effort might be made to impeach such a witness in any one of the three methods above prescribed, yet no one would contend that a jury would be compelled under the law to believe a narrative bearing a falsehood upon its face. While the statute prescribes but three methods of impeachment, it clearly does not mean thereby that for no other reason can a witness be discredited. This is too well established by legal principles relating to the credibility of witnesses, and especially the power given by the law to the jury in passing upon the weight to be given human testimony, to require further argument. We do not think there was any intention of this court to declare a contrary principle in the case of *Jones* v. *State*, 48 *Ga.* 163. In that case, as it appears from page 164, the charge of the court below to this effect was sustained: "That every witness in the case is to be believed until impeached in some one of the modes known to the law. A jury can not arbitrarily, of their own motion, set aside the evidence of any witness; the presumption of innocence attaches to witnesses, which remains until removed by proof." We think the language in that case clearly needed a qualification to make it strictly accurate, but, in the light of its facts, it evidently worked no harm to the complaining party, and was, therefore, not reversible error. The language in this case is quite different in that the judge specified the three methods of impeachment prescribed in the code, and charged that unless a witness was impeached by one of those methods, it was the duty of the jury to believe him. There is nothing in the *Jones* case, in the light of the qualification that the judge gave his charge to the effect that the jury could not arbitrarily, of their own motion, set aside the evidence of a witness, which would authorize the conclusion that this court ever intended to rule that a jury could not discredit a witness unless there had been a formal impeachment of him by methods prescribed by the statute. While the charge of the court complained of is not correct as an abstract proposition of law, we do not mean to say that, were it the only error of law committed, it would necessarily work a new trial in this case, for, in another portion of the charge, the court very fully and fairly stated to the jury what other circumstances or facts they might consider in passing upon the credibility of witnesses; for instance, their manner upon the stand, their bias or prejudice, their interest or feeling in the case, their opportunity for knowing the facts about which they testified, etc. In the light of these further instructions, we doubt very much whether the charge complained of misled the jury. It should not, however, have been given without, in the same connection, calling the attention of the jury to the means by which they might otherwise discredit a witness.

4. Another ground of the motion excepts to the following charge of the court : "Slight evidence that the crime was committed by the defendant and identifying him with it will corroborate the accomplice and warrant a finding of guilty." As

a proposition of law it is true that slight evidence corroborating the testimony of an accomplice may be sufficient to authorize a jury in finding the accused guilty. *Roberts* v. *State*, 55 *Ga.* 220; *Evans* v. *State*, 78 *Ga.* 351. But it does not follow that this was a proper instruction for the trial judge to give to the jury. The question as to whether or not there is sufficient corroboration of the testimony of an accomplice to produce conviction of a defendant's guilt is peculiarly one for the jury. If founded upon slight evidence of corroboration connecting defendant with the crime, as a matter of law the verdict would not be illegal as being contrary to evidence; and this is all the court meant by a declaration of the principle decided in the above-cited cases. But as to whether the corroborating evidence should be slight or strong in order to carry conviction of defendant's guilt to the mind of the jury is a question alone for them to decide. The use of the language in the charge above quoted may have had a tendency to mislead the jury by causing them to infer in this particular case that if the testimony of the accomplice was corroborated by any evidence, however slight, it was their duty to convict; especially as the court did not in the same connection caution the jury with the further instruction that such corroboration, whether in their opinion slight or strong, considered in connection with the other evidence, should be sufficient to satisfy the jury of the guilt of the accused beyond a reasonable doubt.

5. There are several other grounds in the motion for a new trial, complaining of errors of law committed on the trial of the case; but we do not see, after a careful review of them, that they present sufficient merit to authorize the consumption of any time or space in their discussion; especially in the light of the judge's explanatory notes attached to the motion. Except as hereinbefore indicated, there was no error of law committed that would require a new trial.

Judgment reversed. All the Justices concurring.

BARNETT v. CITY OF ATLANTA.

A prosecution for the violation of a municipal ordinance punishable by fine or imprisonment is a criminal case within the meaning of the statute requiring that, "in all criminal cases, the bill of exceptions shall be tendered and signed within twenty days from the rendition of the decision."

Argued October 5, — Decided November 1, 1899.

Bill of exceptions.   Practice in the Supreme Court.

Samuel N. Evins, for plaintiff in error.
J. A. Anderson and *J. T. Pendleton,* contra.

FISH, J.   Samuel Barnett, an attorney of the Atlanta bar, was summoned before the recorder's court of that city to answer to the charge of "doing business as a money-lender and negotiating loans on real estate for commissions, without registering and paying registration tax on such business in the City of Atlanta."   Barnett contended before the recorder that the City of Atlanta had no authority to tax an attorney at law, either as license fee or otherwise.   The recorder adjudged him guilty and imposed a fine of $100, with an alternative sentence of thirty days confinement in the city stockade.   Barnett excepted to this judgment and took the case by certiorari to the superior court, where the certiorari was overruled.   By writ of error he brought to this court for review the judgment overruling his certiorari.   According to instructions previously given by the court in similar cases, the clerk of the Supreme Court entered the case on the criminal docket.   Upon the call of the case in its order, counsel for plaintiff in error moved to have it transferred to the civil docket, upon the ground that it was a civil case.   Counsel for defendant in error contended that it was a criminal case, and moved to dismiss it because the bill of exceptions was not tendered and certified within the time required by law.   It appeared from a note to the judge's certificate that the term of the court during which he rendered the judgment overruling the certiorari adjourned on January 28.   The bill of exceptions was tendered to and signed by him March 6.   He certified that he left the city February 5, and returned March 3.   The question here presented for our decision is, whether the prosecution for a violation of a municipal ordinance punishable by fine or imprisonment is such a criminal case as that a bill of exceptions therein, in which the accused complains of a judgment overruling his certiorari, shall be tendered and certified within twenty days from the rendition of such judgment.

In *Cranston* v. *Augusta*, 61 *Ga.* 572, it appeared that Cranston, who was charged with the violation of a municipal ordinance, was acquitted in the recorder's court. Upon certiorari by the city, the decision of the recorder was reversed by the judge of the superior court, and direction given that Cranston be punished in accordance with the ordinance of the city which he was charged with having violated. To this ruling he excepted, and the judgment of the superior court was reversed; this court holding that, as the power of a municipal corporation to exercise police jurisdiction is a power delegated by the State, the corporation as a party to a criminal proceeding stands in the place of the State, and inasmuch as the State can not have a writ of certiorari or a writ of error to revise a judgment of discharge by its courts, it follows .that a corporation can not have a writ of certiorari to revise a similar judgment rendered by the corporation court on final trial of the accused. In *Mayor etc. of Hawkinsville* v. *Ethridge*, 96 *Ga.* 326, Ethridge was convicted before the police court for the violation of an ordinance. He took the case by certiorari to the superior court, where a motion in behalf of the corporation to dismiss the certiorari was overruled. To the judgment overruling the motion to dismiss the mayor etc. excepted. This court held that the municipality could not prosecute the writ of error, and dismissed the same. Atkinson, J., in delivering the opinion, said: "Towns and cities, in the administration of those functions pertaining to the police department, which by their charters are conferred upon them, represent, in a qualified sense, the sovereignty of the State;" and "The code provides, in express terms, that either party in a civil case, and the defendant in a criminal proceeding, in the superior court of this State, may except to any sentence, judgment or decree. The right of exception is limited to the defendant in criminal cases. This court

can only review the judgment of the lower court by a bill of
exceptions; and inasmuch as no provision is made by the law
by means of which the State can present and have transmitted
here a bill of exceptions in a criminal cause, if there were no
other legal or constitutional impediment to the reversal of a
judgment rendered in favor of the defendant in the court below,
this one difficulty is insurmountable."

In *Mohrman* v. *Augusta,* 103 *Ga.* 841, where one was convicted
in a police court for the violation of a municipal ordinance, and
carried his case by certiorari to the superior court, the case was
recognized as being in its nature a criminal proceeding.   In
Mayor etc. of Macon v. *Wood,* ante, 149, the facts were similar to
those in *Ethridge's* case, supra, and the court held that "The decision of the superior court on certiorari, reversing the judgment
of a municipal court convicting one of a violation of a municipal
ordinance, is not subject to review by this court."   Again, in
Phillips v. *Stone Mountain,* 61 *Ga.* 386, it appears that Phillips
and other liquor-dealers doing business in the town of Stone
Mountain filed their bill against the municipal authorities,
praying that they be restrained from trying, convicting, and
fining them for a violation of the provisions of an ordinance
which the complainants alleged to be void.   The injunction
was denied, and complainants excepted.   This court held that
the injunction was properly refused.   In the opinion rendered
Bleckley, J., said: "Injunctions or orders in the nature of injunctions are not granted by courts of equity to restrain proceedings in criminal matters. . . Chancery takes no part in
the administration of criminal law.   It neither aids the criminal courts in the exercise of jurisdiction nor restrains or obstructs them."   This case was followed in *Garrison* v. *Atlanta,*
68 *Ga.* 64, and in *Paulk* v. *Sycamore,* 104 *Ga.* 24, in each of
which it was sought to enjoin the enforcement of a municipal
ordinance; and this court held that injunction will not be
granted to restrain a criminal proceeding.   The statute in reference to the time within which bills of exceptions shall be tendered and certified provides for only two general classes of
cases, civil and criminal.   Prosecutions in police courts for
violations of municipal ordinances punishable by fine or im-

prisonment must, as to the provisions of such statute, be assigned to the one or the other of these classes; and, according to the rulings above cited, we think they must be classified as criminal cases. They certainly partake more of the nature of criminal than of civil cases. A municipal ordinance is a law for the protection of the public in a qualified sense, it being designed for the protection of the municipality; and while a civil statute of a State is enacted for the protection of the whole State, the punishment for the infraction of the ordinance, as well as of the statute, is for the violation of a public law. If the State itself, directly, should make the act an offense and prescribe the punishment, there could be no question that the act would be a crime, and the prosecution of it a criminal case. How can it make any difference in principle whether the State does this itself, or delegates the power to the municipality to enact the law and inflict the penalty for its violation? Moreover, if the violation of a municipal ordinance punishable by imprisonment is not a crime, then under the provisions of the constitutions of the United States and of this State, forbidding involuntary servitude except as a punishment for crime, one convicted for such violation could not be required to labor upon the public works of the corporation during the term of his imprisonment, and municipalities would be deprived of what has been from time immemorial their most efficient and salutary means of preserving order and enforcing obedience to their ordinances. See State v. West, 42 Minn. 147.

Counsel for plaintiff in error cited the cases of *Williams* v. *Augusta*, 4 *Ga.* 509, and *Floyd* v. *Eatonton*, 14 *Ga.* 354. While there may be some expressions in the opinions in those cases which upon a cursory reading may not seem to be in entire harmony with the ruling herein announced, yet upon a careful examination of those decisions it will be seen that they are not in conflict with what we now hold. What was really decided there was, that the term "criminal cases," as used in that clause of the constitution of 1798 giving to the superior court exclusive jurisdiction in all criminal cases except as therein provided, had reference to violations of the public laws of the State, and not to the infraction of municipal ordinances; and that the declaration in that constitution that "Trial by jury, as heretofore used in this State, shall remain inviolate," did not apply to trials before police courts where pecuniary penalties were imposed. We may say further, in reference to the point ruled in the present case, that there is much reason for applying the rule for the speedy disposition of other criminal cases to prosecutions for the violation of municipal ordinances punishable by fine or imprisonment.

As the bill of exceptions was not presented to and signed by the judge within twenty days from the judgment overruling the certiorari of the accused, the writ of error must be dismissed.

Writ of error dismissed.   All the Justices concurring.

CROSS *v.* SOUTHERN RAILWAY COMPANY.

A railroad company is not liable for damages for a personal injury to a boy more than seven years old, when the evidence shows that the boy was running along a path six feet from the track, with a rope tied around him and trailing behind, and that, after the engine and half of the train had passed him, the rope was by some means drawn under the train and the boy pulled thereunder and injured. Such an occurrence was an accident which could not have been guarded against by any reasonable degree of diligence on the part of the servants of the company.

Argued October 9, — Decided November 1, 1899.

Action for damages.   Before Judge Janes.   Haralson superior court.   January term, 1899.

J. M. McBride and *Daniel W. Rountree*, for plaintiff.

Dorsey, Brewster & Howell, Head & Head and *Hugh M. Dorsey*, for defendant.

SIMMONS, C. J.   The Southern Railway Company was sued for personal injuries to a small boy by one of its trains. After the close of the plaintiff's evidence, the court granted a nonsuit, and to this the plaintiff excepted. From the evidence and the admitted facts it appears that the injury occurred within the limits of an incorporated city, at a point on the company's tracks which was between two public crossings but more than three hundred yards from either of them. The

boy, not quite eight years old, had been "playing horse" with
a little playmate, and, in lieu of harness and bridle, a piece
of rope had been tied to his arms.   Having "gotten loose"
from his driver, he ran away and, entering the shallow cut in
which the track lay, ran along a path parallel to the track
and about six feet from it.   A train of the defendant company
came up behind him, but did not frighten him.   He looked
back at it but continued down the path, and even after the
engine had passed him he kept his course, the rope trailing
behind him.   At a point some seventy-five yards from where
he had run into the path, and when about half of the train
had passed him, the rope by some means, whether as a result
of the disturbance of the air by the train or of the motion im-
parted to the rope itself by the boy does not appear, caught on
a passing car.   The boy was thrown from his feet and drawn
partly under the wheels of the train, both of his legs being cut
off between the knee and ankle.   The evidence also showed
that, when the train was approaching the boy, the engineer
did not ring the bell or blow the whistle, and that the speed
of the train was from eighteen to twenty miles an hour.

Under these facts the company could not properly be held
to have been in fault and liable in damages, and it was, therefore, not error to grant a nonsuit. The company was not liable
unless it had been negligent, and it was not negligence to fail
to do what it was under no legal duty to do.   Simply because
the boy was running along and keeping within a path parallel
with the railway-track and some six feet from it, the law did
not make it the duty of the company's servants to slow up the
train, ring the bell, or blow the whistle.   Had the boy been
running at an angle with the track and been apparently about
to cross it, the case might have been decidedly different.   As
it was, the boy was not on the track and did not appear to be
in any appreciable danger, and the proximate cause of the injury was the engagement of the rope with some part of the
passing train—something which the company's agents could
not have foreseen and have been expected to guard against.
For this reason, we think the injury is shown by the evidence

to have been the result of an accident for which the company can not be held liable.

Judgment affirmed.   All the Justices concurring.

GENTRY *v.* BARRON, administrator.

1. There was no error in allowing the petition in an action upon a promissory note apparently barred by the statute of limitations to be so amended as to allege facts showing that it was not so barred, and, to this end, to set forth a copy of a valid written contract, signed by the defendant, whereby he not only recognized the note as a valid subsisting obligation, but agreed with the plaintiff upon an extension of the time for its payment to a given date, after which less than two years had elapsed before the bringing of the action.

2. That an amendment of this character had been allowed without notice to the defendant afforded no cause for striking the same. If he was surprised upon first learning of its allowance, he was, at most, entitled to no more than a continuance of the case.

3. Evidence supporting the allegations of such an amendment was properly admitted; nor was there any error in admitting in connection therewith the note sued on, notwithstanding "it appeared on its face to have been barred by the statute of limitations."

4. One who procures an adjudication that an action against him upon a promissory note not under seal was prematurely brought, for the reason that the note was not due and payable until after a designated day which had not arrived before the filing of the plaintiff's petition, is estopped from setting up the statute of limitations in defense to a second action on the same note brought after a dismissal of the first and within less than six years from the day above indicated.

5. It plainly appearing that this case could not have been brought to this court except for delay only, damages are awarded against the plaintiff in error.

Argued October 9. — Decided November 1, 1899.

Complaint. Before Judge Janes. Haralson superior court. January term, 1899.

J. M. McBride, S. L. Craven, and *Price Edwards,* for plaintiff in error.   *E. S. & E. D. Griffith,* contra.

LUMPKIN, P. J. It will be seen by reference to the case of *Gentry* v. *Walker,* 101 *Ga.* 123, that the former, in defense to an action upon a promissory note brought against him by the latter, filed a plea setting up that the action had been prema-

turely brought, that the trial court struck this plea, and that
its judgment was reversed, this court holding that the. allegations of the plea, if true, would constitute a complete defense
to the action, it having been brought on January 1, 1895,
and the allegations of the defendant's plea showing that the
time of payment had been by written agreement extended
until November 6, 1895.   The record now before us discloses
that Walker, in view of the judgment of this court, dismissed
his action, but immediately renewed the same.   Thereupon
Gentry filed an answer setting up that the plaintiff's action
was barred by the statute of limitations.   On the trial of this
issue, the plaintiff introduced evidence establishing beyond
controversy the truth of the allegations contained in Gentry's
answer to the first action, and a verdict against the latter was
directed by the court.   He excepted to this, and also to certain
rulings made during the trial, the nature of which is sufficiently indicated in the headnotes.   While the case was pending here, Walker died, and Barron, his administrator, was
made a party defendant in error in his stead.

As will be seen, without discussion, Gentry's special assignments of error are frivolous and entirely without merit.   His
main contention, viz., that the plaintiff's cause of action was
barred by the statute of limitations, is preposterous.   He himself procured from this court an adjudication that, upon a given
state of facts set up by himself, the plaintiff's original action
was prematurely brought, and that upon this state of facts the
plaintiff had no right to sue until after the 6th day of November, 1895.   It resulted that upon Gentry's own theory the
plaintiff had a right to bring his action at any time within six
years from the date last mentioned.   The action was promptly
renewed within this time, which has not even yet expired, and
the plaintiff on the trial proved the truth of Gentry's former
plea.   In the face of this, he deliberately insisted that the present action was brought too late, and not only sought from the
trial court a ruling to that effect, but persists in asking this
court to hold that, under the evidence as stated, the plaintiff's
action was barred, notwithstanding its previous solemn adjudication, invoked by him, to the contrary.   Clearly, this is a

case for damages, and they are accordingly awarded to the defendant in error.

Judgment affirmed, with damages.   All the Justices concurring.

WHITTON *v.* REID.

Though an order setting a motion for a new trial for a hearing in vacation and directing that "the brief of evidence be presented for approval on or before the date aforesaid, or in default thereof the motion will be dismissed," may confer upon the judge authority to approve the brief at the hearing; and though in case of such approval this action of the judge may be treated as the equivalent of filing the brief in the clerk's office, yet where the judge distinctly declines to approve the brief at the hearing and dismisses the motion on the ground that the brief of evidence was not duly filed in the clerk's office, the judgment will not be reversed.

Argued October 9,—Decided November 1, 1899.

Motion for new trial.   Before Judge Janes.   Haralson superior court.   February 11, 1899.

E. S. & G. D. Griffith, for plaintiff in error.

COBB, J.   The case of Reid *v.* Whitton was tried at a term which lasted longer than thirty days.   During the term and within thirty days from the trial a motion for a new trial was filed by the losing party, and an order was passed of which the following is a copy: "Ordered that the plaintiff show cause before me at such time and place as the court may fix, after notice of ten days to each party or their attorneys, why the foregoing motion should not be granted.   Let the brief of evidence be presented for approval on or before the date aforesaid, or in default thereof the motion will be dismissed."   The motion came on for a hearing on a day more than thirty days from the date of the trial.   A brief of evidence was presented for approval on that day, but, the same not having been filed within thirty days from the date of the verdict, the judge declined to approve it, and upon motion dismissed the motion for a new trial on this ground.   To this ruling the movant excepted.

There being nothing in the order passed by the judge in regard to the hearing of the motion for a new trial which allowed the movant more than thirty days in which to file the brief of evidence in order to perfect the motion for a new trial, it was essential that the brief should be filed within thirty days. When thus filed it was in a condition to be presented for approval under the terms of the order. Until it was actually filed in the clerk's office or some action taken by the judge which would be equivalent to a filing, the brief of evidence was not ready to be presented for approval, and when presented in this condition the judge was not required to approve the same or to pass any order concerning it. It is true that in the cases of *Hightower* v. *George*, 102 *Ga.* 549, and *Malsby* v. *Young*, 104 *Ga.* 205, it was held that if the judge approved the brief and passed an order directing it to be filed, this was the equivalent of a filing. In the present case the judge did not approve the brief or pass any order directing it to be filed, but declined to do either. The brief when presented not having been filed, and the judge having taken no action which would, under the rulings above referred to, dispense with the actual filing in the clerk's office, there was no error in dismissing the motion for a new trial for the want of a brief of evidence filed according to law.

Judgment affirmed. All the Justices concurring.

CHEROKEE IRON COMPANY *v.* BARRY.

When a motion for a new trial was duly filed and the court passed an order in effect allowing the movant until the hearing of the motion to obtain the judge's approval of the brief of evidence, it was erroneous to dismiss the motion merely because the brief, which had within the time prescribed by law been filed in the clerk's office, was not presented for approval before the hearing.

Argued October 9,— Decided November 2, 1899.

Motion for new trial. Before Judge Janes. Polk superior court. February term, 1899.

W. C. Bunn and *F. A. Irwin*, for plaintiff in error.
W. J. Harris and *Sanders & Davis*, contra.

LUMPKIN, P. J. The error complained of in the bill of exceptions now under consideration is the granting of an order dismissing a motion for a new trial. It appears from the record that the motion and the brief of evidence accompanying the same were filed within the time prescribed by law, but that the brief had not been approved by the judge when the motion came on to be heard. The case was tried at the August term, 1898, of Polk superior court. At that term the judge signed an order presented to him by counsel for the movant with a view to fixing a day in vacation for the hearing of the motion. It was by this order directed that the motion be heard "on the ....day of............1898." The order also contained the following: "Let the brief of evidence be presented for approval on or before the date aforesaid, or in default thereof the motion will be dismissed." The blanks in the order were not filled at the time the judge signed it, he informing counsel that he would fill the same at a later day, or that, in case of his failure to do so, the hearing of the motion would go over to the next term of the court. In point of fact these blanks were never filled, and the motion came on for a hearing at the February term, 1899. Counsel for the respondent then moved to dismiss it, "because the brief of evidence had not been approved by the court within the time fixed by the order nisi," and, after argument had, the motion to dismiss was granted.

It was insisted in the argument here that the order above referred to in any event required the movant to procure an approval of the brief of evidence on some day during the year 1898, and that after the expiration of that year it was too late to obtain such approval. In this view we can not concur. Under the facts above recited, it is clear that at the time the order was signed no date was fixed or intended to be fixed; and it is equally clear that under the terms of the order the movant was to have until the hearing actually took place to have his brief of evidence approved. Furthermore, it was actually contemplated that the hearing might not take place until the February term, 1899. But, independently of the assurance given to counsel by the judge, the result of his failure to fix a day in vacation for the hearing of the motion was to carry the same over to the next term by operation of law. In *Central Railroad* v. *Pool*, 95 *Ga.* 412, it was distinctly ruled that "the filing of a motion for a new trial together with a brief of the evidence within the time prescribed [by law] is sufficient to make the motion, for the purpose of keeping it alive till the final hearing, a valid and legal one. The approval of the brief of evidence is not indispensable to this purpose, and may be obtained after the time for filing has expired." The decision in that case is controlling here.

Judgment reversed. All the Justices concurring.

WINGARD v. SOUTHERN RAILWAY COMPANY.

109 177
f112 153

1. The mere fact that a magistrate who tried a case entered upon a certiorari bond a certificate that the costs in the case had been paid is not, without more, sufficient evidence of his approval of the bond to warrant the clerk of the superior court to issue the writ of certiorari.
2. The certiorari having been issued·in the absence of a duly approved bond, the writ was void, and the motion to dismiss the same ought to have been sustained.

109 1:
h115 7(
o115 7(
109 1
124 414
109 177
125 453

Submitted October 9,—Decided November 1, 1899.

Certiorari.   Before Judge Janes.   Polk superior court.   February term, 1899.

C. E. Carpenter and *H. M. Wright*, for plaintiff.
Shumate & Maddox and *Fielder & Mundy*, contra.

LEWIS, J.   When the petition for certiorari in this case came on for a hearing before the judge of the superior court, a motion was made by counsel for defendant in certiorari to dismiss the same, because it did not appear that the bond filed by the plaintiff in certiorari was approved by the justice of the peace in whose court the case had been tried.   It appears from the record that a bond was executed by the plaintiff in certiorari and a surety, and attached to the original petition.   The execution of that bond does not appear to have been attested at all.   Following the signatures of the obligors to the bond was a certificate of the justice that the Southern Railway Company had paid all costs in the case.   The judge overruled the motion to dismiss, and this is one of the grounds of error assigned in the bill of exceptions.

12

The question as to whether or not a failure of a justice of the peace to accept or approve a certiorari bond renders void the issuing of the writ of certiorari is not an open one in this court. It has been repeatedly decided that such an approval by a magistrate is essential to the validity of the writ. See *Hamilton* v. *Ins. Co.*, 107 *Ga.* 728, and the opinion of Lumpkin, Presiding Justice, with authorities therein cited. There is nothing in the record which indicates that the justice of the peace ever accepted or approved the bond filed with the petition for certiorari. While the law does not require any formal certificate of such approval, or any special method of showing an acceptance by the magistrate of the bond, yet it must appear from the record that such acceptance and approval were had. The only thing relied on by counsel for defendant in error as showing the bond in this case was approved by the justice of the peace is the fact that his certificate of the payment of costs was entered on the bond on the same day that the bond was executed. There being nothing in the certificate referring to the bond, or even intimating that the security had been approved by the justice, it constitutes no evidence whatever that the bond itself had actually been approved by the justice. We do not think the following cases cited by counsel for defendant in error at all in point: The case of *Kelly* v. *Jackson,* 67 *Ga.* 274, simply held, "if the bond itself, duly and properly executed and approved by the justice, be incorporated in the record, the case will not be dismissed." The justice in that case had entered a certificate of the payment of costs, but in that certificate said nothing about the bond. The record showed, however, that the bond was actually approved by the justice, and its approval bore date before the writ of certiorari was granted. Had the record in that case simply showed a certificate of the payment of costs, the petition for certiorari would doubtless have been dismissed. In the case of *Hendrix* v. *Mason,* 70 *Ga.* 523, the question involved was whether or not the certiorari should have been dismissed because the bond was executed before a commercial notary public. It was simply decided there, where proper bond was given to the justice and accepted by him, the fact that the signatures were attested by a mere notary would not require the dismissal of the certiorari. There was no question raised touching the failure of the magistrate to accept or approve the bond in that case. On the contrary, it appears from the case itself that it was actually accepted, and we presume, of course, that this in some way was shown by the record. We conclude, therefore, that the judge erred in refusing to sustain the motion to dismiss this petition for certiorari.

Judgment reversed. All the Justices concurring.

BROWN *v.* DRAKE, receiver.

1. A contract by a manufacturing corporation to deliver to an individual its products at specified prices and to purchase from him designated agricultural products at so much per bushel, it being in contemplation that he would sell the former at an advance and purchase the latter for less than he was to receive therefor, but which designated no quantity either of the manufactured goods or of the agricultural products, was not broken until the individual ordered goods of the corporation or offered products to it and it thereupon failed to comply with the terms of its agreement.
2. The evidence introduced to sustain the plea failed to establish the allegations thereof, and consequently the court did not err in directing a verdict against the defendant, the plaintiff having made out a prima facie case.

Argued October 9, — Decided November 1, 1899.

Complaint. Before Judge Janes. Haralson superior court. July term, 1899.

Price Edwards, for plaintiff in error.
W. F. Brown and *E. S. & G. D. Griffith*, contra.

COBB, J. When this case was here before (101 *Ga.* 130), it was held that the pleas filed by the defendant set up matters which, if established by competent evidence, constituted a good defense to the action, and it was therefore erroneous to strike such pleas on general demurrer. Upon the trial the only evidence offered was in support of that plea which alleged an agreement between the defendant and the company of which the plaintiff was receiver, under the terms of which the company was to furnish him cottonseed meal and hulls in exchange for cottonseed and to sell him farm fertilizers at a given price, which it is alleged the company failed to do. While there was evidence of a written agreement to this effect, there was no evidence whatever showing that there had been a failure by the company to furnish to the defendant, upon request, any of the articles specified in the agreement, or that it had refused to accept from him when tendered any of the articles which it had agreed to buy. Treating the plea as setting up a valid defense to the action (and for the purposes of this case it must be so treated), the evidence failed to support the allegations of the same; and, there being no evidence offered to establish any of the other pleas, the court did not err in directing the jury to return a verdict in favor of the plaintiff.

Judgment affirmed. All the Justices concurring.

HILES CARVER COMPANY *v.* KING.

180
217

1. When a sheriff's entry upon an attachment recites that he levied it upon a certain tract of land, prima facie there was a lawful seizure, and consequently where an execution issued upon a judgment rendered in an attachment case was subsequently levied on the same land and met by a claim, it was error to dismiss the latter levy on the ground that the entry upon the attachment did not *recite* that the sheriff had actually seized the property or had given written notice to the tenant in possession.
2. It would, on the trial of such a claim, be competent to prove affirmatively that the levy of the attachment was lawfully made, by showing the manner in which the seizure was effected.

Argued October 9, — Decided November 2, 1899.

Levy and claim. Before Judge Janes. Haralson superior court. July term, 1899.

Price Edwards, for plaintiff. *Oscar Reese*, contra.

LEWIS, J. Hiles Carver Company sued out an attachment against McBurnett, on the ground of his non-residence. Upon this attachment was an entry of levy in usual form upon a certain house and lot in the town of Waco, Ga., as the property of the defendant, the entry containing a full description of the property seized. A judgment was afterwards rendered for the plaintiff against the defendant, subjecting the property attached;

and to the levy of a fi. fa. issued upon this judgment the defendant in error interposed a claim.   On the trial of the claim
the plaintiff submitted evidence tending to show a due seizure
of the property under the attachment, and written notice given
to the tenant in possession by the levying officer.   The attachment was duly entered on the attachment docket.   After plaintiff closed the case, the court, upon motion of counsel for claimant, dismissed the levy of plaintiff's fi. fa., upon the ground
that the levy of the attachment did not *recite* that a seizure of
the property levied on was made by the officer making the levy,
or that written notice of such levy was given by the officer to
the defendant or the tenant in possession, and because the court
had no jurisdiction to render judgment on the attachment.

The question raised by this record is whether or not the levy
of an attachment on land is void simply because the officer
does not describe in his entry of levy upon the fi. fa. the particular manner of the seizure, and does not recite that he had
given either the defendant or tenant in possession notice of the
levy.   We know of no law requiring the officer to make any
such recitals in the levy.   The statute simply requires the officer
to enter his levy on the process by virtue of which such levy
is made, and such entry shall plainly describe the property
levied on, and the amount of interest of the defendant therein.
Civil Code, § 5421.   This provision was fully complied with
by the entry of the officer made in this case.   The expression,
"I have this day levied," implies a legal seizure by the officer
of the property described in his entry, and raises the presumption in favor of such officer of a valid and legal seizure of the
property described.   The burden of showing an omission of
duty which renders the seizure illegal or invalid in any particular case is on the party making such an attack upon the
levy.   As stated in the opinion of Simmons, C. J., in the case
Greer v. *Fergerson*, 104 *Ga.* 555, in speaking of a levy of a
tax fi. fa. upon land by an officer, "The law presumes that the
owners of the land had the notice prescribed, for it presumes
that public officers will do their duty."   The attachment in
this case, therefore, together with the entry of levy by the officer thereon, was upon its face regular and valid.   The claim-

ant had a right to introduce evidence showing that for any reason it was void, and having failed in this case to show an illegal seizure of the land under the levy of the attachment, the court erred in dismissing the levy of plaintiff's fi. fa. *McCrory* v. *Hall*, 104 *Ga.* 668_9. The case just cited and that of *Smith* v. *Brown*, 96 *Ga.* 274, turned upon what actually occurred, and not upon the form of the sheriff's entry.

Judgment reversed.   All the Justices concurring.

MOZLEY *v.* REAGAN.

1. A plea by a defendant that the note sued on "does not appear as it did when it was signed, having been altered by marking and scratching over the same with pen and ink," and that he did not execute the note "in the shape it now is," is not such a plea of non est factum or of alteration as to put on the plaintiff the burden of proving the execution of the note by the defendant.
2. The evidence demanded the verdict for the plaintiff, and the trial judge did not err in so directing.
3. Damages are awarded for bringing this case to the Supreme Court for delay only.

Argued October 9, — Decided November 2, 1899.

Complaint. Before Judge Janes. Haralson superior court. July term, 1899.

E. S. & G. D. Griffith, for plaintiff in error.
W. R. Hutcheson and *Beall & Johnson*, contra.

SIMMONS, C. J. 1. Reagan brought an action against Mozley, in a justice's court, on a promissory note. The defendant filed various pleas to the action,—a plea of not indebted, a plea of payment, a plea of fraud and collusion between the original payee and the plaintiff, and a plea that the note had been so altered that it "does not appear as it did when it was signed, having been altered by marking and scratching over the same with pen and ink," and that he did not execute the note "in the shape it now is." The defendant seems to have prevailed in the justice's court, and Reagan appealed to the superior court. On the trial in the latter court, when Reagan offered the note in evidence, it was objected to by Mozley on the ground that the execution of the note had not been proved. The court overruled the objection and admitted the note in evidence, to which ruling Mozley excepted. We think that the plea filed by the defendant as to the alteration of the note was not sufficient to put on the plaintiff the burden of proving the execution of the note. A plea of this kind should state that the note had been altered intentionally, and in a material part thereof, by a person claiming a benefit under it, with intent to defraud the defendant. Civil Code, § 3702. The plea filed states none of these things, and if demurred to should have been stricken. It was therefore not necessary, under such a plea, for the plaintiff to prove the execution of the note before its introduction as evidence.

2.   There was a total failure on the part of the defendant to establish by proof any of the pleas he had filed. It was shown by the plaintiff that he had purchased the note, for a valuable consideration, before it was due and before the defendant had made any payments on it to the original payee. The defendant's testimony shows that the lumber which he claimed was delivered to the original payee in payment of the note was delivered subsequently to the transfer of the note by the payee to Reagan; nor was there any evidence whatever of fraud or collusion between the payee and Reagan. The evidence, therefore, demanded a verdict for the plaintiff, and the court did not err in directing the jury to so find.

3.   The writ of error being palpably without merit and it being manifest that this case was brought here for delay only, damages are awarded against the plaintiff in error.

Judgment affirmed, with damages.   All the Justices concurring.

COLE et al. v. McCLENDON, ordinary.

109 183
115 272

1. Even if examination of folded ballots by the managers of a prohibition election did have the effect of intimidating qualified voters from casting their ballots, it will be no ground of contesting the election, unless the petition for contest sets forth the names of the persons thus deterred from voting, and alleges that they would have voted on the losing side of the question submitted at the election, and that the number of voters

so intimidated was such that the result of the election would have been different if they had voted.

2. In a prohibition election held under the provisions of section 1541 et seq. of the Political Code, qualified voters of the county, residing in portions of the county where the sale of liquor is already prohibited under local or general laws operative in territory less than the limits of a county, may nevertheless vote.

3. Where the names of voters appear upon the official registration lists, even though there may have been irregularities in the entering of their names thereon, they are nevertheless entitled to vote, if qualified voters and entitled to register; and a contest which merely brings in question the regularity of putting their names on the registration lists is not sufficient, unless it alleges facts showing that they could not in any event have been properly so entered.

Argued October 10, — Decided November 2, 1899.

Contested election. Before Judge Harris. Coweta superior court. March term, 1899.

W. Y. Atkinson and *H. A. Hall,* for contestants.
A. D. Freeman, R. W. Freeman, and *W. A. Turner,* contra.

Cobb, J. An election was held under the provisions of section 1541 et seq. of the Political Code, in the county of Coweta, to determine whether the sale of liquor should be allowed in that county. The ordinary declared the result of the election as being "against the sale." A contest was instituted in the superior court, the petition setting forth various grounds as the "cause of contest." Upon demurrer all of the grounds of contest, except three, were stricken. Upon the hearing of the grounds not stricken, the judge determined them against the contestants and approved the action of the ordinary. The contestants excepted to the judgment sustaining the demurrer. Only those grounds which were insisted on in the argument in this court will be dealt with in this opinion.

1. The contestants alleged that at one of the precincts a manager of the election opened and inspected all the folded ballots as they were received, so as to ascertain how each person voted; and that this had the effect of intimidating other voters and deterring them from voting according to their individual convictions; it being further alleged that many voters had been told by their employers that if they voted "for the

sale," they would be discharged. Neither the names nor number of the voters claimed to have been thus prevented from voting were set forth. The policy of the law of this State requires that each qualified voter shall be allowed on a day of election to deposit a ballot expressive of his individual views on the question involved, and that no one shall ever, under any circumstances, either at the election or afterwards, examine his ballot for the purpose of ascertaining how he has voted, save only in case of a contest of the election. Any and all means that are capable of being resorted to which have or may have the effect of destroying the right of the individual elector to vote as he desires are unlawful and reprehensible in the extreme, and when the person guilty of such conduct is himself a manager of the election, no words of condemnation are too strong when used to characterize his conduct. Such conduct will not, however, vitiate the election, nor will it have the effect of changing the result, unless it be clearly shown who were the voters thus deterred from voting, and that if they had voted they would have voted on the losing side and that their votes would have changed the result of the election. The allegations of the ground of contest not being in conformity to this rule, there was no error in striking the same on demurrer.

2. Construing the general local option liquor law (Political Code, §§ 1541-1550) as a whole, the conclusion is necessarily reached that the legislative intention was that the people of the different counties of the State in which the sale of liquor was then authorized should in each county be permitted to determine whether the sale of liquors should be allowed within the limits of the county. No provision is made for an election in territory less than that embraced within the limits of a county. The petition for election must be signed by a designated number of voters of a "county;" license to sell liquors in the "county" shall not issue after the petition is filed and before the result of the election has been declared; the notice of the election, as well as the result of the election, is published in the "official organ of the ordinary or sheriff of the county"; elections shall not be held "in the same county" oftener than once in four years; and if the result of the elec-

tion is "against the sale," liquors can not be lawfully sold
"within the limits of such county." The scheme of the act
being to submit the question to the people of the different counties, all persons qualified to vote for members of the General
Assembly are entitled, by the very terms of the act, to vote.
As no person can so vote who has not resided six months in
the county, the proviso to section 1543, fixing the qualifications of voters, which declares that a voter must "have actually resided within the territorial limits to be affected, at least
six months next preceding the election," is mere redundancy.
It is conceded that the election can only be held for counties,
but it is contended that in such election no person can vote
who resides in any portion of the county where the sale of liquor is prohibited by high license, local option, or other legislation. The following section of the act is cited as authority
for this contention: "No election shall be held under the provisions of this Chapter for any county, city, town, or any other
place in this State where by law the sale of spirituous liquors
is already prohibited either by high license, local option, or
other legislation, so long as these local laws remain of force."
It is contended that the words "county, city, town, or any
other place in this State," and the use of the words "within
the limits of such designated places" in section 1541, as well
as the words "within the territorial limits to be affected" in
section 1543, all indicate that the legislature intended that localities where the sale of liquor was already prohibited were
not to be affected, and therefore that persons residing in such
localities should not be allowed to participate in any election
held under the act. This contention is easily disposed of when
we keep in view the scheme of the act as above indicated. The
words "city, town, or any other place" must be rejected as
meaningless surplusage. The expression "designated places"
can only refer to counties, and the other phrase relied on
is, as we have seen, a mere redundancy, and can not mean
other than a county. This view of the matter is strengthened when we refer to the journal of the General Assembly,
where it appears that the original bill provided for elections in
counties, cities, and districts, and by amendment the scheme

of the act was changed to elections by counties only. See House Journal 1884, pp. 505, 531; House Journal 1885, p. 81. The language now relied on to change the scheme of the law is such as is consistent with the scheme of the original bill, and was evidently left in the act by inadvertence or mistake. The law as it now stands authorizes elections by counties, and when such elections are held any person can vote who is qualified to vote in a county election. A local law which antedates the law under consideration, prohibiting the sale of liquors within a county, will prevent an election from being held, but neither a local law prohibiting the sale of liquors within territory less than a county, nor a general law having the same effect, will prevent an election under the general local option liquor law from being held, nor be any obstacle in the way of any elector in the county voting at such election, notwithstanding he may reside in a part of the county in which the sale of liquor is already prohibited by virtue of either a local or general law operative in territory of less extent than the whole county. It follows, therefore, that an election under the general local option liquor law could be lawfully held in the county of Coweta, and that at such election every person in the county qualified to vote for members of the General Assembly could vote, notwithstanding under the operation of local and general laws the sale of liquor was prohibited in every district in the county save the one in which the city of Newnan was located, there being in existence no local law of older date than the general local option liquor law which had the effect of prohibiting the sale of liquor throughout the entire limits of the county of Coweta. See in this connection the opinion of McCay, Judge, in Weil v. Calhoun, 25 Fed. Rep. 865.

3. The qualifications of an elector are set forth in the constitution of this State, and that instrument declares that the General Assembly may provide for the "registration of all electors." Civil Code, §§ 5737-8. The law carrying into effect this grant of power is contained in the act of 1894 (Political Code, § 35 et seq.). The first section provides that no person shall vote in any election in this State "unless such person

shall have been registered as [therein] provided." The plan
for registering the voters therein provided is, in substance, as
follows: Each person is required to sign in the "voters book,"
or on a separate sheet, an oath administered by the tax-collector
or his clerk, setting forth that the person signing is, or will be
on the day of election, qualified to vote, so far as age and residence is concerned, and that he has paid all taxes required by
law to qualify him as a voter, and that he is not disfranchised
from voting by reason of any offense committed against the laws
of the State. The tax-collector furnishes to the county registrars
a list of names appearing on the voters books, and separate sheets
for the year. The tax-collector, ordinary, and clerk of the superior court, on or before July 1 of each year, furnish to the county
registrars a list of all persons living in the county the first day of
the year, who are shown by the public records of the county, or
otherwise known to them, to be disqualified from voting for any
cause. The county registrars are required to examine the list of
voters, as well as the list of persons claimed to be disqualified, and
determine (hearing evidence, if necessary) whether any person whose name appears as having taken the oath required by
law is not qualified to vote, as well as whether persons not allowed by the tax-collector, or his clerk, to sign the oath were
in fact disqualified from voting. The county registrars, after
determining these questions, make up a list of the registered
voters in each militia district and city ward in the county, and
the lists thus made up are furnished to the managers of the
election. The law distinctly declares that "All persons whose
names appear on the list of registered voters placed in possession of the election-managers, and no others, shall be allowed
to deposit their ballots according to law, at the voting precinct
of the militia district or city ward in which they are registered."
Political Code, § 60. The list of registered voters furnished
by the registrars to the managers of the election absolutely controls the managers, and they have no power or authority to allow any one to vote whose name is not on the list, nor to refuse any one the right to vote whose name is on the list. The
purpose of the registration law is to obtain a list of the qualified voters, in order that such voters may exercise the privilege

of voting on the day of election. If the name of a person who is undoubtedly a qualified voter is irregularly or even fraudulently entered upon the list furnished by the tax-collector to the county registrars, and his name is placed upon the list of registered voters by the registrars, his right to vote, as well as to have his vote counted, would be complete. The judgment of the registrars on the question as to whether or not he was entitled to be entered as a registered voter would be conclusive, certainly in a case where they acted in perfect good faith and ignorantly of the fraud perpetrated upon the tax-collector or his clerk.

Section 625 of the Penal Code provides that any person "who shall vote without having signed the oath provided by the tax-collector in said voters book, unless his name shall have been entered on the lists of legal voters as provided by law, shall be guilty of a misdemeanor." The latter clause of the section, saving a qualified voter who has improperly entered as a registered voter from indictment for voting as such, is strongly indicative of a legislative intention to make the judgment of the registrars conclusive on such matters. If the name of a person who is not a qualified voter is entered upon the list of registered voters, he would not become a qualified voter. While the managers of the election would be authorized to receive a ballot from him, on a contest of the election the vote would not be counted; and the person so voting would be subject to indictment for illegal voting (Penal Code, § 629), as well as for a violation of the registration laws. Penal Code, § 625. It was claimed in the present case that the names of a number of persons were entered on the voters book without the authority of the tax-collector or his clerk, some by the tax-receiver and some by persons unknown; that some of those whose names were on the voters book never took the oath prescribed by law, but that the tax-collector included those names on the lists furnished to the county registrars, and such registrars, in ignorance of how they were entered on the voters book, included their names in the list of registered voters, and that such illegally registered persons voted at the election and voted against the sale, and that their number was such that if their votes were thrown out the result of the election would be changed. The name of each person claimed to have been thus illegally entered as a registered voter is set forth in the ground of contest, but there is no allegation that these persons did not possess all the qualifications required by the constitution, nor is it alleged that any of them were disqualified from voting for any reason. The failure to make such allegation was fatal to the ground of contest, and there was no error in dismissing the same on demurrer.

Judgment affirmed. All the Justices concurring.

CONYERS *et al. v.* BRUCE.

1. In a contest between a creditor and the heirs at law of an intestate as to the necessity of administration, the creditor claiming a debt against the estate and the heirs denying it, it is not necessary for the creditor to establish conclusively the existence of the debt. Prima facie proof is all that is necessary.
2. Under the evidence as disclosed by the record, the creditor established prima facie the existence of his debt, and there was no error in appointing an administrator on the estate.

Argued October 10, — Decided November 2, 1899.

Application for administration—appeal. Before Judge Harris. Carroll superior court. October term, 1898.

W. F. Brown, for plaintiffs in error.
Oscar Reese and *Sidney Holderness,* contra.

SIMMONS, C. J. Bruce, claiming that he had two judgments against the estate of Conyers, obtained during the life of Conyers, applied to the ordinary to have an administrator appointed on the estate of Conyers. The heirs at law of Conyers contested the appointment of an administrator, on the ground that Bruce had no legal judgments against the estate, and that the judgments he held were, even if legal, barred by the statute of limitations. A great many questions were made in the record which the view we take of the case renders it unnecessary to decide.

1. Under our code it is almost a necessity to have administration where a person dies intestate leaving debts; and in our

opinion it is not necessary for a creditor who claims a debt against the estate of the intestate and who applies for administration thereon to prove conclusively the existence of the debt. If he makes a prima facie case, that is sufficient to authorize and require the ordinary to appoint an administrator. On such an application, it is not the duty of the ordinary to go into a regular investigation of all the details as to how the debt in question arose, or, if it has been reduced to judgment, whether the judgment has become dormant. It is not his duty to determine whether the creditor has the right to maintain an action upon his judgment, if dormant, or whether such right has become barred by the statute of limitations. These are all questions to be passed upon by another tribunal which the law has provided. *McLaren* v. *Bradford*, 52 *Ga.* 648.

2. In the case now under consideration, Bruce's judgments had apparently not become finally barred at the time of the death of Conyers. They may have been dormant, but the three years in which he had the right to revive them by scire facias, or to sue upon them as debts, had apparently not expired. The fact that the judgments were dormant did not prevent their being debts. Bruce could still have maintained an action upon them. *Lockwood* v. *Barefield*, 7 *Ga.* 393. In *Ex parte Craig*, *T. U. P. Charlton's Rep.* 159, the ordinary refused to appoint an administrator, on the ground that the debt upon which the application was based had become barred by the lapse of time. On certiorari it was held that "The application should not have been dismissed upon that principle, for it was not competent for the court below thus to destroy the remedy by action which the applicant might have possessed. That was a subject of ulterior investigation, which could not take place before the ordinary." In the case of *Ray* v. *Strickland*, 89 *Ga.* 840, it was held that "Although the judgment was then not only dormant, and the right to revive or sue upon it barred, the debt was not extinguished; and as the bar attached after the debtor's death, his administrator could waive it." If, in the present case, there is any merit in the contentions of the heirs at law, the judgment appointing an administrator will not prevent the administrator from contesting the

justness or the legality of the claims of Bruce, although these questions have been passed upon by the ordinary and by the superior court. *Judgment affirmed. All the Justices concurring.*

LOWERY *et al. v.* POWELL.

Under the provisions of the code, administration upon an alleged unrepresented estate can not be vested in the clerk of the superior court, when the decedent left no estate at all.

Argued October 11, — Decided November 2, 1899.

Petition for administration — appeal. Before Judge Hart. Laurens superior court. January term, 1899.

J. H. Martin, John M. Stubbs, and *B. B. Cheney,* for plaintiffs in error.

T. L. Griner and *Anderson, Felder & Davis,* contra.

LITTLE, J. Powell petitioned the ordinary of Laurens county, setting out that there was then pending in the superior court of said county the case of Powell *v.* Cheney, J. M. Lowery senior, et al., and that since the bringing of said suit J. M. Lowery senior has died and that there is no representation on his estate, nor is it likely to be represented, and that the suit can not proceed for want of parties; that it is necessary that an administrator be appointed on the estate of Lowery senior, in order that the suit may proceed. He then prayed that the ordinary should vest the administration of the estate of Lowery in the clerk of the superior court of Laurens county, after the requirements of the law had been complied with. This petition was caveated by the heirs at law of Lowery, on the ground that the deceased left no estate exceeding in value the sum of five hundred dollars. After the usual citation, the ordinary granted the petition and vested the administration of Lowery's estate in W. J. Hightower, clerk of the superior court. An appeal was taken from that decision to the superior court. On the call of the case in the superior court, it was admitted that Lowery senior died intestate in the county of Laurens and left no property, and by consent it was agreed that the presiding judge should pass on the questions involved and render final judgment in the case. After consideration, the judge affirmed the judgment of the ordinary appointing the clerk of the superior court administrator of the estate of Lowery, and the caveators excepted.

The only question raised is, whether the administration of an unrepresented estate can be vested in the clerk of the superior court when such intestate left no property. It appears that the only object of Powell in having the estate represented was to have the pending suit proceed against the administrator of the intestate. Section 3390 of the Civil Code prescribes that, "If from any cause an estate be unrepresented and not likely to be represented, the ordinary may vest the administration in the clerk of the superior court of the county, or any other person whom he may deem fit and proper—a citation being first published for four weeks, as in other cases; and such clerk, if appointed, shall be compelled to discharge the duties of the office." That section further provides that, "If, however, such estate does not exceed in value the sum allowed by law to the widow and children, no administration shall be necessary, but the ordinary shall, by order, set apart the same to the widow and children." Section 3465 of the Civil Code provides, in relation to setting apart a year's support to the family of decedents, that "if it shall appear upon a just appraisement of the estate that it does not exceed in value the sum of five hundred dollars, it shall be the duty of the appraisers to set apart the whole of said estate for the support and maintenance of such widow and child or children," etc. So that, taking these two sections of the code in pari materia, it would seem that if an estate which is unrepresented does not exceed in value the sum of five hundred dollars, no administration of that estate shall be necessary, but that the widow and child or children of the decedent (or the child or children, if there be no widow) shall be entitled to have the estate without administration.

The ownership by the decedent of personal property was the foundation of the grant of letters of administration, and the object of appointing an administrator was to use this property in paying debts and then to distribute what remains among those who are entitled to it. Croswell on Executors

13

and Administrators, § 54.   Formerly, in England, the amount
of personal property of which the estate consisted settled the
jurisdiction of a particular court to grant administration.   In
some of the States, there are statutory provisions that jurisdiction shall not be granted unless the estate of the deceased is
of a certain value.   The provision in Maine is, that the estate
must amount to twenty dollars, or there must be debts to that
amount and real estate enough to pay them.   22 Me. 549.
Mr. Croswell in his work on Executors and Administrators
says, in § 58, that "it may be considered, perhaps, to be probably the law, that if an application for administration was resisted and conclusive proof offered that there was no estate on
which the grant could operate in the State, administration
would be refused."   In Grimes v. Talbert, 14 Md. 172, it was
ruled that prima facie evidence of personal property belonging
to the intestate is all that is necessary for the administration
to be granted.   In California it was held that an administrator
would not be appointed merely to enter an appearance in a
suit to quiet title, there being no property to be administered.
Murray's Estate, Myrick's Prob. 208.   In a Connecticut case
the question was considered, whether a claim given by statute
against a railroad for the negligent killing of the intestate was
property in such a sense as to give the probate court jurisdiction
to grant administration upon the estate of a non-resident.   The
Supreme Court, after investigation, decided to maintain the
jurisdiction of the probate court.   36 Conn. 214.   Our statute
which authorizes administration to be vested in the clerk of the
superior court confines the appointment to cases where *estates*
are unrepresented and not likely to be represented.   An estate
is defined by Anderson, to be "the quantity of interest which
a person has, from absolute ownership down to naked possession," and by Black, in his Law Dictionary, to be "the interest which any one has in lands or in any other subject of property."   Therefore it would seem from the terms of the statute
that administration will be vested in the clerk only when the intestate died possessed of some character of property in which, as
we understand it, is to be included any claim or right which
might thereafter be made productive.   Indeed, such was the

evident intention of the lawmakers, because in the last paragraph of the section it is declared that if such estate does not exceed in value the sum allowed by law to the widow and children, no administration shall be necessary. So that the same authority which gives to the ordinary the power to appoint the clerk administrator of an estate declares that there shall be no administration except where the estate of a decedent is valued at a named sum.

It is said, however, that the case of *Johnston* v. *Tatum*, 20 *Ga.* 775, is authority to support the judgment rendered in the court below, vesting the administration in the clerk. We have examined the original record in that case, and find that there was no question made as to whether the intestate died seised and possessed of an estate, but that it was a ruling made on the application of the ordinary to the judge of the superior court to compel the clerk to take the administration of an unadministered estate, where no person would apply for or accept the same; and the ruling of the court simply was, that the ordinary had the power in a proper case to force such administration on the clerk against his will. Inasmuch as the statute does not require administration to be vested in the clerk except in a case where there is an unrepresented estate, and declares that no administration shall be necessary unless the estate is of a given value, and it was admitted in this case that the intestate left no property of any character, we are constrained to rule that the court below erred in vesting administration. It is claimed that such an action as that which was pending against the intestate at the time of his death survives against his personal representative. Admitting this contention to be sound, it affords no reason against the plain provision of the statute to require administration to be vested in the clerk. It may be that the lawmakers did not take into consideration the desire of a plaintiff to have a judgment against an intestate who left no property. In any event, in following the plain mandate of the code, we can not, as against the admission made, find any authority which authorizes the administration in this case to be vested in the clerk of the superior court; and the judgment of the court below is

Reversed. All the Justices concurring.

OSBORN & WALCOTT MFG. COMPANY *v.* BLANTON.

196
556

1. In order to render an award a "statutory," as distinguished from a "common-law," award, there must be strict compliance with the statutory provisions by virtue of which an award may be made the judgment of a court. A submission to two arbitrators, with power to select an umpire only in the event of their disagreement, followed by an award signed by one of these two and an umpire, does not amount to such compliance, and such an award is not a statutory one.

2. Inasmuch as an award is vitiated by nothing save fraud, accident, or mistake, and therefore not by a mere error of judgment on the part of the arbitrators, either as to the law or the evidence, an award can not be set aside as being contrary to evidence if there is any evidence to sustain it.

3. There was, in the present case, ample evidence to support the verdict, whereby the jury in effect found that the award was correct and that there was no fraud, accident, or mistake on the part of the arbitrators; and damages are awarded against the plaintiff in error for bringing the case to this court for delay only.

Submitted October 11, — Decided November 2, 1899.

Arbitration and award. Before Judge Reagan. Spalding superior court. January term, 1899.

Robert T. Daniel, for plaintiff in error.
Lloyd Cleveland, contra.

LUMPKIN, P. J. The bill of exceptions in this case assigns error upon certain rulings made at the trial. None of the questions thus sought to be raised can, however, be considered by this court, for the reason that exception to the rulings complained of was not taken within the time prescribed by law. We therefore confine ourselves to the material questions presented by the motion for a new trial, exception to the overruling of which was made in due time.

1. The action was upon an award. One of the contentions of the defendant was that it was a statutory award, while the plaintiff, on the other hand, insisted it was a common-law award. As to this issue, we hold that the trial judge rightly sustained the position of the latter. It appears that the written submission to arbitration distinctly contemplated that the two arbitrators selected by the parties should not choose an umpire save only in the event they failed to agree upon an award. Under the repeated rulings of this court, an award

resulting from a submission of this kind is to be treated as a
common-law award, and not as an award under the act of 1856,
the provisions of which are now embraced in various sections
of the Civil Code; that is to say, it should not be treated as a
statutory award where the terms of the statute have not been
strictly adhered to.　See *Halloran* v. *Bray*, 29 *Ga.* 422; *Crane*
v. *Barry*, 47 *Ga.* 476; *Phipps* v. *Tompkins*, 50 *Ga.* 641, 644;
Cherry v. *Smith*, 51 *Ga.* 558; *Price* v. *Bynes*, 57 *Ga.* 176;
Sheffield v. *Clark*, 73 *Ga.* 92.

2. Another question in the case arises upon an exception to
an instruction by the court to the jury, to the effect that if the
arbitrators acted honorably and fairly, and there was any evidence to sustain the award, it should be upheld.　That this instruction was correct can not, at this late day, be reasonably
doubted.　See *Anderson* v. *Taylor*, 41 *Ga.* 10; *Tomlinson* v. *Hardwick*, Ibid. 547; *Akridge* v. *Patillo*, 44 *Ga.* 585, 587; *Overby*
v. *Thrasher*, 47 *Ga.* 10; *Forbes* v. *Turner*, 54 *Ga.* 252; *Black* v.
Harper, 63 *Ga.* 752; *Hardin* v. *Almand*, 64 *Ga.* 582; *Lester* v.
Callaway, 73 *Ga.* 731.

3. There was ample evidence sustaining the correctness of
the award and fully warranting the conclusion that there was
no fraud or mistake on the part of the arbitrators.　The questions of law raised in this case have been so long and so definitely settled ·by the repeated decisions of this court, it is
plainly apparent that the writ of error is not only devoid of
merit but that it must have been sued out for delay only.　We
therefore award damages against the plaintiff in error.

Judgment affirmed, with damages.　All the Justices concurring.

HUDGINS *v.* BLOODWORTH & COMPANY.

1. A witness can not be impeached by proving contradictory statements
previously made by him as to matters not relevant to his testimony and
to the case.
2. The amendment in the present case offered by the plaintiff during the
argument was properly allowed.　It was subject neither to the objection
that it was "too late," nor that it set up a cause of action different from
that set forth in the original petition.　The only effect of the amendment

was to adjust the pleadings to the case made by the evidence already before the jury.

3. In a case where one of the controlling issues was whether a note made by two persons had been settled by the making and delivery of a note signed by one only of these persons, which note was still unpaid, and the evidence upon this issue was directly conflicting, a charge, "that the giving of a note in lieu of an old one is not payment of the old one until the new one is paid, unless there is an express agreement that it shall be," was inapplicable and so misleading as to require the granting of a new trial.

Argued October 11, — Decided November 2, 1899.

Complaint. Before Judge Reagan. Pike superior court. April term, 1899.

Hammond & · Cleveland, for plaintiff in error.
S. N. Woodward, O. H. B. Bloodworth, R. L. Berner, and *Alexander & Lambdin,* contra.

COBB, J. This was an action upon a promissory note by Bloodworth & Company against J. T. Green and J. J. Hudgins. Green filed no defense. Hudgins set up the following defenses: (1) that since the date of the note sued on the plaintiffs had delivered up the note to defendant Green and had taken another note from Green, thereby discharging him (Hudgins) from all liability; (2) that since the giving of the second note just referred to, plaintiffs and Green had entered into an agreement by which Green was discharged from all liability, and thereby he (Hudgins) was also discharged; (3) that he signed the note as surety only, and that his risk as such had been increased because the payees had, without his knowledge or consent, released a mortgage lien embraced in the note upon the property therein described, and had taken instead of the note and in settlement thereof a new note not signed by Hudgins, which embraced a mortgage on other property. There was a verdict for the plaintiffs, and Hudgins's motion for a new trial having been overruled, he excepted. The following brief discussion will dispose of the material questions raised in the case.

1. While Green was on the stand as a witness, the court, over objection of counsel for Hudgins, allowed plaintiffs' counsel to ask the witness questions by which they evidently sought to show that Green had stated to divers persons that the above-

indicated substitution of notes and of the mortgaged property had been made with the consent of Hudgins. The witness denied having made any such statements. The court then allowed the plaintiffs, over defendant's objection, to prove by several witnesses that Green had told them that Hudgins did consent to the change of notes and mortgages. It is not contended that Hudgins would be bound by the declarations of Green, but it was said that the evidence was admissible as tending to impeach Green. It was inadmissible for this purpose, as it related to matters not relevant to his testimony or the case. Civil Code, § 5292. The evidence being inadmissible and of a nature calculated to prejudice the claim of the defendant on one of the controlling issues in the case, the error in admitting the evidence is of a character requiring the granting of a new trial. The conversation between Green and one of the plaintiffs, in which Green stated that Hudgins would agree to the substitution of notes, was admissible to explain the conduct of the plaintiffs in surrendering the note sued on to Green, it appearing during the progress of the trial that the note had been surrendered to Green and by him delivered to Hudgins, in whose possession it was at the date of the trial.

2. After the evidence was closed and during the argument, the plaintiffs offered an amendment setting up that they had never accepted the new note, that it was to take effect only in the event that Hudgins agreed to the substitution and signed the new note, and offered to deliver the same up for cancellation. The effect of the amendment not being to add a new cause of action, but merely to adjust the pleadings to the case as it was made by the evidence, there was no error in allowing the same, either on account of the time it was offered, or of the subject-matter of the amendment.

3. The charge referred to in the third headnote was not applicable to the present case, and being calculated to confuse and mislead the jury on one of the controlling issues, upon which the evidence was directly conflicting, the giving of such a charge was an error requiring the granting of a new trial.

Judgment reversed. All the Justices concurring.

· VELVIN *et al. v.* AUSTIN.

1. When two or more joint defendants against whom a judgment has been rendered apply for a writ of certiorari, and only one of them verifies the petition as prescribed in section 4638 of the Civil Code, he alone should be treated as a plaintiff in certiorari.
2. The original petition in the city court set forth a cause of action as against the motion to dismiss which was filed by the defendants, and it was therefore not error in the judge of the superior court, on certiorari complaining of the overruling of such motion, to refuse to order the case dismissed in the city court.
8. The case as tried in the city court involved issues of fact and did not necessarily depend upon a controlling question of law, and therefore no error was committed in remanding the case for a new trial, instead of making a final judgment therein.

Argued October 10, — Decided November 4, 1899.

Certiorari. Before Judge Harris. Carroll superior court. April term, 1899.

W. C. Hodnett, for plaintiffs.
Sidney Holderness, for defendant.

COBB, J. Suit was brought in the city court of Carroll county, on a sheriff's bond. The petition alleged that Mrs. Austin, the plaintiff's usee, was the transferee of a certain fi. fa., issued from Carroll superior court, in favor of G. W. Austin against Rodahan and against certain town lots; the amount due on the fi. fa. being between three and four hundred dollars. In July, 1893, Hewitt, the sheriff, sold certain of the property described in the above-mentioned fi. fa., under executions for State and county taxes. After deducting from the proceeds of the sale the amount due on the tax executions, there remained in the sheriff's hands the sum of $140, which was alleged to be subject to Mrs. Austin's fi. fa. In 1896 Mrs. Austin procured against the sheriff a rule absolute from the superior court, requiring him to pay over to her the sum of money in his hands on her execution, which he failed and refused to do. It is alleged that this action is a breach of the sheriff's bond, and that he and his securities are liable to petitioner in the sum of $140, with interest and costs. The petition was amended by alleging that at the time the rule was brought against the sheriff he had in his hands the $140 referred to, and that he still has it in his hands. The securities at the appearance term filed a written motion to dismiss the case, on three grounds: (1) because there was no averment that the fi. fa. of Mrs. Austin was ever put in the hands of the sheriff, together with written notice that she claimed the money; (2) because there was no averment that the fi. fa. was ever levied upon any of the property of the defendant in fi. fa., or was put in the hands of the sheriff for this purpose and that he failed and refused to levy the same; (3) because there was no allegation that the balance of the property described in the petition as subject to the fi. fa., and which was not sold under the tax executions, was not sufficient to satisfy the fi. fa. The demurrer was over-ruled, and the case went to trial and resulted in a verdict for the plaintiff for the amount sued for against the sheriff and the sureties on his bond. Five of the sureties applied for and obtained a writ of certiorari to the superior court. When the certiorari came on for a hearing, a motion was made to dismiss the same, because only one of the applicants therefor had made the affidavit required by section 4638 of the Civil Code. The following is a copy of the affidavit attached to the petition for certiorari: "I, James P. Moore, do solemnly swear that the foregoing petition for a certiorari is not filed in the case for the purpose of delay only, and I verily believe that we have good cause for certiorari; and the facts stated in the foregoing petition, so far as they come within my own knowledge, are true, and so far as derived from the knowledge of others I believe them to be true." The motion to dismiss was sustained as to all of the defendants except the one making the affidavit, and as to him the certiorari was sustained and a new trial granted. To this order all of the defendants excepted; the petitioner for certiorari who made the affidavit complains that the judge did not order the case dismissed as to him, under his motion to dismiss filed in the city court; the others complain of the dismissal of the certiorari as to them.

1. Section 4638 of the Civil Code provides that "No writ of certiorari shall be granted or issued, except to the court of ordinary, unless the party applying for the same, his agent or

attorney, shall make and file with his petition" the affidavit
therein prescribed and which is in almost the exact language
of the one set forth above.   The question arises, therefore, as to
whether the affidavit of one of the petitioners for certiorari is
sufficient to relieve the others from making an affidavit of similar character.   Fairly construing this affidavit, it can not be
said that the affiant intended to bind any one but himself.   It
is true he uses in one place the pronoun "we," but in two
other places he uses the singular pronoun.   Moreover, there is
nothing to show that he was the agent of the others.   The
simple fact that he was a joint promissor with the other defendants would not relieve each of them from making the affidavit required by the section.   While the defendants made
common cause with each other in the defense of the suit, they
did not for this reason constitute one legal entity, but each was
a separate and distinct party and subject to a several liability
in the event the defense failed.   One of the purposes of the
affidavit is to prevent petitions for certiorari from being filed
merely for delay, and while one petitioner might swear that *he*
did not sue out the writ for this purpose, this nevertheless
might have been the motive which actuated the others.   Again,
the affiant in the present case makes affidavit only to facts
which come within his own knowledge, and says that they are
true as stated in the petition; whereas the others, or some of
them, might know that some of the statements made in the
petition were untrue, and hence not be able to make the affidavit.
There was no error in dismissing the certiorari as to those who
failed to make the affidavit.   It is true that in the case of *Taylor* v. *Gray*, 20, *Ga.* 77, it was ruled :   "That the affidavit in
support of a petition for a certiorari is insufficient, is no ground
for dismissing the certiorari on a motion made after the certiorari
has been answered, if the answer supports the petition."   But
at the time that case was decided (1856) there was no law requiring that the applicant for certiorari should swear that the
petition was not filed for the purpose of delay only.   It was
not until 1857 that this statement became an essential part of
the affidavit.   Acts 1857, p. 104.   The reason for the rule announced in the case just referred to is stated in the opinion of

Judge Lumpkin in the following language: "But when the motion was made, the answer was in, and that showed the statements in the petition to be true. Of what consequence was it, therefore, at that time, whether the affidavit was insufficient or not?" Even if the answer of the judge whose decision is sought to be reviewed by the certiorari would cure a defect in that part of the affidavit which is intended to verify the averments of the petition, it could not, in any event, have the effect of curing a defect arising in the fact that the applicant had failed to swear that the petition was not filed for the purpose of delay only.

2. The plaintiff in error, Moore, who was the petitioner for certiorari, and who secured a hearing on the same by filing the affidavit required by the statute, complains that the judge erred " in ordering a new trial as to [him] instead of ordering the case dismissed under the written motion to dismiss as filed, and as set out in the petition for certiorari;" and "in not sustaining the certiorari and ordering the case against the petitioners dismissed." To determine whether the first of these assignments of error is well taken, it is necessary to decide whether the judge of the city court erred in overruling the written motion to dismiss filed by the defendants, the substance of which is set forth above. The original petition in the case alleged, in substance, that the usee of the plaintiff was the holder of an execution against a named defendant, which was a special lien against certain described property; that there had been a sale by the defendant sheriff of a portion of the property, and that after discharging certain taxes there was in the hands of the sheriff a specified sum that was subject to the execution first above referred to; that, at her instance, a rule nisi had issued against the sheriff in the superior court of the county of which he had been sheriff, and that a rule absolute had been obtained against him, requiring him to pay over the money on her execution, which he failed and refused to do; that the sum specified in the petition was in the sheriff's hands at the date of the rule absolute and was still in his hands; and these facts were alleged to constitute a breach of the sheriff's official bond. As against the motion to dismiss which was filed in the present

case, the petition set forth a cause of action, and there was no error in refusing to sustain the certiorari and order the case in the city court dismissed.   It was not necessary in such a case to allege that the execution was placed in the sheriff's hands, there being an averment that there had been a rule absolute obtained against him in the county where he had been sheriff, presumptively, therefore, the county of his residence, and that at the time the rule was made absolute, as well as at the time the suit was brought, there was in his hands a fund which was subject to the execution, which he had failed and refused to appropriate to the payment of the same.   For the same reason it was not necessary to allege either a failure and refusal to levy the execution, or that there was no other property upon which the execution could be levied.   If the fund in the sheriff's hands was subject to the execution and was not claimed by liens of higher dignity, a failure to pay the same over to the usee of the plaintiff, under the circumstances alleged in the petition, would be a breach of the bond.

3. The judge of the superior court, having refused to order the case in the city court dismissed because no cause of action was set forth in the petition, sustained the certiorari on other grounds and remanded the case for a new trial; and plaintiff in error, Moore, complains that this was error, as the case was one in which a final judgment should have been made.   An examination of the record showing that there were issues of fact involved in the case, and that it did not necessarily depend upon a controlling question of law, there was no error in refusing to make a final judgment in the case.   *Mathis* v. *Bagwell*, 101 *Ga.* 167, and cases cited; *Almand* v. *Georgia R. R. Co.*, 102 *Ga.* 151, and cases cited; *Holmes* v. *Pye*, 107 *Ga.* 784.

Judgment affirmed.   All the Justices concurring.

SUTTON *v.* ROSSER.

1. One who seeks under the constitution of 1877 to have an exemption on the ground that he or she has "the care and support of dependent females" must apply for the exemption out of his or her own property.

Neither a wife nor a widow can, under this clause of the constitution, exempt property belonging to the husband or his estate.

2. Were it otherwise, there can be no dependency on a person who is dead, and the homestead would not survive for a beneficiary coming under this clause of the constitution after the applicant for the homestead had ceased to live.

3. A homestead allowed to a widow out of her husband's estate for the benefit of herself and minor beneficiaries ceases when the widow dies and the minors arrive at majority.

4. Though a widow, in applying for a homestead out of her deceased husband's property, may include in the list of beneficiaries adult daughters, they do not become beneficiaries of the homestead, and, after the death of the widow and the arrival of the minor beneficiaries at age, the fact that such adult females were attempted to be included in the application does not render it a subsisting homestead.

Argued October 10, — Decided November 4, 1899.

. Levy and claim. Before Judge Spence. Meriwether superior court. August term, 1899.

John W. Park and *Park & Gerdine,* for plaintiff.
McLaughlin & Jones, contra.

LEWIS, J.   At the August term, 1879, of Meriwether superior court, John R. Jones obtained judgment against Nancy Rosser as the executrix of Asa Rosser, deceased.   The fi. fa. issued upon this judgment was kept alive by proper entries thereon, and in 1897 was levied on a certain lot of land in Meriwether county as the property of the estate of Asa Rosser, deceased. Mrs. Nancy Rosser, the widow of the deceased, applied for and had set apart a homestead in this land as property of the estate of her deceased husband, claiming that she was the head of a family consisting of her single daughter Mattie Rosser, 31 years of age, her single daughter Emily, 28 years of age, and her two grandchildren aged respectively 18 and 19 years.   In her petition for homestead she alleged that all the family were dependent on her for support, that she was an aged and infirm person 61 years of age, that she was the widow of Asa Rosser, and that the family were his children and grandchildren.   The application was approved by the ordinary on March 5, 1897.   At the time of the levy of plaintiff's execution upon this land the widow was not in life; all the minor beneficiaries had arrived at age, and none were living on the place except Mattie Rosser, who was an adult when the homestead was set apart, and who filed a claim to the land levied upon. Upon these facts the court directed a verdict for the claimant. Plaintiff in fi. fa. assigns error on the judgment of the court below in overruling his motion for a new trial.

1. It was contended in behalf of claimant, that the homestead had not terminated when the levy was made, but that she was still a beneficiary thereof, and it was, therefore, not subject to levy and sale for the debts of her father, the original owner. One ground in the application for homestead by the widow in this case was that the beneficiaries named in her petition were dependent upon her for support. The constitution of 1877 (Civil Code, §5 912), and the act of the legislature passed in pursuance thereof (Civil Code, §§ 2827–8), did not contemplate a homestead or exemption for the benefit of dependent females, except in the property of the person upon whom they were dependent. In the present case the application for exemption on this account was not made by the owner of the land in which the homestead was sought. The land belonged to the estate of the applicant's deceased husband. Manifestly neither the constitution nor the statute intended to confer upon the widow such a right; for if it did, she would, under some circumstances, have the power to create a homestead encumbrance upon the property of her husband's estate in favor of dependent females who have no interest in the property as heirs, and thus deprive the heirs at law of their legal inheritance. In order for an adult person to be the beneficiary of a homestead solely upon the ground of being a dependent female, this dependency must be upon the person who owns the property sought to be exempted, and the application for such exemption must be made by the owner himself.

2. Were it otherwise than as above stated, we think there would be a necessary termination of the homestead upon the death of the person on whom the beneficiary was dependent; for the law contemplates a dependency for support, not on any particular property, but upon some particular person, and grants to such person the privilege of exempting his own prop-

erty for the charitable purpose of taking care of such dependent beneficiaries. From the very nature and purpose of the exemption, then, it can not last longer than the applicant lives. In the case of *Towns* v. *Mathews*, 91 *Ga.* 546, it was decided by this court that "A homestead set apart in 1873 by the head of a family for the benefit of his wife and a minor granddaughter terminated on the arrival at majority of the granddaughter, the family having been previously dissolved by the death of both the other members. The condition of the granddaughter as a dependent female would not extend the duration of the homestead, the person on whom she was dependent being no longer in life." On page 549 Lumpkin, Justice, in his opinion, distinguished that case from one of a widow who by reason of her widowhood alone remains beneficiary of the homestead. He says, "No such right belongs, after her majority, to a dependent female who was entitled to be a beneficiary because of the homestead having been granted to the applicant for the reason that the female was dependent on him, and not for her own sake. Moreover, there can be no state of dependency upon a *person* after that person is dead."

3. Another ground of the application seems to have been based upon the fact that the applicant was the widow of deceased, and also the head of the family consisting of the beneficiaries. There is no question about the fact that the widow is entitled to homestead and exemption out of her husband's estate for her own benefit, and also for the benefit of the family consisting of the minor heirs of the deceased. Such a homestead, however, is terminated upon the death of the widow and the arrival at age of the other beneficiaries. *Lee* v. *Hale*, 77 *Ga.* 1; *Vornberg* v. *Owens*, 88 *Ga.* 237.

4. It follows from the above, that while this homestead was no doubt valid during the lifetime of the widow and the minority of the grandchildren, the adult daughters, including the claimant in this case, derived no legal benefit from the homestead, and that if the object was also to set apart an exemption for their benefit during their dependency, the petition to the ordinary showed upon its face that he was without jurisdiction to grant such relief. It is contended by counsel for

the claimant that the homestead continues so long as any
female for whose benefit it was set apart lives and remains
single; and the case of *Gresham* v. *Johnson*, 70 *Ga.* 631, is relied on to sustain this contention.   The expression of the court
in that case, that "If females are members of a family for
whose benefit the homestead is set apart, the property remains
exempt from levy and sale so long as one of them lives and
remains single," is purely obiter.   It will be seen from a report
of the facts in that case that when the exemption in question
was made the family of the applicant consisted only of himself and one minor son.   At the date of the levy of the execution the son had arrived at majority.   It was there decided
that the homestead was at an end, and subject to levy and sale.
In that case no right of females as beneficiaries of the homestead was in any manner involved.   The decision in *Hall* v.
Matthews, 68 *Ga.* 490, is not at all in conflict with our ruling
in this case.   There a homestead was taken by one as head of
a family consisting of his wife and a minor female grandchild,
who lived with him and was dependent on him.   It was simply
decided that the death of the wife did not terminate the homestead estate, but it continued so long as the minor grandchild
remained so dependent.   A later case directly in point is *Vornberg* v. *Owens*, 88 *Ga.* 237, above cited.   In that case a homestead was set apart to the head of a family consisting of himself and four minor children.   The mother and father had
died, and the children had arrived at age.   The property was
levied on under a fi. fa. against the head of the family, and
was claimed by one of the children who was still living on the
land and depending upon it for support.   It was held by the
court, that, after arriving at full age, the fact that she was still
a dependent female would not extend the duration of the homestead estate beyond the death of the head of the family and
his wife, and beyond the arrival at majority of all the children.
Judgment reversed.   All the Justices concurring.

BELL v. BOWDOIN.

1. Where an affidavit of illegality is filed to an execution from a justice's court on the ground that the judgment from which it issued is too vague and uncertain, the judgment may be amended at a regular term of the justice's court, even after the case has been appealed to the superior court.

2. After a suit in a justice's court upon a note has proceeded to judgment and execution issued thereon, the summons, service thereof, and pleas, if any, are office papers, and if lost may be established in that court instanter on motion. Certified copies of such established copies are admissible in evidence in the superior court in the trial of an illegality to an execution issued on the judgment.

3. When on the trial of an illegality in the superior court, appealed from a justice's court, the defendant alleges in the affidavit of illegality that he had never been served with process from the justice's court, it is not error to admit the testimony of the magistrate, that he served the defendant with process at the request of the constable, and that the defendant accepted it as such.

Argued October 10, — Decided November 4, 1899.

Illegality — appeal. Before Judge Reagan. Butts superior court. March 18, 1899.

J. R. L. Smith, for plaintiff in error.
B. P. Bailey and *Y. A. Wright*, contra.

SIMMONS, C. J. It appears from the record that Bowdoin obtained a judgment against Bell in a justice's court, upon a promissory note. Execution was issued thereon and levied upon the property of Bell; whereupon he filed his affidavit of illegality on numerous grounds, one of them being that the judgment entered by the magistrate was too vague and uncertain. The record discloses that the judgment entered on the docket of the magistrate was, "Judgment for plaintiff for his principal sum, and interest at eight per cent. after maturity, and all future interest and cost of suit." The note sued on was for $61.10 principal. The execution issued for this amount, together with interest thereon, and costs. Another ground taken in the illegality was, that the defendant had never been served with any summons, nor had he acknowledged or waived service or authorized any one to do so for him, and that he did not appear and plead at the term of the court at which the judgment was entered up against him. There seems to have

14

been a trial upon this illegality in the justice's court, but whether the illegality was sustained or not the record does not disclose. It does show, however, that there was an appeal taken from that court to the superior court. It also shows that after the appeal had been entered in the superior court the justice of the peace, at a regular term of his court, amended the judgment so as to set out the amount therein.

1. When this amended judgment was offered in evidence on the trial in the superior court, the defendant objected to its admission, on the ground that the judgment was void, and that, even if it was not, the justice of the peace had no power to amend the judgment after the case had been appealed to the superior court, as the trial of the case in that court was a de novo investigation. We do not think there was any merit in this objection. The judgment rendered for the plaintiff, for principal, interest, and costs, was not void. It was merely irregular, and we know of no law which prevents a justice of the peace from amending such a judgment so as to make it speak the truth as to the amount thereof. If the jury believed the evidence for the plaintiff, as they had a right to do, there was a trial before the justice of the peace, or, at least, there was a judgment by him as to the liability of the defendant upon the note sued on. He adjudged that the defendant owed the plaintiff the amount of the note, with interest and costs of suit. By inadvertence he failed to state the amount. Good sense and the ends of justice would require that he be allowed, at a regular term of his court, to amend this judgment so that the amount could be stated therein. Nor do we think there is any law which would prevent the justice of the peace from amending the judgment after the case had reached the superior court by appeal. It was not an appeal from the judgment entered by the justice of the peace, and therefore did not carry up to the superior court the papers in the original suit and the judgment thereon, but the appeal brought in question only his decision upon the illegality, whatever that was. Under section 5113 of the Civil Code a judgment may be amended in conformity to the verdict even after execution issues; and this court has held that it may be amended even after the execu-

tion has been paid off. In the case of *Saffold* v. *Wade*, 56 *Ga.*
174, a judgment was rendered against the defendant and execution issued thereon. He filed an illegality to the levy, which
was sustained. After this the judgment was amended and
execution again levied upon the defendant's property, and this
court held that the plaintiff in fi. fa. had a right to amend his
judgment and fi. fa. and have it again levied upon the defendant's property. The case of *Reeves* v. *Graffling*, 67 *Ga.* 512,
was a suit in a justice's court, appealed to the superior court.
On the appeal counsel for defendant moved to dismiss the case
because there was no legal process or summons, the summons
stating no county or district. The trial judge allowed the
summons to be amended by supplying this omission, and this
court affirmed that judgment.

2. Pending the trial in the superior court certified copies of
established copies of the pleadings in the justice's court were
tendered in evidence and admitted over the objection of the
defendant; the objection being, that it did not appear that the
original papers were lost by the magistrate while in his hands
or while in the hands of some one else, and if lost in the hands
of some person other than the magistrate, then no affidavit appeared of that fact, as required by section 4753 of the Civil
Code. We do not think that these papers were established
under this section, but under section 4743 of the Civil Code,
which provides that office papers may be established instanter
on motion. The first section prescribes the method of establishing copies of papers in a pending suit, which have been lost
or mislaid either by the magistrate or some other person. In
the present case the suit upon the note had been ended some
two years, and the summons, entry of service, etc., were "office
papers" belonging to a case which had been fully disposed of
by the justice of the peace, and not one which was pending.
The copies were doubtless established under the section last
above referred to. When so established, they took the place of
the original papers which had been lost, and certified copies of
these established copies were, under sections 5214, 5215 of the
Civil Code, admissible in evidence in the superior court.

3. One of the grounds of the affidavit of illegality, as before

stated, was that the defendant had never been served with the
summons.   On the trial of this issue the justice of the peace
was offered as a witness, and testified that he issued the original
summons and placed it in the hands of the constable, and that
the constable handed it to him and requested that he serve it
upon the defendant, if he would accept it as service.   He met
the defendant and told him of the request of the constable, and
the defendant agreed to accept service from him.   This testimony was objected to on the ground that, by means thereof, it
was sought to prove a waiver of service of process, which was
not in writing.   We do not think that was the object of the testimony.   The copy summons which the justice of the peace
handed to the defendant was the process of the court, commanding him to appear at the time and place therein designated to
answer, etc.   The testimony did not seek to establish the fact
that he waived this process, but it was simply to show that he
received the process through an irregular channel, and that he
accepted it as service.   We see no reason to hold that a process thus served and accepted would not bind the defendant.
While it is true that the law appoints a particular person to
make this service, still the defendant can waive service by this
particular person and accept it from another.   This summons
informs him that a certain suit brought by a certain plaintiff
against him is pending in a certain justice's court.   That is the
information that the law desires to give him by having him
served with a copy summons.   If he accepts it from a person
other than the one appointed by law to convey it to him, there
is no good reason why he should not be bound thereby; and,
on the trial of a traverse to an entry of service by the constable
on the summons, we think such testimony is admissible to show
in what manner the defendant was served.

Judgment affirmed.   All the Justices concurring.

WILLIAMS, administrator, *et al. v.* MERRITT.

1. The fact that one in whose favor a judgment has been obtained is a minor does not prevent the dormancy statute from running against such judgment.

2. If a judgment in favor of a minor becomes dormant during his minority, he is entitled to bring an action upon the same at any time within three years after his legal disability is removed.

3. Where a judgment obtained by several persons, some of whom are minors, is not divided into separate parts in favor of the respective plaintiffs therein, but is for one entire sum in favor of all of them, if it becomes dormant, the time prescribed by law within which suit may be brought upon a dormant judgment does not begin to run against any of them until the disability of each of such minors has ceased to exist.

Argued October 18, — Decided November 4, 1899.

Action on judgment. Before Judge Hart. Greene superior court. August term, 1899.

Samuel H. Sibley, for plaintiffs.
Park & Merritt, for defendant.

FISH, J. 1. In this case the judge below sustained a demurrer to the plaintiffs' petition and dismissed the same; and to this ruling they excepted. The suit, which was filed January 24, 1898, was upon a judgment obtained in the court of ordinary of Greene county, on December 9, 1878. The ground of the demurrer was, that it appeared from the petition that the plaintiff's right of action on the judgment was "barred by the statute of limitation in such cases made and provided." At the time that this judgment was rendered, two of the parties in whose favor it was rendered, Alice and Antoinette Merritt, were minors. When the present suit was brought, Alice Merritt was twenty-four years old, and Antoinette Merritt was still a minor. Execution was issued upon this judgment on March 28, 1879, but there is nothing in the plaintiffs' petition which shows that any entry was ever made upon the fi. fa. Presumably, therefore, the judgment became dormant in March, 1886, unless, as contended by the plaintiffs in error, the dormancy statute did not run against it, by reason of the minority of some of the plaintiffs. It is contended by the plaintiffs that the dormancy statute did not begin to run against Alice Merritt until she attained her majority, and had not run at all against Antoinette Merritt when the present suit was instituted. The plaintiffs further contend that the minority of any one of the several plaintiffs in whose favor this judgment was rendered prevented the statute from running against any of the plaintiffs. To support these contentions, sections 3779 and 3784 of the Civil Code are cited. The former section provides that "Infants, idiots or insane persons, or persons imprisoned, who are such when the cause of action accrues, shall be entitled to the same time, after the disability is removed, to bring an action, as is prescribed in this Code for other persons." The latter section provides that, "If there is a joint right of action, and some of the persons having such right are under any of the foregoing disabilities, the terms mentioned herein shall not be computed against such joint action, until all the disabilities are removed, but if the action might be severed, and each sue for his own share, those free from disability shall be barred, and the rights of those only protected who are under such disability." If both of these contentions of the plaintiffs are sound, it is apparent that they are suing upon an old judgment, in order to obtain a new one, when the old judgment has never become dormant, but still subsists in all of its original force. There would, therefore, be no necessity to revive it, or to sue upon it. In our opinion, however, this judgment is dormant. Our law in reference to the dormancy of judgments is as follows : "No judgment shall be enforced after seven years from its rendition, when no execution has been issued upon it and the same placed upon the execution docket, or when execution has been issued and seven years have expired from the time of the record, upon the execution docket of the court from which the same issued, of the last entry upon the execution made by an officer authorized to execute and return the same. Such judgments may be revived by scire facias or be sued on within three years from the time they became dormant." Civil Code, § 3761.

It will be observed that there is no exception here in favor of a minor who has obtained a judgment. Unless there is elsewhere in our law some provision which exempts minors from the operation of this section of the code, it is very evident that a judgment in favor of an infant will become dormant under the same circumstances that would render dormant one in favor of a person sui juris. We know of no such provision. As already stated, it is contended that under the provisions of section 3779 of the Civil Code a judgment rendered in favor of an infant can not become dormant until seven years have elapsed after he has attained his majority. As we have seen, this section provides that persons who are infants when the cause of action accrues "shall be entitled to the same time, after the disability is removed, to bring an action, as is prescribed in this Code for other persons." Under this section, the statute of limitations with reference to the bringing of suits does not run against a minor. If a cause of action accrues to him, he can wait until he becomes of age and bring a suit thereon at any time thereafter within the statute of limitations. But if after his cause of action has accrued he brings a suit upon it and obtains a judgment, there is nothing in the language of this section which gives him the right to wait until he has attained his majority before taking any steps toward enforcing such judgment, or keeping its lien alive. When he has sued upon the cause of action which has accrued to him, he has already brought the action which the law says he is not compelled to bring during his minority; and if he persists in the suit until he has obtained a judgment, the cause of action which accrued to him is extinguished by the judgment. "To bring an action" implies the institution of a suit—the taking of the initial step, or steps, toward beginning a proceeding in a court—not an effort to enforce a judgment already in existence and which is the result of an action which has already been brought. We have never heard the issuing of a fi. fa. upon a judgment, the recording of the fi. fa. upon the execution docket, the act of the proper officer in making an official entry upon it, nor all of these things combined, called "bringing an action." These things follow and result from an action previously brought, in which a judgment has been obtained. While, in a general sense, perhaps, proceedings after judgment, for the purpose of enforcing it, or preserving its lien, may be considered as a continuance of an action already brought, they can not be considered as the bringing of an action.   Therefore, the law which gives to a minor to whom a cause of action accrues the same time after his disability is removed "to bring an action, as is prescribed in this Code for other persons," does not have the effect of suspending, during his minority, the running of the dormancy law against a judgment in his favor. When a cause of action accrues to him, he is not bound to institute a suit upon it during his minority, but if he brings a suit and persists in it until he has obtained a judgment, his judgment becomes at once subject to the operation of the law in reference to dormancy.

2. When a judgment is obtained the precedent cause of action is merged into and extinguished by the judgment.   2 Black on Judg. §§ 674, 675, 677; Freeman on Judg. §§ 215, 216.   The judgment is a debt of record, a new cause of action, upon which a new suit may be maintained.   Whether a suit may be brought, in this State, upon a judgment before it becomes dormant, it is unnecessary to determine.   In the great majority of other jurisdictions in which the question has been decided, it has been held that an action upon a judgment may be brought at any time after its rendition.   As we have seen, in this State it is expressly provided by statute that such a suit may be brought within three years after the judgment has become dormant.   Certainly, therefore, within this period after dormancy, a judgment is a cause of action.   Whether the new cause of action arises when the judgment is obtained or only comes into existence when the judgment becomes dormant, is, as above indicated, immaterial in the present case.   In either event, the cause of action accrued while Alice and Antoinette Merritt, two of the parties in whose favor the judgment was rendered, were minors, and Antoinette Merritt had not attained her majority when this suit was brought.   Each of them was entitled to the same time, after the removal of her disability, in which to bring an action upon the judgment, as is prescribed for persons laboring under no disability.   As persons sui juris are entitled to bring an action upon a judgment at any time within three years after it becomes dormant, each of

these minors had three years after her disability ceased to exist in which to sue upon the judgment. Clearly, so far as Antoinette Merritt is concerned, the right to bring this action was not barred, as she was still a minor when it was instituted.

3. The judgment sued upon is for one entire sum in favor of all the plaintiffs therein. Their interests in the judgment are not separated. Their rights in the judgment are joint, not several. The judgment, as a basis for suit, is an entire cause of action; no several rights to sue upon it ever existed in either of the persons in whose favor it was rendered. Two of them being minors when the judgment was obtained, the term of three years after dormancy, prescribed by the statute, within which the plaintiffs could bring an action upon the judgment, could not be computed against such joint right of action until the disability of each of these minors was removed. One of them being still a minor when the present suit was instituted, it is clear that the right to sue upon the judgment was not barred as to any of the plaintiffs under section 3784 of the Civil Code. It follows, therefore, that the court erred in sustaining the demurrer to plaintiffs' petition.

Judgment reversed. All the Justices concurring, except Lewis, J., who was disqualified.

WILLIAMS, administrator, *et al. v.* MERRITT, executor.

1. The judgment sought to be amended was dormant, but not dead.
2. A judgment which, although dormant, still survives as a debt of record, enforceable by suit, may be so amended as to cure a mere irregularity therein.

SIMMONS, C. J., and LITTLE, J., dissenting. A dormant judgment can not be amended until it has been revived as prescribed by law.

Argued October 18, 1899. — Decided January 26, 1900.

Motion to amend judgment. Before Judge Hart. Greene superior court. August term, 1899.

Samuel H. Sibley, for plaintiffs.
Park & Merritt, for defendant.

FISH, J. This was an application, by petition, to the court of ordinary of Greene county, to amend a judgment of that court. The petition to amend was filed on July 25, 1899. A demurrer was filed to the petition, the grounds of which were, that the petition showed that the judgment was "null and void in law," as more than ten years had elapsed since execution issued upon the same, and there was "no entry or levy on said fi. fa. within ten years next preceding said application;" and that the plaintiffs were "guilty of laches." The case was appealed to the superior court, where the demurrer was sustained and the petition dismissed. In the bill of exceptions this ruling of the court is assigned for error. From the petition it appears that the judgment sought to be amended was rendered upon a citation, at the instance of the legatees under the will of Thomas Merritt, to James Merritt, the executor of such will, to appear for a settlement of his accounts as such executor. This judgment was, as appears from the copy of the record from the court of ordinary, as follows: "Whereupon it is considered and adjudged by the court, upon a calculation and settlement of the accounts of said James Merritt, executor of the estate of Thomas Merritt, that the said James Merritt, executor as aforesaid, is indebted to Susan E. Merritt, Marietta M. Merritt, Martha Clements, Sarah V. Merritt, and Ellis Clements, guardian ad litem for Alice Merritt and Antoinette Merritt, in the sum of one thousand and fifty-five 98/100 dollars ($1,055.98), and that execution issue for that amount when called for. Judgment rendered this December 9th, 1878. Joel F. Thornton, Ordinary." The amendment prayed for and insisted upon was to add at the end of the judgment the words, "to be levied of the goods, lands, and tenements of the testator in the hands of said James Merritt to be administered." The petition also prayed that A. L. Williams, as administrator of the estates of two of the parties in whose favor the judgment was rendered, should be made a party to the judgment "in the stead of his deceased intestates," and that "the name of Ellis Clements be stricken from said judgment as guardian ad litem." But it is stated by counsel for the plaintiffs in error that these prayers were abandoned at the trial in the court below, and they are not insisted upon here.

We are of opinion that the court erred in sustaining the demurrer. For the reasons stated in the opinion in the case of *Williams* v. *Merritt*, ante, 213, the judgment sought to be amended was dormant, but not dead. Dormancy destroys the lien, but not the judgment. Notwithstanding dormancy, the judgment, as an adjudication of a court, fixing the legal liability of the judgment debtor, still survives and continues of force until it is absolutely barred by lapse of time. It is still a debt of record, upon which a suit may be maintained. "Every court is vested with inherent power to control and amend its records, judgments, and processes, and to correct errors and mistakes in them." *Brady* v. *Brady*, 71 *Ga.* 71. If, after it becomes dormant, a judgment is alive for any purpose, we do not see how dormancy can deprive the court of its inherent power to amend it. If the judgment still survives, for the purpose of fixing a legal liability, enforceable by suit, it seems to us that the power of the court to amend it has not been lost. So long as it exists for the purpose of establishing and defining a fixed legal obligation of the judgment debtor, the mere fact that it has lost its power to enforce this obligation is not sufficient to defeat an application to make it, upon its face, clearly express its true legal meaning, as a debt of record, when construed in the light of the pleadings upon which it was founded. Dormancy, which merely destroys the lien, but not the settled legal liability created by the judgment, can not prevent an amendment which will make the judgment in and of itself, without reference to the pleadings which preceded it, plainly express the exact nature and amount of this liability. This judgment, when construed in the light of the precedent pleadings, is, and could only be, a judgment de bonis testatoris. So this court has decided in a claim case arising upon the levy of an execution which issued from it. See *Merritt* v. *Merritt*, 66 *Ga.* 324. To add to it the words proposed by the amendment would be to cure a mere irregularity in the judgment. *Leonard* v. *Collier*, 53 *Ga.* 387 ; *Pryor* v. *Leonard*, 57 *Ga.* 136.

We do not think there is any merit in the ground of the demurrer which alleges that the plaintiffs have been guilty of laches. Notwithstanding the long period of time which has elapsed since the judgment was rendered, we do not see how the executor could have been hurt by the failure of the plaintiffs to apply for the amendment sooner.

Judgment reversed. The other Justices concurred, except Simmons, C. J., and Little, J., who dissented, and Lewis, J., who was disqualified.

BANK OF FORSYTH *v.* GAMMAGE, for use.

220
420
220
1030
220
110

The due and unresisted foreclosure of a chattel mortgage, followed by a regular sale of the mortgaged property under the mortgage execution, concludes the mortgagor, as to the property sold, from setting up any defenses, including usury, which he might have set up by counter-affidavit; and is also binding upon him as the head of a family, so as to estop him, as such, from setting up that a waiver of homestead contained in the mortgage was void because of alleged usury in the debt it was given to secure.

Argued October 11, — Decided November 7, 1899.

Trover. Before Judge Clark. City court of Forsyth. July term, 1899.

R. L. Berner and *Bloodworth & Rutherford*, for plaintiff in error. *Stone & Williamson*, contra.

LEWIS, J. N. H. Gammage gave to the Bank of Forsyth a mortgage on certain realty and personalty to secure a loan of money, and in it waived all right to homestead and exemption. The bank foreclosed this mortgage on the personalty therein described, by making the usual affidavit as required by statute, upon which a mortgage fi. fa. issued, and was duly levied upon a horse and mule embraced in the mortgage. To this action no defense by affidavit of illegality or otherwise was made by the defendant, who had full knowledge of the proceeding. Pending the levy the defendant, as the head of a family consisting of his wife and minor children, applied for a homestead and exemption in his property, including that embraced in the levy of the mortgage fi. fa. The application was pending at the time of the sale, and it was announced at the sale that whoever purchased would buy subject to the homestead. Nothing was said indicating any defense to the foreclosure, or any reason why the property was not subject to the debt. The property was bought in by the plaintiff in fi. fa. The ordinary afterwards granted the homestead and exemption applied for, and the defendant, as the head of his family, brought an action of trover against the bank to recover the property sold. The case was tried before the judge of the city court of Forsyth without the intervention of a jury, and a judgment was rendered in favor of the plaintiff in the trover case. Whereupon the bank moved for a new trial, and excepts to the judgment of the court overruling its motion. It appears from the record that the judgment of the trial judge was based upon the idea that the debt secured by the mortgage was tainted with usury, and that therefore the waiver of homestead in the mortgage was of no effect. There is no question that this court is committed to the proposition, that usury in a debt will defeat any waiver of homestead by the debtor. It is equally true that when such a debt is reduced to judgment upon which final process is issued for its enforcement, without any plea or defense of usury filed thereto, the judgment is binding upon the debtor, and estops him, even as the head of a family, from setting up that his waiver of homestead was void because of alleged usury in the debt. *McLaws* v. *Moore*, 83 *Ga.* 177 ; *Stewart* v. *Stisher*, 83 *Ga.* 300 ; *Lowry* v. *Parker*, 83 *Ga.* 343 ; *Barfield* v. *Jefferson*, 84 *Ga.* 609. This is not a case where a general judgment was obtained against a defendant, nor where there had been any adjudication by a court touching the question of usury. The question then arises, as to whether the process issued upon the foreclosure of a mortgage on personalty ever becomes final between the parties where there has been no defense or resistance by the defendant to the foreclosure proceedings. When a chattel mortgage is given, the statute prescribes a certain method by which the mortgagee may assert and enforce his lien. It is a summary proceeding instituted by an affidavit of the plaintiff, prescribed by statute, upon which a summary process issues to be levied upon the personalty described in the mortgage. The law also prescribes a remedy for the defendant in the event he wishes to avail himself of any defense to the proceeding. If he files his counter-

affidavit setting up a legal defense, the fi. fa. then simply becomes and remains mesne process until the issue thus made is
finally determined. When, however, no such defense is filed,
and no resistance whatever is made to the proceedings, we
think the process, after a fair, regular, and legal sale of property thereunder, should be treated, as to the property seized,
as final and conclusive between the parties, especially as to any
defenses the mortgagor had, and which he had ample opportunity of asserting.

Were the rule otherwise, then we would be met with an
anomaly in the law which prescribes the particular method for
the enforcement of a certain legal right, but which can never
become final between the parties, unless the defendant, at his
own option or discretion, sees proper to file a defense, and thus
raise an issue for adjudication. Such a rule, in the sales of
personal property under mortgage foreclosure, would certainly
work great wrong to purchasers at public sales; for a title that
a purchaser would thus acquire would always be open, within
the period of statutory limitation, to an attack by the mortgagor upon any ground of which he may have availed himself in resisting the proceedings to enforce the payment of his
debt. In the case of *Smith* v. *Green,* 34 *Ga.* 180, Lyon, J., in
his opinion, treats a distress warrant as "final process of itself,
under which the property of the tenant may be levied and
sold to satisfaction 'as in cases of other executions'; unless the
tenant shall make oath that 'the sum, or some part thereof
distrained for, is not due.'" See also *Rountree* v. *Rutherford,* 65
Ga. 444_8. The same rule has been applied by the court to a
foreclosure of a mortgage upon personalty. *Dawson* v. *Garland,* 70 *Ga.* 447; *Hart* v. *Hatcher,* 71 *Ga.* 717. In the opinion in the case last cited the court analogizes the foreclosure of
a chattel mortgage to a distress warrant, and quotes and ap-
proves the language used in the case of *Rountree* v. *Rutherford,*
65 *Ga.* 444, above cited. Again, in the *Rountree* case, Justice
Jackson, in treating the subject as to when such mesne process
becomes final, after advancing the idea that it is only mesne
when the counter-affidavit is filed, says, "It is true that if the
counter-affidavit had not been taken, the property would have

been sold under the distress, and in that case, and in one sense, might be deemed final. But it became only mesne process when arrested by the counter-affidavit, and the lien was gone." It is in the power, then, of the defendant to make the process either mesne or final, and if he elects to treat it as final, ignores a defense that he has ample opportunity of making, he should be estopped from setting it up against the purchaser after the sale.

Testimony was introduced upon the trial pro and con upon the subject of usury, but, in the above view taken of this case, it is unnecessary to consider the question as to whether or not there was any evidence showing usury in the debt.

Judgment reversed.   All the Justices concurring.

STRAUSS *et al. v.* MADDOX *et al.*

Where the code provides that a mortgage may be attested by "a notary public or justice of any court in this State," the word "justice" is used as being interchangeable with "judge," and under this provision a judge of the superior court of this State is authorized to attest mortgages.

Argued October 11,—Decided November 7, 1899.

Money rule.   Before Judge Estes.   Butts superior court. July 24, 1899.

Frank Z. Curry, Marcus W. Beck, and *J. M. Terrell,* for plaintiffs in error.   *C. D. Maddox,* contra.

SIMMONS, C. J. The only question in this case is, whether a judge of the superior court of this State is authorized to attest a mortgage so as to admit it to record. Section 2724 of the Civil Code declares that a mortgage "must be executed in the presence of, and attested by or proved before, a notary public or justice of any court in this State, or a clerk of the superior court (and, in case of real property by one other witness), and recorded." We think that the word "justice" in this section is broad enough to include the judge of any court in this State. Anderson, in his Law Dictionary, says that the word "justice" is used interchangeably with "judge." And in the Standard Dictionary a justice is defined as "a judicial officer; a judge."

A "justice" is "a person duly commissioned to hold courts or to try and decide controversies and administer justice;" and "this title is given to the judge of the common law courts in England and in the United States, and extends to judicial officers and magistrates of every grade." Webster's Int. Dict., "Justice." The words "justice of any court in this State" include others than justices of the peace, and included justices of the inferior court when that court was in existence. The codifiers evidently meant that the judge of any court in this State should have authority to attest a mortgage, and used the word "justice" as being interchangeable with judge, as does our present constitution. The constitution of this State declares that the Supreme Court shall consist of a "chief justice and five associate justices," yet, when the same instrument undertakes to fix the salaries of these officers, it terms them "judges of the Supreme Court." In the case of *Helms* v. *O'Bannon*, 26 *Ga.* 132, in construing a statute which authorized "any Governor, Chief Justice, Mayor, or other Justice of either of the United States" to attest a power of attorney, this court said: "The words '*other Justice of* either of the United States' are very broad. They include all others than the Chief Justice in either of the States; and, consequently, a justice of the peace."

We are strengthened in the construction we put upon this section of the code, by the uniform practice of the judges of the superior court in attesting mortgages. Our information and experience would indicate that judges of the superior court in this State have never hesitated to attest mortgages, but have uniformly believed that the code gave them authority to make such attestation. During my experience of eight years as judge of the superior court, I never refused to attest a mortgage presented to me for that purpose, and, so far as I am informed, other judges of the superior court did, and still do, likewise. This court is of opinion that the attestation of a mortgage by a judge of the superior court in this State is valid, and that the mortgage should be admitted to record thereon.

Judgment affirmed.   All the Justices concurring.

FOUNTAIN *et al. v.* NAPIER BROTHERS.

1. A writ of error will not be dismissed upon the ground that the trial judge caused the clerk to alter a marginal note entered by the former upon a motion for a new trial, when the alleged alteration was not of a character to affect the merits of the case here.

2. The mere fact that the sheriff officially attested such a bond as that prescribed in section 2766 of the Civil Code would not make the same a binding contract upon the parties whose names were thereto signed. His acceptance of it would be essential to giving it this effect.

3. The charge complained of was, at least, susceptible of a construction contrary to what is above laid down, and was calculated to mislead the jury. For this reason, and in view of the evidence in the record, the verdict in the plaintiffs' favor should have been set aside.

Argued October 18, — Decided November 7, 1899.

Action on bond. Before Judge Seabrook. Wilkinson superior court. April term, 1899.

J. W. Lindsey, for plaintiffs in error.
George S. Jones, contra.

COBB, J. One of the grounds of the motion for a new trial contained an assignment of error upon a lengthy extract from the judge's charge. In the record transmitted to this court it appears that the judge added to this ground the following note: "This is not the complete charge given in this case, but covers, I think, all that I said upon the point excepted to." When the case was called in this court a motion was made to dismiss the writ of error, upon the ground that, at the time the motion for a new trial was heard and decided, the note appended to the ground in question was in the following words: "The charge, or portion of the charge set forth herein, is correctly set forth so far as it goes, but·it by no means gives the charge full and complete. A great deal of it has been omitted;" and that after the bill of exceptions was certified the clerk of the superior court, under the direction of the judge, erased the note last referred to and substituted the one contained in the record. After a judge of the superior court has overruled a motion for a new trial and certified a bill of exceptions assigning error on that decision, he has no power to change in any way any part of the record in the case; but, under the view we have taken

15

of the present case, the alleged alteration was not of a character to affect the merits of the case, and would therefore be no ground for dismissing the writ of error, or of refusing to consider the ground of the motion which is alleged to have been altered, even if the facts relied on in the motion were made to appear to this court in the proper way, that is, by a certified copy of the motion for a new trial, as it was before the alleged alteration, transmitted by the clerk of the superior court to this court under an order issued under the authority of the act of 1892.   Civil Code, § 5536, par. 4.

The suit was on a forthcoming bond apparently complying in terms with the provisions of section 2766 of the Civil Code. The defense was, that although the bond was signed and attested as required by law, the same was never accepted by the sheriff as a forthcoming bond in the case therein referred to, and that therefore there was no liability on the part of the defendants for the failure to comply with the terms thereof.   In order to make such a bond a binding contract between the parties and to render the person signing the bond as an obligor liable thereon, it is essential, not only that the bond should be signed by the obligors, but that the same should be accepted by the levying officer as a forthcoming bond; and the mere fact that the levying officer officially attested the bond would not be conclusive evidence that he had accepted it.   There being in the present case evidence from which the jury might have inferred that the bond was never accepted by the sheriff, as well as evidence from which it might be inferred that it had been so accepted, and the charge complained of, whether dealt with in the light of the note by the judge which it is claimed was in the motion for a new trial at the time the bill of exceptions was signed, or in the light of the note in the transcript transmitted to this court, being susceptible of a construction contrary to what is above ruled, and therefore calculated to mislead the jury on the controlling issue in the case, a new trial ought to have been granted.

Judgment reversed.   All the Justices concurring.

SMITH *v.* THE STATE.

A brewing company which paid to the State a tax of $200 for the year 1897 did not, by establishing in a county other than that in which its plant was located an agency for the sale of beer manufactured by it and selling thereat such beer during that year, become liable to the State for any additional tax; nor was its employee in charge of such agency subject to State taxation for that year as a dealer in beer.

Argued October 4, — Decided November 8, 1899.

Certiorari. Before Judge Smith. Irwin superior court. June 30, 1899.

D. B. Jay and *Estes & Jones,* for plaintiff in error.
J. F. DeLacy, solicitor-general, and *W. F. Way,* contra.

LUMPKIN, P. J.   This case presents for decision here but one question, viz.: Did a brewing company, by making to the State, in 1897, a single payment of $200, acquire, so far as related to the tax imposed upon "brewing companies" by the 23d paragraph of the 2d section of the general tax act for 1897 and 1898, approved December 24, 1896, the right to establish in a county other than that in which its plant was located an agency for the sale of its product and engage thereat, during the year 1897, in selling beer of its own manufacture?   We have reached the conclusion that this question should be answered in the affirmative.   The paragraph above referred to reads as follows: "Upon all brewing companies, two hundred dollars, and upon all others who are engaged in the sale of beer, whether on consignment or otherwise, who have not paid the tax as liquor-dealers imposed by paragraph fifteen (15) of this section, in each county where they carry on business, two hundred dollars."   See Acts of 1896, p. 26.   The legislative design evidenced by the language just quoted was to divide dealers in beer into two general classes, and impose upon each member of one class a single tax of $200, and upon each member of the other a like tax for each county in which such member engaged in selling beer.   The first of these classes included all persons who both manufactured and sold beer, and the second class embraced all other sellers of beer who did not pay the

tax of $150 imposed upon liquor-dealers by the 15th paragraph
of the same section of the act in question.   We say the first
class included all "persons" who both made and sold beer, because the words "brewing companies" were evidently intended
to cover not only corporations and partnerships, but also individuals engaged in the business of brewing and selling beer.
See *Singer Manufacturing Company* v. *Wright*, 97 *Ga.* 114.   And
we say this class included all who "both manufactured and
sold" beer, for otherwise the word "others," in the phrase "all
others who engage in the *sale* of beer," would be totally without significance.   It follows, we think, as an inevitable conclusion, that the General Assembly did not undertake to impose upon "brewing companies," merely as manufacturers, a
tax of $200 each, but that it was intended to deal with these
concerns as "manufacturing-sellers," if we may use this term
to express the exact idea we wish to convey.   In other words,
a specific license tax was imposed upon the *business* carried on
by brewing companies, a necessary incident of which is, of
course, the selling of the product which such companies usually manufacture.

The authority of the General Assembly to classify objects of
taxation, if the same be done reasonably, is well settled.   See
Singer Manufacturing Co. v. *Wright*, supra, and cases therein
cited.   We are unable to say that the classification above
pointed out was either unreasonable or arbitrary; and, giving
to the words employed their plain and ordinary meaning, we
are forced to hold that a brewing company which paid the State
tax of $200 for 1897 was not obliged to pay to the State an ad-
ditional sum of $200 for each county in which it did busi-
ness.   It is worthy of notice that in the very act now under review the legislature was, whenever it desired to impose a tax
for "each county" or "each place of business," careful to say
so.   For instance, it is expressly provided in par. 3, sec. 2, that
the tax imposed upon photographers "shall be required of
them in only one county;" while, on the other hand, as to the
tax upon "each agent or firm negotiating loans," the same paragraph expressly declares that this tax is imposed "in each
county in which they carry on business."   The 4th paragraph

contains a like provision as to the tax upon auctioneers; paragraph 5 imposes upon the keeper of a billiard hall a tax "for each table" used in conducting the business, while the following paragraph, which lays a tax upon the proprietors of certain other places of public amusement, provides in terms that such tax shall be paid "in each county." The keeper of a tenpin alley is taxed "for each place of business" (par. 7); vendors of proprietary medicines, soap, etc., must pay a license tax "in each county where they may offer such articles for sale" (par 8); local insurance agents are taxed "ten dollars for each county in which they shall solicit business," whereas a "traveling or special or general agent" of an insurance company "doing business in this State" is at liberty to solicit business anywhere within its limits, upon payment by his company of a general tax of fifty dollars (par. 9). An examination of the succeeding paragraphs of this section will likewise show that the General Assembly evidently had under consideration the expediency, in given instances, of levying a tax for each county, for each town or city, or for the whole territory of the State generally, and took especial pains to expressly prescribe the precise locality which each particular license tax should refer to and cover. Manifestly it was not contemplated that every line of business made the subject of taxation should, when carried on in more than one county, be liable to taxation for each county wherein the business was conducted. For illustration, while it is a well-known fact that practitioners of law or medicine do not usually confine their practice to the county in which they reside, yet, in the act under review, no attempt was made to tax such practitioners upon the basis of the number of counties in which they did business, but a general tax of ten dollars was imposed upon each practicing attorney and upon each practitioner of medicine, without regard to the locality or the extent of the territory wherein the professional zeal of such attorney or practicing physician might be exercised. See par. 2 of sec. 2.

If the brewing company, by making a single payment of $200 to the State, was, so far as relates to the question now in hand, entitled to sell its beer in any county of the State, it fol-

lows, of course, that its mere agent or servant was protected
from the payment of the $200 tax.   See 11 Am. & Eng. Enc.
L. (1st ed.) 646, and Black on Intox. Liquors, § 132.   We do
not think the language of the paragraph of the act of 1896 now
under consideration will bear the construction that a brewing
company, upon paying the $200, could sell at its plant only,
and that if it sold elsewhere, either in the county of its location
or in some other county, it would lose its distinctive character
as a brewing company and fall within the class described by
the words "others who are engaged in the sale of beer."   A
brewing company which also sells is a brewing company of this
character at home and abroad, and can not be properly designated as something other than such a company, no matter
where it does business.   It may be that it did not occur to the
legislative mind that a brewing company would sell elsewhere
than at its plant or in the city or town of its situs, and that consequently the tax law was not framed with reference to such a
contingency.   Be this as it may, we have no alternative but to
enforce the law as it is written, and in so doing we are constrained to adjudge that the conviction of the plaintiff in error
was unlawful and must be set aside.

Judgment reversed.   All the Justices concurring.

BLOCKER v. BOSWELL.

1. Under the constitution of this State (art. 6, sec. 7, par. 2, Civil Code,
   § 5856), defining and limiting the jurisdiction of justices of the peace, a
   justice's court has no jurisdiction in actions of trover.   This question was
   not involved in *James* v. *Smith*, 62 *Ga.* 345, and consequently what was
   there said concerning it was obiter.
2. This case turns on the ruling above announced, and, in view thereof, the
   presiding judge erred in sustaining the certiorari.

Submitted October 12, — Decided November 8, 1899.

Certiorari.   Before Judge Hart.   Greene superior court.
February term, 1899.

George A. Merritt, for plaintiff in error.
James B. Park Jr., contra.

LEWIS, J. Boswell brought suit in trover against Blocker in a justice's court, for the purpose of recovering certain personal property. An appeal was had to a jury in that court, and a verdict was rendered for the defendant; whereupon plaintiff brought his petition for certiorari in Greene superior court, alleging, among other things, that the verdict was contrary to law and the evidence. The judge sustained the certiorari, and granted petitioner a new trial. The defendant in certiorari filed his bill of exceptions, alleging error in this judgment of the court.

The controlling question which arises in this case is whether or not, under the present constitution of this State, a justice's court has jurisdiction to try an action in trover. That constitution declares: "Justices of the peace shall have jurisdiction in all civil cases arising *ex contractu*, and in cases of injuries or damages to personal property, when the principal sum does not exceed one hundred dollars." This provision was evidently intended to define and limit the jurisdiction of a justice's court in civil actions. The simple question for consideration, then, is whether, by a fair construction of these words in the constitution, an action of trover is embraced in the class of cases mentioned. Obviously such an action is not a case arising *ex contractu*, but it is an action *ex delicto* founded upon a tort committed by a direct invasion of the owner's legal right to the possession and use of his chattels. It is based upon the title of the plaintiff to the property sued for, and upon the wrongful conversion thereof by the defendant, and is, strictly speaking, an action *ex delicto*. We think it is equally clear that such a suit can not properly be classified among "cases of injuries or damages to personal property." The words "injuries or damages" were evidently intended to be synonymous; and, when applied to property, they mean some physical injury to the property itself, some trespass upon it, by virtue of which its value has become diminished or destroyed. Conversion implies no such injury. An action of trover, therefore, has no reference to any injury or damage which the property itself may have sustained. Indeed, after its conversion, it may actually be enhanced in value by the wrong-doer; yet even if this

were done at his expense, it would have no effect upon the
owner's right to recover back his property by trover.   On the
other hand, if the personalty, while in the unlawful possession
of the defendant, should be materially injured or damaged by
him, and the plaintiff should discover this fact after recovering the property itself by an action of trover, we see no reason
why he would not have the right to institute another and an
independent action for damages resulting from such physical
injuries.   His recovery in trover would be no bar to such an
action, for the simple reason that the two causes of complaint
would be entirely distinct and separate.   It would be just as
reasonable to contend that a suit in ejectment, or an ordinary
complaint for the recovery of land, could be properly designated as an action for injuries or damages done the freehold,
as to say that a suit in trover is an action for damages done to
personalty.   The main issues in an action of ejectment and of
trover are practically the same; both involving title to the
property in the plaintiff, and a wrongful possession thereof by
the defendant.   Applying, then, the ordinary and natural
meaning of the words employed in the constitution, they necessarily deprive a justice's court of jurisdiction over any civil
case arising *ex delicto*, except in suits for injuries or damages to
personal property; and trover not being an action to recover
such damages, it follows that a justice's court has no jurisdiction in such a case.

It is a cardinal rule, in the construction of language, that
words are presumed to be employed in their natural and ordinary meaning.   This rule almost invariably is a legal and
safe guide in the construction of the constitution of a State, as
well as all other written instruments, whether relating to legislation or contracts.   6 Am. & Eng. Enc. L. (2d ed.) 924.
The correct doctrine is also announced on page 925 of the
same work, that "where a word has acquired a fixed technical
meaning in legal and constitutional history, it will be presumed
to have been employed in that sense in a written constitution."
In an able brief and argument before us, filed on this question
by counsel in another case involving the same question, it is
contended, in effect, that the words of the constitution we have

been considering, construed in the light of the legal history of this State bearing on the subject, have a technical meaning, and were intended to embrace an action of trover. In this connection our attention has been called to the stenographic report of the proceedings of the constitutional convention of 1877, a printed copy of which is before us. In sec. 7, par. 2 of the report, page 163, appears the report of the judiciary committee on the subject. This committee recommended to the convention that the jurisdiction of a justice's court be limited to civil actions arising *ex contractu*. When this particular clause in the report was before the convention, it seems three amendments were offered to it; one to strike it out, and leave the matter of the jurisdiction of a justice's court entirely with the legislature. Another was to retain the broad jurisdiction conferred by the constitution of 1868, which gave a justice's court jurisdiction over all cases without any exceptions as to actions *ex delicto*. The third amendment, introduced by Mr. Moore, was to add to the report of the committee the words, "and in cases of trespass or injuries to personalty." The last amendment finally prevailed. We see nothing in the argument of Mr. Moore, in the stenographic report referred to by counsel, at all in conflict with our views as to the meaning of the words, "injuries or damages to personal property." We quote the following from his speech, explaining what would be the result if the report of the committee were adopted without his proposed amendment: "The slightest damage to personal property would have to go to the superior court. The amendment is to provide that when your ox or cow has been killed by the railroad, you can go to a justice of the peace and have redress, and not be forced to go to the superior court." Hence, if the views of any debater in a deliberative body, as to the meaning of a measure which he advocates, should have special weight with the courts in construing the words of the measure finally adopted, then we may gather from the language above quoted a very clear idea of what is meant by the words, "injuries to personal property." From the illustration used in reference to the killing of stock, physical injury to the property was in the mind of the speaker, and he evidently was not contemplating a tort which did not involve any direct injury to the property itself.   It seems, however, from this same stenographic report that a day or two after the adoption of this amendment offered by Mr. Moore, it was reconsidered by the convention, and during its reconsideration another effort was made by members not to restrict the jurisdiction of a justice's court to such narrow limits, and also to provide for appeals of cases in that court.   The result of this reconsideration was the final adoption of the clause that now appears in the constitution, which it will be noted embodies the appeal feature.   But a significant fact is that, as finally adopted, the word "trespass," used in the original amendment, was omitted, and the words "injuries or damages to personalty" employed.   We do not mean to say that even if the word "trespass" had remained, it would have given a justice's court jurisdiction in trover cases; but a wrongful conversion could be more properly called a trespass upon property than it could be designated as an injury to property.   Hence we think it more reasonable to presume the constitutional convention of 1877 acted advisedly, instead of inadvertently as contended, by omitting the word "trespass," and substituting the words finally adopted.   We therefore conclude that there was nothing in the proceedings before the constitutional convention of 1877 authorizing the view that the members of that convention entertained any different idea with reference to the meaning of the words they finally adopted on this subject than what is herein expressed.

We are not aware of any legislation in the history of this State which would authorize the conclusion that an action of trover was ever treated or classified as a case involving injuries to personal property.   Prior to the constitution of 1868, there appears to have been no constitutional restriction upon the jurisdiction of a justice's court in civil actions, but that matter was regulated by legislative enactment.   By the act of 1810 (Cobb's Dig. 638) the jurisdiction of a justice's court in civil cases was confined to suits on liquidated demands or accounts for a sum not exceeding thirty dollars; but no jurisdiction was by that act given to entertain any action involving a trespass upon or an injury to the person or property of a plaintiff.   By the act of

March 5, 1856, the jurisdiction of a justice's court was extended to the sum of fifty dollars principal, but it was still limited to actions ex contractu, that is, to "promissory notes, accounts, and all other evidences of debts." See Cobb's Statutes and Forms, 277 ; Acts 1855_6, p. 254. Under the act of December 9, 1861 (Acts 1861, p. 63), a justice's court of this State was given power to try all cases of trespass upon personal property where the amount claimed did not exceed the jurisdiction of the court. Thus it seems that the jurisdiction of a justice's court as to civil actions was regulated entirely by the legislature until the adoption of the constitution of 1868. In that constitution they were given jurisdiction "in all civil cases where the principal sum claimed does not exceed one hundred dollars." A broader latitude in civil cases was thus given these courts by the constitution of 1868 than was ever conferred upon them before by statute. The evident purpose of the constitution of 1877 was to restrict this jurisdiction as to actions *ex delicto*, and confine it only to such cases as involved injuries to personal property. It is a significant fact that the words of the present constitution not only have no reference to a wrongful conversion of personal property, but the words "trespass on personal property," used in the act of 1861, are not even employed. Our attention has been called to the further fact that in our codes, beginning with that of 1863, the action of trover has been embodied by the codifiers in chapters headed, "Of injuries to personalty generally." The particular heading given by the codifiers to the various chapters of the code can not be considered as part of the legislation of this State. Were we to treat it as such, it would unquestionably give rise to great confusion, render uncertain the law, and nullify some previous adjudications of this court. The codifiers undertook to give in general terms the subject-matters of different chapters of the code, but in many of these chapters will be found a treatment of kindred subjects which would not fall strictly under the general and concise terms used in the caption of the chapter. In fact, it would be next to impossible to form a comprehensive and condensed code of laws without such occasional occurrences in its arrangement and classification.

It was further contended that the statute of limitations, as embodied in the Civil Code, § 3899, on the subject of injuries to personalty, was intended to include an action of trover; for it is insisted this court has recognized, by its decisions, that a suit in trover is barred in four years after the right of action accrues, and that it must have been based upon this provision in the code, and, if so, this court has recognized that an action of trover is properly classified as a suit for injuries to personalty. It is true this court has, in a few of its decisions, indicated that a suit in trover is barred after the lapse of four years from the time the right of action accrues. The earlier decisions on this subject, before the adoption of the first code, were evidently based upon the statute itself. By the act of 1767 (Cobb's Dig. 561_2) it was expressly declared that actions of trespass, detinue, actions of trover, and replevin shall be brought within three years. By the act of December 7, 1805 (Cobb's Dig. 563–4), the limitation for actions of trespass, including in express terms detinue and trover, was extended to a period of four years. Under the act of March 6, 1856 (Acts 1855_6, p. 233), the legislature, in dealing with the subject of limitations, in section 2 of the act, provided for limitations of *"suits for the recovery of personal property,* or for damages for the *conversion* or destruction of the same." In a separate and distinct section, to wit section 4 of the same act, it provided the same limitations for "all suits for injuries to personal property." From this classification of acts of limitation relating to the rights of personalty, it was clearly not the idea of the legislature that suits for the recovery of personal property were included in the expression, "injuries to personal property." Otherwise they would not have been embodied in two different provisions and sections of the same act prescribing the same period of limitation in each case. In this chapter of the code on the subject of the limitations of actions *ex delicto*, it was evidently not the purpose of the codifiers to embody all the different provisions of the act of March 6, 1856, on this subject. For instance, the first section of that act provides, in effect, that suits for the recovery of real estate shall be brought within seven years after adverse possession under written evidence of title commences, and not after. That section is not embodied in the code, and, strictly speaking, we have no statute of limitations as to suits for realty in the code. Its provisions, however, on the subject of prescriptive title to realty under adverse possession practically supply the place of this limitation act. The same is true of suits to recover personalty, or actions of trover; and section 2 of the act of 1856 was for the same reason not embodied in the code; for, by virtue of section 3592 of the Civil Code, adverse possession of personal property within this State for four years shall give a "like title by prescription," the words "like title" referring to previous sections in regard to prescriptive title to land. We think, therefore, that the codifiers purposely left out the statute of limitations as to trover, considering it was for all practical purposes embodied in the section of the code on the subject of adverse possession of personalty for four years. There is as much reason in saying that section 3898 of the Civil Code, fixing a limitation for actions of trespass upon or damages to realty, applies to suits for the recovery of realty, as there is to say that the following section, with reference to injuries to personalty, applies to suits for the recovery of personalty. While this court, as above indicated, has recognized that an action of trover is barred in four years, yet none of these decisions were based upon the fact that the question was controlled by the section of the code relating to injuries to personalty. We think it quite evident, therefore, that neither in the legislative nor constitutional history of this State do the words, "injuries or damages to personal property," have such a fixed and technical meaning as to make them necessarily include actions of trover founded upon the wrongful conversion of property.

It is contended that this issue has been decided in favor of the jurisdiction of a justice's court by the decision in the case of *James* v. *Smith*, 62 *Ga.* 345, and that therefore the question should remain as *stare decisis*. It will appear from the facts of that case that it was not an action of trover. The plaintiffs sued the defendant on an account in a justice's court, for the value of a bale of cotton which he had sold. While in a trover action the plaintiff, at his election, may recover a money verdict for the value of his property converted, yet the suit is brought for the recovery of the property itself, and the verdict in his favor would necessarily be for the property, unless he sees fit to take its money value. But where suit is brought on an account for the proceeds of the sale of property, the tort is thereby waived, as was decided in that case, and the suit treated as brought upon an implied contract for money had and received by defendant for plaintiff's use. In that case, then, the right to recover the property itself was not insisted upon by the plaintiff; his action amounted to a waiver of this right, and the court seems to have considered it was in the nature of an action *ex contractu;* and any judgment thereon could have been pleaded against him as an estoppel in an effort to recover the property itself, the title and right of possession to which he had thus waived. But on the question as to whether the jurisdiction of a justice's court over actions of trover was involved in that case, we can add nothing to the lucid opinion of Justice Little in the case of *Dorsey* v. *Miller,* 105 *Ga.* 88, in which he reached the conclusion that that case can not be held as authority that a justice's court has jurisdiction to entertain suits sounding in tort other than for damages to personal property. In the case last cited, while the question of the jurisdiction of a justice's court in actions of trover was not directly made before this court, we think the *principle* declared in the decision, when followed to its logical result, is applicable to the case at bar, viz., that a "justice's court has no jurisdiction of an action of tort unless the alleged wrong consisted of injuring or damaging personal property belonging to the plaintiff." In *White Star Co.* v. *County of Gordon,* 81 *Ga.* 47, it appeared that the plaintiff instituted in a justice's court a suit for damages against the defendant, by reason of the detention of one of its steamers at a certain bridge upon the Oostanaula river. The contention of the plaintiff in the case was, that the damages to the company by reason of this detention were injuries to personal property, and that therefore the case was within the constitutional grant of jurisdiction. It is true Chief Justice Bleckley, in his opinion on page 48, undertakes to distinguish it from *James* v. *Smith,* 62 *Ga.* 345, inasmuch as the detention of the steamer did not imply a conversion of it; but the complete reply to this distinction sought to be drawn by the learned Chief Justice is, that the constitution no more gives jurisdiction to a justice's court for the trial of an issue involving the conversion of property than it does in a case involving its wrongful detention. It was accordingly held in the 81 *Ga.*, above cited, that the mere detention of a steamer involving *damage to the owner* did not imply any injury or damage to the property itself, and therefore the right of action for such damages did not fall within that class embraced by the words of the constitution on the subject. Damage to the *property*, and not simply *to the owner*, was made the constitutional test of jurisdiction in that case. A wrongful *conversion* of property no more implies an injury or damage done to it than a wrongful *detention* of it; and hence, if no action lies in a justice's court for damages growing out of such detention, it necessarily follows it would have no right to entertain actions of trover for a wrong that simply grows out of the conversion. It is true the two cases last cited above did not involve actions of trover, and left the question we are now considering an open one in this court. Yet the *principle* decided in these later cases, we think, necessarily sustains the construction herein given to the constitutional provision under consideration, and logically leads to the conclusion reached in this case.

If, then, the court where this case originated had no jurisdiction of its subject-matter, none could be conferred by consent or waiver of the parties litigant; and the entire proceeding in the justice's court should by a court of review be treated as an absolute nullity. *Cutts* v. *Scandrett*, 108 *Ga.* 620, and cases cited. Our conclusion, therefore, is that the court erred in sustaining the certiorari, and in remanding the case to be tried again in a court which, under the constitution, has no jurisdiction over the matter. Direction is given that the judgment excepted to be set aside, and that the court below enter in lieu thereof a judgment remanding the case to the justice's court, with instructions to dismiss the action.

Judgment reversed, with direction. All the Justices concurring.

BERGER *v.* SAUL & COMPANY.

Under the constitution and laws of this State, a justice's court has no jurisdiction to hear and determine an action of trover. When, however, such
a case was tried in the justice's court and an appeal entered from the
judgment rendered therein to the superior court, and a judgment in the
latter was rendered in favor of the plaintiff, a motion to arrest such judgment, made at the term at which it was rendered, should have been
granted, because the jurisdiction of the superior court as to the subject-
matter on appeal was no larger than the jurisdiction of the justice's court
in which the suit was first instituted.

Argued December 11, 1899. — Decided January 26, 1900.

Bail-trover.   Before Judge Lumpkin.   Fulton superior
court.   March term, 1899.

S. C. Crane and *J. K. Hines*, for plaintiff in error.
Arthur Heyman, contra.

LITTLE, J. Saul & Company instituted an action of trover
with bail against Berger, in a justice's court in Fulton county,
to recover certain articles of personal property. A verdict and
judgment were rendered for the defendant, and the plaintiff
appealed to the superior court. On the trial of the case in the
latter court a verdict was rendered for the plaintiff, and judgment followed. At the same term the defendant moved in arrest of the judgment so rendered, on the ground that, as the
justice's court had no jurisdiction over an action of bail-trover,
the superior court acquired no jurisdiction by appeal. The
judge of the superior court overruled the motion in arrest, and
ruled that a justice's court had jurisdiction in a case of bail-
trover, and second, because of the time and manner of making
the point. To this judgment the defendant in the court below excepted. That a justice's court has no jurisdiction in an
action of trover has been settled by the decisions of this court
in the cases of *Dorsey* v. *Miller*, 105 *Ga.* 88, 90, and *Blocker* v.
Boswell, ante, 230. Having no jurisdiction, an appeal to the superior court gave to the latter no larger jurisdiction than was
possessed by the justice's court, which was none at all. *Hufbauer* v. *Jackson*, 91 *Ga.* 301; *Greer* v. *Burnam*, 69 *Ga.* 734 ;
Stansell v. *Massey*, 92 *Ga.* 436. By section 5363 of the Civil

Code it is provided that a motion in arrest of judgment must be made during the term at which such judgment was obtained. See also *Hartridge* v. *Wesson,* 4 *Ga.* 101. So that the motion to arrest was in time; and as the justice's court had no original and the superior court no appellate jurisdiction over the subject-matter of the suit, the judgment rendered in the superior court should have been arrested.

Judgment reversed.   All the Justices concurring.

JEWELL v. WALKER, executrix.

1. A debtor may in this State execute an absolute deed to his creditor for the purpose of securing a debt, without receiving from the creditor a bond to reconvey the property described in the deed upon payment of the debt.
2. Upon failure of the debtor to pay the debt at maturity, the creditor may institute suit thereon and may pray for and obtain a special judgment subjecting the property described in the deed to the payment of the debt.
3. In answer to a plea of non est factum it is only necessary for the plaintiff to make out a prima facie case of the execution of the instrument sued on, in order to authorize its admission in evidence.
4. A deed which recites that it was made "for and in consideration of —— dollars" is not inadmissible in evidence merely because the particular number of dollars is not expressed in the consideration clause.
5. In the present case the evidence was sufficient to show that the deed introduced in evidence was given to secure the payment of the note sued on.
6. On the trial of an action upon a promissory note, brought by the personal representative of a deceased payee, in which a plea of non est factum has been filed by the defendant, he is an incompetent witness to testify that alterations in the note were made after the execution and delivery of the same to the payee.

Argued October 12, — Decided November 8, 1899.

Complaint. Before Judge Hart. Baldwin superior court. January term, 1899.

Rufus W. Roberts and *Dessau, Bartlett & Ellis,* for plaintiff in error. *John T. Allen* and *Hardeman, Davis & Turner,* contra.

SIMMONS, C. J. Mrs. Walker as executrix of the will of Samuel Walker brought her action in the superior court of Baldwin county, against Jewell, upon a promissory note for $4,057 principal. In her petition she prayed for a general judgment on the note, and set out a deed to certain described

16

real estate, which she alleged was made and delivered contemporaneously with the note and as security for the payment thereof, and prayed that she have a special judgment against the land described in the deed.   To this action Jewell filed a general and special demurrer, the grounds of the special demurrer being as follows : (1) "Because paragraphs 2, 3, 4, and Exhibit 3 of said petition (the truth of the allegations therein being admitted for the purposes of this demurrer only) show that the alleged security deed was not executed under or in pursuance to section 2771 of the Code of 1895 ; that no bond to reconvey was given to the defendant, the same being, therefore, in law, an equitable mortgage and subject to foreclosure as such." (2) "The petition being complaint upon a promissory note, the prayer for a special lien and judgment against the property described in said deed could not be lawfully granted."   This demurrer was overruled by the court, and the defendant excepted and assigns error thereon in this court.   The case proceeded to trial, and resulted in a verdict for the plaintiff.   The defendant filed a motion for a new trial upon grounds which will be hereinafter referred to, and this motion being overruled, he excepted.

1, 2. We agree with the trial judge that there was no merit in any of the grounds of demurrer filed to the plaintiff's petition.   It is as well established by the decisions of this court as any principle can be, that a debtor has a right to make an absolute deed to his creditor to secure a debt, without any defeasance clause therein, and without requiring the creditor to execute to him a bond to reconvey the property when the debt is paid.   The trouble under which counsel for plaintiff in error labored in filing these demurrers, and which led them to the erroneous conclusion that an absolute deed could not be made to secure a debt without a bond to reconvey being given by the creditor, grew out of a misapprehension of cases decided by this court in regard to the remedy of a creditor when he had taken a deed from his debtor to secure the debt and had given him a bond to reconvey upon payment of the debt.   In other words, when the creditor undertook to follow the act of 1871 (Civil Code, § 2771 et seq.), this court held him down to the remedy prescribed by the act.   This act provides that when the debtor gives his creditor a deed to secure the debt and the creditor gives the debtor a bond to reconvey, title shall pass to the creditor, and he may sue the debtor in case of default in payment of the debt, recover a judgment, file a deed in the clerk's office, and levy on and sell the land as the debtor's property. As before remarked, this court in frequent decisions has held the creditor strictly to the terms of the act when he took a deed and gave a bond to reconvey thereunder.

In *Biggers* v. *Bird*, 55 *Ga.* 650, it was held that an absolute deed conveying land in fee simple passes the legal title, though made and delivered as security for a debt. In the opinion Bleckley, Judge, says: "An absolute deed, not for any cause illegal, passes title, even if given as security for money. This is the way it serves for security. The legal title is the security contracted for and given, and why should the courts not treat it and enforce it as the parties intended? Surely there is no law against putting the legal title in pledge for a debt—against passing that kind of title into the creditor by a *bona fide* conveyance, to abide in him, with all the incidents of ownership, until the debt is paid? If the parties wish to do such a thing, contract to do it, and proceed to carry their purpose into effect, we are aware of no obstacle in the law. It is not only innocent but in a high degree virtuous to secure honest debts; and equally so to stand to the agreed measure of security until they are paid. It does not follow, because a mortgage is only security, that every security is only a common mortgage. For instance, when negotiable paper is delivered as collateral, the legal title passes. Land is just as much the subject of transfer as negotiable paper; the only difference is, that title to land passes by deed, and title to negotiable paper passes by indorsement; or, if payable to bearer, by simple delivery. In respect to neither class of property is it essential for what purpose the transfer is made. Land, like notes, may pass as a gift, or as a sale, or as mere security. When, for any one of these objects, the owner wishes to convey the title, the law furnishes the appropriate instrumentality for the accomplishment of his design." See also *Roland* v. *Coleman*, 76 *Ga.* 652, and cases cited. In *Williamson* v. *Orient Ins. Co.*, 100 *Ga.* 791, this court held that if a deed executed under the provisions of section 2771 of the Civil Code had no defeasance clause therein, it conveyed the title, whether there was a bond to reconvey or not. In many other cases the court has held that a debtor had a right to give an absolute deed to his land to secure his debt, before the passage of the act of 1871, and that that act did not deprive him of the right which every man has of dealing with his property as he pleases. When, therefore, a debtor makes an absolute deed to his creditor to secure his debt and fails to pay the same, the creditor may sue upon the debt, and in the same action, under our system of pleading, pray for a general judgment on the debt and for a special judgment subjecting the property embraced in the deed to the payment of this particular debt in preference to other debts contracted by the debtor. In the earlier cases this court held that a judgment did not bind the property specially unless there was a prayer in the declaration for a special judgment against the property; but subsequently it was held that while that was the proper practice, it was not absolutely necessary to pray for a special judgment, inasmuch as a general judgment would bind it. But that is no reason why a creditor, under our system of practice, should not pray for a general judgment on the debt and for a special judgment binding the property in the same action.

While a creditor who took an absolute deed as security for his debt and gave to his debtor no bond to reconvey could not pursue the remedy pointed out in the act of 1871 (Civil Code, § 2771 et seq.), the act of 1894 (Civil Code, § 5432) made this remedy applicable to him as well as to those creditors who took their securities under the act of 1871. *Williamson* v. *Orient Ins. Co.*, supra, and cases cited; *Coleman* v. *Maclean*, 101, *Ga.* 303. In the latter case Lumpkin, P. J., said that the act of 1894 (Acts 1894, p. 100) "extended this remedy to cases where land has been conveyed as security for debt, whether a bond for reconveyance was given to the debtor or not."

3. The demurrers having been overruled, the case proceeded to trial, and the plaintiff tendered in evidence the note sued on. It seems from the record that the defendant had filed a plea of non est factum. This plea put the burden upon the

plaintiff to prove the execution of the instrument sued on, before it could be admitted in evidence. The plaintiff assumed this burden and proved by a witness the signature of the defendant to the note. It appeared from the note that it had been originally dated May 15, and changed to May 25, 1894. This witness who testified as to the genuineness of the signature of the defendant also gave it as his opinion that the figure 2 was in the handwriting of the defendant. This certainly made out a prima facie case which authorized the judge to admit the note in evidence, and it was for the jury to say, under proper instructions from the court, which were given in this case, from the whole evidence whether the execution of the note had been fully proved. While it is the common practice in this State to file an ordinary plea of non est factum to an instrument in which an alteration has been made, I think the pleader should go further and state what the alteration consisted of, who made it, and that it was made with intent to defraud, etc., as prescribed in the code. A plea of non est factum proper simply denies the execution of the instrument sued on. The code declares that a party may deny the original execution of the contract sought to be enforced, or its existence in the shape then subsisting. Civil Code, §3701. The plea in this case, properly construed, simply denies the execution of the note sued on, when it appears from the evidence, and is admitted by the defendant, that he signed the note, and his defense is that when tendered in evidence it was not in the shape it was when he signed it. He should have pointed out in his plea in what this difference consisted.

4. When the deed was offered in evidence it was objected to because the number of dollars in the consideration expressed therein was not specified, the expression being "for and in consideration of —— dollars." We agree with the court below that this was not a valid objection. While there must always be a consideration for a deed, yet it may or may not be expressed in the writing. In 2 Devlin on Deeds, §809, it is said: "A deed was held to be a good bargain and sale deed where no. amount was mentioned, but it was recited that the deed was made for 'a certain sum in hand paid'; so where the deed recites that it is

made 'for value received.' " In section 823 the same author says: "The only effect of this consideration clause in a deed is to estop the grantor from alleging that the deed was executed without consideration. For every other purpose it is open to explanation, and may be varied by parol proof."

5. A further objection was made to the admissibility of the deed, on the ground that there was not sufficient evidence to connect the note with the deed or to show that the deed was given to secure the payment of the note. From a careful reading of the testimony, we think there was sufficient evidence to show both of these facts. It was argued here that the parol evidence introduced for this purpose was inadmissible under the statute of frauds. We have read the record carefully, and do not find any such question made therein, or even an intimation of it. So far as appears from the record, no objection was made to the introduction of the evidence. Not being in the record, we decline to pass upon the question although laboriously argued.

6. As before remarked, the defendant had filed a plea denying the execution of the note. He tendered himself as a witness to prove certain alterations in the note and deed. His testimony was objected to by the plaintiff, on the ground that Walker, the payee in the note and the grantee in the deed, was dead. The trial judge rejected the defendant's testimony, and this ruling was excepted to and made one of the grounds of his motion for a new trial. It was sought to prove by this witness that the alterations in the note and deed were made after they had been executed and delivered to Walker. The plaintiff's evidence established the fact that Walker was in possession of these papers at the time of his death, that they were in his safe in the same receptacle and were in the same condition when found as presented in court. This evidence, therefore, would make a direct conflict between Walker and the defendant, if Walker were in life. The effect of the defendant's testimony would have been that Walker made the alterations in the papers. Walker being dead, he could not testify and therefore deny that the alterations were made after the instruments were delivered to him. The presumption of law is that they were

made at the time the papers were executed.   The object of the law in refusing to allow a party to a case to testify as to "communications or transactions" with a deceased person whose personal representative is a party to the case on trial is to meet just such a case as this.   It would give the living party every advantage.   If the alterations were material and made with fraudulent intent, Walker's estate could not recover, and would thereby suffer a great loss upon the testimony of the defendant, when the dead man, had he been living, could have denied it. The reasoning in the case of *Neely* v. *Carter*, 96 *Ga.* 197, is controlling when applied to the facts of this case.   We think there was no error in rejecting the defendant's testimony.

Judgment affirmed.   All the Justices concurring.

PAILLE *v.* PLANT.

A debt barred by the statute of limitation will not be revived by a promise in writing which does not plainly and unmistakably refer to the debt in question.

Argued October 9, — Decided November 9, 1899.

Certiorari.   Before Judge Janes.   Polk superior court. February term, 1899.

F. A. Erwin, for plaintiff in error.
William Janes and *Joseph A. Blance*, contra.

SIMMONS, C. J.   In the year 1897 A. & J. Plant brought suit in a justice's court, upon an open account against Paille.   The account was dated May 17, 1884, and was due four months after date.   Paille filed a plea of the statute of limitations, alleging that more than four years had elapsed between the time the account became due and the time when suit was instituted thereon.   To meet this plea and to show a new promise in writing, the plaintiffs introduced in evidence two letters written them by Paille.   The first of these was dated in October, 1896, and stated: "You have presented a claim for $43.50. I do not remember of having any business with you.   If you have a claim against me, you certainly can collect it by prov-

ing that I owe it. I am perfectly solvent. Please enlighten
me in regard to this matter." The other was dated Nov. 3,
1896, and contained nothing which could possibly connect it
with the account of the plaintiffs, except the opening sentence:
"Your statement to hand and correct." The plaintiffs testified by interrogatories,.that the account was due and unpaid,
that the reason suit had not been earlier brought on the account was that Paille had absconded, and that as soon as they
ascertained his whereabouts they put the account into the
hands of an attorney for collection. On the trial of the case
the justice found in favor of the defendant. The plaintiffs, being dissatisfied with that judgment, carried the case by certiorari to the superior court, where the judgment of the justice
was reversed and a new trial granted, instructions being given
the court that the debt had been revived by the acknowledgment contained in the two letters introduced in evidence.
Paille excepted to this judgment, and brought the case by bill
of exceptions to this court for review.

We think the exception of the plaintiff in error is well taken.
In order to revive a promise barred by the statute of limitations by a new promise in writing, as required by our code,
the new promise must so plainly and clearly refer to or describe the original promise in question as to identify it with
reasonable certainty. Neither of the letters here relied upon
as constituting a new promise described the account so as in
any manner to identify it. Indeed, the first letter seems to
refer to another and different account, the account referred to
being one for $43.50 and that sued on being for but $23.48.
Nor did the letter contain any promise to pay the account sued
on, or any other account which the plaintiffs held against the
defendant. It was rather a denial of indebtedness than a
promise to pay. The other letter acknowledges the correctness of some statement, but without any definite promise to
pay it, and without disclosing what statement or account is
referred to. Whether the writer acknowledged the correctness
of the account sued on, or of the account mentioned in his
former letter, or of some other and entirely different account,
does not appear. It is true the plaintiffs, in their interroga-

tories, testify that the account sued on was the only bill of goods they had ever sold to defendant, but this testimony does not connect the account sued on with that mentioned in the second letter. It may be true, and doubtless was, that the account sued was the only one ever made with the plaintiffs by the defendant, but still it does not appear that the letter referred to this particular account. There is no evidence that the account sued on was ever in fact sent to the defendant, and the letter certainly does not "so plainly and clearly refer to or describe the very [account] in question as to identify it with reasonable certainty." *Gartrell* v. *Linn*, 79 *Ga.* 700, and cases cited. In the brief of counsel for the defendant in error it was argued that the judgment was right, because the evidence showed that the debtor had absconded from the place where the contract was made. It is asserted in the brief that the debt was contracted in Ohio, and that the defendant absconded and removed to Georgia; but there is nothing in the record to show this. The record does not show whether the debtor, at the time of contracting the debt, resided in this State or in some other. Nor does the evidence show how long the debtor had been absent before his new place of residence was discovered. If the account was made in this State, and the defendant, though he changed his place of residence, did not remove beyond the limits of the State, the statute of limitations did not cease to run. Under the code a change of residence works a suspension of the statute only where the removal is beyond the limits of the State.

Judgment reversed. All the Justices concurring.

McELVEEN & HARDAGE *v.* SOUTHERN RAILWAY COMPANY, and *vice versa.*

1. Bills of lading belong in the class of written contracts and come within the rule which prohibits the introduction of parol evidence to contradict or vary their terms.
2. When under the terms of a contract for carriage a carrier obligates itself to carry freight to one of the termini of its railroad and there deliver the

same to a connecting line of railroad or steamers, to be transported to destination, evidence of a parol representation that the freight would be delivered to a connecting railroad and not to a steamer is inadmissible to vary the terms of the written agreement; and if in fact such goods were delivered to a carrier by water and transported to destination and placed in the warehouse of such carrier by water, subject to the order of the consignee, such goods were not in fact at that time "lost" so as to afford a right of action in favor of the consignor against the initial carrier for failing to trace such freight, under the terms of section 2318 of the Civil Code, as lost goods.

Argued October 11, — Decided November 9, 1899.

Action for damages.   Before Judge Reagan.   Pike superior court.   April term, 1899.

J. J. Rogers, S. N. Woodward and *Alexander & Lambdin,* for plaintiffs.   *C. E. Battle* and *E. F. Dupree,* for defendant.

LITTLE, J.   McElveen & Hardage instituted an action against the Southern Railway Company.   One part of the petition clearly shows that it was sought to recover the value of certain goods shipped by them, under the provisions of sections 2317 and 2318 of the Civil Code, making it the duty of the initial carrier, on notice, to trace lost, damaged, or destroyed goods, when in order to reach destination the freight must be transported by two or more common carriers of a connecting line.   The defendant filed a demurrer, which the court sustained, to a part of the petition, leaving the case to proceed as an action to recover for a failure to trace the goods. It appears from the brief of evidence, that the plaintiffs in error, on November 5, 1897, delivered to the defendant company at Concord, in Pike county, a number of fruit-trees consigned to Gilham, Ft. Gaines, Ga., for which they received a bill of lading.   One of the consignors testified that, previously to and after the issuing of the bill of lading, the agent of the railroad company at Concord told him that the boats were not running between Columbus and Ft. Gaines, and he would not bill the trees by boat from Columbus for that reason.   It was also shown that the other of the consignors, on November 15, 1897, went to the railroad depot in Ft. Gaines, Ga., and called for the trees, and was notified that they had never arrived. The trees were subsequently found in the river warehouse in

Ft. Gaines, Ga., and had never been called for there, nor at the wharf of the steamboats running to Ft. Gaines. It also appears, from a letter in evidence, that the trees arrived at Ft. Gaines by boat from Columbus on the 15th or 16th of November. It was also shown that the defendant company, on the 15th of November and subsequently thereto, was notified by the consignors that the trees were lost, and it was asked that they be traced, to which notice and request no response was made. It was further shown that the trees should have been in good condition on the 16th of November. The bill of lading was introduced in evidence. It acknowledged the receipt of two boxes of fruit-trees consigned to C. W. Gilham, Ft. Gaines, Ga., to be shipped by the defendant railroad company from Concord to Columbus, Ga. It was an ordinary contract of affreightment, containing a stipulation that the goods were to be transported as specified, and at the end of the initial carrier's line to be delivered to the agents of connecting railroad companies or steamers, to be again so delivered until they should arrive at the place named as the point of destination in the bill of lading. At the conclusion of the evidence, the defendant moved for a nonsuit, which was granted, and the plaintiffs excepted. Defendant also, being dissatisfied with certain rulings of the court, filed a cross-bill of exceptions. The two writs of error were heard together in this court, and will be here considered and disposed of together. It is difficult to determine, from an examination of the seventh and tenth paragraphs of the petition as originally filed, whether by the allegations made in those paragraphs it was sought to recover damages from the defendant railroad company for a breach of duty in failing to transport the goods within a reasonable time, or for the loss of the goods in transit, or for a diversion of the freight from a specified route of shipment. Being thus confused, it was not error to strike these paragraphs on demurrer made thereto. The other allegations made set out a cause of action, and the case was properly allowed to proceed as an action to recover the damages prescribed by law for a failure on the part of the initial carrier to trace goods which had been lost en route to the point of destination.

The plaintiffs complain because the court at the conclusion of their evidence granted a nonsuit. The position taken is, that by agreement with the railroad company, when the goods arrived at Columbus, which was a terminus of the defendant's railroad, they were to be delivered to another railroad line for the purpose of being transported to Ft. Gaines, and that they, therefore, were under no duty to seek the trees at the warehouse of a water carrier in Ft. Gaines, and that when they enquired at the railroad depot in Ft. Gaines and found that the trees had not arrived by rail, they were in fact lost as to the consignors, and it was the duty of the defendant company, on notice of loss and a request to trace the trees, to do so; that they had no right to expect that they would be delivered to a steamer at Columbus, and that such a delivery was a violation of the contract, and, notwithstanding the trees had in fact been transported to Ft. Gaines by steamer, they were not chargeable with any laches in their failure to discover the fact until after they had become worthless by being kept out of the ground. It therefore becomes important to ascertain what was the contract of carriage. McElveen, one of the consignors who shipped the goods for his firm, testified that on the day the trees were shipped he had a conversation in Concord with the railroad agent. He had a similar conversation before and after a delivery of the bill of lading. In these conversations the agent stated that boats were not running between Columbus and Ft. Gaines, and that he would not bill the trees by boat on that account. McElveen also testified that he accepted the bill of lading as the contract between the railway company and his firm as to the shipment of the trees. If it be contended that this evidence supports a theory which would entitle the plaintiffs in error to recover because of a contract subsequent to the issuance of the bill of lading that the trees should reach Ft. Gaines by rail and not by boat, it will be seen that that theory is not supported by this evidence, because it is shown that the trees were shipped on the day of the issuance of the bill of lading, and it would be too late then for the railroad agent to have billed the goods by any route, as they must necessarily have already been billed; and, fairly interpreted, the evidence in relation to what the agent said as to the route by which he would bill the goods must have occurred prior to the issuance of the bill of lading, and so interpreted it is entirely consistent with the other evidence that the agent should have stated after the shipment that the trees would go by rail and not by boat. Such statements could become no part of the contract of shipment, because the trees had already been shipped; and if these subsequent statements are to be relied on as furnishing a right of recovery, then they must be treated as a misrepresentation of the route by which the goods were shipped, rather than any part of a contract stipulating as to the route by which the trees would be shipped. As this action is not brought to recover because of such misrepresentation, but is confined to a claim for failure to trace the goods, it is not necessary to discuss the legal effect of such misrepresentations, if any were made. So, therefore, to determine whether there was error in granting the nonsuit under the allegations made in this case, it is only necessary to ascertain the terms of the contract as to the route by which the goods would be forwarded after reaching the terminus of the defendant company. The evidence, as before set out, shows that before the issuance of the bill of lading the agent of the railroad company told the owner of the trees that they would not be carried by boat from Columbus, because at that time the boats were not running. But the bill of lading thereafter issued, in terms, provides for the transportation of the trees by the initial carrier to Columbus and the delivery in good order there to a connecting railroad or steamer, to be forwarded to destination. Confessedly, the literal terms of the bill of lading were complied with, inasmuch as the goods were transported to Columbus and there delivered to a line of steamers which reached Ft. Gaines by the Chattahoochee river. As a matter of fact the goods were transported by river and delivered at the wharf or warehouse of the steamer, subject to the order of the consignee. There can be no question that the stipulations contained in the bill of lading must govern. These instruments are written contracts.

In the case of *Central Railroad Co.* v. *Hasselkus*, 91 *Ga.* 385, our present Chief Justice said, in delivering the opinion of this court, that: "The office of a bill of lading is to embody the contract of carriage, as well as to evidence the receipt of the goods; and when the shipper accepts it without objection before the goods have been shipped, and permits the carrier to act upon it by proceeding with the shipment, it is to be presumed that he has accepted it as containing the contract, and that he has assented to its terms." To the same effect, also see *Western & Atlantic R. R. Co. v. Ohio Valley Banking & Trust Co.*, 107 *Ga.* 512. Mr. Hutchinson in his Law of Carriers, § 126, in referring to this class of contracts, says: "Except, however, in the recital or acknowledgment of the receipt of the goods and of their quantity and condition when received, bills of lading are strictly written contracts between the parties, and come within the general rule which prohibits the introduction of parol evidence to contradict or vary such contracts." From these rules it must follow, as a corollary, that if no mistake or fraud is charged in the execution of the contract, it will be conclusively presumed that all oral negotiations and representations, not only as to the terms and conditions on which the goods were received, but also as to the route by which they are to be forwarded, are merged in the bill of lading, which will be received as the sole evidence of the agreement between the parties. 109 Ind. 422. See also *Richmond & Danville R. R. Co. v. Shomo*, 90 *Ga.* 498; *Bedell v. Richmond & Danville R. R. Co.*, 94 *Ga.* 22. The bill of lading, then, must in this case be taken as the evidence of the contract between the parties, and by its terms the contract of carriage was complied with when the railroad company delivered the goods to the connecting water carrier at Columbus. It must follow that the plaintiffs could not assume that the goods were lost on November 15, when they enquired for them from the railroad-agent in Ft. Gaines and found that they had never reached that point by rail. It appears as a matter of fact that at that time the goods were being transported by the connecting water carrier, and on the 15th or 16th of November reached Ft. Gaines and were ready for delivery to the consignee. Inasmuch as the contract authorized the shipment by the water route, it was the duty of the consignee to enquire for his goods from that carrier. The goods were not lost at all, and, not being so, the consignor had no right to require the initial carrier to trace them.   These facts appear from the evidence of the plaintiffs, and under it they had no right of recovery, and a nonsuit was properly awarded.   It must not be understood that we intend in any way to qualify the application of section 2276 of the Civil Code.   That section declares that a common carrier may not limit his liability by any notice given either by publication or by entry on receipts given or tickets sold.   He may do so by an express contract.   Where the effect of any notice or entry made on a bill of lading is to limit the legal liability of the carrier, and the contract embodied in such bill of lading has not been expressly assented to by the consignor, such a provision is void.   This statute does not at all conflict with what we have above said.   In the case at bar the liability of the carrier for the value of the goods, for their prompt and safe delivery, is in no way limited.   This being so, the doctrine that a written contract can not be varied by parol evidence governs.

A cross-bill was filed by the defendant below, alleging certain rulings of the judge to be error, and raising the question of the constitutionality of the act under which the suit was brought, as codified in section 2317 of the Civil Code.   But under the rule established by this court, that where the judgment complained of in the original bill of exceptions is affirmed the cross-bill will not usually be considered, the cross-bill is dismissed.

Judgment on main bill of exceptions affirmed; cross-bill of exceptions dismissed.   All the Justices concurring.

WYNN *et al. v.* WYNN *et al.*

109
f114
114

Under the act of 1897 (Acts 1897, p. 35), a defendant may, as a matter of right, amend his answer if he attach the affidavit therein prescribed.

Argued October 12, — Decided November 9, 1899.

Complaint for land.   Before Judge Seabrook.   Wilkinson superior court.   April term, 1899.

F. Chambers and *J. W. Lindsey*, for plaintiffs in error.
Evans & Evans, contra.

SIMMONS, C. J.   An action of complaint for land was brought in the court below, against the present plaintiffs in error.   They filed their pleas in accordance with the pleading act, but inadvertently admitted what they intended to deny and denied what they intended to admit.   Pending the trial, they moved the court to allow them to amend their answer, and filed an affidavit as required by the act of 1897 (Acts 1897, p. 35).   The court refused the amendment, and they excepted.   We think the court erred in not allowing the amendment.   Under the act of 1897, the defendants had the right to amend at any stage of the case, provided they made the affidavit required by the act.   We regret to say that the trial judge, under this act, has no discretion in allowing or refusing an amendment when the affidavit is made in accordance with the act.   The only discretion given him by the act is that he may allow an amendment, if the circumstances of the case or substantial justice between the parties require that it be allowed, without an affidavit.   Under this act the right to amend exists although by the amendment an admission is stricken from the answer first filed.   Of course, striking the admissions made does not prevent the plaintiff from offering them in evidence against the defendants.   Whether the amendment offered in this case would make the answer a good and sufficient one is not now decided, because the question is not made by the record.   All we decide is that the defendants had the right to amend their answer at the time the amendment was offered.

Judgment reversed.   All the Justices concurring.

BURCH *v.* DANIEL.

1. A plaintiff who brought suit upon a promissory note, the legal title to which was not in him when his petition was filed, could not maintain the action by proving that before trial he had procured an indorsement of the note to himself from the person in whom such title had vested at the time the action was begun.

2. In view of the foregoing, and of the facts appearing in the record, the court erred in directing a verdict for the plaintiff.

Argued October 18, — Decided November 9, 1899.

Complaint. Before Judge Hart. Laurens superior court. July term, 1899.

Roberts & Milner and *Anderson, Felder & Davis*, for plaintiffs in error. *A. F. Daley* and *Ira S. Chappell*, contra.

LEWIS, J. When this case was here before (see 101 *Ga.* 228), it was decided that the plaintiff could not maintain an action upon the note sued on in his own name. It is, therefore, unnecessary to enter into any discussion of the question then involved and decided. Upon both trials below it appeared that the notes sued upon were originally written payable to John A. Fretwell or order, and that the word "order," after the execution of the notes, was, without any consent or knowledge of the makers, erased, and the word "bearer" substituted in its place. Fretwell, the payee, transferred the notes by written assignment thereof to C. S. Pope. On the first trial of the case there was no indorsement or other written transfer of the notes to the plaintiff; and it was accordingly held by this court that the plaintiff had no legal title to the notes sued upon, and consequently could not maintain an action in his own name. On the second trial of the case now under review, it appears, when the original notes were introduced in evidence, Pope's indorsement to the present plaintiff did appear thereon. Hence it was evidently made after the filing of plaintiff's suit. In the copy of the notes attached to the petition no such indorsement of Pope appears, nor was there any motion made to amend these exhibits to the petition by making them conform to the original notes introduced in evidence. Defendant's counsel moved to dismiss the petition, on the ground that the notes sued upon showed no title in the plaintiff to the same. At the conclusion of the testimony the court directed a verdict for plaintiff; whereupon the defendants filed their motion for a new trial, and except to the judgment overruling the same. Besides the general grounds of the motion, that the verdict was contrary to law and evidence, error is assigned in over-

17

ruling movant's objection to the admission of the notes in evidence on the following grounds: 1st, because the explanation of the alterations of the note was insufficient.   2d, because the entry of the indorsement thereon, which bore no date, from C. S. Pope to plaintiff, was made after the suit was brought and during the pendency of the litigation.   The motion also assigns error on the judgment of the court directing a verdict for the plaintiff.

There was no error in refusing to dismiss the petition, as a copy of the notes sued upon, attached as an exhibit to the petition, showed that upon their face they were payable to bearer. When the suit was originally instituted the plaintiff had no title to the note sued upon, on which he could maintain an ordinary action at law in his own name.   A simple and a controlling question in this case is whether or not, pending this litigation, he could acquire such title, by a due transfer of the notes, and upon such a transaction with the holder of the legal title maintain his present action.   That the plaintiff, upon the trial of his case, can not insist upon any right or cause of action that did not exist at the time of filing his suit is an axiomatic principle of pleading and practice, so well established as to require no discussion.   We can not see how the present case presents any exception to the rule.   Plaintiff's right of action depended upon his title to the contract declared upon at the time he brought the suit.   Not having title then, he could not afterwards acquire such title and maintain his original action.

There seems to have been no question in this record that the notes were really delivered to the defendant in error for value before suit thereon was filed, and that Pope, who held the legal title to the note, recognized this fact.   For these reasons it may be plausibly urged that the suit should have been maintained in the name of the party who really had such an equitable title to the notes, and that no harm could, under the facts and circumstances of this case, have resulted thereby to the makers who were sued ; but such an answer can be no reply to an established rule of law and of pleading and practice. The law prescribes that when a note is payable to one, or order, a transferee thereof can not acquire legal title without written indorsement. When the maker of the note makes a contract to pay to a certain person, or order, he places himself under no obligation to make payment to any one save the payee named, or to some other person to whom the payee has, by written authority, directed payment to be made. It follows, therefore, that to allow an action maintained merely by the holder of a note not clothed with such legal title might result in loss to the makers, for they could be held liable by a subsequent suit instituted by the payee, or his indorsee. The fact that there is no possibility of such a result in the present case does not change the rule of law. In regard to actions of ejectment, it seems to be uniformly held by the courts of this country, that in order for the plaintiff to recover he must have title at the commencement of his suit; and that he can not avail himself of title thereafter acquired. 10 Am. & Eng. Enc. L. (2d ed.) 494, and authorities cited. We see no reason why a different rule should apply where plaintiff's right of action on a note depends upon his title thereto. In view of the foregoing, and of the facts appearing in the record, the court erred in directing a verdict for the plaintiff.

Judgment reversed. All the Justices concurring.

HOWARD *v.* POPE, guardian.

1. When a year's support in lands is set apart for a widow and a minor daughter, the title vests in the widow *and* the minor, but the widow has the exclusive control and management of the property. A guardian appointed for the minor has no right, as guardian, to demand or to receive the interest of the daughter in the lands set apart or her portion of the rents and profits of such lands. [109] [120] [120]

2. If the guardian should marry the widow and, as the agent of the latter, take possession and control of the lands and from the proceeds thereof support and educate the daughter, the latter can not, after her marriage and majority, maintain an action against him, *as guardian,* for the unexpended balance of such proceeds.

Argued October 12, — Decided November 9, 1899.

Exceptions to auditor's report. Before Judge Hart. Laurens superior court. July term, 1899.

Charles Z. McCord and *Howard & Armistead*, for plaintiff.
A. F. Daley and *P. L. Wade*, for defendant.

SIMMONS, C. J. Some sixty-seven acres of land were set
apart by the ordinary of Laurens county, as a portion of a year's
support for Mrs. Kea, the widow, and Annie L. Kea, the minor
daughter, of James W. Kea. Included also in the year's support was a note due the deceased husband and father by a third
party. In order that this note might be more readily collected,
C. S. Pope was appointed guardian of Annie L. Kea. He had,
after the setting aside of the year's support, married the widow,
and he was by her placed in possession and control of the lands
set apart. He rented out the land and collected the rent. The
minor daughter lived with him and his wife, and was supported
and educated by him until she was married. After she had
married and had become of age, she cited him to appear before the ordinary of the county to make a settlement as her
guardian. The ordinary adjudged that Pope was, as guardian,
indebted to his ward in a certain sum. From this judgment
Pope appealed to the superior court, where the matter was referred to an auditor. The auditor, after hearing evidence as
to the value of the board, clothing, and education given the
minor, the amount Pope had received from the land, etc.,
found that Pope was, as guardian, indebted to his ward in a
sum somewhat smaller than that found by the ordinary. To
this report Pope filed exceptions both of law and of fact. On
the hearing before the judge of the superior court, he sustained
the exceptions, and decided that Pope was not, as guardian,
indebted in any amount to the plaintiff.

It is unnecessary, in the view we take of the case, to pass
seriatim upon the exception filed to the auditor's report, or to
set them out at length; for the exceptions, both of law and of
fact, depend upon one question alone. Under our code, when
a year's support is set aside for a widow and a minor child, or
minor children, jointly, each of them has an equal undivided
interest in the property so set aside, but the widow has the entire control and management of it all. When the property
has been set aside jointly to the widow and minor children, a
minor can not, even after marriage or majority, force a divi-

sion. The entire property, or so much as has not been already used for the support of the beneficiaries, still remains for the support of the widow and other minors, if there be any, and its management and control are still entirely in the hands of the widow. When, therefore, Pope was appointed guardian for the minor child, although his guardianship was as to both her person and property, he had no right as guardian to claim or to receive any portion of the year's support. When he married the widow and was by her placed in custody and control of the land, he did not receive it or any part of it as guardian of the minor, but received it as the agent of his wife. To his wife alone was he responsible for the disposition of the rents and profits. Having received them as agent of his wife, he can not be called upon as guardian of the minor to account for them to his ward. The facts of this case are quite different from those of the case of *Vandigrift* v. *Potts*, 72 *Ga.* 665, cited and relied upon by counsel for the plaintiff in error. In that case the widow married again, and she and her husband sold the land which had been set apart as a year's support for her and her minor children, and, with the proceeds of the sale, bought other land to which they took title in their own name. The children after becoming of age brought suit for their interest in the land. In the present case, the daughter does not bring suit for her interest in the land but only for the rents and profits, over and above her support, collected, as she claims, while she was a minor; and the suit is against Pope in his capacity as guardian. The record discloses that she sold her interest in the land itself to Pope. Even if the case of *Vandigrift* v. *Potts* was well decided, it was very different from this, and could not aid in the present decision. We think that the court below was correct in sustaining the exceptions to the auditor's report and deciding that the plaintiff was not entitled to recover against Pope as guardian. See, in this connection, *Whitt* v. *Ketchum*, 84 *Ga.* 128; *Roberts* v. *Dickerson*, 95 *Ga.* 727; *Miller* v. *Miller*, 105 *Ga.* 305; *Miller* v. *Ennis*, 107 *Ga.* 663.   *Judgment affirmed.   All the Justices concurring.*

GORDON v. GORDON.

1. When upon a petition to enforce by attachment the payment of a judgment for alimony previously granted the judge passed an order directing that out of a fund in court, which had been raised upon a garnishment sued out against a debtor of the respondent, the applicant be paid
   a specified amount less than that to which she was, under the original
   judgment, entitled, providing, in effect, that compliance with this order
   should fully satisfy the former judgment, and taxing the applicant with
   one half the cost of the application thus disposed of, a bill of exceptions
   sued out by her and assigning error upon the granting of this latter order
   did not fall within the provisions of section 5540 of the Civil Code relating to fast writs of error. Such order was not made upon an application
   for discharge in a contempt case, nor was it, in effect, a judgment either
   granting or refusing an application for alimony.
2. It is the duty of the clerk of this court to properly docket all cases brought
   here, and to this end it is, under the provisions of sections 5540 and 5558
   of the Civil Code, incumbent upon him to inspect all bills of exceptions
   filed in his office, with a view to determining upon what dockets the cases
   shall be placed; his actings and doings in the premises being, of course,
   subject to review by the court.
3. In the present instance the clerk dealt with the bill of exceptions as a
   fast writ of error, and accordingly entered the case upon the docket of
   the present term. The question is certainly one admitting of some doubt,
   and, having solved it as above indicated, an order has been passed directing the case to be transferred to the docket of the next term.

Argued October 18, — Decided November 9, 1899.

Motion to transfer to docket of next term.

James P. Brown, for the motion.
Samuel H. Sibley and *Park & Merritt,* contra.

COBB, J. Ellen Gordon applied to the superior court for a
rule nisi against George Gordon, calling upon him to show
cause why he should not be attached for contempt for failing
to pay an amount alleged to be due to her as alimony and attorney's fees under an order previously passed by the superior
court directing him to pay the sums mentioned.   A corporation which had been served with process of garnishment, founded on the judgment against George Gordon for alimony and
attorney's fees, had answered that it was indebted to him in a
given sum.   In answer to the rule served on him George
Gordon set up that his failure to pay the amount which he

had been ordered to pay was due to the fact that he was unable to pay the same, and he prayed for a revision of the judgment fixing the alimony and that the same might be reduced. The judge reduced the amount which was due under the previous order fixing the alimony and attorney's fees, directed that the amount so reduced should be paid out of the fund brought into court under the garnishment above referred to, and ordered that the costs of the rule be divided equally between the parties. To this decision Ellen Gordon excepted.

When the case was called in this court a motion was made to dismiss the writ of error, because the subject-matter of the proceeding before the judge was such that a fast writ of error should have been sued out to review his judgment in this court, and as the bill of exceptions which was sued out was not tendered to the judge within twenty days from the date of the decision complained of, the same was not tendered within the time prescribed by law. The plaintiff in error contends that the subject-matter of the proceeding was such that the ordinary writ of error would lie to review the decision of the trial judge, and that as the bill of exceptions was tendered within thirty days, the case should be ordered transferred to the docket of the next term of this court.

1. The cases which must be brought to this court by fast writ of error are, (1) where an application for an injunction or receiver is granted or refused; (2) applications for discharge in bail-trover cases; (3) applications for discharge in contempt cases; (4) granting or refusing applications for alimony, mandamus, or other extraordinary remedy; (5) granting or refusing applications for attachment against fraudulent debtors; (6) all criminal cases; (7) all habeas corpus cases; (8) all cases where there has been a judgment rendered validating the issuance of bonds by counties, municipalities, and other political divisions of the State. Civil Code, §§ 5540, 4881; Acts 1897, pp. 53, 84. While the present case involves questions relating to contempt as well as questions relating to alimony, it is neither an application for discharge in a contempt case, nor is there involved an original application for alimony, which was granted or refused. Such being true, the case does

not fall within the terms of the law above referred to, and therefore it was properly brought to this court under the rules governing ordinary writs of error.

2. The law requires the clerk of this court, upon receipt of any fast writ of error, to place it immediately on the docket of the circuit to which it belongs. Civil Code, § 5558. The purpose of this is to insure a speedy hearing, if the court is then in session. Civil Code, § 5540. In order to determine how to docket each case, it is absolutely necessary that the clerk should inspect the bill of exceptions filed in his office; and it is not sufficient that he should simply inspect the certificate of the judge, in order to determine to what term the case is returnable. The law, and not the certificate of the trial judge, determines at which term a case shall be heard in this court. *DeLoach* v. *Trammell*, 72 *Ga.* 198. The inadvertence of the trial judge in signing a certificate to a bill of exceptions making a case returnable to a term to which it is not by law returnable should not result in having the case improperly docketed. Of course the action of the clerk in docketing the case is subject to review by the court, but upon him in the first instance devolves the duty of determining from an inspection of the bill of exceptions in each case whether a case should come to this court by a fast writ of error or by the ordinary writ of error.

3. The question as to whether the present case should have been brought to this court by a fast writ of error or by an ordinary writ of error is, to say the least of it, doubtful, and the clerk, therefore, took the safe course and placed the same on the docket of the present term, treating it as involving a question reviewable on fast writ of error. It being now determined that it was not proper to so docket the case, no harm has resulted to the parties, as an order will be passed directing that it be entered upon the docket of the next term. *Kaufman* v. *Ferst*, 55 *Ga.* 350; *Jones* v. *Warnock*, 67 *Ga.* 484; *Smith* v. *Willis*, 105 *Ga.* 840. If the clerk had docketed the case as one brought here by an ordinary writ of error, and it had been determined that the case should have been brought to this court by a fast writ of error, on the call of the case at the next term the same would have been dismissed because not heard at the

term to which it was by law returnable. See, in this connection, *Bleyer* v. *Distillery Company,* 70 *Ga.* 724; *Davis* v. *Bennett,* 72 *Ga.* 762. *Motion sustained. All the Justices concurring.*

CLEVELAND *v.* THE STATE.

109
.112

A motion to quash an accusation in a criminal case, on account of defect in the affidavit made as the basis of such accusation, is in the nature of a demurrer, and error alleged to have been committed in overruling such motion can not be considered upon a motion for a new trial.

Argued November 6, — Decided November 28, 1899.

Accusation of larceny from the house. Before Judge Calhoun. Criminal court of Atlanta. September term, 1899.

R. R. Shropshire, for plaintiff in error.
J. F. O'Neill, solicitor, contra.

LEWIS, J. On the 5th day of July, 1899, plaintiff in error was placed upon trial in the criminal court of Atlanta, under an accusation charging him with the offense of larceny from the house. After issue was joined, and a jury sworn in the case, the accused moved the court to quash the accusation and direct a verdict of not guilty, on the ground that "the affidavit upon which said accusation was based was not sworn to before an officer authorized by law to issue an accusation or warrant." It appears the affidavit was sworn to before a commercial notary public. This motion to quash was overruled by the court. A verdict of guilty was rendered, and in the bill of exceptions error is assigned on the judgment of the court overruling the defendant's motion for a new trial, one ground of which assigns error in the judgment of the court refusing to quash the accusation. There were no other grounds in the motion save the general ones, that the verdict was contrary to law and evidence, which were not insisted on by counsel for plaintiff in error before this court. While the bill of exceptions recites the ruling of the court refusing to quash the accusation, no error is directly assigned in the bill on such ruling, nor does it appear that any exceptions pendente lite were

filed thereto.   The bill of exceptions was presented to the judge
over two months after his ruling on the motion to quash the
accusation, and hence too late for direct exceptions to that ruling, even if such exceptions had been made.

The motion to quash the accusation in this case was in the
nature of a demurrer.   *Cedartown* v. *Freeman,* 89 *Ga.* 451.
Overruling a demurrer to a petition is not good ground in a
motion for a new trial.   *Shuman* v. *Smith,* 100 *Ga.* 415.   The
same doctrine has been applied by this court to procedure in
criminal trials: *Taylor* v. *State,* 105 *Ga.* 847; *Gaines* v. *State,*
108 *Ga.* 772.   Even, therefore, if the ground of the motion
to quash this accusation was well taken, it can not be considered by this court, for the reason that no exception thereto
has been properly made.

Judgment affirmed.   All the Justices concurring.

CRAVEN *v.* THE STATE.

The only person indictable under section 420 of the Penal Code, for the running of a freight or excursion train on the Sabbath day, is the superintendent of transportation, or the officer having charge of the business of
that department of the railroad company.   Accordingly, where an excursion-train was run on the Sabbath day by order of the superintendent of
transportation, he alone having authority to give the order, a trainmaster
who, in pursuance of such instruction, merely directed the "making up"
of the train, selected its crew, and provided whatever was necessary for
its safe and proper running, was not guilty of a violation of such section.

Argued November 6, — Decided November 28, 1899.

Indictment for running excursion-train on Sunday.   Before
Judge Sheffield.   Quitman superior court.   September term,
1899.

W. D. Kiddoo, for plaintiff in error.   *J. R. Irwin, solicitor-
general,* by *King & Anderson* and *Lewis W. Thomas,* contra.

FISH, J.   The indictment charged, in substance, that the
accused, being in the employ of the Central of Georgia Railway Company, and having under his charge the transportation
department of such company, on a given Sunday permitted

and ordered the running of an excursion-train over the line of the company's road in Quitman County.   Section 420 of the Penal Code, upon which the indictment was based, is as follows: "If any freight-train, excursion-train or other train than the regular trains run for the carrying of the mails or passengers, shall be run on any railroad on the Sabbath day, the superintendent of transportation of such railroad company, or the officer having charge of the business of that department of the railroad, shall be liable to indictment in each county through which such train shall pass, and shall be punished as for a misdemeanor."   It is quite apparent that this section means to provide a punishment for only the officer who is primarily responsible for the running of a freight or excursion-train on Sunday, that is, the officer having charge of the business of the transportation department of the company, who is usually the superintendent of transportation.   The various subemployees who, under the orders of such an officer, arrange for and actually engage in the running of the train are not subject to indictment under this statute.   Applying this construction of the law to the facts of the case under consideration, we are of opinion that the verdict was unauthorized.   The evidence was, that the transportation department of the railroad company was in charge of a superintendent of transportation, and that he alone had the power to order that extra passenger or excursion trains should be run; that the accused was a trainmaster of the company, and that his duties were, when an extra passenger or excursion train was ordered out by special instruction of such superintendent, to direct what engine and cars should constitute the train, to select a crew for the same, and to provide everything that was necessary for its safe and proper running; that whenever it became necessary to move freight which had accumulated on his division of the road, the accused had the right and it was his duty, without any special order from the superintendent of transportation, but under his general orders, to order out and have run extra freight-trains; that the accused had no such authority, however, as to extra passenger or excursion trains; that as to the running of the excursion-train for which the accused was in-

dicted, the superintendent of transportation ordered him to
have it run, and that, in pursuance of such order, the accused
directed the making up of the train, selected its crew, and provided whatever was necessary for its safe and proper running.
These facts were insufficient to sustain the charge, and the
court erred in overruling the motion for a new trial.

Judgment reversed.   All the Justices concurring.

JOHNSON *v.* THE STATE.

An indictment based on section 233 of the Penal Code and charging the
forging of an order for a thing not money is fatally defective and will
not support a conviction if it fails to allege that the thing in question
was of some value.

Argued November 20, — Decided November 28, 1899.

Indictment for forgery.   Before Judge Henry.   Floyd superior court.   July term, 1899.

G. A. H. Harris & Son and *R. L. Chamlee*, for plaintiff in
error.   *Moses Wright, solicitor-general*, contra.

LUMPKIN, P. J.   The indictment in this case was founded
upon section 233 of the Penal Code, which makes felonious
the act of forging "an order for money or other thing of value"
with intent to defraud.   The accused was charged with forging
"an order for meat on Dowdle & Watkins, who were running
a meat-market in the city of Rome,   .   .   with intent then
and there to defraud the said Dowdle & Watkins."   After conviction, he moved in arrest of judgment and also for a new
trial.   Both motions were overruled, and he excepted.   In the
view we take of the case, it is necessary to deal with one point
only, and it is presented in the motion in arrest of judgment,
viz., that the indictment was fatally defective in that it failed
to allege that the forged order was for a thing of value.   We
think this point was well taken.   It was within the power of the
General Assembly, if it had seen proper so to do, to make criminal the fraudulent forging of an order for any article or thing,
whether the same was valuable or not.   If the law had been thus

framed, an indictment thereunder would have been sufficient
if it had charged the forging with intent to defraud of an order
for anything, without alleging that the same was of some value.
But the law was not thus framed. It plainly and unmistakably contemplates, as an essential element of this particular
kind of forgery, that the article mentioned or described in the
forged order must have intrinsic value. Two things, therefore, are requisite in a case of this kind, viz., an intent to defraud, and value in the thing sought to be obtained by means
of the forgery. It is conceivable that a man might, with such
an intent in his breast, forge an order with the design of fraudulently getting possession of something of no pecuniary value;
but the lawmaking power did not choose to declare an act of
this kind indictable. Accordingly, it is impossible to escape
the conclusion that there can be no criminal forgery, under
that particular portion of section 233 of the Penal Code with
which we are now dealing, unless the article named or referred
to in the forged order be "money or other thing of value."
There being, in the absence of this element, no criminality, it
is indispensable that an indictment should distinctly aver that
the article to which the forged order related had 'some value.

It will not do to say that a court can take judicial cognizance
of the fact that "meat" is a thing of value. As to some kinds
of meat, this may not be true; as, for instance, decayed meat,
or such as has not been properly prepared for food, or for any
other reason is not useful. The order set forth in the present
indictment was for "spirribs" and "poke rose." Most probably, as was contended by the State's counsel in the argument
here, these words were intended to mean "spare-ribs" and
"pork roast"; or, in other words, the fresh meat of a hog, such
as is usually kept in a butcher's shop. But granting all this,
it could not, in the absence of an allegation that meat of this
character really had value, be arbitrarily assumed, as matter
of law, that such was the fact. In a particular instance, indeed
in one like the present, a court might, if permitted so to do,
be able to say with considerable confidence, upon the strength
of private knowledge, that the article in question was necessarily a thing of value, because quite generally so regarded among

men of all classes. But the difficulty would be in drawing the line between the cases in which this could be done without grave misgivings and those in which it could not. If meat like that described in the order set forth in the present indictment was in fact valuable, it was an easy matter to so allege, and the omission to do so was inexcusable and fatal. We can not undertake to cure a blunder of this kind by arbitrarily assuming a fact of which we have no authority of law to take judicial cognizance. We have no power to substitute our private knowledge, however accurate we might esteem it to be, for something which the law has made essential in an indictment. Were we to do so now, it would be establishing a precedent which would soon lead to the utmost difficulty and embarrassment, if not, indeed, to an actual miscarriage of justice. The next forged order we were called upon to construe might have reference to an article which we confidently and honestly believed was of great value, though as matter of fact it was something utterly worthless. In such a case, counsel might differ among themselves as to the question of value, and in that event we certainly could not be safely guided in arriving at the truth by their statements and contentions pro and con. The only rule which we can, with any degree of consistency, follow in testing the sufficiency of an indictment is, to take nothing for granted which is not alleged therein. As the indictment against the plaintiff in error, conceding that every averment in it was proved, did not necessarily establish his guilt of the offense with which he was charged, the judgment ought to have been arrested.   *Judgment reversed. All the Justices concurring.*

WADE *v.* GARRETT.

1. A sheriff's deed to land, made in pursuance of a sale under a justice's court execution, accompanied by possession, is good as color of title, although there was upon the execution no entry of a search and failure to find personalty upon which to levy the same.

2. Title by prescription based on such color of title will authorize a recovery against one who shows no evidence of title other than naked possession for a period less than twenty years.

Argued October 30, — Decided November 28, 1899.

Complaint for land.   Before Judge Littlejohn.   Taylor superior court.   October term, 1898.

R. S. Foy and *C. J. Thornton*, for plaintiff in error.
O. M. Colbert, contra.

LITTLE, J. Garrett instituted an action to recover from Wade possession of lot of land number fifty-nine in the fifteenth district of Taylor county.   It was proved on the trial that Garrett purchased the lot of land from McCants in 1880, and went into possession of it; and that the title of McCants was a deed from the sheriff of Taylor county, dated January 5, 1875, founded on a sale of the property, which had been levied on as belonging to Ogletree, under a judgment obtained against the latter in 1874.   Garrett claimed, and testified, that he sold the lot of land in question to Wade and put him in possession.   Wade, on the contrary, testified that he never bought the land from Garrett, nor ever made any agreement for the purchase of the same, but that his wife held under John C. Maund, who put her in possession under a statement that if he never called for the land it was hers.   The jury returned a verdict for the plaintiff, and a motion for a new trial was made, on the grounds that the verdict was contrary to law and the evidence, and that the court erred in refusing to charge the jury, in effect, that a levy and sale of land under an execution issuing from a justice's court, in the absence of an entry of no personal property to be found on which to levy the execution, was void, and a sale made under such an execution passed no title.   The motion for new trial was overruled, and the defendant excepted.

The evidence in the record is not conclusive that any of the parties claiming the land had a valid paper title to it.   Ogletree was never shown to have been in possession.   The defendant attempted to set up no title whatever.   Evidently the jury believed Garrett, who testified that he sold the land to Wade and put him in possession.   The deed from McCants to Garrett was dated February 19, 1880.   The deed from Pope, sheriff, to McCants, was dated January 5, 1875, and possession under this deed was shown in McCants until he sold to Garrett, and in Garrett until he sold to Wade about the year 1886, according to the testimony of Garrett. So that, under the testimony, Garrett had a prescriptive title which, in the absence of a better one in some one else, authorized him to recover. Plaintiff in error, however, contends that McCants took no title, because the land was sold under a justice's court fi. fa., and there was no entry at the time on the execution that the defendant in fi. fa. had no personal property on which to levy the fi. fa., and that the court erred in refusing to charge, on his request, that a sale made under such execution was void. Without controverting the proposition of law so raised, it is sufficient to say that the plaintiff in the court below recovered on his prescriptive title, and whether a sale under the execution was valid or not, yet the deed made by the sheriff to McCants was color of title, no bad faith being shown, under which possession was held for more than seven years. The question then being, whether possession under color had ripened into a prescriptive title, it was not error to refuse to give the charge as requested. The evidence, as against the plaintiff in error, authorized the jury to return a verdict in favor of Garrett, his being the only title shown; and the judgment overruling the motion for new trial is therefore

Affirmed. All the Justices concurring.

THOMPSON *v.* THE STATE.

1. There was ample evidence to show that the defendant was guilty as charged, and his conviction was not contrary to law.
2. A challenge to the array is an objection to all of the jurors collectively, because of some defect in the panel as a whole. If for any reason the impartiality of any one or more of the jurors whose names appear on the panel is suspected, the proper method of determining the state of feeling of such juror or jurors is by a challenge to the polls, and when thus challenged they may be put on their voir dire. And this is the rule not only in the trial of criminal cases where the charge amounts to a felony, but in the trial of misdemeanors as well.

Argued November 20, — Decided November 29, 1899.

Indictment for selling liquor. Before Judge Russell. Walton superior court. August term, 1899.

A. C. Stone and *George & George*, for plaintiff in error.
C. H. Brand, solicitor-general, contra.

LITTLE, J. The plaintiff in error was indicted for making an unlawful sale of spirituous liquors. On being arraigned, he filed a challenge to the array of jurors put upon him. The court overruled the challenge, and he excepted. Having been convicted, he made a motion for a new trial on several grounds, among others that the verdict is contrary to law and without evidence to support it. The motion was overruled, and he excepted.

1. It appears from the evidence that in the county of Walton, in a room connected with a storehouse, there was constantly and notoriously carried on, contrary to the law, repeated sales of spirituous liquors. The method of procuring such liquors, on the part of the public, as detailed in the brief of evidence, was, that there was a hole in a partition large enough to put a bottle or a jug in it; that when a person went to that hole and knocked on the partition and put in his bottle or jug, together with a sum of money, the bottle or jug would in a very short time be returned and placed in front of the hole with such a quantity of liquor as the money deposited would pay for. This was done by some person in the room, and no opportunity was afforded to the person purchasing to see the face of the one who furnished the liquor. An exceedingly lax administration of the criminal law is shown in the fact that sales conducted in this manner were allowed to go on month after month, in open violation of the statute. The evidence shows that this place was habitually visited by people, was notorious, and was in effect but a clumsy concealment of the identity of the persons making such sales. As an instance, one person who visited the place for the purpose of purchasing liquor declared that he put in said hole forty-five cents and that there was given him in return but twenty-five cents worth of liquor, and that the person purchasing and the person selling stood there for a considerable length of time quarreling as to the amount of money which had been really deposited. But if the good citizens who are interested in the enforcement of law permit in their immediate locality such repeated violations to exist, it is their fault and their fault alone. The question which concerns us as a judicial tribunal is whether the defendant, who was convicted, was guilty under the evidence as it ap-

18

pears in the record. He is clearly so, we think. He freely and voluntarily at different times confessed that he had been staying at this place known as "the tiger," and that he received for his services there twenty dollars a month; that his contract bound him to stay until the first of April, and that he was employed there for the purpose of selling whisky. This confession was corroborated by the evidence of more than one person, which showed him to have been repeatedly in the vicinity of this place of sale. To one witness he stated that "the tiger" took in a lot of money, and to a question asked by this witness if he ever took in money there, he answered by bowing his head. The defendant, according to another witness, rented certain land in the vicinity of "the tiger," on which to live and make a crop; but did not work the land a single day until April the first. He was absent from his land every week until Sunday morning. He told his landlord that he was engaged elsewhere in cutting cord wood. When this was ascertained not to be true, and being accused of staying at "the tiger," he admitted it and promised that he would quit the first of April. It is proved by this witness that the defendant said he knew he had been fooling some people, but that he also knew that he had not been fooling the witness. In addition to this evidence, it was shown by another person who testified for the State, that he knew the defendant well, had known him for fifteen or twenty years, that witness frequently bought liquor from "the tiger," that in making a purchase on one occasion he distinctly recognized the voice of the defendant. So that, by his own voluntary confession amply corroborated, the defendant is guilty, and the conviction was in accordance with law and fully sustained by the evidence.

2. In addition to other grounds which appear in the motion, the plaintiff in error complains that a challenge which he made to the array of jurors was overruled by the court. It appears that one Aycock was indicted for selling spirituous liquors, that the plaintiff in error was the sole witness for the State, and that after he had delivered his evidence the solicitor-general stated to the court that he would give the defendant a verdict of not guilty, but that the witness had sworn exactly

contrary in his evidence before the grand jury; and then proceeded to state to the judge in open court what the testimony was, which the witness, the plaintiff in error here, had given; and thereupon the court replied to the solicitor-general that there ought to be an investigation of the matter, as perjury goes to the root of all justice and undermines it, and instructed the solicitor-general to draw a bill against the witness for perjury and send it before the grand jury. All this transpired in open court and in the presence of the jurors who constituted the panel for the trial of misdemeanors. Immediately after these occurrences, the solicitor-general called up the case against the plaintiff in error; and it was then that his counsel made and filed a challenge to the array, on the ground that the statements and direction of the court, made in the presence of the panel of jurors, tended directly to the prejudice of the defendant and to discredit any statement which he might make in his own defense. It is now urged that the court committed error in overruling said challenge. It must be freely admitted that the remarks of the judge, and the direction which he gave to the solicitor-general, were sufficient to cause some prejudice, at least, on the part of the jurors against the good faith and integrity of the plaintiff in error; and if by a proper proceeding he had sought to test the fairness and impartiality of the jurors constituting the panel which had been put upon him and had been refused this privilege, we would, under the authority of previous rulings of this court, have sustained his right to purge the panel of all persons who were prejudiced against him. We are quite sure that the presiding judge was actuated by one motive and a single desire to suppress crime and enforce the law in the protection of society, when he openly directed the solicitor-general to prefer a bill of indictment against the plaintiff in error for perjury, assuming that the statements made to him were true. Yet, we ought not to refrain from calling attention to the fact that if a judge has any power to direct a bill of indictment to be laid before the grand jury, such direction should not be given in a manner which would be prejudicial to the witness in the minds of the persons who as jurors were then present in court and who might by any probability be called to pass on his case. We might say, in passing, that as a general proposition we know of no legal authority which a presiding judge has, to give any direction whatever concerning the laying of a bill of indictment before the grand jury for their action. A bill of indictment does not originate either with the court, the solicitor-general, or with the grand jury themselves as a body. Such a bill can not go to the grand jury without the endorsement of a prosecutor, who in certain instances is liable for costs, and, for a want of good faith and probable cause, may be liable for damages, if the prosecution be malicious. If, for any reason in the opinion of the presiding judge, any matter in the interest of the public at large requires an investigation by the grand jury, it is perfectly within his power and prerogative to call that body before him and in open court give such instructions, in relation to their duty as to the investigation of any particular matter, as he may see proper and right, and the grand jury on their own motion, whether they are so charged or not, may investigate any supposed violation of law, and may after such investigation make a special presentment of any person who has been shown to have violated any of the penal laws.

As before said, we are perfectly assured that in what was said and done the presiding judge only desired and intended to have such investigation made as the interest of justice demanded; and while we can not agree with him that such action did not tend to invade any right of the defendant, we do agree with him that the challenge to the array of jurors should not have been sustained. Under section 972 of the Penal Code it is provided that the accused may, in writing, challenge the array for any cause going to show that it was not fairly or properly impaneled, or ought not to be put upon him; and under this provision it has been held that a challenge to the array must be on some ground which taints the whole body of the jurors. *Eberhart* v. *State*, 47 *Ga.* 598; *Dumas* v. *State*, 65 *Ga.* 475; *Blackman* v. *State*, 80 *Ga.* 785. There are, in the trial of criminal cases, two general divisions of challenges: challenges to the array, and challenges to the polls. The only ground of challenge to the array, at common law, was an exception to the whole of the panel because of the partiality or default of the sheriff, coroner, or other officer making the return. This form of challenge is also divided into two kinds, principal, and to the favor. A principal cause of challenge was based upon facts which produced such a manifest presumption of partiality, that, being conceded or proved to be true, the challenge must as a matter of law be allowed. The challenge to the favor, on the contrary, was grounded upon facts giving rise rather to a suspicion of partiality than to a positive presumption or belief. Thompson and Merriam on Juries, § 126. But it must be noted that, whether principal or to the favor, the challenge to the array is and must be on account of the partiality or defect of the officer summoning the jury. In practice, a challenge to the array is said by Bouvier, under the title "Challenge," to be that which applies "to all the jurors as arrayed or set in order by the officer upon the panel. Such a challenge is, in general, founded upon some error or manifest partiality committed in obtaining the panel, and which, from its nature, applies to all the jurors so obtained." By Mr. Clark in his Criminal Procedure, § 162, a challenge to the array is defined to be "an objection to all the jurors collectively, because of some defect in the panel as a whole." By Mr. Chitty in the first volume of his Criminal Law, 536, it is said that "Challenges for cause are of two kinds: 1st, to the whole array; 2d, to individual jurymen. To challenge the array is to except at once to all the jurors in the panel, on account of some original defect in making the return to the venire." In 1 Thompson on Trials, § 31, it is declared: "As the entire office of selecting the panel was, at common law, committed to the sheriff or other summoning officer, the usual ground of challenging the array under that system related to the partiality, 'unindifferency,' as it was called, or other disqualification of this officer." It is true that in the section of the code, supra, after the provision that the defendant may challenge the array for any cause going to show that it was not fairly or properly impaneled, there are the added words, "or ought not to be put upon him." But, from the very nature and character of a challenge to the array, it is evident that such challenge questions the legality of the panel as organized, and for some cause which extends to the illegal arrangement of the jurors put upon him; and while in some of the books it may be found that a challenge to the array may be on account of favor, yet, as before stated, such favor extends not to the individual jurors but to the person summoning the same, from which it may be inferred that improper jurors were selected and impaneled;—and such is the ruling of this court. In the case of *Schnell* v. *State*, 92 *Ga.* 459, it was held that it was no cause of challenge to the array that twelve out of eighteen jurors had just served as a jury for the trial of another person indicted for a like offense growing out of the same transaction, and that if the challenge was good at all, it would not set aside the panel, but would be available only by challenges to the polls. A similar ruling was made in the case of *Jones* v. *State*, 90 *Ga.* 616. In the case of *Humphries* v. *State*, 100 *Ga.* 260, this court held, that a challenge to the array goes to the form and manner of making up the panel, without regard to the objections to the individual jurors which compose it; while the challenge to the polls is directed solely to an objection which is inherent in the individual juror; citing 80 *Ga.* 785.

Under the authority of these cases construing the words found in our Penal Code, it must be held that the challenge to the array was properly overruled. If,· however, it be said that there should be some method of ascertaining the impartiality of jurors put upon the defendant in the trial for a misdemeanor, where he has reason to believe that any of the jurors put upon him are prejudiced, it may be replied that in the case of *Schnell*, supra, it was virtually held that the right to examine a juror upon his voir dire in a trial for a misdemeanor existed in the defendant. The ruling there was in terms that the challenge must be made before the juror is sworn, unless the cause of challenge be unknown until afterwards. In the case of *Wells* v. *State*, 102 *Ga.* 658, it was held that, under our constitution, every person accused of an offense against the laws of this State is entitled, when he demands it, to be tried by an impartial jury. It appeared that in the trial of that case the commission of a misdemeanor was charged jointly against two persons. They were tried separately. One was convicted. In his statement, the person convicted implicated the other. When the second person was arraigned, the same jurors who had tried the case against the first were put upon him as part of the panel of twenty-four. To this panel he made a challenge to the polls, and not to the array, on the ground that the jurors put upon him had formed and expressed an opinion, and were, therefore, not impartial jurors; and the court was requested to put them upon their voir dire that their impartiality might be determined. There the court refused to do so. This court held that such refusal was error, and that the jurors should have been examined on their voir dire, in order that their impartiality might be determined. If any ground of challenge existed in this case, it was because the jurors were prejudiced against the defendant by the remarks of the judge and the solicitor-general made in open court. If in fact such jurors were not prejudiced, they were competent. In order to determine whether they were competent or not, a remedy was afforded, not by challenge to the array, but by challenge to the poll and each separate juror put upon his voir dire to ascertain his state of feeling toward the defendant before he assumed his public duty as a juror in the trial of the case. This was not done, and the partiality of the jurors was not questioned in any legal way; and it must therefore be held, in the absence of the exercise of his right by the defendant, that the jurors were competent.

Several other grounds of the motion assigned error in the rulings and charge of the trial judge. An examination of these grounds fails to disclose that any error requiring a reversal of the judgment was committed; and the judgment of the court in overruling the motion for new trial is

Affirmed. All the Justices concurring.

HARRIS *v.* THE STATE.

1. Recitals of fact in a motion for a new trial filed in a criminal case, relating to occurrences alleged to have taken place in the presence of the judge while the trial was in progress, though verified by the affidavit of movant's counsel and admitted to be true by the solicitor-general, can not be taken as true in this court when it affirmatively appears that the trial judge expressly declined to certify the same. It follows that points made in a motion for a new trial and which depend upon such recitals are not properly here for determination.
2. Words spoken by a person, some of them within an hour and others within twenty-four hours of the time when he took the life of another, capable of being understood as conveying a threat to take the life of some one, are admissible in evidence on the trial of the person speaking them, for murder.
3. The evidence warranted the verdict, and it does not appear that any error was committed in denying a new trial.

Argued November 20,—Decided November 29, 1899.

Indictment for murder. Before Judge Henry. Floyd superior court. July term, 1899.

George A. H. Harris & Son, for plaintiff in error.

J. M. Terrell, attorney-general, *Moses Wright,* solicitor-general, and *M. B. Eubanks,* contra.

COBB, J. Bud Harris was put upon trial upon an indictment charging him with the offense of murder. Having been convicted, he made a motion for a new trial, which was overruled, and he excepted.

1. In two grounds of the motion complaint is made that the solicitor-general was permitted by the judge to use language in his concluding argument which was improper and prejudicial to the accused. Another ground complains that the judge, though requested to do so, declined to charge the jury in such a way as to do away with the injurious effect of the language complained of. That the solicitor-general used the language attributed to him is alleged in an affidavit of one of the counsel for the accused, and was admitted by the solicitor-general himself. The judge declined to certify these grounds of the motion, and appended a note stating, in effect, that the language alleged to be objectionable must have been used by the solicitor-general while he was preparing his charge to the jury, and that he

neither heard the same nor had any recollection of such language having been used; that his attention was not called to the language at the time the same was used, nor at the time the request to charge above referred to was made. The judge further states in his note that one of the counsel for movant made an affidavit verifying the facts recited in the ground, and that the solicitor-general admitted having used the language therein set forth. But the grounds of the motion are not verified by the judge himself. The recitals of fact in a motion for a new trial must be verified by the judge who presided at the trial. The judge could, if he had seen proper to do so, have verified the recitals of fact in the grounds of the motion under consideration, basing such verification upon the affidavit of counsel and the admission of the solicitor-general, but he was not bound to do so. Having refused to so verify them, no other course is open to us than to treat the grounds as not verified; and therefore the questions sought to be raised therein are not properly before us for decision.

2. Complaint is made in the motion for a new trial that the court erred in not ruling out the testimony of a witness for the State, to the effect that he saw the accused the night the dance took place, about three hundred yards from the house where the dance was held and about thirty minutes before the homicide took place; that when witness met him he had a pistol in his hand; that he was laughing and going on, and said "he was going to get him a man." Objection was also made to similar testimony of another witness; this witness stating that the accused said to him, on the day before the homicide occurred, that he "was gwine over to the dance and get him a negro," that "a negro took my woman, and I am gwine over there and get me a negro." Objection was made to the testimony of these two witnesses, on the ground that the language used by the accused was irrelevant, as it was not directed against any particular person, and the statement made to the witness first above referred to was made in a jocular and not in a vindictive manner. We do not think there was any error in refusing to rule out this testimony. What weight it was entitled to was a question entirely for the jury. It was certainly capable of being

understood as conveying a threat to kill some person who was expected to be present at the dance on the night the homicide took place. The statement that a negro had taken his woman, that he was going to the dance to get him a negro, coupled with the fact that he was present at the dance, that he shot and killed a negro about a woman, would indicate that the declarations made had some connection with the homicide charged against him.

3. The finding of the jury was fully supported by the evidence, and the record does not disclose the commission of any error which would authorize us to reverse the judgment of the trial judge refusing to grant a new trial in the case.

Judgment affirmed. All the Justices concurring.

TEASLEY *v.* THE STATE.

Even if a minor is, under any circumstances, liable to a prosecution for vagrancy, the evidence in this case was not sufficient to show that the accused was without means of support during the period in which the State insisted he was a vagrant.

Argued November 20, — Decided November 29, 1899.

Indictment for vagrancy. Before Judge Reese. Hart superior court. September term, 1899.

Asbury G. McCurry, for plaintiff in error.
R. H. Lewis, solicitor-general, by *Harrison & Bryan,* contra.

LEWIS, J. Plaintiff in error was tried on an indictment in Hart superior court, charging him with the offense of vagrancy. The indictment was evidently founded upon section 453, par. 3, of the Penal Code, as it charged that the defendant was "a person able to work, and, not having some visible and known means of a fair, honest, and reputable livelihood, and having no property to support him, did not work." It appears from the record that the defendant was a minor, and that his mother was still living in the county where he was tried. It further appears that this minor had been to Atlanta, Ga., where he had been staying with his brother, and while there for a few months was engaged in work, from which he had accumulated some money. He came home from Atlanta on a visit to his relatives in Hart county. He had a brother and sister in Hartwell, and a mother in the country a few miles distant. The testimony in the case, even on the part of the State's witnesses, is conflicting and confusing as to what length of time he spent in Hart after returning from Atlanta and before being indicted; this being the period of time in which the State insisted he was a vagrant. The evidence relied on for a conviction was to the effect that during this period for several months his time was spent mainly in idleness upon the streets, the witnesses not knowing of any visible means he had of support. On the other hand, the testimony was uncontradicted that while in Hartwell he was taken care of either by his brother or sister, occasionally made visits to his mother in the country, spent his nights and ate alternately at the home of some of these relatives, and was always welcome there. There was also evidence showing that he brought with him from Atlanta some money; what amount does not appear. The minor's father was dead. There was no testimony in the record showing that his mother was not able and willing to support the defendant. She had married the second time a man with property. The jury returned a verdict of guilty. The accused moved for a new trial, and excepts to the judgment overruling his motion.

We question very much whether the penal law on the subject of vagrancy was intended to apply to one who is a minor. The law makes other provision for the care of minors who are without visible means of support. Section 2605 of the Civil Code makes it the duty of the judge of the county court or ordinary to bind out all minors whose parents are dead, or whose parents reside out of the county, the profits of whose estates are insufficient for their support and maintenance; and also, all minors whose parents, from age, infirmity, or poverty, are unable to support them. If a minor, therefore, be found in this situation idle, doing no work, and without means of support, the law contemplates, if he is able to work, that he should be bound out by the county official, and in this way be forced to work and earn a livelihood. In such cases we think, to say the least of it, this is a much wiser course to pursue than a prosecution for vagrancy. But we are quite clear that when it is shown a minor has a parent who has not forfeited or surrendered the right of dominion and control over him, and who could not, under the law, escape the duty of supporting and maintaining him; and where there is no evidence that such parent is not able and willing to support the minor child, there can be no conviction under the allegations in this indictment. The existence of such a parent is itself in law a visible and known source of a livelihood to the minor. In the light of the testimony, therefore, in this case, we think the court erred in not granting a new trial upon the ground that the evidence was insufficient to support the verdict.

Judgment reversed. All the Justices concurring.

McDANIEL *v.* COLUMBUS FERTILIZER COMPANY.

1. Upon a suggestion by counsel here that the clerk of a trial court has made a mistake in certifying as to the date upon which a bill of exceptions was filed in his office this court will direct the clerk to recertify as to this matter, to the end that the actual truth in regard thereto may be ascertained.
2. Causing a bill of exceptions to be actually placed in the hands of the clerk of a trial court within the time prescribed by law for filing the same in his office is all that is, in this respect, required of a plaintiff in error or his counsel.
3. A verdict finding a tract of land subject to an execution as the property of the defendant therein named can not be upheld when it appears that he was the owner of only an undivided one-third of the land and held the same as tenant in common with two other persons who interposed a claim thereto.

Submitted October 30, — Decided November 29, 1899.

Levy and claim. Before J. H. Worrill, judge pro hac vice. Taylor superior court. January 18, 1899.

C. J. Thornton and *A. A. Carson,* for plaintiff in error.
O. M. Colbert, contra.

LUMPKIN, P. J. 1. The bill of exceptions in this case was certified January 27, 1899. The clerk of the trial court certified upon it that it was filed in his office February 15, 1899.

On the call of the case in this court, a motion was made to dismiss the writ of error, on the ground that the bill of exceptions was not filed in the office of the clerk of the superior court within the time prescribed by law. Thereupon one of the counsel for the plaintiff in error stated in his place that the certificate entered by the clerk on the bill of exceptions did not correctly state the date of the filing, the true date being February 7, 1899; and accordingly requested this court to grant an order directing the clerk below to certify the truth in this regard. Acting upon this request of counsel, this court passed an order of the nature just indicated. This was in accord with the provisions of section 5567 of the Civil Code, which declares that "No writ of error shall be dismissed in the Supreme Court of this State on any ground whatever which can be removed during the term of the court to which the said writ of error is returnable, and said Supreme Court shall give such time, during said term, even to the end of the same, as may be necessary to remove said ground, if it can be removed during the said term." While we could not, of course, accept as evidence the mere statement of counsel, it was undoubtedly not only the right but the duty of the court, upon the suggestion that the date named in the clerk's certificate was incorrect, to call upon him to recertify in this regard, to the end that we might have official information from the proper source upon which to predicate action. See, in this connection, *Strong* v. *Atlanta Consolidated Street Railway Co.*, 97 *Ga.* 695, citing approvingly *Jones* v. *Rountree*, 96 *Ga.* 230, 232.

2. The clerk of the trial court, in response to the order above mentioned, certified that he received the bill of exceptions by mail on the 7th day of February, 1899; that he was at the time sick in bed, unable to attend to any business, and did not get to his office until the 15th day of February, and then marked the bill of exceptions "filed of that day, when in truth and in fact it should have been filed on the 7th of Feby., 1899, the day it was actually received." In view of the facts stated in this certificate, we hold that counsel for the plaintiff in error duly complied with every obligation resting upon them under the provisions of section 5554 of the Civil Code,

which requires bills of exceptions in such cases to be filed in the office of the clerk of the court where the cause was tried, within fifteen days from the date of the certificate of the judge. It was not incumbent upon counsel to do more than place the bill of exceptions in the hands of the clerk within the time limited by the statute. This they did, for the bill of exceptions was actually in his hands on the 7th day of February, which was within fifteen days from the date of the judge's certificate. It was the duty of the clerk, on receiving the bill of exceptions, to immediately file it in his office and to certify that he had done so. His failure in this respect, being in no way attributable to any fault or omission of duty on the part of counsel, should not be permitted to work any injury to the plaintiff in error. Section 5125 of the Civil Code declares that: "The mistake or misprision of a clerk or other ministerial officer shall in no case work to the injury of a party, where by amendment justice may be promoted." The spirit, if not the letter, of this section is certainly applicable to a case like the present.

3. It only remains to deal with this case upon its merits. An execution in favor of the Columbus Fertilizer Company was levied upon land as the property of P. E. McDaniel, who, in behalf of his two minor children, interposed a claim. The property was found subject, and the sole question presented by the motion for a new trial is whether or not the evidence warranted the verdict. It appears that the title to the land in controversy was originally in one Ingram, who, on January 19, 1883, conveyed it to McDaniel by a deed which was immediately recorded and which purported to have been based upon a valuable consideration. On July 27, 1883, McDaniel reconveyed the land to Ingram, who, on August 28 of the same year, conveyed it to his daughter, McDaniel's wife, by a deed which was recorded on July 28, 1886. The record does not disclose upon what considerations the two deeds last mentioned were executed, nor does it appear whether the deed from McDaniel to Ingram was ever recorded or not. The judgment in favor of the plaintiff in fi. fa. was rendered February 28, 1889, after the death of Mrs. McDaniel. The debt upon which that judgment was based was contracted in the spring of 1886, or, perhaps,

earlier. There was some evidence which slightly tended to support the theory that the Fertilizer Company extended credit to McDaniel upon the idea that he was the sole owner of the land in question, but this evidence was quite vague and indefinite, and it is certain that the company made no effort to obtain a contract lien upon the premises or ever acquired any sort of a lien upon the property of McDaniel until the date of its judgment in 1889. Upon the facts thus appearing, we are constrained to hold that the verdict was unsupported. The legal title to the property at the time the judgment against McDaniel was rendered was in him and his two minor children, as the heirs at law of Mrs. McDaniel, then deceased, each having an undivided third. No more, then, than McDaniel's third was subject to the execution levied on the land, and the verdict, so far as it affected the two-thirds belonging to his children, was manifestly wrong. It does not appear that their mother had ever said or done anything to mislead the Fertilizer Company into the belief that the property belonged to her husband; nor was any evidence introduced in behalf of the company going to show that his deed to Ingram or that of the latter to his daughter, Mrs. McDaniel, was in any sense fraudulent. This being so, it will not do to say that the children's interest in the property levied on could be subjected to the satisfaction of the judgment merely because of the loose testimony offered to show that credit was extended to their father on the faith of his supposed ownership of the land.

Judgment reversed. All the Justices concurring.

WYNN *v.* IRVINE'S GEORGIA MUSIC HOUSE, and *vice versa.*

An execution against S. J. W. as agent for Mrs. M. W. is against S. J. W. alone, the words, "as agent for," etc , being merely descriptio personæ. Where such an execution is levied and a claim is filed by S. J. W. in his own right, the claim should be dismissed, as only a third person not a party to the execution can interpose a claim.

Submitted October 30, — Decided November 29, 1899.

Certiorari. Before Judge Butt. Marion superior court. October term, 1898.

George P. Munro, for S. J. Wynn. *Simeon Blue,* contra.

FISH, J. An execution, issued from the county court, in favor of Irvine's Georgia Music House against "S. J. Wynn as agent for Mrs. Minnie Wynn," was levied upon a certain piano "as the property of defendant." S. J. Wynn interposed a claim to the piano. Upon the trial of the case in the county court, the levy, upon motion of counsel for S. J. Wynn, was dismissed. Plaintiff in fi. fa. took the case by certiorari to the superior court, where, upon the hearing, it was "ordered that the certiorari be sustained and the case remanded to the county court for a new trial." To this judgment S. J. Wynn excepted, and assigned the same as error. There were numerous points made in the certiorari proceedings, and the record is very voluminous. From the view we take of the matter, however, the case may be readily disposed of by applying a few plain principles of law. The execution against "S. J. Wynn as agent for Mrs. Minnie Wynn" was an execution against S. J. Wynn. The words, "as agent for Mrs. Minnie Wynn," were merely words of description. *Irvine's Ga. Music House* v. *Wynn,* 107 *Ga.* 402, and cases cited; *Lester* v. *McIntosh,* 101 *Ga.* 675; *Jones & Co.* v. *Newman,* 110 *Ga.*; Civil Code, § 2998. S. J. Wynn, being the party defendant in the execution, could not claim the property upon which it was levied. Only a third person, not a party to the execution, could interpose a claim. Civil Code, § 4611. Accordingly the county judge erred in dismissing the levy at the instance of S. J. Wynn, the defendant, who was posing as claimant. The judge of the superior court rightly sustained the certiorari, but erred in remanding the case for a new trial, as, under the peculiar circumstances, there could be no question of fact involved which made it necessary to send the case back for a new hearing before the county court, and the case depending upon a question of law which must finally govern it. The claim should have been dismissed by the superior court, for the reasons above stated.

Judgment affirmed, with direction. Cross-bill dismissed. All the Justices concurring.

PARKMAN v. DENT, for use, etc.

Where a bill of exceptions was on May 6, 1898, returned by the judge to the plaintiff in error for correction, and the same was not finally presented for the certificate of the judge until September 3, 1898, the delay was unreasonable and inexcusable, and the writ of error should be dismissed.

Submitted October 30, — Decided November 29, 1899.

Motion to dismiss writ of error.

C. J. Thornton, for plaintiff in error.
Brannon, Hatcher & Martin, contra.

Lewis, J. It appears from the record that plaintiff in error tendered a bill of exceptions to the judge within the time required by law, but the judge returned the same to his counsel for correction on May 6, 1898. It further appears that the defect in the bill of exceptions as first presented consisted in an omission therefrom of certain documentary evidence, the original of which was on file in the clerk's office. After counsel for plaintiff in error was returned the bill of exceptions for correction, he complained to the court that he was unable to obtain the record necessary to make the correction from the clerk, and the court passed an order at once requiring the clerk to deliver the necessary record. This was sent to the court on August 18, 1898, turned over to counsel for plaintiff in error on that day, and the bill of exceptions, properly corrected, was presented to the judge on September 3, 1898. The record discloses no reason whatever for this delay of over four months after the adjournment of court before a correct bill of exceptions was presented to the judge for his certificate. It seems that an original paper which belonged on file in the clerk's office had been introduced in evidence on the trial. When the clerk refused to allow this original to be taken from his office, it was certainly in the power of the plaintiff in error to have procured a copy thereof, and, with that, supplied the defect in his bill of exceptions. The record fails to disclose how long it was after the bill was returned to him by the judge before he applied for an order requiring the clerk to deliver up the original document. No reason whatever is presented why it was

19

necessary for him to have a period of four months for this purpose.   It was the duty of counsel, under the law, to tender the
judge a correct bill of exceptions to the rulings complained of
in this case, within thirty days from the adjournment of the
court.   There is a failure to meet the requirements of the statute.   If, in any event, counsel tendering a bill of exceptions
can ever be allowed any greater length of time for correcting
the same than that given him by statute for presenting it in
the first instance, it should appear that the delay was occasioned by imperative necessity.   In the case of *Joseph* v. *Ry.
Co.*, 92 *Ga.* 332, where a bill of exceptions was handed back
to counsel by the judge on August 18th for correction, and the
counsel did not tender a correct bill until November 22d, it
was held that "the delay was inexcusable and unreasonable,
the same, so far as appears, not having been occasioned by prov-
idential cause."   See also the case of *Allison* v. *Jowers*, 94
Ga. 335, where it appeared the bill of exceptions, after being
returned by the judge, was kept by counsel from November 11th
until the following January 27th, a much shorter time than
the delay in this case.   It was there held, no sufficient reason for the delay appearing, that the bill was tendered too late.
The principle announced in the cases cited necessarily controls
the judgment in this case, and the motion of counsel for defendant in error to dismiss the bill of exceptions is accordingly sustained.

Writ of error dismissed.   All the Justices concurring.

PRESTON v. WALKER et al.

"The obligee in a bond for titles, who has paid a part of the purchase-
    money for the land to which the bond relates, may, when sued by the
    maker of the bond upon a note given for the balance, recoup his dam-
    ages resulting from a breach of the bond, notwithstanding he retains
    possession of the land, he having at the maturity of the note offered to
    pay the same and demanded compliance with the terms of the bond, and
    by his plea offering to surrender possession and to account for rents dur-
    .ing the time of his occupation of the premises."

Argued October 30, — Decided November 29, 1899.

Complaint. Before Judge Butt. Marion superior court. April term, 1898.

Miller & Miller, for plaintiff in error.
C. J. Thornton and *A. E. Thornton*, contra.

SIMMONS, C. J. It appears from the record, that Lucy, Emma, Ida, and William Walker sold a tract of land to Preston, for which he gave them his three several promissory notes, each for $533.33, due at the time specified therein, and that the Walkers made him a bond for titles conditioned to make him a good and sufficient title in fee simple on the payment of the notes. Preston went into possession of the land, made valuable improvements thereon, and made payments on the notes to the amount of $913.00; and then went to the plaintiffs to pay the balance, and demanded of them a deed in accordance with their bond for titles. They failed and refused to make him a deed upon his tendering the balance due on the land. The Walkers subsequently brought suit against Preston on two of the promissory notes; to which action he filed his plea setting up the above-stated facts, and asking to recoup the damages which he had sustained by reason of the breach of the contract in failing to make him a deed. On the trial of the case he testified to these facts, and as to the improvements made, and that he had asked a rescission of the contract upon the payment by the Walkers to him of what he had paid them and for the improvements he had put upon the place, at the same time offering to pay rent for the land for the time he had occupied it. He also testified that the plaintiffs were insolvent. He introduced his bond for titles, wherein the plaintiffs obligated themselves to make him "good and sufficient titles in fee simple." He also introduced a deed from one Johnson to Lucy Walker, Ida Walker, and Emma Walker, "for their sole and separate use during their natural lives, without the power of alienation by them, or either of them, and at their deaths to their children, and at the death of any or either of them, then to the child or children of the deceased, and at the death of survivor the land to be equally divided among their children." On this state of facts, the trial judge directed a verdict for the plaintiffs against the defendant for the balance due on the notes. To which ruling and judgment the defendant, Preston, excepted, and brings the case here for review.

This case is controlled by the case of *Sanderlin* v. *Willis*, 94 *Ga.* 171. The facts are very similar, but those in this case are stronger in behalf of the defendant than the facts were in behalf of Sanderlin in that case. Here defendant shows absolutely that the plaintiffs can not make him a title in fee simple to the land; because three of them, Lucy, Emma, and Ida, according to the deed under which they claim the land, have only a life-estate, and William, the brother and one of the plaintiffs in the suit upon the notes, has no title at all, as his name is not mentioned in the deed from Johnson to the three sisters. Another difference between this case and that of *Sanderlin* is, that it was alleged in the plea and proved at the trial that these plaintiffs were insolvent; which would bring this case somewhat under the decision of *Black* v. *Walker*, 98 *Ga.* 31, and *Johnson* v. *Dorough*, 99 *Ga.* 644. The reasoning of Mr. Justice Lumpkin in the *Sanderlin* case fully covers the questions involved in this case, and it is unnecessary to elaborate them. *Judgment reversed. All the Justices concurring.*

CADE *v.* LARNED.

That a married woman in writing consented to and approved a security deed executed by her husband, conveying land to which he had title, did not estop her from subsequently setting up that this deed was void for usury, she having, before the bringing of an action against her husband on the secured debt, taken a conveyance of the land from him and having filed a claim thereto in resistance to a levy made at the instance of the holder of the security deed after obtaining judgment against the husband.

Argued October 30, — Decided November 29, 1899.

Levy and claim. Before Judge Butt. Chattahoochee superior court. September term, 1898.

C. J. Thornton, for plaintiff in error.
L. F. Garrard, *E. J. Wynn*, and *Vasser Woolley*, contra.

LUMPKIN, P. J. The record discloses that Julius A. Cade borrowed money from Charles Larned, giving therefor promissory notes the payment of which was secured by a deed to land dated April 10, 1886, and receiving from the latter a bond for reconveyance upon the payment of the indebtedness thus contracted. Upon the security deed was the following entry, dated June 28, 1886, signed by Mrs. Cade: "I, Claudia Cade, wife of Julius Alford Cade, having had the foregoing deed to said Charles Larned read over to me and being fully informed of its contents, hereby freely and voluntarily consent to the same and approve the conveyance thereby made." On December 21, 1890, Julius A. Cade conveyed to his wife the land described in the above-mentioned deed, his deed to her purporting to have been based upon a valuable consideration. Subsequently Larned brought against Cade an action upon the notes already referred to, and, on January 15, 1892, obtained judgment. Thereupon Larned reconveyed the land to Cade and caused the same to be levied on. Mrs. Cade then interposed a claim, and on the trial of the claim case the property was found subject. The only question with which we are now called upon to deal is, whether or not the trial judge was right in holding that Mrs. Cade was estopped from attacking the security deed on the ground that the same was void for usury. Counsel for the defendant in error earnestly insisted here that she was so estopped, (1) because the judgment against her husband concluded not only him but her also on the question of usury, and (2) that even if this position was not maintainable, the above-quoted entry on the security deed signed by Mrs. Cade constituted a binding estoppel upon her.

Conceding that the judgment against Cade was a final and conclusive adjudication, as between him and his creditor, Larned, that the deed given to the latter was free from usury, and that, if Cade's deed to his wife had been executed either while Larned's action was pending or after the date of the judgment therein rendered, she also would have been precluded from attacking the security deed on the ground of usury, it by no means follows that under the facts above recited she is estopped from so doing. On the contrary, it is perfectly clear that Mrs.

Cade was not cut off from making such an attack, either on
the ground that she was a purchaser from her husband, lis pendens, or had acquired title from him subsequently to the rendition of the judgment in favor of Larned; for the conveyance
from Cade to his wife was executed prior to the commencement
of legal proceedings by Larned and long before he obtained
judgment. See, in this connection, *Ryan* v. *Mortgage Co.*, 96
Ga. 322, followed in *Marshall* v. *Charland*, 106 *Ga.* 42, and
in *White* v. *Building & Loan Association*, Id. 146. In view
of the cases just cited, the first contention of Larned's counsel must fall.

Was there any merit in the second contention, viz., that Mrs.
Cade was estopped by the acknowledgment which she signed
on the security deed? We are quite sure there was not. If
Larned was in fact taking a deed tainted with usury, he knew,
or ought to have known, that it would be open to attack on
this ground either by Cade himself or by any other person entitled to raise that issue. If, therefore, Mrs. Cade knew that the
deed was void for usury, and at the time of indorsing her consent thereon secretly intended to attack it on that ground, she
was, in a legal sense at least, perpetrating no fraud upon Larned,
and accordingly had a right to sign the deed with a mental
reservation of this kind. Indeed, we may safely go a step far-
ther. If the deed had been a conveyance of her own property
and she had executed it for the purpose of securing a loan made
to herself, it would still have been her unquestionable right to
subsequently attack it for usury. Surely she was not estopped
by merely consenting to the execution of a deed by her husband, when she would not have been estopped by the much
more solemn act of making in her own name a similar deed
to her own property. It follows that the trial judge erred in
rejecting evidence offered in behalf of Mrs. Cade for the purpose of showing that the security deed relied on by Larned
was infected with usury and therefore void.

*Judgment reversed. All the Justices concurring, except Cobb, J.,
who was disqualified.*

WILEY *v.* CITY OF COLUMBUS.

When the charter of a city distinctly specifies the manner in which the municipal authorities shall contract in its behalf, a petition which in loose and general terms alleges that "the city" employed plaintiff to do a certain thing, and which does not set forth the terms of the alleged contract with him, or contain allegations showing that such contract was in fact made in the manner prescribed by the charter, is demurrable.

Argued October 31, — Decided November 29, 1899.

Complaint. Before Judge Butt. Muscogee superior court. May term, 1899.

James H. Worrill and *Samuel B. Hatcher*, for plaintiff.
Francis D. Peabody, for defendant.

LEWIS, J. Wiley brought suit against the City of Columbus, presenting by his petition substantially the following facts: In August, 1897, he was employed by the City of Columbus to tend upon and treat cases of smallpox, the patients then being confined in the pest-house of the city. He faithfully performed his duties in tending upon the smallpox patients, whereby the city became indebted to him in the sum of $275.00. Attached to the petition is a bill of particulars, being an account in favor of plaintiff against the defendant for "fifty-five visits to small-pox patients at five dollars per visit, $275.00." To this petition defendant demurred on the general ground that there was no cause of action set forth therein; and on the further special grounds, that the petition does not set out how, and by whom, and in what manner the alleged employment was made on be-half of the city; that the petition fails to show such contract was made as by law provided, and fails to allege what defend-ant was to pay for the services mentioned; that the bill of par-ticulars sets out a quantum meruit, and the petition does not allege that the items and sums set forth in the bill had been contracted for and agreed to be paid by the defendant; and that it was not alleged in the petition that the contract of "em-ployment" with the City of Columbus was made through its mayor and board of aldermen, in its corporate capacity. To the judgment of the court sustaining this demurrer plaintiff excepts.

The charter of the City of Columbus declares: "The said corporation, through its mayor and board of aldermen, shall have special powers in its corporate capacity to make all contracts which they may deem necessary for the welfare of the city or its citizens." Acts of 1890–1, vol. 2, p. 490. As a general rule of law, when authority is delegated by the legislature to a municipality to enter into contracts in a certain specified manner, it becomes the duty of any person dealing with such municipality in a contractual relation to see that there has been a compliance with the mandatory provisions of the law limiting and prescribing its powers. It would follow from this principle, that when a suit is instituted by one against a municipality upon a contract, it should be clearly shown in the petition setting forth the cause of action that the contract was valid under the charter powers conferred upon the city. While the suit in this case is properly brought against the City of Columbus, yet the petition alleges no fact which shows through what agency the city acted in making the alleged contract of employment. Under the charter, it could only be made through its mayor and board of aldermen. Besides, the petition does not set forth the terms of the contract; nor does it even set forth facts indicating whether it was an express or implied undertaking on the part of the city, and, if express, what compensation, if any, was agreed upon between the contracting parties. We think the defendant had the right to be put upon notice, by allegations in plaintiff's petition, of the exact nature of this contract relied upon for a recovery, so as to enable the court to judge of its legal effect. No amendment having been offered to meet the special grounds of the demurrer, the court committed no error in sustaining the same, and in dismissing the petition.

Judgment affirmed. All the Justices concurring.

MARCRUM *v.* WASHINGTON.

1. The act of the ordinary in receiving and recording a schedule of property sought to be set aside as a homestead, under the provisions of section 2866 et seq. of the Civil Code, is ministerial only, and the validity of

such exemption may be collaterally attacked in a court of competent jurisdiction in a case involving the right of a plaintiff in execution to subject the same to the satisfaction of his execution.

2. The affidavit required by section 2850 of the Civil Code, in order to authorize a seizure, under execution, of property set apart as a homestead, applies only to homesteads set apart under the provisions of section 2828 of the Civil Code, and not to property sought otherwise to be exempted.

Argued October 31, — Decided November 29, 1899.

Levy and claim. Before Judge Butt. Muscogee superior court. May term, 1899.

J. H. Worrill, S. T. Pinkston, and *Goetchius & Chappell,* for plaintiff. *Charlton E. Battle* and *A. A. Dozier,* contra.

LITTLE, J. W. E. Marcrum obtained a judgment against R. L. Washington for the principal sum of $137, at the January term, 1898, of the city court of Columbus, on which execution issued and was levied upon the south half of lot number ten in block thirty-nine in the city of Columbus. A claim was interposed by R. L. Washington as head of a family. It was shown that on the 10th of July, 1897, Washington filed a petition and schedule under section 2040 of the Code of 1892 (section 2866 of the Code of 1895). In his schedule was set out the south half of lot number ten in block thirty-nine in said city, and he prayed that the same, and the articles of personal property enumerated, might be set aside as a homestead exemption. The petition was sworn to, filed, and approved by the ordinary of Muscogee county on the 10th day of July, 1897. It appeared from the evidence that the consideration of the debt on which the judgment was founded was an open account. There had been a previous levy of this execution on the same lot in March, 1899, which was dismissed on the 20th of March, 1899. The plaintiff in fi. fa. told the sheriff he could not make the affidavit required by the code as a protection to a levying officer in seizing homestead property, but gave him an indemnifying bond, and the levy was made. When these facts were shown, the claimant moved to dismiss the levy, on the grounds, first, that the homestead exemption of personalty could not be attacked collaterally in the superior court, but that the schedule having been approved by the ordinary, that officer alone had jurisdiction to try the question of the validity of the homestead ; second, that no affidavit had been made by the plaintiff, as required by law, which authorized the sheriff to levy upon homestead property.   After argument the court sustained the motion and dismissed the levy.   The plaintiff in fi. fa. excepted.

1. The first question which arises for our determination is, whether an exemption authorized to be made under section 2866 of the Civil Code can be collaterally attacked under proceedings to make the property named in the schedule subject to a judgment against the owner of the property.   It is contended by the defendant, that the court of ordinary being a court of record and having exclusive and original jurisdiction in granting homesteads, its judgment can not be attacked collaterally ; and the case of *Dunagan* v. *Stadler*, 101 *Ga.* 474, is cited as authority to sustain this contention.   It must be noted, however, that there are two classes of exemptions allowed under the laws of this State, and that the manner in which they may be set aside is essentially different.   Under section 2828 of the Civil Code, a person seeking the benefit of the exemption of real and personal property of the value of a sum not exceeding sixteen hundred dollars, to be regularly set aside, must apply by petition to the ordinary of the county where he resides, or where the minor beneficiaries reside.   The petition must on its face make a case authorizing a homestead to be set apart.   This petition must be accompanied by a schedule containing a minute and accurate description of the real and personal property sought to be exempted.   When the application has been made and the schedule filed, notice in a prescribed manner is given to each of the creditors of the applicant or owner of the property, of the time of the hearing of the same.   Any creditor interested has the right to appear and object to the schedule for want of fullness, or for fraud of any kind, or to dispute the valuation of the personalty as made by the applicant, or the value of the premises platted as the homestead.   When such an issue is raised, it is the duty of the ordinary to hear evidence in relation to the same and to judicially pass upon that issue, and from his decision a right of appeal to the superior court is given.   So that, in all respects, the granting and setting apart

of a homestead under this provision of the code is a judicial proceeding; and it was accordingly held in the case cited, that in so passing on the application, schedule, and objections made thereto, the ordinary constituted a court, and his judgments were entitled not only to the force and effect to which judgments of courts of original jurisdiction were entitled, but also to the same incidents, one of which is that such judgment can not be set aside in a collateral proceeding.

By section 2866 of the Civil Code, provision is made for setting apart another and a different character of homestead, which is colloquially termed the "pony homestead." In having an exemption made under this provision of the law, it is only necessary that the party seeking the same shall make out a schedule of the property claimed to be exempt. No application is required, nor is it necessary that there shall be any publication of the filing of such schedule, nor any notice to creditors. This schedule is required by the act to be recorded by the ordinary. One of the items which may be exempted in this manner is real estate, in a city, not exceeding $500 in value; but in order to exempt it, it must on the application of the debtor be platted by the county surveyor and returned to the ordinary. If a creditor disputes the propriety of the survey or the value of the improvements, it becomes the duty of the ordinary, on the application of any creditor, to appoint appraisers to value such real estate. In *Banks* v. *McLeod*, 63 *Ga.* 162, it was ruled that the appointment of appraisers in such a case is but preliminary to judicial action. In this case it does not appear that appraisers were appointed to value the real estate described in the schedule. In *Davis* v. *Lumpkin*, 106 *Ga.* 585, it was said in the opinion that in recording the schedule of property and the plat of the realty the duties of the ordinary were purely clerical. Such proceedings bear no resemblance to a suit. No provision is made for hearing and determining in a judicial way the merits of the case—no notice of any hearing in relation thereto is prescribed—no judgment is required, and no discretion is invoked to determine any right. It is obvious, therefore, that the proceedings designated by the statute to be held can not have the effect of a judgment

of a court. If they do not, no presumption which arises in
favor of the judgments of a court of competent jurisdiction
can attach. Because of the difference between the method
prescribed for setting aside property as a homestead under section 2827 of the Civil Code, and that which we are now considering, must the former be held to be a judicial investigation,
and the latter merely the act of a ministerial officer. The
former is only granted after notice with due opportunity of
objection by any one interested, before a tribunal which passes
on questions raised, and determines the merits of the case,
with the right of appeal to a jury. The latter gets vitality
because of the record of the schedule prepared by the applicant, which follows its presentation as a matter of law, and
seems to amount to no more than a claim that the property is
exempt under the statute because of certain conditions which
attach to the applicant. It is true that section 2872 declares
that any officer knowingly levying on or selling any of such
property shall be guilty of a trespass, that is to say, a levying
officer when he seizes such property does so at his peril; but
it never could have been intended that mere preparation of a
schedule and filing the same should conclusively determine
the value of the property named and the right of the applicant to have it set apart. If such property is not exempt under
the law, or the applicant is not included in the class of persons to whom the law gives the right of exemption, then, notwithstanding a schedule which contains it has been filed and
recorded by the ordinary, that act can not make it exempt;
and we know of no other way of testing the legality of an exemption of this character than by having the same seized
under execution and the question as to whether it is or is not
exempt enquired into and determined; and while the levying
officer may not arbitrarily seize the same, yet, if he takes the
risk and does so, and for any reason it shall be finally determined that the property is not legally exempt, no penalty attaches to him, because as a matter of law the property is not
homestead property and is therefore not exempt.

2. It was sought to dismiss the levy because no affidavit had
been made by plaintiff in fi. fa., as required by law, to author-

ize a sheriff to levy upon homestead property. By the constitution of this State, art. 9, sec. 2, par. 1, which provides for an
exemption of property of the aggregate value of sixteen hundred dollars to the persons named therein, it is declared that
such homestead exemption when set apart is not valid as
against a judgment or decree for the purchase-money of the
same, for taxes, for labor done thereon, for material furnished
therefor, or for the removal of incumbrances thereon; and
by section 2850 of the Civil Code it is prescribed that when a
plaintiff in execution is seeking to proceed against the property
set apart, on the ground that his debt falls within some one of
the classes named, it shall be lawful for the plaintiff, his agent
or attorney, to make affidavit that the debt on which his execution is founded is one from which the homestead is not exempt, which being done, the levying officer is authorized to
proceed to levy and sell such property. It is apparent that this
affidavit is not required to be made in order to effect a valid
levy on property set apart under the short homestead. The
object of filing the affidavit is not to enquire as to the right
to have the property set aside, nor to determine its value.
Both are admitted. But the office of the affidavit is to determine the question whether the property which has been duly
set aside as a homestead is exempt from the debt sought to be
enforced, because it falls within one of the classes from which
the homestead property is not exempt from levy and sale by
the constitution. It is admitted in this case that the execution
sought to be enforced issued from a judgment founded on a
debt due by open account. It was not for purchase-money,
nor taxes, nor for labor done on the homestead, nor for material furnished, nor for the removal of incumbrances thereon;
and, besides being untrue, the affidavit would have been entirely
inapplicable in a case such as we are now considering. Its interposition could have added nothing to the validity of the levy
here. Inasmuch as the act of setting apart the homestead
claimed was ministerial and not judicial, and for the reasons
given no affidavit was necessary to authorize the levy of an
execution, the court erred in dismissing the levy; and the
judgment is   *Reversed. All the Justices concurring.*

EPPS, executor, *v.* STORY.

1. A contract between a father and a daughter, by the terms of which she was to pay to him annually a stated sum, and also to board him four months of each year while he lived, and, in consideration of so doing, was to have as her own a designated parcel of land belong to the father, of which she and her husband were in possession, was, though in parol, irrevocable by the father after substantial performance by the daughter during a considerable period of time.
2. If, in lieu of the annuity due to the father under such a contract, the daughter in one or more years boarded him for a time in excess of the stipulated four months, he not demanding from her any cash, and if his board during such period was worth more than the amount of the annuity, these facts would warrant a finding that there had been a novation of the terms of the original agreement, satisfactory to the parties.
3. Where a contract of the nature above indicated has been made and mutually carried out for a considerable space of time during which the daughter, upon the faith of the contract, has caused valuable and permanent improvements to be placed on the land, her failure to continue to board the father, if due to no fault on her part, would not of itself operate as a rescission of the contract.
4. The charges complained of were substantially correct, and were applicable to the undisputed facts disclosed by the record.
5. The verdict was sufficiently supported by the evidence, and there was no error in denying a new trial.

Argued October 31, — Decided November 29, 1899.

Ejectment. Before Judge Spence. Marion superior court. April term, 1899.

Brannon, Hatcher & Martin, for plaintiff.
W. D. Crawford, for defendant.

LEWIS, J. This action of ejectment was brought by J. W. Epps, as executor of C. W. Epps, against Ada F. Story and Joseph Story. Joseph Story disclaimed title to the land sued for; and Ada F. Story filed an answer, denying the allegations in plaintiff's petition, and claiming title to the property by virtue of a parol contract. The jury returned a verdict for the defendant, and the plaintiff excepts to the judgment of the court overruling his motion for a new trial.

1. There is no material conflict of evidence bearing upon the issues of fact in this case. The evidence was amply sufficient to authorize the conclusion by the jury that the defend-

ant and her father, the testator, entered into the following contract: The father manifested a desire to divide equally among his three children certain lands of his estate, and for this purpose laid off these lands into three equal parts. He placed each child in possession of his and her respective portions. This was done with the understanding between the father and children that each child, including the defendant, should pay to the father thirty dollars a year, and keep him four months, that is one third of each year, as long as he lived. On the faith of this agreement, the defendant entered into possession of her portion of the land, and complied with her agreement by supporting her father and providing board for him at her home for a longer period of time than that required by the contract. She did not, however, pay him the annuity of thirty dollars per year, for the reason that she took care of him at her own home for a longer period of time than she was obliged to do under her contract, and at an expense largely in excess of that annuity. For this reason he demanded no cash from her. On the faith of this contract valuable and permanent improvements, in the way of houses, etc., were erected on the place. The land was fertilized, much of it cleared at considerable expense, thus making the land more productive, and other repairs were made on the place which enhanced its value. The performance of her part of the contract continued for a considerable space of time, when her father, without any cause so far as is developed by the testimony, left her home, and sought a rescission of the contract, instituting proceedings by dispossessory warrant to oust the defendant. It appears from the record that the evidence on the trial was sufficient to establish such a contract as contemplated and described in the foregoing headnotes. There can be no question that a contract of this sort between a father and child is irrevocable by him. Section 4037 of the Civil Code, in reference to parol contracts for land, declares: "Full payment alone, accepted by the vendor, or partial payment accompanied with possession, or possession alone with valuable improvements, if clearly proved in each case to be done with reference to the parol contract, will be sufficient part performance to justify a decree." Section 4039 declares, in effect, that if possession of lands has been given under a parol agreement, upon a meritorious consideration, and valuable improvements made upon the faith thereof, equity will decree a specific performance of the agreement. It appears in the present case that there has not only been partial performance of the contract, accompanied with possession, but upon the faith of it valuable improvements have also been made, and that any failure to fully perform the contract was without any fault whatever on the part of the defendant.

This is not a case, then, where the defendant insists upon her right of possession and her title to the premises in dispute by a mere voluntary agreement or gratuitous promise on the part of her father. It is well recognized that a specific performance of such an agreement could not be decreed. Yet it is equally well established that if possession be delivered in pursuance of such agreement, upon a meritorious consideration, and valuable improvements made on the land by reason of faith in that promise or agreement, the father, at his option, can not rescind his agreement or revoke the gift. *Hughes* v. *Hughes*, 72 *Ga.* 174. Title by prescription growing out of adverse possession by a child of lands of the parent for seven years is based upon the conclusive presumption of a gift. That provision of law has no application to this case, for the principle above cited applies although the donee has not held seven years. See 72 *Ga.* 178, where a charge of the court below enunciating that principle was affirmed. The facts in *Denson* v. *Denson*, 94 *Ga.* 525–6, are very similar to those developed by the record in the present case. It appeared there that the parents, husband and wife, divided their land among their children and a daughter-in-law, allowing each his and her portion ; caused the land to be divided into separate parcels, and placed the daughter-in-law in possession of one of them, she agreeing to pay the owners annually a fixed sum for their support, and she occupied the land for several years, complying with the terms of her agreement. The original owners evicted her from the premises. It was held that although the actual value of the premises for rent greatly exceeded the annuity she was to pay, she could maintain an action for the recovery back of the land against the husband and wife for the purpose of carrying out the original agreement.

The contention in this case, that the evidence tended to show the parent did not intend for the gift of this land to go into effect until his death, and that therefore the scheme of the agreement was testamentary in its character and could not be enforced, we do not think is at all sustained by the record. There is some testimony to the effect that the father intended to treat the land as a home for himself during his life, but the agreement actually made clearly explains what he meant by such a home; each child being obligated to furnish him for a specified time annually a support, and a place of abode on the premises. Besides, a reservation by a grantor of a certain limited interest in property for his life does not prevent the conveyance of property from taking effect in presenti. For example, one person can deed land to another and reserve in himself a life-estate, yet the deed would convey an immediate interest and title to the fee in remainder.

2. It is contended in this case, however, that there was no compliance by the defendant with her contract, in that she did not pay the annuity of thirty dollars per annum stipulated in the agreement. The reason why this annuity was not paid is because the defendant furnished her father a home, and took care of and provided for him at considerable expense, he being at the time blind, and needing more than usual attention, and this service extended over a much longer period of time than the contract required. It was shown that this extra expense amounted to more than the annuity, and that for this reason the father made no demand on his daughter for the cash payment stipulated in the contract. We think there was sufficient evidence for the jury to infer a novation of the terms of the original agreement to the entire satisfaction of both the parties.

3. It appears from the testimony that after the father had boarded with his daughter for a space of fourteen months upon the faith of the contract that he had made with her, and after she had fully complied with all her obligations, as above indicated, he left her home of his own accord, without any cause or provocation whatever so far as was developed by the evi-

20

dence. There is no pretence that the defendant did not stand ready to continue the faithful discharge of her duties under the contract during the lifetime of her father. Her failure to continue to board the father, it appearing that it was due to no fault whatever on her part, but was solely the result of his voluntary act in leaving her home, would not, of course, itself operate as a rescission of the contract.

4, 5. There are several grounds in the motion complaining of certain charges of the court. After a review of these alleged grounds of error, we are satisfied that the charges complained of were substantially correct, and that the charge, taken as a whole, was full and fair, and clearly applicable to the undisputed facts disclosed by the record. The verdict was sufficiently supported by the testimony, and hence the court did not err in denying a new trial.

Judgment affirmed. All the Justices concurring.

MARSHALL *v.* CHARLAND, administratrix.

1. After a judgment has been rendered in favor of one merely described as "administratrix," without adding the name of any person as intestate, it is too late for a claimant of property levied on under such judgment to attack the same on the ground that the plaintiff therein was a foreign administratrix and had not filed a copy of her letters of administration in the clerk's office before bringing suit. Indeed, such a judgment is really one in favor of the individual so described, and not in her favor in any representative capacity.

2. Though a judgment may give to the plaintiff therein a special lien upon described realty to which under the pleadings she was not entitled, this affords no cause for dismissing the levy upon that realty as the property of the defendant in the execution issued upon such judgment, when it appears that the same embraced not only the special lien but also a general lien on all the property of that defendant.

3. Upon the questions of usury involved this case upon its undisputed facts is controlled by the decisions of this court in *Hughes* v. *Griswold*, 82 *Ga.* 299, and *Stansell* v. *Georgia Loan Co.*, 96 *Ga.* 227.

Argued November 1,— Decided November 29, 1899.

Levy and claim. Before Judge Butt. Talbot superior court. March term, 1899.

J. J. Bull and *C. J. Thornton*, for plaintiff in error.
J. H. McGehee, contra.

COBB, J. This case appears here now for the second time. When before this court the first time (106 *Ga.* 42), it was held that, as the year's support proceedings were complete before Mrs. Charland's suit was begun, the claimant should have been allowed to introduce evidence for the purpose of showing that the debt of the plaintiff in execution was infected with usury. When the case came on for trial again, the court directed the jury to return a verdict finding the property subject to the execution. The case is here upon a bill of exceptions sued out by the claimant, complaining that the court erred in directing a verdict against her, and of other rulings made during the progress of the trial.

1. The claimant moved the court to dismiss the levy, because no exemplification of the letters of administration of the plaintiff in fi. fa. had been filed with the clerk of the court either before the commencement of the original suit or at any other time. A foreign administrator appointed at the domicile of a person who is a non-resident of this State at the time of his death may sue and enforce, in the courts of Georgia, any right of action in the estate of his intestate, if there be no administrator appointed here. Civil Code, § 3521. When, however, such foreign administrator sees fit to take advantage of the privilege thus granted, it becomes necessary that he should, pending the action, file with the clerk of the court in which the suit is brought a properly authenticated exemplification of his letters of administration. Civil Code, § 3522. It is the right of the defendant in such a case to raise an objection to the suit proceeding, upon the ground that the exemplification of the letters was not filed as required by law. *Mansfield* v. *Turpin*, 32 *Ga.* 260. But we know of no decision of this court which authorizes the defendant or any one else to collaterally attack the judgment upon the ground that the plaintiff had failed to comply with the law in regard to filing an exemplification of his letters of administration. Even if the court should render a judgment without requiring such exemplification to be filed, it would be a mere irregularity and would not make the judgment void, and therefore would not be a proper ground for collaterally attacking it. Moreover, in

the suit brought by Mrs. Charland in which she styled herself
"administratrix," the cause of action was upon a negotiable
promissory note, which was not payable to the plaintiff's intestate but to another person, and was by such person transferred to the plaintiff as "administratrix," without adding the
name of any person as intestate, and the plaintiff brought the
suit upon the note as transferee of the same.   The suit was
therefore in fact one brought by the plaintiff in her individual
capacity, and the law above referred to in reference to suits by
foreign administrators was really not applicable.

2. It appeared that Marshall, the husband of the claimant,
had in his lifetime made and executed a promissory note payable to the Georgia Loan & Trust Company, and to secure the
payment of the same had executed and delivered to that company a deed to the lands in controversy; that the note had been
transferred to one Johnson, who had in turn transferred the
same to Mrs. Charland; that the execution under consideration
in the present case was issued upon a judgment rendered in
favor of Mrs. Charland upon this note; and that the judgment
provided for a special lien upon the property.   At the conclusion of the evidence the claimant moved to dismiss the levy, on
the ground that no deed from the Georgia Loan & Trust Company to the plaintiff in execution to the lands in controversy
had been made and executed prior to the bringing of the suit,
and the plaintiff was therefore not entitled to a special lien upon
the lands in controversy.   The court refused to sustain the motion, and this is one of the errors assigned.   While the transfer
of the note by the Georgia Loan & Trust Company to Johnson
and the subsequent transfer by him to Mrs. Charland did not
convey to her the legal title to the land embraced in the deed
from Marshall to the trust company, the transfers of the note
had the effect of vesting the legal title to the note in Mrs. Charland, and she thereby became in equity entitled to use the title
held by the trust company to enforce the payment of the debt
represented by the note.   Mrs. Charland was entitled to a judgment against the administrator of Marshall upon her debt, and
she was also entitled to a judgment declaring that she should
have a special lien on the land upon condition that she pro-

cured a proper conveyance to be made by the trust company to the administrator of Marshall in conformity to the bond for titles delivered to Marshall by that company. An unconditional judgment in her favor declaring that she should have a special lien upon the land was irregular, but such irregularity would be no ground for dismissing the levy, provided the Georgia Loan & Trust Company had, after the rendition of the judgment in favor of the plaintiff in fi. fa. and before the levy, executed and filed a deed to the defendant in fi. fa. for the purpose of enabling the plaintiff to enforce the special judgment against the land. *Henry* v. *McAllister*, 93 *Ga.* 667. The record shows that this was done.

Again, the holder of a security deed, who has given bond for titles to his debtor, has a right to obtain judgment against the debtor, file a reconveyance, and levy upon and sell the land, and his judgment is a lien upon the land superior to all liens against the debtor which are subsequent in point of time to the date of the security deed. This priority may be established by recitals in the pleadings and in the judgment, or it may be established whenever necessary by evidence aliunde, when the pleadings and the judgment do not show upon their face the facts necessary to establish the existence of the special lien. *Allen* v. *Sharp*, 62 *Ga.* 183; *Coleman* v. *Slade*, 75 *Ga.* 61; *McAlpin* v. *Bailey*, 76 *Ga.* 687. Under the ruling made in the case of *Henry* v. *McAllister*, supra, the transferee of a note the payment of which is secured by a deed would have the same priority, provided he obtained from the obligor in the bond a reconveyance to the debtor and filed the same at the time and in the manner prescribed by law. While it would be the better practice in such a case to set out in the pleadings and in the judgment all the facts necessary to sustain a special lien, if the failure to do so may be remedied by evidence aliunde in the one case there seems to be no good reason why it may not be in the other. It follows from the foregoing, that all that is absolutely essential to the establishment of a special lien in favor of the holder of the note the payment of which is secured by a deed is, that there shall be an execution issued upon a judgment rendered on the note, a deed from the original creditor to the defendant in fi. fa. made, filed, and recorded, and a levy upon the property therein described. Such being the case, where in a claim case the facts necessary to show the existence of the special lien appear, the mere fact that the special lien has been attempted to be set up in the judgment and the same does not appear in all respects regular is no reason for dismissing the levy at the instance of the claimant, when it appears that the judgment rendered on the debt was one setting up a general lien upon all of the property of the debtor, as well as what purported to be a special lien upon the property described in the pleadings.

3. There was no error in directing the jury to return a verdict finding the property subject. The evidence failed to show any usury in the debt upon which the judgment of the plaintiff in fi. fa. was founded. On this question the case is absolutely controlled by the decisions of this court cited in the third headnote.

Judgment affirmed. All the Justices concurring.

WEAVER *v.* COSBY *et al.*

1. When an action at law has been referred to an auditor, it is error to overrule exceptions to his findings of fact properly set forth, and to withhold the case from the determination of a jury.

2. The possession by a child of a note, reciting a valuable consideration, and a mortgage under seal purporting to secure such a note, raises a presumption that the same were founded upon such a consideration ; and heirs or legatees seeking to defeat the collection of such note, and the enforcement of such mortgage, on the ground that they were without consideration, carry the burden of proving that such is the fact.

3. Exceptions of law to an auditor's report, alleging error in admitting irrelevant testimony, ought to be sustained, when it appears that the testimony in question was irrelevant, and was objected to on this account at the time of its introduction before the auditor.

4. In a case referred by a judge of the superior court to an auditor, he can only pass upon such issues as are made by or grow out of the pleadings. It follows, therefore, in a proceeding to foreclose a mortgage given by a decedent upon lands of his estate, of which the petitioner is executrix, when the only defense made to the action by the heirs and legatees of the mortgagor is that the mortgage had not been delivered and was without consideration, that it is error for the auditor, to whom the case has been referred, to find that the plaintiff had no right of foreclosure until

she had accounted for the rents and profits she had received as executrix; and hence the court erred in overruling plaintiff's exception to this ruling of the auditor.

Argued November 1, — Decided November 30, 1899.

Exceptions to auditor's report. Before Judge Butt. Talbot superior court. March term, 1899.

A. P. Persons and *J. M. Mathews*, for plaintiff.
J. J. Bull and *A. J. Perryman*, for defendants.

Lewis, J. On the 20th day of January, 1890, John C. Maund executed his promissory note payable to his daughter, now Mrs. Ida J. Weaver, for the sum of $1,142, due on the 20th day of January, 1891, and bearing interest at eight per cent. from date. This note purported to be for a valuable consideration. Contemporaneously with the giving of this note, Maund, for the purpose of securing same, executed a mortgage upon certain tracts of land. Afterwards the mortgagor died, and the mortgagee, the plaintiff in error in this case, instituted proceedings at law to foreclose her mortgage upon the property, making party defendant thereto herself as executrix of her father's will; and the remainder of his heirs upon their own motion were made parties defendant. These heirs at law filed an answer, denying the giving of the note by the testator, and alleging that if it was given it was without consideration; and admitting the execution of the mortgage set forth in the petition for foreclosure, but denying that it was ever delivered to the plaintiff. On March 18, 1898, the judge of the court where the case was pending granted an order referring it to an auditor to hear and report upon the same, with full power to subpœna witnesses, and to order the production of books and papers; and further requiring the auditor to make his report at the next term of court. The auditor accordingly made and filed his report, giving a brief of the evidence taken before him, and his conclusions on the law and facts. Within the time required by law the plaintiff filed various exceptions, both of law and fact, to the auditor's report, whose general finding was in favor of the defendants. These exceptions were overruled by the court, and the report of the auditor and his findings were made the judgment of the court.   Upon this ruling and judgment the plaintiff assigns error in her bill of exceptions.

1, 2.   It appears from the record that the auditor in his report substantially found, as a conclusion from the testimony before him, that there was no evidence of any express contract made by the testator with his daughter, the plaintiff, to the effect that in consideration of services he would pay her a specific sum.   The auditor further found in his report that the note and mortgage were without consideration, and constituted a mere nudum pactum upon which there could be no recovery. To this finding of the auditor the plaintiff filed her exceptions; and in the bill of exceptions it is recited that the plaintiff's counsel asked the court "that the exceptions of fact, to wit numbers one and two, be submitted to the jury," and that the court overruled this motion.   On this ruling plaintiff assigns error in the bill of exceptions.   This was an ordinary proceeding at law by the plaintiff to foreclose in the superior court her mortgage upon the lands therein described.   There was nothing whatever in the pleadings, either in the petition or answer thereto, which had any relation whatever to seeking any equitable relief.   Section 4595 of the Civil Code provides that, "In all law cases where an auditor is appointed, exceptions of fact to his report shall be passed upon by the jury as in other issues of fact, and in equity cases by the jury when approved by the judge."   In the case of *Hudson* v. *Hudson*, 98 *Ga.* 147, it is decided: "In all cases strictly in the nature of common-law actions, which are referred to an auditor, it is the constitutional right of either party to have his exceptions of fact to the auditor's report passed upon by a jury, unless this right be expressly waived."   The announcement of the above-quoted principle is but a repetition of repeated rulings of this court previously made, and since adhered to.   See *Poullain* v. *Brown,* 80 *Ga.* 28.   From these provisions of the statute and the decisions of this court it follows as a necessary consequence that the court erred in overruling the exceptions of fact.   When such exceptions are filed to an auditor's report in an action at law, the court has no power under the statute to disallow them and himself pass upon the issues therein presented, without the intervention of a jury, unless the parties expressly waive such right to trial by jury. Even if there be no material conflict in the evidence, and the same should demand the auditor's finding thereon, the court has no right, when exceptions of fact are filed, to strike the same and enter up a judgment without the verdict of a jury. Should a verdict in favor of the report be demanded, then we think the court could properly direct a verdict, as in other cases, but a judgment without such a verdict would simply be illegal. With much more force can this rule be applied in actions at law where there is a conflict in the evidence upon material issues of fact between the parties, and where the testimony reported by the auditor consequently does not demand a finding for either party.

After a careful review of the evidence reported by the auditor in this case, we have reached the conclusion that the testimony not only did not require his findings of fact excepted to by the plaintiff, but to our minds it is exceedingly doubtful whether the evidence was sufficient to authorize the conclusions he reached. In the evidence reported by the auditor the following material facts appear: The plaintiff introduced her note and mortgage, the latter being a sealed instrument, and the former being an unconditional contract in writing purporting to be for a valuable consideration. Section 3656 of the Civil Code, in treating of the consideration of contracts, declares: "In some cases a consideration is presumed, and an averment to the contrary will not be received. Such are generally contracts under seal," etc. *Rutherford* v. *Executive Committee*, 9 *Ga.* 54. In *Smith* v. *Smith*, 36 *Ga.* 190, Harris, J., in the opinion declares that "the solemnity of a sealed instrument imports consideration, or, to speak more accurately, it estops a covenantor from denying a consideration, except for fraud." The plaintiff opened her case before the auditor by the introduction of her note and mortgage. It necessarily follows, from the principles above announced, that these instruments raised a strong presumption of law that they were founded upon a valuable consideration, and that when the want of such consideration is set up as a defense in the answer of the defendants, the burden of proof is upon them to sustain the

truth of their plea. How was the presumption in plaintiff's
favor met in this case? The only testimony on this point in
behalf of the defendants, appearing in the record, as reported
by the auditor, was that of one Dr. Cosby, from which it appears that he had a conversation with John C. Maund, the deceased, after the execution of the note and mortgage he had
given to the plaintiff; that he spoke about giving his daughter
the mortgage and why he had done so; that he had considerable
land in the loan association, and said, if the land was sold and
did not bring enough to pay it, that his other property would
be levied upon, and for fear of that he gave his daughter the
mortgage. The witness further testified that the deceased told
him he was going to destroy the mortgage he had given to his
daughter, and give her a note for $100 per year up to the time of
her marriage; but it appears from the auditor's report that the
objection of plaintiff's counsel to this portion of the testimony
was sustained. Even conceding that the balance of the testimony of the witness was admissible (and it does not appear
that any objection was made thereto by the plaintiff), we think
it utterly fails to overcome the presumption raised by law in
favor of the validity of the note and mortgage.

In the first place, this declaration of the deceased was made,
not in the presence of the plaintiff, after the execution of his
contract importing a valuable consideration, and was not supported by any evidence tending to show that the mortgagee
had any notice or knowledge whatever of this intention of delaying or defrauding creditors. In the next place it appears
from the mortgage itself that the loan association evidently referred to by the witness was mentioned in the instrument, and
it was therein recited that a prior mortgage in favor of this association, and two other prior mortgages in favor of one Sherwood, covered some of the lands mentioned in the mortgage
to his daughter, and therefore these lands were not intended
to be embraced in her lien. Certainly such a recital was sufficient to rebut any idea of an intention to defraud these creditors. Besides this, had the suit been instituted against the
testator in his lifetime, he evidently would have been estopped
from setting up the defense of intending to defraud a creditor;

and while creditors might make such an attack, as a general rule of law, what would estop a mortgagor in such a case would likewise work an estoppel upon his legal representatives and heirs after his death. But, if possible, a more complete answer to overcome this evidence in rebuttal is that it does not appear that any defense of this sort was set up by the heirs in their answer, and the auditor, in his finding against the mortgage, did not base it on this idea, but, on the contrary, as appears from his report, reached the conclusion that the real consideration of giving the note and mortgage was that "plaintiff rendered services to her father that were highly appreciated, and for which he desired that she should be compensated; there can be no doubt, under the evidence, the motive was present and he attempted to carry out the intention." In reply, the plaintiff introduced several witnesses who testified substantially to declarations and admissions made by the deceased, both before and after giving the mortgage, in which he stated a purpose to compensate his daughter for her great care and assistance rendered him, and in which he recognized an indebtedness to her of about $1,000, saying that she had done more for him than all his other children, and that he intended to secure this debt either by deed or mortgage, and, after the execution of the mortgage, declared, in effect, that he had thus secured the payment of such indebtedness. There is not a particle of testimony contradicting this additional evidence in support of a valuable and meritorious consideration which prompted the execution of the contract sued on in this case.

The auditor seems to have based his conclusion upon this parol testimony alone, and concluded that the execution of the contract by the deceased was a mere gratuity, prompted by the affection of a parent to a child, growing out of the latter's attention to her father. While it is possible that, if there had been no written contract between the two, the parol evidence introduced might have authorized the jury to reach the same conclusion, yet, in the light of the record before us, we do not think that even this portion of the testimony, not considered in connection with the written contract, would have *demanded* such a finding. But this case is to be distinguished from those

in which it is sought to imply a contract in which the parent
was to pay for services rendered by a child, and in which it
has been decided that such an implied promise does not usually arise in cases between very near relatives, when the services performed are in the nature of care and attention bestowed by a son, for instance, upon an old and infirm father.
For adjudications on this subject, see *Hudson* v. *Hudson*, 87 *Ga.*
678, s. c. 90 *Ga.* 581; *O'Kelley* v. *Faulkner*, 92 *Ga.* 521. All
these cases related to an implied promise, without any proof
whatever of an express contract; and even in such cases a recovery could be had, if the nature of the services rendered
was such as to authorize an implied obligation to compensate.
But how much stronger is the case when there has been an
express contract to pay, evidenced by an unconditional note,
and an instrument under seal to secure its payment. We conclude, therefore, that there was clear error in the judge's decision overruling the exceptions of fact, and refusing to submit the issues thus made to the jury. In the order granted by
the judge overruling the exceptions, the following words appear: "Exceptions of fact being submitted to the court without the intervention of the jury." There was no contention
before this court by counsel that they had agreed to submit issues of fact to the court and waive a trial by jury. On the
contrary, as above indicated, it appears from the bill of exceptions itself, certified to by the judge, that plaintiff's counsel
asked that his exceptions of fact be submitted to the jury, and
that the court overruled this motion, and upon this error is especially assigned. We infer, therefore, the judge, by the language quoted from his judgment, simply meant to say that the
exceptions were submitted to him for approval or disapproval
before going to the jury, and did not mean that a jury trial
was waived. No such waiver should be presumed in the light
of what the judge has otherwise certified to in the record, and
proof of such waiver should be clear and positive. See opinion of Justice Atkinson in case of *Hudson* v. *Hudson*, 98 *Ga.*
148. For the above reasons we conclude that the overruling
of these exceptions of fact, and refusal to submit the same to
the jury, were a direct deprivation of the plaintiff's constitutional right to trial by jury.

3. On the trial of the case before the auditor, testimony was introduced in behalf of the defendants as to what the lands of the estate were worth per year for rent while in possession of the plaintiff as executrix, and also what amount of rents she had received from the lands since her administration. This testimony was admitted over the objection of plaintiff's counsel, made on the ground that it was not covered by the pleadings, and was immaterial. The auditor overruled the objection, exception thereto was filed by plaintiff, and error is assigned on the judgment of the court sustaining this ruling of the auditor. We think the admission of this testimony was clearly error of law, and that the exception of plaintiff's counsel should have been sustained. Even granting that in an action by one to foreclose a mortgage against an estate of which the plaintiff is executor a plea of this sort could under certain circumstances in equity be set up by the heirs, and that an account of the plaintiff's administration could thus be had in a proceeding at law of this character, there was no such defense set up in the answer; the only defense being that there was no consideration for the note and mortgage, and no delivery of the mortgage by the mortgagor to the mortgagee. The auditor found there was such a delivery, as he was obliged to do under the positive proof on this subject. The only other issue for him to pass upon was whether or not there was a valid consideration for the contract entered into between the parties. The question, therefore, of the proper administration of the estate by the plaintiff was not involved in the pleadings, and was necessarily not submitted to the auditor by the court. It is well settled that, in passing upon issues of fact, the auditor must be governed by such testimony as will throw light upon the matters specially referred to him. *McMahon* v. *Paris*, 87 *Ga.* 660. It follows from the above that the court erred in overruling exceptions of law filed by the plaintiff's counsel to the auditor's report; such exceptions being numbered in the record 1st, 2d, 4th, and 5th. The exceptions of law covered by the 6th, 7th, and "7th" grounds relate mainly to the auditor's conclusions in reference to the consideration of the note and mortgage given, and are fully covered by the views hereinbefore set forth relative to the facts in this case.

4. The auditor in his report also found that this suit was by the plaintiff against herself as executrix, and that, even if this is allowable, the burden is on her to account for the property that went into her hands, and the rents and profits thereof, before she would be allowed a judgment of foreclosure; and, having failed to make any account for the rents, profits, and personal property, she is not entitled to a judgment of foreclosure, even if otherwise entitled. In the 8th ground exception is taken to this finding, and plaintiff assigns error in the judgment of the court overruling the same. For the reasons above indicated, we think the court erred in not sustaining this exception. In the first place, the auditor was passing upon an issue that had not been submitted to him. In the next place, there was no definite finding by the auditor as to what amount the executrix was liable for rents and profits. There was some testimony as to the specific amount of money she had received, which was much less than the amount sued for in this action; but even if such rents etc. had been a proper set-off, that would have constituted no reason why the plaintiff was not entitled to a judgment of foreclosure for the balance. The question as to whether it was permissible for the plaintiff to bring the action against herself as executrix was not before the auditor, not embraced in the pleadings, and is not made in this court. On the contrary, the heirs themselves, upon their own motion, were made parties defendant, filed their answer, and the case should have gone to trial upon the issues thus presented. Even if there was any irregularity in this proceeding, it was cured by appearance and pleading to the merits. Under the rule, however, in the case of *Groves* v. *Williams*, 68 *Ga.* 598 (4), it does not follow that a suit is void because the same party is both the complainant and the defendant.

Judgment reversed.   All the Justices concurring.

JOSSEY v. RUSHIN.

A payee of a non-negotiable paper does not become liable thereon as an indorser merely by writing his name on the back of it, but proof may be made of the actual agreement under which the indorsement was made. If the agreement was that he should be responsible for its payment, such agreement, if for a sufficient consideration, may be enforced.

109
e12

Submitted November 1, — Decided November 30, 1899.

Petition for certiorari. Before Judge Butt. Marion superior court. August 11, 1899.

Simeon Blue, for plaintiff.

SIMMONS, C. J. It appears from the record that Rushin, the sheriff of Marion county, obtained an order from the judge of the superior court on the county treasurer, for his insolvent costs in certain cases tried in that court. It further appears that he sold this order to Jossey for eighty-five per cent. of the face value thereof. Jossey presented the order to the county treasurer on two different occasions, who refused to pay it for the want of funds. Jossey brought suit against Rushin in the county court of said county, and alleged in his petition "that it was understood and agreed verbally at the time of said indorsement that said Rushin was and is liable for the aforesaid sum, with interest." It was also alleged that at the time of the indorsement there were no funds in the county treasury, nor had there been up to the time of the filing of the suit. Rushin filed a demurrer to the petition, upon the several grounds mentioned therein, which are not necessary to be here set out. This demurrer was sustained by the county judge. Whereupon plaintiff presented a petition to the superior court of said county, for a certiorari, alleging as error the sustaining of the demurrer by the county judge. The court refused to sanction the petition, and he excepts and brings the case here for review.

The law seems to be well settled, that if a payee of a non-negotiable instrument merely writes his name on the back thereof, he is not liable as indorser thereon. It seems also to be well settled by the weight of authority, that if he induces the transferee to purchase such non-negotiable instrument, and transfers or indorses the same to the transferee by writing his name thereon in blank, and receives valuable consideration therefor, the transferee may recover of him the amount which the instrument calls for, or, at least, the amount which the transferee paid him therefor. Shaffstall v. McDaniel, 152 Pa. St. 598, s. c. 25 N. W. Rep. 576; Cromwell v. Hewlitt, 100 Am. Dec. 527 ; Frevall v. Fitch, 34 Am. Dec. 558; 4 Am. & Eng. Enc. L. (2d ed.) 480. We think, therefore, that if Jossey can establish, at the trial before the jury, to their satisfaction, the fact alleged in his petition, he would be entitled to recover. If, upon the other hand, Rushin can prove to the satisfaction of the jury that he made no such promise, but only wrote his name on the back of the order for the purpose of assigning the title to Jossey to enable him to collect it out of the county treasurer, he would be entitled to a verdict. We think that it is a question of fact for the jury; and inasmuch as Rushin admitted the allegation in the petition that he agreed to pay it, the judge of the county court erred in sustaining the demurrer, and the judge of the superior court erred in not sanctioning the petition for certiorari.

Judgment reversed. All the Justices concurring.

FELTON v. GRIER.

1. It being legally possible for the owner of realty to sell and convey it to another at an agreed cash price, and at the same time secure the right to repurchase, and become bound so to do, at a higher price payable in the future, the law will enforce such a transaction when actually made.

2. Though the transaction now under review in many respects very closely resembled a mere loan of money at a usurious rate of interest, secured by a deed to land, yet as there was direct and positive evidence warranting the special findings of fact to the effect that it was a bona fide case of bargain and sale with a contemporaneous agreement by the vendee to resell to the vendor, and a binding contract by the latter to repurchase, the verdict must be allowed to stand.

3. The requests to charge were substantially covered by the general charge given to the jury ; and the instructions complained of, construed in the light of that charge, afford no cause for a new trial. Indeed, it is manifest that the jury clearly understood and deliberately, passed upon the issues presented by the evidence.

Argued November 1, — Decided November 30, 1899.

Reargued January 17, — Opinion filed February 26, 1900.

320\
830\
320\
503\
320
838

Complaint. Before Judge Butt. Muscogee superior court. September 1, 1899.

Goetchius & Chappell, for plaintiff in error.
Charlton E. Battle, contra.

LUMPKIN, P. J. This was an action by Grier against Felton, upon 51 promissory notes of $14 each, and the plaintiff had a recovery for the full amount apparently due thereon. On the trial below, there was a "special verdict of the facts." It was supported by clear, positive, and direct testimony; and, as a necessary consequence of the findings of the jury, it must be assumed in this court that the actual truth of the case is as follows: Felton applied to Grier for a loan of $600, proposing to secure the payment thereof by a deed to certain land. Grier positively refused to lend Felton the money on any terms. Some days subsequently, they entered into an agreement to the effect that Felton was to sell and convey the land absolutely to Grier at the price of $600, Felton reserving the right to repurchase, and becoming bound to do so, by paying to Grier $14 monthly for 60 consecutive months. Accordingly, Felton executed and delivered to Grier a deed to the land, and received therefor $600. He then made and delivered to Grier 60 purchase-money notes of $14 each, payable as above indicated, and took from Grier a bond conditioned to make him a title to the land upon the payment of these notes. All the foregoing stipulations were parts of one and the same transaction. Nine of the notes had been paid before the action was begun. Felton's answer set up the defense of usury, it being therein alleged that the transaction between himself and Grier was a mere loan of money, at a usurious rate of interest, secured by deed with bond for reconveyance upon payment of the indebtedness evidenced by the notes. There was some testimony in support of the answer, but we must deal with the case upon the facts established by the special verdict. Without stating and discussing separately the several grounds of the motion for a new trial, it is enough to say that they present for decision the naked question: Is it legally possible for an owner of realty to sell it outright for cash, and at the same

21

time and as a part of the contract of sale secure the right to repurchase, *and become bound to do so*, at a higher price payable
in the future; or, must such a transaction necessarily and inevitably be treated as one of borrowing money and securing
its payment by a deed in the nature of a mortgage? After deciding this question favorably to the defendant in error, we
granted the plaintiff in error a rehearing. Upon further deliberation, we are still of the opinion that the judgment we rendered was right. It may, without careful consideration, seem
contrary to a great current of respectable authority, but, after
examining many text-books and scores of cases, we feel confident that our decision is in accord with the true law, and not
really in conflict with the best considered views we have en-
countered in our search for light. It is certain that there can
be such a transaction as a sale with an agreement for a repurchase. All the books recognize the correctness of this proposition, and every man of common sense knows it is true.

Says Chancellor Kent: "The case of sale, with an agreement for a repurchase within a given time, is totally distinct
and not applicable to mortgages. Such conditional sales or
defeasible purchases, though narrowly watched, are valid,"
etc. 4 Kent's Com. (14th ed.) *144. The real difficulty, so
frequently arising, is to determine whether, in a given instance,
the parties intended a sale or a mortgage. In a note to the
text-book from which we have just quoted is the following,
and the same will be found copied in many judicial opinions
and made the basis of the conclusions therein announced:
"The test of the distinction is this: If the relation of debtor
and creditor remains, and a debt still subsists, it is a mortgage;
but if the debt be extinguished by the agreement of the parties, or the money advanced is not by way of loan, and the
grantor has the privilege of refunding, if he pleases, by a
given time, and thereby entitle himself to a reconveyance, it
is a conditional sale." See also 3 Pom. Eq. Jur. (2d ed.)
§ 1195. In a note the author cites a large number of "cases
in which the transaction has amounted to a mortgage," and
also numerous others which were "cases of sale and contract to
repurchase." We have examined most of these cases of both

classes. Many of them and others of like kind are cited by counsel for the plaintiff in error, and some of both classes apparently sustain without qualification their contention that if, after the transaction has become complete, the relation of debtor and creditor still exists between the parties, it must necessarily be regarded as a mortgage. There is a long line of cases supporting the proposition, that where a grantor executes an absolute conveyance and at the same time reserves the option or privilege of repurchasing, without being under a binding obligation to do so, the mere retention of the right to repurchase is not, of itself alone, sufficient to render the transaction a mortgage. We of course assent to the correctness of this doctrine, but we do not concede that if the grantor bound himself to repurchase, as in the present case, it would inevitably follow there was no sale. Cases of the class last referred to are not really in point, but, as the opinions in quite a number of them refer approvingly to the test above referred to, they are frequently cited as authority by those seeking to maintain a position similar to that now occupied by counsel for the plaintiff in error. We do not think the rule as stated goes to the extent often claimed. An analysis of it will, in our judgment, bear out this assertion. The first proposition embraced in it is: "If the relation of debtor and creditor remains, and a debt still subsists, it is a mortgage." This language is applicable, and we are sure was intended to apply, to cases wherein it appeared that one person, being already indebted to another, had made to the latter a conveyance of property, and the question for determination was whether the conveyance was executed for the purpose of paying the debt or merely securing its payment. The use of the words "remains" and "still subsists" strongly, if not necessarily, implies that there should be a subsisting indebtedness at the time of executing the conveyance; and all the judges and law-writers agree that if that indebtedness is not absolutely discharged by the conveyance, the instrument should be regarded as a mortgage. In other words, if that same debt, in any form, "still subsists," the conclusion must follow that the only object which the parties had in view was to secure its payment, and, this being so, the conveyance could not be treated as effectuating a sale. Thus viewing the first clause of the rule, we accept it without hesitation and freely admit that in most, if not in all, of the numerous cases we have examined it has, upon the facts appearing, been properly invoked and enforced.

The second clause is as follows: "but if the debt be extinguished by the agreement of the parties, or the money advanced is not by way of loan, and the grantor has the privilege of refunding, if he pleases, by a given time, and thereby entitle himself to a reconveyance, it is a conditional sale." The phrase "if the debt be extinguished" applies, as was said respecting the first clause of the rule, to a debt already subsisting. Certainly it can not be understood as aptly referring to a debt coming for the first time into existence as a result of the very transaction by which this same debt is immediately to be extinguished. Relatively, then, to a case like ours, the pregnant and all-important language of the rule is embraced in the phrase, "or if the money advanced is not by way of loan." The words just quoted and those following them manifestly relate to a case where two parties come together for an original transaction in which one advances and the other receives money, and the latter executes to the former a conveyance of property with right of repurchase. If the money advanced is "by way of loan," the conveyance is, in effect, a mortgage only. If not "by way of loan," but as the purchase-money of the property on the resale, the conveyance evidences an actual sale to him who agrees to resell. In case the original seller binds himself to repurchase and gives promissory notes accordingly, the relation of debtor and creditor will, of course, exist between him and the other party; but it will be a newly-created relation and not an old one which "remains" or "still subsists." In other words, the real test, in a case like the present, is whether the consideration of the notes is money loaned or the purchase-price agreed upon in the contract of resale. If the former, the deed made by the party receiving the loan should be treated as a mere security deed; if the latter, such deed should be treated as one of bargain and sale.

We have not in our investigation overlooked or ignored the

fact that many judges and authors, in citing and applying the rule under discussion, have gone so far as to say, literally or in substance, that if after the execution of the deed the relation of debtor and creditor, for any reason arising out of the transaction of which such deed is a part, exists between the parties, it must be regarded as only a mortgage. Our reply is, that the distinguished jurists and commentators here referred to have extended this rule beyond its true intent and meaning. After much deliberation and careful study, we are satisfied that our analysis and interpretation of it is correct, and that, thus understood, "the test of the distinction" is free from the objections which are naturally suggested by an attempt to strain it so far as to defeat purposes which contracting parties deliberately seek to accomplish. We can not believe the author of this rule ever meant to assert that if two sane persons, legally capable of contracting, knowingly, voluntarily, and actually intended to make an agreement by the terms of which one should sell property to the other for cash, receive the money, and bind himself to repurchase at a higher price payable in the future, they could not possibly accomplish their design. Our quotation from the text of the great chancellor unquestionably sustains what we have just said; and in this connection we extract the following from the opinion of Chief Justice Marshall in Conway v. Alexander, 7 Cranch, 236, 237, which has been quoted and followed in dozens of opinions: "To deny the power of two individuals, capable of acting for themselves, to make a contract for the purchase and sale of lands, defeasible by the payment of money at a future day, or, in other words, to make a sale with a reservation to the vendor of a right to repurchase the same land at a fixed price and at a specified time, would be to transfer to the court of chancery, in a considerable degree, the guardianship of adults as well as of infants. Such contracts are certainly not prohibited, either by the letter or the policy of the law." The renowned Chief Justice further says: "But as a conditional sale, if really intended, is valid, the inquiry in every case must be, whether the contract in the specific case is a security for the repayment of money, or an actual sale?" Herein lies the key to the whole matter; "for the ques-

tion finally turns, in all cases, upon the real intention of the
parties, as shown upon the face of the writings or as disclosed
by extrinsic evidence." See Pom. Eq. Jur., supra. The correctness of this statement is so well recognized and accepted,
we regard it as altogether useless to multiply citations in support of it. The only proper course, therefore, to pursue in any
given case is to ascertain what the parties actually intended,
and then effectuate their intention. There is, perhaps, no rule
of such universal application as to afford in every instance an
absolute and conclusive test for finding out what the intention
really was. Thomas on Mortgages, 23. "No conclusive test
can be suggested to determine whether such transactions are
mortgages or conditional sales, because the question arises under such varieties of circumstances that slight differences in
these would make it inapplicable." 15 Am. & Eng. Enc. L. 780.

Mr. Pomeroy claims no more for the "criterion" he lays
down than that it "furnishes a sufficient test in the great majority of cases." Our case is not one of the great majority, but
of the small minority. We have endeavored to find and examine all the cases decided by this court from which we could
hope to derive any aid in properly disposing of the case in
hand. In numbers of them the cardinal rule that intention
must control is stated and recognized, but none of them are
strictly in point; for the precise question with which we are
now dealing has never, so far as we can ascertain, been distinctly made in and ruled upon by this court. As above indicated, that question, reduced to its last analysis, is simply
this: Is it a legal impossibility for two parties to agree between themselves that one shall buy property from the other
for cash and contemporaneously contract to resell in consideration of the original seller's binding undertaking to repurchase on time at an advanced price? The question was certainly not passed upon in either *Spence* v. *Steadman*, 49 *Ga.* 133,
or *Monroe* v. *Foster*, Id. 514, the two Georgia cases mainly relied upon by counsel for the plaintiff in error. In both, however, it was expressly ruled that it was legally possible for one to
actually and truly sell to another unwilling to lend money but
willing to purchase and allow the seller the privilege of repur-

chasing at a specified advance in price. We shall not refer to other Georgia cases, because, for the reason given, none of them are specially helpful in arriving at a solution of the exact question now for determination. The facts of the present case were stated at the outset. Those facts, let it be remembered, were absolutely established by special findings. We have no alternative but to accept them as the true and correct version of what transpired between Grier and Felton. The transaction certainly resembled very closely a mere loan of money at a usurious rate of interest, secured by a deed to land. The criteria, tests, etc., laid down in many of the authorities to which we have referred, suggest excellent reasons why the jury might have found that it was a transaction of that kind. But they did not. On the contrary, with strong evidence so warranting, and in answer to specific interrogatories designed to bring out the actual and precise truth of the matter, they found otherwise. It is settled for us that Grier and Felton did exactly what the jury said they did, and we simply hold that it is within the power of rational and independent adults, if they really desire and intend to do a thing of this kind, to legally accomplish their purpose. We can not undertake to say it is absolutely out of the question for such a transaction to take place. It would be tantamount to holding that a fact actually accomplished was an impossibility.

Judgment affirmed. All the Justices concurring.

TAYLOR *et al. v.* JAMES, and *vice versa.*

1. Where a parol agreement between the head of a family and another for the exchange of parcels of realty was so far executed that the former took possession of the land he thus undertook to acquire, dealt with it as a part of his homestead, and relinquished possession of that portion of the homestead exchanged therefor, one who undertook to purchase from the head of the family the entire homestead as such did not acquire any better title to the land added thereto in the manner above stated than to the remaining part of such homestead.

2. An order having been granted by the judge of the superior court authorizing a sale of the homestead for reinvestment and distinctly providing that it should be sold at a designated price, one who undertook to pur-

chase such homestead or a part thereof was chargeable with notice of the terms embraced in the judge's order. Certainly so when a deed to him from the head of the family expressly recited that the sale was made under and in pursuance of such order.

3. Where the sale was not in accord with the terms of the order, the purchaser did not acquire a valid title to the homestead property, and it was the right of the beneficiaries of the homestead to recover the same, together with mesne profits; but subject in equity to the right of the purchaser to offset against the same so much of the purchase-money paid to the head of the family as was actually used or expended by him in providing necessaries for his family; and also to set off against such mesne profits any additional value to the homestead property brought about by reason of permanent improvements by the purchaser, such additional value to be computed, not at the time the improvements were erected, but at the time of the recovery.

4. A petition brought in the name of the beneficiaries of a homestead estate, seeking to recover realty embraced therein which the head of the family wrongfully attempted to convey, is not void, and is amendable by adding his name as a party plaintiff. It follows that where such a petition is brought within seven years from the date of the attempted conveyance, the law of prescription has no application, notwithstanding more than seven years may have elapsed before the filing of the amendment.

5. In such a case the plaintiffs are not entitled to recover mesne profits for a longer period than four years prior to the filing of the suit.

6. Even if the title to the reversionary interest in homestead property passes under a deed made, while the homestead is in existence, by the person out of whose property the homestead estate was carved, such title can not be asserted in any way until the homestead estate has expired.

7. Some of the foregoing rules were not applied in the trial of the present case, and as this was not done, it should be tried again in the light of what is here laid down.

Argued November 1, — Decided November 30, 1899.

Equitable petition. Before Judge Sheffield. Early superior court. October term, 1898.

W. C. Worrill and *P. D. DuBose*, for plaintiffs.
R. H. Powell and *W. D. Kiddoo*, for defendant.

Cobb, J. On October 11, 1897, Mary E. Taylor, in behalf of herself and as next friend for her five minor children, filed an equitable petition against D. W. James and E. T. James, in which she prayed for a recovery of certain described realty which it was alleged had been set apart to her husband James H. Taylor as a homestead, and which had been illegally sold and was in the possession of E. T. James. By an amendment filed October 8, 1898, James H. Taylor was made a party plaintiff to the case. E. T. James answered the petition, setting up that he was the owner of the property in dispute, by virtue of a deed from James H. Taylor and his wife, dated October 14, 1890. The case came on for trial, and during the progress thereof the plaintiffs announced that they would not ask any decree against D. W. James, and that his name would be stricken from the case. At the trial the following state of facts was disclosed: On January 31, 1871, James H. Taylor filed his application addressed to the ordinary of Early county, praying that an exemption of personalty and a homestead in certain described realty be set apart to him as the head of a family. The realty described in the petition was as follows: Lot number 3, and all that part of lot number 38 lying east of Dry creek in the 28th district of Early county, and an undivided one-half interest in lots numbers 2, 3, and 4 in the 6th district. The surveyor having returned to the court a plat and having filed with the same the affidavit required by law, the ordinary, on February 10, 1871, entered his approval upon the application. On May 16, 1872, James H. Taylor, with the consent of his wife, made an exchange of lands with R. B. Taylor, whereby R. B. Taylor received the lots above referred to in the 28th district and James H. Taylor received the undivided one-half interest of R. B. Taylor in the lots above referred to in the 6th district, and thereafter James H. Taylor and his wife abandoned possession of the lots in the 28th district to R. B. Taylor and took possession of his interest in the lots in the 6th district, and this interest of R. B. Taylor was thereafter held and treated as a part of the homestead estate. On February 26, 1890, James H. Taylor and his wife made application to the judge of the superior court for leave to sell the real estate which had been set apart as a homestead. The application did not describe the property, but referred to the petition for homestead for a description thereof. In this application it was alleged that petitioners "can sell said homestead lands for $3,000, and that they can reinvest said sums in other real estate that will yield a much better income and be worth a greater sum to petitioners and their family." The prayer of the petition was, that an order be passed allowing a sale of the homestead and a reinvestment upon like uses.   D. W. James was appointed guardian ad litem for the minor children, and united with the petitioners in the prayer for a sale of the homestead.   On February 26, 1890, upon this application the judge passed an order directing a sale of the homestead property and that the proceeds thereof be reinvested upon like uses.   After this order had been granted, James H. Taylor entered into an agreement with Elbert Teatt and Gus Thomas, who were negroes, whereby he agreed to sell the homestead lands to them for $3,000 upon credit, and take their notes for the purchase-money, and give them a bond for titles.   Thereafter, the negroes having failed to pay the purchase-money, Taylor entered into an agreement with E. T. James, whereby James was to pay him $2,000 in cash, and he was to deliver to James the purchase-money notes of the negroes above referred to, and also to convey to him the homestead lands, James agreeing to protect Taylor against any rights which the negroes might have under the bond for titles which Taylor had given to them.   James paid to Taylor the amount stipulated, and on the 14th day of October, 1890, Taylor and his wife executed a deed to him conveying lots numbers 2 and 3 and the east half of lot number 4 in the 6th district of Early county, upon an expressed consideration of $2,000; the deed reciting that the lands therein described, with others, had been theretofore set apart as a homestead to Taylor for the benefit of his wife and minor children, and that an order had been granted, after due application in terms of the law, on the 26th of February, 1890, to sell and reinvest, and that the sale was made by virtue of that order. Subsequently to the execution of the deed, James made an arrangement with the negroes to whom Taylor had sold the property, by which the sale to them was rescinded and their notes delivered up to them, and they surrendered the bond for titles to James, which was by him delivered up to Taylor.

The present suit is brought to recover the lands described in the deed from Taylor and his wife to James.   There was evidence tending to show that Taylor had used a portion of the $2,000 paid him by James, in the purchase of necessaries for the support of his family, and that another portion of the

money was used in making a payment on the purchase-price
of certain lands in Randolph county and a house and lot in
Cuthbert, Georgia, but that no title was ever obtained to either
piece of property, for the reason that Taylor, not being able to
pay the balance of the purchase-money, surrendered the possession of the house and lot to the person from whom he had
attempted to purchase the same, and transferred his bond for
titles to the lands in Randolph county to a person to whom he
was indebted for supplies for his family, and that neither he
nor any one of the beneficiaries is now in possession or entitled
to any interest in or possession of either of the pieces of property referred to; that his family did for some time reside in the
house in Cuthbert; that he attempted to farm on the lands in
Randolph county while he was in possession of them, but that
he did not make anything on the same.   The judge submitted
to the jury three questions of fact: (1) How much was paid
by E. T. James to Taylor for the land sued for, at the time it
was delivered?   The answer was, $2,000.   (2) How much was
the land in dispute worth for rent in each of the years, beginning with the year 1891, down to and including the year of
the trial (1898)?   The answer was for various amounts, aggre-
gating $2,972.80.   (3) What is the value of the improvements
put on the land for each year since James took possession?   The
answer was, $75 for each year, aggregating $600.   Upon this
verdict the judge entered a decree, which was in substance as
follows: (1) That upon the payment by E. T. James to the
commissioner of the court, named in the decree, of the sum of
$1,000 principal, and $576.55 interest, within a specified number of days, the sale of the homestead to James be confirmed.
(2) That the commissioner named, or his duly appointed successor, should reinvest the amount paid to Taylor by James under
the order and direction of the judge.   (3) In the event James
fails or refuses to pay over the sum above named, within the
time stated, the plaintiffs recover of the defendant an undivided one-third interest in the lands in his possession, and the
sum of $983.64 mesne profits, and that the title to the other
two-thirds interest in the property be confirmed in James.   The
decree then proceeds to provide for a partition of the land be-

tween the owners of the homestead and James.   (4) In the
event that James should not permit the partition to be made,
then the plaintiffs shall recover the lands described in the petition, without mesne profits, and that writ of possession issue
accordingly. (5) That James pay the costs of the case.   (6)
In the event that paragraph 3 of the decree goes into effect,
the mesne profits therein provided for shall be collected by execution and the money paid into court, to be disposed of or re-
invested as the court may direct.   (7) That no recovery be had
against D. W. James, as the plaintiffs during the trial abandoned the right to proceed against him.   The defendant made
a motion for a new trial, which was overruled.   The case is
here upon a bill of exceptions sued out by the plaintiffs, as well
as upon a bill of exceptions sued out by the defendant.   The
errors assigned in the bill of exceptions of the plaintiffs are as
follows: (1) The court erred in allowing certain amendments
to the defendant's answer pending the trial.   (2) The court
erred in allowing the defendant to amend his answer after the
verdict had been rendered and published.   The amendment
thus allowed in effect set up that the defendant had a prescriptive title to the lands in controversy, and a plea of the statute
of limitations against all rents that had been collected prior to
four years before the filing of the suit.   (3) That the decree
rendered was erroneous, and that upon the verdict and pleadings a decree should have been rendered directing that the
plaintiffs recover the lands in controversy, together with mesne
profits after the value of the improvements as found by the
jury had been deducted therefrom, and the cancellation of the
deed from Taylor and his wife to James.   The errors assigned
in the bill of exceptions of the defendant are: (1) The court
erred in entering any decree at all in the case, as the questions
submitted to the jury were not sufficiently explicit to determine
all of the issues in the case.   (2) The court erred in not holding that James had a perfect prescriptive title to the lands in
controversy.   (3) The court erred in refusing to hold that the
right of the plaintiffs to recover mesne profits was limited to
those accruing within four years prior to the bringing of the
suit.   (4) The court erred in refusing to enter a decree in

favor of James for the reversionary interest of Taylor to the lands in controversy. (5) The court erred in overruling the defendant's motion for a new trial.

1. One of the grounds of the motion for a new trial filed by the defendant assigns error upon the ruling of the court in permitting James H. Taylor to testify that, after the homestead was set apart, he exchanged the interest in the lots in the 28th district for the undivided half-interest of Robert B. Taylor in lots 2 and 3 and one half of lot 4 in the 6th district, and that after such exchange the interest of Robert B. Taylor thus acquired had been held and treated as a part of the homestead estate. The objection to this testimony was, that title to the undivided interest could not be shown by parol, but must be shown by a deed, and that the homestead in that undivided interest could not be shown by parol. We do not think there was any error in admitting this evidence. While Taylor and his wife had no authority to make the exchange without an order of court authorizing it, yet if they thus secured possession of the property which formerly belonged to Robert B. Taylor and treated it as homestead property, it became impressed with the homestead character. The deed under which James claims describes this property as homestead property, and recites that it was made under an order of court to sell it as homestead property; and hence it does not lie in his mouth to complain of the manner in which this fact is proved. If the fact sought to be proved was established, the exchange would certainly be treated as valid as to him, and the property would be regarded as homestead property. It is settled law of this State, that when personalty set apart under the homestead and exemption laws has been sold and the proceeds of the sale invested in other property of like character, the property in which the reinvestment is made becomes impressed with the exemption, and is not subject to levy and sale, notwithstanding the sale is made by the head of the family or the beneficiaries without any authority derived from an order of court. *Wade* v. *Weslow*, 62 *Ga.* 562; *Johnson* v. *Franklin*, 63 *Ga.* 378; *Dodd* v. *Thompson*, Id. 393; *Kupferman* v. *Buckholts*, 73 *Ga.* 778. While we know of no case where this prin-

ciple has been applied to a sale of land, we see no reason why the same is not applicable to that class of property. It has been held, that, if a homestead is sold under proper order, and the proceeds of the sale invested in other lands to which title is taken in the name of the wife, the property is to be treated as homestead property as against one who deals with the same with knowledge of the facts. *Broome* v. *Davis*, 87 *Ga.* 584. As long as Taylor and his wife and the other beneficiaries of the homestead saw proper to deal with the property acquired from Robert B. Taylor as a part of the homestead, it will, as to all other persons who had knowledge of the facts, be treated as properly a part of that estate.

2.   Dealing with the order passed by the judge, authorizing the sale of the homestead, in the light of the allegations in the petition, it can not be otherwise construed than as authority to sell the property only at the price designated in the petition, that is $3,000; and there being nothing in the petition or order indicating that the sale was to be upon credit, or that the land was to be sold in parcels, the order will be construed as authority to sell the property as a whole for $3,000 cash.   Any one dealing with Taylor or his wife in regard to the sale of the land would be bound by the terms of the order.   Especially would this be true when it appears, as it does in the present case, that the deed under which the defendant claimed title to the homestead estate expressly recited that the sale was made under and in pursuance of the order above referred to.

3.   No matter whether we treat James as a direct purchaser from Taylor of the homestead property at the price of $2,000, or as the purchaser of the notes which Taylor had taken from the negroes Teatt and Thomas, the same result is reached, and that is, that James is attempting to set up a contract made with Taylor which is in direct violation of the judge's order, and therefore void.   If James bought a portion of the land for $2,000, when the order authorized only the sale of the land as a whole and for $3,000, of course it needs no argument to demonstrate that Taylor violated the order of the court, and that James is seeking to take advantage of this breach of trust, of which he had at least constructive notice.   If he is simply the

transferee of the notes of the negroes, he stands in no better position; for the sale to the negroes was void, being on credit when the order authorized a sale for cash only. But even if it be conceded that a credit sale was authorized under the order, Taylor had no authority to sell the notes for less than their face value; and hence if James claims as the transferee of these notes, he claims under an unauthorized transfer of the same by Taylor. There is but one way for a person to acquire title to a homestead estate, and that is, under a conveyance made in direct accord with a proper order passed by the judge of the superior court. No matter how we view the status of James in the present case, no one would for a moment contend that he occupies the position which the above rule would require. Such being the case, his possession of the property is wrongful and unauthorized and he may be ejected therefrom at the suit of the beneficiaries, or even at the suit of the head of the family himself, although a party to the proceedings by which the wrongful act was done. If the plaintiffs had sued at law, it is possible they would have been entitled to recover the premises and also mesne profits without abatement or offset; but as they have elected to proceed against the defendant in a court of equity, they must be required to give effect to all of the rights to which in equity and good conscience the defendant may be entitled, notwithstanding the fact that he is himself a wrongdoer. If the sale had not taken place and the beneficiaries had remained in possession of the homestead property, the annual profits of the estate would have gone to their support; and therefore, if it be shown that any part of the money paid by James to Taylor was used in the purchase of necessaries for the family, the amount so appropriated would be in equity a legitimate set-off against the plaintiffs' claim for mesne profits. If it be shown that any portion of the money was used in the purchase of other real property and such real property was still in possession of the beneficiaries, it would not be equitable to allow them to hold such property and also to recover the homestead property which had been sold. *Timothy* v. *Chambers*, 85 *Ga.* 267; *Bazemore* v. *Davis*, 55 *Ga.* 504. The mere fact that there **was** an attempt to acquire property and a payment made on the same out of this money would not raise any equity at all in favor of James, notwithstanding part of the money paid by him had been used in making one of the payments under this contract of purchase. If, however, during the time that Taylor and his family were in possession of this property which they attempted to purchase it afforded a home to the beneficiaries, James would be entitled to a deduction from the mesne profits to be recovered, of whatever amount would be a reasonable rental of the home thus furnished to the beneficiaries during the time they occupied the same. In other words, if James's money furnished to the beneficiaries of this homestead that which the income from the homestead would have furnished them had they been in possession of it, then these beneficiaries must not require of him to pay as mesne profits for that which he has already furnished to them with the money which he has paid to Taylor. If while James was in possession he made improvements of a permanent nature upon the homestead estate, which improvements are still subsisting and their presence upon the homestead estate makes the same more valuable, he would be entitled to a deduction from the mesne profits of such an amount as would represent, at the date of the trial, the increased value of the homestead estate brought about by the erection of such permanent improvements. The plaintiffs are entitled to recover the land in any event. They are entitled to recover mesne profits, but these are subject to the set-offs above referred to.

4. When the suit was filed by Mrs. Taylor and her children, James had been in possession of the property under the deed made to him by Taylor and his wife less than seven years, but at the time that Taylor was made a party the term of James's possession exceeded seven years. It is contended by James that he has a good prescriptive title to the land sued for. When a homestead is set apart to the head of a family, he stands in relation to this property as a trustee clothed with the legal title; and it is not only his right but his duty to protect the homestead estate, and to this end bring an action to recover the same from any one wrongfully in possession. The beneficiaries of the homestead, however, have such an interest in the property

that they may bring an action in their own name to recover the same from any one who is in possession holding adversely to them.   While it is more regular for the head of the family to bring the suit, an action brought by the beneficiaries in their own name is not void, but an amendment adding the name of the head of the family as a party plaintiff is allowable. *Braswell* v. *McDaniel*, 74 *Ga.* 320; *Eve* v. *Cross*, 76 *Ga.* 693; *Pritchett* v. *Davis*, 101 *Ga.* 236, 242, and cases cited.   The cases of *Zellers* v. *Beckman*, 64 *Ga.* 747, and *Shattles* v. *Melton*, 65 *Ga.* 464, in which it was held that the suit must be brought by the head of the family or some good reason shown why this was not done, were dealing with the question as to who was the proper party to bring suit under the act of 1876 (Acts 1876, p. 51), and not with the general homestead law.   The suit by Mrs. Taylor and her children was merely defective; and when an amendment was made adding Taylor as a party, this defect was cured, and being cured, the amendment related back to the beginning of the suit, and the same stood as if it had originally been brought in the name of Taylor.   Such being the case, the question whether James might have acquired a prescriptive title is not involved in the case, as the original suit was filed within seven years from the date that James went into possession.   Especially would this be true in the present case, when the original plaintiffs distinctly allege in their amendment to the petition that at the time of bringing the original suit Taylor refused to sue for the land or to allow the use of his name by them for that purpose, and that the amendment adding him as a party was offered as soon as his consent was obtained.   This seems to bring the case even within the rule laid down in the *Zellers* and *Shattles* cases cited above.

5.   The amendment to the defendant's answer which set up that the plaintiffs would have no right to recover for mesne profits further back than four years from the date of the filing of the suit was demurred to and the demurrer was overruled. Plaintiffs in their bill of exceptions except to the overruling of the demurrer, but as the decision complained of was made on October 13, 1898, and the bill of exceptions was not tendered and certified until February 6, 1899, it is apparent that the ex-

22

ception above referred to is too late to be considered by this court. We must therefore treat the amendment as having been properly allowed. The judge in his decree allowed the plaintiffs to recover mesne profits for the entire time that James had been in possession of the property sued for, and in his bill of exceptions he assigns error upon this decision. The question, therefore, as to whether the four years limitation was properly applicable to the plaintiffs' suit for mesne profits is before us for decision. The code declares that all actions for trespass upon or damages to realty shall be brought within four years after the right of action accrues. Civil Code, § 3898. This section has been held to apply to suits for mesne profits which the plaintiff in an ejectment case is allowed to recover against the defendant by way of damages for the wrong done him. *Lopez* v. *Downing*, 46 *Ga.* 120. The beneficiaries of a trust estate are barred by the statute of limitations in every case where the trustee would be barred. Civil Code, § 3773. The right of action is in the trustee, and the mere fact that he fails to enforce his right and that of his beneficiaries within the time prescribed by law would not give them the right to do so after that time has elapsed. In such a case, if they have any right at all, it is to proceed against the trustee himself for the failure to perform his duty. We see no good reason to hold that this principle would not be applicable to the beneficiaries of a homestead estate. Such an estate is in the nature of a trust estate, and the head of the family is the trustee thereof. The legal title to the property is vested in him, and the beneficiaries have only an equitable interest therein. It is true that, under the decisions of this court, this is such an interest as authorizes the bringing of a suit in their own names to recover the homestead property wrongfully sold, and as a necessary incident of such a suit they can recover for mesne profits; but this is all the more reason for holding that the statute of limitations would run against them. If the statute applies to the beneficiaries of an ordinary trust estate, who have no right of action in themselves but are absolutely dependent upon the will of their trustee in this respect, it would seem for a stronger reason to apply to the beneficiaries of a homestead estate, who can bring suit in their own name. The plaintiffs' right of action in the present case to recover the land was not barred, as we have seen, but the right to recover for mesne profits for a period further back than four years from the time of filing the suit was, and hence the court erred in holding otherwise. See in this connection *Barfield* v. *Jefferson*, 84 *Ga.* 609.

6. The judge committed no error in refusing to decree that title to the reversionary interest in the homestead was in James. While the defendant in his answer prayed for a decree vesting the title to the reversion in him, he was not entitled to such a decree. Even conceding that he acquired title to the reversion under the deed from Taylor and his wife, he can not set up or enforce in any way such title as long as the homestead estate is in existence. It has been held that pending the existence of the homestead estate the reversionary interest of the person entitled to the same is not subject to levy and sale. *Jolly* v. *Lofton*, 61 *Ga.* 154. The case of *Love* v. *Anderson*, 89 *Ga.* 612, seems to rule that a sale of the reversionary interest by the head of the family would not pass the title thereto; and in *Blacker* v. *Dunlop*, 93 *Ga.* 819, it is said that even if a deed made by the head of a family conveying the reversionary interest in the homestead estate passes title, such interest can not be asserted by the vendee during the pendency of the homestead estate.

7. The questions submitted to the jury were not sufficiently full to determine all of the issues made in the case, and the judge should have granted a new trial. Let the case be tried again in the light of what is herein ruled to be the law of the case.

Judgment on each bill of exceptions reversed.　All concurring.

CENTRAL OF GEORGIA RAILWAY CO. *v.* RICKS.

One who purchased a railway-ticket having upon its face an express stipulation that it would be good for passage only during a specified period of time, and who in consideration of its being sold to him at a reduced rate assented to this stipulation, had no lawful cause of complaint against the railway company for ejecting him from a train, after the expiration of that period, upon his refusal to pay fare.

Argued November 2. — Decided November 30, 1899.

Action for damages.   Before Judge Butt.   Sumter superior court.   November term, 1898.

William D. Kiddoo, for plaintiff in error.

LUMPKIN, P. J.   The defendant in error, Ricks, purchased from the agent of the railway company at Americus a ticket, known as a "Sunday excursion ticket," from that point to Macon and return, paying therefor a reduced rate of fare.   Upon the face of this ticket was a stipulation that it was "good for one continuous passage returning to destination until Monday noon next following date of sale, as indicated in margin below, [and] beyond the station scheduled up to that time, conductor will collect fare."   The final limit of the ticket, as indicated upon the margin thereof, was 12 o'clock noon on Monday, March 21, 1898.   The purchaser boarded the train of the railway company leaving Macon at 11:20 a. m. on the day last mentioned, which was scheduled to arrive at Americus at about 2 o'clock that afternoon.   After the hour of 12 o'clock had arrived, the conductor demanded fare of Ricks for the remainder of his journey, and, payment being refused, ejected him from the train at an intermediate station.   He subsequently brought an action against the company and obtained a verdict, and the question here presented is, whether or not the recovery was lawful. In addition to the facts above stated, it appeared at the trial that Ricks was fully aware of the character of the ticket he purchased, and that he assented to the above-mentioned stipulation thereon.   This conclusion was demanded by his own testimony as a witness in the case.   He had, upon a previous occasion, while holding a similar ticket, been ejected from a train of the company because of his refusal to pay fare after the expiration of the time limit of that ticket; and, among other things, testified at the trial now under review that he purchased the very ticket then in question at a reduced price from the regular rates, because of the fact that it was cheaper — necessarily meaning that it was sold at a lower rate than tickets unlimited as to time.   Ricks, therefore, is simply in the attitude of having entered into a contract with the railway company that this ticket should not be good for passage on its trains after 12 o'clock noon of the day upon which he was expelled from the train. Manifestly, therefore, his recovery was contrary to law, for it was in the face of his own agreement, by which he was certainly bound.

This case is clearly distinguishable from that of *Boyd* v. *Spencer*, 103 *Ga.* 828, for the company's defense did not, in this instance, rest upon the idea that it had a right to limit its liability by a mere printed stipulation upon a ticket of which the purchaser did not know and to which he did not assent, but upon the widely different proposition that it was simply enforcing against Ricks an express contract, based upon a valuable consideration, and mutually binding upon him and upon it.

Judgment reversed. All the Justices concurring.

BLUE & STEWART *v.* COLLINS *et al.*

1. The sureties on a constable's bond are not liable for his failure to levy and sell under an execution, when the judgment on which the execution was founded was dormant when placed in his hands.
2. Receipts of payments entered on an execution by the plaintiff therein are not such entries as will prevent the judgment from becoming dormant.

Submitted November 3, — Decided November 30, 1899.

Action on bond. Before Judge Littlejohn. Schley superior court. April term, 1899.

Simeon Blue, for plaintiff.   *C. R. McCrory,* for defendant.

SIMMONS, C. J. It appears from the record, that Blue & Stewart obtained a judgment on the 24th day of May, 1887, against A. J. and I. J. Harrold. Execution was issued on the 19th day of May, 1887. As far as the record discloses, it was not placed in the hands of an officer until sometime in the year 1895, when it was placed in the hands of Barfield, a constable. He failing or refusing to make the money thereon, Blue & Stewart brought suit upon his bond against the sureties, Collins and Lightner, for a breach by the constable of his bond. To this action the sureties filed several demurrers. One of them was, that they were not liable for their principal's failure to execute the process, when the judgment on which it was founded was dormant when placed in his hands. The judge sustained this demurrer, and plaintiffs excepted.

1.   It is clear from the facts disclosed by the record that the judgment was dormant when the execution was placed in the constable's hands. More than seven years had elapsed from the rendition of the judgment, to wit, May, 1887, to January, 1895. It being dormant, the constable had no right or authority to levy the execution issued thereon, and if he failed to do so, the sureties on his bond are not liable for his failure.

2.   But it is alleged that the judgment was not dormant, because the execution had several entries thereon which would serve to keep it alive. The copy in the record does show that there are several entries thereon, and if made by an officer authorized to execute the execution, the judgment would not have been dormant. But, in an amendment to the petition, it is alleged that the entries were made by the plaintiffs in the execution, acknowledging the receipt of certain payments made by the defendant thereon. These entries were not made by an officer authorized to execute the process. The Civil Code, § 3761, requires these entries to be made "by an officer authorized to execute and return the same," in order to prevent the judgment from becoming dormant. The entries, not having been made by an officer authorized to execute and return it, but by the plaintiffs themselves, are not such entries as will prevent the dormancy of the judgment.

Judgment affirmed. All the Justices concurring.

BIVINS *v.* BANK OF RICHLAND.

1. Under the constitution of this State the General Assembly is empowered to provide by law for the appointment of a proper person to preside in cases where the presiding judge of the superior court is disqualified. An act of the General Assembly which makes it the duty of the clerk of the superior court to select some competent attorney practicing in that court to preside in such a case, where the parties do not agree upon some other person to preside, is a due exercise of the power given by the constitution, and is in harmony therewith; and a judgment rendered in a case thus tried is the legitimate outcome of "due process of law."

2. There was no error in refusing to further postpone or continue the case, and the verdict is supported by the evidence.

Argued November 8, — Decided November 30, 1899.

Complaint. Before C. C. Duncan, judge pro hac vice. Dooly superior court. September term, 1898.

Allen Fort, for plaintiff in error. *E. A. Hawkins*, contra.

LITTLE, J. The defendant in error instituted an action against W. W. Shipp as principal, and J. E. Bivins and J. E. D. Shipp as securities, on a promissory note. The defendant Bivins alone pleaded to the action. It appears by the bill of exceptions that the wife of the presiding judge of the circuit, then present, was a sister of W. W. Shipp and J. E. D. Shipp, two of the defendants to the action, but that he was not in any way related to the defendant Bivins. It also appears that when the case was reached the parties failed to agree upon an attorney to preside in the case, and that the clerk of the court designated and appointed C. C. Duncan, a practicing attorney at the bar of said court, to preside as judge pro hac vice. The case proceeded to trial, a verdict was returned against the defendants, and a judgment was entered accordingly. The defendant Bivins made a motion for a new trial, which was overruled, and he excepted.

1. It is complained, in one of the grounds of the motion for new trial, that when the presiding judge announced his disqualification on account of relationship to two of the defendants, the other defendant, Bivins, refused to agree on some member of the bar to preside as judge pro hac vice, and objected to the appointment of an attorney to preside in the place of the judge, by the clerk, for two reasons; first, that the presiding judge was not disqualified, because he was not related to the defendant Bivins, and that the defendants W. W. Shipp and J. E. D. Shipp, to whom he was related, filed no defense to the action; second, because, if the presiding judge was disqualified from presiding in the case, the law under which the clerk acted in appointing the judge pro hac vice was unconstitutional and void. There can be no serious question, in our opinion, that Judge Littlejohn was disqualified from presiding in the case,

Section 4045 of the Civil Code prescribes that no judge of any court can sit in any cause . . where he is related to either party within the fourth degree of consanguinity or affinity, etc. . Two facts are perfectly apparent: J. E. D. Shipp and W. W. Shipp were related to the presiding judge by affinity within the fourth degree, and they were parties to the case. That they filed no defense did not alter their relation to the suit. With or without a defense they were parties, and therefore the judge could not, without the consent of all the parties at interest, preside or give judgment either for or against them; and the plaintiff in error must fail in this contention. He insists, however, that, even if the disqualification existed, the act of the General Assembly which makes it the duty of the clerk of the superior court to select a competent attorney practicing in the court where the case is pending is unconstitutional and void, and the attorney so selected has no power or authority to preside and render a judgment therein, because the constitution provides certain qualifications to be possessed by the judge of the superior court, and the act is in violation of the constitution of the United States because it deprives defendant in this case of his property without due process of law.

It is not necessary for us to enter into a discussion of the abstract question, whether, when the constitution fixes the qualification of a judge of the superior court, and prescribes the manner of his appointment or election, and requires of him an oath of office, some other person not so selected, and without taking the oath of office, may preside as judge of said court. Did the question rest in this case upon such facts alone, it might become a serious one, although this court in former rulings has declared legal the acts of an attorney selected by the parties to preside in a case where the presiding judge was disqualified; and it has also recognized as legal the acts of an attorney selected by the clerk to preside in a disqualified case. *Henderson* v. *Pope*, 39 *Ga.* 361; *Clayton & Co.* v. *Wallace*, 41 *Ga.* 268. In *Drawdy* v. *Littlefield*, 75 *Ga.* 215, it was expressly held, that where both parties agreed upon an attorney to preside as judge pro hac vice in place of the regular judge of the circuit, who was disqualified from presiding, a judgment rendered by such judge pro hac vice was constitutional, although rendered prior to the constitution of 1877. In *Beck* v. *Henderson*, 76 *Ga.* 360, it was held, where the judge was disqualified and the parties had not tried or made any effort to agree on an attorney to preside, that it was proper for the clerk to appoint a competent attorney to do so. See also *Steam Laundry Co.* v. *Thompson*, 91 *Ga.* 47. By the constitution of this State, art. 6, sec. 4, par. 9, it is expressly provided that "The General Assembly may provide by law for the appointment of some proper person to preside in cases where the presiding judge is, for any cause, disqualified." By section 4329 of the Civil Code, which is a codification of the act of 1878, the General Assembly has provided that in such cases when the parties do not otherwise agree, the clerk of the superior court, or in his absence the deputy-clerk, may select some competent attorney practicing in that court to preside. So that the selection, as provided in the code, is based on direct authority of the constitution itself. It is no reply to say that the constitution fixes the qualification of a judge of the superior court, because the person presiding is not a judge of the superior court; he is an attorney at law, vested with the power to preside in a case in which the judge of that court is disqualified, when selected by the clerk. In our opinion, therefore, a judgment rendered by a judge pro hac vice, selected by the clerk under the circumstances named in the section of the code, has, in the case in which he presides, the same validity and effect as would a judgment rendered by the judge of the court in a case where he is not disqualified, and the exercise of the power given to the judge pro hac vice in no way contravenes the constitution of this State; and an attorney pro hac vice, deriving his authority so to preside directly from the constitution of the State, exercises the powers of a judge strictly in accord with law and in the due exercise of its process; and the act which authorizes his action is not in any way obnoxious to the constitution of the United States.

2. There was no error in refusing to further postpone or continue the case, and the verdict is supported by the evidence.

Judgment affirmed. All the Justices concurring.

HANESLEY v. BAGLEY.

1. One who contracted, for a stipulated commission, to obtain for another a loan of money to be secured by a mortgage upon land belonging to the latter, is not entitled to compensation for services rendered in finding a person willing and ready to make the desired loan on condition that the applicant therefor had a good title to the land in question, when it appears that the latter in fact had such a title, and that the loan was refused because of an alleged cloud thereon which was in law no cloud at all.

2. Applying the above rule to the undisputed facts of the present case, the verdict was right and ought to stand, whether the charges complained of were correct and applicable or not.

Argued November 2, — Decided November 30, 1899.

Complaint. Before Judge Littlejohn. Sumter superior court. May term, 1899.

R. L. Maynard, for plaintiff.

COBB, J. Hanesley sued Mrs. Bagley in a justice's court upon an account for commissions in negotiating a loan for $1,000. The defendant filed a plea alleging that she was not indebted to the plaintiff in any amount whatever. The case went by appeal to the superior court, and upon the trial there it appeared that Mrs. Bagley had employed Hanesley to procure her a loan of $1,000, to be secured by a first mortgage upon a tract of land owned by her, and that Hanesley had procured a lender who was ready to advance the money, but that on account of an alleged cloud on the title of Mrs. Bagley to a portion of the land offered by her as security, which she declined to remove, the lender refused to complete the contract of loan. Hanesley contended that he had performed every service which his contract with the defendant required of him, and that for this reason he was entitled to his commission. The jury returned a verdict in favor of the defendant, and the plaintiff's motion for a new trial having been overruled, he excepted. If Hanesley complied with his part of the contract and secured a lender who was willing to advance the money to Mrs. Bagley upon the property which she tendered as security, and she without just cause declined to accept the money, Hanesley would be entitled to recover. If, on the other hand, the failure to com-

plete the contract was not due to any fault on her part or to
any real defect in her title, then Hanesley would not be entitled
to recover simply because, for reasons satisfactory to himself,
the lender procured by him declined to consummate the loan.
See in this connection *Davis* v. *Morgan*, 96 *Ga.* 518. It therefore becomes necessary to determine whether the failure to complete the loan was due to any reason for which the defendant
could be properly held responsible. It appears from the record
that the title of Mrs. Bagley to all of the land offered by her
as security, except a tract of fifty acres, was satisfactory to the
lender. The defendant and those under whom she claimed had
been in uninterrupted possession of this fifty acres for thirty-
seven years, the paper title under which she claimed originating in 1861 in a deed in which Charles A. Walker was the
grantor. In 1887 the administrator of Charles A. Walker sold
and conveyed to one Clay as the property of his intestate a lot of
land which embraced the fifty acres in question. It is claimed
that this deed is a cloud upon the title of Mrs. Bagley which
it was her duty to remove, and that, having failed to do so,
the lender was justified in law in refusing to make the loan,
and hence that Hanesley was entitled to recover his commission. We do not think that, under the facts disclosed by the
record, the deed from the administrator of Walker to Clay constitutes such a cloud upon the title of the defendant as would
render her liable under her contract with the plaintiff upon
her failure to remove the same. It would not be necessary to
invoke the aid of a court of equity to remove it, and therefore
such a deed would be no obstacle in law to the completion of
the loan by the lender, the undertaking of the defendant being simply to tender as security a tract of land of which she
was the owner.

In *Thompson* v. *Etowah Iron Co.*, 91 *Ga.* 538, it was held
that, "In order for outstanding conveyances to be a cloud upon
title, it is necessary that they of themselves, or in connection
with alleged extrinsic facts, should constitute an apparent title;
that is, one upon which a recovery could or might be had
against the true owner were he in possession and relying upon
possession alone. Anything which would force him to attack

the adverse title, or to exhibit his own, would be a cloud; anything which would not have this effect, would be no cloud." Applying this rule to the facts of the present case, it becomes at once apparent that the outstanding conveyance in Clay was no cloud whatever upon the title of Mrs. Bagley. He took the same at a time when there was in possession a person who was holding adversely to the grantor in the conveyance to him. He has never been in possession under the deed; and if he were to bring an action of ejectment against Mrs. Bagley, or any one else in possession of the fifty acres of land, his action would necessarily fail, as he could in no event recover upon this deed, there being no evidence whatever of any facts which, taken in connection with the deed he holds, would make out a prima facie case in his favor. Moreover, his case would fail for the reason that, at the time of the administrator's sale under which he holds, the administrator was not only not in possession of the land but the same was in the possession of another person holding adversely to such administrator; and for this reason, if for no other, Clay acquired no title under his deed. Civil Code, § 3457; *Heard* v. *Phillips*, 101 *Ga.* 691. In any view of the case, therefore, the deed held by Clay was not such a cloud upon the title of the defendant as that a court of equity would entertain an application to remove the same; and therefore when she tendered the property as her own she complied with her contract with the plaintiff, and it was due to no fault of hers that the loan was not consummated. Of course, the lender procured by Hanesley had a right to demand a title which was satisfactory to himself; and if he declined to make the loan merely on account of a supposed defect in the title of the person applying for the loan, it was Hanesley's misfortune. He can not demand his commission from his client, under his contract with her, until he either actually obtains the money or shows that the failure to complete the loan is due to some reason for which she alone is in law responsible. The verdict was demanded by the evidence; and if any errors in charging were committed, they were immaterial.

Judgment affirmed. All the Justices concurring, except Simmons, C. J., who was disqualified.

BIRCH, executor, *v.* ANTHONY *et al.*

109
121

A contract between husband and wife made with the intention of promoting a dissolution of the marriage relation existing between them is contrary to public policy, illegal and void, and will not, after the husband's death, bar the widow's right to a year's support and dower.

Argued November 6. — Decided November 30, 1899.

Petition for injunction. Before Judge Felton. Bibb county. August 1, 1899.

Dessau, Harris & Birch and *W. H. Harris*, for plaintiff.
Harris, Thomas & Glawson, for defendants.

FISH, J. W. B. Birch, as executor of the will of E. R. Anthony, brought his equitable petition against Mrs. Belle Anthony, the widow of his testator, and others, in which he sought, by injunction, to prevent Mrs. Anthony from obtaining a year's support and dower from the estate of her deceased husband, upon the ground that she had entered into the following contract with her husband:

"Having positively determined to leave my husband, E. R. Anthony, and deny him all marital rights whatever, I hereby in consideration of four hundred dollars ($400) this day paid me by him I relinquish all claims of any kind whatever I have on him as wife.

Witness my hand and seal this day of   1894.
          Legal   L. S.

Providing this is a divorce granted said Anthony by 1st of April, 1895.   Mrs. F. B. Anthony.
                                        David Milne.
                                        Isabella Milne." ·

It appeared from the evidence that David Milne and Isabella Milne signed the instrument as witnesses.

The trial judge refused to grant the injunction, and the executor excepted. While there were several points made in the case, we think it necessary to deal with only one of them, and that is, whether the contract above set forth barred the widow's rights to a year's support and dower. It was contended by counsel for plaintiff in error, that the four hundred dollars

mentioned in the contract was paid, upon the separation between Anthony and his wife, as permanent alimony, and that
she was therefore not entitled to a year's support or to dower,
as under our law, in a case of voluntary separation, the husband may voluntarily by deed make an adequate provision for
the support and maintenance of his wife, and thus bar her
right to permanent alimony and any further interest in his
estate, in her right as wife. This contention might possibly
be sound but for a part of the contract, which, in our opinion,
renders the whole of it illegal and void.

Whatever else may have been contemplated by the parties
to this contract, it manifestly appears that it was their intention to promote a dissolution of the marriage relation existing
between them. By reference to the contract it will be seen
that it was apparently complete and ready to be signed when
the condition was added providing, in effect, that it should be
legal if a divorce should be granted to the husband on or before a fixed date. This provision renders the whole contract
illegal, as it is well settled that a contract intended to promote
a dissolution of marriage is contrary to the policy of the law,
illegal and void. 2 Am. & Eng. Enc. L. (2d ed.) 127; 9 Id. (1st
ed.) 920; 1 Bish. Mar. & Div. § 76; 2 Id. § 696; Adams *v.*
Adams, 25 Minn. 72; Weeks *v.* Hill, 38 N. H. 199; Everhart
v. Puckett, 73 Ind. 409; Sayles *v.* Sayles, 21 N. H. 312; Goodwin *v.* Goodwin, 4 Day (Mass.), 343; Cross *v.* Cross, 58 N. H.
373; Muckenburg *v.* Holler, 29 Ind. 139; Hamilton *v.* Hamilton, 89 Ill. 349; Phillips *v.* Thorpe, 10 Oreg. 494. In Sayles
v. Sayles, supra, Wood, J., said : "The object of the agreement
was to bring about a dissolution of the marriage contract, and
to put an end to the various duties and relations resulting
from it. Any contract having any such purpose, object, and
tendency, can not be, in law, sustained, but must be regarded
as being against sound public policy, and consequently illegal and void. The marriage relation is one to be encouraged
and maintained, when formed. Such is the well-settled policy
of the law, and its dissolution or determination is not to be left
to depend upon the caprice of the parties. If determined, it
must be done in accordance with some positive enactment of

law, and in due course of judicial proceedings." We can not see that it matters at whose instance the proviso was added to the contract between Anthony and his wife, or that it was, as claimed by the plaintiff in error, impossible for the divorce to have been obtained within the time specified therein, as the illegality of the proviso entered into and permeated the whole contract and rendered it void. It follows, therefore, that such an illegal and void contract could be no bar to Mrs. Anthony's right to a year's support, or her right to dower, out of the estate of her deceased husband; and that there was no error in refusing to grant the injunction.

Judgment affirmed. All the Justices concurring.

MORRIS *v.* THE STATE.

The act proved in this case did not constitute a violation of so much of section 390 of the Penal Code as makes criminal a "notorious act of public indecency." To render any act notorious and public it must have been committed at a place where it might have been seen by more than one person.

Submitted November 6,—Decided December 1, 1899.

Certiorari. Before Judge Russell. Gwinnett superior court. September term, 1899.

Oscar Brown, for plaintiff in error.
C. H. Brand, solicitor-general, contra.

SIMMONS, C. J. Morris was put upon his trial in the city court of Gwinnett, on an accusation charging that he did "publicly and indecently expose his secret or private parts of his person in the presence of one Mrs. Ella Benton." He was convicted, and sued out a writ of certiorari to the superior court. Upon the hearing of the writ in that court, the certiorari was overruled and the conviction affirmed; whereupon he filed his bill of exceptions to this court, alleging error in the judgment of the superior court overruling the certiorari. There are various allegations of error set out in the petition for certiorari; but, in the view we take of the case, it is only necessary to discuss the one which alleges that the verdict is contrary to the

law and the evidence. The evidence of the offense, in substance, is that the accused was plowing in a field 175 yards
from the house wherein Mrs. Benton resided; that there was a
railroad embankment between the house and where the accused
was plowing, waist high; that the ground between the house
and the field was not cleared; that the accused stopped his
plow, leaned against the plowstock, unbuttoned his pantaloons,
pulled up his shirt, exposed his private parts to her view, and
made a gesture for the purpose of calling attention to the same.
Several witnesses testified that she could not possibly have seen
the private parts of the accused from where she stood in the
house to where she said he stood when the act was committed.
But she swore positively that she did see him expose his private parts. It is contended by the counsel for the plaintiff in
error that, admitting her evidence to be true, the evidence did
not make out the offense as defined in § 390 of the Penal Code.
That section reads as follows: "Any person who shall be guilty
of open lewdness, or any notorious act of public indecency, tending to debauch the morals, or of keeping open tippling-houses
on the Sabbath day, or Sabbath night, shall be guilty of a misdemeanor." It will thus be seen that this section embraces
three offenses: open lewdness, a notorious act of public indecency, and keeping open tippling-houses on the Sabbath. In
order to constitute the offense of which Morris was convicted,
the evidence must show that it was notorious and public. This
definition of public indecency seems to have been taken from
the common law. We find the same definition in the Penal
Code as early as 1817, when the penal laws were codified by
the legislature. Schley's Digest, 380. The construction put
upon this clause by the English courts was, that the act must
be in a public place and where more than one person could
have seen it; and that the crime was not committed by expos-
ing the person to only one individual.

Some of the cases hold that it was sufficient if one person
saw the exposure and others might have seen it. In the case
of R. *v*. Webb, 1 Den. Cr. C. 345 (*338), it was held, "An indecent exposure in a place of public resort, if actually seen only
by one person, no other person being in a position to see it, is

not a common nuisance." Parke, B., said: "In 1830, a French master was tried before me at York on an indictment, averring an indecent exposure, and charging a common nuisance. It was proved that he was seen from an opposite window by a maid servant, but there was no proof of his having been seen by any one else. I thought the exposure to the girl only did not amount to an indictable offence, and directed the jury to consider whether he was in such a position that the passers-by in the street could have seen him had they happened to look; if the jury were of that opinion they ought to find him guilty." Page 351 (*344). In a note to this case it is said: "With regard to the point decided in the principal case, it seems that the law does not consider public decency to be represented by one person in a public thoroughfare. The presence of one person only is not deemed the presence of the public; and the possible presence of others is too remote a possibility for the law to recognize. But if others be actually present, even though they do not see the offence actually committed, the law recognizes the risk of their seeing it as sufficiently proximate to be dealt with as a reality." Page 354 (*347). See also R. v. Watson, 2 Cox Cr. Cas. 376; 12 Am. & Eng. Enc. L. (2d ed.) 538; 1 Bish. Cr. L. §§244, 501, 1125, et seq. According to these authorities, the facts in this case do not make out the notorious and public indecency which the statute makes a criminal offense. The act, if committed at all, was in a field, not on a public road or near by. Only one person saw the indecent exposure, and there is no evidence in the record that others could have seen the same. Indeed, the accusation charges that it was committed in the presence of Mrs. Benton, without charging that it was in a public place; or, if in a private place, that others could have seen the exposure as well as Mrs. Benton. We do not mean to hold that this offense can not be committed elsewhere than in a public road or street, or a place where the public usually resort; but we do hold that the act must be notorious and public, and it can not be so before one person alone. Nor do we mean to hold that the act proved would not be indictable as open lewdness under the section above cited. See in this connection

Com. *v.* Waddell, 128 Mass. 52, s. c. 35 Am. Rep. 357; State
v. Juneau, 88 Wis. 180; Williams *v.* People, 67 Ill. App. 344.
Judgment reversed.   All the Justices concurring.

CENTRAL OF GA. RWY. CO. *v.* BRINSON & INGRAM.

It is indispensable to the rendition of a valid and binding judgment against
a garnishee, condemning a debt which he owes to the plaintiff's debtor,
that the situs of the debt should be within the jurisdiction of the court.
As a general rule the situs of a debt is at the place where the creditor is
domiciled.

Argued October 31, — Decided December 1, 1899.

Garnishment.   Before Judge Butt.   Muscogee superior court.
May term, 1899.

Little & Burts, for plaintiff in error.
J. H. Martin and *W. H. McCrory,* contra.

COBB, J.   Tony Tarver Sr., a resident of the State of Alabama, owed Brinson & Ingram, residents of Muscogee county,
Georgia, a debt which was contracted in that county and State
and was to be paid there.   They instituted proceedings by attachment, in a justice's court of Muscogee county, against Tarver as a non-resident, and on October 4, 1897, without having
served him personally, caused summons of garnishment to be
served upon the Central of Georgia Railway Company, seeking
to condemn a debt due by that company to Tarver on a judgment which the latter had recovered on September 22, 1897,
in the circuit court of Russell county, Alabama.   This judgment was affirmed by the Supreme Court of Alabama in the
fall of 1898, and thereafter Brinson & Ingram took judgment
by default against Tarver in the attachment proceeding in
the superior court of Muscogee county, to which the garnishment and the attachment proceedings had been by consent appealed.   The Central of Georgia Railway Company is a corporation created and existing under the laws of this State, but
operates lines of railway in the State of Alabama by its permission, one of which lines extends through the county of Rus-

sell in that State. After the affirmance of the judgment against it recovered by Tarver in Alabama, the railway company paid to Tarver the amount of such judgment. On the trial of the garnishment proceeding it was agreed that the only issue to be heard and determined by the court was whether or not the debt represented by the judgment which was recovered by Tarver against the railway company in Alabama was subject to the process of garnishment served upon it in this case. The judge decided that it was, and the railway company excepted.

It is a necessary prerequisite to the rendition of a judgment in a garnishment proceeding, condemning a debt, that the situs of the debt should be within the jurisdiction of the court. The question as to what is the situs of a debt in a given instance has become involved in some confusion by the numerous decisions upon this point. Mr. Rood in his work on Garnishment lays down the rule, which seems to be supported by numerous decisions, that, "Wherever the garnishee could be sued by the defendant for the demand, he may be charged as garnishee on account of it." § 245, and cases cited. On the other hand a large number of cases hold that the situs of a debt is the place where the debt is due and payable, which is impliedly the residence of the creditor. 2 Shinn, Att. & Gar. § 626, and cases cited; Waples, Att. & Gar. § 100. See also the able opinion of Mr. Chief Justice Brickell of the Supreme Court of Alabama, in the case of Louisville & Nashville Railroad Company *v.* Nash, 23 So. Rep. 825, and the authorities therein referred to. While this court has never held that this was the only rule for determining the situs of a debt, it applied this test in the cases of *Kyle* v. *Montgomery*, 73 *Ga.* 337, and *Wells* v. *East Tennessee Railroad Company*, 74 *Ga.* 548. In the latter case it appeared that Wells resided in Tennessee, and the railroad company was indebted to him for labor performed in that State. His creditor sued out in this State an attachment proceeding against him as a non-resident, and garnished the railway company. The company answered that it owed Wells for services performed wholly in Tennessee, that he had brought suit in that State to recover the amount due him for these services, and that, notwithstanding it had pleaded the pendency of the garnish-

ment proceeding, he had recovered judgment against it. While
it appeared that the railroad company was acting under charters from each of the States through which its road passed, it
was dealt with as constituting but one corporation ; and it was
held that the garnishment proceeding could not be maintained,
because the debtor had neither effects nor a debt due to its creditor in this State, nor had he any effects on which an attachment could be levied or to which the jurisdiction of the courts
of this State could attach.   In the opinion Justice Hall distinguishes the case of *Kyle* v. *Montgomery,* supra, saying that in
that case "the defendant in attachment rendered service to a
Georgia corporation under a contract entered into and wholly
performed here.   The debt was due to him from a party in this
State over whom our courts had jurisdiction; he had effects
here subject to attachment for his debts.   In the case at bar,
however, the very foundation for the attachment is wanting; the
debtor has neither effects nor a debt due to him from the garnishee in this State; he has not and never had here any effects
on which an attachment could be levied; there is nothing to
which the jurisdiction of our courts could attach."   It follows
necessarily from this decision that the superior court of Muscogee county was without jurisdiction to render a judgment
against the plaintiff in error in the present case.

Judgment reversed.   All the Justices concurring.

KNOWLES v. COACHMAN.

1. When a case in a justice's court is appealed to and tried by a jury in that
   court, and the losing party carries it by certiorari to the superior court,
   no ruling made by the magistrate in the trial from the result of which
   the appeal to the jury was taken can be reviewed by the superior court.
2. Where in a petition for certiorari it is alleged that the magistrate erred
   in overruling certain specified objections to the introduction in evidence
   of the depositions of a named witness, and the answer of the magistrate,
   which is not excepted to, while stating that objections were made to such
   depositions and overruled, fails to disclose that these objections were those
   set forth in the petition, or what they were, such assignment of error can
   not be considered by the reviewing court.
3. The case not being one the determination of which necessarily depended
   upon a question of law which must have finally governed it, and there

being disputed issues of fact involved, the superior court erred in rendering a final judgment therein.

Submitted November 2, — Decided December 1, 1899.

Certiorari.   Before Judge Sheffield.   Randolph superior court.   May term, 1899.

W. C. Worrill, for plaintiff in error.   *Arthur Hood,* contra.

FISH, J.   1. Coachman sued Knowles upon a promissory note, in a justice's court.   The magistrate rendered a judgment in favor of the plaintiff.   The defendant appealed the case to a jury.   The jury found a verdict in favor of the defendant, and judgment was entered accordingly.   The plaintiff took the case by certiorari to the superior court, and upon the hearing in that court the judge sustained the certiorari, set aside the judgment of the court below, and rendered a final judgment in favor of the plaintiff; whereupon the defendant excepted.   In the petition for certiorari the plaintiff alleged that the justice of the peace, who presided at the trial, erred in overruling a demurrer to a plea filed by the defendant.   It was not alleged whether this ruling was made by the magistrate when he tried the case or when it was tried by the jury, but it is perhaps fairly inferable from the allegations of the petition that the ruling was made in the latter trial.   But from the answer of the magistrate it appears that this ruling was made by him, not when the case was tried by the jury, but when it was tried by the magistrate himself.   As the answer was neither excepted to nor traversed, the statements contained therein are to be taken as true.   A trial upon an appeal to a jury in a justice's court, like other appeal cases, is a de novo investigation.   Everything which occurred in the preceding trial, from which the appeal is taken, is wiped out, and the case proceeds as though it had never been tried before, no ruling therein upon the previous trial being of any binding force or effect.   When this case came on for trial by the jury, neither the plaintiff nor the magistrate was bound by the ruling made on the previous trial.   The only rulings of which the plaintiff could complain in his petition for certiorari were such as were made when the case was tried, upon appeal, by the jury.   As it does not appear from the answer to the certiorari that on the trial by the jury any ruling in reference to the defendant's plea was made or invoked, the superior court could not consider that ground of the petition for certiorari which alleged that the magistrate erred in overruling the motion of the plaintiff to strike the defendant's plea.

2. The petition for certiorari alleged that the magistrate, when the case was before the jury, erred in not sustaining certain specified objections made by the plaintiff to the introduction in evidence of the depositions of a witness named Browne Cornelison. While the petition for certiorari states what these objections were, the answer of the magistrate simply states that objections were made, by the plaintiff, to the interrogatories of this witness, without stating, or in any manner indicating, what these objections were. This court can not, and the judge of the superior court could not, legally know what objections the plaintiff made to the depositions of this witness, because the statements in the petition for certiorari, with reference to what these objections were, are not verified in any way by the answer of the magistrate. *Gartrell* v. *Linn*, 79 *Ga.* 700. Upon the trial of a certiorari case, it is to the answer of the magistrate, or judge of the lower court, and not to the petition for the writ of certiorari, that the superior court must look, in order to ascertain what occurred upon the trial of the case below. If the answer is not full enough, the plaintiff in certiorari, by pursuing the course provided for by the law, can have it perfected. If the plaintiff desires to controvert any statement contained in the answer, his remedy is to traverse the truth of the same. In the present case, in order to have got the objections which he made to the depositions of this witness before the superior court, the plaintiff should have filed exceptions to the answer of the magistrate, specifying the defects in the same, and in this way have procured an order requiring the magistrate to perfect his answer. The decision in *Marchman* v. *Todd*, 15 *Ga.* 25, is not authority to the contrary of what is now ruled. The actual holding there both by the superior court and this court was, that the answer was sufficient, and therefore further answer was unnecessary. The remark that the petition should be assumed as true if not fully answered was really obiter.

3. The case not being one the determination of which necessarily depended upon a question of law, which must have finally governed it, and there being disputed issues of fact involved, the superior court could not lawfully render a final judgment therein.

Judgment reversed. All the Justices concurring.

MIZE v. AMERICUS MFG. & IMPROVEMENT CO.

109
116

There was no error in overruling a motion to set aside a judgment on the ground that one of the jury by whom the verdict upon which such judgment was rendered was disqualified, the remedy in such a case being to file in due time a proper motion for a new trial.

Submitted November 8, — Decided December 1, 1899.

Motion to set aside judgment. Before Judge Littlejohn. Sumter superior court. February 23, 1899.

Blalock & Cobb, for plaintiff in error.
E. A. Hawkins, contra.

LEWIS, J. Plaintiff in error filed his motion, in the superior court of Sumter county, to set aside a judgment which had been rendered against him in that court, the ground of the motion being, the jury that rendered the verdict in said case was an illegal one, because one of the jurors was related to a stockholder in the plaintiff company within the fourth degree. It appears from the record that the judgment sought to be set aside was rendered upon a verdict in favor of the Americus Manufacturing and Improvement Company against R. J. Mize, at the May term, 1897, of Sumter superior court. A motion was made by the defendant below for a new trial, and one of the grounds in the motion was the relationship of the juror, which is relied on in this case to set aside the judgment. That motion was dismissed by the trial judge, whose judgment was affirmed by this court. 106 *Ga*. 140. On the hearing of this motion to set aside the judgment, the court overruled the same, and error is assigned thereon. Section 5362 of the Civil Code declares: "When a judgment has been rendered, either party may move in arrest thereof, or to set it aside for any defect not amendable which appears on the face of the record or pleadings." The grounds of this motion were not based upon any defect which appears upon the record, but upon the alleged fact touching the disqualification of a juror, upon which the record throws no light whatever. The motion was really an objection to the verdict itself rather than to the judgment, and the remedy for attacking such a defect in the verdict is by motion for a new trial. This remedy was actually adopted by the plaintiff in error, and his effort thus to set aside the verdict failed by a dismissal of his motion. In *Pulliam* v. *Dillard*, 71 *Ga.* 598, it was decided that a motion to set aside a judgment, like a motion to arrest it, must be based on some defect apparent on the face of the record. The two differ only in respect to the term at which each must be severally made. In *Hamilton* v. *State*, 97 *Ga.* 216, it appeared that a motion was made in arrest of judgment, based on the ground that only seventeen grand jurors acted in finding the indictment. It was held that the motion was properly dismissed, because it was not predicated upon defects appearing on the face of the record. See also *Rountree* v. *Lathrop*, 69 *Ga.* 539; *Clark's Cove Co.* v. *Steed*, 92 *Ga.* 440. The fact that a juror who tried a case was disqualified on the ground of relationship does not render a verdict void, but only voidable, and the verdict can be set aside only in the method prescribed by law. In the *Hamilton* case above cited there was, we think, more reason to hold that the indictment was a nullity, not being found by the requisite number of grand jurors, than there is to declare that this verdict was a nullity because one of the jurors finding the same was disqualified. We conclude, therefore, the court did not err in overruling this motion, and the judgment is accordingly affirmed. *Judgment affirmed. All the Justices concurring.*

ROBERSON v. SIMONS.

1. Where land is rented to a tenant for one year at a stipulated rental, and after the expiration of the term the tenant, without further contract, remains in possession and pays the rental annually at the agreed rate, a tenancy from year to year is created.

2. If at the end of a given year, without giving the landlord any notice of an intention to terminate the tenancy, the tenant abandons the premises, but leaves in possession another, who has previously been his subtenant, and if the latter then remains on the property for an entire year and a portion of the succeeding year, the original tenant is liable to pay the landlord rent for these two years, at the contract rate.

Submitted November 3. — Decided December 1, 1899.

Certiorari. Before Judge Spence. Stewart superior court. April term, 1899.

B. F. & G. Y. Harrell, for plaintiff in error.

FISH, J. In March, 1888, Simons sued Roberson, in a justice's court, for the rent of certain land, for the years 1896 and 1897, at the rate of $23.00 per annum. The magistrate rendered a judgment in favor of the plaintiff; there was an appeal to a jury in the justice's court, and a verdict rendered for the plaintiff. The defendant took the case, by certiorari, to the superior court, where the certiorari was overruled and dismissed, and he excepted. As the verdict was for the plaintiff, in considering the questions involved, wherever there is a conflict in the evidence, we take the case as made by his testimony. In 1888 Simons rented the land to Roberson, for $23.00 per annum. The contract between the parties was in parol, and the duration of the tenancy was not specified. Roberson went into possession of the premises and, without any further contract, remained in possession of the same for a number of years, annually paying to Simons the rent agreed upon. Some years prior to 1895 Roberson put his son in possession of the land as his tenant, and still continued to pay the rent to Simons until the beginning of the year 1896, after which he paid no more rent. He never gave Simons any notice whatever of a desire to terminate the tenancy. Roberson's son remained in possession of the premises until April, 1897. Under these circumstances, was the defendant liable to the plaintiff for the rent of the land for the years 1896 and 1897? No time being specified in the contract for the duration of the tenancy, the law construed it to be for the calendar year. Civil Code, § 3132. When, after the expiration of the tenancy created by the express contract of the parties, without any further agreement the tenant, with the consent of the landlord, remained in possession of the rented premises, paying for the same the rent stipulated in the contract for the first year, a tenancy from year to year arose by operation of law.   Woodfall's Landlord and Tenant, 358, *222; Taylor's L. & T. §§ 55, 56; Wood's L. & T. § 26; 12 Am. & Eng. Enc. L. 675 et seq.   See also Brown v. Kayser, 60 Wis. 1, in which Cassoday, J., cites many cases.

As far back as Wright v. Darby, 1 T. R. 161, Lord Mansfield said: "If there be a lease for a year and by consent of both parties the tenant continue in possession afterwards, the law implies a tacit renovation of the contract.   They are supposed to have renewed the old agreement, which was to hold for a year.   But then it is necessary, for the sake of convenience, that if either party should be inclined to change his mind, he should give the other half a year's notice before the expiration of the next, or any following year."   Tenants from year to year have always been held entitled to notice.   See cases cited in monographic note to Stedman v. McIntosh, 42 Am. Dec. 126.   Indeed, at the ancient common law such tenancies were the only ones in which a notice was required.   Ib.   In 12 Am. & Eng. Enc. L. 679, it is said: "A tenancy from year to year, or other term having periodicity, is terminated by notice to quit."   See also 2 Taylor's L. & T. § 467; 1 Wood's L. & T. §§ 26, 28; 1 Woodfall's L. & T. 534, *335.   In tenancies from year to year the giving of notice is mutual, and the tenant can not leave without giving the same notice of his intention that is required of the landlord to end the tenancy. See cases cited in the note to Stedman v. McIntosh, supra, on page 139; also Critchfield v. Remaley, 21 Neb. 178.

So it is beyond question that a tenant from year to year, in order to terminate the tenancy, must give notice of his intention to quit.   Whether in this State such notice must be for six months as required at common law, or for one month as required in section 3133 of the Civil Code from tenants at will, it is not necessary to decide, as in this case no notice whatever was given to the plaintiff by the defendant of an intention to terminate the tenancy.   In the absence of such notice, the plaintiff certainly had the right, under the law, to treat the tenancy as continuing, and to recover of the defendant the rent for the year 1896, at the agreed rate. We think he also had the right to recover rent for the year 1897. While, without actual notice to the landlord, mere abandonment of the premises, at the expiration of any year of the tenancy, might perhaps be sufficient to bring home notice to him of the tenant's intention to terminate their relationship, so as to prevent the landlord from holding him liable for rent beyond the year immediately succeeding such abandonment, we think in this case the landlord was entitled to recover the rent for both the years 1896 and 1897; for until April, 1897, there was nothing to put the landlord upon even implied notice that his tenant had abandoned the rented premises. Roberson's son, who was put in possession of the land by his father, as his tenant, some years before 1895, held possession of the same until April, 1897, and up to 1896 Roberson continued to pay his landlord, Simons, the annual rent. So far as Simons knew, the son was still the tenant of the father in 1896 and 1897. With the son, who presumably still held for his father, in possession of the land, the mere non-payment of rent to Simons for the year 1896 was not sufficient to put him upon implied notice that his tenant had abandoned the premises. We apprehend that it is not unfrequently the case that a tenant remains in possession of rented premises for a year or more without paying the annual rent for the same. There was no error, therefore, in overruling and dismissing the certiorari.

Judgment affirmed. All the Justices concurring.

RALPH *et al. v.* WARD.

1. The notice which the Civil Code, § 4790, requires partitioners of realty to give to all parties of the time of executing the writ need not be in writing.
2. While tenants in common of realty may agree among themselves to divide the same and assign to each his proportionate part, and while, if such a division is made and each tenant takes possession of the part assigned to him, such agreement will bind them, their heirs and privies, yet if such an agreement is made and not fully executed by each one taking possession of his part, and thereafter some of the tenants in common execute mortgages upon their undivided interests in the whole tract, and these

mortgages are foreclosed and the undivided interests sold by the sheriff under the mortgage fi. fas. to the mortgagee who had no notice or knowledge of the division, he is not bound by such division ; nor can a tenant who did not mortgage his interest set up as against the purchaser, or a vendee of the latter, his long and uninterrupted possession of that part of the land of which he had taken possession under the agreement of division.

Argued November 4, — Decided December 1, 1899.

Partition.   Before Judge Spence.   Stewart superior court. April term, 1899.

J. B. Hudson and *B. F. Harrell & Son,* for plaintiffs in error. *Arthur Hood* and *Clarke & Harrison,* contra.

SIMMONS, C. J.   Mrs. Ward filed her petition for partitioning a certain tract of land in Stewart county, claiming that she owned a three-fourths interest in it, and that the heirs of Isham Ralph owned the other one-fourth interest.   Partitioners were appointed in accordance with the code by the judge of the superior court ; and they proceeded to partition the land and set aside to Mrs. Ward her three-fourths interest.   They made their return to the superior court in accordance with the provisions of the code, and in that return they stated that all parties at interest had received the notice required by law.   At the term at which the return of the partitioners was to be made the judgment of the court, the administrator of Isham Ralph, and his heirs at law, moved to set aside the return of the commissioners, on the ground that they had not received the eight days notice provided for in the code.   Testimony was taken upon this question, which shows that they had received verbal notice of the time and place when the partitioners were to meet and partition the land ; but none of them had received written notice.   The trial judge overruled the motion to quash the return of the partitioners, holding that it was not necessary that parties should have written notice, but that verbal notice of the time and place, etc., was sufficient.   To this ruling the defendants excepted.

1. Section 4790 of the Civil Code requires that partitioners, after they have been appointed by the order of the court, shall give all the parties eight days notice, if possible, of the time

of executing the writ.   The section is silent as to whether the
notice shall be verbal or written; but inasmuch as there is no
provision made for any return of such notice, or any entry
thereof on any of the papers in the proceedings, we think that
verbal notice was sufficient when the return of the commissioners alleges that notice was given.   If written notice had been
given, it would have been just as easy for the defendants to
have said that they had not received that, as it was for them
to have said that they had not received verbal notice.   The
section provides no means nor any manner for the making of
any return, or the entry thereof, by the partitioners.   It is not
like the service of process in a suit, where the original is retained in the office, the clerk issues a copy, and the sheriff
serves the copy and makes a return on the original.   We therefore think that the verbal notice given by the partitioners to the
defendants was sufficient, especially when they appeared and
moved to set aside the return because of the want of written
notice.   They at least had notice sufficient to cause them to
attend the court and make the objections above alluded to.   If
defendants appear in accordance with the notice they have received and contest with the plaintiff, that notice is sufficient.
We therefore think the trial judge was right in denying the
motion to set aside the return of the partitioners, and to have
them to re-execute the writ of partition and give the defendants written notice.

2. It seems from the record that J. L. Wimberly and C. M.
Lowe conveyed these two lots of land now in dispute to Isham
Ralph, Nelson Ralph, Stephen Ralph, and Wilson Wright, by
a deed dated 31st day of December, 1879.   It further appears
that Wilson Wright, one of the tenants in common, had mortgaged his undivided one fourth interest in the land to E. H.
Keese; that Keese had foreclosed the mortgage upon Wright's
undivided interest, and the fi. fa. was levied upon Wright's
undivided interest, which was sold by the sheriff and purchased
by Keese, the mortgagee.   It further appears that Stephen
Ralph had mortgaged his one-fourth undivided interest to
Keese; that the mortgage had been foreclosed and this interest
sold, and purchased by Keese; and that Nelson Ralph had also

mortgaged his one-fourth undivided interest to Keese, which
had been sold, and bought in by Keese.   Keese sold and conveyed his three-fourths undivided interest to Mrs. Ward, the
plaintiff.   On the trial of the case the defendants proposed to
show that, after they purchased from Wimberly and Lowe,
Wright failed to pay his part of the purchase-money, and Isham
Ralph paid it; that they made a division of the lands among
themselves; and that lot 95 was assigned in the division to
Isham Ralph, the intestate of Hawes, administrator, and the
father and grandfather of the other defendants; and that he
went into possession thereof, and remained in possession until
his death.   They also proposed to show that Keese, the mortgagee, knew that Isham Ralph was in possession of lot 95.   The
court excluded this evidence, and defendants excepted.   In our
opinion, there was no error in rejecting this evidence.   While
it is true that tenants in common may agree among themselves
to divide the land and assign to each tenant his proper portion
thereof, and that a division so made, if acquiesced in, will bind
them, their heirs and privies, yet if they make a private or
secret division among themselves, and after this division some
of them execute mortgages to their undivided interest in the
whole tract, and these mortgages are foreclosed, and at the sale
under the mortgage fi. fas. the mortgagee becomes the purchaser without notice or knowledge of the division which has
been made, he is not bound by such division; and the administrator of the tenant in common who did not mortgage his interest can not set up this division against the purchaser, and
show that in accordance with the division his intestate entered
upon a part of the tract and remained in possession from that
time until his death.   And this is especially so where the mortgaged property was advertised by the sheriff as being the one-
fourth undivided interest of the mortgagor, and the sale was had
in accordance with this advertisement.   Each tenant has a
right to occupy his proportionate part of the land owned by
him as tenant in common, and his long and uninterrupted possession of that part of the tract so owned by him would not be
notice to a purchaser that a division had been made, and that
he occupied it under the division, especially when no deed

passed between the tenants in common, and the deed under which they claim as such tenants was on record, granting the land to them as such tenants in common. Under the views above expressed, the proper result was reached, without regard to the character of the evidence.

Judgment affirmed. All the Justices concurring.

CENTRAL OF GEORGIA RAILWAY CO. *v.* HALL.

.109 86
f114 76

1. It is within the discretion of the judge on the trial of a civil case to allow the jury to disperse at dinner and at night while the evidence is being submitted, and before they retire to make up their verdict, without the consent of the parties to the case, no motion being made contra, or cause shown for not allowing the separation.
2. In the trial of an action against a railroad company for injuries done to property at a public crossing which was half a mile from the depot where the train started, it was not error to give in charge to the jury "the crossing law" as contained in §§ 2222 and 2224 of the Civil Code.
3. The verdict, as written off under the order of the court, is not so excessive as to require a new trial.

Argued November 4, — Decided December 1, 1899.

Action for damages. Before Judge Littlejohn. Sumter superior court. May term, 1899.

J. B. Hudson and *W. D. Kiddoo*, for plaintiff in error.
L. J. Blalock, *W. P. Willis*, and *J. A. Hixon*, contra.

SIMMONS, C. J. At a point some half a mile below the depot in the city of Americus, Hall's team and wagon, which was loaded with one ton of guano, were run over by one of defendant's engines at a public crossing within the city limits. The wagon was destroyed, one of the mules rendered entirely useless for service, and the other so badly injured that he was of very little use thereafter. The ton of guano was practically scattered to the winds, very little of it being saved. The evidence is clear that the servants of the company did not observe the "crossing law" contained in §§ 2222 and 2224 of the Civil Code, so far as the checking of the speed of the train was concerned. There is a conflict in the testimony as to whether the bell was rung or not.   Hall brought his action to recover damages for the injury which he alleged he sustained on account of the negligence of the servants of the railroad company. Upon the trial of the case, before the testimony was concluded, the judge allowed the jury to disperse for the purpose of procuring their dinners, and also at night to allow them to return to their homes.   This was done, as the motion for new trial alleges, over the protest of counsel for the defendant at the dinner hour, and without his consent when they were allowed to disperse at night.   The trial resulted in a verdict for $400 for the plaintiff; and a motion for a new trial was made, which was overruled, and the defendant excepted.

1. The motion complains that the judge allowed the jury to disperse, over the protest of counsel and without his consent. When this case was being argued on these two grounds, it was admitted that the protest mentioned in the motion for new trial was a private protest to the judge.   This court has held that private communications between the judge and counsel are not matters that can be reviewed here.   *Grant* v. *State*, 97 *Ga.* 790 ; *Stancell* v. *Kenan*, 33 *Ga.* 56.   So we will consider the motion merely as if the jury were allowed to disperse without the consent of the counsel.   This is not an open question in this court. As early as the case of *Stancell* v. *Kenan*, supra, decided August, 1861, this court held that it was a matter of discretion for the trial judge as to whether he would allow the jury to disperse or not during the trial of the case.   In discussing this question, Jenkins, J., said : "Is it, then, erroneous in the court to permit a special jury, engaged in a protracted trial of a civil cause, to separate whenever the court takes a recess for necessary refreshment, no motion being made contra, or cause shown for not doing so?   We think not.   It is a matter of practice that may well be submitted to the sound discretion of the court, the usual caution being given to the jurors not to converse with any one touching the case during such separation."   And this seems to be the practice in other jurisdictions. 2 Thompson on Trials, § 2548, and cases there cited; 12 Am. & Eng. Enc. L. (1st ed.) 374, and cases cited.   It may be argued, however, that to make a motion to the court to keep the

jury in their room during the trial would prejudice counsel and his case before the jury. That, perhaps, is true, but counsel, if he desired to make such a motion, could request the court to have the jury retire, and then make it, and show his reasons for desiring the jury to be kept together. If the reasons were sufficient, no judge, in our opinion, would deny the motion. If he should refuse it, then it would be a subject-matter of review in this court; because it would have been made in open court and a decision pronounced thereon.

2. Under the facts disclosed by the record, there was no error in giving the law in relation to the duties of railroad companies in approaching public crossings. It was argued here that this law was inapplicable to the facts of the case, as the crossing was so near the starting-point of the train that it would be impossible to comply with the law. We understand from the record and the argument of counsel that this crossing where the injury was inflicted was some half a mile below the depot from which the train started. It was held in the case of *Harris* v. *Central Railroad*, 78 *Ga.* 526 (5), that the statute does not require that a train started at or upon a public crossing should be checked and kept checked while passing over that crossing. This was held for the reason that the train could never pass over the crossing if it was checked and kept checked. Where the crossing is a sufficient distance from the starting-point of the train to allow it to get under way, we think that the law is applicable, as was held in the case of the *E. T., Va. & Ga. Ry. Co.* v. *Markens*, 88 *Ga.* 60. We agree with the learned counsel that this law which requires trains to check and keep checking when approaching crossings is a hard one, and that it is impossible for the railroads of the country to transact the business of the country and obey it. It was passed about fifty years ago, before the people appreciated the necessity of rapid transit in travel and in freight. If the law were duly obeyed by the locomotive engineers, I am informed that it would take twelve hours, or more, to run a passenger-train from Atlanta to Macon, a distance of about one hundred miles. Still, it is the law of the land, and the courts must enforce it, however hardly it may work upon the business in-

24

terests of the country if it should be observed, or upon the railroads when they violate it. Where the servants of the railroad company fail to observe it and any person or property is injured upon the crossing, the company can make no defense except that the injury was done by the consent of the person injured; or that he could have avoided the injury by the observance of ordinary care; or that his negligence contributed to it, in the way of mitigation of damages. *A. & W. P. R. R. Co.* v. *Newton,* 85 *Ga.* 517. Two of these defenses were set up in this case: 1st, that the driver of the wagon could have prevented the injury by the exercise of ordinary care. 2d, by his own negligence he contributed to the accident. These matters were, doubtless, submitted to the jury under proper instructions from the court, and they must have found that the driver did observe proper care, and that no negligence of his contributed to the injury.

3. The jury found a verdict for $400. This was forty dollars more than the highest proved value of the property, including expenses in curing the mule, etc. The court directed this amount to be written off, which was done by the plaintiff. The amount thus written off left the amount of the verdict within the proved value of the property, including expenses, etc. The trial judge being satisfied with the verdict as written off, this court can not say that it is so excessive as to require a new trial.

Judgment affirmed.   All the Justices concurring.

MAYOR etc. OF MOULTRIE v. PATTERSON.

A court of equity will not interfere by injunction to restrain the execution of a municipal ordinance of a criminal nature, on the ground of the invalidity of such ordinance, nor on the further ground that the plaintiff is exempt from the operation of the same. The person affected has a full and adequate remedy at law to test the validity of the ordinance, as well as the question of his exemption from its operation.

Submitted November 8,—Decided December 1, 1899.

Injunction. Before Judge Hansell. Colquitt superior court. September term, 1899.

McKenzie & McKenzie, and *J. A. Wilkes,* for plaintiff in error.

LITTLE, J.　Patterson presented his petition to the judge of the superior court, alleging that in June, 1899, the Mayor and Aldermen of the City of Moultrie passed an ordinance prohibiting the sale of beef, mutton, pork, and fish within the limits of the City of Moultrie, except in the city market, and a violation of the terms of said ordinance was punishable by a fine in the discretion of the mayor.　Petitioner alleges that he is a disabled, indigent Confederate soldier, and was possessed of the necessary certificates which allowed him to peddle and do business in this State without a license; that in August, 1899, he was arrested by the marshal of the City of Moultrie for a violation of the terms of said ordinance, was tried, convicted, and fined.　He further alleges that the ordinance is invalid, and, if it is not, that the certificates issued to him empowered him to sell meats in the incorporation of the City of Moultrie and to be immune from arrest and interruption in his business.　He further alleges that if he continues to ply his said business he will be constantly arrested and fined.　He prays for an injunction restraining the Mayor and Aldermen of the City of Moultrie from in any way interfering with his business, and from arresting him, from arraigning him in the police courts, or from fining or imprisoning him, and from the collection of such fines as have already been imposed.　Defendant demurred to the petition, among other grounds, because a court of equity has no jurisdiction to restrain the enforcement of a criminal ordinance by injunction, and because a court of equity has no right to prevent prosecutions for any criminal offense in the violation of municipal ordinances by injunction.　These are the only questions which we find it necessary to consider.　The doctrine is laid down in the 2d volume of High on Injunctions, § 1244, that "A court of equity will not, therefore, interfere by injunction to restrain municipal officers from prosecuting suits against complainants, or from interfering with their business because of their violation of municipal ordinances which are alleged to be illegal, since the question of the validity of such ordinances does not properly pertain to a court of equity, when complainants have a perfect remedy at law, if the ordinances are invalid, by an action to recover damages for the injury sustained." Citing 10 Paige, 539; 77 N. C. 2. In 2 Beach on Injunctions, § 1289, it is declared, that "An injunction will not be granted to prevent the enforcement of a municipal ordinance on the ground of its alleged illegality; for if a criminal prosecution should ensue upon its violation, its validity would then come directly before the courts." Citing 109 N. C. 21.

In the case of *Phillips* v. *Stone Mountain*, 61 *Ga.* 386, the plaintiffs in error filed their bill against the municipal authorities, praying that they be restrained from trying, convicting, and fining them for the violation of the provisions of an ordinance which the plaintiffs alleged to be void, and which materially restricted their business. It was charged and admitted that it was the intention of the municipal authorities to strictly enforce its provisions. Justice Bleckley, in delivering the opinion in that case, said: "Injunctions, or orders in the nature of injunction, are not granted by courts of equity to restrain proceedings in criminal matters," citing Eden on Inj. 66; 2 Vesey Sr. 396; Hilliard on Inj. 2, 269; Kerr on Inj. 2; 30 Ala. 135. Further in the opinion he says: "Chancery takes no part in the administration of criminal law. It neither aids the criminal courts in the exercise of jurisdiction nor restrains or obstructs them." In the case of *Garrison* v. *Atlanta*, 68 *Ga.* 64, an injunction was sought to restrain the municipal authorities of the City of Atlanta from enforcing an ordinance which declared that no cattle of any kind should be allowed to run at large upon the streets, for the enforcement of which a penalty by fine or imprisonment was provided against the owner upon conviction. The chancellor held that injunction did not lie to restrain proceedings of this character; and the court in that case held that: "Injunction will not be granted to restrain a criminal proceeding." See also 1 Spelling on Extraordinary Relief, § 71. In the case of *Gault* v. *Wallis*, 53 *Ga.* 677, this court said: "We know of no principle of equity jurisprudence which confers upon a court of equity jurisdiction to interfere with the administration of the criminal laws of the State by injunction or otherwise. For a court of equity to assume jurisdiction in criminal cases, and enjoin the judgments of the courts, would be a novel and dangerous precedent to establish." See also *Paulk* v. *Sycamore,* 104 *Ga.* 24. In the case of the *City of Atlanta* v. *Gate City Gas Light Company,* 71 *Ga.* 106, which was also a case wherein it was sought to enjoin the enforcement of a municipal ordinance, this court ruled that equity would not interfere by injunction with the prosecution of a criminal proceeding not touching the enjoyment of property; that it would do so where it was evident that private property and civil rights were invaded by such means; and, to sustain the ruling there made, quoted from Kerr on Injunctions, 2, as follows: "But if an act which is also criminal touches also the enjoyment of property, the court has jurisdiction, but its interference is founded solely on the ground of injury to property." In this case the validity of the ordinance is attacked, and it is urged also that the defendant has a license to engage in the business, notwithstanding the municipal ordinance. Neither of these questions is or ought to be cognizable in a court of equity. The plaintiff in error can have his rights adjudicated otherwise than by seeking the interposition of the restraint which equity imposes only in cases where it is necessary to do so in order to protect some right which is in jeopardy and which can not otherwise be fully protected.

Judgment reversed. All the Justices concurring.

HENDERSON, marshal, *v.* HEYWARD.

What is known as the "general welfare" clause in a municipal charter does not authorize the passage of an ordinance making it penal for one who has lawfully purchased, without the limits of the municipality, alcoholic liquors, to receive the same therein without paying a specific tax of a given amount for the privilege of so doing. The above is true notwithstanding the sale of such liquors is absolutely prohibited within the limits of such municipality.

Argued November 20, — Decided December 1, 1899.

Habeas corpus. Before Judge Harris. City court of Cartersville. July 1, 1899.

109
116
116
———
109
e124

John W. Akin, for plaintiff in error.

James B. Conyers and *Bennett J. Conyers,* contra.

COBB, J. Heyward was arrested under a warrant charging him with the violation of an ordinance passed by the municipal authorities of the City of Cartersville, of which the following is a copy:

"Whereas, this being a prohibition city and county by a vote of the people, and, after their best efforts to protect themselves from the curse of intoxicants, the shipment of vinous, malt, and distilled liquors continue to be made into our community, to the injury and detriment of the morals, good order, prosperity and general welfare of this community, and should be prevented or controlled; therefore the Mayor and Aldermen of the City of Cartersville, in the exercise of the general welfare, police, and other powers vested in them by the laws and the charter of the said city, and to accomplish the purposes heretofore enumerated, do enact and ordain as follows:

"Section 1. That on and after the 4th day of March, 1899, it shall be unlawful for any person or persons, corporation or company, to receive from any common carrier or person any package, jug, demijohn, or bottle of vinous, malt, or distilled liquors in said city, until he, she, or they have paid a specific tax of five dollars on each gallon or fraction thereof. Said specific tax must be paid to the treasurer of the city, and a receipt of the treasurer must be presented to any common carrier or person before the delivery of such packages of intoxicants.

"Section 2. Be it further ordained by the authority aforesaid, that any person or persons, company or corporation, who shall receive or have delivered to them any package or packages of distilled, vinous, or malt liquors, without first procuring and exhibiting the receipt of the treasurer for the specific tax on such package or packages of intoxicants aforesaid, shall, on conviction thereof, pay for each violation of this ordinance a fine of fifty dollars or be worked thirty days in the chain-gang of the city, either or both at the discretion of the court.

"Section 3. Be it further ordained that any express company, railroad company, or other carrier public or private, or any agent or employee thereof, who shall deliver to any person in said city any of the packages hereinbefore enumerated, without having produced to such carrier the receipt from the treasurer hereinbefore provided for, shall also be subject to the same penalties prescribed herein for violation of this ordinance.

"Section 4. Provided, that this ordinance shall not apply to the bringing and delivery, by one citizen of said city, to another citizen of said city, of not exceeding one quart of spirituous liquors for medicinal purposes, to be furnished only upon the prescription of a sober, reputable physician that the same is necessary and to be used for medical purposes only."

Section 5 repeals conflicting laws.

While in custody Heyward applied to the judge of the city court of Cartersville for a writ of habeas corpus, alleging in his petition that the ordinance which he was charged with having violated was invalid, for the reason that the municipal authorities had no power to pass the same, and that therefore he was held in illegal custody. Upon the return of the writ a hearing was had, and a judgment rendered discharging the petitioner from custody, on the ground that the ordinance was void. To this judgment the marshal excepted.

Counsel for plaintiff in error did not expressly concede that the ordinance in question could not be upheld as an exercise either of the taxing or license power of the municipal authorities of Cartersville, but his entire argument was directed to the establishment of the proposition that the passage of the ordinance was a legitimate exercise of the police power. If we regard the amount required by the ordinance to be paid, as a condition precedent to the reception and delivery of the liquors therein enumerated, as a tax upon property, it must fail as such; for it is neither ad valorem nor uniform. Nor can it be regarded as a specific tax or the imposition of a sum in the nature of a license fee, because under its charter the City of Cartersville has authority to impose such a tax or license fee only upon an occupation or business, and the buying of a single vessel containing whisky certainly can not be properly regarded as an occupation or business. We pass, therefore, to a discussion of the question as to whether the ordinance can be upheld as a valid exercise of the police power of the municipality.

It is conceded that the authorities had no express charter authority to pass the ordinance in question; but it is contended that it had the power under the general welfare clause of its charter, which is in the following language: "The mayor and aldermen shall have power to pass all ordinances that they may consider necessary to the peace, good order, health, prosperity, comfort and security of the city and the citizens thereof, not inconsistent with the constitution and laws of this State and of the United States." The police power of a State may be exercised by the General Assembly directly, or indirectly through the medium of the subordinate public corporations of the State. It may be that the State would have a right to prohibit the purchase of whisky. That the State has a right to prohibit absolutely the sale of whisky is no longer an open question, either in this court or in the Supreme Court of the United States. *Perdue* v. *Ellis*, 18 *Ga.* 586; *Hill* v. *Dalton*, 72 *Ga.* 314; Mugler *v.* Kansas, 123 U. S. 623. None of the decisions of this court, however, go to the extent of holding that a law prohibiting the sale of liquor in a designated territory has the effect of destroying entirely all property right in alcoholic liquors which may be brought into such territory. On the contrary, it has been expressly held that the fact that the sale of liquor was prohibited in a designated part of the territory of the State does not destroy the right of a person to own such an article within such territory. *Fears* v. *State*, 102 *Ga.* 274.

It may be contended with great force that if the State, notwithstanding it recognized a property right in alcoholic liquors, can under its police power entirely destroy the right of the owner of such liquors to sell or dispose of the same within the limits of the State, which would, in some instances, be a practical confiscation of the property, it has the power to declare that no person shall by purchase come into possession of such property within the limits of the State. Laws prohibiting the sale of whisky are upheld as constitutional upon the ground that its sale is against the best interests of the public at large, and is a business which, if not inherently evil, is of such a nature that its presence is a constant menace to the peace and

good order of society, as well as the welfare of individuals.
If this be true, it would seem to follow that the State might
enact any law which would effectually prohibit the traffic.   A
law prohibiting the sale would, if effectually enforced, prohibit
the buying; and so also the prohibition of the purchase would
likewise prohibit the sale.   The prohibition of the sale, therefore, puts a ban upon the entire traffic.   Of course a law making penal the sale would not, without more, make penal the
buying; but the practical effect of such a law, if enforced would
be to prohibit the buying.   It would seem to follow, therefore,
that the State might go further than it has already gone, and
make penal the buying.   But be this as it may, we are clear
that a municipal corporation can not, without express legislative authority so to do, pass any ordinance making penal the
buying of alcoholic liquors from one lawfully authorized to
sell the same.   It may be laid down as a general rule, that, in
addition to its express powers, a municipal corporation can
only exercise those which are necessarily or fairly implied in or
incident to its express powers, and those that are indispensable
to the declared objects and purposes for which the corporation
was created.   1 Dill. Mun. Cor. § 89.   The power to pass a
law making penal the purchase of intoxicating liquors is certainly not indispensable to the purpose for which the City of
Cartersville was incorporated; there is no express grant of authority to this effect; and hence the power is wanting, unless
it can be implied from its general welfare clause above quoted.
A municipal corporation has no power to adopt ordinances for
the prohibition or regulation of the sale of liquors, unless expressly authorized to do so, or unless such ordinances fairly
and legitimately fall within the scope of the powers conferred
upon them in general terms.   Black, Intox. Liq. § 220.   As
an instance of the strictness with which the powers of municipal corporations over the subject of liquors have been construed, see *Hill* v. *Decatur*, 22 *Ga.* 203.   In that case, notwithstanding it appeared that the commissioners of the town of
Decatur had authority "to restrict, prohibit, and regulate the
sale, vending, and distribution" of intoxicating liquors; "provided, no license to retail spirituous liquors shall exceed fifty

dollars," it was held that the commissioners had no power to prohibit absolutely the sale of liquor, and that they had authority only to grant a license upon the payment of a fee not exceeding fifty dollars. In *Sanders* v. *Commissioners*, 30 *Ga.* 679, it was held that the power "to regulate the rates of tavern licenses" does not confer the power to grant licenses; there being in existence a different system of issuing such licenses. It was further ruled that the power to grant tavern licenses was not embraced in a general clause of a town charter conferring upon it the power of general legislation for itself; Judge Stephens assigning as a reason for the latter ruling that "The courts will not infer that the legislature intends to authorize a local departure from a general policy of the State, unless the local exception is expressed in specific terms."

In the case of *Mayor of Leesburg* v. *Putnam*, 103 *Ga.* 110, it was held that neither the general welfare clause usually found in municipal charters, nor the special power "to license and regulate the management of barrooms, saloons," etc., includes the power to establish and operate under municipal agency a dispensary for the sale of spirituous and malt liquors. This decision was made at a time when it could not be said to have been against the general legislative policy to operate dispensaries; for a number were being operated in the State under direct sanction of the General Assembly. But the court construed the grant of power strictly, and said that a dispensary was neither a barroom nor a saloon in legislative contemplation. If the general welfare clause of a municipal charter would not authorize the city authorities to establish and operate a dispensary as a means of regulating and restricting the sale of liquors, it is difficult to see upon what principle such a clause would authorize the passage of an ordinance prohibiting the purchase of such liquors, or interfering with the right to receive the same after a purchase from one who was lawfully authorized to sell. The one would be no less a regulation than the other. It would seem, therefore, to follow from these decisions that municipal corporations would not, without express legislative sanction, have authority to prohibit either the selling or buying of intoxicating liquors within their limits. They may, of course, regulate to a certain extent the traffic in such liquors, but even then their powers, under the decisions above referred to, are not very broad under the usual general welfare clauses found in municipal charters. If the rule is so strict as regards the sale of whisky, which the General Assembly has seen fit to deal with as being within the police power of the State, and which under the settled public policy of the State has been either prohibited altogether or allowed under the most rigid regulations, how much stricter ought it to be as regards a subject with which the General Assembly has never seen fit to deal in any way whatever. Whenever the General Assembly has by direct enactment, or by its settled public policy derivable from the various statutes passed from time to time, brought within the police power of the State any particular subject, then the municipal authorities of a town or city would seem to have the power, under the usual general welfare clause in municipal charters, to deal with such subject by proper ordinance, limited only by the established rule that they can not deal with an act which is declared to be a violation of the criminal laws of the State. See in this connection 1 Dill. Mun. Cor. § 329. The sale of liquor is absolutely prohibited in some of the counties of this State. In other counties its sale is only permitted under licenses granted by the proper authorities; in still others liquors are sold under governmental agency. In each of such localities the General Assembly directly brings within the police power the subject of the sale of this article, by expressly prohibiting it on the one hand, or by regulating its sale on the other. Having thus declared that the sale of liquors is a matter legitimately within the police power of the State and having passed regulations in reference to the same, it necessarily follows that when it grants to a municipal corporation the power usually conferred upon such corporations, they may deal with the sale of liquors within their limits as a subject which is within the police regulation of the State; and therefore ordinances passed for the purpose of furthering this end are legitimately within the authority of a municipal corporation under its general welfare clause. Such is what we understand to be the reason at the foundation of the decisions of this court in *Paulk* v. *Syca-more*, 104 *Ga.* 728, *Brown* v. *Social Circle*, 105 *Ga.* 834, and *Papworth* v. *Fitzgerald*, 106 *Ga.* 378. These decisions were departures from the strict rule of construction employed in the earlier cases, and we think, under the principle announced in them, a municipal corporation may, under authority of its general welfare clause, pass ordinances, within reasonable limits, dealing with the subject of the sale of intoxicating liquors.

But the General Assembly never has seen proper to deal in any way whatever with the subject of the purchase of intoxicating liquors, except as such subject may grow incidentally out of the subject of the sale. The General Assembly has never passed any law making penal the purchase of liquors. The policy of a State is to be ascertained from its published statutes and laws. There never having been in force any law making penal the purchase of intoxicating liquors within this State, it may fairly be said that such a law would be a departure from its settled public policy; and any such departure must commence with the General Assembly itself, either by a direct law to this effect, or by granting to some subordinate public corporation of the State express authority to make such a departure. The purchase of liquor from one who is himself violating the law in making the sale is, although not a crime under the law of this State, certainly such a transaction as is contrary to public policy. However, the purchase of liquor in this State from one who is lawfully authorized to make the sale is an act which in its nature is neither criminal nor contrary to public policy. It therefore follows that the reception by the purchaser of liquor so bought is not an act which can be legitimately dealt with by the authorities of a municipal corporation as an act within the police power of the State, in the absence of express power so to do. It necessarily follows from the foregoing, that when the General Assembly gave to the City of Cartersville the power embraced in its general welfare clause above quoted, it did not confer upon it authority to pass the ordinance now under consideration. It is true that the ordinance does not in express terms prohibit absolutely the buying of liquor; and even if the condition annexed to the privilege of buying does not practically amount to prohibition, it certainly has the effect of deterring a person from exercising and hampers a person in the exercise of a right which is neither prohibited by express law nor which can be said to be in any way contrary to the public policy of the State, as it is at this time established. The ordinance does not purport to deal exclusively with the subject of the reception of liquor from one who has no authority to sell the same. On the contrary, taking into consideration the entire ordinance, the conclusion is inevitable that the purpose of the ordinance is to deal with the subject of the reception of liquors by one who has lawfully purchased the same without the limits of the city. So construing it, it is void for want of authority in the municipal legislature to pass it. The judge of the city court did not err, therefore, in ordering that the petitioner be discharged from custody.　*Judgment affirmed. All the Justices concurring.*

HAMILTON *v.* MUTUAL BENEFIT LIFE INS. CO.

1. Where upon default in the payment of a premium due upon a policy of life-insurance, the company, as was its right to do under the terms of the policy, applied the net reserve, less certain indebtedness due the company, to the credit of the insured at the date of such default, to "the purchase of non-participating term insurance for the full amount insured by" the policy, and the insured lived longer than such term insurance had to run, no recovery can be had upon the policy.

2. When under the terms of such a policy it appeared that the "non-participating term insurance" would be in force a period of time fixed by the "company's rate published and in force at" the time such term insurance was to be granted, an objection to parol evidence offered to show what were the company's published rates for such insurance, on the ground that "the construction of the contract was for the court," was not meritorious.

Argued October 30,—Decided December 2, 1899.

Action on insurance policy. Before Judge Butt. Muscogee superior court. November term, 1898.

C. J. Thornton, A. E. Thornton, and *O. M. Colbert,* for plaintiff. *Brannon, Hatcher & Martin,* for defendant.

COBB, J. This was an action upon a policy of life-insurance issued by the defendant on October 2, 1891, upon the life of John C. Hamilton, in the sum of $2,000, payable to Caroline Hamilton, the wife of the insured and the plaintiff in the present case. The uncontradicted evidence establishes the following facts: The insured died March 13, 1895. Two annual premiums were paid on the policy, but default was made in the payment of the third premium due September 19, 1893. On this date the "net reserve" to the credit of the insured on the books of the defendant company was $38.04. The company had loaned the insured on his policy $14.22, and this amount, together with the agreed rate of interest thereon, deducted from the net reserve left to his credit the sum of $18.04. The policy provides that when after two full annual premiums shall have been paid it shall become void solely on account of non-payment of any premium, the net amount due the insured at the date of the default shall, upon surrender of the policy and request by the insured, be applied to the purchase of "paid-up" insurance, that is, insurance upon which no further premiums are to be paid, in whatever amount the sum due him will purchase under the terms of his policy. The policy further provides that if no request for paid-up insurance is made, the sum due the insured "shall be applied by the company, as a single premium at the company's rate published and in force" at the date of the default, "to the purchase of non-participating term insurance for the full amount insured." The evidence showed that the insured did not surrender his policy and request a paid-up policy in compliance with that provision of the policy first above referred to; and it further shows that, under the company's published rates, extended or term insurance was granted to the insured for a period of 328 days from September 19, 1893.

1. From the above-recited facts it will be seen at once that the controlling question to be decided is for what period of time under the terms of the policy the insurance continued in force after the default in payment of the premium. The only portion of the policy bearing upon this matter is that set out above, which provides that the period of time the term insurance shall be granted is determined by the "company's rate

published and in force" at the time the policy became void for non-payment of premium. There being uncontradicted evidence that according to this rate the insurance was in force for only 328 days after this time, and the insured having lived until March 13, 1895, the insurance was not in force at the date of his death. There could, therefore, be no recovery for the plaintiff, and the granting of a nonsuit was proper.

2. The defendant introduced parol evidence to show for what period of time under the company's published rates the extended or term insurance granted to the insured was in force. The plaintiff objected to this evidence, on the ground that "the construction of the contract was for the court." The policy did not undertake to set out the periods of time for which extended insurance would be granted, and hence there was no room for construction as to this matter. The objection urged to the admissibility of the evidence was, therefore, not meritorious. Whether or not it should have been excluded for any other reason we do not decide.

Judgment affirmed. All the Justices concurring.

CENTRAL OF GEORGIA RAILWAY CO. *v.* HAMMOND.

Where, pending the trial of an action against a railway company, the jury, with the court's permission, had dispersed for the night, and one of them was treated to a drink of intoxicating liquor and a cigar, and was also slept with by a person who had not only assisted the plaintiff's counsel in striking the jury and in conducting the case but who was also a witness therein for the plaintiff, and himself directly interested in its result, for the reason that he had a case against the same defendant, in which he claimed damages arising from the same alleged act of negligence upon which the plaintiff's action was predicated, the court, on having its attention called to these facts, ought to have sustained a timely motion for a mistrial, made by the defendant's counsel. Upon principles of sound public policy, and to the end that the purity of jury trials may be preserved unimpaired, any verdict against the defendant should, under such circumstances, be set aside, whether the same is affirmatively shown to be wrong or not.

Argued November 4. — Decided December 2, 1899.

Action for damages. Before Judge Littlejohn. Sumter superior court. November term, 1898.

William D. Kiddoo and *J. B. Hudson*, for plaintiff in error.
Blalock & Cobb, W. P. Wallis, and *J. A. Hixon,* contra.

LEWIS, J.   Upon the trial of this case in the superior court of Sumter county, the plaintiff in error moved for a mistrial, on the ground of misconduct of the jurors, and especially on account of the courtesies and favors received by Howard, one of the jurors, from one Hall.   The court took cognizance of the fact that Howard was a juror, and that Hall had been declared disqualified as a juror, because he had a case pending in the same court against the defendant for damages that he claimed accrued to him out of the same railroad accident for which plaintiff, in his suit, claimed damages, Hall's suit being for damages to his mules, wagon, and other personal property injured at the same time and place.   It further appears from the record that the plaintiff below, by his counsel, asked that Hall be allowed to remain in the court-room to assist them in the management of the case, which the court permitted, and Hall did remain, and assisted in the conduct of the case and in the selection of the jury.   All these things occurred in the presence of the court. It further appeared in testimony that the jury were allowed to disperse when court adjourned on a certain day during the trial, with instructions to communicate with no one about the case. Hall was in court at the time, and at night after the adjournment he extended an invitation to one Pounds to go and get a drink with him, and Howard, who was standing near, accompanied them by invitation of Pounds.   They went into an open barroom, and there ordered drinks and cigars, Hall paying for the treat.   Afterwards Hall and the juror retired to the same room in the hotel, and slept together in the same bed. The next morning a motion for mistrial was made by counsel for the railway company, and was overruled by the court; and upon this ruling error is assigned in the bill of exceptions.

In the administration of law there is perhaps nothing that is guarded with more vigilance by the judiciary than the conduct of the jury pending the trial of a litigated case.   For the sake of public policy, and for the purpose of maintaining and protecting the purity of the jury-box, and to insure a fair and impartial trial to litigants, it is the policy of the law that each juror should be kept entirely and absolutely free from any influence which might tend to prejudice or bias his mind in favor of either party to the case on trial. In *Rainey* v. *State*, 100 *Ga.* 82, it appeared that during the trial of a criminal case the jury dispersed, and one of them was entertained at dinner free of charge by an attorney for the State. It was held that such conduct was cause for a new trial, although counsel for the accused knew of the same before the verdict had been returned. It was further ruled by this court that the trial judge should not, and this court will not, inquire whether injury resulted to the accused or not, but the verdict, upon principles of sound public policy, will be set aside, to the end that the purity of jury trial may be preserved unimpaired. In *Springer* v. *State*, 34 *Ga.* 379, it was held that the conduct of one of the counsel engaged in the prosecution, in protecting for a night, free of charge, the horses of some of the jurors, necessitated the grant of a new trial. *Salter* v. *Glenn*, 42 *Ga.* 64; *Shaw* v. *State*, 83 *Ga.* 92; *Robinson* v. *Donehoo*, 97 *Ga.* 702. The above citations are only a few among the many cases decided by this court in which verdicts have been set aside on the ground of misconduct of the juror, in some of the cases not as reprehensible as the conduct of the juror in this case. This ruling is based upon the idea that the court will, at all hazards, protect the purity of the jury-box; and although the court might be satisfied that there was no fraudulent intent on the part of the juror in his improper associations with the party interested in the case on trial, the general rule is that the question as to whether injury has actually resulted will not be inquired into by the court. In this case it is true that the person who treated the juror in the barroom and associated with him as a bedfellow during the night pending the trial was neither a party nor an attorney for either of the parties to the case on trial; but having a case against the same defendant company, founded upon the same facts, there was certainly as much to excite his interest in the result of the trial as if he had been a regularly employed attorney for one of the parties. Besides this, he aided the plaintiff below during the conduct of the trial, going to the extent of assisting him in striking the jury. The motion for a mis-

25

trial was made immediately upon the discovery of the fact by counsel for plaintiff in error. We think he clearly had a right to insist upon a trial before a jury of twelve men kept entirely free during the trial from any improper associations or dealings involving favors shown the juror by one so directly interested in the result of the issue as the evidence discloses Hall was in this case. We think, therefore, the court erred in overruling this motion for a mistrial.

Judgment reversed.   All the Justices concurring.

BARFIELD *v.* MACON COUNTY.

Following the decision of this court in *Smith* v. *Floyd County*, 85 *Ga.* 420, a right of action exists against a county for damaging private property for public uses in causing public roads to be worked or drained in such manner as to injure or damage the adjacent realty of a landed proprietor.

Submitted November 7,—Decided December 2, 1899.

Action for damages. Before Judge Littlejohn. Macon superior court. November term, 1898.

W. G. Harrison, J. W. Haygood, and *J. M. DuPree,* for plaintiff. *Greer & Felton,* for defendant.

COBB, J. Mrs. Barfield brought suit against Macon County, alleging in her petition, in substance, as follows: She is the owner of certain described lots of land which lie adjacent to a public road of the county. In 1897 the hands summoned to work the public road under the control of the road overseer, who was representing the County of Macon and under its direction, so changed the public road as that the water which had been accustomed to pond in the road overflowed her land and damaged her crops in a sum named. She complained to the commissioners of Macon County, but they paid no attention to her complaint. In 1898 the hands were again summoned to work the road, and, under the supervision of the road overseers, who were representing the County of Macon and acting under its direction, made further changes in the road, whereby her property was damaged, and by reason of such changes the water, which would not otherwise have flowed upon her land, has overflowed the same and injured the land and thereby greatly reduced the market value of her property. It is alleged that she presented her claim for damages to the county commissioners within twelve months from the time such damage accrued, and they refused to pay the same. To this petition the defendant demurred upon the grounds, that it set forth no cause of action, and that there was no allegation that the defendant either did or authorized to be done by others the acts complained of, and that if any one was liable for the damage sustained by the plaintiff it was either the overseer or the road hands, or both, and not the defendant. The demurrer was sustained, and the plaintiff excepted.

In the case of *Smith* v. *Floyd County*, 85 *Ga.* 420, it was held that, "Construing the constitution of 1877 and the code together, a right of action exists against a county for damaging private property for public uses in constructing the approaches to a county bridge, thereby elevating the roadway above an adjacent lot so as to hinder access to the lot from the road." In the opinion Chief Justice Bleckley says: "Had the plaintiff's property been damaged in the mode alleged in his declaration, prior to the constitution of 1877, whether done by a city or a county, he would have had no right of action (*City of Atlanta* v. *Green*, 67 *Ga.* 386); but under that constitution, cities, counties, and all other public organizations are denied any power or right to cause such damages for public purposes without making compensation. In this respect they are all upon an equal footing, and there is no reason for holding a county exempt from suit for acts done by it for objects within its legal competency, when a city, for like acts done within its legal competency, would not be exempt. The constitution is no less directly applicable to the one than to the other." The petition in terms alleges that the changes made by the road hands have diminished the market value of the plaintiff's property, and in effect alleges that these changes were made by the road hands under the direction and authority of the board of county commissioners of the county. Such being the case, under the principle of the decision above cited the petition set forth a cause of action and should not have been dismissed

upon the demurrer filed thereto.   Whether the county would
be liable for acts of the character complained of, when the
same were done by the road hands under the direction of the
road overseer, who derived his authority for giving such direction from the road commissioners of the district, and was not
authorized in any way by the county commissioners of the
county, is a question not·presented in the record.   See, in this
connection, *Smith* v. *Wilkes County*, 79 *Ga.* 127.   The allegations in the petition are that the work was done by the road
hands and overseer under the authority of the county commissioners themselves.   If the county commissioners authorize a change to be made in a public road whereby the property
of an adjacent landowner is damaged, the county will be
liable; and such is the case made by the plaintiff's petition.
In such a case the measure of damages is the actual depreciation of the market value of the property caused by the work
complained of; and in holding that the petition in the present
case sets forth a cause of action, we desire to apply the rule
laid down in the case of *Smith* v. *Floyd County*, cited above; and
to that end we adopt the following language of Chief Justice
Bleckley: "In holding that the declaration sets forth a cause of
action, we are to be understood as sustaining it, not for the purpose of treating the work or its results as a nuisance to the
plaintiff's premises, but only for the purpose of recovering
damages for the exercise of the power of eminent domain.
The work done is to be treated as rightful in all respects save
in the omission to pay compensation.   And the measure of
compensation is the actual depreciation in value (in the market
value) of the plaintiff's premises, resulting from the work done
and its effect upon the property."   See also, in this connection,
Moore v. *Atlanta*, 70 *Ga.* 611; *Campbell* v. *Street Railroad
Company*, 82 *Ga.* 320.

> *Judgment reversed.   All the Justices concurring.*

DAWSON v. EQUITABLE MORTGAGE COMPANY.

1. A ground of demurrer to a petition, stating in general terms that "there are no proper parties," is too vague and general. Such ground is itself defective, in that it fails to point out who would be proper parties to the proceeding.

2. Where a levy of a fi. fa. upon land has been met by a fraudulent and frivolous claim of an insolvent person, made in forma pauperis, an equitable petition in aid of the levy will lie in the superior court of the county in which the claim case is pending, notwithstanding the claimant may not reside in that county; the object of the petition being to prevent such interference by the claimant with the progress of plaintiff's execution, and to have a receiver appointed to take charge of the land, with the view of applying the rents and profits thereof to plaintiff's execution; the petition making a case that the claimant had not only filed the one claim, but, for the purpose of delay, had previously forced a continuance of the case, and had, before the filing of the claim, been instrumental in defeating the collection of the fi. fa. by dilatory tactics; the petition also making a case showing that, but for such equitable interference, the rents and profits would be appropriated by the claimant who was in possession, and the plaintiff's power to collect its money, to that extent, would be defeated.

3. The several objections to the admission of evidence presented no legal reason for excluding the same, save perhaps in one or two instances where the evidence admitted was not of such importance or materiality as to affect the result. In view of the testimony submitted pro and con on the interlocutory hearing, there was no abuse of discretion in granting the injunction and appointing a receiver.

Argued November 7, — Decided December 2, 1899.

Injunction. Before Judge Littlejohn. Macon county. June 24, 1899.

R. D. Smith and *J. M. DuPree,* for plaintiff in error.
Payne & Tye, E. A. Hawkins, and *J. W. Haygood,* contra.

LEWIS, J. At the May term, 1894, of Upson superior court a verdict was rendered in favor of the Equitable Mortgage Company against E. R. C. Dawson for $2,867.50, besides attorney's fees and costs, and a special judgment was rendered on the verdict against certain lands. A fi. fa. was issued on the judgment, and levied upon these lands; whereupon J. M. Dawson interposed a claim. This claim was returned to Macon superior court, in which county the lands were located. At the May term of that court, in aid of the levy made in the case,

an equitable petition was filed in behalf of the plaintiff in fi.
fa. against J. M. Dawson.   The following facts, in brief, were
set forth in this petition: When the lands were first levied on
by the sheriff of Macon county a claim was filed thereto by
one Atwater, which was dismissed on May 13, 1895; and on
June 24, 1895, another claim was filed by Atwater, which was
dismissed on November 10, 1896.   After this the lands were
again advertised for sale, when an affidavit of illegality was
filed by E. R. C. Dawson on June 5, 1897, which illegality
was dismissed on November 9, 1897.   After this the lands were
again advertised for sale, when an affidavit of illegality was
filed by J. M. Dawson (the claimant in this case) as agent for
E. R. C. Dawson, and this affidavit was dismissed on November 15, 1898.   The property was again advertised for sale on
the first Tuesday in January, 1899, and a claim to the lands
was filed by J. M. Dawson under an affidavit in forma pauperis,
no bond and security being given by the claimant, who procured a continuance at the trial term.   The petition charges,
among other things, that J. M. Dawson has no valid legal or
equitable title to the lands, superior to plaintiff's judgment;
that he has resorted to dilatory tactics for no other purpose
than to retain possession of the property and enjoy the rents
and profits thereof; that previously to filing the claim Dawson
requested petitioner that he be allowed to pay the amount due
on the judgment in certain instalments annually until the debt
was discharged in full, and no claim was then made by J. M.
Dawson of any title to, or interest in, the property, but he
recognized the validity and superiority of plaintiff's judgment,
and his only desire was to gain time; but Dawson wholly
failed to comply with this contract.   It was further alleged
that, after the making of this contract, J. M. Dawson interposed an affidavit of illegality as agent for E. R. C. Dawson,
and that after the dismissal of this illegality he filed a claim
to the property, with a pauper's affidavit thereto attached; that
J. M. Dawson was then in possession of the land, receiving
the rents and profits therefrom, and was insolvent; that neither
he nor E. R. C. Dawson paid taxes since 1892, and tax fi. fas.
for the various years since that date have been issued and trans-

ferred to various parties who are holding the same against the property as outstanding liens; that no part of the plaintiff's debt has been paid, and if the frivolous claims are not stopped, and the property brought to sale, the plaintiff will not realize its debt out of the same; and that the claim filed by J. M. Dawson, which was returnable to the May term, 1899, of Macon superior court, was interposed by said claimant for the purpose of further delaying and hindering petitioner in the collection of its debt. The petition prayed for the appointment of a receiver to take charge of the property, rent out the same, and hold the proceeds subject to the further order of the court; and that J. M. Dawson be enjoined from further interfering with or hindering the enforcement of plaintiff's fi. fa., or occupying, renting, or having anything to do with the property; and that the fi. fa. be allowed to proceed and sell the same. Dawson filed his answer to this petition, denying, in effect, its material allegations, setting up title to the property, and admitting that the same had been in his possession before and ever since the rendition of the judgment.

After hearing evidence, the court rendered a judgment on the 24th day of June, 1899, restraining the defendant as prayed for in the petition, and appointing a receiver to take charge of the lands mentioned therein, hold the same as receiver of the court, rent out the lands, collect the rents until the further order of the court, and hold the same subject to its order. The judgment of the court further provided that if J. M. Dawson should, within fifteen days from the date thereof, file with the clerk of Macon superior court a good and solvent bond to be approved by the clerk, payable to the plaintiff, conditioned to pay into court an amount equal to the value of the rents and profits of the property for the year 1899, and all future rents, judgment to be entered up on the bond against principal and securities as in cases of appeal, then the order appointing a receiver should be vacated. To this judgment the claimant excepted, and assigns the same as error in his bill of exceptions.

1. On the hearing of the case before the judge below, Dawson demurred to plaintiff's petition, on the ground that there was no equity in the same; that there were no proper parties;

and that the remedy at law is complete. It is insisted in the argument of this case that the defendant in fi. fa., E. R. C. Dawson, should have been made a party defendant to the equitable proceeding filed by the plaintiff in fi. fa., and that the court erred in not sustaining the demurrer on this ground. But the demurrer itself fails to point out who would be proper parties defendant to the case; and even if the defendant in fi. fa. were a necessary party, there was no reversible error in the court overruling the demurrer as presented, on account of its vagueness and uncertainty.

2. The respondent also filed a plea to the jurisdiction of the court to try the case, on the ground that both he and the defendant in fi. fa. resided in Upson county, and that jurisdiction of the case was vested solely and exclusively in the superior court of that county. The present constitution of this State requires cases in equity to be brought in the county where one of the defendants against whom substantial relief is prayed resides. But it has often been decided by this court that this provision in the several constitutions of the State does not apply to equitable proceedings ancillary to suits already pending, which, for purposes of injunction, may be brought in the county where such suits at law or in equity are pending. *Dew* v. *Hamilton*, 23 *Ga.* 415; *Carswell* v. *Macon Mfg. Co.*, 38 *Ga.* 403; *Ray* v. *Home Co.*, 106 *Ga.* 492. In the last case cited Mr. Justice Cobb, in his opinion, expresses the principle applicable to this case in the following language: "One who goes into the court of a county other than that of his residence, to assert a claim or set up an equity, must be content to allow that court to determine any counter-claim growing out of the original suit which the defendant sees fit to set up by cross-action." As declared in *Caswell* v. *Bunch*, 77 *Ga.* 504, this principle "rests on the idea that the plaintiff, by voluntarily instituting his suit, gives the superior court of the county where it is so instituted jurisdiction of his person sufficient to answer all the ends of justice respecting the suit originally instituted,— such proceedings in equity being ancillary to or defensive of the pending suit." See also *Markham* v. *Huff*, 72 *Ga.* 874 (3); *James* v. *Sams*, 90 *Ga.* 404; *Rounsaville* v. *McGinnis*, 93 *Ga.* 579–581; *Moore, Marsh & Co.* v. *Medlock*, 101 *Ga.* 93.

The original proceeding in this case arose upon the levy of a fi. fa. upon land situated in Macon county. This levy was resisted by the filing of a claim which, under the law, was made returnable to the superior court of the county in which the land was located. The plaintiff in error, therefore, by filing this claim, voluntarily submitted to the jurisdiction of that court as to all matters pertaining to the issue which he had thus submitted by the filing of his claim. Directly involved in this issue was the title to the land levied upon. Claim cases, by adjudications of this court, have repeatedly been regarded as in the nature of equitable proceedings; and the right of a claimant to support his contention, in an ordinary claim at law, by filing equitable proceedings and seeking equitable relief touching the subject-matter of the controversy, can no longer be questioned. When a claim is filed to the levy of a fi. fa., the same right necessarily exists in the plaintiff in fi. fa. to file equitable proceedings in support of his levy, and to enforce all equities pertaining to his rights as such a judgment creditor. While it is true, in the present case, the plaintiff in fi. fa. had no lien upon the rents and profits of the land levied upon, yet, under its allegations and the proof submitted on the trial, it had an equitable interest in such profits from the land, and by the conduct of the claimant, in his repeated efforts to delay frivolously the enforcement of this lien upon the lands, the rights of the plaintiff had become jeopardized. It was in danger of suffering loss of at least a portion of its debt, unless equity intervened by the granting of an injunction and appointment of a receiver, for the purpose of holding up the rents of the land until the issue between it and claimant was finally determined. This equitable proceeding, then, was clearly not an independent one, but was ancillary and in aid of plaintiff's rights involved in the claim case that was pending in court. In the case of *Hart* v. *Respess*, 89 *Ga.* 87, it appeared that a mortgage fi. fa. was levied upon land insufficient in value to pay the debt; that the plaintiff had been delayed by claims interposed by a third person, which were adjudicated against the claimant; and that a sale under the levy was prevented by another claim interposed by a person to whom the first claimant conveyed title.

It was held that a receiver might be appointed to take and hold possession of the land, and receive and preserve the rents and profits until the second claim should be determined; both claimants being insolvent, and having claimed by affidavit in forma pauperis without giving bond or security. It was further recognized in that decision that while the mortgagee had no legal title to the rents and profits, he had an equitable claim upon the same, so far as they were needed to discharge so much of the mortgage debt as could not be realized out of the corpus of the property; the facts in the case indicating that the debtors were insolvent, and the creditor was likely to sustain loss.

3. There were several objections to the admission of evidence which presented no legal reason for excluding the same, except perhaps in one or two instances, where the evidence admitted was not of such importance or materiality as to affect the result; and even if there was error on the hearing of an application for a temporary injunction in admitting testimony of such a character, this will not work a reversal of the judgment of the court granting the injunction. We think there was sufficient testimony before the judge to authorize the conclusion that the material allegations in the plaintiff's petition were substantially sustained; and hence this court can not say that there was any abuse of discretion in the judgment granting an injunction and appointing a receiver, particularly in view of the fact that the judge in his order gave the defendant below the opportunity of vacating the order as to the appointment of a receiver by giving bond and security.

Judgment affirmed. All the Justices concurring.

LUMPKIN, P. J. I concur in the judgment, but not without some doubt on the question of jurisdiction.

DODGE *v.* AMERICAN FREEHOLD LAND MORTGAGE COMPANY OF LONDON LIMITED.

394|
7|
103|

1. For the purpose of admitting to record a deed executed in another State, the attestation of a commissioner of deeds for Georgia in that State is sufficient without a certificate verifying his identity and official character.

2. A power of attorney from a corporation, authorizing an agent to convey land by deed in this State, signed by two directors and the secretary, and unaccompanied by the seal of the corporation, or by proof that the directors and secretary were authorized by the charter to sign for the corporation, is insufficient to authorize the agent to convey land by deed in this State.

3. Where an affidavit for the probate of such a power of attorney before a consul of the United States recites that the affiant is known to the consul as the "individual whose signature is affixed to the annexed deed as one of the witnesses thereto," that this individual was present at the time the writing was executed, that he saw it signed and sealed and delivered by the makers thereof, and that the other subscribing witness was also present and witnessed the execution of the instrument, but the affidavit is signed by another and different person from the one mentioned therein, it is not sufficient to admit the instrument to record in this State.

Argued November 9,— Decided December 2, 1899.

Levy and claim. Before Judge Smith. Dodge superior court. September term, 1898.

DeLacy & Bishop, for plaintiff in error.
E. Herrman and *J. E. Wooten*, contra.

SIMMONS, C. J.   The record discloses that Rawlins made a deed to Sherwood to secure borrowed money.   Sherwood conveyed the land to the American Freehold Land Mortgage Company of London Limited. Rawlins failing to pay the money borrowed, the mortgage company sued him and obtained judgment.   In order to reconvey the land to Rawlins, the borrower, the mortgage company undertook to make a power of attorney to Sherwood, authorizing him to reconvey the land to Rawlins, so that it might be levied upon and sold for the payment of the debt.   Sherwood, under the power, did reconvey.   The sheriff levied upon the land, and Dodge claimed it.   On the trial of the case, this deed from Sherwood to Rawlins and the power of attorney to Sherwood were offered in evidence, and were objected to by the claimant's counsel.   The deed was objected to because the certificate of the commissioner of deeds for Georgia in New York was not such as required by the code. The power of attorney was objected to on the ground that it was signed only by two directors and the secretary of the mortgage company, that the seal of the company was not affixed to the power, and there was no evidence offered to show that the directors and secretary had the right to sign the power of attorney authorizing the agent to convey land. The court overruled the objection and admitted the deed and the power of attorney. To this ruling the claimant excepted, and made it one of the grounds of his motion for new trial.

1. The objection to the deed on account of the certificate of the commissioner of deeds for Georgia in New York was not tenable, under the case of *Hadden* v. *Larned*, 87 *Ga.* 634.

2. The power of attorney was signed by two directors and the secretary of the company. It recites that the seal of the company is affixed; but the original was offered in evidence, and there was no seal impressed thereon or attached thereto. Corporations, in making contracts or in conveying land, act generally by their presidents and secretaries, unless the charter authorizes some other officer or officers to act for the company. If the seal of the company had been attached to the power of attorney, the law would have presumed that when the directors and the secretary signed it they were authorized so to do by the company. *Carr* v. *Ga. Loan & Trust Co.*, 108 *Ga.* 757. The seal not being attached, it was necessary for the plaintiff to show when he offered it in evidence that these persons were either authorized by a vote of the company to sign the power, or that they were authorized by the company's charter. No such proof being offered, the court erred in admitting the power of attorney in evidence.

3. It is claimed, however, by the counsel for the defendant in error, that inasmuch as the power of attorney had been recorded in the clerk's office, the recording of it by the clerk cured the defect. Perhaps this would be true if the clerk had the right to place such an instrument on the record. We do not think that he had. This power of attorney, under our law, must be recorded with the deed made by the attorney in fact. But it is said that the execution of the power was proved by the affidavit made before the United States consul in London. We do not think that this affidavit, even if the power had been sealed, was sufficient to admit it to record. The affidavit appears to have been made in London, England, before Martin B. Waller, Vice and Deputy Consul General of the United

States; and Waller recites therein as follows: "Before me, Martin B. Waller, personally came Tobias Gainsford Ridgway, of London, Notary Public, to me known to be the individual whose signature is affixed to the annexed deed [power of attorney] as one of the witnesses thereto, who being sworn says," etc. The affidavit then recites that this person was present when the deed was executed; that he saw it signed, sealed, and delivered as the act of the company by Blake and Hoare, directors, and Bullock, secretary; that Joseph Cox, the other subscribing witness thereto was also present and witnessed the execution of the deed; and that he, the said Tobias Gainsford Ridgway, and the said Joseph Cox then and there signed the same as attesting witnesses. Naturally, under the recitals made in this affidavit, we would expect to see the signature of Tobias Gainsford Ridgway, but instead thereof we find the signature of W. B. G. Ridgway, who, from the initials of his name, is quite a different person from Tobias. The consul certifies his personal acquaintance with Tobias, and certifies that his name is affixed to that deed, or power of attorney; but he certifies nothing as to his knowledge of W. B. G. Ridgway. While the latter's name is signed to the affidavit, the recitals show that Tobias was the one before the consul making the affidavit. We have no certificate or attestation of the consul that W. B. G. appeared before him at all, or that he was sworn to the truth of the facts stated in affidavit. The power of attorney is not even attested by W. B. G., but by a different Ridgway from either Tobias or W. B. G. It is attested by W. C. G. Ridgway. So it appears that neither Tobias nor W. B. G. witnessed the execution of the paper; and not having done so, neither had any right to make the affidavit for probate. We think, therefore, that for this reason the court erred in admitting this power of attorney.

We have carefully examined the other alleged errors in the motion for new trial, and find no error in any of the other grounds taken in the motion.

Judgment reversed.   All the Justices concurring.

GRISWOLD v. RUTHERFORD.

A judge of a county court has no authority under the law to administer the
  oath necessary for a warrant to issue against a tenant at sufferance, nor
  to issue such warrant.

Argued November 10, — Decided December 2, 1899.

Dispossessory warrant. Before Judge Smith. Pulaski superior court. August term, 1899.

J. H. Martin, for plaintiff.
W. L. & Warren Grice and *George Bright*, for defendant.

LITTLE, J. Aaron Griswold appeared before L. C. Ryan,
judge of the county court of Pulaski county, and made an affidavit authorized by section 4813 of the Civil Code, for the removal of Fannie Rutherford from certain land as a tenant at
sufferance. Under this affidavit the warrant provided for in
section 4814 of the Civil Code was issued by said judge of the
county court. The proceedings were arrested as provided for
in section 4815 of the Civil Code, and an issue formed. On the
call of the case in the superior court, the defendant made a motion to dismiss the case on the ground that only a judge of the
superior court or a justice of the peace could under the law administer the oath and issue the warrant. The court sustained
this motion and dismissed the case, and to his judgment in so
doing the plaintiff in said proceedings excepted. The only
question to be considered is, whether the judge of the county
court had jurisdiction to administer the affidavit and issue the
warrant. Section 4813 of the code provides, that the owner of
the land, or his agent or attorney, may go before the judge of
the superior court, or any justice of the peace, and make oath to
the fact; and section 4814 of the same code provides, that
when such affidavit shall have been made, the officer before
whom it was made shall issue the warrant. When the execution of the warrant is arrested by the counter-affidavit as provided in section 4815 of the Civil Code, the proceedings must
be returned to the superior court of the county where the land
lies. Civil Code, § 4816.

It will thus be seen that the statute only gives jurisdiction to the judge of the superior court, or a justice of the peace, to administer the oath prescribed and issue the warrant. The validity of these proceedings rests alone on the statute, and a well-recognized rule is, that such proceedings can have no effect unless the statute is strictly pursued; and unless jurisdiction to administer the oath and issue the warrant is by some other law given to the judge of the county court, the process issued by that officer is void. By section 4208 of the Civil Code, jurisdiction is given to the county judge to hear and determine all applications for the eviction of intruders, tenants holding over, to issue and dispose of distress warrants, etc. It is clear that this language does not give the jurisdiction in question to the judge of the county court. By section 4 of the act of 1875, amending the Code of 1873, so far as it relates to the county court of Pulaski county (Acts 1875, p. 64), it is provided that the county judge shall have jurisdiction to hear and determine, according to law, all matters and issues arising out of the relation of master and servant, landlord and tenant, for the eviction of trespassers, intruders, and tenants holding over, etc. If it be claimed that the language of this act confers jurisdiction on the county judge to administer the oath and issue the warrant against a tenant holding over, it will be found, by reference to section 4213 of the Civil Code, that it has been repealed, as none of these provisions are embraced in the act of 1879. See Acts of 1878-9, p. 132. Inasmuch, then, as the proceedings authorized are entirely statutory, and the statute only authorizes a judge of the superior court or a justice of the peace to administer the oath and issue the warrant, it must be held that a judge of a county court can not lawfully do either; and the judgment of the court below is

Affirmed. All the Justices concurring.

DRAKE *et al. v.* DREWRY, ordinary.

Under the provisions of the "local option liquor law," embodied in section 1541 et seq. of the Political Code, the ordinary has the power, and it is his duty, before declaring the result of an election held under that law, to entertain and pass upon a contest respecting such election which may

109
s112

109
s112
s113

109
131　7

be presented to him by any qualified voter or voters of the county wherein
the same was held, and his jurisdiction extends to a decision of all questions and grounds of contest affecting the validity of the election or its
result, thus brought to his attention. It follows, that the superior court
has no jurisdiction or authority to prohibit the ordinary from performing
the duties thus imposed upon him by the statute.

FISH and LEWIS, JJ., dissenting. The ordinary of a county where an election has been held under the statute known as the " local option liquor
law " has no jurisdiction to hear and determine a contest, arising under
a petition by one or more voters of the county, which impeaches the
validity and fairness of the election by seeking to go behind the returns
of various managers of certain precincts in the county, with the view of
examining and having a recount of the ballots, for the purpose of throwing out certain votes alleged to have been illegally cast. Under the act
in question, the duties and powers imposed upon the ordinary are of a
ministerial or political nature, and not judicial. The questions presented
by such a petition are of a judicial nature, over which the act itself gives
the superior court of the county original and exclusive jurisdiction.

Argued November 6, — Decided December 6, 1899.

Petition for prohibition, etc.   Before Judge Reagan.   Spalding county.   October 24, 1899.

J. S. Boynton, W. C. Beeks, Lloyd Cleveland, F. D. Dismuke,
and *Searcy & Boyd,* for plaintiffs.   *R. T. Daniel, M. W. Beck,*
T. E. Patterson, and *J. J. Flynt,* for defendant.

LITTLE, J.   Drake and others presented to the judge of the
superior court of the Flint circuit a petition setting out the
following facts : Petitioners are citizens, taxpayers, and registered voters of Spalding county.   On the 19th day of October,
1899, an election was held in said county under the local option law.   At the election a majority of the votes was cast in
favor of the sale, and the managers of the election made returns to the ordinary, and it was the duty of that officer to
immediately consolidate the vote and declare the result of the
election.   Certain persons (naming them) have filed with said
ordinary a paper claiming to be a contest of the election, in
which are set out various grounds, and a prayer that the ordinary hear the grounds of the contest therein made.   The
ordinary, on receiving such paper setting out the grounds of
the contest, refused to consolidate the return and declare the
result.   The ordinary also refused the motion of petitioners
to dismiss the contest, but held and decided that he had juris-

diction to judicially hear evidence and pass upon all the grounds of the contest. The petitioners allege that the ordinary has no legal authority or jurisdiction to hear evidence touching such contest, nor to pass any order or judgment thereon; that such pretended contest does not contain the names of one tenth of the voters voting at the election; and that it is not in form or substance such a contest as would authorize the ordinary or any other court to hear the same. Thereupon the petitioners prayed that the writ of prohibition should issue, directed to said Drewry, ordinary, prohibiting him from hearing and passing upon said contest, and that he be prohibited from opening the ballot-boxes and counting the votes therein, etc. After considering the petition, the judge of the superior court refused to grant the writ of prohibition, and to such refusal the plaintiffs excepted.

The only question raised for our determination is, whether under the provisions of sections 1541 et seq. of the Political Code, which embody the local option law, the ordinary of a county has jurisdiction to hear and determine questions affecting the fairness and legality of such an election, on a contest made before him. This court has found it necessary on more than one occasion to consider the question here made, without having determined the same; and in the case of *McMillan* v. *Bell*, 105 *Ga.* 496, it took occasion to say that some of the provisions of the code in relation to such contests were involved in so much obscurity and uncertainty that it is difficult, if not impossible, to ascertain their true intent and meaning, and it was suggested that such provisions needed legislative revision. Without any legislative action in this direction, we are now called upon to construe and, if possible, harmonize those sections of this law which in the consideration of that case we found to be apparently so inharmonious. In doing so we call to our aid certain rules for the construction of statutes, which have been laid down for ascertaining the proper meaning to be given to their various provisions.

Citing 38 N. J. Law, 64; 9 Cow. 437, Mr. Sutherland in his work on Statutory Construction, § 325, says: "Every part of a statute must be viewed in connection with the whole, so as to make all its parts harmonize, if practicable, and give a sensible and intelligent effect to each. It is not presumed that the legislature intended any part of a statute to be without meaning." It is also a well-recognized rule to be adopted in the construction of statutes, that general words should receive a general construction, unless there is something in the statute to restrain them. In the case of *State* v. *Atkins*, 35 *Ga*. 319, it was said that, "in order to arrive at the intention of the lawgiver, the whole and every part of the statute should be considered in determining the meaning of any of its parts; taking the words to be understood in that sense in which they are generally used by those for whom the law was intended, and discarding all subtle and strained construction for the purpose of limiting or extending their operation or import." It is provided by section 1545 of the Political Code, and as a part of the local option law, that " All managers of elections held as by this Article provided shall . . deliver one list of the voters, . . ballots, and tally-sheets to the ordinary, who shall carefully consolidate the returns, and decide all questions and contests arising under elections held by virtue of this Article." It is further provided by section 1546 of the same code that, "Within twenty days from the day on which the ordinary declares the result, one-tenth of the number of voters having voted at such election may petition the superior court, setting out plainly and distinctly the cause of contest, when, if the cause set out is such as impeaches the fairness of the election, or the conduct of the ordinary, the judge shall grant an order directed to three justices of the peace of the county, requiring them to recount the ballots on a given day, and report the result to the next term of the superior court of that county, or the term of the court to which the petition may be returnable, at which term the case shall be heard." It is further provided in this section that, "If the election shall appear to have been fraudulently conducted, or the votes fraudulently counted, the judge shall have power to declare the result and overrule the action of the ordinary in the premises." It seems, from a literal reading of these two sections, that as a matter of law two contests of an election held under the local option law are provided. But it is urged in behalf of the plaintiffs in error, that the words in section 1545, which authorize the ordinary to decide all questions and contests, only vest in that officer authority to hear such questions and contests as under the general laws of the State are vested in the managers of elections; and we are cited to section 72 of the Political Code, as prescribing those questions and contests. Attention, however, is called to the fact, that the section cited refers to the elections of officers for the administration of the government, and provisions for contesting the election of any one of the persons declared to be elected are expressly made, by statute, essentially different from the provisions in the case of elections under the local option laws. In the cases contemplated by that section, the managers consolidate the returns, and contests which involve the fairness of the election, or which seek to reject illegal votes, are by the statute provided to be made after the vote has been consolidated and the result announced. There is, under section 72, but one provision which may be regarded as a question which the managers of elections may decide. After providing that the election shall be held by ballot, and the method of receiving the ballots, and providing for challenges, and giving the managers power to preserve order, and prescribing the method of the returns and the consolidation of the votes, it is provided that: "If any voter shall vote who has not paid his taxes, and been registered, his vote shall be illegal, and the commissioners who consolidate their returns of the election shall not count such votes in making out the returns."

In cases of elections under the local option laws, the words used in the code make it imperative that the ordinary *shall* decide all questions and contests. These are very much broader in signification than those which direct the commissioners to reject from the returns the ballot of an illegal voter. Fairly interpreted, they imply that the ordinary shall not only reject illegal votes, but shall make an investigation in the nature of a judicial proceeding on the merits of such questions, affecting the final result, as may be brought before him. It will also be found that, by the provisions of section 72, the managers or superintendents shall not examine the ballots, but shall de-

liver them carefully sealed to the clerk of the superior court,
that the latter officer shall retain the same until after the next
term of the superior court, when, if a *contest* is not begun, the
ballots shall be destroyed, etc.; evidently showing that it was
not intended, by the terms of the section which gives the commissioners the right to reject from the returns an illegal vote,
or contemplated, that those officers should have any power in
relation to a contest; while the provision which we are considering, in terms, makes it the duty of the ordinary, after the
ballots, tally-sheets, and list of voters have been returned to
him, to decide all contests, that is to say, where the result of
the election for any supposed legal cause, either of law or fact,
comes into dispute—is called in question, the ordinary shall
decide the questions thus raised, and the duty to decide must
carry with it the antecedent duty of hearing.   It is further
contended that no contest can be instituted except after the
result has been declared.   This position, however, can not be
tenable.   It must be borne in mind that this is a special election to determine simply whether a regulation forbidding the
sale of spirituous liquors shall be enforced within a given county,
thus differing essentially from an election of State or county
officers.   It is made the duty of the ordinary to declare the result, and he by the words of the act is directed to hear all
questions and contests.   Necessarily the result referred to is
the true result.   After having declared the result, no power is
given to him to set it aside.   On the contrary, the result as declared must stand, unless set aside in a manner which we will
presently consider.   It must then be true that, with the power
of deciding questions and contests given, and it being made his
duty to declare the result, the questions and contests must be
determined antecedently to the declaration of the vote or result of the election.   See *Dyson* v. *Pope*, 71 *Ga.* 209.   The
main contention upon which the case of the plaintiffs in error
must rest, if there is any merit in it, is, that the jurisdiction to
entertain a contest of an election under the local option law
rests, by the statute, in the superior court and not in the ordinary; and in furtherance of that view it is claimed that if it
be held that the ordinary has jurisdiction to entertain a con-

test, then provision is made for two contests of the same election. It is further urged, notwithstanding the language used in section 1545 of the Political Code, conferring the power on the ordinary to decide questions and contests, that necessarily the jurisdiction of that officer is limited to ministerial acts, because full provision for the contest is made, in the subsequent section, by petition to the superior court. When we look to the terms of the act, however, as embodied in the statutes, we find it not only plainly written, that the ordinary shall decide all questions and contests concerning the election, and that it is his duty to declare the result, but the statute prescribes that if the result of the election thus declared is against the sale, the ordinary shall publish the same in the newspaper in which notice of the election was given, and the provisions of the act shall take effect as soon as the publication directed has been made. Hence it would seem logically to follow, that whatever questions and contests the ordinary is empowered to hear must be heard and determined anterior to a declaration and publication of the result. It is hardly reasonable to insist that the act should take effect as soon as the publication of the result has been made, and that no license to sell liquors shall be granted after such publication, when in fact the result is in doubt and dependent upon the questions and contests to be decided after such publication. Again, the provision of the next section of the code is, that within twenty days from the day on which the ordinary declares the result, one tenth of the number of voters having voted at the election may petition the superior court on grounds which impeach the fairness of the election or the *conduct* of the ordinary. What conduct? Surely not that of a ministerial officer whose duty it is to simply aggregate the number of votes as returned by the managers of the election. When the statute, in this connection, gives to the superior court a right to review the conduct of the ordinary, such language necessarily implies a review of the action of that officer, and it necessarily follows from the context that the conduct to be reviewed relates to his decision on such questions and contests as may have arisen before him.

Again, it is directed by the act that the superior court may review such conduct, and in doing so may require a recount of the ballots by three judicial officers of the county; evidently implying that any count of the ballots which may have been made by the ordinary in his decision of the questions and contests made before him shall, on a proper case made, not be accepted as final, but that the superior court, in order to determine the truth as to the vote, may have the ballots *recounted.* Now, it will not do to say that such recount refers to the consolidation of the votes cast at the various precincts, for a consolidation of the votes does not involve a count of the ballots —a contest may do so,—and, as has been seen, by the provisions of the act the ordinary shall not only carefully consolidate the returns made to him, but shall also decide questions and contests. Further than this, it is provided that the ordinary shall have ten days notice of the filing of the petition. If this is a mere contest as to the result of the election which has been held, why is the ordinary to be given notice of the filing of the petition? As a judicial officer, it is to be presumed that he stands impartial, and it seems to us that the only reason for giving to that officer notice of the filing of the petition is, that he may have an opportunity of defending his action in deciding the questions and contests which were made before him, and defending himself against charges of fraud and corruption in a case where his action is directly in issue, as well as to furnish the court the reasons for his action; for the last paragraph of the section declares that if the election appears to have been fraudulently conducted, or the votes fraudulently counted, the judge of the superior court shall have power to declare the result and overrule the action of the ordinary in the premises. It would seem, in view of the words of the act fixing the duties of the ordinary, taken in connection with the declaration that if on investigation had in the superior court it appears that the votes were fraudulently counted the judge shall have power to overrule the action of the ordinary, that necessarily the fraudulent count of the votes in the first instance refers directly to the action of the ordinary. Now, if this reasoning be correct, then both of these provisions of the code can stand in entire harmony, that is to say, that when in the first instance the ordinary comes to consolidate the returns, he shall decide all questions and contests made before him at that time, that, having done so, he shall declare the result, make publication of the same, and immediately thereon the act takes effect, and no license for the sale of liquors shall thereafter be granted; but, notwithstanding his publication and putting in force the prohibitions named in the act, if within twenty days as many as one tenth of the voters allege causes which impeach the fairness of the election or the conduct of the ordinary in his determination as to the result of the election, the fairness of such election and the conduct of the ordinary in the first instance may be reviewed, and as a result of such a review, if the election has been fraudulently conducted, or the ordinary has unfairly acted, a power is given to the judge to overrule such action of the ordinary and to declare the proper result. This seems to be the scope of the act, and expresses the intention of the lawmaking power. It is a well-settled rule that in ascertaining the purpose and intention of the legislature in the enactment of a law, if such intention is not clearly expressed in the statute, the court will take notice of the history of the terms of the statute when it was enacted. 3 How. 9; 91 U. S. 72. As said by Mr. Sutherland in his work on the Construction of Statutes, 383: "It is needful in the construction of all instruments to read them in view of all the surrounding facts. To understand their purport and intended application, one should, as far as possible, be placed in a situation to see the subject from the maker's standpoint and study his language with that outlook. Statutes are no exception." Citing 108 U. S. 526; 94 Pa. St. 450; 4 N. Y. 140.

It appears from the journals of the General Assembly of Georgia, at a session held in July, 1885, when the act from which the sections of the code which we have been considering were codified was passed, that the original act was introduced and passed in the Senate; that it passed the House by a substitute, and went to the Senate for consideration by that body; that when the 4th section of the substitute was reached, it did not contain the provisions which authorized a review by the superior court, but did contain the direction to the ordi-

nary to hear and determine contests, and that an amendment
was offered to that section in the Senate, providing for this review of the fairness of the election and the conduct of the ordinary by the superior court.   The original amendment to this
section provided that such review might be had on the petition of any qualified voter.   This amendment was itself amended
by striking out the words "any qualified voter" and inserting
in the place thereof the words, "one-tenth of the number of
voters having voted at such election."   Senate Journal, 1885,
p. 41.   This amendment to the amendment was agreed to, and
the substitute of the House, as amended, was passed by the
Senate.   Senate Journal, 1885, p. 109.   So that it appears
that when the substitute for the original Senate bill was passed
by the House and came up in the Senate, it did not provide
for a review of the fairness of the election and the conduct of
the ordinary by the superior court, but that section 4 only provided, in relation to contests, that the ordinary should decide
all questions and contests arising under the election; that the
Senate amended this section, not by striking out or changing
the powers given to the ordinary, but by simply adding thereto a provision which authorized the superior court, on the petition of one tenth of the voters, to investigate the fairness of the
election and the conduct of the ordinary; and the amendment
thus offered and adopted is the provision which we now find
in our code, without change.   No proposition was made to
curtail, qualify, or explain that portion of the 4th section
which made it the duty of the ordinary to hear contests, but
to this was simply added this provision for a review.   If, therefore, we can arrive at the intention of the lawmakers by reading this law in view of the surrounding facts, we are constrained to rule that the powers given to the ordinary must be
construed to be entirely independent of the power of the superior court to entertain jurisdiction and review the fairness of
the election.   When properly construed, the conflict between
the two sections is more imaginary than real, and the true construction of the act in relation to contests must be, that the ordinary is given jurisdiction, when he goes to consolidate the vote,
to hear all questions and to determine all contests which may

be.made before him concerning the fairness and legality of the election; that notwithstanding his determination, and without regard to the published result, if subsequently a considerable number of those who voted in the election, not less than one tenth, should in a petition to the superior court assign causes, whether made before the ordinary in the first instance or not, why the election was not fairly conducted, or why the ordinary had improperly acted and proclaimed the wrong result, the superior court might take up these questions, in the interest of fairness and justice, and on proper evidence might overrule the action of the ordinary, and declare a different result; and further, that the superior court has this jurisdiction even when no contest is made before the ordinary, or, if made, then on the same grounds as there urged, or different ones. Thus interpreting these provisions of our code, it must be held that the ordinary of Spalding county has jurisdiction to determine the contest made before him, and, having such jurisdiction, the judge of the superior court committed no error in refusing to grant the writ of prohibition.

Judgment affirmed. All the Justices concurring, except Fish and Lewis, JJ.

LEWIS, J., dissenting. It appears from the record in this case that a petition was brought by nineteen persons, claiming to be residents and legal voters of Spalding county, before the ordinary, for the purpose of contesting an election held in that county under the "local option liquor law." One ground for this contest was an allegation made only in general terms, that the result declared by the managers of the Griffin precinct was not a fair and just count; and there was a prayer for a recount of the ballots in that box. The other grounds in the petition alleged that in various other precincts in the county illegal votes were cast; and the purpose of the petition was to go behind the returns of the managers of these precincts, with the view of instituting an examination into the ballots that were cast, for the purpose of throwing out a number of voters alleged to be illegal·for various reasons. The purpose, therefore, of this petition was to have the ordinary, as a judicial tribunal, hear and determine a contested-election case involving issues

which for their proper determination and investigation necessarily involved going behind the returns of the election managers, an examination of the ballots cast, and the hearing of
testimony upon the various issues touching the qualifications
of a number of voters who had participated in the election. It
is claimed that the ordinary has authority to entertain, hear,
and determine such a contest, by virtue of the provisions of
section 1545 of the Political Code.   By this section it is made
the duty of the managers of the election "to deliver one list
of the voters and tally-sheets to the clerk of the superior court,
to be filed in his office, and one list of the voters, ballots, and
tally-sheets to the ordinary, who shall carefully consolidate the
returns, and decide all questions and contests arising under
elections held by virtue of this Article."   This is the only language in the entire act that gives the ordinary any power whatever to decide questions and contests arising under such an
election.   There is nothing in the act which expressly or by
implication prescribes any procedure by which such a contest
shall be heard and determined by the ordinary.   It nowhere
specifies who may file a petition for such a contest, what number of voters have a right to present to him such a judicial
question, and, after presented, what notice, by service, publication, or otherwise, should be given of the proceeding; and if
an effort be made to go into the ballot-box for the purpose of
attacking and throwing out certain votes as illegal, no means is
prescribed for the accomplishment of such an end.   It does not
even give the power to subpœna witnesses or to take depositions,
and no provision whatever is made for the payment of costs of
officers of court, however the contest may terminate.   It would
certainly be an anomaly in law to endeavor to enforce a statute giving in such general terms power to an official to decide
questions and contests relating to a public election, and not
prescribing any method whatever by which such contests shall
be instituted, how issue may be joined thereon, and how or
when the questions involved shall be heard and determined.
In all the laws of this State, of which I am aware, upon the
subject of contested elections involving regular judicial proceedings in court, the means of making, investigating, and de-

termining such a contest are prescribed by the statute. For instance, sections 107 to 109 inclusive of the Political Code, relating to contests over the election of any person requiring a commission from the Governor, prescribe minutely and particularly the form and manner of instituting such a contest, notice that shall be given, how, when, and before whom the case shall be tried, how testimony shall be taken, and particularly what proceedings shall be instituted when the election is contested on the ground of illegal votes. Section 111 of the Political Code adopts these regulations, and makes them applicable to contests arising over the election of the various officers therein mentioned.

Even, then, if it had been the intention of the legislature to confer upon the ordinary the power to judicially hear and determine a contested-election case, especially of the character presented by this record, the act has left that official powerless to accomplish its purpose, in that it does not provide him with the means, or in any manner indicate by what procedure his work may be accomplished. It will be noted that in public elections ordinarily the managers of the various precincts in the county, or a certain number from each precinct, assemble at the county-site for the purpose of consolidating the vote. These managers necessarily at times have questions arising before them, touching the returns, and relating to a consolidation of the votes. In the local option act in question it will be observed that the general rule of elections touching the conduct and duties of managers who meet to consolidate the vote of a county does not prevail; for, under section 1545 of the Political Code, it is made their duty to deliver the returns to the ordinary, and made his duty to consolidate such returns. Manifestly, then, as to this duty, the ordinary occupies very much the position that managers would occupy generally under other elections in Georgia; and the fact that the section cited confers the power upon the ordinary to "decide all questions and contests arising" can not imply that he can enter into a regular judicial contest, when the law nowhere makes any provision as to how he shall conduct such a contest. Therefore, the "questions and contests" mentioned in the act must

refer to such questions as may arise touching the consolidation
of the returns, and which have to be decided before the result
can be declared.   This by no means makes the provisions of
the act as to the ordinary's powers meaningless.   Many questions may arise which a board of managers, even in ordinary
elections held in the State, would necessarily be called upon to
determine before completing the consolidation.   For instance,
the returns of certain managers might show upon their face
that an election was not held at any precinct at all, but that
the votes were cast at an improper place, not recognized by
law; or they may show upon their face that an election at a
precinct was held at an improper time not authorized by law.
Manifestly, it would be the duty of the managers to discard
such returns.   Accordingly, it was held in *Walker* v. *Sanford*,
78 *Ga.* 165, the ordinary acted properly in refusing to count
the vote of a precinct where one of its managers was disqualified.   Other instances might be cited where mere ministerial
officers, in order to consolidate and declare a result, would have
to determine questions; but it by no means follows that in any
event, without special grant of legislative authority, can such
officials constitute themselves into a judicial tribunal for the
purpose of entering into an investigation of a contested-election case.   Even, then, if we construe the provisions of the act,
embodied in section 1545 of the Political Code, without any
reference whatever to other portions of the act relating to contests over such elections, I do not think the ordinary could
assume the power of hearing and determining the contest he
has undertaken in this case.   If the legislature in this instance
intended to create a new court for the purpose of hearing such
contests, it abandoned its wish before the job was completed,
and left it an incomplete judicial structure unsupplied with
such machinery as is essential to its active operation.

If that provision of the statute touching the powers of the ordinary stood alone and unmodified or unexplained by any other
provision in the act, he would have been left practically with
the same powers delegated to that officer in the act regulating
elections for no fences.   The latter part of section 177 of the
Political Code provides that "The returns of said election [that

is, election on the fence law] shall be made to the ordinary of said county, who, after examining the same and deciding upon all questions which may arise out of said election, shall proclaim the result by notice as aforesaid." The act further provides that if a *lawful majority* is for "no fence," then the provisions of the law shall go into effect. It is true the word "contest" is not used in that act, but words are used equally as broad and as comprehensive, giving power to the ordinary to decide upon all questions which may arise out of the election; and besides it seems to contemplate that it is the "*lawful*" *majority* the ordinary must ascertain; and perhaps with more force may it be implied, under the terms of this act, that one has a right to contest the election before the ordinary, if such a contest be necessary to show the *lawful* majority. I infer from the learned argument of Mr. Justice Little, in support of the views of the majority of this court, that it is concluded that the ordinary, under the act in question, is constituted a judicial tribunal, and, as a court, has the power to determine a contested-election case under this local option law. As to the fence law, this court is committed to a contrary proposition in regard to the powers and duties conferred upon the ordinary by virtue of the provisions of that act. In *Seymour* v. *Almond*, 75 *Ga.* 112, it is decided: "The ordinary, in respect to an election to decide the question of fence or no fence, is not a court, but an officer of the body politic of the State, to whom is confided the ordering, supervision, and announcemen tof the result of an election on that issue." It is further decided: "If he acted in these matters as a court, the writ of prohibition would issue only to stop him from acting as such, if the subject-matter was beyond his jurisdiction." But this particular question, so far as concerns powers of an ordinary under the fence law, was directly decided by this court in *Harris* v. *Perryman*, 103 *Ga.* 816. It was there held that the language which we have above quoted from the fence law "does not authorize or provide for any contest before the ordinary as to the result of such an election." It appears from the facts in that case that application was made to the ordinary for the purpose of contesting an election that was held on the question of fence or no fence. The ordinary refused to entertain the contest. A petition for mandamus was filed by the contestants, in the superior court, for the purpose of compelling the ordinary to entertain and pass upon the contest presented in the form of a petition by citizens and taxpayers. The mandamus was refused, and this judgment was affirmed by this court; the ground of its affirmance being based upon the principle above noted, that the act itself did not authorize or provide for any such contest. The reason for the decision is fully and clearly set forth by Mr. Justice Fish in his opinion on page 818, in the following language: "If the legislature intended by this language to confer upon any one the right to contest an election of this kind and to make it the duty of the ordinary to hear and decide such a contest, it seems very strange, indeed, that none of the usual provisions in reference to contested elections are found in the section of the code relating to these elections. How an issue shall be formed, who shall be necessary parties to it, what notice of the contest shall be given, upon whom and how long prior to the hearing it shall be served, before whom evidence shall be taken, the authority to examine suspected ballots, etc., are all questions upon which the law applicable to these elections is absolutely silent."

In this connection attention is called to the case of Echols *v.* State, 56 Ala. 136, cited in the opinion of Mr. Justice Fish. By reference to the facts reported in that case it will be seen that, under the charter for the city of Opelika, the city council were authorized to examine and count the votes; made judges of the election, with full power to determine all matters in relation thereto, ascertain the legality of voters, reject illegal votes, take testimony, examine witnesses, send for persons and papers, and decide who were legally elected mayor and aldermen of the city. Certainly this provision in the Alabama statute is a much more comprehensive one, and enters more minutely into detail, with reference to passing upon all issues that might grow out of a contest over an election, than is embodied in the local-option liquor law of this State, in so far as concerns the powers it confers on the ordinary. Yet it was decided by the Supreme Court of Alabama, that there was "nothing in the statute which gave to this proceeding the form, solemnity, or sanction of a contested election, no provision for instituting any such investigation by any dissatisfied elector, and nothing said about notice, or issue to be formed." This is the reason assigned by the court for its conclusion. It was, therefore, held that the provision in the statute referred to "the primary count and reckoning of the ballots." The same principle, that no such judicial power has been conferred on the ordinary, has in effect by this court been applied to the local-option liquor law in *Scoville* v. *Calhoun*, 76 *Ga.* 263. That was also a petition for a mandamus to the superior court, made with the view of preventing the ordinary from declaring the result of an election held under the local option act of 1885, until he had passed upon a petition, which the plaintiffs had presented to him, contesting the election. It was held that the court properly refused to grant the mandamus; and the reason for the decision was, that the election and the supervision thereof by the ordinary was the exercise of political and police powers incidental to legislative and executive government, and not, in their general political and police effect, at all judicial. It was therefore decided that it was proper to refuse a mandamus on the application of a few persons, less than one tenth of the voters, to compel the ordinary of a county, where an election had been held, to receive and hear a contest made and offered to be filed with him touching the election. If the local option act of 1885 were intended to create the ordinary a court, or to give him power, as a judicial tribunal, to decide such a contest; and if, according to the opinion of the majority of the court in this case, it would be not only his right but his duty to hear and determine such a contest, a mandamus would certainly lie to compel a hearing and disposition of the case in the event the ordinary refused to entertain a petition for such a contest.

The above views are based upon what I think would be a proper construction of section 1545, even if it stood alone in the act, so far as providing for a decision of questions and contests arising under the election. But when considered in the light of the section that follows, the conclusion reached is, if possible, the more irresistible. Section 1546 expressly provides for

a contest of this nature in the superior court of the county where
the election was held.   It prescribes when such contest may be
made; how and by whom it shall be made, to wit, by petition
of one tenth of the voters who voted at the election, and within
twenty days from the time the ordinary declares the result;
what the petition shall contain; what direction the judge shall
give the case; the means by which testimony can be taken, or
the ballots recounted by three justices of the peace under an
order of court; and when the case shall be heard and determined.   In short, it goes into minute details as to what procedure shall be adopted in order to bring about a hearing and determination of such a contest.   This section makes it a judicial question, and specifies the particular court that shall have jurisdiction over the contest.   If a literal, broad and comprehensive
meaning is given the language employed in section 1545, as has
been placed thereon by the majority of my brethren, then we
have the anomalous and perhaps unparalleled feature in a law
touching a particular public election, wherein two judicial tri-
bunals are created and clothed with the jurisdiction of hearing
a contest over the election.   In the one case the ordinary,
whose jurisdiction is limited in law, can hear such a contest
upon the petition even of *one voter*, and can, at his own option
or discretion, if he can do so at all, prescribe the manner of
procedure, fix the time and place of hearing, and what notice
shall be given.   In the other case, power is given to a court of
general jurisdiction, prescribing who and what number shall
have a right to make the contest by petition, and the steps that
shall be taken throughout the prosecution of the case.   There
is nothing in the section giving jurisdiction to the superior court
which in the least indicates that it is only of an appellate nature.   It is virtually conceded, however, by the argument of
the majority of the court that the superior court's jurisdiction is
not of an appellate nature; that questions of contest may be
made before it that were never heard or passed upon by the ordinary; that both, so to speak, are courts of original jurisdiction.   In other words, that the ordinary may decide the result
of the election on one ground of contest made before him, and
the superior court may reach an opposite conclusion on a con-

test made before it on an entirely different issue.　Another difficulty about forcing such a construction of section 1545 is, that any number of contests might be instituted before the ordinary declares the result, and, pending one contest, another may file a petition before him, contesting the validity of the election on entirely different grounds; whereas the act with reference to the jurisdiction of the superior court manifestly provides for but one contest, which must be instituted by at least one tenth of the number of voters who voted at the election.　It is worthy of note in this connection that the general law upon the subject of ballots guards with sacred vigilance the sanctity of the ballot-box, and never sanctions or authorizes any examination or tampering with ballots unless expressly authorized by statute. This contest necessarily involves an investigation into the ballot-box, an examination of ballots, and a recount of votes.　The only provision in this act that authorizes such an investigation is that given in section 2546, to three justices of the peace, under an order granted by the judge of the superior court, requiring them to recount the ballots on a given day, and report the result to the next term of court, or to the term to which the petition for contest is made returnable.　How, then, can it be implied from this act, or any other law upon the subject, that the ordinary has such a power, when it is specifically given to an entirely different tribunal?

Our attention is called to the fact that the contest before the superior court relates to impeaching the fairness of the election, or the *conduct* of the ordinary.　But the same power is granted to the superior court by the same section with reference not only to the conduct of the ordinary, but also with reference to the *conduct of the managers of the election;* and therefore there is no reason for inferring that the judge, in reviewing the conduct of the ordinary, is any more considering the act of a judicial officer, or a court, than he is when he reviews the conduct of the managers of the various precincts in the county. It is further insisted by Mr. Justice Little, in his opinion, that as the act requires a recount of the ballots by three judicial officers of the county, it evidently implies that any count of the ballots which may have been made by the ordinary in his

27

decision of the questions and contest made before him shall not be accepted as final, but that the superior court, to determine the truth of the vote, may have the ballots recounted; and it is contended that as such a recount can not refer to a consolidation of the votes cast at the precincts, it must refer to a count of these votes that has been made by the ordinary under a contest. I think, on the contrary, that the *recount* there clearly has reference to the count that has been made of the votes by the *managers of the various precincts;* for whatever count of the ballots cast at any one or more of the precincts is made after the managers have acted is necessarily a recount of the vote cast at the precincts in question.

I can see nothing in the action taken by the General Assembly in reference to the passage of this act which is at all in conflict with the views herein expressed. Upon examining the journal referred to by Mr. Justice Little in his opinion, I discover that the act originated in the Senate. When it reached the House, a substitute was proposed by that branch of the legislature, which omitted the provision with reference to conferring jurisdiction on the superior court to hear and determine contests over the election. When this substitute was returned to the Senate, it seems that body insisted upon giving that court jurisdiction over such questions, and hence amended the bill from the House by embodying therein the provisions of section 1546 of the Political Code, and the act became a law in its present shape. I infer from this simply that the original purpose of the House was to make the action of the ordinary in declaring the result of the election final, and not open to review by any court, just as has been decided by this court as to his powers in fence elections. The Senate, however, was not willing that such should be the status of law as to the liquor question, and therefore its amendment made all contests of the character presented to the ordinary in this case judicial in their nature, and specifically provided how such contests should be made, heard, and determined by the superior court. As before indicated, even without such special provision in the act in reference to the superior court, I think the powers conferred upon the ordinary were not at all judicial in their nature, and did not confer upon him jurisdiction to hear such a contest as was presented to him by the petition in this case. But this conclusion becomes more irresistible when we construe together the entire provisions of the act relating not only to the powers conferred upon an officer who acts merely in a ministerial or political, and not a judicial capacity, but also to powers conferred upon a court by virtue of which specific provisions are made for the hearing and determination of a judicial question. I recognize, therefore, the doctrine that "every part of a statute must be viewed in connection with the whole, so as to make its parts harmonize, if practicable, and give a sensible and intelligent effect to each;" but the only way of which I can conceive to harmonize the provisions of this law, and give an intelligent effect to the same, is to give the act the construction herein indicated. For the above reasons, I feel constrained to dissent from the decision of the majority of my brethren.

FISH, J. I concur in the dissenting opinion of Mr. Justice Lewis.

McDANIEL v. COWART et al.

Where a security deed to two grantees embraces a power of sale with authority for the exercise thereof upon failure by the grantor to pay at maturity a described promissory note, a court of equity will not, when the grantor has defaulted in making payment, enjoin the exercise of the power, merely because one or both of the grantees may be indebted on an open account to the grantor in a sum nearly or quite equal to the amount of such note, there being in the petition for injunction no allegation of their insolvency, or of other facts showing any good reason why the grantor should not, by payment of the note according to its terms, have thus defeated the exercise of the power.

Argued November 8, — Decided December 6, 1899.

Petition for injunction. Before Judge Spence. Calhoun county. September 9, 1899.

J. L. Boynton, *W. C. Worrill*, and *D. H. Pope & Son*, for plaintiff. *R. H. Powell & Son*, for defendant.

LEWIS, J. On the 9th day of September, 1899, Mrs. Fannie E. McDaniel presented to the judge of the superior court of

Calhoun county her equitable petition against J. S. and J. W. Cowart, in which she alleged, in substance, that on the 9th day of September, 1890, she purchased from one Rheinhardt a certain tract of land in Calhoun county for the amount of fifty bales of cotton, payable in five annual payments, and that she gave her five promissory notes for the cotton. Rheinhardt delivered to her a bond for titles, conditioned to convey to her the land upon the payment of the notes. She failed to pay off all the notes as they fell due, and Rheinhardt proposed to settle same for $1,200.00. She arranged with defendants and Rheinhardt for him to accept their notes for said sum, $600.00 to become due December 1, 1897, and $600.00 January 1, 1898, and upon the payment of said notes Rheinhardt would surrender to her a deed to the land, Rheinhardt to hold the deed until the conditions were carried out. The notes were accordingly given by the defendants to Rheinhardt, the first of which they paid, but failed to pay the latter until reduced to judgment, when they also paid that one. To secure the Cowarts for the sum assumed by them for her, petitioner delivered to them her two promissory notes, one for $648.00 due December 1, 1898, and one for $696.00 due December 1, 1899, and to secure these notes she deeded to them all her interest in said lands, with power to advertise and sell the same upon her failure to meet. promptly the payment of the notes. Petitioner failed to pay off the note for $648.00 given to the defendants, for the reason that J. S. Cowart refused to give her credit for cotton and melons which would have amounted to enough to have fully or nearly paid off the note, and for the further reason the defendants failed to surrender her the Rheinhardt five promissory notes he held against her. Under the power of sale conferred upon the Cowarts, they were advertising the lands for sale, which was to occur in three days after the petition was presented. The last of her two notes not being due, and the first being nearly paid off, as appears from the bill of particulars attached, she claims they had no right to sell. She also makes allegations in her petition to the effect that both defendants were responsible for the cotton and melons, but no explanation is given of the conflict in her allegations on this subject; she having previously alleged that only one of the defendants owed the debt. She prayed that defendants be enjoined and restrained from offering or selling the land on Tuesday, September 12, 1899. On presentation of the petition, which had never been served upon the defendants, the judge granted the following order: "September 9, 1899. Read and considered, and the injunction is refused." Exception is taken to this judgment of the court, and error assigned thereon.

It does not appear that any supersedeas was granted to the plaintiff on her writ of error, nor that defendants had any knowledge of the petition before sale day. If, therefore, the land was sold on the day it was advertised for sale, a judgment of reversal by this court would appear to be nugatory. But as it does not appear from the record or otherwise that such sale has taken place, the case is decided on its merits. The only question for consideration is whether or not the allegations in the petition present a case for the equitable relief sought. There is no charge of insolvency of defendants, or either one of them, and no reason given why she should have the extraordinary remedy of injunction for which she prays. The contract between her and the defendants gives them the power to sell the land in case of default on her part in the prompt payment of either note. The only way in which she could have defeated the exercise of this power was to pay the notes; and the fact that she had an account against one or both the defendants to the amount of her indebtedness to them could not operate per se as a cancellation of their contract touching the sale of the land. The remedy on her account is by suit at law, and no reason is assigned in the petition why it is not ample and sufficient. The remedy of the defendants for the recovery of their money on the land is under contract, which, it appears from the petition, they were pursuing. The court, therefore, did right in refusing to grant the injunction prayed for.

Judgment affirmed.   All the Justices concurring.

122
321

ELLIS, for use, etc., *v.* POE & BROTHER.

There was no error in refusing to allow the introduction in evidence of a voluminous document, tendered as a whole, which contained much irrelevant matter and but little that was pertinent to the issue in controversy, when there was nothing to prevent the party offering the same from pointing out and tendering separately the relevant portion of the paper.

Argued November 10,— Decided December 6, 1899.

Action on contract. Before Judge Smith. Montgomery superior court. April term, 1899.

Williams & Williams, for plaintiff.

J. H. Martin, for defendants.

LUMPKIN, P. J. This was an action by Ellis, for the use of Greig & Jones, against J. W. Poe & Brother. The petition made, in brief, the following case: A firm composed of Ellis and Ludlam, manufacturers of naval stores, had extensive dealings with Greig, Jones & Wood, of the city of Savannah, in the course of which the latter firm made advances to the former. Having thus become indebted to Greig, Jones & Wood, the firm of Ellis & Ludlam entered into a written contract with the Savannah partnership, embracing stipulations of divers kinds and including a mortgage upon much property, both real and personal, and also an agreement whereby Ellis & Ludlam bound themselves to ship to Greig, Jones & Wood certain naval stores which the latter were to handle for stipulated commissions and out of the proceeds of which they were to reimburse themselves for money advanced to Ellis & Ludlam. Subsequently Wood retired from the Savannah partnership and a new firm was formed, composed of Greig and Jones, who succeeded to all the contract rights of the original partnership. Ludlam, the partner of Ellis, fraudulently, and in violation of so much of the above-mentioned contract as related to the shipment of naval stores, sold and delivered to Poe & Brother designated quantities of turpentine and rosin of a stated value, they receiving the same with knowledge of the contract rights of the Savannah partnership and of the fact that Ludlam had no right or authority to sell and deliver these goods to them. The prayer of the petition was that Ellis recover of

Poe & Brother, for the use of Greig & Jones, the value of the said turpentine and rosin. When the case came on for trial the plaintiff offered in evidence the instrument above mentioned, to the introduction of which the defendants objected on numerous grounds, one of which was that the paper was irrelevant. The court thereupon rejected the same, and the plaintiff, offering no further testimony, was nonsuited. The only complaint in the bill of exceptions is that the court erred·in not allowing him to introduce in evidence the contract between his firm and the Savannah firm. We are not now called on to pass upon the merits of the plaintiff's case as laid, and shall therefore confine ourselves to a decision of the single question presented for determination.

An examination of the written instrument tendered in evidence discloses that much of it—indeed, the greater part of it —was totally irrelevant. It was exceedingly voluminous, and embraced detailed stipulations as to numerous matters which had no possible bearing upon the alleged misconduct of Ludlam and of Poe & Brother. In fact, the only portion of the same at all pertinent was that portion setting forth the agreement of Ellis & Ludlam to ship naval stores to Greig, Jones & Wood. This portion was not offered in evidence separately, but the instrument was tendered as a whole. The part just referred to was entirely distinct from, and perfectly intelligible without reference to, the other contents of the paper. It could have been easily tendered alone. We can not, therefore, say that the court erred in rejecting the entire instrument. Certainly, by so doing much irrelevant matter was excluded; and, as we have just remarked, the plaintiff made no effort to get before the jury the only part of this lengthy document which was admissible. Under the circumstances, it was his duty to select and point out the relevant part and tender this part by itself. Failing to do this, he has no good cause for complaining of the action taken by the court. The principle upon which our present ruling is based was stated in *Skellie* v. *Railroad Co.*, 81 *Ga.* 56, and in *Herndon* v. *Black*, 97 *Ga.* 327, and has been discussed and recognized as correct in *Harris & Mitchell* v. *Amoskeag Lumber Co.*, Ibid. 465; *Smalls* v. *State*, 99 *Ga.* 26;

Georgia Railroad Co. v. *Lybrend*, Ibid. 431; *Walker* v. *Maddox*,
105 *Ga.* 255.

> *Judgment affirmed.   All the Justices concurring.*

REID *v.* WILSON BROTHERS.

424
1147
424
147

1. An amendment to a petition, which was offered at the time of the hearing of a demurrer to the petition, and which was disallowed by the court, forms no part of the record, and can only come to the Supreme Court by being incorporated in the bill of exceptions, or by being referred to therein and attached thereto as an exhibit and duly authenticated by the court.
2. A demurrer to an equitable petition which prays for no extraordinary relief, upon the ground that there is an ample remedy at law, has not been sustainable since the uniform procedure act of 1887.
3. A parol agreement by a member of a partnership, made after its dissolution, to pay a debt of the firm, contracted while he was a member thereof, is not, within the meaning of the statute of frauds, a promise to pay the debt of another.
4. The existence of an indebtedness by A to B, and an extension of credit to B by A by reason thereof, constitutes a mutual account. The statute of limitations only runs against such an account from the date of the last item on either side thereof.
5. The petition, although somewhat indefinite, substantially set forth a cause of action.

Argued November 10, — Decided December 6, 1899.

Equitable petition.   Before Judge Smith.   Wilcox superior
court.   June 7, 1899.

Bankston & Cannon, for plaintiff.
Cutts & Lawson, for defendants.

FISH, J.   In February, 1899, G. W. Reid brought an equitable petition against Wilson Brothers, which alleged, in substance, that on May 25, 1890, he entered into a written contract with Wilson, Pryor & Co., for the sale of the sawmill timber on certain lots of land in Wilcox county, at the rate of $3.00 per acre for all the timber cut, one half to be paid in cash and the balance in installments of $200.00 per month; that immediately after entering into the contract Wilson, Pryor & Co. commenced cutting, sawing, and carrying away the timber, and continued so to do "until about the   189 ," when the firm

of Wilson, Pryor & Co. was dissolved and was succeeded by
the firm of Wilson Brothers, composed of two of the members
of the old firm; and that Wilson Brothers, as the successors of
Wilson, Pryor & Co., assumed all the liabilities of that firm and
carried on the business as before, telling him that they would
be responsible to him for the balance due him on the contract
with Wilson, Pryor & Co.; that at the time of the dissolution
of the firm of Wilson, Pryor & Co. it had not cut near all of
the timber purchased from the plaintiff, and Wilson Brothers
continued to cut, saw, and carry away the timber and to pay
the plaintiff, "along, part of the amount due on said timber."
The petition alleged that Wilson Brothers were indebted to the
plaintiff, on the contract for the timber, in the sum of $1600.00
or other large sum. It further alleged that "Your petitioner
further shows that from the   of August, 1890, up to a short
time ago, a space of seven years or more, said Wilson, Pryor &
Co. and said Wilson Brothers paid to your petitioner amounts
on said contract from time to time, and also from time to time
sold your petitioner goods and merchandise out of the commis-
sary kept by them, upon the amount due on said contract. All
moneys paid your petitioner and all goods sold your petitioner on said contract were charged up to him on books kept
by said Wilson, Pryor & Co. and said Wilson Brothers, and,
on account of numerous items so charged, it is impossible for
your petitioner to tell how much is actually due and owing him
by said Wilson Brothers on said contract, without the aid of
said books of account, your petitioner and said Wilson Brothers
having never had a settlement, and the account having run
through a number of years. . . The said Wilson Brothers
never paid your petitioner as per their contract, but petitioner
was forced to take what he got in small and numerous items
and moneys, and therefore the accounts between petitioner and
said Wilson Brothers are very complicated, and it is impossible for petitioner, without the aid of the books, to prove the
amount due him, or to find out the status of affairs between the
parties to this suit, and it has been and is still impossible, from
the few rendered accounts, to come anywhere near knowing the
amount due your petitioner." The petition prayed that Wil-

son Brothers be required to produce their books of account, in order that the standing of the accounts between the parties might be ascertained, and for an accounting and settlement between them, and for judgment for the amount ascertained to be due the plaintiff.

The defendants demurred to the petition, upon the following grounds: "(1) The suit is barred by the statute of limitations, more than six years having intervened from the time when said claim became due and the filing of this suit. (2) The declaration sets forth no cause of action. (3) There is an ample remedy at law by suit on the contract, without the interposition of equity. (4) There is no allegation that there was any writing signed by these defendants, nor any such performance or other circumstances as would make these defendants liable for the debt, default, or miscarriage of Wilson, Pryor & Co. (5) The suit should have been filed against Wilson, Pryor & Co., and other members of said firm should have been served besides defendant R. A. Wilson, or some effort to serve them or reason why they were not served should be alleged, which has not been done. (6) The alleged mistake or mistakes set forth in par. 12 are stale, and no diligence is shown by plaintiff in correcting or endeavoring to have corrected said errors or mistakes; wherefore said paragraph is demurred to." An amendment to the petition was offered, but, upon objection by the defendants, was disallowed. The demurrer was sustained, upon the first, second, third, fourth, and sixth grounds thereof, and the plaintiff excepted.

1. The amendment offered by the plaintiff and which was disallowed by the trial judge can not be considered, because plaintiff in error sought to bring it here as a part of the record, it not being set out in the bill of exceptions, nor in any way made a part thereof. An amendment disallowed by the court is no part of the record, and can only come to the Supreme Court by being incorporated in the bill of exceptions, or by being referred to therein and attached thereto as an exhibit and duly authenticated by the court. *Sibley* v. *Mutual Reserve Fund Association*, 87 *Ga.* 738.

2. It has been several times ruled by this court that, since the

uniform procedure act of 1887, a demurrer to an equitable petition which prays for no extraordinary relief, on the ground that the petitioner has a complete and adequate remedy at law, is not sustainable. *Conley* v. *Buck*, 100 *Ga.* 187, and cases there cited.

3. Both members of the firm of Wilson Brothers were partners in the firm of Wilson, Pryor & Co. at the time of its dissolution, and at the time the indebtedness to the plaintiff was contracted, and were therefore liable for this debt, without any new agreement to pay it. The debt of a partnership is the debt of each of its members, and a new promise by one or more of the partners, made after the dissolution of the firm, to pay a partnership debt, is not, within the meaning of the statute of frauds, a promise to pay the debt of another. *Wilson* v. *Dozier*, 58 *Ga.* 602; *Weatherly* v. *Hardman*, 68 *Ga.* 592.

4. Was the claim of the plaintiff, under the allegations of the petition, barred by the statute of limitations? We think not, as, under the facts alleged, there was a mutual account existing between Wilson Brothers and Reid. *Gunn* v. *Gunn*, 74 *Ga.* 555. In Angell on Limitations (6th ed.), § 149, it is stated that "Mutual accounts are made up of matters of *set-off*. There must be a mutual credit founded on a subsisting debt on the other side, or an express or an implied agreement for a set-off of mutual debts. A natural equity arises when there are mutual credits between the parties, or where there is an existing debt on one side which constitutes a ground of credit on the other, or where there is an express or implied understanding that mutual debts shall be a satisfaction or set-off pro tanto between the parties." In Buswell on Limitations and Adverse Possession, § 195, the doctrine is stated as follows: "The principle runs through all the cases that there must, in order to bring the case within the exception, be a mutual credit founded on a subsisting debt on the other side, or an express or an implied agreement for a set-off of mutual debts." To the same effect, see Bouvier's Law Dict., "Mutual Accounts;" Catling *v.* Skoulding, 6 T. R. 189; Green *v.* Disbrow, 79 N. Y. 1. The petition in the case under consideration, in effect, alleged that the firm of Wilson Brothers was indebted to Reid, and,

by reason of such indebtedness, sold him various items of goods and merchandise, until within about two years prior to the bringing of the suit, thus making the debt due by Wilson Brothers to Reid the ground of credit extended by that firm to him, and clearly bringing the account between them within the meaning of a mutual account, as defined by the authorities cited above. Being a mutual account, the statute of limitations began to run against it only from the date of the last item on either side thereof. Civil Code, §3769.

5. While the petition was somewhat indefinite, it substantially set forth a good cause of action, as under its allegations, nothing being shown to the contrary, the plaintiff would be entitled to recover of Wilson Brothers whatever balance might be due him upon an accounting.

Judgment reversed. All the Justices concurring.

PENN TOBACCO COMPANY *v.* LEMAN & COMPANY.

1. A waiver of process cures the absence of process or the irregularity of the same.
2. Original undertakers by written order for merchandise, who have failed to pay for the same at maturity, are not necessary parties to an action brought against a person on a contract in which he undertook to pay for the goods in the event the parties to whom credit was extended failed or refused to do so. Nor in such a suit is the solvency or insolvency of the original undertakers material.
3. When the terms of such a contract are in writing and are set forth in the petition, as well as the material portions of the order the payment of which is guaranteed, it is not necessary to attach as exhibits to the petition either the contract or the order for the goods.
4. When a suit was brought on such a contract as that above indicated, and the petition alleged that the defendants signed the order for the goods, which was the foundation of the contract sued on, it was not necessary to allege that an invoice of the goods was sent to the defendants.
5. A petition alleging that the letters "O.K." written on an order for goods, and followed by the signature of the person writing them, constituted a contract on the part of such person to pay for the goods in the event the person sending the order failed and refused to pay at maturity, set forth a cause of action. These letters being ambiguous, their meaning may be explained by parol evidence.

Argued November 9,—Decided December 7, 1899.

Complaint. Before Judge Smith. Pulaski superior court. February term, 1899.

W. L. Grice & Sons and *L. L. Brown*, for plaintiff.
J. H. Martin, for defendants.

COBB, J. The plaintiff sued the defendants, alleging in its petition that on the 30th day of September, 1897, petitioner received from George D. Mashburn & Company, merchants of Hawkinsville, Georgia, a written order for 20 boxes of tobacco to be sent to them, the price of which was $204.08; that, before the order was accepted and the goods shipped, the defendants guaranteed to petitioner the payment at maturity of the bill for the tobacco so ordered; that "upon this guarantee of said [defendants] said tobacco was by your petitioner forwarded to and received by said Mashburn & Co.;" that the guaranty was based upon a valuable consideration, that is, the promise of petitioner to allow the defendants two cents per pound on the order in question, as well as on all other orders for tobacco so guaranteed, and that petitioner has actually allowed the defendants a credit on their account of two cents per pound on the bill shipped to Mashburn & Company, which they knew was allowed them in consideration of the guaranty above referred to;. that the guaranty referred to was both oral and in writing, the written part being expressed by the letters "O. K.," followed by the signature of the defendants upon the order above referred to; that the agreed meaning of the letters with the signature of the defendants was that they thereby became responsible for the order in case Mashburn & Company failed to pay the same at maturity; that the bill and order referred to is now past due, and both Mashburn & Company and the defendants have failed and refused to pay the same. The defendants demurred to the petition, upon the following grounds: (1) No cause of action is set forth. (2) There is no process against the defendants as a firm, the capacity in which they are sued. (3) Mashburn & Company should have been made parties defendant to the petition. (4) "The alleged guarantee contract in writing and the account guaranteed should have been attached to the suit now sued upon." (5) There is no allegation that any invoice was

ever sent to defendants, or that the tobacco was shipped through
the defendants, or that the tobacco was shipped on the strength
of the guarantee. (6) It is not alleged that Mashburn & Company are insolvent, or any cause shown why they have not been
sued or the money made out of them.   The demurrer was sustained, and the plaintiff excepted.

1. As the record discloses that there was an acknowledgment of service and a waiver of process, signed by the attorney
for the defendants, it was not necessary that any process should
be issued; and therefore there was no merit in the objection
that the process actually issued by the clerk was irregular.

2. The defendants were to be liable to the plaintiff upon
the failure of Mashburn & Company to pay the bill at maturity.
Upon the happening of this, the only condition provided for
in the contract, the plaintiff had a right to bring suit against
the defendants for the amount due under the contract, and it
was not necessary to make Mashburn & Company parties to
the suit.   The defendants guaranteed not that Mashburn &
Company could pay at maturity, but that they would pay;
and hence their solvency or insolvency was immaterial.   The
rule requiring that the principal debtor should be sued to insolvency or shown to be insolvent, before the guarantor can be
held liable, does not apply to an undertaking of the character
involved in the present case.

3, 4. As the petition set forth in effect the contract relied
upon and also the account guaranteed, it was not necessary to
attach as an exhibit to the petition a bill of particulars of the
account nor a copy of the order with the letters "O. K." and
signature thereon, which were alleged to constitute the contract.
As it was alleged that the defendants had signed the order for
the goods which were shipped to Mashburn & Company and
entered upon such order the letters which it was agreed between the parties meant that payment of the account at maturity would be made by the defendants in case Mashburn &
Company failed to pay the same, it was unnecessary to allege
in the petition that an invoice of the goods was sent to the
defendants.   It was expressly alleged that the tobacco embraced
in the order was shipped to Mashburn & Company and shipped

on the faith of the contract entered into by the defendants. There was no merit in the fourth and fifth grounds of the demurrer.

5. The contract relied on by the plaintiff, evidenced by the letters "O. K." and the signature of the defendants, was ambiguous, and therefore parol evidence will be heard to explain the patent ambiguity appearing upon the paper. If the parties agreed among themselves, as alleged, that this signature and these letters should have a definite meaning as between themselves, then the signature and the letters so entered upon the order would constitute a contract between them, and the defendants would be liable to the plaintiff if the contract thus entered into was of the character alleged in the declaration. Civil Code, § 5202; *Foley* v. *Abbott*, 66 *Ga.* 115. The petition set forth in substance a cause of action, and was not subject to special demurrer on any of the grounds set forth in the demurrer filed thereto. It was error, therefore, to dismiss the action.

Judgment reversed. All the Justices concurring.

BROWN *v.* HOLTON.

109
111 41

Letters written by an attorney at law, in whose hands claims against a merchant had been placed for collection, to the creditor and to a collection agency, in which letters the attorney stated, in effect, that the merchant debtor had failed and refused to pay his debts, when in truth and in fact the merchant had paid to the attorney the debts referred to, were libelous, and an action could be maintained thereon without an allegation of special damage.

Submitted November 10, — Decided December 7, 1899.

Action for libel. Before Judge Smith. Wilcox superior court. June 23, 1899.

It appears from the petition that the plaintiff paid the defendant certain debts, which the defendant, as an attorney at law, had been employed to collect from him, and that the defendant retained the money collected and, after several months had elapsed, wrote and sent letters to certain of the creditors, and to a firm of collecting agents from whom he had received

one of the claims, which letters were received by them, in which
he said, in regard to the indebtedness collected for them: " I
have not collected anything on the claim against M. A. Brown."
" M. A. Brown has not paid anything on the claim against
him." Others of the creditors received letters from him to the
effect that only a part of their claims had been paid. The plaintiff was at that time engaged in business as a merchant. The
petition alleges that the statements thus made were false, malicious, defamatory, and libelous, and were intended to and did
injure the plaintiff in his business and character as a merchant,
and were also intended to conceal the fact that the defendant
had wrongfully and fraudulently kept the money he had collected. It is also alleged that the firm of collecting agents referred to had branch offices in numerous cities named, and at
frequent intervals published lists of delinquent debtors, and
that the statement to them above mentioned was published to
all of these offices and to their customers, and therefore had
the effect of illegally and unjustly blacklisting plaintiff in the
principal markets of the country. There is a general allegation of damages to the amount of $3,000. It is further al-
leged, that, in consequence of the libelous statements mentioned,
certain of the creditors named, who were manufacturers of
and dealers in goods indispensable to the plaintiff in his business as a merchant, refused to fill his orders for goods, and, his
stock being exhausted, his customers had to go elsewhere to
buy their goods, and his business and profits were thus de-
creased to the amount of $200 before he could get such goods
from other dealers; also, that in lieu of the goods ordered and
not sent as aforesaid, he had to order others from dealers whose
goods were not so salable and were of higher price than those
manufactured and sold by the dealers first mentioned, and cost
him $50 more than the goods of those dealers would have cost;
so that, in addition to the general damages claimed, he sustained special damage to the amount of $250.

A demurrer was filed by the defendant, the grounds of which
were: No cause of action is set out. No facts are alleged which
constitute malice or tend to show that the defendant had ill will
toward the plaintiff or intended to injure him. The damages

alleged are too remote and indefinite, and are not capable of
exact proof. The facts alleged would not authorize the finding of punitive damages ; and as no actual damages are alleged,
the petition is fatally defective. There is no allegation that the
plaintiff was a trader, or that he was dependent on the creditors
named for credit, or had credit with no one else. The damages
alleged are speculative; there can be no recovery for profits
that the plaintiff might have made. The court sustained the
demurrer and dismissed the case, and the plaintiff excepted.

Bankston & Cannon and *Cutts & Lawson*, for plaintiff.
Thomson & Whipple, for defendant.

SIMMONS, C. J. The facts alleged in the declaration were,
as against the demurrer, sufficient, in our opinion, to entitle
the plaintiff to a trial by the jury. These facts will be seen in
the official report. It appears that the defendant in the court
below, and the defendant in error here, was a practicing attorney, and as such received several claims against the plaintiff.
According to the allegations in the declaration, he was paid
these claims by the plaintiff, and, after receiving payment therefor, he wrote his clients, and also a collecting agency, in effect,
that the plaintiff had failed and refused to pay them. Plaintiff was a merchant engaged in business in the county of Wilcox. The letters reflected upon the trade or business and business character of the merchant. It is well settled, and is declared in our code, that "charges made on another in reference
to his trade, office, or profession, calculated to injure him therein," are actionable. When such charges are made against the
trade, business, or profession of another, it is not necessary to
allege special damages. The law is sensitive in regard to charges
made against the business of a merchant. It will not permit
any one to make false charges against a merchant's credit or
his financial standing. Newell, in his work on Slander and
Libel, 2d ed. § 35, says: "Of merchants, tradesmen, and others
in occupations where credit is essential to the successful prosecution, any language is actionable without proof of special damages which imputes a want of credit or responsibility or insolvency." And for example, he says it is actionable without proof

of special damages to say of a tradesman, "He is not able to pay his debts." "I have heard of no failures, but understand there is trouble with S." "He will lose his debt; M. is unable to pay it." And other illustrations may be found in that section. In § 33 the author says: "The law guards most carefully the credit of all merchants and traders. Any imputation on their solvency, any suggestion that they are in pecuniary difficulties, is therefore actionable without proof of special damages. In actions of slander for words affecting the pecuniary credit of a merchant it need not be averred nor proved that they were spoken in relation to his occupation as a merchant; for in their nature they strike at the root of the mercantile character."

' *Judgment reversed. All the Justices concurring.*

LITTLE ROCK COOPERAGE COMPANY v. HODGE.

1. When a plaintiff brought to this court for review a judgment sustaining a demurrer to a petition and dismissing the same, and there was nothing, either in the bill of exceptions or transcript of the record specified as material, to indicate that there was any demurrer other than a general one, it was, if there was also a special demurrer and if the judgment excepted to was really predicated upon it, incumbent upon the defendant in error to take the proper steps for causing to be sent up the portions of the record disclosing these facts.

2. Where in such a case this was not done, and this court reversed the judgment, holding that the petition was good " as against the demurrer thereto, which was not only general in its nature but vague in its terms," and further, that "the defects in the petition, if any, should have been specifically pointed out by an appropriate special demurrer," it was erroneous, when the case came on for another hearing, to allow the special demurrer to be again "submitted," and to thereupon dismiss the petition. As the first writ of error ought to have brought under review here all questions arising upon the action of the court below in rendering the judgment to which exception was taken, and as this would have been done if the defendant in error had exercised the proper diligence, and as a consequence this court could and would have passed upon the questions made by the special demurrer, he was concluded by its former judgment and estopped from reopening, either in the trial court or here, the questions last mentioned. The principle upon which this court based somewhat similar rulings in *Story* v. *Brown,* 98 *Ga.* 570, and *Hodgkins* v. *Marshall,* 102 *Ga.* 191, is applicable to and controlling in the present case.

3. Where to the petition in an action upon a foreign judgment copies of

the verdict and judgment were actually attached, an amendment allowed at the trial term, which merely added to a paragraph of the petition, referring to such verdict and judgment, the words, " as will fully appear by reference to an exemplification of the proceedings in said case," was not so material as to open the petition as amended to demurrer. Civil Code, §§ 5659, 5068.

Argued November 10,—Decided December 7, 1899.

Action on judgment. Before Judge Smith. Pulaski superior court. August term, 1899.

The Little Rock Cooperage Company sued Hodge upon a foreign judgment.   The defendant demurred to the plaintiff's petition, and the demurrer was sustained.   Plaintiff sued out a writ of error, and upon review here the judgment sustaining the demurrer was reversed. *Little Rock Cooperage Co.* v. *Hodge,* 105 *Ga.* 828.   When the case came on for trial again in the lower court, "counsel for defendant stated in his place that only the general demurrer went to the Supreme Court, and that the special demurrer did not go up and was not passed upon by the Supreme Court at all.   The presiding judge confirmed the statement that there was a special demurrer, and that it was upon this special demurrer that he sustained the demurrer, and not upon the general demurrer that went to the Supreme Court. Counsel for the plaintiff admitted that there was a special demurrer argued to the court in the former trial.   The court stated that, as the special demurrer did not go to the Supreme Court, and that as it was upon this that he based his former judgment, he would permit the original general demurrer and amended special demurrer submitted again; and then counsel for plaintiff amended the original petition or declaration of the plaintiff, which was allowed by the court, and immediately counsel for defendant reintroduced the original general demurrer and amended special demurrer to the original petition and amended petition of plaintiff, and the court sustained the demurrer after the plaintiff had amended its petition and the defendant tendered the original and amended demurrer to the plaintiff's amended petition."   The third paragraph of the petition was as follows: "That on the 13th day of January, 1897, in said circuit court of Pulaski County, Arkansas, the Hon.

Joseph W. Martin, judge of the second division of said court, being present and presiding, a verdict and judgment in said suit was rendered against the said M. T. Hodge in the sum of two hundred and sixty dollars and twenty-seven cents ($260.27), together with fourteen dollars and seventy cents ($14.70) costs of said suit, in favor of petitioners." Copies of a verdict and judgment were attached to the petition. Upon this second trial plaintiff amended its petition, "by adding at the end of paragraph 3 thereof the words, 'as will fully appear by reference to an exemplification of the proceedings in said case.'"

The court rendered the following judgment:

"Little Rock Cooperage Co. } Suit on judgment, in Pulaski
              vs.   } superior court, on appeal from
      M. T. Hodge.   } county court.

"The above stated case having come on for trial and both sides announcing ready, and it appearing to the court that on the former trial of this case in this court that the defendant had a special demurrer to the plaintiff's petition by way of amendment to original demurrer which was general, and that it was on the special demurrer that this court sustained the demurrer, and it further appearing to this court that when the judgment of this court was appealed to the Supreme Court by writ of error that the special demurrer upon which this court based his judgment in sustaining the demurrer was not transmitted to the Supreme Court, not having been copied in the transcript of the record, and that said special demurrer on which this court based his judgment was inadvertently omitted and not copied in the transcript of the record as was ordered and intended, and was never sent to the Supreme Court and was never reviewed or passed upon by the Supreme Court, and the plaintiff having amended its petition and the defendant having renewed his original general demurrer and special demurrer to the original and amended petition of plaintiff, it is ordered, considered, and adjudged by the court that the defendant's demurrer be and the same is hereby sustained on the grounds set forth in the special demurrer."

To this judgment the plaintiff excepted, assigning as error the rulings of the court "in allowing and considering the special demurrer, and in afterwards sustaining the demurrer and dismissing the petition."

W. L. & Warren Grice, for plaintiff.
J. H. Martin, for defendant.

FISH, J. The above headnotes and the full official report of the facts of the case, which follows them, are amply sufficient to show the precise rulings of the court and the reasons upon which they are based.

Judgment reversed. All the Justices concurring.

ASPINWALL *v.* CHISHOLM & COMPANY.

Parol evidence is not, unless the proper foundation be first laid, admissible to prove either affirmatively what books of account or private writings do contain or negatively what they do not contain.

Argued November 10, — Decided December 7, 1899.

Complaint. Before Judge Smith. Pierce superior court. January 31, 1899.

W. G. Brantley and *Estes & Walker*, for plaintiff in error.
John C. McDonald and *Hitch & Myers*, contra.

LUMPKIN, P. J. The determination of this case in the trial court depended upon a closely contested issue of fact as to which the testimony was directly conflicting. To an action upon promissory notes brought by W. W. Chisholm & Co. against Aspinwall, he set up the defense of payment, and introduced in evidence a receipt, signed by the plaintiffs, a copy of which is as follows: "Whereas E. Aspinwall has had several years business with our firm, covering various transactions, and whereas several notes given by said E. Aspinwall have been paid, and the same can not be found, now this is to certify that we have received payment in full of said E. Aspinwall for all claims of every character whatever to this date. This December 20th, 1889." Though the giving of this receipt was subsequent in point of time to the maturity of the notes sued on, the plaintiffs contended that these notes had never been paid, and that they were neither referred to nor intended to be covered by the receipt in question.   The court, over the objection of defendant's counsel, permitted W. W. Chisholm, a member of the plaintiffs' firm, while on the stand, to testify that the notes in suit had never been charged against Aspinwall upon the books of the firm, that a written paper which the witness held in his hand was correctly copied from the plaintiffs' books, and that this paper was a correct copy of a statement used and referred to when the settlement resulting in the giving of the receipt above mentioned was made between the plaintiffs' firm and the defendant.   The materiality of this copy statement lay in the fact that upon it there was no entry whatever respecting the notes in controversy.   It will thus be seen that the court allowed the witness to testify not only as to the contents of books of account, but also in effect to testify that certain entries did not appear upon an original statement forming the basis of the very settlement the terms and conditions of which were directly involved in the controlling issue as to which the parties were disputing.   No attempt to account for the absence of the plaintiffs' books or of the original statement was made, and the objection urged to all of the above testimony was that these books and that statement were the highest and best evidence of their contents, and that parol evidence as to what appeared or did not appear upon the books and upon this paper was inadmissible without accounting for the originals.

This court, in *Holliday* v. *Griffith*, 108 *Ga.* 803, ruled explicitly that "proving by parol what a given writing does not contain is as much forbidden as proving in this manner what it does contain."   The error of the court in admitting the evidence objected to in the present case constrains us to order a new trial; for it is impossible to say that the testimony thus illegally allowed to go before the jury had no effect upon their finding.   *Judgment reversed.   All the Justices concurring.*

JOSSEY *v.* GEORGIA SOUTHERN AND FLORIDA RAILWAY COMPANY.

One who signs a contract which recites that in consideration of a stated sum
   paid him by a railroad company he releases it from all liability for a personal injury, which he contends was caused by its negligence, will be estopped from claiming that the release is not binding upon him, because
   he thought when he signed the contract that it related only to the time
   he lost in consequence of the injury and did not cover damages caused
   thereby, when it appears that no fraud of any kind was practiced upon
   him, and that having ample opportunity and capacity to read and understand the contract before he signed it, he negligently failed to do so.

109
123
109
129
130

Argued November 8, — Decided December 8, 1899.

Action for damages, etc. Before Judge Littlejohn. Dooly
superior court. February term, 1899.

R. M. Jossey brought suit against the Georgia Southern and
Florida Railway Company, to rescind a contract signed by him,
releasing the company from liability for a personal injury sustained by him, and to recover damages for the injury. So
much of the evidence as is material to the consideration of the
case was as follows :

"RELEASE VOUCHER.

"Whereas I, R. M. Jossey, of the County of Bibb, State of
Georgia, have a claim against Georgia Southern & Florida Railway Company, for the alleged mashing of my right arm while
coupling cars, occurring at or near Cordele, Ga., on or about
the 17th day of July, 1896, under circumstances which I
claimed renders the said Georgia Southern & Florida Railway
Co. liable to me in damages, which claim is denied by said
company; and whereas both parties desire to adjust, compromise, and settle the matter: Now, therefore, I hereby acknowledge receipt from said Georgia Southern & Florida Railway
Company of the sum of forty dollars, and in consideration of
said payment I hereby compromise said claim, and acquit, discharge, and release said Georgia Southern & Florida Railway
Company, its officers, agents, and employees, of and from any
and all liability for said injury or any results, direct or indi-
rect, arising therefrom, and acknowledge full accord and satis-

faction therefor. And I hereby expressly state that the above
consideration is in full for this release, and that there is no understanding or agreement of any kind for any further or future
consideration whatsoever, implied, expected, or to come to me,
in money, employment, or otherwise. This the 17th day of
August, 1896.

"Witness: M. R. Meadows. [Signed] R. M. Jossey.

"Approved for payment.

[Signed] William Checkley Shaw, Vice-President.

"Correct.   Audited.

[Signed] W. M. Craven,   [Signed] A. T. Sherwood,
              M. of T.   Auditor.

"Approved.   [Signed] J. Lane.

A rule for the government of the railway company's employees, taken from its book of rules, and which was introduced in evidence, was as follows: "If an employee should be
disabled by sickness or other cause, the right to claim compensation will not be recognized. An allowance, if made, will be
a gratuity justified by the circumstances of the case and the
employee's previous good conduct."

Jossey, the plaintiff, testified as follows: "My full name is
Rufus M. Jossey. I was employed by the defendant about two
years and a half. In July, 1896, I was in the employment of
the defendant as flagman on a local freight-train. Part of my
duties were to couple cars. About that time I received an in-
injury to. my right arm at Cordele, Dooly county, Georgia. I
was injured while cutting off a car. I was caught between the
dead-blocks, and the bones were broken extending to the elbow. The bones were dislocated, cracked, crushed unto my
elbow." The testimony of the plaintiff as to how the injury
occurred is omitted. He identified his signature to the release
voucher or contract, and testified: "When I got so I thought
I was able to work, I went to Mr. Craven and asked him if he
intended to pay me anything for lost time; he said yes. He
fixed up a paper, handed it to me, and told me to take it to
the cashier, Mr. Austin. I did not know what the paper had
on it. I did not read it. I just thought it was a voucher for
my lost time. I never signed but one paper in reference to

this injury. I signed this one Mr. Craven handed me to sign. He told me to take it to the cashier. The cashier gave me $40.00 at the time the paper was signed. Nothing was said between me and Mr. Craven in reference to my injuries. I agreed with him about the lost time; the only conversation I had with him was in reference to my lost time. We had no talk whatever about the injuries I had received, and the settlement for it. I never knew until you [Mr. J. H. Hall] told me that the railroad claimed that I had released them from the claim for my injuries. You told me about it in Macon. I had no idea up to that time that I had given a receipt for my claim for injuries. I would have earned about one month's wages, about $40.00, from the time I was hurt up until I settled. Craven was trainmaster of defendant. I will be twenty-four years old next August. I can read and write. I took the paper in my hands to sign it, and did sign it. I could have read it and could have known what was in it. I did not read it, and I guess it was my own fault that I did not read it. The month's wages would have amounted to about $40.00; that would be about the average of it. I was paid by the mileage. I was needed on every run, unless I stopped for sickness or something. I was under the impression that I had a regular run at that time. I do not remember exactly how many trips I made before the 17th of July. I do not remember exactly whether I made regular trips that month or not. My pay depended upon the trips I made; if I did not make a trip, I did not get any pay. Q. If you made a trip every day in the month except Sunday, it would amount to about $40.00 per month? A. I mean to say that was just about the salary on the road. Q. Did you get any salary? A. I guess you will call it a salary, what I got every month. Q. You know what I mean; you know the distinction between a salary and paid by the trip—a salary is so much a month, a certain amount. A. No, sir, I did not get any certain amount. If I made a trip, I got pay; if I did not, I did not get any pay. . .

I signed the release voucher on the 17th of August. I do not remember whether I went to work the next day or not; I think not; I think it was a week or two afterwards. I do

not remember exactly how many trips I made in August, 1896.
I can not say whether I made a single trip or not.   I went
back to the road as baggage-master, not as flagman.   I first
went back as baggage-master on the 'shoo-fly.'   As baggage-
master I had to handle large trunks.   It is not true that hand-
ling baggage is harder work than putting on brakes, it depends
on how you handle it.   Baggage-masters have to throw up
wood on the 'shoo-fly'; on the other trains they burn coal.
They have to handle baggage and to throw it out.   Mr. Lane
and I had a dispute about a trunk, and I quit, and then sued.
It is true that I never knew anything about having signed
that paper until I sued.   I was paid by the trip after my injuries.   I made $45.00 a month, if I went every trip.   The pay
of a baggage-master was a little more than that of a flagman.
.   .   From the time that I was injured, on the 17th of July,
until the 17th day of August I made no trips at all, but I think
possibly it was about two weeks after drawing that money that
I didn't make any.   I think it was quite a while after signing
that paper before I went back to work.   .   .   Mr. Lane was
the superintendent of the Georgia Southern & Florida Railway at the time I made settlement.   Q. Did you know at the
time that you went to Mr. Craven, to whom you went for your
lost time, that he had authority to make settlements for injuries?   A. No, sir, I just mentioned it to Mr. Craven.   Q.
If you had wanted to have settled for your injuries, whom would
you have gone to?   A. Mr. Lane, the general manager.   Q.
What authority had Mr. Craven for making settlements for injuries?   A. None at all.   .   .   Q. Did you not talk with Mr.
Lane about getting your claim for damages?   A. No, sir, I
never spoke to him, never but once in my life.   Q. When was
that, before or after the accident?   A. That was just after this
accident, just before I quit the road, in reference to a trunk."
    Joseph H. Hall, counsel for the plaintiff, testified as follows:
"On the date that the notice was dated, I tendered to the Georgia Southern & Florida Railway Company, in cash, the amount
of $40.00 and the amount of two dollars and something interest
for Mr. Jossey, and they refused the tender, and I demanded
the release and they did not surrender it."   Plaintiff put

in evidence a tender in writing of the amount received by him under the release contract, and a demand in writing for a surrender of the release. At the conclusion of the evidence submitted for the plaintiff, the defendant moved for a nonsuit, on these grounds: "1st. That the plaintiff signed the release contract, which is in evidence, of his own volition, without fraud having been practised upon him. 2d. That the plaintiff's evidence shows that by the exercise of ordinary care and diligence he could have avoided the injury to himself. That he was an employee at the time of the injury, and he must show that he was without substantial fault." The court sustained the motion to nonsuit; whereupon the plaintiff excepted.

Guerry & Hall and *J. T. Hill*, for plaintiff. *John I. Hall*, *Thomson & Whipple*, and *Busbee & Busbee*, for defendant.

FISH, J. (after stating the facts.) Under the view we entertain of this case, it is necessary to consider only the first ground of the motion for a nonsuit, and therefore the evidence for the plaintiff as to how the injury occurred has been omitted from the statement of facts. If the release signed by the plaintiff was binding upon him, in view of the evidence submitted, it would not matter whether the defendant company was originally liable or not. The plaintiff contends that he is not bound by the release, because, at the time he signed it, he thought it was merely a voucher for his lost time, and that nothing was said between him and Craven, the trainmaster of the defendant company, in reference to the plaintiff's injuries, and the plaintiff had no conversation with Craven whatever about the injury the plaintiff had received and a settlement for it, and that he never knew until shortly before the suit was brought that the paper he had signed was a release to the railway company for liability for the injury which he had sustained. It does not appear from the evidence that Craven, or any other agent of the railway company, made any representations to the plaintiff as to what the paper contained, or that there was any device or artifice resorted to by the agents of the defendant to induce the plaintiff to sign the paper. The evidence shows that, after the plaintiff and Craven had discussed

the matter as to whether the defendant would allow the plaintiff anything for lost time, Craven wrote the release, handed it
to the plaintiff and told him to take it to the cashier of the
defendant company; that the plaintiff took the paper, carried
it to the cashier, and signed it when he received the money;
that he could read and write, but did not read the paper, and
he testified that it was his own fault that he did not do so.
Should the release be set aside under such circumstances? We
think not. The plaintiff was not employed by the defendant
by the month or by the year, or for any definite period of time
whatever. Whenever his services were needed, he was called
upon to go out with a train, as flagman, and was paid for the
"trip." When he made a "trip," he was paid for it; and
when he did not, he received no pay. There is nothing in the
evidence to show that the railway company was under any
contract to give him regular employment. Therefore he had
no legal right to expect pay for the time lost by reason of the
injury, so far as such lost time concerned any services which he
was under contract to render the company and which he might
have rendered but for this injury. Besides, the rule of the
defendant company which he put in evidence, from its book
of rules for the government of its employees, expressly provided that if any employee should be disabled, by sickness or
other cause, the right to claim compensation would not be recognized, and any allowance, if made, would be a mere gratuity.
This being true, when the plaintiff went to Craven, the trainmaster of the defendant, and asked if he intended to pay him
anything for lost time, it was reasonable for Craven to think
that plaintiff wanted some compensation for the damages which
he had sustained by reason of the injury, of which damages
lost time would necessarily be an element. Not having the
right to demand any pay for lost time, unless it was a right
founded upon and growing out of a general liability of the
company to him for whatever damages he had sustained in
consequence of the injury he had received, when he asked for
pay for lost time it might naturally follow that Craven thought
that all the damages which he claimed against the railway
company was for lost time. Therefore, the simple fact that

Craven gave the plaintiff the release contract in question and told him to take it to the cashier does not show that Craven was trying to perpetrate a fraud upon him, by throwing him off his guard and procuring his signature to a contract releasing the railway company from all liability on account of the injury. Craven did not act like a man who was trying to fraudulently procure the plaintiff's signature to the paper. He did not tell him that the paper was a voucher for lost time, nor make any representation to him whatever in reference to its contents. He did not even ask the plaintiff to sign the paper, but simply handed it to him and told him to take it to the cashier, Mr. Austin. He turned over to the plaintiff, an intelligent man who could read and write, to be taken by him to another, an unsigned paper, which contained the catchwords, "release voucher," printed in large letters at its top, and which in plain and unmistakable language showed its true import. Surely this does not look like the act of a man who was trying, by a trick or artifice, to induce the plaintiff to sign such a paper in ignorance of its true character. The plaintiff, from his testimony, was, as we have said, evidently a man of intelligence. No fraud was practiced upon him. He had ample opportunity to read the release before signing it, and his gross negligence in failing to do so should estop him from having it set aside.

In *Radcliffe* v. *Biles*, 94 *Ga.* 480, G. W. Radcliffe presented his equitable petition against J. S. Radcliffe and J. B. Biles & Brother. It appears from the official report of that case, that J. B. Biles and J. S. Radcliffe requested the petitioner, G. W. Radcliffe, to go on J. S. Radcliffe's note for $2,000.00, as security. This the petitioner refused to do, but agreed with Biles that he would stand the security and guarantee that J. S. Radcliffe should fully account with Biles & Brother respecting any mules J. S. had sold on their account, or turn over to them any notes or mortgages for which the mules might have been sold. Biles agreed to this arrangement; and the petition further stated that "it was then and there agreed that J. S. and Biles should draw up a paper to carry out this agreement. Biles and J. S. left petitioner in order to do so, and soon returned presenting a paper signed by J. S., stating that the matter had been fixed up. Believing the paper contained the agreement he had made with J. S. and Biles, petitioner signed it; whereas it did not contain the agreement, but, as he afterwards learned, was two promissory notes for $1,000 each. This was a fraud upon him, as defendants well knew. He believed, when he signed, that he was only signing an agreement that J. S. should turn over the unsold mules and all notes and mortgages he took for mules sold, and account for all money he received from sale of mules." The petition prayed a reformation of the contract and that a suit in the city court on the notes be enjoined. The judge of the superior court refused to sanction the petition, and upon a writ of error to this court the judgment of the lower court was affirmed, this court holding that "One who executes and delivers a promissory note without reading or knowing its contents can not avoid liability thereon because he acted ignorantly, without showing some justification of his ignorance, either by his inability to read or by some misleading device or contrivance amounting to fraud on the part of the person with whom he was dealing." To the same effect, see *Haley* v. *Evans*, 60 *Ga.* 157; *Bostwick* v. *Duncan*, Id. 383; *Massey* v. *Cotton States Life Ins. Co.*, 70 *Ga.* 794; *Fuller* v. *Buice*, 80 *Ga.* 395; *Boynton* v. *McDaniel*, 97 *Ga.* 400; *Chicago Building & Mfg. Co.* v. *Summerour*, 101 *Ga.* 820. In Wallace *v.* Railroad Co., 25 N. W. Rep. (Iowa), 772, it was held: "A party who, having the capacity and opportunity to read a release of claims for damages for personal injuries, signed by him, and, not being prevented by fraud practiced upon him from so reading it, failed to do so and relied upon what the other party said about it, is estopped by his own negligence from claiming that the release was not legal and binding upon him according to its terms." See authorities cited in the opinion in that case. "One who, having opportunity and ability, neglects to read all of a receipt releasing a railroad company from any and all claims on account of or arising from an accident, and signs the same, can not claim that he thought it only related to time lost in consequence of the accident, and did not cover damages for the personal injuries sustained thereby." Matteer *v.* Mo. Pac. Ry.

Co. (Mo.), 16 S. W. Rep. 839. "Relief will not be given against a mistake, where the party complaining had within his reach the means, or at hand the opportunity, of ascertaining the true state of facts." Barker v. Northern Pac. Ry. Co. (Mo.), 65 Fed. Rep. 460, citing Brown v. Fagan, 71 Mo. 563; Railroad v. Shay, 82 Pa. St. 198; Pederson v. Railway Co. (Wash.), 33 Pac. Rep. 351, and other cases. While it is provided in sections 3982, 3983 of our Civil Code that equity may rescind and cancel a contract upon the ground of mistake of one party only, when the mistake is as to a fact material to the contract, and provided the complaining party applies for such relief within a reasonable time, yet section 3984 says: "If the party, by reasonable diligence, could have had knowledge of the truth, equity will not relieve; nor will the ignorance of a fact, known to the opposite party, justify an interference, if there has been no misplaced confidence, nor misrepresentation, nor other fraudulent act." From Jossey's own testimony it appears that he was the only party laboring under a mistake, that his mistake was caused by his own gross negligence, and not from the fault, fraud, or misrepresentation of the defendant's agents; and under such circumstances equity will not relieve him by rescinding the release. The case of *Werner* v. *Rawson*, 89 *Ga.* 619, was decided upon its peculiar facts, and, even if the judgment therein rendered was correct, the doctrine there laid down should not be so extended as to control a case like the present. Section 3974 of the Civil Code, properly construed, does not entitle a party to relief against the consequences of gross and inexcusable negligence in signing his name to a plain and unambiguous written instrument, when no fraud, artifice, or misrepresentation was employed to induce him to sign it, and when there is nothing to show that it did not embody the identical agreement which the other party actually intended to make.

Judgment affirmed. All the Justices concurring.

RYAN v. RICE.

1. A mortgage on land given to secure the payment of promissory notes can not, after they have been paid, be foreclosed.
2. Accordingly, where a creditor held such notes secured by such a mortgage, and his agent also held a deed embracing a power of attorney executed by the debtor, authorizing the agent to sell the land for the purpose of paying the notes in case of any default in the payment thereof, and this power was exercised, and from the proceeds of the sale the notes were satisfied in full, it was no longer the right of the creditor to foreclose the mortgage.
3. Under the rules above laid down, the original answer and the amendment thereto set up good matters of defense to the plaintiff's proceeding.

Argued November 9, — Decided December 8. 1899.

Foreclosure of mortgage.   Before Judge Evans.   Pulaski superior court.   February term, 1899.

L. C. Ryan and *J. H. Martin*, for plaintiff in error.
Steed, Ryals & Stone and *Jordan & Watson,* contra.

Lewis, J.   Ira A. Rice brought his petition in Pulaski superior court, against Mrs. Eleanora Ryan, for the purpose of foreclosing his mortgage on certain lands in that county.   It was executed on September 2, 1889, to secure her note of $1,250.00 principal, besides interest represented by coupon interest notes, and attorney's fees.   At the appearance term of the case the defendant filed her answer in which she set up substantially the following facts: She borrowed the money mentioned in the petition through the Guarantee Company of Georgia. The notes were delivered to this company, which acted as the agent of Rice, and also as the agent of defendant in negotiating the loan.   The company, as a part of the transaction, took from defendant a deed to all the land mortgaged to Rice, with power, should there be any default in the payment of the principal and interest, to sell the land so mortgaged to Rice and deeded to the Guarantee Company, and to apply the proceeds of the sale to the payment of said notes and mortgage, said company having guaranteed the payment, and being the authorized agent of Rice.   In pursuance of this power of sale, defendant having defaulted in the payment of the notes, the Guarantee Company sold the land at public outcry, and it was purchased by Howard M. Smith, general manager of the Guarantee Company, at the price of $1,405.00, and a deed made to Smith accordingly. The Guarantee Company being the agent of Rice, it was its duty to pay over the money arising from the sale of the land to Rice, and the sale operated as an extinguishment and settlement of the note and mortgage made to Rice. It was prayed in the answer that the Guarantee Company and Smith be made parties in the case, and be required to produce into court the deed with power of sale, made to the company, and the deed made under the power of sale by the company to Smith, and that the notes and mortgage of the defendant held by Rice be delivered up and cancelled. To this answer a demurrer was filed by the attorney for petitioner, which was sustained by Judge Smith. To this judgment exceptions pendente lite were filed, and duly certified by the judge. Subsequently, at the same term, the case was called for trial by Judge Evans, who was then presiding in the place of Judge Smith, and an amendment to the answer was then offered, to the effect that the Guarantee Company was, at the time of making the loan set out in the petition, the agent of Rice, petitioner, and guaranteed to Rice prompt payment of the principal and interest on the notes described in the petition, and, as additional security, Rice procured from defendant a power of attorney to the Guarantee Company, authorizing it, in the event of a failure to pay any of the interest notes, or principal, when the same should become due, to sell the land and pay off and settle up the notes; and defendant failing to pay one of the notes, the land was sold by the company and bought in by Smith for $1,405.00, which sum the Guarantee Company received as the agent of Rice, and paid off and settled the notes described in the petition. The notes and mortgage described in the petition were not delivered by defendant to plaintiff, but were delivered to the Guarantee Company, which acted as the agent for both plaintiff and defendant, in all matters pertaining to the loan. When the case came on for trial before Judge Evans, objection was made to the amendment by counsel for plaintiff below, on the ground that it set up the same defense which had been overruled and stricken by Judge Smith.

29

Judge Evans sustained plaintiff's objection, and refused to allow the plea.   This ruling is excepted to, and assigned as error in the bill of exceptions.   The case proceeded to trial, and
after the introduction of the notes and mortgage plaintiff closed.
Defendant then offered to prove the sale of the land, and payment of the note, which the mortgage was given to secure, by
the money arising from the sale.   The court ruled that, under
the pleadings as they then stood, proof could not be made, to
which defendant likewise excepted.   The court directed a verdict for the plaintiff, and defendant excepted to the form of the
verdict, claiming that it was a "general verdict."

There is nothing in the contention of counsel for the defendant in error, that the ruling of Judge Smith in sustaining
the demurrer to the plea can not be considered by this court,
upon the ground that it has not been properly excepted to.
Exceptions pendente lite were filed to this judgment, and duly
certified by the judge, ordered filed and made a part of the
record in the case, as is recited in the main bill of exceptions,
and as appears of record.   The main bill specifically assigns
error on this judgment of the court in sustaining the demurrer
and striking the plea and answer.   As to the amendment to
the plea offered before Judge Evans during the same term, it
being demurred to on the ground that the same allegations
were contained in the original plea stricken by Judge Smith,
we will treat the case in the light of the allegations in the
original and amended plea, and will consider the question as
to whether these allegations set forth a valid defense to the
foreclosure of the mortgage.

It will be observed from the recital of facts above that the
Guarantee Company had guaranteed to the mortgagee payment
of the loan made by him to the plaintiff in error, and that the
company, to secure itself against loss on this guaranty, took a
deed from the mortgagor to the same land, with power of sale
in the event of default in the payment of the loan.   It is specifically alleged in the answer that this power was executed
by the Guarantee Company selling the land, that in the sale
it was acting as agent for the mortgagee, that it realized a sufficient sum from the proceeds of the sale to pay the debt, and

that the amount due on the notes given by the mortgagor to the mortgagee was actually paid the latter by the Guarantee Company. If this be true (and the demurrer admits the facts), then this necessarily operated as a cancellation of the mortgage which the defendant in error was seeking to foreclose. The simple question for decision then is, whether, at law, a mortgagee can foreclose his mortgage upon land given to secure a note which has been paid off. To state the proposition is to answer it in the negative. The only reason urged why the court did not err in striking the plea of payment in this case is, that the answer of the defendant to the petition to foreclose shows that by virtue of the sale on the part of the Guarantee Company the title to the land has passed to another, and she, therefore, had no interest whatever in the property, and a foreclosure of the mortgage and a sale of the property thereunder could in nowise cause any injury or damage to her.. While it is true that the judgment obtained upon this foreclosure constitutes only a lien upon this property, and can be enforced only by a sale of it, yet it is also a proceeding against the plaintiff in error. The verdict, though general in its terms, must be construed in the light of the pleadings; and it simply means a finding of so much money, to be made by a levy and sale of the land described in the petition for foreclosure. By the rule nisi, the mortgagor is called upon to pay into court, on or before the first day of the next term thereof, the amount due upon the notes. Whether the mortgagor has been divested of the title to the property since the giving of the mortgage can not affect her right to answer and deny any indebtedness whatever on the notes. If they have been paid, the mortgagee certainly has no right to annoy and harass her by a suit calling for their repayment. She is, moreover, interested in seeing that a judgment is not entered against her, finding the notes still unpaid, although the enforcement of the judgment itself might not operate to her injury; for in the event the land should be sold under the foreclosure, and not bring enough to pay the amount found due, to say the least of it, there would exist the danger of a suit for a general judgment for the balance against her, and a claim on the trial of such a suit that the judgment of foreclosure fixed the amount of the indebtedness. We therefore think the court erred in striking the pleas of the defendant below, and that the issues of fact therein presented should have been submitted to the jury.

Judgment reversed.   All the Justices concurring.

CROSBY *v.* KING HARDWARE COMPANY.

Inasmuch as section 2779 of the Civil Code allows the plaintiff in a judgment obtained in any court of this State ten days from the date of its rendition within which to have the execution issued thereon entered upon the general execution docket of the county, the plaintiff in a county court judgment may properly delay applying for an execution with a view to having the same entered on such docket until after the four days allowed the defendant for entering an appeal have expired; and inasmuch as the entering of the appeal during four days prevents the issuance of the execution by the county judge, the lien of the judgment appealed from, relatively to one who purchased from the defendant pending the appeal, is not affected by a failure on the part of the plaintiff to have execution issued and entered within ten days from the date of such judgment.

Submitted November 11, — Decided December 8, 1899.

Levy and claim.   Before Judge Bennet.   Appling superior court.   March term, 1899.

G. J. Holton & Son, for plaintiff in error.
Parker & Thomas, contra.

COBB, J.   The King Hardware Company sued J. D. Dunn & Company, J. D. Dunn, W. D. Dunn, and Mary C. Johnson, in the county court, and obtained judgment on the 29th day of June, 1896.   The defendants entered an appeal to the superior court.   The trial of the appeal resulted in a judgment against J. D. Dunn & Company and J. D. Dunn as principals, and W. M. Stone as security on the appeal, on the 5th day of March, 1897.   The execution issued on the latter judgment was levied upon a tract of land, and Crosby interposed a claim to the same. Upon the trial of the claim case the above facts appeared, and it further appeared that the claimant relied upon a deed to the property in controversy from J. D. Dunn and W. D. Dunn, dated November 11, 1896, and that J. D. Dunn acquired title on the 25th day of March, 1896, under a conveyance from W.W. Graham. It also appeared that if any execution was ever issued upon the judgment in the county court the same was never entered upon the general execution docket of the county of the defendants' residence. The case having been submitted to the judge to be determined without the intervention of a jury, he rendered a judgment finding the property subject to the execution, and the claimant excepted.

When a money judgment is obtained in a county court against a person residing in that county, the plaintiff in the judgment has ten days from the date of the judgment to have execution issued and entered upon the general execution docket which is required by law to be kept by the clerk of the superior court. The lien of such judgment is a valid and binding lien as to all persons within the ten days, although not entered upon the general execution docket. Civil Code, § 2779. The judge of the county court can be compelled to issue an execution as soon as the judgment is rendered, but if he fails to issue the same within the time allowed by law for an appeal to be entered, the power to issue the execution is taken away by the entering of the appeal. Civil Code, § 4205. The plaintiff has ten days within which to have an execution issued and entered upon the general execution docket. The defendant has four days in which to enter an appeal. The plaintiff is under no obligation whatever to apply for an execution within the four days, and as the power to issue the execution is taken away from the judge after the entering of the appeal, no loss must be allowed to fall upon the plaintiff in execution simply because he has failed to do what he might have done but what he was under no legal obligation whatever to do. The judgment of the county court is a lien upon the property of the defendant, and this lien is not discharged by the entering of an appeal, but is merely suspended, and the judgment entered on the appeal is a lien upon property of the defendant, and is to be treated as being of the date when the judgment appealed from was entered. *Watkins* v. *Angier*, 99 *Ga.* 519. The lien of the judgment rendered in the county court attaches to the property of the defendant the moment the judgment is entered, but it is lost, as against a purchaser without notice, if the plaintiff in execution fails to have execution issued and entered upon the general execution docket within ten days from the date of the judgment, if no appeal is entered. As the entering of an appeal prevents an execution from being issued, the lien of the judgment which has already attached to the defendant's property adheres to the same; and purchasers from him buy at their peril if they fail to examine the records of the county court in the county where the defendant is liable to be sued.

It follows from the foregoing, that one who purchases from the defendant in execution while the appeal is pending takes subject to whatever judgment may be rendered on the trial of the appeal. While the case of *Dodd* v. *Glover*, 102 *Ga.* 82, was dealing with a case arising prior to the time that the registration act of 1889 took effect, the principle of that decision is applicable here, for the reasons above stated.

Judgment affirmed. All the Justices concurring.

WOODSON *v.* JOHNSTON & COMPANY LIMITED.

1. An employer is liable in damages for physical injuries to an employee resulting from the negligence of one who was the general superintendent of the business of the former, and who, on the occasion when the injuries were sustained, was acting as the employer's alter ego and not in the capacity of a fellow-servant of the person injured.

2. Though the petition in an action for such injuries alleged that they were received while the plaintiff was working in the hold of a ship, it was not essential to set forth its name or the names of his colaborers, or to aver that the defendant was responsible for the negligence of the latter, the time, place, and manner of the occurrence giving rise to the cause of action being by means of other allegations sufficiently stated.

Submitted November 11, — Decided December 8, 1899.

Action for damages. Before Judge Atkinson. City court of Brunswick. May 20, 1899.

Max Isaac, for plaintiff.   *W. G. Brantley*, for defendants.

LUMPKIN, P. J. An action for damages was brought in the city court of Brunswick, by Woodson against William Johnston

& Company Limited.   The petition made, in substance, the following case: The defendants were engaged in running a line of steamships from Brunswick to European ports, in the course of which they employed the plaintiff to work as a laborer in loading with cotton one of their ships at their dock in the city of Brunswick.   They employed a superior officer, known as the "walking boss," who had power to hire and discharge men, and who also exercised a general superintendence over the hands engaged in loading the defendants' ships.   It was his duty, when about to change the working crew of any steamer from one position to another in the course of loading a vessel, to first notify the gang working in the hold of his intention to make such change, in order that one of the laborers in the hold, known as the "header," might have an opportunity to notify the new crew of laborers, employed on the deck above, not to throw down or lower any cotton until directed so to do —to the end that the gang below might not be subjected to injury.   On a day named in the petition, a bale of cotton was thrown into the hold of the ship, and the plaintiff was thereby crushed and seriously injured.   The hurt thus occasioned him was caused by the negligence of the "walking boss" in the "changing of the crew on deck . . without notice or warning to the men in the hold below, . . and in replacing said deck crew with a new crew that was composed of green men who knew nothing of the work that they were about," one of whom threw down the bale of cotton by which the plaintiff, who was one of the men employed in the hold, was injured.   The conduct of the "walking boss" in this respect was in gross violation of his duty and the direct cause of the injury inflicted upon the plaintiff.

The defendants demurred to the petition generally and specially; their demurrer was sustained, and the plaintiff excepted.

With respect to the general demurrer, we think it sufficient to say that the petition set forth a cause of action.   The case closely resembles that of *Cheeney* v. *Ocean Steamship Company*, 92 *Ga.* 726, 95 *Ga.* 381, and the principle of the decision therein rendered is controlling here.

The grounds of the special demurrer were, that the petition

failed to allege the name of the ship in the hold of which the plaintiff was engaged at work; that it failed to state the name of the "walking boss" referred to therein; and also that it failed to give the names of the "green" men composing the new crew, or to aver how the defendants were in any way responsible for the carelessness of these men.　The plaintiff amended his petition, alleging that he did not know the name of the particular vessel upon which he was injured, for the reason that, being an ordinary laborer, he paid no attention to the names of the various ships of the defendants' line coming into and departing from the port of Brunswick; also, that he did not know the full name of the "walking boss," but that he was generally known as "Charleston" and was so called by the laborers; and further, that the plaintiff was unable to ascertain the names of any of the "green" men composing the new crew.　In view of the amendment, we do not think there was any merit in any of the grounds of the special demurrer.　The name of the ship was entirely immaterial, for the occasion upon which the plaintiff's alleged injuries were sustained was sufficiently identified by the other allegations of the petition as to the date of the occurrence and the location of the vessel at the time thereof.　Omitting to give the name of this vessel was of no more consequence, indeed, than would be a failure to give the name or number of a particular locomotive belonging to a defendant railway company, where an action for damages was brought for injuries caused by its running or that of a train propelled by it.　Certainly, the defendants were clearly enough informed of what "walking boss" was referred to, after the filing of the amendment alleging that he was generally known as "Charleston."　Nor were the names of the "green" crew, or of the particular member thereof who threw down the bale of cotton upon the plaintiff, essential to be alleged.　As already remarked with reference to the name of the ship, the defendants could not, taking the declaration as a whole, have been left in uncertainty as to the time, place, and manner of the wrong complained of.　The plaintiff alleged his inability from ignorance to give the names of the men; and in view of the evident good faith with which he endeavored to give to, the defendants all the specific information within his power, his petition as amended should certainly be regarded as sufficient. The pregnant fact, to wit, that the plaintiff was injured by the act of a "green" employee against whose negligent or thoughtless conduct the defendants had failed to take proper precautions to protect the plaintiff, as it was their legal duty to do, was distinctly alleged. The names of all the employees engaged at work, at the time specified, upon the vessel then loading at their dock were, in contemplation of law at least, fully known to the defendants; and whether or not, as alleged, one of these employees actually injured the plaintiff in the manner described could, doubtless, have been easily ascertained by the defendants, to the end that they might be able to properly prepare their defense to the action. Besides, it is pertinent to remark in this connection, the plaintiff's cause of action was not predicated upon this man's negligence, but upon that of the "walking boss," who was, under the circumstances alleged, the alter ego of the defendants, present at the time and representing them on the occasion when the plaintiff suffered the injuries of which he complains.

Judgment reversed.   All the Justices concurring.

STIGER v. MONROE.

1. Although a deed conveying a leasehold estate contained a clause of general warranty, which necessarily embraced a covenant of quiet enjoyment, the lessee, if he suffered himself to be ousted from the premises, could not maintain against the lessor an action for a breach of such warranty without showing that the person to whom possession was yielded had title paramount to that of the lessor.
2. One can not be evicted from premises of which he has never had possession, either actual or constructive.
3. In no view of the evidence disclosed by the present record was the plaintiff entitled to a recovery.

Argued November 11, — Decided December 8, 1899.

Action for breach of warranty. Before Judge Bennet. Ware superior court. April term, 1899.

Hitch & Myers, for plaintiff in error.
L. A. Wilson and *J. L. Sweat*, contra.

LUMPKIN, P. J.   The petition of W. F. Monroe alleged that
J. M. Stiger executed to the petitioner a warranty deed to "all
the timber suitable for turpentine or sawmill or lumber purposes" on two described lots of land in Ware county, for the
sum of four hundred dollars paid by petitioner to Stiger, that
"petitioner has been evicted from said lots of land, and that
the said J. M. Stiger refuses to indemnify your petitioner for
his damages in that behalf."   On the trial, the plaintiff introduced a warranty deed, duly recorded, from Stiger to himself,
conveying for a term of ten years all the timber suitable for
turpentine, sawmill, or lumber purposes on ten lots of land, including the two lots described in the petition, and proved that
the price paid to Stiger was two hundred dollars per lot.   As
a witness in his own behalf, the plaintiff testified that he had
never been in possession of the two lots in controversy, that two
or three years after taking possession of some of the other lots
he found that one Rozier had entered upon and taken possession of these two lots, and that the latter, upon demand, refused to yield possession of the same.   Monroe then called upon
Stiger to oust Rozier, and, upon his failing so to do, requested
Stiger to deliver to him (Monroe) "the title" so that the latter
might himself institute proceedings to recover possession of
the premises.   In response to this demand, Stiger failed to deliver to Monroe any deeds or muniments of title whatever.

Whether any one or more of the lots of which Monroe actually took possession adjoined either of the two lots in dispute
was not shown.   It did appear at the trial that Stiger, in response to a notice calling upon him to produce his chain of
title to these lots, brought into court only one conveyance,
which was a deed to himself, covering the premises, executed
by one Daniel Lott about four years prior to the date of the
lease from Stiger to Monroe; but there was no evidence showing whether either Stiger or Lott had, or had not, ever been
in possession of the two lots held by Rozier, nor did it appear
that Rozier had any right or title to the same other than such
as was evidenced by his bare possession.   The defendant introduced no testimony, but, after the plaintiff closed, moved for
a nonsuit.   This motion was overruled, and the court there-

upon directed a verdict in favor of the plaintiff; to which action on the part of the court Stiger excepted.

As will have been seen, the plaintiff was a lessee of Stiger for a term of ten years, and depended for a recovery upon the theory that he had been evicted by Rozier. The evidence leaves it in doubt whether Monroe ever had even constructive possession of the lots entered upon by Rozier; for it does not affirmatively appear that any of the lots of which Monroe took actual possession under his deed from Stiger adjoined either of these two lots, so as to place Monroe in the position of one who, claiming under a registered deed covering one entire tract or body of land, entered into actual possession of a part thereof and thus acquired constructive possession of the remainder. But even if Monroe had constructive possession, it would seem clear that, as the same began prior to Rozier's entry, and as it did not appear that the latter was more than a mere-trespasser, it could not be said that Stiger's covenant of warranty was broken by his failure or refusal to oust Rozier; for if he was a mere intruder, Monroe could and ought to have evicted him, instead of yielding to his tortious entry, and suffering him to remain in possession. This remedy was open to Monroe irrespective of the question whether Stiger did or did not comply with the request made of him to furnish the chain of title under which he held the premises, for the reason that, as against a mere wrong-doer, Monroe could recover by simply showing his prior possession under a claim of right. In this view of the case, therefore, it is manifest that the plaintiff signally failed to show that there had been any breach of Stiger's general warranty of title, upon the theory that he (Monroe) yielded possession because of a paramount outstanding title in Rozier and could accordingly claim to have properly submitted to the eviction.

We have said this much respecting the question of constructive possession on the part of Monroe, for the purpose of showing that, even upon this view of the case, he fell far short of establishing a right to recover.

But the case has another aspect. As stated above, Monroe testified without qualification that he had never been in possession of either of the lots in question. If, as is most probably true, he thus meant to assert that he had never entered, either actually or constructively, into possession prior to the entry of Rozier, then clearly no basis for a recovery against Stiger on the ground of eviction was shown to exist; for " It would seem to be the rule that there can be no eviction without an antecedent possession by the tenant, and therefore a failure or refusal of the landlord to deliver possession of all or a part of the premises leased, while a wrong for which the tenant has his remedy at law, does not amount to a technical eviction." 11 Am. & Eng. Enc. L. (2d ed.) 460. The necessary conclusion is that the court below ought to have granted a nonsuit, and erred in directing the jury to find for the plaintiff.

Judgment reversed. All the Justices concurring.

GIBSON *v.* INTERSTATE BUILDING AND LOAN ASSOCIATION.

Where a building and loan association brought an action to recover an amount alleged to be due it, by one alleged to be a member of such association, for money loaned or advanced to him and for dues and fines, and prayed that the judgment which it might obtain should be declared to be a special lien upon certain land conveyed by the defendant to it as security for the debt, and the defendant filed an answer denying all the allegations of the petition, and also special pleas setting up usury and want of consideration in various items of the plaintiff's claim, it was erroneous to sustain a general demurrer to such special pleas.

Argued November 1, — Decided December 9, 1899.

Complaint. Before Judge Butt. Muscogee superior court. May term, 1899.

Cameron & Hargett, for plaintiff in error.
W. A. Wimbish, contra.

Fish, J. The Interstate Building and Loan Association sued Gibson, alleging that he was indebted to it in the sum of $908.60, besides future interest and installments of dues upon certain shares of stock in said association. The petition alleged that Gibson, being a member of the building and loan association and the holder of twenty-two shares of its installment stock, procured from the association, in anticipation of the ultimate value of the said twenty-two shares of stock and in liquidation thereof, an advance of $1,100.00, and executed and delivered to the plaintiff his bond in the sum of $2,200.00, whereby, in consideration of the said advance, he agreed, in accordance with the by-laws of the association, which by express stipulation were, in so far as applicable, made a part of the contract, to pay the association, on the first Wednesday in each month, the sum of $13.20 as a monthly installment on said shares of stock, and the further sum of $5.50 as a monthly payment of interest on said advance, such payments to continue until such a time as each of the shares so advanced upon should mature. It was alleged that in the bond it was further stipulated that should default be made in the payment of the monthly installments on the stock, or of the monthly installments of interest on the advance, for the period of six consecutive months, the full amount of said advance, with all interest thereon, and all fines imposed under the by-laws, should become immediately due and payable, and the association should have the right to proceed to collect the same and enforce the conveyance given to secure the same, and finally cancel the shares of stock advanced upon; and that in said bond the shares of stock advanced upon and redeemed were transferred to the association to be held by it until the shares of stock should mature, or until the advance should be repaid, when the same should be finally cancelled, but as to the rights of Gibson the same should be considered as cancelled and redeemed from the date of the advance. The petition further alleged that, as security for the performance on his part of the stipulations and obligations contained in the bond, Gibson executed and delivered to the plaintiff a deed to certain described real estate. Default by Gibson in the payment of the installments due upon the shares of stock and installments of interest due, for and during the nine months next preceding the institution of the suit, was alleged. There were other allegations in the petition, which we do not deem it necessary to state. We have simply stated so much of the substance of the petition as is material to the question to be decided. Attached to the petition as an exhibit was a statement of an account, showing various items of charges and credits and the balance claimed to be due.   No written contract was set forth in the petition, nor was the bond which was referred to therein, nor any of the by-laws of the association; nor were any of these things set forth by exhibits attached to the petition and referred to therein. The petition prayed for a judgment for the amount sued for, and that the judgment be declared to be a special lien upon the land conveyed to the association as security.

It appears from the record that the defendant filed what the judge below calls a "plea of general denial."   We presume this was a plea denying all the allegations contained in the various paragraphs of the petition.   In addition thereto, the defendant filed certain amended pleas, in which he alleged that he had paid to the plaintiff $22.00, "ostensibly as admission fees into said so-called association," which payment was made without consideration, and "was but a trick or device on the part of plaintiff to cover an illegal rate of interest, greater than the legal rate"; that he paid to the plaintiff $28.60 as fines, which payment was without consideration, and "was a trick or device on the part of plaintiff" to cover usury in the trans-action.   He asked that these sums should be allowed as credits against his indebtedness to the plaintiff.   He further pleaded that he borrowed from the plaintiff $1,100.00 and no more, that he had paid on said sum the sum of $910.80, that the rate of interest agreed upon was six per cent. per annum, and after deducting the sum which he had paid he would be due the plaintiff, at the time of filing the suit, the sum of $299.33 and no more, and that $609.27 of the sum claimed by the plaintiff was usury.   In another amended plea the defendant alleged that he borrowed from the plaintiff $1,100.00 and no more, and had paid on this indebtedness the sum of $910.80, and that the excess charged by the plaintiff against him, over and above the sum so borrowed, with lawful interest thereon, "is with-out consideration, and therefore null and void."   The plaintiff demurred orally to these amended pleas, and the court sustained the demurrer.   After this ruling of the court, the defendant withdrew his plea of general denial.   The bill of exceptions alleges that the court erred in sustaining the demurrer to the defendant's amended pleas.

In our opinion, it was clearly erroneous for the court to sustain the demurrer. The demurrer necessarily admitted the allegations in these amended pleas to be true. Admitting these allegations to be true, the plaintiff could not recover of the defendant the full amount sued for, nor could the plaintiff obtain a special lien upon the land conveyed to it as security for the indebtedness, for a deed infected with usury is void. In passing upon the demurrer, it mattered not what the allegations of the plaintiff's petition were, for these allegations were neither expressly nor impliedly admitted by the defendant, but, on the contrary, he generally denied them all, and in so far as these allegations could be construed as tending to show that there was no usury in the claim of the plaintiff, they were expressly denied by the pleas which were demurred to. The answer to the defendant's pleas should be evidence, not a demurrer.

Whether, upon the question of usury or no usury, the case, in all its aspects, was controlled by the principle which generally governs transactions between a building and loan association and one of its members, could only be ascertained by resorting to evidence.

Judgment reversed. All the Justices concurring.

ACME BREWING CO. *v.* FLETCHER, tax-collector, *et al.*

This case in principle is controlled by the decision rendered at the present term in the case of *Smith* v. *State*, ante, 227. The court erred in denying the injunction.

Argued November 10, — Decided December 9, 1899.

Petition for injunction. Before Judge Smith. Irwin county. July 20, 1899.

D. B. Jay and *Estes & Jones*, for plaintiff in error.
J. F. DeLacy, solicitor-general, and *James Bishop Jr.*, contra.

Cobb, J. The Acme Brewing Company filed a petition to enjoin the tax-collector of Irwin county from levying and collecting a tax execution issued against it for the purpose of enforcing the payment of a specific tax alleged to be due by it as a brewing company for the year 1899. The petition alleges that the plaintiff is a brewing company having its principal place of business in Bibb county; that it has paid to the tax-collector of that county three hundred dollars, the amount required of it under the general tax act of 1898; that it has established a depot or branch warehouse in Irwin county, from which orders are filled when it is more convenient to do so than from its warehouse in Bibb county; but that, having paid the tax-collector of Bibb county the amount required of it under the general tax act of 1898, it has a right to do business as a brewing company in Irwin county without paying any additional tax. The judge refused to grant the injunction, and the plaintiff excepted.

The tax required of brewing companies for the years 1899 and 1900 is prescribed in the 23rd paragraph of the second section of the general tax act of 1898, and is in the following language: "Upon brewing companies, three hundred dollars, and upon all others who are engaged in the sale of beer, whether on consignment or otherwise, who have not paid the tax as liquor-dealers imposed by paragraph 15 of this section, for each place of business in each county where they carry on business, two hundred dollars." The only difference between the section just quoted and the section of the act of 1896 relating to this matter is as to amount; and in reference to the latter section it was held in *Smith* v. *State*, ante, 227, that "A brewing company which paid to the State a tax of $200 for the year 1897 did not, by establishing in a county other than that in which its plant was located an agency for the sale of beer manufactured by it and selling thereat such beer during that year, become liable to the State for any additional tax." Following the principle of the ruling just quoted, it is manifest that the plaintiff in error in the present case is not liable to pay a tax as a brewing company for the year 1899 in Irwin county, it having already paid the tax to the tax-collector of Bibb county. It was error, therefore, to refuse to grant the injunction prayed for.

Judgment reversed. All the Justices concurring.

RAY v. RAY.

It is not necessary that a petition by the wife for alimony for the support of the family of her husband dependent upon him, consisting of herself and a minor child, pending a suit for divorce, should be filed during term time. Under section 2461 of the Civil Code, such a petition can be made to the judge of the court in which the divorce suit is pending, as well as heard by him, in vacation.

Submitted November 10, — Decided December 9, 1899.

Petition for alimony. Before Judge Smith. Telfair county. July 19, 1899.

E. D. Graham, for plaintiff.
B. M. Frizzell and *Eason & McRae*, for defendant.

·Lewis, J. When this case was here before, it was decided that, where a suit for divorce is pending, application for temporary alimony may be heard and determined by the judge in vacation. 106 *Ga.* 260. Since that decision the application for temporary alimony again came on for a hearing before his honor Judge Smith, who, after the introduction of testimony, passed an order refusing to grant the alimony and counsel fees, on the ground that, there being a suit for divorce pending between the parties, the application for temporary alimony should have been filed during term time, and not in vacation. To this order and judgment the plaintiff excepts.

The judge based his ruling upon the provisions of section 2457 of the Civil Code. It will be noted that this section provides only for temporary alimony for the wife when there is an action for divorce pending, or a suit by a wife for permanent alimony. But by the act approved October 28, 1870 (Acts 1870, p. 413), it will be seen that provision is made not simply for the support of the wife pending suits for divorce, but also for the support of the family of the husband dependent upon him, and who as well as the wife have a legal claim upon him for support. The first section of the act is embodied in Civil Code, § 2461. The application for temporary alimony in this case alleges that the applicant has in her custody one girl child aged one year and five months, the issue of her marriage, and that she is several months advanced in pregnancy, the re-

30

sult of her marriage with the defendant. She prays an order granting to her and her said child temporary alimony pending the suit for divorce, and also her expenses of litigation. She is manifestly proceeding under section 2461 of the Civil Code, not only for her own support, but that of the family of the husband dependent upon him; and hence section 2457 of the Civil Code has no application to the case. The statute under which she is proceeding declares: "In suits for divorce, the judge presiding may, either in term or vacation, grant alimony." It says nothing about when the application should be filed. It manifestly follows that, in the absence of any special provision in the statute requiring such application to be filed during term time, if the judge has power to hear and determine the case in vacation, the application may likewise be presented to him in vacation.

We rest our decision in this case on the law contained in section 2461 of the Civil Code, and do not wish to be understood as holding or intimating that, if the proceeding had been filed for the benefit of the wife alone, this section would not apply. Indeed, we see no good reason to the contrary, and it may be that the right referred to by the words, "at any regular term," in section 2457, was enlarged by the provisions of the act of 1870, as embraced in section 2461, and that, construing these two sections together as they now stand in the code, the latter gives to the wife a cumulative remedy, by allowing her to file the application for temporary alimony, even for the benefit of herself alone, in vacation as well as in term.

Judgment reversed. All the Justices concurring.

THOMPSON *v.* WRIGHT.

1. When a petition is demurred to both generally and specially, and upon the plaintiff offering to amend so as to meet the special grounds of the demurrer the court refuses to allow him to do so and enters an order in effect sustaining the general demurrer, the question is presented whether or not the petition in substance sets forth a cause of action.

2. A petition alleging negligence on the part of an employee in and about a matter falling within "the regular discharge of his duties within the

scope of his employer's business," and consequent injury to the plaintiff, sets forth a cause of action against such employee's master.

Submitted November 10,—Decided December 9, 1899.

Action for damages. Before Judge Atkinson. City court of Brunswick. February term, 1899.

Max Isaac, for plaintiff. *D. W. Krauss*, for defendant.

LEWIS, J. Thompson brought his suit for damages in the city court of Brunswick, against Wright, presenting substantially the following case: Petitioner was engaged as a drayman in the transportation of freight, merchandise, and the like, from place to place in the city of Brunswick, for the purpose of which business he had a horse and dray, and in pursuit thereof frequented the wharves, docks, and depots in said city for the purpose of soliciting business. While engaged in this business, on August 29, 1898, the defendant was at the time, and still is, the owner of the steamer "Hessie," engaged as a common carrier in running a steamboat line between the ports of Brunswick and Darien, Ga. At the time mentioned, petitioner was at the landing-place of this steamer, and while there contracted with one Watkins for the transportation of certain hides from the dock of the steamer to Watkins' place of business in the city ; the hides at the time being aboard the steamer "Hessie." For the purpose of facilitating the loading and discharging of the steamer's cargoes, the officers and employees would lay its gangplank from the deck of the steamer to and on the body of the wagon bringing or carrying away merchandise or other freights. On the occasion mentioned the mate of the steamer placed the gangplank from the steamer's deck to the rear end of petitioner's dray, and kept the same in this position for the purpose of transferring the hides from aboard the steamer to the dray. When the loading was completed, petitioner went to his seat on the wagon, and started to drive off, when suddenly, and without any warning to him, the mate of the steamer, being defendant's employee, having neglected to take in the gangplank, wrongfully and negligently caught hold of one of the rear wheels of the dray, simultaneously uttered a tremendous yell, causing petitioner's horse to become fright-

ened, from the effect of which the horse backed himself, hides,
and dray overboard into the waters of the bay, carrying petitioner, who was on the dray at the time, along with him, drown-
ing the horse, sinking the wagon, losing the hides, and physically injuring petitioner. The petition further charged that
the mate was, when discharging the cargo of said steamer, in
the regular discharge of his duties within the scope of his employer's business, and the duty devolved upon him to take in
and otherwise attend to the keeping of said gangplank, and
that petitioner was in no way connected therewith. In consequence of this negligent conduct, petitioner sues for the loss of
his horse and dray, loss of time occasioned by his injuries, and
damages resulting from his physical injuries; all of which were
caused without any fault or negligence on his part, and were the
result of the negligent conduct of the defendant's servant. To
this petition a demurrer was filed, both on general and special
grounds. Petitioner offered to amend to meet any special
grounds of demurrer, but the court refused to allow the same,
and in effect sustained the demurrer on the general grounds.
To this judgment of the court plaintiff excepts.

The rule of law governing the liability of a master for the
negligent acts or voluntary torts of his servant or agent is well
settled, and can not be embodied in clearer language than is expressed in section 3817 of the Civil Code: "Every person shall
be liable for torts committed by his wife, and for torts committed by his child, or servant by his command, or in the prosecution and within the scope of his business, whether the same be
by negligence or voluntary." It follows from this that a master is not liable for the acts of his servant which are not done
within the scope of his employment. In this case the allegation of the petition is specific, that the negligent acts of the servant complained of were committed while he was in the regular discharge of his duties within the scope of his employer's
business. A part of the business of the servant in this case was
evidently to arrange to take care of and protect the gangplank
belonging to his master, when the same was being used for the
purpose of loading or unloading the vessel. It is clearly inferable from the charges in the petition, that at the time of the
negligent acts of the servant which resulted in plaintiff's in-

jury, he was engaged in an effort to save the master's property.
In Wood's Law of Master and Servant, § 300, it is declared:
"When a servant finds himself, or the subject-matter of his labor, in such a situation that, in order to preserve his master's
interests, he must do an act that will most likely result in injury
to others, the master can not escape liability upon the ground
that it was purposely done by the servant. If it was done in
the course of the servant's employment and in furtherance
thereof, the law will regard the act as having been impliedly
authorized by the master." Several instances are given by that
authority which show the principle is equally as applicable to
the facts in this case as it is to the cases cited in the text. In
14 Am. & Eng. Enc. L. 810, the same principle is recognized in
the following language: "It is also well settled that a master
is ordinarily liable for injuries caused by his servant in preventing damage or loss to property of the master." In Cooley
on Torts (2d ed.), *538, it is declared: "The master who puts
the servant in a place of trust or responsibility, or commits to
him the management of his business, or the care of his property, is justly held responsible when the servant, through lack
of judgment or discretion, or from infirmity of temper, or under
the influence of passion aroused by the circumstances and the
occasion, goes beyond the strict line of his duty or authority,
and inflicts an unjustifiable injury upon another." This text
is supported by a number of adjudications cited by the author,
and is directly applicable to the facts relied on by the plaintiff
for a recovery in this case.

Judgment reversed. All the Justices concurring.

MOUNTAIN CITY MILL COMPANY v. BUTLER.

The breach, by a purchaser, of a contract to pay a draft for the price of goods
and remove the same from a railroad depot, the title to the goods remaining in the seller until such draft should be paid, did not involve the purchaser in liability to the seller for loss occasioned by the destruction by
fire of the goods in the depot; and more especially is this so when the
seller's agent for the collection of the draft extended the time for the
payment thereof until the day upon which the fire occurred.

Submitted November 11,—Decided December 9, 1899.

Complaint. Before Judge Williams. City court of Waycross. March term, 1899.

W. C. Holmes, for plaintiff.   *L. A. Wilson*, for defendant.

Lewis, J.   The Mountain City Mill Company brought suit against H. F. Butler for $46.45 damages, which case was tried in the city court of Waycross.   To plaintiff's petition the defendant filed a general demurrer, which was sustained by the court, and error is assigned thereon in the bill of exceptions.

The petition alleged, in brief, that on April 20, 1897, defendant entered into a contract with plaintiff for the purchase of ten barrels of flour at the price of $5.06 per barrel, less the freight; the contract further being that the flour should be shipped by rail to the city of Waycross, there to be received by defendant on presentation to the railway company of the bill of lading, which was to be indorsed to defendant, and attached to a draft for the net amount of the purchase-money due petitioner.   This draft and bill of lading was to be sent to the Bank of Waycross, and by it presented to defendant for payment, the title and possession of the flour to remain in plaintiff until paid for by the defendant.   The flour was shipped according to contract.   Plaintiff drew upon the Bank of Waycross a sight draft for the purchase-money, attaching to the draft the bill of lading indorsed by petitioner.   The flour arrived in Waycross on May 3, 1897, and was unloaded and received by the S., F. & W. Ry. Co., at its freight-depot in Waycross.   On May 8, 1897, the bank presented the draft to defendant and demanded payment.   Defendant recognized that the draft was correct, but, being short of funds, requested the bank to hold the draft until the following Monday, when she would pay the same.   On May 10 the depot in which the flour was stored was destroyed by fire.   It is charged that this loss was the direct result of the non-performance by defendant of her contract, in failing to pay the draft, obtain the bill of lading, and receive the flour in compliance with the contract.

When a contract of purchase has been made and there has been full performance thereof by the vendor, he can recover any damages growing out of the breach of the contract by the vendee. In case of a contract of sale and purchase of personal property at a stipulated price, if the vendor comply with the contract and tender the property in accordance therewith, and the purchaser refuse to accept the goods and to pay the price, the seller may retain them, and for such a breach of the contract his measure of damages is, not the purchase-price agreed to be paid, but the difference between the contract and the market price at the time and place of delivery; or, as agent of the vendee, he may sell the property, and recover the difference between the contract price and the price on resale; or he may store or retain the property for the vendee, and sue him for the entire price. Such are the provisions of section 3551 of the Civil Code. We do not think that the right of the seller to sue the purchaser for the entire price of the goods applies to this action. It appears from the terms of the contract set forth in the petition that the title to this property never passed from the seller to the purchaser, but was in the former when the property was destroyed. The possession of it was also constructively in the seller, and it was designed that it should so remain until the purchase-money was paid. In *Randle* v. *Stone*, 77 *Ga.* 501, a conditional sale of an engine was made, and in the note given for the purchase-money it was stipulated that the title should remain in the seller until the note was paid in full. The property sold was destroyed by fire while in the actual possession of the defendant, but before the maturity of the note or contract. It was held that the title remained in the vendor and the loss fell on him. In one view, the case we are now considering presents a still stronger defense to this action; because, in the present case, the title to the property was not only retained in the vendor, but also the right of possession, which had never passed at all to the vendee. See also *Gunn* v. *Knoop*, 73 *Ga.* 510, where it appears that a factor had agreed to sell cotton to the agent of a certain firm. The cotton was weighed, and price agreed upon. It was to be a cash sale, and the cotton was to remain in the warehouse of plaintiff's factor until the next morning, when it was to be paid for and turned out for shipment. The bill containing the amount of the cotton and its price was handed the defendant, upon which he indorsed "O. K." and signed his name. The cotton was destroyed by fire during the night of the day on which the bargain was made. It was held by this court that the title to the property as well as its actual possession remained in the seller, and he could not recover its value from the purchaser.

Also in the case of *Sparrow* v. *Pate*, 67 *Ga.* 352–3, it appears that the owner of cotton left it with a warehouseman to sell, leaving the warehouse receipt, on presentation of which alone the cotton was deliverable. The agent of certain buyers contracted for its purchase, indorsed on the receipt the price and his initials; returned it to the warehouseman for the purpose of collecting the purchase-price from the buyers. Before the price was paid, the warehouse was burned and the cotton in it. It was there held that the title had not passed to the purchasers. On the trial of the issue a verdict was rendered for the plaintiff below. This verdict was set aside by the judge, and the judgment affirmed by this court, upon the ground that the title had not passed to the purchasers, and that therefore there could not be any recovery from them of the purchase-price. Under the provisions of section 3551 of the Civil Code, where a vendee refuses to accept and pay for goods which he has contracted to buy, it seems that the vendor can not recover the entire price, unless he stores or retains the property for the vendee. There is nothing in this case to indicate that the plaintiff elected to take this step, even if it had a right to do so under the facts, but it simply retained the possession and title to the property for plaintiff's own protection. Besides, construing the petition most strongly against the pleader, it is clearly inferable from its allegations that the time for the payment of plaintiff's draft was extended by the plaintiff's agent, the bank, until the following Monday, when the flour was destroyed before it was presented on that day for payment. The mere failure of the defendant to pay the draft promptly could not, of course, have been the cause of the fire and the destruction of the flour; and it being destroyed while title and possession remained in the plaintiff, and during the extension of the time in which the defendant was allowed to pay the purchase-money, we think the loss fell upon the plaintiff, and that therefore the court did not err in sustaining the demurrer to the petition. *Judgment affirmed. All the Justices concurring.*

MILBURN *v.* GLYNN COUNTY.

Under the law now embraced in section 343 of the Political Code, and in view of the construction placed upon the provisions of section 527 of the Code of 1868 by this court in *Pritchett* v. *Inferior Court*, 46 *Ga.* 462, relating to the same subject-matter, a petition in an action against a county, founded upon an alleged contract, is not good unless it affirmatively avers that such contract was entered upon the minutes of the proper authorities in charge of the financial affairs of the county.

Argued November 11, — Decided December 9, 1899.

Complaint. Before Judge Atkinson. City court of Brunswick. July 6, 1899.

William E. Kay, for plaintiff.
F. E. Twitty and *J. D. Sparks,* for defendant.

LEWIS, J. Plaintiff brought suit against Glynn County on a written contract made September 12, 1897, between himself and the commissioners of roads and revenues of that county. By virtue of the terms of this agreement, he was employed as an architect to make plans and specifications for a court-house for the county, and to supervise the construction of the building, for which he was to be paid a certain percentage of the cost of its erection. It appears from the petition that the terms of this contract were practically agreed upon by parol between the parties in February, 1897; and before the written contract was entered into, plans and specifications of a building had been made by the plaintiff, accepted by the commissioners for the county, and he had received a cash payment of $500.00. The petition alleges that the plaintiff fully complied with the contract as to his part thereof, except in so far as he was prevented from so doing by the failure of defendant to proceed with the work in accordance with the terms of the contract. The commissioners, after bids by contractors were made for an

amount within the limits fixed by the contract and according
to its terms, decided not to build a court-house, but bought for
this purpose another building already constructed. For this
reason plaintiff did not render the service of supervising the construction of the court-house building. A demurrer was filed by
defendant to this petition, and plaintiff in error excepts to the
judgment of the court sustaining this demurrer and dismissing
the action. One ground of the demurrer is, that the petition does
not show the alleged contract sued on was recorded on the minutes of the board of commissioners of roads and revenues, or that
any action of said board authorizing said contract was entered or
recorded on the minutes of said board of commissioners. There
is no question that the petition does not contain any allegation
from which it can be even inferred that the contract sued on in
this case was entered upon the minutes of the board of county
commissioners. It is contended, however, by counsel for plaintiff in error, that the entries on the minutes set forth in the
petition, relative to the construction of a court-house, were a substantial compliance with section 343 of the Political Code, which
declares: "All contracts entered into by the ordinary with
other persons in behalf of the county must be in writing and
entered on their minutes." The petition alleges that on the
2d day of February, 1897, a resolution was adopted by the
commissioners authorizing the chairman of the board to invite
plans, specifications, etc., from competent architects of court-
house buildings, to be submitted to the board for its inspection
and information, and that this action was entered upon the
minutes of the board. It further alleges that on the 1st day
of June, 1897, the board adopted a resolution to the effect that
the notice inviting sealed proposals for the erection of a court-
house in the county be published as required by law, the notice
specifying that the commissioners invited sealed proposals for
the erection and completion of a new court-house building,
agreeably to the plans and specifications prepared by Frank P.
Milburn, architect, of Charlotte, N. C., which were of file in the
office of said commissioners, and open to the inspection of all
during the continuance of the notice. It further specified in
the notice that the work was to be done under the supervision

of the county architect, and payments made in accordance with his specifications. This resolution of the board was likewise entered on its minutes. It further appears from the petition that the cash payment of $500.00 was allowed by the board on September 7, 1897, and entered upon its minutes of that date. These are all the entries on the minutes insisted on by petitioner, as conforming to the section of the code above cited. We can see nothing in them that even indicates an effort on the part of these county officials to comply with the statute which, in plain language, requires that the written contract must be entered on the minutes. There is no allusion whatever to any *contract* made between the plaintiff and defendant, in any of these entries. No reference is made as to the terms of this contract, the amount to be paid the architect, the terms and conditions of the payment, the service he was to render, etc. The written contract sued on in this case is quite a lengthy one, and goes into minute details as to the duties of the contracting parties, and as to the services to be rendered by the plaintiff, the amount to be paid, the terms and conditions of payment, etc. There is not on the minutes even a memorandum relating to any of these terms and stipulations.

The object of the law requiring an entry of such contracts upon the minutes is to give information, easily accessible to the public, as to the character of contracts being made by county authorities. The entries referred to could not possibly have given such information, not only for the reasons above stated, but for the reason that they were made before the written contract sued on in this case was executed. A party examining those entries on the minutes at the time or directly after they were made, even if they had led him to inquire into the nature of the contract with the architect, would have discovered that no such contract was in existence; the parol agreement that may have been had between the parties being a mere nullity, as the statute requires the contract to be in writing. We therefore conclude that there was an utter failure to comply with the provisions of the statute requiring the record of such contracts.

The only question left for consideration, therefore, is whether or not this omission to enter of record this contract renders the same absolutely void, and prevents a recovery thereon by the plaintiff.   If it were an original proposition before this court, the writer, speaking for himself alone would not be prepared to say that such an omission of duty upon the part of county authorities in failing to comply with the statute requiring the record of a contract made with the county would operate to render the contract absolutely void.   A distinction should be drawn between the exercise of powers by municipal or county authorities that are ultra vires, and the omission of such officers to conform strictly to the law touching the execution of a contract they clearly have power to make.   In this case the duty imposed by the law to enter the contract upon the minutes devolves upon the county officials themselves.   The party contracting with the county has no custody or control over its minutes, and after making his contract in accordance with law, and complying strictly with its terms, it would indeed seem a hard rule that he should be deprived of his compensation, simply because of an omission of duty on the part of a county official.   I am inclined to think that a safer rule to adopt in the adjudication of such a case would be to construe the failure to comply with such a provision of the law a mere irregularity, especially as to persons who have acted in good faith; and, from the limited investigation made on the subject, think that the weight of authority sustains this view.   In 2 Dillon's Municipal Corporations (3rd ed.), 936, the proposition is announced that "A municipal corporation, as against persons who have dealt with it in good faith and parted with value for its benefit, can not set up mere irregularities in the exercise of power conferred."   Among the irregularities referred to by the author is given, as an instance, a failure to make publication in the newspapers of a resolution involving the expenditure of moneys; and he declares, "as respects a bona fide contractor with the city who had expended money for its benefit, in respect of a matter within the scope of its general powers, the contract would not be ultra vires in the proper sense of that term; and the city would be estopped to set up as a defense its own irregularities in the exercise of a power clearly granted to it." Among the number of authorities cited in the text is that of the case of Moore *v.* Mayor etc. of New York, 73 N. Y. 238, where Allen, J., draws the distinction between a total want of power and mere irregularities in the exercise of powers conferred. See also 7 Am. & Eng. Enc. L. (2d ed.) 984–5, where it is stated that the statutes requiring the record of certain proceedings by a municipality have been held to be directory merely, and not to have the effect of rendering invalid an ordinance properly passed and not recorded. See also a number of authorities cited in the text.

But the question involved in this case is not an open one before this court. In *Pritchett* v. *Inferior Court*, 46 *Ga.* 462, it appears that a suit was brought against a county on a bond given, after the adoption of the code, by the justices of the inferior court. It was there held that the pleadings must show affirmatively that the contract was entered upon the minutes of the inferior court, and that the contract would not be valid under section 527 of the code, if good in other respects. Section 527 of the Code of 1868, referred to in that decision, is in the exact language of section 343 of the present Political Code, except that the word ordinary is substituted for justices of the inferior court. The decision in the case of *Akin* v. *Ordinary of Bartow County*, 54 *Ga.* 59, does not indicate any modification of this rule laid down in the *Pritchett* case above cited. On the contrary, it is expressly declared that contracts with the county must be in writing and entered on the minutes of the court of ordinary; and it will be seen in the opinion, on page 69, that the principle decided in the 46th *Ga.* was adhered to and reaffirmed. In that case it was held that there had been a compliance with the 493d section of the code. That was an action brought on certain bonds of the county. It appears that the inferior court of Bartow County had authority to issue the bonds, and that they were issued in pursuance of an order so directing, which was entered upon the minutes of that court. They were delivered to the plaintiff, who paid to the county the money therefor, which was received and appropriated to its use. It was held that this was a compliance with section 493 of the code, and that those bonds were valid obligations of the county. The difference between that case and this is, that the record as to these bonds referred to and practically embodied the contract sued upon, while in this case there was an absolute lack of any compliance, or effort to comply, with this statute. It will be noted in that case that the county actually received and got the benefit of the money paid on the bonds, while in the present case no such additional equity is presented in favor of the plaintiff's claim, the county failing to receive any benefit from his services. The right of equitable relief for the recovery of money actually paid to a county, and, after being so paid, legitimately used by it in defraying expenses which were a proper charge upon the treasury, has been held by the courts as an estoppel against the plea on the part of a county that the money was illegally borrowed. This additional equity does not exist in this case, for the reason that the county abandoned its contract before deriving any benefit from the services rendered.   *Judgment affirmed.   All the Justices concurring.*

₄₇₈
_{4 828}

BRANTLEY COMPANY *v.* LEE *et al.*

A defense by one sued for a trespass, that he gave his promissory notes in settlement of the claim for damages, is not sufficient to prevent the plaintiff from recovering upon the original cause of action, unless it is shown that the notes have been paid or that there was an express agreement between the parties that the notes should be received by the plaintiff as payment of his claim for damages. The evidence shows that there was no such express agreement in this case, but that the understanding of the parties was to the contrary, and that the notes were never paid. The verdict was contrary to law and the evidence, and the court erred in refusing to set it aside.

Argued November 11, — Decided December 9, 1899.

Complaint in trover. Before Judge Bennett. Ware superior court. April term, 1899.

Hitch & Myers, for plaintiff.

SIMMONS, C. J. The Brantley Company sued W. P. Lee and H. J. Reed, administrator of D. H. Lee, for a trespass upon its land. W. P. Lee pleaded that he had made a settlement with the agent of the Brantley Company by giving his notes for $125.

There was a dispute as to the authority of the agent to take the notes, but the view we take of the case renders it unnecessary to decide that question. The evidence clearly shows that, when the notes were received by the agent, the understanding between the parties was that unless the first note was paid, the agent's principal would insist upon the $200 claimed. Lee did not dispute this. He failed to pay the first note, or any of them. The Brantley Company brought suit on its original cause of action. The jury returned a verdict in favor of the defendants. Motion for new trial was made, and overruled by the court, and the plaintiff excepted. It is well settled in this State, by the code and by the decisions of this court, that a note given by the debtor is not an extinguishment of the original cause of action, unless there is an express agreement by the parties that it should be received as payment. The code provides that "promissory notes are not payment until themselves paid." There being no express agreement between the parties that these notes would be received by the agent of the Brantley Company as payment of the amount claimed against the Lees, simply taking these notes, presenting them for payment, or placing them in a bank for collection did not extinguish the original cause of action unless the notes themselves had been paid. The notes not being paid, and no express agreement having been made that they should be received as payment, the verdict was contrary to law and evidence, and the judge erred in refusing a new trial. *Norton* v. *Paragon Oil Can Co.*, 98 *Ga.* 468, and cases cited in the opinion of Mr. Justice Lumpkin.

Judgment reversed.   All the Justices concurring.

SMITH v. THE STATE.

1. A verdict finding one tried upon an indictment for murder guilty of "manslaughter" is, in legal effect, a verdict convicting him of "voluntary manslaughter."

2. Giving to the word "impeached" its strictly proper signification as applied to witnesses, a witness whose "unworthiness of credit is absolutely established in the mind of the jury" is impeached and ought not to be believed unless corroborated. It is, however, always a question for them whether or not any witness has been impeached. The word "im-

109
f112
j112
109
116
109
*l18
l18
109
l21
1(
1:
le
10(
d1

peached," appearing in section 5295 of the Civil Code, is not there used
in the sense above indicated, but as being synonymous with "attacked."
The charge relating to the impeachment of witnesses, to which exception
is made in the present case, is not, when taken in its entirety, out of harmony with what is now ruled.

3. When one on trial for murder sets up as his sole defense that the homicide was accidental, and supports the same both by sworn testimony and
his statement, and the judge delivers to the jury an elaborate charge
adapted throughout to a case of intentional killing, without in any manner alluding to this defense until about to conclude his instructions, and
then, after very briefly referring to the contention of the accused and the
law applicable thereto, adds: "I see I have got that noted here, but in
my charge I did not think to call your attention to it," a verdict against
the accused should be set aside.

Argued October 5, 1899. — Decided January 24, 1900.

Indictment for murder.   Before Judge Littlejohn.   Webster
superior court.   April term, 1899.

J. B. Hudson, S. R. Stevens, and *Allen Fort,* for plaintiff in
error.   *F. A. Hooper, solicitor-general;* contra.

LUMPKIN, P. J.   1. In this case the jury, upon an indictment
for murder, returned a verdict finding the plaintiff in error
guilty of "manslaughter."   One ground of his motion for a new
trial alleges that this verdict "is too vague, indefinite, and uncertain to authorize sentence and judgment," but in his bill of
exceptions, which assigns error upon the overruling of the motion, he says the jury rendered a verdict of guilty of "voluntary manslaughter."   The construction thus finally placed on
the verdict by the accused himself is in exact accord with the
decision of this court in *Welch* v. *State,* 50 *Ga.* 128.

2. The court charged as follows, on the subject of the impeachment of witnesses: "Under the law of this State, there
are three ways of impeaching a witness.   One of the ways for
impeaching a witness is by disproving the facts that may be
testified to by the witness.   Another way is by proof of contradictory statements previously made that are material to the testimony of the witness and to the issue of the case.   Whenever
testimony is introduced for the purpose of impeaching a witness, then the question arises for the jury, and it is a question of fact, whether or not the witness has been impeached.

Whether or not the witness has been successfully impeached, to what extent, if any, such witness or witnesses have been impeached, is a question entirely for the jury, a question of fact that is to be determined from the testimony on that question. *Whenever a witness has been successfully impeached, you have the right to disregard the witness's testimony and exclude it entirely if you see proper to do so.* But whenever testimony is introduced for the purpose of impeaching a witness, still the jury has a right to believe such witness's testimony, if they believe the witness has testified to the truth. *If you believe the testimony of a witness is true, you have the right to believe it.* In passing upon that question, gentlemen, should you find any testimony offered in this case, offered for the purpose of impeaching a witness, then you are to inquire and see whether the testimony of such witness has been corroborated, and if corroborated, whether it is corroborated in a material or immaterial part, and the weight and credit to be given to the witness or any witness in the case is a matter entirely for the jury." In the motion for a new trial error is assigned upon the two sentences of the charge which we have italicized, the second being copied immediately after the first, with nothing to indicate that there was any intervening language. As will be readily seen, the omitted sentence had a vital bearing upon the subject which the court was presenting to the jury. The obvious and proper purpose of the judge in using the words thus left out of the motion was to allow the jury to determine the question whether or not any witness sought to be impeached had been in fact impeached; that is, actually rendered unworthy of credit. If there could possibly be a doubt that this was the judge's purpose, a reading of the entire extract which we have made from the charge will certainly remove it.

The portions of the charge set forth in the motion in the manner we have pointed out, and which it is needless to say we do not approve, are alleged to be erroneous, "because if a witness be successfully impeached and not corroborated, such witness is unworthy of credit and it is the jury's duty to disregard such testimony." Taking the two sentences by themselves, they might convey the idea that it was the right of the

31

jury to believe an uncorroborated witness who had been shown
to be totally unworthy of belief; but taking the language excepted to in connection with all the judge said on this subject, no
such idea could be derived.   So the criticism upon the charge is
neither fair nor well founded.   If the real meaning of the charge
was that ascribed to it, we would pronounce it erroneous.

It is surprising that so much confusion should have arisen
over a matter apparently so simple as the true rule relating to
the impeachment of witnesses.   In *Duncan* v. *State*, 97 *Ga.* 181,
the writer undertook to throw some light on this subject, and
in *Powell* v. *State*, 101 *Ga.* 19, 20, 21, 22, Mr. Justice Little discussed it ably, satisfactorily, and convincingly.   His definition
of an impeached witness is concise, but strong and lucid.   It
is: "When a witness is impeached, his unworthiness of credit
is absolutely established in the mind of the jury."   He here
used the word "impeached" in its proper signification.   Can
any one with good reason assert that such a witness ought to
be believed when his testimony is uncorroborated, or that a
judge would be right in instructing a jury to this effect?   Surely
not.   It can not matter by which of the legal methods the impeachment is accomplished, if it is effectual and complete.   If
it absolutely establishes to the satisfaction of the jury that the
witness is unworthy of credit, they ought to disregard his testimony, unless it is corroborated.   It is, of course, always a matter for them to determine whether any witness is really impeached; that is, completely broken down as to credibility;
and until this point is reached, they may or may not believe
him, as they see proper.   As remarked by Mr. Justice Lewis in
Huff v. *State*, 104 *Ga.* 524, "The jury have a right to believe
the witness who is attacked rather than the witness brought
to impeach him."   He evidently used the word "impeach"
here as synonymous with "attack," for he added: "Hence it
does not follow that while testimony may be submitted for the
purpose of impeaching a witness, his testimony is thereby
necessarily destroyed."

The last sentence of section 5295 of the Civil Code is invoked
to sustain the negative of the proposition that a witness impeached by proof of bad character or of contradictory state-

ments (it being understood that we here use the word "impeached" in its true sense as above pointed out) ought never to be believed without corroboration. That sentence reads as follows: "It is for the jury to determine the credit to be given his testimony where impeached for general bad character or for contradictory statements out of court." We do not, of course, undertake to say that this is not the law. We know it is, for the section has the force of a statute and is binding as such. The only thing to do is to ascertain what the language just quoted really means, and then enforce it. The whole question turns upon the meaning of the word "impeached" as employed in this section. We are confident that it was in this place used in the sense of "attacked," or "sought to be impeached." By giving it this signification, all difficulty vanishes and the well-reasoned doctrine of the *Powell* case stands intact and unimpaired. The word "impeached" has often been used in this sense, and it seems quite natural that it should have been so used in this particular instance. Thus treating it, the law will have just such a wise and proper operation as we may well believe the codifiers and the General Assembly intended; but if we give to this word in this section its technically correct signification, it would follow that the distinguished lawyers who last revised the code, and our lawmakers, deliberately declared that a jury might capriciously believe, without corroboration, a witness whose "unworthiness of credit" had been "absolutely established" in their minds. We find ourselves unable to reach such a conclusion. Nor can we see how the next preceding sentence of this code section militates against what we now rule. It reads thus: "But if a witness swear willfully and knowingly falsely, his testimony ought to be disregarded entirely, unless corroborated by circumstances or other unimpeached evidence." That a jury ought to disregard entirely the uncorroborated testimony of a witness when they know that he has committed perjury, affords no help in construing the word "impeached" appearing in the next sentence. The statute does not tell us how the jury are to know that a witness has committed perjury, but we can conceive of no better way of being satisfied that a witness is capable of so doing than ! y

being absolutely convinced of his total unworthiness of credit.
A witness shown to be capable of perjury is not, morally, the
superior of a witness shown to be guilty of perjury. If, therefore, the word "impeached," in the sentence last referred to, relates to witnesses who are absolutely unworthy of belief, the
two sentences are inharmonious. In one it is declared that a
perjurer must not be believed unless corroborated, while the
necessary meaning of the other would be that a witness capable
of committing perjury may be believed without corroboration.
But all this trouble instantly disappears if we give to the word
"impeached" in this last sentence the meaning for which we
have herein contended. In the recent case of *Mitchell* v. *State*,
110 *Ga.*, the writer, for two reasons, purposely refrained from
elaborating our views as to the construction which should be
placed upon this word as used in the sentence just mentioned;
1st, because our present question was not directly made in that
case, and 2d, because the trial judge, taking as a whole his
instructions on the subject of impeachment, evidently understood this word as there employed to mean what we now hold
it does mean.

3. We grant a new trial in this case on the ground which we
will now discuss. The accused set up as his sole defense that
the homicide was accidental, and he supported it by sworn testimony and by his statement. The judge gave to the jury an
elaborate charge, every word of which, down to the very last
of it, was adapted to a case of intentional killing. He did not,
till just about to conclude his instructions, remotely allude to
the defense relied upon. Just as he was about to finish, he
told the jury in a single sentence that if the killing was accidental, the accused would not be guilty of any offense, and
added: "I see I have got that noted here, but in my charge
I did not think to call your attention to it." This was almost
saying to the jury that the judge thought there was very little
in the defendant's contention that the killing was the result
of an accident. It was really more harmful to the accused
than not to mention his defense at all. He was entitled to have
it fully and fairly submitted to the jury at the proper time and
in the proper connection, and not in a manner calculated to

impress them with the idea that thé judge scarcely deemed it worthy to be mentioned. In' a note entered upon the motion for a new trial, his honor certifies, in this connection: "At the close of the charge, which was quite lengthy, I examined my notes and found that I had failed to charge on the accidental theory. The remark complained of was made for the purpose of impressing upon the jury that I did intend to instruct them on that theory and had overlooked it." We do not see how this statement helps the matter. It simply shows that the judge attached so little importance to the "accidental theory" he almost forgot to mention it although he had made a written note of it, and it is not to be supposed that the jury lost sight of a thing of this much consequence. The only defense of the accused, which, we repeat, was supported by evidence and by his statement, was worse than ignored. It was chilled by judicial oversight or blighted by implied judicial disapproval.

Judgment reversed.   All the Justices concurring.   Little, J., concurring specially.

DOVER *v.* THE STATE.

1. The fact that some of the jurors constituting the panel for the trial of a felony case were summoned in an irregular way is no ground for a new trial, when such irregularity was known before trial and no objection was made to the panel.
2. Upon the trial of a person charged with the offense of murder, where the defense set up is that the accused was a member of the posse of an arresting officer, and that when he killed the deceased he was acting under the fears of a reasonable man that his life was in danger, a charge that in order for such fears to justify the killing they must have been the fears "of a reasonably courageous man, not the fears of a coward, but the fears of a brave man who wants to do his duty and is trying to do it," will not be held sufficient cause for ordering a new trial.
3. Where in such a trial there was evidence from which the jury might infer that the arresting officer was not actuated by a purpose to discharge his duty but had in mind a design to do a wrong to the deceased, as well as evidence warranting the inference that the members of the posse shared in the officer's unlawful intention, it was not error for the judge to instruct the jury, in effect, that they should weigh and take into consideration all the facts and circumstances tending to throw light on the motives and conduct of the officer; and that if the officer had an unlaw-

ful design and his associates shared in it, each would be accountable for the motives actuating them as a body:

4. Nor in such a case was it error for the judge to charge the jury as follows: "If you believe from the evidence in this case that the arrest could have been made and should have been made without taking the life of the party to have been arrested, it ought to have been done, and it was a crime to take his life."

5. The law as embodied in sections 70 and 71 of the Penal Code, and the law requiring that to justify the killing the danger must be urgent and pressing at the time, as embodied in section 73 of the Penal Code, may both be appropriately given in the same case, provided they are not confused or made applicable to the same theory or state of facts, that is, there may be in the same case one theory calling for instructions on the first subject and another theory calling for and making proper instructions on the latter subject   In the present case it does not appear that the judge confused these different branches of the law of homicide, or that any injury was done to the accused by giving in charge the law contained in section 73 of the Penal Code.

6. The charge as a whole was a correct exposition of the law of the case. The evidence amply warranted the verdict, and there was no error in refusing to grant a new trial.

Submitted December 4, 1899. — Decided January 24, 1900.

Indictment for murder. Before Judge Estes. Habersham superior court. September term, 1899.

George P. Erwin and *Howard Thompson*, for plaintiff in error. *W. A. Charters*, solicitor-general, contra.

Cobb, J. Dover was placed upon trial, charged with the offense of murder, and was convicted of voluntary manslaughter. He made a motion for a new trial, which was overruled, and he excepted.

1. When the sheriff was making up the panel from which the jury to try this case was to be selected, the judge called upon four persons who were sitting in the court-room and asked each the following questions: "What is your name? Are you related to Mr. Dover?" He then said to the sheriff, "Why don't you put his name down as tales juror?" The sheriff did take the names of such four persons and placed them upon the panel, and two of them were selected as jurors to try the case. It seems that all this took place in the presence of the accused and his counsel, and that no objection was made at the time to the proceeding. While the manner of

selecting these jurors was irregular, it is certainly not a ground
for granting a new trial, when no objection was interposed until
after the verdict had been rendered.

2. Complaint is made that the judge erred in charging the
jury as follows: "The defendant claims in this case that the
circumstances that surrounded him at the time of the shooting,
if he did shoot, and it is admitted in this case that he did shoot;
he claims that the circumstances that surrounded him at that
time were sufficient to excite the fears of a reasonable man. I
charge you, gentlemen of the jury, that means the fear of a reasonably courageous man, not the fears of a coward, but the fears
of a brave man who wants to do his duty and is trying to do it."
The error assigned upon the charge is, that the law does not require that the slayer should be a *brave* man, or that he should be
actuated by the fears of a brave man; the law requiring only
that the killing should be done under the fears of a *reasonable*
man. In the case of *Teal* v. *State*, 22 *Ga*. 75, it was held that
to justify the homicide the fears of the slayer should be those
of a reasonable man — "one reasonably courageous, reasonably
self-possessed, and not those of a coward." In the case of *Price*
v. *State*, 72 *Ga*. 441, this court approved a charge on the subject of reasonable fears, which stated that such fears, in order
to relieve the slayer, must be those of a "courageous man."
In *Gallery* v. *State*, 92 *Ga*. 463, a charge on the subject now
under consideration, that the law "means the fears of a man
reasonably courageous," was held not to be erroneous. In the
present case the judge charged the jury that the accused at the
time of the killing must have been actuated by "the fear of a
reasonably courageous man, not the fears of a coward"; then
adding, by way of explanation of what was a reasonably courageous man, "the fears of a brave man who wants to do his
duty and is trying to do it." We will not because of this
charge reverse the judgment. We do not approve of the use
of the word "brave" in this connection. A jury might understand it to imply something more than "reasonably courageous" or even "courageous." This opinion must not be regarded as a precedent sanctioning the employment of the term
brave in a charge on reasonable fears. We simply hold that

in this particular case, as the accused was acting as a member
of the posse of an arresting officer, the charge complained of
is not cause for a new trial.

3, 4. The charges referred to in the 3d and 4th headnotes
were certainly not erroneous. If the arresting officer and his
posse used the authority which the law gave them, as a cloak
to avenge the private grievance of one of the number, and all
participated in this unlawful purpose, certain it is that the law
would not allow a homicide committed by such party to be justified merely by the fact that the slayer was nominally, at the
time of the killing, a member of the posse of the arresting officer. If the accused killed the deceased from motives of revenge,
the fact that he was a member of the posse of the arresting officer would not avail him as a defense. It is certainly sound
law, that if an arrest can be accomplished without taking human life, it is murder to take the life.

5. In the case of *Powell* v. *State*, 101 *Ga.* 9, Mr. Justice Little, in the opinion on page 26, in referring to sections 71 and
73 of the Penal Code, said: "It is entirely proper that these
two sections of the code and these two theories of justifiable
homicide should have been given in charge to the jury by the
presiding judge in this case. It would not have been proper
for him to have assumed, under the contentions raised, that
this homicide occurred under circumstances which would make
it justifiable under either one of the theories contended for;
that was a question exclusively for the jury; and having been
charged with the law applicable to justifiable homicide under
the two theories, the jury could and would have applied the
same according to the evidence as they believed it to be." It
thus being clear that it was the duty of the judge to charge the
law embraced in both sections, and it appearing from an examination of the record that the charge upon this subject was clear
and explicit and not calculated in any way to confuse the jury,
the assignments of error upon such portion of the charge must
be held not to be well taken.

6. The foregoing deals with such of the assignments of error
as require treatment at length. The charge as a whole was a
correct exposition of the law of the case, and nothing in the

same has been brought to our attention which could be characterized as an error requiring the granting of a new trial. The evidence not only fully justified the jury in finding the accused guilty of voluntary manslaughter, but under the record before us a verdict for murder would not have been unwarranted. There was no error in refusing to grant a new trial.

Judgment affirmed. All the Justices concurring.

TRIPP et al. v. THE STATE.

109 480
f113 1081

109
f127

To commit the offense of riot the joint action of two or more persons is required; and where in a given case it is shown that while two persons were in company one was guilty of an unlawful act of violence, and the evidence fails to disclose any participation by the other in such act, and there were no circumstances from which a common intent to do the act might be inferred, a conviction can not lawfully stand.

Submitted December 4, 1899.—Decided January 24, 1900.

Certiorari. Before Judge Hart. Morgan superior court. October 30, 1899.

W. R. Mustin, for plaintiffs in error.

H. G. Lewis, solicitor-general, and *E. W. Butler,* contra.

LITTLE, J. Tripp and another presented a petition to the judge of the superior court, for certiorari, which was sanctioned; and it appeared by the answer of the judge of the county court, that Henry Tripp and Albert Tripp were indicted in the superior court of Morgan county for the offense of riot; that the same was transferred to the county court where the defendants were tried. The bill of indictment charged the defendants with committing "an act of a violent and tumultuous manner," by riding by the dwelling-house of L. T. Osborn and firing off pistols and shooting into a tenement-house of said Osborn. The evidence tended to show that the defendants were in a buggy traveling the public road in front of the house of Osborn; that Mrs. Osborn was standing in the porch of her residence, when the two defendants drove rapidly by; that two children were in the road, and Mrs. Osborn found it necessary to call them to get out of the way of the rapidly passing vehicle. After the defendants had driven one hundred or more yards beyond the house, the one who was not driving fired a pistol in the air, and a little further on fired a pistol at a tenant-house on the place. The horse was being driven as fast as he could trot. The one who was seated on the left side of the buggy did the firing. They did not seem to be drunk, nor were they boisterous other than in the driving and shooting. The defendants were convicted, and the question presented by their petition for certiorari is, was the conviction lawful under the evidence submitted? We think not. The conduct of the defendant who did the shooting was most reprehensible, and we have no doubt that the good lady who witnessed these occurrences was not only shocked but frightened, and there ought to be found a way to put a stop to such conduct; but are clear that neither of the defendants was guilty of the offense of riot, which by section 354 of the Penal Code is thus defined: "If two or more persons do an unlawful act of violence, or any other act in a violent and tumultuous manner, they shall be guilty of a riot, and be punished as for a misdemeanor." There can be no question that the firing of a pistol towards a tenement-house is an unlawful act of violence, but in the commission of the offense of riot there must be a joint action of two or more persons. *McPherson* v. *State,* 22 *Ga.* 488; *Prince* v. *State,* 30 *Ga.* 27; *Robinson* v. *State,* 84 *Ga.* 680; *Stafford* v. *State,* 93 *Ga.* 207; *Perkins* v. *State,* 78 *Ga.* 316; *Stokes* v. *State,* 73 *Ga.* 816; *Bolden* v. *State,* 64 *Ga.* 361.

The act charged in this case is the rapid driving on the public road and the firing of the pistol. The evidence shows that the horse which was being driven went as fast as he could trot. This is not itself unlawful, nor an act of violence, nor necessarily an act done in a tumultuous manner. If it be said that coupled with such driving was the firing of the pistol, the reply is that the evidence in no way connects the driver with the discharges of the pistol, and there is nothing in the evidence which tends to show that the firing was done in pursuance of a common intent. While we are prepared to condemn such conduct in the most emphatic terms, we can not, as a matter of law, rule that the defendants committed a riot. If the evidence connected both parties with the firing of the pistol, it might be otherwise; but as it was not shown that the driver of the horse had any connection with the act of firing, and as the joint action of at least two persons is required to constitute the offense, it is manifest that the conviction can not stand, and on the hearing the certiorari should have been sustained.

Judgment reversed. All the Justices concurring.

KASSELL *v.* MAYOR & ALDERMEN OF SAVANNAH.

A municipal corporation can not, without express legislative authority so to do, enact a valid ordinance for the punishment of an act which constitutes an offense against a penal statute of the State. It follows from this principle that if, on the trial of one charged with the violation of a municipal ordinance, it appears from the evidence, that the accused has committed no act, save what would constitute a violation of a penal statute of the State, over which no express authority has been by the legislature delegated to the municipality, a decision finding the accused guilty, and imposing a punishment for the alleged crime, is contrary to law.

Submitted December 4, 1899. — Decided January 24, 1900.

Certiorari. Before Judge Falligant. Chatham superior court. October 20, 1899.

Saussy & Saussy, for plaintiff in error.
Samuel B. Adams, contra.

LEWIS, J. The plaintiff in error, on May 29, 1891, was tried before the police court of the City of Savannah for the following offense: 1st. "Violating city ordinance, having her place of business, a barroom, open on Sunday, April 19, 1891." 2d. "Violating 2d section ordinance passed February 25, 1891, by selling liquor on Sunday, April 19, 1891." On May 25, 1891, this trial was concluded, and the police court entered the following judgment: "Fined one hundred dollars, or thirty days imprisonment, for violating section second of ordinance passed in council February 25, 1891, by selling liquor on Sunday, April 19, 1891." An appeal was entered from this decision of
· the mayor, who presided in the police court, to the Mayor and

Aldermen of the City of Savannah.   This appeal was tried in June, 1891, and a majority of the council trying the appeal confirmed the decision of the police court.   Whereupon the plaintiff in error filed her petition for certiorari to the superior court of Chatham county; and she excepts to the judgment of the court overruling her petition.   It appears from the record that on February 25, 1891, the Mayor and Aldermen of the City of Savannah adopted an ordinance entitled, "an ordinance to provide for the observance of the Sabbath or Lord's day," prescribing, in substance, that any person who kept within the city limits a barroom, or other place for the sale at retail of intoxicating liquors of any character, should keep such place of business shut and closed from twelve o'clock Saturday night until twelve o'clock the following Sunday night.   It was further provided in the ordinance that it should not be lawful for any person, within the limits of the City of Savannah, to sell in any quantity, or by any sort of device, any spirituous or intoxicating liquors of any character from twelve o'clock Saturday night to twelve o'clock Sunday night, except that a druggist or apothecary might sell the same as medicine under prescription of a regular physician.   It seems, therefore, that while the defendant below was tried for violating both the provisions of the ordinance above mentioned, to wit, 1st, keeping open her barroom and place of business on Sunday; and second, violating the city ordinance against selling liquor on Sunday, she was convicted upon the latter charge only.   It appears from the evidence in the record that, if she was guilty of selling liquor in violation of the ordinance, this sale took place from her barroom, and, therefore, must have been in pursuit of her business, or the work of her ordinary calling, on the Sabbath.   One defense made on the trial of the case below, and insisted upon in the petition for certiorari as a reason why the judgment of conviction should be set aside, was, that the mayor and aldermen of the city had no jurisdiction to try the defendant under the charges set forth, which constitute a violation of penal laws of the State.   Another ground of error alleged is, that the verdict is contrary to evidence, and if any offense was committed it was in violation of a State law.

It may be considered as a principle well established by the adjudications of this court, that a municipal corporation can not, without valid legislative authority, pass an ordinance for the punishment of an act which constitutes an offense against a penal statute of the State. *Rothschild* v. *Darien,* 69 *Ga.* 503; *Kahn* v. *Macon,* 95 *Ga.* 419; *Keck* v. *Gainesville,* 98 *Ga.* 425; *Moran* v. *Atlanta,* 102 *Ga.* 840. The prosecution in this case is based upon the ordinance of February 25, 1891, above mentioned. In behalf of counsel for defendant in error it is contended that this ordinance is justified by virtue of the powers conferred upon the municipal authorities of the City of Savannah by the act of December 22, 1857. Acts 1857, pp. 166_7. Under section III of that act, there was conferred upon the City Council of Augusta the power " to pass all ordinances in relation to keeping open tippling-houses on the Sabbath day in said city, and in relation to lewd houses, or houses of ill fame, for the purpose of suppressing them in said city, and in relation to selling or purchasing intoxicating liquors to slaves or free persons of color in said city," etc. The next section extends the provisions of the act to the City of Savannah. It does not appear, therefore, from this act that any power was delegated to these cities to pass such an ordinance as was adopted by the City of Savannah in reference to the sale of intoxicating liquors; so far as the sale or purchase of liquors was concerned, the act only relating to slaves or free persons of color in said city. This act, therefore, confers no express legislative authority authorizing the passage of such an ordinance; and it follows that if the facts relied upon for a conviction of the defendant in this case constitute an offense against the penal law of the State, the municipal court had no jurisdiction of the case, and the decision now under consideration is unauthorized. That the facts relied on for a conviction constitute a penal offense against the State law we think there can be no doubt. It appears from the record that the defendant below was engaged in the business and regular occupation of keeping a barroom for the purpose of retailing spirituous and other intoxicating liquors. Even if the evidence were sufficient to authorize the conclusion that she sold liquors on the day charged, this sale took place from her barroom, and was necessarily in the pursuit of her ordinary daily vocation.   The State law in existence when this conviction was had is embodied in section 4579 of the Code of 1882, and provides that "Any tradesman, artificer, workman or laborer, or other person whatever, who shall pursue their business or work of their ordinary callings upon the Lord's day (works of necessity or charity only excepted), shall be guilty of a misdemeanor." The same provision is substantially embodied in the present Penal Code, § 422.

The prosecution in this case relied upon the case of *Hood* v. *Von Glahn*, 88 *Ga.* 405.   We do not think that decision is in point.   It appears there that the plaintiff in error was the keeper of a barroom, and a retail liquor-dealer, and he was tried before the recorder's court of Augusta on the charge of "keeping open his bar on Sunday, July 19, 1891."   The ordinance of that city, it is true, contained a provision against retailing, selling, or furnishing liquor to any person on Sunday; but it likewise contained the further provision that they should not open, or have or keep open, the doors or windows of their retail shops.   The defendant was tried and convicted for a violation of the last provision mentioned.   The only question before this court then was, whether or not that portion of the ordinance against keeping open such tippling-shops was authorized by the act of December 22, 1857.   That is an entirely distinct offense from selling liquors.   Keeping open a tippling-house on the Sabbath day is made penal under a separate and distinct section of the code.   Code of 1882, §4535; Penal Code, § 390.   This question, therefore, as to whether or not a barkeeper engaged in his regular vocation of selling from his barroom liquor on Sunday was amenable to a municipal court for such a violation of a State law against pursuing one's ordinary vocation on the Sabbath, was not made in that case; the only question being whether, under the act of 1857, the City Council of Augusta could try him for violating an ordinance passed in pursuance of that act, which authorized specifically that council to pass all ordinances in relation to keeping open tippling-houses on the Sabbath day.   The case of *Hill* v. *Dalton*, 72 *Ga.* 314, is also relied upon by the prosecution as authority which upholds the validity of a municipal ordinance providing that no person shall be allowed to sell spirituous or other intoxicating liquors within the limits of the City of Dalton in any quantity. It appears in that case that the charter of the City of Dalton gave to the municipality absolute authority over the whole liquor question (see p. 318). It was there simply decided that the ordinance against selling the liquor did not provide for the same offense as that prescribed by the code, which prohibited the keeping of a tippling-house or the retailing of spirituous liquors without a license. The violation of the Sunday law in question was in nowise involved in that case. In *Strauss* v. *Waycross*, 97 *Ga.* 475, it was decided that "Although a given act was, by a valid municipal ordinance, made an offense against the corporation, at a time when such an act was not indictable under the criminal laws of this State, the subsequent enactment by the General Assembly of a statute making the identical act a crime or misdemeanor deprived the municipal authorities (they having no jurisdiction over State offenses) of the power to try and punish offenders for committing the act in question." The decisions in the cases of *Paulk* v. *Sycamore*, 104 *Ga.* 728, *Brown* v. *Social Circle*, 105 *Ga.* 834, and *Cunningham* v. *Griffin*, 107 *Ga.* 690, contain nothing in conflict with our ruling in this case. The cases cited uphold an ordinance of the city making it an offense against a municipality to keep for sale spirituous or intoxicating liquors. Those decisions were based expressly upon the idea that there was no provision in the State law making such acts of keeping liquor for the purpose of an illegal sale a penal offense.

We do not mean to say that the second section of the city ordinance in question should be treated as absolutely a void enactment. That portion of the ordinance simply provided generally against the sale of any spirituous or intoxicating liquors of any character on Sunday. If a person who committed such an act was not one whose business or ordinary calling involved the work of retailing spirituous or intoxicating liquors, the principle herein decided would not apply to his case. In the present case, however, it appears from the record that if the accused was guilty of any offense at all, it consisted in pursuing her business, or the work of her ordinary calling, on the Lord's day within the meaning of the penal law of the State on that subject.

Judgment reversed. All the Justices concurring.

McCOMBS *v.* THE STATE.

1. Upon the trial for forgery of one indicted under the name of "Anna McCombs" and who was known as "Nannie McComb," the circumstance that two letters were found in her possession, one of which was addressed to "Dear Sister" and was unfinished and unsigned, the other not addressed to any one and signed "Unhappy Nan," was not of itself sufficient to prove that the accused wrote such letters, and thus establish the handwriting thereof as a standard with which to compare the handwriting of the alleged forged instrument.
2. The circumstance that shoes precisely similar to those delivered by a merchant to an unidentified person upon a forged order were found, more than four months thereafter, in the possession of one charged with the forgery, was not, without more, sufficient to authorize a finding that the accused wrote such order.
3. The verdict was not warranted by the evidence, and the refusal of a new trial was erroneous.

Submitted December 18, 1899. — Decided January 24, 1900.

Indictment for forgery.   Before Judge Henry.   Floyd superior court.   July term, 1899.

Anna McCombs was convicted of the crime of forgery, and upon her motion for a new trial being overruled, she excepted. The evidence for the State was, in substance, as follows: The order alleged to have been forged, viz.: "Mr. Kuttner,—Please send by this girl two pair of shoes, No. 5 1/2, E last, one suitable for every-day wear and one Sunday pair, the latest styles in vici kids.   I am busy cooking cake.   Send the bill & I will send back the money by the girl, and oblige, Mrs. Blunt Hamilton."   Admission by counsel for the accused that Mrs. Hamilton did not sign or write, or authorize the signing or writing of this order.   Kuttner testified, that the order was presented to him, in Floyd county, in March, by a negro woman, and that he then delivered to her four pairs of shoes on it, of the value

of $12. He did not know this woman and did not remember
how she looked. She said she was working for Mrs. Hamilton,
and that Mrs. Hamilton sent her to get the shoes. He never
saw the accused before she was arrested. She was arrested four
months after he furnished the shoes upon the order. As to the
identification of the shoes found in her possession after her arrest, he testified: "I saw defendant after her arrest. I recognize the shoes on her feet. She had a pair of shoes I furnished
on this order, wearing them. It was a Bolton shoe. We sell a
thousand pair yearly. I don't know where she got them shoes.
I can't begin to name all my shoe customers. Have sold that
shoe four years; no other dealer in Rome sells it. It is widely
known and sold by merchants in other cities throughout the
South. I swear that shoe went out of my store. I swear by the
number on it; don't remember the number now, did at the
time. The regular number is 6704. I think hers was either
6705 or 6706. I do not remember exactly what number it was.
The number of the shoe was either 5 or 5½. The lot number
I don't know; can give no idea what it was. We handled a lot
of shoes of different numbers. I remember this one by number, because it was a pair given on that order. I remember distinctly four pairs were given, and this was one of them. I can
not remember what the number was. This bill of shoes came
in September or October. This was one pair of the order she
had on. I remember that from my knowledge, but don't remember who had the order. I remember the four pairs of shoes
I gave her; these I have seen since her arrest. I remember
the number of the shoe from my own knowledge, I don't remember the number of the shoe exactly. I do not remember
what number it was then. I don't attempt to say to whom I
furnished these shoes, except it was to a negro girl." Wimpee
testified that he was present after the arrest of the accused,
when search was made of her property; that he found a trunk
claimed to be hers at the residence of Lizzie Davis, in which
he found letters directed to Annie McCombs, also photographs
of herself, and two pairs of new shoes, never worn. The pair
of shoes shown witness in court much resembled a pair he found
in the trunk. He could not say the letters shown him in court

32

were found in the trunk.   He identified the trunk shown him as the one found at Lizzie Davis's.   Lizzie Davis testified, that the accused lived with her; that she did not know her as "Annie McCombs," but as "Nannie McComb."   She identified the trunk in court as belonging to the accused.   It is stated in the brief of evidence that "The State introduced in evidence trunk and its contents as contained in the tray thereof, which contents consisted, among other things, of a photograph, letters directed to Nannie McCombe, and a letter signed 'Unhappy Nan,' and an unfinished letter beginning 'Dear Sister,' which the State used for the purpose of identifying the handwriting of the letter signed 'Unhappy Nan' and the unfinished letter with the handwriting of alleged forged order.   Also, the State introduced in evidence the shoes presented to the different witnesses, and about which they testified."   The accused, in her statement, said she got the shoes from a man named Charley Brown, who left them with her to keep until he could send them to his mother and sister.

J. S. Crawford and *Henry Walker*, for plaintiff in error.
Moses Wright, solicitor-general, contra.

FISH, J.   1. The evidence, in our opinion, was not sufficient to show that the accused was guilty of the offense charged. Therefore we deem it unnecessary to pass upon the numerous exceptions, in the motion for a new trial, to the admission of evidence and to instructions given to the jury.   The mere fact that the two letters referred to in the official report were found in the possession of the accused was not of itself sufficient to show that she wrote them, and thus establish the handwriting thereof as a standard with which to compare the handwriting of the forged order.   The mere possession of such letters would not even prove that she could write.   Section 5247 of the Civil Code provides that "Other writings, proved or acknowledged to be genuine, may be admitted in evidence for the purpose of comparison by the jury."   As said by Atkinson, J., in *McVicker* v. *Conkle*, 96 *Ga.* 595, "Where a paper is offered for the purpose of comparison, its execution by the maker must be either proved or acknowledged by him.   Before it could be set up as a standard by which to judge of the genuineness of another paper, the handwriting must be established as being that of the alleged maker of the collateral paper. Its force as evidence can not be made dependent upon inference; because, in order to determine by comparison the identity of makers by similarity of handwriting, it is of prime consequence that we first establish a genuine standard; otherwise, it would be impossible to reach even an approximately correct conclusion." In Van Sickle v. People, 29 Mich. 61, it was held that the mere finding of a diary on a party, with an admission by him that it was his, is not a sufficient authentication of the writing to justify its use as a standard. Graves, C. J., in delivering the opinion, said: "The circumstance, if such was the truth, that the plaintiff in error owned the book and claimed it as his, might have helped to show, that the writing in it was actually made by him, but standing alone and by itself it was inadequate to show that fact. It is certainly possible that he wrote the matter contained in the diary, but the probability that he did so is not sufficiently assured by evidence of his ownership to warrant the assumption which was made. It would, I think, be a very unsafe rule to hold that the possession and ownership of a book or document may authorize an inference that the owner can write, that he did write the matter contained in it, and then, on the foot of these inferences, charge him as the author of other and wholly disconnected writings." The letters in the case under consideration should not have been admitted in evidence, had they been properly objected to. Although it is not clear that a proper objection was made to their introduction, yet, as it is manifest that they were neither proved nor acknowledged to be in the handwriting of the accused, they furnished no standard with which to compare the handwriting of the forged order.

2. The only other circumstance that the State could have relied upon for a conviction was, that shoes exactly similar to those delivered by Kuttner to the bearer of the forged order— whose identity with the accused was not established — were found, more than four months after such delivery, in the possession of the accused. Considering the fact that the testimony

of the only witness who undertook to identify the shoes found in the possession of the accused with those delivered upon the forged order does not, in our opinion, establish such identity beyond a reasonable doubt, the facility with which such articles can pass from hand to hand, and the time which had elapsed from the delivery of the goods upon the order to the finding of them in possession of the accused, and her statement in explanation of her possession, which, if true, was consistent with her innocence, we do not think that this circumstance alone was sufficient to authorize the jury to find her guilty. See *Johnson* v. *State*, 48 *Ga.* 117; *Tarver* v. *State*, 95 *Ga.* 222; *Brooks* v. *State*, 96 *Ga.* 353; *Jones* v. *State*, 105 *Ga.* 649.

3. The evidence introduced for the purpose of connecting the accused with the forgery was wholly circumstantial, and, while it may have been sufficient to raise a strong suspicion of her guilt, it was not sufficient to exclude every other reasonable hypothesis; and hence her conviction was unauthorized.

Judgment reversed.   All the Justices concurring.

McCOMBS *v.* THE STATE.

1. On the trial of an indictment founded upon section 233 of the Penal Code, charging the forgery of an order for goods but containing no allegation that the goods described in the order had value, evidence showing that such goods were valuable was not admissible.

Submitted December 18, 1899. — Decided January 24, 1900.

Indictment for forgery.   Before Judge Henry.   Floyd superior court.   July term, 1899.

J. S. Crawford and *Henry Walker*, for plaintiff in error.
Moses Wright, solicitor-general, contra.

COBB, J.   The indictment in the present case was framed under section 233 of the Penal Code, and purported to charge the defendant with the offense of forgery. While it alleged that she forged an order for certain described goods, it failed to allege that they were of any value. Under the ruling made in the case of *Johnson* v. *State*, ante, 268, this indictment was fatally defective. There being no allegation that the goods were of any value, there was nothing to authorize proof of their value; and it was therefore error in the court to admit evidence going to show that the articles referred to in the order were valuable. See 2 Bish. New Crim. Pro. § 187.

Judgment reversed. All the Justices concurring.

LOWMAN *v.* THE STATE.

1. Evidence that one on trial for crime had done an act calculated to excite prejudice and ill will against him and which had no connection with the charge under investigation is inadmissible. Error in allowing such evidence to go to the jury is cause for a new trial, when there is reason for apprehending that it operated injuriously to the accused.

2. It is not competent for a witness, while testifying to the particulars of a difficulty which he had seen take place between two other persons, to express his opinion that at a given moment the time had come for one of them "to either run or fight."

3. The law embraced in section 73 of the Penal Code was not applicable to this case and ought not to have been given in charge. In other respects, the charge of the court was free from error.

4. As there is to be another trial, no opinion as to the merits of this case is expressed.

Argued December 18, 1899. — Decided January 23, 1900.

Indictment for murder. Before Judge Estes. Dawson superior court. August term, 1899.

W. F. Findley and *H. H. Dean,* for plaintiff in error.

J. M. Terrell, attorney-general, W. A. Charters, solicitor-general, contra.

LUMPKIN, P. J. At the August term, 1899, of the superior court of Dawson county, Morgan Lowman was convicted of the murder of Benjamin Anderson, and sentenced to be executed. The accused made a motion for a new trial, which was overruled, and the case is here for review. The material points presented by the record will be briefly stated and discussed.

1. The court permitted a witness for the State to testify that the accused had "reported a still." This act, if committed at all, shed no light on the charge of murder, and proof of it was

therefore clearly irrelevant. Did it injure the accused? We
are not at a loss for an answer to this question. Aside from
our knowledge derived from oral tradition that in the mountain districts of this State a revenue spy is held in very general contempt, there is in the record of this identical case evidence tending to show that one of the jury who tried the accused
was quite hostile to reporters of stills, and on this ground had
expressed the opinion that Lowman ought to be hung. In the
motion for a new trial this juror is, for the reason just indicated,
attacked as incompetent. There was counter-evidence tending
to show that he was upright, unbiased, and impartial; but the
fact of his antipathy to those who informed against illicit dis-
tillers was clearly established. This is enough to demand another trial of this case. No man should be deprived of his life
when illegal testimony has been admitted against him and there
is such good reason to apprehend that it operated to his hurt
in the mind of one of his triors.

2. A witness for the accused, who was present at the homicide and who had given his version of what had occurred, was
asked if at a certain juncture the time had not come for the
accused "to either run or fight." The answer would have been
in the affirmative, but it was properly rejected. Allowing this
testimony to go to the jury would have been permitting the
witness to express his mere opinion as to a matter which did
not fall within the domain of "opinion evidence." The nature
of the emergency in which the accused was placed by the conduct of the deceased, and the manner in which it should have
been met, were matters for determination by the jury and not
by the witness.

3. The motion for a new trial alleges error in charging section 73 of the Penal Code. We do not think this section was
applicable to the case. It is not our purpose to discuss the
evidence. Suffice it to say it was not a fight begun and carried
on in hot blood, with opportunity to either party to recede, reflect, and endeavor to decline any further struggle before the
mortal blow was given. Mr. Justice Little elaborately discussed
the law of this section in *Powell* v. *State*, 101 *Ga.* 9, and the
writer in *Teasley* v. *State*, 104 *Ga.* 741, undertook to present a

condensed view of its applicability. It has since been referred to in *Parks* v. *State*, 105 *Ga.* 242, *Glover* v. *State*, Id. 597, and *Smith* v. *State*, 106 *Ga.* 673.

Complaint is also made that the court failed to charge sections 70 and 71 of the Penal Code. Much of the former section was entirely inapplicable and therefore properly omitted, and the court did give in charge the law embodied in section 71. Aside from the error above pointed out, we find nothing objectionable in the charge as a whole.

4. Though many witnesses were sworn, there was little conflict in the evidence pro and con. Indeed, we do not recall any case of like importance where there was such harmony in the testimony of persons who had so much apparent reason to be biased one way or the other. As the case is to be tried again, we express no opinion as to what should be the finding of the next jury to whom it is submitted.

Judgment reversed. All the Justices concurring.

CHENEY v. THE STATE.

The evidence as a whole was entirely insufficient to establish the guilt of the defendant.

Submitted December 18, 1899. — Decided January 24, 1900.

Indictment for rape. Before Judge Henry. Walker superior court. September term, 1899.

Copeland & Jackson, for plaintiff in error.
Moses Wright, solicitor-general, contra.

LITTLE, J. Cheney was indicted for the offense of rape; was tried, convicted, recommended to mercy by the verdict of the jury, and sentenced to a term of imprisonment for twenty years. He made a motion for a new trial, because the court committed error in charging the jury, and because the verdict was contrary to law and the evidence. A careful examination of the evidence in the case convinces us that the conviction of the plaintiff in error was contrary to law. The main witness for the State was the girl upon whom the rape was alleged to have been committed. While in her evidence she makes a statement of facts concerning the assault, amply sufficient to support the charge, she, at the same time, gives such an account of her actions when she was assaulted and while the offense was being committed as entirely negatives the force of her evidence that the plaintiff in error assaulted her. In relating the circumstances under which the assault was committed, she testified, among other things, that on Sunday morning in July, 1899, her father and mother went to church, leaving her two little brothers and her sister, nine years old, with herself at home; that previously to this time she had a conversation with the plaintiff in error, who had told her that he was coming to the house on that Sunday and would bring her a pound of candy; that the accused was near the house when her parents left, and she watched them until they got out of sight; that the accused then came to the house, and caught her by the arm; that she jerked loose and ran up-stairs, and he followed her; that in the room up-stairs he asked her to have intercourse with him; that she refused, and ran down-stairs into a little room, when he caught her, overpowered her, threw her on the floor, and violated her person. Witness resisted and screamed, and told her sister to scream and to tell her brother, who lived near, to come and make the accused leave. Had the witness stopped here, her evidence would have been sufficient to make a prima facie case; but, as her evidence appears in the brief, she further testified that the accused was on top of her for a half an hour; that she had a watch with her, and looked at it when he commenced the intercourse and when he desisted; that during the progress of the assault she laid the watch on the floor by her; and that it was half past ten o'clock when he commenced and eleven when he quit; that she consulted the watch because she desired to know how long it took a man to do that way with a woman; that the house in which the assault occurred was on a public road; that while the accused was committing the act, Mr. Bailey, a white man, passed on the road, and at that particular time the accused had her down on the floor forcing her person. She saw Bailey pass, but did not call to him, because she didn't desire him to see her in that kind of a fix. In a very short time after the accused left, one Farmer came to the house, and witness told him what had happened. During the progress of the case Farmer was sworn as a witness for the State, and on this subject testified that, on the day in question, on his way to church he went by the house; that he didn't hear any one scream, or make any noise before he reached the house. When he got there he saw the girl alleged to have been raped, and had a conversation with her. She told him that the accused had been there, but said that he had done nothing while he was there. It is, however, but fair to say, in this connection, that it was shown that the girl sent for her father and mother immediately after the occurrence, and communicated what had happened; and that it was also shown by the evidence of a physician, who examined her soon afterwards, that penetration of her person had been made. The girl testified that she was twelve years old; and it was also shown that she was of sufficient age and development for the menstrual period to occur.

There is a statement made in the record that the evidence of the girl in relation to the watch and her consulting it from time to time was drawn out on cross-examination, and by monosyllabic answers to the questions of counsel. For these reasons counsel for the State urges that it should have no weight. If the man accused is to undergo a term of penal servitude for the commission of rape, he must do so on evidence sufficient to show his guilt. Necessarily, the person alleged to have been raped is the most important witness against him, and whether her evidence comes in the shape of a voluntary narrative of the facts, or is elicited by the cross-examination of counsel, makes but little difference. All of it is her evidence alike, and her narration of the facts which occurred; and we are not at liberty to presume that that part of her evidence which establishes the guilt of the accused is true and the other part which repels the idea of force, and seemingly shows acquiescence, is not true. We take the evidence as a whole, and so considering it, it is wholly insufficient to establish guilt. The court therefore erred in overruling the motion for new trial. *Judgment reversed. All the Justices concurring.*

ROBINSON *v.* THE STATE.

506
181
506
52
369
506
370
761
506
19
107
506
431
506
788

1. If in a trial for murder the law of voluntary manslaughter is not involved, the court should not charge thereon, but so doing will not, in such a case, be cause for a new trial, if the accused be rightly convicted of murder, or if, though he be convicted of voluntary manslaughter only, a verdict of murder was really demanded. If, however, in such a case, the accused be convicted of voluntary manslaughter when there was evidence which would have warranted an acquittal, or when his statement, if believed, would have so warranted, there should be a new trial.

2. Setting aside a juror for cause after the panel of forty-eight has been made up in a felony case and the selection of the jury to try the same has been begun is not cause for new trial. *Doyal* v. *State*, 70 *Ga.* 134, 142.

3. After the original panel of forty-eight has been exhausted, it is a matter of discretion with the judge as to what numbers of jurors shall compose the succeeding panels to be put upon the accused.

4. Inaccuracies in explaining to jurors the meaning of the questions propounded on their voir dire will not, in a plain case of guilt and when no injury to the accused is affirmatively shown, require a conviction to be set aside.

5. When in his charge the judge informs the jury that the contentions of the parties are so and so, it will, in the absence of a certificate from him to the contrary, be presumed that his statement of such contentions was correct.

6. Objectionable remarks by a solicitor-general in his argument to the jury afford no cause for a new trial when no exception was taken thereto and no ruling of the court invoked thereon. It does not, in the present case, appear that the argument of the solicitor-general was in any respect unfair or prejudicial to the accused.

7. Irregularities in the conduct of jurors trying a criminal case, such as the separation of some of them from their fellows, and the like, is not cause for a new trial, when it affirmatively appears that no injury resulted therefrom to the accused.

8. It is too late to poll a jury after the sentence of the court has been pronounced. There is in the record evidence warranting a finding that the request to poll in this case was made after sentence.

Argued December 18, 1899. — Decided January 24, 1900.

Indictment for murder. Before Judge Brinson. Burke superior court. October 23, 1899.

Phil. P. Johnston, for plaintiff in error.
W. H. Davis, solicitor-general, by *A. H. Davis,* contra.

LUMPKIN, P. J.　The accused, James Robinson, a white man, was indicted for the murder of Gilbert Ellison, a colored man. A verdict of voluntary manslaughter was returned, and a motion for a new trial, embracing many grounds, was made and overruled. We do not think that any of these grounds, or that all of them together, would justify us in reversing the judgment denying a new trial. The law announced in the first headnote presents in condensed form the result of numerous adjudications by this court. We do not care to cite the cases, for the doctrine laid down should by this time be familiar to all who are concerned with the administration of the criminal law. The attorney for the plaintiff in error who argued the case here recognized the correctness of this doctrine, and had no objection to it. His position was, that the proper application of it would entitle his client to a new trial; for he contended that the evidence for the State made a case of murder, the statement of the accused one of self-defense, and that there was no middle ground or any basis whatever for the verdict of voluntary manslaughter. If his premises were correct, his conclusion would follow; but, after a thorough and careful study of the evidence and the statement, we are unable to agree with him as to these matters. A long and tedious discussion of the facts would be of no practical benefit to any one, and we shall therefore simply state the result of our examination and consideration of the evidence and the statement. The testimony offered in behalf of the State would well have warranted a finding that the accused committed a cold-blooded and wanton murder, and such, we believe, is the truth of the case; but, for reasons to be presently stated, a verdict of murder was not absolutely demanded. The statement of the accused would have warranted, but did not demand, an acquittal. There was some little evidence, and a portion of the statement, sufficiently bringing into the case the theory of mutual combat to authorize a charge on voluntary manslaughter and a conviction of this offense at the hands of a jury who wished to lean strongly to the side of mercy. We therefore approve the charge on voluntary manslaughter, and, on the merits of the case, decline to disturb the jury's finding. There was too much of righteousness in it for us to set it at naught.

The foregoing disposes of the main contention of the plaintiff in error, and our rulings upon the other questions involved

in the case are briefly stated in the headnotes.   We do not think
further comment necessary, except to make a brief reference to
the point decided in the last note.   The well-settled rule that
a request to poll a jury should be made before the members of
it disperse and mingle with the bystanders is, of course, based
upon the idea that it would be dangerous to allow a juror who
might have heard something calculated to change his mind to
have an opportunity to recede from a verdict to which he had
really agreed.   Certainly, nothing would be more likely to have
such an effect than a sentence of which a juror did not approve.
In this case, the punishment inflicted was, we are informed, a
a term of fifteen years in the penitentiary, and it would not
have done to allow the jury to be polled after they knew what
the judgment of the court was.   We think it was a proper one,
but no man can tell how the jurors may have regarded it, or
that, after it was announced, some of them might not have desired to annul a verdict to which they had deliberately assented.

Judgment affirmed.   All the Justices concurring.

ECHOLS *v.* THE STATE.

1. In giving in charge so much of section 1036 of the Penal Code as relates
   to recommendations by juries concerning punishment, the judge should
   not omit to state that the recommendation of a jury, made under its provisions, will be effectual only in case it is approved by him.   He should
   not, however, give in charge the last sentence of that section, which relates to the power which the judge, independently of any action by the
   jury, has over penalties.
2. Though the charge in the present case did not, in all respects, conform
   to what is above laid down, a new trial will not be ordered ; for the guilt
   of the accused was strongly and conclusively established, and the conviction was fully approved by the trial judge.
3. Nothing will be heard from a juror which can have the effect of in any
   manner impeaching his verdict.
4. Counsel for the accused can not, as matter of right, when he is making
   his statement to the court and jury, ask him questions or make suggestions to him.   It is entirely a matter of discretion with the judge whether
   or not such things shall be allowed.

Argued December 4, 1899. — Decided January 25, 1900.

Indictment for assault with intent to murder.   Before Judge
Candler.   Newton superior court.   September term, 1899.

L. L. Middlebrook, F. C. Foster, and *J. M. Pace,* for plaintiff in error.　*W. T. Kimsey, solicitor-general,* contra.

LUMPKIN, P. J.　In *Johnson* v. *State,* 98 *Ga.* 78, this court held that, on the trial of a person indicted for the commission of a felony other than one of those enumerated in section 1036 of the Penal Code, it was the duty of the court, whether so requested or not, to inform the jury of so much of the provisions of that section as related to their power, in the event of conviction, to recommend that the accused be sentenced as for a misdemeanor. To properly give in charge the provisions just indicated necessarily, we thought, involved telling the jury that "when such recommendation is approved by the judge presiding at the trial," the offense must be punished as a misdemeanor.　In other words, we intended to lay down the proposition that the judge ought to instruct the jury concerning their power to make the recommendation, and also let them understand that it would be effectual to reduce the penalty only when approved by him. In *Cunningham* v. *State,* 103 *Ga.* 239, we were undertaking to deal with another and entirely different matter.　The above-cited section, after declaring that the jury might make the recommendation mentioned and when it should have the effect of mitigating the punishment, embraced an additional provision in these words:　"If the judge trying the case sees proper, he may, in his punishment, reduce such felonies to misdemeanors." We held in the case last cited that the judge should not give in charge to the jury that part of the section which we have just quoted.　In the opinion (page 240) it was said we did not think that the judge should "instruct the jury that, with or without a recommendation on their part, he could, if he saw proper, punish the accused as for a misdemeanor."　We did not mean to convey the idea that it would not be proper for the judge, in a case to which this section is applicable, to inform the jury that their recommendation would, if approved by him, reduce the punishment to that of a misdemeanor.　Indeed, we think he ought to so inform them, in order that they may understand exactly what the law says with reference to their recommendation and its effect.　Our idea in the last case was to lay down the rule that the judge should not inform the jury what his power was

in such cases independently of their action in the premises.
We did not, perhaps, express ourselves with sufficient distinctness. Candor constrains the writer to admit that his language
was not as perspicuous as it might have been. We hope that
we have this time made the matter clear.

The application of the foregoing to the case in hand will
now be made. Echols, the plaintiff in error, was tried and
convicted under an indictment charging him with the offense
of assault with intent to murder. The judge charged the jury:
"In all cases of assault with intent to murder, the jury may,
in the event of their finding the defendant guilty, recommend
that he be punished as for a misdemeanor." He did not add
that such a recommendation would be effectual only in the
event of its approval by the judge, but followed the above-
quoted instruction with the words: "If you find the defendant
guilty in this case, the form of your verdict will be: 'We, the
jury, find the defendant guilty.' And that would mean of an
assault with intent to murder. If you find the defendant guilty
and see fit to recommend that he be punished as for a misdemeanor, the form of your verdict will be: 'We, the jury, find
the defendant guilty, and recommend that he be punished as
for a misdemeanor.'" There was a verdict of guilty, with a
recommendation that the accused be punished as for a misdemeanor. The judge very properly declined to approve this
recommendation, and sentenced the accused to a term in the
penitentiary. In his motion for a new trial, he complains that
the effect of the instructions above quoted was to mislead the
jury into the belief that their recommendation would constrain
the judge to impose upon the accused a misdemeanor sentence,
and that but for this belief they would not have found him
guilty. We are not prepared to say that the jury were misled
as claimed. The issue in the case was a simple one. It was
not disputed that an outrageous assault with intent to murder
had been committed. The only question in controversy was:
Did the accused perpetrate the crime? With the determination of this question, that of punishment had not the slightest
connection. Whether the accused was, in case of conviction,
to be fined one dollar or sent to the penitentiary for ten years

could have no bearing upon the question of his guilt or innocence. It was upon the jury to say whether or not the evidence satisfied them beyond a reasonable doubt of his guilt. Its sufficiency for this purpose could not be affected by the result to follow the verdict. They said under their oaths that the accused was guilty, and did so upon testimony fully warranting their finding. If any juror consented to this verdict under the belief that the punishment must be as for a misdemeanor, but would not have done so had he known the judge had the power to sentence as for a felony, he occupies the position of saying in effect: "Though not satisfied beyond a reasonable doubt of the guilt of the accused, I am willing to find him guilty if he is to receive a light punishment;" or, "Though fully satisfied that the accused committed a terrible crime for which he deserves a term in the penitentiary, I will not agree to convict him unless he escapes with the penalty prescribed for misdemeanors." A juror capable of assuming either of these positions would be equally capable, after solemnly agreeing to a verdict, of swearing that he had not done so, or that he would not have done so if he had not believed his recommendation would be controlling in the matter of punishment. In this very case an attempt was made to show by the affidavits of some of the jurors that they would not have consented to the verdict if they had not believed from the judge's instructions that he would be compelled by the recommendation to inflict a misdemeanor penalty. The judge rightly declined to consider these affidavits. He could not, nor can we, do otherwise than ignore them entirely; for if anything is settled in this State, it is that nothing will be heard from a juror which can have the effect of impeaching in any manner his verdict. It results that the verdict in this case must stand. The evidence in support of the finding of fact embraced therein, viz., that the accused was guilty, is supported by strong and conclusive proof and fully approved by the trial judge. In the absence of any legal reason for so doing, we can not and will not assume that the jury would have found otherwise if the judge had informed them that their recommendation as to punishment would not be binding upon him. In a weak or doubtful case, the charge complained of might be cause for a new trial; but we will not, in one like the present, reverse the judgment merely because of a possibility that the jury would have failed to make a correct finding of fact if the charge on the subject of punishment had been in strict accord with the law.

It will, of course, be understood that much of the foregoing discussion is not applicable to a case where the recommendation of a jury on the subject of punishment is compulsory.

The only verified ground of the motion for a new trial not already dealt with alleges error in not allowing counsel for the accused to make to him, while making his statement to the court and jury, a suggestion for the purpose of calling his attention to a matter to which he had omitted to refer. This would have been the same thing, in effect, as allowing the counsel to ask the accused a question, and this court has ruled that counsel can not, as matter of right, do such a thing. "In making his own statement to the court and jury, the prisoner is not under examination, and his counsel has no right to ask him questions. Doubtless the court might, at the prisoner's request, permit questions to be put to him, as matter of discretion." Bleckley, J., in *Brown* v. *State*, 58 *Ga.* 214, 215. Doubtless this discretion will, on all proper occasions, be exercised favorably to the accused.

Judgment affirmed.   All the Justices concurring.

MILLER *v.* THE STATE.

From the preliminary examination of the child on whom a rape was alleged to have been committed in this case, it does not appear that she sufficiently understood the nature and obligation of an oath or of the responsibilities attaching to a witness who is sworn to tell the truth. On another trial, when she has advanced in age and been the subject of proper moral training, she may appear to be competent.

Submitted December 18, 1899. — Decided January 25, 1900.

Indictment for rape. Before Judge Henry. Johnson superior court. September term, 1899.

William Faircloth, for plaintiff in error.
B. T. Rawlings, solicitor-general, contra.

Cobb, J. Miller was placed upon trial under an indictment charging him with the offense of rape, and was convicted. He made a motion for a new trial, which was overruled, and he excepted. In one ground of the motion for a new trial complaint is made that the court erred in holding that the child who was the victim of the alleged rape was a competent witness. The preliminary examination as to the competency of this witness was as follows: "By the solicitor-general—Q. Do you know what it is to swear? A. Yes sir. Q. If anybody was to tell a story what would become of them? A. The bugger man would get them.

"By the defendant's counsel—Q. Do you know what the solemnity of an oath is? A. No sir; I don't know what an oath is. Q. Do you know what you are doing when you come into the court-room to swear? A. No sir. Q. You don't know what you are required to do? A. No sir. I am required to tell the truth. Q. Do you know what would become of you if you were to tell a story? A. Yes sir; bugger man would get me. Q. Did anybody tell you that? A. No sir. Q. Did not you swear in this case in the justice court? A. Yes sir. Q. Do you remember what you swore down there? A. No sir. Q. Didn't you swear down there that you did not know what would become of you if you told a story? A. Yes sir. Q. Who told you that the bugger man would get you? A. Nobody. Q. Didn't your pa tell you? A. No sir. Q. Didn't your mamma tell you? A. No sir. Q. You don't know what you swore to in the justice court? A. No sir. I don't know anything about it. Q. Do you know how old you are? A. No sir. Q. Are you ten years old? A. I don't know sir.

"By the court—Q. Is it right to tell a lie or the truth? A. The truth."

While questions of this character are to be left largely to the discretion of the trial judge, we feel constrained, in the present case, to hold that the judge should not have held the witness competent. In the light of the rulings heretofore made by this court, we do not think it appeared that the witness sufficiently understood the nature and obligation of an oath to testify in the case. The case of *Johnson* v. *State*, 76 *Ga.* 76, seems to be almost controlling upon the point. What is said by Chief Justice Jackson in that case in reference to the child becoming a competent witness thereafter, when it had increased in age and been under proper moral training, will apply here. The record in the present case shows that the child was eight years of age when the trial was had, and it is probable that on another trial she may appear to have sufficient intelligence and to have been the subject of such training as to understand the responsibilities attaching to a witness in a case where human life is involved. *Judgment reversed. All the Justices concurring.*

BROZNACK *v.* THE STATE.

514
132

1. An allegation in an accusation, that a given representation was made to one member of a firm with a view to procuring credit, is not supported by evidence showing that such a representation was made solely to another member of that firm.

2. A charge of cheating and swindling alleged to have been committed by making false representations as to financial condition, thereby obtaining credit, is not sustained when it affirmatively appears that the goods sold on the faith of those representations were actually paid for. Such representations not repeated or reaffirmed do not, for purposes of the penal statute, apply to credit given at a subsequent period, unless the person to whom the credit was extended knew or had reason to believe that the latter credit was extended solely on the faith of the representations previously made.

3. It was improper for counsel representing the State to say, in his argument to the jury, that he would not appear in the case if he "did not believe the defendant to be as guilty as any man that was ever tried in the courthouse;" and the court should not have approved of such argument as legitimate.

Argued December 18, 1899. — Decided January 25, 1900.

Accusation of cheating and swindling. Before Judge Calhoun. City court of Atlanta. October 28, 1899.

Mozley & Griffin, for plaintiff in error.
James F. O'Neill, solicitor, contra.

Cobb, J. Broznack was arraigned in the criminal court of Atlanta, on an accusation charging him with cheating and swindling, and was convicted. He made a motion for a new trial, which was overruled, and he excepted.

1. The accusation charged that the accused made certain false representations as to his financial standing to T. J. Stovall, a member of the mercantile firm of W. W. Stovall & Brother, and that upon the faith of these representations credit was extended. The evidence introduced showed that representations of the character alleged in the accusation were made to W. W. Stovall, and there was no evidence showing that any of the representations were made to T. J. Stovall. Proof of representations made to W. W. Stovall did not support the allegation made in the accusation; and a verdict finding the accused guilty was contrary to law, and should have been set aside.

2. It appeared from the evidence that on October 6, 1897, the accused made certain representations as to his financial standing to a member of the firm of Stovall & Brother, and purchased from them a bill of goods amounting to $60.35. On October 20, he made another purchase, and still other purchases on November 15 and December 1. On November 15, he paid the amount of the first bill; and on December 1, the amount of the second. He therefore still owes for the purchases made on November 15, and December 1. The only representations as to his financial standing which he ever made to the firm from which he made the purchases were those made on October 6, and these were never reaffirmed by him. In the case of *Treadwell* v. *State*, 99 *Ga.* 779, it was held that statements made by a merchant to a mercantile agency to be used as a basis for obtaining credit, but which were not acted on by any one until some time after the same had been made, could not be the foundation of a prosecution for cheating and swindling, unless the person making such statement expressly reaffirmed the truth of the same, or at the time of obtaining the credit knew, or had reason to believe, that he was obtaining the credit on the faith of the representations made in the previous statement. Applying the above to the facts of the present case, there is no evidence to show that Broznack knew or had reason to believe that the credit obtained by him on November 15, and December 1, was extended solely on the faith of the representations made by him on October 6. For aught that appears, the sole purpose of those representations was to

obtain the credit extended on that date; and it was not unreasonable for the accused to suppose that the subsequent credits were extended to him by reason of his prompt payment of the first two purchases.

One of the grounds of the motion for a new trial complains that error was committed by the judge in allowing counsel who had been employed to assist the solicitor in the prosecution to make the following statement to the jury in his argument: "I would not appear in this case, if I did not believe the defendant to be as guilty as any man that was ever tried in the courthouse." The court not only declined to stop counsel, but expressly ruled that what is above quoted was "legitimate argument." We think this was error. Counsel "is never justified in expressing the opinion, however he may entertain it, that one whom he is pursuing is guilty. Such opinion is not legal evidence, and in no circumstances, and at no step of the proceedings, is he entitled to thrust it into the case, either by direct words or by implication." 1 Bish. New Crim. Proc. § 293 (3). Upon this subject the same author says: "The opinion of counsel, as to the guilt or innocence of the defendant, should not, we have seen, be by them expressed to the jury. Within this principle, a prosecuting lawyer ought not to assure the jury of his belief that he has made out a case against the defendant; for this is the exact question which they, alone and unbiassed, are to decide. Yet one may well argue, and he should, that the testimony has established his client's cause." 1 Bish. New Crim. Proc. § 975 a (2). See also in this connection, Hopkins's Pen. Code, § 454; p. 115, citing 1 Bish. Crim. Proc. § 311.

Judgment reversed. All the Justices concurring.

ROSS *v.* THE STATE.

The evidence in this case was not sufficient to authorize a verdict of guilty.

Submitted December 18, 1899. — Decided January 25, 1900.

16|9|

Indictment for arson. Before Judge Felton. Crawford superior court. October term, 1899.

M. G. Bayne, for plaintiff in error.
Robert Hodges, solicitor-general, contra.

SIMMONS, C. J. Ross was indicted for arson, in burning an outhouse or crib upon the farm of the prosecutor. The only evidence connecting the accused with the burning was that of some tracks made in a sand-bed thirty feet from the house burnt. The weather was very dry, and the ground in other places was, in consequence of the drought, so hard that the tracks could not be followed. When the tracks were made, no distinct impression was left, the sand running in the track and partially filling it. While the witnesses testified strongly to their belief that the tracks found were those of the accused, still it seems to us that under the circumstances it would be very difficult to distinguish one man's track from another, and almost impossible to do so with any great degree of certainty. And even admitting that the tracks were those of the accused, the evidence does not show when he made them. Frequently in similar cases, involving the proof of guilt by means of tracks, the testimony discloses that just before the commission of the crime a rain had obliterated all old tracks and thereby enabled the witnesses to be positive that the tracks discovered were *recent.* In this case, there had been no such rain, and there was no evidence tending to show when the tracks were made, whether they were recent or old. The accused had been for several months a laborer on the prosecutor's farm, and it was possible, even probable, that the tracks discovered had been made before his employment had ceased. Certainly the evidence does not negative the idea that the tracks were made before the evening on which the house was burned.

There was some attempt to show motive on the part of the accused, from the fact that the prosecutor had not fully settled with him. The prosecutor had offered to give him provisions in lieu of the money due, but the accused, it seems, had supplied himself with provisions and preferred payment in cash. The prosecutor thereupon agreed to carry to town, within a day or two, some corn, from the proceeds of which he was to pay the accused. We think that the failure to pay the balance due could hardly, without more, have been a sufficient motive

for the arson.   There was also some evidence tending to show
that the accused said that if the prosecutor did not pay him all
he owed him, he (the prosecutor) "would lose the worth of it
twice."   This, however, was considerably before the time of
the burning and before the accused knew whether the prosecutor would settle on demand or postpone or refuse payment.   It
was weak evidence, and though it tended to show something in
the nature of a threat, it was not sufficient, though taken in connection with the proof as to the tracks, to support a conviction.
The evidence as a whole may raise a suspicion of the guilt of
the accused, but it does not prove that guilt beyond a reasonable doubt.   It is circumstantial, and does not exclude a reasonable hypothesis of the innocence of the accused.

Judgment reversed.   All the Justices concurring.

DELEGAL v. THE STATE.

1. A private person is authorized to make an arrest for a misdemeanor only
   where the offense is committed in his presence or within his immediate
   knowledge.   It was, therefore, error on the trial of a person charged with
   the homicide of one who had attempted to arrest him, where the evidence
   clearly showed that the deceased and another attempted to arrest the accused for a misdemeanor two days after the commission of the offense.
   and that the deceased and his companion were private persons acting
   without a warrant, to give in charge to the jury the law authorizing officers to make arrests without warrants ; and it was especially erroneous to
   instruct the jury in effect that a private person might arrest where "it
   was reasonably proper to do so in order to prevent a failure of justice for
   the want of an officer to issue a warrant."   For the same reason it was
   error to charge: "Whether under all the circumstances, including the
   facilities for obtaining a warrant, according to the spirit of the law, there
   was or was not cause for attempting the arrest, is a question, after all, for
   you to determine."
2. It was error in such a trial to allow a witness to give his opinion as to
   what would have been the result to him and the sheriff if they had per-
   sisted, two days before the homicide, in an effort to remove a prisoner
   from the jail to the railway-station against the will of a mob of which the
   accused was alleged to have been a member.
3. Where there was no evidence of any mutual combat between the deceased
   and the accused preceding the homicide, it was error to give in charge to
   the jury the provisions of section 73 of the Penal Code.
4. Though in the statement of one on trial for murder he may have used an
   expression which, at most, was merely susceptible of the construction that

he had consented for the deceased and another, who at the time of the homicide were threatening without lawful authority to take him into custody, to enter his house for that purpose, yet where it affirmatively and positively appeared from the evidence that neither the deceased nor the other entered the house in consequence of any such alleged consent, it was error to submit to the jury any question as to whether or not their entering the house was upon the invitation, tacit or otherwise, of the accused.

Argued January 15, — Decided January 25, 1900.

Indictment for murder. Before Judge Seabrook. Effingham superior court. September term; 1899.

Robert J. Travis, Twiggs & Oliver, and *John L. Travis,* for plaintiff in error. *J. M. Terrell, attorney-general,* and *Livingston Kenan, solicitor-general,* contra.

SIMMONS; C. J. The record discloses that on August 23, 1899, there was an alleged riot in the town of Darien, Georgia. On the next day the mayor of Darien swore in Hopkins and Townsend for the purpose of making the arrest of one of the rioters. They subsequently saw the sheriff of the county, informed him what the mayor had done, and told him that they intended to arrest John Delegal. The sheriff told them to "go ahead." They left Darien sometime on the afternoon of the 24th, stopped for the night at Hopkins's house, and at two o'clock in the morning started for the residence of Delegal, which was eighteen miles from Darien. They arrived at about daylight, aroused the occupants of the house, announced who they were, and stated that they had come to arrest Delegal. He inquired as to the reason for his arrest, and was told that it was because of his participation in the riot in Darien. He asked if they had a warrant; they replied that they had not, but that they had been sent by the sheriff. Delegal refused to be arrested, but proposed that he be allowed to take the train to Darien at 11 o'clock on that day and surrender himself to the sheriff. They declined to agree to this, and informed him that they intended to carry him to Darien with them, assuring him at the same time that they would do him no personal injury. Townsend told him they intended to arrest him, and would not "have any long talk" about it. Delegal replied, according to the evidence for the State, "We will see about that." In his statement, made on the trial, Delegal said that he finally told Hopkins and Townsend, "I guess I will go. Let me get my pants," and then told his brother to unlatch the door that he might "see what he is going to do." His offer to go with them, if the remark made amounts to that, seems not to have been heard by Hopkins, the survivor. As the door was unlatched, Hopkins pushed it open and stepped into the house with the remark, "I am not afraid of you." At this time Delegal appears to have been still at the window through which he had been conversing with Hopkins. As the latter entered the house, Delegal left the window, retreated to the back of the room, and seized his gun. As Hopkins entered the house, Townsend, the deceased, came up the steps and upon the porch or piazza, when Delegal shot and killed Townsend and shot at Hopkins, wounding him slightly. Delegal, in his statement, said that when he reached the corner of the room he heard some one say "I done killed one son of a bitch, and I don't mind killing another." He claims that he then saw Townsend throw up his gun as if to shoot, whereupon he shot Townsend. This is, in substance, the material part of the testimony. Under this evidence and the charge of the court, the jury returned a verdict of guilty. A motion for a new trial was made and overruled, and the accused excepted.

1. The court charged the jury upon the law which authorizes officers to arrest persons for misdemeanors or felonies with or without a warrant. This was excepted to and made the basis of two grounds of the motion for new trial. The evidence clearly showed that neither Hopkins nor Townsend was an officer of the State or county. They were not legally appointed, by any person authorized to make the appointment, as officers to make arrests. We have no knowledge of any law which authorizes the mayor of Darien to appoint deputy-sheriffs to make arrests, or to administer the oath of office to deputy-sheriffs. Nor do we know of any law which authorizes the sheriff, after an oath has been administered by such mayor, to send the persons thus sworn in to make arrests for a misdemeanor. Under all the evidence, these men were nothing more than private individ-

uals. It is a well-settled principle of the law of this State, and, as far as we are advised, of all other jurisdictions, that a private individual can not make an arrest for a misdemeanor, unless the offense is committed in his presence or within his immediate knowledge. Our Penal Code, § 900, declares that "A private person may arrest an offender if the offense is committed in his presence or within his immediate knowledge; and if the offense is a felony, and the offender is escaping, or attempting to escape, a private person may arrest him upon reasonable and probable grounds of suspicion." The offense for which the accused was sought to be arrested was a misdemeanor. It was not committed in the presence of either Hopkins or Townsend, nor, as far as appears from the evidence, did either of them have any immediate knowledge of the offense. Hopkins, the survivor, was doubtful, according to his own testimony, as to whether he was in Darien at all on the day of the alleged riot, but in the latter part of his testimony states he believes he was there in the afternoon when the troops arrived. At that time it appears that the riot, if there had been one at all, was over. We think, therefore, that it was error to give in charge the law relative to the authority of officers to make arrests. There is a difference between the power of an officer and that of a private individual to arrest without a warrant. An officer may make an arrest without a warrant, "if the offense is committed in his presence, or the offender is endeavoring to escape, or for other cause there is likely to be a failure of justice for want of an officer to issue a warrant." Penal Code, § 896. It was especially erroneous to give in charge the law and circumstances under which officers are authorized to make arrests, when the court in the charge made some of the instances of the power of an officer apply to private individuals. Thus, in the charge complained of in the eighth ground of the motion for new trial, the judge instructed the jury that Hopkins and Townsend had no legal authority to make arrests without a warrant, "unless it was reasonably proper to do so in order to prevent a failure of justice for want of an officer to issue a warrant." As before remarked, unless the offense is committed in the presence of a private individual or within his immediate knowledge, he can not make any arrest for a misdemeanor. He has no power or authority to do so whether he has time to sue out a warrant or not. Where an offense is committed in his presence, he must arrest the offender then and there, and if he fails to do so immediately, his power to do so at all is gone. He has no power to arrest in order to prevent a failure of justice for the want of an officer to issue a warrant. This power is given to public officers only, and not to private individuals. An officer·may arrest when the offense is committed in his presence or within his immediate knowledge, or if there is likely to be a failure of justice for the want of a proper officer to issue a warrant. The charge above quoted instructed the jury that a private individual had, under such circumstances, the same power as is possessed by an officer. This we think was erroneous. The charge complained of in the next ground of the motion for new trial was, for the same reason, also erroneous. In it the jury was instructed as follows: "Whether, under all the circumstances, including the facilities for obtaining a warrant, according to the spirit of the law, there was or was not cause for attempting the arrest, is a question, after all, for you to determine." This was in effect telling the jury that if there were no facilities for obtaining a warrant, a private individual had power to make the arrest without one. This charge seems to have been taken from the opinion in the case of *Thomas* v. *State*, 91 *Ga.* 207, where Bleckley, C. J., said: "Whether, under all the circumstances, including the facilities for obtaining a warrant, according to the spirit of section 4723 of the code above cited, there was or was not cause for attempting the arrest without a warrant, was a question for the jury." It will be seen from a reference to that case that the learned judge was discussing the powers and duties *of an officer* under that section of the code, now section 896 of the Penal Code, and not the powers of a private individual; so the charge, although extracted from one of the decisions of this court, was erroneous because not applicable to the facts of the present case. In the *Thomas* case the officer had been informed that a larceny had been committed in the forenoon, and he undertook, in the afternoon or evening, to make the arrest, and was resisted. The trial judge stated to the jury, as a matter of law, that the officer had sufficient probable cause to attempt to make the arrest without a warrant, and this court held that this was error, and that the matter should in that case have been submitted to the jury.

2. Upon the trial of this case a witness was allowed to testify, over objection of counsel for the accused: "If I had undertaken to carry Henry Delegal down to that train, the result, in my opinion, would have been that Mr. Blount and I would both have been killed." This we think was error. It was simply the opinion of the witness, giving what he thought would have been his fate and that of the sheriff had they attempted to remove the prisoner from the jail to the railway-station for the purpose of taking him to the jail of another county. It was clearly irrelevant and immaterial, and was calculated to prejudice the minds of the jurors against the accused. In this connection, there was another exception to a ruling of the judge in admitting evidence as to the character and details of the alleged riot with which such evidence directly connected the accused. This ground, however, does not set out the evidence to which objection was made, referring instead to certain pages of the brief of evidence where the objectionable evidence is set out. This court has frequently ruled that it will not look to the brief of evidence to ascertain what was the evidence objected to. The proper way of making such a ruling the basis of a ground of a motion for new trial is to embrace the evidence objected to in the ground of the motion or to attach it as an exhibit to the motion. While we think it was probably erroneous to admit this evidence, we can not deal with it in an authoritative way without violating our former rulings. As this case is to be tried again, I will say for myself that I am inclined to think the true rule as to the admissibility of such evidence to be that where the arrest is made by a private individual when the offense has been committed in his presence or within his immediate knowledge, and he is resisted and injured by the party he seeks to arrest, he may give in evidence the fact that an offense was committed in his presence. If, however, the offense is not committed in his presence and he subsequently undertakes to make an arrest

for it, he can not justify the arrest or attempted arrest by proving that an offense was committed. Nor can he justify by showing that an offense was committed in his presence and that he then waited two days before attempting to make the arrest.

3. The judge charged the jury section 73 of the Penal Code, which declares "If a person kill another in his defense, it must appear that the danger was so urgent and pressing at the time of the killing, that, in order to save his own life, the killing of the other was absolutely necessary; and it must appear, also, that the person killed was the assailant, or that the slayer had really and in good faith endeavored to decline any further struggle before the mortal blow was given." The record discloses that there was no mutual combat between the accused and the deceased prior to the killing. Under these circumstances this court has frequently held that it is illegal and hurtful to the accused to give this section in charge. The matter has been so clearly discussed and settled in the following cases, that it is not necessary further to elaborate the question : *Powell* v. *State*, 101 *Ga.* 9, 22; *Teasley* v. *State*, 104 *Ga.* 738; *Parks* v. *State*, 105 *Ga.* 242; *Smith* v. *State*, 106 *Ga.* 673, 680.

4. A portion of the defendant's statement was as follows: "The third time he [Hopkins] said he did not have any warrant, I said I would not go. He said: 'There is not a dam bit of use to talk that way.' I said: 'I will come on the 11 o'clock train to-day.' He said: 'No use to talk that way; you got to go.' I said: 'I guess I will go. Let me get my pants.' Before I stepped back I said: 'Eddie, take the night-latch off; let me see what he is going to do.'" In regard to this, the judge charged as follows: "If . . Messrs. Hopkins and Townsend were engaged in executing an illegal arrest, if the defendant, after having demanded of them whether or not they had a warrant for his arrest and receiving a reply in the negative but was informed that they had come for the purpose of arresting him and they assured him that no violence would be done him and made other statements to him of a reassuring character, and notwithstanding these he declined to submit to arrest but subsequently (if you find from the evidence such to be the case) consented to go with these alleged officers, and in

pursuance to such consent they entered his house, after the latch had been taken off by some one within, they would be authorized in believing that they had a right to enter, and, if no demonstration was made by them of a character calculated to excite the fears of a reasonable man that bodily harm would be done him, and acting, not under the influence of such fears, but in a spirit of revenge, defendant fired upon these gentlemen, which resulted in the death of the deceased, it is for you to determine whether such shooting was or was not murder, in the light of the law heretofore given you in charge." This charge seems to have been based upon the words, "I guess I will go," and the fact that the door was unlatched by some one within the house. It could not have been based on any part of the evidence, for there was no evidence tending to show that the accused ever consented to the arrest or to the entry into his house. We are very doubtful as to whether the words used, even when taken in connection with the unlatching of the door, were sufficient to authorize a finding that the accused consented to the arrest or to the entry. They were scarcely intended as an invitation, for the next sentence, after instructing that the door be opened, was: "Let me see what he is going to do." Taking the whole of the statement together, these words are at least susceptible of a different construction from that placed upon them by this charge; but be that as it may, we are clear that it was erroneous to allow the jury to find that the entry was made in pursuance of this request. According to the testimony of Hopkins, the only witness testifying on the trial who was present at the time of the homicide, he did not hear the words and neither he nor the deceased acted upon them. Hopkins testified, in substance, that he heard the latch of the door raised and he immediately pushed the door open and entered the house, remarking as he did so, "I am not afraid of you." Townsend was closely following him when shot. Hopkins further testified that he had in his testimony detailed all the conversation that he and Townsend had with the accused, and all that was said by the accused. His testimony does not show that these words were used by the accused. Indeed he testified that it seemed to him that the accused was refusing to go when the witness entered the house. It was, therefore, impossible, according to the testimony of Hopkins, that he could have acted upon any invitation or consent, tacit or otherwise, on the part of Delegal. If Hopkins and Townsend had understood that the accused was ready to surrender and willing to go with them, they would not have acted in the belligerent manner which they did, nor would Hopkins have been likely to use the expression, on entering, "I am not afraid of you." The evidence clearly showing that they neither heard nor acted upon any invitation or expression of consent, it was error to submit to the jury the question as to whether they had done so or to instruct that if Hopkins and Townsend were acting upon such invitation or consent and the accused shot and killed the deceased, it was murder. This charge was harmful and prejudicial to the accused, because it is the only theory deducible from the facts appearing in the case which would have authorized the jury to find him guilty of murder.

Judgment reversed. All the Justices concurring.

HAINES *v.* THE STATE.

1. Even if a writing purporting to be a certified copy of the testimony of a witness given at a commitment trial be admissible in evidence, when it appears that the testimony was not taken down while the witness was on the stand, but was afterwards written out by the magistrate from memory, yet allowing such copy to be introduced against that witness on his trial in the superior court for perjury will not be cause for setting aside his conviction, when, in his statement to the jury, he admits that such copy in substance correctly sets forth what he swore at the commitment trial, and when the magistrate testifies to the same effect.

2. That the court on a trial for perjury, in giving in charge section 991 of the Penal Code, instead of reading to the jury the concluding clause of that section as written, stated that "corroborating circumstances may or may not dispense with another witness," was certainly not erroneous as against the accused. The interpolation of the words, "or may not," was favorable to him. Nor was there any error in adding the words, "it must take two witnesses or other strong corroborating circumstances to establish the fact that the testimony given was false." The use of the word "strong" was in this connection more favorable to the accused than he had a right to demand.

3. There was no error in admitting testimony; the evidence, though conflicting, was sufficient to warrant the verdict; and the same having been approved by the trial judge, this court will not interfere.

Submitted January 15, — Decided January 25, 1900.

Indictment for perjury. Before Judge Butt. Muscogee superior court. December 2, 1899.

J. H. Worrill, for plaintiff in error.
S. P. Gilbert, solicitor-general, contra.

Lewis, J. J. T. Haines was by the grand jury of Muscogee county indicted for the offense of perjury, and at the May term, 1899, of that court, was placed upon trial under this indictment, and convicted. It appears, both from the allegations in the indictment and the evidence in the record, that on the 2d day of January, 1899, a commitment trial was had before a justice's court in Muscogee county, upon a State warrant which charged one Jarvis with the seduction of Lizzie Russell; and on that trial in the magistrate's court J. T. Haines, plaintiff in error in this case, was introduced as a witness in behalf of the accused, Jarvis, and testified, in substance, before the magistrate, after being duly sworn, that he had carnal knowledge of Lizzie Russell at Wildwood Park in Columbus on Christmas night, 1896. The magistrate made a memorandum of Haines's testimony during the trial, and, in a short while after the trial terminated, reduced his testimony to writing. Upon the trial in the superior court of the perjury case against Haines, the State introduced the magistrate, J. E. Crenshaw, who testified in reference to the commitment trial, identified the written statement he had made of Haines's testimony, and swore that it was correct. The State then offered in evidence the written statement of Haines's testimony, which was admitted over the objection of counsel for the accused. After making proof of the testimony delivered by the accused in the magistrate's court as charged in the indictment, the State then introduced Lizzie Russell, who, in positive terms, denied the truth of this evidence, denied seeing him at all at the time and place he stated, and further denied ever having been illicitly intimate with him. She admitted having been at Wildwood Park on Christmas day of 1896, but testified that she left there before dark, in company with friends and certain persons with whom she was living. These persons to whom she referred were likewise introduced in behalf of the State, who corroborated her statement to the effect that she was in their company during her whole stay at Wildwood Park at the time mentioned, and left the place before dark, going to her home, where the evidence tended to show she remained all night. In behalf of the defendant there were a number of witnesses who swore to the lewd character of Lizzie Russell, and to certain acts of lewdness on her part. The accused, Haines, in his statement, substantially admitted what he swore to in the magistrate's court, just as detailed by the State's witnesses, and claimed in his statement that he swore the truth. Jarvis, the person who was charged with seduction, likewise testified in the perjury case in favor of Haines, his testimony tending to show lewd character of Lizzie Russell; admitting that he had illicit intercourse with her, and denying the seduction. There was testimony also introduced in rebuttal by the State, some in support of the character of Lizzie Russell, and impeaching some of the defendant's witnesses. There was, for instance, testimony to the effect that Jarvis had admitted having sexual intercourse with Lizzie Russell, and stated he believed he was the only one who had anything to do with her, and that he had "fooled her." The jury returned a verdict of guilty; whereupon the accused filed his motion for a new trial, which was overruled, and in his bill of exceptions he assigns error in the judgment of the court overruling this motion.

1. One ground in the motion for a new trial is, that the court erred in admitting, over defendant's objection, a certified statement of the evidence taken by Justice Crenshaw, because the evidence discloses that this certified statement was reduced to writing some time after the trial, and then certified to by the justice; and because the evidence admitted was not taken down in writing as required by law. On the trial of a felony before the magistrate, the law requires that the court shall cause an abstract of all the evidence to be made, and returned to the proper court, in the event of a commitment. Penal Code, § 911.

The purpose of this requirement of the law was doubtless to aid the solicitor-general in the prosecution of the accused in the superior court; and we think the proper method of taking the testimony on a commitment trial would be to write it out as it is delivered from the stand. But it does not follow from this that if, after trial, it has been reduced to writing, and has been identified as a correct statement of what the witness swore to, it would not be admissible in evidence. In fact, if the testimony were not reduced to writing at all, it would be perfectly competent for the State to prove what the witness swore to, from the memory of any one who may have heard his testimony, and who recalls what it was. Indeed, testimony before a court of inquiry, when offered to impeach a witness, may be shown by such oral testimony, notwithstanding the magistrate may have reduced all the evidence to writing. *Brown* v. *State, 76 Ga.* 626 (2). We think, therefore, the court committed no error whatever in admitting the written statement under the facts in this case. But if it were not strictly admissible under the rules of law, it certainly worked no harm to the accused; for, in the statement made in his own behalf on the trial under this indictment for perjury, he did not deny having made the statement introduced, but, on the contrary, in substance, related the same facts that appeared in the written statement of his testimony before the magistrate, and affirmed that he had there told the truth. His defense was not based at all upon the idea that he did not testify as charged in the indictment, but that the testimony he gave was the truth.

2. Another ground in the motion for a new trial is alleged error in the following charge of the court: "The testimony of a single witness is generally sufficient to establish a fact. Exceptions to this rule are made in specified cases, such as to convict of treason or perjury, and in any case of felony where the only witness is an accomplice; in these cases (except in treason) corroborating circumstances may or may not dispense with another witness. Now, gentlemen, as I have stated to you before, it must take two witnesses or other strong corroborating circumstances to establish the fact that the testimony given was false." In the first portion of the charge excepted to it will be

34

noted that section 991 of the Penal Code was correctly quoted
by the judge below, except that he interpolated into his charge
the words, "or may not," which do not appear in the statute;
the statute declaring, "corroborating circumstances may dispense with another witness." If there was any error, then, at
all in the interpolation of these words, it manifestly inured to
the benefit and advantage of the accused, and, of course, constitutes no ground of legal complaint that would entitle him to a
new trial. The same is true of the last sentence of the charge
quoted. The statute nowhere declares that the corroborating
circumstances should be "strong" in order to base a conviction
upon the testimony of a single witness.

Another ground in the motion for a new trial complains that
the court erred in admitting, over objection of defendant, the
testimony of J. E. Crenshaw, the same being objected to upon
the ground that neither the indictment nor the certified paper
showed that a legal oath had been administered to John T.
Haines at the time he testified in the committal court. There
was no demurrer offered to the indictment for want of proper
allegations as to the oath. Even if there had been, we see
no defect in the indictment in this particular; for it charges
that John Thomas Haines appeared at the commitment trial
as a witness in behalf of the defendant in a case which the
indictment specified, "and then and there was in due manner
sworn to speak the truth, the whole truth, and nothing but
the truth, as such witness aforesaid." The certified statement of Haines's evidence before the committing court was not
offered to show that the oath was properly administered, but the
testimony of Crenshaw himself was offered to this effect, and
shows that, in point of fact, there was a legal oath administered
before the testimony of Haines was delivered. Even if the testimony of Haines had not been taken down at all, it would not
have affected the legality of the oath which he actually took.

3. After a careful review of the entire testimony in this case,
the main facts in which we have substantially recited above,
we have reached the conclusion that, while there is considerable conflict in the evidence between the witnesses for the State
and accused, there was sufficient evidence to support the ver-

dict; and we therefore refuse to interfere with the discretion of
the trial judge in overruling the motion for a new trial.

Judgment affirmed. All the Justices concurring.

COLLUM *v*. THE STATE.

A "church" is not a "public building" within the meaning of section 725
of the Penal Code.

Argued January 15,—Decided January 26, 1900.

Indictment for misdemeanor. Before Judge Reece. City
court of Floyd county. December 23, 1899.

George A. H. Harris & Son, for plaintiff in error.
Moses Wright, solicitor-general, contra.

LUMPKIN, P. J. The plaintiff in error was indicted under
section 725 of the Penal Code, which reads as follows: "If
any person shall designedly destroy, injure, or deface any public building, its appurtenances or furniture, or shall use the
same for an indecent purpose, he shall be punished as for a misdemeanor, besides being liable for the damages." The specific
charge against the accused was, that he "did enter the Silver
Creek Presbyterian Church, a public building, . . and did use
the same for an indecent purpose," the particulars as to which
were sufficiently set forth. There was a demurrer to the indictment, the ground of which was that a church is not a "public building" within the meaning of the above-cited section of
our Penal Code. We think the demurrer was well taken, and
ought to have been sustained. Although the house referred to
in the indictment was therein designated as a "public building," the accused did not by demurring admit that it was a
building of that character, if it could not be such within the
meaning of the statute. It can never be held that a demurrer
admits a legal impossibility. We have no doubt at all that the
words "public building," as used in this code section, relate exclusively to buildings owned by the public as such; as, for instance, the State capitol, court-houses, city halls, and the like.
These words can not possibly refer to a "church" building,

for under our constitution, which forbids any union of church and State, neither the State nor any political division thereof, such as a county, militia district, or municipality, can own or control a "church," and if a church building should become the property of the public, it would instantly cease to be in any sense a "church." It makes not a particle of difference from what source or sources the means for erecting a church edifice are derived, or whether, after it is erected, it belongs to a church corporation or to an aggregation of individuals holding as tenants in common. It is, at last, in any view of the matter, only private, and not public, property, and therefore not a building which the language used in section 725 of our Penal Code was designed to protect from injury, destruction or defacement. The case of *Smith* v. *State*, 63 *Ga.* 168, cited by the solicitor-general, which was decided in 1879, has no application at all to our present question; for the indictment in that case was framed under a section of the then existing code which is now embraced in section 729 of the present Penal Code, relating solely to the offense of malicious mischief.

Judgment reversed. All the Justices concurring.

WILCOX LUMBER COMPANY *v.* BULLOCK.

1. The "perfect title" which will, under section 4927 of the Civil Code, relieve an applicant for an injunction from averring and proving the insolvency of the defendant or that the threatened damages will be irreparable, must be a duly executed paper title, the exhibition of which will show both the "right of possession" and the "right of property" in the plaintiff. A paper title not meeting these requirements, or a title resting in parol, will not bring an injunction case within the provisions of this section.
2. Under the facts disclosed by the record, the plaintiff below was not, either under the general rules of equity jurisprudence or the special provisions of the code, entitled to an injunction.

Argued January 18,—Decided January 25, 1900.

Injunction. Before Judge Smith. Wilcox county. December 29, 1899.

Thomson & Whipple and *J. M. Terrell*, for plaintiff in error. *J. G. Jones* and *DeLacy & Bishop*, contra.

LUMPKIN, P. J. An equitable petition was filed by Bullock against the Wilcox Lumber Company, to enjoin it from cutting for sawmill purposes the timber growing upon four lots of land. An interlocutory injunction was granted, and the defendant excepted. There was no allegation in the plaintiff's petition that the defendant was insolvent; and though it was in loose and general terms averred that the damages to the former would be irreparable unless the injunction issued, it plainly appears from other allegations in the petition that the damages which would flow from the threatened injury were of a character easy of computation. Indeed, it was specifically averred that the damage to each lot would amount to $500. It is clear, therefore, that the court erred in granting the injunction, if the case, upon its facts, does not fall within the provisions of section 4927 of the Civil Code, which in cases of this class dispenses with the necessity of alleging or proving insolvency, or that the damages will be irreparable, when "the petitioner has perfect title to the land upon which the timber is situated and shall attach an abstract of his title, stating name of grantor and grantee, date, consideration, and description of property, names of witnesses, when and where recorded, to his petition, and produce the original titles before the judge." As to one of the four lots in controversy, the plaintiff's case manifestly did not come within the provisions of this section. He certainly did not show a "perfect title," to this particular lot, nor did he attach to his petition any abstract of title to it, though the absence of such an abstract was made a ground of demurrer to the petition. The only evidence of title offered at the hearing was an imperfectly executed lease which had never been recorded and which purported to have been executed by persons who, so far as appeared, had no title whatsoever. As to the remaining lots, the following appeared: Attached to the plaintiff's petition was a copy of a contract, executed April 20, 1893, by the plaintiff and one Bush, conveying to the defendant for sawmill purposes all the timber on a large number of specified lots of land, including the three lots just referred to. This instrument provided that Bush and the plaintiff were "to have six years from January, 1894, in which to turpentine or to finish turpentining the timber on such of said lots as they have not yet boxed or finished turpentining, and the said Wilcox Lumber Company agreeing not to cut the timber on such lots until the expiration of said six years or until the turpentining thereof is finished, if finished within said six years, said parties of the first part agreeing to box as many as six lots a year after this year." The contract contained the further recital that "three years from the time of boxing [was] the time to be allowed to finish turpentining." At the hearing there was evidence tending to show that Bullock, the plaintiff, at some time after the execution of this instrument, succeeded to all the rights reserved therein. There was a dispute between Bullock and the Lumber Company as to the true intent and meaning of the contract as written, the former contending that under its terms he had the right to use the timber for turpentine purposes after the first day of January, 1900, and the latter insisting that all of Bullock's rights terminated with the year 1899. Looking merely to the terms of the writing, it would seem that the contention of the company was correct. But be this as it may, the matter is left free from doubt by parol evidence, admitted without objection and as to which there was practically no dispute, showing that the rights of Bullock, under this contract as it was understood by the parties, were to end with the year 1899.

He however had another contention, the substance of which, very loosely stated in his petition, was, that after the execution of the written contract there had been between himself and the company a parol agreement, his part of which had been fully performed, extending the time for working the timber for turpentine purposes another twelve months. The evidence adduced as to this matter was decidedly conflicting, the preponderance being apparently in favor of the company. But even upon the assumption that the verbal agreement was entered into as alleged, we have, without serious difficulty, reached the conclusion that the plaintiff failed as completely on this branch of his case as upon the other, in so far as bringing it within the provisions of the above-cited section of the code is concerned. According to section 3209 of the Civil Code, a "perfect title" exists where the same person has both the "right of

possession" and the "right of property." Though a grantor
may be said to have such a title against one who holds exclusively under him by virtue of a written lease, yet where in a
given instance a particular conveyance shows upon its face that
the grantor has parted with his title to and interest in the property thereby conveyed, and accordingly is forced to rely upon
a subsequent parol agreement in order to show that a right of
possession still remains in him, he can not be said to have a "perfect title" within the meaning of section 4927 of the Civil Code.
It is evident to our minds that the words just quoted, as employed in that section, mean a complete and perfect paper at
least capable of being recorded, if not actually recorded. The
use of the terms "grantor," "grantee," "date," "consideration,"
"description of property," "names of witnesses," and "when and
where recorded," and the requirement that the plaintiff shall
"produce the original titles before the judge," are incom-
patible with any other idea than that which we have just expressed. Certainly, it never could have been the intention of
our lawmakers to so greatly vary the existing rules relating to
the granting of injunctions as to allow an alleged landowner,
without averring and proving insolvency or that his damages
would be irreparable, to enjoin a threatened trespass of the kind
mentioned in this section, unless he was able to attach to his
petition and exhibit to the court written evidence showing on
its face that he had complete ownership of the property, or at
least of an interest therein which could by injunction be protected from injury. When his claim to ownership rests entirely
upon an alleged verbal agreement, the very existence of which is
stoutly denied by his adversary, it is impossible for him to meet
the requirements of the statute and thus be relieved of the necessity of averring and proving all that would have been essential before it became a part of our law.

As Bullock did not allege or prove insolvency on the part of
the Wilcox Lumber Company, and in his petition practically
admitted that his damages would not be irreparable, he was
not entitled to an injunction under the general principles of
equity jurisprudence; and having failed to show that he was
so entitled under the special statute upon which we have herein

commented, we are constrained to hold that the trial judge erred in granting the injunction.

Judgment reversed.   All the Justices concurring.

GREEN *et al. v.* THE STATE.

1. An indictment alleging that certain named persons "did in a violent and tumultuous manner prevent the sheriff . . from removing from the common jail" a prisoner therein confined, sufficiently charges the offense of riot, as against a special demurrer setting up that the indictment did "not allege any act done in a violent and tumultuous manner, which prevented" the sheriff from removing the prisoner. Aliter, if the point had been made that the act charged was not set forth with sufficient particularity.
2. Evidence warranting a finding that a number of persons, some of whom were armed with deadly weapons plainly exposed to view, suddenly congregated at a given signal for the purpose of preventing the removal of a prisoner from jail by the sheriff and his posse, acted in an excited manner, talked loudly, ran about from place to place, and made use of threatening, profane, and violent language, thereby intimidating the sheriff and his posse and actually preventing the removal of the prisoner until the arrival of military troops sent to his assistance, authorized the conviction of these persons of the offense of riot. All persons connected with and sharing in the common purpose of the assembly were guilty of riot, whether their conduct was violent and tumultuous or not.
3. The judge committed no error in charging, or in refusing to charge as requested. Such of the other grounds of the motion for a new trial as present questions in a manner that can be dealt with disclose no error requiring the granting of a new trial.
LUMPKIN, P. J., and FISH, J., dissenting. The special demurrer above referred to was intended to present, and did sufficiently present, the objection to the indictment that it did not set forth what means the accused employed, or what specific act or acts they did, for the purpose of preventing the removal of the prisoner, and therefore did not with the requisite particularity put the accused on notice of the charge they were called upon to meet. Thus interpreted, the demurrer was good and ought to have been sustained.

Argued December 4, 1899. — Decided January 26, 1900.

Indictment for riot.   Before Judge Seabrook.   McIntosh superior court.   November 2, 1899.

Twiggs & Oliver, Alexander A. Lawrence, R. L. Colding, and *R. L. Travis,* for plaintiffs in error.   *Livingston Kenan, solicitor-general, Walter G. Charlton,* and *Walter C. Hartridge,* contra.

COBB, J. Jonas Green, Moses Miller Jr., Lawrence Baker, and a number of others were arraigned in the superior court of McIntosh county, on an indictment containing two counts, each of which charged the commission of the offense of riot. The first count charged that these persons, on a day named, "having a common cause of quarrel, did violently and tumultuously commit an unlawful act of violence, by preventing the sheriff of said county from removing from the common jail of said county one Henry Delegal, a prisoner therein under the laws of Georgia, to the terror of the people and contrary to the laws of said State," etc. The second count charged that the persons named in the indictment, "with a common cause of quarrel, did in a violent and tumultuous manner prevent the sheriff of McIntosh county from removing from the common jail of said county one Henry Delegal, therein confined under the laws of Georgia." The accused filed demurrers, both general and special, to the indictment, the special demurrers being as follows: (1) The indictment does not set forth or describe in the first count thereof any unlawful act of violence which prevented the sheriff from removing Delegal from the common jail of McIntosh county. (2) The indictment does not in the second count thereof allege any act done in a violent and tumultuous manner which prevented the sheriff from removing the prisoner. The demurrers were overruled, and exception was duly taken to this ruling. After evidence was introduced, the jury returned a verdict of guilty as to Green, Miller, and Baker, who had elected to sever from the others and were tried jointly. They made a motion for a new trial, which was overruled, and they excepted. It appears from the evidence that the sheriff of McIntosh county and his posse attempted to remove Henry Delegal, a prisoner, from jail and carry him to Savannah. About the time this attempt was being made a church bell was rung, at which signal a crowd of persons, variously estimated at from 75 to 250, among whom were the plaintiffs in error, began suddenly and rapidly to congregate. The members of the crowd ran about from place to place, cursing and talking loudly and in an excited manner. A number of them were armed with deadly weapons plainly exposed to view.

Some members of the crowd were heard to make use of threatening and violent language; one remarking that the sheriff and his assistants were going to remove Delegal to Savannah, and that he was going to "see about it." Another was heard to remark, upon the arrival of troops sent to quell the disturbance, that "they are working a new trick on us; get to your arms." Another said "she would be the first to throw a couple of shots among the white sons of bitches." And still another said that "they intended to kill out all the white people in town." The crowd, however, made no hostile demonstration toward the sheriff or his posse; but, as he testifies, he was prevented by their conduct from removing the prisoner until later on when he was enabled to accomplish this purpose with the aid of troops which were sent to his assistance. It is evident from the testimony that the crowd was in an ugly frame of mind, and that it needed but little to stir them into the commission of open acts of violence and most probably bloodshed. The evidence shows that the plaintiffs in error were connected with the other members of the crowd and shared in their common purpose, and that all of them were armed.

1. The section of the code dealing with the subject of riot is in the following language: . "If two or more persons do an unlawful act of violence, or any other act in a violent and tumultuous manner, they shall be guilty of a riot, and be punished as for a misdemeanor." Penal Code, § 354. Riot at common law is defined by Sir William Blackstone as follows: "A riot is where three or more actually do an unlawful act of violence, either with or without a common cause or quarrel; . . or do any other unlawful act with force or violence; or even do a lawful act . . in a violent and tumultuous manner." 4 Bl. Com. 147. The only material difference between the two definitions seems to be, that at common law the offense could not be committed by less than three persons, and under our statute it can be committed by two. The words "with or without a common cause or quarrel" were originally in the code definition. See Code of 1882, § 4514. But these words were omitted from the Code of 1895. Their omission does not materially change the definition of the offense, and therefore, in substance, it remains

the same as it was at common law. The section of the code above quoted embraces two separate and distinct classes of riot; the first being when "an unlawful act of violence" is committed; and the second when two or more persons commit "any other act in a violent and tumultuous manner." Under the view we take of the present case it is unnecessary to determine whether, as against the demurrer filed in the present case, the first count in the indictment sufficiently charges the commision of an unlawful act of violence. See in this connection, however, Regina v. Gulston, 2 Ld. Raym. 1210; Bonneville v. State, 53 Wis. 680; State v. Brazil, Rice's Rep. (S. C.) 257; State v. Dillard, 5 Black. 365, s. c. 35 Am. Dec. 128.

An examination of the evidence in this case has satisfied us, as will be shown hereafter, that it was sufficient to authorize the conviction of the persons on trial of that class of riot which is brought about by the commission of some act in a violent and tumultuous manner. It is necessary, therefore, to determine whether the second count in the indictment, which attempts to charge such an offense, was a sufficient indictment as against the demurrer which was filed to the same. The indictment charges that the persons accused, with others, " did in a violent and tumultuous manner prevent the sheriff" from removing a certain named person from the common jail of the county, who was lawfully confined therein. The special demurrer makes the objection that this count does not "allege any act done in a violent and tumultuous manner which prevented " the sheriff from removing the prisoner. The question which the demurrer raises is, whether the words in the indictment charge that an act within the meaning of the Penal Code was done by the persons named therein. The demurrer does not raise the question as to whether, conceding such an act to be charged, it is set forth and described with that definiteness which good pleading requires and which would be necessary to put the persons accused on notice as to the exact details of the act which they are charged with having committed, either as to place or manner. What is meant by preventing? Prevent is defined as, to intercept; to hinder; to frustrate; to stop; to thwart. Webster's International Dictionary. To hinder from happening, by means of previous measures; keep from occurring or being brought about as an event or result; ward off; preclude; hinder, as to prevent the escape of a prisoner. To stop in advance, as a person or thing from some act or operation; intercept or bar the action of; check; restrain. Standard Dictionary. An act is defined as "that which is done or doing; the exercise of power or the effect of which power exerted is the cause; a performance; a deed." Webster. "Something done or established." Bouvier. From these definitions it is impossible to come to any other conclusion than that a statement to the effect that one person was prevented from doing something by the conduct of another person embraces the idea that the latter person necessarily committed an act of some character. This being true, when the indictment alleged that the persons accused prevented the sheriff from removing a prisoner from jail, it alleged that such persons had committed an act; and therefore the demurrer, which simply raised the point that the indictment did not charge that an act had been committed, was not well taken. As the indictment charged that an act was done in a violent and tumultuous manner, it was sufficient as against a general demurrer and also as against the special demurrer which was filed to the same. We do not mean to say that this indictment is by any means perfect, or that a special demurrer raising the question as to whether the act alleged should not be described with greater particularity would not have been well taken; but we are clear that as against the demurrers filed to the same the indictment was sufficient, and that there was no error in overruling the demurrers. It is a well-settled rule in this State, that the language of an indictment is to be interpreted liberally in favor of the State. Penal Code, § 929; *Studstill* v. *State,* 7 *Ga.* 2, 16. It follows necessarily from this, that a demurrer raising special objections to an indictment should be strictly construed against the pleader.

2. The evidence establishes that a number of persons assembled together, some of them being armed with deadly weapons; that the expressed purpose for which they assembled was to prevent an arresting officer from removing a prisoner from jail; that they did prevent him from doing so until the arrival of the

military, which overawed the assemblage and aided the sheriff
in removing the prisoner. The evidence further discloses the
use of threatening language on the part of some members of the
crowd, indicating a purpose to resort to the most extreme measures, even to bloodshed, to prevent the prisoner being removed;
that the members of the crowd assembled at a given signal, the
ringing of a bell, showing that the movement must have been
preconcerted; this purpose being further manifested by the fact
that some of the members of the crowd left their occupations and
came from various quarters of the town in response to the ringing
of the bell. Do these facts make out the offense of riot as defined
by our code, which definition, as we have seen, is not materially
different from that of the common law? A consideration of the
adjudicated cases will demonstrate that the conduct of the persons accused in the present case was of such a character as to
warrant their conviction for riot. The exact question to be ascertained, as will have been gathered from the above recitals, is
whether an assemblage of persons who commit no overt act of
violence, but still do some other act in such a way that it is calculated to bring about a breach of the peace or terrify the people, are guilty of the offense of riot. Conceding that neither
the indictment nor the evidence authorized a conviction for
that class of riot which is committed by the doing of an unlawful act of violence, we shall endeavor to show that the evidence
in the present case authorized a conviction under the second
count in the indictment. To sustain a conviction under that
count, it is not necessary to show that the act done was unlawful. *Carnes* v. *State*, 28 *Ga.* 192. In the case of *Jacobs* v. *State*,
20 *Ga.* 841, that portion of the opinion of Lumpkin, J., which
deals with the subject of riot is obiter, but any opinion expressed
by that able jurist is valuable in arriving at a proper conclusion. There the evidence did not show that any of the defendants struck the prosecutor, but it did show that they threatened
to whip him, and otherwise acted in a violent and tumultuous
manner. They, however, committed no specific act of violence.
Judge Lumpkin was of opinion that the defendants could have
been convicted under the second branch of the definition of riot;
saying that "their conduct was violent, tumultuous, and cer-

tainly unjustifiable, if not unlawful." In *Barron* v. *State,* **74** *Ga.* 833, it was held that evidence would not warrant a conviction for riot which showed merely that "though their conduct may have been tumultuous, it was not violent." The use of· the word "conduct" in the two foregoing quotations is significant as showing that under the second branch of the definition of the offense of riot the gist of the offense is the character of the conduct of the persons charged with the offense. In the case of *Sanders* v. *State,* 60 *Ga.* 126, the defendants convicted, with others, assembled at a certain house, all being armed. They were in search of some one, though they had no warrant for his apprehension. The owner of the house, seeing they were bound to come in, invited them to enter and join the family at breakfast. They did so, and behaved rudely at the table. The man of the house was frightened, and tried to pacify them. He had before this made a fire for them in the yard, and on account of their boisterous manner had offered to aid them in their search. The court expressed the opinion that the facts made a weak case of riot, and in this opinion we share; but it can not be seriously contended that the facts of the present case do not make a much stronger case of riot. The cases of *Bolden* v. *State,* 64 *Ga.* 361, and *Fisher* v. *State,* 78 *Ga.* 258, were dealing with the offense of riot as defined in the first part of the section of the Penal Code above quoted; and hence the court properly addressed itself to the question as to whether or not an unlawful act of violence was committed. There is nothing in those cases which could be construed as authority for the proposition that violent and tumultuous conduct, such as threats, the exhibition of arms, menacing gestures, and the like, by means of which a desired object was accomplished, would not constitute riot under the second branch of the definition of that offense.

From 1 Hawk. 515, §5, we quote the following: "However, it seems to be clearly agreed, that in every riot there must be some such circumstances either of actual force or violence, or at least of an apparent tendency thereto, as are naturally apt to strike a terror into the people; as the shew of armor, threatening speeches, or turbulent gestures." It would follow from this that if these things were done, or similar things calculated to terrify the people, the offense would be made out. **In the** case of Clifford v. Brandon, 2 Camp. 358, it was held that "if a number of persons, having come to the theatre with a pre-determined purpose of interrupting the performance, for this purpose make a great noise and disturbance, so as to render the actors entirely inaudible, though without offering personal violence to any individual, or doing any injury to the house, they are, in point of law, guilty of a riot." In State v. Jack-son, 1 Spear (S. C.), 13, it was held that the possession of a club, and the use of threatening language, constituted such a show of force as would make out the offense of riot. In the case of Com. v. Runnels, 10 Mass. 518, it was ruled that, "if the offense consists in going about armed without committing any act, the words 'in terrorem populi'" should be alleged in the indictment; and it was said, in the opinion, that, "To dis-turb another in the enjoyment of a lawful right is a trespass; and if it is done by numbers unlawfully combined, the same act is a riot." Under the Indiana statute the commission of an "act in a violent and tumultuous manner" by three or more persons is riot. In State v. Brown, 69 Ind. 95, s. c. 35 Am. Rep. 210, it was held that "persons conducting a chari-vari, or serenade with bells, horns, tin pans, guns, etc., are guilty of a riot." In this case the evidence did not show the com-mission of any specific act of violence, but showed merely gen-eral conduct of a violent and tumultuous nature. In Bankus v. State, 4 Ind. 114, it was held that where several persons marched back and forth along a highway, blowing a horn and singing songs and hallooing, they were guilty of riot under a statute declaring that a lawful act done in a violent and tu-multuous manner is riot. The court said that they regarded the case as a plain but not an aggravated case of riot. In State v. Acra, 2 Ind. App. 384, it was ruled that an indictment which alleged that three persons did, in a riotous, violent, and tumultuous manner, unlawfully attempt to commit a violent injury on the person named, by violently and unlawfully threat-ening to beat, cut, and shoot such person, stated facts which sufficiently charged the offense of riot. In the old case of Queen v. Soley, 11 Modern, 115, Lord Holt says that, "if a number of men assemble with arms, in terrorem populi, though no act is done, it is a riot." Citing Howard v. Bell, Hob. 91.

Also, " if three men come out of an ale-house and go armed, it is a riot." Citing Year Book 3 Hen. 7, pl. 1. See also 2 Bish. New Crim. L. § 1147; 2 Whart. Crim. L. (10th ed.) § 1540; Clark's Crim. Law, 342; 1 Russ. Cr. 555; 2 Arch. Cr. Pl. & Pr. § 588 (n. 1); Hochheimer's Law of Crimes and Crim. Proc. § 796; May's Crim. Law, § 204; Desty's Crim. Law, § 98 (a). From these authorities we think the principle is plainly deducible, that if a number of persons assemble to prevent an arresting officer from removing a prisoner, and do actually prevent him by intimidation arising from the possession of arms and the use of threats to shoot and kill, it is a riot and an aggravated one at that, though no specific act of violence be committed. This is such violent and tumultuous conduct as amounts to a breach of the peace and is calculated to terrify the people; and hence it can be properly denominated riot.

That the plaintiffs in error could have been convicted, though they had no arms and used no threats, if they were in fact members of the assembly and shared in the common purpose, is well settled by the authorities. Clifford *v.* Brandon, 2 Camp. 358; King *v.* Hunt, 1 Keny. Notes of Cas. 108; State *v.* Straw, 33 Me. 554; Williams *v.* State, 9 Mo. 270; 2 Bish. New Cr. L. § 1153. See also the notes to the case of State *v.* Jenkins, 94 Am. D. 138. The evidence amply warranted a conviction under the second count in the indictment.

3. The motion for a new trial contained various grounds. Those complaining of the refusal of the court to charge certain requests are without merit, for the reason that all of the requests contained propositions which either were not sound law or not adjusted to the facts of the case. Portions of the charge of the judge which were excepted to were substantially in accordance with what is above ruled. The remaining grounds of the motion complain of errors alleged to have been committed in admitting evidence. In three of these grounds the evidence objected to is not set forth, but reference is made to the brief of evidence to ascertain what was the evidence objected to. According to repeated rulings of this court, such grounds will not be considered. Three of the grounds set forth the evidence objected to. This evidence consisted of declarations made by persons in the crowd, other than those on trial. Objection

was made to this evidence on the ground that it was irrelevant and that the declarations were made after the sheriff had abandoned his intention of removing Delegal from jail. It is not necessary to cite authority to establish the proposition, that all persons who compose a riotous assembly are bound by every declaration made by any member of that assembly as long as such assembly continues. The evidence in this case shows that the riotous assembly commenced at the ringing of a bell in the forenoon and continued practically throughout the day; and therefore declarations made by the rioters at any time during the day would, under the principle above referred to, be admissible in evidence against the others. The fact that the riot in the forenoon had taken such shape that the sheriff had determined not to risk removing the prisoner would not render inadmissible declarations made after he had come to this determination, which were calculated in their nature to throw light upon the motive and intention of the assembly at some previous period of the day.

Judgment affirmed. All the Justices concurring, except LUMPKIN, P. J., and FISH, J., dissenting. The only point of difference between ourselves and the majority is, whether or not the demurrer properly raises the objection that the indictment fails to set forth the offense with that degree of certainty which the law requires. We all agree that, as against a demurrer itself sufficient in the respect indicated, the indictment would not be good. The single question at issue should therefore be determined by ascertaining the true intent and meaning of the language used in the demurrer. We of the minority do not think its purpose was merely to set up that the indictment charged no act at all. If we entertained this view, we would not hesitate to concur in the conclusion reached by our brethren; but we do not believe they have given to that language its correct interpretation. Had the words employed in the demurrer simply been that the indictment did "not allege any act done in a violent and tumultuous manner," there would be much force in the position that the sole point of objection was as above stated; but the addition of the words "which prevented" throws a clear and strong light upon the pleader's intention. Giving to the words last quoted the only signification

they could reasonably have been designed to have, the true
meaning of the demurrer is that which would be conveyed by
the words, "the indictment fails to allege that any act was done
by which the sheriff was prevented from removing the prisoner," and this would be the equivalent of saying that the indictment does not set forth the particular act or acts, or specify
the means, by which the prevention in question was accomplished.   We entertain no doubt that this was the objection to
the indictment which the demurrer was intended to present,
and we think it did present it with sufficient clearness.   In
other words, we are of the opinion that the point is well made
that the act charged in the indictment, viz. prevention, "was
not set forth with sufficient particularity."   While a charge
that a person was prevented from doing a designated thing is,
in one sense, undoubtedly the expression of a mere conclusion,
we cheerfully grant that, in another sense, prevention is properly termed "an act."   However, it is an act which can be
done in many and very different ways.   This is certainly true
of the particular act of prevention charged in the present case,
and therefore, if the accused properly demanded specific information as to the kind of prevention with which they were
charged, they were entitled to have it.   As to the doctrine
announced in the last sentence we are all of one faith.   It is
only in the application of it that we divide, two of us going
to the right and the remaining four to the left.

BAPTIST *v.* THE STATE.
DUNHAM, WYLLY, DORSEY, UNDERWOOD, and CURRY *v.*
THE STATE.
GOLDEN, GORDON, and ELVERSON *v.* THE STATE.
McDONALD, THOMPSON, PETTY, and BAILEY *v.* THE STATE.
ROSS, ALEXANDER, SEAGROVES, and JOHNSON *v.* THE STATE.
TIMMONS, TURNER, and MIFFLIN *v.* THE STATE.

COBB, J.   These cases are controlled by the decision this day rendered in
Green et al. v. *The State.*

*Judgment affirmed.   All the Justices concurring, except Lumpkin, P. J., and
Fish, J., who dissent solely for the reason stated in the dissenting opinion filed in
the main case.*
       Argued January 15, — Decided January 26, 1900.   •

McCAIN *v.* SUTLIVE *et al.*

When, for want of an essential party to the bill of exceptions, a writ of error
is subject to dismissal but there is no motion to dismiss, this court, ex suo
mero motu, will allow the plaintiff in error time and opportunity to make
parties and obtain, if practicable, any waiver of service which may be
necessary to a proper hearing of the case upon its merits. If, however,
after such indulgence he is unable to obtain the requisite waiver, dismissal must follow.

Argued November 2, 1899. — Decided January 26, 1900.

Practice in the Supreme Court.

H. C. McCutcheon and *Grigsby E. Thomas Jr.*, for plaintiffs.
Foster & Butler, W. A. Scott, and *J. D. Rambo*, for defendants.

LUMPKIN, P. J.   A petition was filed by John McCain and
numerous others therein named, against Mrs. H. M. Sutlive,
R. D. Williams, and many other natural persons, and also the
Southern Building & Loan Association.   The plaintiffs alleged
that they were tenants in common of described realty with
all the defendants except the one last named, and that it was a
creditor of R. D. Williams, holding a mortgage upon his individual interest in the realty in question.   The prayers were,
(1) for the appointment of an auditor; (2) for an accounting
as to rents and profits; (3) for a partition of the property by a
sale and a division of its proceeds "between the parties according to their respective rights"; (4) for general relief; and (5)
for process.   Upon separate demurrers filed by the Building
& Loan Association and the other defendants, the petition was
dismissed.   Thereupon a bill of exceptions alleging error in
sustaining the demurrers was sued out.   It referred to the case
as that of "John McCain et al. *v.* Mrs. H. M. Sutlive, R. D.
Williams et al.," and did not otherwise name as a plaintiff in
error any person except McCain, or as defendants in error any
persons except Mrs. Sutlive, Williams, and the Building &
Loan Association.   Service of the bill of exceptions was acknowledged by Messrs. Foster & Butler as attorneys for the
corporation defendant in error, and by Messrs. W. A. Scott and
J. D. Rambo as attorneys for the remaining defendants in error.
There was no motion to dismiss the writ of error, and it was

not until after we had, while in consultation, begun to examine the record that we discovered the defectiveness of the bill
of exceptions as to parties.   It is now too well settled to admit
of doubt that those only are parties to a bill of exceptions
who are mentioned therein by their names as such, and that
an acknowledgment of service for "defendants in error" relates to those only who are, at the time it is entered, actually
such defendants.   See *Allen* v. *Cravens*, 68 *Ga.* 554; *Cameron*
v. *Sheppard*, 71 *Ga.* 781; *Anderson* v. *Faw*, 79 *Ga.* 558; *Inman*
v. *Estes*, 104 *Ga.* 645; *Augusta Bank* v. *Merchants Bank*, Ibid.
857; *White* v. *Bleckley*, 105 *Ga.* 173; *Papworth* v. *Ryman*, 108
Ga. 780.   This being so, and the present case being one in
which it was essential to have before this court all the parties
below, we could not properly, with the bill of exceptions in the
condition above indicated, proceed further with a consideration of the case upon its merits.   Not desiring to dispose of it
by a judgment of dismissal without giving to counsel for the
plaintiff in error an opportunity to cure, if they could, the defects in the bill of exceptions, we cited them to show cause
why the writ of error should not be dismissed.   The difficulties could have been remedied by making all the persons who
were plaintiffs below plaintiffs in error and all the persons who
were defendants below defendants in error, *and* by procuring
from all of the latter who had not been served a waiver of service and an agreement that the case be heard upon its merits.
As counsel for the plaintiff in error were unable, after being
allowed ample time for this purpose, to obtain such a waiver
and agreement, we must deal with the case as it now stands.
It would, of course, have availed the plaintiff in error nothing
to merely complete the bill of exceptions as to parties without
also procuring the waiver, etc., from the newly made defendants
in error.   Accordingly, we have before us but one plaintiff in
error and but three defendants in error, although, as has been
seen, there were in the court below many other persons who
were directly interested in sustaining its judgment and who
consequently had an imperative right to be heard here.   Under the cases cited above, a dismissal of the writ of error is the
necessary and only result which can follow.   Indeed, a judg-

ment of reversal, even if we should render it, would be of no benefit to the plaintiff in error. It could in no event be operative except as to him and the three defendants in error, as the judgment below would still bind all the other litigants. With the final and conclusive adjudication embraced therein that none of McCain's coplaintiffs are entitled to the relief sought against any of the defendants, and that McCain could in no event obtain from any of the defendants, except three, the relief for which he prays, it is obvious that the petition, however meritorious originally or however well supported by evidence, can no longer have an effectual standing in court. How, under such circumstances, could there be an equitable accounting, or how a sale of the land at which a purchaser could obtain a good title?

If there is to be a judgment of affirmance, it is, of course, immaterial to the plaintiff in error whether it is rendered upon the merits or as the legal consequence of dismissing his writ of error. There must be a dismissal when a judgment of reversal would be incapable of practical enforcement and therefore useless. Nothing of consequence would be accomplished by correcting errors when so doing would leave the party invoking the exercise of our jurisdiction in no better position than he was before. This court does not sit to render judgments which can have no practical bearing upon litigation. The rule which forbids its so doing finds a pointed application in the present instance. What could the trial court properly do, were we to reverse the judgment now under review and send the case back for another hearing? With our judgment favorable to one only of the numerous plaintiffs and adverse to three only of the many defendants below, and its judgment, still of force, adverse to all the remaining plaintiffs and favorable to all the remaining defendants, no course would be left open except to dismiss the case. An effort to try it on its merits would soon show the utter impracticability of arriving at a judgment which would be lawful and in all parts self-consistent. In this connection, mere suggestion, without elaboration, is sufficient. The truth is, the court below would be in no better condition for dealing with the case than if, as in this court, there was a lack of essential parties; for while it would actually have before it all the parties at interest, they would be so circumstanced that equity and justice could not possibly be meted out to all alike. It seems, therefore, that our disposition of the case at once brings about, in effect, the result which must, in any event, come to pass; and if so, neither delay nor circumlocution would be profitable to any one concerned.

Writ of error dismissed. All the Justices concurring.

ATLANTA CONSOLIDATED BOTTLING COMPANY *et al.* v. HUTCHINSON & SONS.

1. Under the principle laid down in *American Car Co.* v. *Atlanta Street Ry. Co.*, 100 *Ga.* 254, and cases therein cited, one who gives a note with full knowledge of facts which would relieve him from liability for a portion of the debt represented in such note can not, in defense to an action thereon, subsequently set up those facts.
2. A guaranty by a seller, to one who purchases for the purpose of reselling, to maintain for a specified season the price of the goods sold, is not applicable, when it appears that the buyer did not himself sell or dispose of the goods during that season.
3. Applying this rule to the facts alleged in the present plea, the defendant, at the time of giving the notes sued on, either knew with certainty of the acts and conduct of plaintiff, now alleged as a defense, or was not protected by the alleged guaranty.

Submitted December 6, 1899. — Decided January 26, 1900.

Complaint. Before Judge Reid. City court of Atlanta. May term, 1899.

Thomas L. Bishop, for plaintiffs in error.
Slaton & Phillips, contra.

Lewis, J. Hutchinson & Sons brought suit against the Atlanta Consolidated Bottling Company, Lee Hagan, and D. W. Liddell, in the city court of Atlanta, on three unconditional promissory notes, each for $115.53, given on January 10, 1898, and due respectively on July 20, August 20, and September 20, after date. It appears from the record that these notes were signed by the Atlanta Consolidated Bottling Company through Lee Hagan, manager, and that each one was indorsed by Hagan and Liddell. The notes were correctly copied on the original petition; but it seems that the clerk, in the copies served on the defendants, omitted to copy the entry of indorsement by Hagan and Liddell. The following is substantially the defense set up by the defendants' pleas to the action: It was admitted in the answer that notes had been given to plaintiffs in the amount sued for, signed by the defendant company, and indorsed by Hagan and Liddell; but they deny they had been sued upon these notes, but upon three notes executed by the defendant company alone. It was further charged that the notes were obtained by fraud and misrepresentation, in this, that the defendant company purchased a large lot of soda stoppers from the plaintiffs under an express guarantee by the plaintiffs that they would maintain the price, and that they would protect for one year the price for which they sold the stoppers to defendant; that after the stoppers were delivered to defendants and the notes given, they discovered plaintiffs had practiced fraud by not protecting the price as agreed, and by selling to others in violation of their guarantee, and to defendants' damage, stoppers at a considerably less price than the sum charged defendants. It seems this was demurred to on special grounds, and the defendants undertook to meet the demurrer by filing a second amendment, in which it was charged that on July 1, 1895, defendant wrote to plaintiffs that it had ordered large bottles, and that it would be in the market for stoppers for the bottles ordered, but that defendant had been informed that the patent on the stoppers which the plaintiffs were then manufacturing was about to expire, and that the price would be materially decreased; and that it did not wish to buy a large quantity at that time unless protected in the price. It was further alleged in this amendment that on July 5, 1895, in answer to this letter, plaintiffs below made the following reply: "We are in receipt of your order for 10 gross of No. 4, Rubber and I extractor, and the same has our attention, and shipped this day by American Express. In regard to stoppers, will say that the price has not yet been reduced. The patent has not yet expired, and we have not decided at what day the price will be reduced. We will say, however, that we will give you every advantage, and

if you are wanting any large amount we will make it to your
interest to give us your order, and will protect you against any
decline during the present season." The plea as thus amended
was demurred to on the ground that it constituted no defense;
that the notes sued on were made long subsequent to the alleged agreement set up in the amended plea; that the plea fails
to set up any agreement; and that there was no consideration
for such alleged agreement. To the judgment of the court sustaining this demurrer the plaintiffs in error except.

1. The allegation in the pleadings to the effect that the defendants had not been sued upon the notes which they executed, not being sustained by the record, of course amounts to
nothing. The principle announced in the first headnote is
well-settled law. One who gives a note, or makes an unconditional promise in writing for the payment of a debt after the
same has been contracted, waives all defenses of which he had
full knowledge at the time such a settlement by written contract was made. See *Edison Co.* v. *Blount*, 96 *Ga.* 272; *American Car Co.* v. *Ry. Co.*, 100 *Ga.* 254; *Lunsford* v. *Malsby*, 101
Ga. 39; *Blount* v. *Edison Co.*, 106 *Ga.* 197.

2, 3. We think the principle above is clearly applicable
to the facts pleaded in this case. The defendants below, by
their plea, resisted a collection of these notes on the ground of
a failure on the part of the vendors of the goods, for which
the notes were given, to comply with their written guarantee
with reference to maintaining the price. The only paper insisted upon as such guarantee is the letter written by Hutchinson & Sons to the defendant company, dated July 5, 1895.
The only promise embodied in that letter is to the effect that
if the defendants desired any large amount of the goods, they
would be protected "against any decline during the present
season." It does not appear from the pleadings what period
of time the expression, "present season," would include. It is
fair to infer that it would not extend longer than the remainder of the year in which this letter was written. Under the
defendant's plea, it is not pretended it covered a period of time
longer than one year. It will be noted that the notes for the
goods were not given until nearly three years after the making

of this alleged contract guaranteeing a protection against any decline in the price of goods. If, then, the defendant company bought the goods during that season, and placed them upon the market before the expiration of the season contemplated by the parties, it, of course, had thorough knowledge of any decline in price when the notes were given in settlement of the . goods nearly three years thereafter. If it did not purchase the goods which constituted the consideration for the notes sued on, or place the same upon the market during the season referred to in the letter of the vendors of July 5, 1895, then evidently there was no contract binding upon the vendors to protect the vendee against such decline. It is evident that the buyer either did or did not sell or dispose of the goods during the season in which it was promised protection by the letter of the sellers. If it sold the goods at a loss, then it certainly knew of their decline in price when the notes were afterwards given therefor. If it failed to sell during this season, or sold them at a loss subsequently to its expiration, then the defendant disposed of the goods at a time when it had no sort of promise or guarantee on the price from the vendors.

Applying the principles of law above enunciated to these facts, we think there was no error in the judgment of the court sustaining the demurrer to the pleas; and the writ of error being palpably without merit, damages are awarded against the plaintiffs in error for bringing the case here for delay.

Judgment affirmed, with damages. All the Justices concurring.

SIMMONS *v.* COOK *et al.*

When a successful bidder at a sale of property made by the sheriff under execution does not pay or tender the amount of his bid in cash, but, without any knowledge or consent of the plaintiff in fi. fa., relies on an arrangement made with the sheriff to receive the money from another source, he is not, if the arrangement so made is not productive of the amount bid so as to be promptly available to the plaintiff in execution, entitled to restrain a resale of the property, nor to require a conveyance to him; and this is so whether the sheriff acted in good or bad faith in failing to execute the arrangement made.

Argued December 6, 1899. — Decided January 26, 1900.

Petition for injunction.   Before Judge Lumpkin.   Fulton county.   June 8, 1899.

Simmons & Corrigan, for plaintiff.

W. W. Haden, for defendants.

LITTLE, J. Simmons filed an equitable petition against Nelms as sheriff of Fulton county, Sammons, and Cook, the latter of whom was plaintiff in a certain execution against Sammons, which had been levied on certain land of the defendant, which petitioner claimed he had purchased at the sale made by the sheriff. He prayed that the sheriff be enjoined from reselling the property and be required to specifically perform the contract of sale made by him to the petitioner, and that it be decreed that the sheriff should make a deed of conveyance of the land to the petitioner; also for general relief. On the hearing the evidence of the petitioner tended to establish the following facts: On the first Tuesday in April, 1899, Nelms, sheriff, by virtue of the fi. fa. described, after levy and due advertisement put up and exposed for sale certain parts of land lot 190 in the 17th district of Fulton county.   At said sale petitioner was the highest and best bidder, and the same was knocked down to him for the sum of six hundred dollars.   On the same day certain lands belonging to the petitioner, which had been levied on to satisfy certain fi. fas. against him, and which had been duly advertised, were also sold by the sheriff, and the Equitable Loan & Security Company became the purchaser of the land belonging to petitioner for the sum of $28,200, which said last-mentioned sum was paid to the sheriff, on the evening of the day of the sale, in the form of a certified check on a solvent bank.   At the time of said payment, executions to the amount of about eighteen thousand dollars against petitioner were in the sheriff's hands, claiming the fund arising from the sale of his property. Under these circumstances petitioner directed the sheriff to appropriate enough of the balance of the proceeds of the sale of his land to pay the amount of his bid for the Sammons property.   This the sheriff failed to do, although there were several thousand dollars in his hands in excess of the amount of the executions against petitioner which had been lodged with said sheriff as claiming the proceeds of the sale. The petitioner claimed that the evidence also established the allegation made by him, that subsequently to the day of the sale he tendered to the sheriff the amount of his bid and demanded a conveyance. It appears also that the property bid off by petitioner was readvertised for the May sales by the sheriff, at the risk of petitioner, for non-compliance with his bid. The sheriff testified, that on the first Tuesday in April he did offer for sale the interest of Sammons in the two tracts of land, under the execution proceeding in favor of Cook, and that petitioner was the highest bidder and the property was knocked off to him for the sum of six hundred dollars. In the afternoon of that sale day the attorney for the plaintiff in execution called on him for the money, and, being informed that the petitioner had not complied with his bid, he directed the sheriff to resell the property if petitioner did not comply before the close of the legal hours of sale on that day. Thereupon the sheriff demanded of petitioner a compliance with his bid, and petitioner promised to pay the same, but did not. On the next day the attorney for the plaintiff in execution instructed him to readvertise and sell the property at the May sales, and in accordance with said instructions he readvertised said property to be sold at the risk of petitioner. On the same sale day (in April) he did sell at public outcry a piece of real estate belonging to the petitioner, under a fi. fa. which had been issued against him, and that property brought $28,200. In payment of the last sum, after the banks of the city had closed, the purchaser gave him a check, but he did not get the money nor any part of it until after 9 o'clock on the next day. Subsequently petitioner instructed him to appropriate six hundred dollars of this money in payment of his bid. Before the May sales, the attorney for Cook, plaintiff in execution against Sammons, informed him that an error had been made in the execution under which the sale of the Sammons property had been had, and to satisfy which the property was readvertised for the May sales at the risk of petitioner, and instructed him not to proceed further under that execution, but to return it to the clerk of the court that it might be amended and corrected, and to release Simmons from all liability arising from his bid made

at the April sales. All this he did, and withdrew the advertisement to resell the property, and the execution has since
been corrected, and the plaintiff has paid the advertising fees
for both the April and May sales. There was other evidence,
both by the plaintiff and the defendant, on the same line and
tending to support their different contentions. The judge,
after argument, refused to grant the injunction, and dissolved
the restraining order previously issued; and to this judgment
plaintiff in error excepted.

While it was the undoubted right of the plaintiff in error to
have appropriated to his bid any sum of money which remained
in the hands of the sheriff in excess of the legal claims held by
the sheriff against him, it does not appear as a matter of fact
that any sum of money was in the hands of the sheriff belonging to the plaintiff in error on the day of the sale of the property for which he was the highest bidder, but that, as the purchase-price for the property of the plaintiff in error which was
sold on the same day, the sheriff accepted, after banking hours,
a check on one of the banks in the city, and that he really did
not receive the money until the following day. Nor does it
satisfactorily appear from the evidence that, at the time the
check for the purchase of petitioner's property was cashed,
there was any amount in excess of that required to pay off executions and liens against petitioner in the hands of the sheriff;
but even if there had been, the arrangement which the petitioner alleges he made with the sheriff was not such a contract
as would be decreed to be performed. The plaintiff in fi. fa.
was directly interested in the sale and the prompt collection of
the money represented in the petitioner's bid, and had a right
to require the bidder to comply with the obligations the law
imposed on him, and it is not alleged that the plaintiff in fi. fa.
consented or even knew of the alleged arrangement between
the bidder and the sheriff. As was said by Chief Justice Jackson in the case of *McLendon* v. *Harrell*, 67 *Ga.* 440: "Cash,
not credit, is that which the law requires them [sheriffs] to
exact from every bidder, and no man's note, or check, or draft,
is, in the cold and impartial eye of justice, the equivalent of
cash. Once relax the rule, and the gate to collusion and fraud

is swung back so wide that an ocean of corruption would enter, and the fairness of public sales would be at an end." See also *Jones, Drumright & Co.* v. *Thacker & Co.*, 61 Ga. 329. It is certain that the petitioner did not tender to the sheriff, on the conclusion of the sale, the amount of his bid in cash. Had he done so, he would have complied with the obligation which the law requires, to entitle him to a conveyance of the property. Not having done so, whether the sheriff did or did not act in good faith with him, and whether the sheriff ought or ought not to have considered the amount of the bid paid, is a question between the petitioner and the sheriff; but so far as the plaintiff and defendant in execution, who had each a direct interest in having the law of sheriffs' sales complied with, are concerned, it was no complete sale; and while it was the right of the plaintiff in execution to have the property subsequently resold at the risk of the petitioner, he was not obliged to do so, and when he withdrew the advertisement for resale he was acting strictly within his legal rights; and as the petitioner had not so complied with the legal terms of the sale as to entitle him to a conveyance of the land, and as it does not affirmatively appear that the petitioner tendered the amount of his bid before the plaintiff abandoned the intention to resell at the risk of the petitioner, he ought not to be heard to complain. The judge committed no error in refusing to grant the injunction.

Judgment affirmed. All the Justices concurring.

PAGE v. PITT.

The superior court has no jurisdiction to entertain an ordinary claim to a fund raised by a garnishment and which has been properly paid into a city court.

Argued December 7, 1899. — Decided January 26, 1900.

Levy and claim. Before Judge Lumpkin. Fulton superior court. March term, 1899.

Lumpkin & Colquitt, for plaintiff in error.
Robert L. Rodgers, contra.

Cobb, J. Pitt obtained judgment against Mrs. Stiles in the superior court of Fulton county, and caused summons of garnishment to be issued thereon, directed to H. L. McKee and Mrs. Jessie McKee. The garnishees answered that at the time of the service of the summons they owed the defendant nothing, but that since the service they had become jointly indebted to her in the sum of five hundred dollars, which amount had been paid into the city court of Atlanta under a summons of garnishment served upon them prior to the service in this case. On October 8, 1897, the attorney for Pitt agreed in writing that the garnishees should answer instanter and pay the fund of five hundred dollars into the city court, because the first garnishment was returnable to that court, and that two hundred and fifty dollars of the amount might be withdrawn and paid over to the attorneys of Mrs. Stiles as their fees in the case where the recovery had been had against the McKees. On November 13, 1897, Mary J. Page filed in the superior court of Fulton county what purported to be an affidavit and claim bond; the affidavit setting forth that Pitt had obtained judgment in the superior court against Mrs. Stiles and had sued out summons of garnishment directed to the McKees, and that the garnishees had answered that they had paid into the city court of Atlanta five hundred dollars in answer to the summons of garnishment in the case pending in that court. The affidavit further set up that the money referred to in the answer of the garnishees was not the money of Mrs. Stiles, but was the money of Mrs. Page. There also appears in the record what purports to be a bond given by Mrs. Page to dissolve the garnishment in the superior court. This bond recites that two hundred and fifty dollars in the hands of the garnishees had been paid into the city court of Atlanta. When the claim case came on for trial in the superior court the presiding judge dismissed the claim. The claimant filed a bill of exceptions, assigning error upon the judgment of the court dismissing her claim, as well as on various rulings made at the trial.

Under the view we take of the case, it is unnecessary to deal with several of the questions presented in the record. The law authorizing a claim to be interposed to a fund which is brought into court by a garnishment contemplates that such claim shall be filed in the court which has control of the fund. Civil Code, § 4720. At the time that Mrs. Page filed her claim in the superior court there was no fund in that court to which the claim could relate, and, by the agreement made with the attorney for the plaintiff in the garnishment proceeding in that court before the claim was filed, no such fund would ever reach that court. It would have been idle for the superior court to solemnly determine the title to this fund, when it had no power to carry into effect the judgment it rendered; the fund in controversy being, at the date that the claim was filed, under the exclusive jurisdiction of the city court. If the claimant desired to assert her title to the property by claim, it should have been filed in the court which had possession and control of the fund.

Judgment affirmed. All the Justices concurring.

STERLING CYCLE WORKS *v.* WILLINGHAM.

109
s113 968

1. Where immediately after executing a written contract guaranteeing to an amount stated payment for goods to be ordered by a partnership the guarantor made a parol promise to pay for all goods so ordered, and subsequently wrote letters to the other party to the written contract containing promises to pay an indebtedness of the partnership, the nature and extent of which was not in such letters explicitly stated, evidence of the parol promise was admissible for the purpose of explaining the true intent and meaning of the letters.
2. There was, in the present case, sufficient evidence of the making of the promise relied on by the plaintiff, and of a consideration supporting the same, to carry the entire case to the jury.

Argued December 7, 1899. — Decided January 26, 1900.

Complaint. Before Judge Reid. City court of Atlanta. May term, 1899.

Mayson & Hill, for plaintiff. *Culberson & Willingham* and *Westmoreland Brothers,* for defendant.

LEWIS, J. The Sterling Cycle Works brought suit against E. G. Willingham, in the city court of Atlanta, for $1,071.65. After plaintiff had introduced testimony and closed its case the judge below, upon motion of defendant's counsel, granted a nonsuit. To this judgment the plaintiff in error excepts. It appears from the record that the plaintiff was a dealer in bicycles, and that it had established an agency, composed of the firm Cabaniss & Castle, for the sale of its goods in the city of Atlanta. Cabaniss retired from this firm, having sold out his interest to R. F. Willingham. The agency was then represented by Willingham & Castle. R. F. Willingham was a son of the defendant, E. G. Willingham. There was evidence tending to show that the defendant, E. G. Willingham, was instrumental in getting his son into the business, and bringing about an arrangement by which the agency for the sale of these goods succeeded to Willingham & Castle. On the 8th of May, 1897, the plaintiff and "Willingham & Co." entered into a written contract. While this contract was signed "Willingham & Co.," E. G. Willingham, the defendant in this case, was really the party constituting the firm of Willingham & Co. The contract was, therefore, by the parties treated as his individual contract with the Sterling Cycle Works. Under the terms of that agreement, the plaintiff agreed to sell and deliver to Willingham & Castle such goods as it kept in stock, in such quantities and at such prices as the plaintiff and Willingham & Castle might agree upon. In consideration of this agreement, E. G. Willingham, defendant herein, guaranteed to the plaintiff the payment at maturity for any and all purchases from the Sterling Cycle Works, made prior to, or on, or after the date of the contract, May 8, 1897, by and in the name of Willingham & Castle. It was further agreed in the written contract that the liability of E. G. Willingham should not be for a larger sum than $2,000.00, unless made by another special agreement. There is evidence in the record tending to show that the past indebtedness for which Willingham & Castle were liable to the plaintiff amounted to within about $500.00 of the limit fixed in the guarantee contract between plaintiff and defendant. The agency was conducted for a short while by the firm of Willingham & Castle, and Castle agreed to withdraw from the firm for the sum of $65.00. In consideration of this, there is testimony to the effect that E. G. Willingham promised Castle to be responsible for all the indebtedness of Willingham & Castle, including the amounts which were due to the plaintiffs in this case. There was also testimony from which it might be inferred that the assets thus recovered by E. G. Willingham were of value more than sufficient to pay off this indebtedness of Willingham & Castle.

The following is the substance of some letters introduced by plaintiff on the trial: On July 21, 1897, E. G. Willingham wrote the Sterling Cycle Works to the effect that Willingham & Castle had in two months sunk about $1,200.00, and perhaps more; that it was useless for him to go into reasons why he should not allow the business to run any longer in this way; and he concluded that it was best for him to buy out the business, which he had done. He would use his best efforts to place plaintiff's wheels on the market, and he wrote to inquire if plaintiff wished him to keep the agency for the wheel for another year. In his letter he further alluded to the fact that, as the business had been started there, his son might continue, after he had become more experienced, and might possibly make a success of it. Everything had been against him (his son) up to now, and, "while I am the loser, yet in the future he may be benefited." He then asked for an itemized statement of "their" account, referring evidently to the account of Willingham & Castle. To this a reply was made on the 23d of the same month by the Sterling Cycle Works, in which, among other things, it was agreed that E. G. Willingham should retain and have the agency of the business, and in which it enclosed a statement of the account asked for by him. To this, on July 27th, E. G. Willingham replied, acknowledging receipt of the bill against Willingham & Castle, for which he expressed thanks, and stated that he would check every bill, and write in a day or two how the account stood. He also stated that he would get things in such shape as to pay plaintiff some money along, or close the account by note, so that the old business could be settled up. That was replied to by the plaintiff during the same month, in which reply plaintiff indicated that the arrangement proposed by E. G. Willingham to make a cash remittance or note settlement was entirely satisfactory. A few days thereafter plaintiff again wrote the defendant, en-

36

closing statement of account amounting to $2,714.39, recogniz-
ing that there would be certain credits made for items returned
which would reduce this amount slightly. Plaintiff again
wrote to the defendant subsequently during the same month,
asking, in effect, for a partial payment of cash on the amount
due. If he could not do that, to send notes maturing at certain times in the future, with interest, and that would be satisfactory. In September, 1897, plaintiff wrote the defendant
another letter, enclosing a statement of account, after crediting
various items of merchandise it had lately received from defendant; and called attention to defendant's letter of August 24th, in which he suggested that when certain items had
been credited he would send plaintiff check to close the account,
including interest on the notes. Plaintiff then offered that if
the defendant would send a check in settlement by a certain
date, plaintiff would waive the question of interest. Finally,
on September 21, 1897, E. G. Willingham replied by letter to
the Sterling Cycle Works, expressing surprise at the statement
showing Willingham & Castle owing, on account and in notes,
an amount of $1,100.00 over and above the last payment made
by defendant to plaintiff. He further added in his letter, he
was under the impression the balance would be only about
$160.00, but if the account stood as plaintiff reported, he would
comply only with his bond.

In the course of the trial plaintiff offered to prove certain
declarations made by the defendant to plaintiff's representative, in answer to a suggestion that the amount of the guarantee be increased so as to give them (meaning Willingham &
Castle) a sufficient margin of credit to enable them to put in a
fair stock of wheels. Defendant replied that he did not feel
disposed to increase the amount of the written guarantee, as he
did not care to have the young men think they had the liberty
to order to an unlimited extent; but that the plaintiff need
have no hesitancy in filling their orders, as he personally would
be responsible for, and would see paid, any indebtedness which
they might incur, whether the same was in excess of the amount
of the guarantee or not. This matter was referred to by the
defendant more than once, and, after the time when all the de-

tails had been arranged and practically settled, he repeated his
assurance that, in view of the fact that he intended to give the
business his personal attention until such time as his son had
mastered all the details and had shown sufficient ability to handle the financial end alone, he personally would be responsible.
It was sought by this evidence to establish another agreement
separate and distinct from the written contract, and made subsequently thereto.　But the court excluded this testimony (sayings of the defendant) from the jury; to which ruling plaintiff
in error excepts.　There is evidence in the record tending to
show that, on the faith of these verbal promises, goods were
furnished Willingham by plaintiff in error in excess of the
$2,000.00 mentioned in the written guarantee.

Viewing all the testimony introduced and sought to be introduced upon this subject, we think there were facts sufficiently
shown, and offered to be shown, to authorize the jury to infer
that this parol agreement was made and entered into subsequently to the written agreement, and constituted a valuable consideration for the contract sued upon.　These declarations of the
defendant were further admissible in explanation of the letters
subsequently written by the defendant, touching a settlement
of the account that had been made by Willingham & Castle.
It does not clearly appear from those letters to what extent E. G.
Willingham had assumed the indebtedness of this partnership.
Some of his letters on the subject are susceptible of the construction that he contemplated being responsible for the entire
indebtedness, whether it amounted to more than the sum stipulated in his written contract or not.　The verbal statements
sought to be introduced, and which were ruled out by the
court, clearly indicate such was his purpose; and we think,
for that reason, if for none other, they were admissible for the
purpose of explaining the true intent and meaning of the letters.　We have not undertaken above to call attention to all
the evidence introduced in behalf of the plaintiff, which is quite
voluminous, but only to such prominent features in it as tend
to show a valuable consideration for the contract sued on in
this case.　In the light of the entire record, we can not say
that there is not sufficient testimony for the jury to really infer

an original undertaking on the part of E. G. Willingham, made after the written agreement was entered into, to pay the entire account of Willingham & Castle, on the faith of which credit for goods sold them over and above the $2,000.00 limit mentioned in the original contract was really extended to E. G. Willingham himself.   Our conclusion, therefore, is that the court erred in granting a nonsuit.

Judgment reversed.   All the Justices concurring.

ROBINSON *v.* THE STATE.

In order to convict a public officer of the offense of embezzlement, all the elements necessary to constitute the crime must be proved,—among others, the fact that the accused fraudulently appropriated to his own use public funds which went into his hands as an officer.   While positive proof of such appropriation is not required, and, as a general rule, may be legitimately inferred from the acts of the accused, yet a mere failure to pay over the amount with which such officer is chargeable is not, of itself alone, sufficient to establish a fraudulent appropriation to his own use.

Argued December 18, 1899. — Decided January 27, 1900.

Indictment for embezzlement.   Before Judge Reagan.   Hall superior court.   July term, 1899.

J. O. Adams, F. M. Johnson, and *H. H. Dean,* for plaintiff in error.

W. A. Charters, solicitor-general, and *W. F. Findley,* contra.

LITTLE, J.   Robinson was indicted and tried for the offense of embezzlement.   The bill of indictment alleges that, as tax-collector of Hall county, he embezzled money belonging to the county, to the amount of $8,401, collected of the taxpayers on the general county tax due on the digests of the county for the years 1890, 1891, and 1892.   A second count alleges that he embezzled money belonging to Hall county, to the amount of $7,273, being taxes collected from the different railroads located in said county.   He was convicted, and made a motion for a new trial on a number of grounds, the first three of which may be summarized to be that the verdict is without evidence and is contrary to law.   Several were added by amendment, but, in view of the ruling we make on the general grounds of the motion, it is entirely unnecessary to consider these additional grounds.

The plaintiff in error was indicted under section 187 of the Penal Code, which declares that "Any officer, servant, or other person employed in any public department, station, or office of government of this State, or any county, town or city thereof, who shall embezzle, steal, secrete, or fraudulently take and carry away any money, paper, book, or other property or effects, shall be punished," etc.   This offense was unknown to the common law, and is entirely the creation of statutes both in England and in this country.   In its nature it is near akin to larceny, the difference being, that in order to constitute the latter offense the property must be taken from the actual or constructive possession of the owner.   Hence it will be readily seen that the taking of property which belongs to another who has never come into possession of it, by one who acquires possession of that property in the course of business, can not technically be classed as a larceny.   The English statute constituting the offense of embezzlement was enacted because of a decision that a clerk of a banker who had received money from a customer and appropriated it to his own use could not be convicted of larceny, in consequence of the fact that the money had never been in the employer's possession. Rex v. Bazeley, 2 East P. C. 571.   Under the definition of the offense of embezzlement given in our code, it seems that it is necessary that the appropriation shall be made of property belonging to another, or, in case of a public officer, to the public, which rightfully came into the possession of the person charged with its appropriation, and that such person can not be convicted unless it be shown that the money has been fraudulently appropriated by the officer to his own use.   The words of the statute constituting this offense afford no reason why, like other crimes, a guilty intent is not necessary to be shown. Some conflict seems to exist between the adjudicated cases on the question, whether a mere neglect to pay over money which has come into the hands of the officer is sufficient evidence to make out the fact of a guilty misappropriation.   Some of the text-books lay down the proposition that a neglect or refusal to pay over the funds is sufficient evidence of misappropriation to sustain a conviction, and a number of cases are cited to sustain the text.

An examination of some of these cases convinces us that the rule thus laid down is not only unsound, but not supported as a general proposition by the authorities cited. As an instance, we are referred to the case of Reg. *v.* Guelder, 8 Cox C. C. 372. It appears in that case that the person charged with embezzlement of public money obtained from the proper authorities, by fraud, receipts for given sums after he had misappropriated the funds, and then, in the audit of his accounts, furnished these receipts as vouchers. The court held that evidence of these facts was sufficient to support the conviction as against the defense relied on, that the accused had made a true and correct entry, in his book, of the sums at the time that he received them, and that therefore he could not be guilty of this particular offense;—the fact of misappropriation was not even contested. Again, we are referred to the case of State *v.* O'Kean, 35 La. An. 901, where the court held that the neglect to pay over on demand is prima facie evidence of conversion and embezzlement; but it was so held because declared by a statute of the State of Louisiana. The same rule was held in the case of State *v.* Munch, 22 Minn. 67, but in that case also the ruling was made on a statute which declared that an improper neglect or refusal to pay over according to the provisions of law was embezzlement per se. In the case of Britton *v.* State, 77 Ala. 202, a similar ruling was founded on the statutes of the State, one of which declares that any tax-collector who shall fail to *make returns* and *forward the tax money* in his hands, from time to time, to the proper authorities, as provided by law, except for good cause, shall be guilty of embezzlement, etc. The only case to which we have been cited which clearly rules that a failure and refusal of a public officer to pay over money belonging to the county is sufficient evidence of a conversion of such money to his own use, is that of State *v.* Leonard, in 6 Coldwell's Rep. 308. There the point was made that the mere failure and refusal to pay over was not evidence of a conversion in the sense of the statute.　The court held such contention to be without merit, and among other reasons given for the ruling was, that failing and refusing to deliver a chattel on demand is evidence of conversion, in the civil action of trover; and this ruling was sustained in the case of State *v.* Cameron, 3 Heiskell, 78, by the same court.　We can not adopt the reasoning upon which the Leonard case, supra, is founded. Under our law, the evidence necessary to obtain a judgment in a civil case and that necessary to sustain a conviction in a criminal case are essentially different.　As to the former the weight of the evidence authorizes a verdict for the plaintiff, while in the latter it is necessary that the evidence shall be so strong as to leave no reasonable doubt of guilt.

But we are not left without authority to establish what is the correct rule.　In the case of Reg. *v.* Jones, 34 Eng. Com. Law Rep. 393, it was ruled that some specific sum must be proved to be embezzled ; in like manner as in larceny, some particular article must be proved to have been stolen.　In the case of Rex *v.* Hodgson, 3 Car. & P. 422, where the facts showed that a clerk, whose duty it was to receive money at a stage office for passengers and parcels and remit to the head office in another town, failed to remit some of the money with which he had charged himself, it was held that a charge of embezzlement could not be sustained for the appropriation of the money which he failed to remit, the judge saying: "This is no embezzlement; it is only a default of payment.　If the prisoner regularly admits the receipt of the money, the mere fact of not paying it over is not a felony.　It is but matter of account." Mr. Clark, in his work on Criminal Law, 275, citing a number of authorities, says that a mere neglect to pay over funds is not sufficient to sustain the charge.　Mr. Bishop in his New Criminal Law, vol. 2, §376, says:　"The agent's mere neglect to pay over the money is clearly insufficient."　So that we find the weight of authority to be, that the mere neglect or refusal to pay over funds in his hands is not sufficient to sustain a conviction for a misappropriation of the fund, in the absence of a statute making such failure or refusal sufficient evidence of the fact.　Under our statute, we think three things must be shown to authorize a conviction: first, that the accused is a public officer or occupies a fiduciary relation; second, that the money or property which he is charged with appropriating to his own use came into his possession by virtue of his office or employment; third, that he embezzled or fraudulently converted it to his own use.   Necessarily this proof can rarely be made by directly showing the conversion; and the facts necessary to show misappropriation can only be inferentially shown.   Mr. Wharton in the first volume of his Criminal Law, § 1030, says: "The fraudulent appropriation is to be inferred from facts," citing a number of authorities in note 2.   And on page 879 of the same work the author says: "Among these is the denial of the reception or the suppression of the fact of such reception. And it is usual to require, in addition to proof of reception, some proof of attempted concealment, flight, or other facts inferring fraud; among which facts the falsification of accounts is to be noticed as peculiarly significant.   And he further says, on authority, that "to show this [fraud], flight, insolvency, concealment, or evasions form strong elements of proof."   Mr. Bishop in section 376 of the second volume of his Criminal Law, says, on authority, that "the common and sufficient proof is either that the servant wilfully made in his books false entries, or that he denied or purposely omitted to acknowledge the receipt of the embezzled article or fund."   And this court in the case of a defaulting tax-collector, in construing this section, said that he must have collected some money for the county and used it for his private purposes, to be guilty of this offense. *Fuller* v. *State,* 73 *Ga.* 412.

Under the general principles of criminal law, as well as under the authorities we have cited above, as to this particular offense, we think that a public officer can not be legally convicted of the offense of embezzlement by showing a mere refusal or neglect to pay over funds which came to his hands, but that in addition thereto there must be some evidence of other things from which it may clearly be inferable that the neglect to turn over the funds was either in contemplation of a misappropriation or was the consequence of the misappropriation.   Such neglect or refusal affords sufficient grounds for a civil action to recover the money; but when, in addition, there is proof that the officer falsified his accounts, that he was guilty of evasions in explaining his default, that he fled, or other acts indicating guilt, a case is sufficiently made to put the defendant on explanation, and if not satisfactorily explained, a conviction may be upheld. But without some similar evidence, neither the misappropriation nor the guilty intent is sufficiently shown. In the present case it appears that the plaintiff in error was liable for a much larger sum of money belonging to the county than he had paid over; and while the proof seems to be conclusive that he was a careless and entirely incompetent officer, it does not necessarily show that he was a dishonest one. There can be no question that he issued executions for a considerable portion of the general tax; that these executions were placed in the hands of collecting officers. Some of these officers paid at different times different sums of money, on account of these executions, to the county treasurer. It inferentially appears that others did not. The matter seems, from the record, to be in some confusion; the evidence as the amount of the general tax which the plaintiff in error actually collected is not made plain, nor sufficiently so to be a basis for a conviction. To sustain the second count in the indictment, it was clearly shown that a certain portion of the railroad tax due to Hall county was collected by the plaintiff in error; but he contends that that amount so collected was paid over to the county treasurer, and the treasurer's evidence shows that, while no particular amount was paid to him as railroad taxes, he did receive from the accused at different times considerable sums of money. It does not appear that the accused fled the county, that he rendered false statements, or made such evasions in rendering his accounts as to sufficiently indicate that he had secreted the money of the county, or willfully appropriated any portion of it to his own use. Indeed, outside of certain specific amounts received from different railroads, the evidence is unsatisfactory as to what amounts actually went into his hands. The charge of embezzlement must be made out under the rules of the law which obtain in the prosecution for the commission of other crimes. The same presumptions exist in favor of the person on trial; and, taking this evidence as a whole, we are of the opinion that it was insufficient to warrant the conviction of the accused.   *Judgment reversed.   All the Justices concurring.*

BROWN *v.* THE STATE.

1. An accused person can not set up former jeopardy upon an accusation which was quashed on a demurrer filed by himself, and this is true though the judge at the time the demurrer was submitted overruled it and allowed the case to proceed to the extent of introducing testimony, but afterwards recalled his original ruling and adjudged that the demurrer was good and the accusation insufficient in law.
2. It is not essential to the validity of an accusation that a warrant for the arrest of the accused should be issued upon the affidavit on which the accusation is founded, or that such affidavit should minutely describe the offense.
3. The evidence fully warranted the conviction, and there was no error in overruling the certiorari.

Submitted January 15,—Decided January 27, 1900.

Certiorari.   Before Judge Harris.   Troup superior court. November term, 1899. ·

E. T. Moon, for plaintiff in error.

. *T. A. Atkinson, solicitor-general,* contra.

COBB, J.   Garfield Brown was placed on trial in the county court of Troup county, upon an accusation charging him with the offense of larceny from the house, and was convicted.   His petition for certiorari, complaining that certain errors were committed by the county judge during the progress of the trial, having been overruled, he excepted.

1. It appears that the accused was first put upon trial upon an affidavit and accusation to which he demurred; that the court at first overruled the demurrer and ordered the case to proceed to trial; that after the accused had pleaded not guilty and the State had introduced one witness, the court came to the conclusion that the demurrer should have been sustained, reversed his former ruling, and quashed the accusation.   It does not distinctly appear from the record that the accused objected to this at the time.   When he was again placed on trial upon

another accusation charging him with the same offense, he entered a plea of former jeopardy, averring that the first accusation should not have been quashed, and that when arraigned thereon he was put in jeopardy. The plea was overruled, and this is one of the errors assigned. Although the demurrer filed by the accused was at first overruled by the judge, the subsequent ruling sustaining the same was the one that the accused himself invoked, and it does not distinctly appear that he objected at the time to the judge sustaining the demurrer at that stage of the case and ordering the accusation to be quashed. It therefore does not lie in his mouth on a subsequent trial to say that the accusation was good, and that for that reason he was in jeopardy on the former trial. Whether the first accusation was good or bad is immaterial. The accused obtained a ruling that it was bad, accepted the benefit of that ruling, and he will not be allowed to bring in question the propriety of a ruling which he himself invoked. We are aware that a contrary view was taken by the majority of the court in the case of *Black* v. *State*, 36 *Ga.* 447, but the dissenting opinion of Walker, J., which is directly in line with the ruling we make, is, we think, the sounder view of the law. The decision in *Black's* case has never been followed. On the contrary the position of Judge Walker has been recognized by this court as the sounder and better one, though no reference was made in terms to his opinion. *Small* v. *State*, 63 *Ga.* 386. That this is in accord with the adjudicated cases there can be no doubt. See Com. v. Gould, 78 Mass. 171; Von Rueden v. State, (Wis.) 71 N. W. 1048; People v. Casborus, 13 Johns. 350; Gerard v. People, 3 Scam. 362; 1 Bish. New Cr. Law, §§ 998 (5), 1000, and cases cited.

2. Another assignment of error is, that the court erred in overruling the demurrer to the second affidavit and accusation. The points thus raised are, that the affidavit is insufficient to base an accusation on, and that no warrant was issued on the affidavit. This affidavit charged that the accused committed "the offense of privately stealing from the storehouse" of a named person certain described property of a given value, which was the property of the owner of the storehouse. It further

charged that the accused bought of a named person the property above referred to, knowing the same to have been stolen. Upon this affidavit and upon an affidavit for a search warrant, which appears to have been the foundation of the first accusation, and in which the property is described and the allegation made that the affiant has probable cause to believe that it is concealed in the house of the accused, the second accusation was based. This accusation contained two counts; the first charging the offense of larceny from the house, based upon the affidavit first above referred to; and the second charging the offense of receiving stolen goods, basing the same upon the affidavit made for the purpose of securing a search warrant. The requirements of an affidavit upon which a warrant may issue are set forth in section 883 of the Penal Code. It has been held, notwithstanding the apparently plain terms of this section, that an affidavit which is the foundation of a warrant charging a person with larceny was sufficient, notwithstanding it did not describe the property, or state its value, or name the owner, or disclose whether the larceny was a felony or only a misdemeanor. *Dickson* v. *State*, 62 *Ga.* 583. It seems to be the settled law of this State that an affidavit need do no more than name the offense, without describing the way in which it was committed, or its character, with any degree of particularity. See *Franklin* v. *State*, 85 *Ga.* 570; *McAlpin* v. *Purse*, 86 *Ga.* 271. The Penal Code provides that upon the hearing of a search warrant the court may require the person in whose possession the goods are found to give bond for his appearance to answer either a charge for larceny, or receiving stolen goods, as the facts may be. Penal Code, § 1247. As to the description of the property, name of the owner, and such other facts as are necessary to make the offense of larceny, the affidavits in the present case seem to accord substantially with the provisions of section 883 of the Penal Code. Under the rulings above referred to, an affidavit charging the offense of larceny would have been sufficient without any description of the property whatever. An affidavit charging one with the offense of larceny, sufficient to authorize the issuance of a warrant for his arrest, or one upon which a search warrant could lawfully issue, would seem to be a sufficient foundation upon which to base an accusation charging with larceny the person alleged in the first instance to be guilty of larceny, or in the latter instance to be in the possession of the goods claimed to have been stolen; the law simply requiring that the accusation shall be based upon affidavit. If the accused is in custody, it is not necessary that any warrant shall issue on the affidavit which is used as a foundation for the accusation.

3. The evidence warranted the judgment rendered by the county judge, and there was no error in overruling the certiorari.

Judgment affirmed. All the Justices concurring.

CARTER *v.* PEOPLES NATIONAL BANK.

|109
f112
109 573
115 685
115 781
109 573
125 781

1. Where to a rule nisi to foreclose a mortgage on land the mortgagor filed an answer setting up that the debt secured was usurious, and named a given sum as the usury, and prayed that such sum be deducted from the principal of the debt, and both the fact and amount of usury were admitted and the principal of the debt was reduced by the amount so claimed to be usurious, the mortgagor obtained all to which he was entitled under the plea, and the question whether (the creditor being a national bank) the entire interest due on the debt was forfeited, not having been made by the plea nor in any manner passed upon, will not be considered here.

2. A plea interposed to a proceeding to foreclose a mortgage on land, in a superior court of this State, that, pending the proceedings to foreclose, the mortgagor was adjudicated a bankrupt, and praying that such proceedings be stayed for the period of twelve months or until the question. of the discharge in bankruptcy of the mortgagor is determined, is not good, and the court committed no error in sustaining a demurrer to the same.

Argued November 2, 1899. — Decided January 27, 1900.

Foreclosure of mortgage. Before Judge Butt. Sumter superior court. November term, 1898.

J. A. Ansley and *J. A. Ansley Jr.*, for plaintiff in error.
E. A. Hawkins, contra.

LITTLE, J. At the May term, 1898, of Sumter superior court, the defendant in error filed its petition to foreclose a mortgage executed by the plaintiff in error on the 5th day of December, 1892, to secure a promissory note payable December 5, 1893, for the principal sum of $1,120, besides interest, etc., the property described in the mortgage being a certain lot in the city of Americus.   On this petition a rule nisi issued in the usual form, and due service was made.   At the November term, 1898, being the return term of said rule, the defendant appeared and filed a plea of usury, in which he alleged that the amount of usury in said note was $120, and prayed for a judgment deducting said sum from the amount apparently due on the note. While the plea avers that the note was given to a national bank and therefore all interest as well as usury charged is forfeited, it further alleges: "amount of interest and usury in said note is $120, and defendant prays the court that the said amount of $120 in said note is void and forfeited, and prays the court for a judgment deducting the sum of $120 from said note."

1. It is only necessary to say, as to the plea of usury, that the fact of usury having been charged and the amount of the same was not contested, and on motion of plaintiff's counsel the verdict, which was directed by the court, was for the sum of one thousand dollars principal, being the amount due, less the exact amount of usury pleaded and admitted to have been charged.   The defendant, therefore, obtained all that he contended for in his plea, and has, therefore, no right to complain of the verdict and judgment rendered; nor, under the plea filed, can the point that, the plaintiff being a national bank, all interest was forfeited, be considered, because that question is not properly raised, nor does it appear to have been passed on by the trial judge.

2. At the return term of the rule nisi, the defendant amended his plea and averred that, since it was filed and during the pendency of the proceedings to foreclose the mortgage, he had been adjudicated a bankrupt, the adjudication having been made on January 14, 1899, and he prayed that the proceedings to foreclose the mortgage be stayed as provided in the bankrupt act of 1898.   He further alleged that no trustee had been appointed, and no meeting of his creditors had.   This plea was demurred to, and the demurrer was sustained and the plea stricken, and he excepted.   It will be noted that the mort-

gage was executed about six years before the plaintiff in error
was adjudicated a bankrupt, and also that no question arose
in relation to the validity of the debt nor the proper execution
and record of the mortgage which was given to secure it. Section 11 of the bankrupt act, approved July 1, 1898, declares
that "A suit which is founded upon a claim from which a discharge would be a release, and which is pending against a person at the time of the filing of a petition against him, shall be
stayed until after an adjudication or the dismissal of the petition ; if such person is adjudged a bankrupt, such action may
be further stayed until twelve months after the date of such
adjudication, or, if within that time such person applies for a
discharge, then until the question of such discharge is determined." It appears from this provision that a stay of a pending suit against the person adjudged a bankrupt will in any
event only be granted when such suit is founded on a claim
from which a discharge in bankruptcy would be a release.
Assuming that the mortgage was regular, and created a valid
lien on the property of the bankrupt, under the provisions of
the bankrupt act, the mortgagee became a preferred creditor
of the bankrupt.

Section 1 of the act, as found in Collier on Bankruptcy, 3,
subdivision 23, declares that the term "secured creditor" shall
include a creditor who has security for his debt upon the property of the bankrupt, of a nature to be assignable under this act,
etc. Undoubtedly within this definition the bank became in
1892 a secured creditor of the plaintiff in error, which relation
existed at the time of the adjudication of bankruptcy. Section 57 of the act, defining what proofs in bankruptcy may be
made by secured creditors, in subdivision e declares that "Claims
of secured creditors and those who have priority may be allowed to enable such creditors to participate in the proceedings
at creditors' meetings held prior to the determination of the
value of their securities or priorities, but shall be allowed for
such sums only as to the courts seem to be owing over and
above the value of their securities or priorities"; and by subdivision g of the same act it is declared that "The claims of
creditors who have received preferences shall not be allowed

unless such creditors shall surrender their preferences." Subdivision *h* of the act declares that "The value of securities held by secured creditors shall be determined by converting the same into money according to the terms of the agreement pursuant to which such securities were delivered to such creditors or by such creditors and the trustee, by agreement, arbitration, compromise, or litigation, as the court may direct, and the amount of such value shall be credited upon such claims, and a dividend shall be paid only on the unpaid balance"; and general order in bankruptcy No. 28 provides for the redemption by the trustee of the mortgaged property of the bankrupt. It must therefore be evident that it was the intention of Congress in the enactment of the bankrupt law to permit a legally secured creditor to hold to his security, and that its value should be appropriated to his claim, in preference to general creditors. Now, if a suit against a bankrupt can only be stayed when it is founded on a claim from which a discharge would be a release, and a preferred creditor is not allowed, unless he surrenders his preference, to prove his entire claim, but proof of his debt otherwise can only be made in the amount which his debt exceeds the value of the securities, it would seem to follow that there should be no stay of a proceeding which does not seek a general or personal judgment against the bankrupt, but is only instituted to foreclose and establish his lien on property, which in no event, unless he surrenders his lien, can be applied to any other debt.   But suppose it be said that if the property is of greater value than the amount of the debt there would be no provision for controlling this excess in the interest of the general creditors.   It may be replied that the trustee is invested with power to redeem the property, and, by so doing, it, unincumbered, becomes subject to be appropriated to the claims of creditors; but even if this be not done, the excess over the debt which the property brought at the sale by the sheriff would undoubtedly be a part of the bankrupt's estate and subject to the control of the court of bankruptcy.   But in any event, where the creditor does not elect to surrender his security and make proof of his entire claim, and thus become entitled to share in the bankrupt's estate equally with the owners of other proved claims, it would be hardly fair, when he elects to rely on his security, to prohibit him from appropriating its value to the payment of his debt in the manner prescribed by law at the time of the execution of his contract, to wit, by fore-closure in the State court. Nor do we think, properly inter-preted, the provision of the act in relation to granting a stay of pending proceedings applies to a case of this character. A mortgage creditor is not such an one as is contemplated in the bankrupt act when it refers in general terms to creditors. By subdivision *b* of par. 56 of the act, creditors holding security for their debts are not entitled to vote at creditors' meetings, nor are the claims held by them counted in computing either the number of creditors or the amount of their claims, except when the amount of their claims exceed the values of the se-curities held, and then only for such excess; thus excluding from the bankrupt court so much and such part of the debt as the security is of sufficient value to pay. By referring to forms Nos. 43 and 44, prescribed by the Supreme Court of the United States for proceedings in bankruptcy, it will be found that it is clearly contemplated that a trustee in bankruptcy may not only redeem the mortgaged property, but he may sell the equity of redemption in such property, which is all the in-terest in it that the debtor has—in other words, that the bankrupt court recognizes the right of the creditor to have the property on which he has a valid lien pay the debt for which it is bound, to the exclusion of other creditors, and that the excess above the debt secured is all that court will administer where there is no surrender of the lien.

We have thus gone into detail, desiring to show that it is not the purpose of the act that the bankrupt court shall assume custody of property given to secure a debt due by the bank-rupt, as a part of his assets, unless the secured creditor so elects; and if this be true, and if the holder of the mortgage on such property has a claim not provable in bankruptcy, then there can exist no reason why that holder should not resort to the State court to enforce his lien against the property, nor why after such proceedings have been instituted they should be stayed and the enforcement of the lien postponed indefinitely,

37

when the result is bound to be the same. But there is another
view of the question, under which we think this court is committed to the doctrine that the State court has jurisdiction to
foreclose a mortgage after the mortgagor has been adjudicated
a bankrupt under such provisions of law as are found in the
act of 1898.   So far as the rights of preferred creditors are
concerned, there seems to us to be but little difference between
the act of 1898 and that of 1867.   Under section 5075 of the
Revised Statutes of the United States, which was compiled
from the last-mentioned act, it is provided that a creditor who
has a mortgage or pledge of real or personal property, made
by the bankrupt for the purpose of securing a debt, shall be
admitted only as a creditor for the balance of the debt after
deducting the value of the property, and, as in the present act,
there is a provision that this value may be ascertained by
agreement and also that the creditor may release or convey
his claim to the assignee and be permitted to prove his whole
debt.   Practically, the provisions of the two acts in this regard are the same.   Under the act of 1867 it was held in the
case of *Toler* v. *Passmore*, 62 *Ga.* 263, that where, pending a
proceeding to foreclose a mortgage on real estate, a plea was
interposed that the mortgagor had been adjudicated a bankrupt, and a motion made to continue the case to await the discharge in bankruptcy, this court held that the motion to continue was properly overruled, because the discharge when had
would not affect the mortgage lien; and a similar ruling was
made in *Brady* v. *Brady*, 71 *Ga.* 71; and in the case of *Broach*
v. *Powell*, 79 *Ga.* 79, it was held that the fact that mortgaged
property is subject to be administered in bankruptcy will not
entitle the mortgagor to resist the administration of it by foreclosure and sale under proceedings in the appropriate court of
this State.   See also 91 U. S. 521; *Cumming* v. *Clegg*, 52 *Ga.*
605; *Hatcher* v. *Jones*, 53 *Ga.* 208; *Price* v. *Amis*, 58 *Ga.* 604.
We are not now called on to pass any opinion as to whether
any different ruling should be made if the trustee in bankruptcy sought to enjoin either the proceedings to foreclose the
mortgage in the State court, or a sale decreed in conformity
thereto.   That question is not involved here.   The motion to
stay was made by the mortgagor, who was the adjudicated

baukrupt. But as we find no material difference between the bankrupt act of 1867 and that of 1898 as to the rights of a secured or mortgage creditor, nor in the provisions made by the two acts as to the disposition of the property on which the lien exists, and as this court has repeatedly ruled that under the act of 1867 the mortgage could be properly foreclosed in the State court, and also because of the construction we place on the act of 1898, it is our opinion that the demurrer to the plea was properly sustained.

Judgment affirmed. All the Justices concurring.

MOHR–WEIL LUMBER COMPANY *v.* RUSSELL *et al.*

1. An application by a party to a case in equity for the allowance of an attorney's fee for bringing a fund into court is, though the attorney for whom the fee is sought joins therein, to be regarded as a proceeding in the name and right of the party, and not of the attorney.
2. No party is entitled to such an allowance out of the proceeds of property which he, for his exclusive benefit and to the injury of his adversary, causes to be placed in the hands of a receiver; nor can any party, except in cases of bad faith, stubborn litigiousness, and the like, charge against the opposite party as "costs" attorney's fees incurred in litigation.
3. A contract to pay the maximum legal rate of interest compounded monthly is in no event valid unless in writing.
4. Though the main purpose of the owner of a manufacturing plant, in delivering the possession, management, and control thereof to a creditor, may be to enable the latter to obtain from the proceeds of its operation payment of a certain indebtedness, yet where the contract expressly provides that such creditor may, at his option, remain in possession for a specified period, his right to do so would not, if he complied with all of his undertakings, terminate upon the satisfaction of the indebtedness before the expiration of that period.
5. Exceptions to an auditor's report should not be stricken on demurrer when they point out the alleged errors in such manner that the nature of the same can be clearly and readily understood when considered in connection with the findings of the auditor to which such exceptions refer.
6. It is not erroneous to strike exceptions not meeting the requirement just indicated, or cause for reversal to strike exceptions which, though sufficient as to form, are manifestly without merit.
7. It is within the discretion of the court to allow or reject new exceptions to an auditor's report after the time for excepting thereto has expired; but the privilege of filing new exceptions should be denied unless good cause for not duly filing them is shown.

Argued November 10, 1899.— Decided January 27, 1900.

109
a115
115
115
109
e122
1

Exceptions to auditor's report. Before Judge Smith. Wilcox superior court. June 29, 1899.

E. H. Williams, and *Hardeman, Davis & Turner*, for plaintiff. *Eldridge Cutts* and *Hal Lawson*, for defendants.

LUMPKIN, P. J. A motion was made to dismiss the present writ of error, on the ground that Messrs. Cutts & Lawson were not made parties to nor served with the bill of exceptions. This motion was not well taken. Our views upon it and upon the question therewith closely connected, viz., whether or not that portion of the judgment now under review allowing these attorneys a fee of $1,500 was erroneous, will be given immediately after stating the facts of this case; but, as will be perceived, the particular facts pertaining to the two matters just referred to, for the obvious reason that it would have been very inconvenient to present them at the beginning of the following preliminary statement, appear at its conclusion.

During the March term, 1897, to wit, on May 22 and August 7 of that year, we dealt with separate writs of error growing out of the litigation involved in this case. See 102 *Ga.* 563, 593. The decisions rendered on these two occasions related exclusively to preliminary matters. The case is now here on its merits after final judgment in the trial court, and presents questions which we have not heretofore considered or passed upon. The record discloses that Mrs. Martha B. Russell was the owner of a shingle-mill, the operation of which was the subject-matter of several contracts and finally of much controversy between her and the Mohr–Weil Lumber Company. In most of the transactions between her and it, she was represented by her husband, A. B. Russell, as her general agent. We will therefore, for convenience, though both Mr. and Mrs. Russell are parties to the case, hereinafter use simply the name "Russell" when referring to them, and, for the sake of brevity, will allude to the other party as "the company."

On March 13, 1893, the company entered into a written contract with Russell, by the terms of which the former agreed to make to the latter certain advances and to take the entire product of the mill at specified prices, Russell contracting to furnish "at least 40,000 shingles per day on an average." Operations were carried on under this contract until December 25, 1893, when the parties entered into another written contract which purported to be a substitute for the first one. At the date last mentioned, Russell had become indebted to the company a considerable sum and had executed promissory notes for the same, bearing interest at 8 per cent. This fact was recited in the new contract, and it was therein stipulated that the company was to make an additional advance of not exceeding $3,000 "for the purchase and improving of machinery, timber, and running business, to be repaid in 12 months, with interest at 8 per cent.," and that Russell was to furnish and the company to accept the entire output of the mill. A new scale of prices for shingles was fixed in this instrument, and it stipulated that "at least 80,000 shingles were to be furnished per day upon an average," Sundays and legal holidays excepted. This contract was to remain in force for three years, and the scheme of it, as shown by other stipulations therein, was that Russell's existing indebtedness to the company and any further indebtedness to it which he might incur should be discharged by the delivery of shingles, it being expressly provided that all payments therefor, "except sufficient amount for running expenses at mill," were to be applied to such indebtedness. On November 20, 1895, Russell, being still largely indebted to the company on the notes and on open account, made with it a third written contract which recited that it was executed "for the purposes of speedily carrying out agreements already existing between the parties," and stipulated that "It is well understood by both parties that this instrument is but a part and parcel of the contract now existing between the parties and supplementary thereto." By its terms, Russell was to turn over to the company the entire control and management of the shingle-mill, with the right to use and operate the same as it might deem best, "for any length or space of time . . not to exceed five years." The further stipulations of this instrument, now material, were as follows: All the past "transactions" between the parties were confirmed as just and legal. The company agreed to "accept the management and control of said property and to operate the same in conformity with the scope, objects, and purposes set forth in the contract now existing between the parties, for such time as [it] may think proper, not to exceed five years," and was to "furnish all money necessary to carry out this supplementary agreement." "All sums of money advanced or expended in operating said shingle-mill" by the company were to be charged to Russell. There was nothing in the last contract expressly referring to any oral agreements or transactions in parol between the parties.

In January, 1897, Russell took possession of the mill, and discharged all the company's employees. It filed an equitable petition to enjoin him from further interfering with the property. The answer averred that the conduct of Russell in taking possession of the mill was lawful and proper, for the reason that the company had in many ways (the particulars as to which were set forth) violated its contract, to the injury and damage of Russell. The answer was in other respects one in the nature of a cross-bill. It denied that Russell owed the company anything, because, as alleged, the output of the mill, properly and efficiently operated under the terms of the contract, would have been much more than sufficient to pay off all of Russell's indebtedness. It further set up that the company, by its failure to so operate the mill, had greatly damaged Russell, and prayed for an accounting, alleging that the same would show that the company was indebted to Russell a large balance, for which judgment was asked. There was also a prayer for the appointment of a receiver to take possession of and manage the property until the respective rights of the parties could be ascertained and fixed by an appropriate judgment. A receiver was appointed and other interlocutory proceedings were had, but further reference thereto is, for the reason stated at the outset, not now necessary. The case was referred to an auditor, whose report, as will presently more fully appear, was in the main adverse to the company. At the hearing before him much evidence was introduced. To sum the same up very briefly, it may be said that the principal allegations of both the petition and the answer were supported by testimony—in other words, there was much conflict. One of the most important questions at issue was whether or not the company had operated the mill skillfully, efficiently, and according to contract. Aside from the dispute over this, the company contended, and introduced evidence tending to prove, that there had been, while Russell was running the mill, a verbal agreement for a reduction in the price of shingles, and that this agreement was in effect after the company took charge of the plant; and further, that Russell had also orally agreed that the interest to be charged against him should be compounded monthly. Russell admitted that he had at one time agreed to a temporary reduction in prices, but denied that this agreement had any relation to the period covered by the last written contract, and he also denied the alleged agreement as to compound interest, supporting his contentions as to these matters by his sworn testimony as a witness. Still another hotly contested issue was whether or not Russell was properly chargeable with the expenses incurred by the company in making certain improvements which, without consulting Russell, it had decided were necessary to a successful operation of the mill property. It appeared at the hearing before the auditor that the company had converted the mill from a one-story to a three-story building, and had also purchased an entirely new boiler and other appliances, the cost of which was included in its account against Russell, upon the theory that the same was a legitimate charge under the terms of their written contract.

To the auditor's report the company filed six exceptions of fact and twelve of law. One of the latter (the 7th) was, however, subsequently voluntarily withdrawn. The court, on demurrer, struck all the remaining exceptions, both of law and of fact, except the 2d and 3d exceptions of law, which were overruled as being without merit. The company assigns error upon this disposition by the court of its exceptions.

After the trial judge announced that he would sustain the demurrer to the exceptions of fact, the company offered to amend those exceptions and also its exceptions of law. The motion was denied, and this is assigned as error. Before the final judgment was entered, Messrs. Cutts & Lawson presented to the court a petition which, after stating the case, began: "And now come

Cutts & Lawson, attorneys, and A. B. & M. B. Russell, and show to the court the following facts." The petition then proceeded to allege that Cutts & Lawson were the only attorneys for the Russells, and that the receivers had sold a large lot of shingles, "thereby bringing into court a fund out of which taxes, debts for labor, and other expenses of operating said plant have been paid, and out of which court costs and expenses are to be paid." This petition concluded with a prayer in behalf of the "movants" that the attorneys be allowed a fee of $1,500 for filing the cross-petition and bringing said fund into court, and that the receiver be ordered to pay the same. It was signed: "Cutts & Lawson, in propriis personis & Attorneys for A. B. & M. B. Russell." The final judgment, to which numerous exceptions were taken and which was substantially in accord with the conclusions of the auditor as to the matters referred to him, also embraced a paragraph allowing a fee of $1,500 to Cutts & Lawson, it being in that paragraph directed that the receiver pay to them this amount or any part thereof, "if he shall have funds on hand for such purpose," and, if he has no funds with which to pay the same, that this fee be charged against the company and the individual members thereof as "costs," to be collected by execution in favor of A. B. & M. B. Russell for the use of Cutts & Lawson.

1. It is certainly true that, up to the time the petition for the fee was filed, Cutts & Lawson were not parties to this case. Otherwise than as attorneys, they had no interest in the subject-matter of it, and there was nothing in the pleadings in any manner connecting them personally with the litigation. Did the filing of this petition make them parties? We think not. They had not, in their own right, any claim against the company or upon the fund in the receiver's hands for fees. If, for any reason, their clients were entitled to have a portion of this fund appropriated to the payment of any of the expenses of litigation, it was a matter upon which these clients might petition the court. This, we think, is what was done. The Russells were joined in the petition and were the real "movants" therein. Properly, Cutts & Lawson should be regarded as mere usees. The court seemed to take this view, for it ad-

judged that if the receiver had not the funds with which to pay the $1,500, its collection should be enforced by execution in favor of the Russells for the use of Cutts & Lawson. It was insisted here that this petition was an independent intervention presented by Cutts & Lawson, and that the court's favorable action upon it necessarily made them parties to the case and therefore persons interested in sustaining the judgment. The reply is, that the petition shows on its face it was not such an intervention. The Russells were surely petitioners as well as Cutts & Lawson, and if the latter desired to become parties in their own right and independently of their clients, why did they not make the application without joining the Russells? They are good lawyers, and we take it that, as such, they knew a petition of this kind could have no lawful standing unless made by and in the right of the parties they represented. As was remarked by Mr. Justice Cobb in *Morgan* v. *Fidelity Co.*, 101 *Ga.* 391, which was a proceeding in equity: "Counsel have no inherent right in such a case to demand an allowance of fees. The right is in the client to appeal to the court for the allowance of an amount sufficient to pay the expenses which he has incurred." In this connection, Trustees v. Greenough, 105 U. S. 527, and Stuart v. Boulware, 133 U. S. 78, are somewhat in point. Upon the well-founded assumption that our learned brethren who obtained the allowance of this fee knew the law, the insertion of the names of the Russells into the application is easily understood; and, on the whole, we have no great difficulty in holding that it was the Russells' petition, and that, as stated above, the attorneys should simply be regarded as usees, who were not parties to the case. It follows that it was neither necessary nor proper to make them parties to the bill of exceptions nor serve them therewith. The case of *Barksdale* v. *Bunkley*, 26 *Ga.* 398, which they cite, does not help them. An examination of it will show that the attorneys there were in fact parties to the case submitted to the judge for decision, and expressly reserved the right to except thereto.

2. Allowing the fee of $1,500 to Cutts & Lawson was totally unauthorized. The bringing of a fund into court operates for

the benefit of those who share in it.   Compensation for services rendered in placing a fund where the court can administer it may fairly be regarded as an expense chargeable to those among whom it is distributed.   The only just and reasonable basis for paying out of money brought into court the fees of the attorneys by whose services this result was produced is, that by rendering those services they did something of value to the successful claimant or claimants of the money.   If the attorney of one creditor brings into court a fund, and thus aids other creditors of the same debtor in reaching his assets, the client at whose expense such attorney was engaged is entitled to reimbursement out of the fund; for in this way all the beneficiaries are made to share equitably and ratably in an expense which should be common to them all.   Even then, the attorney, though he usually gets the money, is not directly entitled to it; for, strictly speaking, the allowance is for the benefit of the client as an expense incurred in behalf of all interested.   These familiar propositions require no argument or citation of authority to support them.   They have, however, no application to the present case.   Cutts & Lawson did not, by having a receiver appointed, bring anything into court for the benefit of the Mohr–Weil Lumber Company.   On the contrary, this step was decidedly to its injury.   There was a serious controversy as to who was entitled to possession.   The company's claim to possession was defeated by the receivership, and the impounding of the property was sought and obtained by Russell as a thing for his exclusive benefit.   It never was or can be a principle of law or equity that a party who for his own benefit has property placed in the hands of a receiver, to the injury of his adversary and over his protest and objection, can compel the latter to pay counsel fees thus incurred, except in cases of bad faith, stubborn litigiousness, and the like, and then only after it has been adjudged that the party to be charged is, because of his contumaciousness or bad conduct, liable to the person thereby injured for the amount of such fees.   There was no such adjudication, or occasion therefor, in the present instance.   If the money in the receiver's hands derived from sales of shingles belonged certainly to Russell, and if there was enough of it to pay the $1,500, the company was not injured by this portion of the judgment; but here are two very large "ifs," and moreover, the judgment made the company liable for this fee as "costs" in case the receiver had no funds with which to pay it. The judgment in so far as it allowed the fee at all was inappropriate and wrong. The petition for it ought to have been rejected altogether. Not even upon the theory that the proceeds of the shingles belonged to Russell was this the proper manner for his counsel to collect their fee.

We will now deal briefly — for otherwise this opinion would become too greatly expanded — with the company's exceptions to the auditor's report, stating generally in connection with each the facts essential to an understanding of what we rule.

3. The auditor found as matter of fact that the debt of Russell to the company on open account was, on November 20, 1895, a specified amount "after eliminating interest illegally charged in said account," and as matter of law that it was per se usurious to compound interest monthly at the rate of 8 per cent. per annum. The company's first exception of fact, which related to this finding, was, under the rule laid down by this court in *Mason* v. *Commissioners*, 104 *Ga.* 35, too loose and general, except that it made the distinct point that there was no illegal charge of interest. By its 6th exception of law, the question as to usury is likewise sufficiently presented for determination. But we do not think either of these exceptions was, under the undisputed facts, meritorious, and therefore it is immaterial how they were eliminated from the case. The reason for this conclusion is stated in the third headnote. In support thereof we need only cite § 2876 of the Civil Code. There was no contention on the part of the company that Russell's alleged oral agreement to pay interest at the rate of 8 per cent. per annum, compounded monthly, was ever reduced to writing. The written contract between the parties contained a stipulation that the advances made by the company were "to be repaid in 12 months with interest at 8 per cent.;" but certainly, this stipulation could not be tortured into an agreement contemplating the compounding of interest monthly at the rate named or any other. Accordingly, whether a contract in writing to pay the maxi-

mum legal rate of interest, compounded monthly, would or
would not be open to attack for usury, is not now material.

4. The auditor reported as matter of law that the contract
between the company and Russell was not to remain in force after the satisfaction of the latter's indebtedness. Complaint of
this conclusion is made in the company's 2d and 3d exceptions
of law. While, as we have seen, the court did not strike these
exceptions on demurrer, it did overrule them as being without
merit. This was erroneous. Whatever relation was established
between the parties by virtue of their written contract, it was
not by the terms of that instrument necessarily to terminate
when the indebtedness in question had become satisfied. On
the contrary, the company, at its option, was entitled to keep
possession of the mill and operate it for the term of five years
from the date of the last writing, if it complied with its undertakings therein expressed. In this connection it is proper
to refer to the 8th exception of law, which ought not to have
been stricken. It appertains to the question of the company's
alleged right to damages for what it claims was an unwarranted
seizure of the property by Russell. As remarked above, the
right of the company to the possession and control of the mill
did not, under the terms of the contract, terminate upon the
discharge of Russell's indebtedness to it; and this being so, if
the company did not, by failing properly to perform its undertakings in the premises, commit a breach of that contract
before Russell entered upon and resumed possession of the
property, he was guilty of a trespass, and the company was
entitled to recover damages therefor.

5. The auditor further found, as matters of fact, that the
shingle-mill, as turned over to the company on November 20,
1895, was fully capable of cutting 80,000 first and second class
shingles per day, and accordingly that there was no necessity
to change the mill in order to carry out the contract that day
made; that before April 1, 1897, the Russell notes had been
paid off and discharged; and that $1.10 per thousand was the
cost of making shingles of the grades specified at that mill.
In connection with these finding of fact, he reached the following conclusions of law: that the company was bound to oper-

ate the mill in a prudent, economical, and businesslike manner, and was therefore bound to cut on an average 80,000 shingles per day, Sundays and legal holidays excepted, and to account for the same at the prices fixed by the written contract; that, for the purpose of carrying out this contract, it was authorized to make all necessary purchases and expenditures and charge the same to Russell, but that the company was not authorized, at his expense, to change the structure of the mill or to purchase new and expensive machinery not necessary for carrying out the contract. In making his calculations, the auditor refused to allow the company credit for the cost of adding the two stories to the mill and the cost of the new boiler and of other appliances which he deemed unnecessary to an efficient and successful operation of the plant. The 3d, 4th, and 6th exceptions of fact, and the 4th and 5th exceptions of law, present with sufficient distinctness the company's objections to the findings and conclusions of the auditor just enumerated, and ought not to have been stricken; but the legal conclusions were, practically and in substance, right, if the findings of fact were correct. The company was certainly bound to operate the mill prudently, economically, and in a businesslike manner. We do not think the terms of the written contract imperatively required it to produce an average of 80,000 shingles per day, excluding Sundays and legal holidays; but if that was the fair capacity of the mill, the company was bound to make the output come up to it. This is one of the controlling issues in the case.

The company, while authorized to make at Russell's expense all needed improvements and repairs upon the existing plant, was not at liberty to erect practically a new one or to add extraordinary and expensive machinery or appliances, such as the new boiler, and charge the same to Russell's account. It is one thing to keep a mill already built and equipped in good running order, and quite another to erect virtually a new one and furnish it with new machinery.

The auditor's finding that the notes had been paid off did not, of course, mean that they had been actually taken up by Russell, but that, allowing him proper credits for the products of the mill, the same had been satisfied by operation of law. The correctness of this finding depends exclusively, and that as to the cost of making shingles largely, upon what was the real capacity of the mill when properly operated.

Below will be found a ruling that the 2d exception of fact did not properly attack the auditor's finding that there was no agreement in parol, effective after the company took charge of the mill, to reduce the price of shingles. This question is, however, properly raised by one of the exceptions now under consideration, and should be dealt with by the trial court, along with other matters hereinabove pointed out, at the next hearing.

6. The 2d exception of fact complains of the finding of the auditor to which we last referred, on the ground that there was no evidence to sustain it. The record shows clearly that there was testimony which, if true, not only supported but fully authorized this finding. This particular exception was therefore without merit, and striking the same did not operate to the injury of the company; but note what is said above concerning the matter to which this exception relates. The 5th exception of fact alleges error in a finding of the auditor that the purchase of certain chemical fire-extinguishers was unnecessary, and therefore the company had no right to charge Russell with the cost thereof. This exception was, perhaps, sufficient in form, but an examination of the record shows that the auditor's conclusion as to this particular matter was demanded. It follows that striking such exception, whether strictly correct practice or not, would not be cause for reversing the judgment. *Mason* v. *Commissioners*, supra.

In the 1st exception of law the point is made that the auditor erroneously found that there was usury in the notes given by Russell to the company. This exception was not well taken, for the language used by the auditor in the finding therein referred to does not bear the construction thus placed upon it. As matter of fact, the auditor's finding as to usury related exclusively to the debt on open account.

The 9th, 10th and 12th exceptions of law merely present loose and general objections to conclusions which the auditor evidently reached by making calculations upon statements of fact embraced in the testimony and upon figures and amounts thereby disclosed. Nowhere in any of these exceptions is a single error in the calculations themselves, or in the data upon which they were based, pointed out. It was proper, therefore, for the court to strike these three exceptions on the ground that they were not sufficiently clear and distinct. The 11th exception of law deals with the same matter as the 5th exception of fact, of which we have already disposed.

7. There was no error in refusing to allow the amendments to the exceptions. In so far as the proposed amendments presented new questions or sought to make good exceptions totally without merit, it was entirely within the court's discretion to allow or reject them; and the company had no right to invoke a favorable exercise of this discretion, for no reason or excuse for not presenting the exceptions in time and in proper form was given. To the extent that the amendments were amplificatory of valid exceptions already in, they were not needed. See *Lane* v. *Railway Co.*, 96 *Ga.* 630, and cases cited on page 644.

Judgment reversed. All the Justices concurring.

RIDGEWAY v. DOWNING COMPANY.

109 591
115 756
109 591
e124 477

Where the owner of a vacant city lot, who for years has suffered the public to use a thoroughfare over the same, employs an independent contractor to construct a building thereon, according to certain specifications including excavations for piling for the foundation, and the contractor digs a trench for such purpose across the thoroughfare, the owner is not liable for a personal injury sustained by one who falls into the trench by reason of its unguarded condition.

Submitted November 11, 1899. — Decided January 27, 1900.

Action for damages. Before Judge Atkinson. City court of Brunswick. March 3, 1899.

Garrard, Meldrim & Newman and *Johnson & Krauss*, for plaintiff. *William E. Kay*, for defendant.

Fish, J. It appears from the record in this case, that the Downing Company, a corporation, owned a vacant lot near the water front in the city of Brunswick. Pedestrians and vehicles, in going to and from a certain boat-landing or dock, had for several years passed over this lot, and in this way, made a well-defined roadway or thoroughfare across it. The Downing Company employed Leonard, a contractor, to erect for it a building upon this lot, according to certain specifications, including excavations or trenches for the piling for the foundation of the building. Leonard dug a trench for piling across this thoroughfare, and left it open, unguarded on the side next to the boat-landing, and without danger-signals to warn the public of its existence. The plaintiff, on his way up town, at night, from the boat landing, while walking in this roadway across the lot, fell into the excavation and sustained personal injuries. He sued the Downing Company and Leonard for damages. The Downing Company pleaded that the excavation into which the plaintiff alleged he fell was made by Leonard, who was an independent contractor, and the same was wholly and absolutely in his charge, and the Downing Company, other than owning the real estate upon which the excavation was made, "had no part in the work of making said excavation, nor any legal liability for any acts of said Leonard, nor were they charged with any duty whatever to anybody to put out lights or give notice to the public of the existence of such excavation." Upon the trial of the case the jury found a verdict in favor of the plaintiff against Leonard, and the court directed a verdict in favor of the Downing Company. The plaintiff made a motion for a new trial, which was overruled, and he excepted.

Although the contract between the Downing Company and Leonard provided that "the contractor, under the direction and to the satisfaction of A. V. Wood, superintendent, acting for the purpose of this contract as agent of said owner, shall and will provide all the material and perform all the work mentioned in the specifications, and shown on the drawings prepared by the said architect," yet, in the light of the entire instrument embracing the contract, its true intent and meaning as a whole was that the superintendent was merely to "see that the contractor [carried] out his agreement," and had the power of supervision solely with relation to the result to be obtained, and not as to the means by which it was to be accomplished, or as to the time and manner of executing the work. It is not contended by the plaintiff that this is not a sound construction of the contract. His main contention, with reference to the liability of the defendant, is that "The Downing Company was the owner of the lot of land in question," and "the law imposed the duty upon the owner to guard the dangerous excavation dug by him, or his contractor or servants, across the way which had been used by the public for years. This duty upon the owner of the lot was an imposed duty; and could not be delegated to an independent contractor." In other words, the plaintiff contends that the Downing Company having contracted for work to be done which, if proper precautions were not taken, was bound to be dangerous to the public, a duty was imposed upon it to see that such precautions were taken, notwithstanding the fact that the work had been committed by it to an independent contractor. The question of the extent to which an employer is relieved from liability for the acts or negligence of an independent contractor employed by him has been much discussed by the courts, and conflicting decisions have been rendered thereon. The general rule, which is well established, is that an employer is not liable for the acts or negligence of a contractor who has complete control of the work and of the persons employed by him to perform it. To this rule there are certain exceptions, and it is with reference to these exceptions that we find the decisions conflicting. Some of the exceptions seem to be recognized by all the courts, while as to others the authorities are not harmonious. Whatever may be the exceptions to the general rule recognized in other jurisdictions, we think it is clear that, under the previous adjudications of this court and the provisions of section 3819 of the Civil Code, the Downing Company, under the circumstances disclosed by the evidence, was not liable for the consequences to the plaintiff of the negligence of Leonard, the independent contractor. In *Harrison* v. *Kiser*, 79 *Ga.* 588, Harrison sued Mrs. Kiser for damages which he alleged he had sustained by reason of the careless and negligent manner in which she had caused an ex-

38

cavation to be made upon a city lot owned by her which adjoined his brick building, in consequence of which his building was deprived of lateral support and one of its walls under-
mined, causing the wall to settle, the floor to sink, etc.   Upon
the trial of the case, it appeared from the testimony that the
excavation in question was made by one McGilvray, whom
the defendant 'had employed to erect a building for her upon
her lot adjoining that of the plaintiff, that he did the work as an
independent contractor, she having no control over the work
and not giving any directions as to the manner in which it
should be done.   There was a verdict for the defendant, and
the plaintiff excepted.   This court held that, "It not appearing that the contractor was employed to do the work in the
manner in which it was done, but it being fairly inferable that
it was a work which could have been done in a lawful manner so as to have caused no injury to the plaintiff, it is to be
presumed that the contractor was employed to do the work in
a lawful, and not in a negligent or unlawful, manner; and,
under the plea of the general issue alone, there was no error
in charging to the effect that where one has a lawful work to
do, and employs another, who has an independent business of
his own including work of that class, to do it, and where the
employer does not himself exercise any direction as to how it
shall be done, he is not responsible for any wrongs that the
employee may commit in the course of the work."

In *Atlanta & Florida Railroad Co.* v. *Kimberly*, 87 *Ga.* 161, ·
"Kimberly sued the railroad company for damages, and alleged
in his declaration that while the company was constructing its
road, it made a deep cut and piled the trash and earth therefrom near his dwelling-house, and dammed up a small stream
and pounded the water therefrom near the house;   .   .   by reason of which the air in and around the house became infected
with   .   .   malaria and other substances injurious to health,
whereby the plaintiff and his wife both became sick and endured
great pain and suffering and were unable to attend to their daily
duties, etc.   The defense of the railroad company was, that it
did not do the acts complained of in the declaration; that if
they were done at all, they were done by the Chattahoochee

Brick Company, an independent contractor, which it had employed to build the railroad." The jury found a verdict for the plaintiff; a motion for a new trial was overruled, and the case was brought to this court. This court held that, as the facts of the case showed that "the railroad company made a contract with the Chattahoochee Brick Company, whereby the latter agreed to build the former's road from Atlanta to Senoia according to certain specifications, and the railroad company did not retain any control over the contractor as to the method or manner of doing the work," and the contractor was to furnish the labor and all the materials, the railroad company was not liable for the damages sustained by the plaintiff in consequence of the negligent acts of the contractor. This decision was cited and followed in *Fulton County Railroad Co.* v. *McConnell*, 87 *Ga.* 756, where it was held that a street-railway company, which employed an independent contractor to construct its railway along a public street, was not liable for injuries sustained by a person while crossing such street, caused by the negligence of a servant of the contractor who had unnecessarily and improperly laid down loose iron rails in advance of the workmen engaged in constructing the track. In *Atlanta & Florida Railway Co.* v. *Kimberly*, the court stated the general rule of law upon the subject and the exceptions thereto. The general rule was stated as follows: "Where an individual or corporation contracts with another individual or corporation exercising an independent employment, for the latter to do a work not in itself unlawful or attended with danger to others, such work to be done according to the contractor's own methods and not subject to the employer's control or orders except as to results to be obtained, the employer is not liable for the wrongful or negligent acts of the contractor or the contractor's servants." After thus stating the general rule, the court enumerates and defines the exceptions to it. These exceptions are now embodied in section 3819 of the Civil Code, which declares that "The employer is liable for the negligence of the contractor — 1. When the work is wrongful in itself, or, if done in the ordinary manner, would result in a nuisance; 2. Or, if according to previous knowledge and experience, the work to be done is in its nature dangerous to others, however carefully performed; 3. Or, if the wrongful act is the violation of a duty imposed by express contract upon the employer; 4. Or, if the wrongful act is the violation of a duty imposed by statute; 5. Or, if the employer retains the right to direct or control the time and manner of executing the work; or interferes and assumes control, so as to create the relation of master and servant, or so that an injury results which is traceable to his interference; 6. Or, if the employer ratifies the unauthorized wrong of the independent contractor." As this section of the code undertakes to declare when the employer shall be liable for the negligence of the contractor, and specifically enumerates the instances in which he shall be, we think it is exhaustive of the subject—that the only instances in which an employer of an independent contractor is liable for the negligence of such contractor are those therein enumerated and defined. Does the case in hand fall within any of these exceptions to the general rule? We think not. The work which the Downing Company employed Leonard to perform was not wrongful in itself, nor would it, if done in the ordinary manner, result in a nuisance. Nor was the work to be done in its nature dangerous to others, however carefully performed. If reasonable and simple precautions had been taken, the presence of the excavation at the place in question would not have been dangerous to the public. It is also evident that this case neither involves any wrongful act which was "the violation of a duty imposed by express contract upon the employer," nor any wrongful act which was "the violation of a duty imposed by statute." The employer did not retain the right to direct or control the time and manner of executing the work; nor did the employer interfere and assume control of the same, "so as to create the relation of master and servant," or so that the injury sustained by the plaintiff could be traceable to such interference, for there was no interference whatever with the work by the Downing Company. No ratification of the unauthorized wrong of the independent contractor is shown. As, under the evidence, a verdict against the Downing Company could not have been lawfully rendered, there was no error in directing a verdict in its favor. *Judgment affirmed. All the Justices concurring.*

SUWANNEE TURPENTINE COMPANY *et al. v.* BAXTER & COMPANY *et al.*

1. Where pending an action of ejectment the plaintiff conveys the land in controversy, it is legal and proper for him to prosecute the suit to judgment, although his vendee and the defendant have agreed in writing that the vendee be permitted to take judgment, and this agreement has been entered upon the minutes of the court.

2. After the recovery of the land sued for and the due filing by the plaintiff's attorneys of their claim of lien, it is legal and proper for such attorneys to commence a suit for the foreclosure of their liens for fees against the plaintiff. It is not necessary that the vendee should have been given notice of such liens, the pendency of the suit in ejectment constituting such notice.

3. When in a suit for the foreclosure of such liens four different liens for different amounts, each on land different and distinct from that affected by the other liens, were consolidated in one petition and judgment prayed setting up and establishing the liens for the aggregate sum of all the liens on all the land, and such a judgment was rendered by the court, it was irregular but not void. Especially is this true when the defendant appeared in court and resisted the foreclosure of the liens. It was, therefore, not error for the trial judge to refuse to set aside this judgment upon the application of the purchaser from the original plaintiff in ejectment, such purchaser not having been a party to the action wherein the liens were foreclosed.

Submitted November 11, 1899.—Decided January 27, 1900.

Petition for injunction. Before Judge Bennett. Clinch county. August 10, 1899.

S. T. Kingsbery & Son and *Denmark & Ashley,* for plaintiffs.
Toomer & Reynolds, L. A. Wilson, and *S. W. Hitch,* for defendants.

SIMMONS, C. J. The facts of this case, briefly stated, are as follows: Moody brought four actions of ejectment against four different defendants, the suit against each being for certain lands not involved in the other suits. Pending these suits Moody sold his interest to the Suwannee Turpentine Company. Mobley, one of the defendants, bought, pending the suits, the interests of the other defendants. He and the turpentine company then entered into a written agreement compromising the suits. The company was to pay Mobley $600, being then "permitted to take judgment . . for all the lots of land described

in each suit," but without rent.   This agreement was dated
Nov. 24, 1894, and was entered on the minutes of the court
April 17, 1896.   On the latter date, judgment in each of the
four suits was entered in favor of Moody, the original plaintiff,
against the original defendant.   At the same term Hitch and
Wilson, Moody's attorneys, filed and had recorded their claim of
lien against the land, specifying in their claim the lots on which
each lien was claimed, and the amount thereof.   Subsequently
they commenced proceedings to foreclose their liens against
Moody and the land recovered for him.   In this proceeding,
instead of bringing four suits, foreclosing each lien separately,
they combined them all in one suit, and prayed that the liens
be set up and established against all the land for the aggregate
sum.   Moody appeared at the trial and contested the right of
the attorneys to foreclose the liens and their right to a judgment
therein.   He did not demur to the petition on the ground that
the liens could not be foreclosed in one suit, but went to trial on
the merits of the cause.   The jury returned a verdict in favor
of the attorneys, establishing the liens, and a judgment was entered thereon.   Execution was issued and levied upon the lands
specified in the lien.   These lands were advertised and sold by
the sheriff, and were purchased at the sale by a member of the
firm of G. S. Baxter & Co.   Thereafter the Suwannee Turpentine Co. and others filed an equitable petition against G. S.
Baxter & Co., Hitch, and Wilson, seeking to set aside the judgment obtained on the foreclosure of the liens of Hitch and
Wilson.   They alleged the purchase by them of the interest of
Moody, pending the suit, the agreement between the company
and Mobley above referred to, that the agreement was placed
upon the minutes of the court and that Hitch and Wilson assented to it, and that, notwithstanding this agreement and assent, the attorneys proceeded to take judgments in the name of
Moody.   They contended that the agreement, having been
placed upon the minutes of the court, was equivalent to an
order making the turpentine company a party plaintiff instead
of Moody, and that Hitch and Wilson disregarded the understanding between them and took the verdicts and judgments
in the name of Moody in order to secure their liens.   They

alleged that the judgments were, for these reasons, void, and that, the judgments being void, the liens of the attorneys were invalid and the suit to foreclose them and the judgment thereon likewise void as against them and the land which they had purchased from Moody. They also alleged that the judgment foreclosing the lien was void, because Whittington, an attorney at law, presided in the case for the purpose of passing an order to perfect service on Moody who was a non-resident, it appearing that Whittington had been engaged with Hitch and Wilson as attorney for Moody in the prosecution of the ejectment suits, and that the order appointing him judge pro hac vice was signed by a judge who was disqualified in the case. These last points were not insisted on here in the argument. They further alleged in their petition that the judgment was void, because the petition to foreclose the liens embraced in one suit all of the liens, and because the court had no jurisdiction to render a judgment on such a petition. They prayed that G. S. Baxter & Co. be enjoined perpetually from cutting timber or entering upon the land; that the judgments in ejectment be set aside; that the judgment foreclosing the liens of the attorneys be declared null and void; and for general relief.

The defendants, answering the petition, denied that the turpentine company was made a party to the ejectment suits by the entry of the agreement between it and Mobley upon the minutes of the court. They alleged that they and the attorney for the turpentine company understood the agreement differently from the plaintiffs, and that the judgments were therefore entered up in favor of the original plaintiff. With these exceptions, most of the material allegations of the plaintiffs were admitted.

This case, between the same parties, has once before been here, and is reported in 106 *Ga.* 180. It came then from Echols county, wherein the petition was filed and the injunction sought, and the court held in substance that the judgment appeared on its face to be regular and legal, and must be attacked in the court in which it was rendered. The suit was then filed in the proper court, and comes to this court on exceptions to the refusal of the trial judge to grant the injunction prayed.

After a careful consideration of this case, we find no error in the rulings complained of in the bill of exceptions.

1. It was earnestly insisted in the brief of counsel that the court erred in not holding the verdicts and judgments in the original ejectment suits void on the ground that when the Suwannee Turpentine Company had purchased the interest of Moody and entered into the agreement with Mobley under which it paid Mobley $600 and he agreed that the company should be permitted to take judgment in the suits, and when this agreement was placed upon the minutes with the consent of all the parties, it was equivalent to making the turpentine company a party plaintiff, and verdicts and judgments in the name of the original plaintiff were void. We think the court was right in holding to the contrary. Moody was the original plaintiff and the only person who could prosecute the suits to judgment. Although he had sold his land to another, he had still the right to maintain the actions, not only to recover damages for the trespass upon his land, but to secure a title which would inure to the benefit of his vendee. *Wood* v. *McGuire*, 21 *Ga.* 576 ; *Harris* v. *Cannon*, 6 *Ga.* 382; 10 Am. & Eng. Enc. L. (2d ed.) 494, and cases cited. Had the name of Moody been stricken from the petition and that of the turpentine company inserted as the party plaintiff, with or without adding a new demise, the actions would necessarily have failed, for it is a well-settled rule that for a plaintiff in ejectment to recover he must have had title and been entitled to the possession of the land at the time of the commencement of the suit. Had Moody's name been stricken and his vendee made plaintiff, the latter could not have shown that it had title and the right of possession at the time of the commencement of the suit. Besides, it would have been adding a new party and perhaps a new cause of action. The agreement between the turpentine company and Mobley could not amount to making the company a party when entered on the minutes with the approval of the court. We are aware of no law, nor have we been cited to any case, which authorizes the substitution of the name of the vendee for that of the original plaintiff in ejectment where there has been a sale by the latter pendente

lite. Instead, therefore, of its being a fraud on the part of
Hitch and Wilson to take the judgments in the name of Moody,
it seems to us that they acted in the best of faith not only for
the protection of Moody but of his vendee. The verdicts and
judgments taken in Moody's name were not void for any of
the reasons urged by the plaintiffs in error. It is quite likely
that had Hitch and Wilson pursued the course insisted on as
the correct one by the plaintiffs, and obtained judgments in the
name of the turpentine company, such judgments would have
been void.

2. It was also contended by counsel for the plaintiffs in
error, that the judgment obtained in the foreclosure suit was
void because brought against Moody alone; that the turpentine company ought to have been made a party or to have had
notice of the pendency of the suit. This contention, we think,
is not sound. The code gives attorneys a lien upon property
recovered by them in litigation. There is always a contract,
either express or implied, between attorney and client. It is
necessary to serve the client when the attorney institutes suit
to foreclose a lien for fees, the proceeding being against the
client and his property. While it is true that the lien of the
attorney arises by operation of law, it can not arise unless there
is a contract for the services of the attorney and the suit is upon
that contract as well as upon the lien. This being true, Hitch
and Wilson could not have brought their suit against the turpentine company, the vendee of their client. With it they
had no contract, express or implied. Indeed, it seems from
the agreement made by the vendee and Mobley that they sought
to take the case out of the hands of the attorneys. The turpentine company was no party to the contract for services of
the attorneys, could not have been sued on such contract, and
was, therefore, not a proper party to the suit to foreclose the
liens. Nor was it necessary that the attorneys should give notice to the company of the foreclosure proceedings. The officers of the company knew of the pendency of the suits for the
recovery of the land, and when the company bought the land
it did so subject to the lien of the attorneys in the event their
services proved successful. The law gave the attorneys the.

lien, and required them to record their claim of lien within a given time after their services were terminated. The liens were properly recorded. The pendency of the ejectment suit was all the notice to which the vendee was entitled. *Little* v. *Sexton,* 89 *Ga.* 411; *Fry* v. *Calder,* 74 *Ga.* 7; *Lovett* v. *Moore,* 98 *Ga.* 158; Bennett, Lis Pendens, § 264.

3. The record discloses that when Hitch and Wilson brought their action to foreclose their liens, they consolidated in one suit their four claims of lien, each on a separate and distinct tract of land. Moody was served with notice of this suit, and appeared personally and by attorney and resisted the foreclosure. The record does not disclose that he objected to the consolidation of the liens, or filed any demurrer on this ground. The case proceeded to trial, and the jury returned a verdict for the plaintiffs. Judgment was entered up on this verdict, and execution issued. It is contended by plaintiffs in error that this judgment was void because of the consolidation of the claims into one suit. While we think the better practice would have been to bring four suits, one to foreclose each lien, the failure to do so and the consolidation of the liens into one suit constituted at most merely an irregularity or error which did not render the judgment void. To render a judgment void there must be want of jurisdiction of the subject-matter or of the person, or an excess of jurisdiction (1 Freeman, Judgments, § 116), or the judgment must be fraudulent or fraudulent and collusive (Civil Code, § 2689; 2 Freeman, Judgments, § 335 et seq.; 1 Black, Judgments, § 293; *Smith* v. *Cuyler,* 78 *Ga.* 654). For a want or an excess of jurisdiction the defendant in a judgment may have it set aside, but this can not be done by one who is a stranger to the judgment. A creditor or a stranger, when their interests are affected by the judgment, may have it set aside for fraud or fraud and collusion. Under the allegations in this bill we might end the discussion of this case by saying, first, that when this case was here before (*Dixon, Mitchell & Co.* v. *Baxter & Co.,* 106 *Ga.* 180) this court held that the judgment foreclosing the liens was not void upon its face but "was on its face valid and regular, and that the plaintiffs were not, so long as it remained of force, entitled to the injunction for which

they prayed;" and, second, that the vendee and those holding
under it, not having been parties to the action in which the
judgment was rendered and not charging that the judgment
was procured by fraud or collusion, can not properly move to
set it aside. "A third person not a party to the record can not
go into a court and move to set aside a judgment which is not
against him." *Merchants' Bank* v. *Haiman*, 80 *Ga.* 624; Civil
Code, § 5362; *Cathing* v. *State*, 62 *Ga.* 244. But even conceding
that the plaintiffs in error can properly bring the judgment into
question by a bill to set it aside, we still hold that it was not
void for any of the reasons set out in the petition. The court
which rendered the judgment had jurisdiction of the subject-
matter of the suit, — that is, it had jurisdiction of suits to foreclose attorney's liens on lands recovered by the attorneys for
their clients, and had jurisdiction of the parties and unrestricted
jurisdiction as to amount. The judgment was, therefore, not
void merely because the attorneys consolidated in one action
four different claims of lien. The defendant could have objected or demurred at the proper time on this ground, and thus
made this question. Instead of this he acquiesced in the judgment which remains of force to-day, unexcepted to and unreversed. If the liens of attorneys for fees be regarded as arising
out of the contract for services, then sections 4943 and 4944 of
the Civil Code would seem to give attorneys the right to consolidate suits for the foreclosure of such liens. If the liens be
regarded as not founded upon the contract of employment but
arising by operation of law upon the performance of the services,
even then the consolidation would not make the judgment void.
It is true, as contended for by plaintiffs in error, that the liens
were for different amounts and were on different tracts of land.
All, however, were against the same defendant and against the
land recovered for him by the attorneys, and it is not shown
that Moody or his vendee was hurt by foreclosing the liens for
the aggregate sum on all of the land, instead of foreclosing each
lien on that portion of the land which was properly subject to
it. However that may be, the court had jurisdiction of the
parties and of the subject-matter, and we are clear that the
judgment rendered was not void. In the case of Pritchard *v.*

Madren, 31 Kans. 38, it appears that the taxing officer assessed taxes for a gross sum upon land in gross, when by law he should have assessed each tract separately. Suit was brought upon the assessment in gross and for a gross sum, and judgment for a gross sum obtained. The court held that the judgment was not void but only irregular. This decision is quoted with approval in Freeman on Judgments (vol. 1, § 135), wherein it is said that "a judgment against lands for a sum in gross, when it should have been against each parcel separately," though erroneous or irregular, is not void. See also Hukm Chand, Res Judicata, § 192. For these reasons we think the judgment of the trial judge was right.

Judgment affirmed.   All the Justices concurring.

GEORGIA RAILROAD & BANKING CO. *v.* ROUGHTON.

Inasmuch as the amendment to the petition alleged an entirely different act of negligence upon the part of the defendant as the cause of the plaintiff's injury, it set forth a new cause of action, and therefore should not have been allowed.

Argued December 6, 1899. — Decided January 27, 1900.

Action for damages. Before Judge Lumpkin. Fulton superior court. March term, 1899.

Roughton sued the Georgia Railroad & Banking Company for personal injuries alleged to have been sustained by him by reason of the defendant's negligence. Upon announcement by the court that the general demurrer filed to the petition by the defendant would be sustained, plaintiff offered an amendment to the petition, to the allowance of which the defendant objected, on the ground that it added a new cause of action. The court overruled the objection and allowed the amendment; whereupon the defendant excepted. According to the allegations of the plaintiff's original petition, a spur-track of the defendant ran along Badger street and across Borne street in the city of Atlanta, and the defendant had left cars standing on the spur-track in such a position that a pedestrian could not get from Badger street on to the sidewalk of Borne street without going into the middle of the latter street at its junction with Badger, and going around these cars. "Said cars were so left that the light from an electric light, which is placed there, was shut off that portion of said street over which petitioner was compelled to travel, and petitioner, for said reason, could not see his way. The ground at the end of said car where petitioner was compelled to walk was rough and uneven, the ground was covered with snow and ice, and was quite slippery. In going around said car, which petitioner was compelled to do to get to the side-walk, he slipped and fell, breaking two of his ribs and otherwise hurting and bruising himself." There were no other allegations of negligence. The amendment practically reiterated the allegations of the original petition, with the following material addition: "That at the end of said cars defendant company had, during that day and since plaintiff had passed along that morning going to his store, dumped and left unscattered a pile of dirt and old brickbats which had become frozen and hard where plaintiff was compelled to walk around said cars, which made the ground rough and uneven, it being also covered with sleet and ice; and said pile of dirt and brick could not be seen, owing to said light being shut off by the cars as aforesaid, and no signal or warning of any kind left to put persons on notice of the rough place. The sidewalk upon which he had a right to pass, to wit, on Badger street, was smooth and safe, and he could have safely gotten to his destination. That when plaintiff reached said spur-track he found said cars obstructing his way as aforesaid, extending up into and nearly across Borne street, at the junction of said Badger street, which forced plaintiff, in order to pass, to go around said cars to get to the sidewalk on said Borne street, and just as he was passing around said cars he stumbled and fell upon said hard and frozen earth and brickbats left that day by the defendant company, with great force, breaking two of his ribs," etc.

Joseph B. & Bryan Cumming and *Sanders McDaniel,* for plaintiff in error, cited, as to the amendment: 1 Enc. Pl. & Pr. 563; 51 *Ga.* 515; 68 *Ga.* 744; 73 *Ga.* 655; Id. 718; 82 *Ga.* 623; 87 *Ga.* 764; 92 *Ga.* 644; 102 *Ga.* 254.

H. M. Patty, contra, cited, as to amendment, 87 *Ga.* 691.

FISH, J. We think the court erred in allowing the amendment to the petition, over the defendant's objection, as, in our opinion, the amendment manifestly set forth a new cause of action. The negligence complained of in the original petition, as the cause of the plaintiff's injury, was, that the defendant had left cars standing on its spur-track, in such a position that the plaintiff could not get from Badger street, along which he was passing, to the sidewalk of Borne street, without going into the middle of the latter street and passing around the cars, and that the ground on which he was thus forced to walk was rough, uneven, covered with snow and ice, and slippery, in consequence of which, in walking around the cars, he slipped and fell, thereby sustaining the injury for which he sued. The negligence alleged against the defendant was the leaving of its cars across the street. It was not alleged that the defendant was, in any way, connected with, or responsible for, the condition of the street at the point where the plaintiff slipped and fell. The amendment, however, alleged that the defendant "dumped and left unscattered a pile of dirt and old brickbats, which had become frozen and hard where plaintiff was compelled to walk around said cars, which made the ground rough and uneven," and that the defendant left no signal or warning of any kind to put persons on notice of the rough place. This amendment introduced an entirely new item of negligence on the part of the defendant as the cause of the plaintiff's injury, viz., the placing of an obstruction in the street and leaving it unguarded, thus adding a new and distinct cause of action, which section 5099 of the Civil Code forbids. See *Central R. & Banking Co. v. Wood*, 51 *Ga.* 515; *Skidaway S. R. Co. v. O'Brien*, 73 *Ga.* 655; *Henderson v. Railroad Co.*, Id. 718; *Cox v. Murphey*, 82 *Ga.* 623; *Davis v. Muscogee Mfg. Co.*, 106 *Ga.* 126.

Judgment reversed.   All the Justices concurring.

DAVIS SULPHUR ORE CO. *v.* ATLANTA GUANO CO.

If a vendor and vendee make an executory contract whereby the former sells to the latter certain goods for which the latter agrees to pay at a time subsequent to the date of delivery; and if, before the time fixed for the delivery of the goods, the vendee becomes insolvent and the vendor stops the goods in transitu and resells them for less than the contract price, and thereupon brings an action against the vendee for the difference between the contract price and the price realized upon the resale, his declaration is fatally defective, unless it alleges either that he gave the vendee notice of his intention to resell, or that he made a tender of the goods and demanded payment and the vendee refused to take the goods or to pay for them.

Argued December 6, 1899. — Decided January 27, 1900.

Complaint. Before Judge Reid. City court of Atlanta. June 17, 1899.

James H. Gilbert, for plaintiff.
Abbott, Cox & Abbott, for defendant.

SIMMONS, C. J. The Davis Sulphur Ore Company entered into a written contract with the Atlanta Guano Company, whereby it sold to the latter certain sulphur ore, the guano company agreeing to pay for the same at a certain time after delivery at the port of Charleston or Port Royal, South Carolina, or Savannah, Georgia. The ore was purchased in Europe and transported by water to this continent. Before its arrival in this country, the vendor ascertained that the vendee had become insolvent, and it exercised its right to stop the ore in transit. Before its arrival at the port of destination, the vendor resold it for some $1,600 less than the price agreed on in the contract with the guano company. The ore company then brought suit against the guano company for the difference between the contract price and the price received on the resale, alleging in substance the above-stated facts. The declaration showed that the goods were never tendered to the guano company or demand for payment made, and there was no allegation that any notice of the second sale or of the intention to resell was ever given to the guano company, the original vendee. The latter demurred to the declaration on several grounds, one of them being that it set out no cause of action. The trial judge sustained the demurrer, and the plaintiff excepted.

Under our Civil Code (§ 3551) and the common law, the vendor has three remedies when he sells goods and the vendee refuses to take and pay for them: "The seller may retain them and recover the difference between the contract price and the market price at the time and place of delivery; or he may sell the property, acting for this purpose as agent for the vendee, and recover the difference between the contract price and the price on resale; or he may store or retain the property for the vendee and sue him for the entire price." If the vendor elects to take the second remedy, and resells the goods at the vendee's risk, and the sale is properly made after due notice to the vendee of the intention to resell, and the goods bring less than the contract price, the vendee is conclusively bound by the resale and the amount realized by it. Unless the vendee has notice of the intention to resell, he is not bound by the amount realized, and this is right upon both principle and justice. The vendor acts as the agent of the vendee in making the sale, and sells at the vendee's risk; and it would be unjust to hold the vendee bound except where he has had notice of the intention of the vendor to resell. If the vendee has notice he may attend the sale, if a public one, and see that it is fair, or, whether the sale be public or private, he may be able to bring about competition or to secure a purchaser who will give the full value of the goods. He may be able in other ways to prevent loss to himself. Some of the cases hold that the resale is in the nature of an adjudication against the vendee, when he has had full notice, as to the value of the goods at the time of such resale. If this be so, it is certainly necessary that the vendee should have notice of the sale. It is said in the American notes in Bennett's 7 Am. ed. of Benjamin on Sales, p. 826, "Notice to the buyer of the time and place of resale is usual, and is important as tending to prove the sale a fair one; but it is not absolutely necessary in all cases that such notice should have been given. . . But although a notice of *the time and place* of resale may not be absolutely necessary, it is now generally thought that the vendor should inform the buyer that he intends to exercise his right of resale and hold him responsible for the difference in price." It was held in the case of *Green* v. *Ansley*, 92 *Ga.* 647, that it was absolutely necessary to give notice of the intention to resell, but not of the time and place of the resale. In that case it was said: "In order to conclude the defendant in this manner, not only must it appear that the resale was made without unreasonable delay, with the same publicity and as far as possible under the same conditions as the first, and with an honest effort to get the best price obtainable, but it must appear also that the defendant had notice that the sale was to be at his risk. The property resold at his risk is regarded as in some sense his own, and the result of the resale is in the nature of an adjudication against him; and before he should be charged with the deficiency, he should be afforded an opportunity to protect his interest and prevent a sacrifice of the property. Unless notice is given him that the property is held and will be sold at his risk, he has a right to assume, if it is sold again, that the vendor elected to retain and deal with it as his own and at his own risk." It is true that the property resold in that case was land, but it is stated in the opinion that the same principle applies to the resale of personalty. In the case of Leonard v. Portier, 15 S. W. Rep. 414, the Texas Court of Appeals held that, "On a refusal to accept goods tendered in performance of an executory contract of sale, the seller must give notice of his intention to resell, in order to bind the purchaser for the difference between the contract price and the price obtained on a resale, and notice must be alleged in a petition which demands judgment for such difference." In Newmark on Sales it is stated that "in order to entitle the vendor to proceed by resale, instead of by rescission or by action for the whole price, he must manifest his election by preliminary notice of his intention to sell, stating in terms or effect that he will assert his right of resale and bind the buyer by the price obtained and hold him for the loss sustained." See, to the same effect: 2 Sutherland, Damages (2d ed.), § 647, t. p. 1432, and cases cited; 2 Addison, Contracts (Morgan's ed.), § 593. These authorities clearly show that the vendee is not bound for the difference between the contract price and the price on the resale, unless he has notice of the vendor's

39

intention to resell and to hold him bound for the difference, or unless his refusal to take the goods when tendered or to pay for them has rendered the notice superfluous. For this last reason, in the case of *McCord* v. *Laidley*, 87 *Ga.* 221, the vendees were held bound by the price realized on the resale. There the vendor tendered the goods and made demand for payment, and the vendees refused to take the goods or pay for them; while in the present case the goods were never tendered, no demand for payment was ever made, and the goods were resold before the time for payment or that for delivery had arrived. See, on this branch of the subject, Burdick on Sales, p. 230, and cases cited. It may be said that the above cases and citations apply only to the case of a solvent vendee who refuses to accept and pay for goods, and that they do not apply to cases where the vendee has become insolvent after the purchase or where the vendor has exercised his right of stoppage in transitu. We can not see that either of these circumstances should affect the question of notice. If the vendee becomes insolvent, he ought in justice and good morals to refuse to accept goods for which he can not pay. When the vendor stops the goods in transitu, it appears from the authorities that such stoppage does not amount to a rescission of the contract but puts the vendor back in possession of the goods to hold them, not only to protect his lien for the purchase-money, but also as in the nature of a pledge. When he afterwards exercises his right to resell, he does so as the agent of the vendee and at the latter's risk. In 2 Morgan's Addison on Contracts, § 605, in treating of the rights of the vendor where the vendee has become insolvent or bankrupt after the purchase, it is said: "The assignees of the bankrupt purchaser are entitled to call upon the vendor to deliver the goods on being paid or tendered the price; but, if they refuse to take and pay for the goods, the vendor will be entitled to resell them in the same way that he is entitled to resell in ordinary cases after the refusal of a purchaser to take and pay for the things he has ordered and bought." The insolvency of the purchaser may relieve the vendor of the necessity of tendering the goods and demanding payment, but notice of an intention to resell is still required. And where, because of the insolvency of the vendee, no tender or demand has been made, there is nothing which brings the case within the doctrine of *McCord* v. *Laidley*, supra, and does away with the necessity of notice. In the present case the petition did not allege that any notice of an intention to resell or of the resale was given the vendee, and we think the court properly sustained the demurrer thereto.

Judgment affirmed.   All the Justices concurring.

BAGWELL *v.* ATLANTA CONSOLIDATED STREET RAILWAY COMPANY.

An action by a father for the loss of the services of his minor daughter, occasioned by personal injuries, should not be dismissed because she, after reaching her majority, refused to obey an order of the court in which the action was pending, requiring her to submit to a physical examination of her person by a physician.

Argued December 7, 8, 1899. — Decided January 27, 1900.

Action for damages. Before Judge Berry. City court of Atlanta. January 24, 1899.

Dorsey, Brewster & Howell and *Hugh M. Dorsey*, for plaintiff.
Goodwin & Hallman, for defendant.

LUMPKIN, P. J. The record is voluminous and redundant, but, after relegating from it all save that which is really material, we find that the case, as now presented, turns upon the single question on which the ruling announced in the headnote is made. We do not think this question requires elaborate discussion. It would be going a great length to hold that such an action by a father should be defeated by the refusal of a daughter who, though not quite twenty-one years old, was practically a grown woman, to submit her person to a physician for physical examination. Certainly, if as was alleged in this case, the physician, though eminent in his profession and a thorough gentleman, was distasteful to the daughter, it would have been placing upon the father, even if she had still been under his control, a great and painful burden to coerce her to undergo an examination or else give up his cause of action. But that is not the case with which we are now dealing, for the record shows that the refusal upon which the judge's order of dismissal was based was made by the daughter after she had become of age.   At that time her father had no right or authority to control her person or her movements.   His conduct would have been indefensible, if not criminal, if he had undertaken to compel her, against her will, to allow a physician to examine her.   No humane father would, at any cost, attempt such a thing. It may be that if he really desired the examination to take place he might, by perfectly proper means, have induced his daughter to consent to it.   Be this as it may, we are not prepared to hold that he was, in any event, bound to pursue such a course; and moreover, it distinctly appears, as already remarked, that this case was dismissed solely on the ground that Miss Bagwell refused to submit to the examination which the court had ordered to take place.

We have no hesitation in holding that a case should not be thrown out of court because of the conduct of one not a party to it and who was neither legally bound to obey the plaintiff's orders nor subject to his custody or control.   If any court in the world has ever gone so far, we are not aware of it, and we certainly are unwilling to establish such a precedent.   Neither section 4047 of our Civil Code, which confers upon every court of this State the power to control, in furtherance of justice, the conduct of all persons "connected with a judicial proceeding before it," nor the decision of this court in *R. &. D. R. Co.* v. *Childress,* 82 *Ga.* 719, affords any warrant for so doing.   In that case it was simply held that it was within the power of the court, in the exercise of its discretion, to compel *the plaintiff* to submit to an examination.   Referring to a suggestion made in the argument that the rule announced "would operate hardly upon delicate and modest females," Chief Justice Bleckley said (page 722), "we can only say that they would be safely guarded by the discretion of the trial judge.   There would be no danger, we think, in this country, of an examination being ordered needlessly or where an improper shock to modesty or feelings of delicacy would be likely."

We are quite sure the case ought not to have been dismissed.
Judgment reversed.   All the Justices concurring.

CUNNINGHAM *et al. v.* BARKER.

A judge of a court of record in another State is, under the provisions of section 3621 of the Civil Code, authorized to take an acknowledgment of a deed to realty situated in this State, which is executed in the State where the court over which such judge presides is located.

Argued December 11, 1899. — Decided January 27, 1900.

Equitable petition. Before John C. Reed, judge pro hac vice. Fulton superior court. March term, 1899.

W. R. Hammond and *L. R. Ray*, for plaintiffs.
King & Anderson, for defendant.

COBB, J. There is but a single question involved in the present case, and that is, whether a judge of a court of record in another State can take an acknowledgment of a deed to realty situated in this State, when such deed is executed in the State where the court over which such judge presides is located, so as to authorize the deed to be admitted to record in this State under the provisions of section 3621 of the Civil Code. Our learned brother who presided as judge pro hac vice in the court below reached the conclusion that such an acknowledgment would authorize the record of the deed. We agree with him in this conclusion, and the reasons given by him in the opinion which appears in the record are so satisfactory to our minds that we adopt the same as the opinion of the court in the present case. The opinion referred to is as follows: "The deed was made without the State. It was attested by an unofficial witness, and also by Severy, who writes after his signature 'Judge, County Court, El Paso County, Colorado.' Further, there is a certificate by the judge of an acknowledgment of the deed before him, and there is a certificate of the clerk that the court is one of record, and that the signature of the judge to the certificate of the latter is genuine. The deed and the two certificates are dated December 2, 1896. The certificates, it is admitted, are in proper form. The petition contends that as the clerk fails to certify the genuineness of the judge's signature in his attestation, not in the acknowledgment which he took, the execution of the deed is fatally

defective.   On the other hand, the defendant contends that
the acknowledgment makes the execution good.   To decide
this contention we must construe section 3621 of the Civil
Code, which is the act of 1895 (Acts 1895, p. 73).   This act
took the place of the first sentence of section 3706 of the
Code of 1882 and the amendatory act of 1893.   Acts 1893,
p. 37.   The second sentence of the section last cited contains
a provision for the acknowledgment of deeds made within the
State, such provision now appearing in section 3621 of the
Civil Code; while the Code of 1882 and the act of 1893 provided only for attestation of deeds made without the State.
To state this more clearly: before the act of 1895, as the legislature seems to believe, deeds made within the State could be
executed both by attestation and acknowledgment, but deeds
made without the State could be executed only by attestation.
This apparent restriction upon the execution of the deeds last
mentioned was the supposed evil of the old law, and the
remedy given by the act of 1895 is its permission that such
deeds be acknowledged before all officials who have authority
to attest such papers, and so to make the execution both of
deeds made beyond and those made within the State as nearly
alike as possible.   After the act was passed parties to a deed
made out of the State could have the same choice of executing
it by acknowledgment or by attestation as parties to one made
at home and under the former law.   The purpose of the act
of 1895 is declared in its title to be 'to prescribe the method
of attestation and acknowledgment of deeds executed without
the State.'   At. the beginning of the first section it is enacted
that such a deed 'must be attested by or acknowledged before'
named officers.   At the end of the section is a significant
change of certain language of the act of 1893.   The latter required a clerk to certify that the notary before whom the deed
was executed was 'authorized by law to attest deeds,' but the
act of 1895 requires the clerk to certify that such notary is 'authorized by law to attest deeds and take acknowledgments
thereof.'   Thus the title, the commencement, and the end of
the enactment show clearly that its intention is to place acknowledgment on the same footing as attestation.

"It is strenuously contended by the petitioners' counsel that
the use of 'by' in the clause 'or by a judge,' etc., in the 6th
line of the section of the code under consideration, prevents our
supplying from the context any other words before it except
'attested'; that one must needs read 'or attested by a judge'
and not 'attested by or acknowledged before a judge'; and that
'by' correctly goes in construction with 'attested' and never
with 'acknowledged,' which verb demands 'before' and not 'by'
to complete its sense. Such an error of grammar as is shown
by this criticism does not vitiate what we have found to be the
clearly expressed intention of the legislature. That intention
demands that we treat 'by' as redundant. If the act be read
without it, the body and end of the main section are all in harmony with the title as it now stands. But under the petitioners' construction the act of 1895 ought to have borne a title
substantially like this: 'An act to prescribe how deeds executed
out of the State shall be attested by or acknowledged before
commissioners of deeds, and consuls and vice-consuls, and how
such deeds shall be attested by judges, clerks and notaries.'
No reason is suggested why in this matter the powers of one
class of officers should be enlarged and those of another class
be diminished, or why a party should be allowed the convenience of acknowledging his deeds before commissioners accessible only in the larger towns and cities of our country, and
consuls and vice-consuls accessible only in foreign nations, and
be denied it before other officers of at least equal importance,
that is, judges and clerks of courts of record and notaries public, who can be found everywhere. If one construction makes
legislative action foolish and unwise, and another makes it effectually cure an evil and bring all of the law of the subject
into harmony, and if these constructions are equally sustained
by the words of the act, no judge would hesitate to adopt the
latter. But in this case, both the letter and spirit combine in
support of the construction which makes the act a complete
and not a fragmentary and insufficient reform of the old law.
A brief examination will show how the clauses commencing
with 'or by' got into the act of 1895, and what they mean.
The act was evidently composed from materials found in the

first sentence of section 2706 of the Code of 1882, and the act of 1893. The draftsman took the sentence just mentioned entire, interlining in it, after 'attested by,' the words 'or acknowledged before,' which is the only addition of his own. The first 'or by' occurs here, that is 'or by a judge,' etc. He deemed it unnecessary to rewrite between two little words the phrase 'attested by or acknowledged before,' which he had connected so plainly with each of the three officers first named, that is, deed commissioner, consul, and vice-consul; he felt it was just as plainly connected with the next officer he named, that is, a judge of a court of record. And he felt the same as to the two officers next mentioned, namely, clerk and notary, and so he preceded each with 'or by,' not seeing that in order to fitly express his intention he ought to have blotted out 'by' in the clause he took from the Code of 1882 and should not have inserted it later before 'clerk' and 'notary.' This explanation of the sense in which he used these words, and why he so used them, is strongly supported by his carefully adding to the certificate required by the act of 1893 a statement of the notary's authority to take acknowledgments of deeds   I hold that the attestation of the deed attacked by the petition is bad, but that its acknowledgment is good, and I therefore sustain the demurrer."   *Judgment affirmed.   All the Justices concurring.*

CUNNINGHAM v. UNITED STATES SAVINGS AND LOAN COMPANY et al.

An appeal does not lie to the superior court from a judgment rendered by the ordinary sustaining a demurrer to an application for a homestead. In such a case the exclusive remedy for reviewing the judgment is by certiorari.

Argued December 12, 1899.— Decided January 27, 1900.

Petition for homestead.   Before Judge Lumpkin.   Fulton superior court.   March term, 1899.

L. R. Ray and *W. R. Hammond,* for plaintiff.

W. M. Everett, Dorsey, Brewster & Howell, Simmons & Corrigan, King & Anderson, and *James K. Hines,* contra.

LEWIS, J. Anna O. Cunningham presented to the ordinary of Fulton county her petition to have set apart to her as a homestead certain lands belonging to petitioner. At the hearing of this application the defendants in error, her creditors, demurred to the petition. This demurrer the ordinary sustained, and from the judgment dismissing her application petitioner appealed to the superior court. When the case was called for a hearing in the superior court, counsel for defendants in error moved that the case be dismissed, on the ground that an appeal would not lie from the judgment of the ordinary dismissing an application for a homestead upon demurrer, but that the remedy is by certiorari, and not by appeal. The court sustained the motion to dismiss the case, to which judgment plaintiff in error excepts.

We think that not only the statute, but also the adjudications of this court, have recognized the distinction between the court of ordinary and the ordinary. The present constitution of the State declares that "The judicial powers of this State shall be vested in a Supreme Court, superior courts, courts of ordinary, justices of the peace, commissioned notaries public, and such other courts as have been or may be established by law." Civil Code, § 5831. It further declares that "The powers of a court of ordinary, and of probate, shall be vested in an ordinary for each county, from whose decision there may be an appeal (or, by consent of parties, without a decision) to the superior court, under regulations prescribed by law." Civil Code, § 5852. Under section 4251 of the Civil Code, it is provided, "The courts of ordinary shall be held in each county, by the ordinary thereof, on the first Monday in each month." In the jurisdiction conferred upon courts of ordinary in section 4232 of the Civil Code, we nowhere find that they are given jurisdiction over homesteads. The constitution of the State, art. 9, sec. 4, par. 1, provides that the General Assembly shall provide by law, as early as practicable, for the setting apart and valuation of property for homestead. So far as the constitution, therefore, is concerned, the General Assembly was unrestricted as to the manner in which it could by statute provide for the setting apart of a homestead. It could have conferred the jurisdiction of passing upon applications for homestead upon any other officer in the county as well as upon the ordinary. Under section 2828 of the Civil Code, it will be seen that this power was conferred by act of the legislature upon the ordinary of the county in which the applicant resided ; and nowhere upon the court of ordinary, over which he presided. Section 4454 of the Civil Code provides for an appeal from any decision made by the court of ordinary, except an order appointing a temporary administrator. It is true that the ordinary acts in a judicial capacity, not only when he sits as judge of the court of ordinary, but in instances when not sitting as such judge. He certainly acts in a judicial capacity when he passes upon applications for homestead ; but he is no more a judicial officer in that case than the sheriff would have been, had the legislature conferred power upon that officer to determine the same questions with reference to homesteads.

We know of no provision in the law anywhere that gives the right of appeal from a decision of the ordinary when not rendered as judge of the court of ordinary, except the appeal provided for in section 2838 of the Civil Code. It will be seen, however, that the provisions of that section with reference to an appeal from the judgment of the ordinary have no application whatever to the case we are now considering. By the preceding section of the Civil Code (2836) the right is given to any creditor of the applicant for homestead to make objections to the schedule, for want of sufficiency and fulness, or for fraud of any kind, or to dispute the valuation of personalty, or the propriety of the survey, or the value of the premises so platted as the homestead. Section 2838 provides that upon such objections being filed in writing, unless the applicant shall so alter the schedule or plat, or both, as to remove said objections, the ordinary shall appoint three disinterested appraisers to examine the property concerning which the objections are made, and on their return, if either be found to be too large, such alterations shall be made as the ordinary may deem proper to bring the same within the limits of the value allowed by the constitution. Now, that section simply provides that either party dissatisfied with such a judgment as this, rendered by the ordinary, shall have the right to appeal under the same rules, regulations, and restrictions as are provided by law in cases of appeal from the court of ordinary. But no such judgment and no trial embodying these issues were involved in this case. The case at bar presents simply the question as to whether an appeal will lie from the decision of the ordinary sustaining a demurrer to petitioner's application for a homestead, a decision and trial which involved purely a question of law. The very fact, therefore, that no provision appears anywhere in the homestead act authorizing an appeal from such a decision of an ordinary shows that no right of appeal exists in such a case. But there is a section of the Civil Code (4634) which fully presents a remedy for the correction of the errors complained of in this record. That section declares: "The writ of certiorari will lie for the correction of errors committed by justices of the peace, corporation courts or councils, or any inferior judicatory, or any person exercising judicial powers, including the ordinary, except in cases touching the probate of wills, granting letters testamentary and of administration." The jurisdiction of the superior court to correct by writ of certiorari judgments of the ordinary in relation to homesteads was recognized by this court in *Lathrop* v. *Building Asso.*, 45 *Ga.* 483. We think the principle ruled in *Harrell* v. *Pickett*, 43 *Ga.* 271, controls this case. It was there decided that the proper mode of bringing before the superior courts of this State the judgment of an ordinary, rendered in the discharge of duties devolved upon him, in relation to county matters, previously vested in the inferior courts, or of matters not touching the probate of wills, or administration, or otherwise specially provided by law, is by certiorari, and not by appeal. It will be seen from the opinion of Chief Justice Lochrane delivered in that case that the decision of the court was based upon the same provisions of the constitution of the State then in force, to wit, the constitution of 1868, in reference to appeals from the court of ordinary, and upon the same statute with reference to the writ of certiorari from the decision of any person exercising judicial powers, including the ordinary, as are now embodied in the present constitution and laws of this

State. It was there decided that, upon construing these various sections of the constitution and code together, the decision of an ordinary, in the discharge of duties devolved upon him in relation to county matters previously vested in the inferior courts, or of matters not touching the probate of wills, or administration, or otherwise specially regulated by law, under section 3977 of the Code of 1868 can be brought to the superior court only by writ of certiorari. Section 3977 of the Code of 1868, then in existence, is substantially the same as section 4634 of the present Civil Code, above quoted. The only difference is that the section in the present code omits designating the "inferior court, or the justices thereof," from the simple fact that that court has been abolished.

But the case at bar is really a stronger one in support of the position that the appeal from the judgment of the ordinary complained of was not the legal remedy for reviewing his decision, than was the case of *Harrell* v. *Pickett,* just cited; for the constitutions, both of 1868 and of 1877, provide that "The courts of ordinary shall have such powers in relation to roads, bridges, ferries, public buildings, paupers, county officers, county funds, county taxes, and other county matters, as may be conferred on them by law." Under this provision in the constitution, therefore, the question might arise with some force as to whether or not the business of the inferior courts was turned over to the ordinary, or court of ordinary. There is no question in the case now under consideration as to whether the jurisdiction with reference to setting apart homesteads under the present constitution and statutes of the State was conferred upon the ordinary, or court of ordinary. It was clearly conferred upon the ordinary himself, who has power to pass upon the same at any time without regard to any term of the court of ordinary. Our attention has been called to several cases which have been before this court where appeals were taken from similar decisions of the ordinary in homestead matters; for instance, the case of *Marsh* v. *Lazenby,* 41 *Ga.* 153. It appears from the facts recited in that case that it was tried in the superior court on an appeal from the judgment of the ordinary dismissing the petition of the applicant for homestead. See also *Kirtland*

v. *Davis*, 43 *Ga.* 318; *Lynch* v. *Pollard*, 40 *Ga.* 173; *Crawford*
v. *May*, 49 *Ga.* 43; *Blackwell* v. *Broughton*, 56 *Ga.* 390; *Burns*
v. *Chandler*, 61 *Ga.* 385. In the cases cited this court passed
upon issues that were decided in the trial of the case on appeal
to the superior court from the decision of the ordinary. But
in none of these cases, or in any others that we have been able
to find, was the question ever made before this court as to
whether or not an appeal was the proper remedy. The decisions cited by counsel for plaintiff in error only tend to show
that it seems to have been a common practice in the profession
to treat any decision of the ordinary in homestead matters as
a ruling from which the law gave either party a right of appeal; and no question, either on the trial of the appeal, or in
the review of that trial by this court, being made touching the
right of appeal, this court never passed upon the question.
None of these decisions, therefore, can be considered as deciding any principle in conflict with our views in this case.

Judgment affirmed.   All the Justices concurring.

NICHOLAS v. BRITISH AMERICA ASSURANCE CO.

Where a petition setting out a cause of action has been filed and followed
up by the issuance of process and service, the time of the commencement
of the suit is the date of its filing. But where, after such filing, no process of any character was issued and annexed to the petition, nor waived,
before the commencement of the term to which the petition was made
returnable, there was in fact no suit pending. The filing of the petition
without more does not operate to commence a suit; nor has the judge in
such a case authority, at or after the return term, to order a new process
to issue.

Argued December 13, 1899. — Decided January 27, 1900.

Action on insurance policy. Before Judge Lumpkin.
Fulton superior court. March term, 1899.

James L. Key, for plaintiff.
Westmoreland Brothers, for defendant.

LITTLE, J. On the 6th day of July, 1897, the plaintiff filed
in the office of the clerk of the superior court of Fulton county

(margin notes beside case heading:) 109 62 / 115 96 / 109 117 / 109 123 / 109 6 / 127 4

a petition seeking to recover a sum of money from the defendant, on account of the loss of certain personal goods by fire occurring on the 26th day of March, 1897, which were covered by a policy of insurance, on which the suit was based.   A copy of the policy was attached to the petition, and among others contained the following stipulation: "No suit, or action on this policy, for the recovery of any claim, shall be sustained in any court of law or equity, . .   unless commenced within twelve months next after the fire."   The petition prayed process against the defendant requiring it to appear at the fall term of the superior court, which convened on the first Monday in September, 1897.   It appears from a recital in the bill of exceptions that, " through inadvertence in the clerk's office, the petition having been mislaid, process was not attached until the 1st day of October, 1897," which process required the defendant to appear at the spring term, 1898, of said court, which convened on the first Monday in March.   It further appears that, without any order of the court, the clerk, on the first day of October, 1897, attached to the petition the process which required the defendant to appear and answer at the March term, 1898, and it also appears that service of the petition and this process was made on the 4th day of October, 1897, and thus the case stood until the 8th day of March, 1898, when the defendant filed a motion to vacate the service in said case.   At the hearing of this motion, the presiding judge intimated a doubt as to the authority of the clerk to have attached process in the absence of an order so to do.   Thereupon the plaintiff applied for an order making the spring term, 1899, which convened on the first Monday in March in that year, the return term of the case, and requiring process to be attached returnable to that term.   The order was granted, and original process bearing date January 18, 1899, was annexed to the petition, and service was perfected on the 21st of January, 1899.   After the grant of this order the case proceeded, and during the spring term, 1899, the defendant appeared and demurred to the plaintiff's petition, on the ground that the cause of action was barred, and on the hearing it was ordered by the court that the demurrer be sustained and the complaint dismissed ; and to this judgment the plaintiff excepted.

Inasmuch as the contract on which the suit was based carried with it a stipulation, binding upon both parties, that no suit or action on the contract should be sustained in any court unless commenced within twelve months next after the fire, the question arises for our consideration, whether or not, as a matter of law, the proceeding instituted and the action had thereon as above recited constituted a suit or action against the defendant. The plaintiff contends that the filing of her petition in the office of the clerk of the superior court was the commencement of the suit, and that the subsequent order of the court providing for original process returnable to the spring term, 1899, of Fulton superior court, and the service of the petition and copy process thereunder on the defendant, were legal and proper, and being so, the time of the commencement of such suit related back to the date of the filing of the petition, which was within one year from the date of the fire. So that, under her contention, if the court had authority to order the process making the spring term, 1899, the return term of the case, the petition should not have been dismissed. Section 4960 of the Civil Code requires that suits in the superior court shall be commenced by petition. Section 4974 provides that to every petition the clerk shall annex a process, etc., requiring the appearance of the defendant at the return term; while section 4973 provides that upon every petition the clerk shall indorse the date of its filing in office, which shall be considered the time of the commencement of the suit. In the case of *Cherry* v. *North & South Railroad*, 65 *Ga.* 633, 636, this court held that the provision which makes the filing of the petition with the clerk the commencement of the suit must be construed with kindred regulations for suits and the service thereof. So that it is not arbitrarily to be taken that the mere filing of a petition in the office of the clerk is the commencement of a suit. In the case of *McClendon* v. *Hernando Co.*, 100 *Ga.* 223, Mr. Justice Fish, in an able opinion, considered the provision of the code which declares that the date of the filing of the petition shall be considered the time of the commencement of the suit, and cited a number of authorities, both from this and other courts, to support, as a proper construction of that provision, the ruling made by this court in the case of *Ferguson* v. *New Manchester Mfg. Co.*, 51 *Ga.* 609, that "The filing of the declaration in the clerk's office, when service has been perfected as provided by law, will be considered as the commencement of the suit; but the mere filing of the declaration, without more, is not the commencement of a suit, without service on a defendant, as provided by law, of whom the court has jurisdiction." See, in this connection, *F. C. & P. R. Co.* v. *Ragan*, 104 *Ga.* 353.

But the plaintiff in error insists that the defect as to service was cured by the order granted in 1898 for process, and the subsequent service thereunder. It must be noted that no process whatever was attached to the petition in this case, which required the defendant to appear at the term to which the case was made returnable. Of course, the subsequent attachment of process after the return term, by the clerk on his own motion, amounts to nothing, because of an entire want of authority to do so. It is freely conceded that in cases where the process attached is irregular or defective, the same may be cured by amendment under the order of the judge; but the provisions of law which apply to the amendments of process do not obtain in a case where there is an entire absence of any original process. It is provided by section 4994 of the Civil Code that no technical or formal objections shall invalidate any petition or process, but if the same substantially conforms to the requisitions of the code, and the defendant has had notice of the pendency of the cause, all other objections shall be disregarded. But section 5109 of the same Code declares that "Void process, or where there is no process or waiver thereof, can not be amended." That is to say, that where there is no process nor any waiver there can be no amendment; and where there is an entire absence of process, another original process can not be substituted. And such was the ruling of this court in the case of *Scarborough* v. *Hall*, 67 *Ga.* 576, where it was held, "Where the clerk failed to attach any process to the declaration, and it was served alone, it was not competent to amend at a subsequent term by attaching process and ordering service." This ruling was affirmed in *Reese* v. *Kirby*, 68 *Ga.* 825.

Judgment affirmed. All the Justices concurring.

ANGIER *v.* EQUITABLE BUILDING AND LOAN ASSO.

109
f110
f111

1. Allegations in a petition relating to a written instrument executed by a defendant, or to his own actings and doings, are not, without some explanation of his alleged ignorance concerning the same, properly met by a general averment that for want of sufficient information he is unable either to admit or deny the paragraphs of the petition in which such allegations are set forth.
2. A mere written proposal to pay money, with no offer of the cash, is not a tender.
3. That the maker of a plain and unambiguous written contract with a corporation was induced to execute the same by false and fraudulent representations as to its methods of doing business, and as to the probable results of the transaction evidenced by such contract, is not a valid defense to an action thereon, when there is nothing to show that the maker was misled or deceived as to its contents or in any manner prevented from ascertaining the same.
4. Allegations in an answer setting up alleged rights under the by-laws of a corporation are incomplete, unless enough of such by-laws, either literally or in substance, be set out to enable the court to determine to what the defendant is entitled thereunder.
5. The questions in the present case not dealt with in the preceding notes were settled by the decision of this court in the case of *Cook* against the defendant in error, 104 *Ga.* 814.

Argued December 6, 1899. — Decided January 29, 1900.

Complaint. Before Judge Reid. City court of Atlanta. January 31, 1899.

A. R. Bryan and *Robert Zahner*, for plaintiff in error.
J. Howell Green, contra.

LUMPKIN, P. J.   The Equitable Building and Loan Association brought in proper form against Edgar A. Angier, one of its members, upon whose stock an advance had been made, an action for alleged breaches of a bond which he had executed and delivered to the plaintiff and which was of the character usually required in such cases.   He filed a voluminous answer, which was stricken on demurrer, and of this he complains in his bill of exceptions.   We will briefly state and dispose of the questions thus presented for our determination.

1. The petition alleged that Angier was a member of the association ; that, as such member, he owned eight shares of stock of a specified class, evidenced by a certificate ; that he

40

procured an advance of $800 upon this stock; that, to secure
the repayment of the advance, he hypothecated his eight shares
of stock to the association; and that, as further security, he
executed and delivered the bond sued on. The substance
of the bond was set forth in the petition, and a copy of the
same was attached as an exhibit. The 10th paragraph of the
petition was as follows: "That the by-laws of said association
provide that all members in arrears in payments on their stock
shall pay to said association a fine of ten cents per share on
each share of stock so in arrears, for each month of such arrears." The defendant in his answer averred that he could not,
for want of sufficient information, either admit or deny the
foregoing allegations, save only as to the fact that he received
the advance of $800, which was admitted. Certainly, this
much of the answer was without merit. As the allegations in
question related to a written instrument executed by himself
and to matters of which he must, in the nature of things, have
had personal knowledge, and as his answer set forth no explanation of his professed ignorance, the ruling of this court in
Smith v. *Champion*, 102 *Ga.* 92, is applicable and controlling
here. As will appear below, the defendant in portions of his
answer undertook to state what the by-laws of the association
contained with reference to certain matters, and it is therefore
difficult to perceive how he could have been lacking in information as to the truth or falsity of the statements made in the
10th paragraph of the petition. And it is proper to add that,
taking the answer as a whole, we do not understand how the
defendant could have failed to know all about the several matters above mentioned.

2. It was alleged in the answer that the defendant had made
a calculation from which it appeared that he owed the plaintiff
a specified amount, and that he addressed to the plaintiff a letter setting forth his calculation and containing the following:
"I only owe you a balance of $331.46, which I herewith tender
you, and you may consider it a continuing tender." The trial
judge held that this was not a good plea of tender, and we agree
with him. The answer did not allege that any money accompanied the letter, or that the word "herewith" really meant to

signify that the cash was enclosed. There was nothing more than a bare offer or proposition to pay. Nothing was in fact tendered. "A proposition to pay and a tender are by no means the same thing. The former may exist without any element of the latter." McCay, J., in *Sharpe* v. *Kennedy*, 51 *Ga.* 263.

3. In the bond declared upon the contract between the parties is plainly and unambiguously set forth. The defendant in several paragraphs of his answer sought to avoid the contract by alleging that, "to the best of his recollection and belief," the plaintiff (probably meaning some agent of the plaintiff) made to him false representations (which are set forth in detail) as to how the association was operated, what payments he would have to make, what credits he would receive, how his transaction with the plaintiff would result, etc., etc.; that these representations were fraudulent; that they were made for the purpose of deceiving the defendant, and did deceive and mislead him into making the contract. Such allegations of fraud are too loose and general, and, moreover, they do not even suggest a reason why the defendant might not have fully informed himself of the exact nature of the bond he was asked to sign. Had he done so, he would have been sufficiently informed of what he undertook and promised to do when he executed it. There was no averment of misrepresentation as to the character of the bond or of any fraud whereby the defendant was prevented from ascertaining its contents before signing the same. If he was in fact defrauded, it was simply because he did not take reasonable precautions to ascertain what he was doing. *Jossey* v. *Railway Co.*, ante, 439.

4. Another defense which the defendant sought to set up was, that under the by-laws of the association he was entitled to specified credits. In a special ground of the demurrer the point was made that the answer should set forth the portion or portions of the by-laws relied on to support this defense. The trial judge rightly held that this point was good. Certainly, it was incumbent on the defendant to set forth, either literally or in substance, enough of the alleged by-laws to enable the court to determine what were his rights thereunder. It seems that the by-laws were accessible to him; but, though the judge allowed

him additional time to cure the defectiveness of his answer in the respect here pointed out, he did not offer to amend.

5. In numerous paragraphs of the answer the defendant alleged that the plaintiff was not a building and loan association pure and simple, but a complex corporation having under its charter divers rights, powers, and franchises (the particulars as to which were set forth), which took it out of the class of institutions whose contracts exacting more than eight per cent. for the use of money were protected under the laws peculiar to building and loan associations proper. In this connection the defense of usury was set up. There was not, however, in the entire answer any distinct and unequivocal averment that the plaintiff was engaged in any business inconsistent with that of a building and loan association whose contracts, under the doctrine of mutuality, are saved from the taint of usury. There are some allegations which seem to mean that the plaintiff had in its operations gone beyond the scope of such an association, but on close inspection we find that the fact that it has actually done so is not alleged. On this branch of the case, therefore, it is controlled by the decision of this court in *Cook v. Equitable Building & Loan Assn.*, 104 *Ga.* 814. And see *Burns v. Same*, 108 *Ga.* 181.

There are some other questions in this case, but none of them are new. Indeed, they have been heretofore made and ruled upon in other cases decided by this court. It would not be profitable to restate and again discuss them. The answer, taken all together, set up no lawful ground of defense to the plaintiff's action, and the demurrer was properly sustained.

Judgment affirmed. All the Justices concurring.

SCHMITT *v.* SCHNEIDER.

A woman who cohabitated with a man, rendered to him household services, and delivered to him her earnings, under the belief, induced by his fraud, that the contract of cohabitation between them was the equivalent of a lawful marriage, could not, upon ascertaining that such was not the fact, maintain against him an equitable petition to compel a division with her of property acquired with the proceeds of the earnings of both; nor could such a petition, when its manifest and only purpose was to obtain relief of the nature just indicated, be treated as an action of assumpsit entitling the plaintiff to a money verdict, merely because it contained some allegations showing a money liability by the defendant to the plaintiff and a prayer for general relief.

Argued December 6, 1899. — Decided January 29, 1900.

Equitable petition. Before Judge Lumpkin. Fulton superior court. March term, 1899.

Thomas L. Bishop, E. Winn Born, and *J. A. Hunt,* for plaintiff. *David Eichberg* and *Rosser & Carter* for defendants.

LUMPKIN, P. J.   A petition was filed by Wilhelmina Schmitt, in the superior court of Fulton county, against J. T. Schneider, the Maddox–Rucker Banking Company, the Citizens Loan & Building Company, and certain named individuals. Upon a demurrer filed by Schneider, the petition was dismissed, and the plaintiff excepted. In some way not distinctly disclosed by the record brought to this court, the other defendants were eliminated from the litigation. It is inferable that as to them the petition was voluntarily dismissed. At any rate, the only question argued here was whether or not the petition set forth a cause of action against Schneider, and we shall accordingly deal with this question only. In brief, the petition made the following case: Many years ago, the plaintiff and the defendant both resided in the City of New York, she then having a living husband and he a living wife from whom he had separated. They met and "became infatuated with each other." He falsely represented to her that he had been divorced from his wife. They entered into an agreement to be married as soon as her husband died or she obtained a divorce from him. Meanwhile, she was to keep house for Schneider and take care of his two minor children, who were the offspring of his marriage with the deserted wife. They resided together on these terms for some months in New York, and then moved to Ohio, where for a number of years they sustained similar relations until the death of the plaintiff's husband. They then agreed to live together and cohabit as man and wife, and made a contract to this effect, the defendant falsely and fraudulently rep-

resenting, and she believing, that a formal marriage ceremony
was not necessary and that the agreement in question constituted a valid marriage under the laws of Ohio.   Finally they
moved to Atlanta, and some time after arriving in that city the
plaintiff, for reasons set forth, became aware that the alleged
Ohio marriage was not valid, and therefore she requested the
defendant to have a lawful marriage ceremony performed between them.   He refused and she insisted, and at length he informed her that he could not marry her without committing
bigamy, for the reason that he had never been really divorced
from his wife in New York.   She then separated from him, and
has not since cohabited with him.   During the years she lived
with the defendant she rendered him services of a stated monthly
value as housekeeper and in conducting a boarding-house and
rearing and caring for his children, etc., etc.   She also turned
over to him nearly all the money, amounting to a specified
amount per month, which she earned in her profession of nurse
and midwife.   In rendering the services mentioned and delivering to the defendant her money, she fully believed she was his
lawful wife.   From his own earnings and with her means and
assistance he has accumulated considerable property and now
has a named sum deposited with the Maddox – Rucker Banking
Company ; also, stock to a specified amount in the Loan & Building Company, and promissory notes for divers sums mentioned,
executed by the individuals named as codefendants, and secured
by mortgages on realty.   All this property and other assets in
the name of the defendant Schneider were "derived from the
proceeds of the earnings of this plaintiff and of said defendant
jointly."   "She has for all of these years been living with him
in absolute ignorance of the fact [that he was never divorced
from his wife], and now claims that by reason of the fraud he
practiced upon her and his misrepresentations that she is entitled to share in the property owned and held in his name, and
in equity and in good conscience the court should decree that
equal division thereof should be made between them."   The
prayers of the petition were: (1) for process against all the defendants;   (2) that J. T. Schneider be enjoined "from transferring, using, encumbering, or otherwise intermeddling with any

of his assets or property, as hereinbefore specifically set out or otherwise, until the further order of this court;" (3) "that a receiver be appointed to take charge of, preserve, and hold the assets upon which this plaintiff makes claim, that the same may be properly divided when final judgment is rendered in this case;" (4) that the Banking Company and the Loan & Building Company, as well as each of the individuals named as mortgagors, be enjoined "from paying to the said J. T. Schneider, his agents or attorneys, transferees or assigns, anything or any money in their possession, or anything or money upon the said mortgage debts, as set out in this complaint, until the further order of the court;" (5) that the costs of this case be adjudged against J. T. Schneider; and (6) for general relief.

Taking into view all of the above allegations and prayers, it is clear that the scheme of the petition was to obtain an accounting from Schneider and a division in kind of property alleged to belong jointly to him and the plaintiff. Her object seems to have been to obtain a winding up and settlement of a quasi partnership between them, having its origin in the relations they had sustained towards each other during the years of their cohabitation. Manifestly, in this view of the petition, it was without equity or merit. There was no actual partnership, of course; nor did any trust in the property acquired by Schneider arise for the benefit of the plaintiff. She gave him no money to invest for her individual use, nor was there any undertaking or promise on his part, express or implied, to invest for her or allow her any interest whatever in his accumulations. For her services and for her money which went into his hands he may be liable to pay; but the only relation which could, relatively to these matters, arise between them is that of debtor and creditor. That he may have perpetrated a fraud upon her gives her no title, legal or equitable, to property acquired by him in his own right, although it may have been purchased with his ill-gotten gains; for, to compensate a person upon whom a fraud has been committed, the law affords full relief by providing for the recovery of damages. In this connection, the case of *Millirons* v. *Dillon*, 100 *Ga.* 656, is quite pertinent. Counsel for the plaintiff recognized the soundness of the views just stated, and, in support of the petition, argued here that it was good solely upon the idea that it contained enough to entitle the plaintiff to a money judgment against Schneider. We do not think the petition maintainable upon this theory. In the first place, it is not a petition to recover an alleged indebtedness by the defendant to the plaintiff, or one for the recovery of damages. It is a petition of a totally different character and for an entirely different purpose, as has been shown. There is no allegation that the defendant is indebted to the plaintiff in any amount, and there is no prayer for a money judgment. It was earnestly insisted, nevertheless, that as the facts alleged showed a money liability, the prayer for general relief was sufficient to support a verdict and judgment for money. Even if by a strain (and it would require a great one) we could hold that the allegations of the petition gave it a standing in court as an action of assumpsit, or for damages resulting from fraud and deceit, it would have to fall for want of an appropriate prayer on that line. A prayer for general relief is good for much, but not for everything. "Where there is a special prayer and a general prayer, the complainant under the general prayer may have such other relief only as is consistent with the case made in the bill and with the special prayer." *Butler* v. *Durham*, 2 *Ga.* 414. "A prayer for general relief, in addition to specific prayers, in a bill in equity, will only warrant the granting relief pertinent to the case made by the bill." *Peek* v. *Wright*, 65 *Ga.* 638. The following, taken from the opinion of this court in *Empire Hotel Co.* v. *Main*, 98 *Ga.* 183, 184, is also applicable here: "A prayer for general relief covers much, but it can hardly be extended so as to authorize relief of an entirely independent nature from that specifically prayed for and forming the basis upon which the plaintiff's petition was framed." What was said in *Tompkins* v. *Cooper*, 97 *Ga.* 631, as to the scope of a prayer for general relief was simply a statement concerning the practice prevailing in Alabama in a particular class of cases, and moreover is, we think, perfectly consistent with the rule announced in the above-quoted extracts. On the whole, therefore, we are very well satisfied that the court below was right in dismissing the present case. *Judgment affirmed. All the Justices concurring.*

TURNER *v.* FULTON COUNTY.

1. There was not, prior to 1899, any law in this State which authorized county authorities to employ and pay a person for services as an inspector of roads and bridges.
2. The validity of the recent act on this subject is not involved in this case.

Argued December 7, 1899. — Decided January 29, 1900.

Complaint. Before Judge Lumpkin. Fulton superior court. March term, 1899.

This was an action against the county upon an account for work done by the plaintiff as "county inspector of roads and bridges," for a specified number of days in 1896 and 1897, at $2 per day. The case was tried upon an agreed statement of facts, from which it appeared that the commissioners of roads and revenues of the county employed the plaintiff as inspector of roads and bridges, and that the work referred to was necessary and worth $2 per day, and was done under an agreement that he was to be paid for it at that rate. The sole question at issue was whether the commissioners had authority to employ an inspector of roads and bridges for the county and pay him from the county treasury. The court directed a verdict for the defendant.

Frank A. Arnold, for plaintiff.
Luther Z. Rosser, for defendant.

SIMMONS, C. J. 1. Under the facts disclosed by the record, there was no error in directing a verdict for the defendant in this case. Whoever has a claim or demand against a county or city and brings suit thereon must show some law authorizing the county or city to pay the demand; otherwise he can not recover. We have searched diligently the code of this State and the acts of the legislature creating the board of county commissioners of Fulton county, and can find no law which directly or indirectly authorized the county commissioners of roads and revenues to employ and pay the plaintiff as an inspector of roads and bridges. The power to tax for county purposes is limited by the constitution (Civil Code, § 5892), and there is nothing in the constitutional provision which would authorize the county authorities to levy a tax to pay for the inspection of roads and bridges.   We are aware that in a great many of the counties of this State the county authorities do not adhere strictly to this provision.   A great many county and municipal authorities appropriate the public money to purposes not authorized by law.   Demands of this nature are not good as against the county or city.   In the present case, the employment of the plaintiff as an inspector of roads and bridges was certainly not authorized by any law on the statute books in this State.   The very duties which he alleges he performed had already been placed by law upon the road commissioners of the different districts of the county.   Political Code, § 589.   If he was one of those "inspectors of roads and bridges" who appear, in *Collier v. Elliott,* 100 *Ga.* 363, to have performed the duties of county police, then, under that decision, he was clearly not entitled to receive compensation from the county.   There being no law authorizing the commissioners to employ him or to pay him, his suit against the county must necessarily fail.   It was argued, however, by his counsel that it would be a great hardship upon the plaintiff to lose the value of his labor for the time for which he had worked for the county.   That may be, and doubtless is, true; but one who contracts with county or other public officers is bound to know their power and authority to contract.   If they have no power to make the contract, and if he performs the work thereunder, he can not look to the public funds for payment.

2. The services for which the plaintiff sued were rendered prior to the year 1899, and the case must, of course, be decided with reference to the law as it existed at that time.   We were requested by counsel to consider and pass upon the validity of the act of 1899 on this subject, but, as it is not in any way involved in the present case, it would obviously be improper for us to do so.

Judgment affirmed.   *All the Justices concurring.*

ENGLISH *et al. v.* S. P. RICHARDS COMPANY.

1. The petition set forth a cause of action against the demurring defendants, and alleged such performance on the part of the plaintiff, accepted by these defendants, in accordance with the contract sued upon, as took the contract out of the provision of the statute requiring a promise to answer for the debt of another to be in writing.

2. There was no error in overruling the ground of the demurrer, which was filed by two of the defendants, that the petition showed that the debt sued on was the individual indebtedness of another of the defendants, for the payment of which he had given the plaintiff his written obligation.

Argued December 8, 1899. — Decided January 29, 1900.

Complaint. Before Judge Lumpkin. Fulton superior court. March term, 1899.

Daley & Hall, for plaintiffs in error.
Lumpkin & Colquitt, contra.

Fish, J. The S. P. Richards Company brought suit against Harry L. English, W. E. Venable, W. H. Williams, and the Atlanta Soda Company, for the sum of $110.00. The petition made the following case: The plaintiff was the owner of a soda-fountain, which it had leased to Shropshire & Colyar, to be operated by them at No. 60 Whitehall street, in the city of Atlanta. English, Venable, and the Atlanta Soda Company operated two soda-fountains near said location, the business and trade of which was interfered with by the competition of the fountain operated by Shropshire & Colyar. They, therefore, wanted to get control of the latter fountain, move it to some other locality, and put Williams in charge of it. "Shropshire & Colyar were behind in the payment of the rent" for the plaintiff's fountain, "in the sum of $110.00, and were not willing to deliver said fount to petitioner," unless the plaintiff "should release them from paying the said $110.00." English, Venable, Williams, and the Atlanta Soda Company, to induce the plaintiff to get possession of said fountain at once and lease the same to Williams, each and all, promised and agreed to pay the plaintiff said sum due by Shropshire & Colyar. "Because of said promises and agreements, petitioner, to get the immediate possession of said fount, released said

Shropshire & Colyar from their lease contract and the payment
of the said $110.00, . . got possession of said fount, and
leased and delivered the same to W. H. Williams under a
lease contract," a copy of which was attached to the petition,
and Williams was in possession thereof and he and Venable
were operating it in another part of the city. The agreement
of English, Venable, and the Atlanta Soda Company with the
plaintiff, to pay the $110.00, was verbal, and the agreement
of Williams to pay the same was in writing and included in
his lease contract. In the written contract of lease between
the plaintiff and Williams, which was attached as an exhibit
to the petition, it appeared that Williams leased the soda-foun-
tain for five years, at twenty-five dollars per month, and, among
other things, obligated himself to pay the plaintiff "the sum of
$110.00 back rent due them by J. S. Colyar, this amount to be
paid before the apparatus is moved from its present position."
Two of the defendants, English and the Atlanta Soda Company,
demurred to the petition upon the following grounds: "1. Because said petition sets out no cause of action against these defendants.   2. Because the indebtedness alleged to be due is
shown by said petition to be an indebtedness claimed by the
plaintiff as due to it by Shropshire & Colyar, and it is not claimed
in said petition that these defendants assumed said indebtedness, and promised to pay the same, in writing, and these defendants are not bound therefor, in law.   3. Because said petition shows that the indebtedness sued on is the individual indebtedness of one W. H. Williams, which said Williams had
obligated himself to pay to the plaintiff by making a written
contract with the plaintiff therefor. A copy of said written contract between the plaintiff and the said Williams is attached to
said petition, and shows upon its face that these defendants are
not parties thereto nor bound thereby." The demurrer was
overruled, and English and the Atlanta Soda Company excepted.

1. It is clear to us that the petition set forth a cause of action
against English and the Atlanta Soda Company, and such performance on the part of the plaintiff of the conditions upon
which their parol promise was based as to take such promise
out of the statute of frauds. According to the allegations of

the petition, there was not only part but complete performance on the part of the plaintiff of these conditions. The consideration for the promise of the defendants to pay to the plaintiff the $110.00 due to the plaintiff by Shropshire & Colyar was, that the plaintiff should get Shropshire & Colyar to surrender their lease of the soda-fountain and, after obtaining possession of the fountain, lease the same to Williams, who would move it to and operate it in a locality where it would not compete with the fountains of the defendants, English, Venable, and the Atlanta Soda Company. The plaintiff did obtain a surrender of the lease from Shropshire & Colyar, got possession of the soda fountain, and leased it to Williams, who moved it to a different part of the city, where he and Venable, another of the defendants, are operating it. In order to procure from Shropshire & Colyar a surrender of the lease which they held upon the fountain, it was necessary for the plaintiff to release them from all liability for the unpaid rent, which amounted to $110.00. This the plaintiff did, upon the faith of the promise of the defendants to pay this indebtedness. The plaintiff released its original debtors and accepted in their stead the defendants, who, to subserve their own interests, assumed the obligation. Shall the plaintiff now, after having fully complied with the conditions upon which the defendants assumed this debt and having released its original debtors, be denied the right to enforce the debt against the defendants? To state the proposition is to answer it. Taking the allegations of the petition to be true, there has not only been such performance on the part of the plaintiff as would render it a fraud of the parties refusing to comply, if the court did not compel a performance on their part, but there has been performance on the side of the plaintiff, accepted by the defendants, in accordance with the contract. Clearly, then, the statute of frauds does not prevent the promise of the defendants from being binding upon and enforceable against them. Civil Code, § 2694.

2. We do not think there is any merit in the third ground of the demurrer. The petition clearly shows that the promise upon which the defendants other than Williams were sued was their parol promise to pay to the plaintiff the debt due it

by Shropshire & Colyar. There is no effort to make the other
defendants parties to or liable upon the written contract of
Williams to pay the same debt, and the rule relied upon by
counsel for plaintiffs in error, that a written contract can not be
added to or taken from by parol evidence is not applicable.

Judgment affirmed. All the Justices concurring.

HUFF *v.* DONEHOO *et al.* (two cases.)

1. Persons through whose land a proposed new public road will not run are
not entitled to the written notice prescribed in section 522 of the Political Code.
2. Owners of realty abutting upon an existing public road are not entitled to
damages alleged to have been occasioned by the establishment of a new
public road which does not touch their premises; and this is true though
the order for laying out the new road may have been granted upon an
application for an alteration of an old road, if as matter of fact the portion of the latter running by or through the property of such owners is
by the express terms of such order left open and provision is therein made
for keeping the same in repair.
3. Whether or not the law is strictly followed by county authorities in establishing a new public road is a matter of no concern to persons who
merely seek as "injured property owners" to obtain damages alleged to
have been thus occasioned, and who do not appear as taxpayers endeavoring to keep such authorities within the bounds of their legal duties.

Argued December 9, 1899. — Decided January 29, 1900.

Certiorari. Before Judge Lumpkin. Fulton superior court.
March term, 1899.

W. J. Speairs and *E. M. & G. F. Mitchell*, for plaintiffs in error.
Rosser & Carter, contra.

LUMPKIN, P. J. These cases were argued together, and will
be disposed of in like manner. Without setting forth the facts
embraced in the voluminous records in which the few material
questions are buried, we will simply remark that we have un-
earthed them and that our rulings thereon are stated in the
headnotes.

1. When proceedings are had by county authorities for opening a new road, the only persons entitled to the written notice
prescribed by section 522 of the Political Code are those "re-

siding on land which such road goes through," who are not applicants therefor, and their overseers or agents. This is what the section plainly says, and its manifest object is to give owners of realty whose property is to be taken for a new road a fair opportunity to present their claims for damages, if they desire to do so. Even if other persons are in any way injuriously affected by the establishment of a new road, the law does not contemplate that they shall have the notice provided for in this section.

2. Landowners whose premises abut upon an existing public road are not, in legal contemplation, entitled to damages because of the establishment of a new public road which does not touch their lands, if the old road be left open and provision be made for keeping it in repair. Were it otherwise, there would be, in many if not in most instances, great difficulty, expense, and embarrassment in opening a new road, however much the public necessities might demand it. It makes no difference that an application to the county authorities may pray for an "alteration" of an old road, if in fact the action taken thereon be as above indicated. The result in such a case is really the establishment of a new road with no discontinuance of the old one. The law is not much concerned about forms or names. It looks to the substance of things and the results accomplished. It is true that in *Ponder* v. *Shannon*, 54 *Ga.* 187, it was held that "the alteration of an old road involves the discontinuance of that part thereof which is altered." This may be strictly true, but if an application for "alteration" actually results in the establishment of a new road under an order expressly providing that a specified portion of the old road shall *not* be discontinued, there is certainly no discontinuance as to that portion, and the landowners whose property abuts upon it are not, in a legal sense, injured. In *Cotting* v. *Culpepper*, 79 *Ga.* 792, the order of the county commissioners actually contemplated a discontinuance of a part of the old road, and therefore, as to the question we have just been discussing, the case is not in point. It is, however, at least persuasive authority for the proposition that "the county commissioners are not bound to follow the recommendation of the road commissioners, but may, in their judg-

ment, adopt a different scheme or plan from that reported," that is, may decline altogether to alter, but, instead, establish a new road for a given distance and leave the old one intact. If every landowner could claim damages for a diminution in the market value of his property, incidentally occasioned by the laying out of a new public road which merely attracted travel from the road running by or through his land and which was itself kept open as before, endless and grievous burdens would be imposed upon our taxpayers. To allow such damages would be stretching the constitutional clause prohibiting the damaging of private property for public purposes without compensation to an extent never dreamed of by the wise men who framed our organic law.

3. Even if the provisions of the code were not strictly followed in the present instance, it was a matter of no concern to the plaintiffs in error. They were not seeking as taxpayers to keep the county commissioners within the bounds of their legal duties, but in the capacity of "injured property owners," as alleged, were endeavoring to obtain damages which they claimed they had sustained for the public good. They were not entitled to such damages, and therefore had no right to complain of the action taken by the county commissioners. See, in this connection, *Keen* v. *Waycross*, 101 *Ga.* 588, 592.

Judgment in each case affirmed. All the Justices concurring.

CONLEY *et al. v.* REDWINE *et al.*

1. Though notice of a sheriff's sale be published once a week for four successive weeks before the day of sale, the advertisement will not meet the requirements of the law if the last publication be made in the same week as that in which the sale is to be had. Where four publications only are made, each must be in a separate week, and each must precede in point of time the week embracing the day of sale. The decision of this court in *Bird* v. *Burgsteiner*, 100 *Ga.* 486, construed in the light of its facts, does not conflict with what is here laid down, and the language in the opinion which seems to indicate the contrary was obiter.

2. Where, however, the purchaser at a sheriff's sale has no knowledge or notice of insufficiency in the sheriff's advertisement, he will be protected, although he be the plaintiff in execution. It does not in this case appear that the purchasers had such notice.

3. A sheriff's sale under a dormant execution is void, and, being a mere nullity, presents no obstacle to a sale of the same property on the same day under a valid execution.

4. There was no error in explaining to the jury the history and nature of the case as it appeared from the uncontradicted evidence and the pleadings, the more especially when the judge went no further than was essential to a clear understanding of the issues involved at the trial.

5. Contiguous parcels of land forming one entire tract may be levied on and sold as one tract, although the same be composed of fractional parts of different land lots.

6. While the rights of one entitled to the balance of the proceeds of a sheriff's sale after the satisfaction of the lien under which the sale took place should not be prejudiced by the misconduct of a stranger in deterring bidders, yet if it appeared that the person first referred to really acquiesced in such conduct and sought to prevent the property from bringing its full value, such person would not, because of the mere misconduct of the stranger, have the right to invalidate or set aside the sale.

7. The mere fact that a principal and agent bid against each other at a sheriff's sale, though their purpose in so doing was to deter other bidders and get the property at less than its value, would not, in the absence of some proof that the price was really affected by such conduct, be cause for setting the sale aside.

8. There is no error in requiring counsel to confine his argument to the facts and issues involved in the case.

9. The fact that a sheriff's sale embraced a parcel of land belonging to a third person is not a ground for setting the sale aside at the instance of the defendant in execution or one entitled to the balance of the proceeds of the sale after the execution was satisfied.

10. Though a tract of land had in fact been laid off into streets and town lots, yet where there were no visible marks on the surface of the tract to indicate the metes and bounds of the lots, and the only thing in the nature of a street appearing thereon was a recognized public road of the county, a levy upon and sale of the entire tract as one parcel was proper and legal.

11. An entry of levy embracing a description of the property levied on, which of itself is insufficient to locate the same, and referring for a more accurate description to a public record, is sufficient as to matter of description if the property is accurately described in such public record.

12. The charge of the court was full, fair, and explicit. The evidence amply warranted the verdict; and no error was committed during the progress of the trial which would require a reversal of the judgment refusing to grant a new trial.

Argued December 19, 1899. — Decided January 29, 1900.

Equitable petition. Before Judge Lumpkin. Fulton superior court. March term, 1899.

A. A. Manning and *T. P. Westmoreland*, for plaintiffs in error. *Arnold & Arnold* and *Rosser & Carter*, contra.

41

COBB, J.   This case brings under review another phase of a controversy which has been before this court in various shapes and at several different times.   See *Conley* v. *Thornton*, 81 *Ga.* 154; *Conley* v. *State*, 83 *Ga.* 496; *Conley* v. *State*, 85 *Ga.* 348; *Conley* v. *Maher*, 93 *Ga.* 781; *Conley* v. *Arnold*, 93 *Ga.* 823; *Conley* v. *Buck*, 100 *Ga.* 187; *Conley* v. *Buck*, 102 *Ga.* 752; *Conley* v. *Redwine*, 103 *Ga.* 569.   The history of the litigation in all of its phases leading up to the present controversy will be found in the cases cited above, and it is unnecessary to repeat it here.   The pleadings in the present case brought before the court two sheriff's sales of the same property.   The first was had under an execution in favor of D. P. Hill, as executor of Wade Hill, against John L. Conley, and the second was under an execution in favor of Thornton, then controlled by Buck, against John L. Conley.   Redwine, the original plaintiff and the purchaser at the second sale, brought his petition praying that the first sale be set aside.   The wife of John L. Conley, who claimed the property under a deed from her husband, was a defendant in this proceeding, and she by answer in the nature of a cross-bill set up that she was the purchaser under the first sale and prayed that the same be confirmed and that the sale to Redwine be set aside.   At the trial it was conceded that the first sale was void, and therefore the only question for decision was whether the second sale was valid.   The trial resulted in a verdict in favor of Redwine, and Mrs. Conley's motion for a new trial being overruled, she excepted.

1. It was insisted that the sheriff's sale at which Redwine became the purchaser was void, because the sale was not advertised according to law.   The advertisement was published four times in the newspaper, to wit, on Monday, March 15, Monday, March 22, Monday, March 29, and Monday, April 5.   The sale was had on Tuesday, April 6.   Section 5457 of the Civil Code provides that notices of all sales by the sheriff shall be published weekly for four weeks; and section 5458, which embodies an act passed in 1891, provides that it shall be sufficient and legal to publish the notice "once a week for four weeks (that is, one insertion each week for each of the four weeks) immediately preceding the . . day when the . . sale is to take place;

and the number of days between the date of the first publication, and the . . day when the . . sale [is] to take place, whether more or less than thirty days, shall not in any manner invalidate or render irregular the . . advertisement or order of sale." Prior to the passage of the act of 1891, when the law required sheriff's sales to be advertised for four weeks, it was held that the word "week" meant a period of time consisting of seven days, and that to comply with the law it was necessary that twenty-eight days should elapse between the date of the first advertisement and the date of the sale; and that this lapse of time was sufficient whether four complete calendar weeks were embraced therein or not. *Boyd* v. *McFarlin*, 58 *Ga.* 208; *Bird* v. *Burgsteiner*, 100 *Ga.* 486. As was said by Mr. Justice Little in the opinion in the case last cited, "This was the law, as construed, at the time the act of 1891 was passed, and that act was intended to change existing law, so that if a notice of such sale should be made once a week for four weeks, such advertisement would be sufficient, without reference to the number of days which might so elapse. In ascertaining the legislative intent as expressed by the act, we are bound to conclude also that the week of seven days was not intended to be taken as the period in which one publication only of the notice must necessarily be made, because such was the statute as interpreted by the court at the time of the passage of the act; hence the act, in referring to the publication to be made once a week for four weeks, means a calendar week, and if notice shall be made on any day of a calendar week, that shall be counted as a publication for that week," etc. That the act of 1891 intended that the notice in any one calendar week should be a notice for the week is undoubtedly true, but this was not all that that act required. The notice must be at some time in the week, and there must be four calendar weeks in each of which there is a publication of the notice of sale preceding the day of sale. The act declares in terms that there must be "one insertion each week for each of the four weeks immediately preceding" the day when the sale is to take place. The week in which the sale takes place is certainly not a week "preceding" the day on which the sale takes place; and it would therefore follow that the notice published in such week could not be counted as one of the four insertions necessary to a compliance with the statute. Under this construction of the law a period of at least twenty-four days must elapse between the date of the first insertion and the date of the sale. If the first insertion is on Saturday and the subsequent insertions on any given day of the three following weeks, the period of twenty-four days elapses between the two. To illustrate: If a sale was to take place on Tuesday, February 6, the first notice would have to be inserted on Saturday, January 13. Insertions January 13, 20, 27, and February 3 would be a compliance with the law. If an insertion on a day embraced within the week of sale was allowable, a sale could be had after the lapse of seventeen days from the first insertion. For instance, if a sale was to take place on February 6, insertions could be made on January 20, 27, February 3 and 5. Such is not our understanding of the law. It appears in *Bird* v. *Burgsteiner*, supra, that twenty-six days elapsed between the first insertion and the date of sale, and that there were four calendar weeks preceding the day of sale, in each of which notice of the sale had been published. The question now under consideration was not involved at all in that case, and any language in the opinion which conflicts with what we now rule is, therefore, not binding as authority.

2. If what has been said is a correct construction of the act of 1891, it follows that the sale at which Redwine was the purchaser was not properly advertised, for the reason that there were not four insertions in four consecutive weeks immediately preceding the week in which the sale took place. The next question to be considered is, whether or not this defect was such as to render the sale void, or simply an irregularity which would not affect the title of the purchaser, who had no actual notice of the same. In the case of *Sullivan* v. *Hernden*, 11 *Ga.* 294, it was held, that if the sheriff has authority to sell property, a failure in the performance of any duty, for which he would be compelled to indemnify the owner for the injury received, would not destroy the title of an innocent purchaser. In *Brooks* v. *Rooney*, 11 *Ga.* 423, it was ruled, that the purchaser at a sheriff's sale depends upon the "judgment, the levy, and the deed; all other questions are between parties to the

judgment and the officer;" it being sufficient for the purchaser that the sheriff had obtained authority to sell and had executed to him a title. It was further ruled in that case, that an act which made it the duty of the sheriff to advertise the sale of property in a particular way, and to sell between certain hours of the day, was merely directory to the officer; the effect of his neglect being to subject him to a suit for damages at the instance of the party injured, but not to affect the title of the purchaser, unless there was collusion between him and the sheriff. Also, that a purchaser at a sheriff's sale has a right to presume that a public officer, known to possess the power to. sell, has taken every previous step required of him by the law under which he sells. To the same effect are the following: *Hendrick* v. *Davis*, 27 *Ga.* 167; *Johnson* v. *Reese*, 28 *Ga.* 353. See also, in this connection, *Johnson* v. *Reese*, 31 *Ga.* 601; *Solomon* v. *Peters*, 37 *Ga.* 251; *Wallace* v. *Trustees*, 52 *Ga.* 167; *Jeffries* v. *Bartlett*, 75 *Ga.* 230; Maddox *v.* Sullivan, 2 Rich. Eq. 4, s. c. 44 Am. D. 234; Burton *v.* Spiers, 92 N. C. 503; Frink *v.* Roe, 70 Cal. 296; Ware *v.* Bradford, 2 Ala. (N. S.) 676; 12 Am. & Eng. Enc. L. (1st ed.) 210 (note 6). Mr. Freeman in his work on Executions says: "Concerning execution sales, on the other hand, and in the absence of any statute establishing a rule upon the subject, there are some *dicta* and a few decisions indicating that the existence of a notice of sale is essential to its validity. But a very decided preponderance of the authorities maintains this proposition: that the statutes requiring notice of the sale to be given are directory merely, and that the failure to give such notice can not avoid the sale against any purchaser not himself in fault." 2 Freeman, Executions, 953, § 286. The rule is thus stated in the Civil Code: "The purchaser at judicial sales is not bound to look to the appropriation of the proceeds of the sale, nor to the returns made by the officer, nor is he required to see that the officer has complied fully with all those regulations prescribed in such cases. All such irregularities create questions and liabilities between the officer and parties interested in the sale. The innocent purchaser is bound only to see that the officer has competent authority to sell, and that he is apparently proceeding to sell under the prescribed forms."

Civil Code, § 5455.   It is therefore the settled law of this State, that a defect in the advertisement is a mere irregularity and does not affect the validity of a sheriff's sale made to an innocent purchaser.   This does not conflict with the ruling made in the case of *Williams* v. *Barlow*, 49 *Ga.* 530.   In that case the property was advertised for the December sales, and was not sold until the first Tuesday in January.   No other inference can be drawn from the language of Chief Justice Warner in that case than that the purchaser knew at the time of the sale that the property had not been advertised according to law. Neither is the case of *Ansley* v. *Wilson*, 50 *Ga.* 418, in conflict with the present ruling, for the reason that that was a municipal tax sale and the requirements of the charter had not been complied with.   The same is true of the case of *Sawyer* v. *Cargile*, 72 *Ga.* 290.   But even conceding, for the sake of the argument, that the three case just cited are in conflict with those cited above, the earlier decisions, never having been brought under review and expressly overruled, are controlling notwithstanding the subsequent contradictory rulings.

The next question to be considered is, whether the plaintiff in execution can, when he has no actual notice of the irregularity, be said to occupy the position of an innocent purchaser. This question is answered by the ruling made in the case of *Humphrey* v. *McGill*, 59 *Ga.* 649, where it was ruled :   "Where a plaintiff in fi. fa. purchases at the sale of property under his execution, he stands upon the same footing as any other purchaser, in respect to irregularities of the sheriff in levying, advertising, and selling.   If he purchases without notice of these irregularities, he acquires a good title."   Rulings to the same effect were made by the Supreme Court of New York and the Court of Appeals of that State.   Wood *v.* Moorhouse, 1 Lans. 405, 45 N. Y. 368.   The sale in the present case was not void, therefore, whether we treat Redwine as purchasing in his individual capacity or as agent for Arnold and Buck; there being no evidence in the record that this irregularity was known to Arnold, Buck, Redwine, or Curran, the agent of Redwine who made the bid.   The case of *Forbes* v. *Hall*, 102 *Ga.* 47, is not in conflict with this ruling.   While the purchaser there was the attorney for the plaintiff in execution, the sale was not declared void on account of any irregularity, but for the reason that the levy was excessive and therefore void. Such a levy is no authority to sell, and therefore it is immaterial who is the purchaser; he gets no title.

3. The sale under the execution of D. P. Hill was void for the reason that the execution was dormant; and counsel for Mrs. Conley contended in the court below, as well as in this court, that as the sale was made under the forms of law, it was, although void, such an obstacle to another sale that it should be set aside by a direct proceeding before another sale could be had. This contention can not be maintained. A void sale is no sale, and can never be an obstacle in the way of a legal sale. The plaintiffs in execution in the second sale had no connection with the void sale, and did not bring it about for the purpose of deterring bidders and affecting the price of the property at their sale; and hence under no view of the case did it present any obstacle to the consummation of that sale. See *Davis* v. *Comer*, 108 *Ga.* 117.

4. Complaint is made that the judge erred in giving to the jury in his charge a history of the litigation prior to the present trial, between Thornton, Buck, and Maher on the one side and John L. Conley on the other. It appears from a note by the judge to the ground of the motion containing this assignment of error, that this history was derived from the pleadings in the case and from uncontradicted evidence, and that he referred to the same only so far as it was necessary to enable the jury to understand the issues involved in the present case. In the light of the judge's note, it can not be said that the charge complained of in any way prejudiced the rights of the defendants.

5. The land levied upon was in one body made up of contiguous parcels composed of fractional parts of different land lots. We do not think that the fact that the tract was divided by the lines of the land lots would interfere with the right of the sheriff to levy upon the property as a whole and treat the same as one entire tract. Especially would this be true in the present case, where the jury were authorized from the evidence before them to find that the owner had treated the property as one tract so far as the land lot lines were concerned.

6. Mrs. Conley was interested in the sale because under the deed from her husband she was the owner of the property as to every one else except the owner of the Thornton execution, and therefore she was interested in whatever surplus there might arise from the proceeds of the sale after the payment of that execution.   At the sale under the execution of D. P. Hill, executor, against John L. Conley, the property had been bid off by Manning for Mrs. Conley.   It is true that Manning testified that he was not the agent of Mrs. Conley but was representing John L. Conley, at whose request he bid it off for Mrs. Conley.   When the sale under the Thornton execution took place Manning made a statement, as he said, at the request of John L. Conley, in reference to a homestead which had been applied for in the property and to an illegality which was pending; such statement being calculated to deter persons from bidding at the sale.   Mrs. Conley admits in her answer that the statement above referred to was made by her authority.   These facts having appeared, the judge charged the jury as follows : "If you should believe from the evidence that this property did not bring its full value at the sale under the execution controlled by Buck, still if you believe that the inadequate price was brought about by the conduct of Mrs. Conley, or her agent or attorney, or the defendant John L. Conley, in deterring bidders by making announcements or statements, publicly in the hearing of prospective bidders, that the property was covered by a homestead; if in fact there was no homestead, or that an illegality was pending, if such illegality was not pending, or that the levy under the execution controlled by Buck had not been sufficiently advertised, if in fact it had been lawfully advertised, or other like conduct, then I charge you that Mrs. Conley can take no advantage of the fact that the property did not bring its full value." The error assigned on this charge is, that the judge declared that Mrs. Conley was bound by the statements made by John L. Conley, when the evidence showed that he had long before the sale parted with the title.

If John L. Conley was the agent of Mrs. Conley at the time the sale took place (and there was evidence from which the jury might infer that such was the case), of course she would be bound by what he said; but the complaint is made that the judge leaves the impression upon the minds of the jury that although he was not her agent she would still be bound by what he said. If he was a stranger, of course her rights should not be affected by what he said or did. Yet, as it appears that Manning, who had bid the property in at the first sale for Mrs. Conley, and whose right to do so does not appear up to the present time to have been impeached by her, made the statement above referred to, and as the evidence shows that John L. Conley and Manning were in apparent co-operation with each other, there was evidence from which the jury could have inferred that Manning was the agent or attorney of Mrs. Conley in making the statements at the second sale, and she admits that such statements were made by her authority. This co-operation with John L. Conley in attempting to deter bidders and depress the price of the property would prevent Mrs. Conley from attacking the sale on account of the mere misconduct of Conley, even if he was a stranger only and not her agent in any way. In this view of the matter there was nothing in the charge of the court which was prejudicial to the defendants.

7. From the evidence it appeared that at the sale under the Thornton execution there were only three bids, $1,000 by Redwine, $1,500 by Arnold, and $2,000 by Redwine, at which amount the property was knocked down to Redwine. As it appeared that at the time Redwine was the agent of Buck and Arnold, it is contended that the manner of the bidding was such an irregularity as would be ground for setting aside the sale. It is insisted that the last two bids were for such amounts as to deter other persons from bidding, and were so intended, and that this proceeding, if nothing else, would have been sufficient for the jury to have returned a verdict setting aside the sale. Upon this subject the court charged the jury as follows: "As to what would be a conspiracy to lessen or deter bidding, the court charges that the fact, if it be a fact, that two persons may bid together for land at a sheriff's sale, or upon joint account, or upon a mutual understanding that they will buy together, does not alone constitute such a prevention of bidding as would make the sale void. Persons have a right to bid together at a

sheriff's sale, provided they do no act which is fraudulent or which tends to deter other persons from bidding or to depreciate the sale or price brought at the sale. The fact that property may be purchased by one person for another and that both persons may be present at the sale can not alone invalidate the sale or make it void on that account." This charge is assigned as error, because it is claimed that counsel did not contend that there was any conspiracy to deter bidders, and that the court failed to charge that the bidding in large amounts might be considered by the jury; and if the amount of each bid was such as to deter bidders, this would be a reason for setting aside the sale. In a note to the ground of the motion for a new trial in which this assignment of error is contained the judge says: "It was contended that the conduct of Arnold, Redwine, or Curran at the sale, and their bidding and acting as the evidence showed, was a ground for setting aside the sale, whether counsel used the word conspiracy or not. It could not have been submitted to the jury merely whether it was strange. There was no request to charge on this subject." There was no error in the charge as given, nor was there any error in the failure to charge as complained of by the defendant. Let it be conceded that the conduct of Arnold and Redwine was such as to deter bidders desiring to purchase the property which was to be sold, such conduct would not be a sufficient ground for setting aside the sale, unless it was shown that there was at the sale a person or persons who would have, but for this conduct, become bidders for the property, and that by reason of this arrangement they were actually deterred from participating in the bidding. As the evidence does not disclose that any one was actually deterred from bidding in the present case, the conduct of Arnold and Redwine, no matter what their intention may have been, did not prejudice the rights of Mrs. Conley.

8. Complaint is made that the court erred in requiring counsel for defendant to refrain from making certain remarks of a pathetic nature in reference to the widow of John L. Conley, who was present in court, it being claimed that such remarks were not inappropriate as a reply to the vigorous assault which had been made on the life and character of Conley by opposite

counsel. We can not say that in the remarks objected to counsel exceeded the bounds of legitimate pathos, but, as all matters of oratory are necessarily left to the sound discretion of the trial judge, we do not feel justified in holding that the conduct of the judge on this occasion was such an abuse of discretion as to require the granting of a new trial.

9. It was contended that because the levy embraced a certain parcel of land which it was admitted was not subject to the execution, the sale was void. We do not see how the defendant in execution, or one claiming under him, can complain of this. The only effect of embracing in the levy and sale more property than the defendant owned would be to increase the proceeds of the sale, and to this extent benefit both the owner of the property which was being sold, and one entitled to the balance of the proceeds of the sale after the execution had been satisfied.

10. It was further contended that the property levied on was embraced within the limits of an incorporated town, that it had been subdivided into streets and town lots, and that for this reason the levy upon the property as a whole was illegal. It appears from the evidence that the owners of the property had caused a map to be made of the same, upon which appeared streets and lots the usual size of town lots; but there was abundant evidence from which the jury could find that the streets and town lots had not been actually laid out over the property, but that the same was really one tract of land, used as such, and the only thing in the nature of a street through it was a recognized public road of the county. The judge's charge fairly submitted these questions to the jury, and the evidence was sufficient to authorize them to find against the contention of the defendant. As there is nothing in the answer of the defendant complaining of the sale on the ground that the same was defective for the reasons referred to in this and the preceding division of this opinion, even if the position taken by the defendant's counsel in this court be correct, it would avail nothing in the present case.

11. One ground upon which the sale to Redwine was attacked was an insufficient description of the property in the levy. The levy described the property as being in the 14th district of

Fulton county, Georgia, and being parts of land lots 163 and 164, being north half of land lot 163, containing 101 1/4 acres, and being the southeast quarter of land lot 164, containing 52 acres more or less, the same being the property described in the deed dated August 16, 1884, from John L. Conley to his wife, and being described also in the petition of A. E. Buck against John L. Conley and wife, heretofore described, suit 1806, fall term, 1894, Fulton superior court, and being the property found subject in said suit. The levy was dated March 15, 1897. It was contended that this levy did not describe the property so that the same could be identified and located, and therefore the public was not put on notice of what property was being sold. It is not claimed that the description of the property in the deed from John L. Conley to his wife or in the petition in the case of Buck v. Conley and wife was not sufficient to identify and locate the property, but it is contended that a levy is not valid which does not in itself, unaided by extrinsic evidence, disclose an accurate description of the property levied on. An entry of levy which embraces in general terms a description of a tract of land levied on and refers for a more accurate description to a public record is sufficient, if the public record accurately describes the property; and this is true notwithstanding the fact that the description might be insufficient to locate the property in the absence of the record. See, in this connection, *Talmage* v. *Interstate B. & L. Ass'n*, 105 *Ga.* 550; *Cedartown Improvement Co.* v. *Cherokee Imp. Co.*, 99 *Ga.* 122; *Hoffman* v. Anthony, 75 Am. Dec. 701, and note on page 706. The levy in the present case, so far as the description of the property was concerned, was sufficient, and there was no error in so holding.

12. We have given the voluminous record in present case a careful investigation, and the foregoing opinion deals with all of the questions raised which, in our opinion, are of such a character as requires discussion at length. The charge of the court was full, fair, and explicit in every particular; and if any error requiring the granting of a new trial was committed during the entire progress of the case, we have been unable to discover it. The evidence fully authorized the verdict rendered

on all of the contested issues of fact, and there was no error in denying a new trial.

Judgment affirmed. All the Justices concurring.

ASHLEY *et al. v.* COOK.

109
114
09　6
19　6
19　6
109
120
d120

109
129
f130

1. A deed passing title to the grantee therein named, for the purpose of securing a debt, can, after the maturity of the debt, be set up as outstanding title to defeat an action of ejectment brought by one claiming under the grantor, if the possession of the defendant is connected with such title.
2. A purchaser at a void judicial sale had in pursuance of a judgment setting up a special lien under the provisions of a security deed is subrogated to whatever rights the holder of the security deed would have had had he acquired possession under his deed. While this doctrine would not be applicable in a case where there were no equitable pleadings invoking it for the purpose of determining the exact equities between the parties, still the facts that it could be made available for this purpose by proper pleadings is sufficient to connect the claim upon which the possession of such purchaser rests with the security deed in such a way as to authorize him to set up the same to defeat an action of ejectment brought against him by one claiming under the grantor therein.
3. The record of a suit in which a decree is rendered, establishing a copy of a lost deed and declaring that the same is established subject to the judgment and claim of one holding a security deed to the property from the same grantor, will not prevent the grantees in the lost deed, who are not parties, from using the same as evidence of their title, and at the same time attacking a sale thereafter had under the judgment rendered in favor of the holder of the security deed, on the ground that no reconveyance was made before the levy, when there is nothing in the pleadings or decree to show that it was intended that the decree should have the effect of dispensing with such reconveyance.
4. Though the failure of the grantor in a security deed, who is present at a sale under judicial process of the property therein embraced, to object thereto, may estop him from afterwards calling in question the regularity or legality of the sale, this will not preclude the owners of the equity of redemption in the property from so doing, when their right to such equity arose out of a deed from such grantor antedating the security deed but becoming inferior thereto on account of a failure to record.
5. In the present case the defendant did not, under the sheriff's sale, become the absolute owner of the property in controversy, being thereby simply subrogated to the rights of the holder of the security deed. The equities of the parties in the property as against each other are not determined in the present case.

Argued October 12, 1899. — Reargued January 16. — Decided January 30, 1900.

Complaint for land. Before Judge Hart. Laurens superior court. January term, 1899.

John M. Stubbs, Anderson, Felder & Davis, F. H. Burch,
D. M. Roberts, and *Alexander Akerman,* for plaintiffs.
James K. Hines and *T. L. Griner,* for defendant.

COBB, J.   This was an action of ejectment brought by J. H.
Ashley, Augustus Ashley, Lula Kreutz, and J. M. Ashley against
W. J. Cook.   The plaintiffs claimed under a deed from P. A.
Ashley, executed in 1884, conveying the property in dispute to
his wife Kate Ashley during her life, with remainder to her children.   This deed was never recorded.   Kate Ashley is dead,
and the plaintiffs are her children.   The defendant introduced
in evidence a deed from P. A. Ashley to Mary L. Floyd Jones,
dated April 13, 1885, conveying the property in controversy,
and reciting that it was executed under section 1969 of the Code
of 1882 (Civil Code, § 2771), to secure a debt which the grantor
owed the grantee.   This deed was duly recorded, and was accepted by the grantee without any knowledge of the prior execution of the deed above mentioned.   At the time the security
deed was executed the grantee therein made to the grantor a
bond to reconvey the land upon payment of the debt.   The
debt was not paid at maturity, and the creditor, having obtained
judgment, without having executed any reconveyance caused
the execution to be levied on the property now in dispute.   At
a sale of the property, had pursuant to this levy, the property
was bought by Cook, the defendant in this action, and the
amount paid by him credited upon the execution.   The judge
directed a verdict in favor of the defendant, and the only question presented by the bill of exceptions sued out by the plaintiffs, in such a way that we can deal with the same, is whether
or not he erred in so doing.

1. It was contended in the argument here that, although the
defendant failed to prove title in himself, the deed from Ashley
to Mrs. Jones constituted an outstanding paramount title in
Mrs. Jones, and that the court was therefore right in directing
a verdict for the defendant.   According to the universally recognized rule of law, a plaintiff in ejectment must recover on the
strength of his own title, and not on the weakness of his adversary's; and hence, to defeat a recovery by the plaintiffs in the
present case, it was only necessary for the defendant to show an

outstanding title in some person other than the plaintiffs, which was superior to that under which they claimed. *Sutton* v. *Mc-Leod*, 29 *Ga.* 589; *Fletcher* v. *Perry*, 97 *Ga.* 369. To accomplish this purpose he introduced in evidence the security deed above referred to. It therefore becomes necessary to determine whether or not this security deed is such an outstanding title as will defeat a recovery by the plaintiffs.

The sheriff's sale under which Cook bought was absolutely void, because the grantee in the security deed had never made a reconveyance of the property to the grantor. *Upchurch* v. *Lewis*, 53 *Ga.* 621; *National Bank of Athens* v. *Danforth*, 80 *Ga.* 55 (6); *McCalla* v. *American Freehold Co.*, 90 *Ga.* 113 (5). But as Cook was in possession under a claim of right, he can not be properly regarded as a mere intruder, and hence the doctrine that such a person can not defeat an action of ejectment by showing outstanding paramount title in a stranger has no application whatever to him. See Tyler, Eject. 564; Newell, Eject. 654; *Sutton* v. *McLeod*, 29 *Ga.* 589; *Fletcher* v. *Perry*, 97 *Ga.* 369. In reference to the character of title necessary to support the defense of "outstanding title," in an action of ejectment, the author last cited says: "It is incumbent on the defendant, if he relies upon an outstanding title for the purpose of defeating the action, to positively and clearly establish such title as an actual subsisting and better title than the plaintiff's title—such a title as would enable the third party himself to maintain an action for the possession of the lands in controversy against both the plaintiff and defendant." Page 653, § 15, and cases cited. See also Industrial Co. *v.* Schultz, 43 W. Va. 470; Ruesens *v.* Lawson, 91 Va. 226; Wilcher *v.* Robertson, 78 Va. 602; Lessee of Griffith *v.* Bradshaw, 4 Wash. (U. S.) 171. A deed made to secure a debt passes title. *Williamson* v. *Orient Ins. Co.*, 100 *Ga.* 791, and cases cited. It has been held repeatedly by this court, that a recovery in ejectment may be had upon such a deed. *Carswell* v. *Hartridge*, 55 *Ga.* 412; *Biggers* v. *Bird*, 55 *Ga.* 650; *Cameron* v. *Phillips*, 60 *Ga.* 434; *Woodson* v. *Veal*, 60 *Ga.* 562; *Robinson* v. *Alexander*, 65 *Ga.* 406; *Oellrich* v. *Georgia Railroad*, 73 *Ga.* 389. It is true that the statute (Civil Code, § 5432) gives another remedy, that is, to obtain a judgment on the debt, reconvey to the grantor, levy on and sell the land ; but the remedy thus given is by no means exclusive. *Dykes* v. *McVay,* 67 *Ga.* 502; *Hines* v. *Rutherford,* 67 *Ga.* 607.　There are also numerous decisions to the effect that a judgment against the grantor in a security deed executed before such judgment was rendered had no lien upon the land embraced in the deed, which could be enforcèd by levy and sale, until the title became revested by redemption. *Phinizy* v. *Clark,* 62 *Ga.* 623; *Cecil* v. *Gazan,* 65 *Ga.* 689; *Groves* v. *Williams,* 69 *Ga.* 614; *Osborne* v. *Hill,* 91 *Ga.* 137.

Mrs. Jones could certainly, after a default in payment by the grantor, maintain ejectment on this deed against him or any one else who was in possession.　The fact that the property was sold by the sheriff and a sum of money equal to the larger portion of her debt credited on her execution would not have the effect of destroying the title which she held nor of transmitting the same back to the grantor, and therefore would not at law be a sufficient defense in an action of ejectment brought by her. Indeed, a partial payment of the debt by the grantor himself would be no defense to such an action brought against him. *Robinson* v. *Alexander,* 65 *Ga.* 406.　When a security deed is executed and delivered, the legal title to the property therein described vests in the grantee and remains there until the debt is paid and the security deed cancelled in the manner prescribed by law for the cancellation of mortgages (Civil Code, § 2774), or a reconveyance is made by the grantee to the grantor, or there has been a judgment recovered on the debt, a reconveyance filed and recorded, and a sale made by the sheriff under a lawful and regular levy.　Until one or the other of the methods above mentioned is pursued, the legal title remains in the grantee in the security deed.　The fact that the grantee had sued the grantor on the debt and obtained judgment thereon would not of itself revest the title, it being essential to accomplish such purpose that the suit and judgment should be followed by a reconveyance, levy and sale.　It would seem from the foregoing, that a defendant in ejectment might under certain circumstances be permitted to sustain the defense of paramount outstanding title by proof of a security deed.

As the plaintiffs in this case claim under the grantor in the security deed, the question arises as to whether that deed would be available to the defendant as evidence to support a defense of paramount outstanding title.   There has never been a ruling by this court on the question as to how far a security deed can be so used in an action of ejectment; and as such deed and the incidents attaching to the same seem to be peculiar to our law, of course we can not find in other jurisdictions any ruling bearing directly upon the point.   However, as our security deed is very similar in its nature to a mortgage at common law, rulings made by the English courts and other courts in this country dealing with the common-law mortgage may be resorted to as furnishing a guide as to what is the status of the security deed of our statute.   In some jurisdictions in which a mortgage passes title it has been held that an unsatisfied mortgage can not be set up as outstanding title to defeat an action of ejectment brought by the mortgagor or one claiming under him, the mortgagor, until ousted by the mortgagee, being treated, as to all the world except the mortgagee, as the owner of the property.   Peltz v. Clark, 5 Pet. 481; Oldham v. Pfleger, 84 Ill. 102; Emory v. Keighan, 88 Ill. 482; Bartlett v. Borden, 13 Bush, 45.   It has also been held that a defendant in an action of ejectment can not set up as outstanding title an unsatisfied mortgage, when he not only does not connect his title with such mortgage but claims adversely to both the mortgagor and the mortgagee.   Woods v. Hilderbrand, 46 Mo. 513, s. c. 2 Am. R. 513; Johnson v. Houston, 47 Mo. 227; Hardwick v. Jones, 65 Mo. 54.   See also, in this connection, Newell, Eject. 656.

The rulings above referred to seem to be supported by reason.   If the grantor in a security deed should be dispossessed, even by one under a claim of right and therefore not such a person as would be precluded from availing himself of the defense of outstanding title, it would seem that the rule which would allow such person to set up, against an action of ejectment brought by such grantor on his prior possession, that the grantor had no title but that his creditor was the holder of the title, would be unreasonable and unjust.   As to all the world except the grantee the grantor in the security deed is the owner of the

42

property; and not even the grantee himself can maintain ejectment before the debt is due which the deed is given to secure;
and even after the debt is due the grantee is not compelled to
bring ejectment. It would therefore seem right and proper that
no person should be allowed to use this title in any way to interfere with the rights of the grantor in the deed, whatever they
may be, unless the person relying thereon connects himself in
some way with the deed.

2. Treating Cook as being in possession under a claim of right
and not as a trespasser or intruder, the next question to be determined is, whether he has connected himself in such a way
with the security deed held by Mrs. Jones as to avail himself
of the same as a defense to the action. The code declares that
"A purchaser at a void or irregular judicial sale under foreclosure of a mortgage succeeds to all of the interests of the mortgagee." Civil Code, § 5471. The section just cited simply applies to purchasers at mortgage foreclosure sales the equitable
doctrine of subrogation, but the principle upon which it is based,
and the reasoning of the decision from which it is taken (*Dutcher*
v. *Hobby*, 86 *Ga.* 198) is sufficiently broad to include judicial
sales had in pursuance of a judgment rendered setting up a special lien under the provisions of a security deed. See Sheldon,
Sub. § 13; *Merchants & Mechanics Bank* v. *Tillman*, 106 *Ga.* 55.
It is contended, however, that as there is no equitable plea filed
by the defendant, he can not avail himself of this principle.
This objection is well taken so far as it would prevent the defendant from obtaining a decree which would settle for all time
his rights as well as the rights of the plaintiffs in the land in
question; but the fact that he would have a right in a proper
case under proper pleadings to set up this equity of subrogation
to the rights of the holder of the security deed is, we think, sufficient in the present case to connect the claim upon which his
possession is based with the security deed in such a way as to
make the title which the grantee in such deed holds available
to him as outstanding title as against the plaintiffs. Treating
it as now established that a defendant in ejectment who connects his possession with an outstanding title represented by a
security deed can set up the same to defeat an action of eject-

ment, the question arises as to what are the rights of such person who has conclusively established such a defense, when his connection with the outstanding title is brought about by the fact that he purchased the property at a void judicial sale which was had at the instance of the holder of the security deed. The judgment in favor of the defendant on such a defense would certainly not have the effect of establishing that he was the sole owner of the property to the entire exclusion of the plaintiffs, when they are the successors in title to the grantor in the security deed, or when for any reason they are entitled in law to claim the equity of redemption which was in the grantor. The defendant is in possession by virtue of the fact that the amount of his bid at the sheriff's sale has been applied to the extinguishment, pro tanto, of the debt due by Ashley to the holder of the security deed. As he did not acquire title by virtue of his purchase at the sheriff's sale, his possession of the property under the circumstances gives him no more rights in the property than Mrs. Jones would have had if she had acquired possession after the debt had become due. Cook stands in the shoes of Mrs. Jones. He is entitled to hold the possession to the same extent for the same purpose only that she would have held it had she acquired possession. It is not necessary to determine in the present case what would be the exact measure of the rights of the parties inter sese growing out of the purchase by Cook and the application of his money to the partial discharge of the debt secured by the deed.

3. The plaintiffs introduced in evidence the record of a suit brought by Mrs. Kate Ashley against P. A. Ashley and Mrs. Jones. The petition alleged that P. A. Ashley, prior to the making of the deed to Mrs. Jones, executed a deed to the same property, which had been lost and was not recorded, and in which it was provided that Mrs. Ashley should have a life-estate therein and after her death the same was to go to her children, and that Mrs. Jones had notice of this deed when she obtained her deed; and prayed that a copy of the lost deed be established, and that Mrs. Jones be enjoined from selling the land under a judgment which she had obtained against P. A. Ashley. A consent decree was rendered in this suit, which pro-

vided that a copy of the lost deed be established, and that the
title to the land therein described be in Mrs. Ashley during her
life and after her death to her children, but subject to the lien
of the judgment in favor of Mrs. Jones.   The children of Mrs.
Ashley, who are the plaintiffs in the present action, were not
parties to the case.   It was claimed that the effect of this decree
was to declare that the deed of Mrs. Jones was in every way
and for every purpose superior to the deed to Mrs. Ashley and
her children, and that the plaintiffs, having used the record as
evidence of their title, must, although not parties to the suit, allow the record to have its full force and effect.   They were not
parties to the suit, and therefore are not bound by the judgment
as such.   We do not think the record, fairly interpreted, would
have the effect of precluding them from insisting that Mrs.
Jones should proceed in the regular way to condemn the land
to sale.   The decree in effect says that the land is the property
of Mrs. Ashley and her children, but that the same is subject
to the claim of Mrs. Jones.   There is not a hint, either in the
pleadings or decree, that it was the purpose of the parties or
the court to relieve Mrs. Jones from the necessity of complying
with the strict terms of the law.   Such being the case, it would
seem that the plaintiffs, even if they had been parties, could
have raised the objection to Cook's title which they have raised
in the present case.   It was further contended that the decree
and record of the case above referred to obviated the necessity
of a reconveyance from Mrs. Jones to Ashley, and that for this
reason the sale was valid and Cook obtained a good title to the
property.   This contention gives to the decree a construction
which is not authorized by its terms.   But even conceding that
it is, there is not an allegation or a prayer either in the petition
or the answer which would authorize such a decree.

4. As P. A. Ashley was present at the sale and made no objection, and as the proceeds of the sale were applied to a valid
lien against him, he is bound by the sale notwithstanding the
same was void.   Civil Code, § 5472.   But as the claim of the
plaintiffs rested upon a conveyance from him which was made
not only prior to the sale but prior to the date of the security
deed, the fact that he would be bound by the sale would not

affect them. Their claim is simply subordinated to that of the holder of the security deed under the operation of the registry laws. It would indeed be a hardship upon them if, after they have already been so seriously wronged by the conduct of P. A. Ashley, they should be defeated by his conduct at the sale occurring long after he had parted with the title to the property. At the time of such conduct he was neither owner of the property nor had any interest whatever therein. What he did at such a time ought certainly not to affect the rights of the owners of the property.

5. Under the view we take of the case, the defendant is not in possession as the absolute owner of the property, but simply has such rights as the holder of the security deed would have had had she acquired possession under her deed. Our ruling goes no further than to hold that the defendant has failed in all his defenses, save the one which sets up the outstanding title in Mrs. Jones, and that this is available to him to maintain possession only to the extent she could have maintained the same had she been in possession under her deed. What are his equities, and what are the equities of the plaintiffs against him as successor of Mrs. Jones, are all questions not involved in the present case, and they can be hereafter determined in a proper proceeding upon sufficient pleadings.

Judgment affirmed. All the Justices concurring.

TIEDEMAN & BROTHER *et al. v.* IMPERIAL FERTILIZER COMPANY *et al.*

1. Where the owner of notes placed the same in the hands of another for collection, and the bailee, having made collections, failed to remit the proceeds, the claim of the owner of the money collected was, in a general sense, in the nature of a fiduciary debt, but not such an one as entitled him to a priority over the claims of general creditors in the distribution of the assets of the bailee who had become insolvent.
2. The distribution in the present case was that of the assets of an insolvent partnership, and not of the estate of an intestate.

Argued November 9, 1899. — Decided January 30, 1900.

Equitable petition. Before Judge Smith. Wilcox superior court. February 1, 1899.

Cutts & Lawson, *T. L. Holton*, and *Dasher, Park & Gerdine*, for plaintiffs. *Thomson & Whipple*, *D. B. Nicholson*, *T. C. Wells*, and *Harrison & Bryan*, for defendants.

LITTLE, J. The exception taken which raises the question to be decided in this case is to so much of a final decree as gives priority to two certain claims over general creditors in the distribution of funds in the hands of a receiver. Weeks & Reid, a mercantile firm, were indebted to various parties. Weeks conveyed his interest in the firm property to Reid, and Reid then made a conveyance to Nicholson as assignee, for the benefit of the firm creditors. This instrument embraced the entire property and assets of the firm, and made two of its creditors, to wit The Imperial Fertilizer Company and J. S. Woods & Brother, preferred creditors. Certain general creditors instituted an equitable proceeding to set aside the deeds of assignment. Reid having died during the pendency of the case, Nicholson, his administrator, was made a party defendant. It also appears that, under the proceedings instituted, Nicholson was appointed receiver and took charge of the assets of the firm, and under order of the court reduced the same to money. The two preferred creditors, the Imperial Fertilizer Company and J. S. Woods & Brother, set up, by their respective answers, that the firm of Weeks & Reid had bought from them commercial fertilizers, and had deposited with said defendants certain customers' notes of considerable amount, as collateral to secure the payment of the notes given by the firm for the fertilizers; that when these collateral notes became due, the defendants had sent them to the firm of Weeks & Reid for collection, the proceeds of which were to be remitted to the defendants; that the firm collected a very considerable amount on said collateral notes, but failed to pay the proceeds to the defendants, and used the same in their business; that the assets of the firm had been reduced to cash; and that the defendants were in law and in equity entitled to a lien on the firm assets, and the proceeds arising therefrom, superior to the claim of the other creditors, theirs being a trust debt. They also claimed that the deeds of assignment which gave them a preference were legal and valid. At the hearing a bill of sale made by Weeks to Reid was introduced, containing the following clause: " I hereby bargain, sell, assign, and convey to S. J. Reid all my right, title, and interest in the business of Weeks & Reid, and all the goods, wares, and merchandise, store fixtures, notes, and accounts due the business, and all other property owned by said firm of Weeks & Reid ; and said S. J. Reid assumes all the debts due by Weeks & Reid, and agrees to make an assignment of all his property to pay the same. " All questions of law and fact were left to the decision of the judge, who determined that the deeds of assignment made by Reid to Nicholson were void and passed no title out of Reid as against any of the creditors, and that the plaintiffs, who were creditors of the firm of Weeks & Reid, should respectively have judgments for the amounts due each, against Weeks, surviving partner, and Nicholson, administrator of Reid, there being no question as to the amount of the debts due to each of said creditors ; and further, that the debts of Woods & Brother and the Imperial Fertilizer Company were of higher dignity and had priority over the general creditors to whom judgments were thus given. The fund not being sufficient to pay all the debts, the receiver was directed to pay the amount of the debt of Woods & Brother and the Imperial Fertilizer Company in full, before any payment should be made to the other creditors. To so much of the decree as gave this priority the plaintiffs in error excepted.

Evidently the judge framed his decree distributing the money in the hands of the receiver on the theory set up in the answers of Wood & Brother and the Imperial Fertilizer Company, that theirs were trust debts. In support of that contention, we have been referred to sections 2790, 3189, and 3424 of the Civil Code. The first two of these provide that liens against trustees dying chargeable with trust funds take priority over all other liens and claims except funeral expenses. The third is the general statute which fixes the priority of debts against the estate of a decedent, and declares that any debt due by the deceased as a trustee, having had actual possession, control, and management of the trust property, shall take priority immediately after unpaid taxes, and before judgments, liens, and other debts. A trust may arise in different ways. If one uses

the funds of another in the purchase of property, taking title
thereto in his own name, as a general rule it will be held that
the purchaser holds the property, thus acquired, in trust for the
benefit of the owner of the funds.   Such is known as a resulting trust, which is sometimes spoken of as an equitable lien,
and while it is, the lien extends no further than the property
acquired with the money of the other.   Such a lien can only
be enforced against the specific property in which the funds
were invested.   The claim of lien in this case, however, is based
not on any specific item of property bought with the funds collected, but rests on the general proposition that the money was
in law held by the firm in trust for its owners, and being so, a
priority exists in their favor.   We are confident that such a
contention is not sound, and that the facts if admitted to be true
do not create such a trust debt as is contemplated by either of
the sections of the code to which reference has been made.
Weeks & Reid did not hold any property of the defendants in
error in trust, in the sense contemplated by the statute.   The
latter had certain notes which were sent to the former for col·
lection, under a contract that the proceeds were to be forwarded to them.   These facts created an agency.   It seems that the
firm, after collecting certain of the notes, did not observe their
obligations to forward the money, which was, of course, the
money of the defendants in error; they could have recovered a
judgment for it in a suit as for a debt, or, had they been able
to identify the particular funds, separate and apart, they could
have recovered the specific funds; and while in a general way
the debt might be classed as a debt arising out of a fiduciary
relation, it was not such a trust debt as gave priority of payment.   In the case of *Southern Star Lightning Rod Co.* v. *Cleg-
horn,* 59 *Ga.* 782, this court held that, "In the distribution of
the estate of a deceased attorney at law among creditors, a claim
for money collected by him professionally, and never paid over
to his client, is not entitled to rank as a debt due by the deceased 'as trustee having had actual possession, control and
management of the trust property.'"   In the opinion delivered
by Judge Bleckley in that case it was said: "An attorney's possession of the money of his client is more like that of a mere

agent or bailee. It would be deviating from the ordinary use of language to call the client's money trust property; and the sole duty of the attorney, in respect to it, is to pay it over. He has no right to control and manage it as trustee in possession. In this regard, his powers do not extend beyond those of an attorney in fact appointed to collect; and the latter is not a technical trustee.'' In the case of *Bowen* v. *Johnson*, 12 *Ga.* 9, where one had executed a power of attorney to another to sell and convey a tract of land, this court held that such a contract created a mere agency, and, where under it a sale was made and the purchase-price collected by the agent, that the agent held the money for the use of his principal, and the latter could have sued for it at once, and no trust of any kind was created. See also *Schofield* v. *Woolley*, 98 *Ga.* 548.

Under the facts here, the debtors were the agents of their creditors to make collection of the notes turned over to them. Their duty was not only to collect, but to pay over. There was nothing to manage, nothing to control. The statutes which have been quoted can have no application in a case like this; they apply only when the claim for which priority is given is against a trustee proper, one in whom the title is vested in trust for other persons, and whose duty it is to make returns to the ordinary under the provisions of the code. *Lightning Rod* case, supra. It is contended, however, that if the debts of the defendants in error are not such technical trust debts as entitle them to priority of payment over the general creditors, their debts are represented by promissory notes, while the debts of the other creditors are represented only by open account, and that for this reason they are entitled to priority. We think this contention can not be maintained. As a matter of fact, no estate of a decedent was being distributed under the proceedings here. Weeks, one of the partners, is in life; Reid, the other partner, is deceased. If the deeds of assignment were good, they did not have the legal effect of vesting the title conveyed by Weeks absolutely in Reid. On the contrary, he would hold the property conveyed as a trustee for the creditors of the firm. But it was adjudicated in this case that the deeds were void and should be set aside, and no exception was taken to this finding, the effect of which is to leave the title where it was before Weeks made the conveyance, that is, in the firm of Weeks & Reid. And the proceeding is not to distribute the estate of a decedent but of an insolvent partnership, in which case we know of no law which creates a preference in favor of holders of a promissory note without a lien. That the debt has none as being a trust debt we have endeavored to show. The court erred in awarding a preference to the debts of the defendants in error over other unsecured creditors.

Judgment reversed. All the Justices concurring.

PETTY v. BRUNSWICK & WESTERN RAILWAY CO.

1. A contract between an employee and his master, or another acting in the latter's interest, by the terms of which the employee when physically injured, whether as a result of his own negligence or not, or when sick, is to receive pecuniary and other valuable benefits, and which stipulates that his voluntary acceptance of any of such benefits in case of injury is to operate as a release of the master from all liability on account thereof, is not contrary to public policy.

2. That such a contract secured to the employee substantial benefits, and that the master contributed to the fund for the payment thereof, constituted a valuable consideration as to the employee; and this is true though he himself made a small monthly contribution to that fund. A contract of this kind is not wanting in mutuality.

3. One who deals with an "association" as a legal entity capable of transacting business, and in consequence receives from it money or other thing of value, is estopped from denying the legality of its existence or its right to contract.

4. A ground of a motion for a new trial complaining of the admission of written evidence will not be considered unless the evidence objected to is set forth, either literally or in substance, in the motion itself, or attached thereto as an exhibit.

5. A contract will not be set aside on the ground of fraud in its procurement, at the instance of one who has neither restored nor offered to restore the fruits thereof.

6. The acceptance by an injured employee of any benefit under a contract of the kind indicated in the first of the preceding notes is an election on his part to look exclusively to that source for compensation on account of the injury, and amounts to a complete accord and satisfaction of his claim for damages against his master therefrom arising.

7. This court can not, when there is nothing in the record to warrant its so doing, undertake to say whether the formation by a particular combination of railway and other corporations of a "Relief and Hospital Department" was, or was not, ultra vires.

Argued November 11, 1899 — Decided January 30, 1900.

Action for damages. Before Judge Atkinson. City court of Brunswick. May 6, 1899.

W. G. Brantley and *Johnson & Krauss*, for plaintiff.
W. E. Kay, for defendant.

LUMPKIN, P. J.　On July 1, 1896, the Brunswick & Western Railway Company and certain other corporations constituting what was known as the "Plant System of Railways" entered into an agreement in writing which, among other things, recited that they had "determined to establish a Relief and Hospital Department, the scope, character, objects and purposes of which" were set forth in a writing thereto attached, embodying the proposed regulations under which such department was to be conducted. Each of these several corporations obligated itself to contribute ratably to a fund of $12,-000 to be used in the establishment and maintenance of this new department, and further agreed to pay its just proportion of "any sum necessary to make up any deficit which [might] at any time occur in the operations" thereof. Provision was likewise made for the payment of "the salary of the Superintendent and Chief Surgeon of said department," and for meeting the expense of building such hospitals as the parties to the agreement might thereafter determine to erect. Subsequently the proposed "Relief and Hospital Department" was duly organized, and at once began operations in conformity with the regulations above referred to. Provision was therein made for the payment, to such employees as might become members, of certain fixed benefits in the event of their being "disabled by accident or sickness," their families to become beneficiaries in cases of death. The fund out of which payments were to be made was to "consist of contributions from the employees and the" several companies belonging to the Plant System, "income derived from investments, and appropriations by" such companies "when necessary to make up a deficit." These companies were to assume "general charge of the department, guarantee the fulfillment of its obligations, and become the custodian of its funds, with full responsibility therefor," and were also to "contribute to the department twelve thousand dollars ($12,000) per annum, payable in monthly installments of one thousand dollars each." In addition to the specific benefits above alluded to, the regulations declared that: "The hospitals of this department are open at all times for the reception of sick and injured employees and members of their families. The treatment therein shall be free of expense to the employee, other than the monthly assessments" which he undertakes to pay into the general relief fund; "but for care and treatment of members of their families, actual cost will be charged, with an addition of ten (10) per cent." The regulations further provided that: "Membership will be voluntary on the part of agents receiving commissions only, and employees who entered the service prior to July 1st, 1896, and have been continuously therein since that date. All persons in service on or after July 1st, 1896, or promoted therein, must, as a condition of employment or advancement, become full members of the department, entitled to all its benefits, before being permitted to go on duty, with the exceptions noted above." "To entitle an employee to participate in any of the forms of relief afforded by the department," he was required to execute a prescribed form of application and "pass a satisfactory medical examination." "In the event of disability or death from accidental injuries," the stipulated benefits were payable only upon compliance with the express condition that "there be first filed with the Superintendent and Chief Surgeon of the Relief and Hospital Department releases satisfactory to him, releasing" each and all of the several companies constituting the Plant System "from all claims for damages by reason of such injury or death, signed by all persons who might bring suit for such damages, or those legally competent to release for them, and by the beneficiaries named in the respective applications. In case a suit for damages should be filed against any of these companies by a member, his beneficiary, or legal representative, with a view to recovering "damages on account of the injury or death of such member," all claims to benefits were thereby to become forfeited, "unless such suit be discontinued and all costs incurred by the defendant therein paid by the plaintiff before any hearing or trial, on demurrer or otherwise."

On and prior to July 1, 1896, Albert Petty was in the service of the Brunswick & Western Railway Company. Although it was not obligatory upon him to do so, on the 22d of that month he applied for membership in the "Relief and Hospital Department." In his application, which was in the form prescribed by the rules of that department, he agreed to become bound by all its regulations, then of force or thereafter adopted, and consented that $1.25 of his wages should be monthly applied, in advance, as a contribution to its relief fund. He further agreed that his application, when duly accepted, should constitute a contract between himself and each of the several companies forming the Plant system, and that, "in consideration of the contribution of said companies to the Relief and Hospital department, and of the guarantee by them of the payments of the benefits aforesaid, the acceptance of benefits from the said Relief and Hospital Department, either money or medical or surgical attendance, for injury or death [should] operate as a release of all claims against said companies, and each of them, for damages by reason of such injury or death, which could be made by or through" him. Another clause recited that it was understood and agreed "that this application, when accepted by the Superintendent and Chief Surgeon, [should] constitute a contract between [the applicant] and the said companies, and each of them, by which [his] rights as a member of said Relief and Hospital Department and as an employee of said companies, or either of them, [should] be determined as to all matters within its scope." Petty's application for membership was duly accepted, and a certificate was issued and delivered to him, by the terms of which he was entitled to the following "benefits provided by the regulations of the Relief and Hospital Department for a member of Class A, to wit: $500.00 in case of accidental death in discharge of duty; $250.00 in case of death from natural causes or injury off duty; $ —.50 per day for accidental injuries on duty (not including Sundays) for first 26 weeks; $ —.25 for accidental injuries on duty (not including Sundays) after first 26 weeks; $ —.50 for sickness per day (not including first six working days or Sundays) for 52 weeks; and free medical and surgical attendance by com-

pany's surgeons and free care and treatment in company's hospitals." On one or more occasions thereafter, Petty availed
himself of the rights thus accorded to him as a member of the
department and received the benefits to which he was, as such,
entitled. He remained in the service of the Brunswick &
Western Railway Company until September 19, 1897. In the
following year he brought an action for damages against that
company, alleging in his petition that on May 12, 1897, while
in the discharge of his duties as a switchman, he sustained personal injuries occasioned by the negligence of one of the company's employees. To this action the defendant pleaded, as
a special defense, the contract which Petty had made with the
Relief and Hospital Department of the Plant System, alleging
that, soon after he received the injuries complained of, he voluntarily elected to accept the benefits thus provided for, and
actually received not only medical and surgical treatment and
attendance but also various sums of money, thereby fully discharging and releasing the defendant company from all liability
in damages on account of the alleged injuries sustained by him
on the date mentioned in his petition. Petty met this special
defense by a demurrer based on various grounds, but it was
overruled by the court, and the case proceeded to a trial upon
its merits. At the conclusion of the evidence submitted pro
and con, the court directed a verdict in favor of the railway
company. The present bill of exceptions assigns error both
upon the overruling of the plaintiff's demurrer and upon the
refusal of the court to grant him a new trial upon each of the
several grounds contained in his motion therefor. Such other
facts as are essential to an understanding of the questions thus
presented for our consideration will be stated in immediate
connection therewith in the discussion which follows.

1. One of the main points raised by the plaintiff's demurrer
and strenuously insisted upon in the argument here was, that
the contract upon which the defendant company predicated its
defense was void because contrary to public policy, in that it
evidenced an attempt to exempt the company from liability for
negligence. In support of this contention, the plaintiff relied
on section 2613 of the Civil Code, which declares that: "All

contracts between master and servant, made in consideration
of employment, whereby the master is exempted from liability
to the servant arising from the negligence of the master or his
servants, as such liability is now fixed by law, shall be null and
void, as against public policy." As should be readily appar:
ent, the weakness of this position lies in the fact that it is based
upon an entire misconception of the meaning and effect of the
contract thus assailed. It did not, as claimed, in any of its
terms or conditions stipulate that the defendant company should
be absolved from the legal consequences of its own negligence
or that of its servants. On the contrary, it merely provided
an additional remedy to that given by law to an employee who
might suffer injury by reason of the negligence, actual or im-
putable, of his master. The latter remedy was left intact, un-
disturbed and unimpaired, and the injured employee might, or
might not, at his option, take advantage thereof. True, he
could not avail himself of both, but was put upon his voluntary election as to which of the two he would pursue. This
feature of the contract is not only technically permissible, but
is in perfect harmony and accord with that fundamental rule of
law, based upon sound and sensible considerations of public
policy, which contemplates that indemnity, rather than the
mere chance of speculative gain, should be the primordial purpose of every contract designed to afford protection to a party
thereto in the event he sustains loss or injury. Only in case
the injured employee commits an error of judgment in determining whether he will accept benefits which, though comparatively small, are yet sure and easily within his grasp, or will
hazard the less certain result of a suit for damages, can he possibly fail to realize all the fruits of every right given him by law.
That it is conceivable he may make such a mistake does not render the contract essentially and inherently vicious, and therefore opposed to public policy. A much more extended argument on the line just suggested might be presented, but we
deem it wholly unnecessary. The question under discussion
is not a novel one, but has been heretofore thoroughly sifted,
minutely analyzed, and satisfactorily determined by a number
of the ablest courts of this country. For further light there-

on, we refer those entertaining unsatisfied doubts to the following adjudications, wherein the whole subject, in all its various phases, has been fully and exhaustively dealt with: Eckman *v.* Railroad Co., 169 Ill. 312, 38 L. R. A. 750, 9 Am. & Eng. R. R. Cas. (new series) 308; Johnson *v.* Railroad Co., 163 Pa. St. 127; Ringle *v.* Railroad Co., 164 Pa. St. 529, 44 Am. St. Rep. 628; Fuller *v.* B. & O. Employes' Relief Assn., 47 Md. 433; Spitze *v.* Railroad Co., 75 Md. 162; Lease *v.* Pennsylvania Co., 10 Ind. App. 47; Pittsburg Ry. Co. *v.* Moore, 152 Ind. 345, 44 L. R. A. 638; P., C. C. & St. L. Ry. Co. *v.* Cox, 55 Ohio St. 497, 35 L. R. A. 507; Donald *v.* Railway Co., 93 Iowa, 284, 33 L. R. A. 492; Maine *v.* Railroad Co., (Iowa) 70 N. W. Rep. 630; Chicago R. R. Co. *v.* Bell, 44 Neb. 44; Chicago R. R. Co. *v.* Curtis, 51 Neb. 442, 66 Am. St. Rep. 456; Johnson *v.* Railway Co., 55 S. C. 152, 44 L. R. A. 645; Owens *v.* Railroad Co., 35 Fed. Rep. 715; State *v.* Railroad Co., 36 Fed. Rep. 655; Otis *v.* Pennsylvania Co., 71 Fed. Rep. 136; Shaver *v.* Pennsylvania Co., Ibid. 931.

2. The plaintiff, by his demurrer, urged, as further objections to the company's special defense, that the contract relied on was without "any good or valuable consideration given or promised by defendant to the plaintiff," and no "mutuality of contract or agreement between" them was thereby created. In neither of these points is there any merit. This conclusion is in accord with the decisions rendered in several of the cases above cited, wherein identically the same questions were raised and judicially passed upon after much apparently careful and patient consideration. Certainly the contract contemplated that Petty was to receive substantial benefits from some source, and accordingly there was a valuable consideration moving to him. As matter of fact, the defendant railway company contributed largely to the relief fund out of which he was to receive such benefits, upon the express condition that it was to be protected by such contracts as the Relief and Hospital Department might make with its members; and in his application for membership therein, Petty stipulated and agreed that, if accepted, it should constitute a contract between himself and all the companies connected with the Plant system, one of which

was the defendant company. It further obligated itself to join with the other companies in making up any deficit in the relief fund which might at any time occur, and to guarantee the payment of all benefits to which the members were entitled. Petty, in consideration of the nominal contribution made by him monthly and the covenants contained in his application for membership, got the benefit of this guarantee and acquired the right to participate in the enjoyment of the funds which this company and its associates annually paid into the treasury of the department. As was pertinently remarked by Spear, J., when dealing with the same topic in Railway Company *v.* Cox, 55 Ohio St. 516, cited supra: "The promises are concurrent and obligatory upon both; both promise and both pay in consideration of promises and payment by the other; and the fact that third persons are interested does not impair the force of the obligation. If these stipulations do not supply consideration, it would be difficult to frame such as would; and there being express assent to the terms of the contract by both parties, the element of mutuality is not wanting."

3. All the facts necessary to an understanding of the general character and scope of the operations of the Relief and Hospital Department, as well as the objects for which it was established and was being conducted, were succinctly set forth in the 17th paragraph of the defendant's answer. Nevertheless the court was asked to strike that paragraph, because the allegations therein contained failed "to show whether the Relief & Hospital Department of the Plant System of Railways [was] a copartnership, a corporation, or a mutual benefit association; and, if a corporation, when and where chartered." As it was not alleged to be a corporation, surely it was not incumbent on the defendant to state when and where it was chartered. Under the facts presented, it was really immaterial whether this organization was, as matter of law, "a copartnership, a corporation, or a mutual benefit association;" for, by his demurrer, Petty necessarily admitted that he had become a member thereof and had thereby recognized its right to make a lawful contract, and was not, therefore, in a position to question its authority to transact the business in which it was engaged,

especially after he had received the fruits of the contract which
it had made with him, as he also by his demurrer admitted to
be true.   Eckman v. Railroad Co., 169 Ill. 312, 322.   A similar application of the doctrine of estoppel has heretofore been
expressly recognized by this court as eminently proper, both in
the case of *Planters' & Miners' Bank* v. *Padgett*, 69 *Ga.* 159, and
in that of *Imboden* v. *Mining Co.*, 70 *Ga.* 86.   The association
styled the "Plant System Relief and Hospital Department"
may, possibly, be conducting a general mutual benefit insurance business without a charter and without the least shadow
of right, but this is a matter as to which the State alone is concerned.   As it is not attempting to engage in a business without the pale of the law, it stands upon the footing of a de facto
corporation, at least.   *Georgia Southern & Florida R. R. Co.*
v. *Trust Co.*, 94 *Ga.* 306, 313 et seq.   The association itself
would certainly be estopped, under the circumstances, from
setting up its want of authority to engage in the business carried on by it, and thus repudiate its solemn engagements to its
members. .   *Georgia Ice Co.* v. *Porter*, 70 *Ga.* 637.   This being
so, it was not essential to the protection of Petty that he should
be allowed to raise, by demurrer or otherwise, any issue par-
taking of the nature of a plea of nul tiel corporation.

4. Before entering upon a discussion of the merits of the
case, as disclosed by the evidence introduced at the trial, it is
proper to briefly refer to a question of practice which, although
repeatedly ruled upon by this court, was wholly disregarded by
counsel for plaintiff in drafting his motion for a new trial.   In
the 6th ground thereof, complaint is made that certain documentary evidence, therein referred to as "contained and indicated in the brief of evidence as Exhibits No. 1, No. 2, and
No. 5," was admitted over various specified objections urged by
him at the trial.   We take occasion to again repeat that, as was
explicitly announced in each of the cases cited below, a ground
of a motion for a new trial which does not set forth, literally
or in substance, the evidence therein alleged to have been illegally admitted, can not be considered by this court.   *Western
Union Telegraph Co.* v. *Michelson*, 94 *Ga.* 436; *Rucker* v. *State*, 97
Ga. 205; *Baker* v. *State*, Ibid. 452; *Moncrief* v. *State*, 99 *Ga.* 395;

Herz v. *Claflin Co.*, 101 *Ga.* 615; *Huie* v. *McDaniel*, 105 *Ga.* 319; *Reinhart* v. *Blackshear*, Ibid. 799; *Pearson* v. *Brown*, Ibid. 802; *Taylor* v. *State*, Ibid. 847. The only remaining special ground of the plaintiff's motion relates to the direction of a verdict. Error is assigned upon the action thus taken by the court, (1) because, as counsel earnestly contends, there was evidence to warrant a finding by the jury that Petty, "being illiterate and unable to read or write, did not have fully explained to him and read over to him the said relied upon and alleged contract," and accordingly did not voluntarily and understandingly assent to its conditions respecting the release of the defendant company from liability; and (2) this contract being, at most, "purely an agreement of accord and satisfaction," the jury should have been allowed to say whether, under the evidence adduced at the trial, "there had been a full and complete accord and satisfaction" as matter of fact. The case really turns upon a proper determination of these two all-important questions. We shall deal with them separately, in the order in which they are presented.

5. As a matter of course, if Petty was by any artifice or fraudulent misrepresentation on the part of the defendant company or its agents induced to sign a contract the terms and conditions of which he did not understand and voluntarily assent to, the same would not be legally binding upon him, and he would be at liberty to repudiate it at pleasure, provided he offered to restore to the opposite party all fruits received by him thereunder. *East Tennessee Ry. Co.* v. *Hayes*, 83 *Ga.* 558. In the present instance, no such offer was made or excuse suggested why this eminently just and reasonable requirement of the law was not complied with before bringing suit. The position taken by Petty at the trial was, that he had a right to retain all the fruits received by him under his contract, ratifying the same to this extent, but repudiating it in so far as his own obligations thereunder were concerned. That is to say, he claimed the privilege of being arbitrarily inconsistent — a privilege which can not, of course, be properly conceded to any litigant. Nevertheless, in support of this position, counsel rely upon the case of *Butler* v. *Railroad Co.*, 88 *Ga.* 594. There it appeared that

the plaintiff "sought to make the question that the written instrument in the form of a receipt and release which the company produced, showing on its face an accord and satisfaction
touching the cause of action declared upon, was procured from
him by fraud. The instrument was signed with his mark, and
he denied that he ever entered into such a contract or that the
same was read over to him. He admitted that the amount specified as paid to him was paid, but denied that it was paid on
any such contract. He contended that it was paid upon his claim
for wages, and that in signing the instrument he thought he
was subscribing to an ordinary pay-roll only." In other words,
his grievance was, "not that he was induced by fraud to enter
into a contract, but that a fraudulent advantage was taken of
him by procuring his signature to a writing which [purported]
to set forth a contract into which he never entered. On his
theory, the money he received was no fruit of such a contract,
and could not have been, because none such was ever made."
Accordingly, it was held that, taking as true his version of the
transaction, he really received "nothing which he ought not
to have had independently of any agreement, fraudulent or not
fraudulent, touching his claim for damages on account of the
personal injury sued for," but merely what, so far as appeared,
he was strictly entitled to under another and entirely distinct
claim against the company, the contract of settlement concerning
which the writing did not truly and correctly set forth, but actually misrepresented. Clearly, under such circumstances, it was
not incumbent upon the plaintiff, as a condition precedent to
bringing his action for personal injuries, to offer to restore the
fruits of a settlement of an entirely distinct claim which he had
in good faith accepted and was undoubtedly entitled to retain,
notwithstanding the alleged fraud perpetrated upon him in procuring him to sign a release wholly different from that which
he had agreed to execute.

In the present case, it was not shown that the plaintiff had
any claim whatever against the company other than that growing out of the injury he alleges he sustained while in its service. He knew that the benefits he accepted were the fruits of
the contract he now seeks to repudiate. Upon this point, he

himself testified as a witness in his own behalf: " I got treated
for this trouble by Dr. Blanton, and was also furnished medicines; they gave that to me ; I had been paying money to that
hospital department for it. . . I did join the Relief & Hospital Department. I signed my name to some papers to join
that department. . . At the time I took these several small
amounts from Mr. Verdery [the company's cashier], I thought
they were for my half wages during the time I was hurt and
laid off. My understanding was, that, if I got hurt, they would
pay me half wages during the time I was laid off, and give me
my medical attention. That is what I thought I was paying
my dollar and a quarter a month for. I sure didn't take them
understanding that it would be a release of the railroad for the
payment of damages; I would not have taken them if I had
known that was what they were aiming at. . . I knew I was
being paid for the time I was laid off; I did not think they was
just giving me the money just to be generous ; I had been paying my dollar and a quarter every month, and I surely expected to get my benefit when I was damaged ; I didn't expect
just to pay my money in there and not get any insurance out
of it when I got hurt ; that was what I understood,—that if I
would give them that dollar and a quarter a month, they would
give me half pay for my lost time and my medicines and doc-
tor's bills. I was treated by Dr. Blanton, and I didn't pay
anything for it except my dollar and a quarter a month ; I got
this treatment and that money under my contract with the Relief & Hospital Department." Each of the several vouchers
which Petty signed with his mark and presented to the company's cashier recited that the amount therein specified was "in
payment of benefits due from " that department, and was "paid
and accepted under the regulations" thereof. Petty did not
undertake to charge that any of the company's agents in any
manner misrepresented the contents of these writings or by
their conduct led him to believe that payment was made on any
different claim than therein specified. Indeed, his sole complaint in this connection is, that the company's cashier paid
the orders drawn on him without any comment whatever, and
neither he nor any other agent of the defendant volunteered

to explain that, under Petty's written contract with the Relief
& Hospital Department, the acceptance of any of the benefits
provided for under its regulations would have the legal effect
of releasing the defendant company from all claims for damages growing out of the particular injury for which compensation was thus made.

We gather from the plaintiff's testimony, construed most favorably to him, that he really was ignorant of the terms and
conditions embraced in that contract, and never did grasp and
fully comprehend its precise character, import, or practical effect.   But certainly this was the result of no fraudulent act of
commission on the part of the company's agents, as the record
before us clearly discloses; and it would seem that if any un-
conscionable advantage was gained by the company through
the omission of its agents to read over to Petty and explain to
him the precise meaning of the written contract into which he
was called upon to enter as a condition precedent to becoming
a member of the Relief & Hospital Department, he by his conduct really misled them into the belief that he fully understood
the terms and effect of the contract, and subsequently allowed
that impression to remain by the readiness he displayed in ac-
quainting himself with all his rights in the premises and the
uniform promptness with which he asserted his claim to all
benefits accruing to him thereunder.   He did, in contradiction
to positive testimony to the contrary, swear that when he "joined
this hospital department, nothing at all was said to [him] as
to what effect [his] joining it would have upon [his] right to
recover for any injuries sustained by" him, and "no explanation of the contract was given;" but what he "understood was,
that all employees of the road had to belong to it and that they
had to join," as he was told by "a little low chunky man"
who, it is fair to infer from other evidence appearing in the
record, was none other than Dr. Caldwell, the Superintendent
and Chief Surgeon of the relief department, who witnessed the
execution of the contract signed by Petty.   The latter did not,
however, undertake to deny the sworn assertion of Dr. Caldwell and other witnesses introduced in behalf of the company,
to the effect that, before Petty was called upon to sign the in-

strument, he was asked particularly if he fully understood its
meaning, and answered in the affirmative. His omission to
meet this important testimony is significant in view of the fact
that he was thereafter recalled to the witness stand and was thus
afforded a full opportunity to do so, if he could truthfully testify to the contrary. In a case very similar, upon its facts, to
that now before us, the Court of Appeals of Maryland, in discussing an attempt by a railroad employee to repudiate a written contract signed by him, on the ground that "he could not
read English" and "believed he was signing a receipt . . and
nothing more," held that "A person who executes, without co-
ercion or undue persuasion, a solemn release under seal, can
not subsequently impeach it on the ground of his own carelessness, when at the time of its execution he might, had he seen
·fit, have advised himself fully as to the nature and legal effect
of what he was doing." See Spitze v. Railroad Co., 75 Md. 162.
This ruling was put upon the distinct ground that: "Such
person can not invoke his own heedlessness to impeach his solemn release, and then call that heedlessness some one else's
fraud. If he did not know what he was signing, it was his plain
duty to inquire. He had no right to act as one who understood what he was doing, unless he intended to lead those with
whom he was dealing to believe that he did understand the act
that he did." The common justice of the rule thus announced
appeals to us strongly. However, we place our decision in the
case at bar upon the incontrovertible ground that the same does
not fall within the letter or the spirit of the ruling made in Butler v. Railroad Co., supra, and therefore, if Petty desired to rescind his contract on the plea of fraud, it was incumbent upon
him to unreservedly make such election and offer to yield up
the benefits he accepted thereunder, if within his power; or, if
not, to treat it as binding upon him to the extent of releasing
the company from liability to respond in damages for his alleged injury, though not effectual to cut off his right to sue in
tort because of the fraud claimed to have been perpetrated upon
him in procuring his signature thereto. It is to be noted, in
·this connection, that the distinction here made between Butler's
case and one like the present was also pointed out and applied

in *W. & A. R. R. Co.* v. *Burke,* 97 *Ga.* 560, the decision in which controls the case at bar upon this point.

6. It may be true, as contended by counsel for the plaintiff in error, that a jury would have been authorized, under the evidence submitted in his behalf, to find that he did not actually receive all the benefits to which he was entitled as a member of the Relief and Hospital Department. It does not follow, however, that for this reason his action for damages had any standing in court. We do not agree with counsel that the contract relied on by the company was "purely an agreement of accord and satisfaction" which, not having been fully complied with on its part, did not operate to extinguish the plaintiff's cause of action, notwithstanding he had voluntarily accepted the major part of the satisfaction to which he was thereunder entitled. Unquestionably, as was said by Chief Justice Bleckley in *B. & W. Ry. Co.* v. *Clem,* 80 *Ga.* 539: "As long as the accord is executory, although it is partially performed, the original cause of action is not extinguished, and an action may be brought upon it, and the remedy for the defendant is to plead his part performance as satisfaction pro tanto. He gets credit for all he has paid upon it, but the right of action is not extinguished by an accord merely, without complete satisfaction, where the parol contract is that performance, not mere promise, is to constitute the satisfaction; [though] if a promise is to constitute it before performance, then the accord is executed by the promise." But the application of this rule to the facts of the present case which counsel invites us to make would not be justified by anything contained in the written instrument now under consideration. Petty therein expressly stipulated that acceptance by him from the Relief and Hospital Department of any of the benefits provided for by its regulations should operate, without more, to release the defendant company from all claims for damage he might have against it. In other words, the contract put him upon his election to look solely either to the treasury of that department or to the assets belonging to the company, for compensation in the event he sustained injury under circumstances which he thought entitled him to redress from it; and the moment he

gave evidence of his election by proceeding against and actually receiving benefits from the department, he necessarily relinquished his right to call upon the company for anything; for
it was mutually agreed between him and the company that
such conduct on his part should be conclusive evidence of his
acceptance of the department's obligation to pay him stipulated benefits, which obligation was expressly conditioned upon
his first fully releasing the company from all liability.   It is
to be remembered that one of the regulations of the relief department was that, "in the event of disability or death from
accidental injuries," none of the benefits therein provided for
should "be payable or paid until there be first filed" a satisfactory release of that character.   Under those circumstances,
the department made to its members only a conditional promise to pay.   To secure an unconditional promise, it was necessary to release the company.   The release was not itself to be
conditioned upon a fulfilment of the promise, but was to be the
consideration supporting such promise, tendered and parted
with in advance in order to make the promise itself obligatory.
The sum and substance of Petty's agreement, therefore, was
that the mere promise of the department should constitute a
full accord and satisfaction of his claim against the company,
in the event he elected to avail himself of such promise in lieu
of prosecuting his action against the company; and this being
so, he certainly can not be heard to urge that full performance,
rather than bare promise, was what was contemplated by all
parties concerned.

7. That we may not be understood as inadvertently overlooking or deliberately ignoring any of the questions presented
by counsel for the plaintiff in error on the argument here, we
will briefly allude to their further contention that the contract
by which the several corporations belonging to the Plant System undertook to obligate themselves to donate money to the
Relief and Hospital Department, assume the management of
its affairs, and guarantee the discharge of its obligations to its
members, was ultra vires, because its object was entirely foreign to the purposes for which railroad companies are usually
chartered.   In the first place, this question is not properly

raised by any of the special grounds of the motion for a new trial, nor is there in the bill of exceptions the faintest suggestion that the same was ever presented to and passed upon by the court below. Furthermore, a patient examination of the record before us discloses that no evidence whatever as to the nature and extent of the charter powers of any of these corporations was introduced at the trial. The silence of the record in this regard indicates either that this important issue was not raised at all, or else that the plaintiff signally failed to establish his contention by competent evidence, as it clearly was incumbent upon him to do. This being so, we can not, of course, undertake to arbitrarily assume that the corporations just referred to exceeded their charter powers when they entered into the contract which the plaintiff claims was ultra vires. Although it would seem that this self-evident proposition is capable of standing alone, unsupported by authority, an adjudication directly in point is not wanting. See Chicago R. R. Co. v. Bell, 44 Neb. 44.

On the whole, we conclude that counsel came to the assistance of the plaintiff too late to render him any effectual aid or comfort on the lines upon which his case was conducted.

Judgment affirmed. All the Justices concurring.

ATLANTA NATIONAL BANK v. GEORGE.

Where a debtor to several persons had a sum of money on deposit in a bank and gave to one creditor a check for a particular sum to be paid out of the fund, and immediately afterward assigned to another all the funds in the bank to his credit, and the assignment was first presented, no recovery can be had by the assignee, against the bank, for the whole sum of the deposit because it first paid to the holder the amount represented by the check, provided the assignee at the time of the assignment knew that it was the intention of the depositor to assign only the amount left after the payment of the check. Whether such was the intention and known to the assignee were questions of fact to be determined by the jury, and they having so found, which was the second verdict for the defendant, and there being ample evidence to support such finding, and the charge on the subject being legal and pertinent, a new trial should not have been granted.

Argued December 6, 1899. — Decided January 30, 1900.

Complaint. Before Judge Reid. City court of Atlanta.
March 27, 1899.

Abbott, Cox & Abbott, for plaintiff in error.
Candler & Thomson, contra.

LITTLE, J.   George sued the bank, alleging that it was due
him $516.49, because of the following facts: On the 26th of
September, 1895, Archibald Wilson gave to the plaintiff an order on the bank in the following words and figures: "Lithonia,
Ga., Sept. 26th, 1895.   To Cashier Atlanta National Bank:
Please pay Mr. M. M. George the amount you are due me, and
also give him my bank book; and if the Chicago check has not
come in, please place to his credit when it does come in."
[Signed] "Archibald Wilson."   By which paper the deposit
account of Wilson amounting to the sum sued for was transferred and assigned to the petitioner.   He gave notice of the
same on the 27th of September, and on said last-named day he
indorsed the written assignment and delivered it to the bank,
and the bank accepted the same, but only paid him $216.49.
The defendant denied all the allegations in the petition, and
pleaded that the paper given was made to hinder and delay the
creditors of Wilson.   It further pleaded that, previously to the
acceptance of the order, Wilson had given a check to one R. W.
Milner for the sum of $300 on the fund in the bank, which was
paid, leaving only to the credit of Wilson in the bank the
said sum of $216.49, which it paid over on said order to the
plaintiff.   The main question of fact to be determined by the
jury was, whether or not at the time Wilson gave the order to
George the latter was informed that previously to the execution
of the order Wilson had executed and delivered to Milner a
check on the fund for $300, in payment of certain claims held
against him by Milner.   The plaintiff testified that he had no
knowledge of that fact; that Wilson owed his firm an account
of about $800, and that he accepted the order assigning the de-
posit account as a credit on said debt, in good faith and without
any knowledge that the fund had previously been drawn on;
that early the next morning, and before the opening of the bank,
he presented the order, and at the request of the bank officials in-

dorsed it and was told when the bank opened he could get the
amount to Wilson's credit, whatever that was. In the meantime,
however, the check for $300 was presented and paid out of the
fund. Wilson, on the contrary, testified that at the time he
drew the check in favor of the plaintiff he notified him that he
had, a short time before, made a check in favor of Milner for
the sum of $300 and that he wrote the order in favor of George
to cover the balance to his credit, without stating any given
sum, because he was not certain what balance would remain
to his credit after the payment of the check for $300. There
was other evidence supporting the contention of the parties
on this issue. The jury returned a verdict for the defendant.
The plaintiff made a motion for a new trial on various
grounds, and, after consideration, the court granted a new trial,
which was the second, on the ground that the verdict was without evidence to support it, and on the further ground that
the court committed error as alleged in the 6th ground of the
motion. The defendant excepted, and we are to determine
whether or not the court erred in granting the new trial.

We are of the opinion that it did. If George accepted the
order from Wilson with knowledge that the latter had previously drawn on the fund to the amount of $300, and that it
was the intention of Wilson to transfer and assign to him the
amount on deposit to his credit in the bank, less the sum of
$300, then under no circumstances was he entitled to receive,
on the order given, any greater amount than that which remained after the payment of check for $300. Whether this
was so or not was a question of fact. Wilson in clear and explicit terms testified that he gave the check early in the evening; that later George called on him, and he explained to him
that he had drawn a check on the fund, and talked the matter
over with him, and after giving him the information he executed and delivered the order upon which the suit is founded.
This evidence, if the jury believed it—and they had the right
to do so—was amply sufficient to authorize a verdict for the
defendant. The charge of which complaint is made, as set out
in the 6th ground of the motion, is as follows: "If the jury
believes from the evidence that at the time Mr. Wilson gave.

the order to Mr. George he stated to Mr. George that he had
given the $300 check to Mr. Milner, and it was the intention
of Wilson, and this intention was known to Mr. George, to give
the order for the balance of the account after the payment of
the three hundred dollars, then and in that event the plaintiff
could not recover, but you should find for the defendant. That
is to say, gentlemen of the jury, on that issue, if Mr. George
took this paper with notice that Mr. Wilson had already given
a check on this fund for $300 to Mr. Milner with the intention
that the check should be paid out of the fund, and Mr. George
knew that, then the bank had the right to pay that check as
against that order, and having already paid to Mr. George
$216.49, the balance of the deposit account, the plaintiff would
not have the right to recover in this case." We see no objection whatever to this charge. It is clear, legal, and pertinent,
and in our opinion was a proper charge to be given. We find
nothing in the grounds of the motion not mentioned in the order
of the judge which requires the verdict to be set aside, and
we think that the judge committed error in granting a new trial
on the grounds specifically mentioned in his order; and while
this court is reluctant to interfere with the discretion of a trial
judge in setting aside a verdict, we are constrained to rule that
as in our judgment the verdict rendered by the jury was
amply supported by the evidence, and the charge of which
complaint is made was legal and proper, the verdict, being the
second one in favor of the defendant, should have been allowed
to stand.   *Judgment reversed. All the Justices concurring.*

BARGE v. WEEMS.

1. That a prosecution by a landlord of a cropper for selling cotton before
paying in full for advances received from the former to aid in making
the cotton was instituted in good faith and upon probable cause could not
be shown by proving that shortly after beginning the prosecution the landlord obtained against the cropper in a civil action a judgment which must
necessarily have been based upon claims not constituting such advances ;
and the more especially is this so when all the facts and circumstances in
proof tended to show that the main, if not the only, object of the prosecution was to affect the result of the civil proceeding.

2. The evidence in this case not only warranted but amply supported the verdict, and the trial judge was right in refusing to set it aside.

Argued December 11, 1899. — Decided January 30, 1900.

Action for malicious prosecution. Before Judge Reid. City court of Atlanta. July 3, 1899.

Peter F. Smith, R. R. Shropshire, and *Westmoreland Brothers,* for plaintiff in error. *Hunt & Golightly,* contra.

LUMPKIN, P. J.   It would be a mockery of justice to set aside the verdict now under review.   That this is so will sufficiently appear from a statement of the material facts, as to which there is little dispute or difference between the parties.   Weems, a colored man, was a cropper of Barge, a white man, for the year 1897, the contract being that the former was to receive for his services one half of what he made, subject, as is usual in such cases, to the payment of whatever he might owe his landlord for advances.   On about thirty acres of land he made a fraction over fourteen bales of cotton and about one hundred and fifty bushels of corn.   There was positive evidence that this was very good farming, and we are all agriculturists enough to know that such is the fact.   It finally resulted that Barge got thirteen bales of the cotton, the greater part of the cottonseed, most of the fodder raised with the corn, and all of the corn except about ten bushels.   After many unsuccessful efforts to bring Barge to a settlement, Weems sold the only bale of cotton which had not been delivered to Barge, and also brought an action against Barge in a justice's court.   At the time Weems sold this cotton, he and his family were actually suffering for want of food and necessary clothing, and he informed Barge before making the sale of his intention to do so.   A few days before the trial of the action in the justice's court, Barge sued out a warrant against Weems, charging him with a misdemeanor. This prosecution was based upon the theory that in selling the bale of cotton Weems had violated section 680 of the Penal Code, which makes it an offense for a cropper to " sell or otherwise dispose of any part of the crop grown by him, without the consent of the landlord, and before the landlord has received his part of the entire crop and payment in full for all advances made to the cropper in the year the crop was raised, to aid in making it." Weems was arrested and taken before a magistrate; and, being unprepared for trial, waived a hearing. Thereupon he was required to give bond in the sum of $200, conditioned for his appearance at the superior court. Barge was instrumental in having the bond fixed at the amount mentioned, and, but for his insistence, a smaller bond, and one which Weems would have been able to give, would have been exacted. Barge's conduct plainly indicated his desire to have Weems imprisoned. Weems could not give the $200 bond, and was kept in jail about three months before his final trial in the superior court, which resulted, as it should have done, in his acquittal. While he was in prison, Barge appropriated the bulk of the cottonseed, fodder and corn, as above indicated. The present action was brought by Weems against Barge for the damages occasioned him by the above-mentioned prosecution, the plaintiff alleging that it was malicious and without probable cause. The jury, after hearing the evidence, the substance of which is embraced in the foregoing statement, agreed with the plaintiff, and returned a verdict in his favor for $433.33. The trial judge refused to set this verdict aside. The defendant's motion for a new trial was based on alleged error in rejecting evidence and on the general grounds that the verdict was contrary to law and the evidence.

1. The evidence which the court refused to admit was a copy of the entire record of the suit of Weems *v.* Barge in the justice's court, which resulted in a judgment in favor of Barge. It was offered to show that when Barge sued out the criminal warrant Weems was actually indebted to him, and that accordingly Barge, in instituting the prosecution, acted in good faith and on probable cause. This record is a remarkable one. From it the following appears: The suit was upon an open account, in which Weems charged Barge with one half of the value of specified quantities of cotton and cottonseed, and credited him with stated amounts for guano, provisions, and cash, leaving a balance due Weems of $33.71. In defense Barge set up a counter-claim, which was also in the form of an account. He charged against Weems the guano, provisions, etc., embraced

\in the account sued, on, and as to these items their figures were
almost identical.   Barge also charged against Weems some
other items, such as costs in a State case of some kind against
Weems, hire of team for "moving son-in-law,"and use of mules
on Sundays.   He also charged against Weems the full value of
the very bale of cotton which the latter had sold.   But the most
remarkable charges which Barge brought against Weems were
items amounting to $75, predicated upon his alleged failure to
cultivate the crops of cotton and corn ."in a proper and farm-
like manner."   Barge obtained a judgment for $99.95, pre-
sumably upon his own testimony.   The record does not disclose where Weems was when this extraordinary judgment was
rendered.   It is quite probable that his mind was occupied with
the question of meeting the criminal prosecution which had
been begun, though the warrant had not yet been served upon him.   Even if Barge could in any event support his claim
of good faith in suing out this warrant by showing that, in a
civil proceeding between himself and Weems, he had obtained
a judgment against the latter, we are quite sure this record does
not tend to support such a claim.   Indeed it tends the other
way, and therefore, even if it had been admissible at all, rejecting it did Barge no harm.   No one could seriously contend that his claim of damages for the alleged "bad farming"
and the other charges above mentioned constituted "advances"
made to Weems to aid him in making the crop; and surely the
bale of cotton which was a part of the crop was not such an
"advance."   Moreover, as has been seen, Barge charged Weems
with the full value of this bale, when one half of it was the property of Weems.   If the items in Barge's account which could
in no fair sense be treated as advances to Weems had been strick-
en, it would have resulted that when he sold the cotton he was
not indebted to Barge a cent, but that Barge was actually indebted to Weems, and this Barge was obliged to know.

The preposterous claim for damages presented by Barge must
stand, because it has been included wholly or partially in a
judgment rendered by a court of competent jurisdiction ; but,
under the circumstances, we do not think the existence of
this judgment should have been proved on the trial now under

review, as an evidence of Barge's good faith in taking out the warrant. He certainly knew at the time of so doing that Weems did not owe him anything for advances. The conclusion that the warrant was sworn out to defeat the civil suit of Weems is much more plausible, and this, most probably, is the exact truth of the matter.

2. We agree with the trial judge that the verdict in this case ought to stand. It is too righteous a finding to be disturbed. Barge's treatment of his humble cropper was oppressive and wrong from the beginning, and the persecution (called prosecution) which he instituted was totally indefensible. If there is anything wrong about the verdict, it is the amount. The jury might well have made it larger.

Judgment affirmed. All the Justices concurring.

FARMERS MUTUAL INSURANCE ASSOCIATION OF GEORGIA v. AUSTIN.

1. The question of the validity of a contract made by an insurance company during a year in which it had failed to pay its license tax to the State is not made in the present record.
2. As the jury in the justice's court found in favor of the defendant upon evidence demanding a verdict for the plaintiff, the superior court erred in overruling the certiorari sued out by the latter.

Argued December 12, 1899. — Decided January 30, 1900.

Certiorari. Before Judge Lumpkin. Fulton superior court. March term, 1899.

O. E. & M. C. Horton, for plaintiff.
R. J. Jordan, for defendant.

LUMPKIN, P. J. The Farmers Mutual Insurance Association of Georgia was a corporation organized for the purpose of insuring its members against loss by fire, wind, or lightning. Its scheme, under its constitution and by-laws, for raising money with which to pay losses was to make assessments upon its members. J. A. DeFoor was a member, and sustained a loss by fire. J. P. Austin, another member, was assessed $4.70 for his pro rata share of this loss. He refused to pay, and the association

44

brought against him an action upon an account in which the particulars as to this assessment were fully set forth. There was a verdict for the defendant, and the plaintiff sued out a certiorari, which the superior court overruled, and the association excepted.

In the justice's court its secretary testified that "the account sued on was just, true, due, and unpaid; that said account was due on account of J. A. DeFoor loss by fire; that said fire occurred on or about the month of December, 1896; that said DeFoor was a policy-holder in said association," etc., etc., making out a complete case for the plaintiff. It does not appear that the defendant disputed either the justice or the amount of the assessment, and the only defense relied upon was that the association, by reason of its failure to pay its license taxes to the State for the years 1896 and 1897, was not lawfully entitled to transact business during those years, and therefore could not enforce the collection of this assessment. In support of this defense, the defendant proved that the plaintiff had not paid the taxes indicated. The record is silent as to whether the tax for 1895 was paid, nor does it disclose the date of DeFoor's policy. Counsel argued here the question whether or not the contracts of this association were void because of its failure to pay the taxes of 1896 and 1897, but we do not think this question was really involved in the case and can not, therefore, with propriety undertake to decide it. If the association was lawfully entitled to transact business when it issued the policy to DeFoor, it certainly had the right to collect the assessment due by Austin. If it ever became legally bound to pay DeFoor for a loss by fire, Austin at the same time became liable to pay his proportion of such loss, if it occurred during the period covered by the policy. The correctness of this proposition can not be seriously doubted. It does not affirmatively appear that the association was for any reason not so entitled when that policy was issued. The loss occurred in December, 1896, or about that time; and, for aught that appears, the policy may have been executed and delivered in 1895. If so, it was apparently a valid contract, for there was no defense based upon the assertion that the tax for that year had not been paid, nor was it incumbent on the plaintiff to show affirmatively that it had paid its tax for that year. If it failed to do so, the burden rested upon the defendant to allege and prove that such was the fact. Let it be remembered that the evidence for the plaintiff made a prima facie case in its favor. The defendant sought to overcome this evidence by attempting to show that the plaintiff could not lawfully write a contract of insurance in 1896 or in 1897, and did not show that the policy in question was in fact issued in either of those years. In other words, he utterly failed to show that the DeFoor policy was for any reason invalid. This being so, and the positive testimony being that the account sued on was "just, true, due, and unpaid," which could not have been so if the policy on which the assessment was based was void, a verdict for the plaintiff, so far as the record before discloses, was demanded and the court ought to have sustained the certiorari.

Judgment reversed.   All the Justices concurring.

FORD et al. v. GILL et al.

The trial court correctly construed the will involved in the present case, and consequently committed no error in granting a nonsuit.

Argued December 18, 1899. — Decided January 30, 1900.

Ejectment. Before Judge Lumpkin. Fulton superior court. March term, 1899.

Plaintiffs were nonsuited in the court below, and excepted. The only evidence necessary to be set out here is a copy of the will of William Terrell, dated February 19, 1851, which is as follows:

"Georgia, DeKalb County. In the name of God, amen. I, William Terrell, of State and county aforesaid, being impressed with the certainty of death, but of sound and disposing mind and memory, do make this my last will and testament. In the first place I desire that my body be decently buried, and my soul I commit to Almighty God who gave it. With regard to my estate, both real and personal, I make the following disposition:

1st.   I give and bequeath to Sileta Henson, wife of James Henson, of the State of Alabama, three negroes, to wit: Fanny, a woman about thirty-three years of age, and her child, a girl by the name of Frances, about three years of age, and Rhoda, a girl about eighteen years of age, which said negroes I give for the sole and separate use of the said Sileta Henson for and during her natural life, free from the control or management of her husband, and at her death to be equally divided between her children.

2nd.   I give and bequeath to Mary Ford, wife of my grandson William Ford, a negro man by the name of Tom, about thirty-seven years of age, a negro woman by the name of Kate, about forty-one years of age, and her child, a girl about six years of age, by the name of Tabitha Camele, to be held and enjoyed by the said Mary Ford to her sole and separate use, and free from the control of her husband, for and during the time of her natural life, and at her death to be equally divided amongst her children.

3rd.   I give and bequeath unto my grandson Coleman Ford a negro man by the name of George, about thirty-five years of age, and a negro man by the name of Dud, about thirty-three years of age. Also I give and bequeath to him all that part of lot of land number one hundred and forty-four in the fifteenth district of originally Henry, now DeKalb County, Georgia, which lies on the East side of Thurman's ginhouse branch, supposed to be one hundred acres.

4th. I give and bequeath to my friend William Ezzard of the State and County aforesaid, to be held in trust by him for the use and benefit and behoof of my great-grandson William Terrell, alias William Terrell Ford, and to be held by the said trustee and managed for the use and benefit of the said William Terrell Ford, three negro men, to wit, Jack, Ben, and Jim, and all that part of lot of land number one hundred and forty-four which lies on the west side of Thurman's ginhouse branch, supposed to contain one hundred acres, and fifty acres of lot number nine in the fourteenth district of originally Henry, now DeKalb County, adjoining thereto, and upon the death of said Ezzard or his resignation of the said trust, I desire that some other prudent and trustworthy person be appointed by the judge of the superior court of said county to take charge of and manage said property for the use and benefit of said William Terrell Ford during his natural life.

5th. My will and desire is that, as soon after my death as convenient, all the balance of my property not hereinbefore disposed of be sold by my executor hereinafter appointed, and, after paying all my just debts, I desire the proceeds to be equally divided between the said Sileta Henson, Mary Ford, Coleman Ford, Wm. Ezzard as trustee as aforesaid for William Terrell Ford, to be held and enjoyed by the said Sileta and Mary and their children respectively in the same manner and upon the same conditions as they are to hold and enjoy the negroes hereinbefore bequeathed to them, and the said Wm. Ezzard is to hold the said money as trustee and for the use and purposes as hereinbefore specified, to wit, for the use of the said William Terrell Ford."

6th. Appoints Coleman Ford as executor.

Oscar Reese, J. M. McBride, E. M. & G. F. Mitchell, P. F. Smith, and *Anderson, Felder & Davis,* for plaintiffs.

C. W. Smith and *W. M. Everett,* for defendants.

FISH, J. There was no error in granting the nonsuit. In disposing of the case, our learned brother who presided in the court below delivered an able and lucid opinion, which so completely expresses the views which we entertain of the questions involved, and so clearly demonstrates the correctness of the judgment which he rendered, that we have taken the liberty of adopting it as our own. His honor said:

"On the fifth day of June, 1897, Hester Ford and others brought their suit against W. C. Gill and others, in ejectment, using what is known as the John Doe and Richard Roe form of suit. They attached to their declaration an abstract of title under which they claim to recover. Briefly stated, their claim to recover is this: That the land was owned by one William Terrell, and that he died seized and possessed of it; that he left a will which was duly probated on July 7th, 1851; that the plaintiffs are the heirs at law and legatees of William Terrell.

They claim to be the descendants of four grandchildren of William Terrell, to wit, Sileta Ford who became Sileta Henson, William Ford, Mary Ford, and Coleman Ford. At the close of the plaintiffs' evidence, the defendants moved for a nonsuit. There are several grounds in the motion, but the only one which I deem it necessary to discuss at any length is with reference to the construction of the will of William Terrell, deceased. The land in controversy is that covered by the fourth item, in which a devise in trust is made for William Terrell junior, who is frequently termed in the evidence 'Little Billy.' It is conceded by the plaintiffs that William Terrell junior died in 1897, leaving children, and also that there had been a conveyance by his trustee; so that if the devise in the fourth item was one in fee simple, the plaintiffs have no case. Their entire case depends upon the proposition that the devise in the fourth item of the will of William Terrell senior only creates a life-estate in William Terrell junior. If this construction is correct, then there are two possible grounds on which the plaintiffs' claim of recovery may rest: (1) that this would leave an intestacy as to an estate in reversion in the land, and pass by inheritance to his descendants through his grandchildren other than the mother of William Terrell junior, whom the present plaintiffs claim to be; (2) that this reversion might be covered by the fifth, or residuary clause of the will, and that under that such descendants might recover.

Turning now to the will with a view of construing the devise in question, I would first remark that the well-recognized rule is that the intention of the testator governs. Looking at the will, it seems quite evident that the testator intended to provide for the disposition of his entire estate, and did not intend to leave any intestacy as to any part of it. This may be gathered from the whole will. In the beginning of the will he uses this language: 'With regard to my estate, both real and personal, I make the following disposition.' Evidently he meant his whole estate, and not part of it, and he thought he was making disposition of his entire estate. Again, after he had made certain devises or bequests, including that contained in the fourth item, he provided in the fifth item that, 'as soon after

my death as convenient, all the balance of my property be sold
by my executor,' etc.　Thus it is clear that he did not intend
to leave an intestacy as to some balance, because, after providing certain specific bequests, he then provided for all the balance of his estate, and not a portion of the balance.　I think,
therefore, it is evident from the language of the will itself, as
well as from the general tendency of the law in the construction of wills, that the testator intended to dispose of his entire
estate, and to leave no intestacy as to any portion of it.　In the
next place I may remark that there is no universal scheme of
life-estates in this will which would indicate that the testator
intended to leave a life-estate for this great-grandson.　On the
contrary the general trend of the will is to vest the fee simple
when it reached his great-grandchildren.　By the first item,
the testator bequeathed to Sileta Henson (his grandchild) certain
property for the sole and separate use of said Sileta for and
during her natural life, free from the control or management
of her husband, and at her death to be equally divided among
her children.　This vests absolutely an estate in the great-grandchildren of the testator.　By the second item he gave and bequeathed to Mary Ford, the wife of testator's grandson, William Ford, certain property 'to be held and enjoyed by the said
Mary Ford for her sole and separate use, and free from the control of her husband, for and during the term of her natural life,
and at her death to be equally divided among her children,'
thus again vesting that portion of the property absolutely when
it reached the great-grandchildren of the testator.　In the next
item he bequeaths to his grandson, Coleman Ford, certain property without any limitation of a life-estate.　So that, up to this
time, it can not be said that the testator exhibited any general
disposition to create a life-estate, especially not so in his great-
grandchildren.　Then follows the item which specially affects
this property, and which reads as follows: 'I give and bequeath to my friend William Ezzard, of the State and county
aforesaid, to be held in trust by him for the use and benefit and
behoof of my great-grandson William Terrell, alias William
Terrell Ford, and to be held by the said trustee and managed
for the use and benefit of the said William Terrell Ford, [cer-

tain described property including that involved in this suit],
and upon the death of said Ezzard or his resignation of the said
trust, I desire that some other prudent and trustworthy person be appointed by the judge of the superior court of said
county to take charge of and manage said property for the use
and benefit of said William Terrell Ford during his natural
life.' Then follows the fifth or residuary clause already referred to, and finally the clause appointing the executor.

It is to be noted that in the clause of the will now under
special consideration, the provision is, 'I give and bequeath to
my friend William Ezzard, of the State and county aforesaid,
to be held in trust by him for the use and benefit and behoof of
my great-grandson William Terrell, alias William Terrell Ford,
and to be held by the said trustee and managed for the use
and benefit of the said William Terrell Ford,' certain property.
There is nothing in this devise or conveying part of the clause
with reference to any life-estate, or any limitation upon the
estate, but it devised the property absolutely for the benefit of
William Terrell Ford, unlimited by any reference to any life-
estate.   Under the law of Georgia, no words of inheritance are
required to create a fee-simple estate, and a conveyance without words of inheritance will ordinarily carry the fee simple,
unless some lesser estate is expressly limited.   If this item had
stopped at this point, it is quite clear that it would have conveyed a fee-simple estate and not a life-estate.   But it is contended that the latter part of this item limits the former, and
curtails the estate so as to limit it to a life-estate.   Nothing is
said about a life-estate in the conveying part of the item, as
already stated.   In the latter part of this item it is provided
that in case of the death or resignation of Ezzard, the trustee,
the testator desires that some other prudent and trustworthy
person be appointed by the judge of the superior court of said
county 'to take charge of and *manage said property for the use
and benefit of said William Terrell Ford during his natural life.*
It does not say that the title is limited or that the estate is de-
creased, restricted, or limited to a life-estate; but only, in case
of the death or resignation of the original trustee appointed by
the item, that some other person shall be appointed by the

superior court to manage and take charge of the property during his (William Terrell Ford's) natural life. There may be
quite a difference between the time when some person is to
manage the property, and the extent of the title.

Furthermore, I think the fifth item, immediately following,
casts light upon the intention of the testator as to the fourth
item. It provides, as already stated, that, 'as soon after my
death as convenient, all the balance of my property be sold by
my executor hereinafter appointed, and, after paying all my
just debts, I desire the proceeds to be equally divided between
the said Sileta Henson, Mary Ford, Coleman Ford, and William
Ezzard as trustee as aforesaid for William Terrell Ford, to be
held and enjoyed by the said Sileta, Mary, and their children
respectively, in the same manner and upon the same conditions
as they are to hold and enjoy the negroes hereinbefore bequeathed to them, and the said William Ezzard is to hold the
said money as trustee and for the use and purposes as hereinbefore specified, to wit, for the use of the said William Terrell
Ford.' Now, if the testator had intended or supposed that he
was creating only a life-estate in the land devised in the fourth
item, then by the fifth item he was providing that the remainder
of this estate should be sold at once by his executor and the
proceeds divided among the certain named devisees or legatees,
including the trustee for the life-tenant as one of them. It can
hardly be supposed that the testator intended to limit the estate created for his great-grandson to a life-estate, and provide
for the sale of the remainder, which probably could not be reduced to possession for many years, as the life-tenant was then
young, and yet intended that a portion of the proceeds of this
very remainder should go to the life-tenant. This would be a
compounding of estates which could hardly have been in the
mind of the testator. So that the very natural conclusion arising from the fifth item would show the improbability of the
testator intending to create only a life-estate by the fourth item.

It is contended by counsel that the expression, 'the said William Ezzard is to hold the said money as trustee for the use and
purposes as hereinbefore specified, to wit, for the use of the said
William Terrell Ford,' means that he was to hold but a life-

estate, and that the words 'as hereinbefore specified' referred to
the *last* words of the previous item providing for a trustee to be
appointed, in case of the death or resignation of Ezzard, to take
care of and manage the estate for William Terrell Ford during
'his natural life.'   On the contrary, it seems to me that the expression used in the fifth item in relation to the trustee distinctly negatives any such idea.   It does not say that William
Ezzard is to hold this fund in the manner in which some person who might be appointed to succeed him should hold or manage the property under the previous item, but that he should
hold this fund as was provided for him to hold it in the previous item ; and to make sure that there could be no mistake how
William Ezzard was specified to hold it in the previous item,
the testator took the trouble to repeat what he intended, 'to wit,
for the use of the said William Terrell Ford.'   Thus at the close
of the fifth item he explains distinctly what he meant by the
fourth item, and that the devise 'as hereinbefore specified' was
meant by him to be for the use of the said William Terrell Ford,
without any limitation for life or otherwise.   If any regard is to
be paid to the light to be drawn from the evidence dehors the
will, it may be remarked that it appears that William Terrell
junior was a young man who was known or considered in the
family as being weak ; and it is quite apparent that he was weak
in character, whether he was in intellect or not ; and this weakness had extended to the point of landing him in the penitentiary.   Therefore there might be a very considerable reason why
the testator might have thought it necessary to have some person to handle and manage the property for him, and yet not
cut off his inheritance.

It is insisted, however, by counsel for the plaintiffs that there
was no reason shown, and no facts shown, which would in law
authorize a trust for William Terrell junior.   If this be taken
as correct, the result would be, not to destroy or limit his estate,
but to vest in him the estate instead of leaving it in a trustee.
If, therefore, a trust was conveyed to William Ezzard in fee simple, and William Terrell junior, upon becoming of age, was
capable of managing his estate so that no continuing trust could
be made for him, the result would be, not to limit his estate,

but to vest it absolutely in him. It does not appear from the evidence that William Ezzard died or resigned, or any other person was ever appointed in his place under the last clause of the fourth item; so that if, under the contingency of a second appointment, there might have been any limitation placed upon the estate, it never occurred, but the estate stood where it was originally created by the devise creating William Ezzard trustee, and was not changed by any change of trustee or any subsequent appointment. If A. conveys an estate in trust for B. and B. is of age and capable of taking the estate, and not a person for whom a trust can be created, the result is that B. takes in fee simple; and if such a fee-simple estate is created for B., but the creator of the estate undertakes to appoint some person to manage the property for B., either for a limited time or for life, this does not limit, curtail, or destroy any estate in B., but the only result is that B. can manage his own property and take it away from the agent, trustee, or person before appointed. Thus then, regarding the whole will, and what seems to me to be the evident intention of the testator, it is quite clear to my mind that the estate created in this land by the fourth item was a fee-simple estate and not a mere life-tenancy. This being true, there could be no recovery by these plaintiffs as being descendants of William Terrell through his grandchildren on the ground that there was an intestacy as to a remainder interest in this estate; and, for the reasons which I have already given, it is quite clear to my mind that the testator never intended or contemplated that there was any remainder interest in this land which could be covered by the fifth item or residuary clause in his will, and that there can be no recovery under that."

Judgment affirmed.   All the Justices concurring.

McMILLAN *et al.* v. HUNNICUTT *et al.*

1. Where an equitable petition was filed against certain minors who were duly served, and thereafter a guardian ad litem was appointed for them, such guardian could, under section 4848 of the Civil Code, consent to the trial of the case at the first term. Even were this not true, if the court proceeded to trial and the jury returned a verdict under which a decree

was entered, such decree, though it might be irregular or erroneous, was not void.

2. Where the title to realty was thereby decreed to be in the plaintiff, and she thereupon mortgaged it, and, after a default in the payment, the mortgage was foreclosed and the property sold at judicial sale; and where subsequently the minors brought an equitable petition to set aside the sale for fraud and collusion in obtaining the decree, and the only notice of such fraud and collusion alleged against the mortgagee was that when the loan was made by him to the plaintiff he had constructive notice of a trust deed of record, the will of the husband of the mortgagor, proceedings for the latter's appointment as trustee, her appointment as such, and the petition by her to have the title to the trust property to be decreed to be in her; *held*, that this allegation of constructive notice was not sufficient, even if proved, to authorize a court to set aside the decree; *held* further, that, as the mortgagee had no notice of fraud, the purchasers at the foreclosure sale obtained a good title although they may have had full notice of the fraud.

Argued.December 18, 1899. — Decided January 30, 1900.

Equitable petition. Before Judge Candler. Fulton superior court. March term, 1899.

P. F. Smith and *R. R. Shropshire*, for plaintiffs.
Arnold & Arnold, for defendants.

SIMMONS, C. J. 1. One of the main propositions argued by counsel for the plaintiffs was, that a guardian ad litem, duly appointed, could not consent to the trial of an equity case at the first term of the court. Section 4848 of the Civil Code authorizes "parties to proceedings for equitable relief" by consent to try cases at the first term. When infants are brought into a court by proper service, the law presumes that they are incapable of conducting or controlling their side of the case, and therefore wisely provides for the appointment of a guardian ad litem to conduct, control, and direct the case so far as the minors' interests are concerned. While such guardian is not strictly a party to the case, in the sense that the judgment is rendered for or against him personally, he is, in our opinion, such a party as may consent to a trial of the case of his wards at the first term. In consenting to such trial he acts for his wards. There are several cases in our reports where this has been done. It is true this particular question was not ruled in any of them, but this court recognized such a consent and held the judgments obtained at the first term valid and binding.   *McGowan* v. *Luf-burrow*, 82 *Ga.* 523; *Sharp* v. *Findley*, 71 *Ga.* 654.   Other cases might be mentioned where a similar consent by the guardian ad litem was not questioned.   We can not see that such conduct on the part of the guardian ad litem was calculated to injuriously affect the interest of his wards.   He did not consent to a decree against them, but simply that the case might be tried at the first term.   We apprehend that trial judges in equitable proceedings against minors will see to it that nothing is done that is prejudicial to the interests of the minors, whether the case be tried at the first or a subsequent term.   Even were this not true, and even though the guardian ad litem had no right or authority to consent to a trial at the first term, we would still hold that this judgment was not void for that reason.   As we have repeatedly held, there is quite a difference between a void and an irregular or erroneous judgment.   The former is an absolute nullity and confers no rights or interests on any one; the latter is binding until reversed or set aside.   In the present case the court, when the petition was filed and served upon the minors, had jurisdiction of the subject-matter of the suit and jurisdiction of the persons.   The consent to a trial at the first term was, under this view, no more than an irregularity, — such an irregularity as did not deprive the court of its jurisdiction.   Counsel for the plaintiffs cited in their brief many authorities as to the power of guardians ad litem in representing their wards.   We have examined many of them, and in each case have found the doctrine relied on by him as declaring the decree to be void was announced by the different courts upon appeal or writ of error.   In cases where the guardian had failed to answer, or had made an admission, or been guilty of some other conduct detrimental to the interests of his ward, and the lower court had sustained him in what he had done, the case would be, on appeal or writ of error, reversed ; or where the lower court had refused to sanction the conduct of the guardian and the case was carried up, the appellate court would affirm the judgment.   There is no case to be found where it is held that such an irregularity on the part of the guardian ad litem made the judgment or decree void, but all hold upon that subject that

the judgment into which such irregularities enter is simply erroneous.   This court, in the case of *Foster* v. *Jones*, 23 *Ga.* 168,
held :   " If one be appointed by the court guardian ad litem of
a lunatic and accept the trust, a judgment against the lunatic
will be good, notwithstanding the guardian fails to act.   A judgment against a lunatic is not void but voidable ; and a purchaser
at sheriff's sale, under such judgment, would be protected."   In
that case an attachment was issued against Mary White, and
pending the suit it was made to appear to the court that she
had been, in due and legal form, declared to be a lunatic.   A
guardian ad litem was appointed to prepare and conduct her
defense in the case.   He accepted, but did not act or make any
defense.   Judgment was obtained, and the execution levied
upon Mary White's land.   The land was sold.   Ejectment was
afterwards brought to recover the land, and the above-quoted
ruling was made.   It is true Mary White was not a minor, but
she was a lunatic and needed representation as much or more
than a minor.   The same principle would apply to each case.
If in that case a motion for a new trial had been made or proper
exception taken, it is very probable that the new trial would
have been granted and the judgment set aside ; but, inasmuch
as it was not excepted to and remained unreversed, this court
held it was not void but of full force and effect in a subsequent
suit brought to recover the land.

2. The petition alleged many facts tending to show the great
hardship on these minors produced by the conduct of their
mother in the management of this property after she got the
full title.   It seems that McMillan & Snow executed a deed of
trust to McMillan to certain realty.   Under the deed, McMillan
was to hold the property in trust for his wife during her life,
and, after her death, for their children.   He died, and his wife
was appointed trustee in his stead.   She was also made his executrix, and qualified as such.   The trust deed and the will were
recorded.   Subsequently Mrs. McMillan filed a petition in the
superior court, alleging that the property was purchased with
her money, that the legal title was taken in the name of her
husband as trustee for her and the children, but that a trust
in her favor resulted from the fact that the property was pur-

chased with her money. She prayed that both the title and the beneficial interest be decreed to be in her. The case was submitted to a jury, and a verdict returned finding the allegations of the petition to be true. The title was decreed to be in the petitioner, freed of any trust. After this decree, Mrs. McMillan borrowed $8,500 and gave a mortgage upon this property to secure the loan. She failed to repay the loan when it fell due, the mortgage was foreclosed, and the property was sold at judicial sale. Subsequently the present petition was filed to set aside the sale. While the original petition contained numerous charges of fraud and mismanagement between Mrs. McMillan and the guardian ad litem, and specified some acts which were alleged to have been fraudulent, by an amendment to the petition it was declared that the facts recited above constituted the only notice of fraud or irregularity with which the mortgagees were affected. When this amendment was made and allowed, the trial judge sustained a demurrer to the petition filed by the purchasers at the foreclosure sale. We think that the facts shown were not sufficient to put the mortgagees upon notice that the decree was fraudulent and void, even if it were so under the allegations of the original petition. Had the mortgagees searched the records they would have found the original deed from McMillan & Snow to McMillan, the application of Mrs. McMillan to be appointed trustee in her husband's stead after his death, the record of her appointment, and the petition filed by her to put the legal title and the beneficial interest in her, proper and legal service upon the minors who were interested, the appointment of a guardian ad litem, and an apparently regular and proper verdict and decree, had, however, at the first term. Had they read the petition they would have known that ... the court had jurisdiction in a case of the kind and to make a decree such as was prayed. The pleadings, verdict, and decree were all regular on their face and showed no fraud or intimation of fraud in the procurement of the decree. There was, therefore, nothing whatever to put them on notice or inquiry as to any fraud or collusion. When they loaned their money to Mrs. McMillan they relied upon the decree showing both the legal title and the beneficial interest to be in her. She got the money, expended it, and failed to repay it when due; and they foreclosed their mortgage. They had no notice of fraud or collusion, and brought the property to sale through the regular channels. The purchasers at the sale got a good title as against these children, even though such purchasers had notice. It is a well-settled principle, announced not only by outside authorities but in our code, that one without notice can convey a good title to one with notice. When the land was purchased at the judicial sale, the purchasers at that sale succeeded to all the rights and interests of the mortgagees. *Cosnahan* v. *Johnston*, 108 *Ga.* 235; Civil Code, § 3938, and cases cited. We therefore affirm the judgment of the court below, sustaining the demurrer to the petition as amended.

Judgment affirmed. All the Justices concurring, Little, J., for special reasons.

OZBURN *et al. v.* FLOURNOY.

Where a married woman sought an exemption of personalty as the property of her husband, alleging that he refused to apply for such exemption, the proceeding was not subsequently amendable by converting it into an exemption of the property as that of the wife as head of the family, based upon the idea that she was living separate from her husband and had a minor child.

Argued December 15, 1899. — Decided January 30, 1900.

Bail-trover. Before Judge Calhoun. City court of Atlanta. July 8, 1899.

McElreath & McElreath, for plaintiffs in error.

S. D. Johnson and *W. J. Speairs*, contra.

CobB, J. On December 18, 1897, Mittie Flournoy filed and had recorded in the office of the ordinary of Fulton county a paper purporting to be a schedule of property claimed as exempt. The following is an extract from the same, showing such of its parts as are material to the present investigation : "Schedule of personal property belonging to Charles Flournoy, of said county, and claimed to be exempt from levy and sale under section 2866 et seq. of the Code of 1895, and the amendments thereto, by Mittie Flournoy, also of said county, wife of Charles Flournoy, he being a debtor and head of a family consisting of his said wife and his child Willie Lee Flournoy, age 6 years, and her said husband refusing to file a schedule under said laws for the benefit of said family." On January 28, 1898, she filed and had recorded in the office of the ordinary what purported to be an amendment to the paper above referred to, which was in the following words : "Mittie Flournoy petitions for an amendment to schedule filed and recorded on December 18, 1897, as follows: Mittie Flournoy owns the personal property set aside in said schedule and exemption. She is the head of a family (living separate and apart from her husband for about seven years), consisting of herself and child, Willie Lee Flournoy, six years of age; the property mentioned in said schedule being the property of petitioner, and her separate property." On July 2, 1898, she filed in the same office another paper, purporting to be a further amendment to the paper first above referred to, which was in the following words: " The petition of Mittie Flournoy shows, that on Dec. 18, 1897, she filed with you her schedule of property claimed as exempt from levy and sale, which was duly recorded, and by mistake alleged that it belonged to Charles Flournoy, her husband, and that he was the head of the family, etc. Your petitioner now comes and asks to amend her schedule by striking from said petition the words Charles Flournoy in the second line, the word said that immediately precedes Charles Flournoy's name in the fifth line, and all of lines six, seven, and eight down to the word to wit, and inserting in lieu thereof words so as to make the schedule read and be as follows, to wit: Schedule of personal property belonging to Mittie Flournoy of said county, and claimed to be exempt from levy and sale under section 2040 of the Code of Georgia of 1882, and the amendment thereto, by Mittie Flournoy, the wife of Charles Flournoy, from whom she has been living separate and apart for about seven years, she being a debtor and the head of a family consisting of herself and her daughter Willie Lee Flournoy, age six years. " The paper last referred to was recorded by the ordinary on July 19, 1898. On December 23, 1897, certain of the articles of personal property em-

45

braced in the papers above referred to were levied upon as the
property of Mittie Flournoy.   On July 2, 1898, she brought an
action of trover against the constable making the levy, and
against the plaintiff in the execution levied, to recover as her
property the articles which had been levied upon.   Upon the
trial she contended that the property was hers, and was exempt
from levy and sale, on account of the homestead which it was
contended had been set apart to her under the proceedings
above referred to.   The jury returned a verdict in her favor for
the property sued for; and the case is here upon a bill of exceptions sued out by the defendants, complaining that the court
erred in refusing to grant a new trial.

. The paper filed by Mittie Flournoy in the office of the ordinary on December 18, 1897, appears upon its face to be a schedule of property belonging to her husband, which she desired
as his wife to have set apart as exempt from levy and sale at
the instance of his creditors, for the reason that he had refused
to take advantage of the law allowing this to be done.   If the
property belonged to her husband, the schedule filed was sufficient to exempt the same from levy and sale at the instance of
his creditors; but if the property did not belong to him but was
hers, then the fact that it had been set apart as a homestead of
the husband would not prevent its being seized upon lawful
process as her property.   It is not, however, contended that she
is entitled to take anything under it as a homestead in her husband's favor, but that the schedule filed was intended to be in
her own favor and was filed for the purpose of having her own
property set apart as exempt.   This fully appears from what
purports to be the two amendments to the schedule.   It is not
necessary in this case to determine whether there is any law
authorizing the amendment of a schedule filed under section
2866 of the Civil Code.   If a schedule so defective as to be
void is filed and recorded, there would seem to be no good reason why the debtor should not thereafter file a complete and
perfect schedule without regard to such defective schedule; but
even if an amendment could be made in any case, no amendment made could ever have the effect of relating back and making perfect a schedule which would be defective and void but

for the amendment. Certain it is, however, that no amendment can be allowed, which would have the effect of changing a schedule setting apart property of the husband, as exempt, from levy and sale for his debts, to a schedule setting apart the same property as the property of the wife and exempt from levy and sale for her debts. Great hardships would result from any other rule. The facts of the present case make this clearly apparent. The constable levies an execution upon property which is not included in any recorded schedule as the property of the defendant in execution, and after the levy a schedule, which would not have put the constable or any one else on notice that the defendant had filed a schedule seeking to have the property exempted from her debts, is allowed to be amended in such a way as to change it into an exemption in her favor, which is now sought to be used as the foundation for holding the constable liable in an action of trespass for levying upon exempted property.

Judgment reversed. All the Justices concurring.

SUTTLES *v.* SEWELL *et al.*

709 707
f109 805
109 707
117 214
109
128

1. If a purchaser at a sheriff's sale does not comply with the terms of his bid, the officer may, under proper conditions, resell on the same day within the lawful hours of sale, the more especially after giving, in advance, notice of an intention so to do in the event of failure by the successful bidder to make payment by a designated hour; but where, in such a case, the second sale took place after the dispersal of the crowd in attendance upon the first and just before the close of sale hours, when there was little or no competition, and the plaintiff in execution became the purchaser at a price which was not only far less than that brought at the previous sale but so grossly inadequate as to shock even the average man's sense of justice and fairness, the second sale should be treated as void and the property should be readvertised and sold again.

2. One who, with knowledge of the facts, becomes the transferee of the bid made by the purchaser at a sale of the character last indicated, and who by virtue of such transfer and the payment of the amount of the bid acquires a deed from the sheriff, occupies no better footing as to title than such purchaser would have done if the sheriff had conveyed to him.

3. The present case should not have been disposed of by a judgment of nonsuit.

Argued December 15, 1899.— Decided January 30, 1900.

Equitable petition.   Before Judge Lumpkin.   Fulton superior court.   March term, 1899.

R. B. Blackburn, for plaintiff.
Simmons & Corrigan and *Oscar Parker*, for defendants.

LUMPKIN, P. J. On the first Tuesday in January, 1897,
certain realty belonging to Mrs. Suttles was by the sheriff exposed to sale before the court-house door of Fulton county under an execution in favor of Mrs. Powell.   It was knocked off
to Gammage at the price of $3,605.   He did not comply with
the terms of his bid, and the property was resold on the same
day to Mrs. Powell for $1,300, a bid in her behalf for this
amount having been made by C. J. Simmons as her attorney.
Subsequently Gammage filed an equitable petition, whereby he
sought to enjoin the sheriff from conveying the land to the
second purchaser, and to compel the execution of a sheriff's deed
to himself.   This court, in 101 *Ga.* 540, affirmed a judgment
denying an interlocutory injunction upon his petition.   Mrs.
Powell's bid was transferred to Sewell, and the sheriff conveyed
the property to him.   In *Suttles* v. *Sewell*, 105 *Ga.* 129, this
court also affirmed a judgment directing the sheriff to put the
latter in possession of the property.   At that time the present
case, which is an action by Mrs. Suttles to set aside the sheriff's
deed to Sewell, was pending; but as the issues therein involved
were not passed upon or adjudicated in the proceeding instituted by Sewell against Mrs. Suttles to obtain possession, it was
in the volume last cited expressly ruled that our judgment in
the case therein disposed of would not conclude Mrs. Suttles
as to the questions at issue in the case now before us.   See remarks of Mr. Justice Cobb as to this matter on pages 133 and
134.   This much of preliminary history seems to be an essential preface to the discussion which follows.
   1. Mrs. Suttles excepts to a judgment in the nature of an order of nonsuit, whereby it was in the court below adjudged that
she failed to make out a prima facie case entitling her to a cancellation of the sheriff's deed to Sewell.   We will not here re-
capitulate the evidence, but will refer to its salient features as
we proceed.   Taking it as a whole and giving to the plaintiff

the benefit of the inferences therefrom most favorable to her contentions, which is the proper course in dealing with a judgment of nonsuit, the jury would have been authorized to find substantially such a state of facts as those outlined in the first headnote, and that Sewell had knowledge thereof when he took the assignment of Mrs. Powell's bid and the sheriff's deed. We do not mean to say that a finding of this kind was demanded, but merely to assert that it would have been warranted. Upon the assumption that such a state of facts existed, was the second sale a valid and lawful disposition of the plaintiff's property?

This court, in *Humphrey* v. *McGill*, 59 *Ga.* 649, held that, upon failure of a purchaser to comply with his bid, the sheriff might, without readvertisement, sell again, within legal hours, on the same day. It has never, however, held that a resale would be upheld merely because it took place during the lawful hours of sale, if it was not in other respects properly and fairly conducted. In *Sanders* v. *Bell*, 56 *Ga.* 443, Judge Jackson, referring to an administrator's sale, said: "If the bidder, on the day of sale, refuses to comply before the crowd disperses and the hours of sale terminate, that day is the proper time to resell; if that can not be done, just so soon as the property can be readvertised after notice of refusal to comply with the terms of sale." Unquestionably this view, if correct, is good law in the case of a sheriff's sale. It is true that in the case cited there was no question as to the validity of a resale made on the same day on which there had been a failure to consummate the first sale. The language quoted from Judge Jackson was used in arguing the proposition that a resale at the first purchaser's risk should be "as soon as it can reasonably be done," but what he says commends itself to our minds as sound doctrine. Indeed, it seems that this eminent jurist instinctively apprehended the true law which should control our present question. "Before the crowd disperses and the hours of sale terminate." A commentary embraced within a phrase. What is the meaning of it? Why, that the second sale should not only take place within the legal hours, but that it should be a fair one—that it should not occur under circumstances necessarily involving a sacrifice of the property—that it should have not merely the form, but

the substance, of a bona fide sale, with reasonable opportunity
for competition. And is not this consistent with common honesty and fair dealing? A month's delay would ordinarily work
no great damage to the plaintiff in execution. A sale without
bidders might ruin the judgment debtor. There was evidence
in this case tending to show that the property was worth from
$5,000 to $6,000. At the first sale, it was knocked off at $3,605.
At the last, the plaintiff in execution, if the transaction stands,
got it for $1,300. While mere inadequacy of consideration
would not avoid the sale, such gross inadequacy as this ought
to do so if the sale was for any other good reason impeachable.
See 12 Am. & Eng. Enc. L. 237, 238. In *Parker* v. *Glenn*, 72
Ga. 637, this court, in dealing with a bill to set aside a sheriff's
sale, held: "Inadequacy of price is not sufficient per se to set
aside a sale, unless it is so gross as, when combined with other
circumstances, to amount to fraud; but if it be great, it is of itself a strong circumstance to evidence fraud, and this is true
where it is attended by any other fact showing the transaction
to be unfair or unjust, or against good conscience." Indeed,
it has been said to be "the duty of all courts, when satisfied that
sales made under their process are affected with fraud, irregularity or error, wilful disregard of the statutory regulations by
the officer, whereby the rights of either of the parties interested
are seriously affected, to set aside such sale upon a proper showing to the court under whose process the sale was made, and order a resale of the property." Herman on Executions, § 249.
The above is quoted in 12 Am. & Eng. Enc. L. 235, and in a
note, followed by numerous citations, it is said: "This statement of the rule serves to indicate generally the *power*, if not
the *duty*, of the courts, and is supported in its general scope by
the authorities cited by Mr. Herman." In *Johnson* v. *Dooly*, 72
Ga. 301, also a case relating to a sheriff's sale, Mr. Justice Hall,
speaking for this court, said: "It is laid down generally that
the court upon whose judgment the execution issues has full
power to set aside an execution sale whenever the ends of justice and fair dealing require it, and to order a resale, or award
execution anew, at discretion." This statement of the law is
taken verbatim from the text in Rorer on Judicial Sales, § 1081,

and the substance of it now appears in section 5427 of our Civil Code.

The sale now under review occurred but a few minutes before the sale hours expired; and if the property was really worth several thousand dollars, it is evident that the plaintiff in error had no competition. At the morning sale, when bidders were on the ground, some one must have run up the land to about $3,600, for the last bid was $3,605, and presumably the next to the last was but a little less. A recital of such facts shocks even the average man's sense of justice and fairness. There was also evidence to the following effect: The husband of Mrs. Suttles, acting as her agent, and Gammage, representing himself, were in the office of the sheriff shortly after three o'clock, endeavoring to arrange for a consummation of the sale to Gammage, the purpose of Suttles being to prevent a resale, so as to secure for his wife the benefit of the price of $3,605, and that of Gammage being to obtain the property. He was seeking an extension of time for payment. The sheriff agreed to do anything to which Simmons, representing Mrs. Powell, would agree, and the latter was summoned by telephone. Suttles left the office and was absent about ten minutes, the sheriff promising to wait till he came back before making another sale. Gammage, during this interval, was in the sheriff's outer-office. About the time Suttles returned, Simmons and Thomas, a deputy-sheriff, entered the office, and the announcement was then made that the latter had sold the property to Simmons. Neither Suttles nor Gammage was present at the second sale nor expecting it to occur, but were anticipating further negotiations with Simmons, as stated. All this should have been weighed and passed upon by the jury. Granting that there was no moral or intentional fraud, the evidence, interpreted most favorably for the plaintiff, makes a case of legal fraud. See second headnote in *Johnson* v. *Dooly*, 72 *Ga.* 297, cited supra, laying down the proposition that "The fraud which avoids a sale may be legal as well as moral." And, under this evidence, could not the jury have found that it was at least an "irregularity" to expose this valuable property for sale almost at the end of the sale day, with no one present to bid for it except the attorney of the plaintiff in execution, and he in a position to bid any desired amount not exceeding that of the fi. fa., which was considerably more than $3,000, without being called upon to produce a dollar for aught save the costs and expenses of the sale? We must not be understood as saying these are the actual facts of the transaction, for we are merely putting the case as the jury might have viewed it. We recognize that the position of the defendant in error is much strengthened by the fact, appearing in the evidence, that the sheriff announced at the first sale an intention to resell if the successful bidder thereat did not pay for the land by 3 o'clock p.m. It was perfectly proper for the sheriff to make such an announcement, but we do not think the fact that he did so is of itself sufficient to prevent the jury from passing upon the plaintiff's case in its entirety, of course giving to the circumstance just mentioned its proper weight.

One other point on this branch of the case requires notice at our hands. It was urged for the defendant in error that the evidence showed that Gammage, who was a brother of Mrs. Suttles, was not a bona fide bidder, and that his conduct at the sale was simply the result of a conspiracy between the two to prevent any sale at all on that day. If the evidence demanded a finding to this effect, it would of course follow that Mrs. Suttles would have no right to invoke equitable aid to relieve her from loss incurred by the sacrifice of her property which she thus contributed to bring about. But we can not say that the evidence did so demand. This question, like all the others in the case, should be passed upon and determined by a jury.

2. If Sewell took the assignment of the bid and the sheriff's deed thereunder with knowledge of the facts as they are claimed to be by Mrs. Suttles, and if under those facts the sale to Mrs. Powell was void, it requires no argument to show that he is in no better position than she would have been had the sheriff conveyed to her. As to how he would stand if he took innocently and in good faith, we are not now called upon to decide, as no question of this kind was made in the record or presented in the briefs.

3. The court erred in granting the nonsuit.   Let the case in all its bearings be submitted to a jury.

Judgment reversed.   All the Justices concurring.

FOUTE *v.* ELDER.

1. A bond for titles to a tract of land, described as being within certain boundaries and measuring a certain number of feet in width and in depth binds the obligor to make title to the entire tract so described ; and if he has no title to a portion of it, this is a breach of the bond, although he did not have title to such portion at the time the bond was executed.

2. Proof that the obligee in the bond for titles knew or had an opportunity to learn that the obligor was not the owner of the entire tract described in the bond does not relieve the obligor of the consequences of his breach, it not appearing that there was any mistake in the description given in the bond.

Argued December 16, 1899. — Decided January 30, 1900.

Complaint.   Before Judge Calhoun.   City court of Atlanta. July 9, 1899.

John T. Pendleton and *W. T. Moyers*, for plaintiff.
Longino & Golightly, for defendant.

SIMMONS, C. J.   The record discloses that Foute sued Mrs. Elder on a promissory note for about $400, the balance of the purchase-price of a certain lot of land in the city of Atlanta, Georgia.   Mrs. Elder filed a plea of set-off for certain interest and taxes she had paid but which should have been paid by Foute.   She filed also a plea of failure of consideration, in that Foute had sold her a lot of land described as being 64 feet in width and 160 feet in depth, and had obligated himself to make her a good and sufficient title thereto upon payment of the purchase-money.   This plea further alleges that the lot was not 160 but 143 feet in depth, 17 feet less than she had purchased. She prayed that she be allowed to recoup the value of the 17 feet, estimating it at $416, and that she might have judgment against the plaintiff for that amount and for the amount of her claims of set-off.   On the trial of the case the jury returned a verdict for the amount of $142 in favor of the defendant.   The plaintiff made a motion for a new trial.   This was overruled, and he excepted. It was admitted by Foute on the trial that the set-off of the interest and taxes was correct, and he also admitted that there was a deficit of 17 feet in the depth of the lot, but he contended that this 17 feet had been dedicated by him to the city for a street, and that this was known or ought to have been known to the defendant when she purchased the lot; that this part of the lot having been merely dedicated, Mrs. Elder still had title to it, the public having only an easement therein. The bond for titles given by Foute to Mrs. Elder described the land sold as follows: "A certain tract or parcel of land, situated, lying, and being in the City of Atlanta, and known as lot number thirty (30) of the subdivision of block two of land lot no. forty-six, in the 14th district of Fulton county, Georgia, commencing at a point one hundred (100) feet north of East Harris street (now Highland avenue) and fronting on the west side of the Boulevard sixty-four feet, and running back west at right angles with said Boulevard (with uniform width of front) one hundred and sixty feet; being on the southwest corner of the Boulevard and Adam street." It seems from this description that the lot *fronted on the west side* of the Boulevard and was to run back 160 feet from the side of that street. The dedication to the city of the seventeen-foot strip was not mentioned or excepted in the bond for titles, although the dedication had been made and the street widened before the time of the execution of the bond for titles. By his bond the plaintiff bound himself to make good and sufficient titles to a lot commencing at the *west side* of the Boulevard and from that side running back at right angles one hundred and sixty feet. This was his contract, and when it was ascertained that there was a deficit of seventeen feet, the defendant was entitled to recover, for this breach of the bond, the value of the shortage.

Wherever one contracts to sell the land embraced within certain boundaries or measurements, and it afterwards turns out that he can not make titles to all of the land embraced within those boundaries and measurements, he is liable to the vendee for the deficiency. This is true although the vendee knew or ought to have known that the vendor had, before making the bond, disposed of a portion of the tract. The vendee has a right

to rely upon the warranty or the contract obligation of the vendor and to demand compliance with the contract as expressed
in the deed or bond for titles.   This is no new doctrine in this
court.   In the case of *Smith* v. *Eason*, 46 *Ga.* 316, it was said :
"A deed or bond for titles to a tract of land by its number in
the State survey binds the obligor to make title to the land
within the boundaries of such survey, and if a part be sold off
before the date of the deed, this is a breach of the bond, nor is
this breach excused by the fact that the quantity sold off is
small, and the bond describes the number, containing two hundred and two and one half acres, more or less.   Proof that the
obligee in a bond for titles knew that the obligor was not the
owner of the whole of the land described in the bond is no reply to a plea of a breach, unless it appear that there was a mistake in the description."   This case was followed in *Miller* v.
Desverges, 75 *Ga.* 407, and again in *Godwin* v. *Maxwell*, 106 *Ga.*
194.   The fact that Foute had dedicated to the city the strip
of seventeen feet and that the defendant has an easement in it,
and that possibly at some future time the city may abandon
the street, does not, in our opinion, alter the case.   Mrs. Elder
has a right to stand upon the contract as it was made and to
claim 160 feet back from the west side of the Boulevard.   The
shortage is not in front of the lot but at the rear.   The meas-
urement was not from the middle of the street, as counsel for
the plaintiff seem to contend, but from the west side, as is expressly and clearly shown by the bond for titles.   Nor would
it make any difference, in our opinion, that the land was enhanced in value by the dedication of the strip and the widen-
ing of the street.   The defendant contracted for a lot 160 feet
deep; and she is entitled to a lot of that depth, running back
160 feet from the west side of the street, or to a deduction in
the purchase-price.   The court did not err in the charge or refusal to charge of which complaint is made, no error of law appears to have been committed, the evidence fully warranted the
verdict, and the trial judge did not err in overruling the motion for new trial.

Judgment affirmed.   All the Justices concurring.

STATE OF GEORGIA *v.* CENTRAL OF GEORGIA RAILWAY COMPANY *et al.*

1. The competition the defeating or lessening of which par. 4, sec. 2, art. 4 of the constitution (Civil Code, § 5800), so far as applicable to railroad companies, was designed to prevent, was competition between lines of railroad viewed with reference to their general business in and through the territory traversed by them, and not competition which might incidentally exist at mere points or particular places. A combination of railroad lines, whatever the form adopted for bringing it about, is not violative of this paragraph of the constitution, even though it might lessen or defeat competition at some point or points, if, as a general result of the combination, the public at large, as distinguished from the people of special or particular communities, was in consequence benefited.

2. Whether or not the combination of any two given lines of railroad would be contrary to this paragraph of the constitution is a question which can not be settled under any rule of universal application, but one which must be determined in each case upon its own peculiar facts and circumstances.

3. The present record discloses that there was ample evidence to uphold an adjudication that the consolidation of the two lines of railroad involved did not defeat, and was not intended to defeat, competition in the sense in which that word is used in the above-mentioned paragraph of the constitution, and also that such consolidation neither encouraged nor tended to encourage monopoly.

Argued December 4, 5, 1899. — Decided January 31, 1900.

Petition for injunction. Before Judge Hart. Putnam county. September 18, 1899.

J. M. Terrell, attorney-general, Joseph S. Turner, S. T. Wingfield, and *W. H. Burwell,* for plaintiff: Paragraph 4, section 2, article 4 of the constitution (Civil Code, § 5800) makes the common law, so far as relates to the purchase of one corporation by another corporation, a part of the constitution: Small's Debates of the Convention of 1877. As to what is the common law: 40 *Ga.* 583. The purchase of the Eatonton Branch Railroad by the Middle Georgia & Atlantic Ry. Co. was illegal and void. While, under the charter, the Eatonton Branch might buy or sell, no such authority belonged to the M. G. & A.: 69 Texas, 313; 101 U. S. 71. The M. G. & A. could not legally buy stock in another road: 40 *Ga.* 583; 43 *Ga.* 13. Authority to buy stock could not be conferred upon it: Civil Code, §§ 5800, 5780; 49 Fed. Rep. 424; 37 Fed. Rep. 449, 465; 40 *Ga.* 583;

93 *Ga.* 53. The two roads were competing roads: Charter of
M. G. & A. Ry. Co.; 40 *Ga.* 583; 37 Fed Rep. 448; 49 Fed.
Rep. 424; 50 Fed. Rep. 338; 72 Tex. 404, s. c. 1 L. R. A. 849;
24 Neb. 143, s. c. 8 Am. St. Rep. 165–178; 75 Tex. 434; 41
La. Ann. 970, s. c. 17 Am. St. Rep. 445; 37 Ohio St. 590; 97
Ky. 675; 161 U. S. 677–685, and cit.; 139 U. S. 24; 101 U.
S. 71; 7 Atl. Rep. 368; 92 Fed. Rep. 735. For the same reasons the purchase of the M. G. & A. by the Central of Georgia
was illegal and void. The right to construct branch roads does
not carry with it the right to purchase roads already constructed:
23 Ohio St. 168–181; 67 Tex. 692–701. The fact that rates
have not been changed does not affect the question: 161 U. S.
648–676; 15 L. R. A. 159; 6 L. R. A. 102. Equity may interfere by injunction and may appoint a receiver: 52 Am. St.
Rep. 415; 50 N. J. Eq. 50–499; 17 L. R. A. 102.

Lawton & Cunningham, Joseph R. Lamar, Thomas G. Lawson,
and *H. A. Jenkins,* for defendants: Contracts encouraging monopoly, or defeating or lessening competition, are void at common law: 16 Wall. 102; 104 *Ga.* 194–5; 40 *Ga.* 582; 65 *Ga.*
160; 10 *Ga.* 505; Greenhood, Pub. Pol. 670; Clark, Cont. 446;
20 Wall. 67. The incomplete sentence in section 5800 (Civil
Code), "all such contracts and agreements shall be illegal
and void," does not enact new law, but preserves the common-
law rule: 104 *Ga.* 195; 40 *Ga.* 582. The common law preserved by section 5800 prohibits the making of contracts which
are "injurious to the public interest": 104 *Ga.* 194; 161 Pa.
St. 473, s. c. 24 L. R. A. 247; 1 L. R. A. 461; Spelling, Trusts,
75, 158; 52 Fed. Rep. 118, 646; 139 U. S. 89. The contracts
prohibited must not only be injurious to the public, but must
directly affect actual competition, important in amount and of
controlling force in fixing rates. Competition which does not
reduce rates or improve service has neither practical nor theo-
retical value: 171 U. S. 592, 594, 600; Id. 568; 31 Am. &
Eng. R. Cas. 649; 1 Interstate Com. Rep. 631; 168 U. S. 145(6);
5 Am. & Eng. R. Cas. (n. s.) 86; 56 Fed. Rep. 947; 50 Fed.
Rep. 309; 1 Interstate Com. Rep. 31. If section 5800 is not
declaratory of the common law, but enacts a new rule, it needs
subsequent legislation to define its limits or to enforce its pro-

visions. It is not self-executing, because, by the provisions of
5802, the legislature "shall enforce the provisions of this article
by appropriate legislation." 3 Fed. Rep. 740; 31 Am. St. Rep.
626; 10 Fed. Rep. 497; 30 S. W. Rep. 350; 45 S. W. Rep. 988;
Spelling, Trusts, 223. The "appropriate legislation" as to railroads is found in the general railroad acts, each of which has authorized the purchase, sale, lease, or consolidation of connecting
railroads, provided such contracts be not made between "competing lines." Acts 1881, p. 161; Acts 1891, p. 116; Acts 1892,
p. 49; Acts 1894, p. 69; Civil Code, §§ 2173, 2179, 2180; 102
Ga. 436. As to legislative and contemporaneous construction:
98 *Ga.* 813; 55 N. Y. 367; 92 N. Y. 328; 149 N. Y. 367; 115
N. Y. 442. Even if they have competing points, the Middle
Georgia & Atlantic and the Central are not "competing lines"
within the meaning of the Civil Code, §§ 2173, 2179, 3668, nor
is the consolidation prohibited by the constitution (Civil Code,
§ 5800): 40 *Ga.* 582; 102 *Ga.* 436; 46 Fed. Rep. 888; 35 Atl.
Rep. 952; 91 Fed. Rep. 317, 318; 49 Fed. Rep. 419; 37 Fed.
Rep. 462; 62 Fed. Rep. 328. The public policy in this State
is the same as that existing in other States which prohibit the
consolidation of competing lines: 161 U. S. 646; 32 Am. & Eng.
R. Cas. 400; 161 U. S. 677; 7 Atl. Rep. 369; 47 Am. & Eng.
R. Cas. 359; 35 O. St. 590. The constitution (Civil Code,
§ 5799) encourages the building of branch roads. This is equivalent to declaring that a branch road is not a competitor within
the meaning of § 5800 Irrespective of the merits of the case,
a receiver was properly refused: 46 Fed. Rep. 888; 103 *Ga.*
557; 105 *Ga.* 494.

Hoke Smith & H. C. Peeples argued in support of the defense,
for parties not of record but interested in the result.

LEWIS, J. This suit was brought in Putnam superior court
by and in the name of the State of Georgia against the Central
of Georgia Railway Company, the Middle Georgia & Atlantic
Railway Company, and the Eatonton Branch Railroad. It was
founded upon an executive order which was issued in the early
part of the year 1899, upon a petition filed by certain citizens
of Putnam county with the Governor; the main purpose of the

petition being to procure an executive order directing the attorney-general to institute suit in the name of the State to set
aside a certain contract of sale under which the two last-named
roads were purchased by the Central of Georgia Railway Company on the 31st of December, 1896, upon the ground that
this contract of sale was in violation of art. 4, sec. 2, par. 4 of
the constitution of this State.   In the petition it was substantially alleged that these two companies, the Middle Georgia and
the Central, were competing lines, and that the effect of this
purchase by the Central was to destroy competition, and to create
a monopoly in the business formerly enjoyed by both corporations.   It was especially charged that there was great competition between the two companies at Milledgeville and at Machen,
and several points were designated in the petition along the
Middle Georgia & Atlantic Railway where it was alleged that
the result of the contract of purchase by the Central was to defeat competition at such places, and created in most of them a
monopoly in the Central.   The Central, through its counsel,
filed an answer to the petition, specifically denying its allegations that the purchase of the Middle Georgia was designed or
had any tendency whatever to defeat or lessen competition or
to produce monopoly within the meaning of the constitution;
alleging that the two roads were never rivals or competitors in
the sense contemplated by the constitution, and that the effect
of the contract of purchase was really of vast benefit to the
public interests, the same having resulted in the reduction of
passenger and freight rates, in the better equipment of the road,
and in superior accommodations to its patrons and the public
generally.   This case came on to be heard before his honor
Judge Hart, at chambers, on September 11, 1899, upon the
prayer of the petition that the holding and operation of the
Eatonton Branch and the Middle Georgia by the Central
directly or indirectly be enjoined; and that until the final hearing of the case a restraining order be granted prohibiting the
further operation of these two railroads by the Central; and
that a receiver be appointed to take charge of the two roads,
and all the corporate property belonging to them, and to hold,
operate, and manage the same under the directions of the court,

in order that competition may be preserved, and the public interests protected, until the two roads are operated by their respective corporations as separate properties. On the 18th of September, after hearing argument of counsel, the judge below, having held up his decision until that date, passed an order refusing the injunction and receiver as prayed for, to which plaintiff in error excepted, and assigns the same as error in its bill of exceptions.

In 1889 what was known as the Eatonton and Machen Railroad Company was incorporated by an act of the legislature, with authority to build and operate a line of railway from Eatonton to Machen, and extend the same in either direction to Savannah and Atlanta. See Acts of 1889, p. 227. At the same session of the legislature (see p. 281) the name of the corporation was changed to the Middle Georgia & Atlantic Railway Company. During the year 1890 this line had been completed between the towns of Eatonton and Machen, and had been graded north of Machen nearly to Covington. In 1893 the road had been completed to Covington, and was being operated from Eatonton to that point. In 1893 there were in Eatonton two separate and independent lines of railway, namely the Middle Georgia and the Central; the latter, through its receiver operating the Eatonton Branch under a lease made many years previously. It appears from the record that the line from Eatonton to Milledgeville, known as the Eatonton Branch Railroad, was completed about the year 1852, and this branch has never been under any separate or independent operation, but, upon its completion, the Central Railroad & Banking Company of Georgia leased the same; and it went into the hands of the receiver of the Central, by whom it was operated until October, 1893, when, under an order of the United States circuit court, this branch railroad was allowed to withdraw and did withdraw its lines from the control of the receiver, upon the showing made to the court by the receiver that this branch was not earning its operating expenses and annual rental. Upon assuming control of its road, the Eatonton Branch Railroad immediately entered into contract with the Middle Georgia & Atlantic, by which the latter corporation was to operate its line temporarily, the net proceeds to be divided between the two corporations on a mileage basis. The Middle Georgia & Atlantic then began to run its trains from Milledgeville to Covington. On the 1st day of June, 1896, the Middle Georgia & Atlantic purchased by deed of conveyance the railroad and corporate franchises of the Eatonton Branch, and then became the owner of the line from Milledgeville to Covington, until it sold out its road and franchises to the Cen-. tral of Georgia on December 31, 1896. The affairs of the Central Railroad & Banking Company became liquidated under the receivership, and a reorganization was perfected by which all the property and franchises of that corporation passed into the custody and control of the new corporation, the Central of Georgia Railway Company. It owned and operated a line of railway from the city of Atlanta to the city of Savannah via Macon; and from Gordon, in Wilkinson county, to Milledgeville, in the county of Baldwin, besides other lines.

The suit in this case, and the relief therein sought, is based upon the following provision in the State constitution, embodied in section 5800 of the Civil Code: "The General Assembly of this State shall have no power to authorize any corporation to buy shares or stock in any other corporation in this State or elsewhere, or to make any contract, or agreement whatever with any such corporation, which may have the effect, or be intended to have the effect, to defeat or lessen competition in their respective businesses, or to encourage monopoly; and all such contracts and agreements shall be illegal and void." The case necessarily involves the vital question as to what is a proper construction to be placed upon this language in the constitution. Did the convention, in framing that instrument, intend to enact any new law, or declare any new principle in connection with contracts touching the defeat or lessening of competition, or the production or encouragement of monopoly? If so, what is that new principle? Can it be gathered from the words employed as to what sort of competition or monopoly is meant? We are left absolutely in the dark so far as provisions in the constitution are concerned, as no language whatever is used therein to throw any light on,

46

or give explanation touching the matter. We are not, however, in absolute darkness as to the general principles of law that have been in existence from time almost immemorial, touching contracts of this nature; that is, principles relating to the protection of the people against contracts preventing competition or creating monopolies. The common law has always abhorred a monopoly and has encouraged competition in all legitimate businesses of the people, whether followed by individuals or corporations. The purpose of such law is patent. One great object it has in view is to prevent such combination in trade, traffic, or other business as to concentrate it under one management and place it under such control of one person, company, or corporation, as to enable them unreasonably to oppress their patrons by exacting payment of extortionate and exorbitant prices. Such contracts are usually designated as those in restraint of trade, and are referred to in section 3668 of the Civil Code as "contracts in general in restraint of trade."

But it does not follow that the law ever intended to defeat all combinations that might be made in the business affairs of life, or to declare null and void all contracts that might in some particulars have a tendency to lessen competition or to restrain trade. It requires no argument to show that such a rigid construction, instead of being demanded by public policy, would in many instances work great injury to the public, and seriously affect the prosperity of a country. Competition may be so unreasonable as not only to result in disaster to the competitors, but also in injury to the public. For instance, three competitors may be engaged in the same line of business in the fair conduct of which the public in a given community or section of the country is vitally interested. Public patronage may not be sufficient to sustain them all. Each one is engaged in an earnest contest for the mastery of the situation. One may be more powerful than the others, and, on account of financial ability, may reduce charges for accommodations, conveniences, or necessities, furnished the public, lower than the actual expense of operating the business; and, in this way, succeed in an extermination of the other two competitors, and this for the direct purpose of securing a monopoly, and raising prices

to an exorbitant and oppressive amount. Now, suppose the
two weaker institutions should make such an arrangement or
combination as to place the business of both under one management, and under the control of such an owner as would have
the ability to compete with the remaining enemy in the field;
would any court of law or equity declare such a contract void,
though made for the purpose of destroying competition between
the parties thereto? Numerous other illustrations might be
given of unreasonable competition that might prove injurious
to the public interests. By virtue of section 2176 of the Civil
Code, such unreasonable competition, in the case of railroads,
is provided against by requiring a new road constructed under
the provisions of the act to be at least ten miles from the one
already constructed.

When an effort, therefore, is made by a State to set aside contracts of this character on account of public policy, the vital
test is whether or not such a contract is injurious to the public
interests. In the text-books and decisions touching the common law on this subject we can find no well-settled definition
of "restraint of trade"; and it would perhaps be impracticable to give any certain definition of the term which would be
of universal application to every case that might arise involving the question of the validity of such contracts. The difficulty grows out of the fact of failure in the lawmaking power
to specify what acts and agreements shall constitute restraint
of trade, monopoly, trusts, etc. Spelling, in his work on Trusts
and Monopolies, enters into a discussion on this subject, and on
page 224 he uses the following language: "The fatality of
any legislation which does not circumstantially define what
shall constitute restraint of trade, but leaves it to the courts to
determine the question by reference to the common law, is this:
There is no settled or accepted legal definition of restraint of
trade at common law. The rule of public policy which must
be violated by an agreement in restraint of trade is a variable
and indefinable quantity. As an English judge once said: 'It
is an unbridled horse, which, when you have once mounted it,
you know not whither it will go, or where it will land you.'
The Federal judges especially have assumed such liberal dis-

cretion in the interpretation of the rule as to indicate that there
is in fact no rule, but that each decision should turn upon the
exigencies, environment, and circumstances of the parties and
the subject-matter.   In other words, there is no pole-star to
guide the judicial mind, but each judge evokes from his own
breast a proper decree upon the facts as presented in each case."
See also the subject discussed in Clark on Contracts, p. 446.
In the case of Leslie *v.* Lorillard, decided by the New York
Court of Appeals, October 16, 1888, 1 L. R. A. 456, Gray, J.,
in discussing this question on page 461, says: "Where, therefore, the provisions of agreements in restraint of competition
tend beyond measures for self-protection and threaten the public
good in a distinctly appreciable manner, they should not be sustained.   The apprehension of danger to the public interests,
however, should rest on evident grounds; and courts should refrain from the exercise of their equitable powers in interfering
with and restraining the conduct of the affairs of individuals
or of corporations, unless their conduct in some tangible form
threatens the welfare of the public."   The decision in that case
was to the effect that a certain agreement of a steamship corporation to buy out a competing line, which line, for a consideration, agreed to discontinue running vessels between certain ports,
was not void as in restraint of trade.   The reason for that ruling was evidently based upon the idea that the facts and circumstances of that particular case did not show that the public interests were injuriously affected.   In the case of Nester *v.* Conti-
nental Brewing Co. (Supreme Court of Pennsylvania), 24 L. R.
A. 247, it was held: "The true test of the illegality of a combination to restrict business is its effect upon the public interests."
   In Spelling on Trusts and Corporations, 158, it is declared:
"But since the public interest is the controlling consideration
in this class of cases, the rule against restrictive contracts by
public servants does not extend beyond or in conflict with public welfare.   Therefore a court will not declare a contract between common carriers illegal merely because it gives monopoly, where it does not appear that the public is injured, or that
either party to the agreement has exercised any function exclusive of public rights."   And again on page 75, § 52, he says

that "courts are not governed by any hard and fast rule in determining whether a particular contract is in restraint of trade and amenable to the rule of public policy rendering such contracts invalid, the test being whether the restriction is reasonable and necessary to the party's protection, the public interest being constantly kept in view." On page 76 the author advances the idea that it is not strange that decisions upon apparently similar facts are variable, and that it is almost impossible to deduce general abstract rules from them; that the courts have an almost unlimited range of discretion in deciding upon the facts of each case as presented, whether the restriction be reasonable and necessary, or inimical to the public interest, because calculated to stifle competition, and lead to extortion and oppression. In Fowle v. Park, 131 U. S. 97, Chief Justice Fuller, in discussing the question as to when the restraint of trade or the lessening of competition becomes invalid, in his opinion says: "Public welfare is first considered, and if it be not involved, and the restraint upon one party is not greater than protection to the other requires, the contract may be sustained. The question is whether, under the particular circumstances of the case, and the nature of the particular contract involved in it, the contract is, or is not, unreasonable." See also In re Greene, 52 Fed. Rep. 118, where the reasonableness of such a contract is made to depend upon whether it is more injurious to the public than is required to afford a fair protection to the party in whose favor it is secured. The court recognizes there that no precise boundary can be laid down as to when and under what circumstances the restraint would be reasonable, and when it would be excessive. See also Ellerman v. Chicago Co. (Court of Chancery of New Jersey), 23 Atl. Rep. 287–300.

The same doctrine touching the effect such contracts have upon the public has been more than once recognized by this court. It will be noted that the words cited above from section 3668 of the Civil Code refer to contracts in *general* in restraint of trade. It does not undertake to declare contracts in partial restraint of trade void. In *Holmes* v. *Martin*, 10 *Ga.* 503, it was decided : "A contract in general restraint of trade is void ; but if in partial restraint of trade only, it may be supported, provided the restraint be reasonable and the contract founded on a consideration." Lumpkin, J., in delivering the opinion in that case, on page 505 says: "The reason assigned for this difference is, that all general restraints tend to promote monopolies and to discourage industry and enterprise and just competition; whereas the same reason does not apply to special restraints. On the contrary, it may even be beneficial to the public that a particular place should not be overstocked with persons engaged in the same business." In the case of *Western Union Tel. Co.* v. *American Union Tel. Co.*, 65 *Ga.* 160, a contract between a railroad and telegraph company, vesting in the latter the exclusive right to use or occupy the right of way of the former for the erection and operation of its telegraph business, was held to be void. It will be seen that although that decision was made since the constitution of 1877, it was not based upon the provision in that constitution against such contract, but upon the common law; it being ruled that they were in general restraint of trade, tending to create monopolies, and thus against public policy. This question was discussed in the case of *Rakestraw* v. *Lanier*, 104 *Ga.* 188, by Justice Little. The contract in that case involved a restraint upon one of the parties from following his occupation at a given place. Justice Little, in his opinion on page 194, says: "It is, however, satisfactorily established that, as a matter of law, such a contract is to be upheld, if the restraint imposed is not unreasonable, is founded on a valuable consideration, and is reasonably necessary to protect the interest of the party in whose favor it is imposed, and does not unduly prejudice the interests of the public." Further, on page 195, he says: "In determining, however, whether such a contract is reasonable, the court will consider the nature and extent of the trade or business, the situation of the parties, and all the other circumstances." Authorities could be multiplied sustaining the position that at common law the test of validity of agreements relating to a restraint of trade, or, what is the same thing, to lessening competition and encouraging monopoly, is whether or not the public interests have been injuriously affected. But we think the above citations are quite sufficient to establish the doctrine.

The above doctrines of the common law have been repeatedly applied by the courts of this country to transactions between railroad companies. The first time the question was before this court as to whether one railroad could purchase the controlling interest in a competing line, and thus destroy the competition that formerly existed between them when they were operated as independent lines, was in the case of *Central R. R. Co.* v. *Collins*, 40 *Ga.* 582. The Central Railroad & Banking Co., which was chartered to build a railroad from Savannah to Macon, and the Southwestern Railroad Co., which was chartered to build a railroad from Macon to the Chattahoochee river, were about to purchase from the City of Savannah 12,383 shares of stock in the Atlantic & Gulf Railroad Company, which was chartered to build a road from Savannah to Bainbridge. It was alleged that the purpose of these two companies was to use the stock thus purchased to affect the management of the Atlantic & Gulf Railroad. An action was brought to enjoin the purchase of this stock and payment therefor, and to prohibit the two railroad companies from voting the stock, and from controlling the Atlantic & Gulf road, to the detriment of the interest of the complainants and the people of Georgia. There seems to have been no doubt in the case that these two roads were competing lines, each terminating at the seaboard, and penetrating at their extremities, and by their connections, the distant southwest, competing for the traffic and travel in that region of the country. On page 583, 6th headnote, it was decided: "It is part of the public policy of the State, as indicated by the charter of the several railroads from the seaboard to the interior, to secure a reasonable competition between said roads for public patronage; and it is contrary to that policy for one of said roads to attempt to secure a controlling interest in another, and any contract made with that view will be set aside by a court of equity as illegal, beyond the objects of the charter, and contrary to the public policy of the State." The decision was evidently based upon the common-law doctrine that contracts or agreements producing monopoly, or lessening or defeating competition, were void. It will be noted that that decision was rendered prior to the constitution of 1877. It will be observed that Robert Toombs was of counsel for the complainants in that case, and, as such counsel, contended for the doctrine of the common law as therein enunciated. As a member of the constitutional convention of 1877, he is reputed to have drawn up this section of the constitution now under consideration. In construing this section of the constitution with reference to defeating or lessening competition and encouraging monopoly, the question naturally arises as to what was the nature of the competition and monopoly referred to. The constitution itself uses no explanatory language, and there is really nothing in the language employed to give these words any different meaning than what was almost universally recognized by judiciaries and legislatures for ages.

In construing a constitution, a safe rule is to give its words such significance as they have at common law; especially if there is nothing in the instrument to indicate an intention by its framers that the language in question should have a different construction. We think, therefore, that the purpose of the constitution was to declare no new principle. What is therein declared with reference to corporations is equally applicable to individuals. It will be noted that the provision is addressed to the General Assembly of the State, and declares that that body shall have "no power to authorize *any corporation in this State, or elsewhere,*" etc. There was a reason for applying the principle to corporations and not individuals; for the legislature could not authorize an individual to do an act against public policy; whereas the powers which corporations exercise are governed by the stipulations in their charters, and franchises conferred upon them by the lawmaking power. At common law a corporation could not make such contracts as contemplated by the constitution, without special grant of power. The object of the constitution was to restrict the legislature in this particular; and our judgment is that in this provision it was simply declaratory of the common-law principle recognized in the *Collins* case, the purpose being to make that principle, so far as corporations were concerned, the organic law of the State, and thus put it beyond the power of the legislature to grant to corporations any rights or privileges inconsistent with its terms.

Another proper rule to be observed and duly considered in the
interpretation of a constitution is to determine what construction the legislative department of a State thereafter placed upon
such provisions in enacting laws in relation thereto. The legislature of the State has, in several railroad acts passed since the
adoption of the constitution, authorized the purchase, sale, lease,
or consolidation of connecting railroads; but has added *provisos*
that such contracts shall not be made with competing lines.
See Acts 1881, p. 165, sec. 15, where the proviso to this purchasing power is added, that "no railroad shall purchase a competing line of railroad, or enter into any contract with a competing line of railroad, calculated to defeat or lessen competition
in this State." See also Acts 1892, p. 49, sec. 13, where similar power is given with a like proviso which prevents the railroads from making such contracts with a *competing line of railroad*, calculated to defeat or lessen competition. These provisions of law are embodied in the Civil Code, §§ 2173, 2179. In
6 Am. & Eng. Enc. L. (2d ed.) 931, it is held: "A constitutional provision is to be construed with reference to the principles of the common law," and the common law will be upheld
in the absence of an apparent contrary intention. It is also
stated that "a contemporaneous legislative exposition of a constitutional provision is entitled to great deference." See numerous authorities cited in the text. It will thus be seen that the
policy of this State is the same that exists in some other States
of this Union, where there are constitutional and statutory provisions prohibiting the consolidation of competing lines.

In the case of Cumberland Valley Co. *v.* Gettysburg Co., decided by the Supreme Court of Pennsylvania in 1896, 35 Atl.
Rep. 952, it was decided, in effect, that railroad companies whose
roads approach their point of connection almost at right angles
are not competing lines. This question as to what constitutes
competing lines of railway within the meaning of the law was
discussed in the case of State *v.* Montana Ry. Co., 11 Am. & Eng.
R. R. Cases, 353, where it was ruled that two roads were competing lines when their relation to one another was such as to
enable them to cut rates to principal or terminal points. Hunt,
J., in delivering the opinion of the court, on page 365 declares:

"The true rule is, that whether two railroads are parallel or competing is a question of fact, of physical fact. . . Exact parallelism, however, is not what is included in the meaning of the words of the constitution forbidding consolidation of parallel railroads. A reasonable construction must obtain. . . We should say that by parallel railroads are meant railroads running in one general direction, traversing the same section of the country, and running within a few miles of one another throughout their respective routes. They may or may not be competing. That depends upon their termini, and their commands of traffic." Again; on page 266, he says: "Whether lines of road are competitive or not depends upon the business of the companies, the conduct of the roads by their authorities, their channels of traffic, and generally — nearly always — upon whether the roads extend for transportation from and to the same points along their routes." There is nothing in the record in this case to indicate that the Central and Middle Georgia roads are *competing lines,* in the light of the above authorities. The Central purchased a branch road from Gordon to Milledgeville. There it connects with the Middle Georgia. For nearly fifty years has the Eatonton Branch been chartered, and yet at no time has it been operated as an independent road. On the contrary, it was leased and operated by the Central as a continuation of this branch line from Gordon to Milledgeville, and on to Eatonton. In the *Collins* case, 40 *Ga.* 633, the relation of this Eatonton Branch to the Central was considered and discussed by this court. It was there held that the Southwestern, Waynesborough, and Eatonton roads were *feeders* to the Central; their interests were in harmony, and both the public and the stockholders of each road were interested in their acting in concert. If, then, it was treated not as a competitor at that time, we can not see upon what theory or method of reasoning it can be contended that a further extension of this branch, not in the direction of the Central's line nor within its territory, but to a point within the territory of a competing line, namely the Georgia Railroad, would make the line a competitor of the Central. It was also decided in the *Collins* case that a line termed then the Waynesborough line, which connected with the Central at

Millen and ran to Augusta, was not a competing line of the Central, but a feeder; yet it was doubtless true that when the Central purchased that line, it necessarily lessened competition at Millen. But, on the other hand, it increased competition at Augusta after its absorption by the Central, by giving another direct line from that point to the seaboard. There is nothing, however, in this case which shows that, from the location of these two roads, the Central and Middle Georgia, and the direction which each ran from their connecting point at Milledgeville, being almost at right angles, they were competing lines in any legal sense of that word.

It is insisted, however, that Milledgeville was a competitive point for these roads and the Georgia road, and the purchase by the Central of the Middle Georgia had the effect of lessening this competition. But it by no means follows that because the number of competitors in a given business is diminished, that competition is thereby lessened to the injury of the public. The facts in the record really show that prior to this contract of purchase the Georgia Railroad and the Middle Georgia acted in concert and harmony by an arrangement or understanding they had with reference to the transportation of through freight, and that the competition then was really between these two roads on the one hand and the Central on the other. It would seem, therefore, that the effect of the purchase was simply to transfer the competition to the Middle Georgia and Central on the one part and the Georgia on the other. It is further contended that at Machen the Middle Georgia crossed the Central, that road having purchased and operating the road from Macon to Athens, which passes through Machen, and that the effect of the purchase was to diminish competition at Machen. On the other hand, there is overwhelming testimony in the record to show a very marked increase of competition by this consolidation of the two roads in question in Covington, and that this competition was increased at the various stations along the line of the road between Machen and Covington; and the testimony seems conclusive that the general interests of the public along the line of this branch road from Milledgeville to Covington were benefited by its consolidation with the Central. Besides, it seems that the sale of its road by the Middle Georgia was an absolute necessity. It was then in a run-down condition. Its road-bed was in such a fix as to render transportation over the same absolutely dangerous to life and property. Citizens interested in its traffic, it seems, petitioned the railroad commissioners to have the road put in good order, and proceedings in court were actually instituted for this purpose. It appears that over a quarter of a million dollars were lost by the owners of this road, and its president swore on this trial that they could not run it safely to life and property, owing to its physical condition, and that the sale of it to somebody became absolutely necessary. It appears that an effort was made to sell it to the Georgia Railroad, which declined to become the purchaser. Then the Central was approached, became the purchaser, and at once commenced the operation of the road. Its condition was thereafter greatly improved, to the general satisfaction of its patrons throughout the entire length of the line. We quote the following from the learned opinion of Judge Hart, embodied in his decision in this case:

"They [meaning the Middle Georgia] were then charging four cents per mile as their passenger tariff, and the maximum freight charges the railroad commission would allow. Immediately after the purchase by the Central, passenger tariff was reduced to three cents per mile, and the freight tariff, where changed, was reduced from 2 to 50 per cent. The road-bed was put in good and safe condition. Its equipment is full and complete, and the service is generally satisfactory to its patrons. No one complains that the road is not now giving a better, safer, and cheaper service than when the Middle Georgia was operated as an independent line. Scores of affidavits were read on the hearing, and with remarkable unanimity affiants asked that there might be no breaking up of the present system by the appointment of a receiver. The court is of the opinion that the purchase has been beneficial to every business, every shipper, every person living on its line, except perhaps to the merchants of Shady Dale who had their freights delivered to them free of charge from the depot of the Central, or individuals at Milledgeville who had free passes given them as an inducement to route their freight over a particular line. It was competition, no doubt, at these two points which induced these concessions; but the people as a whole have been benefited both in convenience and safety in travel, as well as in saving of freight and passenger tariff. It is susceptible of proof that in reduced freight charges the people of Eatonton and Putnam county save annually over $20,000. A lumber-dealer in Covington swears that he saves annually $1,800 on the single item of lumber handled by his firm." We have read this voluminous record of evidence entirely through, and can say, from the facts developed on the trial, that the above conclusion of Judge Hart touching the beneficial effects of this purchase by the Central to the public at large along the line of this branch road was fully authorized. In determining whether this contract defeated or lessened competition within the meaning of the constitution, we must look at its effects, in the light of all the facts and circumstances of the case, along the entire line of the road in question. The evidence in this case tends to establish the fact that the traffic at Machen and Shady Dale, where it is claimed competition was lessened, does not exceed 2.6 per cent. of the traffic on the whole line; and yet the people of that community reap the same advantage in the reduction of freight and passenger tariffs as the people along the road from one end of the line to the other. It is the policy of this State, both in its constitution and its statutes, to prevent a railroad from purchasing a competing or rival line whenever the effect of such a purchase would be to defeat or lessen competition; but in considering whether or not a transaction has had this effect, we must look at the results in their entirety, and the effect upon the general public interested in the traffic of the road along its line. If that general effect be to increase competition to a far greater extent than it has been diminished at particular points, it can not, with reason, be said that competition has been defeated or lessened. In point of fact it has actually been increased.

But it is insisted in this case that if competition be lessened anywhere, it matters not what may be the general effects upon the public, and it matters not whether any loss has accrued to any one from an increase of charges for transportation of freight or passengers, the constitution has been violated, and the contract is, therefore, void. It is true that the doing of an illegal act can not be justified upon the plea that no harm has resulted; but it is perfectly legitimate to look at the purposes for which a law is enacted, in determining its true intent and meaning. The object of the law against defeating or lessening competition was to prevent it being placed in the power of one, whether individual or corporation, to so control rates of trade and traffic as to increase them to an unreasonable amount. If a transaction, therefore, instead of having such a result, has an opposite effect, it furnishes, to say the least of it, a strong argument that that law has not been violated; and the argument becomes more overwhelming when there is nothing in the environment and business of the parties to place them in the position of rivals, or real competitors. As Judge Hart has correctly said in his opinion: "It is the declared policy of this State to prohibit railroads from purchasing competitive or rival lines, but it is also its declared policy to encourage the great trunk lines to buy, build, and operate branch or feeding lines. Both policies are equally wise. The former is to prohibit contracts in restraint of trade; the latter is to build up our great undeveloped interior. Railroads should be prohibited from doing the first, and should be encouraged to do the last." There is nothing in the constitution indicating any hostility whatever to the extension of lines of railway by the construction or purchase of branch roads, or the purchase of connecting lines. On the contrary, under section 5799 of the Civil Code, it is provided that in the event the charter of any corporation is altered or amended, such corporation shall hold its charter subject to the provisions of this constitution. The object of that was to subject such corporations to the taxing power of the State, although exempted therefrom under their original charters. But so jealous was the convention in protecting the rights of the railroads to construct, operate, or control branch roads, that it was provided that section should not extend to any amendment for the purpose of allowing any existing road *to take stock in or aid in the building of any branch road.* It would seem manifest therefore, that the following provision in the constitution, with reference to preventing the General Assembly from giving power to any corporation to make a contract to defeat or lessen competition, or to buy shares of stock in any other corporation, had no reference whatever to the purchase, ownership, and control of branch roads; and they, therefore, could not have been regarded as competing lines to the main roads with which they might make connection. As the result of this policy, great trunk lines have been extended in this country half across the continent. Doubtless in the purchase of connecting lines and branch roads competition was lessened at given points, but the general effect of these consolidations and connections has really been to increase competition, has added greatly to the public convenience, furnished greater and more commodious facilities for traveling, has operated to reduce the cost of transportation, has brought remote parts of the country in close proximity, as it were, to each other, has developed resources that would otherwise have remained dormant, by opening up the markets of the world to the products of the land, and has generally contributed to work to the welfare and prosperity of the people.

Even if we are incorrect in our position that the provision in the constitution with reference to defeating competition or encouraging monopoly is only an embodiment of the common law upon the subject, and if it contains a new principle unknown to the common law, then the clause in question is evidently not self-acting, for no light is thrown upon the new meaning intended to be given the words used. It would follow, therefore, that appropriate legislation would be necessary to carry into effect such a new principle, whatever it might be. Under the provisions of section 5803 of the Civil Code it is provided that the General Assembly shall enforce the provisions of this article by appropriate legislation. In this case, then, the courts would be constrained to decide that the appropriate legislation contemplated is embodied in the general railroad acts, to which we have above referred, where the purchase, sale, lease, or consolidation of connecting railroads is allowed, provided the contracts were not made between *competing lines.* So at last the judiciary would be driven to the necessity, whenever the contest was made, in determining whether or not such contracts were legal, to decide the question as to whether they were between competing lines, and not simply lines that had competing points where competition was lessened to a degree insignificant when compared to its increase at various other points, and the benefits to the public generally along the line of transportation.   When the State appeals to the courts in such matters, she occupies the position of a representative of the public, whose rights, if they have been infringed by a violation of the constitution or the laws, will be zealously protected by the courts. For the same reason courts should deny her prayer, if it appears on trial that granting the relief sought would be productive of greater injury to the public than the wrongs of which complaint is made.   There was ample evidence in this case to authorize the conclusion of the judge below that the consolidation of the two lines of railroad involved did not defeat and was not intended to defeat or lessen competition, or to encourage monopoly, in the sense in which those words were used in the constitution; that these roads were not competing lines; and that the public interests were in nowise injured by their consolidation.   The judgment of the court, therefore, refusing an injunction and the appointment of a receiver is affirmed.

Judgment affirmed.   All the Justices concurring.

TRUST COMPANY OF GEORGIA *et al. v.* STATE OF GEORGIA.

1. When an action is instituted in the name of the State for the purpose of preventing a violation of the provisions of par. 4, sec. 2, art. 4 of the constitution (Civil Code, § 5800), the questions whether such action is well brought and is maintainable depend upon the pleadings and the evidence introduced in support thereof, and not upon the motives inspiring those at whose instance the Governor was induced to order the suit to be filed, or the arguments presented to him to that end.

2. The remedy for such a purpose may be injunction, and it is not in every instance essential to resort to the harsher proceeding to forfeit a charter.

3. That portion of the above-mentioned paragraph of the constitution which denies to the General Assembly "power to authorize any corporation to buy shares or stock in any other corporation" is not absolute in its terms;

but it was designed only to prevent the General Assembly from authorizing one corporation to purchase shares or stock in another, when doing so "may have the effect, or be intended to have the effect, to defeat or lessen competition in their respective businesses, or to encourage monopoly."

4. This clause of the constitution applies to and includes all corporations; and, consequently, is applicable to street-railway companies, and enforceable as to them whenever they, directly or indirectly, violate its provisions.

5. Under the charter of the Trust Company of Georgia, that corporation has authority to buy the shares or stock of any other corporation; provided that, in so doing, it does not violate the provisions of the constitution of this State.

6. Placing upon the word "competition," as used in this paragraph, the interpretation given to it in the case of *State of Georgia* v. *Central of Georgia Railway Company*, ante, 716, and taking into view the evidence in the present record, the court erred in holding that the proposed purchase of stock would be violative of the constitutional provisions referred to, and in granting, on that ground, the injunction sought.

Argued January 16, 17. — Decided February 27, 1900.

Injunction. Before Judge Candler. Fulton county. November 7, 1899.

King & Anderson, Lewis W. Thomas, Goodwin & Hallman, C. P. Goree, and *Payne & Tye,* for plaintiffs in error: Suits of this kind should not be entertained when inspired by rival interests: 3 Cook, Corp. § 913, p. 2231; 50 N. E. Rep. (Ill.) 158. Governor not empowered to order this suit by virtue of his office only; legislation necessary. The anti-trust law (Acts 1896, p. 68) expressly authorized suit, and the anti-pooling law (Civil Code, § 2085 et seq.) defined a method of procedure. Quo warranto the proper remedy; direct suit in the name of the State for injunction not proper; the proceeding should have been on the relation of the attorney-general: 5 Thomp. Corp. §§ 6133, 6035, and notes; 27 Am. & Eng. Enc. L. (1st ed.) p. 410; High, Extraord. Rem. § 660; 76 *Ga.* 644 (1), 648; 24 N. Y. 261, 268; 79 Mo. 632, 638–9; 157 Mass. 548. The constitutional provision upon which this suit is founded (par. 4 of sec. 2, art. 4, Civil Code, § 5800) is not self-acting; legislation to make it effective is indispensable. Nor does it apply to companies not engaged in the same line of business, e. g. a trust company and a street-railroad company, where the charter of the former authorizes it to buy stock in other companies. 62 Fed. Rep. 328

47

(1), 333, 334; Civil Code, § 5803. Legislation carrying this article of the constitution into effect, as to steam railroads: Civil
Code, §§ 2173, 2179, 2167; as to insurance companies: Id.
§ 2085 et seq.; as to articles of manufacture and agriculture generally: Acts 1896, p. 68. There is no legislation carrying this
article into effect so far as concerns a trust company buying
stock in other companies. Street-railroad companies are expressly authorized to sell or lease franchises; Civil Code, § 2184.
Contracts of sale or lease will not be presumed illegal and enjoined, but will be permitted; and if the business is so conducted
afterwards as to violate the law, the illegal use will be prevented.
The general law as to steam railroads, as far as appropriate, is
made applicable to street-railroads: Civil Code, § 2180. The
legislation embodied in section 2184 was enacted in 1891, at the
time of the consolidation of the companies then brought together
as the Atlanta Consolidated Street Railway Company (now the
Atlanta Railway and Power Company, one of these plaintiffs
in error); and several acts were passed at the same time, authorizing the companies to sell out to each other: Acts 1890–
91, vol. 1, pp. 279, 283, and 340. The legislature has recognized the right of street-railroad companies which have purchased the property and franchises of other companies, and has
imposed on them the duties of the latter: Acts 1890–91, vol.
1, pp. 169, 170. The charter of the Trust Company of Georgia
expressly authorizes it to buy stocks of other companies. A
like provision appears in charters granted to trust and banking
companies, almost universally, after the constitution of 1877
was adopted. This continued legislation shows the construction by the legislature of the clause of the constitution above
referred to. That clause was only declaratory of the law as it
existed prior to that time, and prohibited the legislature from
making contracts unduly restrictive of competition: 104 Ga.
188. If prices are not raised above reasonable amounts, though
the contract be made to prevent competition, it is not void: 66
N. H. 100, s. c. 49 Am. St. Rep. 582, 584, 586. There must
be substantial competition, to render the consolidation illegal.
Incidental competition, or competition insignificant in amount,
when compared to the volume of business transacted by the com-

panies, will not render the combination illegal: 46 Fed. Rep.
888; 91 Fed. Rep. 317; 35 Atl. Rep. (Pa.) 952, 954; 111 N. Y.
64 ; 66 N. H. 100, 127; 49 Am. St. Rep. 582; 40 La. Ann. 8;
Cook, Trade and Labor Combinations, 120. Legislation providing that ten miles shall intervene between railroads, as to
their general routes, and making provision as to their approaching each other at terminal points, shows that ruinous competition is discouraged: Civil Code, § 2176. Not illegal for two corporations engaged in same general lines of business to consolidate: 62 Hun, 269, s. c. 133 N. Y. 336; 127 N. Y. 252. The
leasing of competing lines, or bringing them under one friendly
management, does not violate such a provision as that in our
constitution: 53 Pac. Rep. 623. Street-railroad companies, from
their nature, do not fall within provisions prohibiting combination to defeat competition: Booth, Street-Railroad Companies,
§ 429; 20 Atl. Rep. (Pa.) 399, 400. Corporations with the same
officers can validly contract with each other: 57 *Ga.* 371; 55
Md. 420. Injunction harsh and not necessary; jury on final
hearing can settle the matter: 37 Am. & Eng. R. Cas. 100 (2).

J. M. Terrell, attorney-general, Gray, Brown & Randolph, and
Frazer & Hynds, contra: Suit properly brought in the name of
the State: 79 *Ga.* 61 ; 81 *Ga.* 546; 85 *Ga.* 22 ; 66 *Ga.* 408; 56 *Ga.*
478 ; 25 *Ga.* 374; 43 *Ga.* 605, 656; 71 *Ga.* 106, 120; Civil Code,
§§ 5813, 4933; Pol. Code, § 220, par. 4; 145 N.Y. 267–274; 24
Tex. 80; 4 Minn. 213, s. c. 3 L. R. A. 510; 5 Thomp. Corp.
§ 6614; 58 Pa. St. 45; 67 N. W. Rep. 1, 4; 35 Wis. 530; 134
N. Y. 269; 2 Cook, Corp. § 635; 97 Ky. 675; 161 U. S. 677 ;
Civil Code, § 4878 et seq. The attorney-general the proper officer to bring the action in the name of the State, and injunction and receiver the appropriate remedy: 3 Pom. Eq. Jur.
§ 1093; 35 Wis. 434, § 524; 17 L. R. A. 108–111, s. c. 38 N. J.
L. 286; Angell and Ames, Corp. § 734, p. 793, 795; 10 Mass.
290; 145 N.Y. 267, 274; 5 Wend. 212, 220; 50 N. J. Eq. 50,
s. c. 17 L. R. A. 97; 19 Ala. 514; 67 N. W. Rep. 1; 2 Mora-
wetz, Corp. § 1043; Beach, Monopolies and Trusts, § 221; 5
Thomp. Corp. § 6618; 50 N. J. Eq. 449, s. c. 17 L. R. A. 97; 7
Atl. Rep. 368, 374; Pol. Code, § 220. Under paragraph 4 of
section 2, article 4 of the constitution (Civil Code, § 5800), the

General Assembly can not authorize one corporation to buy shares or stock in another. By the common law one corporation could not own stock in another. The import of the clause of the constitution in question may be regarded as prohibiting the legislature from changing the common law on the subject: 49 Fed. Rep. 424, citing 40 *Ga.* 582; 7 So. Rep. 108; 2 Cook, Stock and Stockholders, §§ 667–672; 139 U. S. 24–61; 37 Fed. Rep. 449–465. A constitutional provision is to be construed with reference to the principles of the common law. The framers of the instrument are presumed to have intended no change of the common law further than is expressly declared: 6 Am. & Eng. Enc. L. (2d ed.) 931, citing Cooley, Con. Lim. (6th ed.) 75; 118 Ind. 366; 9 Humph. 43, s. c. 49 Am. Dec. 697; 76 Ill. 370; 4 Mich. 322; 16 N. J. L. 380, s. c. 32 Am. Dec. 397; 71 Pa. St. 293. As to the power of competing railway corporations to consolidate under one ownership or to unite under one management: 6 Am. & Enc. L. (2d ed.) 825; 24 Neb. 164, s. c. 8 Am. St. Rep. 165–178; 66 N. H. 100, 131; 48 N. H. 325; 1 Tex. App. Civ. Cas. 324; 71 Fed. Rep. 787; 46 Fed. Rep. 152; 130 Ill. 268, s. c. 17 Am. St. Rep. 319; 62 N. H. 537; 36 N. J. Eq. 5; 121 N. Y. 582, s. c. 18 Am. Rep. 842; 86 Tenn. 598; 37 Fed. Rep. 449; 49 Fed. Rep. 412; 139 U. S. 24–63; 92 Fed. Rep. 735, 741–4; 55 N. H. 531; 72 Tex. 404, s. c. 1 L. R. A. 849; 101 U. S. 71; 50 Fed. Rep. 338; 17 L. R. A. 97; 24 N. J. Eq. 46; 41 N. J. Eq. 4; 69 Tex. 313; 161 U. S. 691–2; 48 N. J. L. 559; 118 U. S. 309; 130 Ill. 268, s. c. 8 L. R. A. 497; 77 Mich. 632, s. c. 6 L. R. A. 457; 9 L. R. A. 33; 5 L. R. A. 386; 15 L. R. A. (Ohio) 145; 68 Pa. St. 184; Beach, Priv. Corp. § 305, and cases cited; 92 Fed. Rep. 735; 161 U. S. 698–699; 75 Tex. 434; 1 L. R. A. 849; 41 La. Ann. 970, s. c. 17 Am. St. Rep. 445; 37 O. St. 590; 161 U. S. 648–676; Civil Code, § 2184. As to the right of the Trust Company of Georgia, under its charter, to hold stock in other corporations: Civil Code, § 1831; 40 *Ga.* 582, 620, 624, 625; 43 *Ga.* 13; 101 U. S. 71 (1); 62 Fed. Rep. 342; 139 U. S. 24–63; 49 Fed. Rep. 412; 5 *Ga.* 561; 25 *Ga.* 457; 95 *Ga.* 389; 7 *Ga.* 221; 8 *Ga.* 23; 11 *Ga.* 438; 9 *Ga.* 213; 8 L. R. A. 504–508; act incorporating the

"Commercial Travelers Savings Bank" (Acts 1890–91, vol. 2, p. 310), and amendment changing name to the "Trust Company of Georgia" (Acts 1893, p. 142). The power granted to buy and sell "stocks" was intended simply to clothe the bank with power necessary to accomplish the main purpose of its organization, namely, banking. The court should not only have granted an injunction, but appointed a receiver; 36 Ohio St. 355, s. c. 38 Am. Rep. 594; 68 Me. 46, 28 Am. Rep. 9; 139 U. S: 59; 53 Am. St. Rep. 415; Smith, Receivers, 364, and note; 50 N. J. Eq. 489; Civil Code, § 4900.

LEWIS, J. On the 1st day of July, 1899, certain citizens of Fulton county, Georgia, filed with the Governor of the State a petition charging that certain corporations, namely, the Trust Company of Georgia, the Atlanta Railway Company, and the Atlanta Railway and Power Company (formerly known as the Atlanta Consolidated Street Railway Company) had, by certain contracts and agreements, violated art. 4, sec. 2, par. 4, of the constitution of the State, and were about to enter into other contracts in violation of this clause of the constitution. They prayed for an executive order requiring the attorney-general to bring such suits in the name of the State as might be necessary to set aside such contracts and have them declared null and void. His Excellency, the Governor, passed an order directing a suit to be brought as prayed for, and accordingly the attorney-general filed, in the name of the State, a petition in the superior court of Fulton county against the corporations named. This petition alleged, in substance, that the Atlanta Railway Company for a number of years operated lines of street-railroads extending from the central portion of the city of Atlanta along Forsyth, Fair, Cooper, Richardson, and other streets to McPherson Barracks outside of the city, and in Fulton county, Georgia, in one direction, and by way of Forsyth, Church, Ellis, and other streets, to Decatur, in DeKalb county, Georgia, in another direction; also another line running along Forsyth, Cooper, and other streets to Grant Park, in said city. The Atlanta Railway Company purchased this property at receiver's sale, the former owner being the Atlanta Traction Company. The Atlanta Railway and Power Company during the same time operated competitive lines of street-railroad, running on Decatur street, and other streets in the city of Atlanta, to Decatur; also along Alabama and Pryor streets and Georgia avenue to Grant Park in the city of Atlanta, and also along Fair street and Park avenue to Grant Park. Said company also operated a line out Whitehall street in said city, and had lately applied for a franchise running on and along various streets to McPherson Barracks, for the purpose of constructing a competing line with the Barracks line of the Atlanta Railway Company. It finally changed this franchise, and constructed a line practically to Fort McPherson. This company, the Atlanta Railway and Power Company, also owned and operated a line out Edgewood avenue to Inman Park, and beyond Inman Park to and along Euclid avenue to Moreland Park and the county line, where it paralleled and finally crossed the tracks of the Atlanta Railway Company. It also operated other lines competing with the Atlanta Railway Company at many points. The notable places of competition were in the vicinity of Grant Park, at Decatur, Moreland Park, Edgewood, the intersection of Pryor and Ormond streets, Whitehall and Fair streets, Peachtree and Ellis streets, Ellis street and Courtland avenue, Houston and Hilliard streets, Irwin and Jackson streets, Irwin street and the Boulevard. A map was attached to the petition, showing the various routes of the lines operated by the two companies.

The petition further charged that the Trust Company of Georgia had recently, contrary to the constitution and laws of the State, bought up all the stocks and securities of the Atlanta Railway Company for the purpose of causing said company to convey all its property to the Atlanta Railway and Power Company, or whatever new company should be organized, in order to control both systems of railway, and for the same purpose bought up all, or nearly all, of the stock of said Power Company, and is now practically the holder of all the stock of both companies. The Trust Company caused to be elected for the principal officers of the Atlanta Railway Company the same persons who were managers of the Atlanta Railway and Power Company, namely: Woodruff elected president of each company, Hurt, superintendent of each company, and Glenn, the secretary of each company, so that the Atlanta Railway Company passed under the complete management of the officers who controlled the other company. Practically all the stock and securities of both companies were held and owned by the Trust Company of Georgia; and the Atlanta Railway Company was operated by persons who controlled both the Trust Company and the Atlanta Railway and Power Company. The purpose of the managers of the Trust Company was to have the properties of both these corporations conveyed, so that one corporation would own, control, and operate both properties, to the destruction of competition between the two. The combination results in injury to property along the lines of the railways, and at competing points, and, with the exception of about ten miles of tracks running along Walton and other streets to the Chattahoochee river, and lying mainly outside of the city limits, the other two lines of railway were the only two competing lines in the city. The petition alleges somewhat in detail that the effect of these contracts, which it attacks as illegal, has been to lessen competition at the various points named; that since the reported combination of the two lines, the service and accommodations thereon have not been as satisfactory to the people generally, and especially to those patronizing the street-railways. The petition charges that if the threatened illegal acts of the defendants are not enjoined, and the illegal combination be allowed to stand, the street-railway accommodations and facilities of the city of Atlanta, and the means of transportation for the people of Fulton and DeKalb counties and of the cities of Atlanta, Decatur, Edgewood, and Oakland City, and the people of the State visiting this territory, will be placed in the sole control and power of one corporation, competition will be excluded, and the rates of fare controlled in the interest of those connected with the monopoly. One among the prayers of the petition was, that the Trust Company be enjoined "from voting said stock in the Atlanta Railway and Power Company, and said stock in Atlanta Railway Company," and that two Railway Companies be enjoined from receiving the votes of said stock controlled by the Trust Company; that the Atlanta Railway and Power Company be enjoined from

purchasing or acquiring the ownership, control, or operation of
the lines of railway, franchises, and property of the Atlanta
Railway Company, and that it be enjoined from selling its roads,
railways, franchises, etc., to the Atlanta Railway and Power
Company, or any other corporation, that will have the effect
to defeat or lessen competition, or to encourage monopoly; that
the defendant corporations be enjoined from entering into any
agreement whatever by which the properties of said two railway companies would be consolidated, merged, or combined;
that a receiver be appointed by the court to take possession of
the stocks and bonds of the Atlanta Railway Company, to hold,
manage, and dispose of the same under the orders and direction of the court, in order that competition may be preserved,
which was guaranteed to the public, and the public interests
protected.   There was a prayer that a restraining order be
granted, restraining the defendant corporations from doing or
performing the acts against which injunction was prayed, until
the final hearing of the cause.

To this petition each of the defendant companies filed demurrers upon various grounds; and the Trust Company, the
Atlanta Railway Company, and the Atlanta Railway and Power
Company filed their answers, specifically answering the charges
in the petition; denying its various allegations about defeating
or lessening competition, or tending to defeat or lessen competition; denying that the two railway systems were competing
lines in the sense of the constitution and laws of the State; and
setting up advantages that would accrue to the public generally
if the two systems were consolidated, and particularly in respect to the reduction of fares by transfer tickets from the lines
of one to the other, which would often enable passengers to
travel for one fare on various routes through the city, which
would otherwise require the payment of two fares.   In this way,
expense in the operation of these various lines would be greatly
reduced, accommodations and conveniences to the traveling
public increased, roads better equipped, etc.   At the September
term, 1899, of the superior court of Fulton county, the case
came on to be heard on the prayers above stated, for injunction,
receiver, etc., before Judge John S. Candler, of the Stone Moun-

tain circuit, who presided because of the disqualification of
Judge J. H. Lumpkin, of the Atlanta circuit.   Quite a volume
of evidence was introduced both in behalf of the plaintiff and
defendants.   The decision of the judge on the issues made by the
demurrers and answers was reserved until November 7, 1899.
He enjoined the Trust Company of Georgia from selling or
transferring any of the stock or bonds owned by it in and of the
Atlanta Railway Company and the Atlanta Railway and Power
Company, and from transferring any of the stock or bonds of
the latter company to the Atlanta Railway Company, and from
transferring the stock or bonds of either of the railway companies to any other company or association of persons, the object
of which transfer would bring about the consolidation of the
said street-railroad companies into one company.   The Atlanta
Railway and Power Company was enjoined from purchasing or
in any way acquiring the possession or control of any of the stock
or bonds of the Atlanta Railway Company, and the latter company was enjoined from purchasing or acquiring any of the
stock or bonds of the Atlanta Railway and Power Company.
Both companies were enjoined from taking up any of the tracks
of their respective lines, or from discontinuing the running of
reasonable schedules upon the same, without first obtaining the
consent of the city or county authorities from whom they hold
franchises, or without further order from the court in cases where
said lines of road are not located in the streets of any city or
town, or where the public roads are not occupied under franchises granted by county authorities.   The judge denied the
prayer for the appointment of a receiver, and further provided
in his judgment that, as the interests of the two defendant street-
railroad companies, as well as those of the public, may be subserved by the interchange of business between said roads, and
by transfer of passengers from the lines of one road to those of
the other, they were permitted to make any physical connections
with the rails of each other, and enter into any such traffic
arrangement as may be necessary to enable each of said companies to grant transfers or interchangeable tickets over the
lines of the other.   To this judgment of the court the defendant companies, in their bill of exceptions, assign error.

1. It appears from the record that the defendants' counsel called upon the plaintiff, or its attorneys, to produce, upon notice which had been duly served, the contracts between the parties petitioning the Governor to direct the suit brought, and also the contract under which the attorneys filing the suit were employed. In the bill of exceptions complaint is made that the court erred in not requiring the production of the papers called for. In the argument of the case here in behalf of the plaintiffs in error, it is contended that the contracts made by the parties petitioning the Governor would have disclosed that rival interests were actuating this proceeding, and that the contracts between counsel for defendant in error and their clients would have disclosed that their authority was limited to appearing before the mayor and council of Atlanta to prevent the removal of the tracks on Richardson street alone. It appears from the evidence that a petition was presented by the president of the Atlanta Railway Company to the city council of Atlanta, asking for the privilege of removing the tracks of that company on Richardson street. This was protested against by certain citizens on that street; whereupon the application for removal of such tracks was withdrawn by the president of that company. It further appears that the names of those persons appearing in the petition presented to the Governor for this suit were some of the citizens on that street. We think it was immaterial in this case to have entered into an investigation as to the motives of the parties who petitioned the Governor for the institution of this suit, with the view of determining whether the cause of action was properly brought. That question, as to whether the action is well brought or maintainable, must necessarily depend upon the pleadings before the court trying the case, and the evidence introduced in support thereof. The court trying the issue has nothing to do with the motives actuating the parties who instigated the proceedings before the Governor. The Governor is presumed to take care of himself in such matters; and we do not think that his action is the subject-matter of review by the courts in a case that he has directed to be brought. We are inclined to the opinion that the attorney-general has the power to institute suits necessary to the protection of the inter-

ests of the State; in case, for instance, where the State's property is involved, or where public rights are jeopardized, without direction from the Governor; but when directed by the Governor, as in this case, to proceed, he has no discretion in the matter, but should obey the mandates of the chief executive. Whether or not the action is maintainable is dependent at last upon the pleadings, and the evidence introduced in support thereof, and not upon the motives inspiring those at whose instance the Governor was induced to order the suit filed.

2. Among the several grounds of demurrer, the main one that seems to be relied upon by counsel for plaintiffs in error is, that the suit was improperly brought in the name of the State for injunction, but that quo warranto was the proper remedy for the wrongs complained of, and the proceeding should be on the relation of the attorney-general. Upon this point neither the authorities in England nor in this country are entirely reconcilable, some holding that the remedy by injunction in favor of the State will not lie to restrain a corporation from the exercise of powers ultra vires; and others holding that this is the proper remedy. We have reached the conclusion that the sounder reasoning is in favor of allowing to the State relief by injunction whenever it is proceeding in the interest of the public to prevent a threatened injury. As harsh as the remedy by injunction is generally considered, it is certainly not as severe as would be a proceeding in the nature of quo warranto, instituted for the purpose of forfeiting the charter of a corporation. The one is instituted, not for the purpose of causing a destruction of the corporation, but to prevent it from entering into transactions violative of the public policy of the State, and to protect the interest of the public against a threatened wrong. The other remedy, if enforced, would cause the death of the corporation, thus forever preventing it from serving the public interests, or meeting the public demands upon its business, and often result in a wreckage of the property of its owners. We can, therefore, see no reason why, if the remedy for the wrongs threatened can be as well prevented by injunction, it would not be the more readily and properly applied than the harsher one of forfeiture or confiscation. This question is discussed in 2 Cook on Cor-

porations, § 635, p. 1223. It is there recognized that the State has four remedies for relief against corporations exercising powers ultra vires: 1st. The legislature may repeal the charter of the corporation under the reserved right of the State to repeal; 2d, or the State may institute a proceeding to forfeit the charter for misuser of powers; 3d, or such proceeding may be only to oust the corporation from the exercise of the usurped power; 4th, or, according to some authorities, a suit may be commenced in equity for an injunction restraining the corporation from committing the ultra vires acts. On page 1227, however, the author says, "it is very doubtful whether the State may file a bill in equity to enjoin a corporation from committing an ultra vires act. The remedy of the State is quo warranto." The author recognizes, however, considerable English and American authorities to the contrary. In this same connection he declares: "The State may enjoin a railroad corporation from purchasing a competing line in violation of the constitution." While we gather from the entire text that the author seems to conclude that the weight of authority is that the remedy of the State is by quo warranto, and not by bill in equity for an injunction, we do not think all the authorities cited in support of the text fully sustain it. For instance, in the case of Attorney-General *v.* Great Northern Ry., 1 Dr. & Sm. 154, it was held that the attorney-general can not enjoin a corporate act merely because it is ultra vires. Some injury to the public must be involved. The attorney-general's suit, at the instance of a manufacturer, to enjoin one railroad from leasing its rolling-stock to another failed. This decision probably at last gives the clue by which apparent conflict of authorities on this subject may be reconciled, and we think it is the correct doctrine. The State has no right to an adjudication by the courts declaring void such contracts merely and solely for the reason that they are ultra vires, but she is entitled to this relief when injury to the public is involved.

This question was directly made in the case of L. & N. Co. *v.* Commonwealth, 97 Ky. 675. It was there held: "A court of equity has jurisdiction in an action by the State to enjoin a corporation from exceeding its chartered powers, or doing acts otherwise illegal and injurious to the public. Therefore the State may by injunction prevent a railroad company from consummating the purchase of a 'parallel or competing line' in violation of sec. 201 of the State constitution." This case was carried to the Supreme Court of the United States, and there the judgment was affirmed. See L. & N. Co. v. Kentucky, 161 U. S. 677. In Attorney-General v. Chicago Co., 35 Wis. 425 et seq., this right of the State, acting through the attorney-general, and the remedy by injunction, are clearly recognized. See headnotes 4 and 43. In that case an elaborate opinion was written, thoroughly discussing this subject, which will appear on pages 523 to 553, where the decisions both in England and this country are well considered and analyzed. It was there concluded that the English court of chancery entertains jurisdiction in such cases, and it was declared that the English books leave little room for a denial of such jurisdiction. On page 532 it is stated: "We have not found this jurisdiction as directly and succinctly stated in American treatises as in English, although it is fully recognized by the best of our elementary writers." The author quotes from 2 Redfield on Railways the following principle: "Injunctions in courts of equity, to restrain railways from exceeding the powers of their charters, or committing irreparable injury to other persons, natural or artificial, have been common for a long time, in England and this country." Says the court in the Wisconsin case above cited, on page 524, in speaking of the right to proceed by injunction: "It seems to proceed on the presumption that it may better serve the public interest to restrain a corporation, than to punish it by penal remedies or to forfeit its charter." In Attorney-General v. Delaware Co., 27 N. J. Eq. 631, it was decided: "The attorney-general has the right, where the property of the sovereign or the interests of the public are directly concerned, to institute suit for their protection by an information at law or in equity, without a relator." See also Stockton v. Central Co., 50 N. J. Eq. 52, where the court enjoined lease upon application of attorney-general, when its effect was to create a combination in transportation of coal, and to destroy competition in production and sale. See also State v. Merchants Ins. Co., 8 Humph. (Tenn.) 235–254, where insurance company was restrained from banking. We quote the following from Pomeroy's Equity Jurisprudence, § 1093, p. 1263: "When the managing body are doing or are about to do an ultra vires act of such a nature as to produce *public* mischief, the attorney-general, as the representative of the public and of the government, may maintain an equitable suit for preventive relief." In a note to that text it is recognized that some of the cases seem to hold that the attorney-general may thus interfere to restrain *every ultra vires* proceeding of a corporation, on the ground that the public and governmental rights must necessarily be invaded thereby. But it is declared: "The later decisions, however, have established the limitation as stated in the text."

As far as our investigation has extended in reviewing the authorities cited to the contrary in the text-books, and by counsel for plaintiffs in error, we fail to find such conflict as seems to be contended for. For instance, in the case of Attorney-General *v.* Tudor Ice Co., 104 Mass. 239, it was simply decided that there is no jurisdiction in equity of an information by the attorney-general against a private trading corporation, whose proceedings are not shown to have injured or endangered any public or private rights, and are objected to solely on the ground that they are not authorized by the act of incorporation and are therefore against public policy. Gray, J., in his opinion in that case on page 242, draws a clear distinction between that case and modern English cases upon the subject. He says: "The modern English cases, cited in support of this information, were of suits against public bodies of officers exceeding the powers conferred upon them by law, or against corporations vested with the power of eminent domain and doing acts which were deemed inconsistent with rights of the public." In 2 Johnson's Chancery, 370, it was held that equity had no jurisdiction over offenses against a public statute, or to restrain a person from carrying on the business of banking in violation of a certain act of the legislature, and motion to enjoin by the attorney-general was refused. But in the opinion delivered in that case, on page 377, it was stated that the acts complained of were too much in the nature of a criminal offense, penalty being prescribed therefor by the statute; and on pp. 378–380 of the same opinion it appears that no public mischief was threatened in that case, and hence it was distinguished from several cases cited in which this remedy was recognized as a proper one in case public interests were involved.

Our conclusion, therefore, both from reason and a decided weight of authority, is that the State, in her sovereign capacity, can appeal to the courts for relief by injunction, whenever either its property is involved, or public interests are threatened and jeopardized by any corporation; especially one of a public nature like a railroad company, seeking to transcend its powers, and to violate the public policy of the State. We think this court has clearly recognized this sovereign right of the State. As stated by Judge Warner in *Central Co.* v. *Macon*, 43 *Ga.* 642, "If the State had any interest in the controversy, it was in her sovereign capacity as the representative of the whole people of the State, and should have appeared before the court in her sovereign capacity, by the appropriate mode of procedure in such cases." We are equally well satisfied of the correctness of the proposition that if the State has no interest in the matter in controversy, she will not be heard to ask for such extraordinary relief; and she can have no interest, unless her property rights or the public interests are involved. The allegations in the petition for such relief in this case are sufficiently full, clear, and explicit touching the rights of the public involved to give the court jurisdiction of the complaint, and we therefore think there was no error in overruling the demurrer.

It is further contended by counsel for plaintiffs in error that the constitutional provision in question is not self-active, and that some legislation was necessary in order to give a court of equity jurisdiction to grant the extraordinary relief prayed for. This question was practically decided in *State* v. *Central Ry. Co.*, ante, 716, where it was held that the provision in the constitution in question declared no new principle, but was simply the embodiment of the common law. In sustaining the jurisdiction of courts of chancery in such mat-

ters both in England and this country, the decisions are really
based upon the principles of the common law, and not upon
special legislation prescribing the particular procedure that
should be instituted in court in such cases. This will clearly
appear by an investigation into the cases above cited.

3. It is further contended that under the constitution (Civil
Code, § 5800), the provision in relation to corporations buying
shares or stock in any other.corporation has no reference whatever to the effect of such purchases upon competition or monopoly, and that they are absolutely void, although they have
no tendency to defeat or lessen competition, or to encourage
monopoly. We think this is an entire misconception of this
provision in the constitution. The prohibition against the legislative grant to corporations of power to buy shares or stock in
another corporation is clearly qualified by that portion of the
section cited which restricts such purchases only when they
have the effect, or are intended to have the effect, to defeat or
lessen competition in their respective businesses, or to encourage
monopoly. This necessarily follows from the punctuation of
the clause itself. That portion of it in relation to the purchase
of shares or stock is only separated from the balance of the
sentence by a comma, and the relative clause that follows with
the words, "which may have the effect," we think was evidently
intended to relate to what was said about shares and stock, just
as much as to the words "contract, or agreement." If the convention that framed the constitution intended to enact an absolute prohibition against the purchase of shares or stock by one
corporation from another, their meaning could have been made
manifest and clear by a separation of the first clause either by
a period, or semicolon, from what followed; and if such had
been the purpose of the convention, the construction of the
sentence as to its punctuation would evidently have been quite
different. Besides, the view of an absolute prohibition of such
a sale and purchase would be entirely inconsistent with the
provision in the constitution just preceding, embodied in section 5799 of the Civil Code. In that section the policy is indicated of encouraging "any existing road to take stock in
or aid in the building of any branch road." Our view of this

question has been the uniform construction placed upon this provision in the constitution by the legislature after its adoption. One of the first charters granted by the legislature after adoption of this constitution will be found in the Acts of 1878-9, p. 196, where the power of a corporation to invest its money "in any good stocks" was granted. Various acts were passed by subsequent legislatures delegating to corporations the power of purchasing and selling stock. It is true such acts would be void if clearly shown to be in violation of a constitutional provision; but we think the legislative construction in this matter was reasonable and proper, and if there be any serious doubt as to what the convention meant by the words employed, the benefit should be given to the interpretation placed upon it by the legislative branch of the government, and acted on for over twenty years by the people of the State in transactions involving important rights. See *County* v. *Thompson*, 83 *Ga.* 274-5. We are cited by counsel for plaintiffs in error to the decision of Judge Speer in the case of Hamilton *v.* Ry: Co., 49 Fed. Rep. 412. It will be seen in the opinion on page 422 that Judge Speer endorsed a statement relating to this question, made by Mr. Walter G. Charlton, in which an analysis of the section of the constitution under consideration was made, to the effect that what the provision meant was, that the General Assembly shall have no power to authorize any corporation to buy shares or stock in any other corporation in this State or elsewhere, which may have the effect, or be intended to have the effect, to defeat or lessen competition in their respective businesses.

4. It was further contended by counsel for plaintiffs in error, that street-railway companies, from their very nature, do not fall within the provisions of statutes or constitutions prohibiting combinations to defeat competition. From the language in section 5800, it was evidently the intent to apply the principle to all corporations, for it declares, "The General Assembly of this State shall have no power to authorize *any* corporation to buy shares or stock," etc. There is certainly, then, nothing in the words used to authorize the inference that street-railway companies were not contemplated just as much as any other corporation. This construction of the constitution was placed on it

48

by the legislature under the acts of 1880_1, p. 170, embodied
in the Civil Code, § 2184.   There the power was given street-
railroad companies to lease or sell their road, franchises, and
other property to any other corporation for street-railroad purposes; but it is stipulated that the act shall not be construed to
authorize any such company to sell, lease, or otherwise dispose
of any of its property or franchises so as to defeat or lessen competition, or to encourage monopoly.   The only authority relied
on by counsel is Booth on Street Railways, § 429, which simply
refers to a decision on this subject by the Supreme Court of
Pennsylvania.   The case referred to is Appeal of Montgomery,
which will be found reported in 20 Atl. Rep. 399.   It was simply held in that case that, on account of the meaning in which
the terms "railroad" and "railway" were used in the constitution of Pennsylvania, the word "railroad" applied to steam
railroads, and "railway" to street-railways; and that, therefore,
the provision in the constitution against consolidation of "railroads" with parallel or competing lines did not apply to street-
railway companies, and the latter, though parallel, would not
be enjoined from consolidating.   It is quite patent, then, that
this authority has no bearing upon the question before us, for
the word employed in the constitution of this State is neither
"railroad" nor "railway," but "*any* corporation."   It is true
it may be a much more difficult matter to show that by a consolidation of street-railways in a populous city any effect is had
upon competition and monopoly contemplated by the constitution.   On page 400 in the Pennsylvania case cited, Green, J.,
delivering the opinion, said :   "It is quite clear that the sense
of 'competing,' which is the essential sense of the prohibition,
is not applicable to the travel upon the streets of cities and towns
over passenger railways."   He further said :   "The travel over
parallel streets is not necessarily a competing travel.   Each
street has travel of its own which is conducted upon its own
railway."   But the argument of the court in that case only
tends to show the greater difficulty in showing a defeating or
lessening of competition to the injury of the public by combining
two parallel street-car lines than would be the case between two
steam railroads engaged in competition for traffic between dis-

tant points. The question is, at last, one of fact, and in its adjudication in any particular case the courts should be governed
by the fundamental principle as to whether there was such a
creation of a monopoly or defeating of competition as would result in injury to the public.

5. It is further insisted that the Trust Company of Georgia
has, under its charter, no power to purchase stock in other corporations. It is claimed that it was chartered as a banking
company, and that the investing in stock in railroad companies
has nothing whatever to do with the business for which it was
created. It is true that this Trust Company was incorporated
by an act approved September 21, 1891, as the Commercial
Travelers' Savings Bank. Acts 1890–91, vol. 2, pp. 310–313.
That act was amended so as to change the name and capital
stock. Acts 1893, p. 142. In the original act are incorporated
and made a part of its charter the provisions in sections 6, 7,
8, and 11 of an act to incorporate the Oglethorpe Savings and
Trust Company, approved December 18, 1886. By reference
to the provisions in that act, it will be seen that there was an
unmistakable delegation of power by the legislature to this Commercial Travelers' Savings Bank, now known as the Trust Company of Georgia, to purchase stock. It further appears from
the record that while it was chartered as a banking company,
other powers were given it almost ad infinitum; and that the
main business it has been following is that of a trust company,
rather than a regular banking company. It is insisted by counsel that there was at *common law* no power in any corporation
to purchase stock in another; but it is equally true that at common law corporations had no power to make contracts or enter
into transactions that would defeat competition or promote monopoly. But it has never been questioned that, in the absence
of any constitutional provision on the subject, the legislature
can confer such power upon corporations. The truth is that a
corporation, which is a creature of the State, can exercise no
power except what is delegated to it expressly or impliedly by
its creator, the legislature. This power of purchasing stock the
Trust Company of Georgia has, under its charter, and the only
limitation upon it is that it can not exercise it for the purpose

of creating a monopoly or defeating competition, to the injury of the public.

6. The only question remaining in this case for consideration is whether or not, under the evidence before the judge below on the trial of this application for temporary injunction, such wrong, injury, or damage to the public interests was either contemplated or threatened as would justify a court of equity in granting the prayers of the petition. The interpretation given the word "competition" in the case of *State* v. *Central Ry. Co.*, ante, renders it unnecessary to enter into a further discussion of that subject. It is well enough, however, to bear in mind in this connection the vast difference between the business of street-railway companies, constructed generally simply for the purpose of passenger travel from one portion of a city to another, and steam railroad companies, whose business is the transportation of freight and passengers for long distances, and involving business in extensive territory. The Atlanta Railway and Power Company, formerly known as the Atlanta Consolidated Street Railway Company, owned and operated about 65 miles of street-car lines. This company was formed in 1891 by a consolidation of half a dozen street-car companies, each of which operated independently a line of small mileage, some run by dummy, and some by horse or mule power, and none of them having systems of transfers, or extending through-lines across the city. The evidence shows that in many instances these lines were parallel to each other, running upon streets only a block apart for considerable distances, and at many places crossing or intersecting each other. These systems were in 1891 brought together and consolidated, not only under authority given by the city council of Atlanta, but under general and special legislative enactments of the General Assembly. See Civil Code, § 2184. For the special act on this subject see Acts 1890–91, vol. 1, p. 279, where the Metropolitan Street Railroad Company was authorized to extend and operate its road in any part of DeKalb and Cobb counties, increase its stock to a million dollars, and to sell its railroad property and franchises to any other company; also to purchase property and franchises of any other company, or to unite with the same, and

in such event to change its name to the Consolidated Street
Railroad Company of Atlanta. See also special acts in same
volume on pp. 283_340. After this consolidation the lines
were electrically equipped. It does not appear that there has
been any opposition to this consolidation during the eight or
nine years of its operation, and the record indicates that it was
of great benefit to the public by the connection of disconnected
lines, and affording to the public generally much greater facilities for transportation. The other defendant, the Atlanta Railway Company, comprised a system of about 15 miles of street-
car lines. It was composed of two companies known as the
Atlanta City Street Railroad Company and the Atlanta Traction Company. These two companies, after existing for several
years, became unsuccessful in business, passed into the hands
of a receiver, and were finally consolidated by purchase and
combination as the Atlanta Railway Company. This last-
named company had never paid any dividends to its stockholders, according to the evidence, and had acquired from the
city franchises to enter territory into which no street-car lines
had been built, but for want of means was unable to avail
itself of this privilege.

It is contended in behalf of counsel for the Trust Company
of Georgia, that that company realized that the Atlanta Railway Company was not in a position to complete the lines under the franchises it had acquired, thus making of it a really
important system, and if the lines of that company should
then be connected with those of the Atlanta Railway and Power
Company, and transfers issued to and from all the lines of the
entire system, there would be an increase in the volume of business, because of increase in facilities to the public, and that
the public would even be more benefited by this arrangement
than it had been by the consolidation in 1891. It was made
patent that with the disconnected lines a passenger, by paying
the usual fare of five cents, could only go in one direction, and
only to a point on the line which he first takes; and with the separate lines connected, one could start upon any line of the system, and for the same fare, by procuring a transfer to any other
line in the system, he could reach at the same expense any point

upon any of the lines that are controlled by the entire system. It further appears from the evidence that a street-car company could not be operated except at a loss, unless there was considerable patronage from those resident along the route of line it operated ; that short-trip passengers left a profit with the company which would pay the expenses of transporting the one taking the long trip.   We think the evidence in this record fully sustains the conclusion to say the least of it, that the consolidation of these two lines would probably lead to granting the public generally along their routes greater, and less expensive, facilities and conveniences of transportation.   This is certainly a most important consideration, when a court of chancery is appealed to to restrain by injunction the accomplishment of such an end ; for the only business of street-car companies is the transportation of passengers who patronize their lines.   This record indicates there was on the trial below testimony from over 100 witnesses to the effect that a combination of these two systems, as contemplated, would inure to the general interests of the people interested in the operation of these roads as means of transportation.   After a careful review of the entire testimony in the case, which consumed about one and one half days of our time in its investigation, we have reached the conclusion that there is really no serious conflict among the witnesses touching the general effect upon the public interest of the transactions sought to be enjoined. The main point of conflict' seems to us to be limited to certain intersections and terminal points of these two railway companies.   There was a quantity of evidence introduced in behalf of the State, showing competition at some intersections of these roads within the city, and also at some of their terminal points. There was, on the other hand, much evidence in behalf of the railway companies, showing that whatever competition existed at these points was insignificant in its nature, and amounted to nothing compared to the extent of the business transacted by the companies.   There was testimony in behalf of the State to the effect that while these two lines were running absolutely independently one of the other, schedules at some points were so arranged as to be more convenient to the public ; and on the other hand, there was testimony in behalf of the railway compa-

nies to show that at other points schedules and accommodations
to the public were increased since the two roads were acting
more in harmony one with the other.

In this connection we will allude to the Decatur lines of the
two roads as being the lines which counsel seem to insist upon
were most strongly in competition with one another. This
line of the Power Company runs from near the centre of the
city to Decatur on the north side of the steam railroad. The
other line also runs from near the centre of the city on the
south side of the steam railroad. They both terminate in the
town of Decatur at points about 500 or more feet apart. Under the evidence there was no competition whatever, it seems,
between them after leaving Decatur along their routes to the
city, their distance being about a mile or more apart; and the
evidence shows that the amount of business at Decatur, where
there was some competition for passengers en route to Atlanta,
did not amount to more than eight per cent. of the entire business of the line. We will not undertake to give in this connection a synopsis of the conflicting evidence touching the
competing points on these lines, particularly at Grant Park,
Oakland, Fort McPherson, and some points of intersection on
the streets. Our conclusion is that the evidence, fairly considered, is that the competition at these points is unimportant
and insignificant, when compared to what appears to be the
general interests of the public, and to the amount of business
done by these companies along their lines where no manner of
competition exists at all. Street-car companies, like all other
transportation companies, should be operated in such a way as
to afford the greatest convenience, comfort, and facilities for
traveling to the greatest number of people who live near enough
their lines to want, and to be able readily, to use them for transportation. It is utterly impracticable for the same facilities to
be granted every one, so that the people at every point would
fare exactly alike; and when the question arises whether a few
shall suffer some inconsiderable inconvenience by the inaugu-
ration of a system which is of advantage to the general public,
we know of no safer principle to apply than the old adage of
"the greatest good to the greatest number." In any event, as

we think we·have shown both by reason and authority, whenever the State proceeds in such a matter in its sovereign capacity, in law the foundation of its action must be based upon the
public good, and when it fails to show any danger to the public interests, an action of this sort fails.

The judge below in his decision states that the determination of the matter before him "rests upon the finding as to the
truth of the following questions of fact, viz.: "Does the consolidation of these two street-railroads in question defeat competition at any point, on any of their lines? Does it tend to
defeat competition? Does it lessen competition? If either
proposition, under the evidence offered, is determined in favor
of the petitioner, then such consolidation will be violative of
the organic law of the State, and will not be permitted." It
is true this court has repeatedly decided, and it is unquestionably a sound rule in such matters, that when a decision of the
court below granting an interlocutory injunction is based upon
a conflict of evidence, if there be sufficient testimony to sustain
the judgment of the court below, under the law, its discretion
in granting or refusing an injunction will not be controlled.
The question involved in this case, as well as in nearly all cases
which are litigated, depends upon the facts developed by the
evidence.   But evidently, from the decision itself, we think the
judge below, in reaching a conclusion on the case, has applied
to it a wrong principle of law.   His conclusion is, if the consolidation of the two street-railroads defeats competition at *any*
point on any of their lines, or tends to defeat such competition
or lessen it, the courts will interfere to restrain and set aside
such a combination.   This thought in his opinion, coupled with
the character of the evidence in this record, which we have only
in general terms undertaken to outline above, we think necessarily leads to the conclusion of misconception on the part of
the judge below as to the true meaning and spirit of the constitution and laws of the State on this subject, as construed by
this court in the case of *State* v. *Central Ry. Co.*, supra.   We,
therefore, conclude that the judgment of the court below granting the injunction prayed for should be reversed.

We have said nothing in the foregoing opinion touching the

allegations in the pleadings and the evidence in regard to the Atlanta Railway Company removing its tracks from Richardson street. The judge below, in his judgment, enjoins the street-railroad companies from taking up any of the tracks of their respective lines. In the bill of exceptions the plaintiffs in error expressly "except to so much of the order as prohibits them from taking up any part of the tracks of their respective lines, except the track of the Atlanta Railway Company on Richardson street, particularly referred to in the petition." The effect of not excepting to that portion of the order leaves that part of the court's order unaffected by this judgment.

In giving the reasons for his judgment, the judge below says: "Where these lines are in cities, and where they hold their franchises from city government, it is possible for them to be controlled, but large parts of the lines of each of these companies are located outside of cities and are not even located on public roads." We think, however, in the consideration of this case, although some of the lines run in the country, and in an adjoining county, yet all of them being connected with the lines permeating the city in various directions, constituting a comparatively small portion of a grand system of street-railways, the effect of consolidation upon the public generally should be considered, including not only the interests of the people in the country (and, so far as the record discloses, they do not seem to be complaining) but also the people interested on all portions of the lines. In the latter part of his decision the judge states: "Believing, further, that the interests of the two defendant street-railroad companies, as well as those of the public, may be subserved by the interchange of business between said roads, and by transfer of passengers from the lines of one of the roads to those of the other, said companies are permitted to make any physical connections with the rails of each other, and they are further permitted to enter into any traffic arrangement, as may be necessary to enable each of said companies to grant transfers or interchangeable tickets over the lines of the other." The evidence is uncontradicted that the purpose of the transactions among the defendant companies was substantially to effect this result; that the Trust Company purchased the stock in both companies, and the bonds in one of them, none of which it now holds, but it seems had sold or hypothecated them for the purpose of raising money, partly with the view of carrying out this scheme, and also with the view of aiding the Atlanta Railway Company in completing its contemplated lines through territory and to points in the city where it seems there are but little or no street-car accommodations. While the judge seems to recognize in this connection the public interests, yet the effect of his injunction, it seems to us, would be to restrain the parties in such a way that they could not avail themselves of the means of accomplishing the end which he himself thinks desirable. *Judgment reversed. All the Justices concurring.*

GEORGIA NORTHERN RAILWAY CO. *v.* TIFTON, THOMASVILLE & GULF RAILWAY CO. and *vice versa.*

In view of the facts disclosed by the record and of the questions involved, there was no error in granting the injunction.

Argued November 6, 7, 1899. — Decided January 31, 1900.

Petition for injunction. Before Judge Spence. Brooks county. August 5, 1899.

The Tifton, Thomasville and Gulf Railway Company, by its petition against the Georgia Northern Railway Company, alleged, in substance: Petitioner is a corporation duly organized and doing business under a charter granted August 9, 1897, by the secretary of State, under the laws of this State, and is proceeding, under this charter, to construct a railroad from Tifton, in Berrien county, to Thomasville, in Thomas county, Georgia, having heretofore selected and laid out a route on which the road is being constructed, as shown by a plat and survey attached to the petition. It has already spent considerable sums of money in the building of the road and the preliminary work incident thereto, and has secured valuable franchises therefor; among the latter, terminal facilities in the city of Thomasville, of the value of about $18,000, voted to petitioner by the citizens of Thomasville should it complete the railroad from Tifton to Thomasville inside of two years. The Georgia Northern Railway Company, incorporated under the laws of this State, with its principal office and place of business in Brooks county, started in the early part of this year (1899) to build a tramroad from the north side of the town of Moultrie, in Colquitt county, westerly across the Ochlochnee river, to reach some timber there, which it was under contract to haul to Pidcock, in Brooks county, and laid about a mile or less of the tramroad, using on it old, worn-out, bent, and pieced rails of very light weight, unfit for use on a railroad for ordinary business, and barely fit for use to haul logs over. On February 23, 1899, the Georgia Northern Railway Company, for the purpose of placing itself in position to keep others from building a railroad there, and to keep down competition, applied for and obtained from the secretary of State an amendment to its charter, allowing it to build a railroad from Moultrie to Thomasville; and it proceeded for some distance to mark out a line for, and announced its intention to build, such a road from where its said projected tramroad would lead it, down the west side of the Ochlochnee river; Moultrie and Thomasville being on the east side of the stream. It does not and never did intend in good faith to prosecute the work of building, completing, and operating a railroad from Moultrie to Thomasville, and is only making pretense of so building, in order to annoy and delay petitioner, and possibly others, so as to keep out competition in the county of Colquitt, where it now has almost a monopoly and is doing a large business, hauling logs and lumber to and from sawmills. Its projected line would parallel, within ten miles for the entire distance from Moultrie to Thomasville, the line that petitioner has laid out and begun to construct, the distance being only about twenty-eight miles. This would be a violation of the law of the State and of petitioner's rights, since petitioner's charter is older than said amendment to the charter of the Georgia Northern Railway Company; and it would seriously damage petitioner by having the effect of making petitioner wait till the expiration of the two years allowed by law in which the defendant company, should it be allowed to proceed, could hold said line and keep others from building within ten miles of it. The distances between the principal points are as follows: from Pidcock to Thomasville is seventeen miles, from Pidcock to Moultrie is thirty-two miles, from Moultrie to Thomasville is twenty-eight miles, from Pavo (a place on the line of defendant's road) to Thomasville is about seventeen miles, while from Pavo to Pidcock is fifteen miles. The petition prayed that the defendant be enjoined from building its proposed railroad within ten miles of the petitioner's line of road.

By amendment the petitioner alleged, among other things: The property of the Georgia Southern and Florida Railroad Company was sold by commissioners in equity at public outcry in 1894, under mortgage foreclosure, and bought by a committee of the bondholders, who were, as purchasers, incorporated in 1895, under the general law, as the present Georgia Southern and Florida Railway Company; and petitioner procured from the latter all its rights, property, franchises, grades, surveys, etc., from Tifton to Thomasville (which were obtained in good faith and under a valid charter and are very valuable), and, acting through its incorporators, before any valid organization of the company was had, sent over the line between Tifton and Thomasville an engineer corps for the purpose of following up the grade and proposed route of the Georgia Southern and Florida Railroad Company, which had been laid off and graded before the year 1897; the engineer in charge of this work for petitioner's incorporators made an examination of the entire line and estimate of the cost of building and reported the result to the incorporators, and this line was adopted and laid out by the incorporators as the line they intended to build and upon which subscriptions were asked to the stock of the company. This work was done in December, 1898, before the amendment of the charter of the defendant, authorizing it to build a branch road such as now desired. The defendant answered, denying the material allegations of the petition; and the court, after hearing evidence, granted an interlocutory injunction as prayed. Defendant excepted. Plaintiff filed a cross-bill of exceptions, the grounds of which need not be stated.

Humphreys & Branch and *J. W. Walters*, for plaintiff in error.
N. E. Harris, J. H. Merrill, and *J. Carroll Payne*, contra.

LITTLE, J. In this case the evidence as to the fact of location by the plaintiff in error of its line of railroad was conflicting; and even if, in view of all of its charter powers, the right given to construct a line of railroad from Moultrie to Thomasville was such as was contemplated by the statute which sought to protect one line from the encroachments of another, the judge could, in his discretion, in view of such conflict in the evidence, have legally granted the injunction. Some of the evidence directly negatived the fact that the Georgia Northern Railway Company had selected and marked out a line for its railroad. If this evidence was true (and the judge had a right to believe it), it was in his discretion to grant the injunction. 'There is another reason, however, why it appears to us that the injunction was properly granted. The Georgia Southern & Florida Railroad Company was, by an act of the General Assembly of this State, fully empowered to construct a branch of its railroad from Tifton to Thomasville; and the fact is not questioned that, in pursuance of such charter power, it located a right of way between these two points and did a considerable amount of work in its preparation to receive the line of railroad. It is contended, however, that the act of the legislature which incorporated that company contained a stipulation that the corporation should forfeit its rights and franchises unless the line of railroad was completed within a given time; and by reference to the acts of the General Assembly we find these conditions incorporated in the charter. It further appears that that railroad company did not complete its road within the given time, and that its property and assets were placed in the hands of a receiver, and a sale of all the property of the corporation, including the railroad line, was had under order of the court, and that the purchasers organized a new company and took possession of such property. Under our statute such purchasers succeeded to the rights and franchises possessed by the original corporation, and, having organized under the general railroad laws of this State, they succeeded to the ownership of the right of way procured and laid off between Tifton and Thomasville. The defendant in error procured such right of way and the property thereon by purchase from the

Georgia Southern and Florida Railway Company, who were
the purchasers of the property and franchises of the Georgia
Southern and Florida Railroad Company. And even if it be
true that the defendant in error had not acquired this right
of way before the plaintiff in error located its line, we can not
see how that fact operates to the benefit of the Georgia Northern Railway Company. It can do so only on the theory that
the Georgia Southern and Florida Railroad Company had forfeited its franchises and this right of way. It is true that it
was a condition of its charter·that it should so forfeit, but a
forfeiture for a misuser or nonuser of corporate franchises can
be declared only by the judgment of a court of competent jurisdiction, on a proceeding instituted for that purpose, and the
forfeiture dates from the time of such declaration. Civil Code,
§ 1883. Neither can the plaintiff in error avail itself of the
claim that such right of way and the franchise to construct a
railroad upon it had been forfeited, as it seeks to do in this
case; because neither misuser nor nonuser can be set up collaterally as a defense to the action. *City of Atlanta* v. *Gate City
Co.*, 71 *Ga.* 106, and authorities there cited. So that, if there
had been no legal forfeiture of the franchises given to the
Georgia Southern and Florida Railroad Company to construct
the road, and if it be true that the purchasers of the property
of that corporation acquired the franchises possessed by that
company, together with its property, then it will follow that
there was a selected and laid out line of railroad between the
two points, and that it was so located before the plaintiff in
error acquired any rights to its alleged located line. So that,
irrespective of when the Tifton, Thomasville and Gulf Railway
Company acquired this prospective line, a right of way had already been located, towards which the plaintiff in error must
be held to legally observe the restrictions laid down in section
2176 of the Civil Code. In any event, therefore, there was no
error in granting the injunction.

*Judgment on main bill of exceptions affirmed.   Cross-bill dis-
missed.   All the Justices concurring.*

BARROW, trustee, *v.* SMITH *et al.*

When one makes a money subscription to a corporation, to be expended in
the development of its property in certain named ways, and by the contract is to receive therefor "stock, bonds, or other security," as may be
determined by the board of directors, and the board subsequently declares that the subscriber, by virtue of scrip issued to him on the payment
of such subscription, is entitled to the bonds of the company to the extent of the sum paid in, and that such development fund paid in "is
hereby recognized as an indebtedness for which the holder is entitled at
once to the principal and interest in money, except where he takes
bonds in lieu of money," such subscriber, to the extent of the money
paid in, is a creditor of the company, and the legal effect of the contract
under this action of the board of directors is that the unpaid portion of
any subscription, so made, is cancelled, where the subscriber does not
elect to take therefor the bonds of the company.

Argued December 2, 1899.— Decided January 81, 1900.

Intervention.   Before Judge Candler.   Fulton superior
court.   March term, 1899.

Barrow & Osborne, for plaintiff in error.
Hoke Smith & H. C. Peeples, contra.

LITTLE, J.   Hoke Smith applied to the judge of the superior
court of Fulton county for an order directing Joel Hurt, who
was receiver, to pay him out of the funds in his hands the sum
of five thousand dollars.   The receiver resisted the application
to the extent of asking the court to reduce the amount to be
paid to petitioner, by deducting a claim which he, as receiver,
held against him.   Mr. Barrow, as trustee, prayed the court
that he might intervene in the proceedings, which was allowed,
and he exhibited his petition praying that the amount of the
claim which the defendant in error asked to be paid should be
reduced by setting off against it the same indebtedness which
the receiver had set up, which action, the intervenor showed,
would be beneficial to the estate he represented.   At the hearing it was agreed between the parties that all the allegations in
the petition of Mr. Smith, the allegations in the answer of the
receiver, and the allegations in the petition of the trustee were
true and were to be taken as proved.   As we collect the allegations from these pleadings they are as follows: Mr. Smith

sets out, that in the case of *Moore, administrator,* v. *The Suwanee Canal Company,* pending in Fulton superior court, he
was, by a decree rendered on the 11th day of January, 1899,
awarded five thousand dollars as attorney's fees for representing the defendant, and the receiver was directed to pay the
same out of any funds in his possession and out of the proceeds
of the sale of the property of the defendant, prior to any other
claim or lien except other claims for attorney's fees and court
costs allowed by the same decree; that a sale of the property
was made and confirmed by the court, and the receiver has in
his possession sufficient funds to pay the allowance made, but he
declines to do so unless the petitioner will allow, as a credit on
the same, certain charges against petitioner which appear on
the books of the canal company. Petitioner alleges that he is
not indebted to the canal company in any sum, but on the contrary, in addition to the five thousand dollars allowed him as
fees, the company is indebted to him for borrowed money in
the sum of ten thousand dollars, besides other sums as fees for
professional services. The receiver averred, that on June 9,
1891, the petitioner entered into an agreement with the Suwanee
Canal Company and certain stockholders of said company,
whereby, for sufficient consideration, he undertook and promised to pay to the canal company ten thousand dollars in installments, as the same might be called for by the board of directors, which agreement was and is binding on petitioner; that he
failed to pay of this sum two installments which were called
for; and that he is now indebted on that contract two thousand
dollars, besides interest, which debt and other claims due to the
company are in the hands of the receiver, by order of the court,
for collection; and he asks to set off this indebtedness of the petitioner against the allowance made for fees. The answer set up
the contract referred to, the material part of which is as follows:

"In consideration of these presents, it is agreed that the un-
dersigned will pay to said company the amounts set opposite
their names, in installments, as the same may be called for by
the board of directors of said company, receiving therefor stock,
bonds, or other security, as may be determined by said board.
The money thus raised to be expended in the development of

the property of the company, acquiring right of way for canal, and contiguous lands, as the directors may determine, and shall be called for only as required for the purposes aforesaid. This agreement shall be binding upon the subscribers whether they continue to be holders of the stock or not, but shall not be binding until signed by seventy-five per cent., in amount, of all the stockholders of said company. . .

[Signed] Hoke Smith, June 9, 1891, 10,000.00."

It was not contested that the whole amount had been called for in installments, nor that the agreement had been signed by seventy-five per cent. of the stockholders of the company. The original petition was amended by alleging that the following action was had by the directors of the company: On March 19, 1894, the directors were authorized to sell the first mortgage bonds of the company to stockholders at ninety cents on the dollar, etc., and the following resolution was also passed: "Resolved, second: That the scrip issued for payments to the development fund, with interest thereon, be accepted at par in satisfaction for subscriptions to the issue of bonds, but that the bonds thus purchased be not delivered nor the scrip canceled until such time as may be determined by the president and directors. . ." On February 3, 1897, the following preamble and resolutions were adopted by the board: "Whereas subscriptions have been made by a number of holders of the development fund scrip of this company for the bonds of the company, in pursuance of the resolutions passed at the meeting of the stockholders held March 19, 1894, and whereas a tender has been made of said scrip in payment of said bonds, in pursuance of the terms of said resolution; therefore, be it resolved, first, that the board of directors of this company hereby recognize the right of said holders of development fund scrip to the immediate possession of said bonds, and the possession of said bonds to said amount by the Farmers Loan and Trust Company shall be recognized from this day forward as being for the benefit of said scrip-holders to the amount of the principal and interest of their scrip, according to the terms of the resolutions passed at the stockholders' meeting on March 19, 1894. Resolved, second, that the treasurer of this company shall from

time to time procure said bonds to be actually delivered to said
scrip-holders as said scrip-holders may desire.   Resolved, third,
that from and after this day all development fund scrip is
hereby recognized as an indebtedness for which the holder is
entitled at once to the principal and interest in money, except
where he takes in lieu of money the bonds provided for by the
resolutions of the stockholders' meeting above referred to, and
any such holder who has not already subscribed for and demanded bonds shall have the right at any time hereafter to do
so, with all the privileges covered by this resolution."   Petitioner alleges that said bonds were never delivered, and that
the company, on said loan and on purchases which he has made
of scrip issued to other parties, owes him over ten thousand
dollars.

The intervenor alleges in his petition the indebtedness of the
petitioner to the canal company under the contract as set out
by the receiver, and on information charges that a contract was
made by petitioner and the canal company, by which the former
was employed as attorney for the company, and it was agreed
that his indebtedness to the company should be set off against
his compensation as attorney, and that petitioner accepted employment under those terms, and the only thing left open at
that time was the amount of compensation to be paid the petitioner; that this was subsequently agreed on at the sum of five
thousand dollars, to cover his entire services for the company,
including all its litigation; that petitioner has no connection
with the company as its attorney other than under this contract; that petitioner was never appointed by the court to represent the company, nor his compensation fixed by the court,
but that the court allowed him the sum of five thousand dollars because it had been agreed between petitioner and his
client that he should receive that amount, and the client consented to the allowance, and the action of the court was based
on the idea that the company was provided with counsel by
contract; that the claim against the petitioner is the property of
the trust estate which he, the intervenor, represents, and that
he as trustee was the purchaser of the property of the canal
company at the sale made by the receiver; that the debts due

the canal company were reserved from sale and directed to be collected by the receiver, and, after paying expenses, are to be paid over to the purchaser of the property which was sold, and that the trust estate is entitled to have the indebtedness due by the petitioner to the canal company set off against his claim for compensation as attorney; and he prays accordingly. To the petition of the intervenor was attached as an exhibit an extract from the original decree granted January 11, 1899, as follows: "The fees allowed in item three of this decree are allowed by consent and agreement between the parties to this cause, and are only allowed because the party and parties out of whom they come, and from the proceeds of whose property they are to be paid, have agreed to them, and request their allowance by the court." And also this extract: "It appearing to the court that the appointment of a receiver will remove all the assets of the defendant from its custody, and that the best management of the affairs of the company require the assistance in this litigation of the counsel for the defendant, it is ordered that the fees for services in this litigation of the attorneys for the defendant, Hoke Smith & H. C. Peeples, be made a charge upon the assets of the company, in the hands of the receiver, the amount of such charges to be fixed hereafter."

By further amendment of the original petition, Mr. Smith admitted the execution of the contract set out, alleged that the same was an agreement to loan money, and, the canal company having become insolvent, there was no means for the return of the money if loaned, and he denied, therefore, any liability under the contract. He denied that any contract was ever made between himself and the company, fixing the amount of fees to be paid and as to how such fees should be paid. He denied that they were to be settled by any indebtedness due by him to the company. He alleged that he never had any agreement with the company as to what he was to be paid for appearing in the litigation filed by the administrator against the company; that the canal company owed him for professional services rendered before the filing of the bill, and such sum was in addition to the five thousand dollars allowed him as fees in that case. He sets out that his connection with that litigation occurred under the following circumstances: General Jackson was president of the canal company and the holder of a preferred lien against it, the lien being for an amount of money over one hundred thousand dollars, which General Jackson had advanced for the further management of the company.   The original bill asking the appointment of a receiver was filed by the administrator of the estate of Henry Jackson.   A large number of the stockholders, for satisfactory reasons, employed petitioner to represent the interests of the canal company in the litigation, with an understanding that they should not be liable to him for fees if an arrangement could be made by which his fees should be paid out of the fund in court.   An agreement was reached between the plaintiff in the bill, the representatives of Gen. Jackson, and petitioner, that the latter should appear and represent the interest of the company, and that his fee should be five thousand dollars, and was to be a charge on the property of the company, superior to the lien of Gen. Jackson.   The latter came into the litigation for the purpose of foreclosing his lien, and subsequently transferred the same to himself as trustee of named beneficiaries, and his successor in trust, Mr. Barrow, thus came into possession of the property.   Attached to this amendment is an extract from the decree rendered, as follows: "3. It is further considered, ordered, adjudged, and decreed that Joel Hurt as receiver, in full for his services for such, and for conducting the sale of the property of the defendant, making deeds and delivery of the property, shall receive the sum of $7,500.00; that King & Anderson, as plaintiff's attorneys, shall receive the sum of $5,000.00, that Hoke Smith, as defendant's attorney, shall receive the sum of $5,000.00, that Burton Smith, as attorney for John W. Weed and Frank Coxe, shall receive the sum of $1,000.00, that Glenn, Slaton & Phillips, as attorneys for intervenors represented by them, shall receive the sum of $500.00; that the Farmers Loan and Trust Company, trustee, and King & Spalding, and Turner, McClure & Rolston, as attorneys for the Farmers Loan and Trust Company, trustee, shall receive the sum of fifteen hundred dollars, and the officers of the court, for costs in this case, shall receive the sum of . . . . .

The above sums of money to be paid in full for fees as attorneys and receiver, respectively. The above amounts herein decreed in this clause for receiver's and attorney's fees and costs, as above stated, shall be paid, first, from the proceeds of the sale of the property of said defendant, the Suwanee Canal Company, and are preferred over the first preference lien given in the second clause of this decree to the said Pope Barrow as trustee."

After considering the pleadings and hearing argument, the judge ordered the receiver to pay to the defendant in error the sum of five thousand dollars, with interest from the date of the rendition of the original decree; and to this order and judgment the plaintiff in error excepted. Under the view which we take of this case, it is not necessary to discuss or decide many of the interesting points made in the briefs of counsel representing the parties. The question is, whether an alleged indebtedness on the part of the defendant in error to the canal company should be set off against an allowance of counsel fees, made to him by proper order of the court, for the representation of the corporation in the litigation which resulted in the appointment of a receiver and the sale of the property of the corporation, under the facts as they appear in the pleadings. The contract under which it is shown that this alleged indebtedness accrued can not, in our opinion, be held to be one of subscription to the capital stock of the corporation. It will be noted from the terms of the contract that the plaintiff undertook for a specific purpose — that of the development of the property of the corporation, acquiring right of way for the canal, and the purchase of contiguous lands — to pay to the company the sum of ten thousand dollars, and for the sum so paid he was to be entitled to receive stock, that is to say, shares of the capital stock of the company, or the bonds of the company, or other security, as might be determined by the board of directors. If the board of directors had, in pursuance of this contract, declared that shares of the capital stock should be issued for the payments made, then there is no doubt that the defendant in error would have been a subscriber to the capital stock of the company. But, as executed, the contract was to a certain extent indeterminate, and the legal status of the parties to it was made to depend upon the future action of the board of directors. This action, as appears by the record, was had by the directors on March 19, 1894, and February 3, 1897. At their meeting on the first-named date, it was resolved that the scrip issued for payments to the development fund, with accrued interest, be accepted at par in satisfaction for subscriptions to the issue of bonds, and, by the action of the board held on the last-named date, it was resolved that the board of directors recognized the right of the holders of development-fund scrip to the immediate possession of bonds of the company, for the issue of which authority had been given by a previous resolution; and at the same time it was resolved that the development-fund scrip was recognized as an indebtedness for which the holder is entitled at once to principal and interest in money, except where he takes, in lieu of money, the bonds provided for by the resolution of the stockholders' meeting in March, 1894.

Taking, then, the original contract which expressly provided that the board of directors might thereafter determine what stock, bonds, or other securities of the company should be given to subscribers to the development fund, and the action had by the board of directors under the terms of that contract, it appears that subscribers who had contributed to the development fund should have the amount subscribed and paid in returned to them in money, unless such subscriber preferred to take, in lieu thereof, bonds of the company. It is not disputed that the defendant in error, of the sum subscribed by him to the development fund, had paid eight thousand dollars, leaving to be paid the sum of two thousand dollars; and it would seem, from a proper interpretation of the contract and the subsequent action of the board of directors, that he would be entitled to have the money which he had paid into the development fund returned to him with interest thereon, unless he preferred to take bonds of the company for that sum. The record does not disclose any receipt of bonds by him, and, in the absence of his election so to take, he was entitled to have from the company eight thousand dollars in money, with interest. He was, therefore, under the terms of this contract as executed by the company, a creditor of the company to the extent of eight thousand dollars besides interest. But the same contract obligated him to pay in the sum of ten thousand dollars. He had, therefore, not complied with his obligation to the extent of two thousand dollars, and to this extent he would have been a debtor to the company but for the fact that when the debt was enforced and the money collected, the right immediately inured to the subscriber to have it paid back to him. In view of the action of the board of directors declaring that the holder of the development-fund scrip was entitled to be paid back in money all that he paid on his subscription to that fund, it would seem, as a matter of law, that the indebtedness was canceled. This view of the question disposes of the case, and dispenses with any ruling as to the matter of set-off, which, as we think, is not involved under the terms of the original contract and the subsequent action of the board of directors.

Judgment affirmed. All the Justices concurring, except Lumpkin, P. J., and Cobb, J., who were disqualified.

OTIS BROTHERS & COMPANY *v.* HOLMES.

100
136

1. Relatively to the question dealt with by this court in the case of *Atlanta Railway Company* v. *American Car Company*, 103 *Ga.* 254, there is no material difference between an "express promise" to repair defective machinery and "repeated and continuing promises" to do so. Accordingly the amendment to the defendant's answer was properly allowed.
2. While "a plea of total failure of consideration includes partial failure of consideration," there was in a particular case no error in charging, in effect, that the jury must find for the plaintiff the full amount sued for, or nothing at all, when under the evidence pro and con one or the other of these findings was absolutely required.
3. There was no error in admitting evidence for any reason alleged in the objections made to the same, and the evidence warranted the verdict.

Argued December 11, 1899. — Decided January 31, 1900.

Complaint. Before Judge Reid. City court of Atlanta. April 15, 1899.

Charles A. Read, for plaintiffs.
Gray, Brown & Randolph, for defendant.

Cobb, J. The plaintiffs sued the defendant upon a promissory note for five hundred dollars. The defendant pleaded that he had purchased of plaintiffs an electric elevator for the sum of $2,940; that he had paid all of the amount except the sum represented by the note sued on; that the consideration of the note had totally failed, by reason of the fact that the elevator was so defective and so entirely unsuited for the purpose for which it was intended that it was not worth even the amount already paid on the purchase-price; and that while he knew of the condition of the elevator at the time the note was given, the same was given "upon the repeated and continuing promises" of the plaintiffs to repair the defects in the elevator, which they failed and refused to do. Under this plea there were three issues of fact for determination by the jury: (1) Was the elevator defective as claimed? (2) Was the note given upon the promise of the plaintiffs to repair the defects? (3) Have they complied with that promise? A verdict was returned in favor of the defendant, and to the refusal of the court to grant them a new trial the plaintiffs excepted.

1. The plea alleged that the note was given upon the "repeated and continuing promises" of the plaintiffs to repair the elevator. In the case of *Atlanta Railway Company* v. *American Car Company*, 103 *Ga.* 254, the defendant pleaded, to a suit on a promissory note given for the purchase-price of certain articles of personal property known to be in a defective condition when the note was given, that the same was given "in consideration of an express promise" by the plaintiff to repair the property. It was held that this plea was improperly stricken, and that under such circumstances knowledge of the defects at the time the note was given would not preclude the defendant from setting up the defense that the property was worthless. The objection made to the plea filed in the present case was that it was not sufficiently specific, because the language used was not in terms or in substance the same as that employed in the case just cited. We do not think this contention is well founded. There is no substantial difference between "repeated and continuing promises" to repair a defect in machinery and an "express promise" to do so. The plea was therefore properly

allowed, under the ruling made in the case cited. See also *Blount* v. *Edison Co.*, 106 *Ga.* 197.

2. Complaint is made in the motion for a new trial that the court erred in charging the jury as follows: "You would not be authorized, gentlemen, to allow anything off of the note sued on. You would either find for the plaintiffs the whole amount sued on, or else find for the defendant. There is no plea in this case that the note partially failed, but the plea is that as to this particular note the consideration entirely failed and that they ought not to recover at all." In the case of *Morgan* v. *Printup*, 72 *Ga.* 66, it was held, that "A plea of total failure of consideration includes partial failure of consideration; and, under the former plea, a defendant may obtain an abatement in the sum agreed to be paid, if the evidence shows a partial failure and the extent thereof." See also *Hornsby* v. *Butts*, 85 *Ga.* 694; *Hinkle* v. *Burt*, 94 *Ga.* 506; *Skipper* v. *Johnson*, 21 *Ga.* 310. Under the decisions just cited, the charge of the court above quoted was erroneous if there was any evidence from which the jury might have found that there was a partial failure of consideration and the extent thereof. But there is no such evidence in the record. The defendant contracted to pay $2,940 for an electric elevator of a certain kind and description. He paid all of this sum except the amount sued for. There was evidence that the elevator was worth only $1,500, as well as evidence that certain defects in the same had been remedied by the defendant at an expense of $150. This was the only evidence before the jury from which they could measure the damages of the defendant. Taking the evidence in the most favorable light for the plaintiffs, the jury would have been compelled to find that the elevator was worth only $1,650, and, after having allowed the amount paid out by the defendant for repairs, it would leave $1,500 as the amount due by the defendant. As he had already paid $2,440, it is clear that the consideration of the note sued on had totally failed. There was in the case no question growing out of a partial failure of the consideration of the note sued on. It had totally failed. There was a partial failure of the consideration of the entire contract, and this partial failure was of such extent as to show conclusively that the

consideration of the note sued on had totally failed.   The evidence fully authorized a finding that the elevator was defective, that the defendant gave the note sued on upon the promise of the plaintiffs to repair the defects, that they had failed to do so, and that as to the consideration of the note sued on the consideration had wholly failed.   On the other hand, the plaintiffs insisted that they had not promised to repair any defects, that the elevator completely met the requirements of their contract, and that the entire amount of the note was due and unpaid.   These were the issues upon which the jury were to pass.   There was no evidence tending to show a partial failure of the consideration for which the note sued on was given.   The evidence of the plaintiffs authorized but one finding, and that was for the full amount of the note, they contending that there were no defects in the elevator and that they had not promised to repair any.   The evidence of the defendant, as above shown, authorized a finding that the consideration of the contract had failed to such an extent as, in any event, to amount to a total failure of the consideration of the note sued on.   This being so, we think the charge complained of was not erroneous.

3. It is unnecessary to discuss at length the other grounds of the motion for a new trial.   They complain of the admission of certain evidence.   We think there was no error in admitting this evidence for any of the reasons assigned.   The evidence amply warranted the verdict rendered, and there was no error in denying a new trial.

Judgment affirmed.   All the Justices concurring.

FLOYD *v.* ATLANTA BANKING COMPANY *et al.*

Where one voluntarily enters into a written contract agreeing to pay a municipal corporation a given sum of money as his proportionate share of the cost of paving a street upon which his property abuts, and afterwards seeks to annul and set aside such contract on the ground that the assessment made upon him for such work was neither legal nor authorized, but fails to either allege or prove that the contract executed by him was the result of fraud, accident, or mistake, he is not entitled to equitable relief. If the contract was entered into by him with a knowledge that the corporation could not legally demand payment of the assessment, it was competent for him, nevertheless, to make an agreement to pay the same, and the fact that his property was benefited by the work done is a sufficient consideration to support the contract.

Argued December 12, 1899.— Decided January 31, 1900.

Equitable petition. Before Judge Candler. Fulton superior court. March term, 1899.

H. A. Alexander, for plaintiff. *Payne & Tye, J. A. Anderson*, and *J. T. Pendleton*, for defendants.

LITTLE, J. Floyd filed a petition in the superior court of Fulton county, making the City of Atlanta, A. W. Hill, marshal of the City of Atlanta, Venable Brothers, and the Atlanta Banking Company parties defendant, in which it was sought to permanently enjoin the defendants from enforcing against the petitioner certain alleged contracts to pay a portion of the cost of paving the roadway on North Butler street in the City of Atlanta on which real estate belonging to petitioner had a frontage, said contracts being then held by the Atlanta Banking Company. The evidence and admissions of the parties made this case: On February 25, 1895, an ordinance was passed by the authorities of the City of Atlanta providing for the paving of North Butler street between its intersection with Edgewood avenue and Jenkins street, and assessing two thirds of the cost on owners of abutting real estate. On July 1, 1895, in pursuance of said ordinance, the City of Atlanta entered into a written agreement with the Standard Paving Company for the construction of such paving. The contract was as follows:

"Georgia, Fulton County. This agreement, made and entered into this 1st day of July, 1895, between the City of Atlanta, a municipal corporation under the laws of the State of Georgia, party of the first part, and the Standard Paving Company, a corporation under the laws of Georgia, party of the second part, both of said county, witnesseth, that the said party of the first part, on petition of the citizens owning more than one third of the real property abutting on Butler street between Jenkins and Edgewood avenue, for the paving of said Butler street with vitrified brick, said petition dated January 31st, 1895, and on recommendation of the city engineer, and commissioner of public works, dated February 4th, 1895, passed on the petition aforesaid, favoring the paving of said Butler street between the points named, with vitrified brick, at an estimated cost of $7,884.00, and of which the cost estimated to be paid by the City of Atlanta is $2,628.00, besides the sum of $1,200.00 on account of the Grady Hospital lot. The sum to be paid by the owners of abutting property, $5,256.00. In pursuance of said petition, the general council passed an ordinance, February 18th, 1895, being passed by the requisite majority of councilmen and board of aldermen, prior to approval by the mayor, on the 25th day of February, 1895, and which ordinance provides for the paving with vitrified brick of that portion of Butler street between Jenkins street and Edgewood avenue. And whereas the City of Atlanta, by report of the street committee of the general council, which was adopted by said council and approved by the mayor on the day of February 18th, 1895, let the contract for paving Butler street between the points aforesaid, with vitrified brick, to the said party of the second part, at the price of $2.21 per square yard, being the lowest and best bid, conditioned that the work of paving aforesaid shall be executed in all respects to the satisfaction of the city engineer and commissioner of public works, and in accordance with specifications for said paving, prepared by the city engineer of the City of Atlanta, and inspected by the said party of the second part, before making this bid, upon which said bids were based, a copy of which specifications is attached to, and made a part of this contract, and on the further condition that the said party of the second part should give bond in the sum of $2,000.00, with sureties resident in Fulton county, Georgia, to be approved by the mayor of the City of Atlanta, for the faithful performance of said contract, and the maintenance of said pavement for a period of five years from the completion of the work, on the terms stipulated in the specifications aforesaid, and in such smooth condition or repair as the specifications provide for, and on the further condition that said party of the second part agrees to look to the owners of abutting private property for the payment of the assessments for said vitrified brick paving, made by and in pursuance of the ordinance aforesaid, against the lot of each of said abutting owners, and also agrees to allow each of the owners of said abutting private property the option of paying such assessment in full in cash, or one fourth in cash within thirty days after said work is completed and demand made for payment thereof, and the remaining three fourths in three equal installments, falling due in one, two, and three years, with interest at the rate of seven per cent. per annum on said deferred payments. The bills or executions for the assessment against each of the owners of abutting private property are to be transferred to the said party of the second part or its assigns, and the said party of the second part is to look solely to the collection of these bills or executions for payment for paving said Butler street between the points named, except as to that part of said cost and expense in said ordinance assessed against the City of Atlanta; and the City of Atlanta covenants that it has charter power to do this paving, and that the ordinance passed in pursuance of the charter, providing for the paving in question, is a valid ordinance, and gives to the party of the second part a lien, from the date of its passage, against the property of each of the abutting owners of land on Butler street between the points named, for the amount of the assessment against each parcel of property, made by and in pursuance of said ordinance. The work of paving said street shall be begun on the 1st day of July, 1895, and not before, and shall be carried on and completed in accordance with the specifications, to the satisfaction of the city engineer and commissioner of public works, within   days after said date of beginning.

"In consideration of the due and thorough performance of said contract by said party of the second part, the City of Atlanta covenants to pay said party of the second part, upon the completion of said work and its acceptance by the city engineer and commissioner of public works, the sum of two thousand, six hundred and twenty-eight ($2,628.00) dollars, or such larger or smaller sum as may be chargeable to or against the city, upon the final estimation of said paving, at the contract price aforesaid, and to transfer to the said party of the second part valid bills or executions against the several owners of abutting real estate on the said street within the points named, and also to lend the use of the machinery of the city government to the party of the second part for the collection of the bills or executions so transferred to the party of the second part. This contract is to go into effect when signed by the mayor of the City of Atlanta on behalf of the party of the first part, and by said party of the second part by its president or other duly constituted authority, and upon the giving and acceptance of the bond provided for in this contract. In witness whereof said party of the first part has hereunto set its hand and seal by Porter King, mayor, and the party of the second part has likewise signed and sealed this instrument by B. F. Thomas, its president.

"The City of Atlanta, by Porter King, Mayor.

"Standard Paving Company, by B. F. Thomas, President."

Under this contract, the Standard Paving Company began work about the first of July, 1895, and turned over the street to the agents of the city in a finished condition about the last of August, 1895. On February 20, 1895, Floyd filed a written protest with the city council against the paving of Butler street, and said protest was brought to their notice and acted on by them adversely before the work was begun or the contract with the Standard Paving Company entered into. On or about September 5, 1895, a demand was made upon Floyd by the tax-collector of the city, that he pay his proportion of the said assessment, one hundred and seventy-six dollars and forty-four cents; whereupon Floyd paid one fourth of that amount in cash, and signed three written instruments, a copy of one of which is set out below; the transaction having taken place before the question of the liability of abutting property owners for the assessment had been submitted to the courts. The three writings were similar in all respects, except that the date of maturity was different, that of the first being September 5, 1896, of the second, September 5, 1897, of the third, September 5, 1898; the first of which is as follows: "B. R. No.   Note No.   Atlanta, Ga., Sept. 5, 1895. Whereas, by an act of the legislature approved August 21st, 1891, power was granted to the City of Atlanta to transfer bills and executions against abutting owners for curbing and street-paving, which said act grants to the person so liable for such assessment the privilege of paying 25 per cent. thereof in cash, and 25 per cent. per annum each year for three years thereafter, with interest at the rate of seven per cent. per annum, and provides that if default should be made in a deferred payment, then all the unpaid assessment should become due and payable; and whereas an ordinance approved October 10th, 1891, was passed by said city to carry out said act, and whereas vitrified brick street-pavement has been laid by Standard Paving Company in said city on Butler Street, for which I am liable as an abutting land owner to the amount of $176.44 dollars, according to the assessment made by the city, the said assessment having been duly made and the amount ascertained, fixed, and distributed, after notice by the mayor and council of Atlanta, and the bill or execution therefor has been transferred to Standard Paving Company: now I do elect to pay 25% of said assessment cash, and have the balance postponed according to the provisions of said act, and I agree with Standard Paving Company to waive the right for full time aforesaid, and to pay at　　Bank $44.11 Sept. 5, 1896, with interest at the rate of seven per cent. per annum until paid, payable semi-annually; and if I should make default in any of said payments, then all of the unpaid assessment shall become due and payable.　This election and agreement are made subject to all provisions of said act and ordinance, and nothing herein contained shall be so construed as to impair or affect in any manner anything in said act or ordinance contained, as to the lien in favor of the city against abutting land and the owner thereof, the mode of enforcing said lien, collecting assessments, or any other particular.

　　　　　　　　　[Signed]　B. F. Floyd.　(Seal.)"

　These written instruments were delivered to the tax-collector and were transferred to the Standard Paving Company.　Shortly after, they were endorsed and transferred to a partnership company of W. H. and S. H. Venable, entitled Venable Brothers, the following indorsement being written on the back:　"Pay

to the order of Venable Bros., without recourse.   Standard
Paving Company, J. E. M. Haskell, Sec'y and Treas." Two of
these obligations were transferred to the Atlanta Banking Company, the following indorsement being made on the back:
"Venable Bros." When the first of the obligations matured,
Floyd refused to make any payment on it, and subsequently on
the others. In December, 1897, the Atlanta Banking Company
had an execution issued by the city clerk on the contract, as provided by law, against Floyd, which was levied and the property advertised for sale; then an application was made for a
permanent injunction and cancellation of the writings in question. A temporary restraining order was granted by Judge J.
H. Lumpkin, and extended until the final hearing. Upon that
hearing, the Atlanta Banking Company amended its answer,
and prayed for cross-relief in the form of a judgment against
Floyd on the contract it held. This was granted, and a verdict against Floyd was directed in its favor, and injunction and
other relief were denied. It was admitted that the question of
the legality of the assessment against the property-holders for
paving Butler street had been decided, July 27, 1896, by the
Supreme Court of Georgia and the assessments declared to have
been null and void ab initio, and, as distinctly set out in the
bill of exceptions, the sole question on which the present case
turns is, whether, although the assessment was invalid, Floyd
was liable on these written instruments in the hands of the
Atlanta Banking Company.

If the question as to whether the plaintiff in error was liable
to pay the assessments made on him for the paving of North Butler street was involved, it would, under the authority of *City of
Atlanta* v. *Smith*, 99 *Ga.* 462, be readily answered in the negative. Nor could it be held under the facts of this case that the
defendant in error was such a bona fide purchaser of the obligations of Floyd as would exclude the defenses which existed between the maker of the instruments and the City of Atlanta at
the time of their execution. The form of the instruments does
not give them the character of negotiability by delivery or indorsement, and their nature necessarily puts upon the holders
of them notice of the consideration for which they were given,

as well as the law regulating the same. But, notwithstanding these facts, the plaintiff in error was not entitled to any of the relief which he sought, nor can we extract from the record any legal reason why he should not pay these obligations. As a matter of law he was not liable to pay the assessment, but although he protested against the paving of the street and the same was done over his protest, yet when a demand was made upon him to pay his proportion of the assessment for the paving, he at once complied with the demand and elected to exercise the privilege given him by the act of the legislature, and paid one fourth of the amount assessed against him in cash and gave his written obligations to pay the remainder within the three following years. It is true that these agreements were made before it had been determined that such assessments were illegal, but nevertheless, in consideration of the increased value of his property caused by the paving, for which the assessments were made, he could make a valid and binding contract to pay his proportion of the cost of the same. It is argued by counsel for the plaintiff in error that, the assessment being illegal, the plaintiff in error was under no obligation to pay. This would be true if he were resisting the assessment, but in this case he is the moving party and seeks to have the obligations, freely and fairly entered into by him, cancelled, because he was not legally liable to pay such assessments. Before these obligations can be set aside, he must go further and show that in the execution of the obligations he acted under such a mistake of law or fact as would authorize him to call upon a court of equity to set them aside. So far as the record shows, he acted under no mistake either of law or fact. Neither his petition nor any part of it is found in the record, and, under the exceptions taken, there is no suggestion of mistake. For aught we know, he may have been perfectly cognizant of his legal rights in the premises and equally as well informed that the City of Atlanta had not made such a compliance with the law as entitled it to make a valid assessment against the owners of property on North Butler street for their proportionate part of the cost of paving.

As a general rule, a promise to pay upon a supposed liability and in ignorance of the law binds the party.   See authorities cited in 1 Story's Eq. Jur., note on page 111.   And "a mistake as to a matter of fact, to warrant relief in equity, must be material, and the fact must be such that it animated and controlled the conduct of the party. . . The court must be satisfied that but for the mistake the complainant would not have assumed the obligation from which he seeks to be relieved." 93 U. S. p. 60.   In 1 Story on Contracts (5th ed.), § 528, it is said that, to render a contract voidable because of a mistake of fact, it is essential that the contract be made "under an injurious mistake or ignorance of a material fact"; and, in order for equity to interfere with a contract because of a mistake, Mr. Bishop, in his Law of Contracts, § 711, declares that "the mistake must be material, and such that, but for it, the complaining party would not have assumed the obligation."   As before stated, if he were seeking to resist the collection of the assessments, the law is plain that the plaintiff in error could not be made liable; but when he undertakes to set aside contracts voluntarily entered into by him, he must not only allege but prove that it was the result either of such a mistake of law or fact as authorizes the interposition of a court of equity.   So far as the record shows, the plaintiff in error rests his case on the ground that he was not legally liable for the assessments, and he draws the deduction that, not being so liable, he can not be held to the observance of his promises to pay.   This is not tenable.   It was perfectly competent for him to waive the illegality in the proceedings taken to have the work done, and if, with a knowledge of the irregularity of such proceedings he nevertheless, in consideration of the benefit to his property, undertook and agreed to pay his proportionate part of the expense of the same, such agreement will be held to be a valid and binding contract.   Inasmuch, therefore, as it has been clearly shown that he voluntary entered into these contracts, an absence of liability to pay the alleged debt for which they were given, without more, will not avail, and it must be held that he is not entitled to have the same abrogated or set aside.   The judgment of the court below, in refusing to grant the injunction and in rendering judgment against him under the cross-bill filed, is   *Affirmed.   All the Justices concurring.*

MADDOX *et al.* *v.* AMERICAN TRUST & BANKING CO.   109
121

A bond at the beginning of which was stated the case of a named plaintiff
against a designated partnership as defendant and a third person as garnishee; which on its face purported to bind one of the partners "as principal and as a member of" that firm, and certain persons as sureties;
which, after reciting the facts as to the suing out of the garnishment, was
conditioned for the payment to the plaintiff in the case mentioned of
"the amount which may be recovered and all costs therein in said garnishment;" and which was duly executed by such partner and the sureties,
was, under section 4718 of the Civil Code, sufficient as to form, and, if
solvent as to suretyship, was a good statutory bond for the purpose of dissolving the garnishment.

Argued December 13, 1899. — Decided January 31, 1900.

Garnishment. Before Judge Reid. City court of Atlanta.
March term, 1899.

C. D. Maddox, for plaintiffs. *Ellis, Wimbish & Ellis* and
Gray, Brown & Randolph, for defendant.

LUMPKIN, P. J. If the headnote correctly lays down the law,
this case was rightly decided in the court below. The material
facts are as follows: J. J. & J. E. Maddox brought an action
against E. S. Morris & Co., of which firm N. W. Murphy was
a member, and caused a garnishment to be served on the American Trust and Banking Company. N. W. Murphy, for the purpose of dissolving the garnishment, executed a bond. At the
beginning of the bond were these words: "J. J. & J. E. Maddox *vs.* E. S. Morris & Co., defendant, American Trust & Banking Co., garnishee." It then recited that "N. W. Murphy, as
principal and as a member of the firm of E. S. Morris & Co.,"
and certain persons named as sureties, were bound unto J. J. &
J. E. Maddox in a specified amount; and, after setting forth the
facts as to the suing out of the garnishment, contained a condition that it was to be void "if the said N. W. Murphy shall
pay to the said J. J. & J. E. Maddox the amount which may
be recovered and all costs therein in said garnishment." The
garnishee, upon notice from the clerk of the court that a satisfactory bond for the dissolution of the garnishment had been
filed, paid to N. W. Murphy the money in its hands belonging

to E. S. Morris & Co.   Subsequently J. J. & J. E. Maddox obtained a judgment against E. S. Morris & Co., and, on the facts
above stated and an admission by the Banking Company that
at the time of receiving the summons of garnishment it owed
Morris & Co. a stated amount, moved for a judgment against
the company as garnishee.   The judge denied this motion, and
J. J. & J. E. Maddox excepted.   They claimed the right to have
such a judgment on the theory that the garnishment had never
been dissolved, basing their contention to this effect on the proposition that the so-called "dissolving bond" was insufficient in
law.   The only objection urged to it here was that it was not
made in the name of and signed by E. S. Morris & Co., but by
N. W. Murphy.   Before dealing with this point we will remark,
in passing, that the condition in the bond for the payment of
"the amount which may be recovered and all costs therein in
said garnishment" is, in substance, the same as the condition
specified in the statute for the payment "of the judgment that
shall be rendered on said garnishment."

We do not know why the bond was not made in the name
of E. S. Morris & Co.   This would have been the natural,
proper, and manifestly correct way to frame it, but people will
persist in doing things irregularly when it is easier to do them
rightly.   They thus get themselves into trouble and occasion
the courts much labor and vexation.   However, taking the
bond as actually made, we think it was a good "dissolving
bond," for two reasons.   In the first place, it was really binding on E. S. Morris & Co.   Murphy evidently intended to contract, not only for himself, but for his firm.   The bond refers
to him as principal "and as a member of the firm of E. S. Morris & Co.," and it was plainly designed to dissolve a garnishment which tied up money belonging, not to Murphy, but to
the partnership.   The words quoted could have no significance
except upon the idea that Murphy meant to bind his firm, and
this he certainly had authority to do.   If he had signed to the
bond the partnership name, the act of signing, while it would
have been his individual act, would undoubtedly have bound
the firm.   In view of the recitals in the bond and of its purpose, we think the signature of N. W. Murphy to the bond had

the same effect as if he had signed it "E. S. Morris & Co. by N. W. Murphy." But, secondly, we do not think it was absolutely necessary for E. S. Morris & Co. to sign the bond at all. It is true that the statute gives to the plaintiff the right at the proper time "to enter up judgment upon such bond against the principal and securities as judgment may be entered against securities on appeal," but, in so far as such a judgment affects the principal, there is really no need for it, for the plaintiff must already have obtained a judgment against him before he could enter a judgment on the bond. This court, in *Everett* v. *Westmoreland*, 92 *Ga.* 670, held: "Where a garnishment is sued out pendente lite by the plaintiff and dissolved by the defendant, there can be no judgment rendered on the bond given to dissolve the garnishment until after judgment is rendered in the main action in favor of the plaintiff against the defendant therein. This judgment must be against the defendant alone, and not against him jointly with the surety on the bond." A second judgment against the principal can add nothing whatever to the strength of plaintiff's position, for at the very time he seeks to enter judgment on the bond he actually has the principal's property bound by as efficacious a judgment lien as he could possibly obtain.

The question in hand is controlled by the principle laid down by this court in *Pettee* v. *Flewellen*, 2 *Ga.* 236, in which it was held that: "Under the judiciary act of 1799, allowing appeals to be entered upon the payment of costs and giving security for the eventual condemnation-money, the party appealing need not himself sign the bond." It will be seen from an examination of the opinion delivered in that case, which was not only well considered but supported by authorities, that the court placed its ruling on the idea that a second judgment against the principal debtor was a needless thing. It is to be observed that, at the time this case was decided, it was the right of the plaintiff in an appeal case, when the verdict on appeal was in his favor, "to enter up judgment against the principal and the security jointly or severally" (Cobb's Dig. 498); and this was so although the plaintiff may have already had a verdict against the principal from which the appeal had been entered.   Accordingly, the reasoning of Judge Lumpkin is quite applicable to a case like the present, in which, as we have seen, the plaintiff has the right to enter up judgment "as judgment may be entered against securities upon appeal."

As the garnishment was lawfully dissolved, the court was right in declining to allow the plaintiffs below to enter a judgment against the garnishee.

Judgment affirmed.   All the Justices concurring.

BISHOP *et al. v.* MATHEWS & COMPANY.

A defendant in an action brought against him individually upon a demand for the payment of which he is individually liable can not, without showing some equitable reason for being allowed so to do, set off against the plaintiff's claim a debt due by the latter to a partnership of which the defendant is or had been a member.

Submitted December 15, 1899. — Decided January 31, 1900.

Complaint.   Before Judge Lumpkin.   Fulton superior court. March term, 1899.

Slaton & Phillips and *T. L. Bishop,* for plaintiffs in error.
C. L. Pettigrew and *J. D. Humphries,* contra.

LUMPKIN, P. J.   Exception is taken to a judgment rendered by the judge below, who tried this case without a jury.   The action was by E. H. Mathews, who, for some reason not disclosed, styled himself "E. H. Mathews & Co.," against Malvern Hill and Thomas L. Bishop, upon a promissory note, the former being sued as maker and the latter as indorser.   Hill made no defense.   Bishop pleaded payment, but did not prove it.   His real defense consisted of an attempt to set off against the plaintiff's claim his interest in a fee alleged to be due by the plaintiff to the law partnership of Bishop & Hill, composed of the defendants, but the court gave judgment against both of them. This was right.   There was no evidence that Mathews was insolvent, nor any equitable reason shown for allowing the set-off.   It is in the brief of counsel for Bishop stated that Mathews "became insolvent just before the trial of this case in the court below," but there is nothing to this effect in the record. Plainly, the action was not against the partnership. It was, as to each defendant, a suit upon a demand for which he was individually liable. Assuming that Mathews owed the firm of Bishop & Hill the fee in question, and granting that Hill's agreement, testified to by both him and Mathews, to have the amount thereof credited upon an account due by Hill to Mathews was unauthorized and ineffectual so far as Bishop was concerned, it still remains true that the demand of Mathews against Bishop upon the note and the demand of Bishop & Hill against Mathews for the fee were not mutual demands, one of which could be set off against the other. It further appeared that the partnership between the defendants had been dissolved, but there was no proof of any division of its assets or that Bishop had ever become the owner in his individual right of the whole or of any portion of the claim against Mathews for the fee. The case upon its facts is controlled by the familiar rule laid down in section 3747 of the Civil Code, that "Set-off must be between the same parties and in their own right."

Judgment affirmed.   All the Justices concurring.

STEELE *v.* PARKER.

1. Where a creditor sues his debtor in a justice's court and garnishes a third party, and obtains judgment against the debtor and the garnishee, and the latter pays to a constable the amount of the judgment against him, and the defendant thereupon brings a rule against the constable, alleging that the money paid was exempt from garnishment as it was his daily wages as a laborer, and praying that it be paid over to him, it is not error to make the judgment creditor a party to the rule.

2. When in the answers of the judgment creditor and of the constable it is stated that they can not, for want of sufficient information, admit or deny that the movant is a day-laborer or that the fund in controversy is exempt from garnishment, the burden of proof is on the movant to establish these facts. If, instead of doing so, he relies upon the allegations in his rule and the failure of the respondents to positively deny those allegations, and does not traverse their answers, it is not error for the magistrate to award the fund to the judgment creditor.

Submitted December 15, 1899. — Decided January 31, 1900.

Petition for certiorari.   Before Judge Lumpkin.   Fulton superior court.   March term, 1899.

R. J. Jordan, for plaintiff.   *A. R. Bryan*, for defendant.

SIMMONS, C. J. Byther brought suit in a justice's court against Steele, and garnished the latter's employers. He obtained judgment against the defendant, and also judgment by default against the garnishees. The garnishees paid to Parker, a constable, the amount of the judgment against them, and Steele thereupon brought a rule against Parker, alleging that the money paid was exempt from garnishment as it was his daily wages as a laborer, and praying that Parker be required to turn it over to him. The justice of the peace issued a rule nisi against Parker, and ordered that Byther, the judgment creditor, be made a party to the rule. Making the judgment creditor a party was one of the grounds of a petition for certiorari, which the superior court refused to sanction. We agree with the court below that the magistrate did not err in making Byther a party to the rule. As was said by the learned judge of the superior court in refusing to sanction the petition for certiorari, it appeared "that the real contestant was not the officer but the judgment creditor. . . It would be wholly wrong to require an officer who holds a fund to which two persons lay claim to litigate with them separately. . . The constable had a right to have [the judgment creditor] before the court and to be protected by the judgment, as he prayed in his answer." It is the policy of the law in cases of this character to avoid a multiplicity of actions. Where it is possible and proper, it is always best to have all interested parties before the court, and in one action to determine the respective rights of all. This is especially true where one of the parties lays no claim whatever to the fund in controversy but stands rather in the position of a stakeholder in possession of a fund claimed by the others. We therefore think it was not erroneous, but right and proper, that the judgment creditor should have been made a party to the rule.

In the answers of the constable and of the judgment creditor it was stated that they could not, for want of sufficient information, admit or deny the allegations of the petition for the rule, that the movant was a day-laborer, or that the fund in controversy was the proceeds of his labor and therefore exempt from process of garnishment; but they prayed that movant be required to make strict proof of these allegations. The other allegations in the answers are not here material. The movant filed no traverse to these answers, and introduced no evidence. He moved that the rule be made absolute against the constable, "on the ground that said constable's answer was insufficient in law and was not a denial of the plaintiff's petition." This motion was refused by the magistrate, who then discharged the rule on the ground that no traverse to the answers had been filed. This was also alleged as error in the petition for certiorari, and it was here contended that the judge of the superior court erred in not sanctioning the certiorari on this ground. We again agree with the lower court and with the magistrate. While it is necessary, where a garnishee sets up that the fund in his hands is exempt from garnishment as the daily wages of a laborer, that such answer should be traversed, this case is entirely different. Here the garnishees set up no such claim, but allowed judgment to go against them by default, and paid over the money to the constable to satisfy that judgment. Subsequently the defendant undertook by rule to recover the money from the constable, alleging that it was exempt from garnishment. The constable-and the judgment creditor neither admitted nor denied this in their answers, but asked that strict proof be required. Here then, as was said by the judge in refusing to issue the writ of certiorari, the defendant assumed the position of establishing his claim of recovery. Proceeding by rule, he stood like a plaintiff, and as a plaintiff the burden was on him to establish his claim. To that end he should have traversed the answers of the respondents in the rule. He did not do so, but, instead, relied upon the allegations in his rule and the failure of the answers to deny those allegations positively ; and it was not error to discharge the rule and award the fund to the judgment creditor.

Judgment affirmed.   All the Justices concurring.

794
745
794
382

WILKES v. WESTERN & ATLANTIC RAILROAD CO.

It is the duty of a railroad company to exercise due diligence in the arrangement and maintenance of a station-house, including the floors thereof,
so as to enable its passengers to alight from a car in safety. When in a
given case it is alleged that a passenger in so alighting has been injured
because of the neglect of the company so to perform its duty, the particulars being properly set out, it was error to dismiss the petition on demurrer. On the contrary the same, together with such legal evidence as
was offered, should have been submitted to the jury for a determination of
the questions of fact involved, under proper instructions from the court.

Submitted December 16, 1899. — Decided January 31, 1900.

Action for damages. Before Judge Calhoun. City court of
Atlanta. March term, 1899.

Thomas L. Bishop, for plaintiff. *Payne & Tye*, for defendant.

LITTLE, J. Plaintiff in error instituted her action against
the Western & Atlantic Railroad Company, averring that the
defendant had injured and damaged her in a named sum, by
reason of the following facts: Petitioner was a passenger on
the defendant's cars from Nashville, Tennessee, to Atlanta,
Georgia, to which she paid first-class passage, and by the defendant was transported to the city of Atlanta, and the car
upon which she was riding was brought into the passenger station of the defendant in the city of Atlanta, which was the
place designated for passengers to leave the car. While in the
station-house and as she stepped from the car to the floor, a
large wooden splinter, being detached from the floor of the
house or station, penetrated her foot from three to three and
a half inches; the splinter was broken off in petitioner's foot,
and she was compelled to have the same cut out by a physician. From this injury she suffered great pain, and was confined to her house for a considerable length of time, and incurred a considerable bill for medical services and expenses, etc.
She avers that she was without fault, and that the railroad company was negligent in allowing the splinter of wood to be in
the place where it was, and in stopping its train of cars and
compelling passengers to alight where the splinter had been so
negligently left. The petition was subsequently amended by

an amplification of the cause of the injury, the nature of the loss sustained, etc. The petition as amended was demurred to, and the demurrer was sustained by the presiding judge, because it set forth no cause of action. To this judgment plaintiff in error excepted.

In 2 Shearman & Redfield on the Law of Negligence, § 410, referring to the duty of a railroad company to maintain its stations or depots, the rule is laid down that such shall be made safe and convenient for persons lawfully entering therein for the transaction of business, or under any actual or implied invitation; that as to such persons it is bound to use ordinary care. While laying down the rule on this subject, Barrows, in his Law of Negligence, § 79, says, on authority, that "although the carrier is not held to so high a degree of care in these matters [equipping and maintaining stational facilities] as in the act of transportation, it is still his duty to see that all reasonable precautions are taken to insure both the safety and comfort of persons who are on the premises as passengers. Approaches to the station and platforms must be properly built, and maintained in good order"; citing a number of authorities in note 29 on page 208. In the case of *Central Railroad* v. *Gleason & Harmon*, 72 *Ga.* 742, this court ruled that a railroad company which owns a warehouse or place of deposit for goods and freight which are to be delivered to consignees stands upon the same footing as to liability for injuries to persons and property, by reason of not having safe and secure roads and ways for ingress and egress to and from such freight-house, as any other person, and that it was the duty of the company to keep the yard and flooring in such order for public use as not to occasion damage to the property of those who are compelled to use the same. See also the same case reported in 69 *Ga.* 200. In the case of *Central Railroad* v. *Thompson*, 76 *Ga.* 770, it is said that "undoubtedly it is the duty of a railroad company so to fix its station or depot that a passenger, who gets off at the depot or place to alight, may get off the car without danger." See also *Central Railroad Co.* v. *Perry*, 58 *Ga.* 461. We may therefore safely assume that, as the plaintiff in error was a passenger on the train of the railroad company, it was the duty of the latter to exercise at least ordinary and reasonable care in the maintenance of its station-house, including the floor of the same, to prevent her from being injured and to afford to her a safe place to alight from the car. If it were negligent and failed to discharge this duty, it became liable for such damages as she sustained, unless there was some fault attributable to her, or the injury was occasioned by her own neglect and want of care. In her petition she avers negligence and want of care on the part of the railroad company in so maintaining its station-house, and avers that she was injured in consequence of such negligence. Negligence is a question of fact, and is for the jury; and under the allegations made she was entitled to have her case submitted to the jury. The court erred, therefore, in sustaining a demurrer to the petition; and the judgment is

Reversed.   All the Justices concurring.

McCORD COMPANY v. CALLAWAY & COMPANY.

1. One member of a mercantile partnership has no right, over the objection of another member to (1) execute in the partnership name promissory notes due immediately, in settlement of partnership debts which have not matured, or (2) to execute in the partnership name a mortgage upon its goods to secure the payment of such notes, or (3) to thus mortgage such goods to secure the payment of an individual debt of the partner signing the mortgage, or (4) to execute such a mortgage for the purpose of obtaining his release either from such a debt or from his individual liability upon the debts of the firm.

2. A mortgagee who with knowledge of the facts accepts a mortgage executed in the name of a partnership by one of its members without authority and over the objection of another partner takes subject to the right of the partnership to repudiate the mortgage and resist its foreclosure.

3. When an attempt to foreclose such a mortgage is made, the objecting partner may defend in the name of the partnership, and to this end may in its behalf file a proper affidavit of illegality and the statutory pauper affidavit in lieu of the bond required of solvent defendants in such cases.

Argued December 16, 1899. — Decided January 31, 1900.

Affidavit of illegality. Before Judge Reid. City court of Atlanta. March 31, 1899.

Hunt & Golightly, for plaintiff.
Daley & Hall, for defendants.

LUMPKIN, P. J. The mercantile firm of W. R. Callaway &
Co. was composed of W. R. Callaway and W. F. Lilly. The
former executed and delivered to creditors of the firm a mortgage upon most, if not all, of its goods and chattels, to secure
the payment of specified debts. The mortgage was foreclosed,
and after levy Lilly, in the name and behalf of the partnership,
filed a counter-affidavit, and also the pauper affidavit in lieu of
bond prescribed by section 2766 of the Civil Code. The counter affidavit attacked the mortgage on various grounds, the nature of which is sufficiently indicated in the first headnote, and
alleged that all the facts set up in this affidavit were known to
the mortgagees at the time they accepted the mortgage. On
the trial of the case the plaintiff demurred to the counter affidavit, and moved to strike the pauper affidavit. The court
overruled the demurrer and denied the motion, and the plaintiff excepted.

1. This court, in *Fidelity Banking Co.* v. *Kangara Co.*, 92 *Ga.*
172, held that one partner could not, over the protest of another,
mortgage the firm's assets even to secure the payment of a valid
existing debt of the firm. A brief statement of the reasons for
this conclusion appears on pages 176 and 177. This ruling
was impliedly approved in *Kiser* v. *Carrollton Co.*, 96 *Ga.* 761 (2).
If the law be as above indicated, certainly the defense set up
against the mortgage now under consideration was good, if
true, for it was not only executed over Lilly's objection, but
obviously void for the other reasons alleged.

2. The second proposition laid down in this case needs no
argument to prove its correctness. It accords with the rule universally recognized that he who knowingly takes an instrument
affected with an infirmity fatal to its validity takes nothing.

3. In the argument here, counsel for the plaintiff in error
stressed mainly questions of practice. Their contentions seem
to be, (1) that in filing the affidavits Lilly was acting for nobody but himself; (2) that the defense ought to have been
made by the partnership, which was not done because Callaway did not join in it; and (3) that Lilly could not, without
Callaway's concurrence, make a defense for the firm. It seems
inconsistent to urge that Callaway could mortgage the goods

of the firm without Lilly's co-operation, and yet that the latter can not, in its name and behalf, file and maintain a good defense to this foreclosure proceeding. But both of these positions are untenable, for the reason that Callaway did something which he had no right to do, and Lilly did something which he had a perfect right to do. Of course, the defense had to be made by the firm, and this is exactly what was done. Lilly did not file the affidavits in any professed right as an individual. He filed them for the partnership. This was strictly within the scope of his duties as a partner. "Self-preservation is the first law of nature." If a partner can not do that which is essential to save the concern and its assets from total destruction, there is little, we imagine, which he could do. There was no need of Callaway's concurrence, for it was Lilly's right, with or without the approbation of his partner, to make for the firm the perfectly lawful defense which he set up. He was, in our opinion, fully authorized to protect it from the threatened wrong, and in so doing he was properly representing Callaway's interests as well as his own. There was no need for him to seek aid from a court of equity, as was suggested. The city court has ample power to give the partnership the benefit of the allegations made in the counter-affidavit, if they are sustained by evidence.

Judgment affirmed. All the Justices concurring.

MOORE v. KELLY & JONES COMPANY.

1. When it is in a bill of exceptions recited that the same was tendered within the time prescribed by law, the writ of error will not be dismissed because of the failure of the presiding judge to certify the same within the statutory period, unless it be made to appear that his failure to do so was caused by some act of the plaintiff in error, or his counsel.

2. While a motion to set aside a judgment is addressed to the sound discretion of the judge, it should not, although made during the term at which the judgment was rendered, be granted unless some meritorious reason be given therefor. The failure of the defendant to appear and plead, in consequence of a misunderstanding between it and its counsel, affords no such reason.

Argued December 16, 1899. — Decided January 31, 1900.

Motion to set aside judgment.   Before Judge Reid.   City
court of Atlanta.   January term, 1899.

Culberson & Willingham, for plaintiff.
C. D. Maddox, for defendant.

LITTLE, J.   Moore sued out an attachment against the Kelly
& Jones Company on the 4th day of October, 1898, returnable
to the November term, 1899, of the city court of Atlanta, on the
ground of the non-residence of said company.   A summons of
garnishment was duly issued and served on the Hunnicutt &
Bellingrath Company.   On November 1st thereafter, the defendant in attachment dissolved the garnishment by giving
bond and security as provided by the code, and name of counsel was marked on the docket of the city court as representing
the defendant in attachment.   The declaration was duly filed.
At the January term, 1899, of said court, cases on the appearance docket were called, and, among others, that of Moore against
the Kelly & Jones Company.   No anwer or plea had been filed,
and it was marked in default.   On the 5th day of January of
the term, the case was called for trial, and the plaintiff submitted evidence making the necessary proof to sustain his case.   No
defense being made, a verdict was rendered for the plaintiff,
under the direction of the court, for the sum of $600 principal,
besides interest, against both the defendant and the sureties on
his bond dissolving the garnishment.   Judgment followed accordingly.   Prior to the rendition of the judgment, the garnishees made answer, admitted indebtedness in the sum of
$429.63, which was adjudicated as subject to the garnishment.
During the term at which the judgment was rendered against
the defendant and its sureties, the defendant came and filed a
written motion to set aside the judgment, one of the several
grounds being that the petition in the original case did not set
out any cause of action, nor did it show any valid agreement
between the parties under which the plaintiff was entitled to
have any recovery; and because there was an agreement between
the parties in writing and the writing was kept *concealed* and
not exhibited to the court and jury trying the case; and by so
doing the plaintiff made it appear that he had a just cause,

when in fact he had no right of recovery; and that the with-
holding of this contract operated as a fraud and enabled the
plaintiff to get an unjust verdict and judgment against the defendant, etc.   It was further alleged that the defendant intended to file its defense at a proper time, and an officer of the
company came to Atlanta for that purpose, and, while there,
the garnishment was dissolved, but, owing to a misunderstanding between the company's officer and counsel, the defense was
unintentionally omitted to be filed.   Movant then alleged various reasons why the plaintiff was not entitled to have a judgment against it, and made a recital of facts tending to show a
meritorious defense to the action.   On the hearing the judge
sustained the motion and passed an order vacating and setting
aside the verdict and judgment, on condition that the defendant pay the cost and give bond in the sum of $1,500.00, obli-
gating itself to pay to the plaintiff whatever final judgment
might be rendered against it in the case.   To this order and
judgment the plaintiff in error excepted.

1. On the call of the case in this court, a motion was made
by counsel for defendant to dismiss the writ of error, because
the bill of exceptions was not signed and certified within thirty
days from the adjournment of the court at which the decision
excepted to was made, nor within thirty days from the date of
that decision; and because the plaintiff had incorporated in the
bill of exceptions immaterial and cumbersome matters; and
because the bill of exceptions does not specify plainly any alleged error, and is not made returnable to any particular term
of this court.   The motion to dismiss must be overruled on all
the grounds.   By the act of 1896 it is provided, that no bill of
exceptions in the Supreme Court shall be dismissed upon the
ground that the same was not certified by the judge in the time
now required by law for tendering and signing bills of exceptions; but, if it appears that the same was tendered to the
judge within the time required, a failure on his part to sign the
same within the prescribed time shall be no cause for dismissal,
unless the failure to sign and certify is caused by some act of
the plaintiff in error, or his counsel.   Acts 1896, p. 45.   It is
recited in the bill of exceptions, which was duly approved by

the presiding judge, that the plaintiff in error came within the time allowed by law, and presented his bill of exceptions, and as it does not appear that the failure to sign and certify within the statutory limit was caused by the plaintiff in error, or his counsel, the writ of error can not be dismissed on this ground. An inspection of the bill of exceptions shows that it is not amenable to either of the other grounds on which the motion to dismiss is predicated.

2. We think that the court erred in vacating and setting aside the judgment, although the motion was made at the term at which the judgment was rendered. Motions of this character are addressed to the sound discretion of the court, and, as a general rule, this court will not interfere with the exercise of that discretion, and not at all unless it is abused. *Lambert* v. *Smith*, 57 *Ga.* 25. In order, however, to justify the proper exercise of this discretion and to set aside a verdict and judgment rendered in the due form of law, after service and an opportunity to plead, there must be some other cause than the mere laches of the defendant. In this case, although the plaintiff commenced by attachment against a non-resident and did not contemplate personal service, all the proceedings in attachment were regular. The defendant in attachment acquired notice of the pendency of the suit, and sent one of its officers to the city of Atlanta where the attachment proceedings were pending, and dissolved the garnishment. The effect of this act was equivalent to a personal service on it, and had the effect of changing, to some extent at least, the character of the original proceedings, as well as the judgment to which the plaintiff was entitled under the original proceedings. Civil Code, § 4718; *Walter* v. *Kierstead*, 74 *Ga.* 25; *Buice* v. *Mining Co.*, 64 *Ga.* 769; *Phillips* v. *Collier*, 87 *Ga.* 66. Notwithstanding the notice which the defendant received, and acted on by marking the name of its counsel on the docket and dissolving the garnishment, it suffered the case to be in default, and the plaintiff was entitled, under these circumstances, to a verdict at the trial term, on proper presentation of evidence which authorized a finding in his favor. Civil Code, § 5071; *Stephens* v. *Gate City Gas Co.*, 81 *Ga.* 150.

It appears that evidence of the legality of the claim on which

the suit was founded was presented to the court, in a sufficient
manner to authorize the presiding judge to direct a verdict in
favor of the plaintiff. Several of the grounds of the motion
contest the legality of that verdict, and present reasons why, if
the defendant had duly presented its case, the verdict might
have been different. The fact that there was a written contract
between the parties, which settled their rights, was a fact known
before the trial to defendant; and if the paper afforded any defense to the action, the defendant could have availed itself of
it at the proper time, but that it could have done so affords no
legal ground; after the rendition of the verdict and judgment,
to require that these proceedings be set aside. That defendant
could have presented evidence which was not submitted, but
which, if submitted, would have defeated the claim of the plaintiff, does not entitle it to reopen the proceedings. The facts set
out in the motion are not sufficient to authorize the judgment
to be set aside for fraud. The plaintiff duly and legally instituted his case and followed it up in the manner prescribed by
law. The defendant had notice. When the case was in order
for trial, the plaintiff presented his claim with evidence sufficient to sustain it; and if the defendant desired to contest his
right, or to impeach his evidence, then was the time for it to
have done so. That it did not do so on account of a misunderstanding between client and counsel is unfortunate, but the fact
presents no legal reason why the plaintiff, who acted but in the
exercise of his right, should have the legal results of his suit
set aside and again enter the field of litigation. It is our opinion that the court erred in vacating and setting aside the judgment.   *Judgment reversed. All the Justices concurring.*

HAUNSON *v.* NELMS *et al.*

Where an execution was levied upon property of the defendant in execution,
and he filed an affidavit of illegality thereto, and was, on the day of sale,
informed by the sheriff that the latter had accepted the illegality and that
the property would not be sold on that day; and where the defendant
and his counsel thereupon left the place of sale; and where subsequently
the sheriff reconsidered and determined to sell the property on that day,

and at noon notice was given to the defendant's counsel, who sought to find his client but was unable to do so; and where at three o'clock counsel for the defendant and for the plaintiff and two other persons appeared at the place of sale and the property was sold to the plaintiff in execution for $100, when its true value was $2,000: *held*, that the sale should be set aside on application of the defendant in execution, although his attorney gave notice at the time of the sale of the pendency of an application for homestead upon the property.

Argued December 19, 1899.—Decided January 31, 1900.

Petition for injunction. Before Judge Lumpkin. Fulton county. June 8, 1899.

R. J. Jordan, for plaintiff.
J. E. Wooten and *Culberson & Willingham*, for defendants.

SIMMONS, C. J. Haunson borrowed of Leitch $3,000, and to secure the same gave a mortgage upon certain real estate. Default in payment having been made, the mortgage was foreclosed and execution issued. Haunson made application for homestead on a portion of the mortgaged property, and this application was resisted by Leitch on the ground that Haunson had by the terms of the mortgage waived his right to homestead as against the debt to Leitch. The sheriff levied the mortgage execution upon the property, and made regular advertisement of the sale. Haunson filed an affidavit of illegality on the day prior to sale day. The sheriff accepted the illegality, and on the morning of the next day, at a time when a "very large number of people" were present, informed Haunson that "the property would not be sold, that the sale had been marked off." Counsel for Haunson was present on the same day where the sheriff was selling property, and inquired if the property of Haunson would be sold. He was informed by the sheriff "that it would not be sold, that it had been marked off." About noon of the same day Haunson's counsel was notified that the sheriff would not accept the illegality filed by Haunson, but would sell the property at three o'clock of that day. Haunson, after he had been told that his property would not be sold, left the court-house and could not be found or reached by his counsel before three o'clock, the hour thus fixed for the sale. At that hour the attorney for Haun-

son, in company with another attorney, went to the court-house
to attend the sale, and gave notice of the pending application
for homestead.   Besides the sheriff there were but four persons
present, and the property, worth $2,000, was bid in for $100
by one of Leitch's attorneys, who was the only bidder and who
bid for his client.   Haunson filed an equitable petition against
the sheriff and the purchaser, Leitch, asking that the sale be set
aside and that the defendants be restrained from taking possession of the property.   The petition recited substantially the
facts set out above, and the evidence established them without
contradiction, and showed that Leitch's counsel had, at the
time he bid in the property, full knowledge of them.   The relief prayed was denied by the court below, and the petitioner
excepted.   The contention of the plaintiff in error, that the
sheriff should not have proceeded after the filing of the affidavit of illegality, is, we think, not sound, as the affidavit was
itself without merit.   On the other hand, we can not agree with
counsel for defendant in error that the case should be affirmed
on the ground that the court was without jurisdiction to determine this case, for the reason that Leitch was a non-resident
of the county wherein the petition was filed.   The question of
jurisdiction was argued here, but, inasmuch as the record does
not show that any plea to the jurisdiction or any special demurrer on this ground was filed, and does show that the non-
resident appeared and answered, this court will presume that
he waived the want of jurisdiction.

The sole question to be decided is, therefore, whether the sale,
made under the circumstances above recited, was a valid and
legal one.   We think that it was not.   Misleading the defendant in execution and preventing his attendance at the sale by
informing him that the property would not be sold that day
and that the sale had been "marked off," postponing the sale
from the earlier hours of sale when a large number of people
were assembled to a time later in the day when there were but
four persons present and two of these were the attorneys of the
parties, and selling the property for an amount much smaller
than it was worth, are certainly sufficient to show beyond doubt
that the sale was affected with irregularity if not with fraud,

and that the defendant was thereby injured. The purchaser at the sale was the attorney for the plaintiff in execution, who bid in the property for his client, and who had full knowledge of all the facts. He was not an innocent purchaser, and the sale should have been set aside. This case is controlled by the decision in the case of *Suttles* v. *Sewell*, 109 *Ga.* 707, and is a stronger case even than that. We of course realize that the announcement, made by the attorney for Haunson, that the property was sold subject to a pending application for homestead may have had much to do with the inadequacy of the price for which the property was sold. The pendency of a homestead application would ordinarily make property bring less at a sale, but even this can scarcely account for the gross inadequacy here. Besides, the circumstances of the sale were such as to make it void aside from that consideration. The mere fact that a sheriff sells "at public outcry" when, in addition to the parties' attorneys, there are but two persons present, is sufficient to raise a suspicion of fraud; and when it further appears that the sale was made at three o'clock in the afternoon after the defendant in execution had been sent away with the assurance that his illegality had been accepted and that his property would not be sold that day, we think that the sale should be set aside, when the property was bid in by one who had full knowledge of all these facts. See *Suttles* v. *Sewell*, supra, and authorities cited; Pell *v.* Vreeland, 35 N. J. Eq. 22; King *v.* Platt, 37 N. Y. 155; American Wine Co. *v.* Scholer, 85 Mo. 496; Johnson *v.* Crawl, 55 Tex. 571; Hughes *v.* Duncan, 60 Tex. 72; Roberts *v.* Roberts, 13 Gratt. 639; 2 Freeman, Executions (2d ed.), § 308.

Judgment reversed. All the Justices concurring.

ALEXANDER *v.* THE STATE.

1. A dealer in bicycles, who sold the same on his own account and not as agent, was liable to pay to the State a tax of one hundred dollars for the year 1899, if he sold any bicycles the manufacturers of which had not paid such a tax for that year; but after paying the tax of one hundred dollars for the year mentioned, such dealer had the right during its continu-

ance to sell bicycles of as many different "makes" as he chose without paying any additional tax for that year. The mere fact that his license from the comptroller-general or his registration as a dealer in bicycles purported to limit his authority to sell to "makes" of a particular kind did not render it unlawful for him to sell other "makes."

2. The charge excepted to being in direct conflict with the views above expressed, and it manifestly appearing that the verdict against the plaintiff in error was necessarily controlled thereby, the judgment must be reversed.

Submitted February 5, — Decided February 26, 1900.

Accusation of misdemeanor. Before Judge Calhoun. Criminal court of Atlanta. November term, 1899.

Hamilton Douglas and *D. S. Craig*, for plaintiff in error.
James F. O'Neill, solicitor, contra.

COBB, J. Alexander was arraigned in the criminal court of Atlanta, upon an accusation, the following being a copy of the material portion of the same: "The said W. D. Alexander, in said county of Fulton, on the 11th day of July, 1899, did, being then and there a dealer in bicycles manufactured by the Milwaukee Engineering Company, and said Milwaukee Engineering Company not having paid to the comptroller-general of said State the tax of one hundred dollars for the fiscal year, did, before doing business as such dealer in said bicycles manufactured by said Milwaukee Engineering Company, fail to register his name with the ordinary of said county, and exhibit to said ordinary his license from the comptroller-general of said State, contrary to law." Having been convicted, the accused excepted, assigning as error the rendition of the verdict and judgment against him, and certain charges of the court.

1. The accusation was framed under section 11 of the general tax act of 1898 (Acts 1898, p. 33), which is in the following language: "Every bicycle manufacturer selling or dealing in bicycles, by itself or its agents, in the State, and all wholesale and retail dealers in bicycles selling same manufactured by companies that have not paid the tax required herein, shall pay one hundred dollars for the fiscal year, or fractional part thereof, to be paid to the comptroller-general at the time of commencement of business. Before doing business under this act, all bicycle manufacturers, their agents, and all dealers shall be

required to register their names with the ordinaries of those counties in which they intend to operate, and exhibit to said ordinaries their license from the comptroller-general. All unsold bicycles belonging to bicycle companies, dealers, or their agents, or others, shall be liable to seizure and sale for payment of such fees, license, and tax. Any person who shall violate the provisions of this section shall be liable to indictment for a misdemeanor, and on conviction shall be punished as prescribed in section 1039 of Volume III of the Code of 1895. None of the provisions of this section shall apply to . . merchants buying and selling bicycles upon which a license tax has been paid as herein provided, and who keep the said bicycles and sell and deliver them at their place of business, such sales not being on commission; provided further, that manufacturers, dealers, and agents having paid the taxes herein required shall be exempted from any county or corporation license tax for selling bicycles." The evidence discloses that the accused procured from the comptroller-general, upon payment of $100, a license authorizing him "to sell or deal in the Alexander Special and Kennesaw bicycles" for the year 1899. The bookkeeper for the comptroller-general testified that he issued the license above referred to, and that he would, either at the time the same was issued or since, have inserted therein without the payment of any additional sums the names of any other bicycles which the accused might have requested. There was also evidence that in July, 1899, the accused sold a bicycle called the "Famous," manufactured by the Milwaukee Engineering Company. It was admitted by the accused that he had not registered his name with the ordinary as a dealer in this bicycle, but there was no evidence that he had not registered as a dealer in bicycles generally under the provisions of the act above quoted. The accused made a statement in which he asserted that he was a wholesale and retail dealer in and manufacturer of bicycles in Fulton county during the year 1899.

The accusation above quoted charges the accused with violating that portion of the section of the tax act above quoted which required him to register his name with the ordinary and exhibit his license. There is no evidence that he had not registered as a dealer generally, and exhibited the license which he had received from the comptroller-general; and the question, therefore, to be determined is whether or not it was necessary that he should have procured a license to sell the "Famous" bicycle and should have registered as a dealer in that bicycle and exhibited such license to the ordinary.   We have reached the conclusion that it was not.   The section of the tax act above quoted imposes a tax of $100 upon two classes of persons, viz., bicycle manufacturers who sell or deal in bicycles, whether they do business by themselves or by agents, and wholesale and retail dealers in bicycles the manufacturers of which have not paid the tax of $100.   To the latter of these two classes the plaintiff in error, so far as the transaction involved in the present discussion is concerned, belongs.   We think a proper construction of this law authorizes members of the class last referred to to sell as many different "makes" of bicycles as they see proper, after paying a license of $100 and complying with the further requirements of the law as to registering, etc.   The act contemplates that the manufacturer may pay a tax of $100 and sell his bicycles through as many different agents as he chooses.   The manufacturers of a particular make of bicycles may have an agency in every large town in the State, and yet each one of these agents, if charged with selling that kind of bicycle without a license, could defend by showing that the manufacturer had paid to the comptroller-general $100, procured a license, and registered, etc., as required by the act.   And so a dealer in both that and other makes could defend by showing that each manufacturer had paid $100 tax.   But if the manufacturer fails to pay the tax, then the dealer must pay it; but after paying $100 he can sell as many different makes of bicycles as he chooses.   The State requires of every dealer selling bicycles made by unlicensed manufacturers a tax of $100, and is not concerned with the number of makes of bicycles sold by such dealer. Under this view the law works no unjust discrimination upon either class with which it purports to deal.   The manufacturer can pay one tax and establish as many agencies as he chooses for the sale of such makes of bicycles as he manufactures; the dealer can pay one tax and sell as many different makes of bicycles as he pleases.   The mere fact that the. license issued to the accused purported to limit his authority to sell to certain makes of bicycles, not mentioning the one which the evidence in this case shows he sold, did not of itself render it unlawful for him to make such sale.   The license should have been issued to sell bicycles without reference to name or make, and the insertion in the license of the names of two particular makes of bicycles was unauthorized and will be treated as surplusage.

2. Complaint is made, in the bill of exceptions, that the court erred in charging the jury as follows: "I charge you that a license to a dealer to sell certain bicycles, the names of which appear therein, will not authorize such dealer to sell any other makes or names of bicycles."   Under the ruling made above, this charge was error, and as it manifestly controlled the verdict of the jury, the judgment of the court must be reversed and a new trial ordered.

Judgment reversed.   All the Justices concurring.

FULLER *v.* THE STATE.

1. An incriminating admission is not necessarily, as matter of law, to be treated as involuntary because made by a prisoner confined in jail to the sheriff under such circumstances as the following: The officer had caused the prisoner and his cell-mate to be brought into the office of the jail, when the latter said to the former, "Tell [the sheriff] what you said to me last night."   Thereupon the officer said, "Yes, let me hear what you have got to say."   The admission was then made, and as to it the officer testified that it was not induced by any hope of benefit or fear of injury.

2. While a wife, save as expressly provided by statute, is not a competent witness for or against her husband when he is on trial for a criminal offense, a married woman is not rendered incompetent to testify on the trial of one, not her husband, because the latter may be in jail "under a commitment warrant charging him with" the identical offense for which the other is being tried.

3. The evidence was sufficient to sustain the verdict.

Argued February 5, — Decided February 26, 1900.

Indictment for murder.   Before Judge Felton.   Bibb superior court.   January 3, 1900.

Claud Estes, N. E. Harris, and *Washington Dessau,* for plaintiff in error. *J. M. Terrell, attorney-general,* and *Robert Hodges,
solicitor-general,* contra.

LEWIS, J. Allen Fuller was indicted, tried, and found guilty,
in Bibb superior court, under an indictment charging him
with the murder of Mrs. Eugenia Hamilton Pottle, alleged to
have been committed in that county on November 20, 1899;
whereupon he made a motion for a new trial, which was overruled by the judge below, and upon this ruling he assigns error
in his bill of exceptions.

1. Among the grounds in the motion for a new trial is
alleged error in the court allowing, over objections of defendant's counsel, G. S. Westcott, sheriff of Bibb county, when being examined as a witness for the State, to testify substantially
as follows : Witness saw Allen Fuller for the first time in the
office of the county jail, Thursday before the body of deceased
was found. He had a conversation with defendant, on information received from a fellow-prisoner by the name of Lowe,
who slept with defendant the night before. At the conversation
there were present Lowe and deputy-sheriff Herrington. Witness had Allen Fuller brought into his office in the jail, and
Lowe told the defendant to tell witness what he told him
(Lowe) the night before. Neither witness nor Herrington nor
any one offered any inducement to defendant for him to make
a statement. Lowe said to defendant, "Tell Mr. Westcott what
you said to me last night." Witness remarked, "Yes, let me
hear what you have got to say." Herrington said nothing.
The next person who spoke was Allen Fuller. Nothing was
done or said to him by any one more than what has been stated.
Fuller stated, in substance, that he wanted to tell who had
killed Mrs. Pottle; that he had nothing to do with it. Witness
then asked him who did the killing; and he replied, a negro by
the name of Redd, who was then in jail, had done the killing.
Witness asked him how he knew it. He answered, because
Redd had told him so. Witness then asked him how came
Redd to tell him so; and he replied: Redd came to him on a
previous occasion, and wanted him to go with him and kill
Mrs. Pottle; that he would get $200.00 for doing the deed, and

that if defendant would help him he would divide the money with him. Defendant stated that he refused to do it, and had nothing to do with it. On the next day after Mrs. Pottle disappeared, defendant stated, Redd came to him, and told him, "I got her last night." He told him he had killed her, and said, "Keep your mouth shut about what has passed between us, and you will get what I promised you." Witness then asked defendant if Redd told him how he killed her. Defendant replied: "He told me she come to his house and wanted him to go home with her, and that he didn't like her no way, that she owed him for some corn she borrowed from him; and he said that he consented to go, and went out in the yard and got the axe and taken the blade off and sorter held it under the arm or coat, and made it appear as if he was walking with a walking-stick, and led her to the side of the little hill near the house, and as he was going down the hill he knocked her down with the axe, and she hollowed one time and he struck her four or five blows." Witness then asked the defendant if Redd told him what he did with the body. He replied, yes, he did; that he took the body, carried it behind his house to a little charcoal-kiln, chopped her up and burned her up, and said, speaking to defendant, "If you will look about there you will find her or some of her remains." Redd said he had a fire for several days, and, if he had not got it plowed over, you will find where he burnt her up.

It is contended by counsel for plaintiff in error that this testimony should not have been admitted under the circumstances set forth in the motion for a new trial, and substantially given above, for the reason that this conversation, or incriminating statement by the defendant, was not freely and voluntarily made. There is no question about the statement of the defendant admitted in evidence not being a confession. It was, on the contrary, an exculpatory statement in which the defendant evidently sought to place the crime on another, and insist upon his own innocence of any particular crime. It is introduced, however, by the State as a circumstance, taken in connection with other facts proved, which tended to incriminate the prisoner. We think the sounder view of the law touching the admissibility of such declarations on the part of one charged with crime is to exclude them, if not voluntarily made, upon the same principle as the defendant's statement would be excluded if it amounted to a direct confession of guilt. But it is not necessary to decide directly this question, or to undertake to reconcile authorities, or determine the weight of authority upon the subject ; for under the facts of this case, we think there is nothing in the record which indicates that this statement of the defendant was not freely and voluntarily made to the sheriff, without being induced by any hope of reward, or fear of punishment ; or that the will of the defendant was to any degree coerced, or unduly persuaded. It is true this court has, in its adjudications upon the subject, attempted to impress upon sheriffs and other officers the gross impropriety of improperly obtaining confessions from prisoners in their custody ; but there is nothing in the law, or in any of the decisions of this court or any court of last resort, of which we are aware, which would exclude a confession or an incriminating statement made to an officer simply because the prisoner was in his custody under arrest at the time. In the case of *Smith* v. *State*, 88 *Ga.* 627, it was decided that a self-criminating admission made to the sheriff by a prisoner in jail, in response to the sheriff's admonition in these terms: "You know you are the man ; they got your cap, and you might as well own up," is of doubtful admissibility. The court did not grant a new trial in that case, because the other evidence showed the defendant's guilt beyond question ; but the point we make on the decision is, that if in that case the confession made under the circumstances narrated was only of "doubtful admissibility," we can not see that there can be any possible doubt about the admissibility of the evidence objected to in this case. Here, it will be noted, the sheriff received information from another prisoner of a statement made by this defendant, inculpating another person as the guilty party, and simply remarked to him, "Yes, let me hear what you have got to say." We see nothing improper in the sheriff's conduct. He had received information that this defendant would relate facts to show the guilt of another party, and doubtless had no idea whatever of getting from him anything like a confession of guilt; and he did receive simply the information that he evidently expected. There was really nothing more in this statement made by the sheriff tending to incriminate the defendant, if as much, than the statement the defendant himself made before the jury on his trial. This is not near as strong a case for excluding the statement of the defendant as *Miller* v. *State*, 94 *Ga.* 1, where it was held: "That a fellow-prisoner in jail with the accused, who was charged with murder, asked him about the killing and 'told him he better tell the truth, the white folks were going to break somebody's neck,' did not, as matter of absolute law, render inadmissible confessions then and there made in the presence and hearing of fellow-prisoners only." Nor do we think it as strong a case as *Willis* v. *State*, 93 *Ga.* 208, where it was held: "Where one who has killed another surrenders himself to an arresting officer, the fact that the latter told the prisoner that giving himself up was the best course he could pursue did not render inadmissible confessions then made to the officer, it appearing that they were free and voluntary, and that the officer neither said nor did anything, other than as above mentioned, before the confessions were made."

But the case relied upon by counsel for plaintiff in error is *Bram* v. *United States*, 168 U. S. 532. By reading a report of the facts in that case, it will be seen they were entirely different from what the record in the case at bar presents. That was an indictment for murder alleged to have been committed on an American vessel on the high seas. On arrival at Halifax, a policeman and detective in the government service at that place had a conversation with defendant, who was indicted at Boston for the commission of the crime. The prisoner had been brought to the office of the policeman, where he stripped the defendant, examined his clothing, told him to submit to an examination, and searched him. Defendant was then in custody, and did everything the witness directed him to do. When defendant came into the policeman's office, the officer said to him, "We are trying to unravel this horrible mystery. . . Your position is rather an awkward one. I have had Brown in this office, and he made a statement that he saw you do the murder." In the course of the conversation, he further told defendant: "Now, look here, Bram, I am satisfied that you killed the Captain, from all I have heard from Mr. Brown. But some of us here think you could not have done all that crime alone. If you had an accomplice you should say so, and not have the blame of this terrible crime on your own shoulders." The prisoner replied: "Well, I think, and many others on board the ship think, that Brown is the murderer; but I don't know anything about it." He was rather short in his replies. A recital of the facts will show without argument the vast difference between the circumstances under which the defendant in that case made his statement, and those disclosed by the record in this case. The conversation of the officer himself was calculated to impress upon the mind of the defendant the importance of his telling about an accomplice, if he had any, and the fear of having the blame of the horrible crime on his own shoulders. It will be noted, however, in that case that notwithstanding these facts, which might with reason be said to create in the mind of the prisoner some hope that a statement from him about another's guilt would be of some advantage to him, three of the Justices, to wit, Justice Brewer, Chief Justice Fuller, and Justice Brown, dissented, holding that under the facts, the statement of the prisoner was admissible. We conclude that the court below did right in overruling the objection to this evidence; and there being no complaint made of the charge to the jury on the subject, the presumption is the judge fairly and fully instructed them on the law touching this issue; and the evidence was sufficiently strong to submit to the jury, for its determination, the question as to whether the statement made by the defendant was free and voluntary.

2. Another ground in the motion for a new trial is, that the court erred in refusing to rule out the testimony of Anna Redd, a witness for the State, which motion was made by defendant's counsel before the conclusion of the case to the jury, it being substantially as follows: She was the wife of Alfred Redd. The night her husband went to see Woolfolk up at the old Small place, there didn't anything happen at her house. Redd went to George's house and came back home, and witness heard Mrs. Pottle's voice three times. She called him three times,

and asked him was he in bed, and he said, "Yes, ma'am";
and that was all she heard of her at all. The voice seemed
like it was at the ginhouse, a short distance from her house.
Witness's husband was in bed with her when she heard the
voice; and she supposed it was a quarter of an hour after her
husband came in the house when they heard Mrs. Pottle's
voice. She further stated she knew Allen Fuller; saw him
the day he was arrested. He came to her house the day before that, and saw Redd, her husband. It appears from the
evidence that this man Redd was the person whom Fuller, the
defendant, tried to incriminate in his statement to the sheriff.
It was contended by counsel for plaintiff in error that, Redd
being also under indictment for the murder of Mrs. Pottle, the
testimony of his wife was introduced to corroborate him, and
was therefore inadmissible. There was not even a joint indictment in this case against this defendant and Redd, but separate indictments against each. In the case of *Williams* v.
State, 69 *Ga.* 13, this court decided: "The restriction of a wife's
testimony in a criminal case is confined to giving testimony on
issues involving the guilt of her husband. Although he may
be indicted jointly with others, yet on the several trial of one
of the others she may testify as to matters not affecting his guilt
or innocence." In the opinion on page 30, the case of *Stewart*
v. *State*, 58 *Ga.* 577, is cited, where it was ruled that a wife
might corroborate her husband though an accomplice and in-
dited for the same offense, — the issue being the innocence or
guilt of another than her husband. In *Whitlow* v. *State*, 74 *Ga.*
819 (2), it was held: "The wife of one of two persons charged
with a crime may testify against the other, he being severally
and separately tried. The State could sever on the trial for
the very purpose of introducing her testimony." These decisions, and authorities cited, necessarily control this question;
and the court committed no error in refusing the motion to
rule out this woman's testimony.

3. The only other ground to be considered is the general one,
that the verdict is contrary to law and the evidence. There is
quite a volume of evidence in the record; but the main testimony relied upon for a conviction we will undertake to give,

as it was very earnestly argued that, the testimony being purely circumstantial, it did not authorize a conviction. It appears that the deceased was last seen alive on the night of November 20, 1899, while walking on the public road leading from Macon to Clinton, in Jones county. She was seen by several witnesses after dark, from 6.30 to 8 o'clock. The last person seen in her company on this road was Allen Fuller, the accused. Several witnesses saw them on the road, some of them locating him a very few feet behind the deceased. There was evidence of a clot of blood having been found in this road. The witness Redd, who was also arrested for this murder, testified that he saw deceased that night passing by or near his house in the road, with Fuller a few feet from her, following her. She seemed to indicate some fear of defendant Fuller, and asked Redd if he knew this man. Redd assured her that "he was a neighborhood man, and would not hurt her at all." She then went on walking slowly along the road towards Clinton, it appearing that road was in the direction of her house in Jones county, some few miles distant. Redd said he went into his house, went to bed, and some few minutes thereafter he recognized Mrs. Pottle's voice calling for him. He answered. She asked him if he had gone to bed. He replied in the affirmative. He then turned over and went to sleep. Mrs. Pottle was not seen afterwards until about December 7, 1899, when her body was found floating in the Ocmulgee river. The body was identified by witnesses. There was evidence showing several blows made upon her head, supposed to be by a stick or bludgeon. The river was about a mile or a mile and a half from where the blood in the road was found. There was testimony showing that the defendant, Fuller, had a father-in-law living on or near this road, with whom his wife was staying, and that he often went to his house. Mrs. Pottle had in her hands, on the night she is alleged to have been killed, a small hand-satchel. Fuller, shortly before his arrest, carried his household goods, including two valises, to the house of one Lucas, and deposited them in a room. A day or two after his arrest, witnesses inspected this property of the defendant, and in one of the valises was found a small hand-satchel, which was identified as the property of Mrs. Pottle that she had on the day she is alleged to have been killed.

These witnesses further testified that the house, when they got to it, was not occupied, was open, and anybody could have had access into it. In that satchel was also found a pair of scissors, the testimony indicating they were very similar to those owned by the deceased. We have hereinbefore given the statement made by defendant to the sheriff. After this it seems search was made for the body claimed to have been burned, but no sign of such burning was found. The body was found in the river. The sheriff had another interview with the defendant Fuller, and told him that he had misled him, and that defendant had not told the truth; that Mrs. Pottle's body was not where he said it was; that they looked everywhere. Then defendant stated, they had plowed over the place, and Redd certainly told him he put it there, and it was there somewhere, certain. The sheriff remarked, "You sent me off on a wild-goose chase; she is not there," and then told defendant they had found Mrs. Pottle's body about three miles up the river, designating the place in the river where it was found. Defendant then admitted that he did not tell the truth, but stated he would then tell it. In this statement defendant said, he was coming up the road and overtook Redd and Mrs. Pottle. As he was passing, Redd spoke to him in a whisper, and told him, "I am going to kill her to-night, and you come and go with me; if you do, I will pay you for it." He said, "We went on up the road away up about the ginhouse somewhere, and Redd a little bit behind her with an axe in his hand, and before I knowed it Redd struck her from behind with the axe one blow, and that knocked her to the ground, and he repeatedly struck her again, and she screamed and hollered." Redd then took her up and put her on his shoulder, the defendant going with him, carried her to the river, resting one time only, and threw her body into the river. The evidence showed that the deceased only weighed about ninety-three pounds. The next day the sheriff had a conversation with the defendant about the hand-satchel. At that time it had not been found; and he asked him about the hand-satchel. He said, "Yes, she did" have the satchel; it was not thrown in the river; that when Redd knocked her down she dropped it; and when defendant and Redd came back from the river, he wanted to go and get it, and Redd picked it up; that defendant had nothing to do with the satchel, and Redd carried it off. After the satchel was found in defendant's valise, the sheriff again asked him about it. Defendant remarked: "If you did find it there, Redd put it there." Defendant stated that he had nothing to do with it. One witness for the State testified that while they were hunting for the body of Mrs. Pottle he and Mr. Dodd met defendant Fuller, who asked him if he had heard or seen anything of Miss Genie (meaning Mrs. Pottle). Witness said, "No, I have not yet. I wish you gentlemen could find her." Then defendant told witness to get a crowd of men and go and ramble the woods and help look for her, so she could be found; and, after Mr. Dodd left, defendant said to the witness: "You are a damn fool, what business have you got looking for Miss Genie? She is a white woman; let the whites look for her."

The defendant made the following statement: "I was going on home one night, one Monday night, from town. I had been to town at work on Monday, and I was going home from town, and I got up there in the road against old man Redd's house, and Mrs. Pottle and old man Redd was standing in the road talking, or right at the edge of it, and I walked right by them, and old man Redd says, 'Who is that?' and I says, 'It is Fuller,' and he says, 'Hold on a minute, Fuller, and go up the road with me a piece. I am coming right back. I have got some particular business to talk to you'; and I went on with him, and Mrs. Pottle turned around and says, 'Is you going a piece the way with me, Redd?' and he says, 'Yes,' and he turned around and went right on, and me and him and her went on up the road together, and we got such a distance, and he hit her with a stick, and she fell and hollered, and I hollered too, and says, 'What are you doing?' and he jumped around to me, and he says, 'Shut up, you are just as much into this as I am,' and he says, 'If you make any talk about this at all, they will break your neck as quick as they will mine,' and I was naturally scared to tell it to anybody, because I was with him when he did it, and I didn't know what to do, and I didn't tell it to any one. There is nothing else that I desire to say, no more than I reckon that is all I have to say about it."

In the light of this evidence, we can not say that the jury were not authorized to draw the conclusion that the defendant's guilt was proved beyond a reasonable doubt, and to the exclusion of every other reasonable hypothesis. The verdict having been approved by the trial judge, we will not interfere with his discretion in overruling the motion for a new trial.

Judgment affirmed. All the Justices concurring.

In re KENAN, solicitor-general.

1. Since the passage of the act of March 20, 1866, riot is a misdemeanor, and for representing the State in this court in such a case a solicitor-general is entitled to only $15.
2. The phrase "all other cases," as used in section 1099 of the Penal Code, prescribing the fees of solicitors-general, allows but one fee for services performed in connection with each bill of exceptions, though there may be more than one plaintiff in error therein. LITTLE, J., dissenting.
3. The clerk of this court should furnish a solicitor-general with a certificate that he has represented the State in this court in as many "cases" as there are bills of exceptions, without regard to the number of plaintiffs in error. LITTLE, J., dissenting.
4. Unless a solicitor-general presents to the proper officer a certificate of the clerk of the trial court, that each plaintiff in error in a bill of exceptions is insolvent, he is not entitled to receive compensation from the State for services performed in this court in connection with such bill of exceptions.

Submitted January 16, — Decided February 26, 1900.

Motion to tax costs.

Livingston Kenan, solicitor-general, for movant.

FISH, J. Green and twenty-one others were jointly indicted for the offense of riot. Various of these parties were tried together, there being six trials in all. All were convicted. Six bills of exceptions were sued out to this court, the plaintiffs in error in each being respectively the parties convicted in each of the six trials. The solicitor-general prays this court to direct its clerk to deliver to him a certificate for services rendered in as many cases as there are plaintiffs in error, and that his costs be taxed by this court.

1. Section 1099 of the Penal Code provides, that for services performed in this court the solicitor-general shall receive, "in capital cases," $50; in "other felonies," $30; in "all other cases," $15. The phrase "all other cases" necessarily includes misdemeanors. Prior to March 20, 1866, riot was a felony in this State. By an act passed on that date, several offenses, among which was riot, were reduced from felonies to misdemeanors. Nothing was said in that act about the solicitor-general's fees for prosecuting for the offenses therein referred to. It would follow, therefore, that, in the absence of any other law on the subject, he would be entitled only to the fee allowed by the section of the code above referred to, for prosecuting persons guilty of a misdemeanor, which fee is $15. See Acts 1865–6, p. 233. On December 15, 1866, however, the act just cited was amended by adding a proviso, that the fees allowed to solicitors for the prosecution of the offenses referred to in the original act "in the superior courts" should remain the same as they were before such offenses were reduced below felonies. Acts 1866, p. 153. This amendatory act, as will have been noticed, applies in terms only to prosecutions in *superior courts*, and has no application whatever to services performed in this court. The fees for such services remain the same as they were before the passage of the act, and the solicitor-general is entitled to only $15 for representing the State in this court in a case reduced to a misdemeanor by the act of 1866.

2. The movant contends that he is entitled to a fee for each plaintiff in error in the six bills of exceptions. We do not think a proper construction of section 1099 of the Penal Code warrants this contention. The language used is, that in "all other cases" $15 shall be received. The original act prescribing the fees of solicitors-general in this court provided that, "in all cases where the punishment is less than confinement and labor in the penitentiary, the sum of fifteen dollars" shall be received. Acts 1850, p. 375. The bill of exceptions constitutes "the case" in this court. It is the only medium through which "a case" can reach this court, and each bill of exceptions is "a case"

within the meaning of the section of the Penal Code, notwithstanding there may be more than one plaintiff in error in such bill of exceptions. If two persons are indicted jointly for an offense and tried together, there is but one case. The definition of the word case does not depend upon the number of persons involved. The case of *Jack* v. *Kehler*, 55 *Ga.* 639, is somewhat analogous. The code provides that every attorney who argues or presents "a cause" for a plaintiff in error in this court shall be liable to the clerk for costs, except in a pauper case. Civil Code, § 5513. In that case it was held that the bill of exceptions was "the case," and that hence costs should be taxed against the attorney for plaintiff in error in a cross-bill of exceptions. It has been the uniform practice of the clerk of this court to collect costs in each bill of exceptions without regard to the number of plaintiffs in error therein.

The construction which we have given to section 1099 of the Penal Code would seem to be the more reasonable. The services to be performed by the solicitor-general in this court are no more onerous or exacting where there are several plaintiffs in error in one bill of exceptions than when there is only one. They all usually complain of the same rulings, and but one argument is needed to reply to the contentions of all. It is true that the statute allows a fee "for each person" prosecuted in the trial court. In that court both a defendant and the State have the right to sever, in which case the same service must be performed in the case of each person. And even where two or more are tried jointly, it is manifest that the prosecuting officer performs a greater amount of service for the State than in the trial of one person. We conclude therefore that the movant is entitled to but one fee for each bill of exceptions, and the costs are taxed accordingly.

3. The clerk of this court furnished the movant with a certificate which, in effect, states that the latter represented the State in this court in as many cases as there were bills of exceptions. It would follow from what is said above that this was the only certificate to which the movant was properly entitled.

4. Section 1101 of the Penal Code provides that the fees of the solicitors for services rendered in this court shall be paid by

the State, on the warrant of the Governor, in all cases when the solicitor shall present the certificate of the clerk of this court as to services, and of the clerk of the superior that the defendant was acquitted or "was unable to pay the costs." If a defendant is convicted, no fee can be paid the solicitor unless he presents a certificate from the clerk of the trial court that the defendant is insolvent. The statute contemplates that a prosecuting officer shall collect his fee out of property of a solvent defendant who has been convicted. There being but one "case" embraced within each bill of exceptions, and the solicitor-general being entitled to but one fee for each bill of exceptions, he should present a certificate from the clerk of the trial court that each plaintiff in error in the bill of exceptions is insolvent. If there be one solvent plaintiff in error in a bill of exceptions, the fee of the prosecuting officer must be made out of his property.   *All the Justices concurring, except*

LITTLE, J. While concurring in the propositions announced in the first and fourth headnotes, I dissent from those laid down in the second and third.

TINSLEY *v.* THE STATE.

1. While the offense of selling spirituous liquors without a license can not be properly charged against one who sells such liquors in a county where prohibition exists under a valid statute, the offense in question can be committed in a county where prohibition does not exist for the reason that a special act attempting to provide for prohibition therein was itself unconstitutional.

2. Under the principle of the decision of this court in the case of *Papworth* v. *The State*, 103 *Ga.* 36, the special prohibition act of 1883 for Whitfield county is unconstitutional, nor was it rendered otherwise by the amendatory acts of 1888 and 1892. Even if an unconstitutional act can be vitalized by subsequent amendment, these two acts could not thus affect the act of 1883, because, even if they themselves are sufficiently comprehensive to legalize the sale of domestic wines to the extent allowed by the act of 1877, there was at the time they were enacted an existing general law of force on the subject with which they undertook to deal.

3. In view of the rulings above announced, there is no constitutional prohibitory act of force in Whitfield county, and therefore the conviction of the accused for selling spirituous liquors therein without a license, the same being supported by evidence, was lawful.

LITTLE and LEWIS, JJ., dissenting.

Submitted February 5. — Decided February 27, 1900.

Indictment for selling liquor.   Before Judge Candler. Whitfield superior court.   October term, 1899.

R. J. & J. McCamy, for plaintiff in error.
Sam. P. Maddox, solicitor-general, contra.

COBB, J. Tinsley was tried in the superior court of Whitfield county, upon an indictment charging him with the offense of selling liquor without a license, and convicted. His motion for a new trial having been overruled, he excepted. It was contended by the accused that he could not be legally convicted of the offense charged, because there was at the date the sale was alleged to have taken place a valid local law which prohibited the sale of liquor in Whitfield county. If his premise is correct, his conclusion would follow under the decision of this court in *Brown* v. *State*, 104 *Ga.* 525. The State contended that this local law was unconstitutional, under the decision of this court in *Papworth* v. *State*, 103 *Ga.* 36, and that therefore the accused was properly indicted under the general law prohibiting the sale of liquor without a license from the proper authorities. To determine which of these contentions is correct it is necessary to take into consideration the general laws of force in this State in reference to the sales of domestic wines, as well as the local laws passed for the purpose of prohibiting the sale of liquor in Whitfield county. The act of 1877 (Acts of 1877, p. 33) provided that it should "not be unlawful for any person who shall manufacture, or cause to be manufactured, in this State, any wine from grapes, the product of any vineyard in this State, belonging to such person, and to sell or offer to sell, anywhere in this State, such wine at wholesale, or in quantities not less than one quart"; and expressly repealed all provisions of laws relating to the sale of domestic wines. This act was, in *Papworth* v. *State*, supra, held to be a general law within the meaning of that provision of the constitution of this State which declares that "Laws of a general nature shall have uniform operation throughout the State, and no special law shall be enacted in any case for which provision has been made by an existing general law." Civil Code, § 5732. In 1885 (Acts 1884–5, p. 121) the general local option liquor law was passed, and it was therein provided that nothing in that act should "be so construed as to prevent the manufacture, sale, and use of domestic wines; . . *provided,* such wines . . shall not be sold in barrooms by retail." The policy of the law in reference to domestic wines, as indicated by the act of 1877, is thus expressly recognized in the act of 1885. In 1887 (Acts 1887, p. 21) an act was passed which provided that in every county in this State where either under the general local option liquor law or under any other general or local law the sale of liquor was prohibited, but with exceptions in relation to any kind of wines, a tax of ten thousand dollars should be annually levied and collected from every dealer in domestic wines, but with the proviso that nothing in the act should "be so construed as to levy a tax on dealers in or producers of wines manufactured from grapes or berries purchased by them or grown on lands owned, leased, or rented by said dealers; and *provided* further, that said wines shall not be sold in quantities less than one quart, and shall not be drank on the premises where sold." The policy indicated in the acts of 1877 and 1885, not to interfere with the sale of domestic wines made in this State, with certain exceptions noted in those acts, is thus again recognized by the act just referred to, and that policy is by this act extended to wines made from berries; the act of 1877 relating exclusively to wines made from grapes. In the light of this legislation, no other conclusion can be reached than that it is the settled policy of this State not to interfere with the sales of domestic wines manufactured in this State from grapes or berries grown in this State, on lands owned or leased by the person manufacturing such wines, save only that they shall not be sold in quantities of less than one quart, and shall not be drunk on the premises where sold.

The local law for Whitfield county is to be now considered in the light of this established policy of the State. In 1883 (Acts 1882-3, p. 603) an act was passed providing that "the sale of spirituous, malt, vinous, or other intoxicating liquors" in the county of Whitfield should be prohibited until the same was authorized by a majority of the legal voters of that county. No exception whatever in regard to domestic wines was therein made. This act is therefore, under the decision in the *Papworth* case, unconstitutional; and, in the absence of other legislation on the subject applicable to Whitfield county, the case would be absolutely controlled by the decision made in that case. In 1888, however, (Acts 1888, p. 314) the act just above referred to was amended so as to provide that any person in Whitfield county who should "manufacture wine from grapes raised on lands owned or rented by him in said county shall have the right to sell said wine in quantities not less than one-half gallon" at the place where such wine is manufactured. Even if an unconstitutional law can be vitalized by being amended, this act did not have the effect of rendering the act of 1883 constitutional; for it is itself unconstitutional, for two reasons. In the first place, it attempted to regulate the sale of domestic wines in Whitfield county in a different way from that in which the sale was regulated by the act of 1877; the local act providing that the wine could not be sold in quantities less than one-half gallon, whereas under the act of 1877 it could be sold in quantities of one quart. In the second place, if the act was vitalized by the amending act, it became operative only from the time the amending act was passed, and this was at a time when the General Assembly had no power to pass a local prohibition law, by reason of the fact that it was a special law in a case for which provision had already been made by the general local option liquor law, which was, in *Crabb* v. *State*, 88 *Ga.* 584, held to be a general law within the meaning of the constitution. In 1892 (Acts 1892, p. 249) the local act of 1883 for Whitfield county was further amended by adding a proviso, "that the provisions of this act shall not be construed to apply to the sale of domestic wine made from grapes or berries grown in said county, when sold by the makers thereof; *provided*, that said wines shall not be sold in quantities less than one quart and shall not be drank on the premises where sold." As the act of 1883 was unconstitutional at the time of its passage, and as in 1892 the General Assembly had no power to pass a local law prohibiting the sale of liquor in one county, the act of 1892 would not have the effect of rendering the act of 1883 constitutional, even if it should be held that the act of 1892 was not in conflict with the act of 1877. The act of 1883 being itself unconstitutional, and the General Assembly neither in 1888 nor in 1892 having the power to pass a local law on the subject dealt with by the act of 1883, it follows that the three acts are inoperative, and that therefore there is no law prohibiting the sale of liquor in the county of Whitfield.

It was contended in the argument here that the *Papworth* case was not controlling, because in that case the local law for Irwin county provided for absolute prohibition without a vote of the people, and that in the cases of *Patton* v. *State*, 80 *Ga.* 714, *Bell* v. *State*, 91 *Ga.* 227, and *Redding* v. *State*, 91 *Ga.* 231, this court had held that acts similar to the one for Whitfield county, which provided that there should be an election on the question of prohibition, were valid laws. In the *Patton* case the indictment charged the violation of a local law passed for Habersham county in 1884. In the *Bell* and *Redding* cases the indictment charged a violation of a local act passed in 1882, providing for an election in Monroe county on the question of the sale of intoxicating liquors. In none of these cases was any question raised as to the constitutionality of the laws under which the indictments were framed, the decision dealing with the case as if the indictments were under valid laws; and therefore the cases, even if the acts then under consideration were in all respects identical with the one we are now dealing with, are not precedents on the question under consideration. As was remarked by Judge Bleckley in *Kaufman* v. *Ferst*, 55 *Ga.* 353, " A precedent which has no characteristic but that of being a physical fact is of very little consequence."

The charge of the judge was in accord with the views above expressed, and, as the evidence fully authorized the verdict, there was no error in refusing to grant a new trial.

Judgment affirmed. All the Justices concur, except Little and Lewis, JJ., who dissent.

WAYCROSS AIR-LINE RAILROAD COMPANY *v.* OF-FERMAN & WESTERN RAILROAD COMPANY.

1. Contracts made by one corporation are not binding upon another corpo-ration merely because the stock in both is owned by the same persons.
2. When the charter of a railroad company authorizes the construction of the railroad "to" a given town, the company may construct its line of road "into" the town; and if in constructing its road into the town it is necessary to cross the line of another railroad in order to reach its termi-nal point, it may cross such other railroad under the provisions of section 2167 (6) of the Civil Code, which declares that railroad companies incor-porated under the general law of this State for the incorporation of rail-road companies may cross another railroad "at any point in its route."
3. The rulings on the admission of evidence which were complained of were not erroneous. So far as the case turns on questions of fact, the finding of the judge is amply supported by the evidence, and his discretion in re-fusing to grant an interlocutory injunction will not be controlled.

Argued February 5, — Decided February 27, 1900.

Petition for injunction. Before Judge Bennet. Ware county. December 16, 1899.

J. L. Sweat and *L. A. Wilson*, for plaintiff.
W. E. Kay and *J. C. McDonald*, for defendants.

COBB, J. The Waycross Air-Line Railroad Company made application for an injunction to prevent the Offerman and West-ern Railroad Company from crossing its tracks in the town of Nicholls. The judge refused to grant the injunction, and the plaintiff excepted. At the hearing it appeared that the line of the Waycross Air-Line Railroad Company ran from Waycross in a northwesterly direction through the town of Nicholls to the town of Douglas; that the distance from Waycross to Nich-olls was 29 miles; that the town of Offerman was on the line of the Plant System of Railways, at a point about 21 miles northeast of Waycross; and that the Offerman and Western rail-road ran from Offerman in a westerly direction to Nicholls, a distance of about 40 miles. The defendant company had fixed as its terminus within the town of Nicholls a point south of the line of the plaintiff company, and in order to reach the same it was necessary that its tracks should cross those of the plain-tiff company. The plaintiff introduced testimony which it is

claimed established that in 1896 an agreement was entered
into between the plaintiff, the Southern Pine Company, and
the Plant System of Railways, that in consideration that the
Offerman railroad, then a tramroad, would not be extended
either south from Offerman or further in a westerly direction,
and thus not invade "the legitimate territory of petitioner for
freights," etc., certain sums would be paid monthly by the Plant
System and the plaintiff to the Southern Pine Company, and
that under this agreement, within the period beginning July 1,
1896, and ending in June, 1899, sums of money amounting in
the aggregate to more than $14,000 had been paid to the South-
ern Pine Company.   It was claimed that the road now being
constructed by the defendant railroad company went into territory which the Southern Pine Company had agreed should
not be entered by the railroad from Offerman.

  1. The petition alleged that the contract relied on by the
plaintiffs was not made by the Offerman and Western Railroad
Company but by the Southern Pine Company, another corporation ; and it was alleged that the same persons were the stockholders in the two companies, and that therefore a contract
made by the Southern Pine Company was, in legal effect, the
same as if made by the Offerman and Western Railroad Company.   Even if the plaintiff had succeeded in establishing by
proof the allegations above referred to, a contract by the Southern Pine Company would not be, in legal effect, a contract by
the Offerman and Western Railroad Company.   One person
may own all of the stock of a corporation, and still such individual shareholder and the corporation would, in law, be two
separate and distinct persons.   *Newton Mfg. Co.* v. *White,* 42
Ga. 148.   One corporation may own all the stock in another
corporation, but notwithstanding this the two corporations would
not become merged but would remain separate and distinct
persons.   *Exchange Bank* v. *Macon Construction Co.,* 97 *Ga.* 1 ;
Sparks v. *Dunbar,* 102 *Ga.* 129.   It would necessarily follow,
from the rulings in the cases cited, that two corporations would
not become merged into each other merely because the stock in
each was owned by the same persons.   Therefore the contract
made by the Southern Pine Company was not the contract of

the Offerman and Western Railroad Company, even if the stockholders in each were identical. While the evidence showed that these two corporations had many of the same stockholders in each, they were not altogether identical. But even if the contract set up by the plaintiff company was binding upon the defendant railroad company and was otherwise valid, the finding of the judge that such contract, if ever made, had ceased to be operative, was abundantly supported by the evidence. .

2. It was contended that the Offerman and Western Railroad Company had no right to cross the line of the Waycross Air-Line Railroad Company within the limits of the town of Nicholls. The charter of the Offerman and Western Railroad Company authorized it to construct its road "to the town of Nicholls." It is well settled that a charter authorizing a railroad company to construct its line "to" a city empowers it to construct its line "into" the city. *Hazlehurst* v. *Freeman,* 52 *Ga.* 244. It is contended, however, that although under such a charter a railroad company will be allowed to carry its line into the town designated as its terminus, it will not, in the absence of express authority, be authorized to cross the tracks of another company for the purpose of reaching a place selected by it for its depot, when the depot could have been as well selected on the opposite side of the railroad sought to be crossed. The point at which a railroad company shall locate the end of its line within the town fixed by its charter as its terminus is a matter left entirely to the judgment and discretion of the corporation, when there is nothing in the charter fixing the point at which the end of the line shall be located. A railroad company will locate the end of its line at such point as will be to the best interest of those interested in the enterprise; and where such location does not interfere with the rights of the public, another corporation will not be permitted to bring in question the propriety or the wisdom of the location, when the corporation making the location proceeds in accordance with the law to ascertain the damages which the other corporation may suffer by the appropriation of any part of its property to the uses of the railroad company in reaching its terminal point, and, after they are so ascertained, pays or tenders the amount then fixed to the corporation whose property is taken.

The Offerman and Western Railroad Company has authority
"to cross, intersect, or join or unite its railroads with any railroad heretofore or hereafter to be constructed, at any point in
its route, or upon the ground of any other railroad company,
with the necessary turnouts, sidings, and switches, and other
conveniences necessary in the construction of said road, and may
run over any part of any railroad's right of way necessary or
proper to reach its freight-depot, in any city, town, or village
through or near which said railroad may run, under the limitations hereinafter named; but in crossing another railroad,
either over, under, at grade level, or otherwise, it shall be at
the expense of the company making the crossing, and in such
way and manner, at the time of construction, as not to interfere
with said railroad in its regular travel or business."   Civil Code,
§ 2167 (6).   It is further provided in the law of this State, "that
any railroad company shall have the right to cross the track of
any other railroad company."   Civil Code, § 2219.   The Offerman and Western Railroad Company had, under the general
law under which it was incorporated, the authority, as appears
from the section of the code first above quoted, to cross any
other railroad "at any point in its route."   It will not be seriously contended that the route of a railroad ends when the corporate limit of the town or city which is fixed as its terminus
has been reached.   If a railroad company has authority to go
into a town, that part of its line which is within the limits of
such town is certainly "in its route."   Such being the case, the
defendant railroad company has undoubted authority to cross
the track of the plaintiff company within the town of Nicholls.
There is nothing in the case of the *City Council of Augusta* v.
Port Royal & Augusta Railway, 74 *Ga.* 658, to conflict with the
view here presented.   It was there held that a railroad company which was authorized by charter to construct its line to
the city of Augusta, and also, with the assent of the railroads
in Georgia, to join its tracks to theirs on such terms as might
be agreed on, did not have authority to construct its line of road
"through" the city of Augusta for the purpose of connecting
its tracks with those of another company.   An examination of
the record in that case discloses that, in order to make the con-

nection desired, it was necessary for the company to lay its tracks longitudinally upon at least one of the streets of the city. This can not be done in the absence of express legislative authority. *Davis* v. *Railroad Co.*, 87 *Ga.* 605, and cases cited.

3. It was further contended that the crossing sought to be made by the defendant railroad company could not be made except under the order and direction of the Railroad Commission. The general law for the incorporation of railroads provides that a railroad constructed under its provisions shall be at least ten miles from an existing railroad, but that this shall not prevent the new railroad from running as near to the other railroad as the interests of the new company may require for a distance of ten miles from either terminus. And it is further provided that whenever, on account of the physical formation of the country surrounding the initial or terminal point, or by reason of the number of railroads centering at an initial or terminal point, the conditions above referred to are impracticable, and the companies can not agree among themselves as to the location of the new road, such road shall be located under the order and by the direction of the Railroad Commission. Civil Code, § 2176. These provisions of the law can only apply to railroads which run practically parallel with each other; and when it is kept in mind that the line of the defendant railroad company is about forty miles long, and that the lines of the plaintiff company and of the Plant System constitute the other two sides of a triangle, twenty-nine and twenty-one miles long respectively, it needs no argument to show that the law above referred to has no application whatever.

The evidence before the judge authorized the finding that the defendant railroad company was duly organized at the time the proceedings were instituted to condemn the property of the plaintiff company for the purpose of making a crossing. The rulings on the admission of evidence which were complained of were free from error. The case turns to a large extent on questions of fact, and, there being ample evidence to sustain the view taken by the judge, his discretion in refusing to grant the injunction will not be interfered with.

Judgment affirmed.   All the Justices concurring.

DONALDSON *v.* ROBERTS *et al.*

If an equitable petition filed for the purpose of setting aside a judgment
overruling a motion for a new trial and of obtaining a new trial of the
original case will lie at all, it certainly is not maintainable when it shows
that the petitioner was guilty of any default or neglect on his part.

Argued February 1, — Decided February 27, 1900.

Equitable petition.   Before Judge Candler.   DeKalb superior court.   February 3, 1899.

R. J. Jordan, for plaintiff in error.
Candler & Thomson and *W. J. Albert*, contra.

SIMMONS, C. J.   Roberts and Kirkpatrick brought an action
of ejectment against Donaldson, to recover possession of a certain tract of land in DeKalb county, Georgia.   After evidence
for both sides had been submitted, the trial judge directed the
jury to return a verdict for the plaintiffs.   Donaldson moved for
a new trial.   By agreement the motion was submitted to the
judge without argument.   The judge held up his decision for
more than ten months, when, in open court and in term, he
overruled the motion.   Counsel for the movant was not present,
and did not learn of the decision until too late to bring the case
by bill of exceptions to this court.   He thereupon filed what
he calls a "bill of review," asking that the judgment overruling the motion for new trial be set aside and that a new trial of
the ejectment suit be granted.   This petition was mainly predicated upon what is alleged to have been the understanding
between the judge and the counsel for the petitioner.   It was
alleged that the judge, at the time the motion was submitted,
agreed that when he decided the motion he would notify counsel for the movant in time for a bill of exceptions to be sued
out in case of an adverse decision; that he held up his decision
a long time; and that when the decision was made he failed
to notify counsel, and thus by the action of the judge the movant lost his right to bring the case to this court.   The petition also
alleged that there was error apparent on the face of the record
of the ejectment suit, the error consisting in the direction of the
verdict for the plaintiffs under the facts disclosed.   The petition was demurred to on the following grounds: "1. That the

facts in said petition set forth give no cause of action to the plaintiff against these defendants. 2. That upon said case made by said petition the petitioner is not entitled to a review of the order and decree of the court therein set forth, and to have set aside the judgment and order of the court refusing a new trial." The judge sustained the demurrer, and Donaldson excepted.

The pleader in his petition styles it a "bill of review," but we think that it is not such a bill. A technical bill of review or a bill in the nature of a bill of review, according to our understanding, lies only to review a decree of a court of equity, not a judgment at law. The present bill is really a petition to set aside a judgment overruling a motion for a new trial, and to obtain a new trial. Such petitions are not favored by courts of equity. The law has provided ample remedies to the parties, by giving them the right to move for a new trial in the court below, and by giving them the right to a writ of error to this court. Where the losing party fails to avail himself of his proper legal remedies, courts of equity will be slow to grant him relief, unless he shows that he has exercised all diligence, or that from some unavoidable cause he could not pursue his legal remedies. If his petition shows that there has been any default or neglect on his part or on the part of his counsel, equity will not aid him. *Stroup* v. *Sullivan*, 2 *Kelly*, 275; *Robuck* v. *Harkins*, 38 *Ga.* 174; Civil Code, §§ 3987, 3988. Applying this rule to the facts set out in the present petition, we find that the petitioner did not exercise full diligence in the assertion of his rights at law. He relied altogether upon an understanding with the trial judge that the latter would inform petitioner when the decision was made on the motion for a new trial. We think that such an understanding did not relieve the petitioner or his counsel of the duty of ascertaining the progress of the case and when the judge was likely to decide it. Counsel should not have relied entirely upon such a promise by the judge. He should have recognized the fact that a judge has more cases than one, and that this particular judge had many cases and was a very busy man. He ought also to have recognized the fact that the judge might in good faith forget the promise, as was doubtless the case in this instance, if the allegation be true that the judge made the promise in question. It was the duty of counsel to keep himself advised of the progress of his case, to attend court when his case was likely to be decided, and to inquire whether it had been decided. In this case counsel seems to have relied exclusively upon the judge's promise. He ought instead to have kept himself advised as to his case, especially after the judge had held up the decision so long a time. He ought to have attended the term of the court in which the motion for new trial was pending, or at least to have made inquiry within thirty days after the adjournment of the term. The decision was rendered in open court and during term, and such an inquiry would have afforded timely information of the decision. Nor should counsel have relied upon promises made in vacation while the case was held up by the judge and before the decision. In the case of *Parker* v. *Belcher*, 87 *Ga.* 110, Bleckley, C. J., said: "A suitor in the superior court has no right to consult the judge while off the bench for his opinion as to when the case will come on for trial, or as to what will be done with it when it does come on. The sayings and doings of the judge in such an interview are extrajudicial and can not be treated as announcements or rulings of the court." See also *Farley* v. *Bloodworth*, 66 *Ga.* 349. Even where the promise is made from the bench, we still think, for the reasons given above, that counsel should not rely entirely upon it. In the present case counsel did not exercise full diligence in looking after his case. It seems to us that, after the adjournment of the court wherein the motion was pending, the movant or his counsel ought at least to have made some inquiry as to whether or not the decision had been made. While the judgment overruling the motion for new trial may have been erroneous, yet, as the petitioner does not show that he exercised full diligence in the pursuance of his legal remedies but does show that he was in laches, we think he is entitled to no relief in a court of equity. The court was therefore right in sustaining the demurrer to the petition. Upon the subject of laches in such proceedings see *Bryan* v. *Walton*, 33 *Ga. Supp.* 11; *Rogers* v. *Kingsbery*, 22 *Ga.* 60; *Central Ga. Bank* v. *Iverson*, 73 *Ga.* 19; *Sharp* v. *Loyless*, 39 *Ga.* 678.

Judgment affirmed. All the Justices concurring.

WARREN *et al. v.* BRANAN *et al.*

109
128

1. "Owing to their nature and the purpose of their creation, it is essential that the territory included in municipal corporations should be well defined and clearly bounded."

2. In so far as the act of December 20, 1899, "to incorporate the town of Kirkwood, in DeKalb county," undertook to establish "the corporate limits of said town," the provisions looking to that end were so indefinite, uncertain, and incomplete that the legislative intent can not be ascertained and given effect, even by a resort to all competent extrinsic evidence available.

Argued February 2. — Decided March 2, 1900.

Petition for injunction. Before Judge Candler. DeKalb county. January 20, 1900.

John L. Hopkins & Sons, for plaintiffs.
Arnold & Arnold, for defendants.

FISH, J. By an act approved December 20, 1899, the General Assembly of this State undertook "to incorporate the town of Kirkwood, in DeKalb county, to confer certain powers on the municipal authorities of said town," and to prescribe the territorial limits thereof. See Acts of 1899, p. 233. The present proceeding was instituted by certain citizens and taxpayers of that town, with a view to testing the validity of this enactment, they contending, among other things, "that the description contained in the act relative to the property to be granted for municipal purposes" was so indefinite and uncertain that the territorial limits and boundaries of the proposed corporation were incapable of ascertainment.

1. It is unquestionably true, as was conceded by counsel for the defendant in error on the hearing before us, that: "Owing to their nature and the purpose of their creation, it is essential that the territory included in municipal corporations should be well defined and clearly bounded." 15 Am. & Eng. Enc. L. 1001. "Since the leading object of an American municipal corporation is to invest the inhabitants of a defined locality or place with a corporate existence, chiefly for the purposes of local government, it is obvious that the *geographical limits* or boundaries of the corporation *ought to be defined and certain*. . . Because residence within the corporation confers rights and

imposes duties upon the residents, and the local jurisdiction of
the incorporated place is, in most cases, confined to the limits
of the corporation, it is necessary that these limits be definitely
fixed." 1 Dillon's Municipal Corp. § 182. So the only question to be determined is whether or not the act under consideration was sufficiently full and explicit in the respect just indicated.

2. The second section of that act undertakes to describe by
metes and bounds the territory to be embraced within "the
corporate limits of said town" of Kirkwood. On the hearing
in the court below it was shown that while the description given
of the boundaries in contemplation was reasonably accurate up
to a certain point, from thence different surveyors disagreed as
to the line really intended by the legislature to be followed to
the point next designated, and that the course prescribed from
thence as the means of reaching the starting point so far di-
verged therefrom that the same could not be reached without
arbitrarily ignoring the direction indicated and supplying an
entirely new and independent boundary line. The diagram
which follows will, in connection with the accompanying explanation thereof, furnish a better idea of the situation than we
could hope otherwise to give.

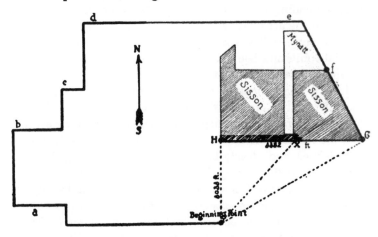

From the "Beginning Point," the location of which is made
definite by the act of incorporation, the contemplated boundary

may be traced with reasonable certainty along the course indicated by the letters a, b, c, d, e, and f. From a stake the position of which on the diagram is at e, and which is described in the act as being "immediately opposite the eastern line of the land of Mrs. P. L. Mynatt," the course directed to be followed is "thence in a southerly direction along said Mynatt line to a stake east of and opposite the *southern line* of the lands of Mrs. V. P. Sisson," (the point, most probably, indicated on the diagram by the letter G), and "thence in a *westerly* direction, *along the southern line of said Sisson*, to the beginning point." Were the course last prescribed strictly adhered to, the nearest approach of the line to the starting point would be at H, over half a mile (3033 feet) distant therefrom. After arriving at the point marked f, one surveyor undertook to run the boundary directly west for a considerable distance, and thence due south, along the land lines of the Mynatt property, ending at the point on the diagram marked X. From there he could only suggest that a line be arbitrarily run to the "Beginning Point" along the dotted line indicated. Other experts were of the opinion that the boundary could be made complete only by wholly ignoring the last course specified in the act and substituting therefor the course indicated on the diagram by the dotted line drawn from G to the "Beginning Point," or else undertaking to arbitrarily supply another and entirely new and distinct course, not hinted at in the act and over half a mile in length, from the southwest corner of the Sisson tract of land, along the dotted line running between H and the point of beginning.

It was earnestly insisted by counsel for the defendants in error, in a brief filed in behalf of their clients, that: "It can not be said that this act leaves a hiatus or gap, because the very language of the act in the concluding sentences fills it up by demanding a line to the beginning;" and "the mere difficulty in selecting the line will not prevent the court from finding it." In reply, we may say that the mere fact that the language of the act manifests an intention on the part of the legislature that the prescribed boundary should effectually encompass the territory designed to be set apart for municipal purposes, and that the last course run should connect with the boundary line at the point of beginning, is of really little aid in determining *how* this result was intended to be accomplished.   Indeed, it is difficult to imagine a case where the legislative intent to bound on all sides, without any gap, the territority set apart to a municipality would not be self-apparent when the purposes of the enactment were taken into consideration.   But when the corporate limits of a municipality are not described otherwise than by metes and bounds, and the specification thereof is so indefinite and uncertain that the same can not be traced and followed from point to point, the means thus afforded of ascertaining the legislative intent as to the precise extent and location of the territory sought to be described must necessarily prove wholly inadequate; and counsel are in error when they assume that "the mere difficulty of selecting the line" which the General Assembly had in contemplation " will not prevent the court from finding it," — presumably by a resort to pure conjecture.   It is to be noted, in this connection, that so far as the present difficulty is concerned, counsel fail entirely to suggest any plausible theory whereby we would be warranted in saying which of the three dotted lines indicated in the above diagram was the course the legislature intended to be followed in locating the southeastern boundary of the town of Kirkwood.   So far as appears from the record before us, that town had not, prior to the passage of the act in question, any definitely established boundaries; nor is there anything in the act to indicate that, were this otherwise, the corporate limits of the contemplated municipality were to be determined with reference to any old boundaries or lines of demarkation which had previously existed.   On the contrary, it would seem that the legislature undertook, irrespective of all subsisting landmarks or recognized lines, to definitely prescribe the boundaries within which the territory set apart for municipal purposes should be embraced.

The case in hand is totally unlike that which would be presented if a landowner, after stating generally in a deed of conveyance his intention to convey all of a certain tract of land upon which he resided or which was locally known by a designated name, should, in attempting to describe the premises by metes and bounds, fail to connect all of the several boundary lines, or inaccurately define the location of one or more of the same. In that event, the intention to convey a tract of land which had previously been laid out and which had existing boundaries capable of ascertainment being manifest, a court of justice would be warranted in endeavoring to give effect to such intention, even though such course involved disregarding to some extent the description contained in the deed of conveyance and fixing the correct boundaries through the aid of extrinsic evidence making clear the exact location of the same. The propriety of so doing in a case calling for an application of the maxim, falsa demonstratio non nocet, was fully recognized in *Rogers* v. *Rogers*, 78 *Ga.* 688. At the same time, however, this court took pains to point out that all the authorities agreed that this doctrine had no application to a case where the instrument under consideration did not refer in sufficiently definite terms to specific property the precise location and extent of which was capable of ascertainment by a resort to aliunde evidence.

In the case now before us, the extent and boundaries of the territory to be included within the corporate limits of the town of Kirkwood were, by the act of 1899, for the first time sought to be determined and established. A resort to extrinsic evidence as an aid in endeavoring to arrive at the legislative intent with regard to the contemplated location of the southeastern boundaries of that town would therefore be futile, as was evidently recognized by the parties to this litigation; for no attempt to show that Kirkwood was enclosed by definitely established lines previously run or recognized by its inhabitants was made on the hearing below. Nor would it benefit the defendants in error were we, in compliance with the suggestion of their counsel, to apply the maxim above alluded to, and thus expunge from the description contained in the act of incorporation so much thereof as refers to the course to be run "in a westerly direction, along the southern line of said Sisson," upon the idea that this was an erroneous specification, inasmuch as a line so run could not possibly connect with the beginning point, as was the result manifestly contemplated. To eliminate this part of the description would have no effect other than to leave the last course definitely fixed by the description in the act as running no further than the point marked G on the diagram presented above, in the event that point, rather than that indicated by the letter X, correctly indicates the location of the "stake east of and opposite the southern line of the lands of Mrs. V. P. Sisson," which is a matter we are not now called upon to decide; for even if the stake last referred to was really intended to be understood as being at X, there would still remain a very considerable distance from thence to the starting point, to traverse which no boundary line would be specified. We can not undertake arbitrarily to supply so grave an omission. Were we to attempt to do so, we are firmly of the belief that the legislative intent would be defeated rather than given effect. It is reasonable to presume that, in prescribing the course "in a westerly direction along the southern line of" the Sisson estate, the General Assembly acted deliberately and advisedly, with a view to excluding some portion, at least, of the lands lying immediately south of that line. Exactly what portion, or its precise extent and location, we can, however, at best only vaguely surmise. How far the course "in a westerly direction" was to run along the southern boundary of the Sisson property is not remotely specified, or indicated otherwise than by the somewhat casual expression of a purpose to eventually arrive at the beginning point. Whether this course was designed to extend to the southwestern corner of Mrs. Sisson's property, or beyond, or only to some intermediate point, before turning southward in the direction of the beginning point, is a matter left wholly to abstract speculation. This being so, we are constrained to hold that the provisions of the act seeking to establish the territorial limits of the town are so indefinite, uncertain, and incomplete that the legislative intent can not be ascertained and given effect, and that therefore the act is wholly inoperative. The court erred in not granting the injunction prayed for.

Judgment reversed.   All the Justices concurring.

APPENDIX.

MEMORIAL OF HON. CLIFFORD ANDERSON.

On March 7, 1900, the Committee previously appointed to
prepare a report commemorative of the life, character, and
services of the Honorable Clifford Anderson, submitted the
following

REPORT.

Death has once more invaded the ranks of the bar of this court, and, this
time, has struck down Clifford Anderson, one of the oldest, most beloved,
and most honored of our members.

Clifford Anderson was born in Nottoway county in the State of Virginia,
on the 23d of March, 1833. While yet a boy he left his native State and
came to Macon, Ga., where he continued to reside, and where he died on
the nineteenth day of December, 1899.

At the age of nineteen he was admitted to the bar of the superior court
of Bibb county. Very soon after his admission he entered into a partnership with Col. R. S. Lanier, and this partnership continued until the death of
Col. Lanier, in 1893, a period of forty years. The first case in which he appeared before the Supreme Court of this State, to the bar of which he was
admitted in March, 1854, is the case of *Bibb County Loan Association* v. *Alexander Richards*, 21 *Ga.* 592. This is the first case in our reports concerning
the law governing building and loan associations in relation to their stockholders and borrowers; and the contentions set up by Mr. Anderson, who
was of counsel for the plaintiff in error, were maintained, and the rules for
which he contended as since been maintained as the law of this State.
In the opinion written by Judge Lumpkin in the case he refers to "the
learning exhibited in its discussion." Thus early in the career of Mr. Anderson did his power as a lawyer, and his familiarity with the great fundamental principles of the law, make a serious and permanent impression upon
our Supreme Court. From this time on to the last case in which he appeared before this court he was of counsel in numbers of cases, and still continued to make his power and learning as a lawyer felt and appreciated. It
is no exaggeration to say that it is likely that no other lawyer at this bar
has had so much to do with shaping the opinions of the court by his
arguments. Shortly after his admission to the bar of the superior court he
was appointed judge of the city court of Macon, which office he filled with
distinction. The last case in which he appeared before this court was that
of *Lamar* v. *McLaren*, 107 *Ga.* 591, involving the construction of a will and
the doctrine of election under it. During all his long and successful career

841

at the bar of this court he met the members of the bar from every quarter of the State. He was recognized, and justly so, as a leader in his profession; the court respected him, and his brethren loved him, not only for his ability and his masterful powers of analysis, buttressed with wide, varied, and exact learning, but also for his uniform courtesy and his sterling integrity. He was a member of the Georgia House of Representatives during the years 1859–1860.

At the commencement of the war between the States he volunteered as a private in the Floyd Rifles, a company from Macon. In 1863 he was elected to the Confederate Congress. At the close of the war he returned to Macon, his home, and began again the practice of his profession. In 1880 he was nominated and elected attorney-general of the State of Georgia, and continued to hold this office for five consecutive terms covering ten years. He brought to the discharge of the duties of attorney-general all the power of a well-trained lawyer. His opinions are models of professional style, and his judgments upon the many and perplexing questions submitted to him were almost uniformly accepted as conclusive upon the matters of law involved. He appeared many times in the argument of cases before the Supreme Court of the United States, and the opinions of the court in the cases in which he appeared show that he impressed himself upon that court as forcibly and successfully as he was accustomed to do in the other courts in which he practiced.

He was appointed with Judge John L. Hopkins and Mr. Joseph R. Lamar as one of the commissioners to codify the laws of this State under the act of December 19, 1893, and his work appears in the present Code of 1895. The particular work assigned to Judge Anderson in this last official labor of his was the annotation of the Supreme Court decisions not relating to criminal laws or practice, and the distribution of the annotations under their appropriate sections. Not until the full history of the work involved in the preparation of this code has been written will the public in general know of the vast amount of labor which fell to his lot. Its accomplishment required more than three years of persistent effort, and during a large part of this time as many as three clerks were employed by him. The problem of sifting out of 95 volumes of reports covering 71,250 pages of printed matter, and obtaining from these the point or points decided, and arranging these points, correctly phrased, in their appropriate places, and under appropriate sections of the code, would stagger even the highest order of mind. There are more than 20,000 annotations, and the proper and successful arrangement and distribution of these are all embraced in his work. How well he did it time and trial will more and more develop. This work stands as a monument of his learning and industry, and his marvelous powers of unerring analysis and discrimination.

With all of his mastery of men and law and learning, he steadfastly declined any wide field of political effort. The reward in this region of endeavor would have been certain, but his regard for the law, his jealous mistress, so filled the purpose of his life that he preferred the honor and the glory of the courts to that of the executive chair or legislative halls.

Early in life Mr. Anderson attached himself to the Presbyterian church, the church of the faith of his fathers, and he continued in this church until his death, a zealous, pure, and prominent member. In every field of duty in which he engaged he was successful, and his success not only brought to him the just rewards which follow merit, but at the same time reflected credit upon the community in which he lived, and upon the State itself. And so he did not live unto himself. He was a many-sided man, and his efforts and accomplishments in the many labors he undertook made him a broad, strong, and well-developed worker. His private as well as professional career is without shadow of stain, and he leaves to his family and to posterity a memory which will always be revered.

Judge Anderson was nominated in the summer of 1880, by the State Democratic Convention, for the office of attorney-general, and was elected the following fall. He assumed the duties of that responsible office, for which he was peculiarly well fitted from every standpoint, in November, 1880, and faithfully discharged the same for ten years, having been re-elected four times without opposition. During Judge Anderson's incumbency of the office of attorney-general there were many cases of considerable magnitude which were fought to the finish in both State and Federal courts, and in all these he not only faithfully represented the State's interest, but did so with signal skill and ability. The many cases in which the State was a party, involving intricate questions relative to taxation of corporations, appearing in the reports of both this and the U. S. Supreme Court from 1881 to 1891, are splendid witnesses of the painstaking care and ability with which he represented the State's interest in the courts. Probably the two cases which best illustrate the force and learning of Judge Anderson are those of Cunningham v. Macon & Brunswick R. R. Co., 106 U. S. 446, and Georgia R. R. Co. v. Georgia R. R. Commission, 128 U. S. 174, which involved questions of greatest moment to the State and the people. In both of these cases he practically single-handed met before the courts some of the ablest lawyers of his time, and succeeded in having all of the contentions in his briefs and arguments upheld by the U. S. Supreme Court. His official opinions to the Governor and the several State-house officers were always clear and concise; many of them bear evidence of much study and research. They continue to be relied upon by the various officers who are charged with administering the affairs of State. In a letter addressed to the writer, Gov. Henry D. McDaniel, who was the chief executive during four years of the time that Judge Anderson was attorney-general, speaks of him in the following manner: "Our official relations were cordial and unreserved. There were frequent calls upon him for legal advice without the formality of written opinions. He was always prompt to discuss the matter in question in a clear, comprehensive, and masterly manner. Where questions of greater difficulty were submitted for formal treatment, he made exhaustive research, and rendered opinions which are models of sound judgment and learning. He was eminently practical in applying constitutional principles to the construction of the statutes affecting the duties of the different departments of the State government, and always adopted enlightened and conservative views. His candor and sincerity in dealing with such questions could not be surpassed. In that office he was a great lawyer. It has not been my good fortune to have known any one who better deserves that encomium."

Judge Anderson was not only a faithful officer in the discharge of his duties before the courts and in the rendition of official opinions. but he fully met every other requirement of the law relative to his official duties. His re-

ports to the Governor contain many valuable recommendations for legislative action. These suggestions were always so practical that hardly without
an exception the legislature enacted the same into law. The act of September 7, 1891, providing for a speedy determination of criminal cases in this
court, was passed in pursuance of a recommendation made by him in his
last official report to the Governor in November, 1890. This act and similar legislation growing out of the same has caused this State to take the
front rank amongst the States for the speedy determination of criminal cases.
The faithful and able manner in which for ten years Judge Anderson discharged every obligation assumed by him when he took the oath of office as
attorney-general entitled him to the great distinction of being known and
referred to as a model officer.

On account of the sickness of his successor, Judge George N. Lester, Judge
Anderson was frequently called upon for advice by the Governor and other
State officials for a year after he had gone out of office, and these requests
were always cheerfully answered. He was specially retained by Governor
Northen to represent the State's interest in making a settlement of the differences between the State and the lessees of the Western & Atlantic Railroad, whose lease expired in December, 1890, and in doing so he appeared
as leading counsel before the Western & Atlantic Commission appointed
under the act of 1890. In this case he made a most masterful presentation
of the State's side of the questions, and his contentions were unanimously
upheld by the commission, which was composed of eight prominent citizens
of Georgia, recognized as men eminent for their integrity and ability, the
late Hon. N. J. Hammond being the chairman of that commission. Judge
Anderson was also specially retained by Governor Gordon, and continued
by Governor Northen, as leading counsel in the litigation growing out of
the legislation relative to the county taxation of railroads. He succeeded in
sustaining the constitutionality of this legislation, both before this court
and the United States Supreme Court.

In part our brother has been portrayed in tracing his career, and it only
remains to add such descriptive touches as may likely aid in completing the
representation. In one way, at least, Nature is a respecter of persons. She
may have a secret and concealed system of compensations by which she
equalizes her gifts to all her children ; but even if she endows them respectively with the same amount of goods in the aggregate, she certainly discrim-
inates largely in kind and quality, and also in the quantity of each kind.
Her show of favoritism extends to and embraces all three classes of wealth
which it is her province to apportion and distribute,—moral, intellectual,
and physical. The allotment of our brother Anderson in the first and second of these classes was in a high degree generous and bountiful; and in
the third his legacy was much superior to the average, for, though there
were considerable intervals when he lacked full bodily strength and vigor,
his person was comely, commanding, and dignified, fitted always for association and companionship with his mind and character. In form, features,
bearing, and deportment he was a gentleman. But his physical advantages
were not such as to play any part in gaining for him the eminence and distinction to which he attained. His real opulence lay in his moral and intellectual characteristics, and these were the capital on which his life and
all its ventures were conducted   Indeed he was remarkable and peculiar in

the apparent detachment of his mind from his body, and in the little use he seemed to make of the latter in performing his most arduous and intense labor, especially in the practice of law. During the examination of witnesses by associate or adverse counsel, or the delivery of argument to which he was to make reply, he often appeared to be utterly inattentive and not to take the slightest notice of what was going on; yet, when it came his turn to discuss the evidence or to speak in reply, he knew with minute accuracy all that had been said, and could detail it with more precision, perhaps, than any other person present. And in the progress of his strongest and most animated speeches this apparent detachment of the spiritual from the physical man seemed even more complete. His mind would glow with the refined heat of internal fires, as if a thought furnace were stationed in the centre of it, while the whole bodily form, including face and countenance, would wear an aspect of marble repose and appear to be scarcely more a part of the speaker than a part of the audience. At such times the orator was condensed, or seemed to be condensed, into a spirit and a voice. His eloquence was the evangelism of thought, unmixed with that of the imagination or the senses; and yet it was not cold—far from it. It derived warmth not only from weighty import but from thrilling tones and delicate modulations of voice, and from a noble earnestness that pervaded every sentence. At his best our brother had no superior in serving the artillery of pure thought, and his effectiveness was great both in producing conviction and giving pleasure. It was not his wont to speak for the mere purpose of pleasing or entertaining. He was eminently practical, and always meant business. Perhaps no man ever lived who spent less time or bestowed less labor on useless or only agreeable things. Utility was a prime, an indispensable element in anything that occupied his serious attention or enlisted his exertions. He regarded life as a scene and a period for work, and he regarded work, so far as he was called to share in it, as an agency for serving useful purposes. And he worked nobly and energetically. He did his full part in a willing, manly way, under the joint incitement of duty and inclination. He was no reluctant vassal to the ordinance of labor, but a ready, eager, and devout coworker with God and his fellow men. Under a sense of duty to his domestic obligations he adhered steadfastly to his chosen field of labor, the practice of law, though perhaps more than once a seat upon the bench was open to his acceptance. It is certain that he declined the opportunity of being Chief Justice of this court on the death of Chief Justice Jackson in 1887. This he did because of the inadequacy of the salary and his need for a larger income.

His mind was strong, broad, and admirably well-balanced. Its power of penetration was that of strength rather than of astuteness, and while it reached all the niceties that belong to substance, it rarely, if at all, had any contact with those impalpable trifles in the recesses and crevices of form that sometimes attract and delight the over-sharp practitioner. He lacked both relish and capacity for magnifying trivialities, or for seeing something in the utter vacuity of nothing. His common sense was so dominant that he could not shake it off or take leave of it; and there is not the least probability that he ever tried or wanted to do so. Intellectually, he was normal, symmetrical, healthy, alert. and vigorous; and while he was deliberate and not given to mental hurry, all his resources were generally at the ready

command of his will. His aptitude for work was abreast with his capacity
for thought, and he would have found it no less hard to be a drone than to
be a dunce. The memory which he left to us is saddened with no regret for
wasted powers or misspent time. We feel that he translated into conduct
all of himself that could be so rendered. Much of his work survives him,
and some of it, especially that done on the Code of 1895, will bless posterity
and go down the ages. While Georgia lives Clifford Anderson will not be
forgotten. First of all and last of all, he was an upright, conscientious, pure
man. In principle and practice he was morally sound. His law and fact
harmonized and coincided. Both in will and deed he was worthy and ex-
alted. Nature gifted him with refined instincts, a mild and equable temper,
a virtuous disposition, noble aspirations, the love of right, truth, and justice.
And the munificence of nature was confirmed and reinforced in the days of
his youth by the graces of Religion. He thus had throughout his active life
the united safeguards and support of Earth and Heaven — Nature and God.
What greater felicity could be the lot of a mortal being!

Peace to his ashes! Rest everlasting to his soul!

L. E. BLECKLEY,	WASHINGTON DESSAU,
JOEL BRANHAM,	ALLEN FORT,
JOSEPH B. CUMMING,	J. M. TERRELL,
N. L. HUTCHINS,	JOHN D. LITTLE,

W. E. KAY.

ADDRESS OF JUDGE JOEL BRANHAM.

I first met Mr. Anderson, about the year 1859, in Americus, Georgia. He
was then a slender, youthful-looking man, about twenty-six years of age.
At the time he was engaged in the prosecution of a murder case. McCay
and Hawkins, both of whom were afterwards members of this court, represented the defendant. Mr. Anderson was a stranger to the community.
His argument in the case was masterly, logical, and eloquent, and his delivery, at times, was like a resistless torrent, bearing everything before it. Occasionally his voice would become soft, slow, and subdued, and then it would
sink into an audible whisper, as he denounced the defendant, and his conduct, as inspired only by a "guilty and bloody heart." His audience was
surprised and spellbound by his eloquence. When the recess of the court
came at the conclusion of his address, a member of the bar suggested that
"the young man" was more than a match for defendant's counsel. Judge
Hawkins realized the effect of his speech, and, with some chagrin, said, "He
is not as young as he appears to be."

During the eight years of my own residence in the city of Macon, I was
frequently thrown into business and social relations with him, and his partner, Col. Robert S. Lanier. Their association was not simply a legal or business one; their daily intercourse towards each other was like that of affectionate brothers, so strikingly so, that it was a source of observation and
comment by all who came in contact with them.

In 1863, when Mr. Anderson was nominated for a seat in the Confederate
Congress, and when he accepted the nomination, he announced to the public that he would make no canvass for the place, nor would he spend any
money, or resort to any combination or scheme to secure his election, and

he kept his word. He was opposed by the Hon. A. H. Kenan, who, to some extent, canvassed the district, but public sentiment favored Anderson, and he was elected. Sam. Hunter, a member of the Macon bar, and one of the firm of Speer and Hunter, said to me on that occasion, "Aside from Clifford Anderson's legal ability, and the excellency of his character, he seems to have been born under a lucky star. Choice fruit falls, of its own accord, into his lap," and this seems true, for the offices he afterwards held, and which he so ably filled, sought him out, and fell gracefully upon him.

He had a fine sense of humor. I trust I may be excused for relating two anecdotes I heard him tell.

Around the camp fire, at Sewell's point in Virginia, while talking of Phil. Tracey, as he was called by his familiar friends, one of Georgia's eloquent and brilliant sons, who had been recently elected major of his regiment, he said, Major Tracey told his regiment, before his election, that he was not a military man, and had no knowledge of military tactics, and that afterwards, while he was drilling his regiment in the manual of arms, he gave the order, "present arms," when the men were at order arms, and the regiment was so well drilled that not a man moved his gun from the ground, or a muscle of his body. Major Tracey, seeing he had committed an error, said, "Men, I told you, before you elected me major, that I was not a military man, and knew nothing of military tactics. Now, that you have elected me, I want you all to understand that when I tell you to do a thing I want you to do it!'"

On another occasion, immediately after the surrender of the Confederate Army, a group of lawyers, standing in front of Hunt's drug-store in the city of Macon, on the corner of Cherry and Second streets, were discussing the situation, and the gloomy condition of the country, on account of the emancipation of the negro, and the attempt the Federal government would likely make, by enfranchising them, to rule the white people of the South by them. The outlook was very dark, and many of the lawyers present were full of apprehension and fear. One of them had a badly worn and defaced one-dollar greenback bill, which was pasted on a piece of newspaper to preserve it. It was handed around and examined by each one of the lawyers present. I remember it was the first greenback bill I ever saw. There was not another cent of current money in the party. One of them said, "Well, there is nothing but ruin and despair ahead of us. I shall take my family and move into a State where there are no negroes." Mr. Anderson laughed heartily, and said, "That reminds me of a man who was sitting on a cart tongue, on a hot summer day, when the steers were running away at full speed to get into a shade some half a mile distant. A man on the roadside called out, ' Why in the world don't you jump off?' The answer came back, from the cloud of dust that enveloped the fast disappearing team and cart, ' Why, my friend, it is all I can do to hold on.'"

He was a lawyer in the true sense of the word. He mastered his cases, seemingly, with the greatest ease, was never off his guard, confused, or intemperate in language, in the court-room. Once only I antagonized him myself, and sank beneath the weight of his heavy hand. I have often heard him in the conduct of his causes, and in debate with other learned and able members of the bar. He conducted and argued the Bank of Rome cases before me, when I occupied the bench. I have had ample opportunity to judge

of his powers, and I have never known him, in any case, to fall below the
standard of a great lawyer. It has been my good fortune to know many of
the common-law lawyers of Georgia. I have listened to learned and eloquent speeches from Judges James A. Merriwether, Eugenius A. Nisbet,
Barnard Hill, Augustus Reese, Francis Cone, O. A. Lochrane, A. R. Wright,
John W. H. Underwood, Colonels Samuel T. Bailey, W. K. deGraffenreid,
L. N. Whittle, W. H. Dabney, Seaborn Jones, William Dougherty, Nathan-
iel J. Hammond, and many others of like ability, who have finished their
life's work, and who have gone before us to the silent and unknown land;
but the argument of Mr. Anderson, in the murder case to which I have already referred, has not, within my memory, been excelled by any of them.
He had hardly run the allotted course of man. Life has been strikingly typ-
ified by the flight of a bird, that, fleeing from the storm without, flies in to
the brilliantly lighted banquet-room, where the happy guests are seated,
feasting at the table. The bird, dazed and bewildered, tarries but a moment,
then passes from the scene, out at the other window, into the darkness and
storm again. But whence it came, and whither it went, God alone knows.

Judge Anderson was a few years my senior, and yet I have lived long
enough to have the honor and pleasure of a personal acquaintance with every
member of this court. My memory does not extend back to its organization, but I have known all the judges. Excepting the present occupants of
the bench, I believe there are only three survivors. Life and death are mys-
teries; the one is as natural as the other. One brings us into active being,
and subjects us to the pleasures and pains of existence; the other is nature's
relief law, which exempts us from all its toils and burdens, when they are
no longer endurable. Plotinus, in his dying agony, in answer to a friendly
question, said, "I am struggling to liberate the divinity within me." Another, greater than he, in his last speech, after sentence of death had been
passed upon him, said, "It is now time that we depart, I to die, you to live;
but which has the better destiny is unknown to all, except God." We are
not without hope. I believe in immortality, and take comfort in nature's
evidences of the resurrection, of which that expressed in the beautiful lines
of William Herbert Carruth, is but one :

> "A carpet all of faded brown,
> On the gray bough a dove that grieves ;
> Death seemeth to have his own,
> But the spring violets nestle down
> Under the leaves.
>
> "A brow austere, and sad gray eyes,
> Locks in which care her silver weaves ;
> Hope seemeth tombed, no more to rise,
> But God he knoweth on what wise
> Love for love's sunshine waiting lies
> Under the leaves."

RESPONSE OF CHIEF JUSTICE SIMMONS.

In responding for the court I can but reflect upon the number of those whom death has, within the past two or three years, claimed from among the members of this bar. Death is ever in our midst, and it is perhaps natural that those who have lived longest should be first selected by the dread destroyer, and that among the older members of the bar will be found a majority of those who are most prominent; and yet, even then, it would seem that this bar has recently lost an unusually large number of those who had attained to eminence in the profession. And none more valued or more worthy of esteem than Clifford Anderson. In all that has been said of his ability and his virtues I most heartily concur. Myself for years a member of the Macon bar, and afterward judge of that circuit, I had ample opportunity to observe and note his merits and his shortcomings; and while the recollection of his many virtues rushes to my mind, my memory fails to record a fault. He was a true and loving husband, a kind and affectionate father, and a consistently good man. He possessed great oratorical and persuasive power, and before juries the influence of his speeches was remarkable. Through great natural ability, honest and faithful application and hard study, he became one of the most eminent jurists of this State. Relied upon by this court as one of its most efficient and valued advisers, he never failed to respond promptly and helpfully to all requests made upon him for information and assistance. Much of his kindness, his courtesy, his faithfulness, and his ability will doubtless pass with time, but some of his works will endure in the memory of a grateful people. He held many positions of trust and honor, and discharged acceptably his every duty and responsibility. His last official work, and one in which he displayed great skill and industry, was assisting in the revision of the Georgia code. He was appointed one of the commissioners, and to him was entrusted the annotation of the Civil Code, a work of lasting worth.

To him, whose abilities and virtues invoke the greatest admiration, we pay our tribute of affection and respect; and to his bereaved family we extend our sincerest sympathy. Let the memorial be filed, and a certified copy thereof be transmitted to the family of the deceased; and let a page of the minutes be inscribed to his memory.

INDEX.

ACCORD AND SATISFACTION.

Mistake as to contents of contract of release, when not ground for rescinding. *Jossey* v. *R. Co.* 439.

Note given in settlement, no defense to original cause of action, unless paid or unless expressly agreed' to be received as payment. *Brantley Co.* v. *Lee,* 478.

Release of master from liability for injuries to employee, acceptance of benefits under contract for, operates as, when. *Petty* v. *R. Co.* 666.

ACCOUNT. See *Limitations*.

ACTIONS. See *Administrators; Jurisdiction; Limitations; Parties; Pleading*.

Amendment, cause of action changed by. *Ga. R. Co.* v. *Roughton,* 604. Not changed by. *Hudgins* v. *Bloodworth,* 197.

Assumpsit, equitable petition here not treated as action of. *Schmitt* v. *Schneider,* 628.

Commencement of, filing petition is not, where process is not attached or waived. *Nicholas* v. *British America Co.* 621.

County, allegations sufficient to show liability of, for damages from work done on public road. *Barfield* v. *Macon County,* 386.

County sued on contract, petition must show compliance with law as to entering contract on minutes. *Milburn* v. *Glynn County,* 473.

Dismissal for conduct of one not a party and not subject to plaintiff's control, improper. *Bagwell* v. *R. Co.* 611.

Ejectment; sale of the land by plaintiff pending suit, not prevent him prosecuting to judgment, though vendee agreed that defendant take judgment. *Suwannee Turp. Co.* v. *Baxter,* 597.

Filing not commencement of, when. *Nicholas* v. *British America Co.* 621.

Guarantor, when sued without joining principal debtor or showing insolvency of principal. *Penn Tobacco Co.* v. *Leman,* 428.

Libel; allegation of special damage not necessary where charge was that a merchant had not paid his debts. *Brown* v. *Holton,* 431.

Municipal corporation sued on alleged contract, but no allegations showing terms of contract or that it was made in manner prescribed by charter, demurrer sustained. *Wiley* v. *Columbus,* 295.

Note sued on not indorsed to plaintiff before suit, no recovery. *Burch* v. *Daniel,* 256.

Process, failure to attach, to petition, not remedied by attaching it at or after return term. *Nicholas* v. *British America Co.* 621.

Process, irregularity in, or absence of, cured by waiver of. *Penn Tobacco Co.* v. *Leman,* 428.

Restitution as prerequisite to. *Petty* v. *R. Co.* 666.

ACTIONS — *continued.*

Same person both plaintiff and defendant. *Epps* v. *Story*, 318.

Services rendered and earnings delivered by woman to man while cohabiting with him under contract which, through his fraud, she believed to be equivalent of lawful marriage; remedy. *Schmitt* v. *Schneider*, 631.

Sheriff's bond, sufficiency of allegations in action on. *Velvin* v. *Austin*, 200.

Title of plaintiff not acquired until after suit brought, not support action. *Burch* v. *Daniel*, 258.

Trover, justice's court has no jurisdiction of. *Blocker* v. *Boswell*, 230; *Berger* v. *Saul*, 240.

ADMINISTRATORS AND EXECUTORS.

Action against himself in representative capacity, brought by one as an individual. *Weaver* v. *Cosby*, 318.

"Administrator," added to name, without more, treated as surplusage. *Marshall* v. *Charland*, 306.

Administration, dormant judgment as basis for. *Conyers* v. *Bruce*, 190.

Administration, existence of debt, as ground for, need not be conclusively shown; prima facie proof, sufficient. *Id.*

Administration, what estate necessary to authorize. *Lowery* v. *Powell*, 193.

Clerk of superior court, estate necessary to authorize vesting of administration in. *Id*, 192.

Deed by, to land held adversely by third person, conveyed no title. *Hanesley* v. *Bagley*, 348.

Foreign, action by; failure to file exemplification of letters of administration, not render judgment subject to collateral attack. *Marshall* v. *Charland*, 306.

ADMISSIONS. See *Evidence; Pleading.*

ADVERTISEMENT. See *Levy and Sale.*

AFFIDAVIT. See *Certiorari; Deeds; Homestead; Landlord and Tenant; Levy and Sale.*

AGENCY. See *Principal and Agent.*

ALIMONY. See *Divorce and Alimony.*

ALTERATION. See *Promissory Notes.*

AMENDMENT. See *Constitutional Law.*

Cause of action changed by, not allowed. *Ga. R. Co.* v. *Roughton*, 604.

Cause of action not changed by. *Hudgins* v. *Bloodworth*, 197.

Disallowed, is no part of the record. *Reid* v. *Wilson*, 424.

Discretion of court as to allowing plea amended. *Wynn*, 256.

Homestead or exemption proceeding, when amendment not allowed. *Ozburn* v. *Flournoy*, 704.

Judgment, amendment of, in justice's court, after affidavit of illegality filed and after appeal to superior court. *Bell* v. *Bowdoin*, 209.

Judgment dormant, amendable. (See dissent.) *Williams* v. *Merritt*, 217.

Limitation, action apparently barred by, amendment alleging facts showing it was not so barred, allowed. *Gentry* v. *Barron*, 172.

AMENDMENT — *continued.*

Materiality of, not such as to open petition to demurrer, where amendment was mere reference to exemplification already attached. *Little Rock Cooperage Co.* v. *Hodge*, 434.

Notice of allowance of, not given, no cause for striking. Continuance granted on account of, when. *Gentry* v. *Barron*, 172.

Party; head of family added as plaintiff to petition brought in name of beneficiaries of homestead. *Taylor* v. *James*, 328.

Schedule of property for exemption, whether amendable. *Ozburn* v. *Flournoy*, 706.

Time of; when not too late after evidence closed and during argument. *Hudgins* v. *Bloodworth*, 197.

APPEAL.

Homestead application, appeal not lie to ordinary's decision on demurrer to; certiorari is remedy. *Cunningham* v. *U. S. Loan Co.* 616.

Jurisdiction of subject-matter wanting in justice's court, that of superior court on appeal is no larger. *Berger* v. *Saul*, 240.

Lien of judgment, relatively to purchaser from defendant pending appeal, not affected by failure to have fi. fa. issued and docketed in ten days from date of judgment. *Crosby* v. *King Hardware Co.* 452.

Ordinary's decision not as judge of court of ordinary, appeal not lie to, and certiorari the remedy, when. *Cunningham* v. *U. S. Loan Co.* 618.

ARBITRATION AND AWARD.

Strict compliance with statute wanting, held not statutory but common-law award. *Osborn & Walcott* v. *Blanton*, 196.

Umpire; submission to two, with power to select umpire if they should disagree; award was not statutory. *Id.*

ARGUMENT. See *Practice in Superior Court.*

ARREST. See *Criminal Law.*

ASSIGNMENT. See *Banks; Insurance.*

ATTACHMENT.

Jurisdiction to obtain, by garnishment, the situs of the debt must be within the jurisdiction of the court. General rule that situs is where creditor is domiciled. *Central R. Co.* v. *Brinson*, 354.

Notice to tenant in possession, presumed prima facie from entry of levy. *Hiles Carver Co.* v. *King*, 180.

Seizure, entry of levy need not recite. *Id.*

ATTESTATION. See *Deeds; Judge; Mortgages.*

ATTORNEY AT LAW.

Disqualified to act as, on appeal before city council in case tried before him as mayor. *Holliman* v. *Hawkinsville*, 107.

Fee for bringing fund into court, application by party for allowance of, though joined in by attorney, is a proceeding in name and right of the party, and not of attorney. *Mohr-Weil Co.* v. *Russell*, 579.

ATTORNEY AT LAW—*continued.*

Fee for bringing fund into court, when not allowed. *Id.*

Fee for recovery of land, where client sold it pending suit, right of attorney to foreclose lien for, though vendee was not notified of lien. *Suwannee Turp. Co.* v. *Baxter*, 597.

Judge pro hac vice, appointment of attorney as, by clerk of court, not unconstitutional. *Bivins* v. *Bank*, 342.

Lien foreclosure ; whether different liens may be enforced in one proceeding. *Suwannee Turp. Co.* v. *Baxter*, 603.

AUDITOR'S REPORT.

Exceptions, discretion of court as to allowing filed after time for excepting expired. *Mohr-Weil Co.* v. *Russell*, 579.

Exceptions to, when sufficiently definite. *Id.* When not. *Id.* 587.

Jury trial on exceptions of fact, right to, in action at law. *Weaver* v. *Cosby,* 310.

AUGUSTA. See *Municipal Corporations.*

AWARD. See *Arbitration and Award.*

BAILMENT. See *Trusts.*

BANKRUPTCY.

Secured creditor's enforcement of lien in State court, debtor himself can not interfere with, by setting up bankruptcy. *Carter* v. *Bank,* 573.

Vendor's rights where goods sold have not been delivered to bankrupt or insolvent vendee. *Davis Sulphur Ore Co.* v. *Atlanta Co.* 610.

BANKS.

Assignment of deposit after depositor had given check to a different person, facts warranting payment of check first, though assignment was first presented. *Atl. Nat. Bk.* v. *George,* 682.

Cashier, power of, as to discounting paper; knowledge of, when notice to bank. *Morris* v. *Ga. Loan Co.* 21.

Notice to, by knowledge of cashier, as to want of consideration of note discounted by. *Id.* 12.

BILL OF LADING. See *Railroads.*

BILL OF REVIEW. See *Equity.*

BILLS AND NOTES. See *Promissory Notes.*

BOND. See *Title.*

Acceptance by sheriff, not shown by his attesting. *Fountain* v. *Napier,* 225.

Action on sheriff's, sufficiency of allegations in. *Velvin* v. *Austin,* 200.

Certiorari bond not approved, writ void. Approval not shown by magistrate's certificate that the costs had been paid. *Wingard* v. *R. Co.* 177.

Forthcoming, acceptance by sheriff, and not merely his attestation, is necessary, to make it binding. *Fountain* v. *Napier,* 225.

BOND — *continued.*

Garnishment, bond to dissolve, substantial compliance with statute, as to condition of. *Maddox* v. *Am. Trust Co.* 788.

Partner's, "as principal and as a member of" the firm, in case against firm, when good. *Id.* 787.

BOND FOR TITLE. See *Title.*

BROKER. See *Contracts; Principal and Agent.*

BUILDING AND LOAN ASSOCIATIONS.

Representations false as to methods of doing business and probable results of transaction evidenced by contract with, made to induce the making of the contract, no defense, when. *Angier* v. *Eq. B. & L. A.* 625.

Taxation of. See *Taxation.*

Usury and want of consideration, pleas of, here, good against general demurrer. *Gibson* v. *Interstate Asso.* 460.

Usury by, plea of, based on allegation that charter powers were beyond proper scope of such an association, but not alleging operations beyond scope of, bad. *Angier* v. *Eq. B. & L. A.* 628.

BURDEN OF PROOF. See *Evidence.*

CARRIERS. See *Railroads.*

CARTERSVILLE. See *Municipal Corporations.*

CERTIORARI.

Affidavit sufficiently followed the statutory form though "only" was omitted after "delay," and "verily" before "believe." *Elhridge* v. *Forsyth,* 156.

Answer of magistrate stating that objections were made and overruled, but not that they were those stated in petition, nor what they were, court should not consider them. *Knowles* v. *Coachman,* 356.

Bill of exceptions alleging merely that court erred in overruling, covers all errors distinctly set forth in the petition for certiorari. *Holliman* v. *Hawkinsville,* 107.

Bill of exceptions to refusal of, from conviction in municipal court, must be tendered in time required in criminal cases. *Barnett* v. *Atlanta,* 166.

Bond, approval not shown by magistrate's entry thereon that the costs had been paid. *Wingard* v. *R. Co.* 177.

Bond not approved, writ void. *Id.*

Error on trial which preceded appeal, not reviewable on certiorari after trial of appeal case. *Knowles* v. *Coachman,* 356.

Final judgment on, when not rendered. *Velvin* v. *Austin,* 200; *Knowles* v. *Coachman,* 356. When proper. *Wynn* v. *Irvine,* 288.

Jurisdiction of subject-matter wanting in lower court, case should be remanded with instruction to dismiss action. *Blocker* v. *Boswell,* 239.

Municipal court, conviction by, reversed on certiorari, reversal not reviewable by Supreme Court. *Mayor* v. *Wood,* 149.

CERTIORARI — *continued.*

Objections not verified by answer, not considered. *Knowles* v. *Coachman,*
        358

Ordinary's decision not as judge of court of ordinary, appeal not lie to,
        and certiorari the remedy, when. *Cunningham* v. *U. S. Loan Co.*
        618.

Verification of petition, where by but one of joint petitioners, he alone
        will be treated as plaintiff in. *Velvin* v. *Austin,* 200.

Void where issued in absence of duly approved bond. *Wingard* v. *R. Co.*
        177.

CHARGE OF COURT.

Accomplice, corroboration of, erroneous charge as to. *Chapman* v. *State,*
        158.

Arrest without warrant, error in charging as to. *Delegal* v. *State,* 518.

Contentions of parties presumed to have been correctly stated by, in ab-
        sence of certificate of judge to the contrary. *Robinson* v. *State,*
        506.

Corroborating circumstances, instruction as to, here, not error as against
        accused. *Haines* v. *State,* 526.

"Crossing law," as to checking speed of train, not error to give in charge,
        though crossing was only half a mile from starting-point. *Central
        R. Co.* v. *Hall,* 367.

Declarations, dying, error in charging as to. *Bush* v. *State,* 125.

Defense not given due prominence. *Smith* v. *State,* 480.

Delivery of deed, what ineffectual as, charge as to, discussed. *Jenkins* v.
        R. Co. 35.

Evidence not warranting, error to give. *Delegal* v. *State,* 518.

Evidence "tending to show" a certain fact, error here to charge that there
        was. *Chapman* v. *State,* 160.

Evidence, what sufficient to corroborate accomplice, erroneous charge as
        to. *Id.* 158.

History of the litigation prior to the trial in progress, when not error to
        give to the jury. *Conley* v. *Redwine,* 641.

Homicide, fears as defense, charge that they should be the fears of a brave
        man, not approved, but no reversal under facts here. *Dover* v.
        State, 485.

Homicide in resisting arrest, erroneous instructions as to. *Delegal* v. *State,*
        518.

Homicide: Penal Code, §§ 70, 71, properly given in charge with § 73, when.
        Dover v. *State,* 486.

Homicide: Penal Code, § 73, error to give in charge, under facts here.
        Lowman v. *State,* 501 ; *Delegal* v. *State,* 518.

Impeachment; error to tell jury they should believe witness if not im-
        peached by one of the three methods prescribed in the code.
        Chapman v. *State,* 158.

Impeachment of witnesses, instructions as to. *Smith* v. *State,* 480.

Inapplicable, required new trial. *Hudgins* v. *Bloodworth,* 198.

Manslaughter, facts not authorizing charge on. *Channell* v. *State,* 152.

CHARGE OF COURT — *continued.*

Manslaughter voluntary, charge as to, where not involved, when cause new trial and when not. *Robinson* v. *State*, 506.

Manslaughter voluntary, facts authorizing charge on. *Sumner* v. *State*, 142.

Opinion as to what had been proved, charge that there was evidence "tending to show" a given fact. *Chapman* v. *State*, 161.

Overlooking theory of defense until about to conclude, and manner of referring to it then, required reversal. *Smith* v. *State*, 480.

Prisoner's statement, omission to charge as to theory presented by, when not error. *Channell* v. *State*, 153.

Punishment, error in charge as to discretion in regard to. *Echols* v. *State*, 508.

"Tending to show," used in reference to evidence, when error. *Chapman* v. *State*, 160.

Theory of defense not mentioned until about to conclude, and then briefly, with remark that court "did not think" to call attention to it; reversal. *Smith* v. *State*, 480.

Threats, charge as to, not warranted by evidence; also intimation as to what was proved. *Chapman* v. *State*, 160.

CHARTER. See *Corporations; Municipal Corporations.*

CLAIM. See *Garnishment.*

Injunction against, when granted. *Dawson* v. *Eq. Mge. Co.* 389.

Party to execution can not claim the property on which it is levied. Rule applied where fi. fa. was against A "as agent for" B, and A claimed personally. *Wynn* v. *Irvine's Ga. Music House*, 287.

CODE.

Heading of chapter, by codifiers, not treated as part of the legislation of the State. *Blocker* v. *Boswell*, 235.

CODE SECTIONS — CIVIL.

35 et seq. Irregularities in registration, when not disqualified from voting. *Cole* v. *McClendon*, 187.

60. See 35.

72. Not apply to contest of election under local option liquor law. *Drake* v. *Drewry*, 403.

229, par. 5. Demurrer because it did not appear that alleged removal had been judicially ascertained, held good. *Channell* v. *State*, 150.

343. Action against county on contract, dismissed on demurrer where petition did not show that the contract had been entered on the minutes of the proper authorities. *Milburn* v. *Glynn County*, 473.

400. Failure of county authorities to comply with, by making required financial statement to grand jury, not affect validity of tax levy. *Atl. Nat. B. & L. A.* v. *Stewart*, 82.

522. Persons through whose land the road will not run are not entitled to the notice here prescribed. *Huff* v. *Donehoo*, 638.

589. Employment of inspector of roads and bridges for county, not authorized prior to act of 1897 as to. *Turner* v. *Fulton County*, 634.

CODE SECTIONS—CIVIL—*continued.*

1541 et seq. Who entitled to vote at election held under. Sufficiency of allegations in petition contesting election. *Cole* v. *McClendon*, 184.

The words "city, town, or any other place," treated as surplusage. *Id.* 186.

Ordinary, before declaring result of election, must pass on contest and decide all questions affecting validity of election. (See dissent.) *Drake* v. *Drewry*, 399.

1543. That liquor-selling is already prohibited in part of county, not prevent residents of that part from voting at election held under this law. *Cole* v. *McClendon*, 186.

The proviso in, treated as surplusage. *Id.*

1545. See 1541.

1546. See 1541.

1642. Ordinary's certificate, prima facie evidence for defendant in prosecution or doing business without license. *Holliman* v. *Hawkinsville*, 107.

Ordinary's certificate need not state that the disability resulted from service in the Confederate army. *Id.* 110.

Person entitled to certificate under, may conduct different lines of business under, without paying license tax to municipal corporation; and his agent may operate under. *Hartfield* v. *Columbus*, 112.

1883. Forfeiture not allowed to be set up collaterally. *Ga. Nor. R. Co.* v. *Tifton, T. & G. R. Co.* 766.

2114. Insurable interest, beneficiary need not have, when. *Union Frat. League* v. *Walton*, 3.

2116. See 2114.

2167, par. 6. Where charter authorizes construction of railroad "to" a city, the road may enter the city and cross another railroad. *Waycross A. L. R. Co.* v. *Offerman & W. R. Co.* 827.

2173. Cited in construing constitutional provision as to defeating or lessening competition. *State* v. *Central R. Co.* 729.

2176. See 2173.

Injunction against interference with route by locating another line within prohibited distance. *Ga. No. R. Co.* v. *Tifton, T. & G. R. Co.* 766

Applies only to railroads which run practically parallel with each other. *Waycross A. L. R. Co.* v. *Offerman & W. R. Co.* 828.

2179. See 2173.

2184. Sale of stock and combination of street-railroads, not illegal here. *Trust Company* v. *State*, 754.

2219. See 2167.

2222. Applied though crossing was only half a mile from starting-point. *Central R. Co.* v. *Hall*, 367.

2224. See 2222.

2276. Did not affect stipulations here as to delivery to-connecting carrier. *McElveen* v. *R. Co.* 255.

2317, 2318. Question as to constitutionality of, not decided. Facts not warranting recovery under. *Id.* 249.

CODE SECTIONS—CIVIL—*continued.*

2388. Cited in discussing tax act as to building and loan associations. *Atlanta Nat. Asso.* v. *Stewart,* 101.

2398. See 2388.

2457. Petition for alimony for support of wife and family dependent on husband, pending divorce suit, may be filed in vacation. *Ray,* 465.

2461. See 2457.

2605. Doubtful whether minor is subject to prosecution for vagrancy. *Teasley* v. *State,* 283.

2613. Release in consideration of benefits to be received by employee when injured, when not in conflict with this section. *Petty* v. *R. Co.* 670.

2689. Cited in enumerating grounds upon which judgments may be treated as void. *Suwannee Turp. Co.* v. *Baxter,* 602.

2693, par. 6. Letters here did not amount to new promise; debt not described with reasonable certainty. *Paille* v. *Plant,* 248.

2694. Performance here took promise out of the statute. *English* v. *Richards Co.* 637.

2724. "Justice," in this section is used as being interchangeable with judge. *Strauss* v. *Maddox,* 223.

2766. Sheriff's acceptance of bond, and not merely his attestation, is necessary, to render it binding. *Fountain* v. *Napier,* 225.

2771. Security deed passed title though no bond to reconvey given; mode of enforcing rights under. *Jewell* v. *Walker,* 242.
Levy and sale without reconveyance of land conveyed as security, void, but purchaser was subrogated to grantee's rights, and could defeat ejectment by setting up possession under the deed. *Ashley* v. *Cook,* 654.

2779. Lien of judgment, relatively to purchaser from defendant pending appeal, not affected by failure to have fi. fa. issued and entered in ten days from date of judgment. *Crosby* v. *King Hardware Co.* 452.

2790. Priority not given to bailee in distribution of assets of insolvent bailee entrusted with notes for collection and who failed to turn over proceeds. *Tiedeman* v. *Imp. Fert. Co.* 663.

2814. Lien of attorney for plaintiff in ejectment, not defeated by plaintiff's sale of the land pending suit. *Suwannee Turp. Co.* v. *Baxter,* 601.

2827. Ordinary acts judicially in setting apart homestead under, and his judgment is not subject to collateral attack. *Marcrum* v. *Washington,* 300.

2828. See 2827.
Exemption for support of dependent females can be taken only from applicant's own property. *Sutton* v. *Rosser,* 206.
Confers jurisdiction upon the ordinary, not the court of ordinary. *Cunningham* v. *U. S. Loan Co.* 618.

2836. Cited in discussion as to when appeal lies from decision of ordinary. *Id.*

2838. See 2836.

2850. Not apply to "pony homestead." *Marcrum* v. *Washington,* 297.

CODE SECTIONS — CIVIL — *continued.*

2866 et seq. Receiving and recording schedule under, is ministerial, not judicial act; validity may be collaterally attacked. *Id.* 296.

Amendment of schedule not allowed, when. *Ozburn* v. *Flournoy*, 706.

2872. On trial of issue formed where property levied on is claimed to be exempt as "pony homestead," the validity of the exemption may be collaterally attacked. *Marcrum* v. *Washington*, 300.

2876. Oral agreement to pay maximum legal rate compounded monthly, invalid. *Mohr-Weil Co.* v. *Russell*, 579.

2998. Fi. fa. against A "as agent for" B, treated as against A personally. *Wynn* v. *Irvine's Ga. Music House*, 287.

3027. Knowledge of officer of bank that note discounted by it was without consideration, when notice to bank. *Morris* v. *Ga. Loan Co.* 21.

3077. Applied to insurance policy. *Id.* 20.

3132. Facts constituting a tenancy from year to year; notice necessary to terminate tenancy. *Robinson* v. *Simons*, 361.

3133. See 3132.

3189. See 2790.

3209. Cited in discussing meaning of "perfect title" as used in § 4927. *Wilcox Lumber Co.* v. *Bullock*, 534.

3390. Estate necessary to authorize vesting of administration. *Lowery* v. *Powell*, 193.

3424. See 2790.

3447. One sued individually on his personal debt can not set off debt of firm of which he is a member, when. *Bishop* v. *Mathews*, 790.

3457. Possession held adversely to administrator, purchaser got no title, *Hanesley* v. *Bagley*, 348.

3465. See 3390.

3521. Failure of foreign administrator to file copy of letters of administration before bringing suit, not render judgment subject to collateral attack. *Marshall* v. *Charland*, 307.

3522. See 3521.

3551. Damages for breach of purchaser's contract to pay draft and take goods from depot; value not recoverable where burned in depot while title was in seller. *Mountain City Mill Co.* v. *Butler*, 471.

Notice of intention to resell not alleged, nor tender of goods to vendee, demand for payment and refusal, demurrer sustained. *Davis Sulphur Co.* v. *Atlanta Co.* 607.

3592. Operates as limitation of actions of trover. *Blocker* v. *Boswell*, 237.

3621. Authorizes judge of court of another State to take acknowledgment of deed. *Cunningham* v. *Barker*, 613.

3656. Burden of proof on parties seeking to show that note and mortgage under seal, reciting valuable consideration, had none. *Weaver* v. *Cosby*, 313.

3668. Cited in construing constitutional provision as to defeating or lessening competition. *State* v. *Central R. Co.* 722, 725.

3701. What sufficient as plea of non est factum. *Jewell* v. *Walker*, 245.

3702. Non est factum, requisites of plea. *Mozley* v. *Reagan*, 193.

CODE SECTIONS — CIVIL — *continued.*

3720. Accord and satisfaction by giving note, no defense to original cause of action, unless paid or expressly agreed to be received as payment. *Brantley Co.* v. *Lee*, 479.

3761. Dormancy not prevented by minority of plaintiff. *Williams* v. *Merritt*, 214.
Dormancy not prevented by receipts of payments, entered on fi. fa. by plaintiff. *Blue* v. *Collins*, 342.

3769.. Indebtedness by A to B, and an extension of credit to B by A by reason thereof, constitutes a mutual account. *Reid* v. *Wilson*, 428.

3773. Applied to beneficiaries of homestead. *Taylor* v. *James*, 338.

3779. See 3761.

3784. See 3761.

3788. See 2693, par. 6.

3817. Liability of master for servant's acts in preventing damage or loss to master. Petition here good against demurrer. *Thompson* v. *Wright*, 466.

3819. Enumeration of exceptions in, is exhaustive. *Ridgeway* v. *Downing Co.* 595.

3837. Allegation of special damage not necessary where charge was that a merchant had not paid his debts. *Brown* v. *Holton*, 433.

3898. Applied to suit for mesne profits. *Taylor* v. *James*, 338.

3898 - 9. See 3592.

3938. Purchasers at foreclosure sale here obtained good title, though they had notice of fraud by which defendant had acquired title. *McMillan* v. *Hunnicutt*, 704.

3974. Rescission for mistake as to contents of writing, not granted, under facts here. *Jossey* v. *R. Co.* 447.

3982. See 3974.

3983. See 3974.

3984. See 3974.

3987. Want of diligence, as bar to relief. *Donaldson* v. *Roberts*, 832.

3988. See 3987.

4037. Title under parol agreement, when good defense to ejectment. *Epps* v. *Story*, 303.

4039. See 4037.

4045. Mayor before whom case tried, disqualified from appearing as attorney in the case on appeal before city council. *Holliman* v. *Hawkinsville*, 107.

4047. Action for loss of service of daughter from injury, error to dismiss because she refused to submit to court's order for examination of her person. *Bagwell* v. *R. Co.* 611.

4205. See 2779.

4208. Does not authorize judge of county court to administer oath for warrant to remove tenant at sufferance, nor to issue such a warrant. *Griswold* v. *Rutherford*, 399.

4213. See 4208.

4232. Jurisdiction over homesteads was not conferred on court of ordinary, but on ordinary. *Cunningham* v. *U. S. Loan Co.* 617.

CODE SECTIONS — CIVIL — *continued.*

4251. Cited in discussing distinction between the ordinary and court of ordinary. *Id.*

4329. Constitutional. *Bivins* v. *Bank,* 345.

4334. Evidence "tending to show" a certain fact, error to charge that there was. *Chapman* v. *State,* 161.

4454. Not apply to decision of ordinary not as court of ordinary. *Cunningham* v. *U. S. Loan Co.* 618.

4595. Error to refuse to allow jury to pass upon exceptions to auditor's report in law case. *Weaver* v. *Cosby,* 312.

4611. Applied where fi. fa. was against A "as agent for" B, and claim was filed by A in his own right. *Wynn* v. *Irvine's Ga. Music House,* 287.

4634. Certiorari, not appeal, the remedy for error in sustaining demurrer to application for homestead. *Cunningham* v. *Loan Co.* 619.

4638. Form here prescribed was sufficiently followed though "only" was omitted after "delay," and "verily" before "believe." *Ethridge* v. *Forsyth,* 157.

Petition joint but verified by one only, he will be treated as sole plaintiff in certiorari. *Velvin* v. *Austin,* 200.

4718. Bond in case against a firm, executed by one "as principal and as member of" the firm, good. *Maddox* v. *Am. T. & B. Co.* 787.

Substantial compliance with, as to condition stated in bond. *Id.*

Non-resident defendant's act in dissolving garnishment was equivalent to personal service. *Moore* v. *Kelly & Jones Co.* 801.

4720. Claim should be filed in the court which has control of the fund. *Page* v. *Pitt,* 559.

4743. Establishment of copy of lost pleadings in justice's court under. Admissibility of certified copy as evidence in superior court. *Bell* v. *Bowdoin,* 211.

4753. See 4743.

4790. Notice required by, need not be in writing. *Ralph* v. *Ward,* 363.

4813. Judge of county court can not administer oath provided for in this section. *Griswold* v. *Rutherford,* 398.

4814. See 4813.

4815. See 4813.

4816. See 4813.

4848. Guardian ad litem of minor defendants could consent to trial at first term. *McMillan* v. *Hunnicutt,* 700.

4881. Cited in enumerating sections which provide for fast writ of error. *Gordon,* 262.

4927. "Perfect title," meaning of. *Wilcox Lumber Co.* v. *Bullock,* 532.

4943–4. Seem to give attorneys the right to consolidate suits for foreclosure of their liens. *Suwannee Turp. Co.* v. *Baxter,* 603.

4960. Time of commencing suit is date of filing, if law as to process and service is complied with; filing alone does not commence. *Nicholas* v. *Assurance Co.* 623.

4973. See 4960.

4974. See 4960.

CODE SECTIONS — CIVIL — *continued.*

4994. Absence of process not remedied by attaching process at or after return term. *Nicholas* v. *British America Co.* 624.

5057. Discretion of court as to allowing plea amended. *Wynn*, 256.

5068. Amendment by mere reference to exemplification attached to petition was not so material as to open petition to demurrer. *Little Rock Cooperage Co.* v. *Hodge*, 435.

5071. Verdict against defendant in default ; error to set aside because default was due to misunderstanding between him and his counsel. *Moore* v. *Kelly & Jones Co.* 801.

5099. Amendment here as to manner in which injury occurred added new cause of action. *Ga. R. Co.* v. *Roughton*, 604.

5109. See 4994.

5113. Judgment amended in justice's court after affidavit of illegality filed and after appeal to superior court. *Bell* v. *Bowdoin*, 210.

5125. Mistake of clerk of trial court in certifying as to date of filing bill of exceptions, how rectified. *McDaniel* v. *Columbus Fert. Co.* 285.

5179. Declarations of alleged principal, when not admissible against alleged accessory, as res gestæ. *Howard* v. *State*, 141.

5202. Parol evidence admitted to explain meaning of "O. K." in writing. *Penn Tobacco Co.* v. *Leman*, 431.

5214–15. See 4743.

5247. Handwriting offered as standard of comparison, not proved genuine by circumstances here. *McCombs* v. *State*, 498.

5292. Admitting proof of contradictory statements as to irrelevant matter here required new trial. *Hudgins* v. *Bloodworth*, 199.

5291–5293. These methods of impeachment are not exclusive ; error to confine jury to them. *Chapman* v. *State*, 163.

5295. "Impeached," in this section, is used as being synonymous with "attacked." *Smith* v. *State*, 480.

5362. Disqualification of juror is not proper ground of motion to set aside judgment. *Mize* v. *Americus Co.* 359.
One not a party can not move to set aside judgment. *Suwannee Turp. Co.* v. *Baxter*, 603.

5363. Arrest of judgment in appeal case, for want of jurisdiction, motion for, in term when rendered, was in time. *Berger* v. *Saul*, 240.

5421. Lawful seizure and notice presumed prima facie from entry of levy, though not recited. *Hiles Carver Co.* v. *King*, 181.

5427. Gross inadequacy of price at sheriff's sale, and other facts shown in proceeding to set aside sale, which rendered nonsuit error. *Suttles* v. *Sewell*, 711.

5432. See 2771.

5455. Purchaser without notice protected where advertisement of sale insufficient, though he be plaintiff in fi. fa. *Conley* v. *Redwine*, 646.

5458. Advertisement insufficient where the fourth publication was on the Monday preceding sale day. *Conley* v. *Redwine*, 641.

5471. Applied to purchaser at void sale under judgment in favor of grantee in security deed. *Ashley* v. *Cook*, 658.

5472. Estoppel to attack sale as void, when applied to grantor in security deed but not to owner of equity of redemption. *Id.* 660.

CODE SECTIONS—CIVIL—*continued.*

5513. Each bill of exceptions constitutes one "case." *In re Kenan*, 821.

5536, par. 4. Alteration of record, when shown by ordering transcript sent up, under this section. *Fountain* v. *Napier*, 226.

5540. Duty of clerk as to docketing. When case docketed to wrong term will be transferred, and when dismissed. *Gordon*, 262.

Fast writ will not lie to order granted on petition to enforce by attachment a previous judgment for alimony. *Id.*

5554. Placing bill of exceptions in hands of clerk within time prescribed for filing was sufficient, though clerk did not mark it filed. *McDaniel* v. *Columbus Fert. Co.* 284.

5558. See 5540.

5567. See 5125.

5659. See 5068.

5729. No recovery by landowner for erection of jail on adjacent lot. *Long* v. *Elberton*, 30.

5732. Special act prohibiting sale of liquors, and not excepting domestic wines, violates. *O'Brien* v. *State*, 51; *Embry* v. *State*, 61; *Tinsley* v. *State*, 823.

5733. Duty to declare unconstitutional act void. *Atlanta Nat. B. & L. Asso.* v. *Stewart*, 97.

5737-8. See 35.

5799. Cited in construing § 5800. *State* v. *Central R. Co.* 734; *Trust Co.* v. *State*, 752.

5803. Cited in construing § 5800. *State* v. *Central R. Co.* 735.

Construed with reference to competition between railroad companies. *State* v. *Central R. Co.* 716. Purchase of stock of corporation by another corporation. *Trust Co. of Ga.* v. *State*, 736.

Motives of those at whose instance the Governor ordered suit filed to prevent violation of, not considered. *Id.*

5831. See 4251.

5850. See 4329.

5852. See 4251.

5856. Justice's court has no jurisdiction of trover suit. *Blocker* v. *Boswell*, 230.

5862. Not apply to case from municipal court of violation of town ordinance. *Holliman* v. *Hawkinsville*, 108.

5883. Tax on stock of building and loan association which had not been advanced on, imposed in lieu of other taxes, unconstitutional as to the latter provision. *Ga. State B. & L. A.* v. *Savannah*, 63.

Tax on gross premiums of insurance companies, not property tax so as to require ad valorem system applied. *Mut. Reserve Fund Life Asso.* v. *Augusta*, 73.

City ordinance imposing tax only on non-resident companies, void. *Id.*

5884. See 5883.

5886. See 5883.

5887. See 5883.

5892. Does not authorize levy of tax to pay for inspection of roads and bridges. *Turner* v. *Fulton County*, 634.

CODE SECTIONS — CIVIL — *continued.*

5912. See 2827.

5913. See 2850.

5974, par. 3. Not prohibit taxation by State of choses in action, wherever owned, though debtor be a non-resident. *Atl. Nat. Asso.* v. *Stewart*, 82.

CODE SECTIONS — PENAL.

64. Facts authorizing instruction on voluntary manslaughter. *Sumner* v. *State*, 143.

65. See 64.

70. Partly inapplicable to facts here, and not error to fail to give in charge. *Lowman* v. *State*, 503.

70–71. When properly given in charge with § 73. *Dover* v. *State*, 486.

·73. Error to give in charge, under facts here. *Lowman* v. *State*, 502; *Delegal* v. *State*, 524.

136. One may be convicted as accessory before the fact to an attempt to commit arson. *Howard* v. *State*, 137.

137. See 136.

187. Mere refusal or neglect to pay over funds is not embezzlement. Discussion as to what constitutes the offense. *Robinson* v. *State*, 564.

233. Indictment under, for forging order for a thing not money, and not alleging that the thing (meat) was of some value, fatally defective. *Johnson* v. *State*, 268. See *McCombs* v. *State*, 500.

354. Joint action of two or more necessary to constitute riot. Common intent not shown by circumstances here. *Tripp* v. *State*, 489.
Facts constituting riot; sufficiency of indictment. *Green* v. *State*, 538.

387. Seduction by persuasion and promises of marriage, "and by other false and fraudulent means," alleged, without specifying what the latter means were, demurrer good. (See dissent.) *Langston* v. *State*, 154.

390. Act must take place where may be seen by more than one, to warrant conviction under this section. *Morris* v. *State*, 351.
Authority of municipal corporation to punish for sale of liquor at barroom on Sunday. *Kassell* v. *Savannah*, 494.

420. Trainmaster acting under orders from superintendent was not indictable under this section. *Craven* v. *State*, 266.

422. Prevents, except where authorized by express legislation, municipal corporations from punishing keepers of barrooms for selling liquor thereat on Sunday. *Kassell* v. *Savannah*, 494.

438. Keeping liquor in buggy, near church, though for sick wife, illegal. *Bice* v. *State*, 117.

441. See 438.

453, par. 3. Doubtful whether applicable to minors. Facts not warranting conviction under. *Teasley* v. *State*, 282.

625. Irregularity in registration, as affecting right to vote. *Cole* v. *Mc-Clendon*, 187.

629. See 625.

CODE SECTIONS — PENAL — *continued.*

670. Offense committed by promise, combined with pretense as to existing title to land, inducing giving of note, though maker insolvent. *Holton* v. *State*, 129.

725. Church is not "public building," within meaning of this section. *Collum* v. *State*, 531.

883. Affidavit need not minutely describe offense ; what sufficient in larceny case. *Brown*, 570.

896. Error to give this section in charge on trial for homicide committed in resisting arrest attempted by private person without warrant. *Delegal* v. *State*, 521.

900. When private person may arrest without warrant. *Id.*

911. Admissibility of writing in which magistrate, after commitment trial, set out from memory what purported to be testimony taken thereon. *Haines* v. *State*, 528.

929. See 387.

Indictment charging unlawful sale of spirituous and intoxicating liquors, too general to cover violation of local liquor laws here. *O'Brien* v. *State*, 52.

Language of indictment is to be interpreted liberally in favor of the State. *Green* v. *State*, 540.

972. Challenge to array, when proper. Challenge on account of feeling of jurors should be to the polls. *Thompson* v. *State*, 272.

991. Additions to language of, in charge here, not error as against accused. *Haines* v. *State*, 526.

998. What admissible as res gestæ, in a dying declaration. *Bush* v. *State*, 123.

1000. Conversation and conduct of the parties, when admissible in a dying declaration. *Id.*

1025–1027. These methods of impeachment are not exclusive ; error to confine jury to them. *Chapman* v. *State*, 163.

1036. Error in charge as to discretion of court in regard to punishment. *Echols* v. *State*, 508.

1076. Not apply to case from municipal court of violation of town ordinance. *Holliman* v. *Hawkinsville*, 109.

1099. Fee of solicitor-general in Supreme Court in riot case, $15. *In re Kenan*, 820.

One fee for each bill of exceptions, though more than one excepting party. *Id.*

1101. Clerk's certificate must show insolvency of each plaintiff in error, though there be more than one in the bill of exceptions. *Id.* 821.

1247. Sufficiency of description of offense, in affidavit for search warrant, as basis for accusation. *Brown* v. *State*, 572.

COLUMBUS. See *Municipal Corporations.*

COMMON CARRIERS. See *Railroads.*

COMPROMISE. See *Accord and Satisfaction.*

CONFEDERATE SOLDIERS. See *Taxation.*

CONFESSION. See *Evidence.*

CONSIDERATION. See *Contracts; Deeds; Promissory Notes.*

CONSTITUTIONAL LAW.

Amendment of unconstitutional act here did not vitalize it. *Tinsley* v.
    State, 822.

Combination agreement between railroads, where general result is benefit
    to public at large, though it lessen or defeat competition at some
    points, is not invalid as tending to defeat competition. *State* v.
    Central R. Co. 716; *Trust Co.* v. *State,* 736.

Common law looked to in construing. *State* v. *Central R. Co.* 728.

Competition, defeating or lessening, provision as to, construed. *Id.* 716;
    Trust Co. of Ga. v. *State,* 736.

Construction of constitutional provisions, rules as to. *Blocker* v. *Boswell,*
    232; *State* v. *Central R. Co.* 728.

Conviction under unconstitutional statute, void, though based on plea of
    guilty. Person convicted should be discharged, on habeas cor-
    pus. *Moore* v. *Wheeler,* 62.

Corporations, purchase of shares of one by another. *Trust Co. of Ga.* v.
    State, 736.

Damage to private property by erection of jail on adjacent lot. *Long* v.
    Elberton, 29.

General and special laws, conflict of, where special act prohibiting sale of
    liquors did not except domestic wines. *O'Brien* v. *State,* 51; *Em-
    bry* v. *State,* 61; *Tinsley* v. *State,* 822.

Homestead and exemption. See cases under that head.

Judge pro hac vice, statute providing for appointment of attorney as, by
    clerk of court, constitutional. *Birins* v. *Bank,* 342.

Jurisdiction of justice's court, not extend to trover suits. *Blocker* v. *Bos-
    well,* 230; *Berger* v. *Saul,* 240.

Jury trial, right to, in law case. *Weaver* v. *Cosby,* 310.

Legislative construction considered in construing. *State* v. *Central R. Co.*
    729.

Monopoly, meaning of constitutional provision as to. *Id.* 716.

Part unconstitutional, rendered whole act void. *O'Brien* v. *State,* 51; *Em-
    bry* v. *State,* 61.

Special act in conflict with general law. *Id.;* *Tinsley* v. *State,* 822.

Taxation, and exemption from. See *Taxation.*

CONTRACTS. See *Insurance; Promissory Notes; Sales.*

Assessment for paving, contract to pay city for share of, binding though
    assessment was illegal. *Floyd* v. *Atl. Bkg. Co.* 778.

Bond for title. See *Title.*

Broker's commission for negotiating loan, contract for, not authorize re-
    covery, under facts here. *Hawesley* v. *Bagley,* 346.

Capacity to contract as an "association," estoppel to deny. *Petty* v. *R.
    Co.* 666.

Cohabitation agreement, recovery of property bought with joint earnings,
    and for services rendered, sought by woman induced to cohabit
    under, by fraudulent representation that it was a lawful marriage.
    Schmitt v. *Schneider,* 628.

CONTRACTS—*continued.*

Combination agreement between railroad companies, when not illegal.
State v. *Central R. Co.* 716; *Trust Co.* of *Ga.* v. *State,* 737.

Consideration, benefit to property-owner from paving street, sufficient to
uphold contract to pay city his share of illegal assessment for.
Floyd v. *Atl. Bkg. Co.* 778.

Consideration, failure of, total, not partial, here. (Machinery defective
and not repaired as promised.) *Otis* v. *Holmes,* 775.

Consideration of contract for release of master by employee from liability
for injuries, when sufficient. *Petty* v. *R. Co.* 666.

Consideration, plea of total failure of, includes partial failure. *Otis* v.
Holmes, 775.

Consideration, presumption as to, where recited in contract under seal.
Weaver v. *Cosby,* 313.

Corporation's, not binding on another corporation because the stock in
both is owned by the same persons. *Waycross R. Co.* v. *Offerman
R. Co.* 827.

County's; petition in action against county on, must show compliance
with law as to entering on minutes. *Milburn* v. *Glynn County,* 473.

Division of land among tenants in common, agreement for, when binding.
Ralph v. *Ward,* 363.

Exchange of products, contract for, not broken where no offer made on
the one side, nor refusal on the other. *Brown* v. *Drake,* 179.

Execution of, denied, or alteration alleged, where sued on; sufficiency of
plea. *Mozley* v. *Reagan,* 182; *Jewell* v. *Walker,* 245. Prima facie
proof of execution sufficient to authorize introduction of. *Id.*

Guaranty by seller, to one buying for purpose of reselling, to maintain
price for specified season, not apply when buyer did not sell during that season. *Atl. Bot. Co.* v. *Hutchinson,* 550.

Guaranty, facts showing. *Penn Tobacco Co.* v. *Leman,* 428.

Indorsement of non-negotiable order, what necessary to render liable on.
Jossey v. *Rushin,* 319.

Interest, contract not in writing, to pay maximum legal rate compounded
monthly, invalid. *Mohr-Weil Co.* v. *Russell,* 579.

Loan, contract to make, if applicant's title to security good, refusal to consummate not justified by alleged cloud on title, under facts here.
Hanesley v. *Bagley,* 346.

Marriage relation, contract intended to promote dissolution of, void.
Birch v. *Anthony,* 349.

Mistake as to contents of, when not ground for rescinding. *Jossey* v. *R.
Co.* 439. See *Petty* v. *R. Co.* 675.

Monopoly, contract tending to create, meaning of constitutional provisions
as to. *State* v. *Central R. Co.* 716.

Municipal corporation sued on alleged contract, but no allegations showing terms of contract or that it was made in manner prescribed
by charter, demurrer sustained. *Wiley* v. *Columbus,* 295.

Negligence, exemption of master from liability to servant for, release contract here did not conflict with law as to. *Petty* v. *R. Co.* 666.

Novation as to annuity, shown by facts here. *Epps* v. *Story,* 302.

CONTRACTS—*continued.*

Offer to comply by one side, or refusal by the other, not shown, no breach of contract for exchange of products. *Brown* v. *Drake,* 179.

Operate manufacturing plant, to collect debt from income, contract that creditor should; rights of parties under. *Mohr-Weil Co.* v. *Russell,* 580.

Parol evidence, as affecting written contract. See *Evidence.*

Parol, for title to land, when irrevocable. *Epps* v. *Story,* 302.

Partnership dissolution, contract for, whether executory. *Phelps* v. *State,* 115.

Performance by one of the parties prevented by the other, failure to perform not operate as rescission. *Epps* v. *Story,* 302.

Pleading; when copy of contract need not be attached as exhibit. *Penn Tobacco Co.* v. *Leman,* 428.

Public policy as to agreements in restraint of competition. *State* v. *Central R. Co.* 723.

Public policy, contract intended to promote dissolution of marriage relation, contrary to. *Birch* v. *Anthony,* 349.

Public policy not contravened by contract here for release of master from liability for injuries to servant. *Petty* v. *R. Co.* 666.

Railroad ticket limitation as to time of use, when binding. *Central R. Co.* v. *Ricks,* 339.

Recording contract with county, effect of failure to comply with law as to. *Milburn* v. *Glynn County,* 478.

Release of master from liability for injuries to employee, contract for, when valid. *Petty* v. *R. Co.* 666.

Representation false, as to corporation's methods of business and as to probable result of transaction with, no defense to action on contract with, when. *Angier* v. *Eq. B. & L. A.* 625.

Rescission, failure to perform, not operate as, where performance prevented by the other party. *Epps* v. *Story,* 302.

Rescission for fraud, when tender back necessary. *Petty* v. *R. Co.* 666.

Rescission for mistake as to contents, when not granted. *Jossey* v. *R. Co.* 439. See *Petty* v. *R. Co.* 675.

Restraint of trade, law as to contracts in, discussed. *State* v. *Central R. Co.* 722.

Sealed, presumption as to consideration of. *Weaver* v. *Cosby,* 313.

Statute of frauds, as affecting. See *Frauds, Statute of.*

Subscription to corporation. See *Corporations.*

Title, bond for. See *Title.*

Usurious. See *Usury.*

CONTRACTOR. See *Negligence.*

CORPORATIONS. See *Banks; Building and Loan Associations; Municipal Corporations; Railroads.*

Capacity to contract as, estoppel to deny. *Petty* v. *R. Co.* 666.

Charter forfeiture not allowed to be set up collaterally; it dates from judgment in direct proceeding for. *Ga. Nor. R. Co.* v. *Tifton, T. & G. R. Co.* 766.

CORPORATIONS — *continued.*

Charter forfeiture, when not resorted to as remedy. *Trust Co. of Ga.* v.
  State, 736.

Combination between, to defeat competition, constitutional provisions as
  to, apply to all corporations. *Trust Co. of Ga.* v. *State,* 737.

Combination between, to defeat competition, State's remedies for. Motives of those who induce Governor to order suit filed, not considered. *Trust Co. of Ga.* v. *State,* 736.

Combination between, when lawful. *Trust Co. of Ga.* v. *State,* 736.

Competition by, defeating or lessening, constitutional provision as to,
  construed. *State* v. *Central R. Co.* 716. See *Trust Co. of Ga.* v.
  State, 736.

Contract of one, not binding on another because the stock in both is
  owned by the same persons. *Waycross A.-L. R. Co.* v. *Offerman
  & W. R. Co.* 827.

Deed, power of attorney to execute, when must bear seal of corporation;
  proof of officer's authority where seal not used. *Dodge* v. *Am.
  Freehold Co.* 395.

Estoppel to deny existence as. *Petty* v. *R. Co.* 674.

Merger of, not result from ownership of stock of one by another. *Waycross A.-L. R. Co.* v. *Offerman & W. R. Co.* 828.

Nul tiel corporation, estoppel to set up. *Petty* v. *R. Co.* 674.

Seal, when must be used; presumption of officer's authority where used;
  proof in absence of. *Dodge* v. *Am. Freehold Co.* 395.

Stock all owned by another, not make them identical. *Waycross A.-L.
  R. Co.* v. *Offerman & W. R. Co.* 828.

Stock of one corporation purchased by another; when not conflict with
  constitution. *Trust Co. of Ga.* v. *State,* 736.

Subscription to; contract construed. Held, subscriber was creditor to extent of money paid, and unpaid part of subscription was cancelled. *Barrow* v. *Smith,* 767.

Taxation of. See *Taxation.*

Ultra vires, question of, not made in record, not considered by Supreme
  Court. *Petty* v. *R. Co.* 666.

Ultra vires acts, State's remedies for; injunction may be had, when. *Trust
  Co. of Ga.* v. *State,* 747.

COSTS. See *Attorneys at Law; Criminal Law.*

COUNTIES.

Action against, on contract; petition must show compliance with law as
  to entering contract on minutes. *Milburn* v. *Glynn County,* 473.

Contract of, effect of failure to record. *Id.*

Estoppel of, to set up invalidity of contract. *Id.* 478.

Inspector of roads and bridges, county not authorized to employ, prior to
  act of 1899 as to. Whether that act is valid, not decided. *Turner*
  v. *Fulton County,* 633.

Liability for damages to private property from working adjacent public
  road. *Barfield* v. *Macon County,* 386.

Power to employ and pay for services, county has only such, as is conferred by law. *Turner* v. *Fulton County,* 633.

COUNTIES — *continued.*

Roads, damages from working and draining, what recoverable by owner of adjacent land. *Griswold* v. *Rutherford*, 398.

COUNTY COURT.

Warrant to remove tenant at sufferance, judge of county court can not administer oath for, nor issue. *Griswold* v. *Rutherford*, 398.

COURTS. See *County Court; Justice's Court; Ordinary; Practice.*

CRIMINAL LAW.

Accessory before the fact, to an attempt to commit arson, one may be convicted as. *Howard*, 137.

Accomplice, corroboration of, erroneous charge as to. *Id.*; *Chapman*, 158.

Accusation, affidavit as basis of, what sufficient. *Brown*, 570.

Accusation valid though no warrant for arrest was issued upon the affidavit on which the accusation was based. *Id.*

Admission by accused, whether admissibility governed by principle applied to confessions. *Fuller*, 811.

Admission, silence as; when not. *Chapman*, 159.

Admission to officer in charge of accused, when not excluded from evidence. *Fuller*, 809.

Affidavit, as basis for accusation, what sufficient; need not minutely describe offense. *Brown*, 570.

Allegata and probata; allegation that representation was made to one of firm, not supported by proof that it was made to another member. *Broznack*, 514.

Arrest, homicide in making or resisting. *Dover*, 485; *Delegal*, 518.

Arrest, when private person may make. *Id.* 521.

Argument improper where prosecuting attorney tells jury he believes the accused is guilty. *Broznack*, 516.

Argument; objectionable remarks of solicitor-general, when not cause new trial. *Robinson*, 506.

Arson, attempt to commit, one may be convicted as accessory before the fact to. *Howard*, 137.

Arson, evidence insufficient to warrant conviction of. *Ross*, 516.

Arson, description of house, sufficient, in indictment here. *Howard*, 137.

Assault, drawing pistol was not, under facts here. *Burton*, 134.

Autrefois acquit, plea of, not good where based on quashing of accusation on demurrer filed by accused, though the demurrer was first overruled and testimony introduced. *Brown*, 570.

Beer-selling without paying tax. See *Taxation.*

Character of deceased, question to witness as to, not in proper form. *Bush*, 122.

Cheating and swindling; allegation that representation was made to one member of firm, not supported by evidence that it was made to another member. *Broznack*, 514.

Cheating and swindling by a promise combined with a pretense as to an existing fact. *Holton*, 127.

Cheating and swindling by inducing another to give his negotiable note, though insolvent. *Id.*

CRIMINAL LAW — *continued.*

Cheating and swindling by representations as to title to land *Id.*

Cheating and swindling; representations which do not make this offense. *Broznack,* 514.

Church is not "public building," within meaning of Penal Code, ₹725. *Collum,* 531.

Commitment trial, writing by magistrate, purporting to contain testimony on, but prepared after trial, from memory, admissibility of. *Haines,* 528.

Confession. See catchword "Admission."

Conduct of accused which was not connected with offense charged, and was calculated to excite prejudice against him, evidence as to, improperly admitted, required reversal. *Lowman,* 501.

Corroborating circumstances, instruction as to, not error as against accused. *Haines,* 526.

Corroboration of accomplice, erroneous charge as to. *Howard,* 137; *Chapman,* 158.

Costs; solicitor-general's fee in Supreme Court; one fee for each bill of exceptions though more than one excepting party. What clerk's certificate as to insolvency must show. Fee in riot case, $15. *In re Kenan,* 819.

Declaration by accused's wife in his presence, to show threat by him, when not admissible. *Chapman,* 157.

Declarations, dying, error in charging as to. *Bush,* 125.

Declaration of alleged principal, when not admissible against alleged accessory. *Howard,* 137.

Declarations of member of riotous assembly, admissible against the others. *Green,* 544.

Demurrer to accusation overruled, no ground for new trial. *Cleveland,* 265.

Demurrer to indictment should be strictly construed against pleader. *Green,* 540.

Dying declaration, what admissible as. *Bush,* 123.

Embezzlement and larceny distinguished. *Robinson,* 565.

Embezzlement by public officer, mere refusal or neglect to pay over funds is not. Discussion as to what constitutes, and authorities as to. *Id.* 564.

Forgery, evidence insufficient to warrant conviction of. *McCombs,* 496.

Forgery of an order for a thing not money, indictment for, not alleging that the thing (meat) was of some value was fatally defective. *Johnson,* 268. See *McCombs,* 500.

Forgery; possession of goods similar to those delivered on forged order, as a circumstance to show guilt, insufficient, when. *McCombs,* 496.

Homicide, charge on, not mentioning theory of defense until about to conclude, and then briefly, with remark that court "did not think" to call attention to it; reversal. *Smith,* 480.

Homicide; fears as defense; charge that they should be the fears of a brave man, not approved, but not cause reversal, where accused was one of posse of arresting officer. *Dover,* 485.

Homicide in making arrest, charge as to. *Id.*

CRIMINAL LAW — *continued.*

Homicide in resisting arrest by private person without warrant. *Delegal*, 518.

Homicide ;· Penal Code, § 73, error to give in charge, under facts here. *Lowman*, 501 ; *Delegal*, 518.

Homicide ; Penal Code, §§ 70,71, properly given in charge with § 73, when. *Dover*, 486.

Homicide : vide catchwords " Manslaughter," " Murder."·

Idem sonans, doctrine of ; " Biggers " and " Bickers " are. *Biggers*, 105.

Identity of person, not of name, as a test of whether indictment applies to prisoner. *Id*. 105.

" Impeached " defined. As used in Civil Code, § 5295, it is synonymous with "attacked." *Smith*, 479.

Impeachment of witness ; statutory methods for, not exclusive ; erroneous charge as to. *Chapman*, 158.

Indecent exposure of person must be where more than one can see it, to warrant conviction of "a notorious act of public indecency." *Morris*, 351.

Indictment defective, not aided by evidence, nor by verdict, when. *O'Brien*, 52.

Indictment, language of, is to be interpreted liberally in favor of the State. *Green*, 540.

Indictment ; power of judge to direct that indictment be laid before grand jury, questioned. *Thompson*, 275.

Indictment too general as to means by which seduction was accomplished *Langston*, 153.

Indictment too general to cover violation of local liquor law. *O'Brien*, 52.

Injunction to restrain violation of penal ordinance, when not granted. *Mayor of Moultrie* v. *Patterson*, 370.

Intent shown by understanding as to meaning of contract, considered, when. *Phelps*, 115.

Jeopardy, former ; plea not good, under facts here. Dissenting opinion in *Black* v. *State*, 36 *Ga*. 447, approved. *Brown*, 570.

Juror can not impeach verdict. *Echols*, 508.

Jurors ; challenge to array because jury commissioner had moved from county ; when not good without showing that the fact had been judicially ascertained. *Channell*, 150.

Jurors ; challenge to array, when proper. Challenge because of feeling of jurors should be to the polls. *Thompson*, 272.

Juror's disqualification ; presumption that juror qualified rightly on voir dire, not rebutted by one witness alone. *Sumner*, 142.

Juror's partiality, how tested ; may be put on voir dire in misdemeanor case. *Thompson*, 272.

Juror set aside for cause after panel of forty-eight made up and selection of jury begun, not cause new trial. *Robinson*, 506.

Jury, irregularities in conduct of, when not cause new trial. *Id*.

Jury, irregularity in summoning, when not cause new trial. *Dover*, 485.

Jury, meaning of questions on voir dire inaccurately explained to, when not cause new trial. *Robinson*, 506.

CRIMINAL LAW — *continued.*

Jury; number composing panel after original panel exhausted is discretionary with judge. *Id.*

Jury, separation of some members of, from their fellows, when not cause new trial. *Id.*

Jury, too late to poll, after court has pronounced sentence. *Id.*

Larceny, accused's understanding as to what contract meant, considered in determining whether guilty of, in appropriating money. *Phelps,* 115.

Larceny; affidavit and accusation sufficient here. *Brown,* 570.

Larceny and embezzlement distinguished. *Robinson,* 565.

Larceny; appropriation by retiring partner of money received in payment of debt to firm, when not. *Phelps,* 115.

License tax law not violated by brewing company's agent here. *Smith,* 227. Nor by bicycle-dealer here. *Alexander,* 805.

Liquor, carrying to church; law violated by keeping in buggy near church, though for sick wife. *Bice,* 117.

Liquor-selling, conviction of, under unconstitutional statute, set aside. *O'Brien,* 51; *Embry,* 61; *Tinsley,* 822. Defendant convicted under, should be discharged on habeas corpus. *Moore* v. *Wheeler,* 62.

Liquor-selling, evidence sufficient to convict of. *Thompson,* 272.

Liquor-selling, indictment for, when too general to cover violation of local law as to. *O'Brien,* 51.

Manslaughter, facts not authorizing charge on. *Sumner,* 142; *Channell,* 150.

"Manslaughter," verdict of, is, in effect, verdict of voluntary manslaughter. *Smith,* 479.

Manslaughter voluntary, charge as to, where not involved, when cause new trial, and when not. *Robinson,* 506.

Minor, doubtful whether law as to vagrancy applies to. *Teasley,* 282.

Misnomer. See catchword "Name."

Motion to quash accusation overruled, matter for direct exception, not ground for new trial. *Cleveland,* 265.

Motive for desiring the crime committed, and an attempt to induce another to commit it, proof of, admitted. *Howard,* 187.

Murder, circumstantial evidence here sufficient to warrant conviction. *Fuller,* 815.

Murder, husband killing for adultery with his wife, guilty of, under facts here. *Channell,* 152.

Murder; past injury, however heinous, no defense. *Id.*

Murder; self-defense, law as to, in Penal Code, § 73, when error to give in charge. *Lowman,* 501; *Delegal,* 518.

Murder, threats by slayer, admissibility of evidence offered to show. *Harris,* 280.

Municipal ordinance violated, criminal case; rule as to bills of exceptions in criminal cases applied. *Barnett* v. *Atlanta,* 166.

Name; "Biggers," "Bickers," are idem sonans; other instances given. *Biggers,* 105.

Name; identity of person, not of name, as a test of whether indictment applies to prisoner. *Id.* 106.

CRIMINAL LAW — *continued.*

Oath, child's understanding of nature of, not shown by answers here. *Miller* v. *State*, 512.

Opinion that the time had come for the accused "to either run or fight," not admitted in evidence. *Lowman*, 501.

Perjury, allegation as to oath, sufficiency of. *Haines*, 530.

Perjury, evidence warranting conviction of. *Id.* 526.

Possession of goods by accused, like those delivered on forged order, when insufficient to authorize conviction. *McCombs*, 496.

Prisoner's statement; discretion of court as to allowing counsel for accused to put questions or make suggestions as to. *Echols*, 508.

Public building, church is not, within meaning of Penal Code, ₰725. *Collum*, 531.

Public indecency, what necessary to constitute. *Morris*, 351.

Punishment, charge as to discretion of court in regard to, when error. *Echols*, 508.

Rape, evidence insufficient to warrant conviction. *Cheney*, 503.

Representations as to title false, cheating and swindling by. *Holton*, 127.

Res gestæ, declarations of alleged principal, when not admissible against alleged accessory, as. *Howard*, 137.

Res gestæ, what admissible as part of, in dying declaration. *Bush*, 123.

Riot; declarations of persons in crowd, other than the accused, when admitted in evidence. *Green*, 544.

Riot, facts constituting; sufficiency of indictment. *Green*, 536.

Riot, fee of solicitor-general in case of, in Supreme Court, $15. *In re Kenan*, 819.

Riot, joint action of two or more required to constitute; common intent not shown by circumstances here. *Tripp*, 489.

Seduction by persuasion and promises of marriage, "and by other false and fraudulent means," alleged, without specifying what the latter means were, demurrer good. (See dissent.) *Langston*, 153.

Statement of accused; discretionary with judge whether counsel for accused shall put questions or make suggestions while it is being made. *Echols*, 508.

Statement of accused, omission to charge as to theory presented by, when not error. *Channell*, 153.

Sunday, running excursion-train on, who indictable for; trainmaster acting under orders from superintendent was not. *Craven*, 266.

Threats, insufficiency of evidence as to ; accused not chargeable with what his wife said in his presence, when. *Chapman*, 157.

Threats, when admissible in dying declaration. *Bush*, 123.

Threats ; words spoken shortly before homicide, and capable of being construed as a threat to take the life of some one, admitted in evidence. *Harris*, 280.

Tracks and threat, evidence as to, here, insufficient to warrant conviction. *Ross*, 516.

Unconstitutional statute, conviction under, void, though based on plea of guilty. Discharge may be obtained by habeas corpus. *Moore* v. *Wheeler*, 62.

CRIMINAL LAW— *continued.*

Vagrancy; evidence not warranting conviction. *Teasley*, 282.

Vagrancy, doubtful whether minors are subject to prosecution for. *Id.*

Value, when indictment for forgery must allege. *Johnson*, 268 ; *McCombs*, 500. Judicial cognizance not taken that meat had. *Johnson*, 268.

Verdict of "manslaughter" is, in effect, verdict of voluntary manslaughter. *Smith*, 479.

Voir dire, inaccuracies in explaining to jurors the meaning of questions on, when not cause new trial. *Robinson*, 506.

Voir dire, jurors in misdemeanor case may be placed on. *Thompson*, 278.

Warrant ; not essential to validity of accusation that warrant be issued upon affidavit on which accusation based. *Brown*, 570.

Wife not incompetent to testify on trial of another than husband, charged with same offense. *Fuller*, 809.

Witness, competency of wife, on trial of one charged with same offense as her husband. *Fuller*, 809.

DAMAGES. See *Actions; Negligence; Railroads.*

Breach of bond for title, recoupment of damages for, when sued on note for purchase-money. *Preston* v. *Walker*, 290.

Breach of purchaser's contract to pay draft and take goods from depot, damages for ; value not recoverable when burned in depot while title was in seller. *Mountain City Mill Co.* v. *Butler*, 469.

County's liability where land is damaged from work done on adjacent road. *Barfield* v. *Macon County*, 386.

Delay, bringing up case for, damages awarded by Supreme Court. *Gentry* v. *Barron*, 172 ; *Mozley* v. *Reagan*, 182 ; *Osborn & Walcott Mf. Co.* v. *Blanton*, 196 ; *Atl. Bottling Co.* v. *Hutchinson*, 550.

Land damaged from working and draining public road ; measure of compensation. *Barfield* v. *Macon County*, 386.

Landowner damaged by character of building erected on adjacent lot or use made of it, when not entitled to recover. *Long* v. *Elberton*, 28.

Libel ; allegation of special damage not necessary where charge was that a merchant had not paid his debts. *Brown* v. *Holton*, 431.

Market value, depreciation in, as measure of compensation for damage to land. *Barfield* v. *Macon County*, 388.

Nuisance caused by manner of maintaining jail, recovery for. *Long* v. *Elberton*, 28.

Release of claim for, when not rescinded for mistake as to contents. *Jossey* v. *R. Co.* 439. See *Petty* v. *R. Co.* 675.

Road, new, damages from establishment of, not recoverable by owners of land abutting on old road, when. *Huff* v. *Donehoo*, 638.

Sale of goods when vendee does not take them or vendor exercises right of stoppage in transitu, damages for which vendee liable. *Davis Sulphur Ore Co.* v. *Atlanta Co.* 608.

DEBTOR AND CREDITOR.

Administration, debt as ground for; what proof sufficient. *Lowery* v. *Powell*, 190.

DEBTOR AND CREDITOR — *continued.*

Contract that creditor should operate debtor's manufacturing plant, to collect debt from income; rights of parties under. *Mohr-Weil Co.* v. *Russell*, 580.

Distribution of assets of one entrusted with notes to collect, who failed to pay over proceeds, priority not awarded to bailor, over general creditors. *Tiedeman* v. *Imp. Fert. Co.* 661.

Guarantor, when sued without joining principal debtor or showing insolvency of principal. *Penn Tobacco Co.* v. *Leman*, 428.

Insurable interest of creditor in debtor's life, limit of. *Morris* v. *Ga. Loan Co.* 12.

Possession of debtor's property, delivered to creditor so that debt might be paid from income, creditor, under contract here, could retain for fixed period though debt paid. *Mohr-Weil Co.* v. *Russell*, 579.

Situs of debt, general rule that it is where creditor is domiciled. *Central R. Co.* v. *Brinson*, 354.

DECLARATIONS. See *Evidence.*

DEEDS.

Acknowledgment in another State of deed to Georgia land, who may take. *Cunningham* v. *Barker*, 613.

Affidavit for probate signed with name different from that given in the body thereof as the affiant's, not admit instrument to record, when. *Dodge* v. *Am. Freehold Co.* 395.

Attestation by judge of court of record in another State. *Cunningham* v. *Barker*, 618.

Attestation in another State by commissioner of deeds for Georgia sufficient without certificate as to his identity and official character. *Dodge* v. *Am. Freehold Co.* 394.

Color of title, sheriff's deed to land sold under justice's court fi. fa., good as, though no entry of "no personalty." *Wade* v. *Garrett*, 270.

Consideration not expressed ("for and in consideration of ——— dollars"), deed good. *Jewell* v. *Walker*, 241.

Consideration, recital of, to what extent an estoppel; how far open to explanation. *Jewell* v. *Walker*, 246.

Corporation's, power of attorney to excute, when must bear seal of corporation, proof of officer's authority where seal not used. *Dodge* v. *Am. Freehold Co.* 395.

Delivery, where grantee is an infant, what ineffectual as. *Jenkins* v. *R. Co.* 35.

Infant, deed to, rule as to delivery. *Id.*

Possession held adversely to administrator at time of conveyance by him, no title passed. *Hanesley* v. *Bagley*, 348.

Power of sale in security deed, exercise of, when not enjoined because grantee is indebted to grantor. *McDaniel* v. *Cowart*, 419.

Recital in, when not binding. *Jenkins* v. *R. Co.* 35.

Record; defect in probate of power of attorney, not cured by recording. *Dodge* v. *Am. Freehold Co.* 396.

Security, as basis of ejectment, or as outstanding title to defeat ejectment. *Ashley* v. *Cook*, 655.

DEEDS — *continued.*

Security; levy and sale without reconveyance of land conveyed, void, but purchaser subrogated to grantee's rights. *Id.* 653.

Security, reconveyance before levy, necessity for, not obviated by decree here. *Id.*

Security, test as to whether conveyance is, where there is a contemporaneous agreement for repurchase by the grantor. *Felton* v. *Grier*, 320.

Security, title passed by, though no bond to reconvey given; mode of enforcing rights under. *Jewell* v. *Walker*, 241.

Subrogation of purchaser at void sale under judgment in favor of grantee. *Ashley* v. *Cook*, 658.

Usurious, deed to realty for cash price and contemporanous agreement to repurchase at higher price, when not. *Felton* v. *Grier*, 320.

Usury in, security deed attacked for, by one who purchased before suit on. *Cade* v. *Larned*, 292.

Usury in, wife's approval written on husband's security deed, not estop her from setting up that it was void for. *Id.*

Warranty, breach of, by eviction, when no recovery for. *Stiger* v. *Monroe*, 457.

DELIVERY. See *Deeds.*

DEMURRER. See *Criminal Law; New Trial; Parties; Pleading; Practice* in *Supreme Court.*

DISPOSSESSORY WARRANT. See *Landlord and Tenant.*

DIVORCE AND ALIMONY.

Fast writ of error will not lie to order granted on petition to enforce by attachment a previous judgment for alimony. *Gordon*, 262.

Vacation, petition for alimony for support of wife and family dependent on husband, pending divorce suit, may be filed in. *Ray*, 465.

DOWER.

Contract between husband and wife intended to promote dissolution of marriage relation, not bar right to dower. *Birch* v. *Anthony*, 349.

EJECTMENT. See *Title.*

Conveyance of land by plaintiff pending suit for, not preclude him from prosecuting to judgment, though grantee agreed that defendant take judgment. *Suwannee Turp. Co.* v. *Baxter*, 597.

Mesne profits, not recovered for more than four years before suit filed. *Taylor* v. *James*, 328.

Paramount title in third person, good defense without connecting defendant's possession with it. *Jenkins* v. *R. Co.* 35.

Parties; substitution of new plaintiff, fatal to the action. *Suwannee Turp. Co.* v. *Baxter*, 600.

Security deed, as basis of action, or as outstanding title to defeat action. *Ashley* v. *Cook*, 655.

Title outstanding, what necessary to support defense. *Id.*

ELECTIONS.

Contest because managers examined folded ballots as they were received, and the effect was to intimidate persons from voting. *Cole* v. *McClendon*, 183.

Contest because of improper registration, petition should show what. *Id.* 184.

Contest of, under local option law, duty of ordinary to pass on, before declaring result of election. *Drake* v. *Drewry*, 399.

Contest; petition here demurrable, not giving names of persons intimidated from voting, nor showing they would have voted on the losing side and thereby changed the result. *Cole* v. *McClendon*, 188.

Liquor, ordinary, before declaring result of, must pass on contest and decide all questions affecting validity of election. (See dissent.) *Drake* v. *Drewry*, 399.

Qualifications of voters at liquor election. *Cole* v. *McClendon*, 184.

Registration, irregularities in, when not disqualify from voting. *Id.*

EQUITY. See *Injunction; Pleading; Receiver; Trusts.*

Attorney's fee for bringing fund into court, when not allowed. *Mohr-Weil Co.* v. *Russell*, 579.

Bill of review, not lie to review judgment overruling motion for new trial. *Donaldson* v. *Roberts*, 833.

Claim in forma pauperis, when enjoined, and receiver appointed to hold land and rents. *Dawson* v. *Eq. Mge. Co.* 389.

Cloud on title, what necessary to authorize court to entertain an application to remove. *Hanesley* v. *Bagley*, 347.

Costs, attorney's fee, when not allowed as. *Mohr-Weil Co.* v. *Russell*, 579.

Criminal matter, when equity has no jurisdiction to interfere in. *Mayor of Moultrie* v. *Patterson*, 370.

First term, trial at, by consent of guardian ad litem of minor defendants. *McMillan* v. *Hunnicutt*, 699.

Fraud, not authorize equitable relief here. *Schmitt* v. *Schneider*, 681.

General relief, prayer for, scope of. *Schmitt* v. *Schneider*, 632.

Homestead property sued for in, effect given to equitable rights of defendant though a wrong-doer. *Taylor* v. *James*, 335.

Jurisdiction of petition to enjoin claim, etc., taken though the claimant was a non-resident. *Dawson* v. *Eq. Mge. Co.* 389.

Laches as bar to relief. *Donaldson* v. *Roberts*, 832.

Levy aided by equitable petition, when. *Dawson* v. *Eq. Mge. Co.* 389.

Mistake as to contents of contract of release, when not ground for rescinding. *Jossey* v. *R. Co.* 439. See *Petty* v. *R. Co.* 675.

Mistake, rule as to when relievable. *Floyd* v. *Atl. Bkg. Co.* 786.

Negligence, as bar to relief, where rescission prayed for. *Jossey* v. *R. Co.* 439.

Remedy at law adequate, injunction not granted. *Mayor of Moultrie* v. *Patterson*, 370.

Remedy at law adequate, not good ground of demurrer, where no extraordinary relief prayed. *Reid* v. *Wilson*, 424.

EQUITY — *continued.*

Rescission for mistake as to contents of contract, when not granted. *Jossey* v. *R. Co.* 439.

Trial at first term, in proceeding against minors, had by consent of guardian ad litem. *McMillan* v. *Hunnicutt*, 699.

ESTATES. See *Administrators; Homestead; Wills.*

ESTOPPEL. See *Judgments; Waiver.*

Capacity to contract, estoppel to deny. *Petty* v. *R. Co.* 666.

Consideration, recital as to, in deed, how far estops. *Jewell* v. *Walker*, 246. See *Jenkins* v. *So. R. Co.* 35.

County, estoppel of, to set up invalidity of contract. *Milburn* v. *Glynn County*, 478.

Deed, approval written by wife on husband's, not estop her from setting up that it was void for usury. *Cade* v. *Larned*, 292.

Existence of corporation, or capacity to do business, estoppel to deny. *Petty* v. *R. Co.* 674.

Inconsistent positions in litigation, when party may not take. *Gentry* v. *Barron*, 172.

Recitals in deed, when not estoppel. *Jenkins* v. *R. Co.* 35. See *Jewell* v. *Walker*, 246.

Ruling invoked, party invoking, and in whose favor it was made, not allowed to question its propriety. *Brown* v. *State*, 571.

Sale, acquiescence and conduct which estopped from attacking because bidding was deterred. *Conley* v. *Redwine*, 641.

Signing contract without reading it, effect of, as estoppel. *Jossey* v. *R. Co.* 439. See *Petty* v. *R. Co.* 675.

Signing as principal, when estops signer to set up that he was surety. *Pirkle* v. *Chamblee*, 33.

Void levy and sale, estoppel to attack. *Ashley* v. *Cook*, 653.

EVIDENCE.

Administration, debt as ground for; what proof sufficient. *Conyers* v. *Bruce*, 190.

Admission by accused to officer, when not excluded. *Fuller* v. *State*, 809.

Admission by accused, whether admissibility governed by principle applied to confessions. *Id.* 811.

Admission in pleading, when may be put in evidence by opposite party, though stricken by amendment. *Wynn* v. *Wynn*, 256.

Admission of alleged principal, admissible against himself, but not against alleged accessory, here. *Howard* v. *State*, 137.

Admission, silence as; when not. *Chapman* v. *State*, 159.

Assignment of error in ruling as to, sufficiency of. See *New Trial.*

Burden of proof as to alteration of note. *Mozley* v. *Reagan*, 182.

Burden of proof as to exemption from garnishment. *Steele* v. *Parker*, 791.

Burden of proof as to seizure and notice, in attachment case. *Hiles Carver Co.* v. *King*, 181.

Burden of proof as to suretyship, as between signers of note. *Pirkle* v. *Chamblee*, 32.

EVIDENCE — *continued.*

Burden of proof on parties seeking to show that note and mortgage under seal reciting valuable consideration had none. *Weaver* v. *Cosby*, 310.

Character, question to witness as to, not in proper form. *Bush* v. *State*, 122.

Child's understanding of nature of oath, not shown by answers here. *Miller* v. *State*, 512.

Commitment trial, writing by magistrate, purporting to contain testimony on, but prepared after trial, from memory, admissibility of. *Haines* v. *State*, 528.

Conduct of accused which was not connected with offense charged and which was calculated to excite prejudice against him, admission of evidence as to, required reversal. *Lowman*, 501.

Confession or admission to officer in charge of accused, when not excluded. *Fuller* v. *State*, 809.

Consideration of deed, recital as to, how far open to explanation. *Jewell* v. *Walker*, 246. See *Jenkins* v. *So. R. Co.* 35.

Corroboration of accomplice, sufficiency of; erroneous charge as to. *Chapman* v. *State*, 158.

Declaration by wife in husband's presence, to show threat by him, when not admissible. *Chapman* v. *State*, 157.

Declaration, dying, what admissible as. *Bush* v. *State*, 123.

Declaration of alleged principal, when not admitted as against alleged accessory. *Howard* v. *State*, 137.

Declaration of member of riotous assembly, admissible against the others. *Green* v. *State*, 544.

Deed reciting consideration of "——————— dollars," admissible. *Jewell* v. *Walker*, 241.

Error in admitting, on hearing of application for temporary injunction, not work reversal. *Dawson* v.*Eq. Mge. Co.* 394.

Execution of instrument, where non est factum pleaded; prima facie proof sufficient to authorize introduction of the instrument. *Jewell* v. *Walker*, 241.

Handwriting, proof of; genuineness of writing offered as standard of comparison, not shown by circumstances here. *McCombs* v. *State*, 496.

"Impeached" defined. When used as synonymous with "attacked." *Smith* v. *State*, 479.

Impeaching; statutory methods for, not exclusive; erroneous charge as to. *Chapman* v. *State*, 158.

Impeachment by proof of contradictory statements as to matters not relevant, not allowed. *Hudgins* v. *Bloodworth*, 197.

Impeachment by proof of testimony on commitment trial. *Haines* v. *State*, 528.

Irrelevant, separation of, from relevant, duty on party offering. *Ellis* v. *Poe*, 422.

Juror's disqualification by prejudice, when not shown by one witness alone. *Sumner* v. *State*, 142.

Lost papers; admissibility of certified copy of established copy. *Bell* v. *Bowdoin*, 211.

EVIDENCE — *continued.*

Motive for desiring crime committed, and attempt to induce another to commit it, proof of, admitted. *Howard* v. *State*, 137.

Oath, child's understanding of nature of, not shown by answers here. *Miller* v. *State*, 512.

Opinion as to what would have been done if a certain thing had happened two days before act for which accused was on trial, rejected. *Delegal* v. *State*, 518.

Opinion that the time had come for the accused " to either run or fight," not admitted. *Lowman* v. *State*, 501.

Parol, as affecting life-insurance policy. *Hamilton* v. *Mut. Ben. Life Ins. Co.* 381.

Parol, to affect bill of lading, when not admissible. *McElveen* v. *R. Co.* 249.

Parol, to explain consideration of deed. *Jewell* v. *Walker*, 246.

Parol, to explain meaning of " O. K.," on written order, admitted. *Penn Tobacco Co.* v. *Leman*, 428.

Parol, to explain writing, admissibility of. *Sterling Cycle Wks.* v. *Willingham*, 559.

Parol, to show land was received in exchange for homestead property and afterwards treated as homestead, admitted. *Taylor* v. *James*, 333.

Parol, to show service of process, when admitted. *Bell* v. *Bowdoin*, 209.

Parol, when not admissible to prove what books of account or other writings contain or do not contain. *Aspinwall* v. *Chisholm*, 437.

Part relevant but the greater part irrelevant, in document offered as a whole, rejection not cause reversal. *Ellis* v. *Poe*, 422.

Possession of goods by accused, like those delivered to him on forged order, when insufficient to authorize conviction. *McCombs* v. *State*, 496.

Presumption as to when alteration in writing was made. *Jewell* v. *Walker*, 246.

Presumption that juror qualified rightly on voir dire, not rebutted by one witness alone. *Sumner* v. *State*, 142.

Presumption that officers do duty, applied where entry of levy did not recite seizure or notice. *Hiles Carver Co.* v. *King*, 180.

Presumptions generally. See *Presumptions.*

Recital in deed, effect of, as evidence. *Jenkins* v. *R. Co.* 40.

Res gestæ, declarations of alleged principal, when not admissible against alleged accessory, as. *Howard* v. *State*, 137.

Res gestæ, what admissible as part of, in dying declaration. *Bush* v. *State*, 123.

Riot; declarations of persons in crowd, other than the accused, when admitted. *Green* v. *State*, 544.

Separation of relevant from irrelevant, duty on party offering. *Ellis* v. *Poe*, 422.

Service of process, admissibility of parol testimony to show. *Bell* v. *Bowdoin*, 209.

Silence, as an admission; when not. *Chapman* v. *State*, 159.

Threats, insufficiency of evidence as to. *Id.* 157.

EVIDENCE—*continued.*

Threats ; words spoken shortly before homicide, and capable of being construed as a threat against some one, admitted. *Harris* v. *State,* 280.

Wife not incompetent to testify on trial of another than husband, charged with same offense. *Fuller* v. *State,* 809.

Witness, competency of. See *Witness.*

Writing attacked by plea of non est factum, what sufficient to authorize its introduction. *Jewell* v. *Walker,* 241.

EXECUTIONS. See *Levy and Sale.*

Agent ; fi. fa. against A "as agent for" B, is against A personally, and not as agent. *Wynn* v. *Irvine,* 287.

Docketing ; lien of judgment, relatively to purchaser from defendant pending appeal, not affected by failure to have fi. fa. issued and entered in ten days from date of judgment. *Crosby* v. *King Hardware Co.* 452.

Dormancy not prevented by receipts of payments entered on, by plaintiff. *Blue* v. *Collins,* 341.

Dormant judgment, officer has no authority to levy fi. fa. issued on. *Id.*

Dormant, sale under, void, and no obstacle to sale on same day under valid execution. *Conley* v. *Redwine,* 641.

EXECUTORS. See *Administrators and Executors.*

EXEMPTIONS. See *Garnishment ; Homestead ; Taxation ; Year's Support.*

FRAUD.

Allegations as to, too general. *Angier* v. *Eq. B. & L. A.* 627.

Notice constructive, of fraud in obtaining decree, not afforded by matters of record here. *McMillan* v. *Hunnicutt,* 700.

Remedy for, when action for damages, and not equitable proceeding. *Schmitt* v. *Schneider,* 631.

Representations as to title, false, cheating and swindling by. *Holton* v. *State,* 127.

Rescission for, when tender back necessary. *Petty* v. *R. Co.* 666.

Sale judicial, circumstances tending to show fraud in. *Haunson* v. *Nelms,* 805.

Title of purchaser at judicial sale, with notice of, when not affected by. *McMillan* v. *Hunnicutt,* 700.

FRAUDS, STATUTE OF.

"Debt of another;" not apply where retired partner agrees to pay debt which firm contracted while he was a member. *Reid* v. *Wilson,* 424.

"Debt of another," performance here took promise out of provision as to. *English* v. *Richards Co.* 635.

FULTON COUNTY. See *Counties.*

GARNISHMENT.

Bond to dissolve, in case against a firm, executed by one "as principal and as a member of " the firm, good. *Maddox* v. *Am. Trust & Bkg. Co.* 787.

GARNISHMENT— *continued.*

Bond to dissolve, substantial compliance with statute, as to condition of. *Id.* 788.

Claim to fund should be filed in court which has control of fund. *Page* v. *Pitt*, 558.

Exemption, burden of proof as to. *Steele* v. *Parker*, 791.

Exemption set up by defendant, by rule against constable to whom garnishee had paid fund; the creditor was proper party to rule. When incumbent on movant to traverse answer to rule. *Id.*

Jurisdiction of claim to fund raised by, and properly paid into city court, superior court has not. *Page* v. *Pitt*, 557.

Situs of debt must be within jurisdiction, to render judgment binding. General rule, that situs is where creditor is domiciled. *Central R. Co.* v. *Brinson*, 354.

GLASCOCK COUNTY. See *Liquor.*

GUARANTY. See *Actions; Contracts; Pleading.*

GUARDIAN AND WARD.

Ad litem guardian could consent to trial of equity cause at first term. *McMillan* v. *Hunnicutt*, 699.

Ad litem guardian, irregularity in acts of, not render judgment void, but merely erroneous. *Id.* 701.

Year's support, ward's share in, when not recoverable. *Howard* v. *Pope,* 259.

HABEAS CORPUS.,

Conviction under unconstitutional statute, void, though based on plea of guilty; discharge obtained by habeas corpus. *Moore* v. *Wheeler*, 62.

HOMESTEAD AND EXEMPTION.

Amendment of proceeding. *Ozburn* v. *Flournoy*, 704.

Appeal from ordinary's judgment sustaining demurrer to application, not lie; certiorari is remedy. *Cunningham* v. *U. S. Loan Co.* 616.

Ceased on death of widow and arrival at age of minors for whom set apart, though adult daughters were included in the widow's application for. *Sutton* v. *Rosser*, 205.

Collateral attack on "pony homestead," allowed. *Marcrum* v. *Washington*, 296.

Dependent female, exemption for support of, not survive applicant's death. *Sutton* v. *Rosser*, 205.

Dependent female, exemption for support of, can be taken only from applicant's own property, not from decedent's estate. *Id.* 204.

Exchange of, without order authorizing, impressed with the homestead character the land received for it, and the land, when afterwards sold without authority, could be recovered as homestead. *Taylor* v. *James*, 333.

Head of family added as a party, by amendment, in suit brought by beneficiaries for recovery of. *Id.* 328.

HOMESTEAD AND EXEMPTION — *continued.*

Improvements allowed to be set off in equitable suit for recovery of homestead. *Id.*

Levy on "pony homestead"; affidavit not required, to authorize levy. *Marcrum* v. *Washington,* 297.

Limitation bar applied to beneficiaries where applicable to head of family. *Taylor* v. *James,* 338.

Mesne profits in suit for recovery of; limitation as to, four years. *Id.*

Notice of terms of order for sale of, purchaser chargeable with. *Id.* 327.

Ordinary's capacity, when ministerial, not judicial, in acting on. *Marcrum* v. *Washington,* 296.

"Pony homestead," levy on, may be made without affidavit. *Id.*

"Pony homestead," receiving and recording schedule for, is ministerial, not judicial act; validity may be collaterally attacked. *Id.*

Recovery of, in equitable proceeding, effect given to equitable rights of defendant though a wrong-doer. *Taylor* v. *James,* 335.

Recovery of land received in unauthorized exchange of, and afterwards sold without authority. *Id.* 327.

Recovery of, suit for, in name of beneficiaries, not void; amendable by adding head of family as a plaintiff. *Id.* 328.

Reversionary interest in, even if it can pass by deed made while homestead estate exists, can not be asserted during that time. *Id.* 339.

Sale not in accordance with order for sale, purchaser got no title. *Id.* 327.

Sale; order authorizing sale for stated price, construed to mean for cash and as a whole, not in parcels. *Id.* 334.

Schedule, amendment of. *Ozburn* v. *Flournoy,* 706.

Set-off, in equitable suit for recovery of homestead from purchaser; what allowed. *Taylor* v. *James,* 328.

Waiver void for usury, estoppel of mortgagor to set up, as head of family, after foreclosure. *Bank of Forsyth* v. *Gammage,* 220.

HUSBAND AND WIFE. See *Divorce and Alimony; Homestead.*

Contract between, intended to promote dissolution of marriage relation, void. *Birch* v. *Anthony,* 349.

ILLEGALITY. See *Levy and Sale.*

IMPROVEMENTS.

Extent to which creditor may make, on debtor's property delivered to creditor for purpose of collecting debt from income. *Mohr–Weil Co.* v. *Russell,* 589.

Set-off, in equitable suit for recovery of homestead land. *Taylor* v. *James,* 328.

INDEPENDENT CONTRACTOR. See *Negligence.*

INDICTMENT. See *Criminal Law.*

INDORSEMENT. See *Contracts; Promissory Notes.*

INFANTS. See *Criminal Law; Deeds; Guardian and Ward; Limitations; Railroads; Witness; Year's Support.*

INJUNCTION.

Claim in forma pauperis, when enjoined, and receiver appointed to hold land and rents. *Dawson* v. *Eq. Mge. Co.* 389.

Criminal prosecution not restrained by. *Mayor of Moultrie* v. *Patterson*, 370.

Municipal ordinance, prosecution under, when not enjoined. *Id.*

Railroad company enjoined from locating its line within prohibited distance from another. *Ga. Nor. R. Co.* v. *Tifton, T. & G. R. Co.* 766.

Resale of property bid off at sheriff's sale, not enjoined, under facts here. *Simmons* v. *Cook*, 553.

Sale under power in security deed, when not enjoined because grantee is indebted to grantor. *McDaniel* v. *Cowart*, 419.

Tax, injunction to prevent collection of, granted. *Acme Brewing Co.* v. *Fletcher*, 463. Refused. *Ga. State B. & L. A.* v. *Savannah*, 63. *Mut. Reserve Fund Asso.* v. *Augusta*, 73; *Atl. Nat. B. & L. A.* v. *Stewart*, 103.

Timber-cutting, injunction against, what applicant must show as to title. *Wilcox Lumber Co.* v. *Bullock*, 532.

Ultra vires acts of corporation, State's remedies for; injunction may be had, when. *Trust Co. of Ga.* v. *State*, 747.

INSOLVENCY. See *Bankruptcy; Sales.*

INSURANCE. See *Taxation.*

Assessment to pay policy-holder, suit by association against member for amount of, defense that contract was invalid because association had failed to pay license tax. *Farmers Mut. Ins. Asso.* v. *Austin*, 689.

Assignment of life-insurance, as security, good only to extent of debt and creditor's expense in keeping up policy. *Morris* v. *Ga. Loan Co.* 12.

Assignment of life-insurance, insurable interest by assignee, not necessary to uphold. *Union Frat. League* v. *Walton*, 3.

Beneficiary, who may be. *Id.* 1.

Benefit society, charter and laws to be looked into, to ascertain contract with member. *Id.* 1, 9.

Benefit society, right of member as to appointing beneficiary. *Id.* 1.

Creditor's insurable interest, limit of. *Morris* v. *Ga. Loan Co.* 17.

Insurable interest of creditor taking assignment of policy, extent of. *Id.*

Insurable interest in life, beneficiary need not have, when. *Id.* 1.

Parol evidence as to rates for, admissibility of, where policy provided for applying net reserve to purchase of term insurance after default. *Hamilton* v. *Mut. Ben. Life Ins. Co.* 381.

Premium, default in payment of, period for which insurance continued in force, under policy here. *Id.*

Wagering, discussed. When want of insurable interest by beneficiary will not defeat contract. *Union Frat. League* v. *Walton*, 1.

INTEREST. See *Contracts; Usury.*

INTERSTATE COMMERCE LAW. See *Taxation.*

INTOXICATING LIQUOR. See *Liquor.*

JUDGE. See *Practice in Superior Court.*

Attestation of mortgage by judge of any court in this State, good. *Strauss* v. *Maddox,* 223.

Disqualification, statute providing in case of, that clerk shall appoint attorney to preside if parties do not agree on another person, constitutional. *Bivins* v. *Bank,* 342.

"Justice," "judge," the former used as being interchangeable with the latter, when. *Strauss* v. *Maddox,* 223.

Pro hac vice, appointment of attorney as, by clerk of court, not unconstitutional. *Bivins* v. *Bank,* 242.

JUDGMENTS. See *Liens.*

Amendable though dormant. (Simmons, C. J., and Little, J., dissenting.) *Williams* v. *Merritt,* 217.

Amendment of, in justice's court, after affidavit of illegality filed, and after appeal to superior court. *Bell* v. *Bowdoin,* 209.

Arrest of, in appeal case, during term at which rendered, for want of jurisdiction. *Berger* v. *Saul,* 240.

Collateral attack because plaintiff was foreign administrator and had not filed copy of letters of administration, not allowed. *Marshall* v. *Charland,* 306.

Conclusiveness of foreclosure of chattel mortgage, as to defenses that might have been made. *Bank of Forsyth* v. *Gammage,* 220.

Conclusiveness; not conclude, as to usury in security deed, one not party to the suit, who bought the property before suit on. *Cade* v. *Larned,* 292.

Conclusiveness of adjudication of Supreme Court upon defendant in error, as to questions which would have been brought under review if enough of the record had been sent up. *Little Rock Cooperage Co.* v. *Hodge,* 434.

Consolidation of different liens on different land in one foreclosure, and judgment establishing the whole on all the land; judgment not void. *Suwannee Turp. Co.* v. *Baxter,* 602.

Default, error to set aside, under facts here. *Moore* v. *Kelly & Jones Co.* 798.

Dormancy, effect of, discussed. *Williams* v. *Merritt,* 219.

Dormancy not prevented by minority of plaintiff. *Id.* 218.

Dormancy not prevented by receipts of payments entered on fi. fa. by plaintiff. *Blue* v. *Collins,* 341.

Dormant, amendable. (Simmons, C. J., and Little, J., dissenting.) *Williams* v. *Merritt,* 217.

Dormant, as basis for administration. *Conyers* v. *Bruce,* 190.

Dormant, in favor of minor, he may sue on, within three years after disability removed. *Williams* v. *Merritt,* 213.

Dormant; where some of plaintiffs are minors and the judgment is in favor of all for an undivided amount, limitation of time of suit on, begins to run when. *Id.*

Final, on certiorari, when not rendered. *Velvin* v. *Austin,* 200; *Knowles* v. *Coachman,* 356. When proper. *Wynn* v. *Irvine,* 288.

JUDGMENTS— *continued.*

Foreclosure of chattel mortgage not resisted, conclusiveness as to defenses that might have been made. *Bank of Forsyth* v. *Gammage,* 220.

Fraud in procuring, constructive notice of, not afforded by matters of record here. *McMillan* v. *Hunnicutt,* 700.

Homestead, act of ordinary in receiving and recording schedule for." pony homestead " has not the effect of a judgment; validity may be collaterally attacked. *Marcrum* v. *Washington,* 296.

Irregular, for gross sum against lands as a whole where should be against parcels separately. *Suwannee Turp. Co.* v. *Baxter,* 597.

Lien special on land, judgment establishing, proper in suit on note secured by deed, when. *Jewell* v. *Walker,* 241.

Lien special on realty, judgment declaring, when irregular. *Marshall* v. *Charland,* 308.

Limitation of time for suit on. *Williams* v. *Merritt,* 213.

Merger of cause of action in. *Id.* 216.

Motion to set aside, can be made only by party to the judgment. *Suwannee Turp. Co.* v. *Baxter,* 602.

Motion to set aside, discretion as to granting; defendant's failure to appear and plead, in consequence of misunderstanding with his counsel, not good ground. *Moore* v. *Kelly & Jones Co.* 798.

Motion to set aside, not remedy where juror was disqualified; remedy is motion for new trial. *Mize* v. *Americus Co.* 359.

Party only may move to set aside. *Suwannee Turp. Co.* v. *Baxter,* 602.

Special, against land conveyed by security deed, when proper in suit on note. *Jewell* v. *Walker,* 241.

Void for uncertainty, judgment for plaintiff for " his principal sum and interest at 8 per cent. from maturity and all future interest and cost of suit," was not. *Bell* v. *Bowdoin,* 209.

Void; irregularity in acts of guardian ad litem, not render judgment void. *McMillan* v. *Hunnicutt,* 701.

Void, rule as to when judgment is. *Suwannee Turp. Co.* v. *Baxter,* 602.

JURISDICTION.

Appeal; where justice's court has no jurisdiction of subject-matter, superior court has none on appeal. *Berger* v. *Saul,* 240.

Claim to fund raised by garnishment and properly paid into city court, superior court has no jurisdiction of. *Page* v. *Pitt,* 557.

Consent not confer, when. *Blocker* v. *Boswell,* 239; *Berger* v. *Saul,* 240.

Debt, situs of, general rule that it is where creditor resides. *Central R. Co.* v. *Brinson,* 354.

Equitable proceeding in aid of levy, when lies in county where claim is pending, though the claimant does not reside there. *Dawson* v. *Eq. Mge. Co.* 389.

Garnishment; situs of debt must be within jurisdiction, to bind garnishee. Rule that situs is where creditor is domiciled. *Central R. Co.* v. *Brinson,* 354.

Justice's court has no jurisdiction of trover. *Blocker* v. *Boswell,* 239; *Berger* v. *Saul,* 240.

JURISDICTION — *continued.*

Non-resident claimant, when subject to be made defendant to equitable petition in county where claim pending. *Dawson* v. *Eq. Mge. Co.* 389.

Subject-matter, jurisdiction of, wanting in justice's court, proper course to be pursued by superior court, on certiorari. *Blocker* v. *Boswell*, 239. On appeal. *Berger* v. *Saul*, 240.

Trover, justice's court has no jurisdiction of. *Blocker* v. *Boswell*, 230; *Berger* v. *Saul*, 240.

Waiver presumed from appearing and answering. *Haunson* v. *Nelms*, 804.

JURY.

Auditor's report, right to jury trial on exceptions of fact. *Weaver* v. *Cosby*, 310.

Challenge to array, when proper. Challenge on account of feeling of jurors should be to the polls. *Thompson* v. *State*, 272.

Commissioner's removal from the county, as a ground of challenge to the array; when it must appear that the removal has been judicially ascertained. *Channell* v. *State*, 150.

Conduct of, as cause for new trial; when court will not inquire whether harm resulted. *Central of Ga. R. Co.* v. *Hammond*, 383.

Conduct of, irregularities in, when not cause new trial. *Robinson* v. *State*, 506.

Dispersal pending trial, discretion of court as to. *Central R. Co.* v. *Hall*, 367.

Disqualification, not proper ground for motion to set aside judgment; remedy is motion for new trial. *Mize* v. *Americus Co.* 359.

Impeach verdict, juror can not. *Echols* v. *State*, 508.

Indictment, power of grand jury as to. Power of judge to direct that indictment be laid before grand jury, questioned. *Thompson* v. *State*, 276.

Irregularity in summoning, when not cause new trial. *Dover* v. *State*, 485. In conduct of jurors. *Robinson* v. *State*, 506.

Number composing panel after original panel exhausted, discretionary with judge. *Id.* 506.

Objections to, how made in criminal cases. *Thompson* v. *State*, 276.

Polling, too late after sentence pronounced. *Robinson* v. *State*, 506.

Prejudice by juror before trial, showing as to, on motion for new trial, when insufficient. *Sumner* v. *State*, 142.

Presumption that juror qualified rightly on voir dire, not rebutted by one witness alone. *Id.*

Purity of trial by. *Central of Ga. R. Co.* v. *Hammond*, 383.

Separation, discretion of court as to. *Central R. Co.* v. *Hall*, 367.

Separation of jurors from their fellows, when not cause new trial. *Robinson* v. *State*, 506.

Setting aside juror for cause after panel of forty-eight made up and selection of jury begun, not cause new trial. *Id.*

Voir dire, jurors in misdemeanor case may be placed on. *Thompson* v. *State*, 278.

JUSTICE'S COURT.

Amendment of judgment in, after affidavit of illegality filed and after appeal to superior court. *Bell* v. *Bowdoin*, 209.

Jurisdiction of, not extend to trover suit. *Blocker* v. *Boswell*, 230; *Berger* v. *Saul*, 240.

Lost papers, how established in. *Bell* v. *Bowdoin*, 211.

KIRKWOOD. See *Municipal Corporations.*

LACHES. See *Equity.*

LANDLORD AND TENANT.

Notice of intention to quit, what necessary to end tenancy from year to year. *Roberson* v. *Simons*, 362.

Warrant to remove tenant at sufferance,. judge of county court can not administer oath for, nor issue. *Griswold* v. *Rutherford*, 398.

Year to year tenancy by operation of law, held to exist here. *Roberson* v. *Simons*, 360.

LAWS. See *Code; Code Sections; Constitutional Law.*

LEVY AND SALE.

Advertisement insufficient where the fourth publication was on the Monday next preceding sale day. *Conley* v. *Redwine*, 640.

Advertisement, insufficiency of, as to time of publication, purchaser without notice protected, though he be plaintiff in fi. fa. *Id.*

Affidavit of illegality, not require sheriff to desist from selling, where without merit. *Haunson* v. *Nelms*, 804.

Bidder's arrangement with sheriff as to payment, not bind plaintiff in fi. fa. *Simmons* v. *Cook*, 553.

Bidding deterred, when not cause for setting aside sale. *Conley* v. *Redwine*, 641.

Bid not complied with, resale on same day proper, when. *Suttles* v. *Sewell*, 707.

Bid, transferee of, when occupies position of bidder, as to matters affecting fairness of sale. *Id.* 712.

Bond, forthcoming, acceptance of, by sheriff, not shown by his attesting it. *Fountain* v. *Napier*, 225.

Contiguous parcels of land forming one tract may be levied on and sold as one, though composed of fractional parts of different land lots. *Conley* v. *Redwine*, 641.

Description of land by reference to public record, when sufficient. *Id.*

Dormant fi. fa., sale under, void, and no obstacle to sale on same day under valid fi. fa. *Id.*

Equitable petition in aid of, where claim in forma pauperis filed, lies when. *Dawson* v. *Eq. Mge. Co.* 389.

Fraud in sale, circumstances tending to show. *Haunson* v. *Nelms*, 805.

Fraud known to purchaser at judicial sale, when not affect title. *McMillan* v. *Hunnicutt*, 700.

Homestead; affidavit not required, to authorize levy on "pony homestead." *Marcrum* v. *Washington*, 297.

LEVY AND SALE — *continued*.

Injunction in aid of levy. ` *Dawson* v. *Eq. Mge. Co.* 389.

Judgment irregular, in declaring special lien on realty, not cause for dismissing levy thereon, when the judgment embraced a general lien on all the defendant's property. *Marshall* v. *Charland*, 306.

Lot lines, when not regarded in levy on contiguous parcels. *Conley* v. *Redwine*, 641.

Notice to tenant in possession, entry of levy need not recite. *Hiles Carver Co.* v. *King*, 180.

Officer's failure to make, where judgment dormant, not render liable. *Blue* v. *Collins*, 341.

Presumption from officer's entry. *Hiles Carver Co.* v. *King*, 180.

Price inadequate, ground for setting aside sale, when. *Suttles* v. *Sewell*, 710; *Haunson* v. *Nelms*, 802. Inadequacy not accounted for here by announcement as to application for homestead. *Id.* 805.

Property of third person included in, not cause for setting aside sale at instance of defendant or one entitled to part of proceeds. *Conley* v. *Redwine*, 641.

Purchaser without notice of irregularities, when protected. *Id.* 645.

Resale on day of original sale, because bid not complied with; when void. *Suttles* v. *Sewell*, 707.

Resale, refusal to enjoin. *Simmons* v. *Cook*, 553.

Sale complete when; sale here was not. *Id.* 553.

Sale set aside where made after affidavit of illegality filed and after sheriff said he would not sell, and where property worth $2,000 brought $100. *Haunson* v. *Nelms*, 802.

Seizure, entry of levy need not recite. *Hiles Carver Co.* v. *King*, 180.

Town lots and streets indicated on map but not on the land, levy on the whole as one parcel, legal. *Conley* v. *Redwine*, 641.

Void, estoppel to set up that sale was. *Ashley* v. *Cook*, 653.

Void sale, because of inadequacy of price combined with other circumstances. *Suttles* v. *Sewell*, 710; *Haunson* v. *Nelms*, 802.

Void, where title to the property had been conveyed by defendant as security and not reconveyed; purchaser subrogated to grantee's rights. *Ashley* v. *Cook*, 653.

LIBEL.

Credit of merchant impugned; allegation of special damage not necessary where attorney who had collected claims for clients against merchant wrote to the clients that their claims were not paid. *Brown* v. *Holton*, 431.

LICENSE. See *Liquor; Municipal Corporations; Taxation.*

LIENS. See *Deeds; Mortgages.*

Attorney's fee for recovering land, right to foreclose lien for, not affected by client's sale pending suit, though vendee not notified of lien. *Suwannee Turp. Co.* v. *Baxter*, 597.

Attorney's, whether different liens may be foreclosed in one proceeding. *Id.* 603.

LIENS — *continued.*

Bankruptcy can not be set up by the debtor as ground for staying enforcing of lien in State court. *Carter* v. *Bank*, 573.

Deed to secure debt, special judgment against land described in, when proper in suit on note. *Jewell* v. *Walker*, 241. When irregular. *Marshall* v. *Charland*, 308.

Docketing; lien of judgment, relatively to purchaser from defendant pending appeal, not affected by failure to have fi. fa. issued and entered in ten days from date of judgment. *Crosby* v *King Hard-. ware Co.* 452.

Foreclosure of different liens on different land in one proceeding, and judgment establishing the whole on all the land, not void. *Suwannee Turp. Co.* v. *Baxter*, 602.

Judgment declaring special lien on realty, when irregular; how lien should be set up. *Marshall* v. *Charland*, 308.

Notice of attorney's lien, purchaser of property takes with, when. *Suwannee Turp. Co.* v. *Baxter*, 597.

LIFE-INSURANCE. See *Insurance.*

LIMITATIONS.

Account mutual, what is. Statute runs from date of last item. *Reid* v. *Wilson*, 424.

Administration not defeated by setting up that a debt, which was the ground of application for, was barred. *Conyers* v. *Bruce*, 190.

Amendment alleging facts showing action was not barred, allowed, though from original petition it appeared to be. *Gentry* v. *Barron*, 172.

Estoppel to set up, after having procured adjudication that a former action, upon same cause of action was prematurely brought. *Id.*

Homestead, suit for recovery of, and for mesne profits as affected by. *Taylor* v. *James*, 328.

Judgment, as basis for administration, though dormant. *Conyers* v. *Bruce*, 190.

Judgment, dormancy not prevented by minority of plaintiff; limitation of time for suit on. *Williams* v. *Merritt*, 213.

Mesne profits not recoverable for longer period than four years before suit. *Taylor* v. *James*, 328.

Minor beneficiaries of homestead, bar applied to, where it was applicable to head of family. *Taylor* v. *James*, 338.

Minor plaintiffs in dormant judgment for lump sum, limitation of time for suit on, begins to run when. *Williams* v. *Merritt*, 213.

New promise, letters here were not; debt not described with reasonable certainty. *Paille* v. *Plant*, 247.

Time of commencing suit is date of filing, if law as to process and service is complied with; filing alone does not commence. *Nicholas* v. *British America Co.* 621.

Trover, limitation in Civil Code, §3899, not apply to; law of prescription (§3592) operates as limitation of. *Blocker* v. *Boswell*, 239.

LIQUOR.

Buying, whether legislature may prohibit. *Henderson* v. *Heyward*, 376.

Church, carrying liquor to ; law violated by keeping in buggy near church, though for sick wife. *Brice* v. *State*, 117.

Domestic wines are intoxicating. *O'Brien* v. *State*, 51 ; *Embry* v. *State*, 61.

Domestic wines, failure to except, in special act prohibiting sale of liquors, rendered it unconstitutional. (See dissent.) *Id.*

Election contested ; ordinary, before declaring result of election, must pass on contest and decide all questions affecting validity of election. (See dissent.) *Drake* v. *Drewry*, 399.

Election contest, sufficiency of allegations in petition. *Cole* v. *McClendon*, 183.

Election, qualifications of voters at. *Id.* 184.

Glascock county, act prohibiting sale in, unconstitutional. *Embry* v. *State*, 61.

License, sale without, conviction of, illegal, where indictment charged merely unlawful sale. *O'Brien* v. *State*, 51.

Ordinance as to sale of, on Sunday, validity of. *Kassell* v. *Savannah*, 491.

Paulding county, act prohibiting sale in, unconstitutional. *Embry* v. *State*, 61.

Police power, as to prohibition or restriction of sale or purchase of. *Henderson* v. *Heyward*, 376.

Property right in, as affected by prohibition law. *Id.*

Receiving by purchaser in city where sale prohibited, ordinance making penal unless tax paid for privilege, unauthorized by charter. *Id.* 373.

Selling unlawfully, evidence sufficient to convict of. *Thompson* v. *State*, 272.

Special act prohibiting sale in county, unconstitutional where domestic wines not excepted. (See dissent.) *O'Brien* v. *State*, 51 ; *Embry* v. *State*, 61 ; *Tinsley* v. *State*, 822 Amendment did not vitalize. *Id.* 822.

Tax on brewing company, under act of 1897, $200, not increased by establishing agencies in different counties for sale of its product. *Smith* v. *State*, 227 ; *Acme Brewing Co.* v. *Fletcher*, 463.

Tax on purchasers receiving, unauthorized, when. *Henderson* v. *Heyward*, 373.

Warren county, act prohibiting sale in, unconstitutional. *O'Brien* v. *State*, 51.

Whitfield county, special acts as to, unconstitutional. *Tinsley* v. *State*, 822.

Wines domestic, held to be intoxicating. *O'Brien* v. *State*, 51 ; *Embry* v. *State*, 61.

Wines domestic ; special act prohibiting sale of liquors and not excepting domestic wines, unconstitutional. (See dissent.) *Id.; Tinsley* v. *State*, 822.

LIS PENDENS. See *Notice*.

LOCAL OPTION. See *Elections; Liquor*.

LOST PAPERS. See *Evidence; Justice's Court*.

MALICIOUS PROSECUTION.
Probable cause and good faith not shown by facts here. *Barge* v. *Weems,*
685.
Prosecution for purpose of affecting result of civil proceeding. *Id.*

MASTER AND SERVANT.
Alter ego of master, employee superintending loading of ships, when
treated as, relatively to injured employee. *Woodson* v. *Johnston,*
454.
Negligence of servant, liability of employer; sufficiency of allegations as
to, in action against employer. *Thompson* v. *Wright,* 466.
Release of master from liability for injuries to servant, contract for, when
valid. *Petty* v. *R. Co.* 666.
Superintendent or "boss," liability of employer for negligence of, causing
injury to another employee. *Woodson* v. *Johnston,* 454.

MESNE PROFITS. See *Homestead; Limitations.*

MINORS. See *Criminal Law; Deeds; Guardian and Ward; Limitations;
Railroads; Witness; Year's Support.*

MISTAKE. See *Equity.*

MISTRIAL. See *Practice in Superior Court.*

MONOPOLY. See *Contracts; Constitutional Law.*

MORTGAGES See *Deeds.*
Attestation may be by judge of any court in this State. *Strauss* v. *Mad-
dox,* 224.
Bankruptcy can not be set up by mortgagor as ground for staying fore-
closure in State court. *Carter* v. *Bank,* 573.
Consideration valuable, presumed, where recited in. *Weaver* v. *Cosby,* 310.
Deed to secure debt, no bond to reconvey, enforcement of rights under.
Jewell v. *Walker,* 241.
Foreclosure after payment, not allowed. Held where the debt had been
satisfied by sale of the property, under power in deed made to
secure guarantor, who was the mortgagee's agent. *Ryan* v. *Rice,*
448.
Foreclosure of chattel mortgage not resisted, conclusiveness as to defenses
that might have been made. *Bank of Forsyth* v. *Gammage,* 220.
Partner's, in firm name for firm debt, when not bind firm. *McCord Co.*
v. *Callaway,* 796.
Power to mortgage, when not included in power of sale. *McMillan* v. *Cox,*
42.
Sale and agreement for repurchase at higher price, test as to whether it is
a mortgage and cover for usury. *Felton* v. *Grier,* 322.
Subrogation of purchaser at void sale under judgment in favor of grantee
in security deed, to grantee's rights. *Ashley* v. *Cook,* 658.

MOTION TO SET ASIDE JUDGMENT. See *Judgments.*

MUNICIPAL CORPORATIONS.

Assessment illegal, for paving, property-owner who contracted to pay share of, held bound by contract. *Floyd* v. *Atl. Bkg. Co.* 778.

Augusta, ordinance of, imposing tax on gross premiums of insurance companies "not located in" that city, void. License tax by, on agents of insurance companies, by what agents payable. *Mut. Reserve Fund Asso.* v. *Augusta*, 78.

Cartersville, ordinance making it penal for purchaser of liquor to receive it without paying tax for the privilege, unauthorized by charter. *Henderson* v. *Heyward*, 373.

Certiorari from conviction in recorder's court is not civil case. *Barnett* v. *Atlanta*, 166. See *Mayor* v. *Wood*, 149.

Charter too indefinite in describing boundary of, invalid. *Warren* v. *Branan*, 835.

Columbus, power under charter as to contracts ; allegations in suit against, on alleged contract here, demurrable. *Wiley* v. *Columbus*, 295.

Contract by, alleged in action against, but no allegations showing its terms or that it was made in manner prescribed by charter, demurrer sustained. *Id.*

Criminal case, prosecution for violation of municipal ordinance was. *Barnett* v. *Atlanta*, 166.

Damage to lot-owner by building jail on adjacent lot, when no recovery for. *Long* v. *Elberton*, 28.

Estoppel to set up invalidity of contract. *Milburn* v. *Glynn County*, 478.

General welfare clause of charter, powers under, as to intoxicating liquors. *Henderson* v. *Heyward*, 376.

Injunction against enforcement of penal ordinance, when not granted. *Mayor of Moultrie* v. *Patterson*, 370.

Kirkwood, act incorporating, invalid because boundaries are too indefinite. *Warren* v. *Branan*, 835.

Limits of corporate territory must be clearly defined in act incorporating. *Warren* v. *Branan*, 835.

Liquor, ordinance making it penal for purchaser to receive, without paying tax for the privilege, unauthorized by charter. *Henderson* v. *Heyward*, 373.

Liquor, powers as to, under general welfare clause. *Id. ; Kassell* v. *Savannah*, 491.

Mayor can not appear as attorney before city council on hearing of appeal from his decision in case tried before him as mayor. *Holliman* v. *Hawkinsville*, 107.

Offense under State law, authority to enact ordinance for punishment of act which is. *Kassell* v. *Savannah*, 491.

Ordinance, validity of, when not assailable by petition to enjoin prosecution under. *Mayor* v. *Patterson*, 370.

Prison, owner of adjacent land can not recover damages for erection of, by city, but may recover where nuisance results from negligent maintenance of. *Long* v. *Elberton*, 28.

Savannah, ordinance of, for punishment of keepers of barrooms selling liquor thereat on Sunday, unauthorized. *Kassell* v. *Savannah*, 491.

MUNICIPAL CORPORATIONS — *continued.*
Sunday sale of liquor, authority of city to punish for. *Id.*
Taxation by, and exemptions. See *Taxation.*
Writ of error not lie to judgment reversing conviction by municipal
    court. *Mayor* v. *Wood*, 149.

NAME. See *Criminal Law.*

NEGLIGENCE. See *Equity; Railroads.*
Contractor's, in excavating for building; when owner not liable for.
    Ridgeway v. *Downing Co.* 591.
Employee's acts in preventing damage or loss to master, liability for.
    Thompson v. *Wright*, 469.
Employee's, when employer liable for; allegations in action against em-
    ployer here, sufficient. *Id.* 466.
Jury question here. *Wilkes* v. *R. Co.* 796.
Nuisance caused by negligent manner in which jail kept, recovery for.
    Long v. *Elberton*, 28.
Premises defective; foot hurt by splinter in depot floor; right to recover
    for. *Wilkes* v. *R. Co.* 794.
Superintendent ("walking boss") in charge of loading ships, liability of
    employer for negligence of. *Woodson* v. *Johnston*, 454.

NEGOTIABLE INSTRUMENTS. See *Promissory Notes.*

NEW TRIAL. See *Charge of Court; Practice in Superior Court.*
Bill of review, not lie to review judgment overruling motion for new trial.
    Donaldson v. *Roberts*, 833.
Brief of evidence, dismissal because not presented for approval before
    hearing, when error. *Cherokee Iron Co.* v. *Barry*, 175.
Brief of evidence presented in vacation, under order in term, but not filed,
    discretion as to dismissal. *Whitton* v. *Reid*, 174.
Certiorari; new trial, instead of final judgment, when proper. *Velvin* v.
    Austin, 200.
Continuance because witness absent, refused, judge saying he would en-
    tertain motion if he failed to procure the witness, motion not re-
    newed, new trial not granted. *Bush* v. *State*, 120.
Demurrer overruled, not considered on motion for. *Cleveland* v. *State*, 265.
Dismissal of motion, for want of previous approval of brief of evidence,
    when error. *Cherokee Iron Co.* v. *Barry*, 175.
Error in overruling demurrer rendered subsequent trial a nullity. *So. R.
    Co.* v. *Dyson*, 104.
Evidence, error in admitting or rejecting, as ground for. See *Evidence.*
Extrajudicial statement of judge in regard to motion, not excuse omission
    of counsel. *Donaldson* v. *Roberts*, 832.
Ground complaining of admission of evidence but not setting it forth, not
    considered. *Green* v. *State*, 544; *Petty* v. *R. Co.* 666.
Ground complaining of refusal to allow question to witness, not consid-
    ered, it not appearing what the answer would have been. *Bush*
    v. *State*, 120.
Judge's private communications with counsel, not matter for review.
    Central R. Co. v. *Hall*, 368.

NEW TRIAL—*continued.*

Judge's promise or statement to counsel as to time when motion would be disposed of, when extrajudicial. *Donaldson* v. *Roberts*, 832.

Juror's disqualification, as cause for. See *Jury.*

Motion to quash accusation overruled, matter for direct exception, not ground for new trial. *Cleveland* v. *State*, 265.

Petition to set aside judgment overruling motion for, and to obtain new trial, when not maintainable. *Donaldson* v. *Roberts*, 832.

Record altered by changing judge's note on motion for new trial, by his direction, after bill of exceptions certified, improper. *Fountain* v. *Napier*, 225.

Verification of recitals in motion; certificate of judge that he did not remember the facts alleged, not aided by affidavit of movant's counsel and admission of opposing counsel. *Harris* v. *State*, 280.

NOTICE.

Amendment to pleadings, want of notice as to allowance of, not ground for striking it. *Gentry* v. *Barron*, 172.

Attachment, notice of, to tenant in possession, presumed prima facie from entry of levy. *Hiles Carver Co.* v. *King*, 180.

Fraud in obtaining decree, constructive notice of, not afforded by matters of record here. *McMillan* v. *Hunnicutt*, 700.

Fraud known to purchaser at judicial sale, when not affect title. *Id.*

Lis pendens, notice afforded by, as to claim of plaintiffs' attorneys for fees. *Suwannee Turp. Co.* v. *Baxter*, 597.

Officer's knowledge, when chargeable to bank, as to want of consideration of note discounted by. *Morris* v. *Ga. Loan Co.* 12.

Order for sale of homestead, purchaser chargeable with notice of terms of. *Taylor* v. *James*, 327.

Partition, notice required by Civil Code, ¿4790, as to time of executing writ, need not be in writing. *Ralph* v. *Ward.* 863.

Presumption from entry of levy, that tenant in possession was notified. *Hiles Carver Co.* v. *King*, 180.

Promise by judge to give, not protect, when. *Donaldson* v. *Roberts*, 832.

Purchaser at foreclosure sale, with notice of mortgagor's fraud in acquiring title, not affected by, where mortgagee had no notice of. *McMillan* v. *Hunnicutt*, 700.

Resale, notice of intention to make, when must be alleged in action against vendee *Davis Sulphur Ore Co.* v. *Atlanta Co.* 607.

Road proposed to be built, persons through whose land it will not run are not entitled to notice of. *Huff* v. *Donehoo*, 638.

Sale, advertisement by sheriff, times when must be made. Purchaser without notice of insufficiency protected, though he be plaintiff in fi. fa. *Conley* v. *Redwine*, 640.

Service. See *Evidence; Practice in Supreme Court; Service.*

Tenancy from year to year, notice of intention to quit necessary, to terminate. *Roberson* v. *Simons*, 361.

NUISANCE.

Jail, adjacent lot owner's right to recover where nuisance is caused by manner of keeping. *Long* v. *Elberton*, 28.

OATH. See *Affidavit.*

OFFICERS. See *Levy and Sale; Presumptions; Solicitor-general.*
Embezzlement by, what constitutes. *Robinson* v. *State*, 564.
Removal from county, when must be judicially ascertained before office
    is vacated thereby. *Channell* v. *State*, 150.

ORDINARY.
Appeal from decision of, not as judge of court of ordinary, not lie, and
    certiorari the remedy, when. *Cunningham* v. *U. S. Loan Co.* 618.
Court of ordinary and the ordinary, distinction between. *Id.* 617.
Election contest under local option law, duty of ordinary to pass on, be-
    fore declaring result of election. (See dissent.) *Drake* v. *Drewry*,
    399.

PARENT AND CHILD.
Parol agreement by father with daughter, that she was to have his land,
    for which she was to board him and pay an annuity in money,
    when irrevocable. *Epps* v. *Story*, 302.

PARTIES.
"Administrator," added to plaintiff's name, without more, treated as sur-
    plusage. *Marshall* v. *Charland*, 306.
Amendment adding head of family as plaintiff in suit for recovery of
    homestead, brought in name of beneficiaries, proper. *Taylor* v.
    James, 328.
"As agent for," etc., in naming defendant, treated as merely descriptio
    personæ. *Wynn* v. *Irvine*, 287.
Attorneys joining in application of party for allowance of fees were not.
    Mohr - Weil Co. v. *Russell*, 584.
Bill of exceptions, dismissal for want of. Time allowed to remedy defect,
    when. *McCain* v. *Sutlive*, 547.
Bill of exceptions, only those named therein as parties are   *Id.* 548.
Claim ; party to fi. fa. can not claim the property levied on. Rule applied
    where fi. fa. was against A "as agent for" B, and claim was by A
    personally. *Wynn* v. *Irvine*, 287.
Demurrer that "there are no proper parties," but not pointing out who
    would be proper parties, too general. *Dawson Eq. Mge. Co.* 389.
Ejectment, substitution of new plaintiff, fatal to the action. *Suwannee*
    Turp. Co. v. *Baxter*, 600.
Guarantor, when sued without joining principal debtor. *Penn Tobacco*
    Co. v. *Leman*, 428.
Homestead, suit for recovery of, proper parties plaintiff. *Taylor* v.
    James, 336.
Interested persons, when should be made parties. *Steele* v. *Parker*, 792.
Rule against constable to whom garnishee had paid fund which movant
    (defendant) claimed to be exempt, the creditor was proper party
    to. *Id.*
Same person both plaintiff and defendant. *Weaver* v. *Cosby*, 318.
Set aside judgment, motion to, can be made only by a party to the judg-
    ment. *Suwannee Turp. Co.* v. *Baxter*, 602.

PARTITION.

Agreement for division, when not bind mortgagee or vendee of an undivided interest. *Ralph* v. *Ward*, 363.

Notice required by Civil Code, §4790, as to time of executing writ, need not be in writing. *Id.*

PARTNERSHIP.

Authority of partner as to making note or mortgage in firm name for firm debt. *McCord Co.* v. *Callaway*, 796.

Bond to dissolve garnishment in case against, executed by one "as principal and as a member of" the firm, bound the firm. *Maddox* v. *Am T. & B. Co.* 788.

Dissolution, contract for, whether executory. *Phelps* v. *State*, 115.

Misappropriation of fund by retiring partner; conviction of larceny set aside. *Phelps* v. *State*, 115.

Note or mortgage, authority to make, in firm name for firm debt; when partner has not. *McCord Co.* v. *Callaway*, 796.

Partner sued on personal debt, can not set off debt to firm, when. *Bishop* v. *Mathews*, 790.

Statute of frauds, not apply to agreement by retired partner to pay debt which firm contracted while he was a member. *Reid* v. *Wilson*, 424.

PAULDING COUNTY. See *Liquor*.

PAYMENT. See *Accord and Satisfaction*.

PLEADING. See *Actions ; Criminal Law ; Equity; Parties*.

Admission in, when may be put in evidence by opposite party, though stricken by amendment. *Wynn*, 256.

Amendment of. See *Amendment*.

Answer, that for want of information defendant can neither admit nor deny, when not good. *Angier* v. *Eq. B. & L. A.* 625.

Bill of particulars, when not necessary to attach as exhibit. *Penn Tobacco Co.* v. *Leman*, 430.

By-law not set out in plea which relied on it to support defense, demurrer sustained. *Angier* v. *Eq. B. & L. A.* 627.

Consideration, plea of total failure of, includes partial failure. *Otis* v. *Holmes*, 775.

Consolidation of different liens on different land in one foreclosure proceeding. *Suwannee Turp. Co.* v. *Baxter*, 602.

Contract insufficiently set out, demurrer good. *So. R. Co.* v. *Dyson*, 103.

Contract, when not necessary to attach as exhibit. *Penn Tobacco Co.* v. *Leman*, 430.

Demurrer erroneously overruled, subsequent trial a nullity. *So. R. Co.* v. *Dyson*, 104.

Demurrer "speaking." (Dissenting opinion.) *So. R. Co.* v. *Dyson*, 105.

Demurrer that "there are no proper parties," but not pointing out who would be proper parties, too general. *Dawson* v. *Eq. Mge. Co.* 389.

Misnomer. See *Criminal Law*, catchword "Name."

PLEADING — *continued.*

Non est factum, requisites of plea. *Mozley* v. *Reagan,* 182; *Jewell* v. *Walker,* 245.

Prayer for general relief, scope of. *Schmitt* v. *Schneider,* 632.

·Railroad ticket insufficiently described. (Dissent.) *So. R. Co.* v. *Dyson,* 103.

Recoupment of damages for breach of bond for title, where obligee is sued for purchase-money. *Preston* v. *Walker,* 290.

Set-off; one sued as an individual, upon his personal debt, can not set off debt due firm of which he was a member, when. *Bishop* v. *Mathews,* 790.

Tender, plea of, showing offer by letter to pay money but not that the money was sent with it, not good. *Angier* v. *Eq. B. & L. A.* 625.

Usury and want of consideration, pleas of, here, good against general demurrer. *Gibson* v. *Interstate B. & L. Asso.* 460.

Usury by building and loan association, allegations in plea here insufficient to show. *Angier* v. *Eq. B. & L. A.* 625.

POSSESSION. See *Criminal Law; Debtor and Creditor; Title.*

POWERS. See *Deeds; Mortgages; Sales; Wills.*

PRACTICE IN SUPERIOR COURT. See *Amendment; Criminal Law; New Trial; Pleading.*

Argument; court not reversed for requiring counsel to refrain from pathetic remarks though legitimate. *Conley* v. *Redwine,* 650.

Argument, discretion of court as to restricting matter of. *Id.*

Argument improper here. *Holliman* v. *Hawkinsville,* 111; *Robinson* v. *State,* 506; *Broznack* v. *State,* 516. When not cause new trial. *Robinson* v. *State,* 506.

Auditor's report, practice as to. See *Auditor's Report.*

Examination by physician, ordered by court, refusal of female to submit to, in action by father for loss of service from injury, not authorize court to dismiss case. *Bagwell* v. *R. Co.* 611.

Extrajudicial promise or statement of judge, not excuse omission of counsel. *Donaldson* v. *Roberts,* 832.

Filing, what constitutes. Date of placing bill of exceptions in clerk's hands, and not subsequent date marked on it by him, was time of filing. *McDaniel* v. *Columbus Fert. Co.* 284.

First term, trial at, in equity cause, by consent of guardian ad litem of minor defendants. *McMillan* v. *Hunnicutt,* 699.

Judge's private communications with counsel, not matter for review. *Central R. Co.* v. *Hall,* 368.

Judge's promise or statement to counsel in regard to case, when extrajudicial. *Donaldson* v. *Roberts,* 832.

Mistrial because of conduct of juror. *Central of Ga. R. Co.* v. *Hammond,* 383.

Trial at first term in equity cause, by consent of guardian ad litem of minor defendants. *McMillan* v. *Hunnicutt,* 699.

PRACTICE IN SUPREME COURT. See *New Trial.*

Amendment disallowed is no part of the record; must come up in bill of exceptions. *Reid* v. *Wilson,* 424.

Assignment of error; allegation that court erred in overruling certiorari covers all errors distinctly alleged in the petition for certiorari. *Holliman* v. *Hawkinsville,* 107.

Bill of exceptions, delay in presenting to judge, after returned for correction, was unreasonable here. *Parkman* v. *Dent,* 289.

Bill of exceptions, dismissal for want of party. Time allowed by court ex suo mero motu ᵗto remedy defect, where no motion to dismiss. *McCain* v. *Sutlive,* 547.

Bill of exceptions, filing; date of placing in hands of clerk of court, and not subsequent date marked on it by clerk, was time of filing. *McDaniel* v. *Columbus Fert. Co.* 284.

Bill of exceptions, mistake of clerk of trial court in certifying as to date of filing, how rectified. *McDaniel* v. *Columbus Fert. Co.* 284.

Bill of exceptions not certified in time, but reciting it was tendered in time prescribed by law, not dismissed. *Moore* v. *Kelly & Jones Co.* 798.

Bill of exceptions to refusal of certiorari from conviction in municipal court; case is criminal, and time for excepting is twenty days. *Barnett* v. *Atlanta,* 166.

Cross-bill of exceptions, rule that it will be dismissed where original bill is affirmed. *McElveen* v. *R. Co.* 255.

Damages for bringing up case for delay, awarded. *Gentry* v. *Barron,* 172; *Mozley* v. *Reagan,* 182; *Osborn & Walcott Mfg. Co.* v. *Blanton,* 196; *Atl. Bot. Wks.* v. *Hutchinson,* 550.

Demurrer not shown by record to be special, though in fact so, and which Supreme Court treated as general in reversing judgment sustaining it, could not be again submitted and sustained. *Little Rock Cooperage Co.* v. *Hodge,* 434.

Demurrer overruled, matter for direct exception, not for motion for new trial. *Cleveland* v. *State,* 265.

Docketed to wrong term, when case will be transferred to proper docket, and when dismissed. *Gordon,* 262.

Docketing, duty of clerk as to. *Id.*

Evidence, assignments of error on rulings as to admissibility of. See catchword "Grounds," under *New Trial.*

Fast bill of exceptions, not lie to order granted on petition to enforce by attachment a previous judgment for alimony. *Gordon,* 262.

Fast bill of exceptions, when held not to lie, case transferred, on motion, to docket of next term. *Id.*

Fee of solicitor-general in riot case, in Supreme Court, $15. One fee for each bill of exceptions, though there be more than one plaintiff in error. *In re Kenan,* 819.

Municipal corporation not entitled to writ of error to judgment reversing conviction for violation of ordinance. *Mayor* v. *Wood,* 149.

Party, dismissal for want of. *McCain* v. *Sutlive,* 548.

58

PRACTICE IN SUPREME COURT— *continued.*

Party, time allowed by Supreme Court, ex suo mero motu, to make party or obtain waiver of service, before dismissal for want of, where no motion to dismiss. *Id.*

Party to bill of exceptions, person not named therein as such, is not. *Id.*

Private communications between judge and counsel, not matter for review. *Central R. Co.* v. *Hall*, 368.

Question not made in Supreme Court, because a material part of the record was not sent up, party concluded as to, on subsequent hearing. *Little Rock Cooperage Co.* v. *Hodge,* 434.

Question not made in trial court, not considered. *Carter* v. *Bank*, 573.

Record altered, how shown; no dismissal where alteration not affect merits of case. *Fountain* v. *Napier*, 225.

Record, failure of defendant in error to have additional part sent up concluded him, how, after reversal. *Little Rock Cooperage Co.* v. *Hodge*, 434.

Record, judge has no power to alter, after bill of exceptions certified. *Fountain* v. *Napier*, 225.

Service, acknowledgment of, for "defendants in error," not include persons not named in bill of exceptions as such. *McCain* v. *Sutlive*, 547.

Service on solicitor-general, when required; not required where conviction was in municipal court. *Holliman* v. *Hawkinsville*, 103.

PRESCRIPTION. See *Title.*

PRESUMPTIONS. See *Evidence.*

Consideration valuable, presumption as to, where recited in note and mortgage. *Weaver* v. *Cosby*, 310.

Officer did duty; presumption protects purchaser at judicial sale, when. *Conley* v. *Redwine*, 645.

Seal of corporation, presumption where affixed to writing, that officer signing had authority to do so. *Dodge* v. *Am. Freehold Co.* 396.

Seal, presumption from, as to consideration. *Weaver* v. *Cosby,* 313.

Surety signing after two persons who signed apparently as principals was presumptively surety for both. *Pirkle* v. *Chamblee*, 32.

PRINCIPAL AND AGENT. See *Taxation.*

A "as agent for" B, execution against, treated as against A personally, and not as agent. *Wynn* v. *Irvine*, 287.

Commission for negotiating loan which, because of alleged cloud on applicant's title to land offered as security, was not consummated, not recoverable, under facts here. *Hanesley* v. *Bagley*, 346.

Knowledge of agent, when chargeable to principal. *Morris* v. *Ga. Loan Co.* 21.

Power of attorney, when must bear seal of corporation; proof of officer's authority where seal not used. *Dodge* v. *Am. Freehold Co.* 395.

PRINCIPAL AND SURETY. See *Bond.*

Burden of proof as to suretyship, as between signers of note. *Pirkle* v. *Chamblee*, 32.

Estoppel of one who signed as principal, to set up that he was surety. *Id.* 33.

PROCESS.　See *Actions; Service.*

PROMISSORY NOTES.

Accord and satisfaction by giving, no defense to original cause of action, unless paid or expressly agreed to be received as payment. *Brantley Co.* v. *Lee*, 478.

Alteration, burden of proof as to; requisites of plea. *Mozley* v. *Reagan*, 182; *Jewell* v. *Walker*, 245.

Alteration, presumption as to when made. *Id.* 246.

Cheating and swindling by inducing another to give, though insolvent. *Holton* v. *State*, 127.

Consideration, failure of, where note was given for machinery, upon promise to repair defects. *Otis* v. *Holmes*, 775.

Consideration, plea of total failure of, includes partial failure. *Id.*

Consideration, presumption as to. *Weaver* v, *Cosby*, 310.

Consideration, want of, known to cashier of bank discounting, bank charged with notice, when. *Morris* v. *Ga. Loan Co.* 12.

Defense known when note given, waived by giving. *Atl. Bot. Co.* v. *Hutchinson*, 550.

Indorsement of non-negotiable paper, what necessary to render liable on. *Jossey* v. *Rushin*, 319.

Indorsement to plaintiff pending suit on, too late to uphold the action. *Burch* v. *Daniel*, 256.

Limitation, action on, apparently barred by; amendment and proof showing it was not so barred, allowed. *Gentry* v. *Barron*, 172.

Non est factum, requisites of plea *Mozley* v. *Reagan*, 182; *Jewell* v. *Walker*, 245.

Partner's, in firm name for firm debt, when not bind firm. *McCord Co.* v. *Callaway*, 796.

Proof of execution, where non est factum pleaded; prima facie proof sufficient to authorize introduction of note as evidence. *Jewell* v. *Walker*, 241.

Purchase-money. See catchwords "Bond for title," under *Title.*

Suretyship on note, burden of proof as to. *Pirkle* v. *Chamblee*, 32.

Title of plaintiff not acquired before suit on, no recovery. *Burch* v. *Daniel.* 256.

PUBLIC POLICY. See *Contracts; Insurance; Railroads.*

QUO WARRANTO.

Remedy for ultra vires acts of corporation; other remedies. *Trust Co. of Ga.* v. *State*, 747.

RAILROADS.

Bill of lading, parol proof, when not admissible to affect. *McElveen* v. *R. Co.* 249.

Cars left standing across street, so that pedestrian had to walk around them, where condition of ground caused him to fall. *Ga. R. Co.* v. *Roughton*, 604.

Child running alongside track and having a rope which trailed behind and was caught by train, no recovery for injury to. *Cross* v. *R. Co.* 170.

RAILROADS— *continued.*

Combination agreement between, where general result is benefit to public at large, though it lessen or defeat competition at some points, not invalid as tending to defeat competition. *State* v. *Central R. Co.* 716. See *Trust Co.* v. *State*, 737.

Combination between, to defeat competition, State's remedies for. *Id.* 747.

Competition by; constitutional provision construed. *State* v. *Central R. Co.* 716; *Trust Co. of Ga.* v. *State*, 736.

Cross another railroad in city, company authorized by charter to construct road "to" the city may. *Waycross A.-L. R. Co.* v. *Offerman R. Co.* 827.

Cross another railroad, when railroad may, without authority from railroad commission. *Id.* 831.

Crossing law criticized, as to requirement to check speed on approaching crossings. *Central R. Co.* v. *Hall*, 369.

Crossings, checking speed on approaching, law as to, applied though crossing was only half mile from starting-point. *Id.* 367.

Defective premises, right to recover for injury caused by. *Wilkes* v. *R. Co.* 794.

Employee's contract for release of company from liability for injuries, when valid. *Petty* v. *R. Co.* 666.

Freight, failure to trace, facts not authorizing recovery for. *McElveen* v. *R. Co.* 249.

Injunction against locating line within prohibited distance from another. *Ga. Nor. R. Co.* v. *Tifton, T. &˙ G. R. Co.* 766.

Location; point where line shall end in terminal city, discretionary when not fixed by charter. *Waycross A.-L. R. Co.* v. *Offerman & W. R. Co.* 829.

Location within prohibited distance from another line. *Ga. Nor. R. Co.* v. *Tifton, T. & G. R. Co.* 766.

Merger of, not result from ownership of stock of one by another. *Waycross A.-L. R. Co.* v. *Offerman & W. R. Co.* 828.

Negligence, exemption from liability for, employee's contract here for release of company from liability for injuries, not in conflict with law as to. *Petty* v. *R. Co.* 671.

Passenger hurt in alighting from train, by splinter in depot floor. *Wilkes* v. *R. Co.* 794.

Passenger, rights of, as affected by limitation in ticket. *Central R. Co.* v. *Ricks*, 339.

Premises dangerous, passenger's foot hurt by splinter in floor of station when alighting from train, right to recover. *Wilkes* v. *R. Co.* 794.

Public policy as to purchase of competitive lines, and of branch lines. *State* v. *Central R. Co.* 734.

Release from liability for injuries, validity of contract for. *Petty* v. *R. Co.* 666.

Release of claim for damages against, when not rescinded for mistake as to contents. *Jossey* v. *R. Co.* 439.

Route within prohibited distance from another line. *Ga. Nor. R. Co.* v. *Tifton, T. & G. R. Co.* 766.

RAILROADS — *continued.*

Signal, failure to give, to child running alongside track on which train was approaching, not negligence. *Cross* v. *R. Co.* 170.

Speed in approaching crossing, law as to checking, applies where train is far enough from starting-point to get under way. *Central R. Co.* v. *Hall,* 369.

Station floor defective, passenger's right to recover for injury from. *Wilkes* v. *R. Co.* 794.

Stock all owned by another, not make them identical. *Waycross A.-L. R. Co.* v. *Offerman & W. R. Co.* 828.

Street-railways, combination of, when not illegal. *Trust Co. of Ga.* v. *State,* 737.

Sunday, running excursion-train on, who indictable for; trainmaster acting under orders from superintendent was not. *Craven* v. *State,* 266.

Terminus; point where line shall end in terminal city, discretionary when not fixed by charter. *Waycross A.-L. R. Co.* v. *Offerman & W. R. Co.* 829.

Ticket in sufficiently described in action by passenger for expulsion, demurrer good. (See dissent.) *So. R. Co.* v. *Dyson,* 103.

Ticket limitation as to time, when binding. *Central R. Co.* v. *Ricks,* 389.

"To" a city means "into" it, in charter authorizing company to build road. *Waycross R. Co.* v. *Offerman & W. R. Co.* 827.

Trace freight, action for failure to, not maintainable under facts here. *McElveen* v. *R. Co.* 249.

RECEIVER.

Land to which claim in forma pauperis filed, receiver to hold, appointed on petition of plaintiff in fi. fa., when. *Dawson* v. *Eq. Mge. Co.* 389.

RECORD. See *Deeds; Executions; New Trial; Practice in Supreme Court.*

Contract of county, petition in action against county on, must show compliance with law as to entering on minutes. *Milburn* v. *Glynn County,* 473.

RECOUPMENT. See *Pleading.*

REGISTRATION. See *Deeds; Elections.*

RELEASE. See *Railroads.*

REMEDIES. See *Actions; Equity; Habeas Corpus; Injunction; Quo Warranto.*

RESCISSION. See *Contracts.*

RES JUDICATA. See *Judgments.*

REVERSION. See *Homestead.*

ROADS. See *Railroads.*

Damages from establishment of new road, not recoverable by owners of land abutting on old road, when. *Huff* v. *Donehoo,* 638.

ROADS — *continued.*

Damages to private property from working adjacent public road, liability of county for. *Barfield* v. *Macon County*, 386.

Inspector of, county not authorized to employ, prior to act of 1889 as to. Whether that act is valid, not decided. *Turner* v. *Fulton County*, 633.

Notice of proposed new road need not be given to persons through whose land it will not run. *Huff* v. *Donehoo*, 638.

Property owners injured by establishment of, complaining as such and not as taxpayers, not heard as to alleged failure of county authorities to strictly follow the law in establishing. *Id.*

RULE. See *Garnishment; Parties.*

SALES. See *Homestead.*

Bidding deterred, when not cause for setting aside. *Conley* v. *Redwine*, 641.

Conditional, distinguished from mortgage. *Felton* v. *Grier*, 322.

Cover for usury, sale and conveyance and contemporaneous agreement for repurchase at higher price, when not. *Felton* v. *Grier*, 320.

Exchange of products, contract for, not broken where no offer made on one side, nor refusal on the other. *Brown* v. *Drake*, 179.

Injunction against resale of property bid off at sheriff's sale, refusal of. *Simmons* v. *Cook*, 553.

Injunction against sale under power in security deed, when not lie because grantee is indebted to grantor. *McDaniel* v. *Cowart*, 419.

Insolvency of vendee ascertained before delivery, rights of vendor. *Davis Sulphur Ore Co.* v. *Atlanta Co.* 610.

Judicial. See *Levy and Sale.*

Loss of goods by fire while in railroad depot and while title was still in seller, after breach of contract by purchaser to pay draft and remove them, not recoverable from purchaser. *Mountain City Mill Co.* v. *Butler*, 469.

Notice of intention to resell, when necessary. *Davis Sulphur Ore Co.* v. *Atlanta Co.* 607.

Power of sale in security deed, exercise of, when not enjoined because grantee is indebted to grantor. *McDaniel* v. *Cowart*, 419.

Power of sale, when not include power to mortgage, nor to convey title as security. *McMillan* v. *Cox*, 42.

Price, inadequacy of, at judicial sale, when cause for setting aside sale. *Suttles* v. *Sewell*, 707.

Repurchase agreement made contemporaneously with sale, when not render transaction a mortgage, or cover for usury. *Felton* v. *Grier*, 322.

Resale by vendor after stopping goods in transit on learning of vendee's insolvency, what allegations necessary in suit against vendee for deficiency in price obtained. *Davis Sulphur Ore Co.* v. *Atlanta Co.* 607.

Resale, notice of intention to make, when must be alleged in action against vendee. *Davis Sulphur Ore Co.* v. *Atlanta Co.* 607.

SALES — *continued.*

Sheriff's arrangement with bidder, to dispense with immediate cash payment, not bind plaintiff in fi. fa. *Simmons* v. *Cook*, 553.

Stoppage in transitu and resale by vendor, what necessary to authorize recovery against vendee for deficiency. *Davis Sulphur Ore Co.* v. *Atlanta Co.* 607.

Tender by one side and refusal by the other, not shown in action for breach of contract for exchange for products, no recovery. *Brown* v. *Drake*, 179.

Tender of goods, demand for payment, and refusal, when must be alleged in suit against vendee after resale by vendor. *Davis Sulphur Ore Co.* v. *Atlanta Co.* 607.

Title wanting, to part of land sold under bond for title, recovery for breach of bond, though vendee knew of the deficiency when the bond was made. *Foute* v. *Elder*, 713.

SAVANNAH.　See *Municipal Corporations.*

SEAL.　See *Contracts; Corporations.*

SECURITY DEED.　See *Deeds.*

SERVICE.　See *Evidence; Practice in Supreme Court.*
Unofficial, of process, when binding. *Bell* v. *Bowdoin*, 212.

SET-OFF.　See *Pleading.*

SETTLEMENT.　See *Accord and Satisfaction.*

SHERIFF.　See *Actions; Levy and Sale; Sales.*

SLANDER.　See *Libel.*

SOLICITOR-GENERAL.

Fee in Supreme Court in riot case, $15. One fee for each bill of exceptions, though more than one excepting party. What clerk's certificate as to insolvency must show. *In re Kenan*, 819.

Service of bill of exceptions on, when required. Not required where case was conviction in municipal court of violating ordinance. *Holliman* v. *Hawkinsville*, 108.

STATUTE OF FRAUDS.　See *Frauds, Statute of.*

STATUTE OF LIMITATIONS.　See *Limitations.*

STATUTES.　See *Code; Code Sections; Constitutional Law.*

STOCK.　See *Corporations; Taxation.*

SUBROGATION.　See *Deeds.*

SUNDAY.　See *Criminal Law; Municipal Corporations.*

SUPERIOR COURT.　See *Practice in Superior Court.*

SUPREME COURT.　See *Practice in Supreme Court.*

SURETY AND INDORSER. See *Contracts; Principal and Surety; Promissory Notes.*

TAXATION.

Ad valorem and uniform, requirement that taxation shall be, discussed. *Ga. State B. & L. A.* v. *Savannah*, 63; *Mutual Reserve Fund Life Asso.* v. *Augusta.* 73; *Atlanta Nat. B. & L. A.* v. *Stewart*, 80.

Agents of insurance companies. taxation of. *Mut. Reserve Fund Life Asso.* v. *Augusta*, 73.

Bicycle-dealer selling different makes, not required to pay more than one license tax, when. *Alexander* v. *State*, 805.

Brewing company employee, in charge of agency for sale of its beer, not subject to tax as dealer, under act of 1897, when. *Smith* v. *State*, 227.

Brewing company paying $200 tax imposed on such companies by act of 1897, not incur additional tax by establishing agencies for sale of its beer in different counties. *Smith* v. *State*, 227. As to act of 1898, see *Acme Brewing Co.* v *Fletcher*, 463.

Building and loan association, obligation of borrowing member to, is an asset which may be taxed to extent of market value. *Atl. Nat. Asso.* v. *Stewart*, 82.

Building and loan association; tax on shares of members, in lieu of all other taxes of the corporation, unconstitutional. *Ga. State B. & L. A.* v. *Savannah*, 63; *Atl. Nat. B. & L. A.* v. *Stewart*, 81.

Building and loan association, tax on stock of, when treated as against property of stockholder and not on franchise of association. *Id.*

Building and loan associations, act of 1896 provides machinery sufficient to bring under taxation the property of. *Atl. Nat. Asso.* v. *Stewart*, 81

Building and loan associations; tax on stock of stockholders, imposed by act of 1896, is on the shares as property of shareholders, and not a tax on property of the corporations. *Id.*

Business, tax on receipts of, when not treated as property tax. *Mut. Reserve Fund Life Asso.* v. *Augusta*, 75; *Atl. Nat. B. & L. A.* v. *Stewart*, 80.

Chose in action owned by resident, though debtor is non-resident, is taxable wherever the evidence of debt may be located. *Id.* 82.

Classification of business for taxation. *Mut. Reserve Fund Asso.* v. *Augusta*, 79; *Atl. Nat. Asso.* v. *Stewart*, 80.

Confederate soldiers, exemption from license tax. *Holliman* v. *Hawkinsville*, 107; *Hartfield* v. *Columbus*, 112. Exemption covers agent or employee of. *Id.*

Constitutionality of general tax act of 1896 as to building and loan associations, express companies and telephone companies. *Atlanta Nat. B. & L. Asso.* v *Stewart*, 81

Corporation, methods of taxing. *Ga. State B. & L. A.* v. *Savannah*, 70; *Atl. Nat. B & L. A.* v. *Stewart*, 80.

Corporation, power to tax stock of, as property of shareholders, while also taxing the property of the corporation. *Id.* 81.

TAXATION — *continued.*

Corporations, legislature can not declare that occupation or business tax on certain classes of, when collected, shall be received in lieu of all other taxes upon the property of the corporation. *Id.*

Corporations, tax on stock of, when not treated as equivalent of tax on property of. *Ga. State B. & L. A.* v. *Savannah*, 91.

Corporations, when tax law provides machinery to tax property of, it may be used to tax property which the same paragraph has unconstitutionally declared shall not be taxed as therein prescribed. *Atl. Nat. Asso.* v. *Stewart*, 81.

Corporations; where tax law provides machinery to bring under taxation all property of an individual, it may be applied to property of corporations. *Id.*

County authorities, law as to statement by, to grand jury, as to county's financial condition and amount of tax required to meet debts, is directory, not mandatory; non-compliance not invalidate tax levy *Id.* 82.

County taxation; query, whether legislature has power to tax certain classes of property and withdraw from counties the power to tax them. *Id.* 81.

County tax without recommendation of grand jury, incumbent on person attacking levy to show it was for purpose for which there was no right to make the levy without such recommendation. *Id.* 82.

Double, not favored, but discretionary with taxing power. *Ga. State B. & L. A.* v. *Savannah*, 71.

Exemption, by failing to provide machinery for collection of tax, not construed to have been intended in tax act. *Atl. Nat. Asso.* v. *Stewart*, 81.

Exemption of Confederate soldiers from license tax. *Holliman* v. *Hawkinsville*, 107; *Hartfield* v. *Columbus*, 112. Covers agent or employee of. *Id.*

Exemptions, invalidity of provisions making. *Ga. State B. & L. A.* v. *Savannah*, 63; *Mut. Reserve Fund Asso.* v. *Augusta*, 73; *Atl. Nat. B. & L. A.* v. *Stewart*, 80.

Express companies, validity of provisions of general tax act of 1896 as to. *Id.* 80.

Insurance companies, tax on agents of, is payable by agent of association which insures on assessment plan, though he be an employee of the company and represent no other. *Mut. Reserve Fund Asso.* v. *Augusta*, 73.

Insurance company, tax on gross premiums of, is not property tax, so as to require ad valorem system applied; municipal ordinance imposing, on non-resident companies alone, void for want of uniformity. *Id*

Interstate commerce clause of constitution of U. S., not prohibit taxing chose in action owned by resident, though the debtor is a non-resident. *Atl. Nat. Asso.* v. *Stewart*, 82.

Liquor, ordinance making it penal for purchaser to receive, without paying tax for the privilege, unauthorized by charter. *Henderson* v. *Heyward*, 373.

TAXATION — *continued.*

Receipts of business, tax on, when not treated as property tax. *Mut. Reserve Fund Life Asso.* v. *Augusta,* 75 ; *Atl. Nat. B. & L. A.* v. *Stewart,* 80.

Stock of corporation, power of legislature to tax, as property of shareholders, while also taxing the property of the corporation. *Id.* 81.

Stock of corporation, tax on, when not treated as equivalent of tax on property of. *Ga. State B. & L. A.* v. *Savannah,* 71.

Stock of corporation, tax on, when treated as against stockholder and not against corporation. *Id.*

Telephone companies, validity of provisions of general tax act of 1896, as to. *So. Bell Tel. Co.* v. *Stewart,* 80.

Value ; query, whether General Assembly has power to declare that certain property has none, and therefore shall not be returned for taxation. *Atl. Nat. Asso.* v. *Stewart,* 82.

TELEPHONE COMPANIES. See *Taxation.*

TENDER. See *Sales.*

Money, letter proposing to pay but not accompanied by, not good tender. *Angier* v. *Eq. B. & L. A.* 625.

Rescission for fraud in procurement of contract, not had without offering to restore fruits of contract.' *Petty* v. *R. Co.* 666.

TIMBER. See *Injunction.*

TITLE. See *Deeds ; Homestead ; Promissory Notes.*

Bond for, breach of ; obligee sued on purchase-money notes, though in possession of the property, may recoup damages, when. *Preston* v. *Walker,* 290.

Bond for, breach of ; when want of title to part of the property is breach, though known to obligee when bond made. *Foute* v. *Elder,* 713.

Bond for reconveyance not essential in order for security deed to pass title. *Jewell* v. *Walker,* 241.

Breach of bond for, obligee sued for purchase-money, though in possession of the property, may recoup damages, when. *Preston* v. *Walker,* 290.

Cheating and swindling by false representations as to. *Holton* v. *State,* 127.

Cloud on, what necessary to constitute. *Hanesley* v. *Bagley,* 346.

Color of title, sheriff's deed to land sold under justice's court fi. fa., when good as, though no entry of "no personalty." *Wade* v. *Garrett,* 270.

Fraud of mortgagor in acquiring, not known to mortgagee, purchaser at foreclosure sale acquired good title, though he knew of the fraud. *McMillan* v. *Hunnicutt,* 700.

Injunction against cutting timber, what applicant must show as to title. *Wilcox Lumber Co.* v. *Bullock,* 532.

Outstanding, as defense to ejectment. *Ashley* v. *Cook,* 655.

Parol agreement for, as defense to ejectment. *Epps* v. *Story,* 302.

Partition by agreement, title by. *Ralph* v. *Ward,* 363.

TITLE — *continued*.

"Perfect title," what is, and when must be shown, under law providing for injunction against cutting timber. *Wilcox Lumber Co.* v *Bullock*, 532.

Possession held adversely to administrator at time of sale and conveyance by him, purchaser got no title. *Hanesley* v. *Bagley*, 348.

Possession of land assigned to tenant in common as his share in division, when not avail as against mortgagee of undivided interest. *Ralph* v. *Ward*, 363.

Prescriptive, under color of void deed, good as basis of recovery against one relying on naked possession less than twenty years. *Wade* v. *Garrett*, 270.

Security deed, as basis of ejectment, or as outstanding title to defeat ejectment. *Ashley* v. *Cook*, 655.

Security deed passes, though bond to reconvey not given. *Jewell* v. *Walker*, 241.

Third person's, good defense in ejectment, without connecting defendant's possession with it. *Jenkins* v. *R. Co*. 35.

TORTS. See *Actions; Damages; Malicious Prosecution; Negligence; Railroads.*

TRESPASS.

Injunction against cutting timber, what applicant must show as to title. *Wilcox Lumber Co.* v. *Bullock*, 532.

TRIAL. See *Criminal Law; Jury; Practice.*

TROVER.

Justice's court has no jurisdiction of. *Blocker* v. *Boswell*, 230; *Berger* v. *Saul*, 240.

Limitation of action. *Blocker* v. *Boswell*, 236.

TRUSTS.

Bailee, when not trustee in such sense as to give priority to bailor in distribution of assets. *Tiedeman* v. *Imp. Fert. Co.* 661.

Fraud of trustee, by which she acquired title individually to trust property, constructive notice of, not afforded by matters of record here. *McMillan* v. *Hunnicutt*, 700.

Homestead is in nature of trust estate; beneficiaries barred by statute of limitations where head of family is. *Taylor* v. *James*, 338.

Power to borrow money and secure it by mortgage, powers conferred by will here construed not to include. *McMillan* v. *Cox*, 42.

ULTRA VIRES. See *Corporations.*

USURY.

Building and loan association, plea of usury, to action by, here, good against general demurrer. *Gibson* v. *Interstate Asso.* 460.

Building and loan association, usury by, plea of, based on allegation that charter powers were beyond proper scope of such an association, but not alleging operations beyond scope of, bad. *Angier* v. *Eq. B. & L. A.* 628.

USURY — *continued.*

Deed and agreement by grantor to repurchase, test as to whether cover for usury. *Felton* v. *Grier*, 322.

Estoppel of wife to set up that husband's deed was infected with, not result from writing her approval on it. *Cade* v. *Larned*, 292.

Forfeiture of entire debt (to national bank) because of ; question not considered by Supreme Court where not made in trial court, though plea of usury filed. *Carter* v. *Bank*, 573.

Sale and contemporaneous agreement for repurchase at higher price, when not treated as cover for usury. *Felton* v. *Grier*, 320.

Security deed subject to attack for, by one who purchased from grantor before suit thereon. *Cade* v. *Larned*, 292.

Too late to set up, as to property sold under foreclosure of chattel mortgage infected with. *Bank of Forsyth* v. *Gammage*, 220.

VENDOR AND VENDEE. See *Sales*.

VERDICT.

Default, due to misunderstanding between party and his counsel, error to set aside. *Moore* v. *Kelly & Jones Co.* 800.

"Manslaughter," verdict of, treated as verdict of voluntary manslaughter. *Smith* v. *State*, 479.

VERIFICATION. See *Certiorari; New Trial.*

WAIVER. See *Homestead; Jurisdiction.*

Defense known when note given, waived by giving. *Atl. Bot. Co.* v. *Hutchinson*, 550.

Process, waiver of, cures irregularity in, as well as absence of. *Penn Tobacco Co.* v. *Leman*, 428.

WARRANTY. See *Deeds.*

WARREN COUNTY. See *Liquor.*

WHITFIELD COUNTY. See *Liquor.*

WILLS.

Life-estate not created by provision here that the trustee should take charge of and manage the property for the benefit of the cestui que trust during his life. *Ford* v. *Gill*, 691.

Power to borrow money and secure it by mortgage, powers conferred by will here construed not to include. *McMillan* v. *Cox*, 42.

WITNESS. See *Evidence.*

Child's understanding of nature of oath, not shown by answers here. *Miller* v. *State*, 510.

Death as affecting competency; personal representative of deceased payee of note sued on, incompetent to testify that it was altered after delivery. *Jewell* v. *Walker*, 241.

"Impeached" defined. When used as synonymous with "attacked." *Smith* v. *State*, 479.

WITNESS — *continued.*

Impeachment by proof of contradictory statements, when not allowed. *Hudgins* v. *Bloodworth,* 197.

Impeachment by proof of testimony on commitment trial. *Haines* v. *State,* 528.

Wife competent to testify on trial of another than husband, charged with same offense. *Fuller* v. *State,* 809.

WORDS AND PHRASES.

"Action," "bring an action." *Williams* v. *Merritt,* 215.

"Administrator," added to plaintiff's name, without more, treated as surplusage. *Marshall* v. *Charland,* 306.

"As agent for," etc., in naming defendant, treated as merely descriptio personæ. *Wynn* v. *Irvine,* 287.

"Assured" and "beneficiary," synonymous. (Per Lumpkin, P. J., dissenting.) *Union Frat. League* v. *Walton,* 11.

"At" a church included a place near it. *Bice* v. *State,* 119.

"Believe," in affidavit for certiorari, is equivalent to "verily believe," as used in Civil Code, §4638. *Ethridge* v. *Forsyth,* 156.

"Cases of injuries or damages to personal property," not include trover. *Blocker* v. *Boswell,* 231.

"Company," in tax act, when applied also to individual. *Smith* v. *State,* 228.

"Consideration of —— dollars;" not essential that amount be stated in deed. *Jewell* v. *Walker,* 245.

"Debt of another" (Statute of Frauds), not apply where retired partner agrees to pay debt which firm contracted while he was a member. *Reid* v. *Wilson,* 424.

"Express promise," "repeated and continuing promises," no material difference between, when. *Otis* v. *Holmes,* 775.

"Impeached," meaning of. *Smith* v. *State,* 479.

"Intoxicating liquors" include domestic wines. *O'Brien* v. *State,* 51; *Embry* v. *State,* 61.

"Justice," "judge," the former used as being interchangeable with the latter, when. *Strauss* v. *Maddox,* 224.

"Lost" freight (Civil Code, §§ 2317–18). *McElveen* v. *R. Co.* 249.

"Manslaughter," verdict of, is, in effect, verdict of voluntary manslaughter. *Smith* v. *State,* 479.

"O. K.," ambiguous, and parol evidence admitted to explain. *Penn Tobacco Co.* v. *Leman,* 428.

"Ordinary," "court of ordinary," distinction between. *Cunningham* v. *U. S. Loan Co.* 617.

"Perfect title," meaning of, as used in Civil Code, § 4927. *Wilcox Lumber Co.* v. *Bullock,* 532.

"Prevent" implies the doing of an act. *Green* v. *State,* 539.

"Public building," when not include church. *Collum* v. *State,* 531.

"Public" indecency, what is. *Morris* v. *State,* 351.

"Restraint of trade." *State* v. *Central R. Co.* 716.

"Tending to show," used by court to jury as to evidence, when error. *Chapman* v. *State,* 161.

WORDS AND PHRASES — *continued.*

"To," in statute prohibiting carrying liquor to church, applied to a place
    near the church. *Bice* v. *State*, 117.

"To" means "into," in charter authorizing construction of railroad "to"
    a named town *Waycross A.-L. R. Co.* v. *Offerman & W. R. Co.*
    827.

YEAR'S SUPPORT.

Contract between husband and wife with intention of promoting dissolu-
    tion of marriage relation, not bar widow's right to. *Birch* v.
    Anthony, 349.

Control of, in widow, though title in her and minor. *Howard* v. *Pope*,
    259.

Division of, when guardian can not compel. *Id.*

Minor's rights in. *Id.*